P9-EES-802

BY THE SAME AUTHOR

World Diary: 1929-1934 (1934)

England Expects Every American
to Do His Duty (1937)

Blood Is Cheaper than Water (1939)

The News and How to Understand It (1940)

A World History of Our Own Times

VOLUME ONE: *The World We Lost* (1949)

VOLUME TWO: *The World Between the Wars* (1953)

VOLUME THREE: *The World We Made* (in preparation)

A WORLD HISTORY OF OUR
OWN TIMES: VOLUME TWO

THE WORLD
BETWEEN
THE WARS

FROM THE 1918 ARMISTICE
TO THE MUNICH AGREEMENT

BY

QUINCY HOWE

19   53

SIMON AND SCHUSTER · NEW YORK

ALL RIGHTS RESERVED
INCLUDING THE RIGHT OF REPRODUCTION
IN WHOLE OR IN PART IN ANY FORM
COPYRIGHT, 1953, BY QUINCY HOWE
PUBLISHED BY SIMON AND SCHUSTER, INC.
ROCKEFELLER CENTER, 630 FIFTH AVENUE, NEW YORK 20, N. Y.

FIRST PRINTING

Quotation from *Science and the Modern World,* by Alfred North Whitehead. New York: The Macmillan Company, 1925. Copyright by The Macmillan Company. Used with the permission of the publisher.

Quotation from *Darkness at Noon,* by Arthur Koestler. New York: The Macmillan Company, 1941. Used with the permission of the publisher.

Quotations from *Der Führer,* by Konrad Heiden. Translated by Ralph Manheim. Boston: Houghton, Mifflin Company, 1944. Used with the permission of the publisher.

Quotation from *I Saw Hitler!* Copyright 1932 by Dorothy Thompson Lewis, and reprinted by permission of Rinehart and Company, Inc., Publishers.

Quotation from *Public Speech,* by Archibald MacLeish. New York: Farrar and Rinehart, 1936. Used with the permission of the author.

Quotation from *Eyeless in Gaza,* by Aldous Huxley. New York: Harper, 1936. Used with the permission of the publisher.

Quotations from *After Seven Years,* by Raymond Moley. New York: Harper, 1939. Used with the permission of the publisher.

Quotation from *Decline of the West,* by Oswald Spengler. Translated by Charles Francis Atkinson. Volume II. New York: 1928. Used with the permission of the publisher.

Quotations from *Prejudices: First through Sixth Series,* by H. L. Mencken. New York: Alfred A. Knopf, 1919–1927. Used with the permission of the publisher.

Quotations from *Fantastic Art, Dada, Surrealism,* by Georges Hugnet. New York: Museum of Modern Art, 1949. Used with the permission of the publisher.

Quotation from *Revolt of the Masses,* by José Ortega y Gasset. New York: W. W. Norton, 1933. Used with the permission of the publisher.

Quotations from *The Coming Struggle for Power,* by John Strachey. New York: The Modern Library, 1935. Used with the permission of the publisher.

Quotation from *The Martyrdom of Spain,* by Alfredo Mendizabal. New York: Scribner, 1938. Used with the permission of the publisher.

Quotations from *Unfinished Business,* by Stephen Bonsal. New York: Doubleday and Company, 1942. Used with the permission of the publisher.

Quotation from *Walther Rathenau,* by Count Harry Kessler. New York: Harcourt, Brace. 1930. Used with permission of the publisher.

Quotations from *The Fateful Years,* by André François-Poncet. Translated by Jacques LeClercq. New York: Harcourt, Brace, 1949. Used with permission of the publisher.

Quotations from *China: The Collapse of a Civilization,* by Nathaniel Peffer. New York: John Day Company, 1930. Used with permission of the publisher.

Quotation from *The Grapes of Wrath,* by John Steinbeck. New York: Viking Press, 1939. Used with permission of the publisher.

Quotation from *The Roosevelt I Knew,* by Frances Perkins. New York: Viking Press, 1946. Used with permission of the publisher.

Quotation from *Freedom's Battle,* by J. Alvarez Del Vayo. New York: Viking Press, 1949. Used with permission of the publisher.

Quotation from *Wooden Titan,* by John W. Wheeler-Bennett. New York: William Morrow, 1936. Used with permission of the author.

Quotation from *New Russia's Primer,* by M. Ilin. Translated from the Russian by George S. Counts and Nucia Lodge. Boston: Houghton, Mifflin, 1931. Used with the permission of the publisher.

All cartoons by David Low reproduced with permission of the artist and copyright in all countries.

Three cartoons by Emery Kelen reproduced with the permission of the artist and copyright by him.

LIBRARY OF CONGRESS CATALOG CARD NUMBER: 49-11858
MANUFACTURED IN THE U.S.A. BY H. WOLFF, NEW YORK

D
421
.H6
vol.2

TABLE OF CONTENTS

494.0

P383

1-22-54

55768

FOREWORD:

THE WORLD BETWEEN THE WARS

· I ·

THE HISTORY of the first two decades of the twentieth century is the history of the world we lost between 1914 and 1918. Europe's civilization never flowered so richly, Europe's power never spread so far as at the moment the First World War began. The next four years saw that civilization laid waste and that power laid low. Britain, France, and Italy paid almost as dearly for victory as Germany and Austria-Hungary paid for defeat, while the Russians, who more than once saved the Allied cause, suffered the heaviest losses of all. By the time the Germans signed the 1918 Armistice the prewar world had gone forever, along with the universal authority Europe once enjoyed. Yet the two chief aspirants for leadership in the postwar world spoke in unmistakably European accents. From the United States the voice of Wilson promised peace for all through world democracy. From Russia the voice of Lenin promised plenty for all through world revolution.

The history of the next two decades of the twentieth century is the history of the world's search for the goals that Wilson and Lenin defined. Both men drew their inspiration from the optimistic nineteenth century. Both shared Europe's faith in progress everlasting. But if they drew their inspiration from Europe's past, their hopes embraced the great globe itself. As children of the nineteenth century Wilson and Lenin both assumed that science had put the good life here on earth within the reach of the common man. As citizens of the twentieth century they also assumed that the common man could not enjoy the good life anywhere on earth unless he enjoyed it everywhere on earth. Drawing upon his own profound religious convictions, Wilson attempted to apply the principles of Christianity to world politics through the League of Nations. Lenin, whose antireligious zeal matched Wilson's religious fervor, offered a program of world revolution based on uncompromising class warfare. Wilson told the American people they must spread democracy everywhere and assure a Christian peace through the League of Nations. Lenin called upon the workers of all lands to unite and establish a Marxist Utopia through the Communist International. Either program had to gain universal sanction to succeed; acceptance of the one required rejection of the other.

In the eyes of their contemporaries Wilson and Lenin embodied the aspirations of the masses. To the peoples of western Europe, the United States, and the British Dominions the world had never before appeared so safe for democracy. The victorious Allies had destroyed the German, Austrian, and Turkish Empires and democracy was breaking out all over the map. The Germans and Austrians had ousted the Hohenzollerns and Hapsburgs and had set up democratic republics. Millions of Slavs had won freedom from Austro-Hungarian rule; millions of Arabs had won freedom from the Turks, who, in their turn, overthrew the Sultan. But the Bolshevik leaders believed that the children of Lenin rather than the children of Wilson would inherit the earth. To the peoples of eastern Europe and of Asia the world had never before appeared so ripe for revolution. The Bolsheviks had gained control of Russia by gaining control of the revolution that overthrew the Tsar and they planned to make that revolution world-wide. Lenin promised a new life to all exploited and backward peoples. To the oppressed majority of mankind he offered more than Wilson.

Speaking at Minneapolis in September, 1919, Wilson called upon his fellow Americans to take the eagle, not the ostrich, as their model: "I mean leaving the mists that lie close to the ground, getting upon strong wing into those upper spaces of the air where you can see with a clear eye the affairs of mankind, see how the affairs of America are linked with the affairs of men everywhere, see how the whole world turns with outstretched hands to this blessed country of ours and says, 'If you will lead, we will follow.' God helping us, we will lead when they follow. The march is still long and toilsome to those heights upon which there rests nothing but the light of the pure justice of God, but the whole incline of affairs is towards those distant heights; and this great Nation, in serried ranks, millions strong—presently hundreds of millions strong—will march at the forefront of the great procession breasting those heights with eyes always lifted to the eternal goal!" What a contrast the rasping tones of Lenin offered. "Only because the revolution is developing throughout the world," he declared in 1921, "is the international bourgeoisie unable to strangle us, although it is a hundred times stronger than we are numerically and from a military point of view." In 1920 Lenin told the Young Communist League of the Soviet Union: "We deny all morality taken from superhuman or nonclass conceptions. We say it is a deception, a swindle, a fogging of the minds of the workers and peasants in the interests of the landlords and capitalists. We say that our morality is wholly subordinated to the class-conscious interests of the proletariat. We deduce morality from the needs of the class struggle of the proletariat."

Wilson described one kind of paradise on earth, Lenin another. But the American people did not lead mankind into the "upper spaces of the air." Lenin's revolution did not develop "throughout the world." Both men died early in 1924, less than a fortnight apart, their missions unaccomplished.

· II ·

BEHIND AND BELOW the Wilson-Lenin conflict lay a crisis of faith which Nietzsche had anticipated when he wrote about the superman, the anti-Christ, and the transvaluation of values. The conflict that tore Nietzsche's generation apart had to do with religion and science. Thirty years later, the men who called themselves Christians were losing their faith in God while the men who called themselves scientists were losing their faith in man. Neither the old-time religion of the churches nor the more recent belief in material progress could compete against the appeals that party, class, nation, and race made to the postwar generation. As the 1920's and 1930's ran their course, Russian Communists, Italian Fascists, German Nazis, Chinese members of the Kuomintang, Indian members of the Congress Party, even American New Dealers discovered in strange and varied forms the kind of faith that moves mountains.

The strange and varied challenges of the twentieth century gave rise to these new cults. Whenever and wherever the human race had to fight for survival against the hostile forces of nature, man turned to the traditional religions for the faith he needed to go on living. But wherever and whenever man subdued and harnessed the forces of nature for his own purposes, the traditional religions lost their hold. Throughout the nineteenth century and on until the outbreak of war in 1914, more and more people, especially in the industrialized countries, took for granted the limitless possibilities of material progress. To help one's neighbor enjoy more of the better things of this life here on earth seemed at once the highest and the most practical form of idealism. Man was regarded as the product of his physical environment and in that environment lay all the causes of good and evil. But these assumptions disintegrated between 1914 and 1918 as the people who had created the most favorable environments for themselves bent every skill they possessed to the extermination of their neighbors.

In so far as Wilson and Lenin offered their followers causes beyond

themselves for which to make sacrifices and work with others, they
provided acceptable substitutes for religion. But Wilson's dream of
world peace never came into being. His chief support lay in western
Europe and the United States, where enthusiasm for the League of
Nations evaporated rapidly after Armistice Day. Wilson also refused
to compromise with his political enemies, preferring no bread to half
a loaf. Lenin, on the other hand, remained a symbol of hope, especially
to the Russian people, even though his dream of world revolution never
materialized. Announcing that it was sometimes necessary to take one
step backward before taking two steps forward, he chose to hold what
he had won in Russia rather than risking all to gain all. Stalin at once
proclaimed himself as Lenin's heir and continued to apply Lenin's
methods. But Stalin had none of Lenin's faith in progress, none of
Lenin's knowledge of Europe, none of Lenin's experience in world
affairs. More important, the situation Stalin faced differed from the
situation Lenin had faced. History assigned to Lenin the task of making
a revolution. History assigned to Stalin the task of consolidating the
revolution Lenin made. Lenin had come forward as a world messiah.
Stalin had to function as a national messiah and preserve in Russia what
Lenin had tried to spread throughout the world. Lenin stopped at
nothing in promoting world revolution. Stalin stopped at nothing in
preserving what Lenin had promoted.

No American called himself Wilson's heir as Stalin called himself
the heir of Lenin. Certain Europeans, notably Masaryk of Czechoslovakia, continued the search for peace along the trail that Wilson
blazed. A League of Nations came into being. Wilson's example inspired
the Kellogg-Briand Pact and a world-wide movement toward disarmament. But the messianic spirit Wilson tried to spread died before he
did. His admirers on both sides of the Atlantic became cynics or skeptics.
This is not to say that the cynics among them all became pessimists and
assumed that the worst had to happen. Neither did the skeptics all
become fatalists and give up hope. During the 1920's the accelerating
progress of science and industry raised living standards and production
well above prewar levels. War never seemed more futile. Abundance
for all never seemed within closer reach.

Meanwhile Asia produced two world messiahs who ministered no less
effectively than Wilson and Lenin to the universal yearning for peace
and plenty that the twentieth century had inspired even in the most
backward lands. Dr. Sun Yat-sen considered himself a Christian revolutionary whose program for China contained a mixture of Christian
and Confucian principles. For the authority of the family around which
Confucius had built one of the most worldly of religious faiths, Dr. Sun
substituted the authority of the Party. The mystical Gandhi brought

religion into politics and thereby made a strong appeal to devout
Hindus as well as to members of the other religious faiths that flourished
in India. Both the Chinese and Indian peoples had a long way to go
before they could hope to win their battles against the hostile forces
of nature. Hence neither Sun Yat-sen nor Gandhi needed to promise a
worldly Utopia, day after tomorrow, as Wilson and Lenin did.

The world depression aggravated the disillusionment that followed
the war. Once again man proved his own worst enemy as millions went
idle and hungry not because of floods or droughts or other natural
causes but solely because of defective human institutions. Gandhi's
prestige soared, not only in India but throughout the world. The heirs
of Dr. Sun, after he died in 1925, extended their power in China. And just
as the war had produced two rival messiahs in the persons of Wilson
and Lenin, so the depression produced two rival messiahs in the persons
of Adolf Hitler and Franklin D. Roosevelt.

· III ·

ALMOST every expression of the spirit of postwar Europe foreshadowed
Hitler's rise. Oswald Spengler's *Decline of the West,* with its emphasis on
inescapable collapse, reflected the first stages of disintegration. The
scientists who became mystics and the religious leaders who embraced
psychoanalysis helped the process along. In the Dada movement
Europe's artists, musicians, and men of letters turned against themselves. In the surrealist movement which followed they turned against
their public. It was not the masses, it was the self-proclaimed elite
who succumbed first. The Freudian approach supplanted the Marxist
approach as novelists dissected the individual instead of depicting
society. James Joyce, D. H. Lawrence, Marcel Proust, and Thomas Mann
indulged impulse and glorified intuition. From the new science of
psychiatry they adopted the technique of the interior monologue. Musicians and painters communicated in an even stranger language with
an even smaller public. Neither religion nor science, neither literature,
music, nor art could adequately explain the world of the twentieth
century to the people of the twentieth century. After losing his faith
in religion, Western man lost his faith in reason and progress. Nothing
remained but faith in himself, in action for action's sake.

Oswald Spengler, who expressed the mood of postwar Europe so
vividly in his *Decline of the West,* later summed up the contrast between
the nineteenth and the twentieth centuries in *Prussianism and Socialism:*
"The nineteenth century was the century of natural science; the twentieth belongs to psychology. We no longer believe in the power of
reason over life. We feel that life governs reason. A knowledge of men

is more important to us than abstract or general ideas; from optimists
we have become skeptics: we are not concerned with what should happen but what will happen; and it is more important to us to remain in
control of facts than to become the slaves of ideals."

Indulgence of the ego, reliance on impulse, and repudiation of all
traditional values found their ultimate expression in Adolf Hitler.
Mussolini and the Fascists had prepared the way for him with their
cult of action, their revolt against reason, intelligence, and free inquiry.
But even before the Fascists had come to power in Italy and long before
the Nazis came to power in Germany, Europe's philosophers, novelists,
artists, and intellectuals had prepared public opinion to accept the
Fascist and the Nazi point of view along with the corollary that Communism offered the only alternative.

Born in the heart of Europe, Hitler rebelled against every humane
tradition that Europe had stood for since the Dark Ages. He reviled
Christianity, repudiated reason, and used science only for purposes of
destruction. Yet Hitler built on the foundations Wilson and Lenin laid.
Like Wilson, he called for the self-determination of nations and invoked
Wilson's ideals to charge that the Versailles Treaty violated the Fourteen Points. Like Lenin, Hitler preached revolution and borrowed his
propaganda tricks and political morality from the Communists. He also
exploited his own anti-Communism to win the tolerance and even the
support of those who rejected the rest of his program.

The nature of Hitler's triumph at Munich confirmed his right to the
title of world messiah. For Hitler had a universal program, consisting
of something more than anti-Communism. He, too, sought a world of
peace and plenty—a world of peace by the sword and of plenty for
Germany first. His program appealed to the emotions of some Germans and to the interests of still more. It also exploited the moral and
material weaknesses of Europe as a whole. Although Europe had led
the world for centuries in the arts of peace, it had also led the world
for centuries in the arts of war. Although the peoples of Europe had
enjoyed more and more political democracy and individual freedom
over the years, they had also, over the same years, subjugated more
and more alien peoples. Nor did the doctrine of racial superiority
originate with Hitler. Nazi racialists borrowed their theories from
British, French, and Russian originals. What distinguished Hitler from
other Europeans was the degree and extent to which he harnessed the
darkest European forces for racial, national, and personal ends.

Eventually Hitler forced Roosevelt into the role of world messiah
that Wilson had needed no prompting to play. During his first term
in the White House Roosevelt functioned only as a national messiah,
putting forth the New Deal as the democratic, American answer to the

depression while Stalin was putting forth the Five-Year Plan as the Communist, Russian way. But the Japanese invasion of China and Hitler's aggressive moves in Europe caused Roosevelt to preach, once again, the Wilsonian doctrines that he had first advocated in 1920 when he sought the Vice-Presidency on a League of Nations platform—and lost. Once again, his own people refused to follow his lead. But even after his proposal, made in October, 1937, to "quarantine" aggressors fell flat, he approached Neville Chamberlain, in January, 1938, with still another plan to assure peace through collective action, only to suffer still another rebuff.

In 1917, when Wilson first essayed the role of world messiah, millions of people in every country at once responded to his leadership. For this supreme opportunity he had prepared himself throughout his life. Roosevelt had not aspired so long or so ardently as Wilson to head a universal, moral crusade, and his first attempts to assert himself and define his purposes did not quite come off. The kind of opportunity that Wilson seized in 1917 had not yet arisen in 1937. The world had been at war for more than two years when Wilson first began proclaiming his universal doctrines. The world still hoped to avoid another general war in 1937 when Roosevelt made his quarantine speech. Nevertheless, no other leader presumed to offer such a program as Roosevelt rather hurriedly improvised. Winston Churchill had warned one section of the British public against one aspect of the war danger, the German aspect. Joseph Stalin talked in Russian accents to certain sections of certain classes inside and outside the Soviet Union. Only Roosevelt even tried to make an essentially universal appeal.

The halfhearted response to this appeal suggested that the West had gone into an even sharper decline than Spengler had predicted. Nor had the East come forward with a dynamic alternative. Dr. Sun Yat-sen and Gandhi inspired revolutions that stirred half the human race, but neither China nor India had the power to attain the goals that Dr. Sun and Gandhi had set, much less to spread that limited power beyond their own borders. The world's twenty-year search for peace and plenty thus ended with Europe in the shadow of war and Asia in the throes of revolution. Although we never found the world we sought, our strivings transformed both ourselves and our world.

Part One

❁　　❁　　❁　　❁　　❁

THE SEARCH FOR
NORMALCY

1

Shell-Shocked Europe

*Weakened, fearful, and suspicious, the people of
Europe stumble from war to peace—sometimes by
way of revolution.*

PREVIEW

THE PROCLAMATION of the 1918 Armistice stirred more nationalist
passion than democratic faith. Little desire for reconciliation existed
in Britain or France, and the continued Allied blockade got democracy
off to a bad start in Germany. Nowhere did nationalist sentiment run so
high as in the succession states of Eastern Europe, where Masaryk's
Czechoslovakia emerged as an island of democracy surrounded by a sea
of turmoil. The Russian Revolution marched on, and from Germany
came a voice of doom that echoed in other lands: Oswald Spengler declared that Europe had entered upon its final period of decline.

· I ·

DURING THE four years from 1914 to 1918 Europe lost the world leadership that it had taken more than four centuries to win. From the time of
Columbus until the Industrial Revolution European explorers, soldiers,
settlers, and traders subjugated or colonized more than half the habita-
ble globe. From the Industrial Revolution on through the nineteenth
century Europe spread its power still further, knitting the whole world
more tightly together. By 1900 Europe could find no new lands to conquer; indeed, most of the Western Hemisphere, which Europeans originally subdued and colonized, had long since won its independence. In
1914 Europe turned against itself the same weapons it had used to conquer or threaten more backward lands. As the conflict went forward it
narrowed down to a struggle between the Germans, who wanted a re-
division of world power, and the Allies, who fought primarily to maintain the status quo. By 1917, however, it became apparent that neither
side could make its will prevail. The Russian Empire collapsed and
within the year the Bolsheviks came to power. At the same time the
United States had to join the Allies to stave off a complete German vic-

tory. The Armistice of November 11, 1918, brought the fighting to a sudden end. Germany's bid for a new and more favorable division of world power had failed utterly and at a cost beyond calculation. But the Allies had paid a very high price for victory, and the status quo which they originally hoped to preserve had vanished beyond recall.

Four years of war had not only bled Europe white. Much of the rest of the world had battened on the catastrophe. The United States, Japan, and the British Dominions all came out of the fighting stronger than they had gone in. Europe had also suffered a fatal loss of face in the eyes of Asia. Some Asiatics turned their eyes toward Wilson, others toward Lenin. All of them had reason to hope for a new and better future. But the people of Asia, and of other undeveloped areas, remained too backward and disorganized to play an immediate role of major importance, whereas the people of Europe, partly because of the war and partly in spite of it, were swept up in a series of decisive events for which neither their prewar nor their wartime experiences had prepared them.

As the fighting ended disillusionment began. The returned soldiers felt that their long agonies set them apart, but those who had remained at home had also endured years of tragedy and strain. Many families had lost at least one member, more often than not the chief breadwinner, and the peace to which they had looked forward brought them neither security nor ease nor hope. A week before the Armistice, the American people elected a Republican Congress which preferred the familiar, intoxicating wine of nationalism to Wilson's strange, new internationalist brew. Public opinion in Britain and France ran in the same direction. The mercurial Lloyd George rode the storm that he dared not breast. As soon as hostilities ceased, he called for a general election and tried to conduct a moderate campaign, only to wind up demanding that Germany pay the whole cost of the war, estimated at some hundred and twenty billion dollars. While the jingo Northcliffe press featured such headlines as "Hun Food Snivel," "The Junkers Will Cheat You Yet," and "How to Smash Lenin," Lloyd George accepted the support of those who promised, in his name, to "hang the Kaiser" and "squeeze Germany until the pips squeak." The Conservative-Liberal coalition that supported him swept the country, and one Tory observer described the new House of Commons as "a lot of hard-faced men who look as if they had done very well out of the war." After the returns were in Lloyd George sighed, "Heaven knows what I would have had to promise if the campaign had lasted a week longer."

At the same time, the French Chamber of Deputies, representing the French people, gave Clemenceau's nationalist Cabinet a four-to-one vote of confidence. Clemenceau wanted Germany dismembered, the Saar Valley permanently annexed to France, and the Rhineland occupied by French troops and set up as a separate state. All this violated the Fourteen Points, but the vote of the French Chamber suggested that a majority of the French people shared his views. Stéphen Pichon, Clemenceau's Foreign Minister, spoke for most of his compatriots when he declared on December 30, 1918, "We have been attacked; we want security. We have been despoiled; we demand restitution. We have been devastated; we want reparation." Clemenceau expressed himself more bluntly: "I do not know whether war is an interlude to peace or whether peace is an interlude to war." Harold Nicolson, one of the brighter young men in the British Foreign Office, paid tribute to the French point of view: "I quite admit that the French cannot see beyond their noses; but after all they are their noses; and my word, what they do see, they see damned clearly."

It did not require 20-20 vision to see, during the winter of 1918-19, a widening breach between Germany and the Allied world. Until the 1918 Armistice, the German people and the people of the Allied lands went through many of the same experiences. Their soldiers had fought under similar conditions on the Western Front. The families of these soldiers had gone through similar anxieties behind the lines. As long as the fighting continued and the outcome remained in doubt, Wilson spoke for most of the people in most of the Allied lands. The signing of the Armistice changed all this. The high cost of victory, when it came, gave rise to a more vengeful mood. The Allied peoples, hoping for restitution, turned away from Wilson; the German people, hoping for reconciliation, turned toward him. They took his Fourteen Points at face value and trusted to one of the Armistice terms under which the Allies promised to "provision" the German people "as shall be found necessary." But most Allied leaders felt their own people had suffered so much and so recently that they refused to lift the wartime blockade of Germany's ports.

As early as November, 1918, Winston Churchill pleaded in vain to rush several food ships to Germany. He did not hate the Germans less; he feared revolution more. Nobody knows to this day how many Germans starved to death during the winter after the Armistice, but the figure certainly ran into the hundreds of thousands. And nobody knew during that winter how the Germans would respond to the consequences of defeat. The abdication of the Kaiser had thrust power into the hands of the Social Democrats, who collaborated with the General Staff in preserving order. How long could this strange, new alliance last? In Russia defeat had come slowly, painfully, at excruciating cost, and the mass of the Russian people held the entire Tsarist regime responsible for that defeat. In the confusion that followed the collapse of that regime, the Bolsheviks found it possible to seize power. In Germany defeat had

UNDERWOOD

Karl Liebknecht

come suddenly, before a single Allied soldier stood on German soil. The popularity of the Kaiser evaporated, but the authority of the General Staff lived on. In addition, Germany had a conservative, respected, and powerful Social Democratic Party, willing and able to take control of the state and to fulfill Wilson's peace terms. But could the authority of the General Staff survive the shame and agony of defeat? Could the Social Democrats adapt themselves to the unfamiliar responsibilities of power? Could the German proletariat be denied its revolution?

By no means, argued a minority faction within a minority party. The minority party called themselves Independent Socialists. The minority faction called themselves Spartacists, and two of this latter group, Karl Liebknecht and Rosa Luxemburg, attracted Lenin's attention and admiration. Karl Liebknecht's father, Wilhelm, had helped found the German Social Democratic Party. The son was the first member of the Reichstag to vote against war credits after the commencement of hostilities in 1914. An increasing minority of Social Democrats gradually followed his example and in 1916 organized the Independent Socialist Party. During the war, Karl Liebknecht took the pen name Spartacus from the leader of the revolt of the slaves in ancient Rome. He founded the little, radical newspaper *Rote Fahne* (Red Flag). His co-editor, wiry, passionate little Rosa Luxemburg, had been born in Poland of Jewish parents. Although she attacked Lenin's dictatorial methods, he called her an "eagle" and looked to her and Liebknecht to lead Germany's proletarian revolution. They attracted some following among the younger soldiers, sailors, and workingmen, but the Social Democrats outnumbered them five to one.

While the Spartacists organized wildcat strikes and street fights, the Social Democrats organized a caretaker government, based on members of the old Reichstag and supported by the Army. Friedrich Ebert, a saddle maker by trade, presided over a Council of People's Commissars and agreed to oppose any revolutionary outbreaks. General Gröner, representing the High Command, supported him. In December, 1918, Ebert and Gröner decided that Liebknecht, Luxemburg, and the Berlin Spartacists might achieve their ambition and do to Germany what

Lenin, Trotsky, and the Petrograd Bolsheviks had done to Russia. "I hate revolution like sin," admitted Ebert as he organized a democratic election to choose a General Assembly that would then write a Constitution and set up a Republic. The Spartacists denounced the Social Democrats as enemies of the revolution and called for a boycott of the election: "The revolution can march forward only over the graves of the Social Democratic majority."

But it was over the graves of Liebknecht and Luxemburg that the German Republic crushed the German revolution. Noske, the Social Democratic Minister of Defense, fought fire with fire. As election day approached, the Spartacist movement that Luxemburg and Liebknecht had organized got out of hand. Its leaders fell behind their followers, who organized for insurrection and for a Bolshevik-style seizure of power. While Rosa Luxemburg tried to apply the brakes and re-establish contact with the more moderate Independent Socialists, Noske winked at the creation of a hastily organized Free Corps of jobless officers who specialized in beating up Spartacists. A few days before the election, members of the Free Corps placed Luxemburg and Liebknecht under "protective arrest" and then shot them "while attempting to escape." The Social Democrats polled eleven million votes; the Independent Socialists two million. The Spartacists, having called for a boycott of the election, polled no votes at all, and lacked both the leadership and the mass support that a successful insurrection required.

LEBENDEN DEM TOTEN . ERINNERUNG AN DEN 15.JANUAR 1919

Memorial to Karl Liebknecht. Woodcut by Käthe Kollwitz

Russia's example did much to prevent Communism from sweeping Germany. The Bolshevik dictatorship had become a bloody legend that the agents of that dictatorship all too vividly confirmed. And while the reactionary extremists of the Free Corps fought the revolutionary Spartacists, the great mass of the German people turned to the parties of moderation. The newly elected General Assembly met at Weimar, where they drew up a Constitution that combined a strong central government with wide individual liberty. Unlike Russia, Germany had a large, vigorous middle class and one of the oldest, most conservative trade union movements in Europe. It was from these two classes that the Weimar Republic drew its mass support, but the Social Democrats furnished the two outstanding leaders—Friedrich Ebert, whom the General Assembly elected President, and Philipp Scheidemann, former Socialist deputy and first Chancellor of Republican Germany.

The Social Democrats not only opposed revolution; they opposed the separatist movements that showed considerable vitality in Brunswick, Saxony, and Bavaria. Local leaders appeared in these German states, seeking to put through social reforms and to decentralize the new Germany along Swiss lines. Once again, however, the Social Democrats and the Free Corps made common cause. Free Corps troops traveled as they pleased throughout Germany, easily crushing the separatists in Brunswick and Saxony, but running into somewhat more opposition in Bavaria, where Kurt Eisner, former member of the staff of the Socialist *Vorwärts*, had become head of a revolutionary government which opposed a federal Reich and a National Constituent Assembly. Councils of workers and soldiers had helped bring Eisner to power, and when his Minister of Defense, a veteran of the Western Front, heard that the revolution had actually seized power in Munich, he exclaimed: "My God, revolution. And I in uniform." But the revolution did not last long. A young Nationalist student shot Eisner dead in a Munich street and his regime collapsed.

Defeat abroad and revolution at home forced the General Staff and the Social Democrats into ever closer association. As symbols of the lost war, Hindenburg and Ludendorff had vanished into the shadows, leaving the thankless task of organizing the retreat and demobilization to General Gröner, the humbly born son of an army paymaster who never held a commission. But Gröner always stood in well with the trade union leaders, and his popularity among the rank and file of the German Army helped him to bring them all home in good order. What General Gröner had done with Germany's soldiers the Social Democratic leaders had to do with Germany's civilians, but the dirtiest job fell to Defense Minister Noske, in whom Gröner said that the High Command possessed "unlimited confidence." Noske had no choice but to reciprocate.

The Social Democrats needed order in the streets during the winter months when revolution always threatened just as the High Command had needed order on the Western Front during the fall months when defeat might so easily have led to mutiny.

The German Social Democrats, during that winter of 1918-19, had reason to consider themselves the saviors of their own country, of Europe, and of world democracy. They had taken the lead in setting up the kind of German government that Wilson had called for in his wartime appeals. They had made the Armistice possible, largely because the terms of that Armistice seemed to promise the German people a new chance. Wilson's wartime appeals had laid no share of the war guilt on the shoulders of the German people. All blame attached to the miserable Kaiser and his defeated generals. The German Social Democrats suddenly faced vast opportunities and still vaster responsibilities. The Russian Bolsheviks and their sympathizers inside Germany therefore sought to prevent Social Democrats from making the country safe for democracy. At the same time, the Bavarian separatists sought to reverse the progress Germany had made since Bismarck's time toward national self-determination. It remained for the Social Democrats to establish German democracy while the High Command preserved German nationalism.

Noske and Gröner, the two men chiefly responsible for this double duty, had their hands full. The war had cost the Germans half their livestock; it had reduced their crops 40 per cent. Inflation had already begun, with ten times as much currency circulating as in 1914. Although Lenin guessed wrong when he predicted that the Allies would impose another Peace of Brest-Litovsk, the Allied attitude toward defeated Germany appeared as stupid if not as cruel as the German attitude toward defeated Russia only ten months before. But if the Allied leaders showed themselves blind to the realities inside Germany, the German leaders and the German people proved equally blind in refusing to see that the war and their country's part in it had embittered the whole Allied world against them and their country. Thus the Weimar Republic got off to the worst possible start.

· II ·

The Empire of the Hapsburgs suffered a more complete defeat than the Empire of the Hohenzollerns. The German Republic lost important territory to France in the west and to Poland in the east. But it was territory inhabited mainly by non-Germans and its loss did not remove the economic base on which Republican Germany had to reorganize itself. The collapse of the Austro-Hungarian Empire not only reduced Austria to misery and Hungary to impotence. It removed the economic base on which the lives of more than a hundred million East Europeans had largely depended for generations.

The Hapsburgs had ignored the national aspirations of their Slavic subjects; they had offended the national pride and threatened the national interests of their Slavic neighbors. But they had made their own empire and the surrounding territories a going economic concern. Most of the leaders of the succession states that burgeoned after the war flouted economic realities as the Hapsburgs had flouted political realities. The stresses and strains of eastern Europe had set off a general war in 1914. The peacemakers of 1919 did little to improve the situation. In many cases they made it even worse.

Austria and Hungary, the favored lands of the old regime, suffered the most under the new dispensation. The imperial city of Vienna, once the symbol and citadel of European reaction, became the chief stronghold of radical Social Democracy. Most of Vienna's two and a half million people voted Socialist. Most of the remaining three and a half million Austrians belonged either to the Nationalist or to the Christian Socialist Party. On November 12, 1918, after the abdication of Emperor Karl, the three groups came together in a coalition that proclaimed Austria a Republic and called for union with Germany. The French pointed out that Austro-German union would reward Germany for having lost the war.

Events in Hungary followed a stormier course. On October 16, 1918, revolutionaries in Budapest proclaimed a Republic. Two weeks later, they killed Count Tisza, the Hungarian Foreign Minister of the Dual Monarchy, and installed Count Michael Karolyi, a pacifist, pro-Ally liberal, as Premier of the People's Republic of Hungary. Karolyi, who came of an aristocratic family, gave up all claims to his own vast estates. But the democratic Republic he headed lasted only a few months. His wartime record of pro-Allied sympathy had failed to persuade the Allies to lift their blockade of Hungary during the first postwar winter. His fellow aristocrats considered him a traitor to their class. The Hungarian Communists considered him a reactionary and seized power in March, 1919, under the leadership of a Jewish ex-Socialist who had taken the name of Bela Kun.

The head of the new Hungarian government came from the disputed province of Transylvania and had fought on the Eastern Front until the Russians captured him. Because he enjoyed wide popularity among his fellow prisoners and then became converted to Communism, Lenin selected him to head the Hungarian revolution. Bela Kun tried to copy Lenin's methods, but his power never extended far beyond Budapest, which he quit in August, 1919, when a Rumanian army of liberation arrived. Only then did the Allies lift the blockade, but the Rumanian troops remained for three months, pillaging the city. Finally, Admiral Nicholas Horthy, wartime commander of the Austro-Hungarian Navy, proclaimed himself Regent of Hungary and released a white terror more ruthless than Bela Kun's terror from the left. The only Communist government outside Russia had collapsed and Hungary became a kingdom without a king ruled by an admiral without a navy.

The Horthy counterrevolution left Hungary's two thousand feudal families still in possession of half the country's farm lands. But the Rumanians who drove communism from Budapest also drove feudalism from the rich province of Transylvania. On November 9, 1918, a pro-Ally liberal government had taken power in Bucharest, declared war on Germany, and proceeded to claim a place among the victors at the peace table. As the officials of this new, Greater Rumania pleaded their case at Paris, their fellow countrymen absorbed the former Russian province of Bessarabia and the former Hungarian province of Transylvania. They had a sound enough case on ethnic grounds. In Transylvania, the Rumanian government also distributed the estates of Hungarian landlords among Rumanian peasants and put through similar measures in Bessarabia and prewar Rumania.

The Serbs had fought harder and longer than the Rumanians and suffered greater losses. Many of their leaders therefore hoped to proclaim a Greater Serbia as their reward when the Central Powers finally went under. They found it more prudent, however, to take the lead in forming the South Slav Kingdom of Serbs, Croats, and Slovenes, known as Yugoslavia, with the Serbian city of Belgrade as its capital and the Serbian Prince Alexander as Prince Regent. The Eastern Orthodox Serbs, who formed little more than half the population of the new Kingdom, had a long tradition of independence, but the Roman Catholic Croats who had lived under Austrian rule scorned the Serbs as a backward race of peasants and shepherds. Smaller minorities of Macedonians and Montenegrins wanted complete independence. The Macedonians waged endless guerrilla warfare against Bulgaria and Yugoslavia. The Montenegrins tried to keep their own king, and when an American diplomat asked Balfour if Britain recognized him Balfour replied, "We do. We pay for him." But hatred of Italy, fear of a Hapsburg restoration, and dislike of outsiders gave the South Slavs a persistent if negative sense of unity that held their new kingdom together.

One real democracy and one real statesman emerged from the ruins of the Hapsburg Empire. On October 28, 1918, the Czechoslovaks proclaimed their Republic at Prague, and Austria's Emperor Karl recognized its independence. They chose as their first President a sixty-eight-year-old professor of philosophy, Thomas Garrigue Masaryk, the son of a Czech servant girl and of a Slovak coachman who, in turn, was born

BETTMANN ARCHIVE

Dr. Thomas G. Masaryk, Czechoslovak President

a serf on an imperial estate in Moravia. Masaryk's parents could not afford to give him an education. At fifteen he went to Vienna and got a job as a locksmith's apprentice, but soon returned to his native village, where the local priest helped him along the road to the higher learning. Masaryk proved a born scholar, with a taste for political action, too. While a student at the University of Leipzig, he fell in love with a well-to-do American girl from Brooklyn. Together they read Buckle's *History of Civilization* and John Stuart Mill's *Subjection of Women*, and when she married him he took her last name as his middle name.

Masaryk did not drink or smoke, and he believed so strongly in monogamy that he did not think a widow or widower should ever remarry. But for all his high, personal standards of conduct he showed the widest tolerance toward others—often to his own hurt.

He chose as his hero the Czech martyr John Hus, who had once said, "I love a good German better than a bad Czech." Masaryk opposed national fanatics of every kind. "A nation that is not founded on truth does not deserve to survive," he declared. Strict Protestants and narrow Catholics abused him as a freethinker, yet he wrote, "Has there ever been a better, more exalted, more divine life than that of Christ? Christ's whole life is Truth. God's son is the highest simplicity. He shows purity and sanctity in the true sense of the word. Nothing external attaches to him and his life, no formalism, no ritualism; everything comes from the inner being; everything is thoroughly true, thoroughly beautiful, thoroughly good." Of himself he declared, "Jesus, not Caesar, is my ideal," and of mankind: "What we need is faith, living faith in something higher than ourselves, something great, something sublime, something eternal." It was Masaryk who chose as the motto for the new state of Czechoslovakia *Pravda Vitezi*—"Truth Shall Prevail."

Masaryk knew and admired Tolstoy, who, in turn, gave up smoking when Masaryk pointed out that peasants could not afford the luxury of tobacco. Masaryk, however, did not accept Tolstoy's doctrine of nonresistance. As professor of philosophy at the University of Prague and as a member of the Parliament at Vienna, Masaryk spoke out against the

Hapsburgs. Soon after war came in 1914, he made his way to Switzerland and then to London, where he spent the next three years, urging Czechs and Slovaks, through underground channels, to support the Allied cause as the best guarantee of their own eventual freedom. In March, 1917, the Russian Revolution brought him to Petrograd, where members of the Czech Legion begged him to become their leader. Within a few months, however, he left for the United States to carry on propaganda and raise funds among Czech immigrants. In June, 1918, he persuaded Secretary of State Lansing to issue a declaration that "America desires that all branches of the Slav race should be completely freed from German and Austrian rule."

Masaryk's own people, recognizing that he embodied Czech and Slovak unity, elected him their President while he was still in New York, and on his return to Prague he installed himself in the Hradshin, ancient palace of the Bohemian kings. Lloyd George, however, scented trouble. In March, 1918, he was fulminating against "the monstrous demands of Czechoslovakia," and in May he warned the Great Powers not to permit "the small states to use them as cat's paws for their miserable ambitions." Yet Masaryk had not wanted Czechoslovakia to include the Sudetenland and its three and a half million Germans and argued in vain for letting this portion of the old Hapsburg Empire join the new German Republic.

If all the East European leaders had shared Masaryk's qualities, Lloyd George need not have worried. Masaryk, however, stood out not only among his neighbors in eastern Europe but among his colleagues from all over the world. Alone among the statesmen of his time, Masaryk possessed the serenity of the humble-hearted. Perhaps Lenin surpassed him in will power; assuredly he surpassed Lenin in power of mind. And where Lenin was cynical and fanatical, Masaryk was tolerant and humane. Masaryk's moral courage ranked with Wilson's, but he possessed a deeper culture, a wider knowledge of the world. Wilson's high ethical principles made him self-righteous. The son of the proud Presbyterian preacher could love humanity only in the abstract; the son of the simple Slovak coachman loved people as such. Masaryk did not talk down to the masses or hold them in low regard. He did not consider himself a messiah, but assumed that others shared his aspirations. His early poverty bred into him sympathy for the downtrodden and hatred of oppression. His emergence from obscurity gave him hope for others and inspired a mellow, even an optimistic, view of life. In 1909 the Austrian writer Hermann Bahr described Masaryk as "the lonely Slovak at Prague who, a mixture of Tolstoy and Whitman, seems to some a heretic, to others an ascetic, and to all an enthusiast."

Circumstance stimulated Masaryk's natural endowments. Born a Slavic subject of the Hapsburgs, he knew from experience what second-

class citizenship means to an individual and to a people. The Czechoslovak Republic that he headed had minority problems of its own, and
one of his first tasks as President was to reconcile the Protestant city-
dwelling Czechs with the Catholic Slovak peasants. Czechoslovakia's
thirteen million inhabitants also included more than three million Germans, nearly three quarters of a million Hungarians, nearly half a million Ruthenians, and about the same number of Jews. As the largest
single national group, with the highest standards of culture and living,
the Czechs might have lorded it over every other minority, but they
had suffered oppression themselves, and when Masaryk—unlike some of
his contemporaries—appealed to his people's highest instincts they responded. Under his leadership Czechoslovakia granted educational,
cultural, and local autonomy to all its many national groupings.

Masaryk's approach to the question of national minorities made
Czechoslovakia internally strong. But his program did not stop there. A
strong, united Czechoslovakia could not exist except as part of a strong,
united Europe. Czechoslovakia lay at the mercy of stronger neighbors,
but Czechoslovakia also lay at the heart of Europe. It was here that the
most highly civilized of all the Slavic peoples came in contact with the
peoples of the West. Masaryk visualized Czechoslovakia as a bridge
between East and West and as a kind of model, or pilot plant, of the
new Europe. In 1920 he recognized and made peace with the Russian
Bolshevik leaders, whom all the other democratic statesmen continued
to shun. Yet he always considered himself and his country "Western,"
not "Eastern."

Colonel Stephen Bonsal, one of the great American correspondents of
the time and personal translator and adviser to Colonel House, visited
Masaryk at Prague early in 1919. In the diary that he published many
years later under the title of *Unfinished Business*, Bonsal quoted Masaryk as follows: "Our purpose is to make Prague the Mecca of Democracy. We have the task to liberate Central Europe. From here we must
radiate the only gospel acceptable to free men. It is a great and noble
task but I am confident my people will prove equal to it—with God's
help!" Looking beyond Czechoslovakia, Masaryk went on: "The era of
imperialism is closed. The self-seeking, ruthless plans of the Germans, of
the Russians, and of their imitators, the Austro-Hungarians, have failed
as did those of Napoleon. The little states are free. The war task is accomplished, but a still greater task lies before us: it is to reorganize not
only eastern Europe but the world as a whole. As I see it, we are on the
threshold of a new era in which the human race feels its unity."

Force of character and force of circumstance made Masaryk a unique
figure. He could not, of course, compete with Wilson or Lenin as a world
messiah. The example of little Czechoslovakia counted for less in the

world than the example of mighty America or vast Russia. Moreover, Wilson and Lenin had made their marks as crisis statesmen; they had shown themselves greatest at moments of catastrophe. By 1919, history had begun to pass both men by. The American people were cooling toward Wilson's leadership; the world revolution Lenin had predicted still hung fire. Germany had become a democratic republic, not a proletarian dictatorship; Europe and America preferred nationalism to internationalism. Masaryk, on the other hand, did not come into his own until the time for reconstruction arrived. If Europe were to have a future, Masaryk had shown how to achieve it. Time might yet work on his side.

· III ·

Six months after Colonel Bonsal listened to Masaryk announce that the future of peace and democracy lay with the small nations of Europe, he heard another wise and equally good European predict something quite different. In the name of democracy and self-determination, many former subjects of the Hapsburgs, the Romanovs, and the Hohenzollerns had carved out new states for themselves in eastern Europe. But Walter Rathenau, Germany's wartime economic dictator, could see nothing but trouble ahead. "What are these states of Poland, Czechoslovakia, and Yugoslavia which you have created?" he asked Bonsal. "Let me tell you: nothing that will last except the shame of them; nothing that will advance humanity; nothing that will redound to the credit of civilization. Should you, Colonel Bonsal, come back here in ten years you will shudder at the sight of the human suffering and the human destruction for which your country will be in a large measure to blame. This is a terrible outlook, and the consequences, the inevitable, tragic consequences of it, I believe, unless the peace conditions are radically changed, will not be borne by us Germans alone. The whole world will be involved and permeated by the lawlessness of the new situation, and the era of our history which began with a laudable attempt (I have no doubt of this) to civilize the Balkans and to bestow civilized government and respect for the law where it is lacking, will end, indeed it has ended by the Balkanization of that Europe from whence came life-giving blood and the heart impulse of the whole civilized world."

But neither the Americans nor the West Europeans had created the peace conditions that Rathenau deplored. It was the people of eastern Europe who took their destinies into their own hands when the Russian, German, and Austro-Hungarian Empires collapsed. The Rumanians, the Serbs, and the Czechs achieved many of their ambitions during the winter of 1918-19. Because the Poles had wider ambitions and faced steeper obstacles, they took longer to establish themselves on the map of the new

Europe. Wilson's Thirteenth Point had pledged an independent Polish state, inhabited by indisputably Polish populations, with access to the sea. Germany quickly ceded some of this territory in the form of the Danzig corridor. Austria ceded more in the form of Galicia. But most Poles, before the war, lived under Russian—not German or Austrian—rule. No matter what conditions the Allies might dictate to the defeated Germans and Austrians, they could not keep their pledges to the Poles without coming to some sort of arrangement with Russia.

Since 1916 the military power of Germany had dominated Poland and under the Treaty of Brest-Litovsk the Bolsheviks gave up all the authority the Tsar had once exercised. At the end of 1918, however, German military power collapsed and the Armistice voided the Brest-Litovsk settlement. The Germans had recognized Poland's nominal independence long since and permitted a Regency Council to operate, at Warsaw, under their supervision. Poles had fought in the German, Austrian, and Russian armies, but most of them regarded Russia as their chief enemy, and Joseph Pilsudski, the outstanding fighter for Polish freedom, had led Polish troops with both the Austrian and German armies. Pilsudski, however, refused to subordinate himself to the Germans, who jailed him in 1917 for the duration. In 1918 the leaders of the German Republic released him and he made his way to Warsaw, where he took over the Regency Council and proceeded to organize a provisional government with himself as chief of state.

Pilsudski was to Poland what Masaryk was to Czechoslovakia, but the resemblance stopped right there. Pilsudski, who came of noble, Lithuanian ancestry, had worked with the Polish Socialists since 1885, when he began to study medicine at the Russian University of Kharkov. He had no use for political doctrines and did not belong to the party of international socialism, affiliated with the Second International, but with a strongly nationalist and strictly Polish group. In 1887 Russian police arrested him in connection with the same plot against the Tsar's life for which Lenin's brother was executed. Although innocent, Pilsudski served a short term of exile in Siberia, where his hatred of Russia deepened. He was a born soldier and self-made revolutionary who believed that Poland had to go through a revolution before it could gain independence. When the Russians did not have him locked up in prison or sentenced to Siberia, he devoted himself to organizing and arming Polish patriots. During the Russo-Japanese War he tried to get the Japanese to back a Polish uprising. In 1908 he led a band of Polish revolutionaries who held up a train in order to raise funds for their party, just as Stalin organized holdups for the Bolsheviks.

In February, 1914, Pilsudski declared, "The problem of the independence of Poland will be solved only when Russia shall be beaten by Germany—and Germany by France. It is our duty to lend our help to that aim." After war broke out six months later, Pilsudski said the Poles had "decided to submit to the destiny of war, and having rendered to God what is God's—a sigh—to render to Caesar what is Caesar's: their lives and property." After his first action against the hated Russians he exclaimed, "For me it had as much moving poetry as my first youthful love affair, my first kisses." But when war began to bring forth revolution his belligerence ebbed. In 1918 he declared that "revolution from the left is always more dangerous than revolution from the right" and sought Socialist support to forestall the spread of Bolshevism. The Allies had meanwhile recognized a rival and more conservative leader, Roman Dmowski, and his Polish National Committee as the Provisional Government of the new Poland. The great Polish pianist, Ignace Paderewski, reconciled the two factions. Paderewski and Dmowski represented Poland abroad and acknowledged Pilsudski, who remained in Warsaw, as head of the new Polish state.

BETTMANN ARCHIVE

Marshal Joseph Pilsudski

Pilsudski cherished extravagant ambitions which the French Foreign Office had reason to indulge. He hoped to bring Lithuania, White Russia, and the Ukraine into a Greater Polish Federation, stretching from the Baltic to the Black Sea, and in the spring of 1919, as a first step toward this goal, he had Polish troops occupy Vilna, his own birthplace and the traditional capital of Lithuania, while other Polish forces invaded the Ukraine. The French egged him on because they hoped to forge a powerful ring of friendly states in eastern Europe—partly as a counterweight to Germany, partly as a *cordon sanitaire* against the expansion of Russian Bolshevism. To most Europeans and Americans, during the first years after the Armistice, the second possibility seemed a more immediate menace than the first.

During the winter of 1918-19, events in Russia had not gone as the Allied leaders hoped: the Bolsheviks remained securely in power. But events outside Russia had not gone as the Bolshevik leaders hoped: the world revolution failed to materialize. Direct intervention by Allied troops rallied the Russian people around the new regime. In like manner, indirect Russian intervention in the affairs of other nations through the newly organized Communist International antagonized the non-Russian majority of the human race. When Lenin learned in late 1918 that the British Labor Party planned to call an international Socialist and Labor Conference, he feared a revival of the Second (Socialist) International and at once set about organizing a Third (Communist) International. Chicherin, as Soviet Foreign Commissar, sent out the invitations and on March 2, 1919, fifty hand-picked delegates and guests from abroad gathered in the Kremlin. Few of them represented large trade unions or strong political parties, but that did not disturb Lenin. He wanted them to obey orders and concentrate for the moment on splitting the Socialist and Labor movement. Gregory Zinoviev, second only to Trotsky as an orator and closer to Lenin than any of his comrades, was chosen president of the new "Comintern."

These doings filled the leaders of the victorious nations with a curious mixture of fear and hope. The fearful ones believed that the world revolution might spread from Russia to other countries. The hopeful ones saw Bolshevik propaganda playing into their hands. The fearful ones supported various expeditionary forces that attacked Russia from without and various ex-Tsarist commanders who fomented civil war from within. But all these efforts failed miserably. French soldiers and sailors, assigned to help the Ukrainians shake off Bolshevik rule, mutinied in March, 1919, and had to be withdrawn. British trade unionists refused to ship military supplies for use against the Bolsheviks. During the summer of 1919 the British evacuated their Expeditionary Force from Archangel and pulled their few remaining troops out of south Russia, too. The Americans lost interest in the Siberian Expedition and when they left they had every reason to believe the Japanese would also withdraw. The one remaining hope of overthrowing Bolshevism lay with the Russian armies of Admiral Kolchak in the neighborhood of Omsk and with General Denikin's troops at Rostov-on-the-Don.

That hope did not survive the year. As War Commissar, the versatile Trotsky put himself through a course in military training and transformed a few experienced officers and not too many experienced troops into a new Red Army. Denikin and Kolchak had plenty of former Tsarist officers and some equipment, furnished by the Allies, but utterly inadequate troops. Denikin's forces disintegrated in the fall of 1919 when he failed to get the support of the Ukrainians. Too late in the day, General Wrangel replaced him. Kolchak lasted a little longer. He helped the last remnants of the scattered Czech Legion move westward, toward home, but in February, 1920, the Bolsheviks caught him and had him shot. Several hundred thousand Russian refugees, both soldiers and civilians, finally made their way to Constantinople.

The Allied interventionists and the Russian anti-Bolsheviks played into the hands of Lenin and Trotsky by acting just as Lenin and Trotsky predicted they would act. If foreign statesmen had not intervened in Russian internal affairs, and if Russian anti-Bolsheviks had not accepted foreign aid and taken orders from former officers of the discredited Tsar, the Russian people might have overthrown Lenin and Trotsky in short order. For the Bolsheviks did not bring Russia the peace or the bread they promised. They brought only bloodier war and worse starvation. Nevertheless, by the end of 1920 the Bolsheviks had crushed all domestic opposition and broken all armed attacks from abroad. They owed their survival less to their own strength than to the folly of their foes. They triumphed at home because Bolshevism offered the only alternative to Tsarism. They failed abroad because too many other leaders of too many other movements offered too many other roads to the peace and security for which so much of the human race yearned.

· IV ·

How the power of Europe had sunk in the world. For more than four years, millions of its strongest, ablest men had devoted themselves all too successfully to killing one another off. Not only had they stopped producing new capital equipment; the war devoured about half their current production, plus untold accumulations of past centuries. It had taken the material resources of the United States and the moral authority of Woodrow Wilson to rescue the Allied cause. But the nations of western Europe still could not impose their will on the nations of eastern Europe; revolutionary Russia survived all attacks. The most beaten and backward peoples in Europe showed more vitality than the peoples of the victorious Allied lands. The despised Bolsheviks outfought and out-thought the leading soldiers and statesmen of western Christendom. But the East Europeans could only declare their independence of the West. Most of them could not govern themselves. The Bolsheviks destroyed an old order but failed to build a new one. The Europe of 1919 lacked the strength and the unity to restore a stable peace.

The fever of rising prices weakened even those nations that appeared to have won the war. Until the Armistice, their civilians had put up with many hardships, counting themselves lucky to escape the dangers of combat. Their earnings, in paper money, increased, but shortages of every kind prevented them from spending these earnings, much of which went instead into interest-bearing government bonds. When the war ended, all the Allied governments owed their people billions of dollars in interest charges as well as principal. The people had accumulated vast savings, but they were paper savings and the shortage of goods continued. Thus, the returned soldiers found trade union members making fabulous wages but living no better than they had in 1914, whereas the salaried workers, whose earnings had not so greatly increased, were living half and less than half as well as they had before the war.

With war industries closing down, jobs were not easy to come by. Some returned soldiers joined or rejoined unions and struck for higher wages. Others threw themselves into nationalist movements and blamed their troubles on foreigners; still others blamed "the enemy within." Many turned their backs on politics, tried to forget the war, sought refuge in escape. Millions of mutilated and wounded men became burdens on their families and communities, forced to accept what crusts the politicians threw their way and to live out blighted lives of solitude, bitterness, and shame. Hordes of war widows, grandparents, and children multiplied the ranks of these forgotten millions. During the closing months of the war and the early months of the peace an influenza epidemic swept the world, claiming an estimated twenty-one million victims—more than twice as many as died in more than four years of combat. The flu did not spare neutrals or noncombatants, but it affected human beings only. It did not destroy past wealth or mortgage the wealth of the future.

The by-products of the war proved as destructive as war itself. The Russian Revolution cost several million lives and untold property damage. But it did give the Russian people the chance to make a new start with a new set of leaders. Defeated Germany bore grievous scars; witness Stephen Bonsal's description of the Unter den Linden in Berlin during the summer of 1919, as recorded in his diary and printed in *Unfinished Business:*

"The great artery was cluttered up with war cripples, who hobbled along as best they could or made imploring gestures for help from vestibules and the entrances to houses. Some of these unfortunates were bold and not a few indulged in menacing gestures. Others, and these were the more numerous, crouched against the cold, damp walls as though ashamed for the stranger to see their distorted leg and arm stumps, their dead eyes, or their faces scarred almost beyond recognition as human beings by flame throwers which one of their great men invented—not thinking it could and would be turned against their ever-victorious army. All these unfortunates were alike in one respect. They were all talking, or rather mumbling, to themselves, their tales of woe, rather than to those callous folk who hurried by as fast as they could. Russian refugees, often barefooted, always in rags, milled round in groups, too. They had escaped the revolution and apparently had no fear of the starvation with which they seem to be confronted. But how unlike they are to the Junker ladies now beaten down upon their long unbending knees. They are not and never have been *hoffähig*, nor can

BETTMANN ARCHIVE

Oswald Spengler

they boast of heraldic quarterings, but they hold high their heads, and if die they must, they will die as free men and masters of their souls —an idea which seems to be beyond the grasp of the average German."

Although Oswald Spengler hardly qualified as an average German, he produced the first expression of the mind of postwar Europe in the first volume of his massive *Untergang des Abendlandes*—or *Decline of the West,* as it became known in English some years later. Spengler taught history at Munich. He had decided upon his title in 1912, and completed his first draft in 1914. During the war he rewrote the entire two-volume work, and when the first volume appeared in 1918 it sold ninety thousand copies in Germany. He called *The Decline of the West* a morphology of world history, *the* philosophy of the future, "in any case the only philosophy which is within the *possibilities* of the European mind in its next stages." Spengler set out to discover and define certain fixed laws of history and to apply those laws to the present in such a way that man could foresee his immediate future and act accordingly.

He announced that the human race had created six or eight great "cultures" which have had life spans of a thousand years before freezing into "civilizations." He discussed at some length Chinese, Indian, Egyptian, Classical, Arabian, and West European cultures, analyzed their distinguishing features, and pointed out parallel developments in all of them. He declared that the culture of western Europe began in the year 900 A.D. and that with the nineteenth and twentieth centuries it had begun to harden into a civilization, just as the Classical culture of ancient Greece hardened into the civilization of Rome. The age of the Caesars had begun with Cecil Rhodes, who coined the slogan "expansion is everything" yet also admitted that "the expansive tendency is doom." Rhodes described the Germans as a "conspicuous example of a people that has become expansive without knowing or willing it."

"We are civilized, not Gothic or Rococo, people," Spengler wrote, "we have to reckon with the hard, cold facts of a *late* life, to which the parallel is not to be found in the Athens of Pericles but in the Rome of Caesar. Of great painting or great music, there can no longer be, for Western

people, any question. Their architectural possibilities have been exhausted these hundred years. Only *extensive* possibilities are left to
them." Spengler considered himself a follower of Goethe and Nietzsche,
not of Kant and Hegel. "There are no eternal truths. Every philosophy
is the expression of its own and only its own time, and—if by philosophy
we mean effective philosophy and not academic triflings about judg-
ment-form, sense-categories, and the like—no two ages possess the same
philosophic intentions. The difference is not between perishable and
imperishable doctrines, but between doctrines which live their day and
doctrines which do not live at all."

Spengler's literary genius did not match Goethe's any more than his
philosophic insight matched Nietzsche's, yet—measured by his own
standards—he spoke for his time as they spoke for theirs. If he was correct and culture had given way to civilization in western Europe, his
own inferiority to Goethe and Nietzsche proved his thesis: the West
had indeed gone into a decline. Because Western man tried, like Faust,
to comprehend everything and achieve the impossible, Spengler called
the spirit of western Europe and the United States "Faustian." Western
man's obsession with time gave him unique insights into both past and
future. No other culture or civilization had developed such a sharp
sense of history. Spengler regarded himself and his book as thoroughly
"Faustian," but since he lived in a "late" period, he addressed himself to
men of action.

"I can only hope that men of the new generation may be moved by
this book to devote themselves to technics instead of lyrics, the sea instead of the paint-brush, and politics instead of epistemology. Better
they could not do." The closing paragraph of his first volume developed
the same refrain: "For us, however, whom a Destiny has placed in this
Culture and at this moment of its development—the moment when
money is celebrating its last victories, and the Caesarism which is to
succeed approaches with quiet, firm step—our direction, willed and
obligatory at once, is set for us within narrow limits, and on any other
terms life is not worth the living. We have not the freedom to reach to
this or to that, but the freedom to do the necessary or to do nothing.
And a task that historic necessity has set *will* be accomplished with the
individual or against him.

> *"Ducunt Fata volentem nolentem trahunt."*

Spengler's fatalism helped reconcile the Germans to their defeat by
making that defeat appear part of a universal European upheaval. He
suggested that the United States might become to Europe what Rome
became to Greece; that Russia might produce a new culture in the shade
of western Europe, as the Arabian world produced a new culture in the

shade of the late Roman Empire. The idea that history repeats itself in cycles did not originate with Spengler. Neither was he the first man to trace parallels between events in western Europe and in ancient Rome. But his attempt to organize and apply past knowledge to present problems earned him, among his contemporaries, a place of his own.

Spengler had almost everything to qualify him as the first of the postwar prophets. His display of esoteric learning made him an expert in the eyes of the half-educated public. His use of such words as "Faustian," "Magian," and "megalopolitan" helped him to become a cult. He combined the authority of the scholar with the vision of the seer. He turned against Darwinism, but did not turn back to religion. He scorned economics, wrote vaguely about "blood" and "race," and called man "a beast of prey." To a generation that reveled in calling itself "lost," Spengler did not offer hope but escape. He had the faculty of making his readers feel that in understanding him they had thereby joined the elect. Of course they could not all become Caesars, but at any rate they would know what to expect and how to adjust themselves to the inevitable. The emergence of Wilson and Lenin appeared to confirm Spengler's prediction about the role great men would play in the twentieth century. His emphasis on practical results appealed to a generation weaned on the pragmatic philosophy of William James. His worship of "technics" suited the scientific temper of the times. But above all Spengler offered a fatalistic formula to replace Western man's lost religious faith. And as his fame spread from defeated Germany to shell-shocked Europe and from shell-shocked Europe to the bewildered United States, it became more and more apparent that nobody had won the war and that everybody had lost it.

· V ·

OTHER VOICES, not speaking from Germany, carried further than Spengler's even before the 1918 Armistice. Although the war had retarded a cultural renaissance in the United States, it had not entirely stifled the creative arts in Europe—especially the art of writing.

By 1917, Europe had already produced three fine, realistic war novels: *Under Fire,* by the Frenchman, Henri Barbusse, depicting the Western Front; *Men in War,* by the Hungarian, Andreas Latzko, depicting the Eastern Front; and the most popular of all war books, *The Adventures of the Good Soldier Schweik,* by the Czech novelist, Yaroslav Hasek. Barbusse and Latzko wrote as revolutionary pacifists. Hasek gave a humorous picture of the typical Austro-Hungarian infantryman, lacking any belief in his superiors or his cause, thinking only of how he could best survive—a sort of Sancho Panza in modern dress. All three of these

*Dada Drawing, 1917, by George Grosz.
From* Fantastic Art, Dada, Surrealism,
*third edition, 1947, Museum of Modern
Art*

books sold by the hundred thousands; their vogue showed how accurately they reflected the popular mood.

The more advanced writers and artists in Europe, addressing themselves to smaller audiences, expressed the same universal sense of confusion, revolt, and anarchy. In Germany, in central Europe, and above all in Paris, which so many Europeans continued to regard as their spiritual home, a new cult that called itself Dada began to attract attention as early as 1916. Some traced the word to the babblings of an infant; others to the Russian word for "yes"—"da." In any case, Dada expressed the mood of many intellectuals—and of a much wider public, too, that saw no sense, no meaning in the war or in the peace; that wanted to defy all authority, all traditions, turn everything upside down, release all suppressions and impulses, and finally turn against even itself. While delegates from all the Allied countries gathered in Paris to write the peace treaties, Dadaists held frantic meetings at which they made speeches, distributed pamphlets, performed plays. Some talent, much humor, and even more egotism went into these affairs. The Dadaist movement had 391 presidents, one of whom, a German, called himself president of the world. The public attended Dadaist meetings chiefly to promote riots, during one of which a Dadaist leader shouted, "You are all idiots. You deserve to be presidents of the Dadaist movement."

Tristan Tzara, a Rumanian poet whose fellow Dadaists called him "the man with the pearl head," read a newspaper at a meeting while an electric bell rang so loud that the audience could not hear a word he said. "All I wanted to convey," Tzara explained afterward in an article in *Vanity Fair*, "was simply that my presence on the stage, the sight of my face and movements, ought to satisfy people's curiosity and that anything I might have said really had no importance." Picabia, a Dada artist, used to execute chalk drawings on a blackboard and then erase them to prove that the picture was valid for only two hours.

In 1916, Tzara had written a Dadaist play, *The First Celestial Adven-*

ture of Mr. Fire-Extinguisher, which he described as "a boxing match with words. The characters, confined in sacks and trunks, recite their parts without moving, and one can easily imagine the effect this produced—performed in a greenish light—on the already excited public. It was impossible to hear a single word of the play."

Tzara cited the following brief sketch as typically Dada. Two people, one carrying a letter, appear from opposite sides of the stage and meet in the center. The one without the letter says: "The post office is across the street."

"What difference does that make to me?"
"Excuse me, I saw a letter in your hand. I thought—"
"It isn't what you think, it's what you know."

The Dada movement produced few books, plays, pictures, or musical creations; it preferred to go in for meetings, magazines, and manifestoes. The Dadaists declared that all true Dadaists opposed Dada. "Dada," they went on, "is against the high cost of living." "Dada is a virgin microbe." When a Paris journalist said Dada was not to be talked about any more, a leading Dadaist replied, "If you must speak of Dada, you must speak of Dada. If you must not speak of Dada, you must still speak of Dada." Prewar futurism brought forth postwar Dadaism and Dadaism, in turn, developed into surrealism, the first of the postwar intellectual movements in Paris. The importance of the Dada movement lay in the very fact that it produced nothing; that it turned against art, against the intellect, against itself. The talented men and women who organized it had reached a small public before the war; they again found that same small public after the war. But during their brief period of complete revolt they expressed, for the first and last time in their lives, an almost universal mood. The mood itself did not—could not—last, but the Dada movement during its short life span reflected the empty anarchy that the war had left in Europe.

Georges Hugnet, a French surrealist painter and critic, contributed an historical essay on Dada to *Fantastic Art, Dada, Surrealism,* published by the Museum of Modern Art in New York. "Dada," wrote Hugnet, "is ageless, it has no parents, but stands alone, making no distinction between what is and what is not. It approves while denying, it contradicts itself, and acquires new force by this very contradiction. Its frontal attack is that of a traitor stealing up from behind. It turns against itself, it indulges in self-destruction, it sees red, its despair is its genius. There is no hope, all values are leveled to a universal monotony, there is no longer a difference between good and evil—there is only an awareness. Dada is a taking-stock, and as such it is as irreparable as it is ridiculous. It knows only itself."

The Dadaists not only rebelled against the realism and naturalism of the nineteenth century; they also turned against those twentieth-century writers and artists who tried to reach the widest possible public through vulgarizing every field of intellectual and artistic creation. The extremes finally met. European Dadaists considered George Harriman's popular American Krazy Kat comic strip an expression of their spirit while the general European public which ignored prewar futurism and postwar surrealism responded to Dada as deep responds to deep—or shallow to shallow. And it was Paris, scene of so many Dada meetings, that witnessed the greatest Dada show of all when the statesmen of the victorious Allies gathered there to write the peace.

SUMMING UP

OF COURSE the outbreak of peace led to a sense of letdown in western Europe, which had stood to lose so much and gain so little from the war. Those leaders who called for a finish fight reaped as they had sown. Farther east, the Allied victory bore more unexpected fruit. Former victims of imperial tyranny used their newly gained independence to settle their own problems in their own way. In spite of the losses they had suffered, their relative strength had increased, not only as compared with their former overlords but as compared with their western allies. Pilsudski and the Poles kicked over the traces and ran off in all directions. In Rumania and Yugoslavia, the application of "self-determination" did not solve the question of national minorities; it simply raised that question in new forms as Rumanians oppressed Magyars while Serbs lorded it over Croats and Slovenes. Only Masaryk and the Czechoslovaks put Wilsonian theory into practice.

No power on earth could have brought peace to the shell-shocked Europeans so soon after the Armistice, yet the statesmen of the victorious Allies tried to write such a peace at once. Although western Europe had little authority in eastern Europe and still less authority in Russia, Wilson nevertheless tried to make a universal League of Nations the cornerstone of a peace structure that he lacked the power to erect. The war had not made the world safe for democracy, or for anything else. The international anarchy that had led to war in 1914 had taken a new and more ominous form.

2

Settlement with Germany

*How the victorious Allies wrote the Covenant of
the League of Nations and drew up the final terms
of the settlement with Germany.*

PREVIEW

THE Paris Peace Conference presented all the victorious Allies with
unique and varied opportunities to achieve conflicting national ambitions. Clemenceau saw France putting Germany permanently in its
place. Lloyd George saw the British Empire sitting permanently on top
of the world. Wilson saw the League of Nations guaranteeing permanent peace for the United States. The Japanese and Italian delegations
hoped to secured permanent possession of the territorial loot that their
allies had promised them during the darkest hours of the war. The
nationalist spirit flared up everywhere—in France, in Britain, and in the
United States, where Wilson's Democratic Party had just lost control
of Congress. Yet Wilson came to Paris with a subservient delegation and
the conviction that he and he alone spoke for all the common people
everywhere. After touring the European capitals for a month, he got
down to the business of peacemaking and during the first month of negotiations persuaded the Conference to approve a draft Covenant of the
League of Nations. He went back for a month to the United States,
where the tide continued to run against him, and on his return to Paris
suspected his fellow diplomats of having let him down. But he and
Clemenceau agreed, for different reasons, to reach a quick German
settlement. While they were completing the details, Orlando of Italy
walked out on them. The Japanese threatened to quit too unless they
got special rights in Shantung Province. On May 7 the Allies handed the
Germans their final terms, which the Germans finally accepted, with a
gulp. The Germans believed that acceptance would at least bring bread.
The Allies began to wonder if acceptance would even bring peace.

· I ·

THE QUALITIES that made President Wilson a great war leader unfitted
him to make the peace. His lofty expression of war aims had unified

27

the American people, boosted the flagging morale of the Allies, encouraged the German people to turn against their leaders, and counteracted Lenin's propaganda for revolution. The signing of the Armistice changed almost everything. Wilson's moral arrogance—a priceless wartime asset—became his principal peacetime liability. He infuriated the Republican opposition at home; he bewildered the Allied leaders in Europe; to the Germans he seemed half dupe and half hypocrite; to Lenin he looked like a Presbyterian Kerensky.

As Wilson saw himself, the Armistice marked the beginning, not the end, of his usefulness to mankind. He—almost alone among the Allied leaders—had felt that the war marked the end of an old era and the start of a new one. Having given the conflict a positive purpose, he stood prepared to lead the world to a new kind of peace, avoiding Europe's bankrupt old order and Russia's bloody new one. "The select classes of mankind are no longer the governors of mankind. The fortunes of mankind are now in the hands of the plain people of the world. Satisfy them and you have not only satisfied their confidence, but established peace. Fail to satisfy them, and no arrangement that you can make will either set up or steady the peace of the world."

President Wilson's immoderate personality put his moderate program in a false light. "What we seek," he declared, "is the reign of law, based upon the consent of the governed, and sustained by the organized opinion of mankind." Like his Fourteen Points, these words could mean much or little, and in the case of the Fourteen Points, they meant what the victorious Allies chose them to mean.

For the Supreme Allied War Council had taken pains, in late October and early November, to agree among themselves and with the President on just what the Fourteen Points really spelled out. Colonel House got Frank I. Cobb, editor of the New York *World,* and Walter Lippmann to prepare a detailed commentary on each of the Points, and after the Allied representatives had approved, Wilson confirmed their understanding. This commentary weakened or qualified all of the Fourteen Points, except the final one proposing the League of Nations. For instance, "open covenants of peace openly arrived at" did not forbid secret consultation and negotiation. It forbade only secret treaties. Freedom of trade did not outlaw tariffs. It merely pledged League members to extend "most favored nation treatment" to all their fellows. The impartial adjustment of colonial claims referred only to the disposition of German colonies. It left all existing colonial empires intact. The evacuation of Russia did not cover all the territory of the former Tsarist Empire. The dismemberment of the Ottoman Empire did not mean that the Sultan's former subjects should all become self-governing. Just the opposite. The commentary declared that France should have mandates

BETTMANN ARCHIVE

Victory: Paris, 1918

over Syria and Lebanon; Britain over Palestine, Mesopotamia, and Arabia. And, to top it all off, the exact definition of "freedom of the seas" and the precise nature of Allied claims upon Germany for reparations were to be settled at some future time. But neither the general public nor the German representatives had any inkling of these interpretations of the Fourteen Points.

This preliminary agreement did not eliminate all conflict among the major Allies. The French saw in the Peace Conference a unique opportunity to protect themselves against German aggression for a long, long time to come. Many living Frenchmen had seen German armies twice invade their country, and only a miracle had saved them the second time. They could not assume that Britain, Russia, and the United States would always and automatically come to their aid, or that such aid would always and automatically protect them. The League of Nations looked well enough on paper. What would it amount to in another twenty or thirty years? The best hope for France seemed to lie in crippling Germany for as long a time as possible. In any event, the French wanted to know where they stood. They demanded a clear conference agenda and a precise, stern treaty. They would take an extreme position at the opening of the Conference and do their best to hold it throughout.

The British, on the other hand, achieved most of their war aims with the signing of the Armistice. German sea power no longer existed. British and Dominion troops had occupied most of Germany's former colonies. Germany no longer threatened to dominate Europe. The chief danger lay farther east, in Russia, where the Bolsheviks were planning to subvert Europe, Asia, the whole world. A lesser danger lay just across the Channel, in France, where certain nationalists seemed to feel that their country could regain the commanding European position it had held in Napoleon's time. For the moment, however, defeat had weakened Germany, revolution had weakened Russia, victory had weakened France.

Britain's leaders recognized that the Peace Conference offered them a unique opportunity. They did not propose to surrender any of their Empire or to reduce their Navy or their merchant marine. Indeed, they planned to add to their overseas territories and to the sea power that held their Empire together. But they did not want to destroy Germany. British exporters had long sold more goods to Germany than to any other European country. British consumers had come to depend on Germany for many low-priced, high-quality imports. A prosperous, peaceful Germany in a prosperous, stable Europe would increase Britain's security and prosperity. During the war—and even before it—some of Britain's most enlightened statesmen had begun to prepare drafts for a League of Nations that would stabilize a world order highly favorable to themselves and at the same time allow some scope for evolutionary change. Winston Churchill, however, warned that "a League of Nations is no substitute for the supremacy of the British fleet."

The Peace Conference also presented a unique opportunity to the United States. The American people needed no foreign territories: the Philippines had already cost far more than they were worth. The American people needed no reparations: they were producing more wealth than they consumed. No foreign country threatened American soil in any future that anyone could foresee. But the war had proved that the American people had an immeasurable stake in world peace and therefore had a vital interest in restoring order in Europe and maintaining stability everywhere. Wilson, however, refused to see this in terms of practical, national interest. He preferred to deal in moral abstractions. He differed from his nineteenth-century British masters in that he believed his own propaganda whereas their moralizing always promoted their Empire's welfare.

The kind of world settlement Wilson proposed called upon the British to give up—in theory at any rate—their claim to control the seas. He demanded that the victorious French respect the defeated Germans' right to self-determination. He demanded that the former subject races of the Austro-Hungarian Monarchy show the same magnanimity to their former masters—and to one another. Although the principal Allied Powers had written their own interpretation of the Fourteen Points in respect to Europe and the Middle East, Wilson's doctrine of self-determination, proclaimed as a universal principle, attacked the very foundations of their colonial empires. Since the United States needed no more territory and possessed no colonial empire to speak of, Wilson's program required Europe's statesmen to make greater sacrifices and take greater risks than he called upon his own country to assume.

Because economics bored Wilson as much as politics interested him, he failed to outline an economic program for the United States as comprehensive as the political program he outlined for Europe. The economic power of the United States had made it possible for the Allies to crush the Central Powers completely. But the war had weakened all Europe to such an extent that only the economic power of the United States could put the Old World on its feet again. In so far as Wilson gave any thought to economic matters, he regarded them as quite secondary to politics. He never understood the necessary part eastern Europe played as a source of foodstuffs for western Europe and as a market for the products of West European factories. Nor did he see that his kind of world settlement required economic action by a prosperous United States to match the political action he demanded of a bankrupt Europe.

Wilson's first published work as a Princeton undergraduate dealt with Bismarck. Forty years on, Wilson could have instructed the Iron Chancellor in the art of popular persuasion. For where Bismarck boasted that blood and iron would cow the German people and crush their neighbors, Wilson promoted the national interests of the United States through sheer moral fervor. But Wilson did not see the connection between moral fervor and national interest. Neither did he know, as Bismarck knew, how to limit his ambitions. Perhaps because Bismarck relied on sheer force, he understood the limitations of force. Wilson, relying on moral fervor, set no limits to his ambition—and there lay his unique strength as well as his fatal weakness. Wilson's ambitions for the United States outsoared Bismarck's ambitions for Germany, and Wilson proposed to achieve those ambitions by asserting moral principles that affected the vital interests of other nations much more than they affected the vital interests of the United States. His personal conviction that through him the voiceless millions of the whole world spoke enhanced his sense of power. Surely the peacemakers must listen and obey.

· II ·

THE 1918 Congressional elections in the United States showed that the American people had turned away from Wilson before the fighting had stopped in Europe. Theodore Roosevelt jubilantly told the world, "Our allies and our enemies and Mr. Wilson himself should all understand that Mr. Wilson has no authority whatever to speak for the American people at this time. His leadership has just been emphatically repudiated by them." Most of Wilson's closest friends and oldest advisers urged him to stay in Washington and fight from there for the League of Nations and the kind of peace treaty he wanted. How little they knew their man. Wilson could no more have stayed away from the Peace Conference, which also drew up the Covenant of the League of Nations, than Lenin could have missed the Bolshevik seizure of power in Petrograd. From boyhood Wilson had specialized in writing constitutions and presiding over debating societies. The opportunity had now come to write a constitution for the whole world and to preside over the greatest conference in history.

When President McKinley appointed a delegation to negotiate peace with Spain, he named two Republican Senators and one Democrat. The delegation that Wilson appointed to assist him in making the peace did not include a single Senator and only one Republican—nice old Henry White, whose lifetime in the diplomatic service had made him, according to Taft, "more of an Englishman than an American." Wilson ignored two outstanding members of the party that now controlled both houses of Congress: ex-President Taft and ex-Senator Root, both of whom had sponsored the League to Enforce Peace. He also snubbed Senator Henry Cabot Lodge, new chairman of the Foreign Relations Committee, who offered the tart comment that Wilson appointed himself four times— and Henry White. This was not quite true. Secretary of State Lansing opposed the League of Nations, but Wilson had to include him because all the other foreign secretaries also attended. The disgusted Taft accused Wilson of wanting to "hog the whole show." Will Rogers remarked that Wilson must have said to the Republicans: "I tell you what, we'll split 50-50. I'll go and you fellows can stay."

Colonel House acted as the President's closest adviser and second in command. General Tasker H. Bliss, a classical scholar, represented the military. Although one critic described his presence at the Peace Conference as "about as fitting as that of an army mule would be in a church choir," Bliss proved the most astute member of the five-man delegation. Of Wilson's decision to go to Paris he said, "Jove should not come down from Olympus." He took a humane if pessimistic view of the prospects. "We are going to vote the proxies of millions of dead men," he wrote Newton D. Baker in December, 1918, "who have died in the belief that what we do now will make it impossible for the same awful sacrifice to be demanded of their children." Bliss had his doubts about the ability of the five-man American peace commission which seemed to Taft "a cheap lot." Bliss observed, "I am disgusted to see how hazy and vague our ideas are. We are going up against the wiliest politicians in Europe. There will be nothing vague or hazy about their ideas."

And so it proved. The prospect that Wilson would attend the Conference as chief of the American delegation distressed the Allied statesmen —at first. Lloyd George warned his fellow delegates that the American President no longer controlled Congress. Clemenceau feared that Wilson's presence might lead Poincaré, as President of the Republic, to take charge of the French delegation. But he felt a lot better when Wilson gladly consented to have the Conference meet in Paris and reluctantly agreed that Clemenceau must therefore preside.

The infatuated American President rarely indulged in self-pity. He assured the experts who accompanied him to Europe on the *George Washington* that "the men whom we are about to deal with do not represent their own people." When it was suggested that Lloyd George might not accept his plans for a League of Nations, Wilson angrily declared that if that happened, "I shall look him in the eye and say, 'Damn you, if you do not accept the League, I shall go to the people of Great Britain and say things to them that will shake your government.'" Wilson ignored the fact that the British people at that very moment were showing more enthusiasm for hanging the Kaiser than for creating the League. The European statesmen at Paris cherished no such wishful illusions concerning the United States. They understood that the American people had just repudiated Wilson's leadership at the polls; he chose to close his ears, eyes, and mind to the spirit of vengeance that naturally possessed so many war-weary people in the victorious lands.

Of his fellow Americans he remarked with a naïveté that did more credit to his heart than to his head, "We would be the only disinterested people at the Peace Conference." He kept impressing on his experts: "Tell me what's right and I'll fight for it." But misgivings, too powerful to suppress, ate at his introverted spirit. "It is a great thing you have done," he told George Creel of the Committee on Public Information aboard the *George Washington,* "but I am wondering if you have not unconsciously spun a net for me from which there is no escape. It is to America that the whole world turns today, not only with its wrongs, but with its hopes and grievances. The hungry expect us to feed them, the roofless look to us for shelter, the sick of heart and body depend upon us for cure. All of these expectations have in them the quality of terrible urgency. There must be no delay. It has been so always. People will endure their tyrants for years, but they will tear their deliverers to pieces if a millennium is not created immediately. Yet you know and I know that these ancient wrongs, these present unhappinesses, are not to be remedied in a day or with a wave of the hand. What I fear to see—

with all my heart I hope that I am wrong—is a tragedy of disappointment."

Wilson, at his best, saw further and felt more deeply than any other
chief of state in Paris. But no other chief of state had surrounded himself with so weak a delegation as the five-man American Commission.
Its strength lay among its expert advisers, and the notion that they knew
nothing about Europe was just as false as the notion that Europe's leaders knew nothing about Wilson's weakened domestic position and the
crucial, treaty-making power of the Senate. The other delegations regarded the American experts as the best in Paris. As for Wilson's shaky
domestic support, it came in for constant discussion in the popular press
as well as among the leading delegates of every country.

Wilson's party landed at Brest on Friday, December 13. "Down the
gangplank," wrote William Allen White, "walked this Yankee knight
errant followed by a desperate crew of college professors in horn-
rimmed glasses, carrying textbooks, encyclopedias, maps, charts, graphs,
statistics, all sorts of literary crowbars with which to pry up the boundaries of Europe and move them around in the interests of justice, as
seen through the Fourteen Points." The President considered thirteeen
his lucky number and therefore welcomed their arrival date as a happy
omen. "If we do not heed the mandates of mankind," he declared upon
landing, "we shall make ourselves the most conspicuous and deserved
failures in the history of the world." The French wanted to rush the
President on an extensive tour of the devastated regions and resented his
refusal. "The French want me to see red," Wilson coolly remarked. What
the French did not know or could not believe was Wilson's other remark: "I could not despise the Germans more than I do." Lloyd George,
who perhaps understood human nature better than Wilson, accepted a
.similar invitation when it came his way. But Wilson preferred to devote
his entire first month in Europe to a triumphal tour of the great capitals—
Paris, London, Rome—soaking up such popular adulation as no man had
ever before received. With his new pretty wife smiling at his side he
found it easy to believe that these crowds represented all of Europe and
accepted all that he stood for. Certainly many, probably most, Europeans admired Wilson as a symbol. But that did not mean that they had
confidence in his ability to put his program through. Nor did it mean
that the mood in which they greeted him would last as long as the mood
in which these same people also supported in their own countries' leaders who favored a vengeful peace.

On January 12 the "Preliminary Conference of the Allied and Associated Powers" finally assembled in Paris. Clemenceau came as close as
any of the Allied leaders to expressing the hopes of the Allied peoples
when he declared in his opening speech as chairman: "The achievement

of our purpose is not possible unless we remain firmly united. Here we have met as friends; from here we must go as brothers. That is the thought that is uppermost in my heart today and I would add that all else must be subordinated to the necessity of a union growing ever closer between the people who have taken part in the Great War." For once, the supreme realist at the Conference had indulged a romantic mood, worthy of Wilson at his wooliest. Everyone wanted the peace Wilson preached. Everyone hoped for the unity that Clemenceau called for. But few of the delegates of the major Powers, and fewer still from the smaller ones, were prepared to make the sacrifices that peace and unity demanded.

More than a hundred years had passed since Europe last tried to make a general peace after a general war. In 1814, the four Great Powers chiefly responsible for the defeat of Napoleon summoned the Congress of Vienna to establish a "firm peace based on a just equilibrium of strength between the Powers." Britain, Prussia, Russia, and Austria all sent their Foreign Ministers. Talleyrand attended as the representative of defeated France, and before the Congress of Vienna ended, Talleyrand had transformed the Big Four into the Big Five. The Vienna settlement paid little attention to the principle of nationality and self-determination of peoples. It partitioned Poland among Prussia, Austria, and Russia. It awarded large sections of Italy to Austria. But it did establish a balance-of-power peace that lasted for a century.

The proceedings at Paris, more than a century later, took quite a different course. The Austro-Hungarian Empire had disintegrated. Defeated Germany played no part in the deliberations. In 1815 the victorious Allies restored the King of France to the throne and dealt with him as an equal. A century later the victorious Allies demanded that Germany set up a Republic and then held the new regime responsible for the actions of the Kaiser. No representative of the new Germany played the part in Paris that Talleyrand played in Vienna. Nobody at Paris called for a balance-of-power peace. Instead, self-determination of nations became the new watchword. Yet Russia, which had lost more men than any of the other Allies, was excluded from the Peace Conference whereas two non-European Powers, Japan and the United States, had two delegates each on the Supreme Council of Ten. The other six came from Britain, France, and Italy. Much of the old diplomacy had gone, and much of Europe's former power had gone with it. But a few Great Powers still tried to decide the fate of the world.

The Supreme Council of Ten, consisting of the head delegates and Foreign Ministers of Britain, France, Italy, Japan, and the United States, put the preparation of a League of Nations Covenant first on their agenda. This commission, with Wilson in the chair, held ten night

BETTMANN ARCHIVE

An American Sentry Stands Watch on the Rhine near Coblenz

meetings, totaling thirty hours, and on February 14 Wilson read the text of the complete Covenant on which his commission representing fourteen nations had unanimously agreed. Long preparation had gone into the final draft, after Wilson and House had spent months drawing up an American blueprint, based on many features of the League to Enforce Peace. The British delegation arrived with the so-called Phillimore Report, which drew from the work of Lord Robert Cecil and General Smuts, of South Africa, who said, "Europe is being liquidated and the League of Nations must be heir to this great estate." All these men as well as Léon Bourgeois of France contributed to the Paris Covenant. No individual, no nation could claim sole authorship. "Practically nothing," wrote Wilson's biographer, Ray Stannard Baker, "not a single idea in the Covenant of the League was original with the President." Wilson, however, could justly claim chief sponsorship. "A living thing is born," he announced as he finished reading. The next day he sailed for the United States, promising to return within a month. He had domestic business to settle and he wanted to present the draft of the Covenant, in person, to the American people.

· III ·

To ALL APPEARANCES Wilson had won the first round. He had got quick unanimous agreement on his cherished League of Nations, while the business of making peace proceeded much more slowly. The Conference suffered chiefly from the lack of a clear program. Back in November, Jules Jusserand, the French Ambassador to the United States, had submitted a memorandum to the White House proposing that the victorious Allies agree at once to impose a preliminary settlement and then arrange for a general congress that would include neutral and enemy countries to work out a wider permanent treaty. Jusserand wanted the Supreme War Council of the five major Powers to agree on a timetable to break up Germany, to partition the Ottoman Empire, and to scrap all their secret wartime treaties. But Jusserand recognized that his bold program meant shelving the Fourteen Points, which the principal Allied Powers had already reinterpreted to suit their own interests. According to Jusserand the Fourteen Points—or "propositions," as he preferred to call them—"cannot furnish a concrete basis for the labors of the Conference." He foresaw them eventually resuming "their full strength in the matter of the future settlement of public law," but for the moment regarded them as "one of the difficulties that might obstruct the Allies." The British did not care for this proposal. It encouraged a peace of revenge, chiefly beneficial to France. Wilson liked it even less. The possible elimination of his treasured Fourteen Points irked him so deeply that he never even replied to Jusserand, thereby missing the chance to scuttle the embarrassing secret treaties and to give the peacemakers both a timetable and a purpose. Wilson's friend Colonel House already showed symptoms of independence. He believed "that it was more important to bring about peace simply than it was to haggle over details." He preferred immediate peace and order to "a better peace and delay."

Wilson had other plans. He regarded himself as the champion of the New Order; Clemenceau and the others as champions of the Old: "The past and present are in deadly grapple." He aimed "to do away with an old order and establish a new one." He resented the implication that he had no program. He insisted that he had defined his principles and had surrounded himself with experts to put those principles into effect. If Wilson erred, it was not in opposing French ideas and French procedures; it was in failing to make his own ideas and procedures more clear. He recognized more clearly than any statesman at Paris that the Conference must take account of public opinion, yet he felt he had only to state a proposition once to lodge it forever in the public mind.

More than five hundred correspondents from all over the world were describing the progress of the Conference. American reporters sent home seventy thousand to eighty thousand words a day by cable and several times as much by mail. Millions of Americans read these dispatches and their opinions, in turn, brought pressure upon Congress. Yet Wilson seldom took the press into his confidence. He did not tell the American correspondents how hard he had fought to make news available to them. He did not make friends easily after the fashion of Taft; he did not turn his own personality inside out after the fashion of Roosevelt, who had specialized in exploiting what the press of the United States could do for the President of the United States.

Wilson made little effort to cultivate individuals or organizations capable of explaining him to the people. Clemenceau and Lloyd George never forgot the importance of the press, and above all of the men and women who work for it. During the war Wilson proved himself a propaganda genius, talking to the German people over the heads of their rulers. He devoted far less effort, during the Paris negotiations, to reaching his own people and the people of Allied lands through the ever-present and all-powerful correspondents who would have liked nothing better than to describe how the new diplomacy worked. But Wilson kept his aspirations under his hat. He wanted no part of the old diplomacy, which specialized in horse trading and reached its decisions by a haggling and balancing of national interests. Wilson wanted the new diplomacy to specialize in fact finding and to reach its decisions on the basis of principle. Experts reported on every disputed area and their findings served as the basis for the final decisions.

Little of this, however, got into the press. The Paris newspapers supported Clemenceau and turned the weapon of ridicule against Wilson. The President had become accustomed to rough treatment in the American press. The attacks of George Harvey and William Randolph Hearst vindicated his confidence in his own virtue. But when the Paris press made fun of him as an irritating, comical professor he became so angry that he threatened at one point to move the whole Conference to Switzerland.

What a contrast to Clemenceau, who thrived on abuse and made copy as instinctively as he breathed. Young John Maynard Keynes, economic adviser to the British delegation, wrote of Clemenceau in his *Economic Consequences of the Peace*: "He had one illusion—France; and one disillusion—mankind, including Frenchmen. . . . One could not despise Clemenceau or dislike him, but only take a different view as to the nature of civilized man or indulge, at least, a different hope." Wilson found Clemenceau a difficult pupil: "We spend an hour reasoning with Clemenceau, getting him around to an agreement, and find when we go back to the original question Clemenceau stands just where he did at the beginning." Of Lloyd George and Wilson Clemenceau remarked, "Lloyd George believes himself to be Napoleon, but Wilson believes himself to be Jesus Christ." Wilson's own words and actions justified this verdict, especially when he analyzed Christianity and the League of Nations for his fellow peacemakers: "Why has Jesus Christ so far not induced the world to follow His teachings in these matters? It is because He taught the ideal without devising any practical means of attaining it. That is why I am proposing a practical scheme to carry out His aims." Lloyd George, who quoted this outburst of Wilson's, also noted that: "Clemenceau slowly opened his dark eyes to their widest dimensions and swept them around the Assembly to see how the Christians gathered around the table enjoyed this exposure of the futility of their master."

During Wilson's month of absence in the United States, an anarchist shot at Clemenceau, leaving a bullet in his lung that pained him the rest of his life. "My enemies could never shoot straight," growled the old Tiger. When the government prosecutor asked Clemenceau about punishment for the would-be assassin he received this reply: "When I think of the men who are continually sniping at me from ambush, I am tempted to say that this brave fellow who faced my walking stick with nothing in the way of a weapon save a machine-gun revolver should have conferred upon him some prize of valor, some Grand Cross or other. But I must not be impulsive, the women and the children and all the innocent bystanders who might have been hurt while the fellow was aiming at my miserable old carcass should be considered. Then his poor marksmanship should be taken into account. We have just won the most terrible war in history, yet here is a Frenchman who at point-blank range misses his target six times out of seven. Of course the fellow must be punished for the careless use of a dangerous weapon and for poor marksmanship. I suggest that he be locked up for about eight years, with intensive training in a shooting gallery." The court finally imposed a ten-year sentence.

Stephen Bonsal included this quotation and other statements Clemenceau made to him privately at the time in his book *Unfinished Business*. "I must make a peace," said Clemenceau, "based upon my belief and upon my own experience of the world in which we live. . . . Mr. Wilson has lived in a world that has been fairly safe for democracy; I have lived in a world where it has been good form to shoot a democrat." Yet Clemenceau came to prefer Wilson to Lloyd George because he "wanted the same things that I did, although we were very far apart as to the ways and means by which we could reach the desired end." He continued, "When he first developed his program, it seemed to be perfectly Utopian. I said to him, 'Mr. Wilson, if I accepted what you propose as ample for the security of France, after the millions who have died and the millions who have suffered, I believe, and indeed I hope, that my successor in office would take me by the nape of the neck and have me shot at daylight before the donjon of Vincennes.' After that we began to get together."

Clemenceau also reported to Bonsal, "I told your President that in my judgment the grave fault of his attitude is that he eliminated sentiment and endeavored to efface all memory of the past. A grave, a very grave fault it seems to me. . . . 'M. le Président,' I said to him, 'I speak for our glorious dead who fell in the two wars. For myself I can hold my tongue, but not for them.'" For Bonsal's personal benefit he added this bit of general advice: "Beware of documents: They are the pitfalls and ambuscades which the crafty jugglers of the day plant in the path of the unwary historian, to waylay, in fact, to mislead him. When you come to write, set down what you have seen with your own eyes and what you

have heard with your own ears, and even if you follow this discreet
policy you may wander from the straight and narrow path."

Looking back, a dozen years later, at his experiences in Paris as one
of the experts attached to the British delegation, Harold Nicolson
found that the impressions of fatigue, haste, and confusion predominated. "One writes the sentence," he says in his book *Peacemaking*, " 'It
was a period of unremitting strain.' The sedative notes of such a sentence, as applied to the scurrying cacophany of the Peace Conference,
forces one to smile. Only through the medium of a sound film could any
accurate impression, that sense of riot in a parrot house, be conveyed."
One evening Nicolson met Marcel Proust, unshaven, but wearing a fur
coat and white kid gloves. Proust inquired how the Conference committees worked. "Well," Nicolson replied, "we generally meet at ten.
There are secretaries behind . . ." Proust interrupted, *"Mais non, mais
non. Vous allez trop vite. Recommencez. Vous prenez la voiture de la
Délégation. Vous descendez au Quai d'Orsay. Vous montez l'escalier.
Vous entrez dans la Salle. Et alors? Précisez, mon cher, précisez."* "So I
tell him everything," Nicolson wrote. "The sham cordiality of it all: the
handshakes: the maps: the rustle of papers: the tea in the next room:
the macaroons. He listens enthralled." But if one impression overshadowed all others, it was the sense of time running out.

Another British observer at the Peace Conference, R. B. Mowat, described the procession of visitors that filed through the lobby of the
Hotel Majestic, headquarters of the British delegation. The passage
appears in *European Diplomacy, 1914-1925:* "Through the revolving
door which kept out the icy blast would come men of all nations and all
ranks, pass over the parquet floor, and disappear to their various desti-
nations and appointments. A British Cabinet Minister in a heavy tweed
overcoat; a French officer in full dress uniform—gorgeous epaulettes and
magnificent wide red trousers with a broad black stripe; an Arab prince
in ample, white flowing robes; British officers in plain khaki, with softly
colored ribbons on their breasts and wound-stripes on their sleeves; an
official from the Quai d'Orsay in plain black, looking businesslike and
neat; American naval and military officers, tall straight men, with the
old-fashioned tunic buttoning up to their necks, always looking smart and
efficient. Russians, Poles, Ukrainians, Czechoslovaks, and Serbs, bearded
bourgeois of the black felt hat, the dark overcoat, and the sallow complexion that comes from lack of exercise; Japanese, trim, impassive,
determined; inquisitive-looking Chinese; ruddy Indian princes with
intelligent faces and pleased expressions, wearing their khaki uniform
with a swinging, soldierly bearing; Portuguese officers in light blue,
Italians in gray, French politicians and statesmen with their portfolios,
their swift steps, and their swifter, intelligent glances—the pageant of

the Hotel Majestic displayed a continual procession." Mr. Mowat's account did not mention the fact that the British delegation included an obstetrician, brought along to cope with "disease."

Many observers frankly gave up when they tried to describe what had happened in Paris. "I don't know," they would say, "I was only there." Paris did not conceal its war scars, the results of long-range shelling by the German "Big Bertha" guns. Many of the people remained almost shell-shocked. Crippled soldiers, mourning men and women filled the streets. So did the uniforms of more than a score of countries, old and new. The sessions took place in thickly carpeted rooms, filled with overstuffed, ornate furniture, the windows muffled with heavy hangings. "I don't believe the air in that room has been changed since the time of Louis Philippe," Lloyd George exclaimed after one unusually trying day.

The Conference got plenty of fresh air of other kinds from many quarters. War, victory, and defeat had smashed down walls as well as windows. Every statesman who represented a democracy had always to take account of public opinion at home. Lloyd George heeded the voice of the British people; Clemenceau heeded the voice of the French people—more closely, perhaps, than Wilson heeded the voice of the American people. And from Moscow, the voice of Lenin challenged all the voices raised in Paris. The Russian Bolsheviks had predicted that the Allies would impose the same kind of peace on the defeated Germans that the Germans had imposed on the defeated Russians at Brest-Litovsk. On March 19, Colonel House wrote in his diary: "Rumblings of discontent every day. The people want peace. Bolshevism is gaining ground everywhere. Hungary has just succumbed. We are sitting on an open powder magazine, and someday a spark may ignite it." Less than a week later Lloyd George warned, "The greatest danger that I see in the present situation is that Germany may throw in her lot with Bolshevism and place her resources, her brains, and her vast organizing power at the disposal of the revolutionary fanatics whose dream it is to conquer the world for Bolshevism by force of arms." Le Temps, organ of the French Foreign Office, agreed: "Either Russia will one day be reorganized by the Germans or the Russians will disorganize Europe."

Winston Churchill, now War Minister in the Lloyd George government, beat the war drums for a combined and large-scale military attack upon the Bolsheviks. Lord Riddell described Churchill as having "Bolshevism on the brain. He is mad for operations in Russia." Lloyd George called Churchill "the most formidable and irrepressible protagonist of an anti-Bolshevik war. . . . His ducal blood revolted against the wholesale elimination of Grand Dukes in Russia." On December 31, 1918, Britain's Imperial War Cabinet voted Churchill down when he proposed a collective attack upon the Bolsheviks by the five Great Powers —including, he hoped, the United States. When Wilson returned to Washington in February, Churchill revived the scheme and found an eager disciple in the person of Marshal Foch, who outlined a plan of attack by "all the peoples that lie along the fringe of Russia—all under Allied direction." Foch counted on Poland as the base of operations, but Pilsudski refused to co-operate: first he must seize Galicia.

Originally Foch wanted the two million American troops who had recently landed in France to invade Russia, but President Wilson had different ideas. Back in July, 1918, he confided to House: "I have been sweating blood over the question of what is right and feasible to do in Russia. It goes to pieces like quicksilver under my touch." In January, at the suggestion of Lloyd George, he invited all the warring Russian factions, Bolshevik and non-Bolshevik, to confer on the island of Prinkipo, near Constantinople, about ending the civil war. The Bolsheviks accepted, to all intents and purposes; the anti-Bolsheviks refused, while the press of London and Paris applauded. Foreign Minister Pichon of France declared that his government "would not come to terms with crime," while Lloyd George still insisted, "It is impossible to make peace in Europe without settling the Russian question." President Wilson, again with the approval of Lloyd George, then decided to sound out the Bolshevik leaders, directly but secretly, on the possibilities of stopping the civil war and restoring economic relations. The day before he returned to Washington with the first draft of the League Covenant he also assured Churchill that the Conference would take some kind of action about Russia. Churchill wanted that action to take the form of military attack and became angry when some of his compatriots let the Americans know that a majority in the British Cabinet had already voted him down.

Meanwhile House took advantage of Wilson's absence from Paris to dispatch a fishing expedition of his own to Russian waters. He told Clemenceau that he "had never been in favor of the Prinkipo proposals" and sought some answers to the question of "how to finesse the situation against the Bolsheviks." Balfour sympathized and proposed taking steps "to put the Bolsheviks in the wrong." Lincoln Steffens urged House to send a secret mission to Russia, and House selected William C. Bullitt of the State Department to go and look things over. Bullitt invited Steffens to come along. According to Steffens, "Colonel House had proposed, Lloyd George had planned the visit." Bullitt's instructions "came from House and from the British Prime Minister." He was to question the Bolshevik leaders on the possibilities of an armistice and assure them that if they would agree to stop fighting, the United States would resume

Trotsky Speaks. Moscow, 1919

UNDERWOOD

normal economic relations and press the Allies to remove all troops from Russian soil. Bullitt, a handsome Philadelphia society man still in his twenties, had radical ideas and some experience as a foreign correspondent. Steffens had witnessed the first stages of the Russian Revolution on the spot and liked it. "I have been over into the future, and it works." The two men returned from a week of hasty conferences with Lenin and other Russian leaders recommending immediate negotiations. Bullitt drafted a proposed declaration of policy to be issued by the Allied and Associated Powers proposing that the Bolsheviks proclaim an armistice and that the Allies lift their economic blockade.

Wilson and Lloyd George both liked Bullitt's proposals, but the British Prime Minister could not endorse them. The Northcliffe press and the less sensational, more reactionary Tory newspapers were featuring Bolshevik atrocity stories, with special emphasis on the nationalization of women. They lumped Lenin and Trotsky together as bloody extremists although Bullitt and Steffens reported that Lenin had turned moderate and seemed prepared to admit foreign capital, whereas Trotsky and the young Red Army leaders had become the new irreconcilables. It was this noisy, ruthless, and boastful type of revolutionary leadership that infuriated such sober journalists as Wickham Steed of the London *Times*. Steed, a good friend of House, assailed the Bullitt proposals in a *Times* editorial that led Lloyd George to comment: "As long as the British press is doing this kind of thing, how can you expect me to be sensible about Russia?" When questioned in the House of Commons about the Bullitt mission, Lloyd George blandly replied that he knew nothing of "the journey some boys were reported to have made to Russia."

Under these conditions, the Paris Peace Conference had to forget about normalizing relations with the Bolsheviks. The best it could do was make it possible for the Norwegian explorer, Dr. Fridtjof Nansen, to get some relief to the Russian people and provide Russian exiles with so-called "Nansen passports." Bullitt reported that the part of Russia under Bolshevik control had no gasoline or coal. Only fifty-five hundred of the twenty-two thousand locomotives the Russians possessed before the war remained in service. Twenty-three separate civil wars had ravaged the farms. The city population simply starved.

It so happened that Admiral Kolchak's anti-Bolshevik armies in south Russia had advanced about a hundred miles when Bullitt and Steffens returned to Paris. The Bolsheviks controlled Petrograd and Moscow, but their authority did not extend over most of the territory the Tsar had ruled. Bullitt and Steffens seemed to be betting on the wrong horse. Their judgment appeared faulty, perhaps even subversive. Steffens, in his autobiography, recalled that "Bullitt asked me in surprise why it was that, having been so elated by the prospect of Russia, we were glad to be back in Paris. I thought it was because, though we had been to heaven, we were so accustomed to our own civilization that we preferred hell. We were ruined; we could recognize salvation, but could not be saved." In May, Bullitt quit his State Department job in disgust. He opposed the decision of the Conference to let the Japanese remain in Shantung and to award the Tyrol to Italy. But it was Russia, he wrote to Wilson, that furnished "the acid test of good will," and the President had failed to meet that test. "I am sorry," his letter concluded, "that you did not fight our fight to the finish and that you had so little faith in the millions of men, like myself, in every nation who had faith in you." He upbraided Wilson for not having made his fight in the open and predicted "a new century of war."

· IV ·

THE FIGHT Wilson had put up for the League Covenant in Paris left him in no mood to conciliate either Bullitt or his Republican opponents. Arriving in Boston, Senator Lodge's home town, the President paraded through the streets, and delivered his first oration in behalf of the League before a cheering audience. He then proceeded to Washington, where, at Colonel House's suggestion, he had invited the two Foreign Relations Committees of Congress to dine with him and discuss the draft of the Covenant. Senator Borah refused to attend because he wanted to feel free to attack it. Senators Lodge and Knox did not utter a single word. After making notes on the questions and suggestions thrown at him Wilson agreed to propose four changes, largely inspired by Taft. They called for specific recognition of the Monroe Doctrine, definite machinery for American withdrawal, exemption of domestic issues, notably the tariff, from the control of the League, and the provision that the United States could not be forced to accept any mandate against its will. After midnight, as the Senators left, Wilson asked Lodge: "Do you think that with these changes and if the Foreign Relations Committee approves it, the Senate will ratify the Covenant?" The wily Lodge spoke for the first time: "If the Foreign Relations Committee approves it, I think there is no doubt of ratification."

Before another week had passed, the Republican leaders in the Senate made it clear that neither the Senate Foreign Relations Committee nor two thirds of the Senate members would give that approval. Thirty-nine Republican Senators—two more than the one third needed to defeat the Covenant—signed a statement declaring that "the Constitution of the League of Nations in the form now proposed to the Peace Conference should not be accepted by the United States"; that "the urgent business of negotiating peace terms with Germany" should receive immediate attention; and that "the proposal for a league of nations to ensure the permanent peace of the world should then be taken up for careful consideration."

Far from mollifying Wilson, this declaration made him all the more determined to weave the Peace Treaty and the League Covenant inextricably together. He assumed that if he tied the League to the Peace Treaty, the Senate would have to take them both, and like it. "When that Treaty comes back," said Wilson as he embarked for Europe again, "gentlemen on this side will find the Covenant not only in it, but so many threads of the Treaty tied to the Covenant that you cannot dissect the Covenant from the Treaty without destroying the vital structure." But Wilson's prestige in Paris had suffered and his temper did not improve when he discovered what had happened in his absence. He had understood that the Council of Ten would prepare a preliminary, military treaty to be imposed on Germany at once and that on his return they would write the rest of the Treaty, combine it with the Covenant, and lay the whole thing before the representatives of Germany. But the military experts needed more than a month to draw up their preliminary terms, and the French discovered that the war had left Germany in far worse shape than they had imagined when they signed the Armistice. The attempt on Clemenceau's life had taken him out of action for several weeks. Lloyd George had returned to England. On February 22, Foreign Secretary Balfour proposed going ahead with the rest of the

German settlement and asked for reports by March 8. President Wilson's own delegation supported Balfour's action.

House had cabled Wilson: "The French have changed their position and now want to hurry the signing of the peace." He added, "I am doing everything possible to hasten the work of the Conference so that upon your return, terms of preliminary peace will be ready for your consideration." When Wilson did return, on March 13, and learned from House what had happened, he said to Mrs. Wilson: "House has given away everything I won before we left Paris." He found that the Supreme Council had not only begun to consider final peace terms of which he disapproved; the Council also seemed to have side-tracked the League Covenant. But Wilson, Lloyd George, and Clemenceau found themselves in agreement on one point, though for quite different reasons. They all favored peace with Germany as soon as possible.

Clemenceau wanted to move fast in order to impose a stern settlement on Germany without discussion. Lloyd George wanted to move fast in order to save Germany from Communism. Wilson wanted to move fast in order to tie the League Covenant to the Peace Treaty. The attitude of the Republican Senators convinced him that he could not force them to swallow the League of Nations except as part of a general settlement which they would not dare to reject. He also found it easy to believe that he, rather than the Republican Senators, knew what the American people really wanted. As General Bliss wrote to his wife from Paris, "Wilson is certainly a most extraordinary man. Ambassador Jusserand described him to me a few days ago as a man who, had he lived a couple of centuries ago, would have been the greatest tyrant in the world, because he does not seem to have the slightest conception that he can ever be wrong."

For instance, when Wilson read, on his return to Paris, that many Republicans did not like the kind of peace he was trying to make, he burst out, "Those people do not know what the people are thinking. They are as far from the people, the great mass of the people, as I am from Mars. Indeed, they are out of touch with the thinking, forward-looking masses of the people throughout the world. Naturally they cannot understand them." Soon afterward the hard-headed Republican editor, H. H. Kohlsaat of Chicago, wrote to Colonel House: "I think the great mass of the American people are still behind the President—but I fear they are very far behind him."

A poll of American newspaper editors, taken in April by the *Literary Digest*, did not entirely bear out Mr. Kohlsaat's judgment. Seven hundred and eighteen of them wanted the United States to accept the League Covenant Mr. Wilson had brought back from Paris; 418 more wanted to join with reservations; only 181 wanted to stay out. Almost

BETTMANN ARCHIVE

The Big Four. Seated, left to right: Orlando, Lloyd George, Clemenceau, Wilson

all the Democratic editors supported the League; most of the Republicans favored the League with reservations. And the President—after two more months of effort—succeeded in getting the Peace Conference to accept the changes that the Republicans had urged. Ex-President Taft assured him that if the Covenant would recognize the Monroe Doctrine, that alone would ensure ratification by the Senate.

A chronological story of what happened in Paris after Wilson's return would convey, at best, only the confusion in which the Conference reached its final decisions. The Big Four—Wilson, Clemenceau, Lloyd George, and Orlando—took over the responsibilities of the Council of Ten, and when Orlando dropped out for a couple of weeks, the Big Four became the Big Three. Here Clemenceau had one advantage over the other two: he alone spoke both French and English. Lloyd George knew no foreign languages, but he did know Europe, and his years of experience in the House of Commons made him an agile debater. Wilson had no speaking knowledge of any foreign tongue; he had visited the European continent but once in his life, back in the eighteen nineties. The wit of Clemenceau and the intuition of Lloyd George left him dizzy. He kept asking to have things repeated, begging time to frame his replies. Soon after his return from the United States he fell seriously ill of influenza; nervous exhaustion gave the left side of his face a permanent twitch. The opposition of the Republican Senators confirmed Europe's impression that he did not speak for all the American people. The fact that he had to request changes in the League Covenant to meet this opposition reduced his bargaining power and his prestige still further.

When the Big Four took peacemaking into their own hands, one question overshadowed all others: what to do about Germany. But before they reached agreement on the German peace terms, they had to take up the secret wartime pledges that Britain and France had made to Italy and Japan; they had to plan the partition of the Austro-Hungarian and Ottoman Empires; they had to do something about reparations and disarmament. They could not take up these matters one at a time; many of them overlapped. But to understand what the peace conference accomplished, its work must be reviewed as if it had fallen into a number of distinct compartments that never existed in fact.

Clemenceau, pressed by Marshal Foch and President Poincaré, wanted to annex the Saar Valley outright; to sponsor a separate Rhineland Republic; to have Allied troops occupy the farther as well as the nearer bank of the Rhine for thirty years. Because these proposals violated the Fourteen Points, Wilson declared: "There will be neither the establishment of an independent state on the left bank nor the occupation of the line of the Rhine, but America and England will sign a treaty with France by which they will engage themselves to support France with all their forces if Germany makes an unprovoked attack upon France." Clemenceau jumped at the offer, on condition that Allied troops should occupy the Rhineland and that the League of Nations should administer the Saar Valley for fifteen years, during which time France should receive the output of the Saar coal mines. Wilson did not like the conditions Clemenceau attached, but he had to accept them to secure approval for the changes he was requesting in the League Covenant. When Poincaré warned Clemenceau that he was promising to quit the Rhineland too soon, Clemenceau replied, "Monsieur le Président, you are younger than I. In fifteen years I shall no longer be. In fifteen years the Germans will not have executed all the clauses of the treaty, and in fifteen years if you do me the honor to come to my tomb, you may say to me, I am convinced, 'We are on the Rhine, and we stay there.'"

Both Houses of the British Parliament quickly ratified the treaty pledging France Anglo-American aid against German aggression. It never got to the Foreign Relations Committee of the United States Senate. This depressed Clemenceau more than it surprised him. At least he had wrung from Wilson concessions that demilitarized the German Rhineland and strengthened the eastern frontier of France. To receive in addition a guarantee of Anglo-American support was perhaps more than he could reasonably expect. Moreover, after weeks of effort, he and Lloyd George had finally persuaded Wilson that the settlement embodied his ideas rather than theirs. It was Lloyd George, not Wilson, who made the most trouble for Clemenceau at this stage of the negotiations, for the volatile little Welshman suddenly decided that they had made too many concessions to France and had penalized Germany too heavily. Too late, Lloyd George tried to persuade Wilson to reverse himself. Wilson "talks a lot of sentimental platitudes," he explained, "but he believes them." As John Maynard Keynes wrote in his *Economic Consequences of the Peace*, "It was harder to de-bamboozle this old Presbyterian than it had been to bamboozle him."

The French at Paris thought chiefly of military security; Wilson thought chiefly of political arrangements; the British delegation concentrated on economics. Lloyd George went along with the political and military settlements that Wilson and Clemenceau reached about the Saar Valley and the Rhineland, but the Big Three failed to come to any agreement on the matter of reparations. Lloyd George had rashly declared during his election campaign that Germany could pay one hundred and twenty billion dollars in reparations. Some French experts put the figure as high as two hundred billions. Wilson agreed with the French that reparations might be extended to include pensions. But when the economic experts sharpened their pencils and got to work, the Big Three recognized that Germany could not possibly pay more than ten to twenty billion dollars over a period of twenty to thirty years.

Norman H. Davis, one of the American financial experts, expressed the problem this way: "Germany can pay only by the labor of its subjects and by becoming prosperous. The imports must be reduced, thereby depriving the Allies of markets, and exports must be increased, thereby causing severe competition with the Allies. The consequence of forcing Germany to a state of maximum efficiency and saving for a long period of years in order to make large reparations payments may cause greater damage to the Allies than the benefits they will receive from the reparation." Or, as Lloyd George put it: "They [the Germans] must pay to the utmost farthing. But the question is how they can be made to pay beyond a certain point. They can pay only by means of gold or goods. We do not mean to take their goods because that would prejudice our trade."

British Treasury experts proposed lumping the payment of German reparations and inter-Allied war debts in a single transaction that would have placed the whole burden, ultimately, upon the United States. The American delegation rejected the plan as firmly as the French opposed any leniency to Germany in any direction. The Big Three therefore fobbed off the whole question of German reparations on a Reparations Commission with almost unlimited power over Germany's economic life. Still more galling to the Germans, Wilson and Lloyd George agreed to include in the final text of the Treaty the following war-guilt clause: "The Allied and Associated Governments affirm and Germany accepts the responsibility of Germany and her allies for causing all the loss and damage to which the Allied and Associated Governments and their nationals have been subjected as a consequence imposed on them by Germany and her allies."

Clemenceau had fought hard for a precise and crushing treaty. He got it—in words. But a spirit of vengeance in the victor hardly encourages a spirit of compliance in the vanquished. It remained for General Tasker H. Bliss of the American delegation to pronounce a more damning judgment on the Paris negotiations than any of his sophisticated, Old World colleagues thought of offering at the time: "Why deceive ourselves? We are making no peace here in Paris. What is there to make it of? We've really seen only five out of another thirty years' war. It looks sometimes as if we were drifting into another dark age."

· V ·

THE Italian member of the Big Four did not allow his three colleagues to spend all their time on the German settlement. Back in January, Wilson had impulsively agreed to support Italy's claim to the Tyrol and its 220,000 German-speaking inhabitants. Wilson liked the cheerful, scholarly Orlando although the two men had to converse through an interpreter. Asked if he spoke English, Orlando replied, "Nothing except these words: eleven o'clock, I don't agree, good-by." But the good-natured Italian Premier kept complaining that his saturnine Foreign Minister, Baron Sonnino, terrorized him.

Having received Wilson's support on the Tyrol, Orlando demanded fulfillment of the rest of the 1915 secret Treaty of London, and more besides. The London treaty promised Italy the Dalmatian coast, the Dodecanese Islands, and an equal share, with Britain and France, in the partition of the Ottoman Empire and of Germany's African colonies. These pledges violated the Fourteen Points, but Orlando had made it plain back in October, 1918, that Italy did not endorse them and that the Austrian settlement did not have to follow the same principles as the settlement with Germany. On the other hand, the British and French could argue that the Italians had violated the Treaty of London long since when they waited for more than a year, after declaring war on Austria, before even breaking relations with Germany.

The British and French also pointed out that the collapse of Austria and the emergence of the new South Slav Kingdom of Serbs, Croats, and Slovenes had changed everything, to which Orlando replied, "As far as these people are concerned, they have merely taken the place of the Austrians." He said the Italians had fought for "*Sacro Egoismo*"—which included naval and economic control of the Adriatic and no nonsense about the Fourteen Points. "After a successful war in which Italy lost some five hundred thousand killed and some nine hundred thousand badly wounded," he argued, "to revert to a worse situation would not be explainable to the Italian people—for, after all, Austria had offered them the Adige and the islands—and they would not understand why Italy had entered the war." Thwarted on the Dalmatian coast, Orlando demanded the port of Fiume, which had an Italian population but which had never been promised to Italy. Wilson showed some sympathy for Orlando's claim but presently changed his mind, and when Orlando refused to back down Wilson appealed over his head, through the press, to the Italian people. Orlando quit Paris in a rage, and the Italian Chamber of Deputies gave him a 382-40 vote of confidence while Italian mobs shouted, "Fiume or death" and "Down with Wilson."

The Greeks and Japanese took quick and simultaneous advantage of the Italian walkout. Premier Venizelos of Greece asked the Big Three to permit Greek troops to land in the predominantly Greek city of Smyrna. Wilson endorsed this appeal to the principle of self-determination. Clemenceau liked the idea of giving the troublesome Orlando his come-uppance. Lloyd George, who did not forget that Venizelos had backed the British cause throughout the war, knew that Britain's strategic position in the eastern Mediterranean required a strong and friendly Greece. When Orlando returned to Paris on May 5, Wilson, Clemenceau, and Lloyd George had already committed themselves. Ten days later, Greek troops went ashore at Smyrna while British, French, and American warships stood by.

While Venizelos persuaded the Big Three to give Greece a share of Turkey's Asiatic possessions, Baron Makino, head of the Japanese delegation, secured a privileged position for his country in the Chinese province of Shantung. Earlier in the Conference he had asked to have the League of Nations Covenant amended to include an endorsement of "the principle of the equality of Nations and the just treatment of their nationals." The British Dominions and the United States opposed the immigration of Orientals. Organized labor feared the competition of Chinese and Japanese workers, and Wilson knew that the Senate would surely reject the Covenant if it included the pledge Makino asked for. Worse yet, he knew that the vast majority of the American people felt the same way. For once, the voice of the people and the voice of his own conscience spoke a different language, and for once he blurted out a rational response: "How can you treat on its merits in this quiet room a question which will not be treated on its merits when it gets out of this room?" It all depended on whose ox was being gored. Wilson never thought to raise such questions in connection with the French attitude toward Germany or the Italian attitude toward Fiume, and when Clemenceau or Orlando raised them he slapped them down. But as presiding officer of the League Commission before which Makino appeared,

Wilson did not have to go on record himself. The unpleasant duty of speaking out against Makino's humane proposal fell to another idealist, Lord Robert Cecil, who, with lowered eyes, rose to remark that the British and Dominion delegates could not support Japan's request. When Wilson called for a vote, only eleven of the eighteen committee members approved, and since every Article of the Covenant required unanimous approval, Baron Makino lost out.

The incident rankled. Japan had lost face, but Japan's delegates did not show the hurt they felt. Baron Makino said nothing until the departure of Orlando threatened to break up the whole Conference and then declared that he, too, would have to leave unless the Allies made good their wartime promise to give Japan all of Germany's prewar rights in Shantung Province, plus the right to maintain troops along the local railway. These demands violated the Fourteen Points and the Open Door, but Wilson, fearful that Makino was not bluffing and might line up with Germany and Russia, gave in. He did, however, persuade Makino to sign a separate declaration promising the eventual return of Shantung to China. The Chinese vainly pleaded that they, too, had declared war on Germany and deserved better treatment. Their delegation finally showed its disgust by refusing to sign the treaty of peace. Whereas Ray Stannard Baker, Wilson's admiring biographer, called the Smyrna deal with Venizelos "the most disreputable intrigue of the Conference," Harold Nicolson described the Shantung compromise as "the worst concession of all." Wilson's capitulation on both issues caused Clemenceau to remark that the American President "talked like Jesus Christ but acted like Lloyd George." In Lloyd George's book, on the other hand, Wilson had "at least one divine attribute. He was a jealous god." And if he never achieved divine omniscience or divine omnipotence, perhaps that arose from what Lloyd George called "his implicit faith in the efficacy of phrases."

On May 7 the Germans got their first look at the highly efficacious phrases of the Peace Treaty that the Allies had drawn up. Count von Brockdorff-Rantzau, a Prussian aristocrat with pro-Russian and even pro-Bolshevist proclivities, headed the German delegation and received from Clemenceau's hands the text of the entire treaty, which filled a book of more than two hundred pages. "The time has now come," said Clemenceau, "for a heavy reckoning of accounts." The Germans had fifteen days in which to put into French and German their written observations, but there would be no discussion, no negotiation, no concession. The arrogant Brockdorff-Rantzau, never rising from his chair, attacked the war-guilt clause and spoke bitterly of the hundreds of thousands of noncombatants whom the blockade had starved to death since the Armistice. His bad taste and bad manners caused such antagonism that the subsequent comments by the official German delegation cut little ice: "Expiring world theories, emanating from imperialistic and capitalistic tendencies, celebrate in it their last horrible triumph. As opposed to these views, which have brought unspeakable disaster upon the world, we appeal to the innate sense of right of men and nations, under whose token the English have developed, the Dutch people freed itself, the North American nation established its independence, France shook off its absolutism. The bearers of such hallowed traditions cannot deny this right to the German people, that now for the first time has acquired in its internal politics the possibility of living in harmony with its free will based on law. A treaty such as has been proposed to Germany is incompatible with respect for this innate right." But the Allied leaders paid no heed, and when Brockdorff-Rantzau resigned his post as Foreign Minister some weeks later, he predicted, "Those who sign this Treaty will sign the death sentences of many millions of German men, women, and children."

The offending document led off with the League Covenant. This ran to some five thousand words and twenty-six Articles, many of which included anywhere from two to ten subsections. The "High Contracting Parties" pledged themselves "to promote international co-operation and to achieve international peace and security." Each sovereign member state had one vote in the League Assembly, which had to meet once a year at the League's permanent headquarters in Geneva. The Assembly was to become a kind of world forum. The League Council of ten nations—with Britain, France, Italy, Japan, and the United States as permanent members—was to serve as the League's executive arm. Like the Assembly, it had to meet once a year, but it could also act at any time on any matter that concerned the League. A Secretary-General, appointed by the Council with the consent of the Assembly, was to direct the permanent Secretariat at Geneva and organize a kind of international civil service.

Article 10, which Wilson called "the heart of the Covenant," read as follows: "The members of the League undertake to respect and preserve as against external aggression the territorial integrity and existing political independence of all Members of the League. In case of any such aggression or in case of any danger or threat of such aggression, the Council shall advise upon the means by which this obligation shall be fulfilled." But if these words expressed the heart of the Covenant, the bone and sinew of the League lay in subsequent provisions to arbitrate all disputes between sovereign states and to invoke economic sanctions against backsliders. Other Articles dealt with mandates, disarmament, health, labor, education, free communications, and suppression of prostitution and the drug traffic. Wilson also put through the major changes that the Republican Senators had demanded, including specific recognition of the Monroe Doctrine.

But the Versailles Treaty to which Wilson had riveted the League Covenant contained provisions that many Americans of recent European extractions detested—notably the Germans, the Irish, and the Italians. Whereas the French counted on the League to enforce and sanctify the terms of the Versailles settlement, Wilson counted on the League to mitigate, in time, some of the harsher features of the Peace Treaty to which it was attached. But he never favored letting the Germans off easily: "I believe, even, that a hard peace is a good thing for Germany herself, in order that she may know what an unjust war means. We must not forget what our soldiers fought for, even if it means that we may have to fight again." If the territorial clauses of the Versailles Treaty sometimes violated the principle of self-determination, they did keep Wilson's pledges to France and Poland. France got Alsace-Lorraine; Poland got a corridor that followed the Vistula River to the sea. Belgium received the townships of Eupen and Malmédy. Plebiscites were ordered in Schleswig-Holstein and Upper Silesia. Germany lost twenty-five thousand square miles of territory and six million people. The Germans also lost their entire overseas empire of a million square miles and twelve million inhabitants. But the Versailles Treaty did not attempt to break up the German state. Just the opposite. It left Germany better able to preserve its national sovereignty in a world where the spirit of national self-determination ran stronger every day.

The severity of the Versailles Treaty lay in its economic penalties, military restrictions, and psychological effect. In the war-guilt clause, Germany acknowledged sole responsibility for the war and for all of the war's damage. The Treaty set no figures for reparations, but postponed that decision to some future time. An Allied Reparations Commission controlled the entire German economy. The Saar coal mines and their output went to France "in full and absolute possession" for a period of fifteen years. At the end of that time the inhabitants would vote whether they preferred to remain part of France or return to Germany, and if they voted to return to the Reich, Germany would have to buy back the coal mines by paying in gold. The Versailles Treaty cost Germany 45 per cent of its prewar coal reserves and 65 per cent of its reserves of iron ore. Britain received all German merchant vessels of more than 1,600 tons and half of those between 1,000 and 1,600 tons. The German shipbuilding industry had to construct up to 200,000 tons of merchant shipping for the Allies during a five-year period, but Germany's own merchant marine was limited to 400,000 tons as compared to five and a half million tons before the war.

A majority of foreigners sat on three commissions that controlled Ger-

UNDERWOOD

German Volunteers Prepare to Fight the Poles, 1919

many's three chief waterways—the Rhine, the Oder, and the Elbe. The German Army was reduced to 100,000 men, conscription was outlawed, and the General Staff dissolved. To prevent the formation of a large, trained reserve, officers had to serve twenty-five years, enlisted men not less than twelve. The Rhineland was demilitarized and Allied troops moved in for a fifteen-year period that might continue indefinitely if the Germans did not behave themselves. Submarines and all types of military aircraft were forbidden. The German Navy was reduced to six 10,000-ton battleships, six light cruisers, twelve destroyers, and twelve torpedo boats. In November, the Kaiser's Grand Fleet had surrendered itself to the British and spent the winter and spring interned at Scapa Flow. On June 21, a week before the signing of the Versailles Treaty, the officers and crews released their pent-up humiliation, boredom, and rage by opening the cocks of every vessel and sending them all to the bottom of the sea.

The mass of the German people applauded their sailors' gesture of protest but could not follow their sailors' example. To refuse to sign the Treaty would have led to blockade, invasion, and more misery, followed by Communism, disintegration, or both. Scheidemann resigned as Chancellor rather than endorse the Versailles *Diktat*. "May the hand wither that signs this Treaty," he exclaimed melodramatically. But another coalition government headed by another Social Democrat, Gustav Bauer, took the responsibility that Scheidemann rejected and that the generals not only avoided but renounced. Indeed, the discredited Nationalists relished the embarrassment of the Social Democrats, whom they held responsible for the bitter consequences of defeat. The Spartacists renewed their attacks on the betrayers of the revolution, the lackeys of the bourgeoisie, the agents of Allied imperialism. Lloyd George and some of the other Allied leaders fell into a panic. What if the Germans refused to sign? But the Social Democrats heeded the desperate cry of the masses: "Sign! Then there will be bread." In a note, dated June 23, 1919, the new German government wrote: "Yielding to overpowering might, the Government of the German Republic declares itself ready to accept and to sign the peace treaty imposed by the Allied and Associated Governments. But in doing so the Government of the German Republic in no wise abandons its conviction that these conditions of peace represent injustice without example."

In May, General Smuts had written to Lloyd George: "I am very anxious not only that the Germans should sign a fair and good peace treaty, but also that, for the sake of the future, they should not merely be made to sign at the point of the bayonet. The Treaty should not be capable of moral repudiation by the German people hereafter." For once it was Wilson who proved the realist. "One of the things that have disturbed me in recent months," he wrote on May 9, "is the unqualified hope that men have entertained everywhere of immediate emancipation from the things that have hampered and oppressed them. You cannot in human experience rush into the light. You have to go through the twilight into the broadening day before the noon comes and the full sun is upon the landscape."

Yet Wilson had done more than any other national leader to stir excessive hope in the masses. Lloyd George described him as "the most extraordinary compound I have ever encountered of the noble visionary, the implacable and unscrupulous partisan, the exalted idealist, and the man of rather petty and personal rancors." He especially deplored Wilson's "pervasive suspiciousness. He believed in mankind, but he distrusted all men." And again: "His face was contorted with unsightly hatred if you mentioned the names of two or three eminent Republicans who had criticized his policies." Harold Nicolson analyzed Wilson's character in further detail in *Peacemaking:* "He possessed no gift for differentiation, no capacity for adjustment to circumstances. It was his spiritual and mental rigidity which proved his undoing. It rendered him as incapable of withstanding criticism as of absorbing advice. It rendered him blind to all realities which did not accord with his preconceived theory, even to the realities of his own decisions. He and his conscience were on terms of such incessant intimacy that any little disagreement between them could be easily arranged. The profound, rigid, and quite justified conviction of his own spiritual rectitude; the active belief that God, Wilson, and the people would triumph in the end, led him to look upon his own inconsistencies as mere transient details in the one great impulse toward right and justice."

Wilson's opinion of the Peace Treaty accorded with Nicolson's opinion of his own character: "I think it will be found that the compromises which were accepted as inevitable nowhere cut at the heart of any principle; the work of the Conference squares, on the whole, with the principles agreed upon as the basis of peace as well as with the practical possibilities." Lloyd George described it as "a stern but just treaty," and Clemenceau convinced himself that "the day has come when might and right—terribly divorced hitherto—have united to give peace to the peoples in travail." Foch took a darker view: "This is not peace; it is an armistice for twenty years." Colonel House would have "preferred a different peace." Will Rogers echoed the views of many Americans with the quip: "I thought the Armistice terms read like a second mortgage, but this reads like a foreclosure."

The Germans could see nothing to laugh at. Matthias Erzberger of the Catholic Center Party warned, "Do not expect us to be our own executioners." *Vorwärts,* mouthpiece for the Social Democrats, sounded like Bethmann-Hollweg at the time of the German invasion of Belgium: "We must never forget that it is only a scrap of paper. Treaties based on violence can keep their validity only so long as force exists. Do not lose hope. The resurrection day comes." On June 28, the fifth anniversary of the Sarajevo assassination, Hermann Müller, the Social Democratic Foreign Minister, and Dr. Johannes Bell of the Catholic Center Party arrived before the Allied war leaders and peacemakers in the Hall of Mirrors of the Versailles Palace, the same Hall of Mirrors in which Bismarck had proclaimed the German Empire in 1871. To Colonel House the scene recalled "what was done in olden times when the conqueror dragged the conquered at his chariot wheels." He found it out of tune with "the new era" and lacking in the "element of chivalry." What nonsense. As Bernard Baruch commented in connection with the reparations clauses, "The Conference was not writing a mere contract of dollars and cents; it was dealing with blood-raw passions still pulsing through people's veins." While the German delegates put their names to the document, a young member of their party murmured, "All things pass. It will seem so different in ten or twenty years." Smuts signed for South Africa under protest: "I feel that in the Treaty we have not yet achieved the peace for which our people were looking." Clemenceau, in tears, accepted the congratulations of Paul Painlevé with the words. *"Oui, c'est une belle journée."*

SUMMING UP

Who had come out on top in the Paris negotiations—Clemenceau, Wilson, or Lloyd George? Clemenceau had disappointed those French nationalists who wanted Germany broken up and a separate republic established in the Rhineland. He did not even secure permanent possession of the Saar Valley for France. He had no guarantee that the Anglo-American pledge to help France against future German attack would ever come into force. The best he could hope for would be to maintain the positions that French troops held beyond the Rhine. Yet Clemenceau had to make the best of a bad bargain. Neither Wilson nor Lloyd George would give him the kind of guarantees he wanted. The bitter truth was that France could not stand up alone against Germany nor count upon Anglo-American aid under any and all circumstances.

Wilson had done far better. He got what he wanted most: acceptance of the League Covenant. Not only that; he persuaded the Conference to make changes in the Covenant to meet the criticisms of certain Republican opponents at home. He had, however, made several concessions. He let Italy have the Austrian Tyrol. He permitted the Japanese to remain in Shantung Province. He sanctioned the Greek occupation of Smyrna. These seemed minor concessions at the time. They also involved parts of the world in which the United States could take no effective action—and in which the United States had no vital interest.

Lloyd George had done the best of all. The British achieved their major war aims before the Paris Conference met: destruction of German sea power and virtual possession of Germany's colonies. Sober second thought convinced him—and an increasing number of his people—that a punitive German settlement ran counter to Britain's best interests. He therefore said nothing more about "squeezing Germany till the pips squeak" and made successful common cause with Wilson against Clemenceau's demand for a stern peace. "The truth is," he admitted at the time, "we have got our way. We have got most of the things we set out to get. . . . The German Navy has been handed over, the German mercantile shipping has been handed over, and the German colonies have been given up. One of our chief trade competitors has been most severely crippled and our allies are about to become her biggest creditors. That is no small achievement." If Lloyd George had any initial doubt about the final treaty it was that Germany did not get off easily enough. For the prospects for the German Republic on which both he and Wilson based their hopes looked black. The natural, logical determination of the French to write a stiff treaty gave rise to an equally natural, equally logical determination on the German side to repudiate that treaty. The war had been fought in such a way as to make future war impossible. Now it seemed that the peace had been made in such a way as to make future peace impossible, too.

The future of the League of Nations looked as black as the future of the German Republic. Republican members of the United States Senate had already shown more than enough strength to defeat both the Treaty and the League, especially with Wilson insisting on tying the Treaty and the League together. Wilson hoped that the League machinery could be used to revise those parts of the settlement he did not like. The French counted on the League to underwrite and sustain the settlement, intact. Other treaties with Austria, Hungary, Turkey, and Bulgaria remained to be written and signed, but Clemenceau, Wilson, and Lloyd George, sitting in Paris, lacked the power to impose their will on these far-off regions as they had imposed their will upon Germany. They had to content themselves with drawing up preliminary arrangements based on accomplished facts beyond their control and subject to change without notice. The war that had just ravaged so much of the world had its origins in eastern Europe, where rivalry between Slav and Teuton set the Austrian and Russian Empires at each other's throats, and destroyed them both. Unless the victorious Powers could re-establish stability in the east and continue it in the west, they could not hope to consolidate the peace.

3

Unsettlement in the East

Why Allied victory over Germany opened a new era in eastern Europe, the Middle East, and India and weakened the power of Europe over the backward majority of the human race.

PREVIEW

THE PEOPLES of the former Hapsburg lands lost no time in making their own kind of peace, which the western European leaders accepted with fairly good grace. Soviet Russia and the new Polish Republic did not compose their differences so quickly: it took them two years of fighting—including some French aid to Poland—to reach a settlement that fenced off Russia behind a *cordon sanitaire* of small, somewhat shaky democracies. The more remote the territory, the less influence the victorious Allies commanded. In Asia Minor the defeated Turks turned and rent the victorious Greeks, splitting Britain off from France, and helping to overthrow Lloyd George's coalition government. Still farther afield, the Arabs and the other Middle Eastern peoples rebelled with varying success against continued European domination. Everywhere native nationalists challenged foreign imperialists. The most momentous struggle took place in India, which had contributed mightily to the Allied war effort and felt entitled to a larger reward than the British held out. A new national leader emerged—Mahatma Gandhi—who not only inspired his people; he transcended his political role to become the first essentially religious world messiah of the twentieth century.

· I ·

WHEN the Allied peacemakers gathered at Paris in 1919, they faced, throughout the former Hapsburg lands, a condition, not a theory; a condition of national and social revolution. Delegates from the new and enlarged Succession States laid their claims, in the forms of accomplished facts, before the Council of Ten and the Big Four. It proved impossible to apply Wilson's doctrine of self-determination to every square inch of the former Dual Monarchy. Too many different nationalities overlapped in too many different places. Too many old scores had to be paid off—in kind. New rivalries replaced the old. The last became first and the first became last as starvation in Vienna and Budapest transformed these former strongholds of Hapsburg power into breeding grounds of revolution.

Not until the close of 1919, after the Big Four had completed work on the Versailles Treaty and scattered for good and all, did the lesser Allied statesmen draw up the final terms of the treaties with Austria, Hungary, Bulgaria, and Turkey. The Treaty of Saint-Germain with Austria, signed on September 10, 1919, forbade union with Germany and set the boundaries of the new Czechoslovak Republic. The Treaty of Trianon with Hungary, signed on June 20, 1920, set the new, enlarged boundaries of Yugoslavia and Rumania. It also ceded considerable territory to Czechoslovakia and forbade any restoration of the Hapsburg Monarchy. The Treaty of Neuilly with Bulgaria, signed on November 27, 1919, gave up some territory to Yugoslavia, Rumania, and Greece, but permitted King Boris, the son of the disastrous Tsar Ferdinand, to remain on his father's throne. The Treaty of Sèvres, signed with Turkey on October 20, 1920, gave all of Thrace to Greece, thus virtually eliminating Turkey in Europe. All in all, the peace treaties, concluded in the name of self-determination of peoples, left about thirty million Europeans living under alien rule.

If the Treaties of Saint-Germain, Trianon, and Neuilly showed less respect than the Treaty of Versailles for the principle of self-determination, they showed no regard at all for the economic needs of the people concerned. Politically, they marked an advance over the prewar order, just as the Treaty of Versailles did. The new order in central and southeastern Europe contained more democracy, more self-determination than the old. Except in Hungary, small farmers divided up most of the great landed estates. But the economic virtues of the vanished Hapsburg Empire had made up for some of its other defects. Austria-Hungary had brought nearly sixty million people together into a single free trade area which also put few restrictions against trade with the rest of Europe. The new frontiers changed all that by laying the groundwork for a new maze of tariff walls behind which the national spirit burgeoned. The settlement in western Europe tried to curb the military power of Germany by curbing the economic power of Germany. But in eastern Europe the war had already destroyed the economic base on which the power of the Hapsburgs had rested, and the settlements in eastern Europe made no attempt to create a new economic base to replace the old. Instead, they aggravated the national rivalries that had just brought the Hapsburgs down.

Europe in 1914

Because the western democracies had little power to impose their kind of settlement on the Succession States of eastern Europe, nothing prevented the people directly concerned from taking matters into their own hands—for better or worse. The Poles, however, faced some unique difficulties and opportunities. Winston Churchill called Poland "the linch-pin of the Versailles Treaty" and visualized it as a buffer between Bolshevism and the west and as a counterweight against future German aggression upon France. Clemenceau always wanted to give the Poles as much as possible. Wilson generally supported him. Lloyd George, fearful of making Germany too weak and driving the German people to

Post-War Europe

despair and Communism, wanted to move a little more cautiously. Clemenceau and Wilson prevailed and for once the principle of self-determination and the security of France went together. But what to do about Poland's eastern boundary with Russia?

Although the answer to that question depended on the Russians and the Poles rather than on the Western Powers, the consequences affected west as well as east. By 1920 the Bolsheviks had fought off their external enemies and defeated their enemies within. They had established—on paper at any rate—the Third Communist International, dedicated to world revolution. In June, 1920, the Comintern held its second world

Congress, which attracted more delegates and adopted a more definite program than the first gathering that had taken place the year before. "No Parliament," declared the second Comintern Congress, "can under any circumstances be an arena of struggles for reforms, for betterment of the conditions of the working classes." All parties that joined the Comintern had to call themselves Communist Parties and submit to Communist discipline and Communist morality. "The Communists," wrote Lenin, "must be prepared to make every sacrifice, and, if necessary, even resort to all sorts of cunning, schemes, and stratagems, to employ illegal methods, to evade and conceal the truth, in order to penetrate the trade unions, to remain in them, and conduct the Communist work in them at all costs."

The establishment of the Comintern weakened the Socialists, split the labor movement, and strengthened reaction everywhere. Because the moderate parties had offered the strongest opposition to the Russian Bolsheviks, Lenin assumed that he had only to weaken the corresponding parties in other countries to assure the triumph of Communism. He did not make nearly sufficient allowance for the swelling numbers and power of the middle classes, which responded to nationalist slogans and promises as fanatically as the industrial workers responded to Communism. Lenin could cite the holy books of Marx as proof that the middle classes steadily lost ground to the proletariat. But the election returns and the distribution of national income told a different story. The middle classes had become a dynamic force in most of the western democracies and it was to their way of life that more and more industrial workers aspired. In eastern and central Europe, the middle classes also proved more militant than the workers.

Nowhere did the most militant, radical nationalism make such an appeal, immediately after the Armistice, as in Poland. In 1919 the peacemakers at Paris had failed to prevent Pilsudski's armies from seizing the Lithuanian capital of Vilna and invading the Ukraine. Pilsudski's success not only went to his own head; it caused some of the more belligerent French leaders to push him still farther east against the archenemy, Bolshevik Russia. In July, 1920, the Bolshevik government announced that the Allies were driving Poland into "an unwanted, senseless, and criminal war with Soviet Russia." For once, the Bolsheviks did not exaggerate. Although they had won the civil war and Allied intervention had fizzled out, their own regime had barely survived. Soviet Russia covered far less territory than Tsarist Russia. Finland, Estonia, Latvia, and Lithuania had all set up independent republics and their armies had defeated the Bolsheviks in the field. One opportunity to overthrow Bolshevism remained, an opportunity that could also become a menace: Poland. For if the Polish attack upon Russia should fail, the Red Army might well overrun Poland and bring Communism to all of eastern and central Europe—including Germany. Pilsudski, however, felt that the moment had come for Poland to protect itself against future aggression from either Russia or Germany by adding to its territories while the adding was good. An opportunity like this might not come again for centuries.

Plenty of Allied statesmen saw the risks Pilsudski was running, but he listened only to the French and to the patriotic promptings of his own heart as he sent the bulk of his armies deeper into Soviet territory until they occupied the Ukrainian capital of Kiev. In July, 1920, young General Tukhachevsky, a former Tsarist officer, attacked Poland farther north. The Red Army went through Poland as easily as the Polish troops, who now retreated in confusion from Kiev, had gone through the Soviet Ukraine. "The destinies of the world revolution will be settled in the West," Tukhachevsky declared. "Our way toward world-wide conflagration passes over the corpse of Poland." The Polish government appealed to the Allies for help and promised to abandon its expansionist program and accept any decisions the Allied Supreme Council might make. Lord Curzon, the British Foreign Minister, then suggested that the Poles and Russians both accept a frontier that gave White Russia and the western Ukraine to Russia, but now it was the Russians' turn to feel their oats and they rejected the proposed "Curzon Line." Foreign non-Communists came to Russia's support. British, Czech, and German workers refused to handle munitions destined for use against the Bolsheviks. So did the Danzig dock hands. France and Britain could supply only a military mission, headed by General Weygand and including Lord D'Abernon, Britain's shrewd new Ambassador to Berlin. Pilsudski still had faith in his armies, but he welcomed Weygand's advice, and under their combined direction the Polish armies turned the Russian flank outside Warsaw on August 16, 1920, in what Lord D'Abernon called "the eighteenth decisive battle of history." As he pointed out later, a Russian victory "would have been a turning point in European history, for there is no doubt at all that the whole of central Europe would at that moment have been opened to the influence of Communist propaganda and to Soviet invasion."

Seven months after the Poles had won the Battle of Warsaw they signed the Peace of Riga with the Russians. In 1920, the Republic of Poland covered ninety thousand square miles and contained a population of twenty millions, mostly Poles. Thanks largely to the Peace of Riga, Poland expanded its territories to one hundred and fifty thousand square miles and increased its population by eight million people, most of them White Russians and Ukrainians. The new Polish-Russian frontier lay far to the east of the proposed Curzon Line and resulted in the partition of White Russia and the Ukraine between Soviet Russia and Poland. The Allied governments, the United States government, and the Soviet government had all tried to prevent Pilsudski from grabbing so much for his country, but once again the peoples of eastern Europe had taken matters into their own hands.

· II ·

IT HAD TAKEN more than two years and many more than two battles for the Poles and Russians to reach a settlement in eastern Europe. It took three years—until the fall of 1922—for Greece and Turkey to reach a Middle Eastern settlement. And before they reached that settlement, Turkey went through one kind of revolution; Greece went through another; they fought a war that cost a quarter of a million lives, a war that finally drove Lloyd George from power in Great Britain.

At the end of 1918, the collapse of the Ottoman Empire appeared complete. Turkish power had once blanketed Asia Minor and North Africa; now it did not reach beyond the suburbs of Constantinople. From October, 1918, until the middle of the following May, Turkish officers quietly demobilized their troops and dutifully surrendered their arms to small groups of Allied officials who journeyed unmolested through Anatolia, which the Turks had regarded as their homeland for five centuries. But the decision of the Big Three to permit Greek troops to land at Smyrna on May 15 brought the Anatolian Turks to sudden life. They regarded the Greeks as inferior intruders, and when the Greeks committed the same kind of atrocities in Smyrna that the Turks had committed upon their own subject peoples for generations, the same spirit of national resistance that the Turks had tried in vain to crush in others now took possession of them in their turn.

Three men inspired and directed the Greek invasion of Turkey: Lloyd George, Venizelos, and a Greek munitions merchant from Anatolia named Sir Basil Zaharoff. Lloyd George acted with his usual impulsiveness, but he had a serious, strategic purpose: to strengthen Britain's position in the eastern Mediterranean. Economically Greece had always belonged to central and eastern Europe. Culturally it had certain ties with Russia, which had received its religion and its alphabet from Greece. But politically and strategically, Greece had looked to Britain. The defeat of Germany, the revolution in Russia, and the collapse of the Ottoman Empire gave Greece and Britain a new and perhaps a unique opportunity to work together more closely than ever. To exploit and control the oil of the Middle East, the British needed a strong and friendly Greece. British sea power and Greek military power, in combination, could stand guard over the crossroads of the world, all the way from the Dardanelles to Suez.

The Tory members of Lloyd George's coalition Cabinet had no quarrel with what he was trying to do, but some of them feared that he had committed himself exclusively to the Greece of Venizelos and Zaharoff. Lord Curzon, who replaced Balfour as Foreign Secretary in the fall of 1919, favored a generous settlement with the Turks, whom the British had always supported against the Russians. Other Tories feared that Lloyd George's pro-Greek policy would antagonize the whole Moslem world, which had always looked to Britain for protection. Meanwhile the Russian Bolsheviks and the Turkish Nationalists, companions in defeat, were beginning to establish cordial relations. British imperialists and Greek expansionists, companions in victory, found themselves drawn together, too.

Venizelos took the initiative. Secretary Lansing had said of him, "The views of M. Venizelos were given greater weight by the Big Four than those of any other single delegate at Paris." Yet Lansing confessed to an "almost heretical doubt" about Venizelos's integrity. Francesco Nitti, who succeeded Orlando as Premier of Italy, wrote of Venizelos: "In asking he always had the air of offering, and in obtaining, he seemed to be conceding something." Venizelos looked like a bearded, bespectacled professor of archaeology. His smile, his voice, his gentle manner radiated virtue and charm. Yet he had a formidable history. Back in the eighteen nineties he had quit the profession of law to join the revolutionary brigands on his native island of Crete in their successful fight for independence from Turkey. After Crete joined itself to the Greek Kingdom, Venizelos went to Athens and in 1910, at the age of forty-six, headed a strong coalition government. As Premier he masterminded Greek strategy through the two Balkan Wars, always showing a talent for compromise and moderation. In August, 1914, he threw himself wholly into the Allied cause and, almost singlehanded, finally brought Greece into the fighting against the Central Powers. At the Paris Peace Conference he presented a stiff bill for services rendered, and Lloyd George endorsed it.

So did Wilson—though for different reasons than motivated Lloyd George. Early in the Conference, Venizelos had arranged for a brief appointment with the busy President of the United States, who begrudged any time not devoted to promoting the League of Nations. Venizelos, alert to Wilson's interests and character, said nothing about Greece when they met but introduced himself as a passionate disciple of the great American President's ideas and offered his services to the cause of the League of Nations. The interview, scheduled to last ten minutes, continued for an hour and from that time on Venizelos had Wilson as well as Lloyd George behind him.

The Venizelos-Lloyd George firm also included an affluent sleeping partner in the person of seventy-year-old Sir Basil Zaharoff, born in Anatolia of Greek parents and originally named Basileos Zaharias. As a youth Zaharoff went to Constantinople, where he made his way from the underworld of money-changers and tourists' guides into the gun-running business. From gun-running he moved into the sale and manu-facture of munitions, and in 1888 joined forces with Hiram Maxim. After the Boer War, Zaharoff and Maxim entered the Vickers armament concern, and by 1919 Zaharoff found himself the holder of British titles and French honors and one of the richest men on earth. He controlled Paris banks and newspapers. He contributed funds to the British Liberal Party, through Lloyd George. He financed the wartime political career of Venizelos. And now that the war had ended he put still more of his swollen fortune behind Venizelos's grandiose scheme to bring all of Thrace as well as the rich Anatolian city and province of Smyrna under the Greek flag.

Once the Big Three had permitted Greek troops to land at Smyrna, the Venizelos program seemed sure to go through of its own accord. Allied war vessels dominated the Dardanelles, and in March, 1920, Allied troops occupied Constantinople. Meanwhile Greek troops had extended their foothold in the province of Smyrna, and other divisions occupied more of Thrace. In the treaties with Austria, Hungary, and Bulgaria, the Supreme Allied Council at Paris approved and recognized a new order that the peoples of eastern Europe had created for them-selves. During the summer and fall of 1919, the Greeks seemed to be creating another new order in Thrace and Anatolia. The Supreme Allied Council therefore prepared to approve and recognize this new order in the Treaty of Sèvres with Turkey.

Not until August, 1920, did the Turkish government at Constantinople get around to signing the treaty that defined this new order. Greece re-ceived eastern and western Thrace, the Gallipoli peninsula, most of the Aegean Islands, and—subject to a plebiscite—the city and province of Smyrna. The Straits were to be placed under international control. The French were to receive Syria, then in a state of revolt; the British were to receive mandates over Mesopotamia and Palestine; the United States, a mandate for Armenia. As soon as the Turks signed the treaty, Britain, France, and Italy were to receive further zones of influence in Anatolia. In September, Venizelos returned to Athens and received a hero's wel-come. He had restored the glory that was Greece.

But not for long. On the throne of Greece sat King Alexander, the second son of ex-King Constantine, who had abdicated in 1917. Alexan-

UNDERWOOD

UNDERWOOD

Premier Eleutherios Venizelos of Greece   *General Mustafa Kemal Pasha of Turkey*

der had supported Venizelos, and between them they had given Greece a stable government for three years. On October 2, 1920, King Alexander was walking in his royal gardens with his spaniel, which nipped a female monkey playing there. The monkey's gallant mate retaliated by nipping the King's leg. Three weeks later Alexander died of blood-poisoning. Although the Constitution did not require him to do so, Venizelos ordered a general election in which the Greek people had a chance to vote on whether they wanted his antagonist, King Constantine, to return to the throne. On November 14 the Greeks voted by a majority of more than two to one to restore Constantine. They had suffered more than enough from the bloody, costly, and risky policies of Venizelos, who did not even win back his own seat in the Greek Parliament. Three days later he sailed for Italy on a friend's yacht.

Once again—as in the fateful assassination of the Austrian Archduke six years before—blind chance forced the pace of history. A monkey's bite had suddenly driven Venizelos from office and restored King Constantine to the Greek throne. Instantly, the French and Italian governments lost all interest in supporting Turkey against Greece—an obliging monkey had eliminated the incendiary Venizelos—while in England Tory opposition to Lloyd George hardened and increased. Constantine then made matters still worse by committing his country to an even more ambitious program than Venizelos had followed. Not only had Constantine lost the Allied support that carried Venizelos so far; he faced new difficulties in Anatolia. For while the shadowy Turkish government at Constantinople made concession after concession to the Allies, it quietly encouraged a new nationalist movement in Anatolia.

General Mustafa Kemal Pasha, the leader of this movement, came of the mixed stock to which so many Levantines owe so much of their vigor. His father, a minor Turkish official in Salonika, claimed Albanian ancestry. This made him a Moslem by religion, a European by descent. Some of Kemal's mother's forebears included Salonika Jews, the descendants of Visigoths who had become converted to Judaism in Spain, and had later been expelled by Ferdinand and Isabella. Kemal himself did not accept any religion; he had little Turkish blood; yet he re-created the spirit of Turkish nationalism at the lowest point in Turkish history. Before the war he quarreled with the leaders of the Young Turk movement, to which he belonged. During the war he proved himself a daring commander at the Dardanelles, by defying his German superiors. After the war, when the Allies jailed the other Young Turks, Kemal escaped and in June, 1919, the Constantinople government appointed him Inspector General of the Turkish troops in Anatolia. Here he began to organize a new army, established friendly relations with the Bolsheviks, and by 1920 emerged as the one national leader able to rally his people against the Greeks.

Rough country, meager supplies, and weary, inadequate armies prevented the Greeks from making the most of their opportunities in 1920. By 1921 Kemal had scraped together sufficient forces to put up a fight. Although the French and Italians withdrew all support from Constantine, he took command of the Greek armies in Asia Minor and opened a drive on Ankara. Crowds in Athens shouted, "To Constantinople." The Greeks had two hundred thousand troops in Anatolia who were costing about a million dollars a week. Some fifty thousand of these troops advanced toward Ankara. Almost the same number of Turks—with more in reserve—opposed them, and the Greeks failed to break through. Both sides lost about eighteen thousand men. In October, 1921, the French government granted Kemal official recognition and made arrangements to provide him with fighting equipment while he used his good offices to support French rule in Syria.

Then, for the better part of a year, Kemal proved that he knew how to wait as well as how to fight. The Greeks had scattered their forces through hostile territory in Anatolia and eastern Thrace. Their morale slumped; their money drained away. The Turks resumed their habit of massacring Christians, especially Greeks, behind their lines. In March, 1922, the Allied governments proposed a Greek-Turk armistice which the Greeks welcomed but the Turks refused. All this time, Kemal accumulated more supplies from France, but made no use of them. In July the Greeks took a long chance, shifted two divisions from Anatolia to eastern Thrace, and asked the Allies for permission to take over Constantinople from the British, French, and Italian troops who had occupied the city since March, 1920. Nothing stood in their way, and if the Greek request had been granted the whole Kemalist movement might have collapsed.

But the Italians did not want the Greeks in Constantinople; the French were already backing Kemal; the British were divided. In August, Kemal threatened the northern end of the Greek line in Anatolia, then threw his main force against the south and broke clear through to Smyrna. As the elder Moltke once said: "The Turk begins to fight only at the point where the Christian would surrender." The whole Greek front collapsed entirely. The Turks took fifty thousand prisoners, burned Smyrna, massacred thousands of its Christian inhabitants. Forty thousand Greek soldiers and refugees escaped by sea. Kemal controlled all of Anatolia and seemed in position to regain Constantinople, the Dardanelles, and eastern Thrace.

Confronted by this threat, the French and Italians withdrew their troops from Chanak, the neutral occupation zone they held, with the British, on the Asiatic shore of the Dardanelles. The British remained, but when they asked the Dominions to support a policy of resistance, they received mixed replies. Again Kemal played it safe. He did not attack the British at Chanak, but moved his troops toward Scutari, across the Bosporus from Constantinople. In October he accepted an Allied invitation to discuss revision of the Treaty of Sèvres—almost entirely at the expense of Greece. In the Treaty of Lausanne, signed on July 24, 1923, Kemal gave up all claims over the Sultan's former Arab possessions, but Turkey regained Constantinople and most of eastern Thrace. For the first time in centuries, Turkey also won complete control over its internal affairs and no longer had to grant foreigners special trading privileges. The Allies even permitted Turkey to establish a kind of trusteeship over the Dardanelles.

The Treaty of Lausanne cost the major Allies little. The Italians had already lost, at the Paris Peace Conference, what little chance they ever had of getting concessions in Anatolia. The British and French had more than enough postwar commitments to keep their hands full. But the Treaty of Lausanne came down as hard on Greece as any of the earlier treaties had come down on any of the Central Powers. Having squandered men and money fighting the Turks, the Greeks now had to make room in their small, barren, overcrowded country for a million and a quarter refugees from Asia Minor. King Constantine abdicated a second time. It is doubtful that he took much comfort in the thought that the final threat of war between Britain and Turkey also overthrew the British government.

Lloyd George resigned as Prime Minister in October, 1922, when a majority of Conservative Party leaders voted to withdraw support from his coalition government. An accumulation of grievances brought him down. Most Conservatives had grown weary of serving under a Liberal. More and more Liberals considered Lloyd George a renegade. He did not show enough firmness toward Ireland to suit the die-hards; he showed too much to win confidence in Ireland itself. In the general election that followed his resignation, the Conservatives won 347 seats in the House of Commons; Labor won 159; the Independent Liberals, 60; the Lloyd George Liberals, 59. The emergence of the Labor Party as His Majesty's Loyal Opposition overshadowed the disintegration of the Liberals. The Conservatives preened themselves on having won their first general election since 1900. Yet all these portents of change inside Britain could not conceal the fact that events in the Middle East had brought the crisis to a head. These events also served as a reminder that Britain had vital interests far from home and that Asiatic unrest had put those interests in peril.

· III ·

THE MAN who helped to end the Lloyd George era in Britain helped to open a new era in the Middle East. Mustafa Kemal Pasha stressed nationalism as heavily as Lenin had stressed internationalism; he practiced dictatorship as effectively as Wilson preached democracy. Lenin and Wilson set themselves up as world messiahs; Kemal set himself up as a national messiah. Wilson had failed to make the world safe for democracy; Lenin had failed to make the world safe for Communism; Kemal achieved his more modest ambitions for the new Turkish Republic. But the whirlwind that he rode in Turkey swept the rest of the Middle East and much of Asia, too.

On March 16, 1920, Kemal had officially informed the outside world, "We are convinced that there is no power on earth that can deprive a nation of its right to existence." Appealing to the national spirit of his hardy people, Kemal had first defeated the Greeks and then forced the Allies to revise the Treaty of Sèvres in Turkey's favor. He also learned from the mistakes of Turkey's past rulers. The Young Turks had led their country to disaster by allying themselves with the Central Powers and trying to keep the backward Arabs under their rule. Kemal laid no claim to any Arab lands. More than 85 per cent of the inhabitants of the new Turkish Republic spoke the Turkish language. But he did not consider his own people ripe for political democracy. He and his right-hand man, General Izmet Pasha, managed to squeeze through the National Assembly a bill that gave him virtually unlimited power as chief of state, commander in chief of the armed forces, and leader of the only political party in the country. On October 29, 1923, the new Turkish Republic proclaimed its existence.

From the failure of the Young Turks, Kemal had learned that the old Ottoman Empire had no place in the twentieth century. From the failure of the Sultans, whose temporal power the Young Turks had broken in 1908, he learned that the old-time religion must also go. Abdul Mejid, the descendant of these Sultans, still held the title of Caliph, or Successor of the Prophet, and lived in Constantinople. Millions of Moslems all over the world still recognized him as their spiritual leader, although millions of others denied his claim. To the Turks, Abdul Mejid symbolized the superstition and corruption that had laid their country low. A few months after the Turkish National Assembly proclaimed the Turkish Republic, Kemal saw to it that the Constantinople papers printed a letter signed by two leaders of the Indian Moslems, including the Aga Khan, demanding that the Turkish Republic show the Caliph more respect. Kemal then quoted this letter to imply that the British were using both the Aga Khan and the Caliph to destroy the Turkish Republic and asked the National Assembly to abolish the Caliphate altogether. He received an overwhelming vote of confidence; Abdul Mejid fled to Europe. Kemal had eliminated the Sultanate in 1923 and the Caliphate in 1924.

"There followed," wrote J. Hampden Jackson in his *Short History of the World Since 1918,* "a general secularization of the Turkish State. The Bill abolishing the Caliphate declared that 'The antiquated religious courts and codes must be replaced by modern scientific civil codes. The schools of the Mosques must give way to secular government schools.' Accordingly, the laws of God, the *Sheriat,* were replaced by civil laws copied from Switzerland, criminal laws from Italy, commercial laws from Germany." The secular schools taught Roman instead of Arabic script. Kemal himself went about the country with a blackboard, giving instruction in the new style of writing which he himself had only just mastered. He forbade women to wear veils. He outlawed the traditional fez, which the Turks had made their national headdress during the nineteenth century, although it originated in Austria.

"Nations that persist in remaining at the intellectual stage of the Middle Ages are destined to disappear from the face of the earth," Kemal told his people. "The Turk must become affiliated with an international civilization and this fact must be plainly shown in his external appearance. Civilized, international garments are the only ones worthy of our nation. We shall wear laced boots, trousers, jackets, collars, ties, and a headgear with a rim or peak. I am naming articles of clothing and I shall even utter an ominous word—this form of headgear is called a hat." Kemal wanted the Turks to dress like Europeans and to mechanize their farms and modernize their factories not in order to make themselves

General Smuts. Drawing by Kelen

over into foreigners or to subordinate themselves to foreign influence, but in order to stand more firmly on their own feet as Turks. The doctrine of "Turkey for the Turks" that Kemal promoted was as European, in its origin, as the scientific techniques that he also borrowed from the West. The Russian Bolsheviks sized up the new Turkey quickly and correctly in March, 1921, when they signed a pact with Kemal's representative in Moscow renouncing all Tsarist claims to Turkish territories and recognizing Kemal's claims to the strategic Kars-Ardahan area in the Caucasus Mountains. Seven months later, the French recognized Kemal, but the British refused to admit his claim to Mosul and its oil fields, although the Kurds who lived there wanted Turkish rule.

The entire Middle East told the same story. From the Persian Gulf to the Black Sea, from the eastern Mediterranean to the Indian Ocean, the ancient lands and peoples of Asia Minor, Arabia, and North Africa rumbled and stirred. The general principles proclaimed by Woodrow Wilson, the specific wartime promises of the British and the French, the propaganda of Lenin, and the guns of Kemal rang in the ears of the common people of the Middle East. The discovery of oil brought new wealth to some areas; European techniques brought the rudiments of a better life to others. Leaders arose who no longer accepted poverty, ignorance, and disease as inevitable parts of the eternal scheme of things. These leaders told their people to oust the foreigner, take charge of their own affairs, and inaugurate a new age.

General Smuts, who had fought against Britain in the Boer War, understood what was at stake. Not Wilson, but humanity failed at Paris, said Smuts, and he tried to repair the damage by warning that the peace of the world and the fate of the League of Nations depended on the attitude of the victorious Allies toward the world's more backward peoples and less developed areas—notably in the Middle East. Smuts and several other outstanding statesmen therefore addressed themselves to incorporating in the League Covenant a new form of modified imperialism known as the mandate system. "Certain communities," the Covenant declared, "formerly belonging to the Turkish Empire have reached a stage of development where their existence as independent nations can be provisionally recognized, subject to the rendering of administrative advice and assistance by the Mandatory until such time as they are able to stand alone. The wishes of the communities must be a principal consideration in the election of a Mandatory."

During the war, the Allied leaders had given various Arab rulers reason to believe that the defeat of Turkey would lead to their freedom and independence. But the Allies entered into a series of conflicting commitments—to the Jews and Arabs in Palestine and to one another elsewhere. Even the most ardent Wilsonian did not demand immediate and complete independence for the illiterate fellahin of the Middle East, but when the Peace Conference awarded League Mandates over Palestine and Mesopotamia to Britain and over Syria and Lebanon to France largely because British and French troops happened to have occupied those countries, Wilson objected. Unable to persuade the British and French to sponsor an Allied commission of investigation, he sent six Americans on a forty-day inspection tour of Palestine and Syria. On their return, they reported that the Syrians opposed any mandate, especially a mandate administered by France. The Americans also recommended the inclusion of Palestine in a "united Syrian state" and called for "only a greatly reduced Zionist program . . . only very gradually initiated." Citing Wilson's principle of self-determination, they pointed out that nine tenths of the population of Palestine was non-Jewish and emphatically opposed the whole Zionist program. "There is nothing on which the population of Palestine were more agreed than this."

The British did not care for this attack on Zionism, which the Balfour Declaration had endorsed. They liked even less the proposed "united Syrian state" which seemed to contemplate their ultimate withdrawal from the Middle East. But instead of challenging the American report, the British countered with a flank attack. President Wilson had begun to show a laudable willingness to accept an American mandate over devastated Armenia, where war and massacre had wiped out almost one third of that country's two and a half million people. If Wilson's sympathy for the distressed and deserving Armenians could lead him to involve the United States more deeply in Middle Eastern affairs, might the British not also convince him that they backed Zionism only because they wanted to help the persecuted Jews of eastern Europe find a national home? Hence the stillborn Treaty of Sèvres provided for a possible American mandate over Armenia.

The Treaty of Lausanne, which superseded the Treaty of Sèvres, provided for no such mandate. From November, 1922 until July, 1923, representatives of Kemal's Turkey negotiated with diplomats from the four chief Allied Powers, from Greece, Bulgaria, and Yugoslavia, with an observer from the United States also on hand. They agreed to restore Turkey's pre-war frontiers in Europe, arranged for more than a million Greeks to evacuate Asia Minor, and gave the Turkish Republic more authority over the Straits than the old Ottoman Empire had enjoyed before the war. At Lausanne, the first of the post-war settlements went by the board as the defeated but resurgent Turks successfully invoked the principles of Woodrow Wilson to amend a settlement originally drawn up in his name.

And the more the Americans learned about the mandate system in general and the Middle East in particular, the less enthusiasm they felt about undertaking obligations in Armenia. They saw the British reverting to divide-and-rule tactics, using the Zionist movement as a club over the heads of the Arabs and the Arabs to club the Jews. The French wasted no time on hypocrisy. When the American Commission of Inquiry returned from Syria, the French used their troops to break the country up into five separate areas which they placed under military administration. But instead of establishing order, this lead to demonstrations, riots, and threats of civil war. Six years later, in 1925, the French invited certain Syrian leaders to a conference, arrested them, and shelled the city of Damascus to crush the uprising that followed. Soon fifty thousand French troops were fighting in Syria, but a year later they had to call it a day and make peace. Between 1918 and 1920 eighty thousand British and Indian troops waged the same kind of war against the natives of Iraq. In 1921 Churchill, as Colonial Secretary, had most of them withdrawn and replaced by Royal Air Force planes. However, the British government decided that the time had come to give Iraq an Arab ruler and prevailed upon King Faisal—whom the French had just driven from Syria—to take the job. Faisal proved a wise ruler and conditions gradually improved.

Faisal's brother, King Abdullah, whom the British installed in Transjordan, had less power. The Arabs in that region and in nearby Palestine objected to the immigration of Jews, who, in their turn, objected to the favoritism that the British showed the Arabs. After Lloyd George had to quit office and join the opposition, he accused the Conservatives of "using the fact that you are doing nothing for the Arabs as an excuse to forbid the Jews to do something for themselves." Dr. Chaim Weizmann, the Zionist leader, had declared at the Peace Conference that the Balfour Declaration meant "that Palestine should be as Jewish as England is English and America is American." And at the same time Faisal wrote to Felix Frankfurter in the United States: "Our deputation here in Paris is fully acquainted with the proposals submitted yesterday by the Zionist Organization to the Peace Conference and we regard them as moderate and proper. We are working together for a reformed and revived Near East, and our two movements complete one another."

The British, on the other hand, were working to establish themselves permanently in this area by divide-and-rule methods. Palestine occupied a strategic position on the map. It commanded the approach to the Suez Canal and lay close to the oil wells of Transjordan and Iraq. Indeed, thirst for oil accounted for most of these efforts by the British and the French to control the former Arab provinces of the vanished Ottoman Empire. In 1916 the British and French governments had signed a secret agreement that awarded the province of Mosul to France. Later, however, the French surrendered this claim and permitted Mosul to be incorporated in Iraq on condition that they receive one quarter of all the profits of the Mosul oil fields. As a result, the oil wells of the Middle East and the pipe lines connecting these wells with ports and refineries on the coast remained in Anglo-French hands.

In Syria, Iraq, and Transjordan the French and the British managed to keep the local nationalists under control. They had less luck in Persia and Arabia. In 1919 British troops forced the Shah of Persia to sign an agreement putting his whole country under British political and military control. But the British could not defend northern Persia from an invasion by Russian Bolsheviks who organized a short-lived Soviet Republic. It remained for a young Persian cavalry officer, Riza Khan Pahlevi, to break up the Soviet Republic, repudiate the agreement with Great Britain, drive out the Shah, and set himself up as Prime Minister. In 1921 he signed an agreement with the Russians, who pledged themselves to keep hands off Persia and to send no troops across the border unless a third power attempted military intervention in its turn. In 1925 Riza Khan had the Constituent Assembly proclaim him Shah and change the name of his country from Persia to Iran.

Shah Riza Pahlevi, as he called himself, played all the powers off against one another. He installed American financial advisers, Belgian custom inspectors, French educational directors. He permitted the Russians to build a railway and the British to organize an air line. But the bulk of the revenues of the new state continued to come from Anglo-Persian Oil Company royalties. The great landowning families and the Moslem religion remained undisturbed by Riza Khan.

If Riza put through fewer reforms in Iran than Kemal put through in Turkey, he looked like a Bolshevik compared to King Ibn Saud of Arabia. Ibn Saud belonged to the fanatical Moslem sect known as Wahhabis who believed that Mohammed sanctioned only three activities: reading the Koran, praying, and waging war. Ibn Saud himself came from a line of Arabian rulers whom the Turks had ousted. In

Post-War Middle East

1900 he seized the throne of Nejd; by 1912, the Turks pitted King Husein of the Hejaz against him, and Ibn Saud had to recognize the authority of the Sultan. But the defeat rankled and Ibn Saud nurtured his hatred of Husein. The British bribed Ibn Saud to remain neutral throughout the war and kept in contact with him through St. John Philby, a convert to Islam. Philby worked through the pro-Moslem India Office, while T. E. Lawrence, who attached himself to Husein's family, worked through the Foreign Office. Although the British rewarded two of Husein's sons by making one of them King of Iraq and the other King of Transjordan, Lawrence accused his country of having betrayed the Arab peoples of the Middle East.

King Ibn Saud felt doubly betrayed, both by the British and by the Husein family. He therefore proceeded to strengthen his authority throughout Arabia, where he had established a unique order of military knights who set up a series of desert colonies combining the functions of farm, religious seminary, and military garrison. They earned the gratitude of their fellow Moslems by wiping out the raiding parties that used to harass pilgrims journeying to the holy cities of Mecca and Medina. They also formed the backbone of an army with which Ibn Saud drove King Husein from the Hejaz and made himself the sole master of the Arabian peninsula.

Except for his gold-rimmed glasses, Ibn Saud looked like a character from the pages of the Old Testament. He observed all the taboos of the Wahhabi sect which sanctioned polygamy and therefore permitted him to marry one hundred and sixty wives. His height—six feet six inches—set him apart from most of his subjects, and in spite of his fundamentalist religious views, he knew how to come to terms with the twentieth century. He signed contracts with foreign oil companies—especially the Americans—and announced, "Moslems today are awakening from sleep. They must take hold of the weapons which are at their hands and which are of two kinds—first, piety and obedience to God; second, such material weapons as airplanes and motorcars." He invoked the religious spirit of Arabia as Kemal invoked the national spirit of Turkey. Like Riza Khan in Persia, he played one foreign power off against another. His career, especially after the 1918 Armistice, showed that even the most backward peoples of Asia had the power to find a new place for themselves in the sun and that the leader who knew his own limitations could go far.

· IV ·

GEOGRAPHICALLY Egypt belonged to the Middle East; in religion it belonged to the world of Islam; historically it had close ties with the Ottoman Empire and the new Arab states. Politically, however, Egypt belonged to the British Empire and the war tightened those bonds. British troops had occupied Egypt since 1882, and in December, 1914, the British government proclaimed Egypt "a British Protectorate." Four years later the British refused to let the Egyptians send a delegation to the Paris Peace Conference. A local Nationalist Party, known as the Wafd and led by Zaghlul Pasha—a self-made member of the oppressed fellahin class—responded by demanding immediate and complete independence. In March, 1919, the British authorities arrested Zaghlul and three other Wafdist leaders and deported them to the island of Malta.

Although the Egyptian masses led as miserable lives as most of the other Middle Eastern people, Egypt had a larger middle class than the more backward Arab lands farther east, and it was from this class—especially from the students—that the Nationalists drew their chief support. The arrest of Zaghlul led to widespread sabotage: Nationalists cut all telegraph wires, roads, and railway lines into Cairo and made no less than two hundred breaks in the railway connecting Egypt with the Sudan. However, surprisingly little bloodshed accompanied these outbreaks; at only one country station did the Nationalists get out of hand, massacring eight Englishmen. The British government wisely sent Lord Allenby, the hero of the campaigns in Mesopotamia and Palestine, to restore order—a man whose experience told him that concessions had to be made to the Nationalist movement.

In 1922 Britain recognized Egypt as an "Independent Sovereign State" and released Zaghlul from prison to become its first Prime Minister. But Zaghlul and the Nationalists objected to certain "reserved points"—including the right to maintain troops in Egypt—that the British refused to concede, and in 1924 Nationalists in Cairo assassinated Sir Lee Stack, the Commander in Chief of the Egyptian Army and the Governor General of the Sudan. Zaghlul had to resign, and for the next two years the unpopular King Fuad ran Egypt's affairs in the old, corrupt, despotic way. The native population showed its feelings by voting Nationalist in the 1926 elections, but Lord Lloyd, the die-hard High Commissioner, refused to let Zaghlul become Prime Minister and carry out the voters' will.

The same nationalist spirit that swept the Egyptian middle classes swept the middle classes of India, too. One million, three hundred thousand Indians had served in the armed forces of the British Empire during the war—more than all the troops of all the self-governing Dominions of the British Empire put together. Indians had contributed half a billion dollars to the British war effort; they had contributed another seven hundred million dollars to British war loans; they had shipped a billion and a quarter dollars' worth of supplies to the Allies. Like the Dominions —like the United States, for that matter—India came out of the war stronger than it had gone in, and the middle classes—the bankers, industrialists, and professional people—felt that their country had earned a more important place in the Empire and in the world. In 1916, before Wilson had called for the self-determination of nations and a world made safe for democracy, the Indian National Congress and the All-India Moslem League adopted Home Rule for India as their common policy. For more than thirty years the Congress Party had been agitating for Indian independence. Although it had attracted individual Moslems as well as Hindus, it remained an essentially Hindu organization. However, the fact that the organized Moslems of India had now formed a united front with the Congress suggested that the national spirit was running stronger than the religious spirit and that the British could no longer rely on their divide-and-rule policy to hold India in subjection.

During the black year of 1917, Britain's rulers recognized that they must make some concessions to the Indian nationalists, and Edwin S. Montagu, as Secretary of State for India, therefore declared, "The policy of His Majesty's Government, with which the Government of India are in complete accord, is that of the increasing association of Indians in every branch of the administration, and the gradual development of self-governing institutions with a view to the progressive realization of responsible government in India as an integral part of the British Empire." The declaration served its purpose: India's war effort did not slacken. When peace came, the native nationalist leaders expected payment for value received.

The British leaders had other ideas. Although victory had liquidated the German menace, the position of Great Britain in the Empire and in the world had declined. The voters who responded to nationalist slogans in the general election of 1918 gave little thought to wartime promises of Home Rule for India; they wanted homes in England for their own heroes. And the Conservatives, who had won control of Parliament, regarded any concession to India as a sign of British weakness.

Early in 1919 the new Parliament passed a new Government of India Act based on a joint report drawn up by Montagu and Lord Chelmsford, the Viceroy of India. The "Montagu-Chelmsford Reforms" promised "gradual development of self-governing institutions" and transferred control of agriculture, education, public health, and public works to the native population in those provinces under British rule. But the British continued to reserve to themselves such vital matters as the police, the courts, the armed services, foreign policy, finance, and taxation. The Indians could spend on agriculture, education, health, and public works only such money as the British made available to them. At the same time, the power of the Indian Princes to rule their own states—comprising about one third of the entire subcontinent—remained intact, subject as ever to British supervision.

Indian extremists retaliated with strikes and demonstrations, whereupon extremists in London hit back by persuading Parliament to pass the Rowlatt Bill permitting Indian police to arrest and imprison suspects without a trial. In April, 1919, British police arrested two Indian leaders who had urged their compatriots to take part in *hartals*, or passive resistance strikes, in the city of Amritsar in the Punjab. An angry Indian mob retaliated by stoning the office of the British Deputy Commissioner. The police fired on the crowd, killing ten persons; the crowd fought back and killed five Englishmen. Within a few days six hundred British regulars arrived, under the command of Brigadier General Dyer, who banned all parades and meetings. Dyer's proclamation coincided with the arrival of ten thousand Hindus who had come from the surrounding countryside to celebrate a religious festival in a walled enclosure. Will Durant, in *The Case for India*, described what followed:

"Without giving the slightest warning, or affording the assemblage any opportunity to indicate its pacific intentions, he [General Dyer] ordered his troops to fire upon the imprisoned mass; and though the crowd made no resistance, but shouted its horror and despair and pressed in panic against the gates, the General ordered the firing to continue until all the ammunition the soldiers had brought with them was exhausted. He personally directed the firing towards the exits where the crowd was most dense; 'the targets' he declared were 'good.' The massacre lasted for over ten minutes. When it was over, 1,500 Hindus were left on the ground, 400 of them dead. Dyer forbade his soldiers to give any aid to the injured, and by ordering all Hindus off the streets for twenty-four hours prevented relatives or friends from bringing even a cup of water to the wounded who were piled up in the field.

"A reign of official terror followed. General Dyer issued an order that Hindus using the street in which a woman missionary had been beaten should crawl on their bellies; if they tried to rise to all fours, they were struck by the butts of soldiers' guns. He arrested five hundred professors and students and compelled all students to present themselves daily for roll-calls, though this required that many of them should walk sixteen miles a day. He had hundreds of citizens, and some schoolboys, quite innocent of any crime, flogged in the public square. He built an open cage, unprotected from the sun, for the confinement of arrested persons; other prisoners he bound together with ropes, and kept in open trucks for fifteen hours. He had lime poured on the naked bodies of *Sadhus* (saints) and then exposed them to the sun's rays that the lime might harden and crack their skin. He cut off the electric and water supplies from Indian houses and ordered all electric fans possessed by Hindus to be surrendered, and given *gratis* to the British. Finally he sent airplanes to drop bombs upon men and women working in the fields.

"The news of this barbaric orgy of military sadism was kept from the world for half a year. A belated commission of inquiry appointed by the government rendered an equivocal report. A committee appointed by the Indian National Congress made a more thorough investigation and reported 1,200 killed and 3,600 wounded. General Dyer was censured by the House of Commons, exonerated by the House of Lords, and was retired on a pension. Thinking this reward insufficient, the militarists of the Empire raised a fund of $150,000 for him and presented him with a jeweled sword."

The Amritsar Massacre ended all hope for Anglo-Indian compromise. Many Indian moderates who had not called for more than Dominion status as a first step toward independence now demanded *Swaraj*, or self-rule, at once. The Rowlatt Bill and the Amritsar Massacre killed the Government of India Bill at birth. The National Congress Party turned to a new kind of leader who outlined a new kind of revolution. The leader's name was Gandhi, and his revolution sought to win power by non-violent means.

· V ·

MOHANDAS KARAMCHAND GANDHI, born on October 2, 1869, had spent the first fifty years of his life preparing himself for this moment of destiny. He was born to the Bania, or tradesman, caste and to the Jain sect of Hindus who opposed any taking of life. His father, grandfather, and great-grandfather had served as Prime Ministers in small princely states north of Bombay. He was the youngest son of his father's fourth wife—a religious woman whose strong personality did much to shape his own. His parents married him off at the age of thirteen to another thirteen-year-old—an illiterate girl named Kasturbai who never did learn to read or write properly. The boy-husband continued his education, spending only the nights with his girl-bride, of whom he was at first jealous and to whom he always remained faithful. He attributed her lack of education to his own "lustful love."

Gandhi was a shy, small, spidery, delicate, bat-eared youth. Under the spell of a husky elder brother, he agreed to go to London at the age of eighteen to study law, leaving his wife and their first-born infant at home. The Bania caste, which forbids its members to cross the sea, expelled him. He promised his mother to eat no meat, and almost starved to death in London until he found a vegetarian restaurant that prepared meals for him without even milk or eggs. Presently he made friends with English vegetarians, met Annie Besant and Madame Blavatsky, learned about nationalism, democracy, and Christianity. The Old Testament left him cold; but when he read the Sermon on the Mount the teachings of Jesus touched his heart. However, when one of his Christian friends told him that Jesus had suffered to atone for the sins of mankind and that Christianity offered a life of peace instead of a life of restlessness, Gandhi—a believer in original sin—replied, "If this be the Christianity acknowledged by all Christians, I cannot accept it. I do not seek redemption from the consequences of my sin. I seek to be redeemed from sin itself, or rather from the very thought of sin. Until I have attained that I shall be content to be restless."

Gandhi had gone to London a timid, provincial idealist of delicate physique, awkward bearing, and uncertain purpose. At first, he tried to adopt English ways, wore a silk top-hat, took unsuccessful lessons in dancing, elocution, French, and the violin. Although he felt uncomfortable, he also discovered—with growing admiration—that the English practiced the tolerance they preached and that he could make real friendships with individuals. After studying law for three years at the University of London, he was admitted to the bar. Two days later he sailed for Bombay.

Gandhi soon found he had entered an overcrowded profession for which he had little aptitude. When he rose to defend his first and only client in a Bombay court he could not speak and had to turn the case over to another lawyer. In 1893—a year after his return from London—he accepted a job with a concern of Moslem merchants who needed a legal expert with a speaking knowledge of English to settle a commercial dispute concerning forty thousand pounds' worth of merchandise in South Africa. They paid all his traveling expenses and gave him a fee of 105 pounds and a year's time to complete the assignment.

Gandhi landed at Durban, in the British colony of Natal, and took a train to Pretoria. As an Indian—or "coolie"—he could not ride in the first-class accommodations for which he had paid; he could not stay in any first-class hotel; he discovered what it meant to belong to a persecuted minority. Behind these restrictions lay a sordid history. Nearly one hundred thousand Indians had emigrated to South Africa as bonded laborers, usually under five-year contracts. They lived in compounds, and when they had served their time they were expected to go quietly home again. But the Indians proved successful as small traders, industrious as cultivators, skillful as workers in handicrafts. Afraid of competition, the government passed laws imposing poll taxes on Indians, restricting the movements of Indians, forbidding Indians to acquire land, compelling Indians to register their children as Christians or have them declared illegitimate. Marriages between Moslems and Hindus were also forbidden in order to keep the Indians divided against themselves. At the same time the vast majority of native blacks received far worse treatment.

Gandhi wound up his business in less than a year, following his own saying that "the true function of a lawyer is to unite parties riven asunder." Almost from the moment he arrived, the condition of his fellow Indians engrossed him and he at once set about applying religious principles. With Christians he invoked the Sermon on the Mount. Of himself he said that the following stanza of Indian didactic verse "gripped my mind and heart" and "became my guiding principle":

> For a bowl of water give a goodly meal;
> For a kindly greeting bow thou down with zeal;
> For a simple penny pay thou back with gold;
> If thy life be rescued, do not life withhold.

Thus the words and actions of the wise regard;
Every little service tenfold they reward.
But the truly noble know all men are one,
And return with gladness good for evil done.

Gandhi urged all the Indians in Natal to make a common front; to avoid violence and hatred; to love and trust the British. He organized the Natal Indian Congress, taking the name from the Congress Party of India, and he became the first Indian lawyer to win the right to appear before the Natal Supreme Court. Most of the British respected him. Middle-class Indians—especially Moslems, who suffered fewer indignities than Hindus—contributed funds. In 1896 Gandhi returned to India for six months and then took his family back to Natal with him. A friendly police chief saved him from a possible lynching after he landed at Durban, where feeling against the Indians persisted. But Gandhi persisted, too, and led thousands of Indians on foot over provincial borders that the British had forbidden them to cross. When police arrested them they made no resistance, and soon the jails could not hold them all. Gandhi always stood trial with his followers; he never asked them to do anything he would not do himself; he did nothing that they, too, could not do. Thus he became the kind of leader who duplicates himself over and over and over again among the entire rank and file of his movement.

Gandhi did more than turn the other cheek. During the Boer War he raised a volunteer Indian ambulance corps that served with the British forces, and he himself tended British wounded in the trenches of Ladysmith. In 1906, when the Zulus attempted an uprising, Gandhi served as a stretcher-bearer with the British, who three times awarded him medals for heroism. He made no secret of his personal sympathy for the Boers and the Zulus, but he considered himself a loyal British subject and acted on the assumption that the British would meet good faith with good faith. "Hardly ever," he said of himself, "have I known anyone to cherish such loyalty as I did toward the British Constitution." It took twenty years for his tactics to justify themselves, but eventually he gained most of the concessions he had demanded and in doing so he won among his fellow Indians the title of "Mahatma," or "Great Soul." His friend Tagore once wrote: "The word 'Mahatma' means the liberated ego which rediscovers itself in all souls, that life no longer confined in individual human beings, the comprehensive soul of the Atman, of the spirit. In this way, the soul becomes 'Mahatma,' by comprehending all souls, all spirit, in itself." Gandhi himself never liked the title, preferring to be called "Babu," or father. "The woes of Mahatmas," he declared, "are known to Mahatmas alone."

UNITED PRESS PHOTO
UNITED PRESS PHOTO

M. K. Gandhi, the Young Lawyer   *Gandhi, the Mahatma*

Gandhi entitled his autobiography *The Story of My Experiments with Truth*—a phrase that gives the key to his personality. He never, for instance, considered himself primarily a political leader. The search for truth always came first and he sought the truth gradually, by trial and error: "My firm belief is that God reveals Himself daily to every human being, but that we shut our eyes to the 'still small voice.' I claim to be nothing but a humble servant of India and humanity." Nor did he attempt to foist his Hindu faith on others: "My faith offers me all that is necessary for my inner development, for it teaches me to pray. But I also pray that everyone else may develop the fullness of his own being in his own religion, that the Christian may become a better Christian, and the Mohammedan a better Mohammedan. I am convinced that God will one day ask us only what we are and what we do, not the name we give to our being and doing." Gandhi never claimed that he saw visions or received privileged revelations: "I have no special revelation of God's will. . . . I have no desire to found a sect." J. Polak, a Jewish friend of Gandhi's in South Africa, said of him: "You cannot say that this is he or that is he. All you can say with certainty is that he is here, he is there. Everywhere his influence reigns, his authority rules, his elusive personality pervades. This must be so for it is true of all great men that they are incalculable, beyond definition. They partake of the Illimitable and Eternal from which they have sprung and to which they are bound."

Gandhi gathered about himself a small band of disciples who had to follow his own strict regime. They performed the humblest tasks, ate no meat, practiced complete nonviolence, loved their enemies, abstained from all sexual activity. Gandhi had no use for people who refused to take vows for fear of losing their independence. He regarded a vow as sacred and necessary. In 1906, at the age of thirty-seven, he vowed himself to lifelong chastity. He had already sworn never to eat meat, eggs, or the milk of a cow or buffalo. "It is my firm conviction that man need take no milk at all beyond the mother's milk that he takes as a baby. His diet should consist of nothing but sun-baked fruits and nuts. He can secure enough nourishment both for the tissues and the nerves from fruits like grapes and nuts like almonds. Restraint of the sexual and other passions becomes easy for a man who lives on such food."

Gandhi's vegetarian diet expressed his hatred of violence: "To my mind the life of a lamb is no less precious than that of a human being. I should be unwilling to take the life of a lamb for the sake of the human body. I hold that the more helpless a creature, the more entitled it is to protection by man from the cruelty of man." And the man who would find truth must cut himself off from his passions: "A man who is swayed by his passions may have good enough intentions, may be truthful in word, but he will never find the Truth. A successful search for Truth means complete deliverance from the dual throng such as love and hate, happiness and misery." He also liked to quote these lines from the Bhagavad-Gita, one of the holy poems of Hinduism:

> For a man who is fasting his senses
> Outwardly the sense-objects disappear,
> Leaving the yearning behind; but when
> He has seen the Highest
> Even the yearning disappears.

Yet these aspirations did not cut him off from a life of political action. On the contrary. Only by participating in the political life of his time did he feel he could apply his beliefs and find truth: "To see the universal and all-pervading Spirit of the Truth face to face one must be able to love the meanest of creation as oneself. And a man who aspires after that cannot afford to keep out of any field of life. That is why my devotion to Truth has drawn me into the field of politics; and I can say without the slightest hesitation and yet with all humility that those who say that religion has nothing to do with politics do not know what religion means."

The outbreak of war in 1914 found Gandhi in London, where he organized Indian students to serve in an Indian ambulance corps on the Western Front. The British had granted the concessions for which he had fought for twenty years in South Africa; as a loyal British subject the least he could do was encourage other Indians to aid Britain in its time of need. He also expected a grateful Empire to give him and his people their reward after the immediate danger had passed. Only part of Gandhi's success lay in his own willingness to turn the other cheek, to meet hatred with love. He understood the kind of people with whom he had to deal. Some Britons, it is true, continued to persecute Gandhi's followers, but most of them responded nobly to Gandhi's own nobility. It may be doubted that he would have received so much consideration at other hands. It can hardly be doubted that he proved himself a political psychologist of genius in using moral weapons against a people who prided themselves on their own virtue.

Early in 1915 Gandhi returned to India, where he began in a small way to adopt the same regime that he had followed in South Africa. In May, he and twenty-five followers established a community at Ahmedabad to follow the practices that he had perfected in South Africa. Soon he startled millions of orthodox Hindus by admitting a family of Untouchables and then he attracted attention by opposing continued emigration of indentured Indian labor and by persuading oppressed sharecroppers and factory workers to adopt his nonviolent tactics. When his little community seemed doomed through lack of funds, a rich Moslem who had watched Gandhi's career with quiet sympathy suddenly came to its rescue.

Although Gandhi held no official position in the Indian National Congress Party, he attended its meetings and easily gained its support in his fight against the emigration of indentured labor to South Africa. The older leaders of the Congress Party favored Dominion status for India within the Empire; the younger ones favored early independence. Gandhi agreed with the older group, but even they did not like it in 1918 when he urged Indians to join the British armed forces in the belief that "it was possible by such services to gain a status of full equality within the Empire."

The passage of the Rowlatt Act followed by the Amritsar Massacre converted the whole Congress Party to the cause of immediate independence for India. It remained, however, for Gandhi, drawing upon his South African experience, to create the necessary strategy. The Indian people had no arms; they had no militant organizations, no violent traditions. Having already proved the uses of nonviolence, he demanded that his people adopt the same tactics against the British in India that they had successfully used, under his leadership, in South Africa. He called first for nonviolent non-co-operation and at the same time attacked the whole factory system. On the surface this seemed like sheer madness. Who, in the twentieth century, could ignore the sanction of force? Who could build a new nation on cottage industries? Gandhi had answers to both questions: "I am not a visionary. I claim to be a practical idealist." Although the unarmed Indians could not overthrow British rule by main force, the working power and buying power of India's millions could destroy the economic base of British rule in India without recourse to violence. At the same time, if the Indians refused to buy any imported manufactured goods and did more to develop homespun yarns and cloth, they could win economic independence while crippling the British still further.

Gandhi did not believe in absolute nonviolence under any and all circumstances: "Where there is a choice between cowardice and violence, I would advise violence. I would risk violence a thousand times rather than the emasculation of the race. I would rather have India resort to arms to defend her honor than that she should in a cowardly manner become or remain a helpless victim to her own dishonor. But I believe nonviolence is infinitely superior to violence." Still more he believed in Indian unity: "If we Indians could only spit in unison, we would form a puddle big enough to drown 300,000 Englishmen." Gandhi also took an elastic view of the evils of the factory system: "I would not weep over the disappearance of machinery or consider it a calamity. But I have no design upon machinery as such." What he did oppose was "the madness of thinking that machinery saves labor. Men 'save labor' until thousands of them are without work and die of hunger on the streets. I want to secure employment and livelihood not only to part of the human race, but for all and I will not have the enrichment of a few at the expense of the community. At present the machinery is helping a small minority to live on the exploitation of the masses." And these words sound more like Marx than the Mahatma: "Machinery must not strive to cripple and stunt human limbs. It must one day cease at last to be a mere tool of acquisitiveness; then the workers will no longer be overstrained and the machine will be a blessing instead of a danger. I am aiming at a change in working conditions of such a kind that the mad race for money will come to an end and the worker will not only be adequately paid but will also find work which is something more than mere slavery."

Gandhi declared that eight Indians in ten had no jobs during half the year and that the hand-operated spinning wheel offered their one hope for a better life: "I claim that in losing the spinning wheel we lost our left lung. We are, therefore, suffering from galloping consumption. The restoration of the spinning wheel arrests the progress of the fell disease." The program of nonviolent non-co-operation that the National Congress Party adopted under Gandhi's leadership proved so successful that in 1922 a British judge finally—and reluctantly—sentenced its instigator to six years in jail. "I hold it to be a virtue to be disaffected toward a Government which has done more harm to India than any previous system," said Gandhi at his trial. "I am here to invite and cheerfully submit to the highest penalty that can be inflicted upon me for what in law is a deliberate crime and what appears to me to be the highest duty of a citizen.

The only course open to you, judge, is either to resign your post or inflict on me the highest penalty." The British judge paid homage to Gandhi's character. Gandhi himself harbored no ill will: "Through love we seek to conquer the wrath of the English administrators and their supporters. We must love them and pray to God that they may have wisdom to see what appears to us to be their error. It is our duty to let ourselves be slain, but not ourselves to slay. If we are cast into prison we must acquiesce in our lot without bad feeling, hate, or any thought of revenge."

Although Gandhi never aspired to become a world messiah in the sense that Wilson and Lenin did, his words and deeds won him a world renown comparable to theirs. "It is true," he once said, "I work for the freedom of India. I inherited its culture, and was created to serve my country. But my love for my fatherland has not only no desire to injure any other nation, it rather aims at serving as best it can all other nations in the truest sense of the word. The freedom of India, as I conceive it, can never be a danger to the world." He also declared, "For me patriotism is the same as humanity. I am patriotic because I am human and humane. My patriotism is not exclusive. I will not hurt England or Germany to serve India. Imperialism has no place in my scheme of life."

The use of ruthless means to achieve noble ends appealed to Lenin's sense of irony. Wilson did not believe that the end justified the means, yet he convinced himself that he could turn the evil of war to higher purposes. Gandhi believed that ends and means are inseparable, that violence serves only to bring forth more violence. He acknowledged the evils of his own Hindu religion, especially the caste system which excluded sixty million Untouchables from intercourse with other Indians. He stretched out the hand of fellowship to the Moslems. Lenin attacked organized religion with the fury of a fanatic; Wilson looked upon himself as a devout Christian who tried to apply his religious beliefs to world politics. Gandhi, on the other hand, once said, "Most religious men I have met are politicians in disguise. I, however, who wear the guise of a politician am at heart a religious man." He spoke the literal truth—and by that truth he lived. There lay his unique genius.

In 1922 the British had sentenced Gandhi to six years in jail. In 1924 they released him in order that he might be operated on—successfully and somewhat against his will—for appendicitis. Already he had consented to drink goat's milk to maintain his strength. He had not violated the letter of his vow not to take cow's or buffalo's milk, but he felt he had violated its spirit. His operation also troubled him because he believed that applications of earth and water could cure all ailments. In spite of his eccentric theories about health—he would have said because of them —he agitated all his life for modern sanitation and personal cleanliness. He had no use for the religion of "pie in the sky, bye-and-bye." Bread seemed to him of greater importance than beauty. "I have found it im-possible," he once remarked to Tagore, "to soothe suffering patients with song. The hungry millions ask for one poem—invigorating food." He came to believe more and more in the virtues of menial, manual work: "A life of labor, the life of the tiller of the soil and the handcraftsman is the life worth living." He spent his time in jail reading, writing, praying, and spinning—and it was the spinning that gave him the greatest refresh-ment. He used the technique of going without food to discipline his body and went on periodic fasts to persuade his followers to compose their differences; none of them dared to be held responsible for his death. Be-cause the British soon understood this, they virtually forced him to go free and submit to the appendicitis operation. They did not like to think what might have happened if he had died in one of their jails.

Meanwhile, more and more Indians adopted Gandhi's tactics with ever-increasing effect. In 1926 the Swaraj (Self-Rule) Party swept the provincial elections. British rule in India had become as outdated as Tsarist rule in Russia ten years before, with this difference. The war ag-gravated Russia's internal tensions. The old order became increasingly corrupt, incompetent, and brutal while at the same time the workers and the soldiers had the arms they needed to make a revolution. The Indian crisis, on the other hand, became acute in time of peace. The British rulers of India showed far more restraint and tolerance than the Tsarist rulers of Russia. Nor did the unarmed workers and peasants of India have the weapons or the organization to fight back. Nevertheless, Gandhi embodied the Indian revolution as Lenin had embodied the Russian Revolution. For Gandhi belonged to a people who were going through a revolution at least as profound as that through which the Russians were passing. Nor was this revolution confined to India. Other Asiatic peoples were following other Asiatic leaders, all the way from China's Dr. Sun Yat-sen to Turkey's Mustafa Kemal, in challenging the old imperialist order and demanding national independence. The war which had de-stroyed so much of Europe had given most of Asia a new lease on life, and almost every student, almost every business and professional man from Suez to Singapore, from Constantinople to Tokyo saw bright, new prospects ahead for himself and his country.

Both Wilson and Lenin had preached the self-determination of peo-ples; it remained for native leaders to apply their principles to Asia. Equally important, the great colonial powers had begun to lose their nerve. India had not only become richer and more productive; Britain's Liberal and Labor parties sympathized with the aspirations of the In-dian nationalists. More and more Britons of all classes and parties re-garded Kipling's effusions about "the white man's burden" as obsolete hypocrisy. Some idealists went so far as to hope that the liberation of

Asia would also break down the barriers that Kipling had apostrophized when he proclaimed that East and West could never meet.

"The most important of all facts in the present world is that East and West have met," wrote Rabindranath Tagore in 1920. "So long as it remains a mere fact, it will give rise to interminable conflicts; it will even hurt man's soul. It is the mission of all men of faith to raise the fact into truth. The worldly wise will shake their heads and say it is not possible —that there is a radical difference between East and West, and that only physical power will have its sway in their relationship." Tagore urged the East not to misunderstand the West as the West had misunderstood the East: "The present age has been forcefully possessed by the West; it has only become possible because to her is given some great mission for man. We of the East have come to her to learn whatever she has to teach us; for by doing so, we hasten the fulfillment of this age."

Gandhi had learned about nationalism and democracy in the West, but he rejected the means that the West had chosen to gain its purposes: "The world war has shown as nothing else has the satanic nature that dominates Europe today. Every canon of public morality has been broken by the victors in the name of virtue. . . . But the cause of all these crimes is the crass materialism." Enough Indians caught enough of Gandhi's spirit to make a success of nonviolent non-co-operation. What most Europeans and Americans failed to grasp was that positive religious faith always animated him. Lenin became a world messiah because he pursued purely material ends with a religious zeal. Gandhi became a world messiah because he applied religious principles to practical politics. And as the star of Woodrow Wilson began to set in the West, the star of Mahatma Gandhi began to rise in the East.

SUMMING UP

ALTHOUGH the Versailles Treaty assigned full and sole responsibility for the war to Imperial Germany, the rest of the settlement gave Republican Germany some chance to earn its way back into a new European community. But whether the Allies agreed to a harder or a softer peace for Germany, they could do nothing to repair the confusion farther east. The collapse of the Hapsburg Empire and the victory of the Russian Bolsheviks demolished two of the main foundations of prewar Europe. No matter what might happen in Germany—unless, perhaps, it went Communist—Europe could not hope to regain any unity in any foreseeable future. And the prospects for world unity seemed still farther off.

The Turkey of Mustafa Kemal went through a nationalist revolution that took similar forms in other countries of the Middle East: everywhere backward peoples rebelled against European domination. This new national spirit ran especially strong among the leaders of the Indian Congress Party—and among these leaders Mahatma Gandhi won a unique position. For more than a century, control over India had helped Britain to maintain a commanding position in the world. Most of the other nations of western Europe—large and small—also depended on their colonial possessions overseas. The war, in weakening Europe, at the same time set off a wave of revolt all the way from North Africa to China.

One nation and one nation only possessed the power to give the world the kind of leadership Europe had lost. The United States of America had ensured the complete defeat of Germany, but only if the United States continued to intervene actively in European affairs and to adopt a more vigorous interest in more backward regions—only thus could the world hope to come together in the near future. Everything therefore depended upon Woodrow Wilson's ability to persuade the Senate and the American people to accept the entire settlement he had brought back from Paris or to persuade himself to meet the rising Republican opposition part way.

4

Back to Normalcy

*How the Senate Republicans defeated Wilson in
his fight for the Versailles Treaty only to disgrace
their party and themselves by sending Harding to
the White House.*

PREVIEW

T HE Senate Republicans played on Wilson's weaknesses until he defeated himself in the fight for the Treaty and the League. But in
outsmarting Wilson the Old Guard also outsmarted itself when it picked
Warren G. Harding to run for the Presidency in 1920. The strain of high
office and the sins of his cronies killed him within two and a half years.
By the time of his death, the postwar depression had ended and the prewar cultural renaissance had revived. Most Americans welcomed Calvin
Coolidge as Harding's successor and gave him credit for the good times
that followed his arrival in the White House. The Democrats, divided
among themselves on Prohibition and the Ku Klux Klan suffered another defeat in the Presidential election of 1924.

· I ·

NOWHERE did the fruits of victory sour so rapidly as in the United States.
By the middle of June, 1919, General Bliss anticipated the public mood:
"What a wretched mess it all is: If the rest of the world will let us alone,
I think we better stay on our own side of the water and keep alive the
spark of civilization to relight the torch after it is extinguished over here.
If I ever had any illusions, they are all dispelled." Early in July, President
Wilson returned to the heat of humid Washington a half-broken man. In
another three months the collapse became complete. His singlehanded
battle against prewar diplomacy and postwar influenza had robbed him
of all his energy. The hostility of the Republican leaders rasped his weary
nerves. Every clause and comma of the book-length Treaty seemed to
him part of his own, intimate personality. The long negotiations at Paris
had drained away all his patience, tact, and politeness; only stubbornness, touchiness, and pride remained. On July 10 he laid the final draft of

the Treaty before the Senate in a brief, strangely halting speech. "Dare we reject it," he asked, "and break the heart of the world?" But his appeal to the Senate to ratify the Treaty made no mention of the Security Pact he had signed with Britain and France and that he had pledged himself to submit to the Senate along with the Treaty of Versailles. He broke that pledge because he felt that keeping it would make the whole issue too "complicated." A man less convinced of his own moral integrity might have felt he had compromised his honor.

Wilson, at the height of his powers, had coined the phrase "Too proud to fight." But assurance had given way to exhaustion; strength had turned to weakness, and a new kind of pride possessed him, the kind of pride that forces a man to seek battle rather than avoid it. It was the kind of pride that made Wilson his own worst enemy and the surest ally of Henry Cabot Lodge. The senior Senator from Massachusetts had earned his Ph.D. at Harvard before Wilson had received his A.B. degree from Princeton. Lodge regarded himself as the original scholar in politics and despised Wilson as an upstart. He deplored the absence of classical allusions in Wilson's prose and criticized the League Covenant on stylistic grounds: "As an English production it does not rank high. It might get by at Princeton, but certainly not at Harvard." Henry Adams found Lodge's enjoyment of hatred typical of Boston, and Senator Chauncey M. Depew of New York compared Lodge to the soil of New Engand—"naturally barren but highly cultivated."

The personalities of Wilson and Lodge affected the American political scene as two papers of Seidlitz powders affect a glass of water. Wilson returned from Paris weary, stubborn, and proud. His conscience told him that he and he alone had put through the only kind of settlement that offered the world any hope for lasting peace. But his conscience blinded him to the facts of arithmetic, history, and politics. The Republicans held 49 Senate seats, the Democrats 47. Every Republican opposed the Treaty Wilson had brought back. So did four Democrats. A treaty to become binding required the approval of two thirds of the Senate. Although Wilson's Treaty did not command even majority support, some Republicans favored it with mild reservations, approved by Taft and Root. Others favored stronger reservations drawn up by Lodge. Only seven Republicans opposed the Treaty in any form. Wilson thus faced a clear but bitter choice. He must compromise something or lose everything.

Emotion, not reason, dictated his decision. He felt that he had already gone the limit when he persuaded the peacemakers at Paris to accept changes that certain Republicans requested. Conscience forbade him from giving any more ground. Viscount Grey, from England, tried to convince Wilson that Britain would gladly accept the additional changes

WILSON DID IT!
WILSON DID IT!
WILSON DID IT!

REPUBLICAN
PRESS

BETTMANN ARCHIVE

*"Teaching Him What to Say": Senator
Lodge as Seen by Rollin Kirby*

the milder Republican reservations proposed. Ambassador Jusserand of France came to the White House in despair, begging Wilson to make enough concessions to assure Senate approval of the Treaty. "Mr. Ambassador," Wilson replied, "I shall consent to nothing. The Senate must take its medicine." More than ten years had passed since Wilson faced a comparable situation at Princeton, where he favored a reform program that a majority of the faculty opposed. "How on earth," he exclaimed to his recalcitrant colleagues, "do you expect me to make this a democratic institution unless I have complete control?"

This attitude conformed perfectly to the plans of Senator Lodge, who aimed to defeat the Treaty in such a way as to make Wilson appear responsible. And hatred possessed Lodge as completely as self-righteousness possessed Wilson. The two scholars in politics both succumbed to emotional orgies that any professional politician would not have dared to indulge. For Lodge was no isolationist. He never joined Borah and Johnson and the irreconcilable "Battalion of Death." Back in 1915, Lodge had spoken for the League to Enforce Peace: "Nations must unite as men must unite in order to preserve peace and order. . . . In differences between nations which go beyond the limited range of arbitral questions, peace can only be maintained by putting behind it the force of the united nations determined to uphold it and prevent war." But Lodge forgot his convictions. He forgot that a majority of the Senate and a majority of the American people clearly favored some compromise that would bring the United States into the League. A single passion consumed him: the passion to destroy Wilson. He therefore stacked his Foreign Relations Committee with members of the irreconcilable minority. One of them, Senator James Watson of Indiana, expressed alarm. "I don't see how we are going to defeat this proposition," he told Lodge. "Eighty per cent of the people are for it. Fully that percentage of the preachers right now are advocating it."

"Ah, my dear James," Lodge replied, "I do not propose to beat it by direct frontal attack, but by the indirect method of reservations." He then explained to the admiring Watson how he planned to defeat the Treaty by debating it to death. Although Watson had no use for either

Wilson or the League, he kept his emotions in hand. Most Republicans felt more envy than contempt for Wilson, who inspired fear as well as dislike among his political enemies. But Alice Roosevelt Longworth, the only child of Theodore Roosevelt's first marriage, kept her father's hatred for Wilson alive. "A murrain on him," she murmured when she first saw him on his return from Paris, giving him at the same time the sign of the evil eye. "How we did cherish and nourish our hatreds in those days," she confessed afterwards.

And how Wilson indulged his own. As soon as Lodge opened his fight on the League with the tactics of delay, Wilson met the attack as he had met all others. He decided to take his case to the people and stump the country. His personal physician, Admiral Cary Grayson, warned him that his delicate, weakened physique could not stand the strain of the projected journey. Friends pointed out that the decision did not lie with the people but with the Senate. Nevertheless, Wilson insisted that he had only to give the people leadership, and the sheer force of public opinion would compel two thirds of the Senate to accept the Treaty, on his terms. He refused to see that wartime unity had given way to postwar disunity; that his own administration was falling apart; that public opinion was turning toward the Republicans.

On September 3, Wilson boarded his special car in a special train for a nation-wide speaking tour, with special emphasis on the Middle West. He covered eight thousand miles in three weeks, delivered thirty-six pre- pared addresses that lasted an hour each and that he typed out huddled over his own portable in the hot, gritty train. He delivered sixty more brief, extemporaneous talks and subsisted on a diet of dining-car and banquet food. The crowds that greeted him grew larger and larger, more and more enthusiastic. The people admired his fighting spirit, his clear style, his polished delivery. But the Battalion of Death fought back. Senator William E. Borah of Idaho and Senator Hiram W. Johnson of California followed on Wilson's trail, and their irreconcilable opposition to him drew as much applause as his irreconcilable opposition to them. Borah and Johnson had loud voices, strong convictions, large vocabu- laries, and progressive records. They also had maintained close contact with the people of the Middle and Far West.

In Pueblo, Colorado, on his way back east, Wilson broke down. A persistent agonizing headache forced him to cancel all further engage- ments and hasten to Washington. Admiral Grayson announced that over- work had produced a nervous collapse. The worst was still to come. Two weeks later, a brain hemorrhage paralyzed his left side. After another two weeks, the doctors warned that they must operate upon his prostate gland within two hours. Mrs. Wilson, convinced that he could not sur- vive an operation, rejected their advice and within three hours the condition cleared up. "For days," wrote Mrs. Wilson afterward, "life hung in the balance."

Mere chance had decreed that Wilson should not die a martyr and a hero; that the Senate should not be shamed into approving the Treaty and the League—at any rate in some form—as it almost surely would have done had Thomas R. Marshall, the popular, easygoing Vice-President, stepped into Wilson's shoes. All this was not to be. Wilson lived on, to continue his proud, stubborn, futile fight. For weeks he saw only his doctors and his wife, through whose hands all his correspondence passed. He grew a white beard. The public, not informed that the President had suffered a stroke, heard that he was paralyzed, insane, dead. Actually he kept possession of his faculties. When a committee of Senators visited Wilson in his sickroom, Fall of New Mexico unctuously declared, "Mr. President, we have all been praying for you." "Which way, Senator?" Wilson replied. His illness had served only to make him more determined than ever to force acceptance of his version of the Treaty and the League.

The attempt failed utterly. On the first vote, a majority of Senators rejected all reservations. In this case, most of the Democrats obeyed Wilson's orders and voted with the irreconcilables against every Republican attempt at compromise. The most drastic of the Lodge reservations would have changed Article X, "the heart of the Covenant," as Wilson called it, by requiring Congress to approve in advance any steps the United States might take to prevent aggression on the part of one League member against another. According to Wilson, the Lodge reservations added up to "nullification," which was just the response Lodge had counted on getting. When the time came to vote on the Treaty in the form Wilson wanted, only 39 Senators favored it, 55 opposed.

Wilson had become so obsessed with the letter of the Treaty that he lost sight of its spirit. He acknowledged imperfections in the German settlement, and counted on the League of Nations to mitigate them in time. But he would stand no tampering with his precious League Covenant. Yet this Covenant did not set up a world government. It did not touch the national sovereignty of any member state. It did not create an international police force. It called only for consultation and arbitration. The Covenant had not come into existence to curb national sovereignty. It had come into existence to fortify and guarantee the national sovereignty of all League members. The essence of the Covenant lay in the fact that it set up new machinery for consultation among nations. It tried to replace the prewar balance of power with a postwar community of power. Nor did Lodge accuse Wilson of subordinating the national sovereignty of the United States to the international sovereignty of the League of Nations. Lodge attacked the Treaty because, in his view, it infringed upon the powers of Congress as guaranteed by the Constitution. The essence of his reservations was that they required the consent of Congress before the United States could fulfill some terms of the Covenant. "I wish," said Senator Lodge in late November before the Senate took a short recess, "to carry over these reservations into the campaign." Some weeks later the President accepted Lodge's challenge in a message to the annual Jackson Day Dinner of the Democratic Party, urging that the Treaty be laid before the voters so as "to give the next election the form of a great and solemn referendum."

Having fought the battle of the reservations to a deadlock in November, the Senate resumed the battle over the entire Treaty in March. More than two thirds of the Senate still wanted some kind of Treaty and some kind of League, with some kind of reservations. Ex-President Taft, originally a mild reservationist, preferred the Lodge reservations to no treaty at all. Bernard M. Baruch, a good Democrat who never broke with Wilson, urged him to accept the Lodge reservations because "half a loaf is better than no bread." But Wilson remained as irreconcilable in one direction as Borah and Johnson in another. The President's opposition to any Republican changes now forced the mild reservationists into the Lodge camp. Wilson again ordered Senator Gilbert Hitchcock of Nebraska, who had led the Democratic fight for the Treaty, to oppose Lodge to the end. As the President said to Mrs. Wilson in November, "Better a thousand times to go down fighting than to dip your colors in dishonorable compromise." When the Treaty, with the Lodge reservations, came up for a final vote on March 19, 23 Democrats obeyed Wilson's orders and joined the 12 irreconcilables in opposition. Forty-nine Senators—including 21 Democrats—voted in favor. The Treaty had failed by seven votes to win the necessary two-thirds majority. As the irreconcilable Senator Brandegee whispered to Lodge: "We can always depend upon Mr. Wilson. He has never failed us."

· II ·

THESE Republican Senators had won more than a personal victory over Woodrow Wilson. They had established their own claim to Party leadership. Wilson's obdurate refusal to compromise not only divided the Democrats, some of whom voted to join the League with reservations; by committing his Party to an extreme position, he forced the Republicans to the opposite extreme. Most rank-and-file Republicans preferred the moderation of William Howard Taft, Charles Evans Hughes, and Elihu Root, all supporters of the League, with reservations, to the immoderation of the Old Guard. But the violence of the fight over the Treaty and the League played into the Old Guard's hands, and by 1920,

55768

EMORY & HENRY LIBRARY

© VANGUARD PRESS

"What's he been doin'?"
"Overthrowin' the guvment."
Cartoon by Art Young

Senators Lodge of Massachusetts, Penrose and Knox of Pennsylvania, Smoot of Utah, and Curtis of Kansas, working with sanctimonious Will H. Hays, chairman of the Republican National Committee, and glib Colonel George Harvey, gained control of the Party machinery. The death of Theodore Roosevelt, in January, 1919, after his return to orthodoxy, left no popular leader in the field.

Public opinion, which had already begun to turn against the Democrats in 1918, swung still further away from them in 1920. Wilson's obsession with foreign affairs lost him much of the progressive, independent vote that had won him his two White House terms. More and more Americans felt that their recent adventure abroad had turned out badly. It was not that they opposed the Treaty and the League. What distressed them was Wilson's intolerance, his disregard of domestic issues, and the support that certain members of his administration, notably Attorney General A. Mitchell Palmer, gave to the home-grown reactionaries against whom Wilson had declared war before he crusaded to make the world safe for democracy.

By 1920 the cost of living in the United States had more than doubled as a result of the war and the subsequent removal of wartime controls. Labor tried to keep wages up, to organize more industries. Employers, free again to do as they pleased, fought back. The great United States Steel Company had successfully staved off unionization and still retained the twelve-hour day and the seven-day week. The work-week of its employees averaged 68.7 hours. When 350,000 of them went out on strike in the fall of 1919, the company circulated instructions among its informers who attended strike meetings: "We want you to stir up as much bad feelings as you possibly can between Serbians and Italians. Spread data among the Serbians that the Italians are going back to work. Call up every question you can in reference to racial hatred between these two nationalities; make them realize to the fullest possible extent that far better results would be obtained if they will go back to work. Urge them to go back to work or the Italians will get their jobs." But the strike did not end until federal troops broke it on the picket line.

William Z. Foster, who led the strike for the American Federation of Labor, had belonged to the I.W.W. He came from Taunton, Massachusetts, where he once drove a trolley car. During the war he sold Liberty Bonds, and two years after the collapse of the steel strike joined the Communist Party of the United States. Of such stuff were the early fathers of American Communism made. But Communism made no appeal to young John L. Lewis, leader of the 450,000 coal miners who quit work in November, 1919. "We cannot fight against the government," said Lewis when a court injunction ordered the men back to their jobs. The miners not only ignored both Lewis and the court; a denunciation by President Wilson left them unmoved. Yet Wilson, from his sickroom, recognized that the country as a whole suffered from the same kind of postwar letdown that had laid him low. His message to Congress, dated December 2, 1919, contained these words of warning: "The real antidote for the unrest which manifests itself is not suppression but a deep consideration of the wrongs that beset our national life and the application of a remedy." During the year 1919 more than four million workers had either gone on strike or been locked out of their jobs. The I.W.W. had tied up the city of Seattle, Washington, for several days with a general strike.

Senator Lodge's Boston furnished the greatest excitement of the year. In September the entire police force quit work after rugged Police Commissioner Edwin U. Curtis refused to deal with their A. F. of L. union. Calvin Coolidge, the canny Republican Governor of the state, ducked into hiding during two days of disorder and was not heard from until Mayor Andrew J. Peters of Boston, a Democrat, asked for help from the State Guard. Coolidge then called upon all citizens to uphold law and order. When President Gompers of the A. F. of L. asked Coolidge to give the strikers their jobs back, Coolidge wired, "There is no right to strike against the public safety by anybody, anywhere, any time." A book of Coolidge speeches entitled *Have Faith in Massachusetts* became a best seller. Its author became a local hero and a national figure.

The violence that accompanied the Boston police strike gave the press a text to warn Americans of Bolshevism. "Bolshevism in the United States is no longer a specter," said the Philadelphia *Evening Public Ledger*. "Boston in its chaos revealed its sinister substance. In their reckless defiance of the fundamentals of morality, in their bullying affront to the structure of civilization, wherein do the police of the New England metropolis differ from the mad minority which overthrew Kerensky and ruined Russia? Only an arrant casuist, a fatuous hair-splitter, can proclaim a shade of contrast. The nation has chosen. If ever it was vague in its conception of the Bolshevist horror, its vision is clear-cut now. So is the issue. Defiled Boston has seen to that." Even the cool and experienced Lloyd George shared these apprehensions, although he expressed himself more soberly. "The next five years," he predicted in February, 1919, "will be a very trying time for the world. Civilization in its present form may be severely strained."

The Wilson administration succumbed to the prevailing mood. The President called the Boston police strike "a crime against civilization" and congratulated Coolidge on his re-election to the Governorship the following year. Attorney General A. Mitchell Palmer opened a national drive against the Reds. He had fifty-three alien Communists arrested for deportation in February, 1919; by December his agents were shipping Reds out of the country at the rate of more than two hundred and fifty a month. A bomb explosion wrecked his home in Washington. On December 2, Wilson's message to Congress urged curbs upon the Reds. In Democratic Georgia the Ku Klux Klan began to ride again, and the hooded fighters against "Koons, Kikes, Katholics" gained tens of thousands of recruits in other Southern states and then in the Midwest. In the summer of 1919 a three-day race riot in Chicago between whites and Negroes took thirty-six lives. Even the Assembly of the enlightened state of New York refused to let five Socialist Assemblymen take their seats, as Alfred E. Smith, the liberal, Roman Catholic, Democratic Governor protested in vain.

Nor did the Constitution itself come through the period intact. The wartime Prohibition Act went into effect on July 1, 1919. By the following January, this gave way to the newly passed Eighteenth Amendment to the Constitution, prohibiting the manufacture, sale, and transportation of intoxicating liquors. The Nineteenth Amendment, granting votes to women, soon joined the Prohibition Amendment to the Constitution. Once the American woman won the right to vote, nobody tried to take

BETTMANN ARCHIVE

NEW YORK WORLD

"I Want to Make Their Flesh Creep."
Cartoon by Rollin Kirby

"Now then, all together, 'My Country
'tis of thee.'" Another Kirby cartoon

that right away from her, but a great many Americans refused to take
Prohibition lying down.

They faced an uphill fight. Even before the Eighteenth Amendment
went into effect, two thirds of the American people had outlawed liquor
on a local option basis. In terms of area, though not of population, more
than ninety per cent of the country had voted itself bone dry. Wilson opposed Prohibition. He vetoed the Volstead Act, which defined as intoxicating any beverage containing more than one half of one per cent of
alcohol, whereupon Congress passed the Volstead Act over his veto,
thanks largely to the votes of the Southern Democrats who favored Pro
hibition because they feared the effects of alcohol on Negroes. The big
city vote ran just the other way. Whereas the South went along with the
President on the Treaty and the League, the voters of Irish, Italian, and
German origin in the big cities supported him on Prohibition but opposed the peace settlement. These conflicts tore the Democratic Party
to shreds and ribbons. Wilson himself lost interest in the reform movement that had swept him to the White House in 1912 and kept him there
in 1916. At the same time, William Jennings Bryan, former champion
of peace by arbitration, took little interest in the League of Nations. The
fight against booze appealed to him more than the fight against war. But
the fight against change stirred the widest popular response. Vice-
President Marshall spoke for most of the professional politicians when
he expressed alarm because students in postwar Radcliffe chose as a subject of debate: "Resolved, that the recognition of labor unions by employers is essential to successful collective bargaining." It was Marshall
also who summed up the mood of the time with his deathless observation: "What the country needs is a good five-cent cigar."

The Republicans appealed far more successfully than the Democrats could to this yearning for a return to the good old days. They addressed themselves primarily to business and professional people, to farmers, to unorganized labor, to the lower middle classes, and to the vast area between the Alleghenies and the Rocky Mountains where native, nationalist-isolationist sentiment prevailed. In addition, they talked effectively against Wilson among the foreign-born and so-called hyphenated-American groups in the big cities, especially the Irish-Americans, the Italian-Americans, and the German-Americans, who saw Europe through the eyes of their relatives overseas. The enthusiasm that Wilson had diverted from reforming the country to reshaping the world turned against itself. New frictions developed inside the United States; old suspicions toward other countries revived. The Senate Republicans had appealed to these fears and suspicions in their fight against the Treaty and the League. They kept right on appealing to them after they had routed Wilson on that issue.

When the Republican National Convention met at Chicago in June, 1920, Senator Lodge declared in his keynote oration: "Mr. Wilson and his dynasty, his heirs and his assigns, or anybody that is his, anybody who with bent knee has served his purposes, must be driven from all control, from all influence upon the government of the United States." But the Old Guard, who controlled the Convention, did not like the two candidates who had received the widest popular support in the primaries —General Leonard Wood and Governor Frank O. Lowden of Illinois, neither of whom belonged to the inner Senatorial circle. The Old Guard cared even less for the independent Herbert Hoover, most popular of the dark horses. He had worked for Wilson, spent far too much time abroad, and—for a while—did not know whether to call himself a Democrat or a Republican.

Samuel G. Blythe, Washington correspondent for the *Saturday Evening Post*, expressed himself pungently on the Old Guard, even at the risk of offending his predominantly conservative readers: "You cannot teach an Old Guard new tricks. Every circumstance, from catastrophe to candor, has taken a hand at it but to no avail. The Old Guard surrenders but it never dies. Right at this minute [Blythe wrote late in 1919] despite conditions, both political and national, that are so changed they bear no relation to conditions whenever precedent, those ancient and archaic Republicans who think they control the destinies of the Republican Party—think they do:—are operating after the style and manner of 1896. The war hasn't made a dent in them. The new aspect of affairs has had no impress. They are proceeding toward 1920 in the same old way. Day after day they are led into the menagerie and shown the ring-tailed gyascutus of the new order; and day after day they chew their straws, shake their hoary heads, and solemnly aver, 'There ain't no such animile.' The pathos of it is obscured in the purblindness of it. You can't teach an Old Guard new tricks."

What happened at Chicago bore out Mr. Blythe's prediction. In Washington Lodge had proved himself a master wrecker when it came to tearing down Wilson and the League. But Lodge was no master builder. If he had hated Wilson less and loved his country, or even his party, more he might have gone to Chicago with a constructive plan. But his passion to destroy Wilson blinded him to the situation that Wilson's destruction created. Lodge and his Senate colleagues had chosen no Presidential candidate of their own and had devised no clear Convention strategy. They had so little leadership that Senator Penrose, sick unto death in Philadelphia, carried more influence over the long-distance telephone than any of his hale and hearty colleagues could command in person. But even Penrose had not groomed any suitable candidate.

Three men dominated the field when Lodge called the Convention to order. General Leonard Wood had the most delegates and the most money. His backers had spent $1,773,303, including a loan of $710,000 that was never repaid from Colonel Procter of Ivory Soap. Governor Frank O. Lowden of Illinois had corralled the second largest group of delegates. He had his strongest support among the farmers, who had no prejudice against the fortune his wife inherited from the Pullman Company. The galleries and the rank and file of the Party liked Herbert Hoover, but Hoover had no backing among the professional politicians. This left the field open to the political genius of Harry Micajah Daugherty of Washington Court House, Ohio. Daugherty had first entered the law and then politics, but the people never elected him to any office. He worked best behind the scenes, and preferred power to fame. He had a mind of his own and knew how to express himself forcibly. "General Wood," said Daugherty, "is backed by a powerful group of rich men who wish a military man in the White House. They are nervous over the social disorders following the war. They are nervous over the growing demands of labor. They wish to entrench themselves behind the invincible force of the bayonet and the machine gun. The scheme won't work. The people are sick of war. The boys who saw it in France have begun to tell tales out of school. They hate war to a man. They'll not vote for a General. . . . There's not enough money in the world to buy the nomination for a man with epaulettes on his shoulders."

Daugherty not only spotted the fatal weakness in the Wood campaign. He had his own candidate—Senator Warren Gamaliel Harding, of Ohio. "I found him," said Daugherty, "sunning himself like a turtle on a log and I pushed him into the water." The friendship between the two men dated back to the turn of the century, when Daugherty decided that any

UNITED PRESS PHOTO

President Warren Gamaliel Harding

man who looked so much like a President of the United States ought to go to the White House, and in 1920 his opportunity arrived. "When the Convention comes," Daugherty predicted, "those two armies [Wood and Lowden] will battle each other to a standstill. When both realize they can't win, when they're tired and hot and sweaty and discouraged, both armies will remember me. . . . They'll be like soldiers after a battle who recall a shady spring along a country road." The wealth of the Wood supporters and a minor scandal among some Missouri delegates pledged to Lowden helped to make Daugherty's prediction come true. The support for Hoover never spread beyond the galleries, and the Old Guard finally turned to the most astute political operator in Chicago who had already selected the ideal dark horse candidate from the ranks of the Senatorial cabal itself.

No man ever looked more like a President than Harding: wisdom, benignity, and strength shone from his Roman features. The appearance belied the man. Harding was born in 1865 in Marion, Ohio, where his father had taught himself to become a horse doctor and, after a course in homeopathy, ministered to human beings. Of his eldest boy, Warren, the father once said, "It's a good thing you wasn't born a girl because you'd be in a family way all the time. You can't say no." Harding had received a desultory education; he played the alto horn in the Marion Citizens Cornet Band; at the age of nineteen, he and two other young men borrowed a few hundred dollars and purchased the only daily paper in Marion, the *Star*. Here he worked happily and successfully for the next sixteen years, marrying the daughter of Amos Kling, the richest man in town. Florence Kling, eight years Harding's senior, had divorced a drunken husband who died before she married again. Her ambition and business ability helped make the *Star* a success.

Harding liked newspaper work better than politics, but he liked people best of all and could not say no when friends urged him to run for the state Senate. He became as popular in the State Capitol at Columbus as he had been at Marion and won election as Lieutenant Governor; in 1915 he went to Washington as United States Senator from Ohio. He soon became known as the Senate's leading slacker, missing almost half the roll calls and failing to vote on more than one third of those he did attend. His name never appeared on any important bill. One of Harding's secretaries observed that his chief "didn't like being a Senator; he liked being in the Senate." Or as Harding himself once declared on the Senate floor: "Mr. President, I like the fraternity of this body. I like to know that when the waters are muddy, I will be considered. I like to participate in the 'booster' proposition."

When the Senate cabal finally met, just as Harry Daugherty had predicted they would, in a smoke-filled room in the Hotel Blackstone and decided at 2 A.M. to select Harding, Colonel Harvey put these words to Harding in private: "We think you may be nominated tomorrow. Before acting finally we think you should tell us, on your conscience and before God, whether there is anything that might be brought against you that would embarrass the Party, any impediment that might disqualify you or make you inexpedient, either as candidate or as President." Harding asked for a little time to think it over. He and the Republican high command knew the rumor that he had some Negro blood. He also knew—but the Republican high command did not—that working at Republican headquarters in Chicago was a young girl from Marion named Nan Britton who had fallen in love with Harding, become his mistress, and recently borne him a daughter. Harding, however, ran true to form. He couldn't say no. It took him only ten minutes to square his decision with his conscience and his God, and when the Convention nominated him the following day he chortled, "We drew to a pair of deuces and filled."

"Harding is no world-beater," said Senator Brandegee of Connecticut, "but he's the best of the second-raters." After the nomination Penrose warned, "Keep Warren at home. Don't let him make any speeches. If he goes out on tour somebody's sure to ask him questions, and Warren is just the sort of damn fool that will try to answer them." Harding followed the advice and campaigned from his front porch in Marion, but even that modest effort had Penrose worried: "Harding isn't as big a man as I thought he was. He should have talked more about the tariff and not so much about playing the cymbals in the Marion brass band." Penrose had advised basing the campaign on Americanism. "I don't know what it means," he confessed, "but it would make a damn fine campaign issue."

Harding used more words than Penrose needed to conceal his meaning. According to William G. McAdoo, Harding's speeches left "the impression of an army of pompous phrases moving across the landscape in search of an idea; sometimes these meandering words would actually capture a straggling thought and bear it triumphantly, a prisoner in their midst, until it died of servitude and overwork."

The oration that restored the word "normalcy" to the English language contained this characteristic passage: "America's need is not heroism but healing, not nostrums but normalcy, not revolution but restoration, not agitation but adjustment, not surgery but serenity, not the dramatic but the dispassionate, not experiment but equipoise, not submergence in internationality but sustainment in triumphant nationality." Frequently Harding's sentences had neither grammar nor meaning: "We have mistaken unpreparedness to embrace it to be a challenge to the realities, and due concern for making all citizens fit for participation will give added strength of citizenship and magnify our achievement."

The Republican Senators who engineered Harding's nomination planned to have the Convention nominate another of their colleagues as his running mate. First, Hiram Johnson of California, who had accepted second place on the Progressive ticket headed by Theodore Roosevelt in 1912, spurned the Old Guard's attempt to make him the tail of Harding's kite. Then the Convention itself rejected Irvine Lenroot of Wisconsin, another former Progressive, and chose instead Governor Calvin Coolidge, whom Lodge barely knew and thoroughly detested. "A man who lives in a two-family house," exclaimed Lodge when somebody suggested Coolidge as a possibility, "Never." But the Convention liked Coolidge's record in the Boston police strike and rebelled against further dictation by the Senate Old Guard, which once again proved its political ineptitude. In point of fact, the contrasting personalities of Harding and Coolidge formed an effective combination. Only Mrs. Harding feared for her husband's future: "I cannot see but one word written above his head if they make him President, and that word is 'tragedy.'"

In 1920, however, that word fitted Wilson better than it fitted Harding. As William Allen White wrote of Wilson afterward in *Masks in a Pageant:* "He went to Europe a God. He sat down at the green baize table in the Room of the Clocks at Versailles a philosophical prig. He arose the incarnation of tragedy." According to White, Wilson hoped to win the Democratic nomination for the Presidency and a third term that would give him a chance to vindicate himself and his discarded and discredited League of Nations. "Ike" Hoover, the observant White House usher, described Wilson as "not only receptive but anxious and expectant" though he made no overt acts. But the rank-and-file Democrats at the Convention wanted no part of Woodrow Wilson, sick or well, and gave the nomination to James M. Cox, three times reform Governor of Ohio. Second place on the ticket went to handsome, young Franklin D. Roosevelt, who had successfully fought the Tammany machine in the New York State Assembly and served as assistant Secretary of the Navy under Josephus Daniels. When Cox and Roosevelt visited Wilson in the White House, the President's appeal for the League moved both men to tears and they promised to campaign for the "solemn referendum" the President had called for. Both kept their word, but Cox devoted most of his speeches to the fifteen-million-dollar "slush fund" that he accused big business of spending to elect Harding.

The Republican irreconcilables did not object to Harding; on the matter of the Treaty he had vacillated between them and the Lodge group. Nevertheless, thirty-one of the "best minds" of the Republican Party—including Hughes, Root, Hoover, President Lowell of Harvard, and President Butler of Columbia—issued a statement calling for the election of Harding as the best means to secure American entrance into the League of Nations. They chose to ignore a passage of Harding prose in his acceptance speech: "With a Senate advising as the Constitution contemplates, I would hopefully approach the nations of Europe and of the earth, proposing that understanding which makes us a willing participant in the consecration of nations to a new relationship, to commit the moral forces of the world, America included, to peace and international justice, still leaving America free, independent, and self-reliant, but offering friendship to the world." The common people understood, even if the best Republican minds did not, and they gave Harding sixteen million votes as against nine million for Cox. The Republicans carried thirty-seven of the forty-eight states, the Democrats carried no state outside the South, and lost Tennessee. The Republicans won the popular election far more overwhelmingly than they had crushed Wilson and the League in the Senate. "It wasn't a landslide," said Joseph Tumulty, former secretary to Wilson, "it was an earthquake." The men who regarded themselves as the only fit rulers of their country had waited eight long years for this triumph. Their opportunity to justify their claim had come at last, and in full measure. They could blame no one but themselves if they failed to make good.

· III ·

"Often as I sit here," Harding remarked after he had moved into the White House, "I don't seem to grasp that I am President." He also failed to grasp almost everything else pertaining to his new job. Knowing that he had no grasp of foreign affairs, he wanted to make Senator Albert B. Fall of New Mexico Secretary of State because of his high regard for Fall's intellect. Wiser Republican leaders overruled this decision and saw to it that Charles Evans Hughes headed the State Department. They could not, however, prevent Harding from making Fall his Secretary of the Interior or from installing Harry Daugherty as Attorney General.

Daugherty, who regarded Fall as a "typical Progressive," said of himself, years later: "I lay no claim to infallibility or sainthood. As a humble member of the Methodist Church I sometimes fall from grace, ask the Lord to forgive, and try again." Daugherty fell from grace with the Old Guard when he persuaded Harding to put Herbert Hoover, who had no standing with the Party regulars, in charge of the Commerce Department. But Daugherty also fell from grace with his chief when he chose as his closest associate a small-time grafter named Jesse W. Smith, who, in turn, surrounded himself with big-time bootleggers, gamblers, and criminals.

Before the 1920 election, Senator Penrose said of Harding, "We are going to put in a man who will listen." Elihu Root took a more skeptical view. After a pre-election conference with Harding he commented: "I have known intimately five Presidents and each of them was eager for counsel—before the election." Harding, however, did not spurn counsel. He did not refuse to listen to advice. He just could not understand what he heard. He accepted shy 'little Andrew W. Mellon, the third richest man in the country, as his Secretary of the Treasury. Mellon and his fellow Pittsburgher, Henry C. Frick, had contributed heavily to Harding's campaign fund and before that had financed the fight against the Treaty and the League. The eastern seaboard bankers saw a golden future for the United States in overseas trade and investment; the industrialists of Pittsburgh and the Midwest looked mainly to the possibilities at home. Yet when Mellon went to Marion to call on the President-Elect, Harding did not know him either by sight or by reputation and did not offer him the Treasury until after he had left—still unrecognized.

In his own appointments Harding displayed a comic genius for the grotesque. The Reverend Heber Herbert Votaw, a missionary of the Seventh-Day Adventist Church who had married Harding's favorite sister, found himself Superintendent of Federal Prisons. Daniel R. Crissinger, who had headed a bank in Marion for a few months, became Comptroller of the Currency and then Governor of the Federal Reserve System. Harding chose as his personal secretary George B. Christian, Jr. —a lifelong Democrat. As chief of the new Veterans Administration, Harding selected Charles R. Forbes, a deserter from the Army with a jail record. The Veterans Administration received larger appropriations than any government department—half a billion dollars a year—and Harding picked the forty-year-old Forbes because he found him such an agreeable drinking companion. Mrs. Harding, known to the inner White House circle as the Duchess, liked Forbes, too. His jokes made her laugh. But what made the people of Marion laugh most at the time was the local quip: "George Washington couldn't tell a lie; Harding can't tell a liar."

The best minds of the Republican Party who had picked Harding as a willing tool found him pliable enough. The trouble was that Harding gladly let anybody use him, and his own taste in friends ran to second- and third-raters in morals, in manners, and in mind. Ike Hoover, in *Forty-Two Years in the White House*, described Harding as "a sporting ladies' man." The new President continued his affair with Nan Britton, spent two evenings a week gambling under his own roof with his "poker Cabinet" of Daugherty, Smith, Fall, and Forbes, and another evening a week in Daugherty's "Little Green House on K Street" which the Ohio gang made into a center of gambling, bootlegging, and wenching. What a contrast with Woodrow Wilson, for whom dissipation meant an evening a week at B. F. Keith's vaudeville theater with its Swiss bell-ringers, performing seals, and soft-shoe dancers.

The contrast between the incoming and the outgoing Presidents extended beyond their different tastes in entertainment. Wilson wrecked his own ambitious plans for a new world order by refusing to delegate authority. Harding had no blueprint for world peace—or for anything else—and left the conduct of foreign affairs entirely in the hands of Secretary Hughes, who took office with the naïve assumption that the United States had to ratify the Versailles Treaty in order to make peace with Germany. But Senator Brandegee soon introduced Hughes to the facts of political life: "Being no more than a country lawyer myself, I would not venture an opinion on the legal side of this question in your presence. Ignorant as I also am of international law, I would not dare to challenge that aspect of the case as you present it. But I do know a little about the Senate, and I must tell you that ratification of the Treaty of Versailles in any form is impossible." "Then I fear," said Hughes, "my usefulness is at an end." "Ah, no," Brandegee reassured him. "No man could be quite so useful to this administration as yourself."

Hughes got the point and during August, 1921, the Senate ratified separate peace treaties that the State Department prepared with Germany, Austria, and Hungary, restoring normal relations with all three countries and leaving any American claims open for negotiation with the Allied Powers. The treaty with Germany, incidentally, included the identical war-guilt clause that appeared in the Treaty of Versailles. Having done what he could to restore normalcy with America's ex-enemies, Hughes adjusted himself to the existence of the League of Nations by creating an "unofficial observer" to represent the United States at the endless succession of European postwar conferences. "This 'unofficial observer' was in attendance wherever European Conferences considered questions in which the United States might be concerned, but always in the guise of night watchman," wrote the distinguished foreign correspondent, Frank H. Simonds. "He could sign no document, express no official opinion. He only whispered hints, which could be denied if they became embarrassingly public, and volunteered advice, which could be repudiated if it came to unfriendly ears. This 'unofficial observer' was invariably on the premises, but the country to which he belonged was invariably absent. He was dispatched to accomplish missions which in the diplomatic hierarchy are reserved for Cabinet Ministers and Ambassadors exclusively, but he lacked the official rank of a filing clerk in the State Department. In that capital where Wilson had proclaimed the will of America from the housetops, the unofficial observer whispered the suggestions of an anxious Administration in a conveniently obscure corner."

Hughes did his best to maintain and encourage some contact with Europe and the League of Nations. He tried still harder and still more effectively to discourage any contamination—official or unofficial, political or economic—with Soviet Russia. In March, 1921, he turned down a Russian proposal to resume normal trade. He would have no dealings with the Bolsheviks until they had made some settlement of American war loans to the vanished Tsarist government and of American claims to property confiscated by the Revolution. Senator Borah of Idaho took a different view. Although Borah had led the irreconcilables in their fight against the League of Nations and the Versailles Treaty, he favored a quick resumption of normal Russian-American relations. Borah distrusted European diplomacy and British imperialism, but saw no reason why America and Russia should not agree to live and let live.

Borah also favored disarmament, though he shared the widespread fear of imminent war with Japan. In December, 1920, a Senate majority —including Harding—had voted down a proposal of Borah's to seek an agreement with Britain and Japan to limit naval construction, but when the Republican administration took office the following March, Hughes persuaded Harding to give Borah's scheme a serious try, and at once received help from an unexpected quarter. Lord Lee of Fareham, the newly installed First Lord of the British Admiralty, got word to Washington that his government would welcome an Anglo-American treaty limiting their navies to the same size. The Wilson administration had started a naval building program that was about to give the United States a larger navy than Britain could build—a prospect that galled the pride of those Britons who looked back yearningly on the dear, dead days of the two-power standard. But as long as the British continued their alliance with Japan, the advocates of a big United States Navy had a strong talking point.

The majority of the British people certainly did not prize the Japanese alliance more highly than they prized good relations with the United States; as for the people of Canada, Australia, and New Zealand, many of them feared and actively disliked Japan. During the summer of 1921 the Dominion Prime Ministers conferred with the British leaders in London and persuaded Lloyd George not to extend the Japanese alliance, which expired that year, but to work instead for an Anglo-Japanese-Chinese-American agreement on the whole Pacific area. Secretary Hughes wanted still more. He insisted that the United States play host to a nine-power conference including Britain, France, Italy, Portugal, Belgium, Holland, China, and Japan, with disarmament at the top of the agenda and "Pacific and Far Eastern Questions" second. Hughes knew what he wanted and knew how to get it. He wanted substantial disarmament; he wanted to end the Anglo-Japanese Alliance; he wanted to re-establish the principle of the Open Door in China; he wanted to get Japan out of Shantung Province; he wanted a general Far Eastern Agreement, including all countries with interests in the Far East—except the outlawed Russians; he wanted the United States to seize and hold real leadership in naval disarmament and stabilization of the Pacific and the Far East. He knew that all peoples everywhere wanted disarmament. He knew that the British government could not defy the United States and that the Dominions actively supported American objectives in the Far East. He knew that the Japanese had overextended themselves and would have to accept his program, no matter how little they liked it. He knew that the European nations with interests in the Far East also had no choice but to go along.

When the conference assembled in Washington, on Saturday, November 12, 1921, Hughes followed the initiative he had already seized. He had the bumbling Harding open the proceedings with an appeal for peace that genuinely moved all the delegates present. Then Hughes arose and flabbergasted the conference by announcing that the United States would scrap most of its naval building program and even many ships already under construction if all the nations with interests in the Pacific would agree to limit their construction programs, too. The suave Balfour, who had done so much to create the Anglo-Japanese Alliance, visibly winced. William Jennings Bryan, in the spectators' gallery, yelled with joy. When Hughes sat down, the conference adjourned until the following Monday, with the result that the press and public spent the whole weekend mulling over the American proposals. It was said at the time that Hughes in a few sentences had sunk more ships than all the admirals of the world had sunk in a cycle of centuries.

After twelve weeks of negotiation, the conference agreed on seven treaties—three of them crucial. America, Britain, Japan, France, and Italy signed a fifteen-year Naval Limitation Treaty restricting the tonnages of their capital ships to 525,000 each for America and Britain, 315,000 tons for Japan, and 175,000 each for France and Italy. Under a ten-year treaty, the United States, Britain, Japan, and France agreed to respect each other's rights in the Pacific, thus terminating the Anglo-Japanese Alliance. Finally, all the delegations at Washington signed a Nine-Power Treaty endorsing the American principle of the Open Door in China. No nation agreed to take any specific measures if any other nation violated the territorial or administrative integrity of China. As A. Whitney Griswold put it in his *Far Eastern Policy of the United States:* "It was a self-denying ordinance rather than a collective security pact. The only sanction behind it was the good faith of its signatories." Mr. Griswold summed up the importance of all the seven treaties:

"They were primarily a recognition of existing, if brutal, facts, a consolidation of the *status quo.* By them the Pacific suffered no peaceful change; it was only partially frozen. The same was true of China. Admitting these limitations, the treaties constituted the most dynamic and the most comprehensive attempt on the part of the United States to uphold the territorial integrity of China and all that it believed to depend upon it; to make the open door in China an enduring principle of international law; to obtain security for its Philippine hostages to fortune, and to confine within the barriers manufactured in Washington the hungry expansion of Japan. The treaties went as far as pen and ink could go to preserve a peace founded on such antithetical elements as those inherent in the *status quo* in the Far East."

For his conduct of the Washington negotiations Secretary Hughes deserved well of the Republican Party—if not of the American people. At last the United States had the power and experience to put into effect some of the policies that the Republicans tried and failed to apply immediately after the war with Spain. The United States played a larger part in the world of 1922 than in the world of 1900, Britain a smaller one. Germany now counted for almost nothing in the Far East; the Bolshevik Revolution had weakened Russia. Japan, on the other hand, had overextended itself. The combination of powers that Hughes organized at Washington forced the Japanese to surrender most of the positions they had seized in Shantung Province. The Twenty-One Demands on China also became a dead letter. But Hughes had not saved the Far East for the United States or for China, either. He had saved the Japanese from themselves. They did not have to scrap any battleships. Instead, because of the Anglo-American concessions, forced by Hughes, they found themselves impregnable in their own waters. The Chinese demanded more than they received, but could they hold their own?

Many of the same Republicans who had fought the League of Nations and opposed any commitments in Europe welcomed the Washington Treaties. Few of them believed that the United States could go it alone in the postwar world. They had rejected Wilson, not because he favored internationalism but because he made his kind of internationalism a party issue. Most Republican leaders had wanted the United States to declare war upon Germany long before April, 1917. They felt a special affinity for Britain's Tory imperialists and they found, in the Far East, more scope for a similar policy than they could find in Europe. At the same time they recognized that the mass of the American people craved peace and distrusted the race for naval supremacy on which the country had embarked.

The 5:5:3 building ratios established among the American, British, and Japanese fleets covered capital ships only. The British refused to limit their construction of cruisers; the French rejected the British proposal to outlaw submarines and resented having to accept parity with the Italians. No less important than the "building holiday" was the nonfortification agreement whereby the Americans and British promised to build no great, new bases in the far Pacific, close to Japan. As a result, the Japanese fleet controlled its own home waters, and the Japanese people stood in no danger of attack from the more powerful American and British fleets. In like manner, the people of the United States and the British Isles could feel equally secure from foreign aggression.

Senate ratification of the Washington Treaties did not reduce antiforeign feeling in the United States. In February, 1921, Congress had passed a bill limiting the admission of aliens during the next fifteen months to three per cent of the number of natives of each of the respective countries dwelling in the United States at the time of the 1910 census. The next year, Congress reduced the annual proportion to two per cent and took the 1890 census as the base. This worked against the recent Slavic and Latin immigrants from the poorer, overcrowded countries of eastern and southern Europe. It favored the Germans, the Scandinavians, the West Europeans, and the people of the British Isles. Then, in 1924, the Senate voted 76 to 2 to revoke the "gentleman's agreement" that permitted a few hundred Japanese, under the supervision of their own government, to enter the United States each year. Now, all Japanese were excluded.

No other action by Congress during the early 1920's created such widespread effect as those two measures curtailing immigration. The total exclusion of the Japanese wounded their pride as a nation and vindicated their most belligerent patriots. The reduction of immigration from Europe did not offend the sensibilities of many Europeans; it did, however, lead to profound changes on both sides of the Atlantic. Throughout the nineteenth century and on until the outbreak of war in 1914, unrestricted emigration to the United States had relieved Europe of its surplus population. The influx of these Europeans had also provided the United States with a steady supply of cheap labor. The ending of the war increased social tensions throughout Europe, but a panicky Congress had discriminated against the most dangerously overcrowded countries. And Congress merely expressed the will of the great majority of Americans. Organized labor had reason to believe that a new wave of unrestricted immigration from impoverished Europe would drive wages down, reduce living standards, and increase unemployment. The middle classes and the farmers, already hit by the postwar depression, also feared the intrusion of unruly aliens during a period of uncertainty and distress.

Not satisfied with cutting down foreign immigration, the Republican Congress also voted to reduce imports. In 1921 it passed an emergency act, raising duties on farm products. Because this did not check the decline of farm income in the United States, Congress in 1922 passed the much more drastic Fordney-McCumber Tariff Act, raising duties on industrial as well as farm products to the highest levels in history. The *Daily Chronicle* of London—referring to the ten billion dollars in war debts that Europe owed to the United States—addressed this warning to Americans: "It is only in goods that the foreigner can pay—and in proportion as you keep his goods out, you make his payments impossible." Harding proposed making the best of both worlds: "The United States should adopt a protective tariff of such a character as will help the struggling industries of Europe to get on their feet."

Immediately south of the Rio Grande lay still another world which President Harding could not and Secretary Hughes would not understand—the world of Mexico. Back in 1917, Wilson had withdrawn Pershing's Expeditionary Force from Mexico and soon had another, far larger, army preparing to save democracy in Europe. The Mexicans, meanwhile, had sought to establish democracy at home by means of revolution. Their first step took the form of a new Constitution which legalized trade unions, abolished child labor, provided various forms of social insurance, vested in the villages the title to any waters, woods, and land that they might need. The most controversial articles came down hard on the Roman Catholic Church and on foreigners: "Churches shall have no legal capacity to acquire, hold, or administer real property or loans on real property." All priests had to register with the government; their number was limited; foreign priests were barred. The government took over public education, and religious teaching was forbidden in the primary schools.

Foreigners howled when they read two other passages in the Constitution: "The nation's ownership of waters and minerals is direct and imprescriptible; only the 'right of exploitation' of the nation's waters and subsoil may be conceded to private parties, and that only on condition that the resources be regularly developed and the right legally exercised." Also: "Only Mexicans by birth or naturalization and Mexican companies have the right to acquire ownership in lands, waters, and their appurtenances or to develop mines, waters, minerals, and fuels in the Republic of Mexico. The nation may grant the same right to foreigners, provided they agree to be considered Mexicans in respect of such property, and accordingly not to invoke the protection of their government in respect of the same."

President Carranza, a strong man in the Díaz tradition, accepted the Constitution but did little to enforce it. Most of the land remained in private hands. Labor received few of the promised benefits. The power of the Church remained largely undisturbed. Other men therefore led uprisings in the name of the Revolution that Carranza had betrayed and the Constitution that he had flouted. Emiliano Zapata, an illiterate peon, organized a ragged army of peasants with a slogan that rang around the world: "Men of the South: It is better to die on your feet than live on your knees." Federal troops finally tricked Zapata into a conference and murdered him. The most effective opposition came from Carranza's own War Minister, the popular one-armed General Alvaro Obregón. By 1919, popular hatred of Carranza increased to such a point that he, too, fell victim to assassins. Some months of general confusion followed; Mexico had no central government for any foreign power to recognize, and when Obregón finally swept the Presidential election of September, 1920, the radical program to which he was committed stirred up so much antagonism outside Mexico that his regime, too, remained unrecognized abroad.

Mexico had stayed neutral throughout the war and had not joined the League of Nations afterward. Nevertheless, leaders of the Republican Party in the United States called the Obregón government "Bolshevistic." The fact was that the Russian and Mexican Revolutions had little in common. In Russia, three years of disastrous war caused the whole social order to collapse. It was not Bolshevism that destroyed the Tsarist regime; it was total collapse that gave Bolshevism its chance. The Mexican Revolution had little to do with war; it did not destroy a traditional social order. The Mexican Revolution amounted, primarily, to a revolt against foreign control. The Díaz dictatorship had made Mexico safe for foreign capital and for the Roman Catholic Church, which many Mexicans regarded as a foreign institution.

A decade of anarchy followed the abdication of Díaz. Madero and Carranza, who succeeded him, belonged to the upper, landowning classes, although both men had Indian as well as Spanish blood. Obregón came of pure Spanish stock but he first made his living as an independent farmer and a dealer in chick peas, not from landownership. "His formal education," wrote Hudson Strode in *Timeless Mexico,* "was limited, but

he had an unusually receptive mind and was an astute judge of men.
He knew values. He was hard to fool. He was not selflessly inspired as
was Madero. He was a practical man of affairs, with ambition, a humanitarian outlook, and a healthy sense of humor. Despite his faith in himself,
he was somewhat surprised to find that he possessed the military genius
to become one of the greatest Mexican generals of all times."

The Wind That Swept Mexico, by Anita Brenner, gives this picture
of the people of Mexico during the early, exciting days of their Revolution: "Artists returning from guerrilla trooping and from war-exhausted
Europe organized a 'Syndicate of Painters, Sculptors, and Intellectual
Workers' headed beamingly by Diego Rivera some of whose Parisian
friends were now high in new Soviet councils. The painters got contracts
for murals, at plasterer's rates, from the Minister of Education, and swag-
gered in overalls up splintery scaffolds to put the meaning of the revolution, thrice human size, on public walls. What they painted was like
nothing any of them had done before. They had something to say that
they felt deeply and wanted to communicate with force. Foreign critics
saw the work in progress and said with awe that this was the first great
modern art created in America, but the best people screamed in the
press and their pious sons ganged up to scratch the walls at night and
throw corrosives on the monumental figures. The painters took that glee-
fully as a tribute, and came to work with pistols in their pockets. The
great Indian faces and the overpowering compositions, linked deliberately to ancient Mexican art and to Italian primitives, taught this religion: beauty is all that is native, active, living, earthly, all that is productive work."

It was not surprising that the America of Harding and Hughes, of
Fall and Daugherty, found it convenient to delay recognition of a government that permitted such abominations to flourish. Nor was it surprising that Mexico refused to accept recognition on the terms outlined
in May, 1921, by Hughes, who demanded in effect that Mexico wipe
out those provisions of its 1917 Constitution that deprived foreigners
of the privileges they had enjoyed. Not until September, 1923, did the
United States finally recognize Obregón after he had occupied the
Presidency for almost three years. Obregón pointed out that he had
never enforced the Constitution in a retroactive fashion and reminded
Hughes that Anglo-American interests controlled more than 90 per cent
of Mexico's billion-dollar oil industry as compared with 1 per cent in
Mexican hands. Obregón also played off American oil men against
American bankers. The more radical Mexicans accused him of selling
out to the United States; the more conservative Americans accused
Hughes of selling out to Moscow.

· IV ·

IF EVER a people got the government they deserved, it was the American people during the Harding years. The puritan element won the greatest of all its triumphs when the Anti-Saloon League lobby got the Prohibition Amendment written into the Constitution. The Prohibitionists fought fire with fire and thus set an even bigger blaze than they had tried to extinguish. To break the corrupt influence of the liquor industry on politics, Prohibitionists used blackmail and bribery to force recalcitrant legislators into line. But Prohibition did not kill the liquor industry; it replaced the relatively honest distiller, brewer, and saloonkeeper with the completely crooked bootlegger, highjacker, and gangster. The drys claimed that Prohibition cut the national consumption of liquor in two. In 1920, deaths from alcoholism dropped almost fifty per cent. Two years later, Dr. Richard C. Cabot of the Harvard Medical School stated: "The rich may for all we know be as foolish as ever, but beyond question the poor are much better off." A few years later, however, the Health Commissioner of New York State reported that bad liquor had caused a "striking rise in the death rate since 1920." The American Brewers' Association estimated that the switch from mild legal drinks to hard illegal ones may have caused fewer drinks to flow but did not cut down the consumption of alcohol.

Plenty of leading citizens followed the example set by the President and his cronies. The poor could not afford to pay bootleggers between five and ten dollars a quart for bad gin and whiskey. The well-to-do, however, could and did, thus helping to create a new financial aristocracy of criminals. And while the illegal liquor trade flourished in the big cities, abstainers in the rural regions poured themselves into a reorganized Ku Klux Klan which attracted four and a half million members by 1924 and dominated the political machines of seven states—Arkansas, California, Indiana, Ohio, Oklahoma, Oregon, and Texas.

Back in Reconstruction days, white Southerners had organized the original Ku Klux Klan to hold the Negro down. Colonel William Joseph Simmons of Atlanta, Georgia, tried to revive it in 1915, but got nowhere until 1920, when the Klan suddenly began to attract thousands of new members, especially in the South and in the Far and Middle West. According to its Constitution, the purpose of the Klan was "to unite white male persons, native-born Gentile citizens of the United States of America, who owe no allegiance of any nature to any foreign government, nation, institution, sect, ruler, person, or people, whose morals are good, whose reputations and vocations are exemplary." The Klan also sought "to cultivate and promote patriotism toward our Civil Government; to

UNDERWOOD

Dr. Hiram Wesley Evans, Imperial
Wizard of the Ku Klux Klan

practice an honorable Klannish-ness toward each other; to exem-plify a practical benevolence; to shield the sanctity of the home and the chastity of womanhood; to maintain forever white supremacy, to teach and faithfully inculcate a high spiritual philosophy through an exalted ritualism, and by a prac-tical devotion to conserve, protect, and maintain the distinctive insti-tutions, rights, privileges, princi-ples, traditions, and ideals of a pure Americanism."

That was the theory. In practice the Ku Klux Klan divided the country into Realms, headed by King Kleagles, and subdivided in-to Domains headed by Grand Gob-lins. Members called themselves Kleagles and solicited new mem-bers at ten dollars a head. Four dollars remained in the Kleagle's pocket; the other six went to the Im-perial Wizard in Atlanta, except for small rake-offs to the Grand Goblin of the Domain and the King Kleagle of the Realm. In 1921 a Congres-sional investigation revealed that the Klan had taken part in so much violence that Simmons had to quit. Hiram Wesley Evans, a Texas dentist who called himself "the most average man in America," succeeded him and the Klan continued to grow. Its members usually met at night, clad in white sheets. They burned fiery crosses on hilltops, paraded through the streets, and continued to tar, feather, and flog Negroes, Jews, Catho-lics, or anyone who asserted the rights of religious and racial minorities. From time to time they killed their victims, especially Negroes. Some Kleagles used the Klan to settle private grudges; in other communities, gangsters took over the whole local organization. Not until the mid-1920's, when the postwar depression had run its course, did the influ-ence of the Klan begin to decline.

By this time the Klan had become more anti-Catholic and anti-Jewish than anti-Negro. Hiram W. Evans's pamphlet, *The Klan of Tomorrow*, published in 1924, set forth the new philosophy: "The Negro is not a menace to Americanism in the sense that the Jew or Roman Catholic is a menace. He is not actually hostile to it. He is simply racially incapable of understanding, sharing, or contributing to Americanism." The Klan drew most of its membership from small businessmen, small farmers, low-salaried employees, and cautious, suspicious, small-town folk. Its growth in the rural districts paralleled the spread of bootlegging in the great cities. The Harding administration had not purged the American people of the poisons generated by the war and postwar years. Normalcy, in practice, did not mean a return to the easygoing freedoms of prewar America. Normalcy freed Americans of many government controls only to release violent opposition to many forces of legal authority. Few politicians dared advocate the repeal of Prohibition; fewer still actually enforced it. As a result, organized crime flourished in the cities while the organized violence of the Ku Klux Klan terrorized wide sections of rural America.

Harding's good intentions did little to ease matters for his troubled people. He released the Socialist-pacifist Eugene Victor Debs from the federal penitentiary in Atlanta, where he was still serving time for having opposed the war. Harding also persuaded Judge Elbert Gary to reduce the working day in United States Steel Corporation plants from twelve to ten hours. But he did nothing to help organized labor at a time when the same respectable businessman who patronized the local bootlegger also used spies and thugs to prevent unionization of his own shop. Nor did Harding awake to the corruption of his closest associates until 1922. Already the duties of the Presidency had worn him down. He often read speeches prepared by other hands, speeches that he had never looked at before he delivered them. In the midst of one of them, he suddenly blurted out: "I never saw this before. I didn't write this speech and I don't believe what I have just read." His mind could not absorb the reports that came to his desk, and his advisers only added to his confusion. "I can't make a darn thing out of this tax problem," William Allen White quoted him as saying. "I listen to one side and they seem right and then—God!—I talk to the other side and they seem just as right, and here I am where I started. I know somewhere there is a book that will give me the truth, but hell! I couldn't read the book. God, what a job! This is a hell of a place for a man like me to be." He sought escape from his troubles at the poker table—only to find that his closest companions had done him the most grievous harm.

The Congressional elections of 1922 brought the year to a gloomy close. The Republicans lost seventy seats in the House and seven in the Senate. The Progressives and farm bloc Senators controlled the balance of power, and often voted with the Democrats against the administration. A few weeks later, Harding received incontrovertible proof that Charles R. Forbes had enriched himself by some two hundred thousand dollars through the sale and purchase of supplies for the Veterans Administration. In January, 1923, Forbes quietly left for Europe and sent in his resignation while abroad, but Harding did not accept it until the end of February. The details of Forbes's misdeeds came out gradually: not until 1926 was he sentenced to the Federal Penitentiary in Leavenworth on the charges of fraud.

Soon after Forbes had resigned, Charles F. Cramer, his assistant and general counsel, shot himself. No evidence ever showed that Cramer profited from Forbes's graft, but their close association reflected further discredit on Harding. The shrewd Daugherty, fearful of a revolt against the man he had put in the White House, at once announced: "The President will be a candidate for renomination." This checked any open rebellion, but the President's troubles still piled up. When he learned that Jesse Smith had accepted bribes totaling fifty thousand dollars in connection with the Alien Property Custodian's office, he dropped him from the poker Cabinet. On the night of May 29, 1923, Smith destroyed all Daugherty's house accounts and personal correspondence and then shot himself through the head. The Department of Justice never held an autopsy, but Harding and all the insiders knew that it was suicide, not foul play.

That summer Harding fled the cares of Washington by taking a "voyage of understanding" to Alaska and showing himself to the people. Mrs. Harding accompanied him, following her own formula for wedded bliss: "Never let your husband travel without you." On their way across the continent Harding conferred for an hour with the wife of Albert B. Fall, who had recently resigned from the Cabinet to go into the oil business. Afterward, the President commented glumly on the train, "In this job I am not worried about my enemies. It is my friends who are keeping me awake nights." Shortly before he left, William Allen White heard him express the same views with more force: "My God, this is a hell of a job. I have no trouble with my enemies. I can take care of my enemies all right. But my damn friends, my God-damn friends, White, they're the ones that keep me walking the floor nights." To another visitor he confided: "I'm not fit for this office, and should never have been here."

Not much time remained. Colonel Edmund Starling, head of the White House secret service detail, had already noted that Harding showed symptoms of heart trouble. He had what Starling called "a high stomach" and although he was pouring less liquor into it, years of dissipation began to tell. Pains in his chest forced him to sleep sitting upright. The sea voyage to Alaska did not refresh his spirits. The fact that he owed his brokers $180,000 on his stock-market speculation added to his gloom. He returned to Seattle in a heat wave and after delivering one speech gave up trying to make any more. He appeared to be suffering from indigestion, but rallied and went by train to San Francisco. There a heart attack carried him off, while his wife was reading aloud Samuel

G. Blythe's article about him in the new *Saturday Evening Post*—"A Calm View of a Calm Man."

Not since the assassination of Abraham Lincoln had the American people mourned the death of a President so effusively. Weeping crowds stood silent and bareheaded as the funeral train carried Harding's body across the continent to Washington. Bishop William T. Manning of New York declared, "If I could write one sentence upon his monument it would be this: 'He taught us the power of brotherliness,'" adding, "May God ever give to our country leaders as faithful, as wise, as noble in spirit as the one whom we now mourn." Some years later, Alice Roosevelt Longworth offered a more succinct obituary: "Harding was not a bad man. He was just a slob."

· V ·

LESS than two and a half years in the White House finished Harding: he tried to bring back the good old days and died in the attempt. Although Wilson broke down trying to create a new world made safe for democracy, he survived Harding by almost six months. Harding went in for poker and people; Wilson, for reading and religion. To Harding, the entire range of human knowledge remained a sealed book; to Wilson, science and technology meant little. Like most of their contemporaries, they did not devote more than passing notice to the British physicist, Sir Oliver Lodge, who declared in September, 1919, that the atomic energy in an ounce of matter could raise the sunken German fleet from the depths of Scapa Flow and pile it on the mountaintops of Scotland.

If the scientific predictions of Sir Oliver Lodge received less attention than they deserved perhaps it was because the world press of 1919 devoted more space to scientific facts no less fantastic and far more real. On June 15 Captain John Alcock, a British pilot, and Lieutenant Arthur Brown, an American navigator, flew a British Vickers-Vimy plane 1,960 miles nonstop from Newfoundland to Ireland in 16 hours and 12 minutes. On July 2 the British dirigible *R-34* flew more than 3,000 miles, nonstop, from Scotland to Long Island and returned safely on July 9. A United States Navy seaplane flew almost 4,000 miles in stages from New York to Plymouth, England, by way of Lisbon. Two other seaplanes that attempted the same journey were disabled on the way. Thanks to the wartime progress of military aviation, a new age of high-speed, long-distance air travel had arrived. No matter how the Senate might vote, science had ended the era of America's physical isolation.

The war had also given the United States a new industrial plant which doubled and trebled the output of millions of workers and taught millions more new skills. Henry Ford had already begun turning out automobiles on a mass production basis. By 1920 more than seven million Americans owned passenger cars and the industry was turning out new ones at the rate of two million a year. The Model T Ford sold for less than $500; the Dodge, the Overland, and the Chevrolet—a product of the reorganized General Motors Corporation—cost a few hundred dollars more. The automobile revolutionized American life in many directions. It ended the farmer's isolation; it led to a boom in suburban real estate; it spread American cities over wider areas; it gave the American people new opportunities to discover their own country. Busses drove street-cars and even railways out of business; the truck rivaled the freight car. Church attendance, which had begun to slump before the war, went into a sharper decline afterward as golf and pleasure riding competed with Sunday services. The closed passenger car which swept the market in 1919 and 1920 broke down more barriers between the sexes. More babies, so ran the folklore of the time, were being conceived in Ford cars than in beds. "For city dwellers," wrote Frederick Lewis Allen in *Only Yesterday*, "the home was becoming less of a shrine, more of a dormitory." During the 1920's, the automobile industry became the biggest in the land and created countless new jobs in related lines. The oil industry at home and the rubber industry abroad expanded many times over. American mass-produced cars undersold European cars on the world market.

Two other new industries—movies and radio—worked more directly on the minds of the American people, and of other peoples too. Newspapers, books, pamphlets, and magazines had carried the bulk of war-time news and propaganda. Only in the United States did the movies reach a universal audience during the war years. By 1920, however, American films had become an important article of export and a challenging form of popular art. The producing and directing genius of David Wark Griffith added new dimensions to the motion picture screen. "His innovations in camera technique alone were formidable," wrote Lloyd Morris in *Not So Long Ago*. "They included the close-up, long shot, vista and vignette; the iris-effect, fade-in and fade-out, high- and low-angle shots. Griffith was the first maker of pictures to overcome the frozen immobility of the camera and move it at will. He originated night photography and modern methods of lighting. He also added many resources to the technique of story-telling, by making radical experiments in the cutting and editing of his pictures."

When Woodrow Wilson saw Griffith's *Birth of a Nation* at a White House preview he is said to have exclaimed that it was "like writing history with lightning." Griffith's glorification of the early Ku Klux Klan caused him to be denounced as a bigot, but his next picture, *Intolerance*, produced in 1916, set forth a more humane theme: the sin of self-right-

eousness through the ages. This he
depicted in thirteen reels and four
stories, told simultaneously, from
the fall of Babylon to a modern
story of industrial strife. *Intolerance* cost more than two million
dollars, and the tale of a hypocritical employer hiring strikebreakers
and factory guards to slaughter his
workers earned Griffith the hatred
of the business community—the
more so as he based the plot on
hearings of the Federal Industrial
Relations Commission. *Intolerance*
also exposed the evil of war so vividly that many cities banned it, and
Lenin arranged to have it widely
shown in Russia. The American
motion picture had begun as an

CULVER

Charlie Chaplin and Jackie Coogan in
The Kid

almost exclusively proletarian art, shown chiefly in nickelodeons, until
Griffith suddenly forced it upon the attention of a wider public, shocking
the life out of the predominantly middle-class audiences that his genius
attracted.

During the war, at the invitation of Lloyd George, Griffith had made
propaganda pictures at the front. Afterward he sought expiation by producing *Broken Blossoms,* based on the tragic love of a Chinese boy for
a white girl. The pathos of Lillian Gish as the heroine and the restraint
of Richard Barthelmess as her Chinese admirer won the praises of the
serious critics and attracted huge audiences. *The New York Times* called
Broken Blossoms a "masterpiece"; the *Literary Digest* hailed the birth
of a new art "as important as music and poetry." And in spite of its tragic
ending, *Broken Blossoms* proved an immense box-office success.

Charles Chaplin's genius as an actor matched Griffith's genius as a
producer-director. After making scores of short, slapstick comedies for
nickelodeon audiences, Chaplin produced his first full-length picture,
The Kid, in 1920, depicting the touching adventures of a hobo (himself)
and a waif (little Jackie Coogan). Chaplin said of his own work: "My
pictures have always been for the underdog. They have always tried to
create pity. I think pity is a great attribute of civilization. Without it we
have no civilization." Certainly he won a success without precedent in
recorded history. Never before had one man's name, face, and personality become so widely known throughout the world. It was a success
achieved because of a new medium of communication and in spite of the

men who largely controlled that medium. Yet those men barely escaped ruin in the pit that they themselves had dug.

Mack Sennett, the outstanding producer of short screen comedies with whom Chaplin had worked for years, once remarked: "You will find your idea for a motion picture comedy either in sex or crime. These two fields are the great feeding-grounds for funny ideas." But Roscoe ("Fatty") Arbuckle—a Sennett-trained comedian with a popularity second only to Chaplin's—did not seem to understand where screen life ended and real life began. In 1921 he was arrested for having killed a young woman under revolting circumstances in a drunken brawl. Preachers, professors, and newspapermen denounced the depravity of Hollywood, which had become the movie capital of the country. Protestant, Catholic, and Jewish organizations issued resolutions condemning immorality on and off the screen. The legislatures of thirty-seven states considered a hundred different bills calling for censorship, and four states set up censorship machinery.

In December, 1921, two representatives of the film industry invited Will H. Hays, Republican National Chairman and Postmaster General in the Harding Cabinet, to become "leader of the industry" at a salary of one hundred thousand dollars a year. Hays reached his decision on Christmas morning when he saw his son and two nephews dressing up in cowboy suits and arguing about which of them would represent the great Western star, William S. Hart.

A quarter of a century later, Raymond Moley wrote in his life of Will Hays: "Tears still come to his eyes when he tells that he stood up, then, in the shadow of the Christmas tree, and silently repeated the vow of St. Paul: 'And this I do.'" Hays himself expressed his purpose this way: "We must have toward that sacred thing, the mind of a child, toward that clean and virgin thing, that unmarked slate—we must have toward that the same sense of responsibility, the same care about the impressions made upon it, that the best teacher or the best clergyman, the most inspired teacher of youth would have."

The vision that Hays saw on his road to Damascus assumed corporate form in the shape of the Motion Picture Producers and Distributors of America, a trade association that proposed self-regulation as an alternative to censorship. The Hays Office also tried to educate the public to enjoy better pictures and the various branches of the industry to work together in close harmony. Hays himself soon got a 50 per cent wage increase, but not until 1930 did he persuade the members of his association to adopt a "production code," drafted by Martin Quigley, leading publisher of movie trade papers and fan magazines, and the Reverend Daniel J. Lord, Jesuit professor of dramatics at the University of St. Louis. Many of the movie producers were Jews; they chose a Presbyterian as their "Tsar"; Roman Catholics laid down the moral code for their pictures.

The pooled efforts of Jews, Protestants, and Catholics did not, however, lead to any measurable improvement in the quality of American motion pictures. They liquidated Fatty Arbuckle; but they did nothing to encourage new Griffiths or Chaplins. Cecil B. De Mille, the most popular director of the 1920's, created such pictures as *Forbidden Fruit, Saturday Night, The Golden Bed, Don't Change Husbands,* and *Why Change Your Wife?* It was De Mille who transformed Sir James Barrie's *The Admirable Crichton* into *Male and Female.* Yet the vitality of the American motion picture survived the hypocrisy of Will Hays, the vulgarity of the industry, and the censorship of the politicians. "There is only one thing that can kill the movies and that is education," said Will Rogers. And again: "A bad picture is an accident and a good one is a miracle."

By the early 1920's few Americans regarded any movie, either good or bad, as a miracle. It was the infant radio industry, not the massive movie industry, that seemed to border on the supernatural. In November, 1920, a single commercial station, KDKA in Pittsburgh, carried the returns of the Harding-Cox election. But within two years radio had begun to grow at a rate that had no parallel in any American industry. Here was another new medium of mass communication that could bring music, news, drama, the human voice to an audience of millions instantaneously. Who should control it? Herbert Hoover, Secretary of Commerce in the Harding Cabinet, told the first national radio conference that he found it "inconceivable that we should allow so great a possibility for service to be drowned in advertising matter." He went on, "The ether is a public medium and its use must be for the public benefit. The use of radio channels is justified only if there is a public benefit. The dominant element for consideration in the radio field is, and always will be, the great body of the listening public, millions in number, nation-wide in distribution." The federal government, however, made no attempt to regulate radio, and radio in its early days made no attempt to regulate itself. Hundreds of stations sprouted up, some financed by the makers of radio sets, but more and more of them looking to advertising revenue to pay their way. By 1926 they had to beg the federal government to intervene and save them from themselves. So many stations had gone on the air that they were jamming one another's signals, and it became imperative for the government in the public interest to assign wave lengths and frequencies.

The most important changes that science and technology set in motion after the war had to do with communication—the physical communication of people and things by means of automobiles and airplanes and the mechanical communication of words and pictures by means of the popular press, the screen, and the radio. In the United States, more than anywhere else, mass production and mass distribution had brought these changes home to virtually the whole people. But what kind of words, what kind of pictures, what kind of ideas and emotions were the American people producing and distributing immediately after the war? What had become of the cultural renaissance that the war had interrupted?

Before the war, that renaissance had not spread far beyond the readers of little magazines that died to make verse free. By 1920 it was reaching a wider public through the columns of the *Smart Set,* a monthly pulp magazine of conventional appearance and unconventional content, edited by H. L. Mencken and George Jean Nathan. In Mencken, to a greater extent than in Nathan, these new writers found a fugleman who trumpeted his own talents and theirs so blatantly that the general reading public began to give ear. Mencken, a self-educated Baltimore newspaperman, was a critic some of the time, a stylist much of the time, a humorist most of the time, and a 200 per cent American all of the time. He strove primarily for laughs; he developed unique mastery of what he called "the American language"; he abused academic critics, conventional writers, and the puritan tradition. He brayed the virtues of the superior man while Bryan and Billy Sunday, both of whom he despised, brayed the virtues of the masses. Nothing delighted Mencken more than to have some of his victims try to shoot back at him, usually with boomerangs.

In attacking the puritan tradition, Wilson's hypocrisy, Harding's prose, the corruption of Congress, the ignorance of the Protestant clergy, the prejudice of the "booboisie" and the small-town *"boobus americanus,"* Mencken was thrashing men of straw. Most of the literate public agreed with him. But for all his destructive talk and antipatriotic diatribe, Mencken performed a constructive task and deserved well of the Republic that he lambasted. Thanks to his crusading, the names and works of Theodore Dreiser, Sinclair Lewis, Sherwood Anderson, and Willa Cather became known to a wider public than they would have been likely to attract unaided. That he overpraised James Branch Cabell and Joseph Hergesheimer and underrated T. S. Eliot and Upton Sinclair did not matter.

Some of Mencken's reflections would have done little credit to a contemporary sophomore: "No article of faith is proof against the disintegrating effects of increasing information." "One might almost describe the acquirement of knowledge as a process of disillusion." But what a comical picture he gave of the Methodist clergy of the time: "What one observes is a horde of uneducated and inflammatory dunderheads, eager

for power, intolerant of opposition, and full of a childish vanity—a mob
of holy clerks but little raised, in intelligence and dignity, above the forlorn half-wits whose souls they chronically wrack. In the whole United
States there is scarcely one among them who stands forth as a man of
sense and information. Illiterate in all save the elementals, untouched by
the larger currents of thought, drunk with their power over dolts, crazed
by their immunity to challenge by their betters, they carry over into the
professional class of the country the spirit of the most stupid peasantry,
and degrade religion into the estate of an idiotic phobia. There is not a
village in America where some such preposterous jackass is not in
eruption."

Mencken quoted a correspondent who asked him why, since he found
so much in the United States unworthy of reverence, he continued to live
there. "Why," Mencken replied, "do men go to zoos?" On other occasions he said he lived in the United States because it provided incomparably the greatest show on earth.

Mencken had always ridiculed Wilson, but it was not until the 1920's
that he found a substantial audience—notably among callow idealists
whose frustrated hopes changed them overnight into callow cynics. "The
Woodrovian style," wrote Mencken in the January, 1921, *Smart Set*, "at
the height of the Wilson hallucination was much praised by cornfed
connoisseurs. I read editorials in those days comparing it to the style of
the Biblical prophets, and arguing that it vastly exceeded the manner of
any living literatus. Looking backward, it is not difficult to see how
that doctrine arose. Its chief sponsors, first and last, were not men who
actually knew anything about writing English, but simply editorial writers on party newspapers, i.e., men who related themselves to literary
artists in much the same way that an Episcopal bishop relates himself to
Paul of Tarsus. What intrigued such gentlemen was the plain fact that
Wilson was their superior in their own special field—that he accomplished with a great deal more skill than they did themselves the great
task of reducing all the difficulties of the hour into a few sonorous and
unintelligible phrases, often with theological overtones—that he knew
better than they did how to arrest and enchant the boobery with words
that were simply words and nothing else. The vulgar like and respect
that sort of balderdash. A discourse packed with valid ideas, accurately
expressed, is quite incomprehensible to them. What they want is the
sough of vague and comforting words—words cast into phrases made
familiar to them by the whooping of their customary political and theological rabble rousers, and by the highfalutin style of the newspapers
they read. Woodrow knew how to conjure up such words. He knew how
to make them glow, and weep. He wasted no time on the heads of his
dupes, but aimed directly at their ears, diaphragms, and hearts."

It may well have occurred to Mencken himself that he was using, in reverse, precisely the same literary and intellectual tricks that he scorned in "the sainted Woodrow." Such heresy did not, however, occur to Mencken's public. Moreover, the humor, talent, and zeal that he poured into his diatribes gave evidence of his passionate love of life in the United States. The same concern about their country also inspired thirty outstanding Americans to contribute to a widely read symposium, edited by young Harold Stearns in 1922, under the title *Civilization in the United States.* "The most moving and pathetic fact in the social life of America today," wrote Stearns in his preface, "is emotional and aesthetic starvation." Experts of every kind—doctors, lawyers, historians, scientists —discussed their specialties. "The chronic state of our literature," wrote Van Wyck Brooks, "is that of a youthful promise which is never redeemed." Of scholarship Professor Joel Spingarn said, "American universities seem to have been created for the special purpose of ignoring or destroying scholarship." Of the American theater, George Jean Nathan said, "Financially it reaches the stars; culturally, with exceptions so small as to be negligible, it reaches to the drains." Mencken, on politics, wrote, "Examine the average Congressman at leisure, and you will find that he is incompetent and imbecile, and not only incompetent and imbecile, but incurably dishonest."

Mark Sullivan suggested that the decline in the relative earnings of American teachers accounted for this mood of doubt and gloom. During the 1920's, the salaries of school and college teachers remained relatively constant while the earnings of the businessman and many other professionals multiplied. It was not that the buying power of the dollar shrank; prices did not fluctuate sharply after the deflation of the early 1920's. But the teachers, with their fixed salaries, found it more and more difficult to keep up with the Joneses whose rapidly rising incomes permitted them to buy automobiles, radios, and electrical household appliances, to join golf clubs, patronize bootleggers, and see the world. The men and women who taught American youth during the 1920's instilled their pupils with their own frustrations, thus preparing the ground for Mencken's cynicism and for the Marxian materialism that followed. In Britain, the astute Lloyd George had long since agitated for higher pay for teachers as the best possible insurance against a revolutionary future.

Nothing like revolution threatened the United States during the 1920's. Nor did American civilization go into a decline during the first three decades of the twentieth century. The fact that so many American leaders took such critical stock of themselves indicated that a national civilization had only just begun. Nor did the war kill the cultural renaissance that roughly coincided with Woodrow Wilson's election to the Presidency; instead, that renaissance continued with a delayed kick.

BETTMANN ARCHIVE

H. L. Mencken as Seen by Ralph Barton
(Woman's Home Companion, *1930*)

BETTMANN ARCHIVE

Sinclair Lewis
A Photograph of the 1920's

For instance, the year 1920 witnessed the publication of three new works of fiction by authors of major talent: *Main Street* by Sinclair Lewis, *Winesburg, Ohio* by Sherwood Anderson, and *This Side of Paradise* by F. Scott Fitzgerald. Lewis came from Minnesota; he had gone to Yale, where he felt his classmates snubbed him. He came briefly under the influence of Upton Sinclair's Utopian Socialism and then made a successful beginning as a writer of popular fiction. But he presently turned against "the bitch-goddess, success," and put his sharp ear for dialogue and his sharp eye for character in the service of social satire. *Main Street* depicted small-town America; in *Babbitt* he moved on to a bustling Midwestern city; *Arrowsmith* followed the career of a doctor; *Dodsworth* the career of a businessman. Having eschewed one kind of success in commercial fiction, Lewis could not resist the appeal of the success that he won with such apparent ease by exploiting his genius for mere observation to the exclusion of his other gifts. But if he never outgrew *Main Street, Babbitt,* and *Arrowsmith* he nevertheless made a unique and valuable contribution to later generations as well as to his own through his realistic and critical appraisal of the America he knew so well.

Sinclair Lewis was the first American author to win the Nobel Prize for Literature; Sherwood Anderson never won comparable acclaim at home or abroad. The short stories of *Winesburg, Ohio* remain his outstanding work. But he possessed that sense of pity which is so lacking in so many American writers of the twentieth century, with the notable exception of Theodore Dreiser. Anderson at the age of forty quit a successful career in advertising to write fiction. He had himself endured the psychological and emotional tortures that his characters went through and that afflict so many Americans. Yet he was no pessimist or decadent; he accepted life—including life in the United States—most of all when he rejected the certainties of commercial success for the uncertainties of literature. He not only made a living; he attracted readers and influenced younger writers to follow a similar course. More talented writers of an earlier day—Melville and Hawthorne, for example—worked under much heavier handicaps. The importance of Sherwood Anderson did not lie entirely in his compassion for the emotionally starved, small-town American. The fact that his insights—so much deeper than Sinclair Lewis's—had so much meaning to so many of his contemporaries showed a new sense of American self-awareness.

Lewis and Anderson both belonged to the prewar generation. F. Scott Fitzgerald was the first American novelist to come to maturity during the war years. He had gone into uniform but did not see service overseas —in which respect he resembled most of his contemporaries who dramatized themselves as the "lost generation." The fact was that only a minority of Americans who entered the armed services ever got overseas and of those a still smaller minority ever saw action. Many half-trained young soldiers regretted the 1918 Armistice; they felt it had cheated them of their chance for glory. The war had interrupted—even dislocated —their lives, but it had not wiped them out as it had wiped out their European contemporaries. They accepted the defeat of the League and the repudiation of Wilson without a fight, without regret. They had no enthusiasm for Harding's normalcy; they turned against the puritan tradition. They came of age to find all gods dead, all wars fought, all faiths in man shaken. And when handsome, twenty-four-year-old F. Scott Fitzgerald, just out of Princeton, wrote *This Side of Paradise* they recognized themselves in this autobiographical picture of the "jazz age." Indeed, the Fitzgerald "flapper" in her "petting shirt" suggested that Mencken had perhaps exaggerated the vitality of the puritan tradition.

Fitzgerald's later books—*The Beautiful and Damned, Tender Is the Night,* and *The Great Gatsby*—as well as the short stories he wrote for the popular magazines depicted the world of the Ritz, the speakeasy, the coonskin coat, and the Stutz Bearcat. Fitzgerald and his young wife went in for everything this world had to offer, though it all tasted of dust and ashes, flavored by synthetic gin. As an artist Fitzgerald also recognized the limitations of his character, talent, and tastes and wisely confined himself to writing about the specialized world that he knew best.

One of the most popular sports writers of the time—born Ringgold W. Lardner of Niles, Michigan—followed the same course of least resistance. He knew the world of professional baseball as Fitzgerald knew the world of the Ritz Hotel, and Lardner's letters of an imaginary bush-leaguer, "You Know Me, Al," which he began as a daily newspaper feature became one of the most widely admired books of the time. Still confining himself to almost stenographic reports of the middle-class Middle-Westerners he knew best, Lardner grew from a humorist into one of the great masters of the short story, and none of his contemporaries depicted the average, typical, striving American of the 1920's with such lifelike savagery. Lardner possessed the rare gift that marks the writer of true classics: he appealed to many different readers at many different levels. The mass-circulation magazines for which he wrote featured him as a humorist; the leading critics regarded him as a great social satirist.

In 1921 came the disillusioned war novel: John Dos Passos's *Three Soldiers*. The author, a recent Harvard graduate still in his twenties, had driven an ambulance in France, where he saw the face of modern war at close range; he also threw himself into the literary and artistic life of wartime and postwar Paris. *Three Soldiers* dealt bitterly and realistically with the war experiences of three typical Americans, reflecting at the same time the disillusionment that most of the younger generation of European writers were already expressing. Dos Passos was not the first American writer to come under European influence; he was the first to find at once a large audience in his own country. Something new had happened under the American literary sun. A high-brow, advance-guard advocate of revolutionary pacifism had reached the general book-reading public.

After *Three Soldiers* Dos Passos continued to experiment. *Manhattan Transfer* borrowed heavily—too heavily—from James Joyce's *Ulysses*. In *Forty-Second Parallel*—the first of the trilogy, *U.S.A.*—Dos Passos at last hit his stride, combining new literary technique with sharp observation and understanding of his own country. He never attracted as large a public as Sinclair Lewis, but he stood out from his contemporaries as the first uncorrupted advance-guard writer to make himself widely understood. The American public had not gone high-brow or Bohemian. E. E. Cummings, also a Harvard graduate and a contemporary of Dos Passos, had less success with his revolutionary picture of the horrors of war, *The Enormous Room*. Cummings, the son of a New England Unitarian minister, wrote only about his own experiences in a French jail, but leading American and foreign critics rated *The Enormous Room* at least as high as they rated *Three Soldiers*. Whereas Dos Passos turned to new experiments in fiction, Cummings experimented far more boldly —and somewhat less successfully—with poetry. He signed himself e. e. cummings and the liberties he took with punctuation, typography, spelling, and every literary convention drove most critics wild.

Before the war the experimental versifiers on both sides of the Atlantic seldom wrote the language of the man on the street. Most of them affected a disdain for the illiterate mob. Cummings, an upside-down snob, preferred the language of the street to the language of the salon—and liked the language of the gutter best of all. He experimented as boldly as any European Dadaist, but behind his perversity and humor lay originality and purpose. It was a sign of the times that while Cummings, the aesthetic product of Harvard, Boston, Paris, and New York, ridiculed most of the traditions and influences to which he had been subjected, Ring Lardner, the sports writer from Niles, Michigan, amused himself by spoofing the high-brows with authentic Dadaist playlets. In Lardner and Cummings extremes met, but it was Lardner whose work appealed to the general public.

Gilbert Seldes, one of the editors of *The Dial*, attempted to reconcile the world of E. E. Cummings and the world of Ring Lardner. In the columns of *Vanity Fair* and in his book *The Seven Lively Arts*, Seldes discovered Charlie Chaplin, Al Jolson, and George Herriman's "Krazy Kat" comic strips with somewhat the same wide-eyed wonder that Molière's bourgeois gentleman displayed when he found that he had been speaking prose all his life. Seldes did not place any of America's popular artists among the immortals, but he wrote about the music of Irving Berlin, George Gershwin, and Jerome Kern, about Mack Sennett's Keystone Comedy Cops, about vaudeville, burlesque shows, and the circus with the same earnestness that other critics brought to discussions of Eleonora Duse, Richard Strauss, or Bernard Shaw. For the end of the war had given the popular American arts a new burst of energy, and the newspapers, the magazines, the movies, and the radio carried them to the millions. This popular culture specialized in laughter, sentiment, and violence. It lacked subtlety, but achieved superb technique. "What Europeans feel about American art," wrote Mr. Seldes, "is exactly the opposite of what they feel about American life. Our life is energetic, varied, constantly changing; our art is imitative, anaemic (exceptions in both cases being assumed). The explanation is that few Europeans see our lively arts which are almost secret to us, like the mysteries of a cult. Here the energy of America does break out and finds artistic expression for itself. Here a wholly unrealistic, imaginative presentation of the way we think and feel is accomplished. No single artist has yet been great enough to do the whole thing—but together the minor artists of America have created the American art."

Add the novels of Sinclair Lewis, Scott Fitzgerald, and John Dos Passos, the short stories of Ring Lardner and Sherwood Anderson, the criticism of H. L. Mencken and George Jean Nathan, and the picture becomes more complete and more coherent. Although the high-brows attacked the normalcy of Harding, they released as much energy as Al

Jolson singing a "Mammy" song: it was because they loved their country so much that they belabored it so fiercely. Nor did they flee from their native land as Henry James fled from the Gilded Age; they did not have to endure the ordeal of Mark Twain, who suppressed his spleen and gave himself over to the accumulation of money. For the first time since New England's golden age, America's creative intellectuals became a national influence and found a national audience.

While Harding's more gifted contemporaries rejected the kind of normalcy that the Republican Party established during the early 1920's, his supporters made out a plausible case for themselves. The business leaders who came to prominence during the early 1920's followed a different code than the robber barons of the late nineteenth century and the monopolists of the early twentieth. None of them dared to echo Commodore Vanderbilt's famous words: "The public be damned." The editorials by George Horace Lorimer in the *Saturday Evening Post*, the articles by Garet Garrett in the same magazine, the books on which Henry Ford collaborated with Samuel Crowther expressed a new philosophy of economics and of life, appropriate to those who regarded themselves as the new leaders of a new America. "Twenty-five years ago," Crowther wrote for Ford in *Today and Tomorrow*, "we heard a great deal about big business. There really was no big business twenty-five years ago. What we had was our first mergers of money. Money is not business. Big money cannot make big business. Men of money, foreseeing the approach of the industrial era, sought to seize and control it by means of their pooled capital. And for a time the country rang with their exploits. Money brokers are seldom good businessmen. Speculators cannot create values. However, the idea got abroad that 'money' had grabbed everything and that 'money' controlled everything." Ford himself once expressed his own business philosophy in these words: "I hold that it is better to sell a large number of cars at a reasonably small margin than to sell fewer cars at a larger margin of profit. I hold this because it enables a large number of people to buy and enjoy the use of a car and because it gives a larger number of men employment at good wages." On May 31, 1921, the Ford Motor Company produced its five millionth Model T car, which contained about five thousand interchangeable parts and did not differ essentially from the original 1909 product. Crowther also quoted Ford to this effect: "The owner, the employees, and the buying public are all one and the same, and unless an industry can so manage itself as to keep wages high and profits low, it destroys itself, for otherwise it limits the number of its customers." But while Samuel Crowther popularized Ford and his ideas, Will Rogers expressed a skepticism that many Americans shared: "I think Mr. Ford is wrong when he says that 90 per cent of the people in this country are satisfied.

Ninety per cent of the people in this country are not satisfied. It's just got so 90 per cent of the people in this country didn't give a damn."

In *My Life and Work*, Ford said, "It is extraordinary how firmly rooted is the notion that business—continuous selling—depends not upon satisfying the customer once and for all, but on first getting his money for one article and then persuading him that he ought to buy a new and different one." Ford spoke as a manufacturer, not as a salesman; Garet Garrett spoke for the rising generation of high-pressure installment salesmen when he wrote in *The American Omen:* "Increasingly, the anxiety of modern business is how to stimulate effective wanting, how to stimulate people to exert themselves more in order to have and consume more. Installment selling has that motive."

Nobody gave such effective expression to the aspirations of American business as George Horace Lorimer, who had made the *Saturday Evening Post* the most popular and influential magazine in the country before the war. Lorimer wrote his own weekly editorial; he inspired and hired others to write longer articles. He paid top prices and attracted top talent in the fiction field. During the early 1900's he published Frank Norris and Jack London. Sinclair Lewis was a successful, prosperous *Post* contributor before he stopped writing to please others and started writing to please himself. F. Scott Fitzgerald wrote many stories for the *Post* after *This Side of Paradise* made him the literary saxophone of the jazz age.

Like many other great editors, before and since, Lorimer could not transcend his limitations; indeed, his limitations made him great, and as long as America's upper middle class prospered, Lorimer and the *Post* prospered too. He reached ten times as many readers as Mencken did and therefore felt it unnecessary to pay too much attention to the increasingly critical, cynical, and skeptical attitude of the more aggressive writers of the younger generation. Even so discerning a critic as Bernard De Voto, himself a *Post* contributor, found much to praise in slick-magazine fiction which Lorimer had done so much to encourage: "The historian is going to recover the surface of American life—at least middle-class life—much more fully and with less distortion from the slicks than from the novel of our day. The slicks render the surface more honestly, more accurately, and with greater respect. The slick writer, unlike the novelist, is penalized if he loads his dice." It may be doubted that this judgment has stood the test of time; it cannot be doubted that De Voto made a valid distinction between popular slick fiction and the serious novel that dwelt on some of the seamier sides of life in the United States.

Lorimer's strong opinions and distinctive tastes mirrored and anticipated—as a good editor's should—the opinions and tastes of his readers.

He defined introspective stories as "stories in which one looks within and finds nothing." He laid down the law, "Nobody can tell a story in less than three thousand words." "Maupassant did," Ben Ames Williams objected. "Maupassant's dead," replied Lorimer.

Lorimer opposed American entrance into the European war, backed the war effort, then fought the League of Nations or any kind of foreign entanglement. In 1919 he sent Kenneth Roberts, one of his crack feature writers, to Europe to get in touch with people who had returned from the United States, to find out how many planned to emigrate—and why. He had Roberts concentrate on central Europe and report fully on the type of European who wanted to come to America. This series and others did much to build up popular sentiment for restricting immigration. One of Lorimer's 1919 editorials entitled "Joyriding and Jaywalking" expressed the fears of many businessmen at the time: "The simply and amply proven fact is that government ownership does not make men and rarely makes money. It makes weaklings, dependents, grafters, bureaucrats, autocrats, and deficits. It is the first lesson in Socialism and Socialism is the first lesson in Bolshevism, and Bolshevism is the last lesson in government. The class graduates from that into Anarchy." Lorimer and the *Post*, not Mencken and the *Smart Set*, spoke for the great American middle class during the early 1920's. Lorimer's culture and Lorimer's politics summed up the culture and the politics of the all-powerful business community which gave the whole decade of the 1920's its unique character.

While the *Saturday Evening Post* flourished, the daily newspaper languished. The trend toward centralization, concentration, and standardization doomed the small-town paper and cut down the number of papers in the larger cities. The syndicated columnist replaced the editorial writer. But the newspapers that did survive won more and more readers. Although Hearst never gained the political power he craved, the newspaper chain he created across the country set an example that others tried to follow. Only E. W. Scripps and Roy Howard succeeded and they did not build so wide or powerful a network as Hearst. William Allen White summed up what many decent newspapermen all over the country felt when he described Hearst as "my idea of a rattlesnake crossed with smallpox." Hearst owed his initial success, in large measure, to inherited money. He entered a business which had generally financed itself and poured into it the profits of his father's gold mines and other properties. As a rich man's son, he knew little and cared less about where the money came from. What interested him was the power that money could buy in the low-paying newspaper field. William James, with his philosophy of pragmatism, has much to answer for, but nothing that he inspired turned out more disastrously, from James's own point of view, than the advice he gave to Senator Hearst's spoiled son from California to start a chain of newspapers.

Frank A. Munsey also smirched the press of his time, but there his resemblance to Hearst ended. Munsey was a poor boy from Maine and made his own way in the world. Instead of spending his father's money, as Hearst did, by founding new papers, Munsey piled up money for himself by purchasing, merging, and annihilating papers that already existed. White had no more use for Munsey than for Hearst and when Munsey died he composed a bitter obituary: "Frank Munsey, the great publisher, is dead. Frank Munsey contributed to the journalism of his day the talent of a meat-packer, the morals of a money-changer, and the manners of an undertaker. He and his kind have about succeeded in transforming a once-noble profession into an eight per cent security. May he rest in trust."

· VI ·

WHEN Coolidge became President of the United States, the country had recovered from the sharp postwar depression. Its people had also acquired a new sense of their own importance and with it a new feeling for their own past. Many of those with money to spare collected antiques or built reproductions of early American houses. The vulgar Harding had failed to restore the world of William McKinley; the ascetic Coolidge —a throwback to pre-Civil War New England—recalled a more austere, dignified past. His dry voice, which William Allen White called a "quack," and his laconic speech came as a reassuring contrast to the expansive Harding, who, in his own version of the English language, loved nothing so much as to "bloviate." Coolidge stories went the rounds. When asked why he dined out so much as Vice-President, he replied, "Got to eat somewhere." At another dinner his partner confided that a friend had bet her ten dollars she could not make him say three words. "You lose," Coolidge replied. Shoveling up a piece of earth at a tree-planting he quacked, "That's a fine fish-worm." When asked what the minister said about sin in his Sunday sermon, he replied, "He was against it." When a messenger from the Treasury handed Coolidge his first pay check in the White House, the new President was said to have remarked, "Call again." And the story is told in Boston that when one of Coolidge's advisers warned him not to endorse a certain Congressman for re-election because he was "a son of a bitch," Coolidge commented, "There are a lot of those fellers in the country and they should have representation."

Coolidge knew far more than the lazy Harding about politics. He had come up step by step during the past quarter of a century from Mayor of Northampton, Massachusetts, to State Legislator, Lieutenant Governor, and Governor. He sought office nineteen times and missed out only once. Yet he had not run with the orthodox Massachusetts Republicans. He entered politics as a protégé of the late Senator W. Murray Crane, a well-to-do businessman who did not share Lodge's hatred of Wilson and the League. Coolidge also remained the close friend of Frank W. Stearns, a Boston merchant, of William M. Butler, a New Bedford cotton manufacturer, and of his

BETTMANN ARCHIVE

Calvin Coolidge

Amherst classmate Dwight W. Morrow, who became a Morgan partner. According to Will Rogers, who knew both men, Coolidge told Morrow in 1923, "Dwight, I am not going to try to be a great President." Coolidge had agreed with the rest of his Amherst classmates that Morrow was the man most likely of them all to succeed. Morrow, however, picked the shy, obscure Coolidge, and in 1919 saw no reason to change his mind. "I have about come to the conclusion," he wrote to Frank W. Stearns, "that the division of the people of the world is not really between conservative and radical, but between the people that are real people and people that are not. Calvin is one of the fellows who is real. He really wants to make things better, not to pretend to make them better."

The night of August 2, 1923, when Harding died, found the Vice-President vacationing in his father's farmhouse at Plymouth, Vermont. He and Mrs. Coolidge had retired at nine, but were wakened at 2 A.M. with the news of the President's death. "Is this information authentic?" cautious Cal inquired, and when he learned it was, he thought to himself: "I believe I can swing it." He then drafted a brief statement, consulted the Constitution, and had his father, as Justice of the Peace, administer the oath of office by the light of a kerosene lamp. The new President placed his hand on a Bible that had belonged to his mother, and visited her grave on his way to take the train to Washington. She had died when he was twelve years old.

Everything about Coolidge and everything he did from this moment on went to the hearts of the American people, if only because he had so little in common with the more raucous symptoms of his time. To Alice Roosevelt Longworth he "looked as if he had been weaned on a pickle." He fished with gloves on and made the secret service men bait his hook and remove his catch. He brought with him to the White House two sons, still in their teens, and a wife as different from Mrs. Harding as he was from his predecessor. The fact that Grace Goodhue Coolidge was teaching deaf and dumb children before she married her taciturn husband caused some humorous comment, but she soon established herself as her husband's better half—and no one knew that better than the President himself. This warm, responsive, charming woman had every sympathy with Coolidge when he informed Ike Hoover, the White House head usher: "I want things as they used to be—before." Neither the President nor Mrs. Coolidge wore the aristocratic airs of the Roosevelts or the Lodges; they had something better—Yankee good taste that restored dignity to the White House overnight.

Their respectability served them well in other connections. On October 23, 1923, Democratic Senator Thomas J. Walsh of Montana summoned Albert B. Fall to testify concerning certain oil leases that Walsh had spent the past eighteen months investigating. It seemed that Fall, when Secretary of the Interior, had leased three of the Navy's richest oil fields to private companies without competitive bidding. The incident had received some slight publicity back in 1922, when the public learned that Secretary of the Navy Denby had given Fall authority to make any disposition he chose of three oil fields at Teapot Dome, Wyoming, and at Elk Hills and Buena Vista, California. When the press expressed some surprise, Harding announced, "These acts have at all times had my entire approval." This reassured the public but did not satisfy Senator Walsh.

It took Walsh almost as long again to reveal the full story as it had taken him to prepare his case. When Fall first testified, in October, 1923, he made a strong impression with his flashing blue eyes, sweeping mustaches, Kentucky drawl, and Western breeziness. He admitted that he had leased the Elk Hills and Teapot Dome fields to private companies, but refused to reveal their names and denied having accepted any money from Edwin F. Doheny, a millionaire prospector, or from Harry F. Sinclair, a big oil operator.

More witnesses followed with testimony that shattered Fall's story, health, and spirit. In February he hobbled before Walsh, supported by a cane, declining to answer any question on the traditional ground that "it may tend to incriminate me." By this time, the oil leases had become the greatest scandal in American political history. Coolidge finally appointed two special investigators to delve deeper: ex-Senator Attlee Pomerene of Ohio, a Democrat, and Owen J. Roberts, a Republican

UNDERWOOD

Albert Fall (left) and E. L. Doheny (right) with their Attorney, Frank J. Hogan

lawyer from Philadelphia. And when Attorney General Daugherty declined to hand over certain documents to the Senate Committee, Coolidge demanded his resignation. Years passed before the courts finally sent Fall to jail for having accepted bribes totaling $100,000 in cash and $260,000 in Liberty Bonds. Sinclair also went to jail when he refused to testify before the Walsh Committee. No other oil man suffered any penalty; nothing was proved against any other member of Harding's official family. Yet Attorney General Daugherty owed $27,000 in debts and had assets totaling $10,000 when he took office and within two years he had a bank account of $75,000 plus $40,000 in bonds. Daugherty not only considered his own conduct in office beyond reproach. He said of Fall, "And to save my soul, I can't bring myself to believe that when he took or borrowed this famous $100,000 from Doheny he realized it was a bribe."

By the summer of 1924, when the Republicans and Democrats held their national conventions, the Democrats appeared to have at least an even chance of winning. The Republicans met first and quickly nominated Coolidge, with Charles Gates Dawes as his running mate. Nicholas Murray Butler told a characteristic story about the selection of Dawes.

It seems that Mellon, Longworth, Senator Harry New of Indiana, and a few others were trying to find the ideal candidate. At last New got up in disgust. "I am going off to bed," he said. "The kind of man you are looking for as Vice-President was crucified nineteen hundred years ago." Dawes, a successful Chicago banker, had held the rank of general during the war when he served as chief supply officer with Pershing in France. Harding had appointed him director of the budget; Coolidge made him head of the American delegation that framed the so-called "Dawes Plan" to restore Germany. The Republicans chose as their slogan "Keep Cool with Coolidge" and took credit for the business revival that had begun six months before Harding died. They said less about the work that Dawes had done abroad. Few Americans knew it—and fewer Republicans admitted it—but the fact was that four years after the United States had rejected the Versailles Treaty, the League of Nations, and the confusing entanglements of Europe, Coolidge and Dawes had quietly eased their country closer to the turmoil of Old World power politics.

The Democrats also ignored foreign affairs in the 1924 campaign. They had three domestic issues that seemed more important: the oil scandals, the distress of the farmers, and Coolidge's lethargy. But the Democrats lacked unity; two irreconcilable leaders split the Party. William Gibbs McAdoo of California accepted the support of the Prohibitionists and the Ku Klux Klan. Governor Alfred E. Smith of New York wanted the Eighteenth Amendment repealed, and his Roman Catholic faith enraged the Klansmen. The Convention met in New York and after three weeks and more than one hundred ballots finally nominated John W. Davis and Governor Charles W. Bryan of Nebraska—William J.'s brother. Davis had served two terms in Congress as a Democratic Representative from West Virginia and had become Solicitor General and Ambassador to Great Britain during the Wilson administration. He then joined a leading New York law firm as legal counsel to J. P. Morgan.

The Republicans offered the American people the close friend of a Morgan partner; the Democrats offered the American people a Morgan lawyer. "The only thing I can see now that divides the two old parties," said Will Rogers, "is who will have the post offices." The Progressives therefore improvised a third party that nominated Senator Robert M. La Follette of Wisconsin—nominally a Republican—and Burton K. Wheeler, junior Senator from Montana, a Democrat. They assailed both the old parties, but Coolidge did not bat an eye: "I am for economy and after that for more economy," he declared, carefully making no reference to the oil scandals. His backers concentrated their fire on Charlie Bryan. "Coolidge or chaos," they proclaimed, warning that the La Follette candidacy might throw the election into the House of Representatives, where the Democrats and insurgent Republicans had enough votes to put Bryan in the White House.

Coolidge luck continued to serve the new President even though it took the form of a personal tragedy. Early in July, 1924, his second son, the fourteen-year-old Calvin, died of blood poisoning after he blistered his toe playing tennis. "When he went," wrote his father five years later, "the power and the glory of the Presidency went with him." But at the time of the boy's death, millions of Americans sympathized with the stricken President, whose bearing showed a grief that he could not put into words. When Election Day came around, Coolidge received more than fifteen million votes to Davis's eight million and La Follette's five. "The result," said Will Rogers, "was just about as big a surprise as the news that Christmas was coming in December." Republican prosperity made a wider appeal than the false insurgence of the Democrats and the real insurgence of the Progressives—combined.

Something more than Coolidge luck accounted for the prosperity that spread across the land in 1924. A large wheat crop in the United States and a partial failure in Canada improved the condition of the American farmer, for the moment. Foreign loans jumped from three hundred million dollars in 1923 to over a billion dollars in 1924. Confidence and prosperity had returned to the United States with such a rush that the country could again afford to interest itself in world affairs. By March, 1925, when Coolidge delivered his inaugural address, the prospects looked so pleasing that he indulged himself in words of assurance and cheer:

"Here stands our country, an example of tranquillity at home, a patron of tranquillity abroad. Here stands its government, aware of its might but obedient to its conscience. Here it will continue to stand, seeking peace and prosperity, solicitous for the welfare of the wage earner, promoting enterprise, developing waterways and natural resources, attentive to the intuitive counsel of womanhood, encouraging education, desiring the advancement of religion, supporting the cause of justice and honor among the nations. America seeks no earthly empire built on blood and force. No ambition, no temptation, lures her to thought of foreign dominions. The legions which she sends forth are armed, not with the sword but with the cross. The higher state to which she seeks the allegiance of all mankind is not human, but of divine origin. She cherishes no purpose save to merit the favor of Almighty God."

To the man who spoke these words and to millions of his fellow citizens they expressed the highest aspirations of a great and mighty people. In Europe, in Russia, in China they had a different meaning—if, indeed, they had any meaning at all.

SUMMING UP

IF ONE man wrecked Wilson's plans for America and the world, it was Wilson himself. The burden that he insisted upon carrying alone in Paris broke his body and his nerves before he returned to face a hostile Senate. He had beaten himself, physically, on the eve of the political battle on which his lifework depended. The final irony lay in the fact that Wilsonism completed the destruction of its creator. Wilsonism stressed self-determination and the extension of democracy. It was Wilson's own propaganda for self-determination that fed nationalist fires everywhere—including the United States—and this nationalist spirit that Wilson encouraged all around the world did not sit well with the new spirit of internationalism that he tried to breathe into the League of Nations. Wilson also found that democracy was a sword that cut two ways. He had become so accustomed to speaking the mind of the American people that he instinctively identified his own aspirations with theirs. Thus, during the fight for the Treaty, it did not occur to him that he no longer spoke for a firm majority, but for a dwindling minority, and his last public statement, uttered on Armistice Day, 1923, a few weeks before his death, showed that this delusion persisted to the end: "I am not one of those who have the least anxiety about the principles I have stood for. I have seen fools resist Providence before and I have seen their destruction, as will come upon these again—utter and complete destruction and contempt. That we shall prevail is as certain as that God reigns."

Even as he spoke, Providence was proving Wilson half right: the same ironic fate that destroyed him was already catching up with his enemies as they succumbed to the same intolerance that had wrecked his own hopes. Lashed on by Lodge, the bitter-end Republican Senators rejected the moderates within their own Party only to find themselves saddled with Harding's Ohio gang. Retribution followed. Death saved Harding himself from almost certain impeachment, but his guiltier cronies and underlings did not get off so easily. The embittered Lodge, who had dominated the 1920 Republican National Convention, snarled in the wings, four years later, as the upstart Coolidge reaped the rewards that caution and moderation sometimes pay. The Wilson Democrats and the Lodge Republicans had destroyed each other and set the stage for American big business to take over.

Yet strong undercurrents in American life were already beginning to run the other way. Rural reformers had put across the Prohibition Amendment, which was proving more and more difficult to enforce in the big cities, to which more and more country people had moved.

Organized crime flourished; middle-class morals broke down; respect for government authority declined. A large and increasing minority of the American people—perhaps even a majority—wanted the Eighteenth Amendment repealed or modified. No such reaction followed the passage of the Nineteenth Amendment, giving votes to women. That had marked a major triumph for the social reformers, and since 1920 the American woman had become more and more important in many fields. The emancipation of the American woman, symbolized by the Nineteenth Amendment, cut across party lines. But an irreversible revolution in morals had run a long, long way in the United States during the war and postwar years.

This revolution expressed itself most sharply in the cultural renaissance that had coincided with the proclamation of Wilson's New Freedom back in 1912 and which neither Harding nor Coolidge could arrest. It was a nonpolitical, nonviolent revolution. The critics who preached it and the novelists who depicted it had as little use for Democrats as they had for Republicans. They turned against Wilson as a hollow phrasemaker; the reality of Harding surpassed the most extravagant flights of satirical fancy; after his two and a half years in the White House there was no alternative to keeping cool with Coolidge. La Follette attracted an impressive protest vote, but he had become a figure of the past. Thanks to expanding business activity, the American writer, artist, and intellectual did not have too hard a time making a living during the mid-1920's, and he busied himself mainly with satirizing and criticizing a civilization that continued to spread its benefits more unevenly than widely. But the fact that the middle and professional classes prospered gave this continuing cultural renaissance a solvent public. The decline of farm income and the exclusion of the factory worker from a substantial share in the fruits of his toil received even less attention than the plight of Europe, which, soon after Harding's death, required the New World once again to redress the balance of the Old.

Europe's First Six Years of Peace

While democracy gained strength in most of western Europe and while Italy went Fascist, the vitality of the Old World reasserted itself in the sciences and the arts.

PREVIEW

BETWEEN 1919 and 1924, German big business first tried to wreck and then helped to rescue the new-born German Republic. During these same years, a nationalist French government under Poincaré's leadership took advantage of German weakness and defiance to carry the victory of 1919 several steps further. But a succession of British governments—headed by Liberal, Conservative, and Labor Prime Ministers—refused to support Poincaré and kept encouraging the Germans to rally around a central, solvent, democratic regime. Eventually the British prevailed, but not until Ramsay MacDonald's Labor government came to power and not until private American bankers supervised and underwrote the Dawes Plan for German recovery and reparations. Germany—and all Europe—had teetered on the edge of collapse and possible revolution, and the disgusted people of France finally voted the Nationalists out of office, replacing them with the Radical Party of Édouard Herriot, who worked with Ramsay MacDonald to pacify Europe and strengthen the League of Nations. The British Conservatives, however, took alarm and used a forged document and a fake Red scare to overthrow the Labor Government. At the same time the renegade radical, Benito Mussolini, established a new kind of dictatorship. To judge from the new writers who emerged in Europe after the war, belief in social reform and material progress had begun to wane. They paid more attention to Freudian psychoanalysis than to Marxian economics. But the scientists had started the greatest revolution of all.

· I ·

THE UNITED STATES had only just begun to recover from its postwar slump when Europe sent out an S O S as if to remind the new Coolidge administration of important unfinished business across the Atlantic.

From the summer of 1919 to the end of 1922 Britain and France had tried to impose a heavy reparations schedule upon Germany. During 1923 Britain and France split apart as French troops occupied the Ruhr and Rhineland valleys. But they drove Germany so close to revolution that in 1924 the United States had to rush dollars and dollar diplomats to the rescue. The steady demoralization of Germany during the first five years of peace had demoralized Europe, too.

Those Germans who signed the 1918 Armistice believed in Wilson's Fourteen Points and in the future of democracy everywhere. They belonged to the Socialist, the Democratic, and the Catholic Center Parties, which received, among them, eighty per cent of the total vote in the 1919 elections. But when the terms of the Versailles Treaty became known, four months afterward, about one hundred per cent of the German people believed that the Allies had violated the Armistice terms and the Fourteen Points. The continuing Allied blockade, during the winter of 1918-19, deepened the disillusionment. Socialist leaders who had demanded peace since 1917 now called in Nationalist generals to preserve order and prevent a revolution that only a small minority of the working class supported. In 1920 some of these same Nationalists attempted a counterrevolution when eight thousand troops in the Berlin garrison seized government buildings, proclaimed the Republic at an end, and installed an almost unknown character named Wolfgang von Kapp as Chancellor. The top officials of the menaced Republic fled to Stuttgart and ordered the arrest of von Kapp while Socialist working-men in Berlin staged a general strike that forced him to flee to Sweden. Communists in the Ruhr organized futile insurrections. A year later von Kapp's supporters made more trouble in Bavaria, which had already crushed Kurt Eisner's seizure of power back in 1919.

Although the Weimar Republic survived revolution from the left and counterrevolution from the right, it had already lost much of its original vitality. The suppression of the Kapp Putsch won general support, but many rank-and-file Socialist workers mistrusted their political leaders for working so closely with former officers in the Kaiser's Army. The more astute Nationalists, in turn, did not commit themselves to von Kapp; they divided their energies between leading regular troops against the Communists and organizing an illegal Free Corps of adventurous reactionary youths who systematically assassinated outstanding supporters of the Republic, beginning with Matthias Erzberger, of the Catholic Center Party, who had signed the 1918 Armistice. The Nationalists wanted a Hohenzollern restoration. They despised the red, black, and gold flag of the Republic, charging that the red represented Socialism, the black Catholicism, and gold the international Jewish banker.

In the 1920 elections the Socialists, Democrats, and Center Party lost

UNDERWOOD

Berlin Communists Parade in Honor of Liebknecht and Luxemburg. Their Placard Reads: "The Day Will Come When We Will Avenge Ourselves. Then We Shall Sit as Judges."

ground to the Nationalists and to the new People's Party, representing big business. The Nationalists had not yet lived down their responsibility for the defeat of 1918. The People's Party, on the other hand, did not appear responsible either for the lost war or for the hard peace. Indeed, the biggest businessman in postwar Germany found the peace anything but hard and thus became a popular hero of sorts. Hugo Stinnes, who celebrated his fiftieth birthday in 1920, had inherited some properties from his well-to-do father, for whom he had gone to work early in life, rising from pit boy to mine foreman and then following the sea until he became a steamship captain. By 1922 Stinnes had acquired control of almost one sixth of all the industries in Germany—coal mines, steel mills, steamship lines, and more than sixty newspapers that supported the new People's Party. He headed half a dozen separate trusts; he had a quarter of a million employees—more than the older Krupp and Thyssen dynasties combined; and he kept adding to his possessions by selling Germany short. Stinnes became the greatest bear market operator in history by mortgaging his properties, paying off his borrowings in depreciated marks, and pouring his profits into new ventures. His fabulous wealth—estimated at more than a billion dollars—forced the German government to admit him to an international conference where he insulted the French delegates. He declared that the French suffered from "the disease of victory" and tried to blackmail his country's creditors by threatening to bring Bolshevism to Germany through further, deliberate inflation.

A contemporary German wrote a vivid description of Stinnes at the height of his power during the early 1920's: "Stinnes was at that time the most powerful man in Germany, a sort of a secret Kaiser, towering above the stricken state on a pedestal of huge, if rather vague, industrial power. For the man in the street, both at home and abroad, he had already become a legendary figure, a wizard, a Klingsor who alone possessed the secret of conjuring forth magic gardens from the stony ruins of German industry, a Cagliostro, an alchemist capable by some sort of sorcery of transmuting paper into gold. But even at close range he was impressive—one half, to be sure, only a big uncanny financier, but the other half a prophet, wont to say his sooth blatantly and bluntly, but yet impenetrable, and thus mysterious to friend and foe alike. He went about among German coal merchants and steel magnates, his colleagues, like a stranger; very dark, looking like a southerner, a Frenchman or an Assyrian, with a thick black beard and eyes that seemed always gazing on some inner vision, moving in what was left of Society with heavy peasant boots and clothes that hung about him as if he had just got them back from the pawnbroker's, always surrounded by a vast family, which he dragged along behind him wherever he went; a cross between a patriarch, a commercial traveler, and the Flying Dutchman. Taken all in all, he was perhaps a man possessed—possessed by the demon of big business, by an unquenchable thirst for supreme power through commercial transactions, as Hokusai was possessed by the demon of painting and drawing. For, at bottom, he was nothing but a company promoter with no other outlook or interest than finance."

This passage comes from Count Harry Kessler's biography of Walther Rathenau, Stinnes's chief antagonist. Stinnes embodied the interests of German heavy industry. He looked east rather than west; he saw German brains and German factories plus Russian manpower and Russian resources dominating Europe. Rathenau looked west rather than east. He did not come from the old world of heavy industry, of coal and iron and steel, but from the new world of light industry, having inherited from his father a controlling interest in the General Electric Company of Germany. Although he favored doing business with the Russians,

Rathenau argued that Germany must make a sincere attempt to fulfill the Versailles Treaty and earn a strong and honorable place in the European community of nations. A substantial portion of the business community—especially the bankers—agreed with him and he had conservative as well as liberal support in 1922 when he became Foreign Minister, in the coalition government headed by Chancellor Wirth of the Catholic Center Party.

By this time Lloyd George's coalition British government was showing less and less sympathy for France. Between January, 1920, and December, 1922, no less than twenty-three international conferences had assembled and broken up in vain attempts to fix a definite schedule of German reparations and to pacify Europe. The "land fit for heroes to live in" that Lloyd George had promised in the first flush of victory had not materialized. Britain had defeated Germany only to lose its prewar position of world predominance. Unemployment, less than one million in 1920, climbed to more than two million by 1922. Coal mines and textile factories shut down. "These are my devastated areas," Lloyd George told a group of visitors from France as he showed them so-called "depressed areas."

The withers of the French remained unwrung. More than a million of their young men had lost their lives in the war. In 1920 the dwindling birth rate sent the population down another 220,000. That same year the Nationalists won a majority of 200 seats in the Chamber of Deputies. The ex-Socialist, Millerand, succeeded Clemenceau as Premier and Paul Deschanel defeated him for the Presidency. Père-la-Victoire (Father Victory), as Clemenceau had been called in wartime, became Perdre-la-Victoire (Lost Victory) because of the popular disappointment about the peace. The United States had rejected the League of Nations and had refused to guarantee France against future German aggression. The French felt they had no choice but to build their own network of alliances in eastern Europe to check the spread of Russian Communism and to keep Germany encircled.

In 1921 France began to enter into a series of alliances with Poland and then, through Poland, with the newly formed Little Entente of Czechoslovakia, Yugoslavia, and Rumania. Here French bankers found investment opportunities; French munition makers found markets. But the revival of German industry had already begun to cause alarm. German coal production had climbed to two thirds of the prewar level and the German steel industry was buying iron ore from Sweden instead of Lorraine, while the French still had to buy coke from the Ruhr. The interests of the French industrialists coincided with the fears of the French people, and the Nationalists exploited both.

In spite of his dislike of French policy, Lloyd George did not turn against his wartime ally. In 1921 a plebiscite in Upper Silesia resulted in a vote favoring union with Germany by a three-to-two majority, yet Lloyd George approved the French solution which awarded the industrial regions to Poland and the agricultural regions to Germany. Not until 1922 did he begin to pry himself loose from France, when he sponsored a momentous international conference at Genoa, the first to which both the Germans and the Russians had also been invited. The move came too late. Poincaré had just reorganized the French government and dropped the conciliatory Briand as Foreign Minister, replacing him with the rigid Louis Barthou. A tragicomedy of errors found Rathenau, at his first meeting of the kind, holding a separate, furtive meeting with Chicherin, the Soviet Foreign Minister, at nearby Rapallo, where they agreed to restore diplomatic relations and encourage trade. Their conduct seemed to confirm all the worst suspicions that the outside world still held about two pariah nations, but the breach between Germany and Russia did not narrow so much as the breach between Britain and France widened.

Rathenau and Chicherin made a curious pair. Rathenau belonged to a Jewish family, but he admired the Prussian virtues. Born to wealth and trained to take over his father's great electrical trust, he quit business for politics and preferred philosophy to power. He regarded himself as a German patriot who hoped to see his country take a leading place among the nations in western Europe. His enemies at home considered him an agent of international high finance; his enemies abroad considered him an agent of Moscow. Chicherin also possessed a dual nature in that he had belonged to the aristocracy of the old Russia, but had thrown in his lot with the Bolsheviks. Lord D'Abernon, British Ambassador in Berlin during the early 1920's, found Chicherin reminding him "of a rather amiable and agreeable snake—not devoid of kindly feeling toward the world in general and toward rabbits in particular, provided they surrender their lives without too much fuss. Like many historical characters accused of wholesale cruelty, he is sensitive and humane almost to exaggeration in regard to minor acts of bloodshed: he will not shoot game as he cannot bear to see animals killed—and he crosses the street to avoid a butcher's shop. At the same time, the fangs are there at the disposal of theoretical conceptions fanatically held."

A few months later, the Rapallo Agreement had its tragic sequel when two young anti-Semitic, Nationalist hoodlums—members of the Free Corps—shot and killed Rathenau. His broken-hearted mother wrote this letter to the mother of one of the apprehended murderers: "In grief unspeakable I give you my hand, you, of all women the most pitiable. Say to your son that in the name and spirit of him he has murdered, I forgive, even as God may forgive, if before an earthly judge he make full and frank confession of his guilt and before a heavenly one repent. Had he known my son, the noblest man earth bore, he had rather have turned the weapon against himself than on him. May these words give peace to your soul."

Although the murder of Rathenau set off a series of working-class demonstrations against the Nationalists, the power of Stinnes and the People's Party increased. Chancellor Wirth continued in office; the mark continued to fall. Between 1914 and 1920 the value of the mark had dropped from four to the dollar to forty to the dollar. By March, 1922, it took 670 marks to buy a dollar; in another six months it took 4,500. The death of Rathenau had left nobody to challenge the invisible dictatorship of Stinnes, and the faster the mark fell, the more pervasive that dictatorship became. In November, 1922, Dr. Wilhelm Cuno, former president of the Hamburg-America Line, replaced Dr. Wirth as Chancellor. Big business had taken over the receivership of the bankrupt Weimar Republic.

· II ·

THE COURSE of events in Germany played into the hands of French big business and of the French General Staff. Germany's industrialists appeared determined to bring themselves and all Europe down in ruins rather than live up to the letter and spirit of the Versailles Treaty. Had not Stinnes threatened to let Germany go Bolshevik and come to terms with the Russians? Premier Poincaré drew the necessary conclusions and worked out the necessary strategy. To most Frenchmen, the security of their country, their homes, their families, and their very lives depended on the complete fulfillment of the Versailles Treaty. Poincaré therefore believed that almost any action he took against any violation of the Treaty would command the widest popular support. Nor was this all. Poincaré also believed that France could not enjoy real security unless French troops occupied the Rhineland indefinitely, and took over the Ruhr Valley as well. "As far as I am concerned," said Poincaré in June, 1922, "it would pain me if Germany were to pay; then we should have to evacuate the Rhineland. Which do you regard as better, obtaining cash or acquiring new territory? I for my part prefer occupation and conquest to the money of reparations. Hence you will understand why we need a powerful army and a vigilant patriotism; you will understand that the sole means of saving the Treaty of Versailles is to arrange matters in such a way that our defeated enemies cannot fulfill its conditions."

André Tardieu, one of Clemenceau's ablest lieutenants, felt much the same way about Germany: "We cannot accept the risk of German industrial revival; therefore we must compel her to pay mountainous indemnities." But of Poincaré he said, "He is a lathe, painted to look like iron." An Italian diplomat once remarked, "Even when Poincaré catches the right train, he misses the right station." Poincaré's strength and weakness lay in his rigid devotion to the principles and policies that had served him and his country so well during the prewar and war years. Detesting the Russian Revolution, despising Wilson's propaganda for democracy, ignoring wartime shell-shock and postwar disillusion, Poincaré cited Germany's failure to pay certain reparations and on January 11, 1923, ordered French troops to occupy the Ruhr Valley in accordance with the terms of the Versailles Treaty. Some Belgian soldiers and a token force of Italians went along too. The British government refused to associate itself with this adventure, for reasons as obsolete as Poincaré's own. Lord D'Abernon, Britain's Ambassador to Berlin, wrote in his diary: "Anyone who supposes that a French government dominating the Continent as Napoleon dominated it after Tilsit will remain friendly to England must be a poor judge of national psychology." In other words, Poincaré's attempt to make French weakness look like strength deceived the tradition-bound D'Abernon; it was not fear of French failure in the Ruhr but fear of French success that caused Britain to hold back.

This line of reasoning accorded with the character of the Conservative government that had just come to power across the Channel. The Lloyd George coalition had finally collapsed, in October, 1922, largely as a result of the fiasco of the Greek-Turkish war; partly because the Conservatives felt that Lloyd George had made too many concessions to the Irish Nationalists when he granted Ireland virtual Dominion status after several years of savage civil war. But it was not what Lloyd George did that irked the Conservatives; it was the way he did it. His demagogic gifts made him a great war leader. His uncanny feel for the popular mood saved him from Wilson's fate. The Conservatives feared his demagogy and distrusted his methods and motives. As soon as they saw a chance to escape from their dependence on so volatile a master they quickly tried to reassert their national leadership. Their calculations proved correct. They won the general election that followed Lloyd George's resignation and rejoiced in the split that paralyzed their Liberal rivals. Asquith, Grey, and the Liberal Imperialists who had feared Lloyd George's radicalism at the turn of the century now regarded him as a renegade. But while the Liberal Party split into two impotent factions, the Labor Party had doubled and trebled its following, polling more than four million votes in the 1922 election and becoming for the first time His Majesty's Loyal Opposition.

Bonar Law, the upright, colorless Prime Minister of the new government, did not have long to live. He retained as his Foreign Secretary

Lord Curzon, who attached more importance to Asia and India than to Europe and Germany and who nourished an intense personal hatred of Poincaré. Curzon had also planted his old friend and protégé, Lord D'Abernon, in the British Embassy at Berlin, and D'Abernon spoke for both men when he defined British foreign policy during the early 1920's in the introduction to his *Ambassador of Peace:* "Resistance to Communistic propaganda, the maintenance of peace in Europe, the avoidance of another Great War, the establishment of security for respective frontiers, the preservation of society on existing lines were the capital objects of British policy. But there was more than this. England's stupendous and vital interests in Asia were menaced by a danger graver than any which existed in the time of the old imperialistic regime in Russia. Hostility to England or jealousy of the intrusion of British civilization into Asia were indeed of old standing. For the last seventy years of the nineteenth century, rivalry between Britain and Russia had been a dominant fact in history. But the Bolsheviks possessed two weapons which Imperial Russia lacked—class-revolt propaganda, appealing to the proletariat of the world, and the quasi-religious fanaticism of Lenin, which infused a vigor and zeal unknown to the officials and emissaries of the Tsar." And again in his diaries D'Abernon wrote: "As long as there is a strong Russia, India is to a certain extent menaced. The Balkanization of Central Europe is bad, but the Balkanization of Central Asia would be an unquestioned relief to English policy."

Lord D'Abernon found an invaluable disciple and ally in the person of the United States Ambassador to Germany—Alanson B. Houghton, president of the Corning Glass Works and one of the ablest businessmen of his generation. He and his Republican friends at home did not need Lord D'Abernon to convince them of the danger of Russian Bolshevism or the importance of Germany to the recovery of Europe. As early as December, 1922, Secretary Hughes urged taking the problem of reparations out of politics and turning it over to a commission of experts who should make recommendations based only on Germany's ability to pay. Hughes and Houghton did, however, need D'Abernon's diplomatic experience. Houghton in particular stood ready to put American business and high finance behind whatever political strategy D'Abernon and the British Foreign Office might suggest, and the two men worked together like partners. Fearing the power of France in Europe and the power of Russia in Asia, D'Abernon and Houghton applied themselves to encouraging a restoration of German power in every direction. Disliking the radical domestic reforms of the Socialists, fearing the adventurous truculence of the Nationalists, they cultivated a new and unique German statesman, Dr. Gustav Stresemann, who belonged to Stinnes's People's Party yet favored good relations with the west.

Stinnes and Rathenau both belonged to the world of business and finance; Stresemann was the first purely middle-class German to become a power in the land. He was the youngest son of a Berlin beer-hall proprietor—and his mother's favorite. His family scraped up enough money to permit him to win his Ph.D. degree in economics at the University of Leipzig, where he wrote his thesis on the development of the bottled-beer industry. In 1901, at the age of twenty-three, Stresemann got his first job as man-

Dr. Gustav Stresemann. Kelen Drawing

ager of the Association of German Chocolate Manufacturers in Dresden. At twenty-eight he was elected to the Reichstag as a member of the middle-class National Liberal Party. He quickly distinguished himself as a debater and during the war his expansionist speeches earned him the nickname of "tree-frog annexationist." At once an optimist and a realist, Stresemann understood, soon after the defeat of 1918, that he had been deceived—along with the millions of other Germans—by the war propagandists, but he still believed in his class and in his country. After the Armistice the National Liberals split into the liberal Democratic Party and the more conservative People's Party. Stresemann joined the latter group, but always supported the Weimar Republic and always welcomed collaboration with the Socialists. Because Stinnes backed the People's Party, Stresemann earned a new nickname—"Stinnes's young man."

Yet Stresemann differed from Stinnes in that he believed politics took precedence over economics; he also differed from Rathenau in that he opposed a paternalistic state. Stresemann often quoted Napoleon's words, "I am certain that the middle ranks of life are much happier than the so-called upper classes." He had a happy temperament himself and his physical gusto and delight in debate reminded Lord D'Abernon of Winston Churchill. Much of Stresemann's power lay in the fact that he had shared the enthusiasms and disappointments of millions of other middle-class Germans. An extraordinarily happy marriage to a Jewish wife and a profound religious faith sustained him, too.

"I believe in Jesus Christ," he wrote at the age of seventeen, "in so far as He is the purest and truest embodiment of the divine nature. His words and teachings seem to me the clearest and noblest manifestation of the divine will and I therefore look on them as the foundation of Christianity." This faith never left him.

D'Abernon and Houghton counted on Stresemann to put German finances in order and to come to some sort of terms with France. But things had to get worse before they could get better. The occupation of the Ruhr united the German people against France and behind the Cuno government, which called for passive resistance and continued the inflation by printing more and more paper money. Between January and March, 1923, Cuno let the German national debt increase from one trillion to six trillion marks. By April his government was meeting only one tenth of its current expenses from current revenues. Paper marks, based on nothing but an empty promise to pay, covered the rest. Figures express but they cannot describe what inflation meant to the German people. One characteristic story illustrates the kind of thing that happened over and over again. A certain rich man had two sons— one a miser, the other a drunkard. The inflation ruined the miser; the drunkard lived well on what he got for selling his hoard of empty champagne bottles. Shoppers needed larger bags to carry their paper marks than to carry their purchases. Only once did the inflation falter: the government printers went out on strike.

Class conflicts sharpened and multiplied. The landowners, large and small, did comparatively well because they dealt, as always, in real wealth rather than paper values. Speculators did even better. Big industry did best of all because it paid off all its accumulated debts in worthless paper. The same process that enriched the industrialist impoverished all holders of bonds, mortgages, fixed-interest-bearing securities, and pensions. The prudent German middle classes saw their savings wiped out, and salaries did not begin to keep up with the rise in prices. Middle-class parents lost authority over their children, who still suffered from the effects of wartime undernourishment and had no funds to get the kind of education they had been brought up to expect. Returned soldiers, cut off from civilian life for four years, found it easy to blame the defeat on the home front—and impossible to lead a normal life in an abnormal world.

Few industrial workers had any savings to lose. Their wages rose faster than the salaries of the middle class, but not so fast as prices. By October, 1923, a suit of clothes cost an industrial worker twenty weeks' pay. The inflation also wiped out the savings of the great trade unions and made all their contracts with employers obsolete. Trade union elections during the summer of 1923 showed that the Communists had more popular support than the Socialists, and members of the two parties served together in the governments of the little states of Thuringia and Saxony. Most German Communists and many German Socialists believed that they could have organized a successful revolution at this time, but the older Socialist leaders opposed violence and the Russian Communists from whom the German Party took its orders preferred to deal with a more or less friendly German Republic rather than take a chance on insurrection. Stalin, as the new General Secretary of the Russian Communist Party, rationalized its line this way: "If today in Germany the power so to speak falls and the Communists seize

"Germany's children are starving." Lithograph by Käthe Kollwitz

hold of it, they will fall with a crash. That is the 'best' case. And at worst they will be smashed to pieces and thrown back." Lenin at this time lay dying of a paralytic stroke, but Stalin's warning tied in with Lenin's new assumption that the world revolution was no longer at hand.

With the wisdom of hindsight, many dissident Communists have since argued that Stalin missed a great opportunity in not encouraging and helping the German Communists to make the revolution that most of them wanted to attempt at this time. The fact was that Stalin and the other members of the Politburo wavered throughout the critical summer of 1923 while events moved too fast for them. In August, the Cuno government gave way to a grand coalition headed by Stresemann who called off the passive resistance campaign in the Ruhr and stabilized the currency, which sank to five million marks to the dollar on the day Cuno quit. The weary, dutiful German people obeyed Stresemann's orders. Panic suddenly seized the Russians, who feared that Stresemann was about to form an anti-Soviet front with the British and the French. Too late, the German Communists received instructions to organize armed uprisings in Saxony and Thuringia as well as in Hamburg and other cities. For a few days insurrections exploded in various parts of Germany, but they all failed for lack of preparation. President Ebert ordered the Communist Party dissolved for the duration of the emergency.

Finally, on November 8, General Ludendorff attempted a Nationalist counterrevolution in Munich. He had discovered and promoted a fanatical Austrian named Adolf Hitler who had served as a corporal in the German Army and had begun to organize a National Socialist German Workers' Party. When Hitler proclaimed his counterrevolution in a Munich beer hall, Stresemann ordered General von Seeckt, Mackensen's former chief of staff, to suppress it. Ludendorff surrendered and got off scot free. Hitler dislocated his shoulder as he ducked bullets fired by Reichswehr troops and then received a five-year prison sentence. Von Seeckt emerged with enhanced prestige. If he and the Bavarian Premier and War Minister had chosen to ignore Stresemann's orders, they might easily have marched on Berlin by way of Thuringia, where the Communists had recently made trouble.

The world press at the time paid more attention to Ludendorff and Hitler than it did to the Communists. Although revolution had more popular support than counterrevolution in the Germany of 1923, the counterrevolution had organized itself more efficiently. But popular discontent in postwar Germany assumed so many different forms that neither revolution nor counterrevolution triumphed. At first, most Germans had blamed the loss of the war on the ruling groups in Imperial Germany: the Hohenzollerns, the General Staff, the Junkers, and the big industrialists. The Weimar Republic came into being because it promised gradual, democratic reform at home and a conciliatory policy, based on Wilson's Fourteen Points, abroad. The Versailles Treaty, the occupation of the Ruhr, and the inflation of the mark then put the Weimar Republic on the defensive. Counterrevolution became a greater threat than revolution as assorted reactionaries, adventurers, and demagogues found new scapegoats to attack: the Socialists, the Communists, and, above all, the Jews.

The Jewish population in Germany numbered about six hundred thousand—or one per cent of the total population—most of whom had lived in the country for generations. The Kaiser's Germany had excluded Jews from diplomacy and from the Army's officer corps. The professions offered German Jews some opportunities, business offered them more. Social discrimination had gradually waned: thanks to intermarriage, some two million Germans had some Jewish blood. After the war a new influx of impoverished Polish Jews arrived in Berlin—some of them fearful of Russian Bolshevism, others fearful of Polish anti-Semitism. They set themselves up in the small businesses that their ancestors had followed for generations.

As the inflation gathered momentum, destitute aristocrats, ruined members of the middle class, and desperate young people found it easy to believe that the Jews had caused all the trouble. The Polish Jews, accustomed to hardship, had survived worse crises than the inflation. The German Jews, experienced in finance, business, and the professions, more cosmopolitan than most of their fellow countrymen, were better equipped than most Germans to ride out the storm. Some of them, of course, profiteered, though none of them on such a scale as Stinnes. But when demagogues blamed Germany's troubles on the Jews, an increasing minority agreed. Ironically enough, Stinnes himself died in 1924 just as the inflation which had made his career came to an end. But thousands of Jewish lawyers, doctors, businessmen, and intellectuals lived on to reap a harvest of hate that others had sown.

As for the Ruhr occupation, it led to comparatively little bloodshed; seventy-six Germans lost their lives in street brawls with French troops— some of them colored Senegalese. The French jailed a few German industrialists who had encouraged passive resistance; French troops also distributed copies of the Communist newspaper *Rote Fahne,* because it called for violent revolution. Propagandists for a separate Rhineland Republic financed by French funds made no headway. Meanwhile, German production declined; German reparations deliveries ceased; consumption of meat, sugar, tobacco, and beer fell off one third; the tuberculosis rate more than doubled; and French occupation costs climbed.

On September 27, 1923, President Ebert signed a decree rescinding all ordinances passed in support of passive resistance. French troops, however, remained in the Ruhr, while the Weimar Republic, defeated abroad, successfully crushed its domestic enemies to the left and right. On November 23 the Stresemann government fell because the Socialists voted against its rough treatment of the Communist insurrection in Saxony. Wilhelm Marx of the Center Party formed a new government, continuing Stresemann as Foreign Minister. Before the year ended the mark had fallen to four trillion to the dollar and lost all use and meaning as a unit of currency. Dr. Hjalmar Horace Greeley Schacht, the newly installed head of the Reichsbank who had acquired his two middle names during a boyhood spent in Brooklyn, devised a new form of paper currency known as the rentenmark, based on Germany's railways and stabilized at the old prewar rate of 4.2 to the dollar. One trillion paper marks got you one rentenmark. Again, as in the summons to drop passive resistance, the German people accepted the new currency at once. German democracy and German big business had survived a storm that menaced the existing order throughout Europe. But neither Germany nor Europe could recover from that storm or from the war that had caused it without substantial aid from the United States. "Currency gone; exchange gone; confidence gone and hatred still left," said Lloyd George at the time. "That is Europe."

That was where Ambassador Alanson B. Houghton came in. Repre-

senting American big business to an even greater degree than Stresemann represented German big business, Houghton made it plain that
a German government committed to financial stability and treaty fulfillment would receive American financial help. As soon, therefore, as
Stresemann had carried out his end of the bargain, the Allied governments set up a Reparations Commission headed by Charles G. Dawes,
the Republican lawyer-banker from Chicago who later served as Vice-
President with Coolidge. At his elbow sat Owen D. Young, a Democrat,
whose position as chairman of the board of the General Electric Company made him the trusted friend of Wall Street. Although the United
States government remained officially aloof from the negotiations, it was
also stipulated that a third American, young S. Parker Gilbert of New
York, who later became a Morgan partner, should remain permanently
in Berlin as collection agent for the Allies. The Germans agreed to
put their railways and the Reichsbank under Allied supervision and to
start paying reparations at the rate of a billion gold marks a year until
1929 and then to increase the annual payments to two and a half billions
for an indefinite period. The Inter-Allied Commission agreed, in turn,
to raise an international loan of eight hundred million gold marks to
restore German industry. It was also understood that the French would
withdraw progressively from the Ruhr when and if the Dawes Plan—
as the new arrangement was called—went into effect.

It all boiled down to this. Germany pledged to pay the equivalent of
about five per cent of its annual national income to the Allies in reparations. These payments would be made in cash, but Germany could
get the cash only if its production, especially its export trade, were permitted to increase. The Dawes Plan loan of eight hundred million gold
marks could not do more than prime the pump of German recovery.
For the Dawes Plan to yield the reparations set by the experts, Germany
had to become a going concern, and Germany could not become a going
concern without substantial private loans by private investors—most
of whom would have to be Americans. And those loans would be forthcoming only so long as the United States had surplus funds to invest
abroad. Whatever the Dawes Plan might eventually mean, it certainly
did not spell "Back to Normalcy" either for the United States or for
Europe.

· III ·

BEFORE Stresemann came to power in Germany, Prime Minister Bonar
Law of Great Britain had died and was replaced for a brief spell
by a new leader: Stanley Baldwin. Then soon after Marx replaced
Stresemann as Chancellor, the British people voted the Conservatives

out of office, and the Labor Party
formed its first government with
Ramsay MacDonald, who had opposed Britain's participation in the
war, as Prime Minister. Baldwin,
far more than any of his contemporaries, embodied the interests and
character of the Conservative Party. MacDonald's humble background and gentlemanly bearing
made him well suited to lead the
Labor Party from opposition into
power. He reassured his supporters without alarming his adversa-
ries.

When the Conservatives in May,
1923, selected Baldwin to replace
the ailing Bonar Law, Lord Curzon had broken down and wept.

UNITED PRESS PHOTO

Mr. and Mrs. Stanley Baldwin

Having served as Viceroy to India and as Foreign Secretary, he hoped
to crown his career with the Premiership. The fact that he belonged to
the anachronistic, unpopular House of Lords stood in his way; so did his
own pride—even his own ability. King George in particular felt that a
Lord must not serve as Prime Minister in the new democratic age. Baldwin, the Commoner, on the other hand, belonged to the industrial rather
than the feudal aristocracy. He had attended Harrow, where one of the
masters said to him, "Baldwin, you'll never do anything wrong; you
haven't the brains, but you'll never do anything big either." From Harrow he went to Cambridge and from Cambridge to his father's great
iron and steel firm of Baldwin's, Ltd. He became a director of the Great
Western Railway and of Lloyd's Bank, but did not enter the House of
Commons until he reached the age of thirty-nine. Here he specialized
in finance, attracting no particular attention until 1922, when he negotiated the debt settlement with the United States. Balfour had muddied
up Anglo-American relations with the proposal that Britain should pay
the United States no more principal and interest on the war debts than
Britain should receive from the nations of Europe. The indignation this
aroused in the United States compelled Baldwin to accept much stiffer
terms than he might have arranged had Balfour held his peace.

Baldwin's character and experience suited him to his role. A gift for
simple, direct speech—he was Rudyard Kipling's first cousin—and a
phlegmatic personality made Baldwin appear the very embodiment of

British common sense. Although he posed as a country squire, puffing his pipe and knee-deep in pigs, he loved power even more than he loved leisure. His business experience gave him some insight into the problems of the urban poor; he drew his income from industry rather than the soil. Baldwin had, it is true, the simplicity of the countryman rather than the complexity of the city dweller, but his unique appeal lay in his combination of innocence and shrewdness, of poetry and practicality, of instinct and experience. And beneath it all lay a deep, modest patriotism: too old to fight when the war broke out, he had quietly turned over one quarter of his personal fortune to the state.

Even as Prime Minister he remained, at first, a shadowy figure. A boyhood friend, recognizing him as they sat together in a railway-car compartment, broke the conversational ice with the question: "We were at Harrow together. What are you doing?" By the autumn of 1923 the limitations of Baldwin's personality and of the party that he led caused him to make a blunder that might have ended the career of a lesser, or a greater, man. Mounting unemployment, declining trade, deepening distress in Germany had brought the condition of Britain from bad to worse. Baldwin and the Conservatives could offer no better remedy than Joseph Chamberlain had proposed more than twenty years before— an end to free trade, and high tariff walls around the Empire. The government called for a general election, which brought the Asquith and Lloyd George Liberals together again, and which benefited the Laborites even more. Labor won almost one third of the seats in the House of Commons, topping the Liberals and causing their leader, Asquith, to make a bold decision. Since no party commanded a majority in the House of Commons and since most Liberals preferred the Laborites to the Conservatives, Asquith agreed that if the Labor Party chose to form a government, the Liberals would support the program that Ramsay MacDonald had outlined of reform at home and collective security abroad. But it was not MacDonald's program that worried King George V during his first interview with the first Laborite ever invited to head a British government. The question that filled the King's mind to the exclusion of all else was whether the members of the new Labor Cabinet would conform to Court etiquette and wear the appropriate dress.

The promotion of Baldwin over Curzon reflected the growing power of finance and industry within the British ruling class. The sudden emergence of MacDonald from oblivion to national leadership reflected the rapid but peaceful revolution in Britain's social order. MacDonald was the illegitimate son of a Scottish servant girl. When his mother and maternal grandmother could not afford to send him to school after he had reached the age of twelve, the local teacher in his little birthplace of Lossiemouth, recognizing the brilliance and eagerness of his mind, helped him to educate himself. Obscure birth, frail health, and early poverty all left their marks on the sensitive boy, who turned first to his womenfolk, then to a schoolmaster, then to religion, and finally to Henry George's *Progress and Poverty* for understanding and guidance.

At eighteen MacDonald went to London, where he found work as a warehouse clerk. He lacked the stamina to take a science scholarship in the University of London, but at the age of twenty-two he got his first break when Thomas Lough, a Liberal Member of Parliament, hired him as his private secretary. Here the young man found scope for his talents. He met politicians and journalists and soon attached himself to the little band of social workers, labor leaders, and intellectuals who created the British Labor Party. Most of them came from the middle class, and one of them—Margaret Gladstone, the niece of the great scientist, Lord Kelvin—married MacDonald in 1896. His skill as a speaker and writer, his charm, his presence, his zeal had already made him an outstanding figure. In 1906 at the age of forty he won his first seat as a Member of Parliament. Five years later his wife died in childbirth, leaving him a widower with four children.

Back in the 1890's MacDonald had delivered a speech on Character and Democracy which summed up the faith that helped him to rise above his personal tragedy. "Character—that power in man which enables him to see what is good in experience and what is bad in experience; that power in man which enables him to link himself with the great past and make himself responsible for the future. Character, that power in man which organizes his life so that the passing moment presents itself to him not as something that is to be seized for its own sake and when done with forgotten, but simply an incident in eternity, something that is going to yield fruit to eternity, never going to be lost, never left behind. Character, which enables man to see himself, not as a reckless or irresponsible individual, but as one of humanity, as a thought of God maturing as the ages go until his humanity becomes divinity itself."

The outbreak of war put MacDonald's character and his faith in democratic socialism to their severest test. He had opposed the Boer War, but so had Lloyd George and Campbell-Bannerman. When the World War broke out most Socialists in most countries supported their governments. Not so MacDonald. After Grey revealed his secret understandings with France, MacDonald replied that Grey had not convinced him that "our country is in danger," or even that its honor was at stake. He continued: "There is a third point. If the right honorable gentleman could come to us and tell us that a small European nationality like Belgium is in danger, and could assure us that he is going to confine the conflict to that question, then we would support him. What is the use of talking about coming to the aid of Belgium when, as a matter of fact, you are engaging in a whole European war which is not going to leave the map of Europe in the position it is in now?"

MacDonald remained in Parliament throughout the war devoting most of his energies to working for a just settlement. He was no doctrinaire pacifist or conscientious objector. The authorities refused to let him drive an ambulance at the front for the Red Cross. He opposed conscription, but riots prevented him from speaking against it in public on two occasions. In 1917 he declared, "I am not pro-German; I am a pro-European, a pro-democrat, and pro-internationalist, and I never want to be anything else. I want not a patched-up peace, a miserable peace which would not stand the strain of six years in the Courts of Europe, but a peace which would never be broken because it would be established on the foundations of a free democracy, no longer assailed by kings, emperors, diplomats, or the military classes." When he tried to take ship for a Socialist conference in Stockholm that same year, the Seamen's Union refused to let the vessel move.

"The Russian Revolution," he declared later, "has been one of the greatest events in the history of the world, and the attacks that have been made upon it by frightened ruling classes and hostile capitalism should rally to its defense everyone who cares for political liberty and freedom of thought." But MacDonald was no communist, no advocate of violent revolution: "The common people in history have been working through violence into politics, and now that they have got there I am in too great a hurry to go back. I know that ancient times had their attractions—the Spartacus revolt, Wat Tyler, John Ball, Oliver Cromwell—that the French Revolution is inspiring in spite of its dirt, and the Commune heroic in spite of its squabbles and its failure before the Versailles troops came to murder it. I prefer to read about them rather than to repeat them, and to use the powers they have given us rather than to neglect them. The disfranchised revolted during the past two centuries in order that their offspring might not have to revolt any more but to govern. I, being a modern creature, believe in government rather than in revolutions or dictatorships."

In the "Hang the Kaiser" election of 1918, MacDonald lost the seat that he had held in Parliament for twelve years. Conservatives and Liberals called him a Bolshevik. Lenin evaluated him quite differently: "Ramsay MacDonald's speeches and articles are the best example that could be given of that smooth, melodious, banal, Socialist-seeming phraseology which serves in all the developed capitalist countries to camouflage the policy of the bourgeoisie inside the labor movement.

UNDERWOOD

Ramsay MacDonald and Aristide Briand

MacDonald remains throughout a bourgeois pacifist and middle-class reformer, cherishing the illusion of a non-class state. MacDonald recognizes the class struggle only as a figure of speech, just as do all deceivers, sophists, and pedants of the bourgeoisie."

The strain of the war years had turned MacDonald's hair white. Widowed and ostracized, he had to draw on resources within himself. The horrors of peace soon vindicated all he had said about the horrors of war, and in the 1922 election he regained his seat in the House of Commons. Here he called for a capital levy to reduce the national debt and for greater reliance on the League of Nations. He pleaded for closer understanding with the Weimar Republic; he warned against Poincaré's Nationalist bloc in France; when the Tories came out for protection he declared that such measures solved nothing. After the general election of December, 1923, some Laborites advised against attempting to create a government. Others proposed that Labor outline a program of immediate socialization, and thus go down to immediate defeat on a matter of principle. Ramsay MacDonald persuaded his colleagues to make an honest attempt to govern by offering the country a program that the Liberals as well as the Laborites could support. He himself had always specialized in foreign affairs and it was in this field that he believed Labor could make its greatest contribution.

MacDonald took the post of Foreign Secretary as well as Prime Minister, and soon one of the permanent Foreign Office officials who had resented Curzon's querulous conceit was heard to remark, "It is good to have a gentleman to deal with again." Nothing about MacDonald except his sympathy for the underdog recalled his proletarian past. His tall frame, noble brow, and courtly manners suggested the born aristocrat. His intellectual interests suggested the scholar in politics. In addition, he had the temperament and talent of a poet, and Thomas Hardy once urged him to abandon politics for literature. He took office shortly after the Marx-Stresemann government had persuaded the German people to begin pulling themselves up by their bootstraps; a few months later the French people turned against Poincaré. The moment for a general European settlement had arrived at last.

· IV ·

As long as the German people supported their government's costly policy of passive resistance, the French people supported Poincaré's costly occupation of the Ruhr. But as soon as Stresemann called off passive resistance and Marx prepared to fulfill the terms of the Versailles Treaty, Poincaré's popularity began to slip. Baldwin and MacDonald both opposed him, though for different reasons. The Conservatives feared that a Nationalist France would upset the European balance of power and dominate the entire Continent. The Laborites had no great fear of France as such. They feared balance-of-power politics of any kind and saw only one hope of peace for Europe: collective security under the League of Nations.

In May, 1924, much the same thing happened in France that had happened in Britain a few months before. The French people elected a new Chamber of Deputies in which the Radical Socialists, plus the Socialists, won an absolute majority. The Radical Socialists, or Radicals as they usually called themselves, did not deserve either of their names. They considered themselves the heirs and protectors of the French Revolution and drew their support from the middle and professional classes. They fought the political influence of the Roman Catholic Church and the economic power of the larger banks and industries. They tried to avoid making any enemies to the left, but the Socialists never fully trusted them. Strong leaders could adapt the Radical Socialist Party to their purposes, and such a man headed the government that took power in France in June, 1924.

Édouard Herriot, like Ramsay MacDonald, rose from the ranks of the common people. His mother had worked as a servant in the household of Maurice Barrès, the celebrated Nationalist writer, who respected young Herriot's gifts and helped him to get an education. Herriot came

ahead fast. He taught literature
in the university of his native
city of Lyon, but soon branched
out into politics. Rejecting the
conservative views of Barrès, he
joined the Radical Socialist Party,
won the position of Mayor of Lyon
at the age of thirty-three and a
seat in the Senate at forty. During
the war Herriot served in one of
Briand's Cabinets; afterward he
traveled in both the United States
and Russia. In 1922 he urged a resumption of Franco-Russian diplomatic and trade relations. The
Socialists agreed to vote for his
government but refused to accept
office in it. Herriot shared Mac-

UNDERWOOD

Édouard Herriot

Donald's confidence in the League of Nations as the best hope of
European peace. Like MacDonald, he held the post of Foreign Minister
as well as Premier.

Unlike Poincaré, Herriot was a true cosmopolitan, a good European,
and as such belonged to the new France. He had written books on
Madame Récamier and Beethoven. During the 1924 election campaign,
he devoted one of his weekly newspaper articles to the Byron Centenary.
Herriot reveled in the pleasures of the flesh: his wide paunch, rough features, bristling hair and mustache, and stubby briar pipe made him a
cartoonist's favorite. Accounts of his exploits with women filled the columns of the gutter press. Yet even his political enemies never challenged
his personal honesty. He suffered from no more serious weakness than
all-too-human vanity.

MacDonald and Herriot lost no time in getting together to build the
new kind of Europe they both wanted. During July they and their experts met in London, where they put the finishing touches on the Dawes
Plan while Secretary of State Hughes toured many of the European
capitals as a kind of oversized, bewhiskered "unofficial observer." Early
in August Marx and Stresemann joined MacDonald and Herriot to accept the reparation terms on which the British and French had already
agreed. The French Premier and the German Chancellor shook hands
with MacDonald's benediction and the Dawes Plan went into immediate
effect. Peace had at last returned to Europe, with the British in their
favorite position as arbitrators between France and Germany—and with
the United States underwriting the whole enterprise. For the arrange-

ment required private American banks to sell Dawes Plan bonds to American investors, at the usual commission, or "spread." Thus private profit as well as national interest played its part in bringing American influence back to Europe.

National interest plus moral principle also caused MacDonald and Herriot to push their countries in new directions. At the Geneva headquarters of the League of Nations they initialed the far-reaching "Geneva Protocol" pledging themselves to work for arbitration, disarmament, and collective security within the League Covenant. Thanks to the statesmen of certain small nations, who had nowhere else to turn, the League had begun to function, and it was young Dr. Eduard Beneš, Foreign Minister of Czechoslovakia, who persuaded MacDonald and Herriot that Article X of the League Covenant should be amplified to require all member states to give some kind of aid to all victims of aggression. In accepting Beneš's proposal, MacDonald was putting the British Navy and Herriot the French Army behind certain decisions the League might make.

The French Chamber of Deputies accepted the Geneva Protocol. The British House of Commons voted against it. Both France and Britain granted diplomatic recognition to the Soviet Union in 1924, but when MacDonald asked the House of Commons to approve a trade treaty and debt settlement he had also worked out with the Russians, he was voted down. However, his government fell on a more limited issue after ten months in office. MacDonald himself believed that the Liberals took such alarm at Labor's success that they ganged up with the Conservatives at the first opportunity. Most Laborites preferred to attribute the defeat of their government to anti-Russian, anti-Communist feeling. Just a few days before the vote in the ensuing general election the Foreign Office published a letter, supposedly written by Zinoviev as head of the Third International, endorsing the treaties, but going on to call for Communist uprisings in the British armed services.

That finished MacDonald. Although the Laborites increased their vote from more than four millions to more than five millions, the Liberals lost a million and a half and the Conservatives won more than two thirds of all the seats in the new House of Commons. Years later, evidence appeared linking the "Zinoviev letter" to the same group of German gangsters who set fire to the Reichstag building shortly before the Nazis came to full power in March, 1933. What connections, if any, there may have been between the fabricators of the Zinoviev letter and the Conservative Party remains a mystery. Dissident Communists have still another theory. They claim that the forgers of the Zinoviev letter were working for Stalin, who hoped thereby to discredit Zinoviev and the Comintern.

· V ·

THE END of the war had brought new classes and new leaders to power throughout Europe. In Russia, middle-class intellectuals put through a successful proletarian revolution. In Germany, big business saved the Weimar Republic that the Socialists had created. In Britain and France, two men of proletarian origin led their people toward social democracy. Italy moved in the same direction. In the general elections of November, 1919, the Liberals, the Socialists, and a new party known as the Populists, or People's Party, organized by Don Sturzo, a Roman Catholic priest, won most of the seats in the Chamber of Deputies. Francisco Nitti, an anti-imperialist, antiwar Liberal, headed a coalition government that the Populists supported and that the Socialists opposed. Half a year later Nitti gave way to another Liberal, the octogenarian Giolitti, who had promoted Italian expansion before the war and then went into semi-retirement.

Both the Nitti and the Giolitti governments met with violent opposition from the extreme left and the extreme right. The Socialists organized general strikes, but Italy's two Liberal Premiers kept hands off, with the result that even the factories seized by workers continued to operate while the moderate Socialists gained the upper hand over the Communist extremists. The strikes, however, gradually collapsed as the workers ran out of the raw materials they needed to keep production going. It was not the Italian working class, it was the middle class, the war veterans, and the young people who made the most trouble. And the first leader to whom they turned was not a politician but the soldier-poet Gabriele D'Annunzio.

Before the war, D'Annunzio had become famous by publicizing his love affair with Eleonora Duse and by adapting some of Nietzsche's romantic nihilism to the Italian temperament. He summed up his new gospel in the meaningless, sonorous phrase:

> "Morire, o giore:
> Giore, o morire:"

which meant that to die is to be happy and that to be happy is to die. One of his tragedies, La Nave (The Ship) kept repeating this refrain:

> "Arma la prora e salpa verso il mondo,"

which meant "Arm the prow and set sail against the world." Although he had passed the age of fifty when Italy joined the Allies, D'Annunzio served with the Infantry, the Cavalry, the Navy, and finally the Air Force. After the war ended he led the agitation to bring the Adriatic port of Fiume under Italian rule and headed the force of volunteers who seized the city in 1919. He remained the self-proclaimed ruler of Fiume until early in 1921, when he finally withdrew and recognized the settlement that the Giolitti government worked out with Yugoslavia, whereby a stopgap neutral administration attempted to make Fiume a free city.

One man and one movement turned the romantic excitement that D'Annunzio had whipped up over Fiume to serious, lasting account. The man was Benito Mussolini; he called his movement Fascism. All the other Europeans who had risen to national leadership since the war came from conventional proletarian or middle-class families. All of them promoted precise, established doctrines—Communist, Socialist, democratic, and the rest. Only Mussolini had received a revolutionary upbringing from birth. Only Mussolini turned against all doctrines and creeds. Only Mussolini appealed to the mounting discontents of the growing middle class. Lenin and Trotsky addressed revolutionary appeals to peasants and industrial workers. They preached Marxism, the dictatorship of the proletariat. MacDonald, Herriot, and Stresemann preached democracy to all classes. Mussolini made as violent an appeal as Lenin and Trotsky, but he addressed it to a different quarter: to young people, to war veterans, and above all to middle-class misfits. But behind this appeal lay no clear program—like Communism; no definite philosophy—like democracy. Mussolini preached action and violence for their own sake.

His early childhood had made him a rebel. During his youth and young manhood he turned to Socialism; the liberal, democratic faith never touched him at all. Mussolini's father, a Socialist blacksmith, had spent three years in prison for consorting with the Russian anarchist Bakunin. He married a schoolteacher and they named their first boy, who was born in 1883, Benito, after the Mexican anti-Clerical, Benito Juárez. The father moved up in the world—from blacksmith to tavern keeper and from tavern keeper to Mayor of the little town of Predappio —giving young Benito a rough and revolutionary education as he went along. The thin-skinned son resented the thick-skinned father, rebelled against rebellion, found some protection and solace with his mother, but spent most of his boyhood by himself. As he approached maturity, he gravitated more and more toward the radical movement, read Marx, Bakunin, Nietzsche, Sorel; delivered revolutionary speeches; found the courage to take part in street fights and strikes. His adventures with women got him into still more trouble. He had two sons and a daughter by Rachele Guidi, the daughter of his father's mistress, but Rachele was a servant girl, and only after they had lived together for some years did Mussolini make her his wife.

Many outstanding men have owed their success in life to their mothers.

Mussolini owed his to a tiny Italian aristocrat, Dr. Angelica Balabanov, who married a Russian, threw herself into the Socialist movement, and eventually helped Lenin and Trotsky organize the Third International. Dr. Balabanov spotted the unhappy Mussolini at a Socialist meeting in Switzerland, where he had fled, in 1904, to escape military service at home. She encouraged the furtive youth with the prominent jaw and the burning eyes to pour his undisciplined energies into the Socialist movement. To her he confided his ambitions to speak and write, his fears of the venereal disease he had inherited from his father. From her he gradually gained belief in himself. He returned to Italy in 1905, took his military training, and by 1910 he was speaking, as a Socialist, against Giolitti's attack upon Tripoli. But Georges Sorel, whom Mussolini admired, wrote of him: "Our Mussolini is not an ordinary Socialist. It is my belief that someday we shall find him at the head of a mighty legion, saluting the Italian flag with a sword. He is a fifteenth-century Italian, a *condottiere*."

In 1912 the Italian Socialist Party decided to found a daily paper, the *Avanti*, in the industrial city of Milan, and Mussolini accepted the post of editor on condition that Dr. Balabanov serve as his assistant. Soon the *Avanti* became the most important radical organ in Italy. On July 29, 1914, it carried a Socialist proclamation that Mussolini signed and helped to write: "It is to the interest of the proletariat of all nations to impede, circumscribe, and limit as much as possible the armed conflict, useful only to the triumph of militarism and the parasitical business affairs of the bourgeoisie." In the *Avanti*, Mussolini himself wrote, "In case of a European conflict Italy does not want to precipitate itself into the ultimate ruin, but has one attitude to take—neutrality."

Before the end of October, 1914, Mussolini had quit the Socialist Party and resigned the editorship of *Avanti*. In November he started a new paper, *Popolo d'Italia*, with funds furnished by the French government through Marcel Cachin, one of the French Socialist leaders, who became a Communist after the war. Its masthead carried two slogans: "Who has steel has bread"—Blanqui; and "The revolution is an idea which has found bayonets"—Napoleon. While D'Annunzio appealed to the middle-class intellectuals in the name of nationalism, Mussolini urged the Italian workers to enter the war on the Allied side in the name of revolution. "Do we wish," he wrote in his first issue, "to drag out a miserable existence under present conditions, content with the status quo of the monarchy and the bourgeoisie, or do we wish instead to break up this wretched combination of intrigue and cowardice?" His former Socialist comrades called him traitor, hireling, assassin. He replied, "You hate me because you still love me."

Popolo d'Italia prospered, and when Italy entered the war Mussolini volunteered for military service. The authorities assigned him to quiet sections of the front, where he served as a private and then as a corporal until February, 1917, when the explosion of a trench mortar in a trial firing sent him to the hospital. He spent the rest of the war editing his paper. In March, 1919, he extended his activities from journalism to politics and organized the first *Fascio di Combattimento,* or union of combat veterans, in Milan. The word *"fascio,"* meaning bundle or bunch, is derived from the Latin *fasces,* which the Roman magistrates used as their symbol of power and strength.

The original Fascist program drew all its proposals from the Socialists: proclamation of an Italian Republic; freedom of speech, religion, education, assembly, and the press; abolition of child labor, of compulsory military service, of secret diplomacy; the eight-hour day; improved public health services; confiscation or taxation of private fortunes, banks, and industries; land reform; reorganized co-operative production; profit sharing. In 1920 Mussolini approved the seizure of factories by workers. As a former Socialist he understood the weaknesses of capitalism and the strength of the labor movement. As a journalist he knew how to appeal to the masses. As a war veteran he had learned that pacifism is not enough, that military organization creates a certain type of morale, that the practical politician in a period of rapid change must know how and when to resort to force. The example of the Russian Bolsheviks guided his own decisions.

While the Socialists ignored or opposed D'Annunzio's Fiume expedition, Mussolini jumped at the chance to put his newly organized, semi-military Fascist squads into action. But his movement appealed less to the industrial workers than it did to the young, uprooted, bewildered members of the middle class. Although Mussolini himself came of proletarian stock and had received the education of a revolutionist, his rebellious, nihilistic nature conformed with frustrations of the demobilized, disillusioned veterans and the vague hopes and fears of the half-educated young who found in the Fascist movement comradeship, organization, and a cause for which to make sacrifices. The more the movement grew, the vaguer its aims became. It offered action for the sake of action and substituted violence for persuasion, force for ideas. War veterans in all countries looked back with a certain nostalgia on the fellowship of army life, but the Italian war veterans looked back on their experiences with a special bitterness. The soldiers of the Kaiser, the Tsar, and the Austrian Emperor had all suffered defeat—and they drew various conclusions from this experience. The soldiers of the Allied Powers had gained the victory, but for most Italians victory proved no better than defeat. Their country gained few material benefits from the war. They returned to even poorer lives than they had lived before they went off to fight.

In July, 1921, Mussolini had declared, "To maintain that the Bolshevist danger still exists in Italy is equivalent to mistaking one's fears for reality. Bolshevism has been destroyed." It was not Fascism that destroyed Communism in Italy; liberal democracy had done the job, whereupon the Fascists proceeded to crush liberal democracy. The Communists, assuming that events in Italy would take the same course as events in Russia, fought both the Fascists and the Socialists, whom they lumped together. When the Socialists began to organize their own squads, known as the Arditi del Popolo, to fight the Fascist squads, the Communists denounced them as allies of the bourgeoisie and formed separate squads of their own. Lenin opposed any Communist attempt to seize power in Italy at this time. "Italy has no coal," he pointed out. But even though the Communists had lost all chance of coming to power themselves, they used what power they had to divide the working class and thus aided the Fascists. Nevertheless, the Giolitti government gradually restored order at home and peace abroad. In the general elections of 1921 the Communists won only 16 seats in the Chamber of Deputies; the Fascists, 35; the Nationalists, 40; the Democratic and Socialist parties a total of more than 400.

After the elections, Giolitti retired in favor of his younger colleague Ivanoe Bonomi, but not before he had permitted the Fascists to continue to organize their private army of black-shirted action squads. Giolitti —and Bonomi to a lesser extent—did not take the Fascist movement seriously. They knew that it had the support of certain industrialists who were using the Fascists to fight Socialists, Communists, and the whole labor movement; it never occurred to them that Fascism could become a power in its own right. Mussolini himself had his doubts and warned against taking unnecessary risks. Finally, in December, 1921, fearful that Bonomi might dissolve the Fascist action squads and outlaw the Party, he announced that "sections of the Party and combat squads form an indivisible whole." Bonomi took no action against the Fascists; in February, 1922, the Chamber of Deputies voted his government out of office and installed a more conservative, less comprehensive coalition headed by a weak, vain protégé of Giolitti's named Facta.

Events in Italy during 1922 showed that economic revival and stable government do not necessarily go together. Although the material condition of the masses improved, political conditions did not. Returned soldiers, teen-agers, and the middle classes felt themselves squeezed between the thin, upper millstone of the well-to-do and the thick, nether millstone of organized labor. The Fascists shouted slogans against the rich and took direct action against Socialists, Communists, and trade unions. Instead of seeking to alleviate the kind of discontent on which the Fascist Party thrived, the Giolitti and Bonomi governments permitted that discontent to take itself out on the labor movement. Facta went further. Encouraged by an ambitious wife, he tried to help the Fascists to power, expecting to receive the Premiership as his reward. In like manner, Queen Elena, a Montenegrin Princess who had spent much time in the court of her cousin, Tsar Nicholas of Russia, persuaded the weak King Victor Emmanuel to rely on the Fascists as the Tsar had relied on the Cossacks and the secret police.

The more rapidly Mussolini's radical program of 1919 withered away, the more liberally big business supported him: deep called unto deep, like unto like. Big business wanted only to increase its power and its profits and to keep labor in line. It had no positive philosophy, no precise program. The Fascist leaders sought power for the sake of power, and they, too, lacked any positive philosophy or precise program. Mussolini reverted to his youthful adventurism, which appealed to a large section of an entire generation that suffered from the same frustrations he had once known. "Our program is very simple," said Mussolini. "We want to govern Italy. They ask us for programs, but there are already too many. It is not programs that are wanting for the salvation of Italy, but men and will power." He called the Fascists "the gypsies of Italian politics, not being tied down to any one goal." Mussolini also glorified war at a time when most liberals, Socialists, and Communists preached peace: "War brings up to their highest tension all human energies and puts the stamp of nobility upon the peoples who have the courage to meet it. Fascism carries this antipacifist spirit over even into the lives of individuals. It is education for combat." And again: "War is to the man what maternity is to the woman. I do not believe in perpetual peace; not only do I not believe in it, but I find it depressing and a negation of all the fundamental virtues of man."

By October, 1922, Facta had lost control of his government and the government had lost control of the country. On the 24th of the month Mussolini told a Fascist Congress in Naples that the time had come to take power—and promptly left for Milan, close to the Swiss frontier. Three days later the Fascists called for the resignation of Facta, who quit when the King refused to invoke martial law. At noon on the following day—October 28—the King summoned Mussolini to Rome from Milan to form a government. Fascist sympathizers who had hesitated to show their colors publicly suddenly appeared on the streets of Rome in their traditional black shirts. Mussolini arrived—by sleeping car—on the 30th and presented himself and his proposed Cabinet list to the King. On Mussolini's orders, the blackshirts in and around Rome broke up, after paying their respects at the tomb of Italy's Unknown Soldier.

Fascists held most of the seats in Mussolini's coalition Cabinet. He himself took the Premiership, the Ministry of Foreign Affairs, and the Ministry of the Interior. Lesser posts went to half a dozen Liberals and

UNITED PRESS PHOTO

Mussolini Prepares to March on Rome

Populists. Not until March did he begin to spell out his program and even then he confined himself to declaring: "Both in Russia and in Italy it has been demonstrated that it is possible to govern outside, above, and against all liberal ideals. Neither Communism nor Fascism has anything in common with Liberty. Fascism is not afraid to declare itself illiberal and antiliberal. It has already passed and will again pass, without the slightest hesitation, over the more or less decomposed body of the Goddess of Liberty."

Count Carlo Sforza, who had served as Foreign Minister under Giolitti and had refused to join Mussolini's government in 1922, defined Fascism in its early years as "a state of mind, explicable perhaps from certain points of view, but deprived of any positive system of thought; and, by that very fact, destined to be able to live exclusively in an atmosphere of uncontested prestige or in an atmosphere of terror. Fascism will be able to fight many kinds of battles; but there is one battle it can never engage in and that is intellectual criticism."

What Sforza regarded as an argument against Fascism, Mussolini regarded as an argument in its favor. "All the problems of life in Italy, all I say, have already been solved on paper," declared Mussolini shortly after he came to power, "but the will to translate them into facts is

missing. The government, today, represents this will, firm and resolved."
"Credare, obbedire, combattere" (Believe, obey, fight), proclaimed
his sloganeers. In place of liberty he set up his hierachy, which "must
culminate in a pinpoint." *"Mussolini ha sempre ragione"* (Mussolini is
always right) became another popular cry. The Leader—the Duce—became the source of all power, but Mussolini moved cautiously at first.
When he attended his first international conference at Lausanne to prepare a peace treaty with Turkey, Lord Curzon inquired, "What is your
foreign program?" Mussolini replied, "Nothing for nothing." Curzon
then asked, "Indeed, very interesting. And what has Italy to offer Great
Britain?" Mussolini made no reply, but a few months later—in August,
1923, he showed he could act. When local bandits killed an Italian general and four members of his staff who were surveying the Greek-Alban-
ian frontier for the League of Nations, Mussolini sent an ultimatum to
Athens demanding, among other things, an immediate indemnity of
fifty million lire. The Greek government rejected some of the terms,
whereupon Italian warships opened fire on the Greek island of Corfu in
the Adriatic and Italian troops occupied it. Mussolini refused to let the
League of Nations settle the dispute, and threatened to take Italy out
of the League if the matter were not referred instead to a Conference of
Ambassadors of the Great Powers. He got his way, and Fascist prestige
rose as much as the prestige of the League went down. The Italians
withdrew from Corfu but got the indemnity they demanded.

During the summer of 1923 the Italian Chamber of Deputies passed a
new law giving two thirds of its seats to whatever party could win the
largest number of votes cast. This did not have to amount even to a
majority of the total popular vote; a plurality, which the Fascists by this
time had achieved, sufficed and Mussolini found himself more firmly
established. In the April, 1924, elections the Fascist plurality became a
Fascist majority as Mussolini's followers received 65 per cent of the
votes cast. They had to use violence and intimidation, especially against
the Socialists, who remained their most powerful enemies. On May 30,
1924, the Socialist leader Matteotti delivered an eloquent attack on the
Fascists. Ten days later, his dead body was discovered in a forest outside
Rome. The five Fascists who killed him received no punishment. Mussolini denied any complicity in the crime, but the opposition press made
such an uproar during the course of the next few months that Mussolini
had all anti-Fascist papers suppressed.

By the end of 1924—when Coolidge had won the American Presidency;
when the Dawes Plan had gone into effect in Germany; when the Mac-
Donald government had fallen in England; when the Cartel des Gauches
had ousted Poincaré in France—Mussolini's Fascists had begun to establish a new kind of state in Italy. Many American tourists approved of

the Fascists; they had made the trains run on time. Richard Washburn Child, the American Ambassador to Rome, praised the new regime. Judge Elbert Gary, president of the United States Steel Corporation, said, "I feel like turning to my American friends and asking them whether they do not think that we, too, need a man like Mussolini." British Tories praised his handling of the labor movement. The British Foreign Office found Fascist Italy a valuable counterweight to French influence in eastern Europe and the Mediterranean. But even by the end of 1924, Italian Fascism remained in the experimental stage. It had borrowed some of the practices of Communism, some of the theories of Socialism, some of the propaganda of nationalism. Where Mussolini might lead Italy, no one knew—least of all the Duce himself. But what had happened gave plenty of food for thought. While proletarian dictatorship had established itself in Russia, while democracy had taken some root in Germany and gathered strength throughout the rest of Europe, a new kind of dictatorship, based on middle-class discontent, had come to power in Italy. The seeds of peace, sowed in the postwar soil, had brought forth strange fruit.

· VI ·

DURING the first six years of peace the literature of Europe revealed that the war had further undermined belief in reason and faith in progress. Emotion became more important than intellect, the subconscious mind more significant than physical environment. The Dada movement started before the fighting ended, spreading rapidly from Paris to other centers of civilization. When Spengler's *Decline of the West* appeared in 1918 it looked like a purely German phenomenon. By 1924 Spengler's influence had penetrated France, Britain, Italy—even the United States. He predicted the inevitable collapse of Europe; he rejected Darwinian evolution, Marxist revolution, and the whole idea of progress which so many Europeans had taken for granted before the war. Up to 1914 good works seemed more important than any doctrinal faith; social reform took precedence over organized religion. Political radicals accepted the dialectical materialism of Karl Marx, who had announced that the proletarian revolution would eventually and inevitably usher in a new Golden Age.

If Marx was the intellectual grandfather of the social reformers who carried so much weight in prewar Europe, Dr. Sigmund Freud was the intellectual father of the postwar generation. This shift of emphasis from Marx to Freud revealed itself most clearly in the art of literature, which retained its cosmopolitan character during the 1920's as James Joyce, D. H. Lawrence, Marcel Proust, and Thomas Mann acquired international reputations. Whereas Marx and the prewar literary realists looked upon man as a social animal whose environment determined his behavior, Freud and the postwar stream-of-consciousness writers directed their attention to the individual's inner life. "Karl Marx made a man of me," Bernard Shaw boasted before the war. According to Marx, "The consciousness of man does not determine his social existence; rather does his social existence determine his consciousness." With Freud it was just the other way around. He stressed the role that instinct, emotion, and the unconscious play in human affairs. He attributed supreme importance to childhood influences and to the suppression and sublimation of the sexual drive. With Marx, environment shaped human destiny; with Freud, the subconscious.

The expressionist writers studied Freud as Shaw studied Marx. Freud himself wrote: "The poets and philosophers before me discovered the unconscious. What I discovered was the scientific method by which the unconscious could be studied." Before the war Freud believed that the "pleasure principle," as he called it, underlay human behavior. After the war, however, he concluded that dreams contain more than wish fulfillment. We rehearse unhappy experiences in our sleep because we suppress them in our waking hours: "These dreams are attempts at restoring control of the stimuli by developing apprehension, the predetermination of which caused the traumatic neurosis." The child at play, he continued, "repeats even the unpleasant experiences because through his own activity he gains a far more thorough mastery of the strong expression than was possible by mere passive experience."

Two Jews originated the rival doctrines that competed for the mind of Europe during the first half of the twentieth century. Two Irishmen applied these doctrines to literature. For more than sixty years George Bernard Shaw preached the virtues of reason, intelligence, and progress. James Joyce, born a generation later, devoted his shorter life to art for art's sake. Shaw proudly called himself a journalist; Joyce dedicated himself to becoming an artist. Shaw received a Protestant upbringing and quit provincial Dublin to seek his fortune in London. Joyce received a Catholic upbringing and quit his native land for a life of Bohemian exile in Paris, Zurich, and Trieste. Shaw drank no liquor, smoked no tobacco, ate no meat, fathered no children. Joyce indulged himself as much as his limited means permitted, marrying happily and raising a small family. Shaw wrote music criticism; Joyce almost became a professional singer. Shaw agitated for social, political, and moral reforms; Joyce took no part in any of the popular movements of his time. Shaw wrote plays, prefaces, novels, and tracts on matters of topical interest. Joyce spent seven years perfecting his masterpiece, *Ulysses*, which dealt with one ordinary day in the lives of a group of ordinary Dubliners. But the war which shattered the beliefs and assumptions on which Shaw's work had rested brought Joyce into his own.

Before the war Shaw wrote such plays as *Major Barbara*, dealing with the Salvation Army and the munitions trade; *Man and Superman*, which depicted modern woman as the pursuer and man as the pursued; *Widower's Houses*, a tract on Henry George's single-tax theory; *John Bull's Other Island*, a tract on the Irish question; *Mrs. Warren's Profession*, a tract on prostitution. As a master journalist Shaw understood that the war had made the causes he used to exploit obsolete and irrelevant; as a creative artist he continued to write plays and prefaces. In *Saint Joan* he went back to the Middle Ages, showing how a French peasant girl gave birth to what eventually became the modern religion of nationalism. In *Back to Methuselah* he dealt with the possibility of immortality, jumping from the Garden of Eden to a future society thirty thousand years away. One play that he published in 1919 summed up the havoc that the war had created among the British intellectuals. *Heartbreak House* brought together more eccentric characters than any play Shaw ever wrote. Never did these emanations of his own personality talk with more brilliance or less purpose. Finally, during a Zeppelin raid, they light up their house hoping that a German bomb will destroy it and them. But the intellectuals survive; only a businessman and a burglar who seek shelter are killed.

In castigating the British intellectuals Shaw castigated himself. *Heartbreak House* had more venom but it also had more tragedy than any of his earlier plays. It depicted the end of a world to which Shaw, the Irishman, had not been born but to which he attached himself when, in his forties, he married an Anglo-Irish millionairess and chose to make his career writing for the commercial London theater.

While Shaw dropped his prewar tracts for his postwar historical dramas and philosophical fantasies, James Joyce completed seven years of labor on his masterpiece, *Ulysses*, which appeared in 1921. *Ulysses* falls into eighteen parts, each of which corresponds to one of the books in Homer's *Odyssey*. In addition, each part stands for a certain hour of the day, a certain symbol, and a certain "technic." Fifteen of the parts correspond to fifteen organs of the human body. Seventeen correspond to seventeen forms of art. Eight represent different colors.

Joyce's friend Stuart Gilbert has written: "James Joyce is in fact in the line of classical tradition which begins with Homer. Like his precursors he subjects his work, for all its wild vitality and seeming disorder, to a rule of discipline as severe as that of the Greek dramatists; indeed, the unities of *Ulysses* go far beyond the classic triad; they are as manifold and withal symmetrical as the daedal network of nerves and bloodstream which pervade the living organism."

Because Joyce used four-letter words, seen more frequently on the walls of toilets than in the more conventional works of English literature, he had to publish *Ulysses* in Paris, but copies gradually reached England and America and received serious attention on both sides of the Atlantic. He parodied every literary style, often surpassing the original; he drew from every field of knowledge. He told a great deal of the story through the thoughts of its hero—Leopold Bloom, a Dublin Jew; most of the rest was seen through the eyes of Stephen Dedalus—Bloom's spiritual son and the replica of the youthful Joyce. The final section consists of an unpunctuated soliloquy: the night thoughts of Mrs. Marion Bloom, awaiting her husband's return.

Joyce was no more a Freudian than Shaw was a Marxist, but the inner life of his characters played as crucial a part in his work as external circumstances played in the work of Shaw. Literary critics have written volumes dissecting *Ulysses*, and the discussion seems likely to continue as long as literary critics exist. That the book is one of the masterpieces of the century is beyond dispute; that its appearance started a new trend is equally apparent. Joyce brought the "interior dialogue" to a technical perfection never before equaled. Superficially he reverted to art for art's sake. At bottom his obsession with the subconscious mind of the individual marked as complete a break with Oscar Wilde's aestheticism as it did with Bernard Shaw's socialism. Joyce offered his readers no social or religious faith. His characters lived life for the sake of living; he wrote about them for the sake of revealing a new, interior reality. In the language of psychoanalysis Joyce belonged among the introverts, Shaw among the extroverts. In the language of the social scientist, Joyce dealt with the individual, the human being, and Shaw with the group and the environment. The realists, who had dominated European literature throughout the nineteenth century and on into the twentieth, suddenly found themselves challenged by a writer who turned his eye inward instead of outward, who accepted religion as one of the fundamental facts of life, no less basic than economics. And to Joyce, unlike Shaw, emotion took precedence over reason.

Joyce did not revolutionize the literature of the twentieth century singlehanded. Several contemporaries struck out in the same direction. In England, for instance, D. H. Lawrence gave himself over to unrestrained indulgence of the emotions. The chief difference between the two men lay in the fact that Joyce lived only for his art whereas Lawrence used his art to popularize a pseudo-religion of sex. Lawrence's first novel of major importance, *Sons and Lovers*, appeared in 1913. It was his own story, told in the naturalistic prewar style, describing his proletarian origins and early struggles with much more in the way of sexual and psychological undertones than Bennett, Galsworthy, or Wells put into their work. *The Rainbow,* which appeared in 1915, dealt so openly with normal and abnormal passions that the British authorities had the book suppressed. Lawrence was the consumptive son of a coal miner; his mother helped him get a good education, but he did not shed her influence until he persuaded Frieda von Richthofen, the sister of Germany's greatest wartime aviator and the wife of an Englishman, to leave her husband and children and live with him for several years before she gained freedom to remarry. It was his life with Frieda that led Lawrence to make a virtual religion of sex and to become the embarrassed idol of a neurotic cult. Aldous Huxley put the Lawrences, thinly disguised, into *Point Counter Point,* a savage satire on the same kind of people Shaw had lampooned in *Heartbreak House.* "I have read *Point Counter Point,*" Lawrence wrote Huxley in 1926, "with a heart sinking through my bootsoles and with a rising admiration. I do think you've shown the truth, perhaps the last truth, about you and your generation with really fine courage."

Of his own beliefs Lawrence wrote: "My great religion is a belief in the blood, the flesh, as being wiser than the intellect. We can go wrong in our minds, but what our blood feels and believes and says is always true. The intellect is only a bit and a bridle. All I want is to answer to my blood, direct, without fribbling intervention of mind or moral or whatnot." On the subject of politics, he added: "Let us have done with this foolish form of government, and this idea of democratic control. Let us submit to the knowledge that there are aristocrats and plebeians, born not made. Some amongst us are born fit to govern, and some are born only fit to be governed. Some are born to be artisans and laborers, some to be lords and governors. But it is not a question of tradition or heritage. It is a question of the incontrovertible soul."

Lawrence's personality transcended his books, but it was an ironic commentary upon the man and his times that he made the greatest impression upon precisely the thin-blooded intellectuals whom he derided. After his marriage he seldom lived in England, where several of his novels were suppressed. *Lady Chatterley's Lover,* his final work, had to be printed in Italy, although bowdlerized versions later appeared in England and the United States. The story dealt with the love affair between the wife of an impotent aristocrat and her gamekeeper and expressed Lawrence's revolt against bourgeois standards of sexual morality and his belief in physical love between man and woman as the supreme experience and reality. His *Fantasia of the Unconscious,* published in 1922, showed the direct influence of psychoanalysis upon his work; indeed, he even set himself up as a kind of authority on the subject, whereas Joyce merely used the findings of psychoanalysis to widen the scope of his greater talent. Both men, however, broke away from pre-

BETTMANN ARCHIVE

UNDERWOOD

Marcel Proust

James Joyce

war naturalism and realism; both men defied bourgeois morality; both spent most of their mature lives in exile; both concentrated their attention on the inner man rather than on environment; both men became the centers of overlapping cults.

The work of Marcel Proust radiated a comparable influence from France. He died in the early twenties just after completing his autobiographical epic, *À la Recherche du Temps Perdu,* which carried the technique of the subjective, interior dialogue to its furthest limits. Proust suffered all his life from asthma and devoted his early years to the intellectual salons of Paris, where he sought out the society of the rich, the fashionable, and the talented. But disgust and illness laid him low, and in the solitude of his cork-lined room he concluded that the greatest pleasure life could afford him would be to recapture, in art, his own past. Seeking personal relief from a personal problem, he made himself the outstanding social historian of the Paris salons during the first two decades of the twentieth century and one of the great literary innovators of the postwar years. In content, Proust's work depicted the decay of high French society. In style, it combined the clinical detail of a professional psychiatrist with the imagination of a poet. Some of his sentences ran for whole pages; he devoted long passages to explaining why time seems to pass more rapidly when one is busy than when one is idle. He dissected the very soul of the homosexual Baron de Charlus; at the same time he also indicated the play of social forces, the rise and fall of certain figures in the world of the Paris salon.

Proust's work exercised wide influence abroad. A beautiful English translation which C. K. M. Scott-Moncrieff did not live to complete made him available to readers—and writers—in England and the United States. Eventually, of course, a reaction set in. Aldous Huxley had one of his characters in *Eyeless in Gaza* exclaim: " 'All this burden of past experience one trails about with one! There ought to be some way of getting rid of one's superfluous memories. How I hate old Proust! Really detest him.' And with a richly comic eloquence he proceeded to evoke the vision of that asthmatic seeker of lost time, squatting, horribly white and flabby, with breasts almost female but fledged with long black hairs, forever squatting in the bath of his remembered past. And all the stale soapsuds of countless previous washings floated around him, all the accumulated dirt of years lay crusty on the sides of the tub or hung in dark suspension in the water. And there he sat, a pale repellent invalid, taking up spongefuls of his own thick soup and squeezing it over his face, scooping up cupfuls of it and appreciatively rolling the gray and gritty liquid around in his mouth, gargling, rinsing his nostrils with it, like a pious Hindu in the Ganges."

The violence with which this character of Huxley's turned against Proust expressed the revulsion of the 1930's toward one of the literary idols of the previous decade. But the sincerest flattery came from Thomas Mann, whose *Magic Mountain* appeared in Germany in 1924. Ponderous, long-winded, obvious beyond the limits of banality, it made its points with all the subtlety of an avalanche. Mann used a community of tuberculosis victims in the Swiss sanatorium of Davos to express and embody the conflicts and decadence of contemporary European civilization. No other German writer of the time rivaled Mann in intellectual power or imaginative sweep. Some of the *Magic Mountain* dialogue recalled Goethe and the Greeks. The fault of the book and the author lay in their lack of what the French call *mésure*. The fact that Mann wrote sentences as long and involved as Proust's with the same stream-of-consciousness style served only to underline his shortcomings. Mann lacked Proust's delicacy of perception but used Proust's methods to convey his murky but original vision of a sick Europe.

None of these four men—Joyce, Lawrence, Proust, or Mann—who set their marks on European literature during the first postwar decade had himself experienced the war at first hand. Nevertheless, they spoke a new language that those who had gone through the war understood. The suffering, waste, and brutality of war had destroyed Europe's prewar faith in automatic material progress. At the same time, the wartime fortitude, comradeship, and devotion of civilians as well as soldiers had revealed an unsuspected capacity for faith and sacrifice. Europe's outstanding postwar writers had no faith—no interest, even—in progress.

They did, however, have considerable faith—and still greater interest—in the indomitable, irrational human spirit that keeps the race and the individual alive. Some of them portrayed the decadence of European society; others portrayed the vitality of the individual European. While the leading American writers continued to follow the realistic, naturalistic tradition of prewar days, the leading writers of Europe broke sharply away from their prewar past.

· VII ·

THE LITERATURE of postwar Europe reflected the revolution that followed the war. The science of postwar Europe foreshadowed a deeper revolution in the attitude of Western man toward the universe around him. This revolution began at the turn of the century when the German physicist, Max Planck, brought forward the mathematical formula known as the "quantum theory" in obedience to which light waves oscillate. Five years later an unknown young physicist named Albert Einstein, still in his middle twenties, combined the quantum theory with the earlier theory that the speed of light is constant to develop his own relativity theory. Planck's quantum theory showed that all waves of radiant energy have the same fixed length. Before him, another German scientist named Döppler originated the theory that the speed of light is constant. Einstein put the two theories together and announced that light, being a substance, acts like all other forms of matter and is subject to the attraction of gravity.

The public first heard the name of Einstein in 1912 when a Viennese newspaper came out with the headline: "The Minute in Danger: A Sensation of Mathematical Science." It appeared that a young scientist named Einstein had suggested that time could expand or contract. Not until after the war did he gain world fame. On May 29, 1919, the British Royal Society and the Royal Astronomical Society put Einstein's theory to the test and showed, through photographs of an eclipse of the sun, that light waves behaved as he had reasoned they must behave. The following November the two Societies assembled to hear the report vindicating Einstein. "The whole atmosphere of tense interest," wrote Professor Alfred North Whitehead, who attended the proceedings, "was exactly like that of Greek drama. We were the chorus commenting on the decree of destiny as disclosed in the development of a supreme incident. There was dramatic quality in the very staging—the traditional ceremonial, and in the background the picture of Newton to remind us that the greatest of scientific generalizations was now, after more than two centuries, to receive its first modification."

What new decree of destiny did Einstein disclose? According to Sir

J. J. Thomson, president of the Royal Society and a research physicist himself: "I have to confess that no one has yet succeeded in stating in clear language what the theory of Einstein really is." The London *Times* reported that "observational science has in fact led back to the purest subjective idealism." In 1921 Lord Haldane, who had studied the sciences, written philosophy, and practiced statesmanship, brought out a book entitled *The Reign of Relativity* in which he declared: "The test of truth may have to be adequacy in a fuller form, a form which is concerned not only with the result of measurement, with the balance or rule, but with value that cannot be measured and that depends on other orders of thinking. What is truth from one standpoint may not necessarily stand for truth from another. Relativity, depending on the standard used, may intrude itself in varying forms."

UNDERWOOD

Dr. Albert Einstein in his Berlin Home

Einstein himself gave this definition of relativity to the newspapermen of New York: "It was formerly believed that if all material things disappeared out of the universe, time and space would be left. According to the relativity theory, however, time and space disappear with these things." Gradually, certain generalities associated with the relativity theory became clear. Because we live in a curved universe, a straight line is not the shortest distance between two points. Time is a fourth dimension and indissoluble from the other three, all of which exist only in time. It is not enough to fix the longitude, latitude, and altitude of an airplane in flight. The time at which it passes a given point in space must also be defined. The faster any object moves, the greater its mass becomes and the smaller its length. The faster a clock moves through space, the more slowly it runs. Energy and matter are one and the same thing. The only absolute in Einstein's universe is the speed of light; everything else is relative. According to Einstein, scientists used to believe that physical laws could be discovered "by a logical process from experiment." The relativity theory proves that the existing physical laws are "the free inventions of the human mind. But these laws cannot be accepted until they have been proven by experimental means."

Einstein's own utterances, sometimes cryptic, sometimes technical, sometimes humorous, sometimes philosophic, excited immense curiosity. His personality and personal history stirred still wider interest. He came of an old South German Jewish family. His father owned a small factory; his mother went in for music. Albert, their only son, received his early education in a little Catholic school. His genius for mathematics led his family to send him to the Polytechnic School at Zurich, one of the leading scientific institutions in Europe. After graduation Einstein took out Swiss citizenship and worked with the Swiss Patent Office until his first paper on relativity made such an impression on the physicists of Switzerland that they persuaded him to become first an instructor at the University of Bern and then a full professor at the University of Zurich. In 1910 he moved to the German University at Prague; in 1912 he was back in Zurich; the next year he joined the Kaiser Wilhelm Institute in Berlin, which he made his home. But he did not become a German citizen again until the establishment of the Republic.

Einstein never regarded his relativity theory or even science as an end in itself. He proceeded from the assumption that we live in an orderly universe. "I cannot believe that God plays dice with the world." He saw no contradiction between science and religion: "The most beautiful thing we can experience is the mysterious. It is the source of all true art and science. He to whom this emotion is a stranger, who can no longer pause to wonder and stand wrapped in awe, is as good as dead: his eyes are closed. This insight into the mystery of life, coupled though it be with fear, has also given rise to religion. To know that what is impenetrable to us really exists, manifesting itself as the highest wisdom and the most radiant beauty which our dull faculties can comprehend only in their most primitive forms—this knowledge, this feeling, is at the center of the true religiousness. In this sense, and in this sense only, I belong in the ranks of devoutly religious men." His own religion, he said, "consists of a humble admiration of the illimitable superior spirit who reveals himself in the slight details we are able to perceive with our frail and feeble minds. That deeply emotional conviction of the presence of a superior reasoning power, which is revealed in the incomprehensible universe, forms my idea of God." Einstein rejected any belief in personal immortality, and said of himself: "My passionate interest in social justice and social responsibility has always stood in curious contrast to a marked lack of desire for direct association with men and women. I am a horse for single harness, not cut out for tandem or teamwork. I have never belonged wholeheartedly to any country or state, to my circle of friends, or even to my own family. These ties have always been accompanied by a vague aloofness and the wish to withdraw into myself increases with the years."

The causes of Zionism and pacifism did, however, enlist his support.

In 1921 Einstein became a wholehearted Zionist. Ten years later he authorized the establishment of the "Einstein War Resisters International Fund." Throughout the 1920's he spoke and wrote in behalf of both these movements. German Nationalists accused him of "Jewish Bolshevism," while a leading Soviet scientist, A. Maximov, attacked the "idealistic atmosphere" surrounding the relativity theory: "It is only natural, therefore, that the announcement of 'general relativity' by Einstein was received with delight by the bourgeois intelligentsia. The impossibility within the limits of bourgeois society to withdraw from these influences led to the circumstance that the relativity principle served exclusively religious and metaphysical tendencies." By the 1930's, however, Cardinal O'Connell of Boston, Massachusetts, found Einstein too materialistic: "Remembering the tremendous excitement over the Darwinian theory of evolution during my boyhood and the furor created less than ten years ago by Einstein's theory of relativity I tell you that these theories became outmoded because they were mainly materialistic and therefore unable to stand the test of time." Maximov clung to Newton's mechanical view of the universe, which Marx and Lenin accepted. O'Connell, believing in original sin, rejected Einstein's attempt to identify the material with the spiritual world.

Einstein's scientific contemporaries accepted his view of the universe because he could prove it. In many cases, too, their own researches were leading them in the same direction and some of them knew, better than Einstein himself, how to explain themselves to the general public. For instance, *The Mysterious Universe*, by the British astronomer Sir James Jeans, became a best seller in 1930. "Forever solid matter melts into insubstantial radiation," wrote Jeans, "forever the tangible changes into the intangible." He also described what had happened in the physical sciences since the turn of the century: "Thirty years ago, we thought, or assumed, that we were heading towards an ultimate reality of a mechanical kind. It seemed to consist of a fortuitous jumble of atoms, which were destined to perform meaningless dances for a time under the action of blind purposeless forces, and then fall back to form a dead world. Into this wholly mechanical world, through the play of the same blind forces, life had stumbled by accident. One tiny corner at least, and possibly several tiny corners of this universe of atoms, had chanced to become conscious for a time, but was destined in the end, still under the action of blind mechanical forces, to be frozen out again and leave a lifeless world.

"Today there is a wide measure of agreement, which on the physical side of science approaches almost to unanimity, that the stream of knowledge is heading toward a nonmechanical reality; the universe begins to look more like a great thought than like a great machine. Mind no longer appears as an accidental intruder into the realm of matter; we are beginning to suspect that we ought rather to hail it as the creator and governor of the realm—not of course our individual minds, but the mind in which the atoms out of which our individual minds have grown exist as thoughts."

Jeans wrote as a scientist with a gift for popular exposition. The philosopher Whitehead, who was also a student of mathematics and religion, probed deeper in his *Science and the Modern World*, which appeared in 1925: "The progress of science has now reached a turning point. The stable foundations of physics have broken up: also for the first time physiology is asserting itself as an effective body of knowledge, as distinct from a scrap-heap. The old foundations of scientific thought are becoming unintelligible. Time, space, matter, material, ether, electricity, mechanism, organism, configuration, structure, pattern, function all require reinterpretation. What is the sense of talking about a mechanical explanation when you do not know what you mean by mechanics?" Yet the great virtue of the scientific method, according to Whitehead, lay in the willingness of the scientists to change their assumptions. Religion, on the other hand, went into a decline because it failed to change with the times: "For over two centuries religion has been on the defensive, and on a weak defensive. The period has been one of unprecedented intellectual progress. In this way a series of novel situations have been produced for thought. Each such occasion has found the religious thinkers unprepared. Something, which has been proclaimed to be vital, has finally, after struggle, distress, and anathema, been modified and otherwise reinterpreted. The next generation of religious apologists then congratulates the religious world on the deeper insight which has been gained. The result of the continued repetition of this undignified retreat, during many generations, has at last almost entirely destroyed the intellectual authority of the religious thinkers. Consider this contrast: when Darwin or Einstein proclaim theories which modify our ideas, it is a triumph for science. We do not go about saying that there is another defeat for science, because its old ideas have been abandoned. We know that another step of scientific insight has been gained."

Yet Whitehead minimized the conflict between science and religion: "Science is concerned with the general conditions which are observed to regulate physical phenomena; whereas religion is wholly wrapped up in the contemplation of moral and aesthetic values. On the one side there is the law of gravitation, and on the other the contemplation of the beauty of holiness. What one side sees, the other misses; and vice versa." The genius of Einstein—what set him apart from his scientific, religious, and philosophic contemporaries—lay in his passion for unity and simplicity, his determination to reduce the greatest number of questions to the fewest number of answers: "The special aim which I have always kept before me is logical unification in the field of physics." Or again: "The theory of relativity is a fine example of the fundamental character of the modern development of theoretical science. The hypotheses with which it starts become steadily more abstract and remote from experience. On the other hand it gets nearer to the grand aim of all science, which is to cover the greatest possible number of empirical facts by logical deduction from the smallest possible number of hypotheses or axioms."

But this logical deduction is the result of pure intuition: "The supreme task of the physicist is to arrive at those universal elementary laws from which the cosmos can be built up by pure deduction. There is no logical path to these laws; only intuition, resting on sympathetic understanding of experience, can reach them." Finally, "cosmic religious feeling is the strongest and noblest incitement to scientific research." He continued: "Those whose acquaintance with scientific research is derived chiefly from its practical results easily develop a completely false notion of the mentality of the men who, surrounded by a completely skeptical world, have shown the way to those fellow spirits scattered wide through the world and the centuries. Only one who has devoted his life to similar ends can have a vivid realization of what has inspired these men and given them the strength to remain true to their purpose in spite of constant failures. It is cosmic religious feeling that gives a man strength of this sort. A contemporary has said, not unjustly, that in this materialistic age of ours the serious scientific workers are the only profoundly religious people."

Nevertheless, an immeasurable gulf separated the materialistic age of Einstein from past ages of faith. The serious scientific worker might, in the twentieth century, follow his calling with a missionary's zeal. The difference was that the missionary had to convert others; the scientist had only to fulfill himself, often without any reference to any other human being. This had not prevented Eddington, Jeans, and other scientists from becoming converts to religious mysticism. Sir Oliver Lodge went still further and accepted the religion of spiritualism. Einstein, on the other hand, belonged among the philosophers and recognized that his theory of relativity needed a philosophy to go with it. His aptitude for mathematics turned him to the sciences, but he had a deeper affinity with the great Jewish prophets, especially such latter-day prophets as Marx and Freud. Marx had stressed the importance of the material world, of environment, economics, and the influence of the group on the individual. The realistic literature of the nineteenth century took the same course. Freud stressed the importance of the individual's inner impulses, and the outstanding postwar writers followed him rather than Marx. Einstein made Euclid's geometry and Newton's physics out-of-date, and his new doctrine of relativity put the conflict between religion and science on a new plane. But Marx and Freud had operated in a philosophic universe that Einstein dissolved.

Einstein embodied all the mystery of modern science. The popular press reported that only twelve people in the world could understand him, thus magnifying his prestige. The more the wonders of science intruded upon the lives of Europeans and Americans during the 1920's, the less they knew about how these wonders—the automobile, the airplane, and the radio—actually worked. And of the theoretical research that had made these inventions possible, they knew next to nothing. Although Einstein symbolized research, the simplicity of his character touched the hearts of simple people everywhere. He had more, perhaps, in common with Gandhi than with any other world figure, and their very differences underlined their similarities. Gandhi spurned the uses to which modern science had been put. He was an Asiatic, not a European; a religious leader who chose a political career. Yet both men rejected violence; both led dedicated lives; both revolted against twentieth-century materialism. Einstein, the physicist, brought a religious fervor to his scientific work; Gandhi, the mystic, brought religion into politics. Each in his own way had attained a condition of saintliness, of other-worldliness, that set him apart from his contemporaries and yet—for that very reason—appealed to a universal aspiration toward a better way of living than any national community in the twentieth century had attained. Both men embodied the hope that Anatole France expressed when he said at Renan's funeral: "Slowly but always humanity achieves what its wise men dream."

SUMMING UP

STRESEMANN in Germany, MacDonald in Britain, Herriot in France, Mussolini in Italy. Within six years after the Armistice four new national leaders had come to power in the four major countries of western Europe. Stresemann did not belong to the old aristocracy that had dominated the Kaiser's Germany. He came from the middle class and believed that a democratic Germany could and should get along with a democratic England and a democratic France. MacDonald and Herriot came of proletarian stock. Their rise in the world seemed to confirm the hopes of the prewar believers in evolutionary progress and social reform. As long as their influence persisted, both Britain and France seemed safe from reaction and revolution. Only Italy, the least of the

Major Powers of western Europe, refused to conform to this pattern of progress. Mussolini turned against liberal democracy in word and deed. He expressed more sympathy for Lenin than for Wilson, yet he treated Communists as his bitterest enemies. He gave his turgid doctrines the name of Fascism. In some respects, Mussolini looked like a throwback to the time of Machiavelli and the Medicis; in other respects, he sought to improve upon Marx and Lenin.

The leading writers of postwar Europe broke still more sharply with their past. While the Fabian Socialism of Ramsay MacDonald made increasing inroads on all its rivals in the political field, the field of literature told a different story. There the influence of Freud prevailed over the influence of Marx as Joyce, Lawrence, Proust, and Thomas Mann replaced Bernard Shaw, Anatole France, and Gerhardt Hauptmann, as the leaders of the new advance guard. It was a literature that broke away from the naturalistic treatment of social themes, turning instead to representing the inner man. Emotion and instinct received more consideration than reason and logic. But the most striking and least understood of all postwar revolutions took place in the field of science, where Einstein overwhelmed Newton more completely than Freud overwhelmed Marx. The old universe of tangible matter dissolved into a new universe of intangible energy. This was not a triumph of idealism over materialism. It was a triumph of Einstein's deductive logic over the inductive logic of an earlier day. He may have reached some of his conclusions in a flash of inspiration. Nobody can define just how the mind of a genius works. But once Einstein reached his conclusions, he showed by test and proof that they stood up better than the conclusions Newton had reached.

At a time when popular education was becoming more and more widespread, at a time when science was making the whole world over, fewer and fewer people could understand the latest findings of the most advanced scientists. Yet something in Einstein's personality seemed to bring science and religion together. He regarded himself as an essentially religious man—or at any rate a philosopher, a seeker for truth—who was devoting his life to simplifying the laws that govern the universe. Few people could follow all the reasoning that Einstein's own mind explored, but his conclusions presented no such difficulty. The question was what impact this new knowledge would have on the human race. Science in the service of war had wrecked nineteenth-century Europe. Now came Einstein and others offering new insights and holding out hope that a new European renaissance might be at hand.

6

New Era

The open assets and concealed liabilities of Coolidge prosperity and why it divided America against itself and weakened America before the world.

PREVIEW

COOLIDGE'S TEMPERAMENT made him the ideal President during a time when America's big business leaders wanted the federal government to let them alone. His administration reduced the national debt, cut the taxes of the rich, encouraged stock-market gambling, installment buying, and the sale of foreign bonds, but denied relief to the American farmer. The political and business leaders of the country held themselves apart from the leaders of a vigorous cultural renaissance and ignored the social implications of the Scopes trial in darkest Tennessee and the Sacco-Vanzetti case in enlightened Boston. The defeat of Al Smith in the 1928 election revealed the power of religious bigotry in the United States; the execution of Sacco and Vanzetti stirred anti-American feeling all around the world. Nor did Coolidge's cautious foreign policy yield many positive results. Dwight Morrow's mission to Mexico marked the outstanding diplomatic achievement of the Coolidge years. Henry L. Stimson also brought peace to Nicaragua and regained some good will in the Philippines. Meanwhile, the people of the United States showed more interest in foreign countries than their government displayed as isolation went the way of normalcy.

· I ·

THROUGHOUT the 1920's revolutions swept most of the earth's surface and most of the earth's people. In Russia, Stalin consolidated the revolution that Lenin had begun. In China, Chiang Kai-shek installed the revolution that Dr. Sun Yat-sen had blueprinted. In India, Gandhi used nonviolent revolution to undermine British rule. National revolutionaries came to power in Turkey, Persia, and Egypt. But the same decade that meant revolution to the depressed majority of the human race who

192

dwelt in Asia and the Middle East meant something quite different to the favored minority who dwelt in western Europe, the British Dominions, and—above all—in the United States. During the first half-dozen years after the Armistice, the victorious Powers concerned themselves mainly with reconstruction and recovery. By 1925, however, prosperity became their main concern. And most of that prosperity originated in the United States, where more and more people believed that they were leading the world into a "new era" of permanent peace and plenty.

Yet the personal character of President Coolidge had little in common with the prosperity to which he gave his name. Only his political lethargy suited the mood of a time which cried out for less government in business and more business in government. Wilson had striven to become a world messiah during a period of general crisis. During the subsequent period of reaction and recovery, Harding and Coolidge strove to bring their country back to normalcy. Wilson ceaselessly extended his power; Harding and Coolidge ceaselessly limited theirs— Harding because he lacked most of the finer qualities that distinguish human beings from the animal kingdom, Coolidge because he lacked the animal spirits that distinguish animate from inanimate matter.

Two and a half years in the White House finished off the flabby Harding; Coolidge husbanded his resources and lasted more than twice as long. He took a two-hour nap almost every afternoon and went to bed at ten almost every night. According to H. L. Mencken, Coolidge possessed but "one really notable talent. He slept more than any other President, whether by day or by night. Nero fiddled, but Coolidge only snored." Asked by Will Rogers how he survived a job that killed Wilson and Harding, Coolidge replied, "By avoiding the big problems." He regarded himself "as the representative of the government and not as an individual. When technical matters come up, I feel called upon to refer them to the proper department of the government which has some information about them and then, unless there is some good reason, I use this information as a basis for whatever I have to say; but that does not prevent me from thinking what I please as an individual."

Coolidge's split personality made him the pliant tool of America's big business leaders. As William Allen White put it in his admirable Coolidge biography, *A Puritan in Babylon:* "President Coolidge pitchforked the muck of oil and petty graft from the Augean stables of the White House, but he let in, all smartly frock-coated, plug-hatted, highcollared, bespatted, and smugly proud, another crew that was to devastate the country more terribly than Harding and his greasy playfellows." Coolidge's favorite White House guests included bankers—Morgan, Baker, Stotesbury, Giannini; railroad presidents—Loree and Atterbury; industrialists—Young and Firestone. William Howard Taft, the only ex-

President ever to become Chief Justice of the Supreme Court, frequently dropped in to talk politics. Andrew Mellon shaped national economic policy. "Why is it," a curious reporter once asked Coolidge at a press conference, "that your White House guests are limited to men of business? Why don't you have artists, musicians, actors, poets around the White House as Wilson and Roosevelt did and sometimes Taft and Harding?" The President replied: "I knew a poet once when I was in Amherst; class poet, name of Smith. Never heard of him since."

"I have never been hurt by anything I didn't say," Coolidge once boasted. Yet he issued more official statements and speeches than the strenuous Roosevelt or the wordy Wilson. According to Nicholas Murray Butler, Coolidge used "more words during his five and a half years in the White House than were used by Theodore Roosevelt and Wilson together in their fifteen years of the Presidency." What did Coolidge say? "I do not favor the granting of a bonus. . . . I am opposed to the cancellation of the war debts. . . . The Fordney-McCumber tariff will be retained. . . . Our government does not propose to enter into relations with Russia." These negative statements from Coolidge's first message to Congress struck a note that he maintained, almost without interruption, until he left Washington in March, 1929. But the descendant of Vermont dirt-farmers reserved his chilliest words for the debt-ridden tillers of the soil the country over: "No complicated scheme of relief, no plan for government fixing of prices, no resort to the public Treasury will be of any value. Simple and direct methods put into operation by the farmer himself are the only real sources of restoration."

Coolidge had all the luck, Harding none. Coolidge did not become President until after the foundation of the prosperity that bore his name had already been laid, whereas a cruel fate put Harding in the White House during the first, difficult period of postwar readjustment. The death of Harding not only broke up the Ohio gang; it finished off the Republican Old Guard. With the succession of Coolidge, the President of the United States became a cipher, the White House a vacuum. The politicians in Washington took their orders from the businessmen in New York. "Economy is idealism in its most practical form" expressed Coolidge's highest aspirations. "The business of America is business" summed up his everyday code.

And the business of America boomed as the 1920's ran their course: industrial wages up 33 per cent, salaries up 42 per cent, corporation profits up 76 per cent, dividends up 108 per cent, real national income up 50 per cent. Two million Americans owned common stocks in 1920. Ten years later their number had increased to 17 million. The number of passenger cars rose from less than 7 million in 1919 to more than 27 million in 1929. Bank deposits increased by 13½ billion dollars; bank loans and investments by 14½ billions. While more and more Americans enjoyed more and more of the good things of life, one formidable item stood out on the debit side of the national ledger. The value of American farm lands dropped from 78 billion dollars to 57 billions. In 1920 the American farmer received 15 per cent of the national income; in 1929 he received 9 per cent. Farm population declined by more than 2 million during the boom years. Yet the American farmers who remained on the land produced more and more. Between 1922 and 1926 while crop acreage remained almost stationary, the number of farmers declined, and agricultural production increased 27 per cent.

The industrial revolution had come to the farm. Between 1918 and 1932, the horse and mule population of the United States dropped about 10 million, releasing 30 million acres of crop land, besides much pasturage. Gasoline and electrical power replaced human and animal labor. Soil chemistry, synthetic fertilizers, and hybrid grain increased the yield per acre. Fewer farmers grew more food with less work at lower cost. But the demand for farm products remained relatively fixed as compared with the demand for factory products. The American people had almost four times as many automobiles in 1930 as in 1920; they could not eat four times as much food. The American farmer also faced increasing competition from abroad as the agricultural revolution spread to Canada, Australia, Argentina, and even eastern Europe. Perhaps the American farmer did not quite understand what had hit him, but he knew he had run into trouble and needed help. Nevertheless, in 1927 and again in 1928 Coolidge vetoed two versions of the McNary-Haugen Farm Bill that would have set up a federal fund to purchase surplus farm products at fixed prices. "Government price-fixing, once started, has alike no justice and no end," he declared. "It is an economic folly from which this country has every right to be spared."

But the weakest link in the chain of Coolidge prosperity did not lie in the farm belt. It lay in the uneven distribution of wealth. In 1929, the peak year of postwar prosperity, only 2.3 per cent of all the families in the United States had incomes of over $10,000 a year. More than 21 per cent had incomes of less than $1,000 a year. Sixty per cent had incomes of less than $2,000. And according to the prudent and authoritative Brookings Institution, "At 1929 prices a family income of $2,000 may be regarded as sufficient to supply only basic necessities." Though a larger number of people and a larger proportion of people were enjoying the highest living standards in recorded history, the number and proportion were still not high enough to put the United States on a full-production, full-employment basis. In theory, mass production plus advertising plus installment buying added up to permanent prosperity. In practice, the men and women engaged in mass production did not receive enough wages to buy back the fruits of their toil. One American in every four still lived and worked on a farm, but the golden twenties passed him by. New England's mill towns resembled Britain's depressed areas as textile factories moved below the Mason-Dixon Line and kept wages at traditional, substandard Southern levels. No labor organizations existed to protect the poor whites who preferred any kind of factory work to slow starvation in their native hills.

It was the same story in Detroit and other centers of the new mass-production industries. The American Federation of Labor had organized certain skilled workers, craft by craft, but it failed to organize the steel industry. The railwaymen and coal miners had strong unions, but the militant I.W.W. had fallen apart and no new movement appeared to organize the workers in the automobile factories. In 1920 more than five million American workers belonged to labor unions; by 1929 the number had fallen to less than three and a half million. But during those same ten years, the productivity of American labor had increased 50 per cent: two factory hands in 1930 did the work of three factory hands in 1920. More and more of the men who found jobs in the new factories belonged among the semiskilled. There were fewer openings for the highly skilled as the new industries recruited their workers from the farms of the Midwest, the hills of the border states, and the foreign-born of the big cities. Each man tended to look on his neighbor or fellow worker with suspicion and thought chiefly of how he could get himself ahead in a bewildering, new world.

· II ·

THE GREAT REWARDS of Coolidge's new era did not go to the farmers and factory workers. They went to the business and professional classes. These classes not only received the bulk of the national income. Their numbers multiplied. College enrollment doubled during the 1920's, rising from half a million to over a million. While the less ambitious and gifted young country people found new jobs in industry, the more affluent and eager went into business and the professions. More doctors had more patients as the life span increased from an average of fifty-one years in 1920 to fifty-nine in 1930. School teachers had twice as many students. More clients sought legal advice—though the supply of lawyers continued to exceed the demand for their services. Bankers and brokers never had so much of other people's money to invest. But the twenties were primarily the decade of the promoter, the speculator, and the plunger.

When Karl Marx coined the phrase "surplus value" he described what happened several generations later in the United States. According to Marx, capital does not pay labor full value for services rendered. Capital, said Marx, withholds what he called "surplus value," which is then reinvested in new capital equipment. In short, capital does not pay labor enough to buy back what labor itself has produced. During the 1920's, the acceleration of American industrial progress gave new urgency to Marx's analysis. American capitalists poured back their rising corporate profits into new plants so fast that existing plants became too outdated to meet the competition. In order to preserve the value of existing plants, American capitalists put more and more of their rising profits into stock-market speculation and foreign investments. And to enable the American people to buy back the products of American industry, American business had to resort to more and more installment selling. By 1929 80 per cent of all automobiles were sold on the installment plan; 15 per cent of all retail trade was conducted on the same basis, with the buyer often having to pay interest rates that would run as high as 20 and sometimes up to 35 per cent a year. Gradually, millions of people were drifting toward the dead end that an unhappy citizen of Oklahoma reached when he found that his installment plan payments for assorted luxuries exceeded his total income.

Only one kind of shortage plagued the American people during the 1920's: a shortage of money to buy the goods and services that the advertisers offered in such profusion. It was a buyer's market all the way, with the sellers competing for the consumer's elusive dollar. But this did not mean that the consumer got his dollar's worth. Selling became an end in itself. Breakfast foods costing two or three cents a pound sold for 68 cents. "Sanatogen," according to one advertiser, "contains over 700 per cent more tissue-building, life-sustaining nourishment than wheat flour." The fact was that a dollar's worth of wheat flour contained as much energy as $197 worth of Sanatogen. The manufacturer of a hot-air furnace sent these instructions to his salesmen: "There are four words in the English language which mean absolutely nothing to us and which we never use in making a sale or interviewing a prospect. They are FURNACE, HOT, COLD, and PRICE. We do not sell furnaces—we sell WARM-AIR HEATING SYSTEMS. We never mention the word hot air, but substitute WARM, MOIST AIR. We never say cold-air returns, but RECIRCULATING FRESH-AIR DUCTS. We avoid the bugaboo price and talk only in terms of investment."

The American people came out of the war with a magnificent industrial plant. Ten years later they had stepped up the efficiency of that plant 50 per cent. They had most of the resources they needed to keep that plant running, and they had easy access to the rest. They had a huge market at home and an almost unlimited one abroad. Americans did not chase dollars any harder than Englishmen chased pounds or Frenchmen chased francs. What set the American of the 1920's apart from the people of other countries was his capacity to produce wealth, and the force that drove him throughout the decade was the determination to sell. "One third of America promotes," said Will Rogers, "two thirds of America provides."

It was the promoting third that gave the twenties their special character. While the advertiser debauched the American consumer, the broker and the banker debauched the American investor. And since the advertiser consumed and the broker and banker invested, everybody had his hands in the other fellow's pockets. Several million Americans had enough spare cash on their hands to speculate or invest, and it sometimes seemed as if there must have been twice as many customers' men from banking and brokerage houses to help them along. Concerns with headquarters in New York maintained branches throughout the country and operated a network of gambling establishments that dealt in securities instead of colored chips. The speculator put up 10 per cent, or less, of the price of the security. The broker, borrowing from a banker, provided the other 90 per cent—or more. This meant that a speculator could purchase $1,000 worth of securities for $100 in cash. If the price of the securities went up to $1,100, the speculator could sell and double his money. If the price went down to $900, he had to put up more cash or lose his $100. The bulls bet the stocks they bought would go up. The bears, by a more complicated process of promising to deliver a stock they did not own, made their profits by betting it would go down. The brokers made their money by charging a small commission for each sale and urging their customers to buy and sell as often as possible.

American investors who wanted high interest rates put their money into foreign bonds. The Fordney-McCumber Tariff prevented foreign countries from selling their wares in the United States, and thus acquiring the dollars they needed to buy American goods. American bankers thereupon discovered that they could provide Europe and South America with the necessary dollars by selling foreign securities in the American market. Nor did the bankers forget themselves. Whether it was the ancient House of Morgan marketing Dawes Plan bonds or the newly arrived Dillon, Reed selling South American securities, the banker always pocketed a "spread" between the price the American investor paid and the price the foreign borrower received. These foreign securities paid much higher interest rates than American securities, and by 1930 the American people had invested 15 billion dollars abroad.

Speculation drove common stocks up so high that many of them yielded no more interest than a bond or a savings bank account. Some of the shakier governments in eastern Europe and Latin America, on the other hand, offered to pay as high as 7 and 8 per cent for the privilege of borrowing dollars. A growing number of frustrated American investors could not resist the temptation to get such handsome returns on their money and found themselves involved in an even crazier process than installment buying or stock-market speculation. The American who bought on the installment plan, even at excessive interest rates, at least had the use of what he had bought and the hope of earning enough money to pay for it in full. There was one chance in fifty that the speculator could beat the law of averages and make money in Wall Street. But the American who invested his money abroad had almost no chance of getting it back. The Fordney-McCumber Tariff raised an insuperable barrier against repayment.

"Lafayette, we are here." Cartoon by Al Frueh, copyright 1927, The New Yorker Magazine, Inc. Reproduced by permission

The Coolidge administration not only stood for high tariffs. It went to unprecedented lengths in the encouragement of stock-market gambling. Coolidge personally practiced the utmost economy in his private life. He had always saved some money every year, having laid away about $25,000 by the time he reached the White House. He saved at least another $50,000 as President and took special pride in the way Andrew W. Mellon reduced the national debt. But "the greatest Secretary of the Treasury since Alexander Hamilton" had not accumulated one of the great American fortunes by practicing the Coolidge type of thrift. According to the New York Times, the Mellons, by 1927, had made 300 million dollars speculating in aluminum and Gulf Oil. The Van Sweringen brothers of Cleveland controlled a two-and-a-half-billion-dollar railway system through their ownership of twenty million dollars' worth of holding-company stock. "A holding company," said Will Rogers, "is a thing where you hand an accomplice the goods while the policeman searches you." The definition did not please the financiers or satisfy the economists, but it expressed a widespread belief.

Not that all the financiers or all the economists approved of the way Coolidge's inaction permitted Mellon to run the country. A mere Harvard professor named William Z. Ripley gave the stock market a brief

UNDERWOOD

Andrew W. Mellon

sinking spell in 1926 when his article "Main Street and Wall Street" appeared in the *Atlantic Monthly*. "The sudden widespread ownership of corporations since the World War," wrote Professor Ripley, "has created entirely new circumstances and conditions in the business world. Main Street and Wall Street have come to cross one another at right angles—Main Street our synonym for this phenomenon of widespread ownership, and Wall Street as applied to the well-known aggregation of financial and directorial power in our great capital centers. This intersection of interest, so often at cross purposes, is marked by an imminent danger of collision at the junction point of ownership and management." Ripley attacked corporate management for divesting the stockholders of their voting rights and for withholding vital financial information. But the investing public did not want to listen to gloomy, impractical professors; it preferred the cheerful, successful man of business. Secretary Mellon, in the spring of 1927, could "see no evidence of overspeculation," and the following August the Federal Reserve Bank dropped its discount rate from 4 per cent to 3½ per cent. Montagu Norman, governor of the Bank of England, and Dr. Hjalmar Schacht, president of the German Reichsbank, favored lower interest rates, and their good friend J. P. Morgan agreed with them. So did about a million American speculators.

These same speculators, moreover, applauded the sentiments of Mellon when he declared that "the man who seeks to perpetuate prejudice and class hatred is doing America an ill service. In attempting to promote or defeat legislation by arraying one class of taxpayers against another, he shows a complete misconception of those principles on which the country was founded. Any man of initiative or energy in this country can get what he wants out of life. But when that initiative is crippled by a tax system which denies him the right to receive a reasonable share of his earnings, then he will no longer exert himself and the country will be deprived of the energy on which its continued greatness depends." The United States came out of the war with a national debt of more than 26 billion dollars. Ten years later Secretary Mellon could take most of the credit for having reduced that debt to 16 billions, without, however, soaking the rich. In 1920 surtaxes on big incomes ran as high as 65 per cent. Mellon persuaded Congress and the administration to cut this rate to 50 per cent in 1921, to 40 per cent in 1924, and to 20 per cent in 1926. But it was not until 1926 that the lower-bracket incomes received substantial relief. "As a matter of policy," Mellon once remarked, "nothing so brings home to a man the feeling that he personally has an interest in seeing that government funds are not squandered, but intelligently expended, as the fact that he contributes individually a direct tax, no matter how small, to his government."

Lesser men of business echoed Mellon's views, translating them into the evangelical language of Rotary, Kiwanis, and Lions Club luncheons. It was no uncommon experience, for instance, for small-town business leaders to hear such appeals as this, delivered by Everett W. Hill, first vice-president of International Rotary, at a luncheon in Springfield, Massachusetts, during the mid-1920's: "Rotarians, trail blazers of honesty and correct business practices, when our tasks of life near completion may we halt a moment on the brink and, turning, look backward o'er the span of life, and, when our eyes shall be turned for the last time to behold the sun in the evening, may they not see a land given over to selfishness. Rather, let their last lingering glance behold the flag of Rotary unfurled full high in the heavens, its arms and its trophies streaming with all their original beauty, not a single spoke erased or polluted and not a single cog removed; bearing for its motto no such miserable interrogatory as 'How much can I get with the least possible effort?' but the beautiful sentiment everywhere shining in characters of living light emblazoned on all its ample folds as they float over the sea and over the land, and in every wind under the heaven, that motto dear to the heart of every true Rotarian: 'Service above self.'"

With the support of such sweet reason and such flow of soul, Mellon's tax policies helped to swell corporate profits, dividend payments, and the incomes of the well-to-do. Prices of common stocks kept climbing until January, 1928, when more economists called attention to greater dangers than Professor Ripley had stressed in 1926. Loans by stockbrokers to stock speculators exceeded six billion dollars—an ominously high level—and once again the market sagged. Whereupon Coolidge put the immense authority of his office behind the statement that brokers' loans were not too high. That, as the British say, tore it. The man whose reputation for parsimony and reticence might have slowed down the speculative boom gave it new impetus. Yet Coolidge did not believe his own advice. "If I were to give my own personal opinion about it," he admitted at the time, "I should say that any loan made for gambling was an excessive loan." The Federal Reserve Bank raised the discount rate back to 4 per cent in February and boosted it to 5 per cent in June, but the horse had long since escaped from the barn. As prices of common stocks went up and up, Governor Roy A. Young of the Federal Reserve Board could only laugh at his predicament, while confiding to a friend: "What I am laughing at is that I am sitting here trying to keep a hundred and twenty million people from doing what they want to do."

Mr. Young exaggerated. At no time did more than a million Americans ever speculate in the stock market, but those who did caused enough commotion, both financial and psychological, to produce far-reaching effects. The fluctuations of one volatile stock showed what was happening. At the end of November, 1928, Radio Corporation of America sold for 400. It fell 72 points in one day, dropped to 94½ in March, 1929, rose to 505 on September 3. A speculator with $1,000 in cash could have bought one hundred shares in March, 1929, by borrowing $8,450 from his broker, who, in turn, got the money from his bank. If the speculator had sold at the top of the market, he would have received $50,500—less an insignificant broker's commission and a few hundred dollars in interest. Within the space of six months he would have increased his original investment fifty times over. Radio stock at that time paid no dividends, but price bore no relationship to yield. It was a speculator's, not an investor's, market, and the speculator sought quick, huge profits.

On at least two counts, the Coolidge years deserved to be called the new era. The United States had not only created the mightiest productive system on earth. The productive power of the country continued to grow at accelerating speed. But America's buying power lagged so far behind America's productive power that manufacturers had to sell more and more goods to the masses on the installment plan while the classes, the well-to-do, felt it necessary to speculate in Wall Street in order to keep up with the Joneses. Few Americans, during the 1920's, speculated for the sake of speculation. They seldom plowed all their profits back into the market. Most of them depended on the proceeds of their stock gambling to buy automobiles, yachts, country estates, and Prohibition booze. Only through the kind of profits that Wall Street yielded during the Coolidge years could they live like the lords of the new era. Meanwhile Coolidge lent the sanction of his parsimonious personality to the prosperity that bore his name, playing all unconsciously the part of the professional gambler in the old West who won the trust of his victims by getting himself up to look like a deacon. But there was this difference. The gambler, having no conscience, never deceived himself. Coolidge, on the other hand, felt that his New England code required him to seek his own salvation and to let his neighbor save himself.

· III ·

THE WAY Coolidge separated his private conscience from his public duty followed the pattern of the time. Government kept hands off business; industry let the farmer go hang; Wall Street scorned Main Street; the state ignored the citizen and the citizen ignored the state. Yet the Coolidge era, equally barren in political leadership from Washington and in business leadership from New York, witnessed a steady outpouring of creative activity in literature, science, and the arts. Business attended to business. The politician stuck to politics. Which gave the more creative professions their opportunity.

In January, 1924, Alfred A. Knopf, who had introduced scores of new writers, both native and foreign, to the American book-reading public, launched *The American Mercury,* edited by H. L. Mencken and George Jean Nathan. Its first issue contained a play by Eugene O'Neill, who had already begun to make a reputation with *The Emperor Jones* and *Anna Christie* and soon added to his fame with *Desire Under the Elms.* In 1924 the jazz-band leader Paul Whiteman made a musical sensation when he first played Gershwin's *Rhapsody in Blue* in New York's Carnegie Hall. In 1925 came Sinclair Lewis's *Arrowsmith,* a mature and sympathetic study of a high-minded American physician. Theodore Dreiser's masterpiece, *An American Tragedy,* appeared the same year. This detailed if ponderous story of how a weak, ambitious young man murdered his sweetheart in the hope of being able to marry his boss's daughter showed that the United States had at last produced an epic novelist whose stature equaled that of many of his European contemporaries. The "lost generation," as the American expatriates in Paris called themselves, found a new voice when Ernest Hemingway's *The Sun Also Rises* appeared in 1926. That was also the year when Professor Sidney B. Fay, then of Smith College, completed his *Origins of the World War,* which struck a judicious balance between the excesses of wartime Allied propaganda and the equally violent reaction of the revisionists.

Two still more impressive creations of American scholarship came out in 1927: *The Rise of American Civilization,* by Charles A. Beard and Mary Beard, and Vernon L. Parrington's *Main Currents in American Thought.* Both these massive works revaluated the American past, borrowing many insights from Karl Marx while avoiding his dogmatism. Ellen Glasgow and Willa Cather showed themselves worthy successors to Edith Wharton. Robert Frost, E. A. Robinson, Vachel Lindsay, Carl Sandburg, Edna St. Vincent Millay, Elinor Wylie, Stephen Vincent Benét, and Robinson Jeffers proved that all poets did not go the way of

Coolidge's obscure Amherst classmate. A new, vigorous school of American painters appeared: Grant Wood, Thomas Hart Benton, Georgia O'Keeffe, George Bellows, Reginald Marsh, Charles Burchfield. The Tribune Tower in Chicago and half a dozen New York skyscrapers fulfilled the early promise of the Woolworth Building. Frank Lloyd Wright experimented as boldly and successfully as any architect in Europe. American science also came of age as Thomas Hunt Morgan of Columbia continued his prewar study of genes and Arthur H. Compton of Chicago applied Einstein's relativity theory to the study of X-rays. The Mayo Clinic at Rochester, Minnesota, became a world-famous center of medical research, and in 1925 Dr. and Mrs. Dick of Chicago developed an antitoxin for scarlet fever. Robert and Helen Lynd of Columbia brought the methods of anthropology to bear on a typical American community, and their book, *Middletown*, published in 1929 and based on a careful survey of the people of Muncie, Indiana, not only revealed new aspects of life in the United States; it became a model for similar researches elsewhere.

The Lynds' book, based on firsthand evidence carefully weighed and interpreted by experts, depicted an America that bore little resemblance to the America that advertisers were spending a billion and a half dollars a year to glorify in magazines, newspapers, and over the radio. Studying an American community as if it were a tribe of aboriginal head-hunters, they confirmed what the leading realistic writers of the time had already revealed. What they depicted was an America of sharply stratified class divisions, an America in which the rich and the poor, the native and the foreign-born, the white and the colored, the Protestant and the Catholic, the city dweller and the farmer lived quite different lives, based on quite different assumptions. In *Middletown* the characters in the novels of Sinclair Lewis, Sherwood Anderson, and Theodore Dreiser found their real-life counterparts. An underlying sense of frustration and fear possessed even the minority of boosters; the majority suffered from loneliness, insecurity, tension. Big business had nibbled away at the power of the federal government while checking its expansion for fear of curtailing its rate of profit. So faithfully, indeed, did big business observe its own individualistic code, so scrupulously did it specialize, that it talked only to itself. The masses did not understand its language any more than big business understood what the writers, artists, and scientists had to say. But it took the glittering talent of F. Scott Fitzgerald to translate the glitter of his time into book form. *The Great Gatsby*, depicting the rise and fall of a society gangster, remains an imperishable allegory of the period, combining as it does the journalist's eye for surface detail with the artist's insight into human motivation.

Two writers whose professional work kept them in touch with the mass audience wrote two books of utterly different character and equally wide appeal. Both appeared in 1925: *The Man Nobody Knows,* by Bruce Barton, and *Gentlemen Prefer Blondes,* by Anita Loos. Bruce Barton, who had made a fortune as an outstanding writer of advertising copy, wrote a best-selling life of Jesus—as "the most popular dinner-guest in Jerusalem," "the founder of modern business," and author of "the most powerful advertisements of all time." Cynics scoffed; serious thinkers viewed Barton's—and the public's—taste with alarm. Yet Barton, like most of his readers, had

UNDERWOOD

Anita Loos

Christianity in his blood. His father, William E. Barton, was a distinguished Congregational minister whose dignified life of Lincoln appeared during the same year as *The Man Nobody Knows.* Both books sold widely, but the greater popularity of the son's suggested that he had caught, more successfully than his father, the spirit of the time. Bruce Barton believed, equally, in Christ and in advertising just as Kipling believed, equally, in Christ and the British Empire.

Anita Loos wrote motion picture scenarios as successfully as Barton wrote advertising copy, and her cynical humor matched his self-serving idealism. *Gentlemen Prefer Blondes,* the imaginary diary of a kept woman, depicted the raucous, vulgar life of the new rich during the mid-1920's. "A kiss on the wrist feels good, but a diamond bracelet lasts forever," summed up the worldly wisdom of Lorelei Lee, who found Paris "devine" and London "really nothing." Anita Loos had none of Ring Lardner's bitterness, none of Scott Fitzgerald's romanticism. Ostensibly she wrote only for laughs, yet in doing so she presented the most widely enjoyed and most devastatingly realistic satire of her time. The same people, tens of thousands of them, who found true spiritual comfort in *The Man Nobody Knows* recognized in *Gentlemen Prefer Blondes* a true picture of themselves and their world.

Bruce Barton and Anita Loos, Charles Evans Hughes and H. L. Mencken, Henry Ford and Sinclair Lewis, Calvin Coolidge and Theodore Dreiser—the United States during the mid-1920's had a split personality—a personality, indeed, split many different ways. At a time of rapid growth and sudden change, the centrifugal forces showed greater strength than the centripetal ones. The country seemed to be flying apart. It became more and more difficult to reconcile violently opposing trends. Prohibition remained the law of the land, yet the abolition of the saloon and the adoption of woman's suffrage failed to arrest the rapid growth of organized crime and the breakdown of sexual morals, especially in the middle class. George Horace Lorimer, creator of the first great mass-circulation magazine, no longer welcomed new talent to the *Saturday Evening Post;* he preferred to romanticize American big business.

While the *Post* appealed more and more directly to conservative, well-heeled middle-class readers, Bernarr MacFadden wooed the proletariat with *True Story* and a variety of confession magazines celebrating his cult of physical and sexual vitality. The quality magazines that tried to keep alive the genteel tradition languished. Only the *Atlantic Monthly* and *Harper's* survived, and both drew their inspiration from the same man. Ellery Sedgwick had served his apprenticeship in the magazine business under S. S. McClure during the early 1900's. In 1908 Sedgwick purchased the *Atlantic Monthly,* which then had a circulation of eighteen thousand copies, chiefly in New England. By the 1920's he had run the circulation up to more than one hundred thousand and one of his young assistants, Frederick Lewis Allen, had joined the staff of *Harper's,* which proceeded to apply the Sedgwick formula. This meant serving up the readers a mixture of human-interest articles, based on the actual experiences of real people, and adult, contemporary reporting. The whimsical essay, the sentimental short story, and nostalgia for nineteenth-century respectability faded away.

The twenties also produced three new magazines that made distinctive places for themselves in American life: the *Reader's Digest, Time,* and the *New Yorker.* DeWitt Wallace, a wounded young war veteran, got the idea for the *Reader's Digest* in a hospital bed where he pasted up excerpts from current magazine articles and passed them on to his wife and friends. He had the eye of a born editor for inspirational writing; he also possessed the born editor's genius for cutting away verbiage. Briton Haden and Henry R. Luce, two young Yale graduates, developed a formula for reprocessing news more drastic than Wallace's formula for condensing magazine articles. *Time* magazine, with its slangy style, cocky point of view, and departmental treatment of the news of the week, became a new force in American journalism. The *Reader's Digest* confounded convention by refusing to accept advertising, and the Wallaces founded it with almost no capital investment. *Time* proved an excellent advertising medium; Haden and Luce kept editorial control in their own hands, but they did raise some Wall Street money to help them on their way. Haden died before he reached the age of thirty, leaving an estate worth more than a million dollars.

The *New Yorker* never reached so wide an audience as *Reader's Digest* or *Time*, and Raoul Fleischmann, who made a fortune in yeast, went several hundred thousand dollars into the red before the *New Yorker* turned the corner. But Harold Ross, who had edited the army newspaper *Stars and Stripes*, in France, proved himself a more creative magazine man than Wallace, Haden, or Luce. *Reader's Digest* and *Time* summarized, rehashed, or reprinted material that other publications had gathered. The *New Yorker* created a new style of journalism, humor, and art. E. B. White and James Thurber contributed an unsigned, introductory section, "Talk of the Town," which combined the basically parochial and the superficially sophisticated. Peter Arno's cartoons of the Whoops Sisters introduced a novelty in comic art: the one-line caption. The old humorous weeklies, *Life* and *Judge*, were dying on their feet, and the *New Yorker* soon acquired Robert Benchley, *Life*'s drama critic. The meterless poems of Ogden Nash, the more disciplined verses of Dorothy Parker, the delicate line drawings of Gluyas Williams and Rea Irvin, the essays and book reviews of Clarence Day, Jr., made the *New Yorker* a national reputation, in spite of, or really because of, its boast that it was "not written for the old lady in Dubuque." The *American Mercury* gave Mencken and Nathan an outlet for their personalities and a vehicle through which many talented young writers first gained national recognition. In the *New Yorker*, the creative spirit of the most cosmopolitan world capital since Byzantium found its natural outlet.

During the 1920's those Americans who continued to prefer their daily paper to any other kind of reading matter lived on a diet of murder, bootlegging, sex, and sports stories. On September 16, 1922, the nude bodies of the Reverend Edward Wheeler Hall and Mrs. James Mills, chief choir singer in his church at New Brunswick, New Jersey, were found beneath a crab-apple tree in the local lover's lane, shot to death. A grand jury failed to indict Mrs. Hall on a charge of first-degree murder and the case lapsed for four years until Hearst's New York tabloid, the *Daily Mirror*, brought forward new information allegedly implicating Mrs. Hall. This time the case did go to trial, and during the eleven days it lasted, reporters sent out five million words of news and comment. Mary Roberts Rinehart, the popular mystery writer, and Billy Sunday, the popular evangelist, covered the story on the spot. Again the case collapsed for lack of evidence.

A few months later, in a Long Island suburb, Judd Gray, a corset salesman, and Mrs. Ruth Snyder, wife of a minor magazine functionary, killed Snyder with a sash-weight in his home. There was no mystery this time, but the trial received even more attention than the Hall-Mills case. In addition to Mrs. Rinehart and Billy Sunday, the reporters included David Wark Griffith, the much-married Peggy Joyce, and Dr. Will Durant, whose *Story of Philosophy* had become a best seller. The most grue-some touch of all came when a reporter who witnessed the electrocution of Mrs. Snyder sneaked a small camera into his trouser leg and emerged with her picture that duly appeared on his paper's front page.

The front pages of all papers always had space to report Chicago's gang wars. During the twenties, Chicago gangsters committed more than five hundred murders, few of which led to any criminal action. On Valentine's Day, February 14, 1929, five members of Al Capone's gang, three of them dressed as policemen, machine-gunned six members of the rival Bugs Moran gang and won undisputed control of the vice and liquor rackets of the whole Chicago area. A few months later, thirty Chicago gangsters held a conference at Atlantic City with gang leaders from other cities and mapped out a division of territories, like so many business leaders or world statesmen. Capone himself, at the age of thirty-two, dominated Chicago's municipal government and headed an organization which was taking in over sixty million dollars a year. At one formal dinner he produced from beneath his chair a baseball bat with which he bashed in the skull of the guest of honor. Federal agents estimated Capone's fortune at twenty million dollars, but the Chicago police never touched him and when he finally went to jail, years later, it was on charges of income tax evasion.

Sports commanded a wider and healthier interest than murder or boot-legging. Throughout the autumn months every college community in the land lived for its weekly football game, and many of the stadiums built to accommodate the crowds held between fifty thousand and one hundred thousand persons. Professor John Dewey and his associates at Teachers College had spread the doctrine of "learning by doing," which sometimes led to curious results. For instance, a press dispatch from Palo Alto, California, reported a characteristic development at Leland Stanford University: "Yelling has been made a subject in the curriculum at Stanford and credit will be given to sophomores trying out for assistant yell leader who register in the new course. 'Bleacher psychology,' 'the correct use of the voice,' 'development of stage presence,' and 'what a coach expects of the yell leader' will be topics of lectures by members of the faculty and by Prof. Andrew Kerr, football coach."

More than one football student soon surpassed the prowess of his master. Red Grange, sometimes known as the Galloping Ghost, sometimes as the Wheaton Iceman, brought fame and fortune to the University of Illinois with his open-field running. He refused a salary of $120,000 a year to work for a real estate firm, but quit college in the fall of 1925 before graduation to play as a professional for the Chicago Bears. He received $12,000 for his first game and two weeks later got $30,000 for playing in New York. The next day he signed a $300,000 movie contract.

UNDERWOOD

Cartoon by Richard Decker, copyright
1932, The New Yorker Magazine, Inc.
Reproduced by permission

Babe Ruth Shakes Hands with
Judge Landis,
Baseball's High Commissioner

Like many other celebrities of the time, Grange's star sank almost as fast
as it rose. By 1930 he was working in a Hollywood night club. Ten years
later he enjoyed a more substantial if more modest success as a radio
sports announcer.

Professional baseball players got a better break. Babe Ruth's annual
salary rose to $80,000 after he had hit sixty home runs, the record for a
single season. He had already played more than ten years in the major
leagues, and almost ten more years of active, high-priced playing remained ahead. The professional prize fighter could not hope for any
such luck. The first Dempsey-Tunney heavyweight championship fight
in 1927 yielded almost two million dollars in gate receipts; the return
match the following year yielded over two and a half millions. But no
other fighter in the 1920's approached the earnings of these two men, and
most of them wound up as punch-drunk derelicts before they reached
the age of thirty. Old-timers warned that Americans were becoming a
nation of spectator-sportsmen. They never stopped to count how many
sons and daughters of horseshoe pitchers took up golf and tennis.

Stuart Chase estimated that the American people spent as much as one
quarter of their national income on recreation. Florida collected more
than a billion dollars from tourists in a single winter. The motion picture
industry took in several times as much money the whole year around.
Three Americans in every four attended a motion picture every week.
In 1927 Warner Brothers produced the first feature-length sound film—

Al Jolson in *The Jazz Singer*. Within another two years almost every movie theater in the country was wired for sound. Clara Bow, the famous "It Girl" of the silent films, went into retirement. John Gilbert, hero of the silent screen, committed suicide because his high-pitched voice seemed to lack virility.

The American people spent less on radio sets than they spent on movie tickets, but American advertisers found radio a more and more rewarding medium. In 1926 the Radio Corporation of America began to create the first national network of stations when it organized the National Broadcasting Company as a subsidiary. The next year, young William S. Paley started putting the Columbia Broadcasting System together. NBC began as an offshoot of a concern that manufactured radio sets. CBS made no sets and went into business for the sole purpose of broadcasting. As the 1920's ran their course, the radio characters of Amos and Andy became as familiar to every American as Charlie Chaplin. Graham McNamee's reporting of sports and news made him as celebrated as Arthur Brisbane, the syndicated editorial pundit of the Hearst press. The combined and parallel development of network broadcasting and commercial sponsorship transformed radio into something more than big business. It created a new means of mass communication.

And this development of mass communications underscored the excesses of the Coolidge era. The American people still went to extremes —witness the story of Prohibition. Before the passage of the Eighteenth Amendment the corner saloon had bred much of the crime and evil that corrupted so many American cities. To rid themselves of this disgrace, the American people chose a drastic and oversimplified remedy which promptly gave rise to more crime and evil than it sought to cure. "Now for an era of clear thinking and clean living," boasted the Anti-Saloon League as Prohibition went into effect. "A new nation will be born." That new nation promptly cultivated the manners of a snooper, the morals of a gangster, and the methods of a highjacker. Eventually, the pendulum swung back and a balance was struck. But the Prohibition era happened to coincide with a new era in mass communications. The magazine, newspaper, movie, and radio industries, ever seeking larger and larger audiences, exploited sensation for sensation's sake. America's business was business; whatever worked was right; success justified everything. As a result, Americans during the 1920's received a grossly exaggerated picture of themselves, day after day and twenty-four hours around the clock. The record of these exaggerations still stands—on film, in print, and in the living memory of most chroniclers of the 1920's who, themselves, experienced those frantic years.

When Rudolph Valentino, the most popular movie hero of the time, died on the same day as President-Emeritus Charles W. Eliot of Harvard, it was Valentino, not Eliot, who got the headlines. But this did not mean that Americans who had twice sent Woodrow Wilson to the White House held university presidents in singularly low esteem. What it did mean was that mass publicity had discovered how to stir mass emotions. More-over, the protests against the new era sometimes surpassed the absurdities of the new era itself. Dr. John Roach Straton, "the Baptist Pope of New York," as H. L. Mencken called him, warned his flock: "Vice and crime are increasing day by day. Sensualism reigns supreme on stage and screen. Many magazines and best sellers are putrid with moral iniquity. The popular dance has descended to the lowest depths of degradation. Churches on every side are lukewarm and spiritually paralyzed, and blatant infidelity is proclaiming its untruths in college halls and even from many pulpits of the land. The marriage vow is becoming a scrap of paper. The foundations of the home have been all but destroyed by commercialized amusements and a money-mad, pleasure-crazed race is rushing toward the precipice!"

From Denver, Colorado, came further proof of the corrosive effect of Prohibition on traditional religious practices in a commercial age. The manufacturers of Whistle, a popular soft drink, flavored with synthetic orange, publicized a testimonial from the Reverend F. H. Rice of the Liberal Church: "In this day of Prohibition you have heard of many churches that have supplanted the communion wine with grape juice, but we claim to be the first to use Whistle for this very important service. At 11 A.M. last Sunday morning, every member of the Liberal Church partook of Whistle at the Lord's Supper and during the ceremony five large Whistle signs and three linen banners were prominently displayed. The purity, quality, and general excellence of your beverage well justify its being used in such a manner and we think that many others will follow our example."

Frederick Lewis Allen, in *Only Yesterday*, cited the solo, nonstop flight of twenty-five-year-old Charles A. Lindbergh from New York to Paris as welcome proof of the fundamental good health and good sense of the United States. Will Rogers commented at the time: "Of all things that Lindbergh's great flight demonstrated, the greatest was to show us that a person could still get the entire front pages without murdering anybody." Lindbergh was a stunt flier, the son and namesake of the late Congressman C. A. Lindbergh of Minnesota. Young Lindbergh's story differed from the stereotyped pattern. His father had been an antiwar, radical Progressive. His mother, a conventional schoolteacher from Nova Scotia, left her husband early in their married life because she hated his extreme views and unconventional ways. The boy stayed with the father, whom he idolized. The father wanted him to go through college, but the boy had a stubborn adventurous streak; he was also a born mechanic who soon made such a reputation for himself as an aviator that a group of St. Louis businessmen financed his flight to Europe, which netted him a $25,000 prize.

The fact that Lindbergh accepted the acclaim of the Paris public with simple modesty and did not at once commercialize his success gave him the aspect of a superman. The American people, eager for an old-fashioned hero, found in Lindbergh the embodiment of all they yearned for. Lindbergh himself disliked publicity; he made no attempt to conceal his hatred of the press; after returning to the United States to be greeted by President Coolidge, he accepted the commission of Colonel in the Army and prepared to devote himself to scientific work, the encouragement of aviation, and occasional public service. The Lindbergh story stood out as the one happy, healthy symptom of a frantic time.

· IV ·

NEITHER the Lindbergh story on the one hand nor the murder-sex-crime stories on the other quite succeeded in blanketing two more serious symptoms of the 1920's—the Scopes trial in benighted Dayton, Tennessee, and the Sacco-Vanzetti case in enlightened Boston, Massachusetts. In March, 1925, the Governor of Tennessee signed a bill, introduced in the state legislature by a Fundamentalist Baptist farmer, forbidding any state-supported school to teach "any theory that denies the story of the Divine Creation of man as taught in the Bible." Mississippi and Arkansas passed similar laws. Billy Sunday, the former professional baseball player who became one of the most popular evangelists of the war and postwar years, declared: "If anyone wants to teach that God-forsaken, hell-born, bastard theory of evolution, then let him go out and let him be supported by men who believe that blasted theory and not expect the Christian people of this country to pay for the teaching of a rotten, stinking professor who gets up there and teaches our children to forsake God and makes our schools a clearing-house for their God-forsaken dirty politics." In Georgia, State Representative Hal Wimberly advocated a bill that would have forbidden any public library or county school to purchase or accept as a gift any book except the Bible, the hymnal, and the almanac: "Those three are enough for anyone. Read the Bible. It teaches you how to act. Read the hymnbook. It contains the finest poetry ever written. Read the almanac. It shows you how to figure out what the weather will be. There isn't another book necessary for anyone to read and therefore I am opposed to all libraries." Mr. Wimberly's bill failed to pass the Georgia House of Representatives by a vote of 63 to 57.

When the American Civil Liberties Union offered to back any schoolteacher who defied the antievolution law, young John Thomas Scopes, a

UNDERWOOD UNDERWOOD

William Jennings Bryan *Clarence Darrow*

biology teacher in the small town of Dayton, Tennessee, agreed to make the test. In July, 1925, he was arrested for having told his class "that the earth was once a hot molten mass, too hot for plant or animal life to exist upon it; in the sea the earth cooled off; there was a little germ of one-cell organism formed, and this organism kept evolving until it got to be a land animal, and it kept on evolving, and from this was man." William Jennings Bryan undertook the prosecution; the agnostic Clarence Darrow headed the defense.

Scopes stood in no danger; at most he risked a fine of one hundred dollars and the costs of the trial. Bryan summed up the Fundamentalist case: "Power in this country comes from the people; and if the majority of the people believe that evolution breaks down a religious faith and threatens Christianity, they have a right to demand that it be suppressed or at least confined to the little group of research men who may study it as a theory not yet proven." He based his case on "The Rock of Ages," not "the age of rocks." The high point of the trial came when Bryan permitted Darrow to cross-examine him on his belief in the literal, historical truth of the entire Old Testament narrative, including the story of the whale swallowing Jonah and Joshua making the sun stand still. Bryan insisted that God created the world in six days in the year 4004 B.C.; that Eve was made of Adam's rib; that differences in languages began with the building of the Tower of Babel. When Darrow accused Bryan of accepting "fool ideas that no intelligent Christian on earth believes," Bryan replied that he was trying "to protect the word of God from the greatest atheist and agnostic in the United States."

None of the scores of reporters at the Scopes trial enjoyed it so thoroughly as H. L. Mencken, who covered the proceedings for the Baltimore *Sun*, and the figure of Bryan inspired him to some of his most effective efforts: "This old buzzard, having failed to raise the mob against its rulers, now prepares to raise it against its teachers. He can never be the peasants' President, but there is still a chance to be the peasants' Pope. He leads a new crusade, his bald head glistening, his face streaming with sweat, his chest heaving beneath his rumpled alpaca coat. One somehow pities him, despite his so palpable imbecilities. It is a tragedy, indeed, to begin life as a hero and to end it as a buffoon. But let no one, laughing at him, underestimate the magic that lies in his black, malignant eye, his frayed but still eloquent voice. He can shake and inflame the ignoramuses as no other man among us can shake and inflame them, and he is desperately eager to order the charge."

The jury found Scopes guilty. A higher court upheld the decision, then freed him on a technicality. Bryan, the practicing Prohibitionist, died a week after the trial ended—a victim of overeating. In his youth he had declared, "No man can make a million dollars honestly." He left behind an estate valued at more than that unholy sum.

The Scopes trial received world-wide attention during the brief time it lasted. The case of Sacco and Vanzetti received greater attention over a longer period. Nicola Sacco was an Italian-born shoe-factory worker; Bartolomeo Vanzetti an Italian-born peddler. Both promoted anarchist propaganda; Vanzetti had something of a reputation as a speaker. The police of Brockton, Massachusetts, picked them up in May, 1920, with anarchist pamphlets in their possession. The prisoners gave evasive answers and found themselves accused of having killed a paymaster and factory guard in South Braintree three weeks previously. Witnesses readily identified Sacco, who had no distinguishing features, as one of the men in the murder car; they had more difficulty with Vanzetti and his sweeping mustaches. But an ambitious District Attorney got him convicted, without evidence, of having taken part in a similar attempted holdup in Bridgewater the year before. Sacco's factory time-card proved he could not have taken part in the Bridgewater affair.

Sacco and Vanzetti went on trial at Dedham, Massachusetts, on May 31, 1921. Communists, no less eager than the District Attorney to have the men convicted, took charge of their defense and brought in a Western lawyer who bungled the case. The Yankee jury found both men guilty; Judge Webster Thayer, who presided at the trial, said to a group of friends afterward, "Did you see what I did to those anarchistic bastards the other day?" The Communists had their martyrs; Judge Webster Thayer had his victims. Not for the first time—nor for the last—the extreme radical and the extreme reactionary pursued the same path toward opposite goals. But William G. Thompson, a liberal Boston lawyer of impeccable social position and professional reputation, took over from the Communists, and a much wider Sacco-Vanzetti defense committee was organized. For seven years, Thompson staved off the execution, while the laws of the Commonwealth of Massachusetts made it possible for Judge Thayer to prevent any other judge or court from passing on his conduct of the trial.

UNDERWOOD

Sacco and Vanzetti

Finally, in the summer of 1927, new evidence implicating known criminals and new information about the doings of Sacco and Vanzetti on the day of the murder forced Republican Governor Alvan T. Fuller of Massachusetts to appoint a three-man advisory group to review the case and make recommendations. They included President A. Lawrence Lowell of Harvard, President Samuel W. Stratton of the Massachusetts Institute of Technology, and Robert Grant, a retired judge of the probate court. The committee, dominated by Lowell, ignored the new evidence, disregarded Judge Thayer's prejudice, and upheld the original conviction.

Meanwhile all over the world Sacco and Vanzetti became the subjects of mass demonstrations. Felix Frankfurter, then a professor at the Harvard Law School, wrote the article in the *Atlantic Monthly* that forced Governor Fuller's hand. John Dos Passos, Edna St. Vincent Millay, and other writers came to Boston to demonstrate their sympathy. Heywood Broun, popular columnist on the liberal New York *World*, lost his job when he described Lowell as a hangman. Most of the best people in Boston reacted to outside interference like any other lynch mob anywhere on earth. Yet it was Vanzetti who had the last word in his last statement, expressed in the broken English he spoke to the end: "If it had not been for this thing, I might live out my life among scorning men. I might have die, unmarked, unknown, a failure. Now we are not a failure. This is our career and our triumph. Never in our full life can we hope to do such work for tolerance, for joostice, for man's understanding of man, as now we do by an accident. Our words—our lives—our pains— nothing! The taking of our lives—lives of a good shoemaker and a poor peddler—all! The moment that you think of belong to us—that last agony is our triumph."

The Sacco-Vanzetti case showed how bitterly the old New England Yankees hated the new Italian immigrants and how much they resented outside interference in their affairs. Local spirit fanned the flames of class prejudice. But the issues of the Sacco-Vanzetti case never played any part in any major political campaign in the United States; only in Europe did the two men become symbols of proletarian righteousness and victims of American capitalist oppression. The Scopes trial, on the other hand, released a spirit of religious bigotry that figured prominently in the Presidential campaign of 1928.

In the summer of 1927, Coolidge reveled in a supreme act of political self-indulgence. While on vacation in the Black Hills of North Dakota he unexpectedly summoned the press and handed out this ten-word statement on twenty-five slips of paper: "I do not choose to run for President in 1928." Neither then nor later did he add a single syllable to this declaration. His refusal to make any move for a nomination that he could have had for the asking—a nomination that the Republican Party and its big-business leaders hoped to confer upon him—finally set the stage for Herbert Hoover, his Secretary of Commerce. Coolidge had no special liking for Hoover. Neither did the professional politicians. But Hoover had a devoted personal following and had built up a strong personal organization during his eight years in Washington. No one else had a chance and he won on the first ballot.

Alfred E. Smith, four times Governor of New York, overcame powerful enemies inside and outside his Party to win the Democratic nomination as easily as Hoover won the Republican. Smith's record in New York had earned him a reputation as a first-rate executive with a genius for dramatizing political issues. He came from the rough-and-tumble Fulton Fish Market section of Manhattan and attended only a few grades of grammar school. His Irish Catholic parents lived in poverty, but from them and from his Church he learned to follow a strict code of personal honesty in his public and private life. He came up through the Tammany organization without a taint of its corruption. He had risked his political future by denouncing Hearst. His knowledge of the State Constitution earned him the praise of Elihu Root. At the 1924 Democratic Convention, Franklin D. Roosevelt, still in the early stages of recovery from a severe attack of infantile paralysis, had described Smith as "the Happy

Warrior" in an eloquent nominating speech. John J. Raskob, of General Motors, took charge of Democratic Party finances and many well-to-do Republicans prepared to jump the reservation and vote for Smith, who favored amending the Volstead Act but not the Fordney-McCumber Tariff. Smith did, however, come out for the McNary-Haugen Farm Bill and conducted a much more aggressive campaign than the constricted Hoover. The words "Let's look at the record" became Smith's trade-mark and caused his audiences to yell with delight. But most Americans did not care too much about the kind of record Smith called to their attention. Babe Ruth's home run record interested them more. And Smith's partiality to such mispronunciations as "raddio" irked the half-educated shabby-genteel, who also resented his stout wife, his brown derby, his cigar, and his Tammany background. His campaign song, "The Sidewalks of New York," made him few friends west of the Hudson or below the Mason-Dixon line.

Almost any Republican could have beaten almost any Democrat for the American Presidency in 1928. Never in history had the party out of power triumphed during a period of prosperity. Moreover, the Republicans nominated their ablest and—next to Coolidge—their most popular man. In 1920 many Wilson men were prepared to vote for Hoover either as a Democrat or as a Republican because his reputation as an administrator and humanitarian transcended party lines. During his eight years as Secretary of Commerce he won the support of the business community and built a strong, personal machine inside the Republican Party. The Democrats selected a more controversial candidate. Al Smith's frank opposition to the Volstead Act and his fine record as a humane administrator in New York State won him the support of the independent progressives to whom Wilson owed his two White House terms. Smith got fifteen million votes—more than any candidate of either party had ever received before. The Democrats also won unprecedented majorities in the big cities. But Hoover got over twenty-one million votes and carried all but eight of the forty-eight states. Smith lost such traditionally Democratic Southern states as Texas, Virginia, North Carolina, and Florida as well as Tennessee and Kentucky. In the North he won only Massachusetts and Rhode Island. He even lost his own state of New York as well as the entire West and Midwest. His challenging personality brought out a record vote; his Roman Catholic faith turned the bulk of that great vote against him.

In the rural South the Protestant Fundamentalists who cheered the conviction of Scopes in 1925 voted Republican for the first time in their lives. Religious bigotry and provincial suspicion overrode party loyalty and traditional tolerance. Harding, Coolidge, and their big-business masters had done so little to encourage any unifying, national spirit that

UNDERWOOD

Alfred E. Smith and Anthony Eden on the Empire State Building Roof

millions of voters succumbed to local prejudice. This was no regional neurosis, peculiar to the more backward regions of the South. The people of New York State who rejected their Roman Catholic Governor for the presidency chose a Protestant Democrat to succeed him at Albany—Franklin D. Roosevelt. The historic importance of the 1928 Presidential election in the United States was not that Hoover and the Republicans won. Nothing could have stopped them. But the 1928 election showed the continuing power of religious bigotry in prosperous America.

Al Smith's fellow Catholics drew the logical conclusions. Up to that time most of them shared the views of Cardinal Gibbons of Baltimore, Archbishop Ireland of St. Paul, and Cardinal Hayes of New York, who had preached and practiced the American ideal of separation of church and state, always assuming that if Roman Catholics loyally accepted that ideal, they would enjoy the same liberties and opportunities as all other Americans. The 1928 election disproved this assumption. It vindicated Pope Leo XIII, who had condemned the heresy of "Americanism" back in 1899. The higher Vatican authorities had always agreed with Pope Leo; so did Cardinal O'Connell of Boston, whose diocese contained a Roman Catholic majority, dominated by an Irish-American priesthood. In the New York diocese of Cardinal Hayes, on the other hand, the Roman Catholics formed a minority and pursued different tactics, and it was in this diocese that Al Smith received his schooling in religious tolerance. Now, the non-Catholic majority of the American people had given the most convincing kind of proof that even a follower of Cardinal Hayes could not expect from his fellow citizens the same kind of tolerance he showed toward them. Henceforth, the Roman Catholic Church proceeded to serve its communicants in the United States by the militant promotion of its own aims in those areas where its influence predominated and by pressure-group tactics everywhere else.

· V ·

AT THE HEART of Coolidge's domestic policy lay his determination to limit the power of the federal government and to give business its head. The same determination possessed him in his dealings with other parts of the world. His *Autobiography* contains no mention of foreign affairs. Other countries held no interest for him; he never traveled outside the United States. What little he achieved for America abroad other men achieved for him. What little he attempted on his own momentum failed. Like Senator W. Murray Crane, his first important backer, Coolidge wanted the United States to join the League of Nations and never shared Lodge's hatred of Wilson. In March, 1925, the House of Representatives voted 303 to 28 in favor of a resolution urging American membership in the World Court. The Senate then added five amendments and likewise approved the resolution by a vote of 76 to 17. Even in its original form, the resolution had the support of the American Bar Association, the American Federation of Labor, and the Federal Council of Churches of Christ in America. The League, however, to which the Court was bound, refused to accept all the amendments that the Senate had added; Coolidge supported the Senate and in December, 1926, announced that the issue was closed. Elihu Root continued to work, without success, on a formula to bring the United States in.

Coolidge next turned his attention to naval disarmament. By 1927 Japan had fourteen cruisers under construction, Britain thirteen, the United States two. To save money and to promote peace, Coolidge urged that the Japanese and British scale down their cruiser-building programs and summoned a conference at Geneva to extend the naval limitation treaty of 1922 to include cruisers as well as capital ships. After six weeks of futile Anglo-American bickering, the meeting ended in a deadlock, as the British remarked that the Americans could have cruiser parity any time they wanted to spend the necessary money. The Senate took the hint and appropriated 250 million dollars to start work on fifteen cruisers. The controversy lent some color to extremists of the right and left, who predicted inevitable war between Britain and the United States. It was a thesis set forth with equal passion by Colonel Robert R. McCormick, editor of the superisolationist Chicago *Tribune*, Leonard J.

Maxse, editor of the super-Tory *National Review,* and Leon Trotsky, apostle of the permanent revolution.

The question of war debts added to the friction between the United States and Europe throughout the 1920's. Coolidge summed up his own views in the classic phrase, "They hired the money, didn't they?" The amount in dispute totaled more than eleven billion dollars—seven of it the result of wartime borrowing, four of it money lent to Europe after the 1918 Armistice. In 1923 the British agreed to settle their debt of more than four billion dollars and to pay interest charges of 3.3 per cent for a period of sixty years. The other Allied Powers slowly, reluctantly, followed suit, but they paid lower interest rates—Italy settling for less than half of one per cent. In 1921 the Germans had agreed in principle to pay reparations of thirty-three billion dollars, but in practice none of the European debtors ever paid the United States more than they received from Germany. Moreover, the Germans never paid in reparations anything like the equivalent of the two and a half billion dollars that Americans lent them during the Coolidge years. Abroad, the United States earned the name of Uncle Shylock. American newspapers preferred Uncle Sap.

In March, 1925, Hughes retired as Secretary of State and Coolidge replaced him with Frank B. Kellogg, for whom he had acquired considerable respect. Kellogg had practiced law in Minnesota, busted trusts with Teddy Roosevelt, served in the Senate from 1917 to 1921, and favored American participation in the League with fewer reservations than Lodge demanded. In 1923 Coolidge appointed him Ambassador to Great Britain after several other people had refused the job and came to like him so much that he made him Secretary of State. Kellogg had a fine head, a noble brow, and deep-set eyes, but his stooped, gnarled figure and fussy, timid ways earned him the nickname "Nervous Nellie." When he succeeded Hughes, Taft wrote: "I am very sorry to have Secretary Hughes leave the State Department. He was a great Secretary, one of the ablest we have ever had, as he was a great Judge and a great Governor. Mr. Kellogg is by no means his equal, but Mr. Kellogg is a hard-working, clear-headed lawyer, with some experience on the Foreign Relations Committee of the Senate, and with his recent experience as Ambassador to England, I doubt not he will make a very safe adviser for the President, though he will not be the brilliant representative of our Nation in the State Department we have had in Mr. Hughes. Mr. Hughes retires for the purpose of amassing a competence for his wife and family."

Kellogg left a single monument to commemorate his four years as Secretary of State: the pact to outlaw war that bore his name and that of Aristide Briand of France. Briand launched the project on April 6, 1927, the tenth anniversary of the American declaration of war upon Germany, when he proposed to Kellogg that France and the United States exchange pledges never to go to war against each other. Senator Borah then urged Kellogg to extend the agreement to all other countries and "Nervous Nellie" finally consented. On August 27, 1928, fifty-three nations, including Britain, France, Germany, Russia, Italy, Japan, and the United States, agreed to "renounce" war "as an instrument of national policy in their relations with one another" and to settle "all disputes or conflicts of whatever nature or of whatever origin they may be" exclusively "by pacific means." The agreement had no force behind it; it called for no economic sanctions; it made no mention of the League of Nations. In the United States it attracted more attention than an international tennis or golf match; not so much as a heavyweight championship boxing bout or a baseball World Series.

Kellogg also claimed credit for the outstanding diplomatic achievement of the Coolidge administration—Dwight Morrow's mission to Mexico City. In 1924 Plutarco Elías Calles replaced General Obregón as President of Mexico and proceeded to infuriate the Roman Catholic Church and the foreign colony by strictly enforcing the 1917 Constitution. "I am an enemy," said Calles, "of the priestly class which considers its position in the light of privilege and not of evangelical service. I am an enemy of the political priest who tries to keep our people submerged in ignorance, the priest who is allied with the landlord to exploit the peasant, and the priest who is allied with the employer to exploit the worker." In 1926 the Archbishop of Mexico declared that his Church rejected the 1917 Constitution in so far as it limited the number of priests and forbade foreign priests to enter Mexico. Calles retaliated by deporting foreign-born priests and nuns and turning monasteries into public schools, whereupon the Church announced that it would hold no services. At the same time, Calles also began to enforce the 1917 land law that forbade foreigners to own rights in the subsoil wealth of Mexico. The smaller foreign oil companies agreed to forfeit their titles to the fields they exploited while still keeping them in production. The bigger companies refused to make retroactive concessions to the Mexican government and closed down.

William Randolph Hearst owned vast tracts of land in Mexico and his newspapers opened a campaign for armed American intervention, even going so far as to publish a collection of forged documents that accused four noninterventionist Senators of having accepted million-dollar bribes from the Mexican government. Doheny and Fall echoed Hearst's war-whoops but the agitation boomeranged as Coolidge invited his Amherst classmate, Dwight Morrow, to go to Mexico City as Ambassador and work out a peaceful settlement. Kellogg mistakenly believed that he originated the Morrow mission—a belief Coolidge never discouraged.

"After Morrow come the Marines," the Mexican press predicted, but Morrow not only resigned his Morgan partnership; he threw himself into public service as he had thrown himself into the law and banking during the earlier stages of his career. To his son he once wrote: "The world is divided into people who do things and people who get the credit. Try, if you can, to belong to the first class. There's much less competition." Morrow had always followed this advice himself, and so, on this occasion, did Coolidge, who gave him a completely free hand in Mexico. As a result, the credit went to Morrow, where it belonged, when his personal approach to Calles and his friendly attitude toward the Mexican people led to satisfactory compromises on the church and land laws. "I know one thing I can do for the Mexicans," commented Morrow just before he left. "I can *like* them."

While Coolidge snored away the afternoons in Washington, Morrow busied himself in Mexico City arranging for good-will visits by Lindbergh and Will Rogers, whose proudest boast was "I never met a man I didn't like." The Mexicans met these evidences of friendship more than halfway, as the new Ambassador by-passed his State Department attachés. "Cookie-pushers," he called them, "with the milk of Groton still wet upon their lips." Morrow, following his own instincts, bought a private house and interested himself in the native arts. After three years, his good offices prepared the way for a settlement of the church-state dispute and a resumption of Roman Catholic worship throughout the country.

Coolidge called in another New York lawyer to ease an equally troubled situation in Nicaragua. Henry L. Stimson had served as Secretary of War under Taft and commanded his own regiment in the war, but never saw action. In the 1920's he returned to his private law practice until Coolidge invited him to go to Nicaragua, where a civil war had raged sporadically for some years. Both the major Nicaraguan parties asked the United States to intervene, and welcomed a small body of Marines as the best hope for peace. Stimson then appeared as arbitrator and arranged for an orderly election in 1928. He seemed to have won an easy success until the troops of General Sandino, a bandit-revolutionary of the Pancho Villa type, attacked the United States Marines. Kellogg called Sandino a Bolshevik and accused Mexico of backing him. Anti-imperialist Senators denounced Coolidge, Kellogg, and Stimson, but the Sandino rebellion presently fizzled out.

Stimson's success in Nicaragua earned him a much more important assignment in the Philippines, where General Leonard Wood had served as Governor General since 1921. Wood had abolished the native Council of State that the Wilson administration had encouraged the Filipinos to create as a further step toward independence. Wood also kept overriding the wishes of the native legislature and at one point the entire native Cabinet resigned. Coolidge ordered an investigation and Wood came home, where he died of an operation for tumor on the brain. The investigation suggested giving the Filipinos a few concessions, and Coolidge appointed Stimson as Governor General. Stimson restored the Council of State, gave the native legislature more power, and generally conciliated the Filipinos. The truth was that American big business did not want to hold on to the Philippines forever. The local land laws had discouraged heavy American investments; importation of duty-free sugar and other raw materials from the Philippines alarmed the protectionists; the Islands had proved useless as a base to promote American exports in the Far East; the cost of administering them increased year by year. By the late 1920's American self-interest and Philippine self-government had become almost identical.

At home and abroad Coolidge took the same line of least resistance to big-business pressure. At home, this meant curtailing the power of the federal government; abroad, it meant curtailing the national power of the United States. Just as Coolidge encouraged—usually by inaction— the speculative boom on Wall Street, the extension of installment selling, and tax reduction for the rich, so in the foreign field he put up no real fight for American membership in the World Court, tried to save money by promoting naval disarmament, and offered as his sole contribution to world peace the Kellogg-Briand Pact, which cost no more than it was worth. On the more positive side, he encouraged American loans to Europe and South America. He backed away from dollar diplomacy in the Western Hemisphere and from imperialism in the Philippines because they cost too much money and entailed too many risks. American businessmen had long since lost faith in the doctrine of "manifest destiny," preached by Roosevelt, Beveridge, and Lodge at the turn of the century. Morrow's Morgan partners did not regard him as a turncoat because he appeased Mexico. Quite the opposite. It seemed to them good business and sound common sense to come to terms with Mexico's revolutionary leaders.

Coolidge inaction at home divided America against itself by encouraging the growth of religious bigotry, local pride, and special interest. Coolidge inaction abroad weakened America in world affairs because the country refused to follow a clear, strong line in any direction. Yet Coolidge's inaction at home had not prevented a nation-wide boom in the arts and sciences any more than his inaction abroad was able to seal off the culture of the United States from the rest of the world. What if Coolidge himself ignored books and authors, paintings and artists, music and musicians? What if he had never contaminated his lungs with foreign air? Sinclair Lewis won the first Nobel Prize for Literature ever awarded to an American. American scientists won similar honors in their specialized fields. The Moscow Art Theater toured the principal American cities. Dr. Coué of France became a household word with his formula of "Every day in every way I am getting better and better." German movie directors and actors taught Hollywood tricks it never knew. Paris still set the styles for women's fashions; London, for fashions for men. Most important of all, American tourists flocked across the Atlantic in ever-increasing numbers.

Congress had cut down immigration from Europe to a trickle. But the steamship companies made up for their loss of steerage revenue by catering to tens of thousands of middle-class, middle-income Americans who could "do" Europe in a few summer months for a few hundred dollars. The United States Senate had rejected the League of Nations; Coolidge made no attempt to overcome its aversion to the World Court. Yet the people of the United States took a growing interest in other countries, and those who could not visit them read and heard more about them through newspapers, books, magazines, movies, the theater, and the radio. Americans invested more money abroad than they borrowed from their brokers to play the market. Exports, during the 1920's, averaged eight billion dollars a year—more than one tenth of the total national income. In theory, the United States had reverted to isolation in 1920. In practice, this isolation proved as elusive as Harding's normalcy, as short-lived as Coolidge's new era. Too few Americans saw, in the 1920's, that their prosperity depended upon other countries as much as other countries depended upon them. Once more, events abroad intruded upon the American dream.

SUMMING UP

The teachings of Karl Marx suffered an ironic fate during the 1920's. The Soviet leaders made Marxism the official state religion while violating Marxist precepts at every turn of the tortuous Communist Party line. The leaders of the United States ignored Marx while American life conformed with many of his predictions. American capitalists withheld so much "surplus value," as Marx called it, from the American people that Coolidge prosperity never reached the masses. Inveighing against class conflict, Mellon put through a tax program that widened the gulf between rich and poor and aggravated social discontent. The surface prosperity of Coolidge's new era concealed and intensified frictions and tensions at home and abroad. The exclusion of the majority of Americans from the boom made little sense morally and still less economically. The nation that invented mass production had failed to solve the problem of mass distribution.

The best that Coolidge could do was keep the petty defects of his petty nature under control and out of sight. His virtues, not his vices, plagued him. Shyness and humility no less than fear and caution kept him isolated from the bold, creative spirits of his time. Frank recognition of his own shortcomings prevented him from giving the American people any sort of lead. American big business gloried in this absence of political constraint—to its own hurt. The wiser men of business wondered where the speculative boom would end. The wiser bankers warned against the overextension of American credits abroad. The leading writers felt themselves virtual enemies of society. Some of them brooded with Anderson and Dreiser; some chose exile with Ernest Hemingway; some sought escape in pleasure with Scott Fitzgerald; most of them preferred to enjoy the show with H. L. Mencken and Sinclair Lewis. But all of them—even the exiles, the rebels, and the cynics—retained pride in their American inheritance. The artists, the scientists, the scholars found plenty to do at home while trying at the same time to become citizens of the world.

The chief distinguishing feature of American life during the later 1920's was also its chief weakness. No common spirit possessed all the people. The individual felt isolated. Lacking any national leadership, Americans tended to split into rival groups. Protestants stressed their differences with Catholics, Fundamentalists fought modernists. Children rebelled against their parents. The divorce rate doubled. Respectable citizens patronized bootleggers, and organized crime took over the city of Chicago as well as many lesser communities. Coolidge's America dissipated its ever-growing vitality, yet the whirling dynamo of its prosperity acted like a world gyroscope that served to stabilize many distant lands.

New Economic Policy

*How Lenin's New Economic Policy saved Russia
from chaos and set the stage for Stalin to consolidate his power when Lenin died.*

PREVIEW

T HE RUSSIAN REVOLUTION survived its final crisis in the spring of 1921
when the threat of complete breakdown forced Lenin to install the
New Economic Policy at home and to abandon world revolution abroad.
In 1922, as Lenin's mind and body began to fail, Stalin began to gain
control of the all-powerful Communist Party. When Lenin died, in 1924,
Stalin applied his master's ruthless methods in new directions, and proceeded to eliminate all rivals, one by one, beginning with Trotsky. In
1928 he announced a Five-Year Plan to replace the New Economic
Policy as the effects of the revolution spread beyond the political and
economic sphere and transformed religion, education, the arts and sciences, even home life. What Lenin had begun Stalin carried forward.

· I ·

THE FIRST new religion of the twentieth century did not originate with
the pious Wilson, the saintly Gandhi, or the inspired Einstein. It remained for the antireligious Lenin and his cynical disciple, Stalin, to
create a faith for which millions were prepared to live and die. The letter
of this faith stressed material progress, especially for the toiling masses,
as devout Communists ridiculed the old-time religion with its promises
of "pie in the sky bye and bye." Yet the failure of the Bolsheviks to provide the Russian people with bread in the here and now served only
to increase Communist zeal. The spirit counted for more than the letter;
the promise outweighed the performance. In 1921 the territory under
Soviet rule was producing only about one third as much food and less
than one fifth as many factory goods as before the war. The productivity
of the average Russian worker slumped to one third of the prewar level.
Revolution, starvation, and disease had taken at least ten million lives,
on top of more than two million soldiers killed in action. In 1921 and

UNDERWOOD

Leon Trotsky (in fur hat) Addressing Moscow Crowd

1922, more famines took another five million lives. Walter Duranty, who had covered the fighting on the Western Front, felt that this experience helped him when he began covering postwar Russia for *The New York Times:* "For all my ignorance of Russia, I believe that I was better equipped for it than I realized. The war in France had taught me a measure of indifference to blood and squalor and fear and pity. Sudden death had become a commonplace and vermin a joke." Yet the Communist leaders under whom the Russian people continued to suffer steadily increased their power and spread their faith.

They had their troubles. On March 5, 1921, the sailors at the Kronstadt Naval Base near Petrograd attempted an anti-Communist uprising. "The autocracy has fallen," they proclaimed. "The Constituent Assembly has departed to the regions of the damned. The commissarocracy is crumbling." But the men around Lenin crushed the Kronstadt mutineers more ruthlessly than the men around the Tsar ever crushed similar uprisings led by prewar Nihilists and Social Revolutionaries. Lenin scornfully dismissed the mutiny as a plot by White Guard generals. Trotsky ordered General Tukhachevsky to send sixty thousand picked Cheka troops and military cadets against the rebellious sailors. On March 17 Tukhachevsky reported that he had crushed the mutiny. "I was in the war five years," he said later, "but I cannot remember such a slaughter. It was not a battle but an inferno."

Bloodshed, as such, had never bothered Lenin. The lives of Mensheviks and Social Revolutionaries meant no more to him than the lives of Grand Dukes. Only the revolution mattered. But the Kronstadt mutiny cost the lives of men who might have become good Bolsheviks. It raised the possibility of mass defections within the Bolshevik movement itself. Lenin drew the necessary conclusions and decided that the time had come to slow down a revolution that might go the way of the French Revolution and destroy itself by devouring its own children. He therefore informed the Tenth Congress of the Communist Party that the government must adopt what he called the "New Economic Policy." He admitted that the peasants had failed to supply the cities with enough bread. "I regret it," he frankly acknowledged, "because our experience, which is not very long, proves to us that our conception was incorrect. Our New Economic Policy means that in applying our former methods we suffered defeat and had to begin a strategic retreat. Let us retreat and construct everything in a new and solid manner; otherwise we shall be beaten." The defeat the Bolsheviks suffered when they "tried to pass over into Communism" seemed to Lenin "more serious than any we ever suffered against the armies of Kolchak, Denikin, and Pilsudski." But, he continued, if any Menshevik rose to remark, "The revolution has gone too far; we have always said what you are saying now, permit us to say it again," Communists must reply, "Permit us to put you up against the wall for saying that."

Lenin spared neither himself nor his hearers: "Some of the things we were compelled to do by necessity. . . . We did much that was simply wrong." He could see no alternative to retreat: "We are living in such conditions of impoverishment and ruin, of overstrain and exhaustion of the principal productive forces of the peasants and the workers that for a time everything must be subordinated to this fundamental consideration—at all costs to increase the quantity of goods. The New Economic Policy means a transition to the restoration of capitalism to no small degree. In what degree we do not know. The fundamental question from the point of view of strategy is, who will the sooner take advantage of this situation? Who will win? The capitalist whom we are now letting in through the door or even through several doors which we ourselves ignore and which will open independently of us and against us? Or the proletarian sovereign power?" It had to be one or the other. Intellectually, Lenin saw the world in blacks and whites only. But as a practical politician he recognized the need for constant compromise. He did not apply the New Economic Policy as he had tried to apply the dogmas of Marx and Engels.

To many of Lenin's orthodox Party comrades, the New Economic Policy seemed like heresy if not treason. It permitted peasants to trade freely in any produce that the government did not claim for tax purposes. It allowed small enterprisers to start workshops and factories employing twenty persons or less. Foreign capital was invited to return to Russia on a short-term basis. Lenin, who had come to power on the slogan "All power to the Soviets," now remained in power with the slogan "Learn to trade." But if he made some compromises in practice, he made none in purpose. The end still justified the means, and the larger factories, the mines, and the heavy industries remained in the hands of the state. A new class of "Nepmen" enriched themselves as production of many consumer goods doubled and trebled in less than a year. Zealous Communists shook their heads; foreign capitalists rubbed their hands. But who would laugh last?

Not the critics or enemies of Lenin. The New Economic Policy, with all its improvisations and compromises, at least served its purpose. It got the workers and peasants producing again. It also ended the agony of War Communism. This was the ruthless, makeshift system the Bolsheviks had set up, during the civil war and intervention of 1918 and 1919, while fighting off their enemies at home and abroad. In the name of War Communism, the Bolsheviks restored compulsory overtime and piecework; they assigned all workers over sixteen to jobs; they requisitioned food from the peasants and set up collective, state farms. But the factory workers stole materials; they stripped their shops of furniture, even of windows; they set up private enterprises of their own, on the side. More than half of these factory workers eventually drifted back to the farms from which they had come, perhaps only five or ten years before, and joined the peasants in withholding food and refusing to work with the new regime. "We have created an atmosphere of general idleness and criminal negligence," Maxim Gorky warned the readers of *Pravda* in 1920. "We have never worked so ill nor so dishonestly as at present."

In replacing War Communism with the New Economic Policy, Lenin merely substituted one stopgap measure for another. Neither of these two emergency devices promised to do more than stave off complete defeat for the revolution. Even after the Bolsheviks began to call themselves Communists, the most they dared promise was not Communism but Socialism, for Communism refers to the classless society that will come into being in some distant future when the power of the state has withered away. Socialism, on the other hand, refers to the transitional period when the state, acting as trustee for the proletariat, takes possession of the whole productive apparatus—the land, the factories, the transport system, and all natural resources—until such time as all classes vanish and humanity moves from the realm of necessity into the realm of freedom. Lenin and his Bolshevik comrades all shared this clear vision of mankind's future destiny. They all agreed, also, that only the Communist Party could lead mankind into this future. But it remained for Lenin to devise and justify the ruthless zigzag tactics the Communists used to reach their goals.

· II ·

AT THE SAME TIME that Lenin put his New Economic Policy into effect at home, Foreign Commissar Chicherin gave Russia a new foreign policy. In April, 1920, he began sending out a series of notes to China, Persia, Turkey, and Afghanistan renouncing all the special privileges, claims, and territories that the Tsars had always demanded. While the British and the French tried to restore the prewar colonial order, the Russians posed as the protectors and liberators of all backward peoples. Chicherin took up Wilson's slogans and signed new treaties with King Abdullah, the shifty ruler of Afghanistan; with the upstart tyrant, Riza Shah Pahlevi of Persia; and with Turkey's President Kemal. These treaties cut some ground out from under the British in the Middle East and made up for some of the losses that the Russians had suffered in the West.

The Comintern took a stronger line. In September, 1920, Zinoviev told a Congress of Eastern Peoples at Baku: "China, India, Turkey, Persia, and Armenia can and must make a direct fight to get the Soviet system. . . . You who are met here together for the first time in a congress of the peoples of the East must here and now declare a true, holy war against the English and French robber capitalists." These words from the president of the Comintern did not send any part of Asia up in flames, but they increased Russian prestige, promoted general unrest, and put the British and French on the defensive.

The Soviet Foreign Office and the Comintern followed the same double policy in western Europe. Local Communists continued to make a nuisance of themselves, especially in Germany, but as capitalism appeared to have survived the war, the rulers of Russia put less emphasis on promoting revolution and tried, instead, to sign trade agreements and win full diplomatic recognition from the West. In March, 1921, the British government ended the blockade that had contributed to the starvation of some ten million men, women, and children and signed a trade agreement with the Soviet government. A year later came the Russo-German Treaty of Rapallo. Russian and German military leaders had begun co-operating in 1920 when the Germans agreed to help reorganize the Red Army after its defeat by the Poles outside Warsaw. By 1926, the German Reichswehr was spending more than one third of its budget in Russia. It chief reorganizer, General von Seeckt, demanded a full Russo-German military alliance. Many German firms built plants in Russia: Junkers put up three airplane factories; Krupp secured an oil concession in the Caucasus; Hugo Stolzenberg built a poison gas plant; Dr. Fritz Haber helped the Russians reorganize their chemical warfare service.

On April 24, 1926, Stresemann and Krestinsky, the Soviet Ambassador, signed a treaty at Berlin that went far beyond the Rapallo agreement of 1922. The two countries pledged each other to remain neutral if either one was attacked and not to join any boycott if war did break out. Lord D'Abernon, who had bet everything on Stresemann and feared a Russian-German combination as he feared the plague, wrote in his diary at the time of the Stresemann-Krestinsky pact "I still hold that prolonged co-operation between the German Right and the Russian Left is unthinkable, but I must admit that the other night at the Russian Embassy, I was somewhat shaken to see how many gentlemen there were with stiff military backs and breasts bedecked with Iron Crosses, all partaking freely of Soviet champagne."

The people of Russia got no champagne and little enough bread. Even by 1926 living standards had not reached prewar levels. Between fifteen and twenty-five million farm workers sought better jobs. Some seven to nine million homeless children wandered through the cities and countryside. A spokesman for one of the villages had dared, in the early 1920's, to blame the Communists and to complain to the Third All-Russian Congress of Soviets: "The land belongs to us, the bread to you; the water to us, the fish to you; the forest to us, the timber to you." By 1926, however, no oppositionist dared raise his voice in public, and in the Politburo the power once wielded by Lenin had fallen into the hands of Stalin, who had already proved himself the one man supremely qualified to apply his master's methods on an ever-widening scale.

· III ·

"REMEMBER MY WORDS," Lenin once told his friends, "I will end in paralysis." In 1920 and 1921 headaches, insomnia, and vertigo affected him more and more. In May, 1922, he suffered his first stroke, which left him unable to speak, although by the end of the summer he had improved so much that doctors allowed him to work five hours a day five days a week and to preside over the Council of People's Commissars that governed Russia and over the Political Bureau that controlled the Russian Communist Party. In December, 1922, he suffered a second and more severe stroke and turned his duties over to a triumvirate of Stalin, Zinoviev, and Kamenev, who, together with Lenin and Trotsky, comprised the all-powerful Politburo. In Lenin's eyes, Stalin and Trotsky overshadowed all other Party leaders, and Stalin had greater claims than Trotsky to preferment. Unlike Trotsky, Stalin had never differed openly with Lenin. Unlike Trotsky, Stalin had belonged to the Bolshevik faction since the early 1900's. Most important of all, Stalin in 1922 proved himself a supreme political realist by maneuvering himself into the position of General Secretary of the Russian Communist Party. To his more intellectual colleagues, it looked like a dull, routine job for which the loyal, industrious Stalin appeared well suited. Even so hostile a critic as Ruth Fischer found good things to say of him in *Stalin and German Communism* at this stage of his career:

"In 1922, Stalin had a good reputation in the Russian Party. He was an intimate friend and pupil of Lenin, he was an 'old Bolshevik,' he came from the rank and file. He had lived in Russia during exile, he neither was nor wanted to be a brilliant writer, theorist, or orator. He was a matter-of-fact organizer with a down-to-earth pragmatism, with vitality and energy, not a socialist tribune in the European style. He was known by the upper brackets of the hierarchy; on the Central Committee he managed a thousand Party affairs with skill, seeking and sometimes finding a common denominator between the Party organizations in the provinces and the center. Since the Party cadres wanted him to be General Secretary Lenin had no serious political or personal reason to force another choice."

By December, 1922, Lenin had begun to regret the appointment: "Comrade Stalin, having become General Secretary, has concentrated an enormous amount of power in his hands; and I am not sure that he always knows how to use it with sufficient caution." But Lenin also had misgivings about Trotsky. Although Lenin described Trotsky as "the most able man in the present Central Committee," he found fault with Trotsky's "too far-reaching self-confidence and a disposition to be too much attracted by the purely administrative side of affairs." What Lenin feared was that Stalin's rudeness and Trotsky's cockiness might "quite innocently" lead to a Party split, and since Trotsky had always held somewhat aloof from the other Communist leaders, concentrating on his job as War Commissar, Lenin approved the selection of a new, ruling triumvirate of Stalin, Zinoviev, and Kamenev, with Stalin as its keystone. Zinoviev possessed oratorical gifts, intellectual brilliance, and international experience. Kamenev had served as Lenin's deputy, and his good nature and good manners made him personally popular. But Zinoviev was a physical coward; Kamenev an intellectual one. Although Stalin lacked their more engaging qualities, he possessed the rudimentary virtues associated with the name he had chosen for himself —steel.

As Commissar of Nationalities since the Bolshevik seizure of power in 1917, Stalin had dealt steadily with almost half the inhabitants of the Soviet Union. He had also been made head of the Workers' and Peasants'

Inspectorate, a gigantic snooping organization set up to combat administrative inefficiency. A new Soviet Constitution, based largely on Lenin's theories and practices, ostensibly transformed the remains of the Tsarist Empire into a confederation of seven Republics, known as the Union of Socialist Soviet Republics. The Russian Socialist Federated Soviet Republic covered more territory and contained a larger population than all the other six put together, but Russia did not impose its language, customs, and culture on all these regions as it had under the Tsars. It was not Russia; it was the Communist Politburo that dominated the new confederation.

The Soviet Constitution did not mention the Communist Party. The Constitution assigned all power to the local Soviets which elected provincial Soviets; the provincial Soviets elected the Congress of Soviets; the Congress of Soviets elected the Council of People's Commissars. Between this hierarchy and the people of the Soviet Union stood the Communist Party. It was Lenin who conceived of the Communist Party as an elite of professional revolutionaries who would establish a temporary, iron dictatorship over the masses as the prelude to final, complete emancipation. Under Lenin's slogan of "All Power to the Soviets," the Bolsheviks had liquidated all classes in Russia except the peasants and workers and had subordinated the peasant majority to the minority of industrial workers. Under Lenin's leadership, the Bolsheviks then liquidated all rival political parties and set themselves up as the new Communist Party, with affiliates all over the world. Still under Lenin's leadership, the Communists extended their control over the Soviets where the peasants and workers voted by a show of hands. Those who did not vote Communist stood in danger of losing their jobs, their living quarters, and their ration cards. Those who threatened opposition found themselves in trouble with the Communist-controlled Cheka, or secret police, which the new Constitution reorganized and enlarged as the Unified State Political Bureau, or OGPU.

The Council of People's Commissars over which Lenin presided gradually faded to a mere puppet government. "All Power to the Soviets" shriveled to a dead slogan. Control shifted from the Council of People's Commissars to the Central Committee of the Communist Party and from the Central Committee to its Political Bureau, or Politburo. The Congress of the Communist Party, not the Congress of the Soviets, shaped the policies of the Soviet Union, and Stalin as the Party's General Secretary became the most powerful individual in the new setup. Bukharin, the official theoretician, described the Russian Communist Party as "entirely apart from and above everything." With a cynicism worthy of Lenin he pointed out: "Under the dictatorship of the proletariat, two, three, or even four parties may exist, but on condition that one of them is in power and the rest in prison." B. D. Riazanov spoke for many of the Bolshevik old guard to which he belonged when he said of the Central Committee: "The English Parliament can do anything except change a man into a woman. Our Central Committee is more powerful—it has already changed more than one extremely revolutionary man into a woman, and the number of these women has increased incredibly."

Lenin on his sickbed saw more clearly than the healthiest of the Old Bolsheviks. The Russian Revolution, under Stalin's leadership, was not turning soft. It was hardening into a new kind of dictatorship. In January, 1923, after rallying from his second stroke, Lenin added a postscript to the "Political Testament" he had written his Party comrades the month before; calling Stalin "rude" and "insupportable," he urged his removal from the post of General Secretary and the substitution of "another man who in all respects differs from Stalin, only in superiority —namely more patient, more loyal, more polite, and more attentive to comrades, less capricious, et cetera." On March 5, 1923, Lenin dictated a note to his secretary declaring that he had broken "all personal and comradely relations with Stalin." But Lenin never recovered sufficient strength to pursue the matter further. A third stroke ended his life on January 21, 1924.

The secret of Lenin's genius lay in his unique capacity for making the lowest methods serve the highest purposes. There also lay the secret of his final failure. Lenin devoted his whole life to promoting revolution, to creating better conditions for human life here on earth. Hatred of capitalism consumed him; hope for socialism sustained him. He despised all forms of organized religion and believed in human perfectibility and material progress. Moses, Jesus, and Mohammed sought to make their fellow men aware of God's kingdom, which is not of this world. Lenin put all the same zeal into convincing his fellow men that they themselves made their own heaven and their own hell in this life on this world and nowhere else. It was not Lenin's materialist philosophy that proved his undoing; it was the ruthless methods he used to carry it out. For Lenin had no faith in democracy as such; he regarded most proletarians as dumb, driven cattle; he despised even the majority of those who called themselves Bolsheviks. He counted entirely on a small group of disciplined, professional revolutionaries to overthrow capitalism, install the proletarian dictatorship, and prepare the way for the ultimate classless Utopia. Among this select company he permitted free discussion, confident that the power of his own intelligence and the purity of his own purpose would always prevail.

The early course of the Russian Revolution vindicated Lenin's theory and practice. Lenin had not hesitated to use criminals, stool pigeons, and gigolos to further the revolution in Tsarist times. During the summer of 1917 he had no scruples about accepting German gold; the following year he also accepted, under heavy coercion, the German Peace of Brest-Litovsk. When the world revolution failed to materialize after the Armistice, he turned first to War Communism and then to the New Economic Policy. The more intellectual of Lenin's colleagues sometimes found his inconsistency hard to rationalize. The more scrupulous found his ruthlessness distasteful. Only Stalin accepted the inconsistency and the ruthlessness as a matter of course. He had no use for hair-splitting intellectuals or for squeamish moralists. Intellectuals used words to convey ideas; moralists used words to convey emotions; Stalin used words to get practical results. Their meaning, their significance, their promise meant nothing.

To the intellectuals—above all to Trotsky—Stalin seemed stupid, mediocre, sullen. Actually, Stalin carried over the theory and practice he had learned from Lenin into a new situation. Before the Bolsheviks gained power, they had to justify and rationalize their actions—and Lenin did just that with a minimum of hypocrisy and a maximum of cynicism. But to gain power was one thing; to hold power something else again. In gaining power the Bolsheviks had championed certain ideas, and the ruthlessness of Lenin's methods matched the sincerity of his faith. But once the Bolsheviks had gained power only one thing mattered: to hold it. This was where Stalin came in. All the leading Bolsheviks, save only Stalin, believed their own propaganda. They regarded the Party as the mere instrument to make their propaganda come true. To Stalin, on the other hand, the Party came first; it was an end in itself. The world revolution, the dictatorship of the proletariat—these were mere words that had but one use, to perpetuate the Party's power.

"You must reach the understanding," Stalin declared on one occasion, "that of all the precious assets existing in the world, the most precious and decisive are the cadres." He referred here to the small fighting units into which Communists everywhere always organize themselves, and it was this party within the party that Stalin considered of supreme importance. His rationalization of the omnipotent one-party state also threw light on his devious mental processes: "We are in favor of the state dying out, and at the same time we stand for the strengthening of the dictatorship of the proletariat which represents the most powerful and mighty of all forms of state which have existed up to the present day. The highest possible development of the power of the state with the object of preparing the conditions for the dying out of the state: that is the Marxist formula." These words may have hypnotized some Communist intellectuals and bewildered some non-Communists. To Stalin, however, and to the men around him these words meant that they did not expect the shadow of the Soviet state to lessen in their time.

· IV ·

THE DEATH of Lenin early in 1924 gave Stalin his first chance to push himself forward as Lenin's successor: he arranged to deliver the official funeral oration. The former student for the Orthodox priesthood understood how to go about making Communism the religion of the twentieth century: "We Communists are people of a special type. We are carved out of special matter. We are those who form the army of the great revolutionary strategist, the army of Comrade Lenin. There is no higher honor than to belong to this army. There is no loftier title than member of the Party of which Comrade Lenin was the founder and director. It is not given to everyone to be the member of such a Party. It is not given to everyone to endure the misfortunes and the storms involved in belonging to such a party. The sons of the working classes, sons of poverty and struggle, sons of incredible privations and heroic efforts—they are the men to be members of such a party. That is why the Leninist Party, the Communist Party, calls itself the party of the working classes."

Having represented the Party leaders and the Party members as a kind of priesthood, Stalin went on to represent Lenin as the founder of a new religion, using language that recalled the litanies he had repeated as a youth in the Tiflis seminary:

"In leaving us, Comrade Lenin commanded us to hold and keep pure the great name of Member of the Party. We swear to thee, Comrade Lenin, to honor thy command.

"In leaving us Comrade Lenin ordered us to conserve the unity of our Party as the apple of our eye. We swear to thee, Comrade Lenin, to honor thy command.

"In leaving us Comrade Lenin ordered us to maintain and strengthen the dictatorship of the proletariat. We swear to thee, Comrade Lenin, to exert our full strength to honor thy command." And so on.

Stalin had lost, long since, whatever faith he may once have had in orthodox Christianity, without accepting orthodox Marxism as the twentieth-century equivalent of religion. For Stalin had no great capacity for belief of any kind. He lacked the necessary imagination. Stalin did, however, have the professional politician's unwavering loyalty to the boss. He had complete confidence in Lenin's methods and understood, better than Lenin's other heirs, how to apply these methods to the Russia that Lenin had done so much to create. In at least one respect, Stalin surpassed his master. He made no attempt to address logical appeals to the minds of the Russian people. He preferred to speak only to their emotions, sometimes in the language of religion, sometimes in the language of the advertising billboard. To glorify the name of Lenin, Petrograd was renamed Leningrad. Smaller cities and towns were given such names as Lenino, Leninsk, Leninskaya, Leninakan. When other Bolshevik leaders had died, their bodies had been cremated. Not so Lenin's. His remains were embalmed and placed on permanent public display in a mausoleum in Moscow's Red Square. Soon devout pilgrims by the thousands, by the tens of thousands, and eventually by the millions made their way to this shrine, as Moslems made pilgrimages to Mecca or Roman Catholics to Rome. Pictures of Lenin replaced the family icon in millions of Russian homes. During his lifetime, Lenin had exclaimed to a friend, "I find it difficult to read the papers. Wherever you look they write about me. I consider

UNDERWOOD

Joseph Stalin (left) and Maxim Gorki

this completely un-Marxist emphasis on an individual extremely harmful. It is bad, entirely inadmissible, and unnecessary. And these portraits? Everywhere! What is the purpose of this?" He had even less use for religion, calling it "a sort of spiritual liquor, meant to make the slaves of capitalism drown their humanity and their desires for a decent existence." Yet in death, Lenin's teachings became holy writ; his mausoleum a shrine.

Lenin's widow, the devoted Krupskaya, protested against the unseemly deification of her dead husband: "Do not let your sorrow for Ilyich find expression in outward veneration of his personality. Do not raise monuments to him or palaces to his name, do not organize pompous ceremonies in his memory." She accepted Lenin at his own valuation, and she was revolted when his former comrades turned the cynicism they had learned from their master against its creator: "In his lifetime, he took little account of that kind of thing, which distressed him. Remember how much poverty and disorder there still is in our country. If you seek to honor the name of Vladimir Ilyich, create crèches, children's playgrounds, houses, schools, libraries, ambulances, hospitals, houses of refuge, etc., and, above all, realize his teachings in your lives." Alas, the heirs of Lenin, with Stalin at their head, realized his teachings only too well. Their master had urged them to have no scruples about what means they used to gain their ends. Now that they had gained these ends, now that they had established themselves in power, the perpetuation of that power became an end in itself, to be held with the same measures by which it had been gained.

Stalin quickly proved his right to succeed Lenin by a series of maneuvers that first split and then annihilated his rivals. He began by warning Zinoviev and Kamenev, with whom he shared power, of the danger of Trotsky. All Russian Bolsheviks, having studied the history of the French revolution, had become obsessed with the fear of military dictatorship, with the prospect of what they called Bonapartism. Because Trotsky, as Defense Commissar, had the support of the Red Army, Stalin encouraged the rumor that Trotsky aspired to become the Russian Napoleon. Yet Trotsky, when Lenin died, resembled Hamlet rather than Napoleon. He was at Tiflis on his way to the Caucasian Riviera for a rest cure when he received a telegram from Stalin informing him of Lenin's death. A mood of doubt and indecision at once overcame him. For reasons never made fully clear, Trotsky could not bring himself to hasten back to Moscow and cut a figure at the funeral. Instead, he continued on his way, leaving the resolute Stalin free to dominate a fluid situation. It seemed as if Trotsky had lapsed back into the same fit of gloom that seized him back in 1919 when Dora Kaplan's attempt to assassinate Lenin caused him to exclaim: "When we think that Lenin may die, our whole life seems useless, and we cease to want to live."

No such doubts afflicted Stalin, who lost no time in poisoning Zinoviev and Kamenev against Trotsky. This he accomplished so successfully that he soon found himself holding them in check, since he believed in making haste slowly. Stalin could also intimidate Zinoviev and Kamenev by reminding them that they had voted against seizing power in November, 1917, just as they could all intimidate Trotsky by reminding him that he had not joined the Bolshevik Party until 1917.

Zinoviev owed his prestige to the fact that he had lived with Lenin in exile and to his position as secretary of the Comintern. He excelled as an orator, but he had a bad reputation for cowardice. Kamenev owed his prestige to his attractive personality and to the fact that he had served as Lenin's deputy since 1922. The Politburo was presently extended to include Tomsky, head of the Russian Trade Unions; Rykov, the most respected Soviet politician; and Bukharin, the top theorist and the most popular man in the Party. These three men all wanted to continue the New Economic Policy, to slow down the tempo of the revolution inside Russia, to soft-pedal world revolution and the Comintern. Zinoviev and Kamenev disagreed. Like Trotsky, they argued that the revolution inside Russia must be speeded up again and that more use should be made of the Comintern. But Stalin had isolated Zinoviev and Kamenev from Trotsky, their natural ally, and thus felt free to proclaim the new doctrine of socialism in one country. "The victory of socialism is possible even in a country relatively undeveloped from the capitalist point of view," said Stalin in 1924.

This marked a clear and clean break with the doctrine laid down by Lenin in May, 1918: "We do not close our eyes to the fact that we cannot achieve the socialist revolution in one country alone, even if that country were less backward than Russia, and even if we lived under easier conditions. . . . We are deeply convinced that in the near future, historic events will bring the West European proletariat to supreme power." When the world revolution hung fire, Lenin adopted emergency measures. "We must learn to trade," he finally advised as he came to terms with the unexpected. It remained for Stalin to define and stabilize the situation that Lenin had helped to create. Stalin therefore proclaimed that socialism in one country must take precedence, for an indefinite period, over world revolution. He did not exclude the possibility of world revolution, perhaps even at an early date, but he did not assume that world revolution lay just around the corner.

At the same time, Chicherin tried to tempt foreign concessionaires to invest money in Russia: "Enrich yourselves. Let us say in the words of Guizot: 'Enrich yourselves.' For in this way we enrich ourselves." The foreigners, however, remained unimpressed, many of them agreeing with what Balfour said to Chicherin at one of the conferences they both attended: "Bolshevism is an excellent method of making rich men poor but a questionable method of making poor men rich." Meanwhile Stalin blew hot and cold with disconcerting frequency. In the fall of 1924 he declared, "The workers are moving toward revolution and demand revolutionary leadership." The following March he changed his tune: "Capitalism has succeeded in recovering from the postwar shock." But within another year he decided that "If the Dawes Plan is pregnant with revolution for Germany, the Locarno Pact is pregnant with a great European war."

When Stalin made alarmist statements, he did so purely for effect and not because he believed what he said. According to his secretary, B. Bazhanov: "Stalin did not confide his innermost thoughts to anybody. Only very rarely did he share his ideas and impressions with his closest associates. He possessed in a high degree the gift of silence, and in this he was unique in a country where everybody talked far too much." Especially Stalin's political enemies of the Trotsky type, who in their intellectual pride mistook his silence for stupidity. For Stalin's reticence, like his other qualities, always served his underlying lust for power. As Lenin lived only to advance the cause of revolution, Stalin lived only to advance himself. "He loves neither money nor pleasure, neither sport nor women," wrote Bazhanov. Stalin's singleness of purpose, no less than his ruthlessness of method, made him Lenin's successor.

In December, 1925, Stalin planted three more supporters in the Politburo—the cautious Mikhail Kalinin, who dressed himself up to look like his peasant forebears; the poker-faced General Klementi Voroshilov, a close associate from the civil war period; and the dogged Vyacheslav Molotov, who had shrewdly attached himself to Stalin since the earliest stages of the revolution. Kamenev was demoted to the position of deputy, and Zinoviev had joined Trotsky in the opposition. The Stalinists now outnumbered the anti-Stalinists in the Politburo seven to two.

Too late, Zinoviev and Kamenev recognized that Stalin had out-maneuvered them. Too late Zinoviev admitted that he made the mistake of his life when he split with Trotsky in 1924. According to popular legend, Trotsky surveyed Lenin's tomb and remarked: "He is alive, though dead, and I am dead though alive." Nevertheless Trotsky argued against Stalin before the Politburo and even wrote pamphlets, of ever more restricted circulation, accusing him of betraying the revolution. Trotsky attacked Stalin's halfhearted support of the German Communists, his preference for coming to terms with the German Republic and even with the Reichswehr leaders. Stalin supported Pilsudski's Polish *coup d'état* in the spring of 1926. He subordinated the Chinese Communists to the Kuomintang from 1924 until 1927, when the Kuomintang exterminated more than one hundred thousand Communists in one of the great social upheavals of the century. Trotsky also called for speeding up Russia's industrialization and collectivizing Russia's farms. His words, of course, made little impression. He was expelled from the Party in 1927, exiled to Siberia, and finally deported to Turkey in 1929. Zinoviev and Kamenev were also ousted from the Party at the same time.

Whereupon Stalin performed another somersault. In 1928 he turned against his moderate supporters—Rykov, Tomsky, and Bukharin—and swung over to an even more radical domestic program than Trotsky had advocated. Ever the nationalist rather than the internationalist, he announced a "Five-Year Plan" to modernize Russian industry and mechanize Russian farming on the theory that the Soviet Union, with its own resources, could overtake and surpass the capitalist world. He stilled the opposition by warning against the immediate danger of war and raising hopes of immediate revolution. "The foremost problem at the present time," said Stalin in 1927, "is the danger of a fresh outbreak of war." And again: "We live on the eve of a new revolutionary upsurge both in the colonies and in the older countries." He did not himself anticipate either war or revolution in the near future. He did, however, anticipate that the changes he kept ordering in the Party line might produce a serious split in the Politburo, and his predictions of war and revolution tended to silence disagreement. The removal of Tomsky, Rykov, and Bukharin from the Politburo also enabled Stalin to promote three more of his hand-picked alternates to full membership and to select new alternates of proven loyalty.

Did Stalin use his power for any other purpose than to increase it? Did he seek any ultimate purposes, hold to any underlying convictions? The record of his performance through the 1920's shows him clinging to a few fixed principles. He had an instinctive distrust of the Party intellectuals—writers like Trotsky, orators like Zinoviev, theoreticians like Bukharin. But to accuse him, as Trotsky did, of suffering from an inferiority complex is to miss the mark. Boris Souvarine conceded in his generally hostile biography, *Stalin,* "When all is said, Stalin had the advantage over his fellow Bolsheviks of knowing in his heart his own shortcomings, a silent modesty which is not incompatible with the self-confidence he displayed in his actions as dictator. He still attached a certain importance to the benefit to be derived from the ideas, talent, and activity of the men he disparaged." In *Stalin: A Political Biography* Isaac Deutscher, an admirer of Trotsky, wrote Stalin down as a revolutionary pessimist: "The revolutionary optimist sets his hope on his frank appeal to the people, even when he may seem to hope against hope. The pessimist in power distrusts those whom he rules. The Communist pessimist treats his own doctrine as a piece of esoteric knowledge. He does not believe that the working classes are really capable of accepting it unless it is, brutally speaking, pushed down their throats."

Stalin's background and character disposed him toward revolutionary pessimism. Unlike Lenin, he had never lived in western Europe and exposed himself to its faith in social progress, its belief in human perfectibility. Stalin learned his Marx from the printed page, but he had known Lenin in the flesh and regarded Leninism as the fulfillment of Marxism: "Leninism is Marxism of the era of imperialism and of the proletarian revolution. To be more exact, Leninism is the theory and tactics of the proletarian revolution in general, the theory and tactics of the dictatorship of the proletariat in particular." Stalin disagreed with the Communist intellectuals who kept looking westward for signs of the approaching world revolution. Stalin preferred to concentrate on Russia and when he looked for symptoms of world revolution, he directed his eyes to the East. In 1919 he wrote two articles, "Do Not Forget the East" and "Ex Oriente Lux." In the first he asserted: "Once and for all you must learn the truth that he who wants the triumph of socialism cannot forget the East," and in the second: "The West with its imperialist cannibals has become the center of darkness and slavery. The task is to destroy that center, to the joy and jubilation of the toilers of all countries."

Like Lenin, Stalin distrusted the Social Democrats, but beneath this distrust lay his hatred, fear, and jealousy of western Europe. When Mussolini's Fascism came along, just as Lenin lay dying, Stalin evolved the mechanical theory that Fascists and Socialists were equally the servants of the capitalists: "Fascism is the militant organization of the bourgeoisie

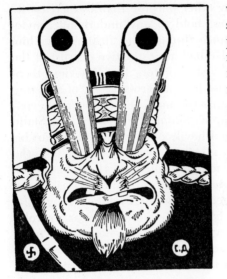

*The "Eyes" of Fascism and Social De-
mocracy Leveled at the Five-Year Plan.
From* Vecherniaia Moskva, *Moscow*

which bases itself on the active
support of Social Democracy. Objectively, Social Democracy is the
moderate wing of Fascism. There
is no reason to suppose that the
militant organization of the bourgeoisie can achieve any decisive
successes without active support
from Social Democracy. There is
just as little ground to think that
Social Democracy could achieve
decisive successes without the active support of that militant organization of the bourgeoisie. Those
organizations do not contradict
but supplement one another. They
are not antipodes but twins." Yet
Stalin's strictures against Social
Democrats did not prevent him
from coming to terms with German generals who supported the
Weimar Republic or with Polish landowners who supported Pilsudski.

This decision proceeded from a logic that Stalin's more brilliant critics
chose to ignore. For the purpose of day-to-day nuisance value—if for no
other—Stalin had to give some support to Communist Parties in other
countries. This meant, as he had learned from Lenin, fighting the Socialists who continued to compete against the Communists for working-class
support. But Stalin did not want and did not expect either widespread
revolution or general war. He assumed that peace among nations and
within nations would continue more or less indefinitely and he decided
to resume the revolution that Lenin's New Economic Policy had interrupted inside the Soviet Union. Kalinin, the cautious peasant leader, had
no real faith in the turn Stalin took toward the left in 1928: "He chatters
about veering to the Left, but in a short space of time he will have to
apply my policy threefold. That is why I support him." Lenin's widow
took a darker view. In 1927 she declared that if her husband were still
alive "he would probably be in a Stalinist prison."

Nor was Krupskaya the only close associate of Lenin who came to
believe that Stalin had betrayed the revolution. First Trotsky, then
Zinoviev, and finally Bukharin broke with the man who inherited Lenin's
power. Although these men expressed horror at Stalin's ruthlessness, all
of them had resorted to equal ruthlessness when it suited their purposes
to do so. They could lay no claim to moral superiority. Neither could

they invoke the principle of majority rule or democratic procedure. They had worked as zealously as Stalin to establish Communism and destroy democracy—all under the leadership of Lenin. Stalin did not, therefore, differ from his rivals in the methods he used to gain his ends. He differed from them in the ends he sought. For Lenin had not only organized the revolution that Stalin inherited. Lenin originated nearly all the theories and practices that Stalin applied and enlarged after his death. And here Stalin showed himself the most clear-sighted of Lenin's heirs. He devoted himself first to securing complete personal control of the whole Party machinery—and thus of the whole Soviet state. Not until he had gained this control did he reveal his own policy. His rivals either let themselves become his pawns or they advocated rival policies that they lacked the power to put through. Before the 1920's had ended, Stalin thus made himself the new master of the new Russia and had announced a Five-Year Plan that aimed, by 1933, to bring Russian factory and farm production up to higher levels than they had reached under the Tsars. Was it for this that the Russian Revolution of 1917 had shaken the world?

· V ·

ALTHOUGH the Russian Revolution set out to improve the lot of the common man, its chief accomplishments during the first ten years of its existence lay in other fields. From the moment the Bolsheviks seized power they waged unceasing war on all organized religion—not as tolerant agnostics, but as militant atheists. The revolution withdrew all subsidies the state formerly paid the Orthodox Church and acquired many Church properties, transforming former places of worship into antireligious museums. Just as many countries gave religious instruction in state schools, so revolutionary Russia instructed its young people in atheism. The Communists exposed fake relics—wax bodies of saints stuffed with cotton that the priests formerly displayed, for a fee, to the faithful. The Communists also held mock festivals at Christmas and Easter, singing familiar hymns with new words, ridiculing Jesus, Mary, and the saints. They paraded in the streets carrying puppets representing Jehovah, Buddha, and Allah which they would finally desecrate and destroy. No child under eighteen could work on any Church property or receive baptism in any faith. Restrictions of this kind applied to Jews and Moslems as well as to Christians; to Protestants and Roman Catholics as well as to members of the Eastern Orthodox Church. Some priests adapted themselves as best they could; others joined the counterrevolutionaries and met death at the hands of firing squads. The Communists never quite dared to liquidate religion by main force as they liquidated the landowners and the bourgeoisie, but their subsidized campaigns against religion won over most of the younger generation and caused unnumbered millions of the suspicious and faint-hearted to lose whatever faith they had.

In place of the old faith in God, Communists preached a new faith in "dialectical materialism." As originally used by the ancient Greeks, the word "dialectic" meant the art of argument by means of questions and answers. But Hegel and Marx used dialectic to describe a process of thesis, antithesis, and synthesis, of action, reaction, and combination, that they detected at work everywhere. Hegel saw history proceeding by a process of trial and error, onward and upward, until the human race finally achieved the perfect synthesis in the Prussian state. But Hegel's glorification of Prussia rested on a philosophy of idealism. Marx turned Hegel upside down and used the dialectical process to justify a philosophy of materialism. Hegel saw history as a series of conflicts between abstract ideas. Marx saw history as a succession of class struggles. According to Marx, the conflicts of feudal society gave birth to bourgeois society, and the conflicts of bourgeois society would give birth to a classless proletarian society. With the triumph of the proletariat all classes would vanish and all class conflicts cease. By calling this line of argument "materialistic," the disciples of Marx convinced themselves that they had cut loose from Utopian idealism. Yet Dante's vision of Paradise, Purgatory, and Inferno in the world to come looked no more fanciful than the visions of this world that the Marxists accepted—not as revealed religion but as scientific fact.

"Our ultimate aim," wrote Lenin, "is the elimination of the state and therewith all organized and systematic power. The state can be entirely done away with if men will only become so conscious of the basic rules of their common life as to work, of their own free will, in accordance with their capacities. We shall then go beyond the narrow horizon of bourgeois law, which, with the hardheadedness of a Shylock, makes a man hesitate to work half an hour longer than his fellows. The distribution of commodities will render unnecessary any fixing by society of the share of the individual. Everyone will be able to take all he wants, freely according to his needs."

In order to liquidate the bourgeois state, Lenin made the proletarian state all-powerful. In order to abolish all existing religions, Lenin established a new religion of his own. Yet he called the Marxist program scientific because it repudiated all existing churches, spurned idealism, and concerned itself with the material world of the five senses. "Modern physics," Lenin wrote, "is in travail. It is bringing dialectical materialism to birth." In mathematics, he continued, it is plus and minus; in mechanics action and reaction; in physics positive and negative electricity; in chemistry attraction and repulsion of atoms; in the social sciences

Russian Posters of Mid-1920's Showing Man and Machine

class war. Ten years before Lenin made these assertions, the most advanced physicists had already denied the assumptions on which they rested. The point is not that the physicists were right and Lenin wrong. The point is that Lenin accepted certain scientific principles not as working tools but as immutable truths. What distinguishes the man of science from the man of faith is not that the man of science is a materialist and the man of faith an idealist. The distinction is that the man of science seeks working principles which he keeps discarding as he pursues his unending search for new and better principles, whereas the man of faith proclaims an eternal principle, and if the facts do not fit that principle, so much the worse for the facts. Lenin and his followers attacked organized religion not with the weapons of science and reason but with the weapons of faith. Hence their power and their success.

This new faith made itself felt in all spheres of Russian life. "Figures of gods and heroes," wrote an architect named Tatlin, "are not consistent with the modern conception of history; they are unfitted to symbolize the present age, which has to do with mile-long columns of proletarians. At the best, they enforce the character, feeling, and method of thought of a revolutionary hero, but they must fail to give expression to the concentrated sentiment of a collective thousand-headed mass." Tatlin recommended "the monument of the machine"; sculpture, he declared, "must go beyond the representation of the individual, and spring from the spirit of collectivism." Tatlin prepared drawings of cylindrical buildings with rotating rooms, and façades that looked like an amusement park roller-coaster. Other architects designed spacious, vast housing projects for the proletariat, but few of them ever took shape for lack of materials, engineers, and skilled construction workers. For the capitalist's pie in the sky, the Communist substituted blueprints on the drawing boards.

The poets, playwrights, and musicians of the revolution did not labor under so many handicaps as the architects. The government and the Party stood ready to subsidize their work. Vladimir Mayakovsky, the outstanding poet of the revolution, won universal fame with his poem, *150 Million.* Before the Revolution, Mayakovsky had shown a certain affinity for the advance guard of Paris writers who later gave birth to the Dada movement. He had written a love story entitled *A Cloud in Trousers* and a collection of satirical verses, modestly entitled *Mayakovsky Laughs, Mayakovsky Smiles, Mayakovsky Makes Merry.* Came the revolution, and Mayakovsky sang a different tune:

> *"One hundred and fifty million:*
> *That is the name of the composer of this poem.*
> *The rattling of shot and shell:*
> *That is its rhythm.*
> *Squalls of fire flung zig-zag,*
> *Fire-damp, booby traps,*
> *Mine explosions, bursting,*
> *House leaping on house—*
> *I am a talking machine.*
> *Paving stones whirl about.*
> *Let your tread press the soil*
> *Jangling like letters of the alphabet:*
> *One hundred and fifty million:*
> *Stamp!!*
> *And thus this edition was printed here."*

The theater, in which the Russians had always excelled, lent itself more readily than literature to proletarian propaganda and the glorification of the collective mass. The Soviet government did not withdraw its support from the classical opera, ballet, and symphony as it had withdrawn its support from the Orthodox Church. Stanislavsky's Moscow Art Theater continued its meticulously realistic performances of Gorky, Chekhov, and Ibsen. But Meyerhold, who had learned all that Stanislavsky could teach him about naturalism in the theater, led a movement in the opposite direction, presenting rewritten versions of the classics and new propaganda plays against cubist backdrops and scenery that moved back and forth to suggest the rhythm of the action. Meyerhold discarded conventional stage furniture for impressionistic scaffolding or for real guns and motorcycles. His actors wore silk hats, bow ties, underwear, and skirts; his actresses got themselves up in hodgepodge clown costumes. The plays dealt with episodes from the Russian Revolution and from Russian history, featuring long quotations from Lenin's speeches and writings. But these plays proved so empty and mechanical that they gave way to dances, pageants, and finally acrobatics. Some theaters eliminated the stage altogether; the performances took place in the middle of the hall and depended more and more on gymnastic equipment. The Dada movement in western Europe burned itself out in a year or two. The disintegration of the Russian stage continued for half a decade. It was not so much a process of decay as a process of breakdown in which new techniques kept succeeding one another, each more absurd than the one before. The audiences, half starved for food, took what pleasure they could from the varied dramatic fare offered by the new regime, and the classics lost none of their popularity as time went on.

While the revolution invaded the Russian theater, the theater invaded the daily lives of the Russian people. The Communists kept staging pageants in the large squares of the large cities and sending propaganda trains and theaters to the provinces. They showed their contempt for monuments of an earlier day by concealing them behind wooden and canvas frames, scrawled with cubist designs and revolutionary slogans. Posters covered the walls of houses and public buildings. Communist Russia, which aspired to equal capitalist America in the field of mechanization, surpassed capitalist America in the field of billboard art. And middle-class intellectuals created the proletarian culture in which Russia's Communist leaders took such pride.

During the 1920's, Russian Communists used the word "culture" as freely and as loosely as the chairman of any program committee of any women's club in the American Midwest. In the Soviet Union, as in the capitalistic United States, culture covered almost every variety of social activity. Ella Winter, for example, quoted in *Red Virtue* a card entitled "Behave Culturally in the Refectory" that she found on the factory dining tables of Nizhni Novgorod:

1. Wash your hands before meals.
2. Don't put your hat or your brief case on the table.
3. Don't eat or drink with anybody out of the same dish.
4. Don't take salt from the saltcellar with your fingers.
5. Don't take mustard with your own knife or fork.
6. Don't scatter on the table bits of food or cigarette stubs.

7. Carry the plate so that you don't dip your fingers in it.

8. Don't spit and don't put rubbish on the floor.

All of which added up to nothing more nor less than a proletarian version of Emily Post's book of etiquette which enjoyed, at the same time, a wide circulation among America's newly rich. Revolutions come and revolutions go; culture marches on.

· VI ·

NOWHERE did the determination of the Communists to create a new, proletarian culture go to such extremes as in the field of music. "When I sit in the Great Theater," wrote Sosnovsky, a leading Communist critic, "and hear the music and look at the red-gold magnificent hall, something rankles in my mind: 'No, no, not that.'" Here was what this good Party man preferred: "A Soviet Congress is one of the greatest symphonies the world has ever known. The composer of the symphony is the hundred and fifty million population of our great country. The performers are the thousands of the best sons of this nation. The soloists—the few really gifted men in the history of the world. Each symphony is different from every other. Who heard Symphony No. 2 on October 26, at the Smolny in St. Petersburg? To my great regret I was unable to be present at this unforgettable and incomparable performance. The Decree of the Peace, the Decree on the Land, and the Repudiation of Foreign Debts—these three chords were enough to shake humanity to the depths of their hearts and to split them into two camps—the friends and enemies of Soviet Russia."

Sergei Prokoviev, one of the few Communist composers with a reputation outside Russia, added to his fame after the revolution, but some of his comrades dashed off in new directions. A group calling themselves "machine worshipers" held a music festival in the Moscow Trade Union Palace, with an orchestra made up of sirens, turbines, motors, and whistles. But even this seemed too constricted. René Fülöp-Miller in *The Mind and Face of Bolshevism,* from which much of this material is drawn, reported that the promoters of "proletarian music" tried to reach the population of a whole district. "The factory whistle was, in their opinion, best adapted to be the new and predominant orchestral instrument, for its tone could be heard by whole quarters and remind the proletariat of its real home, the factory. It was not long before theoretical discussions were put into practice; as early as 1918 experiments with factory whistles of this kind were tried in Petersburg and later in Nizhni-Novgorod. But the first performance on a large scale took place in Baku, on November 7, 1922. The foghorns of the whole Caspian fleet, all the factory sirens, two batteries of artillery, several infantry regiments, a machine gun section, real hydroplanes, and finally choirs in which all the spectators joined, took part in this performance. The festival is said to have been very impressive; it is not surprising that this 'music' could be heard far beyond the walls of the town of Baku."

Neither Lenin nor Trotsky encouraged the more extreme versions of proletarian culture. Trotsky argued that no socialist culture could exist until a socialist society had come into being; meanwhile the proletariat must master artistic techniques. "The bourgeoisie," he pointed out, "understood very well; they used literature and art in the interests of their class, and attained their object by never losing sight of the artistic point of view." Lenin had still less patience with the promoters of "Proletcult." He regarded most of the efforts to create a new, proletarian, Soviet culture as a waste of time and preferred to concentrate on teaching the masses to read and write. Here much needed to be done. In 1900 more than 75 per cent of the Russian people could neither read nor write; by 1918 the rate of illiteracy stood at almost 70 per cent. The Communists therefore resolved to wipe out all illiteracy by 1927.

They made a good beginning. In 1919, Communist Russia had twice as many schoolteachers as Tsarist Russia, but the famines of 1921 and 1922 led to a breakdown of the Russian educational system. In 1920, 75 per cent of all Russian children under the age of eleven were attending school. By 1922, less than half were getting even an elementary education. It took several more years for the Communist crusade against illiteracy to get going again, and during those years millions of Russian children roamed the countryside in homeless marauding bands. The Russian universities soon felt the effects of the new order. Marxist courses in the social sciences replaced courses in philosophy, history, law, and theology, as hundreds of professors who refused to teach the Communist version of Marxism lost their jobs and emigrated. But the government tried to make life as comfortable as possible for distinguished scientists, like Professor Pavlov, provided they did not openly attack the regime. Students gained entrance to universities on the basis of competitive examinations, although the children of workers and peasants received special opportunities. Members of Communist youth organizations received extra instruction as future Party leaders.

In addition to attacking religion and reforming education, the Communists emancipated women. The Soviet Constitution gave women equal political and economic rights with men, including the right to vote in their local Soviet elections, to hold political office, and to receive equal pay for equal work. The Communist Party welcomed women to membership. The attempts to give women social equality had more unfortunate results. Under Soviet law either the husband or the wife could unilaterally declare their marriage dissolved at any time. Remarriage required a divorce, and that could be gained if both husband and wife registered with the same office at which they were married. If one party did not want the divorce, the other could appeal to a judge. Theoretically, this freed the wife from bondage to her husband. In practice, it permitted the husband to abandon his wife although both remained responsible for any children they might have. Soviet law tried to remedy this situation by legalizing abortions.

These new laws covering marriage, divorce, and abortion had no precedent and gave rise to lurid stories in the foreign press about Russia's "nationalized" women. The Russian press preferred the story of the man whose divorced wife haled him into court. The judge ordered him to pay her one third of his earnings as alimony. "I can't," he replied, "I'm already paying it." "Then pay her two-thirds," said the judge. "I can't, I'm already paying it," the man replied. "Then pay her three-thirds." "I can't, I'm already paying it." "Then what are you living on?" shouted the judge in despair. "Oh," the man replied, "I'm living on the alimony my present wife is obtaining from five other men."

Unmarried younger people carried on much more freely than their parents ever had, and a woman contributor to *Pravda* went so far as to declare: "Every young Communist, even every member of a labor faculty whose aim it is to raise the intelligence of the working classes, every man or girl considers it axiomatic that in affairs of love they should put the least possible restraint upon themselves." The strait-laced Lenin disapproved of the new laxity in sexual morals: "Certainly thirst must be assuaged, but does a normal person, under normal conditions, lie in the street and drink from mud puddles? Or even from a glass that dozens of other people have been drinking from? Our future generation disturbs me greatly." Trotsky, in 1925, wrote in the same vein: "Family relations are being shattered. Some big process is going on, very chaotic, assuming alternately morbid or revolting, ridiculous or tragic forms, but they have not yet had the time to disclose their hidden possibilities."

The effect of the Russian Revolution on sexual morals and family life affronted Lenin and Trotsky to the depths of their bourgeois souls. Having met and mastered political and economic breakdown, they lacked any new proletarian morality to take the place of the bourgeois morality which they had encouraged the revolution to destroy. In the name of the revolution, they had justified bloodshed, destruction, crime. They had welcomed the suppression of religion. Meanwhile, years of mass misery, mass famine, and mass migration were turning millions of boys and girls loose on the Russian countryside. The Russian Revolution did not give rise to an orgy of proletarian lust but to a breakdown of family life which the Communists tried to check by the literal application of assorted feminist doctrines imported from the West. The ensuing confusion found

Lenin and Trotsky talking like a couple of bourgeois moralists. It was not the first time their insight into human nature surpassed that of their revolutionary comrades.

· VII ·

MOST REPORTS on Russia that reached the outside world during the 1920's went to one of two extremes. Some listed only the unique achievements of the revolution; others consisted of nothing but atrocity stories. Both contained some truth, almost the same truth. It was that the Russian Revolution had destroyed one civilization and laid the groundwork for another. But it had not yet run its course, nor had the terrible price it cost yet been paid in full.

The 1920's in Russia opened with the New Economic Policy and closed with the Five-Year Plan. The New Economic Policy slowed down and even reversed the progress of the revolution. It gave the small merchant, trader, and manufacturer a brief whirl of prosperity. It eased the pressure on the peasants. The proclamation of the First Five-Year Plan in 1928 brought the New Economic Policy to an official end. It had two purposes: first, to collectivize and nationalize Russian agriculture; second, to build up Russian industry. The farm progam came down hard on the peasants who had prospered under the New Economic Policy. The industrial program came down hard on almost everybody because it called for the diversion of about one quarter to one third of the Russian national income into capital investment. And three quarters of this capital investment went into the development of heavy industry.

In November, 1929, Stalin celebrated the first anniversary of the Five-Year Plan: "We are advancing full steam ahead along the path of industrialization to socialism, leaving behind the age-long Russian backwardness. We are becoming a country of metal, a country of automobiles, a country of tractors. And when we have put the U.S.S.R. in a motorcar and the *muzhik* upon a tractor, we shall see which countries may be classified as backward and which as advanced." But Russia needed many Five-Year Plans to attain the kind of millennium Stalin outlined.

Of the many observers who reported on Russia during this period of transition from the New Economic Policy to the Five-Year Plan, none saw it with a more sensitive and informed eye than Maurice Hindus. Born in a Russian village in the early 1890's, he had emigrated to the United States as a young man shortly before the outbreak of war in 1914. More than ten years later he returned to his native village, which he continued to visit annually. *Broken Earth,* published in 1926, described the first of these trips. "Russia was then a different land from what it is now," wrote Hindus in his preface to a new, 1931 edition. "It was in the throes of preparation for the first Five-Year Plan and the collectivization of the land. Outwardly it was more shabby and

KEYSTONE

Moscow Girl Exhorting Tram-Car
Workers to Fight for Better
Working Conditions

unsightly than now. On the main avenues of Moscow it was still common to see men and women walking barefooted. Building after building showed the ghastly ravages of the civil war. The shortage of manufactured goods was painfully acute." Nevertheless he found the mood of the country "relaxed." He had no difficulty getting a passport and traveling freely.

"Everywhere, especially in the villages, people argued, quarreled, laughed, teased, cried, cursed, and hoped. Nobody, not even the Communists, knew definitely what the next step in the revolution would be. Yet everyone felt its terrific impact. Attacks on God and the church were violent, but defenses of both were no less so. Protestant missionaries trudged around the bazaars of the villages preaching a new Christian gospel. Like them, youthful revolutionaries had embarked on a mission of social evangelism. They preached against alcoholism, against stealing, against bribe-giving and bribe-taking, against beating children, against self-abasement before officials, against race prejudice, and against a host of other old usages. They campaigned for education, for co-operation, for racial tolerance and for class intolerance, for interest in science and all that made it possible, from disinfectants to tractors. It was, in short, a period of universal heart-searching and of romantic adventuring. It was indeed one of the most exciting periods in the history of the Russian village, with comedy and tragedy, sanity and madness, agony and rapture stalking hand in hand."

As the peasants in Hindus' native village discussed the new regime, they reminded him of brash college boys criticizing their professors out of class: "That these peasants mistrusted the Soviet government was clear enough. After all it was a government, something that exacted obligations which they were loath to fulfill, just as the old government did. But—in the old days they accepted the government as a matter of course, just as they did a flood, a storm, an epidemic, something that was not within their power to contol. But now they did not hesitate to berate such governmental rulings as puzzled and incensed them, and even to question the government's right to exist."

Many aspects of the revolution had barely touched the older peasants, and what they knew of it they did not like. The younger generation, however, produced a crop of revolutionaries who had nothing in common with the ignorant provincial boys with whom Hindus had been brought up. "They lived like their fathers and grandfathers, and great-grandfathers before them, in filth, poverty, darkness, with no ambition, no hope, no stimulus, save their one immemorial dream of some day coming into possession of the landlords' estates. Year after year, generation after generation, the same monotony, the same drudgery, the same dullness. But now? Their imagination had been stirred. They were naïve enough in their faith in the miraculous power of the Revolution to rid the world forever of want, inequality, sorrow—of all evil and all woe. They knew so little of the perversity of human nature. They gave no thought to forces which someday would bring them no little disillusionment. They were so young and so inexperienced in the ways of man and the world. But their minds teemed with new concepts, new ideas, new beliefs. They *were* aware of a world outside of their village. They *were* awake to the darkness about them and to the need of ushering in enlightenment. *Science . . . Technique . . . Tractors . . . Atheism . . . Education . . . Culture . . . Electricity . . .* the words rang deafeningly in my ears."

The word that rang longest and loudest was Atheism. A few years later, in *Humanity Uprooted,* Hindus reported that the revolution had won no clearer, quicker, more complete, or more important victory than its victory over religion. His own Russian past had impressed on him the importance of religion in the life of the Russian people under the Tsars: "What is noteworthy in the religious crisis in Russia is that fundamental forces have been set in motion, some loosed by the Revolution, others always latent in the country but formerly held in leash by severe disciplinary measures and now given free play, which are working havoc with the old faith, with all religious faiths, for that matter. What should stir the honest believer is not that hundreds of churches in Russia are still open and are often crowded with worshipers, but that hundreds of others have had to close and, most important of all, that a tide of atheism is engulfing the youth of the country, even the peasant youth." Most peasants resisted the collective farm movement, often to their own hurt. Not all workers joined the Communist Party or supported its program. But the great mass of the younger generation, especially the boys, eagerly accepted the antireligious propaganda of the Bolsheviks. It was just what the doctor ordered.

But atheism is no substitute for faith. Only Communism could fill the gap that the collapse of religion created. A few Communists may have accepted the new religion as cynically as a few Christians accepted the

"Mother, isn't he an arithmetic teacher?"
"Who told you that?"
"He's wearing a plus sign on his chest."
From Crocodile, *Moscow*

old. The great majority, however, accepted the words of Marx and the works of Lenin with the unquestioning devotion of a religious convert. Indeed, it sometimes required a more drastic act of the will to become a Communist than to remain a Christian: "To be born a second time is just as terrible as to die." These words, spoken by a character in a popular Soviet novel, inspired Hindus to add: "Aye, far more terrible. For to be born a second time you must die first, die as completely as though you had never lived, die slowly, lingeringly, with terrible pain. Then you are a new man. Reborn. You are an alien to those who had not been with you in those hours of deathly transformation. Then you can see the goatish beard of your father and his beastly walk. You can run away from the pleas of your uncle whom you have condemned to die."

Yet even the sensitive Maurice Hindus did not quite see, at the time, to how great an extent Communism provided the outlet that religion had once supplied. And to this day, no Communist will admit that he has accepted a faith as irrational as any revealed religion, and rather less satisfying. But the heirs of Lenin, the leaders of the Russian Revolution, had no time for theology or psychoanalysis. They had their hands so full ruling other people that they felt no need to take stock of themselves.

Nor did they feel that they had failed as rulers. During the last years of Lenin's life and during Stalin's first years as the new, unseen master of the Soviet Union, the condition of the masses gradually improved. It could hardly have become worse. Millions of peasants in the Ukraine and along the Volga had died of starvation; those who lived refused to ship what little food they produced to the hungry cities. American relief, administered by Herbert Hoover, afforded some stopgap aid, but it took Lenin's New Economic Policy to turn the tide. Although the mines, the heavy industries, and the larger factories remained in the hands of the state, a minority faction in the Communist Politburo, led by Trotsky, opposed the concessions that Lenin and then Stalin both made to small businesses and independent farmers. It was the old conflict between theory and practice, and the practical men won out. Russia, during the early and middle 1920's, developed a mixed economy of large state-owned enterprises and small private enterprises, while behind the scenes Stalin quietly tightened his hold on the new centers of power.

SUMMING UP

THE LIVES of Lenin and Wilson ran parallel to the end. Both men died of mental and nervous exhaustion—Lenin on January 21, 1924; Wilson less than two weeks later on February 3. Acting in Lenin's name and continuing Lenin's methods, Stalin gave the Russian Revolution a new turn. First he deified its atheist creator; then he surrounded its materialist creed with all the trappings of a new religion. But Stalin himself, intent on enlarging his own power, turned Leninism against the Leninists, destroying all opposition—left, right, and center. Had he betrayed Lenin or given Lenin new life? The Bolshevik intellectuals felt that Stalin had scuttled the world revolution and destroyed democracy within the Party. The new men whom Stalin raised to power were equally convinced that they—not Trotsky or Zinoviev, not Bukharin or Kamenev—were the real heirs of Lenin.

The ironies of history that Lenin relished during his life did not cease with his death. The apostle of world revolution died as his own New Economic Policy reversed the direction of his whole life's work. Stalin, the man against whom he turned at the end, proved his most loyal disciple, but Stalin, too, found himself forced to move in strange, new directions. Having ousted Trotsky by championing socialism in one country against world revolution, Stalin had to speed up the tempo of revolution inside Russia and intervene in the affairs of China, where local Communists, on Moscow's orders, sold the revolutionary movement short.

Wilson suffered an equally ironic fate. His own irreconcilable fight for the League of Nations brought the Republican irreconcilables to power. He left a split in his own party that proved disastrous in the 1924 election. But Wilson lived to see Harding die disgraced and to see the Republican Old Guard discredited. If Wilson left no successor to establish a cult in his name, he also left no one to pervert his teaching. At the time he and Lenin died, Lenin had become by far the bigger man. Within a few years Stalin had transformed Lenin's heritage—in Lenin's name. Wilson's stature remained unimpaired. He came more and more to resemble the hero of a Shakespearean tragedy, destroyed by false friends, strong enemies, and himself.

The Wilson-Lenin cleavage continued after both men had died, spreading to other fields. At a time when the leading creative artists of Europe were turning from social themes to the study of the inner man, the creative artist in Russia ignored the individual and tried to create a mass art for a mass audience. Naturalism and realism, which petered out in Europe before 1914, took a new lease on life in Russia during the 1920's. The scientists and philosophers of postwar Europe, inspired by Einstein's example, rejected the materialist, mechanical view of the universe while Russia's scientists and philosophers rejected the universe of Einstein—not on the basis of scientific evidence, but on the strength of their faith.

8

Revolution in China: Round Two

*The end of the war in Europe led to a resumption
of the revolution in China which wound up with
a Nationalist triumph and a Communist defeat.*

PREVIEW

ROUND TWO of the Chinese Revolution began with the return of Dr.
Sun Yat-sen to China in 1917 and ended in 1929 with Chiang
Kai-shek's establishment of a military, Nationalist dictatorship at Nanking. At first, Dr. Sun tried to establish a national government at Canton
while the young intellectuals led a veritable Chinese renaissance. In
1923 Dr. Sun came to an agreement with Soviet Russia; he reorganized
his Kuomintang Party along Communist lines; he died at Peking in 1925,
leaving behind a program that his supporters at once put into effect.
Chiang Kai-shek, his chief military commander, and Wang Ching-wei,
his closest political adviser, established a revolutionary government at
Canton with the help of Russian military and political experts. In 1926
Chiang ousted Wang and marched his armies north in an attempt to
bring all China, south of Manchuria, under Kuomintang control. The
Left Kuomintang and the Communists set up a rival regime at Hankow
which soon collapsed as Chiang came to terms with the bankers and
secret societies of Shanghai before making Nanking the new Nationalist
capital and himself the one-man ruler of a one-party state. But less than
one quarter of China lay in Chiang's jurisdiction and even in the limited
areas under Nationalist control, Communist guerrilla bands fought on.

· I ·

THE END of the war in Europe accelerated the progress of the revolution
in China. On May 4, 1919, five thousand Peking students demonstrated
against the clause in the Versailles Treaty that awarded the former German concessions in Shantung Province to Japan. They burned the house
of a pro-Japanese Cabinet member and beat up the Chinese minister to
Tokyo. Students in other big Chinese cities went further. Their demonstrations, speeches, and strikes helped to persuade local merchants to

boycott Japanese goods. Labor unions refused to handle Japanese cargoes. It was the widest, most effective display of national feeling since the Boxer Rebellion of 1900, and the leadership came almost entirely from middle-class intellectuals and students who forced the weak Peking government to reorganize itself and reject the Versailles Treaty. The American philosopher John Dewey, who had gone to Peking early in 1919 to lecture at the University, wrote at the time: "To say that life in China is exciting is putting it mildly. We are witnessing the birth of a nation, and birth always comes hard."

Since the death of Yuan Shih-kai in 1916, the authority of the Peking government had steadily dwindled. Yuan's attempt to become Emperor destroyed both himself and the Republic. He left but one vital legacy: resistance to Japan's Twenty-One Demands. A weak president succeeded him. Several dozen war lords ignored and defied Peking and went through the motions of fighting each other. Their troops seldom bled or died in battle. They used their weapons chiefly against unarmed peasants and lived off the countryside as their commanders preferred to settle all differences by negotiation, bribery, and bluff. The armies, untrained, unequipped, unwilling to fight, served as symbols of power not to be risked in anything so costly and risky as physical conflict.

The militant leaders who overthrew the Manchus and set up the Republic in 1912 had soon lost their influence. A year after turning over the presidency to Yuan Shih-kai, Dr. Sun Yat-sen fled to Japan and renewed his contacts with Japanese expansionists who hoped to turn China's troubles to their advantage. Just how much help Sun received from Japan or what pledges he gave in return remains a mystery, but there is no doubt that while certain Japanese were urging Yuan Shih-kai to accept their Twenty-One Demands and become their puppet ruler of China, others were making different propositions to Sun. Because Yuan held the job of President he could not knuckle under to the Japanese without a fatal loss of face. Because Sun held no official position he felt he could use the support of the Japanese for his own purposes and later turn against them.

Dr. Sun Yat-sen's prospects never looked worse than during the war years. He had not yet gained enough popular support to live and work inside his native land; neither could he persuade any foreign country— and he tried them all—to support his cause. Those that were not too busy fighting the war saw little to be gained by meddling in China. He therefore remained in Japan from 1913 to 1916, where he married his second wife, Soong Ching-ling. She was the daughter of his friend and contemporary, Charles Jones Soong, an American-educated, Christian Chinese businessman who had helped to finance the revolution for more than twenty years. Dr. Sun already had one wife living in China and a grown son attending college in California. The young Soong girl's marriage to Sun shocked her fellow Methodists; many Chinese could not understand why she did not accept the customary position of "second wife" inasmuch as Sun's first wife had already justified herself by having borne him a boy. But Sun needed affection to help him through a difficult time and for Soong Ching-ling, the marriage fulfilled all her girlhood dreams of romance.

The entrance of the United States into the war in 1917 seemed to give Dr. Sun his chance. Under American pressure, the Peking government set up a puppet Parliament that declared war upon Germany. Whereupon many members of the legally elected Parliament of 1912 assembled in the revolutionary city of Canton and set up a provisional government under Dr. Sun to repair the wreckage wrought by Yuan Shih-kai and the war lords. "The revolutionary intellectuals who had conspired so fervidly to bring the monarchy down were helplessly sidetracked in the developments that followed," wrote Harold R. Isaacs in *The Tragedy of the Chinese Revolution*. "There had been no authentic movement from which they might have drawn strength. The revolution had occurred almost independently of their efforts. Afterward they became mere appendages of the militarists who seized power. . . . Those intellectuals who did not become secretaries or jobholders under illiterate generals fell away from politics into passive despair. Sun Yat-sen and the remains of his Party, the Kuomintang, wrote on their party banner the slogan, 'Protect the Constitution.' But the only protection they sought was in the camp of one set of generals pitted against another. At this game they lost with consistent regularity. Only the generals won."

The terms of the Versailles Treaty left the intellectuals feeling betrayed by Wilson, democracy, and the victorious Allies. The Bolshevik seizure of power in Russia stirred their interest in Lenin, Communism, and the Soviet Union. The Chinese workers also turned toward the left. Between the years 1916 and 1922, the number of industrial workers in China jumped from one to two millions. "The rise of productive forces," wrote Isaacs of China during this time, "brought on a new contest between aspiring Chinese capital and entrenched foreign interests and the existing structure of foreign economic and political privilege. It also brought the new class of industrial workers into conflict with their employers, foreign and Chinese alike. From these new springs flowed fresh nationalist currents which swept China into the upheavals of the next decade." One important section of the Chinese proletariat went through a memorable wartime experience when the Allies shipped two hundred thousand coolies from China to perform hard physical labor at low pay in the Middle East and behind the Western Front. Many returned with a new outlook on the world, having learned how to read and write and having seen the higher living standards enjoyed by other workers in other lands.

While China's students and workers turned toward revolutionary solutions of their problems, Dr. Sun Yat-sen turned more and more toward maneuver and intrigue. In *China: The Collapse of a Civilization*, Nathaniel Peffer described Sun's goings and comings during the immediate postwar years: "To combat the corrupt imperialism which held the Peking government in its grip, he made alliances with the most predatory military adventurers, duped by their promises of support for his arms. He sought help from first one country and then another, forgetting that when foreign Powers intervened they did so with a motive, and the motive boded China no good. Interference in China's affairs had helped to bring China to the pass in which it was. He surrounded himself with sycophants and parasites, men who erected a wall of flattery around him to screen out the truth. He would arrive at Canton, proclaim a provisional government as the only legal government of China, although he had only a precarious hold on the one city, demand that the foreign Powers recognize his government as the government of China and cease dealing with Peking. Two months later he would be evicted from Canton and have to take refuge in British Hong Kong a few hours away. Then another turn of the political wheel, and he would be back in Canton, and again there would be proclamations, demands, announcements. It was opéra bouffe, but in the meantime, Canton was being impoverished by one military occupation after another."

At the outset of his revolutionary career Dr. Sun had accepted the ancient Chinese saying, "Action is always difficult; knowledge is always easy." By 1918 he came to the opposite conclusion: "Men of action do not at all require to be steeped in knowledge; it is sufficient to be able to carry out what is required." He therefore devoted most of his own time to program writing and emphasized the importance of "knowing what to do." He proposed that the war-weary nations invest in China one quarter as much money as they had spent fighting. To prove that he meant business, he drew up a program that called for foreigners to build one hundred thousand miles of railways, a million miles of macadam roads, innumerable canals, power plants, and factories at a cost of sixty million dollars a day. "I intend to make all the national industries of China into a Great Trust owned by the Chinese people, and financed with international capital for mutual benefit." Almost as an afterthought he appended this comment: "So far there is not a word expressed in disfavor of my proposition. The only anxiety ever expressed is where we can obtain such huge sums of money to carry out even a small part of this comprehensive project." Yet Dr. Sun never entirely lost his peasant shrewdness. In 1920, Thomas W. Lamont told him that President Wilson wanted to know if peace could somehow be restored between north and south China. "Why, yes," Sun replied. "Just you give me twenty-five million dollars, Mr. Lamont, and I'll equip a couple of army corps, then we'll have peace in short order."

Sun Yat-sen always treasured a passage from the Book of Rites, by Confucius, outlining the world ideal to which he hoped to dedicate the New China: "All men everywhere will live for the common good; leaders of worth and ability will be selected; their words will be trusted and they will be makers of peace. Men will not love their own parents to the exclusion of the parents of others, nor their own sons to the exclusion of the sons of others. They will provide sustenance to the aged as long as they live, employment to the able-bodied, opportunity for development to the young, friendly care to widows, orphans, childless men, and the disabled; for each man a task and for each woman a home. Not wishing to be wasteful of their possessions, they will nevertheless not keep them for purely personal use; not wishing to be inactive in the application of their strength, they will at the same time not exert it merely in their own behalf. Thus evil devices will cease or fail to prosper, robbers and traitors will be out of work, and outside doors will not need to be closed."

While Dr. Sun tried to apply some of the teachings of Confucius to new conditions, younger intellectuals worked out new philosophies to meet the changing times. Dr. Sun always wrote in classical, scholarly Chinese; Dr. Hu Shih—his junior by a quarter of a century—led a successful movement to abandon the elaborate written language of the scholars for the much simpler, spoken Chinese. Hu Shih was the son of a scholar who married, late in life, a vigorous, illiterate peasant woman and died soon afterward. The mother saw to it that her son received the education she lacked and at the age of three he had learned eight hundred Chinese characters. Hu Shih always excelled in his studies: first in the local village school, then at Shanghai where he spent six years studying the leading philosophers of Europe, later at Cornell—where he won a prize for an essay on Browning—and finally at Columbia where he became a favorite pupil of John Dewey. "I believe the greatest thing that I have learned since leaving China," he wrote in 1914, "is the optimistic philosophy of life." Hu Shih first broke with the orthodox beliefs of China to embrace Christianity; then he dropped Christianity for a new faith of his own in "Social Immortality," which he defined as follows:

"The individual may die but he lives on in the Great Self which is immortal. All his virtue and vice, all his merit and sin, all his action and thought and speech, significant or trivial, right or wrong, for good or evil—everything lives in the effect it produces in the Great Self. This Great Self lives forever as the everlasting monumental testimony of the principles and practices of the numberless individual selves." Somewhere he had read these words—and never forgot them: "The body is the material basis of the spirit and the spirit is only the functioning of the body. The spirit is to the body what sharpness is to a sharp knife. We have never known the existence of sharpness after the destruction of the knife. How can we admit the survival of the spirit when the body is gone?" And to this he added his own corollary: "*Everything* is immortal. Everything that we are, everything that we do, and everything that we say is immortal in the sense that it has its effect somewhere in this world, and that effect in turn will have its results somewhere else, and the thing goes on in infinite time and space."

Hu Shih returned to China in 1918 and threw himself into the task of language reform. He eschewed political for cultural activity, writing poems and pamphlets in the vernacular and inspiring his whole generation to follow his example. He agreed with Lao-tse that the highest virtue is to resist nothing since water, which resists nothing, is itself irresistible. Europeans called Hu Shih the Voltaire of the Chinese Revolution; they compared his efforts in behalf of a new, popular Chinese language with the efforts of Chaucer in English and of Dante in Italian. Every Chinese university followed Hu Shih's lead, with the result that the common daily speech of China became, within a few years, its common written language. But written Chinese contains tens of thousands of ideograms. It remained for another American-educated Chinese, "Jimmy" Yen, to develop a basic script of one thousand ideograms that could be learned in ninety-six hours. Chih Meng, director of the China Institute in America, summed up the Chinese renaissance that Hu Shih and Jimmy Yen had led: "The goal is democracy, the process is education; the underlying philosophy is live and let live." In the year 1919 alone, some four hundred new Chinese periodicals appeared, mostly written by and for students, mostly supporting the revolutionary movement which Dr. Sun Yat-sen had come to embody.

In some respects Dr. Sun appeared outdated; in others he appeared impractical. Although the full extent of the revolution in which he was participating passed his comprehension, all who met him—Chinese or non-Chinese—at once became aware of a magnetic, dedicated personality whose power lay in his feeling for the past as well as his yearning for the future. Nathaniel Peffer called his famous Three Principles "a combination of sound social analysis, keen comment on comparative political science, and bombast, journalistic inaccuracy, jejune philosophizing, and sophomoric economics. On the other hand, the man had a touching humility; he did suffer little men to come unto him and he listened to them sympathetically. He was studious and continued to develop intellectually to the end. He had a personal magnetism and power of inspiration which would have made him a leader of any race

in any hemisphere. There were men of discernment who could not resist him even when convinced that he was wrong and who followed him
blindly and willingly. For above all there were his sincerity, his integrity,
his sweep of imagination, and a dedication to the interests of his people
which lifted him above the plane of ordinary men. His ambition and
egoism and struggle for power were not vaingloriousness or desire for
self-aggrandizement. He sought power as an instrument to save his
country and make its people prosperous and happy. He was moved by
patriotism in the purest, finest sense. And if his dreams were preposterous by the standards of reality and practicability, it should be remembered that he had made some of them come true."

Dr. Sun needed all his vast capacity for idealism to persevere in his
chosen task. Four Chinese in every five still lived the same peasant
existence that their ancestors had lived for three thousand years and still
chanted this ancient song:

> "When the sun rises, I toil;
> When the sun sets, I rest;
> I dig wells for water;
> I till the fields for food;
> What has the Emperor's power to do with me?"

About half the Chinese peasants farmed their own land; 20 per cent
sharecropped the land of others; the rest combined sharecropping with
working small plots of their own. The great European landowner had
no Chinese counterpart. Feudalism had died out in China at the time of
Christ. But China's millions upon millions of small, peasant proprietors
could not finance themselves and thus fell into the clutches of the village
moneylender to whom they pledged their goods at two thirds of their
value and to whom they paid interest rates of 40 to 80 per cent a year,
and sometimes as much as 200 per cent. China's exhausted soil yielded
meager crops, and when the peasants were not suffering from droughts
they were fighting floods.

The workers in China's shops and factories fared no better. Most of
them had to live on the premises and often did not see their families or
the outside world for months at a time. Their wages ran about two or
three dollars a month, although it cost at least $2.60 a month to buy
enough food for an adult male. The peasants had to make their living on
the most densely populated farm lands in the world. The workers dwelt
in the most overcrowded cities. Primitive, inefficient transport increased
their troubles. If the farmers of Shensi Province had presented their
grain to the Shanghai mills, free of charge, grain fom Seattle would still
have sold for less because of the huge cost of shipping goods from one

part of China to another. Some students of China have estimated that 20 per cent of the working population had some kind of job in transportation—in most cases carrying burdens or hauling carts. During the 1920's work output per head in China averaged less than one twentieth of the work output per head in the United States.

The family, not the state or the church, not the workers' guild or the peasants' commune, had remained the basis of Chinese civilization for more than three thousand years. R. H. Tawney, in *Land and Labour in China,* described the "Chinese ideal" as resting "on the Chinese family uniting, not the living alone, but the living, the dead, and those yet to be born in an undying community; on the stable, patient routine of the Chinese village; on the common heritage of a philosophy which made personal relations and the conduct appropriate to them, not metaphysics or political obligations, the foundation of its scheme; on a tradition and style of behavior which turned each individual into the expression of a whole people, and to perpetuate which in himself and his descendants was happiness and virtue; on a common sense of the insignificance of the present in the great ocean of the past, which even today causes many Chinese to think in terms of centuries where the West thinks in decades. Custom, not law, fixed the framework of existence; ethics, not theology or political interests, gave life its meaning." But the twentieth century was destroying this ancient China and the family on which it rested. The impact of the Western world had knocked the Chinese economy off balance. The impact of Western ideas challenged the assumptions on which China's old civilization had rested.

Because the peasants and the workers suffered the material consequences of this impact, they had no stamina left to fight back. As Tawney put it, "There are districts in which the position of the rural population is that of a man standing up to his neck in water, so that even a ripple is sufficient to drown him." While the Chinese peasants worked as their ancestors had worked, the Chinese students, most of them sons and daughters of the professional classes, responded to the leadership of Sun Yat-sen and if they looked abroad looked to Lenin and Gandhi rather than to Woodrow Wilson. The Chinese student read books, but not to gratify his aesthetic or intellectual senses. As Olga Lang put it in *Chinese Family and Society:* "Books are expected to teach him how to think, how to live, what to do, how to reform his private behavior and the society in which he lives." She also quoted the comments most frequently heard from Chinese students when asked about their ambitions in life. "I think only of freedom and the liberation of the Chinese people." "The aim of my life? To live and struggle for the masses." "I hope to live in a rational society. I want to smash this world where men hate men." The twenty-year-old son of a businessman said he wanted above everything else "a comfortable and tender home, devotion to study." He paused, then added hastily, "and service to society."

In China and India, in Egypt and Mexico—all around the world, wherever the masses had always lived in the blackest poverty—a new faith in material progress was turning the old order upside down. The mass of the people in these backward lands lived in such poverty and ignorance that they could not play any active political role. But many sons and daughters of the well-to-do, many younger business and professional people, most intellectuals, both students and professors, launched crusades against the privileged foreigner and against those members of the native ruling class who collaborated with the foreigner to exploit their fellow countrymen.

A veritable Chinese renaissance, under student leadership, spread the glad tidings of a better life for all. The leaders of this renaissance got their ideas from books, magazines, and newspapers, 90 per cent of which were published in Shanghai, and they spread them by word of mouth, a much easier task in densely populated China than in thinly populated Russia. Even so, however, they reached only a tiny fraction of the people. "The first problem in Chinese politics," wrote Tawney, "is vast and fundamental. It is not who shall govern the state, but whether there shall be a state at all. It is whether public power shall exist." Dr. Sun, for all his fantastic schemes, understood this hard fact of Chinese life. More, perhaps, than any other revolutionary leader of his time, he merged himself with the mass of the Chinese people. "I am a coolie," he declared, "and the son of a coolie. I was born poor and I am still poor. My sympathies have always been with the struggling mass." W. H. Donald, an Australian newspaperman whose sympathy for China won him the affection and trust of the leaders of the revolution, felt the same way, and when a former viceroy of the Manchus contemptuously asked who the Chinese people were, Donald burst out: "Who are the people? I'll tell you who they are. They are the sweat that runs in your rivers. They are the bones that build your mansions. They are the blood of your wine, the meat of your table. They are the quilts in winter, the fans in summer, the tea when you are thirsty. They are the laughter in despair. They are a philosophy unending, untiring, an oasis for the weary such as you." It was as the champion of these people that Sun Yat-sen entered the final, decisive stage of his career.

· II ·

TEN YEARS had passed since the Manchus had abdicated and Dr. Sun Yat-sen had proclaimed China a Republic. The remote authority of the Emperor gave way to the direct tyranny of local war lords. As China's intellectuals saw it, the war to make the world safe for democracy had made their country safe for Japan. But during the early 1920's the Chinese war lords and the Japanese expansionists began to run into trouble. Opposition to the Versailles settlement brought the revolutionary forces in China together again as the victorious Allies discovered they had overreached themselves. The Washington Conference of 1922 checked Japan and gave China new and stronger guarantees from the United States as well as from the major European Powers. In 1923 a terrible earthquake wiped out large sections of Tokyo and Yokohama, taking more than one hundred thousand lives and forcing the Japanese to concentrate on domestic reconstruction for a while.

China, Mexico, and Turkey had all begun to go through national revolutions before 1914. All three of these revolutions continued after the fighting in Europe ended, and similar revolutions shook Egypt, the Arab states, Persia, and India. Wilson's promises of self-determination raised new hopes throughout Asia and among subject peoples everywhere. But the Russian Revolution had more influence on events in China than anything Wilson ever did or said. In 1919 the Bolshevik leaders issued their first manifesto to the Chinese people: "If the people of China wish to become free like the Russian people and be spared the lot prepared for them by the Allies at Versailles, which would make of China a second Korea or a second India, let them understand that their only allies and brothers in their struggle for national freedom are the Russian workers and peasants and their Red Army." The next year, the Soviet government declared the Tsarist treaties with China null and void. It abandoned all extraterritorial rights, relinquished all concessions and seized territories, claimed no more payments under the Boxer Indemnity, proposed writing a new treaty covering trade relations and the Chinese Eastern Railway which Russia and China had jointly controlled. In 1921 one of Lenin's secretaries visited Dr. Sun Yat-sen in Canton and Marshal Wu Pei-fu, the top war lord of the moment, in Peking.

By this time a small Chinese Communist Party had come into existence, founded by Chen Tu-hsiu, professor of literature, and Li Ta-chao, professor of history, at the University of Peking. Like most Chinese intellectuals, these two scholars knew the works of Rousseau, Darwin, Spencer, Nietzsche, Tolstoy, and Prince Kropotkin. Not many Chinese, however, had ever heard of Karl Marx until the Russian Revolution broke, and then Lenin's ideas interested them more. As Benjamin I. Schwartz wrote in *Chinese Communism and the Rise of Mao:* "The Leninist theory of imperialism confronted the Chinese intelligentsia with a grandiose, starkly melodramatic image of the world. Within this theory almost the entire onus for the wretchedness of backward areas is laid at the door of international finance capital." The Communists, continued Schwartz, offered the Chinese student "a spectacular role of leadership in an atmosphere supercharged with the promise of imminent redemption."

Not until 1920 did the two middle-aged professors who founded the Chinese Communist Party accept the teachings of Marx and Lenin. Even as late as December, 1919, Chen Tu-hsiu argued that "in the average Chinese artisan shop, after all, the position of managers and workers is more or less alike." Before another year had passed, Chen saw the light: "I recognize the existence of only two 'nations,' the 'nation' of the capitalists and the 'nation' of the workers. At present the 'nation' of the workers exists only in the Soviet Union. Everywhere else we have the 'nation' of the capitalists." But Dr. Sun's propaganda proved more to the public taste and the Russians therefore tried to establish good relations with him and with other non-Communist leaders, too. What concessions they made cost the Russians little in a material sense and benefited them hugely in a moral sense. Lacking the power to enforce the privileges that Tsarist Russia commanded before 1914, the Bolsheviks won priceless Chinese good will by bowing to the inevitable and identifying themselves with changes that other Europeans resisted. Yet, even so, they managed to maintain effective control over the Chinese Eastern Railway.

The Bolsheviks also managed to maintain good relations with the Chinese government at Peking and with Dr. Sun's in-again-out-again regime at Canton. At a time when all the other major Powers showed their contempt for China by having Ministers represent them, the Russians dispatched to Peking a full-fledged Ambassador in the person of Karakhan, formerly a high official in the Soviet Foreign Office. This boosted Soviet prestige throughout China, but did not prevent Lenin from sending a special envoy named Adolf Joffe to confer with Sun Yat-sen. In January, 1923, they issued a joint manifesto:

"Dr. Sun Yat-sen holds that the communistic order or even the Soviet system cannot actually be introduced into China because there do not exist here the conditions for the successful establishment of either communism or sovietism. This view is entirely shared by Mr. Joffe, who is further of the opinion that China's paramount and most pressing problem is to achieve national unification and attain full national independence, and regarding this task, he has assured Dr. Sun Yat-sen that China has the warmest sympathy of the Russian people and can count on the support of Russia."

Joffe, the diplomat, opened the door through which Michael Borodin, the organizer, entered. Borodin had lived in the United States and, after the Russian Revolution, had worked with Communist leaders in eastern Europe. In *China in the Sun,* the American correspondent Randall

WIDE WORLD

Michael Borodin

Gould described him as "a large, quiet man whose white Russian blouse and drooping mustache somehow assist materially in conveying an impression of force, poise, earnestness." When Gould inquired whether the Chinese would ever accept Communism, Borodin replied, with quiet scorn, "China already has communism, the communism of the family's one rice bowl." Another American correspondent, the younger and more enthusiastic Vincent Sheean, found in Borodin the very embodiment of the "Old Bolshevik," whose "long view" of the events in China during the mid-1920's inspired this passage in *Personal History:* "He seemed to take the 'long view' by nature, by an almost physical superiority of vision. His whole adult life had been lived by a system of thought in which the immediate event was regarded as meaningless unless related to other events on both sides in time; in which the individual was valued by his relationship to his fellow being; in which the most important of processes was held to be the comprehension, however disagreeable, of cause and effect. Disregarding the economic structure (Marxian economics) with which the Bolshevik mind was preoccupied, it could be seen that the method of thought in itself was 'good'—produced, as in the case of Borodin, a clear, calm view of life. Borodin himself would have attributed the quality I call greatness (the quality of being in, but above, the battle) to the political philosophy and to nothing else. He would have said that the philosophy gave 'historical perspective' and that historical perspective, once thoroughly understood, enabled the mind to inhabit a clearer air."

"Borodin's name is Lafayette," exclaimed the ecstatic Dr. Sun, who derived much of his inspiration from the heroes of American history. Sun said he based his famous Three Principles on the democratic doctrines of Abraham Lincoln: "Our three principles of the people mean government of the people, by the people, for the people—that is, a state belonging to all the people, a government controlled by all the people, and the rights and benefits for the enjoyment of all the people." But only the Kuomintang could confer these benefits and they must come to China in three stages—from military conquest to political tutelage to constitutional government. First, during the period of "People's Nationalism" China would have to resort to force to liquidate foreign imperialism and attain national unity. Second, during the period of the "People's Democracy," the Kuomintang would introduce popular government under a temporary one-party system. Third, during the period of the "People's Livelihood," China would establish socialism.

In January, 1924, Dr. Sun told Kuomintang members: "There is one thing of greatest importance in a political party; that is, all members must possess spiritual unity. In order that all members may be united spiritually, the first thing is to sacrifice freedom, the second is to offer ability. If the individual can sacrifice his freedom, then the whole party will have freedom. If the individual can offer his ability, then the whole party will have ability." He also made it clear that China must look toward Russia and that the Russians, in their turn, had cast in their lot with Asia: "So only 250 millions of the tyrannical races are left, but they are trying by inhuman methods and military force to subjugate the other 1250 millions. So hereafter mankind will be divided into two camps: on one side will be the 1250 millions; on the other side the 250 millions."

Dr. Maurice William, a Russian-born Brooklyn dentist, had written a book, *The Social Interpretation of History*, with which he successfully inoculated Dr. Sun against Marxism. Sun did, however, accept in his own way and for his own purposes Lenin's corollary to Marx: that imperialism is the final state of capitalism. Unlike both Marx and Lenin, Sun denied that Chinese capitalists exploited Chinese workers: "The difference between Chinese workers and foreign workers lies in the fact that the latter are oppressed only by their own capitalists, and not by those of other countries. The Chinese workers are not as yet oppressed by Chinese capitalists. They are oppressed by foreign capitalists." Sun all but denied the existence of any ruling, privileged class of native Chinese, saying that there were neither rich nor poor in China—only the poor and the less poor.

Although Sun repudiated Communist ideology, he accepted Communist strategy. Largely under Borodin's guidance he transformed the Kuomintang into a revolutionary organization on the Bolshevik model. Dr. Sun had always dominated the membership from above. He continued to dominate the Central Executive Committee that Borodin devised and that handed down orders to smaller, local groups, just as the Politburo and the Central Executive Committee of the Communist Party did in Russia. This did not mean that Borodin forced an alien, Russian system on the reluctant Chinese. He merely adapted the system that Sun had already created, and Sun in his turn modified the teachings of Confucius by substituting the authority of the Party for the authority of the family. The Kuomintang admitted Communists to full membership, and the Communists agreed to accept Kuomintang discipline.

In 1924 Dr. Sun delivered before his followers in the Kuomintang a series of lectures that became the Bible of the movement. No precise transcipt of what he said exists; he never completed all he planned to say; often he contradicted himself. One day he declared, "Japan is an excellent model." On another: "China's ancient virtues are superior to foreign virtues. Europe looks to China for the fundamentals of political philosophy." He urged foreigners to invest billions in China, asserting that the country could support "at least eight hundred million people." Yet he had also written, just the year before: "The real trouble is that China is not an independent country. She is the victim of foreign countries. She is really in a worse condition than Korea or Formosa. They have one master; we have many. Their master dominates them, but has important responsibilities for the people who are under his subjection. China is equally dominated from the outside, but her masters rule without accepting any responsibility."

Isolated quotations from Dr. Sun's speeches and writings may be made to prove anything, but his ability to hold the devotion of the same group of followers over the years helped to establish him as one of the great prophets of the time. Gandhi possessed that same gift, and in addition knew how to project himself to the masses. The same messianic sense also inspired both men. Dr. Sun called himself "a messenger of God to help men obtain equality and freedom." Like Gandhi, Dr. Sun had a deep respect for the Christian religion. He urged his followers not "to make trouble for the Christians" and said of his own beliefs: "I do not belong to the Christianity of the churches, but to the Christianity of Jesus, who was a revolutionary."

At least two of Dr. Sun's closest disciples did not share his spiritual zeal. Both Wang Ching-wei, his political spokesman, and Chiang Kai-shek, who commanded his armed forces, were essentially children of this world rather than the sons of light. Chiang Kai-shek came of a merchant family in Chekiang Province, just south of Shanghai. At the age of nineteen he decided to become a professional soldier and spent the years from 1908 to 1911 at the Imperial Military College in Tokyo, leaving it to fight in the Chinese Revolution. He put three thousand troops, drawn from the gutters of Shanghai, through stiff training but could not discipline himself and disappeared, sometimes for weeks, on drinking and wenching bouts. He met the leaders of various Shanghai gangs who respected his stubborn will and fiery temper. But when Yuan Shih-kai scuttled the Republic in 1912, Chiang sobered up and followed Dr. Sun Yat-sen to Tokyo. Within another three years he had become one of the

UNITED PRESS PHOTO

The Youthful Chiang Kai-shek

UNITED PRESS PHOTO

Marshal Chang Tso-lin

inner circle of the Kuomintang. According to Harold Isaacs, "Gangsters, bankers, military men, murderers, thieves, and brothel keepers helped draw the original lines of the portrait the world was to come to recognize as Chiang Kai-shek. Far from being effaced as time passed, they deepened. In the years to come Chiang was destined to lean upon and be leaned upon by these early mentors."

For several years after 1913 Chiang leaned principally upon Dr. Sun. In 1917 the two men went together to Canton and the bond that developed between them reflected credit on both. The fact that Dr. Sun commanded Chiang's entire devotion even under desperate conditions revealed the quality of his leadership. The fact that Chiang subordinated his ruthless nature to the visionary Dr. Sun revealed an unsuspected streak of idealism in the sullen young soldier whose ill temper and bad manners made most Party comrades dislike him. In 1920 he broke loose for a while, made an estimated million dollars speculating on the Shanghai exchanges, then turned all the proceeds over to the Kuomintang. Two years later Chiang advised Dr. Sun to crush one of the periodic rebellions that had broken out in Canton. Dr. Sun ignored the advice, but when the revolt drove him from the city he summoned Chiang to join him aboard a gunboat, where they spent two months together. Dr. Sun could not return to Canton until January, 1923, and by this time he had made Chiang his closest military adviser.

In July, 1923, Dr. Sun sent Chiang to Russia to spend six months studying Soviet military and political strategy. Chiang and Stalin exchanged warmly inscribed photographs—like called unto like—and with Borodin's approval Chiang founded a new military college at Whampoa, near Canton, where, with forty Russian instructors to help him, he began to train Chinese officers to know what they were fighting for as well as how to fight. Dr. Sun's Kuomintang Party, which controlled the Canton area, rightly regarded itself as the true custodian of the 1912 revolution and Chiang's job was to give that revolution an army. Two rival centers of power also existed: the weak, corrupt remains of a Republican government, headed by Tsao Kun at Peking, and the outstanding Chinese war lord, Marshal Chang Tso-lin, in the Manchurian capital of Mukden.

Tsao Kun in Peking had amassed a fortune as a local war lord, but did not become President of China until a fortuneteller informed him he must crown his career by making himself titular head of his country's government. On October 10, 1923, Tsao Kun paid a majority of members of Parliament five thousand dollars apiece, in American money, to vote him into office, and it cost him close to eighteen thousand dollars a day in bribes to stay there. Parliamentary debates degenerated into inkwell-throwing contests. The real power in Peking was neither the President nor the Parliament; it was Marshal Wu Pei-fu, the scholarly Minister of Defense, a survivor of the old regime, adored by the foreign colony. The Kuomintang leaders watched with disgust the antics of the Peking officials who betrayed the 1912 revolution. But the Kuomintang had no army to throw the rascals out. Only one man could do that: Marshal Chang Tso-lin, who had begun life as a bandit in his native Manchuria, worked with the Japanese against the Russians in 1905, and since then had organized an army of a quarter of a million men through which he controlled Manchuria, the richest and most productive area in China. Chang was a slender, high-strung man, just turned fifty, who, when he had nothing more important to do, burned up his nervous energy gambling for as long as forty-eight hours without sleep. He had remained on good terms with the Japanese and he certainly had their blessing when he prepared to move in on Peking in the fall of 1924. As Marshal Chang gathered his forces to advance southward, Marshal Wu proceeded northward, accompanied by his forty-year-old protégé, General Feng Yu-hsiang, a burly peasant whom the Methodists had converted to their strenuous form of Christianity. But General Feng had ideas of his own—radical ideas—and to carry them out he did not hesitate to double-cross Marshal Wu. It was what H. B. Elliston, an American newspaperman, called "China's eternal triangle—two generals fighting, whose plans are upset by the treachery of a third." While Marshal Wu continued northward to stop Chang near the Great Wall, the Methodist led thirty thousand picked troops south. Singing "Onward, Christian Soldiers," they entered Peking, took over the city, and left Wu and Chang to fight it out. But Wu and Chang, as good war lords, had never intended to commit their troops to actual battle, and Feng's defection alarmed Chang almost as much as it alarmed Marshal Wu, who slipped away to a scholar's retreat in the distant province of Szechuan, beyond the Yangtze River gorges, where he composed these lines:

"The cold wind from the west stirs my old battle cloak.
To look upon the bloodstains on the coat brings sorrow to my heart.
My only possessions now are my loyal heart and brave soul.
These will be with me forever in spite of ice and snow."

On arriving in Peking, Feng went through the formalities of submitting himself to President Tsao, but the new Cabinet that Feng installed demanded a new deal. On November 1, 1924, it "approved of Tsao's desire to surrender the Presidency" and Feng invited representatives from many organizations to confer with him at Peking on how to revive the Republic. Chang Tso-lin, preferring to play his usual lone hand, pulled back into Manchuria. Dr. Sun, suffering from cancer of the liver, slowly proceeded northward. By the time Sun reached Peking, Feng had already announced a program of his own.

Dr. Sun arrived at Peking in January, 1925, sick unto death. An operation disclosed the fatal liver ailment, and his colleagues gathered in his sickroom, where they spent the next two months drawing up final statements for him to sign. General Feng's reorganization plans fizzled out; the Kuomintang leaders, with Borodin beside them, prepared to exploit Dr. Sun's prestige as the Bolsheviks had exploited the prestige of Lenin. The top military post in the Party went to Chiang Kai-shek. Wang Ching-wei, the Party's foremost intellectual and Dr. Sun's closest collaborator, wrote the manifestoes to which the dying man attached his name.

Wang Ching-wei played somewhat the same part in the Chinese Revolution that Trotsky played in the Russian. Dr. Sun, the self-made professional revolutionary, corresponded to Lenin; Chiang Kai-shek, the self-made professional soldier, corresponded to Stalin. Wang Ching-wei, a born agitator, loved to write, make speeches, and bask in the spotlight. His father, a well-to-do scholar, lived in the revolutionary city of Canton, where Wang passed the old-style provincial examinations so brilliantly that he went to Japan as a government scholar in 1902 at the age of nineteen. Four years later, he helped to found the first official publication of Dr. Sun's newly formed Kuomintang Party and regularly contributed about half of its entire contents. He also wrote romantic poetry, some of which was translated into English. Handsome and idealistic, Wang helped to found the so-called "Six No Society," whose members pledged themselves not to drink, smoke, gamble, accept bribes, hold any office under the Empire, or engage in promiscuous sexual relations. Wang be-

TRIANGLE

Wang Ching-wei

came known as "The Saint," but Manchu officials set a price of fifty thousand dollars for him dead, or one hundred thousand dollars for his capture alive.

While Dr. Sun raised money for the Kuomintang among rich Chinese abroad, Wang Ching-wei helped to organize a more sensational defiance of the Manchu dynasty in Peking itself. He persuaded a small group of men and women, including a Chinese graduate of the Tokyo Normal School for Girls and "chairman of the Department of Assassination," to kill the Prince Regent. In 1910 Wang placed a bomb under a bridge which he expected the Prince to cross, but police traced the plot to his hide-out in Peking, where they arrested him and secured an immediate confession. But Wang's good looks were said to have made such an impression on the Empress Dowager that she had his sentence commuted from death to life imprisonment, to be spent with iron chains locked around his wrists, ankles, and neck. When asked why he had tried to assassinate the Prince Regent, Wang wrote that he wanted "to perform some extraordinary and sensational act in the most important place in the whole world for the purpose of arousing the people." Although the attempt failed, it revived the spirit of Wang's comrades and thereby speeded the revolution of 1911 and his own release from prison that same year.

Wang had everything that Chiang lacked—good looks, good manners, charm, talent. Dr. Sun used both men, respected them both, and they respected each other. Wang knew Dr. Sun's mind so well that the manifestoes and the will he wrote rang true. Every Kuomintang branch has always been required to open every one of its weekly meetings with a reading of the complete text of the will:

"For forty years I have devoted my energies to the cause of the Nationalist Revolution. The object of the latter is to seek a position of independent equality for China. The experience of forty years has caused me to realize that if it is desired to achieve the object, the people is to be aroused, and we must strive in unison with all those nations of the world who treat us on a basis of equality. The revolution has not yet achieved

its object. All those who are of the same purpose as myself must therefore act in accordance with the precepts of my three books, A *Method of
Establishing a Nation, A General Plan for the Reconstruction of the
National Government,* and *The Three People's Principles,* and also the
announcement made on the occasion of the First National Representatives' Conference, and must continue to use every effort to attain the first
two ideals of holding a people's conference and of abolishing all unequal
treaties. It is essential that this should be brought about in the shortest
possible time. My last Will and Testament."

Dr. Sun signed the will on March 11, 1925, the day before he died. At
about the same time, he also signed a letter to the Central Executive
Committee of the Soviet Union, reaffirming the agreement he had
reached with Borodin the year before. Yet Dr. Sun died a Christian, not
a Communist. On his deathbed, he grasped the hand of one of his brothers-in-law, saying, "You are a Christian; I, too, am a Christian." His last
words were: "Peace. Struggle. Save China."

Lyon Sharman's perceptive life of Dr. Sun Yat-sen sums up his character: "Dr. Sun Yat-sen did that presumptuous thing, so rarely done
that we think of it as daring: he assumed a role in history and he played
it to the end, in spots ineffectively, even incompetently, sometimes pomp-
ously, sometimes tragically; but he played it—that is the point. How he
got in touch with the great Director of the drama we call History, and
learned how the play was to be plotted, is the mystical core of his life—
mystical but not mysterious to those who agree with its fundamental
assumptions. If Christianity frequently gave its adherents such a sense
of historic direction, we might say Sun Yat-sen's Christianity helped him
to know."

· III ·

Dr. Sun Yat-sen died a saintly bore whose passing caused no such immediate stir as the death of Lenin had occasioned the previous year. But
the myth of Dr. Sun soon proved as potent as the myth of Lenin. When
several aspiring war lords tried to overthrow the Kuomintang regime at
Canton, Chiang Kai-shek's indoctrinated troops went into action. The
troops of the war lords disintegrated; the Canton workers and the peasants of the surrounding province of Kwangtung welcomed Chiang as
the man who could make Dr. Sun's Utopian promises come true.

Dr. Sun also lived on in the person of his zealous young widow, who
accompanied Wang Ching-wei and Borodin to Canton, where they organized a local experiment in government of the Kuomintang type that
attracted world-wide interest. "Friends who know Canton ask me what
I am doing here," said Borodin. "It seems to them I am at a job for a

Churchill, not a Communist." Of the regime that he had helped to set up in Canton, Borodin said, "Where else in the world today could one have a political program consisting of only two words, 'good government'? And yet this is the principal clause in 'Red' Canton's program today. The one thing which the Kuomintang is endeavoring to bring to the territory under its control is simply—good government. Security; safety for life and property; the assurance that when one wakes up in the morning his life and property will be safe. That is all."

The chief threat to Red Canton came from abroad. In May, 1925, British police shot down several Chinese students and workers demonstrating in Shanghai. In July the Kuomintang organized a protest demonstration in Canton where British sailors and French marines killed 52 persons and injured 117 more. At once, 200,000 Chinese workers in the nearby British Crown Colony of Hong Kong quit their jobs and moved to Canton, which the British blockaded. The Kuomintang ordered a nation-wide boycott of British goods. But blockaded Canton could not long support an army of 100,000 men and care for an additional 200,000 refugees. The Kuomintang faced two alternatives: retreat or advance—and nobody counseled retreat. The Hong Kong strike continued. The nation-wide boycott of British goods spread.

The 1925 strike and boycott put the British Crown Colony of Hong Kong temporarily out of commission. At first the strikers changed the Chinese name of Hong Kong, from Hsiangkang, meaning fragrant harbor, to Ch'oukang, meaning stinking harbor, for the local garbage collectors had gone on strike. Finally, as the Crown Colony showed symptoms of *rigor mortis*, the strikers triumphantly named Hong Kong Szukang, or dead harbor. But Chinese liberals who had supported the Kuomintang became uneasy. They admitted that it was "a good thing" for the labor movement to become aggressive, but added "too much of a good thing is harmful."

They did not need to worry. The Chinese Revolution, at this stage, was no proletarian revolution, on the Russian model, directed by a disciplined high command of professional agitators. It was a revolution of bourgeois nationalists, led by middle-class intellectuals and supported by peasants and workers. The Communists tried to build a mass proletarian party, but most of their leaders came from the student and professional ranks and found it expedient to share Stalin's faith in the "revolutionary bourgeoisie" who had created the Kuomintang. In 1925 the Chinese Communist Party claimed only one thousand members, plus some nine thousand Young Communists. The Kuomintang rode high. Stalin assumed that the Soviet Union would have to remain on the defensive indefinitely. Regarding the British Empire as the chief threat to Soviet security, Stalin saw little chance for a Russian-style revolution in

China. He wanted to help the Kuomintang establish a strong, friendly national government that would work with him to undermine the British position in Asia.

When Borodin arrived in China he ordered the Communists to "do the coolie work for the Kuomintang." Trotsky denounced this submission to a bourgeois, capitalist party as betrayal of the world revolution. The less radical members of the Kuomintang warned against the creation, within their own ranks, of a disciplined minority taking its orders from a foreign power. Within a few years, events justified both warnings, but for the moment all went well. Wang Ching-wei presided over the meetings of the Central Executive Committee of the Kuomintang and won over many of the well-to-do Cantonese merchants to the Nationalist cause. Chiang Kai-shek staffed the army with personal supporters and renewed his contacts with the Shanghai bankers and the secret societies —or gangs—some of which had existed for several hundred years. The Communists, whose numbers increased to fifty-seven thousand by 1927, concentrated on the workers and peasants. But Chiang Kai-shek never batted an eye, and on March 20, 1926, forced Wang Ching-wei to resign all his Party posts and leave the country by alleging that the Communists were plotting against them both. He secured all of Wang's political power for himself and at the same time had himself appointed supreme commander of a so-called "Northern Punitive Expedition" to bring the principal cities of China—Hankow, Nanking, and Shanghai—under Kuomintang rule and to set up a national government at Peking.

Wang Ching-wei gladly quit. He did not want to split with Chiang and he needed to go to Europe for a delicate surgical operation. No other Kuomintang leader dared stand up to Chiang, whose military plans aroused enthusiasm. Borodin feared the worst, but could not openly object without appearing faint-hearted. Moreover, Chiang had not openly broken with the Communists. "We cannot deny that the Chinese Revolution is part of the world revolution," he told his Whampoa cadets. "The realization of the Three Peoples' Principles means the realization of Communism. Knowing that we cannot separate the Chinese Revolution from the world revolution, why should there be any quarrel among us about the Three Peoples' Principles and Communism?" Chiang Kai-shek had learned his lessons in Moscow all too well. He not only knew how to spout revolutionary slogans; he had mastered the Communist art of double-talk and double-dealing.

Seven Kuomintang armies, totaling more than one hundred thousand men, began to fan out from Kwangtung to the northwest, north, and northeast. The army led by Chiang Kai-shek headed northeast for his native province of Chekiang and the city of Shanghai, but it made slow progress. The largest army moved northwest against Hankow, five hun-

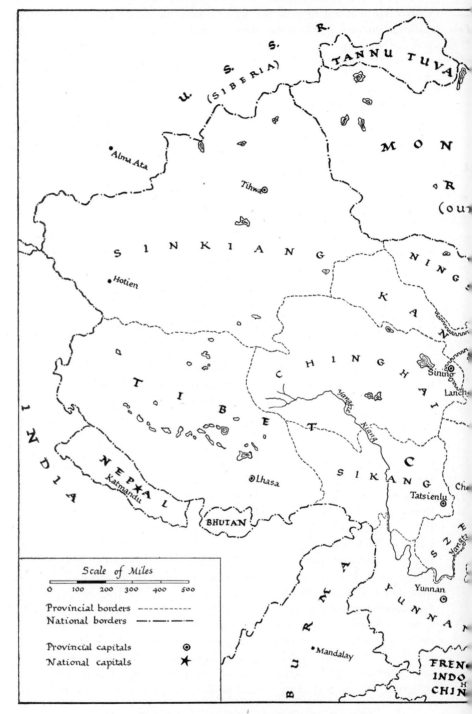

China: Its Provinces, Principal Cities, and Neighbors

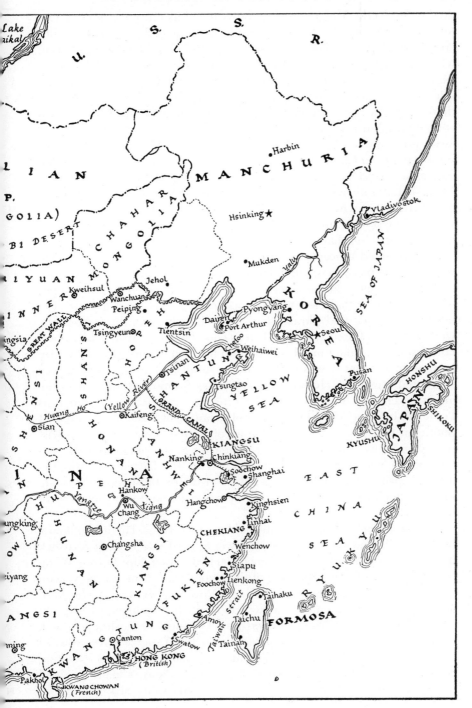

dred miles up the Yangtze River, and reached its objective in early October. The peasants in the countryside welcomed the invaders as liberators; so did the workers of Hankow. The troops of Marshal Wu Pei-fu,
who had again become War Minister for the Peking government, offered
slight resistance. The Kuomintang politicians followed the Kuomintang
soldiers to Hankow and established a provisional national government
there. Borodin tried to persuade the Kuomintang to attack the British
concessions, but Eugene Chen, the Foreign Minister in the new government, preferred to negotiate. Chen was born in the West Indies, a British
subject of mixed Chinese and Negro ancestry. He received his education
in England, studied at London University, and spoke more English than
Chinese. Later he became English secretary to Dr. Sun. Chen's proudest
moment arrived when he persuaded the British to recognize the provisional Chinese government at Hankow and to give up their extraterritorial privileges in that city.

Chen repelled Vincent Sheean as much as Borodin attracted him: "He
was all of a piece, a small, clever, venomous, faintly reptilian man,
adroit and slippery in the movements of his mind, combative in temper
with a kind of lethal elegance in appearance, voice, and gesture. His
talent for grand, bad phrases had made him famous throughout the
world." Sheean found Eugene Chen as complacent as Austen Chamberlain, but at the same time "his delight in his own language and the care
he took to see that it was written down in all its baroque significance
suggested Mussolini. He was as theatrical as Briand, without any of the
old fox's charm; he was as ingratiating as Stresemann, as bitter as
Poincaré. In short, Mr. Chen was a politician." But Chen was a careerist
politician with an ax to grind, the ax of hatred: "As a pure careerist
politician he would normally have gone over to the side of the big bat-
talions. He was prevented from doing so by the hatred that was the
original spring of all his action—a hatred of the pretensions of the white
race, particularly of the British. His hatred made and kept him a revolutionary."

Eugene Chen knew how to hate and how to intrigue. He did not know
how to lead. And with Wang Ching-wei abroad and Chiang Kai-shek
in the field, the Hankow government lacked leadership. Before Wang
had gone abroad, the right wing of the Kuomintang took up the slogan,
"Ally with Chiang to overthrow Wang." Now the left wing of the Kuomintang which dominated Hankow took up the Communist-inspired
slogan of "Welcome Wang to overthrow Chiang." Wang hurried back
from Europe while Chiang hurried down the Yangtze River toward
Nanking and Shanghai. The Kuomintang troops who took Nanking
committed atrocities that alarmed the foreign colony. Chiang pledged
himself to maintain better discipline and moved toward Shanghai. As he

reached the outskirts of the city in March, 1927, the Communists led a workers' insurrection against the local commanders and turned over all power to Chiang Kai-shek, who had meanwhile re-established contact with his banker and gangster friends on the inside. A month later, after the leaders of the workers' insurrection had taken the city for him from the inside, he turned his gangsters loose. Between April and the end of the year Chiang had almost forty thousand Chinese workers killed and more than thirty thousand jailed as political prisoners, most of them in the great cities and the coastal provinces. "The usual methods of shooting and beheading have been abetted by methods of torture and mutilation which reek of the Dark Ages and the Inquisition," reported the *China Weekly Review*, an American-owned, pro-Kuomintang paper published in Shanghai. "The results have been impressive. The peasant and labor unions of Hunan, probably the most effectively organized in the whole country, are completely smashed."

Chiang justified this slaughter by accusing the Communists of plotting against him, especially in the city of Canton. Chen Tu-hsiu, general secretary of the Chinese Communist Party, expressed pained amazement: "Unless the Communist Party is a party of madmen, certainly it does not want to establish a workers' and peasants' government in Canton. Chiang Kai-shek is one of the pillars of the national revolutionary movement. Unless the Communist Party were the tool of the imperialists, it would surely not adopt such a policy of disrupting the unity of the Chinese revolutionary forces." In an open letter to Chiang, the official spokesman for the Chinese Communists protested further: "At this time to conspire for the overthrow of Chiang Kai-shek in Canton—what a help to the reactionary forces this would be! If the Chinese Communist Party is such a revolutionary party, it should be got rid of. If among the comrades of the Communist Party there are any who harbor ideas of such a counterrevolutionary character, you should shoot them without the least ceremony." Chen Tu-hsiu referred here to the Trotskyites who were calling for just such a Communist seizure of power as the Stalinists denounced. The Chinese Communists could not countenance any move against the Kuomintang: "The Chinese Communist Party resolutely recognizes that the Kuomintang and its principles are necessary to the Chinese Revolution. Only those who are unwilling to see the Chinese Revolution advance could advocate overthrowing the Kuomintang. No matter how misguided it is, the Chinese Communist Party could never advocate the overthrow of its ally, the Kuomintang, to please our imperialist and militarist enemies."

These appeals meant just one thing to Chiang Kai-shek. He had gone to school in Moscow, where he learned to trip your enemy when you are in the way with him and, if he stumbles, to kick him and keep on kicking as hard as you can. Chiang therefore turned against the workers of Shanghai and Canton and the peasants of Hunan Province, smashing their organizations, exterminating leaders with any Communist connections, and thus shattering the whole policy that Stalin had followed in China since Sun and Joffe made their original agreement back in 1923. Shortly before Chiang struck, the Comintern announced: "The Chinese Communist Party and class-conscious Chinese workers must not, under any circumstances, pursue a tactic which would disorganize the revolutionary armies just because the influence of the bourgeoisie is to a certain degree strong there." And even after Chiang had turned his gangsters against the Shanghai Communists, Stalin cautioned: "At present we need the Right. It has capable people who still direct the army and lead it against imperialism."

Not until April, 1927, did Stalin reverse the Party line by rushing M. N. Roy, a militant Indian agitator, to Hankow to replace Borodin and organize revolts of workers and peasants. This did not, however, lead to mass uprisings. Instead it caused the leaders of the Left Kuomintang to throw all Russian advisers out of Hankow on July 15, 1927, and ship them back to Moscow. One by one, the Left Kuomintang leaders trooped to Nanking and submitted themselves to Chiang; only Madame Sun and Eugene Chen refused to capitulate, and although they had opposed Roy and the Communists, they finally made their way to Moscow, too. Meanwhile, Chiang Kai-shek turned his troops against all remaining Communist strongholds, finally wiping out the "Canton Commune" where Moscow ordered a bloody, futile last stand in December. The year 1927 thus ended with the Chinese Communists decimated and dispersed, their Russian masters driven back to Moscow, and Chiang Kai-shek at the head of a new national government which had transferred the capital of Republican China from Peking to Nanking.

But the authority of this government did not extend, even in a nominal sense, beyond four of China's eighteen provinces. Everywhere else the war lord system remained. Some of these war lords went through the formality of acknowledging the authority of Nanking. In practice, however, they collected all taxes—sometimes years in advance—and more often than not one rival war lord would overthrow another and tax the people all over again. Two million Chinese remained under arms, and nobody would start disarming for fear of losing face or falling victim to a double-cross. In the part of China that Chiang did control he outlawed all strikes, except those approved by the government. He did nothing about land reform. China remained without adequate transport, without any uniform currency or system of law, without any new system of education to replace the old Confucian system that the revolution had destroyed. For himself Chiang did well. After he took Shanghai he announced his conversion to the Methodist Church, married the youngest of the Soong sisters—May-ling—and made her brother, T. V. Soong, his Finance Minister and their brother-in-law, Dr. H. H. Kung, director of the central bank. "T.V.," a recent Harvard graduate, had some sympathy for the Left Kuomintang; Dr. Kung, who claimed direct descent from Confucius, seized the opportunity to make himself one of the richest men in China. In allying himself with the newly formed Soong dynasty Chiang was following a pattern that every Chinese understood: without strong families, no nation can be strong.

Yet one important member of the Soong family held out. Although the Central Executive Committee elected Madame Sun as one of its members, she refused to serve, preferring to live quietly in the green-shuttered house that her husband had occupied in the French concession of Shanghai. When the new government placed the remains of Dr. Sun in a million-dollar mausoleum outside Nanking, she participated in the ceremonies, but made it clear that she still did not endorse the new regime. An exasperated government official once told her, "If you were anybody but Madame Sun, we'd cut off your head," to which she smilingly replied, "If you were the revolutionaries you pretend to be, you'd cut it off anyway." The remark did less than justice to the calculated ruthlessness of Chiang Kai-shek, who, on his march to power, had approved the slaughter of more than a hundred thousand Communists and Communist sympathizers. Most of them belonged to the younger generation of students, and in a country with so few trained leaders as China the loss was impossible to estimate or repair.

· IV ·

THIS LOSS raked the Communists fore and aft. In the first place, it wiped out most of their young leaders and potential leaders. In the second place, Stalin held the few Chinese Communists who escaped Chiang's firing squads responsible for the failure of his own disastrous policy. But while Moscow kept making and breaking a succession of Chinese Communist leaders in Canton, Shanghai, and Hankow, another group, known as the "Real Power Faction," devoted itself to organizing the peasants, building up its own army, and establishing its own government in Kiangsi Province. From Moscow, Stalin and Bukharin insisted that the urban proletariat must lead the Chinese Revolution, while in China itself, the urban proletariat turned from the Communists, partly as a result of Chiang Kai-shek's systematic terror, partly as a result of Stalin's mistakes. In April, 1929, the Chinese Communists admitted that only 10 per cent of their members belonged to the proletariat. By June the proportion had dropped to 3 per cent. Meanwhile the Real Power Fac-

TRIANGLE

Mao Tse-tung

tion continued to widen its mass base, enlarge its army, and increase the territory under its control by concentrating on the largest and most depressed class in China—the peasantry.

While the Russian Bolsheviks perpetuated the proletarian revolution by sentencing five million Russian peasants to death by starvation, the Chinese Communists tried to create an agrarian revolution by setting up the Chinese peasants on their own land. Because Chinese Communists had no strength in the cities, they could not promote industrialization along Russian lines. Nor did Chinese agriculture lend itself to the mechanized, collective methods that the Soviet government forced on Russia. China possessed no great landowning class for the Communists to despoil and destroy. About all the Chinese Communists could do was distribute some of the larger farms among the poorer peasants, expropriate the village moneylender, and help the individual Chinese to farm his land more efficiently. The Chinese Communists did not nationalize any farm land and did not force the peasants to join giant collectives. The Chinese Communists did, however, offer a military career to young men in rural districts who could not find work or land of their own.

Mao Tse-tung, the brain and spirit of the Real Power Faction, had rebelled against his father, a well-to-do rice merchant, who had tried to indoctrinate the boy with the precepts of Confucius. "I hated Confucius from the age of eight," Mao told a friend. "There was a Confucian temple in the village, and I wanted nothing more than to burn it to the ground." But, like Sun Yat-sen, who also turned against Confucius, Mao remained under the spell of his authoritarian philosophy. Unlike Sun Yat-sen, Mao based his political philosophy on the heroes of Chinese literature and history, especially the leaders of several peasant rebellions that had threatened the very existence of the Empire during the latter half of the nineteenth century. "He approved of the peasants," one of his friends recalled, "he approved of no one else. What he particularly approved of in the peasants was their courtesy and their loyalty to one another. He said the townspeople were not really loyal to one another; and they were not courteous by nature, they simply followed accepted customs. In a sense he was split between his admiration for scholarship and scholars, and his admiration for the peasants. He thought he would be a teacher, and he would spend his time teaching peasants." Although he excelled as a scholar, Mao also had ambitions to become a political and even a military leader. He served briefly as a soldier during the 1911 revolution before taking up the life of a wandering scholar.

The end of the war in Europe found the twenty-five-year-old Mao Tse-tung holding a lowly job delivering and picking up newspapers in the periodical room of the Peking University library. Here he came under the spell of the founders of the Chinese Communist Party, which he joined. But while most young Communists followed Moscow's orders and organized the city workers, Mao returned to his beloved peasants in his native province of Hunan, in behalf of both the Communists and the Kuomintang. Chiang Kai-shek agreed with his Communist allies that the peasantry could be used to further the revolution they were trying to make together: "The task of the peasant is to provide us with information concerning the enemy, food and comfort in our encampments, and soldiers for our armies."

Chiang Kai-shek turned against the Communists, but Mao Tse-tung organized a drastic and extensive peasant revolution in Hunan Province. "No landowner's life was safe," wrote Robert Payne in his life of Mao Tse-tung. "The richer ones fled to the safety of Shanghai; those who were less rich fled to Hankow; others escaped to Changsha. Those who remained, or were caught by the peasants, were compelled to renounce their riches. Those who wore long gowns or owned more than fifty *mou* of land were fined, required to make contributions to the peasant association, and had their sedan chairs smashed before their eyes. The final affront consisted in having their opium pipes taken away from them, and then the pipes were broken. With some relish Mao noted that 'the ivory beds of the daughters of the landlords were stepped upon by the dirty feet of the peasants.'" During the summer of 1926 the membership of the peasant associations in central Hunan Province increased from three hundred thousand to two million.

The next year Chiang Kai-shek crushed the workers' organizations and exterminated the Communist leaders in most of China's cities. Almost alone, Mao Tse-tung held out. He finally assembled three regiments of a thousand men and less than two hundred rifles on Chingkanshan Mountain, on the border between Hunan and Kiangsi Provinces. He allied himself with two local bandits, won support among the nearby peasants, and slowly accumulated more men and arms. Throughout 1928 this one mountain area remained the only stronghold still in Chinese Communist hands, and its survival and growth soon attracted the attention of Chiang Kai-shek. In 1930 and 1931 he sent three annihilation campaigns against the Communists. They all failed and suffered enormous casualties at the hands of much weaker forces. Mao Tse-tung originated his own style of guerrilla warfare, which he summarized in this quatrain:

> *"When the enemy advances, we retreat.*
> *When he escapes, we harass.*
> *When he retreats, we pursue.*
> *When he is tired, we attack."*

Two more annihilation campaigns followed in 1933. All told, Chiang's casualties ran into the hundred thousands. Mao Tse-tung's forces, often outnumbered ten to one, did not suffer one tenth as many losses.

In 1928 Mao Tse-tung acquired an able helper in the person of General Chu Teh, of peasant stock, also an intellectual but not so much of an introvert as Mao, less a theoretician, more a popular leader and born mixer. They worked together in the closest harmony—Mao devising most of the strategy, Chu Teh executing the tactics. "Essentially," wrote Benjamin I. Schwartz, "the Maoist strategy involves the imposition of a political party organized in accordance with Leninist principles and animated by faith in certain basic tenets of Marxism-Leninism onto a purely peasant mass base." By 1928 Mao had evolved a strategy that required these five conditions before it could go into operation. First, a strong mass base, which had to be a peasant base at that time. Second, a strong party, organized in accordance with Lenin's principles. Third, a strong Red Army. Fourth, a strategically located territory. Fifth, a self-sufficient territory.

Mao found all these conditions—or helped bring them about—in Kiangsi Province, and while the Communists in other parts of China suffered one catastrophe after another his Real Power Faction went from strength to strength. On November 7, 1931, the Central Committee of the Chinese Communist Party shifted its headquarters from Shanghai to the city of Juichin in Kiangsi Province, where the first All-China Congress of Soviets met and established the Chinese Soviet Republic with Mao Tse-tung as its chairman. Mao had never openly broken with Moscow and Moscow had never publicly reprimanded Mao. Which added to the significance of his triumph. For years Mao had stubbornly violated Moscow's directives and organized his own kind of revolution, and now Moscow tacitly admitted that he had followed the correct course. "The Chinese Communist Party," wrote Schwartz, "under the leadership of Mao Tse-tung has not been the party of the industrial proletariat nor has it been the party of the peasantry in the Marxist-Leninist sense. It has rather been an elite corps of politically articulate leaders organized along Leninist lines, but drawn on its top levels from various strata of Chinese society."

The outside world had no inkling at the time of what Mao Tse-tung's triumph really meant. The Russian Communists and even Mao himself preferred not to reveal what had happened. As a result, some visitors to Red China, observing Mao Tse-tung's independence from Moscow and his reliance on the peasantry, mistook him for an agrarian reformer. Others, noting the correct relations that continued between the Russian and the Chinese Communists, regarded him as just another puppet of the Kremlin. But the eyes of the world and the eyes of most Chinese, too, looked in other directions and saw that the bloody events of the mid-1920's that brought Chiang Kai-shek to power in Nanking had hastened one fundamental—if negative—change. They inflicted upon all foreign influences in China, including the Russian, the worst defeat they had ever suffered. The results of the war had weakened the European Powers in China; the results of the revolution had weakened Russia; the Tokyo earthquake of 1923 had weakened Japan. The United States, at the Washington Conference, revived the Open Door and restrained the British and Japanese. But the Chinese also made headway on their own account. The Kuomintang organized strikes, boycotts, and antiforeign demonstrations. It created a fighting army, a one-party state, and a terror campaign that smashed the Communist movement in every urban center. But Mao Tse-tung devised a new revolutionary strategy that began to achieve substantial results among the peasants. The same nationalist spirit that had swept the Middle East and India reached China, too. Nor had the triumphant Kuomintang quite extinguished the fires of revolution which it had once fanned. Thus the chief result of the Chinese Revolution during the decade was that it put the foreigner on the defensive at the moment when the feverish prosperity of the 1920's first began to cool.

SUMMING UP

DURING the 1920's the revolution in China on which Dr. Sun Yat-sen had been working since the turn of the century came into its own. Dr. Sun did not, however, live to see the fulfillment of his life's work—which may have been just as well. For the revolution to which he had given so much benefited chiefly a small group of Kuomintang leaders who clung to Chiang Kai-shek and the Soong family. Unlike Lenin in Russia, Dr. Sun inherited no revolutionary tradition. The Kuomintang had no time to organize itself into a small, tight organization like the Russian Bolsheviks —or into a mass democratic party like the German Socialists or the British Laborites. Dr. Sun therefore thrashed about in every direction, seeking aid from every foreign quarter, appealing to every native group.

The Chinese Revolution reached far deeper than the Russian Revolution or any of the attempted revolutions in Europe. It went to the very roots of Chinese life. For thousands of years the Chinese had based their education on the precepts of Confucius, their religion on the authority of the family. The newer nations of eastern Europe had fewer traditions; the more backward nations of the Middle East had a less rich culture. Dr. Sun did what he could to fill the void that the collapse of the old China had left. That his hopes never materialized did not reflect upon his character or ability. All that any mortal could accomplish under the circumstances, he had done. The revolution he proclaimed in 1912 still had a long way to go. At first, it responded chiefly to foreign influences. Then, in the 1920's, it turned against the foreigner. The European Powers and the United States could not halt the avalanche that Dr. Sun had started. They lacked the power; they even lacked the will to act. The war had caused them to lose face in Chinese eyes. Their failure to make good on Wilson's promises sent their stock still lower. And they themselves knew that the old authority and assurance had gone. The Russians, on the other hand, got off to an impressive start. While the Chinese railed in vain against the Versailles Treaty, the Bolshevik leaders freely gave up certain privileges the Tsars had always enjoyed in China. Yet the Russians, under Stalin's leadership, eventually failed as completely as everyone else. The Kuomintang turned against the Communists as it had never turned against the foreigners, and all that the Communists could save was a new leader, Mao Tse-tung, with a new revolutionary strategy based on the peasantry. While the successors of Dr. Sun spent much of their time lining their own pockets, a battered remnant of Communists in the interior refused to capitulate to Chiang Kai-shek.

9

New Europe

*The later 1920's gave promise of a real European
revival, but war-weariness, inertia, and despair
lingered on.*

PREVIEW

BY 1925 the peace and security that the world had vainly sought
since 1918 showed signs of materializing at last. Recovery and democracy went forward together in France. Order and dictatorship went
forward together in Italy and Spain. Germany remained the big question
mark. The election of Hindenburg to the Presidency and the death of
Stresemann, four years later, did not augur well for the future of the
Weimar Republic. Conditions in Poland, Rumania, and Austria remained
disturbed. Over most of the rest of Europe comparative tranquillity
reigned. But the British found the 1920's a consistently discouraging
decade. The Tories put the pound back on the gold standard, thereby
contributing to the outbreak of a general strike. The Laborites won the
1929 general election and gave a better account of themselves in foreign
and imperial affairs. But they played more often from weakness than
from strength.

· I ·

THE "Back to Normalcy" fever that swept the United States presently
affected Europe, too. In 1925 Winston Churchill put Britain back on the
gold standard; the French Radicals installed the orthodox Caillaux as
Minister of Finance; the German people elected Field Marshal Hindenburg President of the Republic. The year 1925 also saw the principal
Foreign Ministers of Europe meeting in the little Swiss town of Locarno,
where they signed a series of treaties that restored peace on the old prewar balance-of-power basis.

On February 28, 1925, Friedrich Ebert, the Socialist saddle maker
who had become the first President of Germany, died in office. Two
months later the German people chose the seventy-seven-year-old Hindenburg to replace him. Hindenburg polled fourteen and a half million
votes; Wilhelm Marx, of the Catholic Center Party, polled thirteen and

a half millions; Ernst Thälmann, the Communist, polled nearly two millions. Hindenburg triumphed because the Communists refused to form a common anti-Hindenburg front with Centrists, Socialists, and the smaller moderate parties. Once again, the extreme left played into the hands of the extreme right. "*Aujourd'hui Hindenburg, demain le Kaiser*," commented a Belgian newspaper. Hindenburg personally favored a return of Hohenzollern rule, but he gave his soldier's oath to uphold the Weimar Republic. Not all his supporters wanted the Hohenzollerns back; not all his opponents wanted the Republic to endure. By and large, the election revealed a widespread yearning for the good old prewar days.

On April 28, 1925, two days after the Hindenburg election, Winston Churchill resumed his accustomed place on the front pages of the world press with the announcement that he was putting the pound sterling back on the prewar gold standard. Since the collapse of the Lloyd George coalition in 1922 Churchill had spent most of his time painting pictures and writing a massive history of the war, but in the autumn of 1924 he returned to the Conservative Party, which he had deserted in 1904, and Prime Minister Baldwin rewarded him with the post of Chancellor of the Exchequer. The plodding Party leaders feared Churchill's brilliance; they feared even more "to let Winston loose in the Opposition." And they cheered his two-hour presentation of the gold-standard budget, especially when he paused to lubricate his oratory with an "amber-coloured liquid," as the official record solemnly described it.

Since August, 1914, the Bank of England had refused to redeem pound notes in gold, and since the 1918 Armistice the value of the pound had dropped about 20 per cent below its prewar level. But now, as in prewar times, the pound could once again "look the dollar in the eye." The return of the pound to gold meant happier days for holders of British war bonds and of all other British securities that paid fixed interest rates. British bankers also had reason to hope that London would resume its traditional place as financial capital of the world. But British exporters gnashed their teeth. Before the war they had lost ground to Germany. Now they found American competition still more formidable. Although the pound might look the dollar in the eye, British industry stood knee-high to America's. The British had to import most of their raw materials from all over the world. American industry procured most of its raw materials at home. The British got most of their power from inefficient coal mines and produced most of their goods in antiquated factories. The Americans possessed abundant supplies of oil, natural gas, and water power. While British industry still concentrated on quality, the Americans concentrated on serving a mass market. The war, which had left the British having to pay the equivalent of one and three quarter billion dollars a year on their national debt, left the Americans with a new industrial plant that they continued to expand during the postwar years.

John Maynard Keynes attacked Britain's return to the prewar gold standard in a witty article entitled "The Economic Consequences of Mr. Churchill." While the romantic Chancellor of the Exchequer foresaw his beloved Empire rising to new heights of glory, the realistic Mr. Keynes foresaw disaster. For Churchill had favored British bankers at the expense of British industry, and British coupon clippers at the expense of British workers. With the pound back at par, British exports could not hope to boom, and British industry could not hope to recover unless British workers toiled longer hours for less pay. The Labor Party lacked the votes to defeat the Churchill budget in the House of Commons, but the trade unions commanded power of another kind. By strikes and threats of strikes they had the power to prevent the Conservatives from carrying the new policy too far.

While the British Conservatives prepared to bring back the good old prewar days at the expense of the British working classes, the French Radicals tried to make everybody happy by easing financial burdens in all directions. They ran into trouble at once. Within less than a year Herriot had to quit as Premier after the Senate discovered that his government had doctored the financial figures to make the picture look deceptively bright. Joseph Caillaux, the only orthodox financier in the Radical Party, could not persuade the Chamber to vote the necessary taxes or the public to buy a new bond issue. Several more governments and half a dozen more Finance Ministers tried in vain to make two and two equal five until the summer of 1926 when Poincaré returned to power at the head of a government of National Union which included members of all the leading parties except the Socialists and Communists. The franc stood at fifty to the dollar when Poincaré took office. By the end of the year he pegged it at twenty-five to the dollar, having increased all taxes except the income taxes of the very rich. For this outcome the Radicals had only themselves to blame. In spite of their wide popular support outside the Chamber of Deputies, they refused even to face economic realities, much less to master them.

In foreign affairs the Radicals performed more creditably. Briand replaced Herriot as Foreign Minister in 1925 and even the return of "*Poincaré la guerre—Poincaré la Ruhr*"—did not alter the conciliatory policy that superseded the policy of revenge in 1924. Lord D'Abernon, the British Ambassador in Berlin, had a hand in shaping this policy when he started backing Dr. Stresemann during the Ruhr conflict of 1923. But when MacDonald came to power in Britain and Herriot came to power in France the following year, they went rather further than D'Abernon contemplated. D'Abernon of course approved the Dawes

UNDERWOOD

Sir Austen Chamberlain

Plan; he welcomed the meeting of Herriot, Stresemann, and Mac-Donald in London. But he and his Conservative friends recoiled with horror when MacDonald first recognized Soviet Russia, then prepared to sign trade agreements with the Bolsheviks, and finally joined Stresemann and Briand in initialing the Geneva Protocol. Apparently, MacDonald wanted to welcome Russia back into the family of civilized nations while committing his own country, under the Geneva Protocol, to renounce some of its national sovereignty to the League of Nations.

When the Conservatives returned to power in England at the end of 1924, they reverted to the original D'Abernon strategy. This meant, first of all, bringing the power of France and Germany into so close a balance that Great Britain could again exercise a determining influence in Europe. The next step called for the formation of a solid bloc of West European states as the best guarantee against the expansion of Russian Communism. Prime Minister Stanley Baldwin entrusted the execution of this strategy to the man he appointed Foreign Secretary—Austen Chamberlain, who looked like a more refined edition of his more robust father, "Brummagem Joe." Unlike the father, the son had attended Rugby and Cambridge, had spent two years of study abroad, and preferred France to Germany. Austen Chamberlain did not have to fight his way to the top of the political ladder; he relied on his name, his industry, and his character. He was less mercurial than his father and a more loyal party man, but he lacked his father's drive.

Early in 1925, Chamberlain made his first appearance at League headquarters, where he announced that his government would not ratify the Geneva Protocol. This hastened the fall of Herriot and set the stage for Briand to assume control of French foreign policy. Chamberlain then spent most of the spring and summer months trying to work out a new agreement to bring the countries of western Europe together and guarantee France against Germany and Germany against France. On June 5 he associated himself with an Allied note demanding that the German government abolish the General Staff and all secret military societies. Yet if the Allies accepted the facts and logic of their own note, they had every reason to assume that the Germany which had just elected Hindenburg chief of state would at once start scheming against the peace of Europe. On the other hand, if the Allies believed that Germany could play a peaceful, honorable part in building a new Europe, why affront German susceptibilities by challenging German good will? The answer was that both the Allies and the Germans were divided. The French had little faith in German integrity. The British had little patience with the fears of the French. As for the Germans, almost half of them had just voted for the monarchist Hindenburg; a smaller number had voted for a genuine Republican; more than one in twenty had voted Communist.

These divisions strengthened Stresemann's position in the Foreign Office. His Nationalist past made him acceptable to many of Hindenburg's supporters. His postwar record commended him to most supporters of the Republic. His policy of treaty fulfillment won general confidence in Britain and the United States. Stresemann did not let the Allied note provoke him; instead, he harked back to the proposal he had first made in February, 1925, for a Three-Power Anglo-Franco-German agreement whereby Britain would guarantee France against German aggression and guarantee Germany against French aggression. Germany would renounce forever all claim to Alsace and Lorraine and would accept as immutable the western frontiers laid down in the Versailles Treaty. "We have first to liquidate the postwar period," said Stresemann, "and for that purpose we must maintain good relations with France."

The Stresemann proposal did not go so far as the Geneva Protocol, but it involved more commitments than the League of Nations required. British Liberals and Laborites favored these commitments and wanted more. So did Briand, who urged extending the scope of the pact to include the eastern as well as the western settlement. But the Germans would not agree to accept the status quo in that quarter for all time, and to the British eastern Europe seemed far, dangerously far, away. As negotiations proceeded during the summer of 1925, chiefly in London, Chamberlain transformed the German proposal into a West European security pact to be signed by Germany, Belgium, France, Italy, and Great Britain, to go into effect as soon as the League of Nations admitted Germany to membership.

The Russians watched the negotiations with a suspicion that Chamberlain reciprocated. After first meeting Litvinov at Geneva, he had written a friend, "Do you think it was pleasant for me to shake the hand of the representative of men who killed the cousin of my sovereign?" The British Laborites, who had no sympathy for Communism, accused Chamberlain of building a western anti-Soviet bloc. He preferred to regard himself as a twentieth-century Castlereagh, who negotiated a

Maxim Litvinov. Drawing by Kelen

balance-of-power peace after the Napoleonic wars. In October, after the West European Foreign Ministers met at the Swiss town of Locarno and signed the treaty that bore its name, King George V awarded Chamberlain the same title, Knight of the Garter, that Queen Victoria had bestowed upon Disraeli when he returned from the Congress of Berlin, bringing "peace with honor" and changing the European balance of power to Germany's advantage. Both the Castlereagh and the Disraeli comparisons held water. Like Castlereagh in 1815 and like Disraeli in 1878, Chamberlain committed Britain to support a balance of power in Europe. The chief difference between Chamberlain and his predecessors was that they looked to the present and future whereas he found inspiration in the past.

Ramsay MacDonald entered a dissenting opinion when he accused Chamberlain of having "engineered Locarno for the purpose of unifying Western civilization against Russia." William Ormsby-Gore, speaking for the Conservative government, preferred to put it another way: "The significance of Locarno was tremendous. It meant that as far as the present government of Germany was concerned, it was detached from Russia and was throwing in its lot with the Western Powers." As for Chamberlain, what he liked best about Locarno was that Britain's obligations were "narrowly circumscribed to the conditions under which we have a vital interest." He emphasized that Locarno was in no sense an alliance but, rather, an agreement among former enemies not to combine against one another: "It is the distinction between an alliance of certain powers against another power or group of powers and a mutual guarantee of the peaceful settlement of disputes between a group of powers interested in a certain area."

Foreign Minister Beneš of Czechoslovakia expressed the most optimistic view of all when he declared: "Settled peace on the Rhine means settled peace on the Danube." His prediction could come true if the "Locarno spirit" spread, and the prospects for a stable Europe did look better in the fall of 1925 than they had since the Paris Peace Conference of 1919. At Locarno Stresemann, in effect, accepted the Versailles settlement in so far as it covered western Europe. Beneš hoped, ultimately, for an "Eastern Locarno" under which the Great Powers as well as the small ones would extend their guarantees to the eastern settlements. Only Briand called for the kind of commitments Beneš wanted, and he showed France meant business by signing mutual-assistance pacts with Czechoslovakia and Poland. Stresemann, on the other hand, would not commit Germany to anything more than arbitration treaties with those two countries, and Chamberlain would not make any commitments for Britain beyond the Rhine. The major statesmen of western Europe went a long way, at Locarno, toward creating a new balance of power, along pre-Wilsonian, nineteenth-century lines. They had their own version of "back to normalcy" even though they called it by another name.

· II ·

DURING the latter half of the 1920's, European culture moved forward toward a postwar new era while European politics moved backward toward a prewar balance of power. Until 1925 the major nations of the West had concentrated on reconstruction and recovery and all had made startling progress. France spent the equivalent of three and a half billion dollars restoring farm lands, roads, and railways and rebuilding more than eight hundred thousand shattered farmhouses and buildings in what D. W. Brogan, author of *France Under the Republic*, called "the greatest economic achievement of postwar Europe." French industry had taken an even worse wartime beating than French agriculture, yet

by 1925 the French had rebuilt more than ten thousand factories, and their automobile industry, the first in Europe, was producing two hundred thousand cars a year, including the economical little Citroën, which even began to rival Ford in the low-price field. As in the United States, the farmers did not enjoy their share of the postwar revival. While most prices went up three or four times over— as the franc went down—land values in France increased only 50 per cent. Peasants kept migrating to the cities and the area of cultivated land dropped a little lower every year.

UNDERWOOD

Dr. and Mrs. Eduard Beneš

Paris became more than ever the tourist capital of the world where more and more Americans spent more and more money. Diaghilev revived his ballets, but the younger French generation followed the American tourists to watch Josephine Baker, the Negro dancer, and to hear Duke Ellington, the Negro jazz-band leader. From this generation also came a new kind of popular, cosmopolitan literature, written in a slang that Frenchmen themselves could not always understand. Maurice Dekobra started the vogue immediately after the war with his potboiling *Madonna of the Sleeping Cars.* In the early 1920's Paul Morand, a young diplomat, wrote two collections of short stories, *Ouvert la nuit* and *Fermé la nuit,* in which the new-style postwar Frenchman made his first appearance, speaking many languages, visiting many countries, adapting himself to many situations, most of them amorous.

"After the war," Morand wrote, "a very curious and surprising kind of life began, a way of living that lasted until about 1925, when currencies were stabilized. It was a kind of life that is hardly likely ever to occur again and I wanted to write the history of this interesting period, to paint its picture. That is how *Ouvert la nuit* and *Fermé la nuit* came to be written." Confusion, immorality, and despair permeated the Europe that Morand depicted. "I am often accused," he commented in 1926, "of keeping to the exceptional and not seeking in my writings to establish the human and permanent elements. Is it possible today, when all the new psychology teaches is that the deepest abysses of our moral life are never revealed on the surface but are revealed by actions that have apparently miscarried—actions that are illogical and unexplainable—is it possible to take young writers to task for commencing on the same lines? For me the study of the exceptional is a way of reaching the permanent." While writing a book on the professional prize-ring, *Champions du monde,* Morand visited New York and proceeded to write another book on that: "All is gay yet terrible," he observed. "The lights and the fanfare of Broadway are not destined to make people forget life, but to intensify it for them tenfold. . . . It is a terrible wearing life; people fall by the way and are removed, and the game goes on."

The United States fascinated Morand; Britain fascinated André Maurois, who had served as liaison officer between British and French armies during the war and won fame in both countries with his *Silences of Colonel Bramble* and *Discourses of Dr. O'Grady.* After the war his novelized biography of Shelley, entitled *Ariel,* attracted even more readers in England and the United States than in France and set a new literary fashion that other writers vulgarized.

French literature during the 1920's specialized as never before in cosmopolitan, exotic themes. Soon after the war the coveted Goncourt Prize

went to an African Negro for a novel about jungle life; another year it
went to Henri Fauconnier for his book on Malaysia, another year to
Maurice Bedel for *The Latitude of Love,* a novel based on Scandinavia.
Thomas Raucat made a huge success with *The Honorable Picnic,* a
masterly study, half humorous, half tragic, of the psychology of Japan.
Jean Giraudoux in *Siegfried* and Maurice Rostand in *The Man I Killed*
used the stage as a rostrum for preaching Franco-German understanding. André Siegfried wrote informed, popular, and original studies of the
United States, England, and South America. A laborer called Dubreuil
described the United States as the paradise of the workingman. The
high-brow Georges Duhamel wrote *America: The Menace.*

Such books and writers as these had little in common with the introspective Proust or the ironic Anatole France. Nor did they recall the
great tradition of French literature. André Gide, the one man above all
others who kept that tradition in his custody, fitted into no category.
He came of a Protestant family; he began to write autobiographical and
literary essays at the turn of the century. His first major novel, *The
Counterfeiters,* appeared in 1925. It deals with an experiment in crime,
attempted by a group of adolescents, as told by another character, the
novelist Édouard. Édouard also kept a journal in which he analyzed
himself and his work: "I am never anything but what I think myself—
and this varies so incessantly that often, if I were not there to make them
acquainted, my morning's self would not recognize my evening's. Nothing could be more different from me than myself. It is only when I am
alone that the substratum emerges and that I attain a certain fundamental continuity, but at such times I feel that life is slowing down,
stopping, and that I am on the very verge of ceasing to exist. My heart
beats only out of sympathy; I live only through others, by procuration,
so to speak, and by espousals; and I never feel myself living so intensely
as when I escape from myself to become no matter who."

In addition to writing an imaginary diary for the imaginary character
of Édouard, Gide kept a real diary of his own, *The Diary of the Counterfeiters,* which duly appeared. Albert J. Guérard, in his biography of
Gide, represented *The Counterfeiters* as the culmination of expressionism: "The paradoxical aim of the expressionists, carried to its extreme
by Joyce, was to abandon 'realism' for the sake of a more realistic imitation of life; to disintegrate the form of the novel until form itself expressed the baffling complexity and disorder of experience. Gide refined on this aim by juxtaposing this disorder and the effort of one of his
characters (the novelist Édouard). But his immediate technical objectives were to describe a series of interpenetrating destinies, and 'to avoid
at all cost the simple, impersonal *récit.*' *The Counterfeiters,* he resolved,

would avoid the narrowness of his earlier books even at the risk of unmanageable excess; it would become a receptacle for everything he observed, for everything he wanted to say."

In *The Counterfeiters*, expressionism and realism met and merged. In carrying the expressionist techniques as far as he could make them go, Gide added a new dimension to realism. He transcended his own introverted nature, turning himself inside out while reporting the outside world as faithfully as he reported the world within. As if recognizing that he had exhausted the possibilities of this technique, Gide struck out in a new direction. He put France behind him and made a slow voyage up the Congo River into French Equatorial Africa. On his return he wrote an exposé, more like a prewar American muckraker than a postwar French expressionist, of the white man's brutality to the Negro. This contact with imperialism in the raw led him to explore Communism and visit Moscow. Again, contact with reality led to disillusionment. Three years later, in *Return from U.S.S.R.*, he wrote, "Three years ago, I declared my admiration and my love for the U.S.S.R. An unprecedented experiment was being attempted there which filled our hearts with hope and from which we expected an immense advance, an impetus capable of carrying forward in its stride the whole human race. It is indeed worth living, I thought, in order to be present at this rebirth, and well worth while giving one's life in order to help it on. . . . A land existed where Utopia was in process of becoming reality." But the means the Soviet leaders used to achieve their ends repelled Gide, as they repelled so many other sensitive observers, and he finally concluded: "There are things more important in my eyes than myself, more important than the U.S.S.R. These things are humanity, its destiny, its culture. . . . The gravest error would be to link too closely the U.S.S.R. to the cause it stands for and make the cause appear responsible for what we deplore in the U.S.S.R." Gide, the embodiment of the twentieth-century pilgrim, did not find salvation in Moscow—or anywhere else.

Meanwhile the Catholic tradition in French literature revived under the influence of such distinguished converts as Paul Claudel, poet and diplomat, Jean Cocteau, artist and Bohemian, and Jacques Maritain, philosopher and man of letters. Some of these writers quarreled with Gide. Henri Massis, who had written a *Defense of the West* in reply to Spengler's *Decline of the West*, accused Gide of corrupting the youth of France by dealing frankly and sympathetically with the problems of the homosexual. Léon Daudet and Charles Maurras made of themselves and French Royalism an unprecedented nuisance. Maurras's cynical perversion of Roman Catholic dogma caused the Pope to place his works on the *Index Expurgatorius*.

The surrealist movement which superseded Dadaism during the early

man Ray · 1932

Surrealist Art: Man Ray, "Object of Destruction." From Fantastic Art, Dada, Surrealism, *third edition, 1947, Museum of Modern Art*

1920's gave further proof that writers and artists sought inspiration inside themselves rather than in the world around them. André Breton, who fought on the Western Front and then joined the Dadaists, wrote the First Surrealist Manifesto in 1924. Georges Hugnet, in his *Fantastic Art, Dada, Surrealism,* summarized and quoted from this document: "Convinced from the start that 'literature is a sad road that leads anywhere,' Breton wishes only to let himself go to unbridled imagination. The more this contradicts all known trends of thought, the better. He attacks *'the hatred of the marvelous wherever it rages.'* He declared that *'the marvelous is always beautiful, in fact only the marvelous is beautiful.'* He puts at the disposal of those who would venture into the realm of the marvelous not only poetic arguments, but the means to investigate modern thought and, above all, the new and decisive interpretation of psychoanalysis. During the course of surrealist development, outside all forms of idealism, outside the opiates of religion, the marvelous comes to light within *reality.* It comes to light in dreams, obsessions, preoccupations, in sleep, fear, love, chance; in hallucinations, pretended disorders, follies, ghostly apparitions, escape mechanisms and evasions, in fancies, idle wanderings, poetry, the supernatural and the unusual; in empiricism, in *super-reality.* This element of the marvelous, relegated for so long to legends and children's fairy tales, reveals now in a true light, in a surrealist light, the immanent reality and our relations to it. Surrealism has never doubted its power 'to resolve the heretofore contradictory conditions of dream and of reality into an absolute reality, a super-reality.' Surrealism will persist in forwarding and consolidating the identification of contraries which every modern discovery proves to be possible and true. The graph which would trace through the course of time the attraction of irreconcilables would be the history of surrealism. Surrealism lowers its barriers against those who consider it impossible to identify reality."

The French, with their passion for programs, had once again announced a principle before carrying it out in practice. It was not a principle that ever lent itself to successful literary use, but Breton at once recognized its applicability to painting: "The narrow concept of imitation as the goal of art is at the source of the serious misunderstanding which we see perpetuated even in our own time. Basing their work on the belief that man is capable only of reproducing more or less happily the superficial image of that which moves him, painters have shown themselves much too conventional in the choice of their subjects. Their mistake was to suppose that the subject could be taken only from the external world, whereas it should not be taken from the external world at all. It is true that human imagination can give to the most ordinary object an unexpected distinction; but the magic power of the imagination is put to very feeble use indeed if it serves merely to preserve or reinforce that which already exists. That is an inexcusable abdication. It is impossible in the present state of modern thought, when the exterior world appears more and more suspect, to agree any longer to such a sacrifice. The work of art, if it is to assist in that absolute revision of values, upon which we all agree, must base itself upon a purely subjective inspiration or it will cease to exist."

More than a decade later, Breton contributed an essay to a symposium on surrealism edited by Herbert Read, who used the word "superrealism" but decided that the public preferred "a strange and not too intelligible word for a strange and not too intelligible thing." But to Breton, the fantastic and the marvelous remained the essence of surrealism: "Above all we expressly oppose the view that it is possible to create a work of art or even, properly considered, any useful work by expressing only the *manifest* content of an age. On the contrary surrealism proposes to express the *latent* content. In the light of the greatest examples of the past we deny that the art of a period can consist of an imitation pure and simple of its external happenings." Surrealists "reject as erroneous the conception of socialist realism which attempts to impose upon the artist the exclusive duty of describing proletarian misery and the struggle for liberation in which the proletariat is engaged."

The principles of postwar surrealism as set forth by André Breton in the 1920's and the 1930's had little in common with the principles of prewar realism. Although he did not mention Marx or Freud by name, his attack on "socialist realism" repudiated Marx just as his emphasis on dreams and obsessions vindicated Freud. Then, too, the development of photography forced the painter, in particular, away from the representation of surface reality while at the same time the development of psychoanalysis opened new, inner perspectives to practitioners of all the arts. But the new techniques and new sciences told only part of the story. Surrealism appealed to the same emotions to which Communism and Fascism also catered. Low-brows as well as high-brows, the masses

Pablo Picasso, "Two Figures on the Beach." From Fantastic Art, Dada, Surrealism, *third edition, 1947, Museum of Modern Art*

as well as the classes turned against reason and logic. Life for life's sake, action for the sake of action became the new order of the day.

· III ·

No POLITICAL LEADER during the 1920's exploited the visceral appeal more effectively than Mussolini. What if his Fascist movement had produced nothing of intellectual or artistic merit? It had made the trains run on time. Isaac Marcosson and Kenneth Roberts wrote articles in praise of Fascism for the one-time isolationist *Saturday Evening Post.* Richard Washburn Child, former United States Ambassador to Italy, worked as a ghost-writer on Mussolini's autobiography, and praised Mussolini as "the greatest man of our sphere and our time." A Fascist Academy came into being in April, 1929, though it failed to include in its list of the thirty greatest living Italians such outstanding names as Gabriele D'Annunzio, Benedetto Croce, Guglielmo Ferrero, Giovanni Papini, and Grazia Deledda, whose stories of Sicilian peasant life won her the Nobel Prize for Literature in 1926. When Mussolini asked

D'Annunzio to join the Fascist Academy, he received this brief reply: "A thoroughbred horse should not mix with jackasses. This is not an insult but a eugenic-artistic fact." Mussolini did, however, persuade Marconi to accept the presidency of the Fascist Academy and to announce: "Italy's soul is growing as its body grows. Arts were never on a higher plane. Intellectual freedom was never so prevalent." His fellow Academician, F. T. Marinetti, had different ideas. He was the author of a Futurist Manifesto which began: "We intend to destroy the museums and burn the libraries. We hate unto death vulgarity, academic mediocrity, pedantry, and the cult of antique and worm-eaten art. We intend to raise love to the sphere of danger. We shall sing the songs of war."

But Mussolini had first to dispose of the opposition, destroy democracy, and set up the one-party corporate state. "The corporate state idea which Fascism has conceived and enforced," wrote Giuseppe Bottai, a member of the Fascist Cabinet, "is an absolutely modern idea. The corporations of the Middle Ages were closed institutions; Italian corporativism, on the contrary, is founded essentially on the idea of syndicates, organizations to which access is on principle freely open to all those who ply the same trade. Italian corporativism preserves the syndical structure likewise in the workers' syndicates as well as in the employers' confederations, the two parallel organizations being united in a higher state which is the corporation." In theory, employers and employes composed their differences around the table, under the eye of the all-wise Fascist state. In practice, Italian Fascism abolished the eight-hour day and the right to strike. It also did away with academic freedom and free speech. "The press of Italy is free, freer than the press of any other country," boasted Mussolini, "just so long as it supports the regime." In 1927 Pope Pius XI denounced the corporate state as "contrary to the Christian conception of the state and individual liberty." Two years later, however, he and Mussolini agreed to settle their differences.

Pope Pius XI, who ascended the throne of St. Peter in 1922 on the death of Benedict XV, had been Cardinal Ratti of Milan, an aristocrat of powerful intellect and an enthusiastic mountain climber. Confinement within the hundred acres of Vatican City irked him so much that his health went into a decline. Mussolini irked him even more. The new Pope knew all about the Duce's atheistic past. "We shall conquer without God," Mussolini had declared during the war. "I love a pagan and warlike people, a people which refuses its allegiance to revealed dogma and which is not fooled by miracles." But Mussolini, in power, needed the sanction of religion; Pope Pius and his advisers wanted to end their anomalous position as "prisoners" of the Italian state. Early in 1929 the two men signed a treaty and concordat. The Fascist state recognized the temporal power of the Pope over Vatican City and proclaimed the Roman Catholic faith as the sole religion of Italy. The Vatican, in turn, declared "the Roman question definitely and irrevocably settled and therefore eliminated" and recognized "the Kingdom of Italy under the Dynasty of the House of Savoy, with Rome as the capital of the Italian state." But within a few months the Pope and Mussolini were wrangling again over the right to teach the young.

During a period of general revival, the condition of the Italian masses under Fascism went from bad to worse. Unemployment rose from 181,-000 in 1926 to 439,000 in 1928. Bankruptcies rose from less than 4,000 in 1922 to more than 8,500 in 1926 and over 11,000 in 1929. After 1925, Mussolini never once balanced the budget. The deficit averaged about five billion lire—a quarter of a billion dollars—a year. Thanks largely to the efforts of the House of Morgan, Fascist Italy raised six hundred million dollars in loans from private American investors. But the living standard of the Italian people failed to rise above its prewar level, and in 1930 the International Labor Office of the League of Nations reported real wages in Italy as among the lowest in Europe.

Such facts and figures as these—like similar facts and figures about Russia—led the liberal world to anticipate the early collapse of both Fascism and Communism. But the assumption that mass misery breeds revolt proved nothing but wishful thinking. The power of Mussolini, like the power of Stalin, rested on a one-party state and a secret police. The Russians called theirs the Cheka, the OGPU, and later the NKVD. Mussolini's Organizzazione Volontaria per la Repressione dell' Antifascismo went by the name of OVRA. But Mussolini felt he had to appear constantly before his public—a risk Stalin saw no reason to run—and in consequence he became the frequent target for the bullets of assassins. The Honorable Violet Gibson, a recent British convert to Catholicism, fired a revolver shot that skinned his nose. The Duce, ever a showman, affixed a piece of sticking plaster, posed for photographers, and told an American journalist, "The bullets pass, Mussolini remains."

· IV ·

IN 1923 another dictator came to power in another Latin country. But different forces gave rise to the Spanish dictatorship and it pursued a different course. As Salvador de Madariaga, the Spanish husband of a British wife, expressed it, "The war drove a powerful current of foreign vitality right into the inmost recesses of the nation." Between 1914 and 1918, King Alfonso XIII of Spain enjoyed telling visiting Britons and Frenchmen, "Here in Spain only I and the canaille are pro-Ally." But his country made the best of both worlds, remained neutral, and waxed comparatively rich. The war enabled Spain to pay off most of its national debt and to increase its gold reserves from about 100 million dollars in 1914 to some 450 millions in 1918. New industries boomed; the labor movement thrived. The end of the war brought a slight slump and a mild strike wave, but times remained fairly good until 1920, when foreign orders declined, unemployment increased, and wages dropped. In 1921 King Alfonso chose the old-fashioned way out of the crisis and sent a large military expedition into the Riff Mountains of Morocco against the local chieftain, Abd-el-Krim, who had rebelled against Spanish rule. In July, at the battle of Anual, Abd-el-Krim routed the Spaniards, killing ten thousand of their soldiers, taking fifteen thousand more as prisoners, and capturing all their equipment.

In many other countries the King, the Army, or the government would have had to answer to an aroused populace. But in Spain the King, the Army, the government, and the people all gave the world a characteristic display of national pride. As the Spanish philosopher José Ortega y Gasset once wrote: "Pride is our national passion, our greatest sin. The Spaniard is not avaricious like the French, nor drunk and stupid like the Englishman, nor sensual and histrionic like the Italian. He is proud, endlessly proud." These words not only expressed the Spaniard's high opinion of himself; they revealed his sense of superiority toward others. For two more years Spain's national pride made it possible for the King, the Army, and the government to cover up their failure in Morocco and continue the futile, desultory war. Finally, to prevent exposure of his own responsibility, King Alfonso forced Alcalá Zamora, the civilian Minister of War, to resign and then dissolved the Cortes, or Parliament. On September 14, 1923, General Primo de Rivera of Catalonia proclaimed a directorship and suspended the Constitution. Alfonso accepted the coup d'état, violated the Constitution, and refused to reconvene the Cortes.

Salvador de Madariaga, who neither opposed nor supported the directorship, called Primo "a Liberal in municipal affairs, a Socialist of sorts in labor matters, a Conservative in constitutional ideas, a reactionary in education, an opportunist (with but scanty opportunities) in military administration, a truly spirited leader in Moroccan affairs, and an indifferent amateur in foreign policy." Primo had charming manners, silver hair, blue eyes, broad shoulders, a red face, and a disarmingly cynical smile. Sisley Huddleston, wandering correspondent of the Liberal *New Statesman* of London, found him "an ordinary sort of man with perhaps a spice of recklessness, a little more vitality than the ordinary man. He is the stuff of which good policemen are made. His limitations are obvious but it is just because he is not really different from the man in the street, sharing his prejudices and his predilections, that the man in the street deems him to be either the worst or the best Prime Minister that Spain has had. Primo de Rivera is then a superior gendarme —superior in power, but not in intelligence."

Primo closed many Spanish universities and drove leading Spanish intellectuals into exile. He censored the newspapers and thus earned the opposition of 90 per cent of them. He left the power of the Roman Catholic Church untouched; indeed, all teachers were forced to attend mass, and the school inspector in the province of Granada lost his job when he failed to attend the official entrance of the Cardinal Archbishop to his diocese. Primo paid one friendly visit to Mussolini, who told him, "You are living through what we are living through; as we have lasted out, you will last out." Primo won his greatest triumph abroad when he joined forces with the French in 1925 and let them bear the brunt

UNDERWOOD

King Alfonso XIII of Spain (left) and General Primo de Rivera

of a campaign against Abd-el-Krim, who was captured and exiled to Réunion Island, four hundred miles from Madagascar. In 1926 Primo organized Spain into a corporate state and created a party of young men of the middle class, known as the Unión Patriótica; but he never captured the imagination of the masses.

The resemblances between Mussolini's Italy and Primo de Rivera's Spain distracted attention from their differences. Italy had gone through the war and emerged a virtually defeated power. Mussolini found his following among disillusioned veterans and frustrated middle-class youth. On this base he climbed to power. Primo de Rivera had even less of a mass base and needed none. King Alfonso placed him in power to meet a crisis of the monarchy, and Primo proved himself exceptionally gifted at getting along with people. He had more humor and suppleness than the conventional military man, especially in so formal a country as Spain, and he did not need to worry about any liberal opposition. As Professor Alfred Mendizabal of the University of Oviedo pointed out: "The great difficulty in Spain has been to find a man who is genuinely liberal. In this difficulty lies the political tragedy of a country where he who claims to be a liberal invokes liberty only when he is oppressed, and then it is only his own liberty he wants and not that of his fellows.". With cynical heartiness, Primo loved to describe his regime as "illegal and patriotic." Quoting the language of an earlier day he also set out to eliminate "the disastrous mania of thinking."

On January 28, 1930, Primo caused something unprecedented to happen in the life of postwar Europe when King Alfonso asked for his resignation and he promptly turned it in. At last a dictator had gone out of business. "And now for a little rest," declared Primo in a final communiqué, "after two thousand three hundred and twenty-six days of continuous uneasiness, responsibility, and labor." Seven weeks later he died in Paris of diabetes and his remains were taken back to Spain for a glorious funeral. Another soldier, General Damaso Berenguer, replaced him and began to restore constitutional government in Spain by releasing political prisoners from jail, ending press censorship, and preparing to reform the schools and to hold elections for a new Cortes.

Salvador de Madariaga in his book *Spain* attributed the rise and fall of Primo to the failure of "the center," as he called it: "Why did the center fail—fail not merely to govern but even to be born? First and foremost because of the unyielding and absolute nature of the Spanish character. This is the psychological root-cause of all Spanish troubles. It determines all that happens in Spain, and explains the periodical failures of Parliamentary government and the periodical rises of dictators; as well as the Separatist movements whose leaders, be they Basques or Catalans, are blissfully unaware of the fact that they reveal themselves the more Spanish the less tractable they are. By nature, the Spaniard gravitates to the farther end of his thought, just as the Englishman gravitates to the near end of it—for thoughts are tricky things, feels the Englishman. So, while Englishmen who think differently are nevertheless always within sight and hearing of each other and of the parting of their ways, Spaniards are always out of each other's mental reach and must shout to each other and run the risk of misinterpreting a gesture of acquiescence or doubt as a gesture of threat, and of mistaking a pipe for a revolver."

To the non-Spaniard, this interpretation may appear farfetched. Would it not be equally true to attribute the special character of Spain to its lack of a substantial middle class? In one respect, however, Spain conformed to the nationalist spirit of the times. In 1926, when Germany was proposed for membership in the League of Nations with a permanent seat on the League Council, the Spanish delegate demanded a permanent seat for his country as the price of his approval of German membership. He was refused. Several months of haggling followed and when the Spaniards finally compromised and agreed to vote for Germany's entrance in the fall, the damage that the Western Powers feared had already been done. Germany and Russia had signed a new agreement that undermined in advance the new balance of power that the British had tried to create.

· V ·

IT DID NOT take long for the weaknesses of the Locarno Pact to reveal themselves. The Parliaments of all the nations concerned ratified it promptly enough, but a Colonel von Rodenberg expressed a view widely held in German military circles when he wrote in a Nationalist magazine: "If the Cabinet has agreed that Stresemann should state his views before the Reichstag Committee on Foreign Affairs, it is merely allowing him the right of defense conceded to any murderer or similarly unprofitable member of society, though there are many members of our party who regard Stresemann as something worse than a murderer." German Nationalists and German Communists voted together against Locarno. A few months later, after Spain blocked Germany's admission to the League of Nations, Stresemann appeased his opponents of the extreme left and the extreme right by signing a far-reaching agreement with the Soviet Union. The two countries not only pledged themselves to "remain in friendly touch with one another"; they went so far as to add that "if a coalition be formed between third parties for the purpose of imposing upon one of the contracting parties an economic or financial boycott, the other contracting party undertakes not to adhere to such a coalition." Germany, in effect, pledged itself not to be bound by any obligations it might later assume as a League member to join any kind of common action against Russia. And to spell this out still more clearly, Stresemann added a personal letter declaring that Germany would automatically oppose any solely anti-Soviet move the League might ever take.

As an embodiment of the Locarno spirit, Stresemann left much to be desired. At best, he carried water on both shoulders; at worst, he remained an unregenerate Nationalist in democratic disguise. The avowed German Nationalists made no pretense of seeking agreement with the Western Powers; they repudiated the Versailles Treaty; they hoped for closer relations with Soviet Russia. The Prussian Junkers had always looked to the east. Some had settled in Russia's former Baltic provinces— Lithuania, Latvia, and Estonia—that had now become independent states. Others had intermarried with the Russian aristocracy. The Bolshevik Revolution alarmed the German Nationalists less than it alarmed the propertied classes in France and England. Partly the Germans felt superior to the Russians, especially after having dictated the Peace of Brest-Litovsk; partly they resented the victorious Western Allies, who had dictated the hated Peace of Versailles.

A more practical, more recent bond brought Germany and Russia still closer together during the postwar years. The Versailles Treaty limited the German Army to one hundred thousand men and outlawed such aggressive weapons as tanks, planes, and heavy artillery. The Versailles Treaty did not, however, prevent the Germans from equipping the Russians with the most modern military equipment and training them in its use. And the Russians welcomed this assistance as eagerly as the Germans gave it. The Socialist and liberal founders of the Weimar Republic chose as their Ambassador to Moscow the haughty Prussian aristocrat, Count von Brockdorff-Rantzau, who had insulted the Allies when they handed him the text of the Versailles Treaty in 1919, and then showed such friendliness to Russia that he earned the title of "The Red Count." While Brockdorff-Rantzau established close personal and diplomatic relations with the Russian leaders, General Hans von Seeckt, Mackensen's former chief of staff, reorganized the German Army.

"A strange man, Hans von Seeckt," wrote John Wheeler-Bennett in his life of Hindenburg; "at first glance a typical Prussian officer, with his thin, red turkey-neck, surmounted by an inscrutable face and the inevitable monocle. Just another general, one thought, as he entered a room, and that impression remained until he took his hands from behind his back, and one was amazed at their beauty. Long, thin, artistic, they might have belonged to Benvenuto Cellini or to Chopin. Not a soldier's hands, and no one who possessed them could be an ordinary soldier. Seeckt was not. He was a genius; a genius at making bricks without straw, and at fashioning a military machine, nominally within the restrictions of the Peace Treaty, which struck admiration and apprehension into the heart of every General Staff in Europe."

Von Seeckt's skeleton army of one hundred thousand included a General Staff of more than a thousand officers, plus another fifty-five generals, thus violating the Versailles Treaty, which had ordered the General Staff dissolved. But the authors of the Versailles Treaty believed they had protected Europe against a resurgent Germany by requiring that the recruits in this new German Army serve for twelve years. The authors of the Versailles Treaty remembered that during the early 1800's Napoleon had tried to reduce the military power of Prussia by reducing the size of its Army. But the Prussians outwitted Napoleon by calling up and training a new army of recruits year after year until they had built up a substantial reserve. Von Seeckt reversed the process and outwitted the victorious Allies by creating an army of noncommissioned officers so thoroughly trained that they could whip an army of over a

million raw recruits into an efficient fighting force in short order.
In 1926 Germany's military budget
came to more than 775 million
marks, or close to 200 million dollars. In proportion to its size it was
the most expensive army in the
world. Its superbly trained corps
of officers and noncommissioned
officers kept the old Prussian tradition alive, and von Seeckt saw
them fighting side by side with the
Russians against the French. Von
Seeckt had served almost exclusively on the Eastern Front, where
he learned to hold the fighting
ability of the Russian foot soldier
in high regard. After the war he
saw to it that a certain number of
German officers went to Russia

General Hans von Seeckt

every year to instruct the Red Army in the use of weapons that the Versailles Treaty forbade in their own country. Under a secret military
agreement, concluded at the same time as the Rapallo Treaty of 1922,
the Russian and German General Staffs worked closely together—not
without certain suspicions on both sides. And this co-operation had
begun even before Rapallo.

The election of Hindenburg to the Presidency led to the elimination
of von Seeckt. First, the Army transferred its loyalty from its commander
to the venerable Field Marshal. Then Oskar von Hindenburg, the Field
Marshal's son, maneuvered General von Heye, a pompous mediocrity,
into von Seeckt's job. Von Heye, in turn, soon gave way as chief of staff to
General Wilhelm Gröner, chief German military attaché in Russia until
September, 1918, when he organized the retreat from the Western Front
and helped stave off revolution in Germany the following winter. Gröner
had studied Bolshevism in action and learned to dread it. The fact that
he did not belong to the Prussian aristocracy had held him down in
Imperial Germany, but under the Weimar Republic this liability became an asset. Gröner's loyalty did not belong to the Hohenzollerns or
to the Prussians, to the Empire or to the Republic. It belonged to the
Army and to the people whom, in his view, the Army served. By an
ironic twist of fate, Seeckt owed his position as chief of staff to Gröner,
who now got the post himself.

Gröner's loyalty to the Army made him serviceable to the Prussian aristocrats, who took advantage of Hindenburg's election to re-establish their authority. Colonel Kurt von Schleicher, an attractive young intelligence officer, started the ball rolling by ingratiating himself with Gröner, who referred to him affectionately as "my son," and secured him the post of Defense Minister. Schleicher also exploited his personal friendship with Oskar von Hindenburg to plant his own adherents in key military positions. The President's son amounted to little on his own account but became an invaluable tool in the hands of Schleicher and other intriguers. Then there was Otto Meissner, whose square head, close-cropped hair, and steel-rimmed glasses made him look like the embodiment of the civil service class to which he belonged. Meissner, the son of a German father and an Alsatian mother, had worked with the State Railways under the Kaiser; in 1918 he reorganized the railroads of the Ukraine; in 1920 he became Secretary of State under Ebert. In this capacity he gained such mastery of administrative detail that Hindenburg kept him in office: "When a lieutenant becomes company commander, he keeps the old sergeant-major." Here Meissner became as important to Hindenburg the civilian as Ludendorff had been to Hindenburg the soldier. While Schleicher saw to it that co-operation between the German and Russian Armies continued as it had under Seeckt, Meissner saw to it that Hindenburg backed Stresemann's foreign policy.

When Hindenburg became President, German industrial production had just about returned to prewar levels. The new era followed fast. Between 1924 and 1929 the Germans received twice as much money from abroad as they paid out in reparations, and more than half of these funds came from the United States. The bulk of German reparations went to France and it was with the French that the Germans did more and more business as the leaders of heavy industry in both countries brought their iron ore, their coke, and their coal together again and organized cartels to limit production and fix prices. German commercial airlines offered the best service in Europe; the new luxury liners *Europa* and *Bremen* set new high standards for ocean travel. German municipalities spent the funds that American bankers pressed upon them erecting handsome, modern public buildings. German factories rationalized themselves along American lines. Mass production became a cult, with a name borrowed from the United States—*Fordismus.*

Germany produced more than material wealth during the later 1920's. The Weimar Constitution permitted wide freedom of expression, and German writers and publishers took advantage of this latitude. Two great publishing combines, Scherl and Ullstein, with headquarters in Berlin, extended their newspaper chains and issued a profusion of books and magazines. The German press flourished under the Republic, with such liberal journals as the *Vossische Zeitung* and the *Berliner Tageblatt*

of Berlin and the *Frankfurter Zeitung* maintaining correspondents all
over the world. Sometimes their dispatches dealt with politics and
economics; more often they discussed books, music, travel, and folk-
ways. While the German press brought the world to the German people,
German books and magazines gave opportunity to many talented men
of letters. Heinrich Mann, a Socialist of long standing, wrote novels that
brought him as high a reputation if not so wide a fame as his younger
brother, Thomas, enjoyed. Many of the younger novelists came of Jewish
families and frequently dealt with Jewish themes. Lion Feuchtwanger's
Jud Süss, published in the United States under the title of *Power,* showed
how a Jewish financier in the medieval court of the Hapsburgs redeemed himself from worldly failure by reverting to the highest traditions of his religion. Joseph Roth retold the story of Job in a modern
setting. Arnold Zweig's *Case of Sergeant Grischa* followed the adventures of a Russian war prisoner in eastern Germany. Erich Maria Remarque, a war veteran of mixed French and German descent, won the
greatest popular success of any postwar German writer with his *All
Quiet on the Western Front,* published in 1929. Other antiwar books by
Ludwig Renn, Ernst Glaeser, and Fritz von Unruh followed. But serious
critics thought far more highly of Franz Kafka, a Jewish citizen of Prague
who wrote introspective novels in German, and of the German lyrics by
another Czechoslovak citizen—Rainer Maria Rilke. Both Kafka and
Rilke, however, died in their prime and did not win serious critical attention until the 1930's and 1940's.

Many German writers under the Republic reported the surface of contemporary life in realistic, almost journalistic, prose; others used historical themes to preach contemporary sermons. Emil Ludwig, a popular
war correspondent, became an even more popular adept at the new art
of novelized biography. He lacked the scholarship and grace of Lytton
Strachey, the delicacy of André Maurois, the seriousness of Gamaliel
Bradford, who pioneered in the same field. But no German writer of the
time did more than Ludwig to revitalize and simplify German prose, and
his studies of Napoleon, Bismarck, and the Kaiser reached wider audiences in his own country and abroad than more scholarly works ever
attracted. Egon Friedell's *Cultural History of the Modern Age,* in three
volumes, borrowed some of Spengler's ideas and added a light touch to
which the master never descended. Count Hermann Keyserling's *Travel
Diary of a Philosopher* made an international success during the early
1920's. Its author, who never let his readers forget that he came from an
ancient Baltic family, founded a pompous "School of Wisdom" at Darm-
stadt where he preached a pseudo-Oriental mysticism. Yet in spite of
Keyserling's affectations and conceit, he showed occasional flashes of insight. Relying on instinct and emotion rather than reason or logic, he

appealed to that large body of Germans who rejected the simpler realism of the younger postwar writers.

Disillusioned by the lost war and ruined by the subsequent inflation, many Germans turned to quack substitutes for religion and science. Astrologists and revivalists flourished. Great numbers of young Germans, both girls and boys, joined the *Wandervogel*, or wander-bird, movement. With compulsory military service abolished, the young men of Germany no longer had to train for war and live apart from the young women. Instead, they hiked and camped together, singing songs and glorifying the strenuous, outdoor life. They had found a moral equivalent for war preparations, if not for war itself. The *Wandervogel* movement broke down the barriers of class and sex, it provided an outlet for group activity, even for a kind of discipline. For a few years it also offered hope that the rising generation might build a new and more peaceful Germany.

But the Weimar Republic had its unlovely aspects, too. While novelists exposed the false glories of the recent war, two outstanding artists depicted the savagery they saw in the present. The sober, tragic lithographs of Käthe Kollwitz displayed the sorrows of the forgotten proletariat with love and understanding. Her work reminded all who saw it that many of Germany's toiling millions found life no better under the Republic than they had under the Hohenzollerns. The paintings and drawings of George Grosz lashed the old aristocracy and the newly rich with ruthless impartiality. "The artist sets up a mirror in which his contemporaries may see their own grimaces," wrote Grosz. "I have designed and painted out of a sense of opposition. I have tried in my pictures to show that the present society is ugly, sick, and hypocritical." Vice, both natural and unnatural, paraded itself in Hamburg and Berlin. Profiteers who had made fortunes selling Germany short during the inflation invested their winnings in real estate, new construction, new enterprises, and stock market speculation.

The warped prosperity that gave Germany a glow of false health during the later 1920's helped to demoralize the generation born between 1900 and 1910. The young Germans who came of age during the twenties had been too young to fight in the war, but they had some recollection of the prewar days and most of them had lost fathers or brothers. Still more had at least one wounded veteran in the family circle. These German boys and girls had gone hungry as children; on some of them the Allied blockade left permanent physical and psychological effects. They went to school during the years when the shock of defeat hit every German home. Then came the inflation, turning all values upside down, rewarding vice and punishing virtue. They reached maturity at a moment when conditions turned temporarily for the better. But they had no assurance that prosperity would last. All their experience had taught them, the girls as well as the boys, that often the greatest rewards went to those with the fewest scruples. Nor was this state of mind peculiar to the younger generation. It extended to all ages and all classes.

The spreading corruption did not spare Hindenburg himself. Although he distressed his Nationalist backers by supporting Stresemann's foreign policy, he proved more amenable in domestic affairs. The President of Germany had less power than the President of the United States, more power than the President of France, and Hindenburg quickly used that power to support two financial decisions that discriminated in favor of the

Woman Welcoming Death. Drawing by Käthe Kollwitz

very rich. On the one hand, he did nothing to compensate the small holders of war bonds that the inflation had rendered worthless; on the other, he approved a measure that fixed the value of mortgages on great estates at one quarter of their prewar value. He also approved a decision of the Reichstag to vote tax relief to great industrial and banking combines. But Hindenburg had also been on record since 1917 in behalf of a plan to break up parts of the large East Prussian estates into small farms for war veterans. Perhaps because his own family's great estate at Neudeck had passed into strange hands with the death of his sister-in-law, he felt a personal bond between himself and other dispossessed survivors of the war.

But the Prussian landowners quickly won Hindenburg over to their point of view. Together with certain industrialists, they bought up his family estate at Neudeck and presented it to him in 1927 on his eightieth birthday. The President himself wanted the old house in which he had spent his childhood left intact, but his son insisted on having it rebuilt as a palace. Moreover, to escape inheritance taxes, the son saw to it that the deed to Neudeck was made out in his name rather than his father's. This shabby transaction did not come to light until three years later, but it did not take three years for Hindenburg to lose his enthusiasm for East Prussian land reform and to throw his personal and official influence behind his feudal neighbors.

Neither the German people nor Hindenburg himself understood the intrigues that surrounded the whole Neudeck affair. The popularity of the President never stood higher, and the boom that American dollars financed continued. But living costs were slowly rising; social services and the salaries of government servants put the budget out of balance. Finally a dispute over state aid to Roman Catholic schools split the coalition Cabinet, headed by Wilhelm Marx of the Catholic Center Party. In May, 1928, came the election of a new Reichstag. By this time Alfred Hugenberg, publisher of a chain of Nationalist newspapers, had gained control of the Nationalist Party and promoted two contradictory slogans: "A Vote for the Nationalists is a Vote for Hindenburg," and "If You Are Discontented, Vote Nationalist." The Nationalist vote fell 20 per cent; the Socialists and Communists scored the biggest gains and, between them, attracted two fifths of the total vote cast. Hermann Müller of the Socialists organized a new coalition government which included Stresemann as Foreign Minister as well as members of the Center Party. Only the Nationalists, the Communists, and a few small, extremist groups like Adolf Hitler's Nazis fought Müller.

Conditions during the winter of 1928-29 gave them unexpected aid. The flow of American dollars into Germany dropped sharply; unemployment rose. Germany's postwar prosperity faced the prospect of an early and sudden death. Schleicher, Meissner, and Oskar von Hindenburg prepared for the worst, working quietly behind the scenes to increase the powers of the President, but they did not join the Nationalists or any other opposition group. At the same time, Chancellor Müller, President Schacht of the Reichsbank, and S. Parker Gilbert, the Agent General of Reparations, celebrated the New Year by preparing a final settlement to replace the Dawes Plan. Müller needed to assert Germany's independence. Schacht could not stand for anything less than Müller proposed. Gilbert, as an American, welcomed the prospect of a firm and final settlement with a stable Germany. Owen D. Young presided over the discussions and in June they revealed their proposals. The Young Plan called for Germany to pay a total of twenty-five billion dollars in reparations over a period of fifty-nine years. It did away with the Agent General of Reparations and in his place created a Bank for International Settlements. The French agreed to speed up the withdrawal of their troops from the Rhineland, provided the Germans made their reparations payments on schedule. It was this feature that commended the proposition to Stresemann, who died on October 3, 1929, a few months before the Reichstag voted final acceptance. Reluctantly but firmly, Hindenburg backed the Young settlement which restored control of the German economy to German hands, but Ludendorff spoke for the Nationalist minority when he said: "Field Marshal von Hindenburg has forfeited the right to wear the field-gray uniform of the Army and to be buried in it. Herr Paul von Hindenburg has destroyed the very thing he fought for as Field Marshal." Hindenburg's original Nationalist supporters seemed to be turning against him while his original opponents in the Center and Social Democratic Parties found him more and more acceptable. Behind the scenes, however, Meissner, Schleicher, the President's son, and others were making their own plans.

· VI ·

THE SAME CONFLICTS that gave Germany such a confusing aspect during the 1920's appeared in simpler form among Germany's neighbor states to the east and south. Among the Poles, for example, long-repressed nationalist emotions ran wild. Having thrown back the Red Army at Warsaw, they proceeded to annex the western Ukraine with an area of 150,000 square miles but only 90,000 "indisputably Polish" inhabitants. Speaking of the predominantly Ukrainian population of this region, a Polish statesman frankly admitted that "75 per cent of them were permanently menaced, 20 per cent were insecure, and only 5 per cent safe." But the acquisition of the western Ukraine did not satisfy a certain General Zeligowski, who took advantage of the general confusion of the time to defy the League of Nations and seize the city of Vilna, historic capital of Lithuania. The new Poland had a population of thirty millions, ten millions of them non-Poles. This meant that only Czechoslovakia had a larger percentage of alien minorities than Poland, and Poland's minorities—especially the Ukrainians, who comprised 14 per cent of the population—received worse treatment than any other minorities in Europe. When the Tsar ruled the western Ukraine in 1913, it had more than twenty-four hundred Ukrainian schools; after the Poles took over, they closed down more than two thirds of them. Representatives of the persecuted Ukrainian minority protested in vain to the League of Nations as liberal journalists wrote horrifying eyewitness stories of Polish atrocities on Ukrainian citizens. The point here is not that the Poles behaved with exceptional savagery. The Germans had behaved just as badly when they had the opportunity—and with less excuse, because they had not lived for a century and a half under foreign rule. Poland's body politic merely proved uncommonly receptive to the nationalist bacillus that infected so much of Europe after the war.

This bacillus proved a welcome ally of Poland's aristocrats, who maintained a landowning system as antiquated as East Prussia's. Aggression against neighboring Lithuania and suppression of the Ukrainian minority inside Poland distracted the attention of the Polish peasants from their own grievances. In 1926, the year after the German people elected Hindenburg President, another Field Marshal became chief of the new Polish state. Joseph Pilsudski, who had begun his career as a revolutionary socialist, wound up as the champion of the landowners, and he did not come to power by peaceful, constitutional methods. He seized power as the commander-in-chief of an army of 250,000 men. French loans supported this army and financed the construction of a great, new port at Gdynia, near Danzig, where the Vistula flows into the Baltic Sea.

Rumania's postwar history paralleled Poland's—for a while. The Liberal Party, which had brought the country into the war on the Allied side, remained in power from 1918 to 1926. It protected the landowners and persecuted the Hungarian minority—not without some previous cause. In 1926, however, the same year that Pilsudski established a virtual military dictatorship in Poland, an altogether different kind of upset took place in Rumania. The National Peasant Party led by Julius Maniu, one of Rumania's few honest politicians, organized a march on Bucharest and drove the Liberals from power in a bloodless revolution. Substantial land reforms followed, but the march of the Rumanian peasants on Bucharest spelled out a warning that hardly anyone in any other country chose to read. Throughout Europe and the United States, the farmer was getting the dirty end of the stick, and the Rumanian farmers were among the first to wrest that stick from the hands of their oppressors.

The little Republic of Austria presented the saddest spectacle in postwar Europe. Its six million people could not possibly support the former imperial capital of Vienna. Moreover, most of the Viennese belonged to the most radical Social Democratic Party in Europe; most of the peasants in the surrounding countryside belonged to the Christian Democrats, whose leader, a Jesuit priest named Monsignor Ignaz Seipel, served three times as Chancellor during the 1920's, and had his disciples rule for him when illness laid him low from 1924 to 1926. An international loan, arranged for through the League of Nations, stabilized the Austrian currency, which had gone the way of the German mark. The same thing also happened in Hungary. But Hungary lived under the dictatorship of Admiral Horthy; Austria became a democratic Republic. Just as the Rumanian peasants staged a march on Bucharest in 1926, so in 1927 the Social Democrats of Vienna demonstrated against a court decision that seemed to them to give too much power to the provinces. Fighting broke out and eighty-five demonstrators and two policemen were killed. Factory workers as well as peasants gave their lives attempting to wipe out certain grievances.

The plight of Austria made a singularly poignant impression on visitors from abroad, and Louis Fischer in *Men and Politics* summed

it all up in these eloquent, precise words: "One third of post-war
Austrians were peasants who could not raise enough food to feed the
nation; one third were industrial workingmen who manufactured too
much for the nation to consume. The last third were officials with no
empire to rule, officers with no army to command, and artists, actors,
musicians, writers, teachers, doctors, lawyers, and intellectuals whom
shrunken Austria could not longer support."

For the most part, however, Europe had recovered from the worst
effects of the war and during the latter 1920's more people lived better
than they had ever lived before. But the prewar balance of power, embracing classes as well as nations, had gone and the new equilibrium
of Locarno had not quite taken its place. No longer did the United
States absorb Europe's surplus population; instead, Americans used
their surplus capital to keep Europe a going concern. Unfortunately,
the United States also raised higher tariff barriers than ever against
European goods while the Europeans played the same suicidal game
against one another. Free trade in ideas remained brisk; new means of
communication brought the common people of all countries closer. But
Russia remained as mysterious as ever—some people regarding it as a
universal menace, others as the hope of the world. The new democracies
on Russia's borders settled down after a fashion; the Balkans no longer
seethed as they had during the early years of the century; the Scandinavians, the Dutch, the Belgians, and the Czechoslovaks adjusted themselves to conditions of peace. One question, however, kept breaking
through the fog that shrouded the island from which it rose: Was
Britain done?

· VII ·

"THE ECONOMIC CONSEQUENCES of Mr. Churchill" against which J. M.
Keynes had warned in 1925 exploded, the following year, in a general
strike that forced the moderate majority of the British people to suffer
loss and hardship at the hands of two extremist minorities. One minority of labor extremists saw the British working class setting the
world an example of revolutionary leadership. The other minority of
die-hard employers and politicians saw themselves reasserting the prewar power of their class and recapturing the prewar glory of their
country. Each of those two minorities did everything possible to confirm the worst fears and suspicions of the other. Both of them refused to
admit that the war had destroyed Britain's world pre-eminence. It was
their one common delusion.

It was also a delusion that British leaders encouraged during and
after the war. Yet the promises and hopes these leaders aroused in the

British masses refused to come true. Throughout the 1920's British exports never rose to more than three quarters of the prewar level. Unemployment never fell below one million and several times rose to more than twice that figure. The return of the pound to the gold standard aggravated this condition because it raised the prices of British manufactures on the world market at a time when other nations had reduced theirs. The French and Germans brought their prices down by debasing their currencies. The Germans then borrowed money from abroad to modernize their industries. The United States went still further in the direction of mass production. British manufacturers could no more meet this kind of competition than British labor could compete against the low-paid Japanese. The Germans and Americans centralized their industries in large combines. In Britain, hundreds of small firms competed against each other in every line. Churchill assumed that the restoration of the pound sterling to its prewar level would restore Britain to its prewar eminence, and when that assumption proved false, he agreed with those British employers who could see but one way out: a pay cut for British workers.

Where to begin? Britain's national economy rested on dwindling coal deposits that ran in narrow veins deep underground. As British mining costs rose, foreign demand declined. Britain's coal exports dropped to half their prewar volume. Between 1924 and 1926 more than five hundred mines employing more than one hundred thousand workers closed down. Back in 1919 the miners, by a majority vote of more than half a million, threatened to go out on strike and kept working only after Lloyd George's government promised to abide by whatever recommendations a Royal Commission, headed by Lord Sankey, might make to reform the industry. The Coal Mines Act of 1919 had already provided for a seven-hour day. A majority on the Sankey Commission then voted in favor of nationalizing the coal mines. No action followed, but in 1921 the Miners' Federation and the Mining Federation, representing the employers, reached the first nation-wide wage agreement in British history. Labor and management agreed on a minimum wage scale, with increases depending on profits. In 1924 they revised the agreement to the advantage of the union.

The arrangement did not outlast the Conservatives' return to power. In the summer of 1925 the operators of the coal mines announced they would have to cut wages by at least 13 per cent to as much as 48 per cent. They also scrapped the nation-wide agreement in favor of separate, local agreements in each district, and eliminated the minimum wage provision. "Not a penny off the pay, not a minute on the day," replied A. J. Cook, the fiery secretary of the Miners' Federation as Prime Minister Baldwin appointed a Royal Commission of Inquiry which issued a report favoring a restoration of the minimum wage. Parliament, at the last moment, voted a temporary subsidy, totaling almost twenty million pounds, to maintain wages at existing levels until May 1, 1926, and appointed still another Royal Commission.

Cook announced that the government and the operators had already capitulated to the power of his mighty union. When Parliament voted the subsidy he announced that "labor could get only what it was strong enough to take," and in August, 1925, he made this further boast: "I don't care a hang for any government or army or navy. They can come along with their bayonets. Bayonets don't cut coal. We have already beaten not only the employers but the strongest government of modern times." Neither the operators nor the government had prepared themselves for a shutdown in the coal mines, much less for the general sympathy strike that the miners and other organized workers threatened. But while labor talked, capital acted. A distinguished group of British citizens, headed by Lord Hardinge, former Viceroy of India, and numerous generals, admirals, and members of the House of Lords, created a voluntary body known as the Organization for the Maintenance of Supplies which enlisted and trained more than a hundred thousand persons to perform essential services, especially transportation, in the event of a general strike. The organizers of O.M.S. made no secret of their plans, which they worked out in co-operation with the government. Churchill, speaking for that government, put the matter bluntly when he announced in December, 1925: "We decided to postpone the crisis in the hope of averting it, or, if not of averting it, of coping with it effectually when the time came." The labor movement, though it knew exactly what to expect, made no corresponding move. It even took pride in its unpreparedness.

On March 11 the Royal Commission appointed by the government came up with its report. It opposed paying any more subsidies after May 1. It recommended that the nation buy the mines from their present owners, who were leasing them on a royalty basis to the operators. But the Commission did not recommend government operation of the mines. The Commission proposed that the same operators remain in business, paying royalties to the government instead of to the private owners. But until the government could arrange to purchase the mines, the Commission called upon the owners to have more steps taken to increase the efficiency of their mines. Although the Commission found that the operators were paying excessive dividends, it suggested that the miners might have to accept some pay cuts. On March 24 Prime Minister Baldwin announced, "We accept the report, provided the other parties do so," and turned the whole matter back to the operators and the union leaders, who spent the next month vainly trying to reconcile their irreconcilable views. For the union leaders laid down these three conditions on which they refused to compromise: there could be no reduction of wages, no lengthening of hours, and no interference with the principle of national agreement. The operators insisted just as stubbornly on a 13 per cent wage cut, an hour's increase in the working day, and regional agreements instead of national ones. As for the government, it refused under any conditions to pay any more subsidies beyond May 1.

As this deadline approached, the leaders of the Miners' Federation turned the matter of further action over to the General Council of the Trades Union Congress. The coal miners and their leaders argued that if the operators got their way, other workers in other industries would soon meet the same fate. Instead of a tie-up in the coal mines only, the Miners' Federation therefore called for a general strike. The leaders of several of the biggest British unions, representing more than three million workers, accepted this line of argument, and the leaders of the miners put the General Council in charge of any general strike that might occur while the Miners' Federation remained free to speak in the miners' behalf.

On Sunday, May 2, with the possibility of a general strike looming close ahead, the pressmen on the London *Daily Mail* refused to run an editorial containing these sentences—among others: "The general strike is not an industrial dispute; it is a revolutionary movement, intended to inflict suffering upon the great mass of innocent persons in the community and thereby put forcible constraint upon the government. . . . We call upon all law-abiding men and women to hold themselves at the service of King and country." Winston Churchill and a die-hard minority within the British government wanted a fight to the finish. They persuaded Stanley Baldwin to denounce the stoppage on the *Daily Mail* as an "overt act" and to call upon the General Council of the Trades Union Congress to call off the projected general strike, unconditionally. Most members of the General Council did not want to proclaim a general strike. Even the extremist leaders—including a handful of Communists—did not expect the strike to take place. But the extremist minority in the Cabinet forced the reluctant labor leaders to act and the procrastinating Baldwin to resist. On Tuesday, May 4, the general strike began.

Kingsley Martin commented in the pro-labor *New Statesman and Nation:* "The Trades Union Council stood as a combatant in a war which had been forced upon it and which it feared to win." *Lansbury's Labour Weekly* wrote: "The Trades Union Council had an almost overwhelming desire for peace. This must not be thought of as betrayal, or selling the pass. In principle and in practice, they were against a general strike and they said so again and again. They were doing their utmost to avoid the necessity of a stoppage. They would have been satisfied with any reason, perhaps with any excuse, to turn back." J. H. Thomas, one of the leaders of the railwaymen's union, said of himself at the time that "he had never disguised and did not disguise now that he had never been in favor of the principle of a general strike." He told the House of Commons: "I have never disguised that in a challenge to the Constitution, God help us unless the government won." But he regarded this as "merely a plain, economic, industrial dispute" and he accused the government of having "declared war."

But Prime Minister Baldwin insisted that the declaration of war had come from labor. He described the strike as "threatening the basis of ordered government and going nearer to proclaiming civil war than we have been for centuries past. . . . It is a conflict which, if fought out to a conclusion, can only end in the overthrow of Parliamentary Government or in its decisive victory." But the Bishops of Southwark and Winchester, in a joint statement, described Britain as "suffering a national humiliation comparable to a defeat in war. We preach peace among the nations, but we fail to attain it at home." Pleading for "the Christian point of view," they urged the government to continue the subsidy. But Winston Churchill seized one quarter of the newsprint supply of the London *Times* and began issuing an official government daily, *The British Gazette,* which headlined the news of the strike: "Hold-Up of a Nation."

Of Britain's six million organized workers, only three million quit work. These included the coal miners, transport workers, railwaymen, printers, builders, and iron and steel workers. Although business as usual came to a standstill, essential services continued. Tanks moved into London. Soldiers guarded docks, freight yards, and bridges. The aristocratic officers of the Coldstream Guards resented, as one reporter put it, "the spectacle of the proudest regiments in the world exulting over moving flour lorries." A quarter of a million volunteer constables patrolled the more densely traveled streets and highways. In the cities, office workers drove busses; Oxford and Cambridge students stoked locomotives. Most newspapers suspended publication while the British Broadcasting Corporation used its monopoly of the radio to preach the government point of view and to refuse to carry the terms of a settlement proposed by the Archbishop of Canterbury. After the strike had lasted a week, Churchill told the readers of the *British Gazette:* "An organized attempt is being made to starve the people and to wreck the state, and the legal and Constitutional aspects are entering a new phase." The government at once had to repudiate the implication that it planned to use force, for the fact was that no bloodshed occurred

UNITED PRESS PHOTO

Armored Car Convoys Food Truck Through Hyde Park, London,
During British General Strike

anywhere. A football game played between a team of strikers and a team of policemen came in for wide publicity and symbolized the spirit in which the majority of the British people met the situation into which two belligerent minorities had forced them.

Two prominent Liberals helped bring the strike to an end. First, Sir John Simon, a former attorney general, created a great stir by announcing on the third day of the strike: "Every workman who was bound by a contract to give notice before he left work, and who, in view of that decision, has either chosen of his own free will or has felt compelled to come out by leaving his employment without proper notice has broken the law." Not only that, but Simon went on to argue that every trade union leader who promoted the strike was liable "to the uttermost farthing of his personal possessions." The issue of illegality caused some misgivings among the law-abiding British people. As for the strike leaders, the threat that they might lose their hard-earned, meager possessions stirred something deeper than misgivings within their breasts. But they could see no immediate solution.

Another Liberal, Sir Herbert Samuel, provided the formula that brought the strike to an end. Samuel had headed the Royal Commission whose recommendations the owners of the coal mines had rejected. At his request, he met the negotiating committee of the General Council of the trade unions and proposed that the strike be called off, negotiations between the coal miners and the mine owners resumed, work continued on the terms that applied up to May 1, and the government sub-

sidy continued until June 1. The miners, however, refused to go back on
these terms, which neither the mine owners nor the government had
officially accepted. Nevertheless the General Council voted unanimously on May 12 to call off the strike, assuming that the government
would enforce the Samuel proposals. That same evening, Prime Minister Baldwin broadcast a message to the British people informing them
that the general strike had ended without conditions but that he
pledged himself to have negotiations between the coal miners and the
mine owners resumed at once and that there would be no reprisals. The
next day the *British Worker*, mouthpiece of the labor unions, published
the text of the Samuel memorandum but did not mention the fact that
the Miners' Federation had rejected it.

"Alarm—fear—despair—a victorious army disarmed and handed over
to its enemies." This message received from Hull at general strike headquarters in London expressed the mood of the rank and file when the
word went out that the strike had ended. John Balderston, representing
the New York *World*, cabled his paper on May 13: "When the strike
was actually called off, the whole government publicity machinery,
which was not under the direct control of the Prime Minister, and almost all newspapers able to print at all, set up a howl of joy over labor's
defeat. The result was immediate. The strike went on. It got worse,
and it is worse now than it was when it started ten days ago." But the
strike fizzled out as suddenly as it had begun. The rank-and-file workers, unprepared by their leaders to carry it through to a successful conclusion, returned to their jobs as dutifully as they had left them. Many
of them had never understood the issues. They had no serious grievances of their own. Fear of losing what security they enjoyed outweighed hope of gaining greater security by strike action. The employers spread further confusion and gloom by forcing many returning
union members to tear up their union cards. Strike leaders came in for
especially heavy penalties.

The nine-day tie-up cost Great Britain about 150 million pounds, or
well over half a billion dollars. But the real damage could not be estimated in pounds, shillings, and pence. Will Rogers summed up American opinion when he pointed out the danger of failing to go through
with what you have advertised: "So all I blame England for was the
billing. It should have been called A Temporary Cessation of Employment Without Monetary Consideration for an Indefinite Period Without Animosity or Hostile Design." But Will Rogers, America, and most
of the rest of the world glossed over some of the uglier scars that the
general strike left. The coal industry, at once the most vital and the most
backward in the British Isles, turned its own crisis against its own workers. Instead of modernizing their equipment and centralizing their or-

ganization, the mine operators cut wages, and went back to the eight-hour day and to district agreements. Although the miners felt rejected and deserted by their fellow workers and fellow unionists, they nevertheless remained out on strike until December, when they, too, had to give in and accept work on the operators' harsh terms.

The Baldwin government not only backed the mine operators. In 1927 it put through a new Trades Disputes Act which pronounced any general strike illegal. The Act also hampered the Labor Party in collecting dues from trade union members, and Party leaders called it "a declaration of war on the whole labor movement." Lord Reading, former Viceroy to India, former Ambassador to the United States, former Lord Chief Justice, and lifelong member of the Liberal Party, offered a scathing and comprehensive analysis of the Trades Disputes Act: "When I take the bill as a whole and look through it as I have done with great care, consider it clause by clause, I say without hesitation that it is a bill which in the language it uses is more vague, more indefinite, more lacking in precision in respect of the crimes which it indicates and the penalties which follow upon them than any bill I have ever seen or any Act of Parliament I have had to construe either as a law officer or as a judge." Like so many other efforts to legislate economic facts and social tensions out of existence, the Trades Disputes Act added to the confusion that it strove to allay.

During the years of Coolidge prosperity in the United States, of Poincaré stabilization in France, of Stresemann fulfillment in Germany, the best that Stanley Baldwin could offer the British people was "Safety First," with capital getting the safety and labor making the sacrifice. In the 1929 general election he reaped as he had sown: the Conservatives won only 260 seats in the House of Commons to Labor's 287. The Liberals, with 59 seats, held the balance of power, and with their tacit backing Ramsay MacDonald once again succeeded Stanley Baldwin as Prime Minister.

· VIII ·

THE CONSERVATIVES had performed more creditably abroad than at home. In the summer of 1926 British and Dominion Ministers met in London at an Imperial Conference which formulated a drastic new definition, phrased by Lord Balfour, of the ties that held the British Commonwealth of Nations together. Britain and the Dominions declared that "They are autonomous Communities within the British Empire, equal in status, in no way subordinate one to another in any aspect of their domestic or external affairs, though united by a common allegiance to the Crown and freely associated as members of the British

Commonwealth of Nations." The British Conservatives wisely recognized that the mother country could best hold the Dominions to some sort of loyalty by freely acknowledging their virtual independence. This concession strengthened the Empire in that it built up good will for Britain among the Dominions. But it also showed that Britain had lost, perhaps forever, the dominance it once enjoyed.

It was one thing to make concessions to people of British descent. It was quite a different matter when it came to coping with the people of India. It cost the Tories hardly any pain at all to produce the Balfour Report; it cost the Dominions no pain whatever to accept it. To offer any such concessions to India, "brightest jewel in the British Crown," was out of the question. It was equally absurd to expect the Indian leaders to accept the kind of settlement that an elder Tory statesman would offer. Yet something had to be done. After the British released Gandhi from jail in 1924, the Congress Party coupled its demand for independence with a sweeping program of internal reform. When the Congress called for a revival of hand spinning in the villages and complete suppression of the drug and liquor traffic, the British did not dare express their opposition; they could only keep silent. And when the Congress Party went on to demand identical moral standards for men and women, Hindu-Moslem unity, and the abolition of untouchability, the British did not dare withhold their approval.

The story of the revolution that swept India during the 1920's and 1930's belongs with the story of the similar revolutions that swept other backward lands. It is sufficient to report here that the same faction in the Conservative government that led the fight against the general strike tried, with less success, to lead a similar fight against Gandhi. They represented, however, a diminishing minority of their own people and could not offer more than a delaying rear-guard action. Moreover, recent events in Ireland gave them little reason to hope for success. In the 1918 elections, the Sinn Feiners, who demanded immediate and complete independence, won 64 per cent of the popular vote. To force a showdown they set up a state within a state. They had their own President, Parliament, and law courts which administered justice over most of Ireland; they also had their own Irish Republican Army, chiefly composed of veterans of the Western Front. Against this Army, the British pitted the Royal Irish Constabulary, better known as the Black and Tans because the supply of Royal Irish Constabulary uniforms had given out and they had to wear black hats and black armbands with the khaki of the regular British Army. Englishmen commanded the Black and Tans, but most of the soldiers were Irish, and they, too, had seen action in France. The I.R.A. specialized in guerrilla fighting; the Black and Tans fought back with terror. The British never dared to wage a full-scale war—they feared world opinion, American opinion, even the opinion of their own people, many of whom sympathized with the aims if not the methods of Sinn Fein. By 1920 Sinn Fein received 80 per cent of the popular vote, and in 1921 the Sinn Fein leaders, including Arthur Griffith and Michael Collins, patched up a peace treaty with Lloyd George, who recognized an Irish Free State with Dominion status.

A third leader who had remained in Ireland rejected the settlement they brought back. Eamon de Valera had been born in the United States of mixed Spanish and Irish parentage, and wanted an independent Irish Republic at once. The Free Staters and the Republicans spent the next year fighting a civil war of their own until 1923, when the Republicans recognized the government established by the Free Staters. After that, the Free State shifted its attention to Ulster, which refused to break its ties with the United Kingdom. But the Irish question had at last ended in a solution of sorts, and nearly all the concessions had come from the British side.

For almost everyone in the British Isles, the decade of the 1920's proved a disappointing one. While Harding had vainly tried to bring the United States back to normalcy, Lloyd George had promised "homes fit for heroes to live in," and Bonar Law sought for "tranquillity." While Americans "kept cool with Coolidge," Baldwin tried to give Britons "safety first." Neither British Liberalism nor British Conservatism met the challenge of the 1920's. The Laborites believed in more radical measures, but they had not yet won the absolute Parliamentary majority they needed to put these measures through. Moreover, even a complete socialist program could not meet all of Britain's difficulties: the war and its consequences had undermined too many foundations of Britain's prewar power.

Yet no country had attained so many of its war aims so quickly. German sea power ceased to exist before the Germans signed the Versailles Treaty. Nearly all Germany's overseas possessions had also fallen at once into British hands. The Versailles Treaty gave the French enough rope to hang themselves in the Ruhr and to prepare the way for the Locarno Treaty, which created a new balance of power in Europe with Britain in the controlling position. Soviet Russia lost much of the territory over which the Tsars once ruled and then abandoned its original program of world revolution. Chiang Kai-shek had defeated Communism in China. The old Anglo-Japanese Alliance had given way to a wider agreement that included the United States. Nor was Britain's domestic picture entirely black. In spite of chronic depression in the coal fields and textile centers, certain new industries had prospered. Production of artificial silk increased 40 per cent between 1924 and 1928. The number of passenger cars increased five times over between

At the Political Magicians' Dinner. The Man Above: "They're all very funny tricks, but where's the magician who can produce some work?" Strube in the Daily Express, *London*

1923 and 1929. London, with its shops and theaters, its docks and railways, its traffic and its new buildings, wore a truly prosperous look. The American tourists who swarmed there every summer saw as little of its slums as they saw of the distressed areas farther north.

It was not, however, necessary to visit Great Britain during the 1920's to find evidences of decline. The books written by England's leading writers showed the kind of decay that had set in. Thomas Hardy, in his eighties, still composed occasional gnarled fragments of rustic verse. Arnold Bennett had written himself out before the war. John Galsworthy brought his *Forsyte Saga* to a somewhat lame and mechanical conclusion. H. G. Wells and Bernard Shaw lost none of their gusto, but they no longer put their best efforts into creative literature. Wells produced his most ambitious and successful work during the early 1920's, *An Outline of History;* a few years later Shaw wrote *The Intelligent Woman's Guide to Socialism and Capitalism.* Two younger writers failed to redeem the early promise of their first autobiographical novels: Compton Mackenzie, who wrote *Sinister Street* in 1913, and W. Somerset Maugham, whose *Of Human Bondage* appeared in 1915. Mackenzie came of a theatrical family; his sister Fay Compton was a popular actress. *Sinister Street* depicted the childhood and early life of a poetic young man who was graduated from Oxford into his first serious love affair. *Of Human Bondage* dealt more brutally with the same period in the life of a young doctor. Mackenzie then turned to romantic, adventurous, and humorous fiction; Maugham frankly set out to make money and won an almost unprecedented success as a popular playwright with six of his plays running simultaneously in London theaters. Robert Graves wrote the outstanding war book, *Good-Bye to All That*, based on his own experiences on the Western Front. R. C. Sheriff's play, *Journey's End*, put the horrors of war effectively on the stage. But Graves lacked the universal simplicity of Remarque; Sheriff's work lacked the vitality of *What Price Glory?* by the American playwrights, Laurence Stallings and Maxwell Anderson.

E. M. Forster's *A Passage to India* remains perhaps the outstanding British novel of the 1920's. It presents a balanced, touching, and convincing picture of the conflict between Indian and Englishman and between Indian and Indian. Yet in spite of its cool, realistic style, *A Passage to India* has little in common with prewar social realism. Forster himself belonged to the so-called Bloomsbury set of writers who combined the aesthetic tradition of the nineties with more serious scholarship. The economist John Maynard Keynes, who married a Russian ballet dancer, belonged to the Bloomsbury group. So did Lytton Strachey, whose *Eminent Victorians* and *Queen Victoria* put half a dozen nineteenth-century worthies in their places. Harold Nicolson, son of the great Sir Arthur Nicolson who died Lord Carnock, showed considerable promise with his book of character sketches, *Some People*, but he finally chose to devote himself to historical and biographical writing. Perhaps the skillful novels of his talented wife, Victoria Sackville-West, made him hesitate to compete in the field of fiction. David Garnett's *Lady Into Fox* and Walter de la Mare's *Memoirs of a Midget* attracted some attention as works of fantasy. Michael Arlen's *Green Hat* and the plays of Noel Coward appealed to the same bright young people who went in for Scott Fitzgerald in the United States and for Paul Morand in France. Aldous Huxley's *Crome Yellow* and *Antic Hay* introduced a more spectacular talent which came into its own with *Point Counter Point* in 1928. Here Huxley borrowed from the technique of André Gide, and several of his characters were thinly disguised real people—notably D. H. Lawrence and J. Middleton Murry, husband of Katherine Mansfield. But the very savagery of *Point Counter Point*, its even-handed satire of Communists, Fascists, Tories, scientists, aesthetes, men of the world, escapists, pleasure-seekers, and puritans, offered the sorriest commentary on the decadence of the British upper and middle classes. Huxley, the grandson of Thomas Henry Huxley and the nephew of Mrs. Humphry Ward, spoke with an authority equal to his talent.

One English novelist who died at the height of his fame during the mid-1920's was not an Englishman at all. Joseph Conrad, a Pole by birth and a sea captain by profession, left his native land as a youth and quit the sea in middle life to become a British subject and one of his adopted country's literary masters. Conrad had little in common with his contemporaries, who had already made their reputations before the war; he also stood somewhat apart from the writers of the postwar school. Although his work won the praises of outstanding critics during the early 1900's, he did not win wide recognition until the war had ended. His tales of action, laid in exotic settings, repelled the high-brows; his emphasis on the inner lives of his solitary heroes repelled the low-brows. It took time for him to establish himself as a romantic, devoid of illusions, a devotee of action, who nevertheless preferred words to deeds.

Conrad took pride in the simplicity of his beliefs: "Those who read me know my conviction that the world, the temporal world, rests on a very few simple ideas; so simple that they must be as old as the hills. It rests notably, among others, on the idea of loyalty. At a time when nothing which is not revolutionary in some way or other can expect to attract much attention, I have not been a revolutionary in my writings. The revolutionary spirit is mighty convenient in this, that it frees one from all scruples as regards ideas. Its hard, absolute optimism is repulsive to my mind by the menace of fanaticism and intolerance it contains." Thus Conrad, in his own way, broke with the revolutionary optimism of the prewar period. But instead of taking up with the new science of psychiatry, he fell back on conventions: "One aspect of conventions which people who declare against them lose sight of is that conventions make both joy and suffering easier to bear in a becoming manner."

Like many other postwar writers, Conrad made a cult of action: "Action is consolatory. It is the enemy of thought and the friend of flattering illusions. Only in the conduct of our action can we find the sense of mastery over the Fates." Conrad's books, as Morton Dauwen Zabel emphasized in his foreword to *The Portable Conrad*, depict "the plight of man on whom life closes down inexorably, divesting him of the supports and illusory protection of friendship, social prestige, and love." As Zabel went on to point out, this made Conrad kin to Gide, Mann, Kafka, and Joyce. He also anticipated the existentialist philosophy of Jean-Paul Sartre, for whom life had no other excuse than itself for being.

If any one distinguishing feature can be said to mark the best British fiction of the 1920's it was the fact that most of it was written by women. Since the death of Queen Victoria and with increasing vitality every year, the women of England were shaking off their bustles, their parents, and even their husbands—if any. The war left Great Britain with two million more women than men. In 1918, women over thirty got the vote provided they or their husbands paid local taxes; not until 1928 was the franchise granted to both women and men at the age of twenty-one. Meanwhile, women novelists assaulted the domain of literature in such force and numbers as to drive many men to the tall timbers of biography and history or to the cooling springs of verse. Consider this formidable array of literary Amazons whose books appeared during the 1920's: Katherine Mansfield, Virginia Woolf, Mary Webb, Rosamund Lehmann, V. Sackville-West, May Sinclair, G. B. Stern, Rebecca West, Margaret Kennedy, Storm Jameson, Sylvia Thompson, Rose Macaulay, Clemence Dane, Edith Sitwell, Sheila Kaye-Smith, and Stella Benson. In quality as well as quantity their work overshadowed the performances of Warwick Deeping, Charles Morgan, Francis Brett Young, John Buchan, J. D. Beresford, Hugh Walpole, and Frank Swinnerton.

At the time of the Armistice, the magnitude of British sacrifices seemed no greater than the magnitude of British victory. Ten years later, the sacrifices loomed larger than ever; the victory had yielded only Dead Sea fruit. But the rise of the Labor Party held out the hope of better things at last. In domestic affairs, its leaders had something more than cautious reform to offer as an alternative to the proven incompetence of the Tories. Abroad, too, they favored something bolder than a return to the prewar balance of power. The war had certainly shaken the British Isles and the British Empire. It had destroyed the delicate equilibrium from which Britain had profited so greatly during the century between Waterloo and Sarajevo.

Although the Versailles Treaty failed to restore the kind of stability that the Congress of Vienna created after the defeat of Napoleon, the Locarno settlement, six years later, marked real progress. Never since the rise of Bismarck had Franco-German relations appeared less strained. Locarno had brought stability to western Europe. The chief threats to peace lay in the east. Stresemann refused to accept Germany's eastern frontiers as he accepted the frontiers in the west; the Russians rightly suspected Briand of trying to bring Germany into an anti-Soviet coalition.

But the situation in Russia had its favorable aspects. Lenin's New Economic Policy had given way to Stalin's Five-Year Plan; socialism in one country had replaced world revolution. Everywhere the common man seemed to be inching into his own. In France, the Radicals had established themselves so firmly in power that they summoned Poincaré to save the franc, and Poincaré, in turn, confined himself to conservative financial measures and dropped the belligerent poses he once struck. In so far as Stanley Baldwin's Conservative government tried to turn the hands of the clock back in Britain, it came to grief, especially in the restoration of the gold standard and the handling of the general strike. The Labor victory in the 1929 election showed how sharply the public reacted against five years of Conservative rule. In every country, the die-hard conservative seemed to be going the way of the dodo. But the world made safe for democracy that Woodrow Wilson had promised as the war ended had not fully materialized. The later 1920's had seen at best some progress toward that world and felt at most some hope that during the 1930's that progress might continue.

SUMMING UP

HELP from the United States saved Germany and Europe from financial collapse in 1924. From 1925 through 1929 more help from the United States permitted Germany and Europe to enjoy prosperity of a kind. The people of Europe had lost little of their prewar vitality; the culture of Europe retained most of its prewar vigor. The chief weakness of Europe lay in the destruction and dislocation caused by the war, and the dislocation caused more hurt than the damage. No foreign armies laid waste any important part of Germany, yet what a weak figure the Weimar Republic cut as compared with the Germany of the Hohenzollerns. The Austro-Hungarian Empire suffered complete dismemberment, and the people who had once traded freely with one another under Hapsburg rule now checked the flow of trade with tariff barriers and burdened themselves with foreign loans that went for military preparations. And the Russian Empire suffered more losses than any other belligerent on either side.

Nor did the other Allies gain any corresponding advantage from their victory. The British had to work so hard avoiding bankruptcy that they could not afford to rebuild and reorganize their backward industries. Inflation and devaluation robbed the French franc of four fifths of its value. The Americans regarded their prosperity as the eighth wonder of the world—the ninth and tenth wonders being how it kept up and how long it would continue. In 1914 discerning observers foresaw trouble; repeated shocks had warned them that war might break out at any moment. But the common man throughout Europe lived in comparative tranquillity. He had only the press to disturb him, and in many countries the common man did not know how to read, though by the 1920's literacy had increased. Now, in addition to newspapers, there were also movies and the radio using still more effective methods to excite an ever expanding public. If the common man in Europe did not expect immediate war or revolution neither did he have much reason to believe that the postwar world was as safe or stable as the prewar world had once seemed.

In Russia, Italy, and Spain, dictatorships denied their people full access to the facts. The Weimar Republic imposed no restrictions on free expression in Germany, but the moderate parties did not know how to use this freedom and the Nationalists and Communists abused it. Only the British, the French, and the smaller democracies expanded their freedoms without harming themselves or threatening their neighbors. To live in freedom, it seemed, took generations of experience. But it took something more than experience with freedom to seize the opportunities the 1920's offered. The United States was certainly the most prosperous and probably the freest nation on earth, yet its record during the first postwar decade hardly inspired confidence. After the Armistice, the American people failed to follow through and consolidate the victory they had won. Ten years later, Europe again looked to them for leadership. The people of the United States had achieved unprecedented prosperity for themselves; they had spread some of this prosperity to others. Could they and their leaders do a better job for world prosperity in 1929 than they had done for world peace ten years before?

Part Two

* * * * *

DESTINATION: DISASTER

10

"Wall Street Lays an Egg"

The above headline from Variety *summed up the first American response to the greatest national disaster since the Civil War.*

PREVIEW

HIGH-PRESSURE PUBLICITY helped propel Herbert Hoover into the White House and for the first few months he lived up to the claims of his press agents. But the Wall Street crash proved his undoing. It was a time of falling idols and the Democrats launched a smear campaign that held Hoover personally responsible for all the nation's ills. By June, 1931, every Presidential cure and remedy had failed, and the depression had spread all over the world. Hoover announced that its causes lay abroad and proposed a one-year moratorium on all reparations and war debt payments as America's contribution to the recovery of all.

· I ·

No INCOMING President of the United States ever took office under happier auspices than Herbert Hoover. After eight years of Harding and Coolidge, the country had attained the greatest prosperity it had ever known, and Hoover towered over Harding in character and intelligence as he towered over Coolidge in ability and experience. But he suffered from one major handicap. His press agents had created a mythical Hoover who embodied a whole world of make-believe that the most popular newspapers and magazines, the most powerful radio stations and motion picture companies had created in the mind of the mass public.

Seen from Washington, as Hoover took his oath of office in March, 1929, the golden twenties presented a panorama of progress from one record to another, year after year—automobile production, department store sales, bank deposits, freight-car loadings—every index of business activity curved steadily upward. Seen from Europe, American prosperity appeared even more remarkable. The French, who had no word for "waste" in their language, asserted that one of their families could live

well on what the average American family threw away. Surplus dollars
for which Americans could find no profitable use at home stabilized the
mark and financed Germany's postwar boom. The British, with all their
experience and effort, could not recapture their financial leadership that
had fallen, unsought, into American hands. A new economic era had
begun, and the beneficent Hoover would not only lead his own country
to new heights. He embodied the world's best hope for security and
peace for all.

The success story of Herbert Hoover from his birth in West Branch,
Iowa, in 1874 to his election to the Presidency in 1928 made Horatio
Alger's heroes look like failures in comparison. One of his aunts quoted
his father as having told her just after his birth, "Well, we have another
General Grant at our house." Both his parents came of Quaker stock.
When their son reached the age of six, his father, a blacksmith, died;
within another four years his mother, too, was dead. Relatives took the
boy in charge, and when he reached the age of eleven one of them told
him, "Thee is going to Oregon." There he lived with one of his mother's
brothers, a country doctor, who gave him this suggestion for dealing
with violent playmates: "Turn your other cheek once, but if he smites
it, then punch him."

In 1891, the year young Hoover finished high school in Salem, Oregon,
Leland Stanford University opened its doors at Palo Alto, California.
Its youthful president, Dr. David Starr Jordan, planned to specialize in
technical and scientific subjects, in line with the progressive ideas of
the time, and Hoover persuaded his uncle and grandmother to let him
take advantage of the chance to get the kind of education he wanted.
He paid his fare to Palo Alto by tutoring the son of the local banker in
mathematics; he put himself through the four-year undergraduate course
by getting an office job in the university. Yet he found time to play
some part in campus politics, siding with the "barbs," or nonfraternity
members, and winning the nickname of "Sosh"—short for Socialist. He
specialized in geology and was graduated, three months before his
twenty-first birthday, with just forty dollars in his pocket.

He at once went to work as an unskilled laborer in a Nevada gold
mine, but soon learned enough to get a miner's job at miner's pay. Moving to San Francisco, he talked himself into the position of assistant mine
manager, and in 1897 the British mining firm of Bewick Moreing and
Company hired him at six hundred dollars a month to take charge of
some new properties in Australia. His initials, "H.C.," earned him the
nickname of "Hail, Columbia"; but his closest associates instinctively
called him "the Chief." Hoover made such a success in Australia that
within three years his employers got him promoted to an advisory post
with the Chinese government at twenty thousand dollars a year and all

expenses. He took time out to travel to California and marry his campus sweetheart, Lou Henry, who proved her mettle during the Boxer troubles of 1900, saving children's lives and helping him keep the foreign colony at Tientsin together. She also accompanied him on many of his trips through the interior of China, one of which took him as far as Urga, in the Gobi Desert, where he met the Dalai Lama.

More promotions followed fast. Hoover became a junior partner in Bewick Moreing but after seven years went into business for himself as a consulting engineer, specializing in mining zinc, lead, and coal and in making abandoned properties pay. In 1909 he reorganized a mining community of more than one hundred thousand persons in the Ural Mountains of Russia. Other assignments led to Burma and South Africa. In their travels—which took them around the world many times—the Hoovers also found time to translate a treatise on mining written in Low Latin in the 1550's by a German scientist who signed himself Agricola. It presented so many difficulties that scholars had given up, long since, any attempt to render it into any modern tongue.

In 1909 Hoover delivered a series of lectures on engineering at both Leland Stanford and Columbia University. Later he made them into a small textbook, *Principles of Mining*, which went into several editions and remains, more than forty years on, a standard work in schools of engineering. One of the most lyrical passages in Hoover's surprisingly eloquent memoirs celebrated the sorrows and joys of the engineering profession: "The great liability of the engineer compared to men of other professions is that his works are out in the open where all can see them. His acts, step by step, are in hard substance. He cannot bury his mistakes in the grave like the doctors. He cannot argue them into thin air or blame them on the judge like the lawyers. He cannot, like the architects, cover his failures with trees and vines. He cannot, like the politicians, screen his shortcomings by blaming his opponents and hope the people will forget. The engineer simply cannot deny that he did it. If his works do not work, he is damned." But he has his compensations. "On the other hand, unlike the doctor his is not a life among the weak. Unlike the soldier, destruction is not his purpose. Unlike the lawyer, quarrels are not his daily bread. To the engineer falls the job of clothing the bare bones of science with life, comfort, and hope. No doubt as the years go by people forget which engineer did it, even if they ever knew. Or some politician puts his name on it. Or they credit it to some promoter who used other people's money with which to finance it. But the engineer himself looks back at the unending stream of goodness which flows from his successes with satisfactions that few professions may know. And the verdict of his fellow professionals is all the accolade he wants."

It was not all the accolade that Hoover himself got. When he reached

UNITED PRESS PHOTO

Herbert Hoover in 1926

his fortieth birthday in August, 1914, he had accumulated a personal fortune of several million dollars earned chiefly in backward countries where he proved that applied Christianity yields rewards in this world. Service to others seemed to his Quaker nature a privilege rather than a duty, and his unassuming zeal in behalf of Belgian relief led Walter Hines Page to write of him: "He is a simple, modest, energetic man who began his career in California and will end it in Heaven; and he doesn't want anybody's thanks." Hoover in turn described Page as "one of those blossoms of American life which justify our civilization." Yet the two men disagreed about the war. Page favored belligerence for the United States at the earliest possible moment. Hoover favored neutrality. But as Hoover was to write afterward, "It was not Page who took America into war; it was the Germans."

As National Food Administrator, appointed by Wilson in 1917, Hoover fought a steady and winning fight in favor of voluntary measures and decentralized controls. "We found in the American people," he wrote in his *Memoirs*, "exactly what we expected—a wealth of co-operation." And one of the statements he issued to the press at the time read: "I hold that Democracy can yield to discipline and that we can solve this food problem for our own people and our allies largely by voluntary action. To have done so will have been a greater service than our immediate objective, for we have demonstrated the rightness of our faith and our ability to defend ourselves without being Prussianized."

Hoover's public service did not end with the Armistice. He attended the Peace Conference and even the caustic John Maynard Keynes spoke kindly of him: "Mr. Hoover was the only man who emerged from Paris with an enhanced reputation." Having fed the Belgians and organized America's food supplies, Hoover distributed relief in Germany, Russia, Poland, and the Baltic States. He had advised Wilson not to attend the Paris Peace Conference and he broke with Wilson over the Versailles Treaty, which Hoover considered too harsh. He opposed letting the Japanese send troops into Siberia in 1918, correctly predicting that intervention would strengthen the Bolsheviks. His prewar experiences in

Russia led him to recall: "Always there was the feeling among us that some day the country would blow up." In 1919 he tried to have some of the neutral nations distribute relief in Soviet Russia, and when his plan failed, he worked through General Yudenich and General Denikin, but the disintegration of their armies prevented him from accomplishing much. He also worked hard to get food to non-Communists in Poland, to anti-Communists in Hungary, and to starving people generally, without regard to politics, in eastern Europe. Later, when the Bolsheviks had crushed their various enemies at home and abroad, Hoover headed a large-scale Russian relief mission that saved some ten million lives. His reputation as a humanitarian in Europe surpassed his reputation as an administrator in the United States.

No disillusioned Wilsonian reacted more sharply than Hoover to the lost peace of 1919. "America, with its skill in organization and the valor of its sons, could win great wars," he wrote in his *Memoirs*, "but it could not make lasting peace. I was convinced that we must keep out of Old World wars, lend measures to preventing war, maintaining peace, and healing the wounds of war." Nor did he forget Clemenceau's farewell advice, spoken during the summer of 1919: "There will be another world war in your time and you will be needed back in Europe."

Although Hoover had joined the National Republican Club in 1909 and supported Theodore Roosevelt in 1912, the postwar leaders of the Party gave him the cold shoulder. Senator Lodge had opposed his wartime relief efforts in Belgium and continued to oppose his efforts to feed the starving children of former enemy nations. After all, the man had endorsed Wilson's appeal for a Democratic Congress in 1918 and favored American membership in the League. During the Republican Convention of 1920 only the galleries wanted Hoover to get the nomination, and soon afterward he almost accepted a position with the Guggenheim copper interests at a minimum guaranteed salary of half a million dollars a year. But rough, tough Harry M. Daugherty affronted the Old Guard by persuading Harding to make Hoover his Secretary of Commerce. According to Mark Sullivan, "One may say that Hoover regarded our entire business structure as a single factory, conceiving himself, as it were, consulting engineer for the whole enterprise. Having this conception, Hoover set about applying to the whole business structure of the United States principles similar to those which Henry Ford applied to the manufacture of automobiles."

As Secretary of Commerce under both Harding and Coolidge, Hoover built the organization that won him unanimous nomination to the Presidency on the Republican ticket in 1928. His greatest strength lay in his ability to inspire intense personal loyalty among the people who worked most closely with him. Throughout the Coolidge years, Hoover got more

publicity than any man in Washington, except the President—and sometimes even the President came in second. At a time when Coolidge
endeared himself to the business community by keeping hands off its
affairs, Hoover endeared himself to hundreds of individual businessmen
by using the Department of Commerce to circumvent the antitrust laws.
From the point of view of the Attorney General's office and of the Supreme Court, Hoover was encouraging restriction of production, price-
fixing, and combinations in restraint of trade. From his point of view,
he was eliminating wasteful competition and promoting economy by
standardization. "I believe," Hoover said, "that we are, almost unnoticed,
in the midst of a great revolution, or perhaps a better word, transformation of the whole superorganization of our economic life. We are passing
from a period of extremely individualistic action into a period of associated activities." Or—as his Department of Commerce phrased it—
"Competition has changed from the contest of merchant with merchant
to a gigantic struggle of industry with industry, for space on the dealers'
shelves and for a place in the consumer's budget."

American business during the 1920's appeared to have solved the problem of production. It was the problem of distribution that made all the
trouble. For the American people never seemed to have enough money to
buy back all the goods they made or to pay for all the services they performed. Advertising thus became a major industry in its own right, levy-
ing a toll of more than two billion dollars a year on other industries. But
it was not enough for Henry Ford to advertise his automobiles or for
John D. Rockefeller to advertise his gasoline. The public also had to see
the man behind the product in a favorable light. Advertising agencies
spent billions of dollars promoting the products of their clients; it took a
new kind of salesman, the public relations counselor, to sell the client
himself. And this was not done through paid advertising but through
free publicity which the client paid the public relations counselor to
obtain.

Hoover's colleagues in the Department of Commerce and his friends
in other walks of life showed the world what this kind of publicity could
do when they sold their chief to the American people as the self-made
Great Engineer who had also made himself the Great Humanitarian.
His engineering achievements proved he had a hard head; his relief
work proved he had a tender heart. But it was always as an administrator
that Hoover excelled. He knew how to issue orders and delegate authority. He had less experience with the world of the businessman who must
deal with the intangibles of human relations or with the world of the
politician who must work through compromise.

Unlike the trained social worker, Hoover saw little connection between the poverty in which the masses still lived and the surrounding

social conditions. He knew how to administer relief to the victims of war and famine. How to attack the causes of war and famine lay outside his experience. He had done well in the world as he found it; he had repaid the world what it had given him, many times over. How, then, could he question a system which had treated him so handsomely? He did not consider that the poverty and struggle of his early childhood handicapped him in later life. Just the opposite: "It is the entry to life which I could wish for every American boy and girl." Charity for the unfortunate and needy by all means and in all abundance. But it must come from the individual, whose generosity wins him favor in the sight of God. For the government to intervene is to deprive the individual of the chance to grow in virtue.

As the right kind of engineer and the wrong kind of humanitarian, Hoover came to bat, as it were, with two strikes against him. In addition, he lacked almost every natural qualification for the job in hand. Harding had at least looked like a President. Although Coolidge neither looked nor acted like one, he made a surprising hit playing the character part that he had devoted his life to perfecting. Hoover did not even know how to act the part of himself. Talking intimately to small groups, he made a favorable impression. Before a crowd, he failed to register. Shy, sensitive, modest, and awkward, he winced beneath the spotlight, froze before an audience. His native honesty, kindliness, and humility worked against him. He hated political shenanigans. He took his high office with the deepest seriousness and always expected others to show him the same respect that he tried to show them. The fact that he had overcome all these obstacles and had won his way to the White House testified to his real ability and—still more—to the skill of his promoters. But now the chips were down. He had to stand and deliver. He was on his own.

· II ·

Hoover walked into the White House as energetic as Theodore Roosevelt and as determined as Woodrow Wilson. Between his election and inauguration, he made a good-will tour of Latin America, preaching what he called the good-neighbor doctrine. His years abroad, especially in lands that export raw materials, had taught him Latin America's importance to the rest of the world, a lesson that his more recent experience in the Department of Commerce confirmed. Perhaps the League of Nations, which he had once urged his fellow countrymen to join, had not fulfilled all the hopes it originally stirred, but there was no doubt that isolation for the United States offered no hope at all.

One passage in Hoover's inaugural address attracted special attention: "One of the oldest and perhaps the noblest of human aspirations has been the abolition of poverty. By poverty I mean the grinding by under-nourishment, cold, and ignorance, and fear of old age of those who have the will to work. We in America are nearer to the final triumph over poverty than ever before in the history of any land." Hoover did not speak the empty rhetoric of the politician; he meant every word of it and took quick action to make every word good. To begin with, he sur-rounded himself with a first-rate Cabinet. Colonel Henry L. Stimson replaced "Nervous Nellie" Kellogg as Secretary of State. Charles Francis Adams, distinguished descendant of two Presidents, became Secretary of the Navy. Dr. Ray Lyman Wilbur left the presidency of Leland Stan-ford University to become Secretary of the Interior. Andrew W. Mellon remained in charge of the Treasury Department, but it did not take Hoover long to show what he thought of the speculative boom that Mellon had sponsored. Two days after the new President delivered his inaugural address he saw to it that the Federal Reserve System stopped lending any more money for stock-market speculation. The precaution did no good. With brokers and speculators willing to pay 15 per cent and 20 per cent interest, they had only to turn from the bankers to the industrialists and borrow the funds they needed from General Motors, Bethlehem Steel, Standard Oil of New Jersey, and similar great enter-prises. As Judge Gary of United States Steel once observed, "A corpora-tion is entitled to 15 per cent on its money."

The growing distress of the American farmer matched the growing prosperity of the American speculator and both conditions set Hoover into action. His attempt to check stock-market gambling through the Federal Reserve came too late to have any effect. So did his farm relief program. In his inaugural address he reluctantly summoned a special session of Congress to write a new farm bill and on June 15, 1929, he signed the Agricultural Marketing Act, which set up a nine-man Federal Farm Board and appropriated half a billion dollars to lend to farm co-operatives and to purchase surplus crops above the market price. But he refused to take any measure to provide subsidies or to control produc-tion: "There is no relief to the farmer by extending government bureauc-racy to control production and thus curtail his liberties, nor by subsidies that bring only more bureaucracy and ultimate collapse. I shall oppose them." As chairman of the new Farm Board he appointed Alexander Legge, president of the International Harvester Company.

Hoover called the Agricultural Marketing Act "the most important measure ever passed by Congress in aid of a single industry." Moreover, the Farm Board did exactly what he had said no government agency should ever do—"engage in buying and selling and price-fixing of prod-ucts." The fact was that the plight of the farmer called for drastic action, and Hoover gritted his teeth and asserted the power of the federal government. Nor did he restrict the exercise of this power to the limited area of farm relief. In July he called a White House conference on child health. In September he appointed a Committee on Recent Social Trends to submit a report that would provide "the basis for the formation of large national policies looking to the next phase of national development." Even Prohibition, the hottest political issue of the day, did not faze him. He appointed an eleven-man commission, headed by George B. Wickersham, former Attorney General, to study the whole subject, report the facts, and offer recommendations. In short, Hoover at once gave the country a new kind of leadership. He broke away from the Coolidge policy of calculated drift. He enlisted outstanding men and women of both parties to study vast matters of national concern. Like Coolidge, he hated bureaucracy and feared any extension of the federal power. Unlike Coolidge, he gladly used the prestige of the White House and the power of the federal government to further certain causes in which he believed. "Progress," he said, "is born of co-operation in the community, not from governmental restraints. The government should assist and encourage these movements of collective self-help by itself co-operating with them." His own temperament and the time in which he held office conspired to make Hoover try to wield his executive power as other strong Presidents had wielded it before him. He differed from Theodore Roosevelt and Woodrow Wilson in that they rode the reform wave whereas Hoover tried to buck it.

At first, he had little choice in the matter. With helpless disapproval, he had watched the Coolidge-Mellon market boom onward and upward. In those days, his charts told him that the Wall Street boom had to end in a crash, and that was that. But the speculator in his greed and the politician in his fear ignored the charts. Emotion put logic to rout. And all the while the public ate its cake and had it too—praising Coolidge prosperity and then welcoming the great engineer as Coolidge's successor. Nor could the great engineer, for all his charts, forget that his political fortunes under Coolidge prosperity had more than matched the financial fortunes of any bull in Wall Street. The new President had no sympathy for that handful of wild men from his native farm belt—"sons of the wild jackass," as Senator George Moses of New Hampshire once called them—who abused Wall Street during the happy summer of 1929. John J. Raskob of du Pont and General Motors, who had become treasurer of the Democratic National Committee, laid down sound Republican doctrine when he declared: "If a man saves fifteen dollars a week and invests it in good common stocks, and allows the dividends and rights to accumulate, at the end of twenty years he will have at least eighty thousand dollars and an income from investments of around four hundred dollars a month. He will be rich. And because income can do that I am firm in my belief that anyone not only can be rich but ought to be rich." The speculators, by this time more than a million of them, wanted to believe Mr. Raskob's advice; so did about another million investors in common stocks; how, then, could the leader of the Party of Prosperity take a less cheerful view? On September 3, 1929, the Tuesday following the Labor Day holiday weekend, the price level of common stocks hit an all-time high as four and half million shares changed hands. What if automobile production during August had fallen more than one third below the figure for August, 1928? What if construction of new buildings had fallen more than one quarter? Business activity had oscillated before. And what if two banks—mostly small ones, to be sure—had been closing their doors every day for the past six years? True, Roger Babson, the business forecaster, had for months past been predicting a major break in the stock market, but Professor Irving Fisher of Yale, an equally respected economist, disagreed. As Fisher described it, stocks had reached "what looks like a permanently high plateau."

And then something happened; something that no expert could explain, that no layman could understand. Confidence, that unknown factor, that immeasurable force, gave way. It did not happen overnight. During the first two weeks in September, prices of common stocks slumped as they had slumped before. On September 19 they rallied, some of them to new highs, but again the decline set in. Meanwhile brokers' loans went up and up, finally reaching eight and a half billion dollars in October. When Charles E. Mitchell, president of the great National City Bank of New York, returned from Europe on October 22 he told reporters, "I know of nothing fundamentally wrong with the stock market or with the underlying business and credit structure." The next day stocks dropped an average of eighteen points as buyers refused to make any bids at all for some of the issues offered for sale. On October 24, over twelve million shares changed hands, but a bankers' pool of $240,000,000 organized in the Morgan offices checked the decline. Richard Whitney, broker for the Morgan firm, loudly bid 205 for 10,000 shares of United States Steel at a time when only 200 were being offered at a price of 193½.

Whitney's gesture not only checked the selling wave. It gave some of the biggest operators just time enough to unload. On October 29 came the deluge. More than sixteen million shares of stock were thrown onto the market for whatever they would bring. Within the space of a few weeks the paper value of American common stocks dropped thirty billion dollars. This was almost as much as the country had spent fighting the recent World War; it was a higher figure than the national debt had ever reached. Nevertheless, all the experts, from President Hoover down, interpreted the crash as a localized affair that hurt nobody except a few speculators. On October 30 Irving Fisher commented, "Yesterday's break was a shaking out of the lunatic fringe that attempts to speculate on margin." John D. Rockefeller did more than talk; he set an example: "Believing that fundamental conditions of the country are sound and there is nothing in the business situation to warrant the destruction of values that has taken place during the past week, my son and I have for some days been purchasing sound common stocks." Chairman Schwab of Bethlehem Steel announced: "The Wall Street crash means nothing in the welfare of business." President Hoover himself let it be known that "the fundamental business of the country, that is the production and distribution of commodities, is on a sound and prosperous basis."

The Music of Triumphant Capitalism.
From Izvestia, Moscow

He then did his best to make these words come true. In November he summoned the leading bankers and industrialists to a conference in the White House, where they pledged themselves not to cut wages and to spend two billion dollars on new construction in 1930. A similar gathering of labor leaders pledged themselves not to seek wage increases or call for strikes. Secretary Mellon foresaw a happy new year: "The speculative flurry is over," he announced on January 1, 1930. "The nation will make steady progress from now on." The measures Hoover took to cope with the results of the crash proceeded naturally from the analysis he and other leaders made of what had happened. They did not want to believe that the society in which they had flourished suffered from any serious defect. They regarded the Wall Street crash as an isolated affair.

The great majority of Americans gladly accepted this view. Never having bought stocks on margin or sold stocks short, they could not see where a crash in Wall Street touched their pocketbooks. The department store clerk in Boston, the assistant professor of French at Leland Stanford University, the Georgia sharecropper, the switchman in the Indianapolis yards of the Wabash Railway, the lawyer in Albuquerque, New Mexico, the doctor in Bismarck, North Dakota, had enjoyed no benefits of the boom. To them, as to most Americans, prosperity was something they read about in newspapers and magazines, heard about over the radio, or saw in the movies. They lived somewhat better in 1929 than they had lived in 1919, but they also lived better in 1919 than their parents had lived in 1909. That was the American way of life. The victims of the Wall Street crash, on the other hand, had violated that way of life. They had tried to get something for nothing and their folly had caught up with them. The safe and sane majority could even feel vindicated and take new confidence from the Wall Street debacle. The hard-working, money-saving mass of the American people who kept their life-insurance policies paid up and never fell behind on the monthly installments for such necessities as automobiles, radios, washing machines, and electric iceboxes had nothing to fear. They did not all, of course, assume that they lived in the best of all possible times in the best of all possible countries in the best of all possible worlds. But they saw no reason to quarrel with Hoover's analysis of the crash or the measures he took to repair the damage. Indeed, his energy and enterprise caused some alarm. Coolidge had done so well just doing nothing at all.

Worse yet, the patient failed to respond to the treatment. The stock market continued to slump; business activity dropped, unemployment increased. For several years the Wall Street boom had distracted attention from existing weaknesses; now the collapse in stocks aggravated weaknesses that the boom had concealed. Henry Ford put his finger on the root of the trouble when he pointed out in November, 1929, "American production has come to equal and surpass not our people's power to consume, but their power to purchase." Dr. Virgil Jordan, of *Business Week*, estimated that during the twelve years before the crash the American people had spent ten billion dollars more than they had received in the form of income. Gilbert Seldes summarized the situation in *Years of the Locust:* "We went into debt in order to build factories which would sell more or less perishable things to people who would go into debt to buy them; when we had built too many factories and people had gone into debt as far as they dared, we could no longer sell what we made; and therefore could no longer borrow money with which to finance new factories and new payrolls; so, with vast stocks of raw materials and finished goods on hand, we collapsed."

The Wall Street crash delivered a one-two punch to the American economy. First, it cut the wealth and buying power of more than a million speculators whose spendings had helped sustain business activity at a high level. Second, the number of bank failures suddenly doubled, partly because brokers defaulted on their loans, partly because the banks' own assets sank along with everything else. Both these blows affected millions of Americans who never played the market. "Wall Street may sell stocks, but Main Street is buying goods," announced the *Saturday Evening Post*. The wish was father to the slogan. "Wall Street" in this particular connection meant the propertied minority whose losses forced them to stop buying new automobiles, extra radio sets, and costlier luxuries. "Main Street" meant the less favored majority who at once began losing their jobs or working shorter hours. They could no more buy goods on the installment plan than the speculators could con-

"Just around the corner." Cartoon by Al Frueh, copyright 1932, The New Yorker Magazine, Inc. Reproduced by permission

tinue to buy common stock on margin. Coolidge and Mellon had balanced the federal budget and paid off one third of the national debt while the American people had gone deeper and deeper into the red.

Hardly anybody at the time saw how fast and how far the consequences of the Wall Street crash would spread. In March, 1930, President Hoover predicted, "The crisis will be over in sixty days." Two months later the market had slumped still further and unemployment continued to grow. "I am convinced," said the President, "that we have passed the worst and that with continued unity of effort we shall recover." Wih pride and conviction, Hoover put the combined authority of his personality and his office behind this effort to convince his fellow countrymen that nothing serious had gone wrong. Never did he give way to fear or panic; never did he attribute the crash to evil, hostile forces at home or abroad. He showed dignity, manliness, courage. But, like so many other Americans of all ages, classes, sorts, and conditions, he could not transcend the familiar world which had so unaccountably come tumbling down.

In the middle of June, 1930, President Hoover moved from words to deeds. The plight of American agriculture during the 1920's left the American farmer singularly unprepared to meet the shock of bank failures, falling prices, and shrinking markets that followed the Wall Street crash. As the *Neue Zürcher Zeitung* of Switzerland pointed out at the time: "The bulk of American farm products are now sold on the American market rather than on the world market, and the American farmer has in consequence been transformed from a fanatical free trader into a fanatical protectionist. Those whose prosperity depends on high prices for pigs, corn, and wheat want to maintain these high prices by means of high tariffs." Hoover therefore found it convenient to take the advice of orthodox Republican leaders and attempt to improve the condition of the American farmer by raising tariffs. Certain industries also wanted more protection; their lobbyists made the usual representations. In mid-June Congress passed and Hoover signed the Smoot-Hawley Tariff Act, which raised the highest tariff wall in American history still higher. Twelve hundred leading economists vainly urged the President to use his veto power. Alfred P. Sloan, Jr., president of General Motors, warned, "You cannot ship out of the country a terrific amount of goods without gettings goods back to pay for them." The leading bankers who had grown so rich selling so many foreign securities in the United States agreed with Mr. Sloan. They, too, stood to profit from lower tariffs. But the President ignored the professors; he ignored the industrialists; he ignored the bankers. He listened only to the professional politicians who persuaded him to apply the sovereign, Republican remedy for all economic ills: a higher tariff. Had he known more about politicians and less about economics, he might have taken a different course. But Hoover had come into politics so recently that the arguments of the professional politicians impressed him unduly. On the other hand, long experience with professors, industrialists, and bankers had taught him that they could all be wrong. But on this occasion it was the politicians who made the mistake, and the Liberal *Manchester Guardian* spoke for a wide public all over the world when it commented, "The Tariff Bill has probably done more to discredit Mr. Hoover's administration than anything else."

If Hoover signed the Smoot-Hawley Tariff against his better judgment, he regarded it as an inexpensive, unimportant sop to the professional politicians and the pressure groups. What stirred his soul was not the tariff, it was relief to the unemployed. As the great humanitarian, he felt an obligation to do at least as much for his own people in distress as he had done for distressed peoples in other lands. But because they were his own people, he also felt constrained, as the self-made engineer, to administer relief in the traditional American way. In October, 1930, he sponsored a President's Committee for Unemployment Relief, and when Republicans as well as Democrats, businessmen as well as social workers, called for direct federal relief to the unemployed, he replied: "This is not an issue as to whether people shall go hungry or cold. It is solely a question of the best method by which hunger and cold shall be prevented. It is a question of whether the American people will maintain the spirit of charity and mutual self-help through voluntary giving and the responsibility of local government, as distinguished from appropriations from the Federal Treasury. My own conviction is strongly

that if we break down this sense of responsibility, of individual generosity, of individual and mutual self-help in the country in times of
national difficulty and if we start appropriations of this character, we
have not only impaired something infinitely valuable in the life of the
American people but have struck at the roots of self-government." As
Gilbert Seldes put it, "A scientifically trained mind was substituting a
memory of the past for the facts of the present."

As usual, Hoover put the whole weight of his office in the service of
his belief. But when he denied the obligation of the federal government
to care for the unemployed, when he called upon individuals and communities to bear the whole burden, he spoke from Washington radio
networks that brought his voice to the whole country. Other eminent
voices delivered the same message—from Hollywood, from Broadway,
even from the great J. P. Morgan himself—urging the American people
to deal with the unemployed on a system of "block aid" whereby each
block in each neighborhood cared for its own. Although nobody in
authority knew the exact relief needs of the American people at this time,
few social workers saw any reason to believe that "block aid" would fill
the bill. In 1930 the Bureau of Labor Statistics in Washington estimated that almost one quarter of all factory workers in the United States
had lost their jobs. If this estimate were true, it meant that unemployment at the end of 1930 totaled some eight millions. Most newspapers,
however, put the figure at closer to five millions and the great engineer-
humanitarian gave out no figures at all.

The outcome of the elections for Congress in November, 1930, suggested that the pessimists were the ones who had erred in the right
direction. A coalition of Democrats and progressive Republicans won
control of the Senate, and the Democrats—for the first time since 1916—
won control of the House of Representatives, though by the narrowest
of margins. Instead of offering a coherent alternative to the Hoover
policies, the Democrats fought the President by turning against him the
same publicity techniques that had contributed so mightily to his own
power and fame. In the summer of 1929 the Democratic National Committee began spending two million dollars in an unprecedented between-
campaigns offensive. Jouett Shouse, a conservative Kentucky politician
who favored outright repeal of Prohibition, planned the grand strategy
which consisted of holding Hoover personally responsible for all the
troubles of the nation. Charles Michelson, former political reporter for
the New York *World,* carried out the tactical details which took the
form of inspired press releases. Thanks to Shouse and Michelson, the
shacks in which more and more of the unemployed had to live became
universally known as "Hoovervilles"; old newspapers became "Hoover
blankets"; jack rabbits became "Hoover hogs." If the Democrats had

been able to foresee the course of the depression, they could not have chosen a more effective line of attack. And the 1930 elections not only showed the Democrats polling more votes than the Republicans. The Democrats ran strongest in the most densely populated regions. In New York State, Governor Franklin D. Roosevelt won re-election with a whopping 725,000 majority. The next day, Roosevelt's two closest political advisers, James A. Farley and Louis McHenry Howe, issued a statement in Farley's name: "I do not see how Mr. Roosevelt can escape being the next Presidential nominee of his party even if no one should raise a finger to bring it about." Having released the statement, Farley asked Roosevelt over the telephone how it struck him. "Whatever you said, Jim," the Governor replied, "is all right with me."

· III ·

HOOVER paid little heed to Roosevelt and the unemployed paid little heed to either. During 1931 four New York hospitals reported ninety-five deaths from starvation—this in the richest city in the richest country on earth. And a routine report by the Welfare Council of New York City gave a picture of the plight of one family in the Brownsville section of Brooklyn: "Family reported starving by neighbors. Investigator found five small children at home while mother was out looking for vegetables under pushcarts. Family had moved into one room. Father sleeping at Municipal Lodging House because he could get more to eat there than at home and frequently brought food home from there in pockets for children and wife. Only other food they had for weeks came from push-carts."

The Democrats, reading the lines Michelson ghost-wrote for them, blamed such conditions as these on Hoover. The President, fearing the outcome of the next election, accused them of "playing politics with human misery." Since neither of the two major parties offered any analysis of the depression, they failed to suggest any cure. The Socialists, on the other hand, explained in detail what had happened, while the Communists went in for direct action. College students flocked to hear Norman Thomas expound Socialism with the same eloquence that he had preached Christianity as a Presbyterian minister. The Communists went in for "organizing the unorganized." They set up skeleton unions in some of the major industries, they staged several abortive strikes, but they made the greatest headway among the unemployed. Neither the Socialists nor the Communists had a mass following. Thomas had polled less than a quarter of a million votes in the 1928 Presidential election. Membership in the Communist Party totaled perhaps fifteen thousand, with at least half of them dropping out every year. Yet a zealous, inner circle of several hundred disciplined fanatics kept the Party alive and growing, and by 1930 and 1931 their influence extended, indirectly, to millions of the depression's victims.

The Wall Street crash found America's intellectuals as unorganized as America's unemployed and left them equally bitter. Sinclair Lewis and H. L. Mencken satirized the twenties; Sherwood Anderson and Theodore Dreiser took a more grim and tragic view of their times; Thornton Wilder, James Branch Cabell, and Joseph Hergesheimer sought escape; Ring Lardner masqueraded as a humorist, Scott Fitzgerald as the spokesman for the jazz age. But all these men rejected the values of their generation. With the crash, a new generation appeared. In 1930 John Dos Passos fulfilled his youthful promise with the publication of *The 42d Parallel*, the first volume of a projected panoramic trilogy depicting life in the United States at many levels and in many regions since the turn of the century. Where Aldous Huxley's *Point Counter Point* copied some of André Gide's tricks, Dos Passos developed new techniques of his own: he embellished his narrative with the autobiographical "Camera Eye" which told his personal story, with the journalistic "Newsreel" which presented crucial scenes from recent history, and with his "Biographies" which re-created the great men of the time. And where Huxley castigated himself, his caste, his country, and his period, Dos Passos reaffirmed the defiant American spirit in revolutionary terms. Occasionally Dos Passos wrote a short piece for the *New Masses*, weekly mouthpiece of the Communist intellectuals, who turned themselves inside out trying to convert him to their dogma. They attracted his interest, but never his faith.

Gertrude Stein, in Paris, called the young people who were coming of age at about the time of the 1918 Armistice "the lost generation"—and they had wallowed in self-pity with the same abandon that the Wall Street plungers had wallowed in self-esteem. Dos Passos was the first member of this generation to command a wide audience. Where Lewis and Lardner depicted the surfaces of life with photographic accuracy, letting the readers draw their own conclusions, Dos Passos originated an individual style and preached a doctrine of social revolt. His contemporary, Ernest Hemingway, also created a style of his own, a style to which the critics applied the words "lean," "muscular," and "athletic." Hemingway had suffered a serious wound while driving an ambulance on the Italian front; he had worked as a newspaperman in the States and in Europe, and the abbreviated "cablese" of the foreign correspondent inspired him to create a prose style of comparable simplicity. His first novel, *The Sun Also Rises*, dealt with a group of American expatriates in Europe, and won some critical success in 1926. *A Farewell to Arms*, a story of love and war laid on the Italian front, appeared in 1929 and

Hemingway's reputation was made. He became at once the most widely imitated stylist of his generation, but his work contained few ideas. Deliberately he bent all his efforts to capture "the real thing, the sequence of motion and fact which made the emotion." Hemingway and Dos Passos both rejected the values of the twenties—Dos Passos as a radical in search of a social philosophy, Hemingway as a nihilist interested in experiencing and recapturing sensation.

Three new Southern writers also began to attract attention as the decade of the twenties ended. In 1929 Thomas Wolfe's *Look Homeward, Angel,* introduced one of the most powerful talents America had produced since Walt Whitman. Wolfe's autobiographical account of his childhood and youth in North Carolina, his postgraduate work at Harvard, writing plays under the guidance of Professor George Pierce Baker, and his early years in New York and Europe achieved a literary and psychological miracle of total recall. Wolfe also had a distinctive style which he used to express his passion for all the richness, vigor, and variety of American life. He neither accepted nor rejected the twenties; something deeper in his country's character and being stirred his passion. William Faulkner, a native of Oxford, Mississippi, who had served with the British Royal Air Force, wrote a less turgid, more difficult prose than Wolfe. He had some of Hemingway's nihilism, but he wrote of the unconscious mind, and the dark, twisted hates of the ingrown people of the Deep South. Georgia-born Erskine Caldwell reached a wider audience than Wolfe or Faulkner with his sordid, sexy novels about poor whites—*Tobacco Road* and *God's Little Acre.* Caldwell shared some of Dos Passos's revolutionary fervor, but his ideas had no more originality than his naturalistic style. But of these three Southerners, more later.

In 1906 the aging Henry James had traveled up and down the land of his birth describing what he saw in *The American Scene.* In 1930 Edmund Wilson, perhaps the most gifted young literary critic in the country, quit his ivory tower and spent more than a year on a similar voyage of rediscovery. He had just finished his most ambitious book of literary criticism, *Axel's Castle,* dealing with Proust, Joyce, Yeats, Rimbaud and other symbolists. He followed it up with *The American Jitters,* which covered the whole range of the American social ladder as well as every important section of the country.

The muckrakers of the early 1900's had also called attention to abuses, but they were professional reporters. Edmund Wilson was a distinguished man of letters who drew radical philosophic and political conclusions from what he had seen: "Capitalism has run its course," he concluded, "and we shall have to look for other ideals than the ones that capitalism has encouraged." He went so far as to express sympathy for the young radicals in the labor movement who "want in fact a Communist dictatorship," as the only possible alternative to a dictatorship of big business: "I, though I am a bourgeois myself and live in and depend on the bourgeois world, have certain interests in common with these prole-tarians. I, too, admire the Russian Communist leaders, because they are men of superior brains who have triumphed over the ignorance, the stupidity, and shortsighted selfishness of the mass, who have imposed on them better methods and ideas than they could ever have arrived at by themselves. As a writer I have a special interest in the success of the 'intellectual' kind of brains as opposed to the acquisitive kind. And my present feeling is that my satisfaction in seeing the whole world fairly and sensibly run as Russia is now run, instead of by shabby politicians and in the interests of acquisitive manufacturers, businessmen, and bank-ers, would more than compensate me for any losses that I might incur in the process."

Wilson had good reason to reject American capitalism. He had less reason, as he soon discovered for himself, to accept Russian Communism. Too many leading Americans during the 1920's had largely ignored poli-tics, economics, and the social sciences, and when the crash came some intellectuals looked to Stalin's Russia because nowhere else could they see any practical alternative to their own broken-down system. It did not take Wilson long to recover from his trance. With more energy, courage, and independence than many lesser radicals displayed, he devoured the works of Karl Marx, learned Russian, visited the Soviet Union, and re-turned disillusioned.

Not all his writing colleagues shared this mood. Like Wilson, many of them soon concluded that capitalism—which Hoover preferred to call "the American system"—was doomed. Like Wilson, they read Marx and Lenin and concluded that the best hope for America's future lay in Mos-cow. Unlike Wilson, they seldom put these new convictions to the test and the few who did dared not admit that they had made a mistake. Will Rogers summed up the low-brow American attitude toward Communism when he described it as "one third practice and two thirds explanation." But in at least one respect Rogers proved himself a better prophet than many of the high-brows. As early as 1930 he observed, "We can't pick up a paper that from one to a hundred don't prophesy that Prosperity is just around the corner. But let me tell you that war is nearer round the corner than prosperity is."

In 1931 young Edward Angly, a reporter on the New York *Herald-Tribune,* made a typical depression killing when his collection of false predictions by the former lords of creation became an immediate best seller under the title *Oh, Yeah?* "I see no reason why 1931 should not be an extremely good year," said Alfred P. Sloan, Jr., president of General Motors in November, 1930. The following March Henry Ford discovered, "These really are good times, but only a few know it." Three days later he added, "There is plenty of work if people would do it." Roger Babson, who had called the turn on the stock market in the summer of 1929, declared, in April, 1931, "Business has now turned the corner." At the same time, Walter S. Gifford, president of American Telephone and Telegraph, predicted, "As sure as I am standing here, this depression will soon pass and we are about to enter a period of prosperity the like of which no country has ever seen before."

It may be doubted that the American people ever took seriously such pronouncements from the lords of creation. Charles Franklin Kettering, president of General Motors Research Corporation, showed his independence when he publicly confessed, "Our chief job in research is to keep the customer reasonably dissatisfied with what he has." Will Rogers owed his unique prestige to his outspoken humor. At the time of the Wall Street crash he commented, "Confidence hasn't left this country; confidence has just got wise." A year later he added, "We are continually buying something we never get from a man who never had it." As the depression deepened, Americans recovered their ability to laugh at themselves. George T. Delacorte, Jr., and Norman Anthony made an enormous killing as publisher and editor of the magazine *Ballyhoo,* which instantly attracted well over a million readers by lampooning the editorial and advertising pages of the conventional periodical press. An editorial entitled "How Long Shall We Stand For It?" contained nothing but the words: "Blah. Blah. Blah. Blah. Blah," and such occasional subtitles as "Whither?" "The People?" "What Next?" "Good Times?" A burlesque advertisement of Old Gold cigarettes displayed a baby's bare bottom and the caption "Keep Kissable with Old Colds." The copy began with the statement: "Old Colds were created to give you . . . Old Colds." It wound up: "Open up a pack of Old Colds. Open up a dozen packs! See if we care! Smell the tobacco . . . You can't! Because there isn't any tobacco in it!" A dozen imitators of *Ballyhoo* sprung up at once, the astute Delacorte launching the first of them himself. Their off-color pictures and jokes caused several of them to be banned from the mails, though *Ballyhoo* itself successfully fought off an obscenity charge.

As usual, nature improved upon art. What Americans actually did and said surpassed the imagination of any contributor to *Ballyhoo.* During the summer of 1930 they spent a million dollars a day playing miniature golf on thirty-five thousand courses that represented an investment of one hundred and thirty-five million dollars. Still crazier than the addicts of miniature golf or the proprietors of the courses were the economists who seriously hailed it as the remedy for the depression. Once again, the economists guessed wrong. The fad collapsed in 1931 as rapidly as

Man on Top: *"I can't see why they want me to get off when we're nearly there."* Strube in the Daily Express, *London*

it had burgeoned in 1930, having provided a brief and inexpensive diversion for the new poor who soon found other uses for their vanishing reserves of hard cash.

By the time miniature golf had gone the way of mah jongg, the lords of creation had more serious worries on their hands. Albert Henry Wiggin, president of the Chase National Bank, showed himself an even worse loser than most of his colleagues when he repudiated the whole American theory of prosperity—that mass production plus high wages equal prosperity. "It is not true," said Mr. Wiggin, "that high wages make prosperity. Instead prosperity makes high wages." While the head of the biggest bank in the world took refuge in word games, the only living ex-President of the United States offered this characteristic suggestion: "If those who have the means," counseled Calvin Coolidge, "would pay all their retail merchandise bills and in addition purchase what they need and can afford, a healthy commerce would be quickly created." Hoover, on the other hand, finally opened his mind to the possibility that orthodox measures might not master the crisis: "If the time should ever come that the voluntary agencies of this country are unable to find resources with which to prevent hunger and suffering, I will ask the aid of every resource of the federal government."

By the summer of 1931 that time seemed to be approaching. The

Smoot-Hawley Tariff Act of 1930 had proved a boomerang: other nations hit back by raising the bars against imports from the United States and world trade shrank in all directions. Surveying the planet from the vantage point of the White House, President Hoover therefore let it be known that "the main causes of this depression came from outside the United States." Clearly the fault did not lie at home. Had he not left the natural laws of economics free to undo the damage of the Wall Street crash? Had he not used all the power and prestige of his high office to make private charities and local communities wholly responsible for unemployment relief? Yet business had grown steadily worse; distress had steadily increased. Nothing could be wrong with his beloved "American system," especially under the guidance of the only political party fit to govern. There could be no doubt about it: the cause of the trouble must lie abroad.

And Hoover's British friends had been explaining for years just where the trouble lay. Back in 1922, the Balfour Note had spelt it all out when the British offered to cancel all the war debts their allies owed them provided the United States would cancel the war debt owed by Britain, thus transferring the burden of the Allied war debt to the American taxpayer. It also made the Germans feel that the reparations they paid to France went on to Britain and eventually to the greedy, rich Americans, who refused to break the vicious cycle. No American political leader ever dared give any encouragement to the Balfour Note, until the depression forced Hoover to accept its underlying principle.

On June 21, 1931, after having talked the whole situation over with the British, but with no one else, the President suddenly announced: "I am suggesting to the American people that they be wise creditors and good neighbors," and went on to call for "the postponement during one year of all payments on intergovernmental debts." This meant no more reparations from Germany as well as no more war debts from Britain, France, and the other Allies. Hoover had adopted the principle of the Balfour Note. The concessions that he offered benefited the British, whom he had consulted, far more than they benefited the French, whom he had not consulted. And if his offer were accepted for even one year, he had no assurance that the beneficiaries of that offer would resume paying either war debts or reparations once their year of grace came to an end. For a few days, however, the great engineer seemed to have turned the tide as stock prices staged their widest, sharpest rally since October, 1929. But those same world forces to which he attributed the depression developed irresistible momentum and the moratorium that bore his name soon became their latest but not their last victim.

SUMMING UP

THE same force that created the Hoover myth also destroyed it. First, a group of Republican ballyhoo artists inflated Hoover until he looked like a superman; then, a group of Democratic smear artists deflated him until he appeared subhuman. Nobody remembered—few people even knew—that he had warned against stock-market speculation during the Coolidge years. Hoover had become identified with the kind of prosperity his predecessor had encouraged. When that prosperity collapsed, Hoover collapsed with it. Others who had benefited from the seven fat years met the same fate. But the real victims of the depression were not the new poor who had once enjoyed the better things of life. The depression often came down hardest on millions who had never enjoyed the benefits of the boom.

When Hoover called upon private charity to care for the victims of depression and when J. P. Morgan urged each city block to take care of its own, they acknowledged that each man was his brother's keeper. What they did not acknowledge was that private charity and block aid were not enough. The relief burden had become too heavy; everybody had become dependent, one way or another, on everybody else. In like manner, the United States found itself at the mercy of world forces. The American people had sought security in isolation. The Wall Street crash not only affected the entire country; its repercussions spread throughout the world, and distress abroad soon led to still further distress at home. President Hoover recognized the national scope and international repercussions of the Wall Street crash, but his countermeasures proved tardy and inadequate. At first, he used all the forces at his command to make private charities and local communities bear the whole burden of relief. And as soon as he saw symptoms of depression in other countries, he held them responsible for America's troubles. Yet the moratorium on war debts and reparations that he proclaimed charged the United States with a responsibility that he had originally laid elsewhere.

Not many Americans knew the extent of this responsibility; not many Europeans understood its nature. Before the war, a million Europeans had migrated to the United States every year, thus relieving population pressure in the Old World and increasing the bonds between the Old World and the New. But the curtailment of European immigration to the United States weakened these bonds, hampered Europe's recovery, and increased Europe's tensions. The common people of Europe, shocked by Woodrow Wilson's defeat at the hands of his fellow countrymen, no longer looked to the United States as the promised land. The Wall Street crash cost America still more good will abroad—not only among the common people but among the ruling classes in all the capitalist lands. Indeed, the depression caused the tide of immigration to reverse itself as more people left the United States than came there to live. Here was something quite new in the history of the Republic. Democracy and capitalism had suffered parallel defeats in the land where both had developed to an unprecedented degree. It remained to be seen whether they could recover, either separately or together.

11

Europe's End Begins

*How the impact of the world depression started a
new kind of revolution in Germany and soon began to tear all Europe asunder.*

PREVIEW

By 1929 the speculative boom in the United States was already absorbing most of the surplus funds that had financed the revival of Germany since 1924. By 1930, as the depression ended all hope of further
aid from abroad, the Hitler movement suddenly zoomed up from nowhere. Yet hardly anyone outside Germany, or even outside the Nazi
Party, saw its full significance at the time. Indeed, the Republican
Revolution that swept Spain in 1930 and 1931 raised the hope that Hitler
might collapse as fast as he had arisen and that democracy had taken a
new lease on life. But successive financial crashes in Austria, Germany,
and England overshadowed events in Spain, while Japan's invasion
of Manchuria put Asia in the spotlight once again.

· I ·

It took the Wall Street crash to destroy America's postwar prosperity.
It took no more than the approach of that crash to shatter Germany's.
Between 1924 and 1928, loans from the United States gave the Germans
their first taste of good times in more than ten years. In 1929 these good
times ended. With Wall Street speculators borrowing billions at interest
rates as high as 15 and 20 per cent, American loans to Germany dropped
from a billion dollars in 1928 to 221 millions in 1929. German business at
once slumped; unemployment climbed. On May Day, 1929, more than
two hundred persons suffered serious injuries in riots and demonstrations throughout Germany. Five months later came the death of Foreign
Minister Stresemann and the beginning of the end of the Weimar Republic.

Stresemann had devoted the last of his failing energies to working
out a final schedule of reparations payments with a committee of experts
headed by Owen D. Young. Under this arrangement the Germans agreed

to pay reparations at a fixed annual rate, 16 per cent below the Dawes Plan level, for the next fifty-nine years in exchange for an Allied promise to withdraw their troops from the Rhineland and to restore Germany's economy to German control. Alfred Hugenberg, leader of the German Nationalists, threw his considerable personal fortune and his powerful newspapers into an attack on the Young Plan, but when Hindenburg invited him to form a new government, Hugenberg refused: he believed he could play a bigger role by letting conditions get worse. Soon afterward, Dr. Hjalmar Schacht resigned the presidency of the Reichsbank and joined the opposition to the Young Plan—which he had helped to negotiate. Meanwhile, Hugenberg was turning over funds to Hitler's National Socialist Party and between them they backed a plebiscite that would have repudiated the whole Young Plan settlement.

R. T. Clark in *The Fall of the German Republic* found one trait Hugenberg shared with Hitler: "Like Hitler, he had been immensely impressed with the achievements of a foreigner who had never hidden his light under a bushel, but had added reflectors and magnifiers; his method of approach to power as a politician was to seek to become Germany's Northcliffe." Hugenberg studied propaganda seriously and lacked "that fundamental contempt for the demagogue that characterized his better born colleagues." Hugenberg also respected businessmen: "Alfred Hugenberg, whose record for political intransigence and political stupidity is almost unique in German politics, combined the appearance of a hoary, genial, but beardless Santa Claus with ruthless greed of power, unscrupulousness in method, and profound contempt for that large section of the Nationalist leaders whose long tradition still inhibited them from adopting the standards of big business."

Hugenberg had more support inside the Reichstag than out. Barely 10 per cent of the German people voted against the Young Plan in the plebiscite that he and Hitler had supported, but the Reichstag approved the Young Plan only by the narrowest margin—226 votes to 224. Hugenberg's papers intensified their attacks on Chancellor Müller's Socialist government. Nazis to right of him, Communists to left of him, volleyed and thundered. The Socialist trade union leaders warned that they could not support him if he ordered cuts in wages or unemployment relief. Müller therefore resigned, whereupon Hindenburg took General von Schleicher's advice and replaced him with Heinrich Brüning of the Catholic Center Party. Schleicher and the court camarilla detested Müller as a matter of course; they distrusted Hugenberg; Hitler they regarded as a joke. Brüning looked like the ideal stopgap, strong enough to preserve order, but not too strong to prevent them from seizing power at some future time. Brüning came from a middle-class family in Münster. He volunteered when the war broke out, but the Army doctors

rejected him because of his poor
eyesight. He therefore continued
his studies at the University of
Bonn, and after winning his Ph.D.
with a thesis on railways he volunteered again and was accepted. As
captain of a machine-gun company
on the western front he won the
Iron Cross, first class, for "unprecedented heroism." Since the war he
had supported the Republic without reserve and had always backed
the foreign policy of Stresemann,
whose successor, Dr. Julius Curtius, he retained in the Foreign
Office. Brüning had traveled in
both France and England and held
the statesmanship of the latter
country in especially high regard.

KEYSTONE

Heinrich Brüning

He was a devout Roman Catholic bachelor with the chiseled ascetic
features of a priest and a determination made, like his spectacle rims,
of steel.

"The experiences of the war," wrote Brüning immediately after the
Armistice in an article for young people, "generally strengthened the
realization of those who participated in those great and terrible events—
unless they were spiritually unsettled by them—that the great tasks in the
world are accomplished only by sacrifice, unselfishness, and voluntary
discipline." In 1920 he told the students of Göttingen: "Our time needs
a hard, determined, and, above all, an uncomplicated kind of man. I
trust that the generation that took part in the war possesses all the qualifications for becoming this strong and hard race of men." Hindenburg
liked and respected Brüning. Baron von Oldenburg-Januschau, eighty-
year-old president of the Herrenklub and embodiment of the Prussian
tradition, called him "the best Chancellor since Bismarck." But never in
his long life had Baron von Oldenburg-Januschau spoken political sense.

The kind of support on which Brüning had to rely and the kind of situation he inherited doomed him from the start. By 1930 private American
loans to Germany had ceased; a general decline in world trade had also
set in. Not to cut wages, not to cut relief to the unemployed meant another inflation—and that was something that even the extremists dared
not advocate. But the court camarilla not only persuaded Hindenburg
to demand economies at the expense of the workers and the unemployed;
they persuaded him to insist on increased subsidies for the East Prussian

landowners. Yet when Brüning put the program before the Reichstag
he failed, by eight votes, to get the necessary two-thirds majority.

At this point Hindenburg invoked Article 48 of the Constitution and
told Brüning to govern by decree. But in July the Reichstag voted against
the government, Hindenburg ordered it dissolved and set new elections
for September. Schleicher and the camarilla congratulated themselves.
They had replaced Müller with the stronger, more conservative Brüning.
They had set the stage for their Nationalist friends to sweep the forthcoming election. But they had reckoned without the growing mass of
unemployed, whose plight most German politicians, except the Nazis
and the Communists, largely ignored. By the early months of 1930, two
million Germans had no jobs; by the end of the year their numbers had
risen to more than three millions—a dangerously high figure in a country that had recently lost a war and then had gone through the wringer
of inflation. What unemployment, this latest scourge of the twentieth
century, meant to its victims, the liberal *Berliner Tageblatt* revealed in
this anonymous monologue by one of them:

"You have two legs, two arms, two very long arms, in fact, two large
hands, two clear eyes without glasses, a sound, healthy skull, and yet you
cannot manage to scrape together food for three people. You are not
succeeding in your efforts. The field is barren. You are working powerfully but you miss your aim every time. You are accomplishing nothing.
You might just as well grub up the soil with your ten fingers, or tear up
the pavement of the streets with your feet and hands, hoping by magic
to cause it to bring forth bread and fruit and life itself. You feeble, impoverished rat! You are getting nowhere. The sparrows have their refuse,
the bees have their pollen, and the earthworms have their crumbs of
black mold, while you sit in their midst vainly racking your brains. Man
is great. He is able to send his spirit on journeys far beyond the stars,
where the day of his life is merged with the night of God. He can dispatch his spirit to Hell, fight with the Devil and overcome him. Man is
mighty. He can do everything. Yet he cannot compress his stomach and
command it not to growl. This most insignificant miracle is denied him.
Let him lie flat upon the road, wringing his hands and peering with his
eyes until they start from their sockets; if he is condemned to poverty,
there is no God and no power of any kind to send him twenty pfennigs
for a bit of bread or a piece of sausage. You are a helpless rat. Go home
where your wife stands gazing into the great, worn pocketbook. Go
home. You are achieving nothing."

Only two political parties in Germany—the Communists and the Nazis
—made their primary appeal to such nameless millions as spoke through
this man's voice. As a result, the Communist vote increased more than
40 per cent between 1928 and 1930, the Nazi vote more than 1,000 per

cent. Between 1924 and 1928 the number of Nazi delegates in the Reichs-tag dropped from 32 to 11; on September 14, 1930, they won 107 Reichstag seats. They had become the third largest party in the country —only the Socialists and the Centrists had wider support. A strange, new force had appeared in Germany—and the world.

· II ·

ONCE BEFORE, in November, 1923, the name of Adolf Hitler and his Nazi Party made world news. But the ludicrous collapse of his attempted beer-hall *Putsch* in Munich appeared to have killed him off for good and all. The German authorities set him free after he had served only eight and a half months of a five-year jail sentence. Nor did they bother to deport him to his native Austria or bar him from political activity when he got out. Did not his whole past history prove his impotence? Even as late as 1929 the generally perceptive Lord D'Abernon could write that Hitler had "faded into oblivion." Yet the paradox of Hitler and the secret of Nazi success lay in precisely those weaknesses and evils that the civilized portion of mankind despised or dismissed.

Adolf Hitler came of sickly, inbred, lower-middle-class stock. His father, Alois, lived for years under his unmarried mother's maiden name of Schickelgruber. At the age of eighteen Alois left his native village and got a job as border policeman with the Austrian customs service in the little town of Braunau, near Salzburg. Here, at the age of twenty-seven, he made his first marriage to a woman fourteen years his senior; here he lived for sixteen years, slowly working his way up in the service. His first wife died of tuberculosis. So did his second. In his late forties he married his first cousin's daughter—a woman twenty-three years younger than himself. His own father and mother had meanwhile married and he had taken the name of Hitler, after his father's name of Hiedler. Alois Hitler had seven children, four of whom died in infancy. His eldest son, Alois, Jr., became a waiter and served two terms in jail for theft. Only two of the five children that his third wife bore him lived to grow up—a daughter named Paula, born in 1896, and a son, christened Adolfus, born in 1889.

At this point, the family moved to Linz, where the father lived on his pension and speculated in real estate. Already irked by the bad start his eldest son and namesake had made, he tyrannized over young Adolf, whom the mother coddled and spoiled. At first the boy proved himself a better than average student with some aptitude for free-hand drawing, but after his father died of a lung ailment in 1903, Adolf's efforts in the classroom subsided. The same kind of lung ailment that carried off his father cut the boy's education short at the age of sixteen, and Adolf spent

"*Hitler, or The Baby Who Grew Too Fast.*" Groene Amsterdammer

two years with his mother at Linz, doing nothing at all. In 1907 he went to Vienna, where he twice tried unsuccessfully to gain admission to the Academy of Fine Arts, but failed both times for lack of talent. He could copy pictures of buildings but could not draw the human face or form. Hitler's mother died in 1908 and the next year his relatives stopped financing his artistic education.

A new and crucial chapter in Hitler's life began. He gave up his furnished room and slept in cafés and on park benches until cold weather forced him to seek shelter in a flophouse. "A light blanket on a hard spring, his own clothes for a pillow, his shoes wedged beneath the leg of the bed lest they should be stolen, to left and right of him companions in misery—thus Adolf Hitler passed the next months." That was the picture Hitler's biographer Konrad Heiden painted of his first, bitter winter in Vienna. "He had no overcoat. He trudged through the snow with his comrades to the suburb of Edberg or the district of Favoriten; there they hung around the 'warming rooms' where the homeless took refuge from the cold and found soup and bread to still their hunger. These warming rooms were a charity of Baron Königswarter, a man of Jewish origin."

Occasionally Hitler earned small sums shoveling snow off the Danube bridges and carrying tourists' luggage outside a railway station until another frustrated artist, Reinhold Hanisch, warned him not to do any manual work if he ever hoped to rise in the world. Hitler took the advice and let Hanisch make a little money for him selling post-cards he had drawn of famous Viennese buildings. A Christmas gift from relatives permitted him to move to a "Home for Men," chiefly frequented by tramps and drunkards. A Jewish friend named Neumann gave him some shirts and a long coat. From beneath a greasy derby, matted hair hung down over his collar; his beard formed a ruff around his chin. "Neither in Adolf Hitler's physical appearance," wrote Konrad Heiden, "nor in the history of his family is there any suspicion of Jewish strain, and yet among the unkempt Jews of Vienna, he looked like an unkempt Jew of Vienna. Such is the force of environment. On the basis of these few who outwardly resembled him, he formed his opinion about them all."

Hitler lived on in the Home for Men, occasionally painting houses as well as post-card pictures of them. Finally he accused Hanisch of embezzlement and got a court judgment against the man. Their partnership ended and three years later, in 1913, Hitler moved to Munich. Here, too, he had no friends, no girls, but he had begun to take a strident interest in politics. His father had revered the Hapsburg Empire. That was enough to make the son a fervent Pan-German who kept repeating three favorite slogans: "Away from Rome," "Home to the Reich," and "Out with the Jews." The Austrian authorities considered Hitler a deserter, but when he reported for military service at Salzburg in February, 1914, the doctors found him "unfit to bear arms." Returning to Munich, he lived an even emptier, more anonymous life than he had known in Vienna, yet he enjoyed it in his fashion. He had left the cosmopolitan atmosphere of the Austrian capital and made his way "home to the Reich."

With Germany's declaration of war, Hitler suddenly came alive. Later he wrote that war "was not forced upon the masses, but desired by the whole people," that thousands of other young men, like him, "overpowered by stormy enthusiasm fell down on their knees and thanked Heaven from an overflowing heart." He at once joined the Bavarian Army and served throughout the war as a dispatch carrier. His obedience and daring eventually won him the coveted Iron Cross, first class, yet he made few friends among his fellow soldiers. He never relaxed; he neither smoked nor drank nor showed any interest in women. With his zeal to obey orders went no corresponding capacity to give them, and he never rose above the rank of lance corporal. In October, 1918, a gas attack blinded him for several days and left a permanent obstruction in his throat. The effort of will that it cost him to overcome this handicap helped transform him into one of the most formidable orators of his time.

But it was not Hitler's speaking ability, it was his willingness to take orders that got him his first postwar job. The District Army Command at Munich hired him as a civilian employee in the press and news bureau of its political department. Here the colorless, dutiful, ex-lance corporal made himself useful as an informer, keeping in touch with the revolutionary and counterrevolutionary currents that swept the bewildered populace this way and that. Hitler presently joined a group of former officers and soldiers who called themselves the "Iron Fist," one of whose trigger men assassinated Kurt Eisner, head of the short-lived revolutionary government of Bavaria. Contacts with the Iron Fist group then led Hitler to a tiny offshoot of the prewar Pan-German movement known as the Workers' Party. In 1920 he and half a dozen comrades reorganized the Workers' Party into the German National Socialist Workers' Party, for which they prepared a twenty-five-point program.

Hitler himself wrote the first plank: "We demand the union of all Germans in a Pan-German state in accordance with the right of all peoples to self-determination." Point four stressed the importance of race: "Only a racial comrade can be a citizen. Only a person of German blood can be a racial comrade without regard to religion. Consequently no Jew can be a racial comrade." Other points in the platform called for the abrogation of the peace treaties, the return of Germany's colonies, abolition of "interest slavery," of "land rent and real estate speculation," and of "all income obtained without work or pains." Still others called for the nationalization of all trusts and chain stores, for greatly increased old age and maternity benefits, for a reorganization of higher education, and for government control of the press. "The common good before the individual good," summed up the platform's underlying principle, and the final plank demanded "the creation of a strong central power in the Reich; the unconditional control by the political central Parliament over the whole Reich." This reference to Parliament suggested that Hitler planned to carry out his revolution within the framework of the Weimar Republic. There could be no doubt, however, that his party stood for a much stronger central government than Germany had ever known before.

The Nazi Party that tried to seize power in 1923 under the joint leadership of Ludendorff and Hitler had only thirty thousand members. By 1927 the Nazi Party that Hitler reorganized after spending eight and a half not unpleasant months in prison attracted forty thousand members. According to R. T. Clark's *Fall of the German Republic,* Hitler's stay in prison "had restored his mental balance. From the high-souled patriot, whose fanaticism had gone perilously near dementia, he had become again the cunning, petty bourgeois, the *rusé* private of the line." He no longer believed in the violent coup d'état as a means of gaining power. He preferred fraud to force. Above all, he believed in himself and proceeded to reorganize the Nazi Party in accordance with the principle of one-man leadership: "He had merely been the leader at the apex of the Party pyramid. In the new Party the leader must be the base. The members, individually or as a party, must have no power except that which was delegated to them by the leader himself. *Le parti c'est moi* is Hitler's contribution to German political theory and practice, the contribution that any gang leader could have made. He, rather than Mussolini who has affinities with the medieval 'tyrant' or Stalin who is the apotheosis of the political 'boss,' is the supreme gangster of modern politics. The essence of Hitlerism, as of gangsterism, is the dominance of the leader. The real cause, to him, of the failure of the *Putsch* was the multiplication of leaders and the absence of a gang. That mistake, at least, must never be made again."

On his release from prison, Hitler announced that the Nazis would come to power legally. But the backbone of his support still lay in the brown-shirted detachments of Storm Troopers, known as the *Sturmabteilung,* and in the elite, black-shirted *Schutzstaffel* men. At first his chances looked dim indeed. If the Munich beer-hall *Putsch* had made a clown even of the mighty Ludendorff, how could the ludicrous Hitler, who looked like a pudgy, pasty-faced Charlie Chaplin, hope to be taken seriously? Hitler did not touch alcohol, tobacco, or meat. In the presence of authority he quailed or ranted. Women filled him with nervous embarrassment, though he did not share the homosexual tastes of some of his followers. All his energies went into writing for the Party newspaper, the *Völkischer Beobachter,* and into making speeches. On large audiences and on close associates his harsh voice and nervous energy produced a kind of hypnosis.

The prosperity that Germany enjoyed during the later 1920's enabled Hitler to enjoy petty luxuries that he could not afford during the lean postwar years. He made contact with a few men and women of means from whom he received contributions. His widowed half-sister and her seventeen-year-old daughter, Angela Rabaul, from Vienna, kept house for him in a little rented villa at Berchtesgaden, not far from Munich. Here a morbid, frustrated romance developed between Hitler and his half-niece. In 1929 he wrote her an obscene letter that never reached her but that others found useful in blackmailing its author. In 1931 "Geli" Rabaul—now a handsome, statuesque blonde of twenty-three—tried to run away to Vienna only to be found shot dead in her Munich apartment. The coroner called it suicide, rather than murder, but her Catholic priest permitted her burial in consecrated ground. That was as close as Hitler ever got to romance during his first forty years.

His tastes and talents lay in other directions. Unable to lead a normal personal life or gratify the normal human emotions, Hitler took to writing and provided his movement with its indispensable bible. Originally, he wanted to call the book *Four and a Half Years of Struggle Against Lies, Stupidity, and Cowardice,* but agreed to the briefer title *Mein Kampf* (My Struggle) instead. Rudolf Hess, who had served as an infantry officer and then as an aviator on the Western Front, helped Hitler write *Mein Kampf.* A psychic, almost an hypnotic, bond developed between the two men. Hess, the son of a prosperous German exporter, had spent the first fourteen years of his life in Alexandria, Egypt, but moved to Germany to complete his education. He served in the same regiment with Hitler during the war, when the two men met briefly and casually.

After the war Hess belonged to the secret society that murdered Kurt Eisner and renewed his acquaintance with Hitler, who, he decided, had a mission to save Germany. Soon Hess became Hitler's closest friend, helped organize his ideas and plan his strategy. It was Hess who first defined the role of the dictator in the Nazi scheme of things: "For the sake of national salvation the dictator does not hesitate to use the weapons of his enemy, demagogy, slogans, street parades, etc. Where all authority has vanished only a man of the people has authority. This was shown in the case of Mussolini. The deeper the dictator was originally rooted in the broad masses the better he understands how to treat them psychologically, the less the workers will distrust him, the more supporters he will win among the most energetic ranks of the people. He himself has nothing in common with the mass; like every great man he is all personality."

The same qualities in Hitler that appealed to the perverted idealism of Rudolf Hess appealed no less strongly to the earthier nature of Hermann Wilhelm Göring, an outstanding war ace and son of the first Governor General of German South-West Africa. After the war Göring got a job as a transport plane pilot and in this capacity met a well-to-do Swedish aristocrat, Count Eric von Rosen, whose sister divorced her husband to marry the young German hero. Göring's wife suffered from epileptic fits; Göring himself had become a morphine addict, a habit he did not break until 1932. But Göring's bad behavior and violent nature did not blight his social career. On the contrary. He remained a friend of the former Crown Prince, through whom he established close relations with the Italian royal family and, through them, with Mussolini. Göring's wife's family also widened his contacts among the leading industrialists of Europe. He might have used these connections to make himself rich and respectable; he preferred to throw in his lot with Hitler, who put him in charge of his private, brown-shirted army—the *Sturmabteilung*—in 1922. Göring believed that the Nazi Party under Hitler's inspired leadership offered the greatest possible scope for his talents and persuaded some of his influential friends to share his enthusiasm.

The third of Hitler's closest associates did not make contact with the inner Nazi circle until 1925. Dr. Paul Joseph Goebbels came of a poor family and attended six German universities before he qualified for a Ph.D. A clubfoot and crippled physique exempted him from military service. He once aspired to become a playwright, but went in for political journalism and speechmaking instead. Goebbels joined the Nazi Party through burly Gregor Strasser, a Bavarian ex-officer who became a drugstore proprietor after the war and then devoted more and more of his energies to promoting social revolution. Strasser won a seat in the Reichstag and set out to replace Hitler as Party leader by demanding a more radical domestic program and, abroad, an alliance with Russia. But when Strasser attempted a showdown with Hitler in 1926, Goebbels thought fast and turned against him. Like both Hess and Göring, Goebbels instinctively felt that Hitler and Hitler alone could give the Nazi movement the kind of leadership it needed.

Although Goebbels broke with Strasser, he continued to tell his friends that the Nazi Party must be both proletarian and revolutionary. In an open letter to a Communist he declared: "You and I are fighting one another, but we are really not enemies. Our forces

UNDERWOOD

Dr. Paul Joseph Goebbels

have split apart and thus we never reach our goal." Hitler showed sporadic sympathy for this point of view. When some of his friends denounced Trotsky's autobiography as "loathsome," he burst out angrily, "Loathsome? Brilliant! I have learned a great deal from it and so can you." One lesson Hitler learned from Trotsky—and from Danton before him—was audacity, audacity, and still more audacity. "All parties, public opinion, take a position against us," Hitler boasted. "But therein lies the unconditional, I might say the mathematical, reason for the future success of our movement. As long as we are the radical movement, as long as public opinion shuns us, as long as the existing factors of the state oppose us—we shall continue to assemble the most valuable human material around us even at times when, as they say, all factors of human reason argue against us."

The valuable human material to which Hitler appealed was precisely the riffraff, the outcasts, the insulted and injured whom the older parties ignored. And Hitler appealed not to their better but to their baser instincts which he so fully shared. Konrad Heiden's invaluable biography, *Der Fuehrer,* from which many of these facts and some of these judgments are drawn, paid a backhanded tribute to Hitler as the first politician to speak primarily for and to the victims of the world depression: "The sentiment that our modern society had arrived at a breaking point, that millions and millions would be crushed in the impending collapse, tormented every man's soul. With unerring sureness Hitler expressed the speechless panic of the masses faced by an invisible enemy and gave that nameless specter a name. He was a pure fragment of the modern mass soul, unclouded by any personal qualities. One scarcely need ask with what arts he conquered the masses; he did not conquer them; he portrayed and represented them. His speeches are daydreams of this mass soul; they are chaotic, full of contradictions, if their words are taken literally, often senseless, as dreams are, and yet charged with deeper meaning." The British historian R. T. Clark stressed the timeliness of Hitler, describing him as "the apotheosis of the mediocre, the *reductio ad absurdum* of democracy, so much, so utterly a product of his age that he had to wait for his hour until 1933."

When Dorothy Thompson met Hitler in 1932, she did not see him in this guise. She had spent most of the 1920's as an American correspondent in Germany and Austria and her impressions, as recorded in her little book *I Saw Hitler!*, reveal how Hitler affected many other intelligent and informed reporters: "When finally I walked into Adolf Hitler's salon in the Kaiserhof Hotel, I was convinced that I was meeting the future dictator of Germany. In something less than fifty seconds I was quite sure that I was not. It took me just about that time to measure the startling insignificance of this man who has set the world agog. He is formless, almost faceless, a man whose countenance is a caricature, a man whose framework seems cartilaginous, without bones. He is inconsequent and voluble, ill-poised, insecure. He is the very prototype of the Little Man.

"A lock of lank hair falls over an insignificant and slightly retreating forehead. The back head is shallow. The face is broad in the cheek-bones. The nose is large, but badly shaped and without character. His movements are awkward, almost undignified and most unmartial. There is in his face no trace of any inner conflict or self-discipline. And yet, he is not without a certain charm. But it is the soft, almost feminine charm of the Austrian! When he talks it is with a broad Austrian dialect. The eyes alone are notable. Dark gray and hyperthyroid—they have the peculiar shine which often distinguishes geniuses, alcoholics, and hysterics. There is something irritatingly refined about him. I bet he crooks his little finger when he drinks a cup of tea. His is an actor's face. Capable of being pushed out or in, expanded or contracted at will, in order to register facile emotions.

"As I saw him I thought of other German faces. The President, von Hindenburg. A face cut out of rock. No imagination in it; no light; no humor. Not exactly an appealing face. But one revealing a character so defined as to determine its owner's destiny. Chancellor Brüning. The head of an eighteenth-century cardinal-statesman. A high-bridged sensitive nose. A finely cut mouth. The convex profile of obstinacy. Quizzical, wise, humorous. A man who will hold on forever. A little too sensitive, perhaps. He ill endures dislike.

"I thought of this man before me, seated, as an equal, between Hindenburg and Brüning, and involuntarily I smiled. O, Adolf! Adolf! You will be out of luck!"

Miss Thompson based her analysis on reason, morality, and historic precedent. Her journalist's eye and ear also caught Hitler's salient physical and emotional qualities. Had she concluded, early in 1932, that Hitler was a man of destiny, she would have had to ignore reason, reject morality, dismiss historic precedent, disregard the evidence of her own senses, forget everything that the culture to which she belonged had taught her. Only ignorant Nazi fanatics believed that Hitler had a future. Sensible people knew better. This alleged war hero had never risen above the rank of lance corporal and he came out of the war as friendless as he had gone in. This would-be leader of the blond, Protestant, beer-drinking, meat-eating, prolific Germans was a dark-haired, renegade Roman Catholic, a teetotaling, unmarried vegetarian of Austrian origin. As Hitler himself repeatedly emphasized, he counted on emotion to triumph over reason and on evil to overcome good. The spectacle produced such bewilderment among the rational portion of the human race that most of the anti-Hitler propaganda boomeranged. Non-Germans also recalled the exaggerated stories of German atrocities that circulated during the war and discounted the attacks on Hitler as more of the same.

The four and a half million young German voters who went to the polls for the first time in the 1930 elections did not discount either Hitler or the attacks against him. They had lived through defeat, inflation, prosperity. Now universal depression had the whole world on the skids. These young Germans had not fought in the war. They had only the dimmest recollections of the war years; of the prewar years they knew nothing. These things, however, they did know because they had heard them repeated again and again and because they seemed to explain the plight of the German people: Germany had not lost the war. Profiteers, Communists, Socialists, and Jews had stabbed the Army in the back. The Allies not only violated the promises they made in the Fourteen Points. They continued the blockade during the winter of 1918-19 and finally they imposed the *Versailles Diktat*, with its insupportable war-guilt clause. Most of the leading statesmen in most of the victorious Powers seemed, to many Germans, to be treating Germany as a pariah nation. All right; if that was going to be the attitude, the Germans would live up to this reputation and in Hitler they found the man who embodied all the vices of which their former enemies accused them.

Konrad Heiden gave a vivid picture of the new German generation and its leaders: "The type which came to the fore in 1930 was rapidly departing from the old class concepts. He was led by the declassed of *all* classes, the armed Bohemians. The worn-out occupational and class concepts had concealed the decisive phenomenon, a new human type, which now revealed himself in a brown or a black shirt, with pistol, club, and torture chamber: the armed intellectual. This total disregard of humanity is born not from bloodthirstiness, but from cold calculation— for the vilest horrors of this age have been perpetrated out of cold intellectual calculation and not out of bestial cruelty."

These words described Communists as well as Fascists; they fitted postwar Russia as well as postwar Italy. But they applied above all to the German Nazis, who combined the worst features of Communism and Fascism, plus a few refinements of their own. Like Italy's Fascists, the Nazis began as a veterans' organization. They stressed the leadership principle and made terror their chief political weapon. The national welfare took precedence over class interest; emotion took precedence over reason. "Reason can treacherously deceive a man," said Hitler, "emotion is sure and never leaves him." To the Communists Hitler owed more than he did to the Fascists. First, he persuaded the frightened rich that contributions to his movement offered the best possible protection against Communism. Then he used the proceeds to fight fire with fire. From the Communists the Nazis learned how to organize subversive cells. Like the Communists, the Nazis used democratic liberty to destroy democratic liberty. Again and again, Nazis and Communists made common cause against Social Democrats, Catholic Centrists, and other moderates. In August, 1931, Aristide Briand asked Bella Fromm, society editor of Berlin's *Vossische Zeitung*, "Did you ever notice the similarity between the National Socialists and the Communists? Just listen to their speeches. The arguments are so alike that you have to wait until the end to see whether the raised hand is open or clenched."

Hitler made one contribution to the politics and morals of his time— a contribution that distinguished him from the Communists. He blamed the Jews for all of Germany's troubles and for most of the world's troubles as well. With a cynicism surpassing Lenin's he observed, "Especially in a people like the German people, it is absolutely necessary for psychological reasons to point to only one enemy, to march against one enemy. By one enemy, if necessary, many can be meant." The Jew whom Hitler attacked wore more than one disguise: "While Moses Kohn sits in the directors' meeting, advocating a policy of firmness—that is, hostility in the face of workers' demands—his brother, Isaac Kohn, stands in the factory yard, stirring up the masses: 'Take a good look at them, all they want is to oppress you. Cast off your chains, etc.' And upstairs his brother is helping to forge these very chains. On the one side, the stock-exchange organ tries incessantly to arouse the fever of speculation; these people speculate on the broadest possible scale with grain and all

Nazi Election Posters

the foodstuffs of the people beyond comparison; on the other hand we find the workers' organ busy getting the masses' hair up." It was against "Moses Kohn" that Hitler inflamed the German workers and peasants; it was against "Isaac Kohn" that he inflamed the middle classes. And to German patriots of all classes he pictured the Jew as the alien enemy within the gates. Having lost more than two million men in the war and most of their savings in the inflation, the Germans felt they had a score to settle with a hostile, unjust world. Many of them therefore seized upon the Jew as the safest and most satisfying scapegoat. A certain Berliner was said to have remarked to one of his friends, "The Jews and the bicyclists are to blame for the depression." "Why the bicyclists?" the friend inquired. "Why the Jews?" the first speaker replied.

· III ·

WHY the Jews? The same irrational forces that made Hitler the natural leader of the Nazi movement made the Jews the Nazis' natural victims. And rational attacks on anti-Semitism proved as futile as moral attacks on Hitler. In both cases the Nazis released passions that went, in Nietzsche's phrase, "beyond good and evil." In both cases they harnessed those subconscious impulses to which Freud traced back so much human behavior. The weaknesses that Hitler's enemies ridiculed and the vices they assailed commended him to his followers, who recognized his

bitterness, ignorance, hysteria, and jealousy as their own. Of their un-
controlled emotions he made a virtue. By identifying the individual
with the party and the party with the state and the state with the people,
he removed moral and social stigmas from immoral and egocentric behavior. His anti-Semitic propaganda not only stirred deep popular emotions. Hatred of the Jews became the cardinal Nazi virtue.

Attacks on Hitler's anti-Semitism therefore proved unavailing. Some
of his halfhearted apologists minimized this aspect of his program; some
of the more radical Nazis urged him to forget the Jews and assail the
capitalists instead. Hitler knew better. Somewhere from the depths of his
neurotic, intuitive personality an inner voice told him to concentrate his
fire on the Jews—and the kind of response he met vindicated that inner
voice. What if the anti-Semitic *Protocols of the Elders of Zion* which the
Nazis publicized had no basis in fact? Where there was so much smoke
there must be some fire. What if the science of anthropology proved
that no such thing as a Jewish "race" existed? Exactly because the word
"race" carried powerful emotional associations, the attempts to redefine
it in scientific terms seemed petty, technical, and suspect. True, the Jews
had a religion and a language of their own. But more and more of them
were abandoning Judaism; fewer and fewer of them spoke Hebrew or
Yiddish. In all the more advanced countries, including Germany, Jewish
citizens had for generations considered themselves "assimilated." Only
in eastern Europe and the Middle East did they remain a race and a
people apart. Only the Zionist colony in Palestine considered itself a
nation. If neither race nor language nor religion nor nationality made
a person a Jew, what did?

"A Jew is anyone who for any reason calls himself such or is called
such in any community whose practices take note of the distinction."
This definition, by Sidney Hook, professor of philosophy at New York
University, makes as much sense as any and more sense than most.
Another professor of philosophy, Jean-Paul Sartre of Paris, got closer to
the roots of anti-Semitism when he observed: "Have we ever stopped to
consider the intolerable situation of men condemned to live in a society
which adores the God they have killed? Originally, the Jew was a murderer or the son of a murderer—which, in the eyes of a community with
a pre-logical concept of responsibility, amounts to the same thing—it was
as such that he was taboo." Goebbels exploited this taboo with characteristic cynicism when he declared, "Christ cannot possibly have been a
Jew. I don't have to prove that scientifically. It is a fact." The child is
father of the man, and religious teachings instilled in our early years
influence us all our lives even if our childhood faith evaporates. As a
Roman Catholic, born and bred, Hitler had of course heard the story

of the crucifixion as far back as he could remember. So had millions of other Germans and Austrians, Russians, French, and English, Protestants, Roman Catholics, members of the Greek Orthodox Church, and members of no church at all. Yet how many devout Christians, or how many Christians who have lost their faith, pause to reflect that the story of the crucifixion may have predisposed them against the Jews?

Just as many Christians, whether active or passive, forget that some aspects of their religious education may have encouraged a latent anti-Semitism, so many Jews also forget the non-Jewish response to the role of "chosen people" associated with their religion. Between the time of Moses and the time of Jesus, the children of Israel preserved their Ten Commandments and their belief in one God against all enemies—defying the whole world and causing some of their own prophets to denounce them as a "stiff-necked people." Indeed, Hitler himself hardly surpassed some of the diatribes the Jews delivered against themselves in the Old Testament narrative. But in regarding themselves as the "chosen people," devout Jews of the pre-Christian era believed that Jehovah had chosen them not so much for their own salvation as for the task of converting the whole world to worship the one true God.

It was among the Jews that Christianity made its first converts and it was from Judaism that Christianity derived its proselyting zeal. But the destruction of Jerusalem by the Romans during the first century of the Christian era revolutionized Jewish history and religion. Some Jews followed the example of Paul and became Christians; the rest, menaced with dispersion if not destruction at the hands of the Romans, drew closer together in sheer self-protection. They could no longer afford the luxury of proselyting others; they faced the stark and simple question of survival. Under the Roman Empire and on through the Dark and Middle Ages, the Jews therefore kept their religion—and with it their culture—to themselves. And anti-Semitism always ran strongest, and still runs strongest right down to the present day, in those parts of the world where the Jewish religion and Jewish culture stand at a higher level than the surrounding religion and culture.

Even in the skeptical twentieth century, religious practices and historic traditions live on outside our churches in our homes and schools. Although Christians and Jews have become more tolerant—perhaps indifferent would be a better word—they continue certain religious formalities and practices, especially in bringing up their children. And our absorption in the history of our own times has not entirely wiped out all memory of earlier times. If, therefore, the story of the crucifixion has predisposed Christians toward anti-Semitism, the older story of the Jews as the Lord's chosen people has predisposed Jews to regard themselves as a race apart—thus playing straight into anti-Semitic hands. This is not to say that Christianity breeds anti-Semites or that Judaism breeds the kind of Jew that anti-Semites vilify. The point is that early influences and ancient traditions predispose certain reactions in communities and individuals.

Perhaps Hitler knew all the time how deep an emotion he stirred and how wide an appeal he made when he singled out the Jews as the unique villains of the world. Certainly nobody else did. The Christians did not recognize fully or in time how successfully Hitler was exploiting certain prejudices of which they had little conscious knowledge. The Jews forgot, among other things, how many anti-Semitic texts the Old Testament contained. But when Hitler chose to make Munich the headquarters of his anti-Semitic movement, he showed that he knew his Bavarians as well as his Germans. In most of Germany, Protestants outnumbered Catholics by more than two to one. Only in Bavaria did the Catholics predominate, and because they felt victimized by Protestants in other parts of the Reich, they cultivated a militant faith which rendered them especially susceptible to anti-Semitism. Moreover, the defeat of 1918 and the subsequent sufferings made most Germans need to feel superior to somebody—and the Jews provided the obvious scapegoat.

Nevertheless, the full secret of Hitler's success did not lie in Bavaria, or in Germany either. It lay in the disintegration of postwar Europe. The victorious Allies had fought to make the world safe for democracy— but where had democracy triumphed? Not in the Russia of Lenin and Stalin, not in Mussolini's Italy, Pilsudski's Poland, Horthy's Hungary, or most of the states that replaced the old Austro-Hungarian Empire. In Germany democracy connoted defeat, inflation, depression, and Allied hypocrisy. Everywhere, especially in the less favored lands, the world was selling democracy short. But during the spring of 1931 events in Spain suddenly aroused the hope that the tide had begun to turn and that Hitler had perhaps arrived too late upon the scene.

· IV ·

SOMETHING unprecedented happened in the life of postwar Europe when Primo de Rivera quit Spain. For the first time, dictatorship had given way to constitutional government, instead of the other way around. Half a dozen questions at once arose. Did Primo's retirement mark the beginning of a general liquidation of all the postwar dictators and—if so— what governments would replace them? Was democracy in for a revival or did the fall of one dictator merely set the stage for another to take his place? Was Spain an exceptional case? For the past several hundred years its power in the world had steadily declined. The Protestant Reformation had left Spain virtually untouched and the Industrial Revolution had passed most of the country by. Spain had kept out of the World War. Why, then, try to read Europe's future in the events of so backward, so exceptional, a country?

To these questions certain answers suggested themselves. Although Spain had remained isolated and backward for centuries, the war and postwar years had brought deep and rapid changes. The war stimulated the growth of industry, and what the war had begun the dictatorship continued. During his six years in office Primo sponsored

"Listen, Mr. Morgan, come to Spain. You can make morganatic marriages there." (Newspapers had just announced that a Morgan loan had been offered to Spain.) Bagaría in Luz, Madrid

the construction of four thousand new schools and of the beautiful University City at Madrid. He speeded up the trains, set big irrigation schemes in motion, put through an extensive program of railway and highway construction. But Primo had no mass following in the middle class or anywhere else. Whereas in Italy Mussolini used the monarchy to make dictatorship appear respectable and legal, King Alfonso of Spain had created the dictatorship to preserve the monarchy. And Alfonso outlasted Primo. When the dictatorship collapsed, the monarchy remained.

But where would Alfonso lead Spain and what might that signify to Europe? The same forces that destroyed Primo soon undermined Alfonso, and many of these forces originated abroad. The effects of the world depression made themselves quickly felt in Spain as the value of the peseta dropped 20 per cent during the closing months of 1929. *"Don Dinero es el mejor informada,"* says an old Spanish proverb—"Mr. Money is the surest guide." Businessmen, landowners, Army and Navy officials, leading Church dignitaries all turned against a regime that had never commended itself to the workers, peasants, or intellectuals. The departure of Primo failed to check the fall of the peseta, the rise of unemployment, or the spread of general strikes from city to city, and Alfonso could not escape a large share of the blame. In October, 1930, when the universities reopened, José Ortega y Gasset, professor of philosophy at Madrid, declared, "The plain people who are not revolutionaries should now say to one another: 'Spaniards, you have no government. Reconstruct your state.' *Delenda est monarchia.*"

While Ortega lent his moral and intellectual authority to the anti-monarchist cause, the younger Army officers provided the most active leadership. They had planned a nation-wide mutiny for December 15, 1930, but two of their members—Captain Firmin Galán and Captain Angel Garcia Hernández—jumped the gun on December 12 when they attempted a premature uprising in the little town of Jaca in the Pyrenees. Salvador de Madariaga, in his history of Spain, branded both Galán and Hernández as Communists and declared they deliberately sabotaged a revolt that the Communists could not easily have controlled. In any event, the government crushed the mutiny at Jaca, both Galán and Hernández were shot, and the wider uprising set for December 15 never took place. But Galán and Hernández became national heroes and support for King Alfonso melted away.

In February, 1931, the King belatedly restored the Constitution and ordered Parliamentary elections to be held in March. But the government headed by General Damaso Berenguer had become so unpopular that it had to resign, the King canceled the elections, and a new government of strong men headed by Admiral Aznar took office and ordered municipal elections in April. The Republicans won most of them and when their leaders called upon Alfonso to abdicate he declared, "I do not wish a single drop of blood to be shed for me." But instead of abdicating, he merely vacated the throne and left the country, after issuing a manifesto written with one eye on history and the other on the main chance: "The elections which took place on Sunday show me clearly that I no longer have the love of my people. My conscience tells me that this indifference will not be final, for I have always done my utmost to serve Spain, and even on the most critical occasions I have made the public interest my sole endeavor. A king can make mistakes, and no doubt I have sometimes erred, but I well know that our country has always shown herself generous to those whose faults are devoid of malice. I am King of all Spaniards and I am also myself a Spaniard.

"I could find ample means to maintain my royal prerogative by making effective use of force against those who contest it. But I desire most resolutely to abstain from any course which might plunge my compatriots into fratricidal civil war. I renounce none of my rights, for they are not so much my own as a trust committed to me by History, for which one day I shall have to render her a strict account. I await the tidings of the authentic and adequate expression of the nation's collective conscience, and, while the nation is speaking, I deliberately suspend the exercise of royal power and leave Spain, thus showing that I recognize her as the sole mistress of her destinies. By doing this I believe I am fulfilling the duty dictated to me by love of my country. I pray to God that other Spaniards may feel it as deeply and may fulfill it as I do."

Nothing in Alfonso's kingship so became him as the leaving of it. He had finally lived up to his reputation as a truly modern, twentieth-century monarch. It was now up to his successors to play their parts as twentieth-century revolutionaries. Francisco Largo Caballero, the leader of the Socialist Party, possessed a personality that made his followers call him the "Spanish Lenin," but the revolution in Spain did not follow the Russian pattern. The Spain of 1931 had a more important middle class, a more vigorous trade union movement, and a less desperate peasantry than the Russia of 1917. In Russia, three years of disastrous war led to a general breakdown. Spain, on the other hand, had prospered more than most European countries until its inefficient dictatorship and obsolete monarchy crumbled under the impact of the depression. The Republic—thanks as much to King Alfonso as to his enemies—came to power without bloodshed. The first provisional government included Socialists, Republicans, Liberals, and several former monarchists. Don Niceto Alcalá Zamora, the Prime Minister and provisional President, came from Cordova and spoke with a strong Andalusian accent. Zamora had served as War Minister under the monarchy and did not share the anti-Clerical fervor of some of his new colleagues. Still in his early fifties, he had a fine head, a weak mouth, and such big feet that he earned the nickname *Botas,* or "Old Boots." He always looked and usually acted like the bourgeois lawyer-politician that he was.

"On the fifth day of Republican rule," Zamora boasted soon after Alfonso had left the country, "a civic procession of over one hundred thousand people made its way through Madrid without the least disorder." According to Professor Alfred Mendizabal of the University of Oviedo, "The Spanish Republic was established without a shot being fired, without a drop of blood being spilt." For four more weeks the calm continued. The Revolutionary Committee—now the Provisional Government of the Second Spanish Republic—issued a triumphant manifesto: "There are civic events in the modern history of Europe comparable with that which took place in Spain on the twelfth of April, but there is none that can surpass it. . . . We invoke those supreme civic virtues which in every cultured nation are respected by the foremost institutions of the state, the official organs of the government, and the armed forces." Lawyers and professors held most of the positions in the new regime, but they talked more like Socialists than like bourgeois intellectuals: "It is quite safe to say," read one of their declarations, "that Spain will not be a bourgeois republic. All signs point, rather, to a nation of workers." But they warned against Communism: "Let students and intellec-

tuals avoid false imitations of what a semi-Asiatic people had to do in
a terrible hour of their history. Let them insist on fulfilling the strict
destiny of Spain and not a false or borrowed one."

The Spanish Republic received a good press abroad. All the Great
Powers, including the United States, recognized the Zamora regime by
April 22, perhaps because it agreed to honor the debts of the monarchy.
Early in May, however, the first signs of violence began to appear. Angel
Pestana, spokesman for the Anarchists, whose greatest strength lay in
Barcelona, had already warned: "Spain has had her political revolution.
Now she must undergo her social revolution. Russia has initiated a cycle
of social revolutions, but in my opinion she has failed because her social
forms are derived excessively from political ones. The syndicates are the
forces that should make a social revolution, and they have sufficient
doctrine and organization to do so." Pestana spoke for the only mass
party capable of revolutionary violence. Cardinal Segura, Primate of
all Spain, spoke with greater authority for the more militant and reactionary supporters of the Church and the Monarchy: "If we remain
'quiet and idle'; if we allow ourselves to give way to 'apathy and timidity'; if we leave the road open to those who are attempting to destroy
religion or expect the benevolence of our enemies to secure the triumph
of our ideals, we shall have no right to lament when bitter reality shows
us that we had victory in our hands, yet knew not how to fight like intrepid warriors, prepared to succumb gloriously." How long could such
militant Clericals and militant Anarchists live together at peace under
the tentative authority of a provisional government?

On Sunday, May 10, a street mob invaded the headquarters of a new
Monarchist club in Madrid. A rumor spread that two members of the
club had yelled, "Long live the Monarchy," and then killed a taxi driver
who had shouted for the Republic. Within a few minutes crowds were
yelling, "Down with the Monarchists! Down with the house! Down with
the balcony!" The Civil Guard failed to disperse the mob, which amused
itself by setting fire to the parked cars of Monarchist club members.
When policemen tried to carry club members to safety in motor vans,
the Monarchists refused their protection and the crowd shifted its attentions to the offices of the Monarchist newspaper, *A.B.C.* Even the Civil
Guard could not check the demonstration until some of its members
entered the newspaper building and discharged their guns out the windows into the air. The demonstrators finally scattered and the government suppressed not only *A.B.C.* but the other leading Monarchist daily,
El Debate.

The next day the demonstrators turned to organized armed attack,
chiefly against churches, monasteries, and convents. The government
took few police measures and the disorder spread from Madrid to other

cities. On May 11 and 12 Zamora's Spain seemed to be going the way of Kerensky's Russia, with the Anarchists stirring up most of the trouble. When the Minister of the Interior prepared to suppress the riots, Manuel Azaña as War Minister ordered him to do nothing: "All the convents in Spain are not worth the life of a single Republican which might be lost during the suppression." On May 13, however, the riots ended as suddenly as they had begun, perhaps because Cardinal Segura had crossed the frontier and set out for Rome. Later in the summer, he quietly returned to Spain, but presently left again as the Vatican put an older, more moderate Cardinal in his place as Primate.

The summer also witnessed elections for a new Parliament. In line with the traditions of liberal democracy, women and priests cast their first votes in Spain, although some liberals feared that the Republic was cutting its own throat by giving its enemies the franchise. The fears proved groundless. Of the 470 deputies elected to the Cortes only one called himself a Monarchist, a "kingless Monarchist in the service of the Republic." Even Zamora's right-wing Republican Party won only 28 of the 100 seats it sought. The left-wing Republican Alliance won 145 seats; the Socialists 114. The occupations of the new deputies showed what classes had turned the revolution and the Republic to good account. Lawyers predominated—123 of them. Professors and teachers, 65 strong, made up the next largest group. After them came 41 physicians, 24 workingmen, 18 businessmen, 16 engineers, 15 authors, 8 soldiers, 8 ecclesiastics, 6 druggists, 3 architects, and 2 veterinary surgeons. In Spain, predominantly a peasant country, only one farm laborer had a seat in the Cortes.

· V ·

THE MEMBERS of the new Cortes spent five months, from July to December, debating a new Constitution. This meant that the provisional coalition government headed by Zamora continued to administer the country. It had its hands full. In May the peseta had dropped to less than half its par value. By July it rose to what it had been when the Monarchy collapsed. It then held steady the rest of the year in spite of constant strikes and riots—some political, some religious. At first the Anarchists formed the largest of the militant, direct-action groups, but they steadily lost ground to the Communists, who had tighter discipline and clearer purpose. Communist leaflets attacked the "Republican illusions" of the masses and called for the immediate organization of workers' soviets, the arming of the proletariat, and the redistribution of land: "The Communist Party has to fight not only against the bourgeoisie and social fascism but against the Trotskyites and the Anarchists. The big landed estates have not been touched, nor have the estates of the Church been confiscated; the living conditions of the working class have not been improved."

The Zamora government, with the support of its Socialist members, ordered the Civil Guard to close Anarchist and Communist headquarters in the larger cities. Thousands of extremist leaders were arrested and jailed. In August the Moscow newspaper *Pravda* observed, "It is true there exists no practical difference between the present Republican-Social-Fascist regime and a military dictatorship. The Civil Guard, the select gendarmerie of ex-King Alfonso, is proceeding ruthlessly against the workers." True enough: the Republic, like the dictatorship and the Monarchy before it, used force to suppress violent enemies, but the resemblance ended there. The Cortes took time out from its Constitutional debates to pass laws establishing the eight-hour day in some industries and the seven-hour day in others. It limited the size of the great landed estates and drew up plans for the peasants to put more land into cultivation. These reforms took time to accomplish; they did not entail outright confiscation. But a beginning had been made.

By October, a majority in the provisional government decided that Zamora had not made this beginning fast enough, especially in whittling down the privileged position of the Roman Catholic Church. Under the Monarchy, the Church had largely controlled education and received vast subsidies, direct and indirect, from the state. Moreover, the power of the Jesuit Order had always run strong in the native land of its founder, St. Ignatius Loyola. The chief opposition to the Catholics and the Jesuits came from the Grand Orient Lodge of Freemasons, which had worked for more than a century against the Jesuits to gain political power in many Latin countries on both sides of the Atlantic. To be known in Italy, France, Spain, or Latin America as a Freemason was to be identified with the anti-Clerical political parties of the left.

The Grand Orient Lodge of Spain had issued a bulletin immediately after Alfonso's departure: "Salute to the Republic. The honor of saluting a new regime, born of the will of the people, has been left by a Supreme Providence for this number of the bulletin. As Spaniards and Freemasons contemplating as an accomplished fact the structure of a new state, the fruit of those immortal principles that shine from the Orient, we cannot but feel keen satisfaction. To the Freemasons who form the Provisional Government and also to the high officials, who are mostly brothers, we promise our support." The Spanish Republic lost little time carrying out one Masonic principle. On May 6 the government invited the exiled Sephardim, or Spanish Jews, to return to Spain for the first time since 1492, thus fulfilling the hope expressed in the 1927 report of the Grand Orient Lodge of Spain, which read: "We are working to form public opinion to obtain the reform of Article II of the Constitution so as to obtain complete religious freedom and to obtain later complete separation of church and state. When we have religious freedom we will set to work to bring to the country many of the descendants of those who in days long past were victims of religious intolerance."

The adoption of the new Constitution permitted the Freemasons to settle accounts with the Vatican and the Jesuits once and for all. And when Zamora refused to go as far or as fast as the anti-Clericals wanted to go, the provisional government voted him out of office and put Manuel Azaña, the War Minister, in his place. Azaña had received an excellent education from the Augustinian monks in the Escorial, only to turn against them. He had translated George Borrow's *Bible in Spain* and had written several novels and plays of his own. As president of the Ateneo of Madrid, the leading literary club in Spain and the chief stronghold of liberal opinion, Azaña possessed great intellectual prestige. But one of his fellow members, Miguel de Unamuno, warned ironically, "Beware of Azaña. He is an author without readers and would be capable of starting a revolution in order to be read."

As head of the provisional government Azaña lived up to Unamuno's words. He also uttered a great many of his own: "The continual influence of the religious orders on the consciences of the young is precisely the secret of the situation through which Spain is now passing and which as Republicans—and not only as Republicans but as Spaniards—we are in duty bound at all costs to prevent. Do not tell me that this is contrary to freedom: it is a question of public health." And he went on to argue that "in the sphere of the political and moral sciences, the Catholic religious orders are compelled, by virtue of their dogma, to teach everything that is contrary to the principles which are the foundation of the modern state." The debate ended with the Cortes voting that "no state religion exists," and ordering complete separation of church and state, regulation of all religious orders, expulsion of the Jesuits, and confiscation of their property.

José Ortega y Gasset, who also belonged to the Ateneo, said that the Catholics had been routed because "there is not and never has been any opposition in Spain. This is the deepest mystery of Spanish history. We are a nation that is loyal to its government, and this explains a great deal of our past. Take our Catholicism, for instance. Spain was anti-Protestant because Protestantism was the opposition and Rome was the government, not because the nation was any more Catholic or anti-Catholic than any other. As the world ceased to be Catholic, so Spain today is no longer Catholic. Contrary to what most foreigners believe, there is probably no European country that has fewer Catholics than Spain."

If the outside world overestimated the number of Catholics in Spain, Ortega underestimated the fervor of the faithful. The new Constitution that the Cortes finally adopted early in December looked like a triumph of Azaña's hopes over Zamora's fears. "Spain is a democratic republic of workers of every category," it began. Unhappy experience with kings and dictators caused the powers of the President to be restricted to the purely ceremonial. Power resided in a single-chamber Cortes elected by all Spaniards over twenty-three years of age, women as well as men. But the lawyers saw to it that a Tribunal of Constitutional Guarantees could review legislation and arbitrate disputes between various regions. The Constitution included wide social provisions. It made the entire wealth of Spain "subordinate to the national economy," but forbade confiscation. "Labor in its diverse forms is a social duty and will enjoy the protection of the state." Yet in spite of these fine words that the radicals had persuaded the Cortes to adopt, misgivings persisted. A majority had voted in favor of every clause, but the number of abstentions and absentees often exceeded the number of affirmative ballots. It was one thing to pass a new Constitution and quite another matter to enforce it, especially in a country that ran so often to extremes as Spain. "The curse of Spain is the pendulum," wrote a British observer, E. Allison Peers, in *The Spanish Dilemma.* "Not the steady tick-tock of alternating Liberalism and Conservatism, but the frenzied rocking of reaction and counterreaction, suggestive of the periodic intervention of some outside agency."

Azaña had dominated the proceedings since October; Zamora had dropped more and more into the background. The Spanish Republic required the support of all its original backers, from A to Z, and if Azaña spoke for the anti-Clericals, Zamora represented that considerable body of Catholic opinion without which the Republic could not survive. The Cortes therefore elected Zamora to the symbolic post of President, at an annual salary of one million pesetas, thus removing him from the arena of political and religious warfare and depriving the Catholics of an effective potential leader. At the inauguration ceremonies the new President wore around his neck the gold and enamel collar of the Order of Isabella the Catholic. He drove in a gilded coach, once used by Alfonso, to a reception at which the Papal Nuncio, as dean of the diplomatic corps, extended official greetings. Military planes dropped four hundred thousand copies of the new Constitution on the assembled throng. Meanwhile, the Anarchists refused to recognize the holiday the government had proclaimed as rank-and-file laborers presented themselves at their jobs, demanding work or wages. And in the cities of Gijon and Saragossa, several workers lost their lives in clashes with civil guards.

In Spain democracy fought a winning battle against dictatorship. In Germany it was the other way around. But in both countries internal tensions increased. In Germany, the Nazis stressed anti-Semitism and the

Communists stressed class war. In Spain, the Communists and the Anarchists assailed the class enemy, but most of the Republican leaders assailed the church. Everywhere in Europe the depression revived old antagonisms and uncovered new ones. More and more Germans reverted to their traditional nationalism. The British turned against the French. Sir Charles Petrie, writing in the Conservative *Saturday Review,* expressed the antagonism many Tories felt toward the Republican regimes of both Spain and France:

"Alfonso in Exile." Bagaría in
Luz, Madrid

"There can be no question but that the chief bulwark of the Spanish Republic is France, for the recovery of Spain under Primo de Rivera gave her northern neighbor a very nasty shock indeed, and so long as the Republican regime does not actually become Bolshevist, it can rely on the support of the Quai d'Orsay. The repeated appeals of France to the sanctity of treaties and Mr. Briand's fantastic schemes for a European federation cannot disguise the fact that France is a revolutionary power and that Paris is the headquarters for every conspirator in Europe." By the time the Cortes completed its work on Spain's Constitution, continuing depression had brought still greater changes to far wider areas.

· VI ·

WHILE Spain spent most of the year 1931 trying to pull itself together, most of the rest of Europe spent most of the same year trying to pull itself apart. It was from Germany that most of the trouble radiated. Nazi gains in the September, 1930, elections threw the Socialists into the arms of Brüning, whom they regarded as the Weimar Republic's last, best hope. Brüning, however, had little hope for the Republic and regarded a Hohenzollern restoration, headed by one of the sons of the ex-Crown Prince, as the only alternative to Hitler. Spain and Germany thus presented this curious contrast. In Spain, monarchy and dictatorship went hand in hand; in Germany, monarchy offered the last frail alternative to dictatorship. For the moment, however, dread of another inflation forced Brüning to order so many cuts in wages and the dole that he earned the bitter nickname of "Hunger Chancellor." Nazis and Communists fought steadily to control the streets. Killings averaged one every other day;

casualties totaled fifteen thousand for the year 1931. "Never in my life have I been as well disposed and inwardly contented as in these days," wrote Hitler at the time. "For in these days hard reality has opened the eyes of millions of Germans to the unprecedented lies, swindles, and betrayals of the Marxist deceivers of the people. In these days great masses have seen, perhaps for the first time, who was right: the Young Plan swindlers or the men of the Young Plan popular protest. In these days, therefore, I have rightly felt happy and content, while conversely fear and consternation have crawled up the necks of the party and newspaper swindlers of the Young Front." Concerning the near future he predicted: "If this process of disintegration lasts much longer, the nation will fall apart. Only egotism will remain."

Unable to raise Germany by its bootstraps, Brüning took a bold chance abroad. In March he and Foreign Minister Curtius announced that Germany and Austria had agreed to establish a customs union: "The aim which we have all set before us of a union of all the European states will be more easily realized if we conclude regional agreements and if we create spheres of influence which it will be much easier later to incorporate into a general Pan-European organization. Germany and Austria have decided to start out on this road in a first practical act." Brüning and Curtius knew—none better—that the proposed customs union meant the first, long step toward complete Austro-German Anschluss, which the treaties of Versailles and Saint-Germain expressly forbade. In Britain and the United States Brüning became a hero; in Paris, Prague, and Warsaw the press and the politicians labeled him a Pan-German, not a Pan-European. Expressing as he often did the French point of view, Frank H. Simonds compared Brüning's declaration to the Austrian ultimatum to Serbia in July, 1914: "The whole French system of alliances, the entire prestige of France in Europe, the security which rested upon both, would collapse if this challenge went unanswered. The Treaty of Versailles in its territorial, financial, and military provisions would be fatally breached."

The French lost no time and missed no opportunity to protect themselves. Three days after the Germans and Austrians announced their projected customs union, France, Czechoslovakia, and Italy filed a joint protest with the World Court, which later outlawed the Austro-German action as illegal, by a majority of two votes. And long before September, when the World Court announced its decision, the French launched a financial flank attack of "golden bullets," suddenly withdrawing deposits from the largest and most reputable banking house in Vienna—the Credit Anstalt für Handel and Gewerbe, founded by the Rothschilds during the 1850's. In May, 1931, the Credit Anstalt closed its doors, but help from the Bank of England permitted it to reorganize and reopen a few weeks

© LOW, ALL COUNTRIES

"Phew! That's a nasty leak. Thank goodness it's not at our end of the boat."
Cartoon by David Low

later. By this time, however, the panic had spread to Germany. Hindenburg appealed to Hoover to save the country from financial bankruptcy and political chaos. Hoover took counsel with his British friends, ignored the French, and announced his moratorium.

The best intentions inspired the American President. At last he had linked war debts and reparations and had offered to sacrifice the former in his country's name for Europe's sake. But his political ineptitude and psychological misunderstanding more than offset his economic good sense and his moral good will. The French received more in German reparations than they had to pay in war debts to Britain and the United States. Hoover not only demanded that France, without advance notice, make this sacrifice. He attacked French vital interests by proposing to aid their hereditary enemy at their expense. "The more one reflects, the more one is stupefied," wrote the conservative historian Pierre Gaxotte, of the French Academy. "In the name of the Young Plan M. Briand made us abandon Mainz on the Rhine. In the name of the Young Plan we renounced the Dawes Plan. In the name of the Young Plan we made enormous advances to the Reich. For more than a year, we have walked, run, and danced, and now a Mr. Hoover appears and says to us: 'All over. Play has stopped.'"

Of course the French fought back with every weapon at their command. And they had the necessary weapons. The success of the moratorium depended upon its immediate acceptance. By stalling for more than two weeks and then demanding some further payments from Germany, the French killed the Hoover Moratorium at its birth. But in killing the Hoover Moratorium the French also killed all hope of collecting another penny in German reparations.

The London *Times* took a wider view. It admitted that Hoover had destroyed the whole postwar debt structure, but only in order to save the world-wide system of credit based on the gold standard: "There is at stake the very basis and maintenance of the gold standard in a world whose members are today so linked one with another, so unitedly caught in the vast web of cosmopolitan dealing, that the effect of a collapse of credit at any one of a number of important points can no longer be localized."

Events soon confirmed this analysis. On July 13, 1931, the Danat Bank of Berlin, one of the four largest in the country, closed its doors, following a six-week run. All the other big German banks refused to honor more than 10 per cent of their deposits and the Berlin stock exchange closed for two days. And it had all begun in Wall Street. After the 1929 crash, Frenchmen had withdrawn the money they had been lending to New York and deposited seventeen billion francs—or close to a billion dollars—in the banks of Great Britain, payable in pounds sterling. The British then used these deposits on which they paid 2 and 3 per cent interest to extend credit to German banks at 5 and 6 per cent. The German banks extended credit to Vienna at 8 and 9 per cent and Vienna extended credit to the banks of Budapest and Bucharest at 12 per cent. But the Hungarian and Rumanian farmers who had borrowed from the banks in their national capitals saw the price of wheat suddenly drop 50 per cent in 1930 and could not repay their loans. Nor could they buy the products of German industry which already had curtailed operations because Americans could no longer afford to buy German goods or lend Germany more dollars.

In July, 1931, the gold standard broke down in Germany. England's turn came next. That spring Montagu Collet Norman, governor of the Bank of England, wrote Governor Moret of the Bank of France: "Unless drastic measures are taken to save it, the capitalist system throughout the civilized world will be wrecked within a year. I should like this prediction to be filed for future reference." One of Mr. Norman's grandfathers had served as a director of the Bank of England for fifty years; the other had served for twenty. True to the traditions of his caste, young Montagu Norman served with distinction in the Boer War, and then earned the right to continue the family tradition in the service of the private bank to which the British government had issued a special charter giving it the sole right to issue currency and fix the interest rate. In 1929 the self-perpetuating Board of Directors of the Bank of England elected Norman governor. He had inspired the return to the gold standard in 1925; he had thrown Great Britain's financial resources behind the revival of Germany throughout the 1920's. His biographer, Dr. Paul Einzig, called him "the greatest statesman in Great Britain since the war."

With his black hat, pointed beard, and shy, furtive manner, Montagu Norman looked like an artist rather than a banker. He hated the spotlight and often crossed the Atlantic, under the alias of Professor Clarence Skinner, for a vacation on the Maine coast, favorite playground of those Morgan partners who did not shoot grouse in Scotland. Between 1923 and 1929 the Bank of England and the British Foreign Office, working in close, informal co-operation, established what came to be known as the "gold exchange standard" throughout most of Europe. Certain countries that lacked large gold reserves acquired, through Norman and his friends, foreign currencies or foreign loans redeemable in gold. The result was that most currencies—and thus all the goods these currencies bought—were tied directly to the value of gold. This gold exchange standard, supervised from London with some assistance from Norman's American friends, meant that London remained the financial capital of the world. Only the more brash American operators aspired to relieve weary British shoulders of the white man's financial burden. The House of Morgan had a saving knowledge of its own limitations and a healthy respect for British experience.

The leaders of France at this time had an exaggerated conception of their own strength and little respect for British methods or purposes. Almost immediately after the death of Stresemann, Briand also had gone into a decline. The short-lived government that he headed gave place to a more conservative regime, with André Tardieu as Prime Minister, Pierre Laval as Minister of Labor, and Briand still in the Foreign Office. But the influence of Briand steadily waned. The French National Assembly, consisting of the Senate and the Chamber of Deputies, failed, by a small margin, to elect him to the Presidency in 1931; a year later he was dead. Tardieu and Laval, on the other hand, showed themselves very much alive. Tardieu, a bachelor and Protestant in his middle fifties, had entered the diplomatic service at the age of twenty-one and at twenty-eight he had his first book, *Diplomatic Questions of the Year*, crowned by the French Academy. Before the war he received funds from Russia for the editorials he wrote in *Le Temps*, as a sideline. He also became involved in financial scandals, one in Africa, another in Turkey. His secretary served two years in jail for stealing documents from the French Foreign Office.

"I do not dispute M. Tardieu's ability to give me lessons in politics and morality," wrote Poincaré, and a fellow deputy once told the Chamber: "There are certain individuals whose dishonesty is universally rec-

"The Course of Foreign Exchange."
Guerin Meschino, *Milan*

ognized but who remain unpunished. You, M. Tardieu, are the last man in the world who has the right to accuse another man of being a thief." Tardieu may have been a knave, but he was no fool. He joined the group around Clemenceau during the war and went to Washington on an economic mission. During the twenties he wrote a book, *The Truth About the Treaty*, and became the intimate of several important industrialists. He dressed elegantly in the English fashion, wore thick eyeglasses, and sported a long cigarette-holder. It was not only because he had the look of a scavenger about him that Tardieu had long been nicknamed *"le requin,"* the shark. "I despise programs," he once declared, "and scruples are nothing but evil outgrowths of the mind."

With characteristic cynicism, Tardieu called his first Cabinet "The Ministry of Good Humor." Of all its members none appeared more miscast than his understudy, Pierre Laval, described by John Franklin Carter in *Our Lords and Masters* as "dopey in appearance, like an overworked headwaiter on his day off." Laval, a dozen years younger than Tardieu, came of peasant stock from the South of France and in 1919 almost broke away from the Socialist Party to join the Communists. Failing to win a seat in the Chamber of Deputies, he temporarily dropped politics for journalism and acquired a number of provincial papers. In 1924, no longer a Socialist, Laval won a seat in the Chamber and got his first Cabinet post as Minister of Public Works in Paul Painlevé's Cartel des Gauches government. By 1929 he had shifted so far to the right that he joined forces with Tardieu, who, however, had to resign as Premier in December, 1930, after becoming involved in a banking scandal. Early in 1931 the forty-six-year-old Laval became the youngest Premier in the history of the Third Republic and in addition took the post of Foreign Minister. He usually wore a white bow tie, in the fashion of the 1890's, and in summer topped it off with a stiff straw hat, associated with the same period and generally known as a boater. His dark skin, full lips, straight black hair, and scraggly mustache gave him a semi-African, semi-Asiatic appearance. To Americans he looked like a miniature Warner Oland, favorite villain of the silent films.

From Poincaré's government of National Union the governments of Tardieu and Laval inherited a large and growing gold reserve that they made into a formidable instrument of national policy. In 1926 Poincaré stabilized the franc at four cents after it had dropped to two. In 1928 recovery had gone so far that he made the franc—like the pound—convertible into gold on demand. But the stabilized pound was convertible into gold at the old prewar rate, whereas the franc had been devalued to only one fifth of its prewar value. This gave French exporters a great competitive advantage over the British, without inflicting too many hardships on the relatively self-sufficient French people. It was not until after illness forced Poincaré to retire in 1929 that his successors had a chance to turn his preparations to account. In the first place, they felt they had a score to settle with the British. As Tardieu saw it, the British had built up Germany—partly as a counterweight to France, partly as a counterweight to Russia—and what had it led to? Stresemann was dead and discredited; Hitler and Hugenberg were alive and kicking; must France therefore make concessions to Brüning and Hindenburg for fear of getting something worse?

Tardieu felt strongly on the subject of Germany. Laval, who came to full power in 1931, felt no less strongly against Britain and the United States. It was under his leadership that French bankers used their gold reserve during the summer of 1931 to drive first Austria, then Germany, and finally Britain to the wall. Having ample supplies of gold themselves, the French called in the loans they had made to their overextended neighbors and, in the case of Great Britain, demanded gold payment for pound notes. British leaders resented this practice of using a financial lever to gain political concessions, just as the French leaders resented the way the British had built up Germany against both France and Russia while extending profitable loans, themselves, at the same time. By August, 1931, the French had smashed the Austro-German customs union, brought the Succession States of eastern Europe into their financial orbit, isolated Italy, wrecked the Hoover Moratorium, weakened Britain, and made Paris the financial capital of the world.

· VII ·

"FRANCE," wrote J. L. Garvin, editor of the London *Observer,* that August, "expects to receive Germany's surrender in three months. The Paris press expects and believes that Britain and America can do nothing without France. The immense withdrawals of French money from the City of London were undoubtedly connected with the idea of making Britain feel that unless she conforms to French policy, it will be the worse for her." The French had deposits in London totaling 150 million pounds, and if they had demanded immediate payment in gold, they could have exhausted the entire gold reserve of the Bank of England. In addition, other foreigners had claims totaling another 350 million pounds, and short-term foreign credits in New York totaled another two and a half billion dollars. So London could not expect much help from that quarter.

The French did not want or intend to wreck either the pound or the dollar. At most, they hoped to use their financial power to modify Anglo-American policy toward Germany and to strengthen the French position throughout Europe. On August 1 the Bank of France therefore joined the Federal Reserve Bank of New York in extending credits of twenty-five million dollars to the Bank of England to withstand the run on its resources that immediately followed the collapse of the mark. Major Walter Elliott, a rising young Conservative Member of Parliament, described the atmosphere in London at the time: "Last Wednesday men came back from the City to the House of Commons like soldiers coming out of the line. There is no mistaking that atmosphere. Men say little, they sit quiet, they are glad to be at peace. They are not able to accept things around them as real. Reality is out there where they left it, where they will have to go to meet it again."

Another kind of reality, to which Major Elliott paid less heed, also existed in England at that time. Textile workers in Lancashire earned an average of twenty-five shillings—barely six dollars—a week. One city spent more on unemployment relief during the 1920's than it would have cost to build new, modern mills. "Before the decline," wrote a correspondent of the *New Leader,* organ of the Independent Labor Party, "children left school and went to the mill as a matter of course. Now that avenue is largely closed, and in any case parents are loath to send children into a trade that is badly paid and irregular. Many children wander about the streets for years—though now and then a job is secured for a few weeks. These children, with such a training, will never settle down to work during the whole course of their lives."

The plight of such people and the power of their sympathizers had brought the Labor Party to office in 1929. But Labor could not protect Britain from the impact of the world depression, and Philip Snowden, Chancellor of the Exchequer in the Labor government, fought the French on the financial front more vigorously than any Tory. Snowden, a middle-class intellectual who had suffered a crippling bicycle accident during his boyhood, had shared Ramsay MacDonald's wartime pacifism. He advocated treaty revision and in February, 1923, told the House of Commons that he did not know what a victorious Germany might have done except that such a Germany could not have imposed a more brutal, dishonest, hate-filled settlement than the Treaty of Versailles. Snowden believed in "democratic" socialism with the same stubborn dogmatism that Marx believed in "scientific" socialism. Snowden also shared Bernard Shaw's curious passion for the gold standard. Never in modern times had the French to deal with so hostile and recalcitrant a British statesman. And no London banker ever fought for sound finance and a balanced budget with such determination as this doctrinaire Socialist.

It did not take long for the financial crisis of August, 1931, to become political as well. The credits from New York and Paris did not stop the run on the Bank of England. Indeed, the day before the credits were granted, the Labor government had issued a report predicting a deficit of 120 million pounds in the current budget unless social services were cut deeply and at once. A special committee, headed by Sir George May of the British Prudential Insurance Company, had spent months studying Britain's economic problems and finally recommended an economy program as the only solution. For several weeks the Labor Party leaders argued and pondered until August 23, when the MacDonald Cabinet held its last meeting. The Bank of England needed more credits from abroad to keep the pound on the gold standard, and the American and French bankers would extend those credits only if benefits to the unemployed were cut 10 per cent. MacDonald's pacifist convictions had cost him almost ten years of political exile. Twice since then he had held the office of Prime Minister and he had no craving to end his life in futile opposition. He wanted to accept the bankers' terms. So did Snowden— not for vainglorious reasons, but on largely financial, almost moral, grounds. Good-natured Arthur Henderson, the Methodist lay reader who had served in Lloyd George's war Cabinet and headed the Foreign Office since 1929, favored rejecting the bankers' terms and most of the other leaders as well as the rank and file supported him.

MacDonald then resorted to a political trick that his Cabinet colleagues never forgave. He asked, and received, their resignations, which he assured them he would present to the King along with his own. But instead of quitting, he agreed to head a new national government consisting of four Laborites, four Conservatives, and two Liberals. Snowden remained Chancellor of the Exchequer, but the power behind the scenes was Stanley Baldwin, who became Lord Privy Seal and let MacDonald enjoy the public glory. The new government cut the salaries of all government servants between 10 and 20 per cent and raised income taxes as well as the taxes on beer, tobacco, and entertainments. A group of American bankers, headed by Morgan, at once found the new government worthy of two hundred million dollars' worth of credits, and other private British and French bankers supplied the same amount.

The break between MacDonald and the bulk of the Labor Party cleared the air and the issues. In spite of his humble beginnings, MacDonald never felt at home with trade unionists, who looked on him, in turn, as an aloof high-brow. From his earliest days as a poor, forlorn, young Scottish boy in London, MacDonald had gravitated toward social

UNDERWOOD

MacDonald's National Government. Front Row, left to right: Philip Snowden, Stanley Baldwin, Ramsay MacDonald, Sir Herbert Samuel, Lord Sankey. Second row: Sir Philip Cunliffe-Lester, J. H. Thomas, Lord Reading, Neville Chamberlain, Sir Samuel Hoare.

workers, writers, and teachers, who also cottoned to him. He came to maturity at a time when the Labor Party responded to the leadership of middle-class intellectuals and he was well equipped by nature, temperament, and training to become head of Britain's first Labor government. In a country where tradition counts as it does in Britain, MacDonald's good looks, his air of distinction, his mellifluous speaking voice and polished literary style produced a reassuring effect. He made the ideal transitional figure with his aristocratic appearance, his middle-class mentality, and his proletarian origins. But by the time the crisis of the gold standard came to a head, he had served his purpose. Labor needed tougher, plainer leadership than MacDonald could give, and MacDonald craved recognition, honors, and ease in his declining years. Life had brought him more than his share of tragedy, both personal and political. Not much time remained for him to make up for all that he had lost or passed by.

The rank-and file trade unionists shed no tears for Ramsay MacDonald. He got no sympathy or support from that quarter. Nor did the intellectuals in the labor movement mourn his loss. They had more urgent problems to attack. H. N. Brailsford, for instance, writing in the pro-Labor *New Statesman and Nation*, estimated that British banks had advanced half a billion dollars to Germany and added this cautionary word: "Don't imagine that 'the City' saved this money or that bankers painfully scraped it together through a lifetime of self-denial and thrift. If anyone did that it was the French peasant. Nor need anyone ascribe philanthropy to the City. What the City did in fact was to borrow from the French at three per cent in order to lend to the Germans at six per cent or eight per cent. Then came the crash in Vienna; the Bank lent money. Next the crash in Berlin; and again the Bank lent money. The French thereupon had a vision: they saw the various banks, Austrian, German, and English, tied together like Alpine climbers above the abyss. Two of them had tumbled over; might they not drag the third with them? Acting on this vision they started a run on the Bank of England; in plain words, they called in their deposits. To save its gold reserves and maintain the exchange value of the pound sterling, the Bank had to borrow. That, then, is the course of events that exposed us to this humiliation. The 'dole' has nothing to do with it. What is at stake is the prestige of the City and its profits as the international usurer."

Within three weeks after the national government took office, the disaster that it had come into being to prevent happened—and happened as a result of the measures taken to fend it off. The pay cuts ordered by the national government led to a threat of mutiny in the Royal Navy. On September 15, the Admiralty Office, fearing trouble, called off the annual autumn maneuvers. A selling panic swept holders of British securities all over the world, and within a few days the Bank of England exhausted its latest, half-billion-dollar infusion of new credits from abroad. The foreign bankers refused to pour any more credits into the bottomless pit, and on September 20 the Bank of England stopped redeeming pound notes in gold. The value of the pound sterling dropped 30 per cent, from $4.86 to $3.49, and the same experts who had called for saving the pound at any price now embraced the fate they had tried so hard to forfend.

It took another month for political appearances to catch up with economic realities. The national government, having come into existence to keep the pound on the gold standard, resigned and its leaders asked for a general election. MacDonald, Baldwin, and their colleagues then went to the people and sought a vote of confidence for having failed to achieve their recently declared purpose. They succeeded magnificently. Although the Labor Party received six million votes, it won only 59 seats in the House of Commons as compared with 553 for the national government. "The trick has worked," commented the Liberal *Manchester Guardian*. "The Conservatives have put on as many votes in the slums as in suburbia. The panic ran through all sections of society. The country will wake up shuddering from its hot fits of patriotism in which, searching for security, it has saddled itself with the worst House of Commons in thirty years."

It took Dr. Paul Einzig's *Behind the Scenes of International Finance* to discover the logic that Britain's leaders followed when the pound went off the gold standard: "There is an old-fashioned game called ombre in which the player who holds no trumps is in a stronger position than the player who holds them all. It sometimes happens that the man who holds all the trumps and triumphantly declares 'grandissimo' is defeated by an opponent who unassumingly declares 'nullissimo.' It was in just such a way that the cards of international finance were called in September of 1931."

Viewed from behind the scenes of international finance, the world wears one aspect. Viewed from beyond the scenes of international finance, it wears another. Dr. Einzig depicted the world as it looked at the end of the summer of 1931 from London, New York, Paris, and Berlin. He did not show how that same world looked from the less developed countries—from the South American republics, from India, Russia, and the Far East. Nor did he take account of how the more backward peoples looked upon the more favored lands. A sudden explosion in the Far East supplied the necessary corrective. On September 19—four days after the threatened mutiny on the British fleet—Japanese troops crossed the borders of China and began to occupy Manchuria. "The Second World War has begun, and Japanese imperialism has started it," announced the Soviet press. The judgment appeared extreme and premature. But it had become evident, long before 1931, that the depression had hit hardest of all those backward regions least able to cope with its assault.

SUMMING UP

WHAT the World War had begun the world depression continued. In 1914 a royal assassination in the Balkans set all the major nations of Europe to fighting among themselves. They did not stop until several of them had fought to exhaustion and all of them had bled themselves white. Only the intervention of the United States assured an Allied victory. Only the intervention of the United States saved Germany from chaos a few years later. Then came the crash of 1929 and once again Europe seemed headed for bankruptcy until the Hoover Moratorium of 1931. But the French refused salvation on Hoover's terms, and the collapse that Hoover had tried to prevent happened anyway.

Ten years after the Allies made peace at Versailles, Europe was again turning against itself—nation against nation and class against class. In 1930 the Hitler movement in Germany began to threaten the Weimar Republic. In 1931 the Republican movement in Spain overthrew the Monarchy. It was an ironic commentary that the kind of democracy the

Allies had fought for found itself on the defensive in the heart of Europe. Only in backward, feudal Spain had it seized the initiative. The defeat of the Hohenzollerns had not made Germany safe for democracy. Defeat had made Germany increasingly safe for Hitler—and the best alternative Chancellor Brüning could offer was a restoration of the same Hohenzollern dynasty that the Allies had overthrown at such a cost. The French blamed this sorry outcome on Anglo-American coddling of Germany. The Anglo-Americans blamed the French for refusing to build up the Weimar Republic while the chance lasted.

If the rise of Hitler signified that something was rotten in the state of Germany, the condition of Germany signified that something was rotten in the state of Europe. The depression had hit the United States sooner and harder than it hit any other major Power, but the United States had sufficient resources not to disintegrate under the blow. Germany, on the other hand, had few resources of any kind, and Hitler successfully appealed to the basest passions and lowest instincts of a distracted people. In Great Britain Montagu Norman, the arch-capitalist, and Philip Snowden, the arch-Socialist, formed a strange alliance to preserve the gold standard, first in Germany and then in England. They failed because the French had the power to wreck their plans on both occasions. It remained to be seen whether the French could now rule Europe as successfully as they had helped to ruin it.

What had the French to show for the victory they had won? Their political influence ran strong throughout eastern Europe, but they got no economic benefit from that part of the world. On the contrary. Much of the trade between the French and their allies in the east took the form of French military equipment, paid for by French loans. Nor did the France of Tardieu and Laval welcome the kind of republic that seemed to be emerging in Spain. The rise of Hitler in Germany caused much greater fear, and yet the French had alienated their mighty wartime ally, Great Britain. More folly than villainy accounted for this state of affairs. Weakness and weariness lay at the root of the matter. And nowhere was this weakness and weariness more apparent than in connection with Europe's new relationship toward the less industrialized parts of the world. There, too, the depression had made itself felt—sometimes in the form of revolutionary violence, sometimes in the form of war or threats of war. But these great events beyond the seas received little attention in a Europe that could no longer save others since it lacked the power and the will to save itself.

12

Depression Everywhere

What happened when the world depression reached South America, India, China, and the Soviet Union.

PREVIEW

Between 1930 and 1931 the depression set off revolutions in five South American republics. Bolivia and Peru ousted illegal dictators. In Argentina a soldier drove a demagogue from office. Brazil and Chile moved a little to the left. Events in India moved faster and more decisively when Mahatma Gandhi's Congress Party won substantial concessions from the British, although not so many as Gandhi himself wanted. Japan took advantage of the general confusion to seize Manchuria and Jehol Province before China had a chance to unify under Chiang Kai-shek. The League of Nations and the United States did little to stop Japan. The Soviet Union did less. Stalin had bet everything on a Five-Year Plan that almost wrecked Russian agriculture but did give Russia an industrial plant second only to America's. Not since Lenin's time had revolution brought so many changes.

· I ·

Wars and depressions have done more than peace and prosperity to unify the world of the twentieth century. President Wilson could not keep the United States out of Europe's war. Europe could not escape the effects of Wall Street's crash. Nor could the New World refuse to redress the economic balance of the Old when Americans drew up the Dawes and Young Plans and when Hoover proclaimed his moratorium. But the great depression confronted both the New World and the Old with a new kind of crisis. Neither Europe nor the Americas could buy the foodstuffs and raw materials that their own people and the people of more backward lands produced in such profusion. Even in the prosperous United States, the boom had passed the farmer by, and when the boom collapsed the Western farmer suffered even more than the Eastern speculator.

In less favored lands the farmers did more than suffer. Their distress became so acute that it led to revolution in South America and to war in East Asia. "It is hard to prophesy what will happen as a result of this agricultural distress," wrote Hans Zehrer, political editor of Berlin's liberal *Vossische Zeitung*, during the summer of 1930. "Once the tillers of the soil mobilize, whether they are Indian or Chinese peasants, South American Indians or East European farmers, all values become fictitious, and capital is the form of value that is chiefly threatened today. If the soil of Asia, South America, and agricultural Europe opens up and swallows this capital, the whole axis of the earth will be shifted."

Europe had to wait until the summer of 1931 to experience the truth of this prediction. Not so South America. Within thirteen months, beginning in June, 1930, Bolivia, Peru, Argentina, Brazil, and Chile all went through revolutions—in that order. Of the one and three quarter billion dollars that United States citizens invested in those five republics, all but one quarter of a billion went into default. The borrower felt no respect for the lender; the lender had no understanding of the borrower. William R. Castle, Under Secretary of State under Coolidge, loftily advised an exporters' convention in Washington to regard Secretary of State Kellogg as "your attorney" and Secretary of Commerce Hoover as "your advance agent." Manifest destiny no longer invaded Latin America on the bayonets of United States Marines; it arrived in the brief-cases of Wall Street's high-pressure salesmen. But this did not allay Latin-American fear and distrust of the Colossus of the North. As the Chilean poetess, Gabriela Mistral, once wrote, "Two things unite us Spanish Americans: our beautiful Spanish language and our distrust of the United States."

Not all the fault lay north of the Rio Grande. Augustín Alvarez, known as the Emerson of Argentina, wrote in the early 1900's: "Work, which in medieval Europe was simply humiliating, descended a few degrees lower and became in Spanish America *shameful*, since it was abandoned to the Indians and Negroes—even to the plebeians who continued to come from the peninsula hastening to buy a wig and a sword in order to play the hidalgo. Employers learned to despise and to exploit the white laborer as well as the Indian and the Negro, treating him like a work animal, under the lash. Degraded by such labor and deprived of the incentive of gain, the indigent white man toiled to keep from starving, and if later he could without working contrive to keep from dying, he immediately gave up the work which he had all the while despised. Placing a premium on suffering, religion had destroyed all the humanitarian motives that might have induced the powerful to abolish or alleviate it, since suffering in the toil of life was a means of redemption."

If an eminent Argentine could generalize so glibly about the nineteen

South America in 1930

Spanish American republics, a North American found it easy to generalize as glibly about just one of them. Francis Herron, of the Institute of Current World Affairs in New York, reported in his book, *Letters from the Argentine*, that the local landowning aristocrats not only despised the manual laborer; they also looked down on the successful businessman: "In a country where individual enterprise is uncommon and where success is difficult to achieve, wealth can most easily be obtained by a quick stroke at the expense of others. Hence a capitalist is not esteemed. He is considered to be a schemer, an opportunist, at times even a thief. A capitalist is not admired, he is more hated than admired. A capitalist is not regarded as one who promotes civilization; he is thought of as a plunderer. If he does good it is regarded as a simulation, and the good he does is presumed to be for the ulterior purpose of placing himself in a position so that he can make another profitable deal at the expense of others. This conception of the capitalist is inherited from the Spanish colonial system, under which a capitalist had no social recognition."

But the poor students in Peru had little in common with these rich Argentine landowners. When Samuel Guy Inman, lifelong expert on Latin America and author of many sympathetic books about its people, visited Peru in 1925 a group of students asked him to transmit this appeal to the outside world in their behalf: "Our country is perishing for the lack of moral stamina, sacrificial service, and practical idealism. Send us men to lead us into this new life. If you come only to develop our material resources, to work our mines, and to cultivate our rich soil, Peru itself will remain poor in the real values of life. We have been trusting for a hundred years in literature and professionalism to save us. We are now disillusioned as to this. But we believe that to go to the other extreme of materialism will bring results just as disappointing. We call on your universities, your great foundations in the social sciences, your leaders in moral and spiritual movements to reach out a hand to the young men of Peru."

Five years later Kasimir Edschmid, a German journalist, made the grand tour of South America which he reported in *South America: Light and Shadow*. On the light side, he quoted a Dutch engineer's observation: "All lads in South America are as astute at the age of nine as other people are at thirty. But when they are thirty they unfortunately have no more intelligence than other people have at the age of nine." Edschmid himself drew a more somber conclusion: "There was nothing durable on this continent. The people were bound to have dictatorships and to smash them each time. They were resolved to have democracies and they always got dictatorships. They put themselves to all pains to organize, to co-ordinate, to construct and to mold—but at long last they were bound to wreck it all again. They were unable to endure anyone or anything set in authority over them. Nor would they even have endured Christ or Napoleon in authority over them."

With the provincialism of the European intellectual, Edschmid passed judgment on the whole continent of South America as he would never have pronounced judgment on the whole continent of Europe. The South American republics did not, it is true, have those ancient traditions that kept Europe so sharply divided into so many sovereign, national states. But the South American republics, because they had fewer traditions, cultivated what they had with all the more fervor. Moreover, these differences tended to become more and more pronounced as the individual South American nations gradually acquired more distinctive characteristics. Consider, for instance, Bolivia, scene of the first revolution that the world depression brought to South America. Like the other five republics which went through their revolutions in short order, Bolivia had recently borrowed large sums of money abroad and then had found it impossible to repay these loans because the prices of the goods it exported had collapsed. But there the resemblance between Bolivia and the rest of the South American republics ended and the differences began.

Only two South American republics—Brazil and Argentina—had a greater area than Bolivia, but nowhere did the mass of the people live in greater poverty. In 1930 not one Bolivian in five could write his name or read a newspaper headline. Bolivia had less than three million inhabitants, two thirds of them poor, diseased, illiterate Indians, who farmed land they did not own or worked in the tin mines which produced more than two thirds of Bolivia's export trade. Other metals accounted for all but 8 per cent of the rest. Most Bolivians dwelt ten, twelve, and fifteen thousand feet above the sea—to which their country had no access.

In 1913 Bolivian borrowings from the United States totaled ten million dollars. By 1929 they had risen to $113,000,000. A three-man fiscal commission, two of them United States citizens, supervised the collection of all taxes, revenues, and customs receipts. The price of tin, which began to slump in 1926, dropped 35 per cent between 1930 and 1931 and it was in June, 1930, that demonstrations of students and workmen in the capital city of La Paz forced President Hernando Siles to quit his job and flee the country. In 1925 Siles had violated the Constitution by establishing himself as dictator, and the Guggenheim copper interests kept him there. The military junta that replaced him supervised national elections in January, 1931, when Dr. Daniel Salamanca, founder of the Republican Party, won the Presidency. Meanwhile the country had to repudiate all its private and government debts, and Salamanca soon recalled General Hans Kundt, the German military adviser who

had served under Siles. In 1932
Kundt led an invasion army of fifty
thousand men into the jungles of
the Chaco, which both Paraguay
and Bolivia claimed. Of the war
that followed a Frenchman remarked, "The struggle between
Bolivia and Paraguay over the
Chaco reminds me of two bald-
headed men fighting over a comb."

In primitive Bolivia the kind
of revolution that the depression
engendered took its simplest possible form. A poor country, specializing in the export of a single product, borrows too much money
abroad. The borrowed funds yield
disappointingly low returns. The
depression cuts down the country's

UNITED PRESS PHOTO

Augusto P. Leguía

only source of outside revenue. A desperate population demonstrates
against a corrupt government, which promptly quits. But no revolution,
no reforms follow. The Army steps in, installs a new President, who
tries to solve the crisis by going to war.

None of the subsequent South American revolutions followed exactly
the Bolivian pattern. Each conformed to the conditions that existed in
each separate republic. Peru, for example, covered somewhat less territory than Bolivia but it had more than twice as many inhabitants. In
both countries people of Indian descent outnumbered people of Spanish
descent, but the Peruvian Indian, perhaps because he was descended
from the rulers of the old Inca Empire, displayed more stamina. Peru had
fourteen hundred miles of Pacific coastline and possessed more oil and
minerals than Bolivia and better farming land. Peru had also lived for
more than ten years under the rule of one of the most remarkable dictators in South America—President Augusto P. Leguía.

"Leguía," wrote United States Ambassador Alexander P. Moore, "is a
greater commander than Caesar, a greater law-giver than Napoleon,
a greater diplomat than Richelieu; after God comes Leguía." But at a
measurable distance. Leguía had won the Presidency of Peru in 1908
and during his first four-year term he balanced the budget and introduced some modern improvements that he had learned about as the
employee of a North American insurance company. In 1919 he seized
power in a coup d'état, backed by organized labor and the middle
classes. During the next ten years he added over one hundred million

dollars to Peru's ten-million-dollar foreign debt, and spent sixty-five million dollars on internal improvements. Within a decade, Peru's school attendance more than doubled and the value of Peru's foreign trade tripled. But Leguía also abolished freedom of speech and of the press. He made Indians build new highways at forced labor. He kept the University of San Marcos in a "state of reorganization" for seven years. His son, Juan, received $415,000 when he helped the Seligman firm in New York float a hundred-million-dollar Peruvian loan. But it was not corruption that brought Leguía down. It was the collapse of raw-material prices. Peru did not specialize in a single product as Bolivia specialized in tin, but Peru did need to export large quantities of sugar, rubber, oil, cotton, lumber, and wool at good prices to pay its debts and give its people work. When the depression cut down these sources of revenue, Leguía's dwindling circle of friends joined his growing throng of enemies and clapped him into jail in August, 1930. There he died, two years later, a broken man of seventy.

Lieutenant-Colonel Sánchez Cerro, head of the military junta that overthrew Leguía, assumed the title of Provisional President, and promoted himself to the rank of General. Having thrown the rascals out, Sánchez Cerro set up a personal regime of his own, no less arbitrary and far less enlightened than Leguía's. He began to fight a war with Colombia over the disputed province of Leticia, but an assassin murdered him in 1933 and a more benevolent despot, Oscar Benavides, replaced him. What chiefly distinguished Peru's revolution from Bolivia's was that Peru developed a revolutionary movement of sorts. During the 1920's Raúl Haya de la Torre, a radical young intellectual, had founded the Alianza Popular Revolucionaria Americana, or APRA for short, but Leguía drove him into exile. Haya had left Peru a patriot and a Socialist; he returned, after the overthrow of Leguía, more impressed with the Communists, whom he had studied in Russia, and with the Nazis, whom he had studied in Germany. But Haya still felt that Peru needed more democracy, not less, and he ran for the Presidency in 1931. Sánchez Cerro won overwhelmingly and threw him in jail. Benavides released him, but he had to live an underground existence in the suburbs of Lima. Peru had failed to make a social revolution to match its political revolution. But at least Peru had tried.

· II ·

ARGENTINA, where the third political overturn of 1930 occurred, did not even try. For Argentina had already undergone a social revolution of sorts. The arrival of the depression found the country living under the rule of President Hipólito Irigoyen, an even more remarkable character than Leguía of Peru. Irigoyen, a bearded, handsome Basque, popularly known as "The Armadillo," had begun life as a schoolteacher, and first won the Presidency in 1916 as the candidate of the Radical Party. His election marked a social as well as a political overturn because he owed his victory to the votes of the industrial and white-collar workers in Buenos Aires and to the landless peons who worked on the great estates of a few wealthy families. Irigoyen distinguished himself during his first term by keeping Argentina neutral throughout the war. Not only that; he embargoed food shipments to the Allies and when a huge majority in the House of Representatives and every Senator but one voted to break diplomatic relations with Germany, he ignored their wishes. The Argentine Constitution forbade any President to succeed himself, and Irigoyen backed another Radical, Dr. Marcelo T. de Alvear, who won the 1922 election. But Alvear did not share Irigoyen's psychopathic fear of the United States nor did he continue Irigoyen's demagogic and dictatorial methods. A split developed within the Radical Party, as Irigoyen organized a new faction who called themselves Personalistas. In 1928 Irigoyen waited until a week before voting day to announce that he would once again, at the age of seventy-five, seek the Presidency. He offered no program, made no promises, no public appearances—and received two thirds of the popular vote.

Raúl Scalibrini Ortiz, a popular Buenos Aires journalist, compared Irigoyen's appeal to Mohammed's: "Nobody knew anything about the way he lived or even what he looked like, for until he was elected, Irigoyen did not permit himself to be photographed. He had the same reluctance as Mohammed toward letting his person be reproduced in pictorial form; indeed, in respect to his life, his conduct in office, his whole personality, and his role as mass leader, he bore much more resemblance to the prophet of Arabia than to any politician of the European type. Like Mohammed, he had spent thirty years in voluntary exile; like Mohammed, he represented himself to the public as an uneducated man yet one who understood everything; like Mohammed, he practiced a confused, bombastic literary style full of sibylline images and had no hesitation in referring to himself as a high point in human history if not an emissary of God. Finally, like Mohammed, he knew how to win the affection and loyalty of his people."

When Hoover visited Argentina in 1929 as President-Elect, Irigoyen received him cordially. Afterward, however, Irigoyen informed the public that Hoover had stopped by in connection with a recently completed cable that permitted telephone communication between Argentina and the United States. According to Irigoyen, Hoover hoped to use these new facilities to receive orders and take advice from the Argentine President. But things did not work out quite that way. Some months later Irigoyen put in the first call only to be informed that Hoover was not available and when Hoover called back, with a formal message, Irigoyen would not answer. All this delighted the Argentine public, as did Irigoyen's refusal to appoint an ambassador to Washington.

The eccentric Irigoyen thrived in predepression Argentina for the same reasons that Leguía thrived in predepression Peru. Both men satisfied the needs of their countries at those times. But the depression finished both men off for reasons arising from the different situations in which they held office. Suffice it to say that the Leguía type of dictator and the Irigoyen type of demagogue suddenly went out of date. Irigoyen, however, faced a more complex set of problems. Argentina's thirteen million inhabitants occupied the richest land and enjoyed the highest living standards of any Latin-American people. Argentina led the world in the export of beef, corn, linseed, and quebracho. It was the second greatest exporter of wheat, lamb, mutton, and wool. It also produced hides, cotton, sugar, tobacco, and wines. But Argentina had no coal, no mineral wealth, little hydroelectric power. Its industrial possibilities therefore remained limited. Most Bolivians and Peruvians had Indian blood. Argentina had few Indians and fewer Negroes. But two million Argentines had Italian ancestors; more than a quarter of a million had German ancestors. Fifty thousand Britishers made their homes in Argentina, although few of them became Argentine citizens. Buenos Aires, with more than three million inhabitants, had as mixed and vigorous a people as Chicago and as rich a cultural life as New York.

Hubert Herring in *Good Neighbors* listed some "typical markings" of the *porteño*, or port-dweller, of Buenos Aires: "He speaks Spanish with the vigor of a pile-driver, a Spanish which has neither the caress of the Mexican nor the cadence of the Colombian. He works hard, idles feverishly. He has little of the leisurely grace of the Brazilian, and does not know how to waste words with the profligacy of the Peruvian. He is alternately maddeningly suave and harshly abrupt. . . . There is a determined sophistication in the cultural life of the capital, as though its contrivers were fiercely intent upon forgetting something and upon seeking escape in other worlds. Argentine painting, with notable but scant exceptions, is synthetic French. Argentine music is almost altogether borrowed. Argentine writing, with exceptions again, is diluted Proust, Molière, and Racine. The *porteño* fancies himself as a cosmopolitan. He dresses the part. I get the impression of more well-dressed men on Buenos Aires streets than in any city in the world. If he aspires to culture, he reads in French and plans another journey to Paris. He turns his back as though in shame upon the pampas which give him life, and reckons himself a citizen of the world which lies east. The *porteño*, no matter how tiny his business or practice, knows himself cut off by ponderable barriers from his uninitiated countrymen."

The *porteño*'s dependence on the pampas brought him down in the world and cast Irigoyen from office. In 1929 Argentine exports, more than half of them products of the pampas, brought more than a billion dollars into the country. By 1930 the depression cut this revenue almost in two and forced Argentina to devalue the peso 50 per cent. The price collapse meant that Argentina suddenly had to get along with half as much money from abroad. The collapse of the peso meant that Argentina had to pay twice as much of its own money for its imports. As the national gold reserve began to melt away, Irigoyen cut wages and salaries. When the railwaymen went out on strike, he ordered the Army to break it. Having antagonized the masses, who had twice voted him into office, he antagonized the landowners by threatening to confiscate their estates. In the Congressional elections of March, 1930, the Personalistas lost two hundred thousand votes. By summer Irigoyen had lost control of himself as well as of his country. He kept dismissing provincial governors, as the Constitution permitted him to do, and replacing them with incompetent toadies. On September 6, supposedly on doctor's orders, Irigoyen delegated his powers to the Vice-President. The next day General José F. Uriburu, Commander-in-Chief of the Army and nephew of a former President, occupied the executive mansion with his staff and proceeded to govern. The droning of military planes early that morning prepared the citizens for the coup d'état that followed, and that might have been bloodless if a company of soldiers, mistaking the sound of a blown-out tire for a rifle shot, had not skirmished briefly with some students at the cost of several lives. Irigoyen resigned and the London *Times* attributed the revolt to an unholy alliance between North American capitalists and Argentine landowners. Uriburu resumed normal relations with the United States but devoted most of his energies to removing Personalistas from office and supplanting them with Conservatives.

Uriburu served as acting President for more than a year, and then reluctantly ordered a general election. The Radicals tried to nominate Alvear, but Uriburu ruled him off the ballot because six years had not passed since his first Presidential term had ended. Radical candidates showed great strength in local elections, but their Party boycotted the Presidential contest, which General Augustin Justo, the Conservative candidate, won by virtual default. Under Justo, Anglo-Argentine relations improved while ties with the United States weakened. After the Prince of Wales visited Argentina in 1932, Justo approved a trade pact that put the country back in Britain's economic orbit. Ex-President

KEYSTONE   UNITED PRESS PHOTO
Hipólito Irigoyen   *Getulio Vargas*

Alvear and Dr. Honorio Pueyreddon, former Ambassador to the United
States, went into exile.

Argentina resembled the other Latin-American republics in that the
collapse of farm prices struck at its vitals. But Argentina differed from
the other Latin-American republics in that it had not overborrowed from
the United States. British, not North American, capital dominated Argentina to the tune of two billion two hundred million dollars. About half
of this money had gone into railway construction. Much of the rest went
into meat refrigeration plants. British investors in the Argentine went
there to live. They made friends among the people. They also saw to it
that Anglo-Argentine trade kept flowing in both directions at a high
level. Few North Americans followed their funds to Bolivia, Peru, and
other outlandish spots and fewer still did anything to promote two-way
trade between the northern and southern halves of the hemisphere. The
British missed few opportunities to aggravate existing frictions between
the United States and Argentina. "You may take Canada from us," they
used to say, "but you will never take Argentina." Argentine and United
States citizens got on each other's nerves because both carried chips on
their shoulders; both suffered from the same inferiority complex of the
newly rich. The British knew how to ingratiate themselves with both
although they defaulted on their war debt payments to the United States
while Argentina did not default on interest payments due to British
investors. But the British had earned Argentine good will. In 1932, after
they built a tariff wall around their Empire at Ottawa, they entered into
a special arrangement with Argentina under which they agreed not to

reduce their meat purchases more than 10 per cent while Argentina agreed to use all the funds thus received on purchasing British goods.

Argentina differed from Peru more than Peru differed from Bolivia. But Brazil differed still more sharply from Argentina. Brazilians spoke Portuguese, not Spanish. The original settlers left a tiny homeland and proceeded to bring almost half the continent of South America under the Brazilian flag. No Spanish American republic ever had as large a population as Spain, the mother country. In the case of Brazil, the tail wagged the dog. The population of Brazil not only exceeded the population of Portugal. In Napoleon's time, the Portuguese court moved from Lisbon to Rio de Janeiro, and during most of the nineteenth century, while the rest of Latin America lived under republican rule, Brazil lived under an Emperor. Not until 1888, when Brazil became a republic, did it also abolish Negro slavery.

In 1922 Brazil estimated its population at 51 per cent white, 22 per cent mixed white and Negro, and 14 percent Negro. Pure-bred Indians came to only 2 per cent of the total. "If the United States is to be thought of as a melting pot," wrote T. L. Smith in *Brazil: People and Institutions*, "Brazil must be considered a cauldron." Brazil not only contained three separate racial strains—white, Negro, and Indian. Like Argentina, Brazil had large Italian and German colonies as well as other European immigrants plus some thousands of Japanese. Unlike Argentina, Brazil had always maintained close ties with the United States. Unlike the Spanish American republics, Brazil preached and practiced real good will in that direction.

Argentina during the 1920's bore some resemblance to the United States of fifty years before. Brazil bore no resemblance to any other land at any time. It was more like a separate continent. The depression hit Brazil harder than it hit Argentina and the revolution to which the depression gave rise caused more bloodshed. In the nineteenth century Brazil's cotton exports led the world. It developed the first rubber plantations. But the Brazilians said of themselves that they gathered the fruit and forgot the tree. Having let several opportunities slip away, they concentrated on coffee-growing with such success that in 1931 they had thirty-eight million bags of coffee in storage although they were exporting only sixteen million bags a year. Some of these bags they had stored back in 1929, when they fetched twenty-five cents a pound. By 1931 they fetched only seven cents. Coffee accounted for three quarters of Brazil's export trade and more than half this coffee went to the United States. The prices of rubber and cocoa, Brazil's other chief exports, also collapsed.

Brazil's political structure soon cracked under the economic strain. According to unwritten law, the Presidency of Brazil had always alternated between a native of the state of São Paulo and of the state of Minas Geraes. But when the term of President Washington Luiz Pereira de Souza expired in 1930, he proposed that the office should again go to a native of São Paulo in the person of its Governor, Julio Prestes. The politicians of Minas Geraes and of Rio Grande do Sul, knowing their man had no chance, nevertheless nominated Getulio Vargas, who had once served as Secretary of the Treasury under Washington Luiz. Prestes won easily, but a number of opposition Congressmen were more successful, and when Washington Luiz refused to recognize them a Liberal Alliance came into being for the purpose of using force against a man who had first violated the spirit and then the letter of the Constitution. The world depression played into the hands of the Liberal Alliance. In past years Washington Luiz had supported coffee prices by buying the surplus with state funds, but in 1930 the funds had shrunk as much as the coffee surplus had grown. The Brazilians found themselves having to spend twice as much of their depreciated currency to meet their foreign debts.

On October 3, 1930, military revolts broke out in three widely separated areas as members of the Liberal Alliance seized control of several state governments. Within three weeks the rebels triumphed everywhere. A group of their generals arrested Washington Luiz, who refused to resign until another month had passed. By that time, Vargas had proclaimed himself provisional President and the new regime received recognition from all the major foreign Powers, led—all too tardily —by the United States. For it was at this time that Secretary Stimson won the unhappy nickname of "Wrong Horse Harry" by supporting Washington Luiz too long against Vargas.

The revolution in Brazil lasted longer and cost more lives than the almost bloodless overturns in Argentina, Peru, and Bolivia. It also pushed the country measurably toward the left. Under pressure from his Liberal Party backers, Vargas adopted a reform program that included an eight-hour-day and minimum-wage law and that created a new Department of Education and Public Health and another of Labor, Industry, and Commerce. He set up a rudimentary system of social insurance and required all foreign corporations doing business in Brazil to give two thirds of their jobs to Brazilian citizens. He restricted immigration. But these measures did not end the depression or mitigate its effects. In October, 1931, Brazil defaulted on all its foreign debts. To nine Brazilians in every ten, this default meant less than nothing. They had lived badly when funds from the United States flowed into their country during the golden twenties. They lived no worse when the flow ceased. Afranio Peixoto, a Brazilian sociologist, summed it all up in a few words: "We do nothing well because we are on a diet—a perpetual diet." Neither during the prosperous twenties nor the depressed thirties did that diet include the drastic changes that the country needed to realize its immense possibilities. And under the enervating equatorial sun, no changes came rapidly.

Only in Chile did the impact of the depression give any promise of hastening the changes which so many South American countries needed. But Chile had other unique claims to fame. It was the only country on earth more than twenty-six hundred miles long and barely one hundred miles wide. For years it had a virtual world monopoly in the production of nitrates. The Germans broke that monopoly during the war when their scientists learned how to make nitrates from the air. Chile enjoyed the longest period of internal peace of any Latin-American country—one hundred and ten years. No single ruling group anywhere in the Western Hemisphere had owned and farmed the same lands so long as Chile's "Forty Families" had owned and farmed the rich Central Valley estates. Many had Basque names; more had English, German, French, or Dutch names. Over the centuries their Spanish ancestors had married and assimilated non-Spaniards—not to a Spanish but to a Chilean way of life. Chile's Forty Families looked to no mother country overseas. They regarded themselves as primarily Chileans, and with this deep sense of national pride went some awareness of social responsibility. If they possessed the feudal vices as well as the feudal virtues, at least they had escaped the curse of social irresponsibility that afflicted the newly rich Argentines. Chile permitted more free speech and greater freedom of the press than Brazil or Argentina. No Latin-American people made so successful an effort to practice the democracy they preached.

Yet the same gulf that separated the rich minority from the impoverished majority divided Chile, too. One third of all the workers in Chile worked on the land, some of them as migrant laborers, most of them as *inquilenos,* who might be described as overprivileged serfs or underprivileged sharecroppers. Chile did not have so large a proportion of pure-blooded Indians as Bolivia or Peru, but in the rural regions, whites and Indians intermarried and produced a hardy *mestizo,* or mixed stock. Another one third of the populace worked for wages—in the copper mines, controlled by the foreign, absentee Guggenheims; in the nitrate fields, controlled by a native trust; in factories, offices, and fisheries. Many of them lived in Santiago, the national capital and fourth largest Latin-American city, with its population of almost a million. Hubert Herring stressed their misery during the depression years in *Good Neighbors:* "The poverty of Santiago hits the traveler in the face from the moment he steps off the train, and finds an old man eager to carry his trunks and heavy suitcases for four cents each to the waiting taxi. There is a life-and-death quality to that poverty unlike any other city in the Americas. It is not New York's misery—where one feels someone is just about to do something about it all. It is not even Brazil's—for the Brazilian, out of wisdom or contrariness, insists upon being happy. It is not Buenos Aires'—her slums have the rather amiable quality which is New York's. Santiago's poverty is that of men who have given up.

"Perhaps the best way to know a people is to catch them on holiday parade. I recall New Year's Eve on the great central Alameda in Santiago. There were gay lights and a mile of booths and side shows. There were thousands of the people who get 30, 40, 50, or 60 cents each working day, who live three or more to the room, who spend 80 per cent of their pay on food alone, and who have 3.2 per cent left for education, amusements, doctors, dentists, savings. (Damn the statistics and the statisticians.) I looked for one well-dressed man of the sort one sees everywhere in Buenos Aires—I did not see him. I looked for one woman having more than a bit of sleazy finery—I did not find her. They were a dull, pasty-faced, driven people, they scarcely laughed. They seemed to say, we are here to enjoy ourselves, and we must—but there was little evidence that they were enjoying themselves. . . . Three fourths of the concessions were gambling devices—cards, wheelers, rings to be thrown over china dolls—and the crowds thronged about them, to take a fling at a fortune of two bits. Cheap drinks everywhere and most of the people had too much. Improvident people, gamblers, drunkards—I am told—people who spend money on lottery tickets and alcohol which should go on milk. These are not attractive people, I reluctantly admitted. Life seems to have passed them on the other side of the street."

The depression did not hit Chile any harder than it hit other parts of Latin America. But Chile reacted more sharply. Bolivia, Peru, Argentina, and Brazil all went through their revolutions during the summer of 1930. Chile's revolution came a year later, with a delayed kick. But its origins went back more than ten years. In 1920 the workers and middle classes of Chile created the Liberal Alliance, which elected a reformist President, Arturo Alessandri, the humbly born son of an Italian immigrant. At that time 40 per cent of the Chilean population was illiterate, and many sons and daughters of well-to-do families joined the mass of university students in agitating for social reforms. Alessandri began to put through a program of higher taxes on the rich, free primary schools, factory inspection, improved sanitation, and public health services. But the professional politicians and the wealthy Senators kept throwing sand in the gears until 1925, when Alessandri put through a new Constitution after two military juntas had tried and failed to establish dictatorships. But Alessandri had moved too fast and too clumsily. A month after the proclamation of the new Constitution, a third military junta headed by Colonel Carlos Ibañez forced him to resign and leave the country.

This government remained in power, except for a brief period in 1926, until the summer of 1931. By this time, however, the consequences of the depression had caught up with every last man, woman, and child in Chile. A student strike in two universities and a demonstration by members of the middle and professional classes led Ibañez to quit and turn over his office to Premier J. E. Montero, a sincere, capable Conservative. Montero won the Presidency in an election in October, 1931, but a group of radical Army and Navy officers ousted him eleven months later, and in October, 1932, Alessandri returned from half a decade of exile to regain the Presidency in still another special election. Soon afterward Chile had to follow the example of its neighbors, proclaim its bankruptcy, and stop payments on all foreign loans. By the time Alessandri came to power, radical leaders had gained so wide a following that the propertied classes came to his support, preferring moderate reform to violent revolt.

Excessive foreign loans contributed to Chile's plight. United States investments in Chile had risen from 15 million dollars in 1913 to 659 millions in 1929, or almost two hundred millions more than had gone into Brazil. But what bothered Chile's politicians and businessmen was not their country's inability to repay past loans; it was their country's inability to raise new ones. For Chile lacked the natural wealth of Argentina, the varied resources of Brazil. Yet leading Chileans had more pride than any Argentine or Brazilian, although the mass of their people lived hardly any better than the people of Bolivia or Peru. This pride not only led to the fall that Chile suffered in the depression. The same pride inspired the subsequent agitation for social reform.

The arrogance and corruption of the favored few, the poverty and misery of the depressed masses, excessive loans, exorbitant interest rates, and collapsing prices brought down five Latin-American governments between the summer of 1930 and the summer of 1931. All these governments could have absorbed, to good purpose, ten times as much money as United States investors made available. But United States investors could not expect quick returns on such capital. Neither could they expect payment in cash. They would have to accept Latin-American products, and their tariff policy ruled that out. Many South Americans blamed the depression on Wall Street and most North Americans agreed with them. Almost nobody in the United States suggested sending the Marines or the Navy to collect South America's defaulted debts, but plenty of South Americans feared Yankee dollars as much as they once feared Yankee guns.

Back in 1923 Manuel Ugarte, of Argentina, sounded a prophetic warning in *The Destiny of a Continent:* "Commercial concessions are for certain peoples of Latin America what revolutions are for others. It is not the official agent who stoops to whisper in the ear of the *caudillo* 'I have rifles and money; you, too, may be president,' but the man of business who is all the while preparing to control the vital energies of the country, though he so arranges things that even those whose interests he threatens exclaim: 'We have never sold our steers at so good a price!' Brazilian coffee and Argentine stock-breeding may suffer the same fate as Cuban sugar. And in mentioning these products, we are referring to them all in general. The evil arises from the fact that the real owners of this wealth do not think of making it productive, and so increasing the common vitality of their efforts; but let it pass into other hands, making a much lower profit, but one sufficient to exempt them from trouble and work. How many railroad concessions, how many businesses of every sort have been acquired with the sole aim of reselling them! And as it is always foreign companies who acquire them, it is our own property, our own country, our very flag which we are handing over to others. Before taking up arms in civil conflicts or sterile warfare, we ought to learn to manufacture them in times of peace. And it is not only in this sphere that we have to begin at the beginning, but in every activity and the whole upkeep of our collective life."

As a result of the revolutions of 1930 and 1931, Chile took more steps than any of its neighbors in the direction Ugarte recommended. No Latin-American republic had yet developed the intense national spirit so characteristic of Europe, but all of them were moving in that direction. They might never build up important industries. Even their own continent might never approach self-sufficiency. But the depression did more than end Latin America's semicolonial era. It opened a new era in other underdeveloped regions, too.

· III ·

THE revolution that swept India during the early 1930's started long before the depression began. And it brought deeper changes than the South American republics experienced during those same years. For centuries India's illiterate peasant majority had subsisted on a single meal a day—or its equivalent. For decades two thirds of the babies born in Bombay died within less than twelve months of birth. To the Indian masses, world depression had no more meaning than world prosperity, and their poverty and ignorance rendered them devoid of political power. The Indian middle classes, on the other hand, steadily became more numerous, more potent, better educated, and more radical. For they multiplied more rapidly than their opportunities for skilled work increased. It was from their ranks that the Congress Party drew most of its support, though the leader of that Party knew how to appeal to the masses as well. "I am just an ordinary human being and full of weaknesses and sins," said Gandhi. "But I have this one thing the poor recognize in me at once: they know that I share their hardships." By assuming command of the Congress Party, Gandhi committed himself to the cause of Indian independence. By accepting this leadership, the Congress Party committed itself to achieving that end by nonviolent means.

The movement for Indian independence could never have achieved anything if the Indian people themselves had not gained new strength. During the 1920's the population of India began to increase at the rate of more than two million a year. What this meant was that public health measures had begun to yield some results and infant mortality had dropped slightly. Although some Congress Party propaganda attributed the poverty of the Indian masses to British rule, the leaders of that Party did not call for a revolt against misery. Just the opposite. The Congress Party depended for its funds and leadership on the rising middle and professional classes, who sought independence from Britain in order to increase their own power and wealth. The Indian masses continued to live on the edge of starvation, but even their lot had improved a little. The middle classes had multiplied more rapidly and their living standards had gone up, too. But they wanted a great deal more of the better things of life for themselves and for their children and they found it convenient to blame all of India's troubles, including their own, on British rule.

The younger members of the Congress Party took a more radical view of India's situation and attacked Gandhi because he stressed spiritual rather than economic matters. Many did not dispute the wisdom of his nonviolent methods; they distrusted his Mahatma aspect. "The asceticism of Gandhi, his simple life, his vegetarian diet, his adherence to truth, and his consequent fearlessness—all combined to give him a halo of saintliness," wrote one of these younger men, Subhas Chandra Bose, in *The Indian Struggle: 1920-1934.* "His loincloth was reminiscent of Christ, while his sitting posture at the time of lecturing was reminiscent of Buddha. . . . Consciously or unconsciously, the Mahatma fully exploited the mass psychology of the people, just as Lenin did the same thing in Russia, Mussolini in Italy, and Hitler in Germany. But in doing so, the Mahatma was using a weapon which was soon to recoil on his head. He was exploiting many of the weak traits in the character of his countrymen which had accounted for India's downfall to a large extent. After all, what has brought about India's downfall in the material and political sphere? It is her inordinate belief in fate and the supernatural—

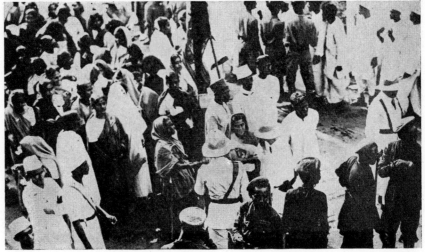

KEYSTONE

Non-Resistance Demonstrators in India

her indifference to modern scientific development—her backwardness in the science of modern warfare, the peaceful contentment engendered by her latter-day philosophy and adherence to Ahimsa (nonviolence) carried to the most absurd length." Bose went on to recall: "In 1922, when the writer was in prison, Indian warders in the service of the Prisons Department would refuse to believe that the Mahatma had been cast in prison by the British Government. They would say in all seriousness that since Gandhi was a Mahatma, he could assume the shape of a bird and escape from prison any moment he liked."

In 1924, when Gandhi finally did emerge from jail to undergo an appendicitis operation, the British permitted him to remain at large. He had failed both as a liberator and as a martyr and the British hoped his release would complete his descent to oblivion. For several years this hope seemed likely to come true. Gandhi retired from political activity, leaving the field free to the more extremist Swaraj, or Independence Party, which demanded immediate Dominion status within the Empire. Calcutta, the largest city in India, and the second largest in the Empire, elected as its mayor the Swaraj leader, C. R. Das, but his death in 1925 checked the further growth of Swaraj. Gandhi, on the other hand, stuck to his spiritual guns, insisting that "the instant India is purified India becomes free, and not a moment earlier." To further this process of purification Gandhi undertook a three-week fast in the home of a Moslem friend, meanwhile urging Hindus and Moslems to end their constant strife and live together as brothers. "I respectfully invite the heads of all communities, including Englishmen, to meet and end this quarrel which is a disgrace to religion and to humanity. It seems as if God has been dethroned. Let us reinstate him in our hearts."

The Hindu-Moslem unity for which Gandhi risked his life did not materialize. Although his fast received enormous publicity and stirred wide sympathy, it had no practical result. Gandhi described India as "disrupted and demoralized" and he decided that only silence, "the true language of cosmic adoration," would meet the situation. During the year 1926 Gandhi therefore kept silent every Monday, remaining as active as ever the rest of the week. From the British he received an unexpected and unintended boost, for 1926 was the year they brought Gandhi and the Congress Party's cause back to life by following up the stabilization of their own currency with the stabilization of India's as well. By raising the value of the rupee from one shilling and four-pence to one shilling and six-pence—an increase of 12½ per cent—they made it easier for foreign goods to enter the Indian market and harder for Indians to sell their goods abroad. The Congress Party denounced the stabilization of the rupee as "the death warrant of millions of Indian farmers." The rich native merchants and the still richer native industrialists also felt the pinch. Thanks to Great Britain, the Congress Party now widened its base from the classes to the masses.

Stanley Baldwin's Conservative government recognized the need for repairing the damage it had done and approached the whole question from both sides of the road as well as down the middle. To appease Indian opinion, Baldwin appointed as Viceroy his saintly friend Lord Irwin, who was later to have another try at appeasement under the name of Lord Halifax. To satisfy his fellow Tories, Baldwin installed the arrogant and cynical Lord Birkenhead as Secretary of State for India, and Birkenhead, in his turn, made a gesture toward the Liberals by naming one of their most distinguished leaders, Sir John Simon, head of a commission of seven British Members of Parliament to draw up a report on India. Baldwin felt that he had proved his good will by placing the future of India in the hands of three such eminent Englishmen. He could not understand why the Indians felt that they deserved some representation, too.

Few Indians objected to the selection of Lord Irwin as Viceroy. He came of an aristocratic and deeply religious family. His father had held conversations at Malines with Cardinal Mercier of Belgium, looking to a possible reconciliation between the Church of England and the Church of Rome. They had reached no agreement, but Irwin—like his father— went in for all the ritual and discipline of the High Church Anglo-Catholic. Arriving in India on a Good Friday, Irwin made an unforgettable impression on both Hindus and Moslems by spending most of the day at religious services. Never before had Indians seen an Englishman of high station follow so strict a religious code. And they soon found that the new Viceroy's religion came from the depths of his character and made itself felt in all aspects of his public and private life. Perhaps a withered left arm, which had not prevented him from becoming a master of fox-hounds, contributed to Lord Irwin's humility. In any case, Baldwin had sent to India, "accidentally on purpose," the one man in British public life capable of meeting Gandhi on the same spiritual ground.

The arrogance of Lord Birkenhead, however, more than canceled off the humility of Lord Irwin. "Humility," wrote Birkenhead's admiring biographer, C. E. Bechhofer Roberts, "is not one of his faults, and he has been heard half seriously to marvel that any man could be so perpetually and consistently in the right about everything." Birkenhead had started life as F. E. Smith, son of a lawyer in the town the name of which he later made his title. Winning a scholarship at Oxford, he proved such a brilliant student that he at first chose an academic career. But ambition soon got the better of him. Abandoning teaching for politics and the law, he became one of the greatest courtroom advocates of his time and a Conservative member of Lloyd George's coalition Cabinet. After the war, Lloyd George appointed him Lord Chancellor and he entered the House of Lords as Lord Birkenhead. Like Austen Chamberlain and Winston Churchill, Birkenhead refused to join the revolt against Lloyd George in 1922, but in 1924 he returned to office as Secretary of State for India in the Baldwin Cabinet.

Birkenhead once said of his good friend Winston Churchill: "He is easily satisfied with the best of everything." The remark also fitted the man who made it, and his resemblance to Churchill did not stop there. Both men had proved themselves successful writers and effective debaters. Both had trained themselves to several different professions. Both possessed exceptional reserves of energy. Churchill had written biographies, histories, and an early novel. He had also mastered bricklaying and landscape painting on the side. But Churchill, the aristocratic amateur, could always count on instinct and influence. Birkenhead, the professional bounder, had to depend on ability and industry alone, and when wealth and success came to him in his middle thirties, they went to his head. He loved to get himself up in his robes of office; he prided himself on his sleek, dark hair, large, dark eyes, and smooth, pale skin. His indrawn lower lip accentuated the perpetual sneer in which his mouth had set, and he took the superiority of the Anglo-Saxon race as much for granted as Hitler took the superiority of the Teutonic. But Birkenhead never stooped to Hitler's brutal methods. Of course, he could not permit any Indian leaders to serve on the Simon Commission, but he proved his good faith by naming Sir John Simon, the outstanding Liberal lawyer of the day, as its chairman and including, among its members, Major Clement Attlee of the Labor Party, who had engaged in social work before the war and had served with distinction in France.

Birkenhead's attempt to exploit the moderation of Sir John Simon backfired. The Congress Party had no objection to Sir John personally or to his position as commission chairman. But the exclusion of any Indian from any position of responsibility rankled—as Birkenhead knew it would—for Indian sensitiveness more than matched his arrogance. The Congress Party boycotted the Simon Commission, whose members on their two trips to India were greeted everywhere by crowds bearing placards that read "Go Back, Simon." While the Simon Commission gathered what information it could, Gandhi preached the program that he had persuaded the Congress Party to accept. Even in country districts crowds of one and two hundred thousand people gathered to see and hear the Mahatma; more often than not they only saw him. When he faced a crowd so large that many of those present could not hear him, he did not try to speak but merely sat in silence and the crowd found inspiration in his physical presence. When he did speak he would take one hand by the other at its wrist and compare its five fingers to the five points in the Congress program—1. Hindu-Moslem unity. 2. The removal of untouchability. 3. Equal rights for women. 4. Prohibition of the drug and liquor traffic. 5. Spinning thread and weaving cloth at home. After explaining each of these five points in simple speech, Gandhi likened his wrist to the trunk of a tree which represented Ahimsa, or nonviolence, the spiritual force binding the separate parts of the program together. In short, Gandhi brought to the common people of India— especially to the Hindus—the essence of a religion which had never spread far beyond the priestly caste. And there was nothing in Hinduism as he taught it that Moslems could not accept, since Gandhi's Hinduism tolerated and even embraced all other faiths.

· IV ·

IF THE Tories' sponsorship of the Simon Report confounded the Indian Nationalists, the victory of the British Laborites in the general election of 1929 confounded the Tories. Whereas most Tories planned to use the Simon Report to justify the continuation of British rule in India, most Laborites hoped to use it to justify concessions to the Indians. Lord Irwin returned to London to consult with the new government and on October 31, 1929, announced that a Round Table Conference of British and Indian delegates would study the Simon Report before it went to Parliament in its final form. The new government, he explained, wanted to "break through the webs of distrust that have lately clogged the relations between India and Great Britain." It had also set India a new goal—

"the attainment of Dominion status." But this did not satisfy Gandhi, who had now adopted the Swaraj point of view and demanded that the Conference commit itself in advance to writing a Constitution that would give India immediate Dominion status, including the right to secede from the Empire. Irwin refused to make any advance commitment and the Congress Party leaders voted to launch a campaign of civil disobedience and nonpayment of taxes in behalf of complete and immediate independence.

On March 2, 1930, Gandhi addressed a letter to Lord Irwin announcing that he would defy the law that forbade any Indian to make salt without paying a tax unless either the Viceroy or the British government promised to grant India Dominion status before the opening of the Round Table Conference. He also announced that the defiance of the salt laws would open a new campaign of nonviolent non-co-operation with the ultimate purpose of gaining India complete independence. "I cannot intentionally hurt anything that lives, much less fellow human beings, even though they may do the greatest wrong to me and mine," Gandhi wrote the Viceroy. "While therefore I hold British rule to be a curse, I do not intend harm to a single Englishman or to any legitimate interest he may have in India." Of nonviolence he wrote: "Many think that nonviolence is not an active force. My experience, limited as it undoubtedly is, shows that nonviolence can be an intensely active force. It is my purpose to set that force in motion against the organized violent force of British rule as well as against the unorganized violent force of the growing party of violence." The Viceroy's private secretary replied to Gandhi's lengthy letter in two sentences: "His Excellency the Viceroy desires me to acknowledge your letter of the second of March. He regrets to learn that you contemplate a course of action which is clearly bound to involve violation of the law and danger to the public peace."

A month later Gandhi carried out his threat. After marching two hundred miles to the Arabian Sea, he and a small band of companions began making salt. Within a week, British soldiers throughout India were using their swagger sticks to flick the white cotton caps from the heads of Gandhi's supporters who were boycotting British goods, refusing to obey British laws, and obstructing traffic by lying down on railroad tracks and public thoroughfares. On May 3, less than a month after the civil disobedience campaign began, the British arrested and imprisoned Gandhi near Bombay.

Shortly afterward, the Laborite journalist H. N. Brailsford described the scene: "A week ago when I landed in India I saw what no one is likely to see again—Bombay obeying two governments. To the British government with all its apparatus of legality and power there still were loyal the European population, the Indian sepoys who wear its uniform, and a few of the merchant princes, and the older generation of the Moslem minority. The rest of Bombay had transferred its loyalty to one of the British government's too numerous prisoners, Mahatma Gandhi." A few months later an English resident of Bombay wrote the Conservative London *Spectator:* "I tell you in all solemnity that Indians are prepared to ruin themselves if necessary, in the same spirit that the Dutch flooded their own land in the fight for freedom. I never realized the Indians were capable of such an effort. Men are not only cheerfully going to prison but are cheerfully allowing their lands to be confiscated in return for nonpayment of taxes. When a country's spirit is like that, how can any real Englishman (who loves his country and thinks what he would do if his own Motherland were in alien hands, however justly it were ruled) help but respect a people who are by nature pacific and nonviolent?"

Rabindranath Tagore, winner of the Nobel Prize for Literature, having turned back his British knighthood and all other British honors and titles after the Amritsar Massacre, warned a *Manchester Guardian* interviewer: "Those who live in England, away from the East, have now got to realize that Europe has completely lost her former moral prestige in Asia. She is no longer regarded as the champion throughout the world of fair dealing and the exponent of high principle, but rather as the upholder of Western race supremacy and the exploiter of those outside her borders. For Europe it is, in fact, a great moral defeat that has happened. Even though Asia is still physically weak and unable to protect herself from aggression where her vital interests are menaced, nevertheless, she can afford to look down on Europe where before she looked up."

The appearance of the Simon Report in May, 1930, confirmed Tagore's strictures. It did not mention Dominion status although the British government as long ago as 1917 had described Dominion status as the "natural issue" and although Irwin had again in 1929 defined Dominion status as Britain's "goal" for India. Yet the Simon Report did contain one eloquent reference to the popular support, at once wide and deep, that the Congress Party attracted: "We should say without hesitation that with all its variations of expression and intensity, the political sentiment which is most widespread among all educated Indians is the expression of a demand for equality with Europeans and a resentment against any suspicion of differential treatment. The attitude the Indian takes upon a given matter is largely governed by considerations of self-respect. It is a great deal more than a personal feeling; it is the claim of the East for due recognition of status."

As if to vindicate this analysis, the first meeting of the Round Table Conference at London in November, 1930, invited no Indian representatives and did not even discuss the Simon Report. But the British government drew the obvious conclusions and turned over a new leaf.

"When Gandhi Comes to Town." Strube, Daily Express, *London*

In February, 1931, Lord Irwin released Gandhi from jail and the two men began a series of talks that led to Gandhi's attendance at a second Round Table Conference in September. The British had acknowledged the power of Gandhi and the importance of the Congress Party. Gandhi, in his turn, agreed to call off the civil disobedience campaign and to bring the Congress Party into negotiations with the British. Irwin promised to let the Indians who dwelt in salt-producing areas make their salt without paying taxes. He also agreed not to prosecute any more nonviolent agitators. The whole performance filled Winston Churchill with repugnance, "to see," as he put it, "Mr. Gandhi, a lawyer, who had become a seditious type of saint well known in the East, striding half-naked up the steps of the Viceregal Palace, while he was organizing a defiant campaign of civil disobedience, to parley on equal terms with the representative of the King-Emperor."

By the time Gandhi arrived in London as the sole delegate from the Congress Party to the second Round Table Conference, Churchill had more urgent worries. Baldwin and MacDonald had omitted him from their national government and were preparing to meet the Indian Nationalists part way. Although Labor, when in opposition, had urged the Tories to make large concessions to India at once, Labor in office had made only slight concessions, and those had come slowly. Most of the Labor leaders and almost all rank-and-file members of the Labor Party opposed the national government, which saw no need to make further concessions to the Indians in such troublesome times. After all, it had dropped Churchill and Birkenhead and had invited Gandhi to London.

The British people greeted Gandhi with a hospitality that accorded with their finest traditions. Nowhere did he receive such ovations as among the unemployed textile workers in those stricken cities on which the Congress Party's boycott of British goods had inflicted such misery. The grandchildren and great-grandchildren of the same British working people who had supported Lincoln and the Union cause in the American Civil War, even at the expense of their jobs, now supported Gandhi and the cause of Indian independence that he symbolized. At the conference table itself, Gandhi contributed little. When he disliked the trend of the discussion, he withdrew into an obstructive "day of silence." All the other delegates assumed that India would become a British Dominion with a British system of parliamentary democracy. Gandhi rejected the limited Dominion status offered by Britain; as spokesman for the Congress Party he called for "complete control over the Army, over the defense forces, and over external affairs." Although he frankly described his program as a "dream" that would take time to come true, he insisted that the control of the Indian Army "in its entirety" must pass into Indian hands: "I have told you that I know the risk that is attendant upon it. That Army will not accept my command. I know that very well. I know that the British Commander-in-Chief will not accept my command; nor would the Sikhs, nor the proud Rajputs—none of them would accept my command. But I expect, even so, to exercise that command with the good will of the British people; that they will be there at the time of transferring the command to teach a new lesson to these very soldiers, and to tell them that they are after all serving their own countrymen."

The Congress Party, according to Gandhi, did not demand complete independence but wanted to become a member of the British Commonwealth of Nations, with the right to withdraw at any time, and with the British also free to terminate the connection at their pleasure: "Time was when I prided myself on being called a British subject. I have ceased for many years to call myself a British subject; I would rather be called a rebel than a subject. But I have aspired—I still aspire—to be a citizen, not in the Empire but in a Commonwealth; in a partnership if possible—if God wills it an indissoluble partnership—but not a partnership superimposed by one nation upon another. Hence you will find that the Congress claims that either party should have the right to sever the connection, to dissolve the partnership."

Differences between the Hindu and Moslem delegates spared the British the embarrassment of having to turn Gandhi down, and the conference broke up on December 1. Gandhi mournfully confessed his own failure to bring the Hindus and Moslems together: "It is with deep sorrow and deeper humiliation that I have to announce utter failure." The British did not share his gloom and announced that they would have to impose their own solution if the Indians could not agree among themselves. Taking heart from the split among the Indians, the national government followed up the failure of the second Round Table Conference by appointing the coldly hostile Lord Willingdon to succeed the warmly human Lord Irwin as Viceroy. Gandhi returned to India to find a "no rent" campaign in progress. He called for a resumption of civil disobedience and Willingdon clapped him into jail. This strengthened the party of violence, against which Gandhi had warned both his own people and the British. The world depression intensified the crisis by curtailing India's export trade and cutting the prices of the raw materials that formed the bulk of those exports. India thus found itself in the same economic squeeze that had led to so much political violence in South America.

Gandhi never paid much attention to economics, but he recognized that India faced new problems that demanded some action on his part. Ignoring, for the moment, his British jailers, he therefore opened a campaign against the Hindu practice of untouchability, and when the British proposed segregating the untouchables in a separate electorate, Gandhi declared a perpetual "fast unto death," refusing to let any substance but water pass his lips. Hindu leaders rushed to his jail in Poona. Rabindranath Tagore knelt in prayer at his bedside. Within a week, the Hindus patched up a compromise, known as the Poona Pact, renouncing untouchability, which the British government accepted "with great satisfaction." In November, 1932, a third Round Table Conference assembled in London, without Gandhi or any Congress Party delegate, and on Christmas Eve completed work on a draft constitution.

Meanwhile the India League, representing British supporters of Indian freedom, sent a small commission of its own to India to make an on-the-spot report. The findings appeared in 1933 in a book entitled *The Condition of India* with a foreword by the League's president, Bertrand Russell. One Englishman, two Englishwomen, and an Indian spent nearly three months traveling all over India, interviewing all kinds of people wherever they went. The peasants, who lived the closest to starvation, interested them most because they comprised more than 80 per cent of the population. "We tested for ourselves," they wrote, "in a number of places the extent to which the villager has appreciated the issues, and understood the causes, in the pursuit of which his property and person is being subjected to losses and risks. In a Madras village, we spent quite a long time in questions and cross-examination of villagers, individually and in a gathering, and in talking with a village official. We found that the economic and social issues were very live ones. We heard about poverty, taxation, foreign exploitation, neglect of education, and all the other factors that are at the back of India's resistance. We found out that the villagers knew what the Congress stood for, and also that they had no illusion about the enormity of the task before the country. They knew it would mean suffering, perhaps for a long time.

"We went on to talk about Swaraj and why they wanted it. We suggested in great detail that their conditions would be better if they had more schools, roads, and other facilities, if their taxes were lightened, and that to win Swaraj was merely a political business. We expected this to go down and to be told that the material improvements we suggested were all that they really wanted. Instead, an old man who was a working agriculturist himself, told us that Swaraj was a matter of self-respect, freedom, and self-power. Also he felt quite sure that without 'self-power' the conditions which we had mentioned would not be obtained."

The authors of *The Condition of India* found no sign of any Hindu-Moslem conflict in any village: "Even in places where one of the communities was in a small minority it exhibited no fear of the majority." In the towns, on the other hand, they found evidences of "acute tension." The facts, as gathered by these British sympathizers with Indian independence, did not clash with the facts as presented in the more massive and dispassionate Simon Report. But the authors of the Simon Report received little co-operation from the Indian people and the same findings could have been compiled from reference books. The authors of *The Condition of India* got their facts and opinions from the people of India, at first hand.

Yet the Indian peasant did not lead quite so hard an existence as the Chinese. His country had somewhat better land, a considerably warmer climate, and much less savage rivers. Both, however, lived always on the edge of starvation and both went into debt to the village moneylender, who sometimes charged interest rates as high as 100 per cent a year. Before the British came to India, most villages managed their own affairs; afterward, the head man in the village no longer led his people but merely collected taxes for the British who appointed him to his job. These tax collectors gathered the equivalent of almost 150 million dollars a year from the Indian peasantry, or one fifth of India's total tax revenue. The landlords passed on their burden to the tenants. But more than taxes, primitive, inefficient farming methods accounted for India's misery. Although the Australian farm laborer received twenty times as much pay as the Indian for an hour's work, Australian wheat undersold Indian wheat on India's own market. And one American farmer, equipped with modern machinery, could do the work of forty-five Indian peasants. Few of these peasants could afford to let their children attend school for more than two or three years. Many of their children did not get any education at all.

In 1935 India finally received a new constitution, based on the work of the third Round Table Conference which assembled in London in 1932. Churchill fought it because it gave India too much self-government; Gandhi attacked it because it did not give enough. The dyarchy, or division of authority, continued. A British Viceroy, appointed by the British Crown, remained in charge of defense, foreign affairs, and finances. Provincial legislatures, some of them elected by popular vote, others appointed by native Princes, controlled domestic affairs and had some representation in a federal legislature from which the Viceroy selected an advisory Council of Ministers. Burma—which the French had always called *L'Indo-Chine anglaise*—was separated from India and received a similar constitution of its own.

India's revolution and the revolutions in South America had followed quite different courses. The South American republics had resorted to the violence that usually goes with revolution, but the new governments that came to power did not tamper with the existing social order. In India, the Congress Party attempted something new—revolution by nonviolence—and the British met these tactics halfway by offering compromises. But the new constitution that the British granted marked the beginning of a new era in India. The Congress Party had proved its ability to gain real concessions. It now had the opportunity to show its popular strength in local elections and to assume new responsibilities in local government. And Indians of all parties found new opportunities at almost every level of public life as the British relinquished more and more authority. The course that India's national revolution followed during the difficult depression years reflected equal credit upon the Indian and the British leaders chiefly concerned. Bloodshed accompanied most of the great changes that had shaken the world during the first three decades of the twentieth century. India stood out as the great exception—all the more striking because of the events that took place in two other revolutionary areas during these same depression years.

· V ·

THE world depression produced opposite reactions in Britain and Japan and different results in India and China. Chastened by hardship and fearful of more hardships to come, the British leaders made concessions to India. The leaders of Japan, on the other hand, released their frustrated energies attacking China. And while Gandhi tried to promote national revolution in India by nonviolent opposition to British rule,

Chiang Kai-shek tried to put the brakes on the Chinese Revolution. Chiang fought native Communists harder than he fought native war lords and offered no opposition when Japanese troops attacked Manchuria in 1931. In the Anglo-Indian conflict, the initiative lay with Gandhi and the Congress Party. In the struggle between Japan and China, the initiative lay with the Japanese militarists.

In spite of their deepening distress, the British still had some accumulated fat on which to draw. They had also remained true to their traditional belief in peaceful compromise and evolutionary change. The Japanese had no accumulated fat, and their ancient tradition of the sword inspired them in the twentieth century to seek frequent recourse to the machine gun. Their victory over Russia in 1905 proved the efficacy of force. They also recalled that they had imposed their Twenty-One Demands upon China as long as the other major Powers were busy fighting one another in Europe. When peace came it was a different story. The authors of the Versailles Treaty denied Japanese claims to racial equality, even on paper, and at the Washington Conference the invincible Europeans and Americans formed a solid front behind the powerless Chinese and forced Japan to promise to quit Shantung. It had become more apparent than ever that force and force alone ruled the world.

Yet doubts persisted. The national policy of the United States lacked both logic and consistency. The abrupt and total exclusion of Japanese immigrants led Dr. Inazo Nitobe, an internationally renowned scholar, to comment: "Japan felt as if her best friend had, of a sudden and without provocation, slapped her on the cheek. Each year that passes without amendment or abrogation of the law only strengthens and sharpens our sense of injury which is destined to show itself, in one form or another, in personal and public intercourse." Nitobe spoke for a minority of Japanese intellectuals who took the loftiest expressions of American idealism at face value. The more practical politicians were content to use the exclusion issue merely as a bargaining point. But neither the intellectuals nor the politicians could understand it when the Americans, who had snubbed Japan on the matter of exclusion, contributed so generously to the relief and reconstruction of Tokyo after the 1923 earthquake had cost 160,000 lives and two and a half billion dollars in property damage. If you hate and fear a man, you do not help him when he is down, you hit him.

Japanese official behavior appeared just as unaccountable in foreign eyes. The same militarists who had backed the Twenty-One Demands on China considered themselves mortally offended when the Chinese refused to let them exploit the country for its own good. And this perplexity turned to rage in 1928 when the Chinese retaliated against the special privileges Japan still enjoyed in certain parts of China by proclaiming a boycott of Japanese goods that cut down Japanese exports to China by as much as 90 per cent. As the Japanese saw it, they had to export or die. Their archipelago covered only half of 1 per cent of the earth's surface, yet 5 per cent of the earth's inhabitants lived there. With 85 per cent of their islands too barren to yield any crops, the Japanese had to make their country the manufacturing center of the Far East and live by trading factory products for food and raw materials.

By 1930 the population of Japan was increasing at the rate of a million a year. The countries to which the Japanese wanted to emigrate would not let them in, and the Japanese people would not leave their homeland to settle in nearby Manchuria, which had absorbed two million Chinese between 1927 and 1929. And more Koreans moved to Japan than Japanese moved to Korea. In Manchuria, the Japanese could not compete against the more rugged Chinese. Korea presented fewer opportunities than Manchuria. It had less natural wealth and more people, per square mile, trying to make a living. But Korea, once known as the Hermit Kingdom, did not have to trade in order to live. Neither did Manchuria, or China proper. Japan, with its crowded cities, tiny farms, and growing population, had to find space in the sun. The only question was whether to seek that space with the weapons of peace or the weapons of war. The Mitsui network of holding companies and the conservative Seiyukai Party that it controlled favored a warlike policy. The Mitsubishi network of holding companies and the liberal Minseito Party that it controlled favored a peaceful policy.

In a book entitled *Survey of Crimes Committed by Political Parties,* the Japanese economist T. Tachibana drew a distinction between Mitsubishi and Mitsui and hence between the Minseito and the Seiyukai Parties: "Mitsubishi is more engaged in financial operations and heavy industry than in commercial deals. It controls only a few commercial firms whereas it directs a decidedly larger number of banking institutions and insurance companies. Consequently Mitsubishi always covets a financial policy that affords more protection to the financial capitalist than to the industrial capitalist. But this partiality to the financial capitalist is unwelcome or even detrimental to the interest of Mitsui, which has its predominant concern in commercial enterprise and controls a very large number of major and minor industries of various kinds. It is for this reason that Mitsui favors more intense protection of home industry and that the Seiyukai Party promotes tariff policies that directly or indirectly benefit domestic production." In foreign affairs, Mitsubishi and the Minseito Party favored the peaceful penetration of Asia and sought the aid of foreign capital to develop Manchuria. Mitsui and the Seiyukai Party preferred the "positive policy" of Baron Tanaka, who, in 1927, allegedly submitted to the Emperor a famous memorandum that bore his name. "The way to gain actual rights in Manchuria and Mongolia," it read, "is to use the region as a base and under the pretense of trade and commerce penetrate the rest of China. Armed by the rights already secured, we shall seize the resources all over the country. Having China's entire resources at our disposal, we shall proceed to conquer India, the Archipelago, Asia Minor, Central Asia, and even Europe."

Baron Tanaka served as Prime Minister in 1927 and 1928. He had to step down in 1929 when the Minseito Party, which had governed Japan during most of the 1920's, again won control of Parliament and installed in Tanaka's place Yuko Hamaguchi, whose courage had earned him the nickname of "The Lion." Minseito leaders had negotiated the Washington Naval Treaty of 1922. They had kept hands off China in 1926 when British and American warships bombarded Nationalist troops in Nanking. And in 1930 Hamaguchi overruled the admirals representing Japan at the London Naval Conference and agreed to limit new naval construction. Several months later, as soon as the treaty went into effect, a fanatical young assassin shot Hamaguchi dead.

The death of Hamaguchi hastened the inevitable. Between 1929 and 1930 the world depression had cut Japan's export trade by almost one third. Two fifths of this trade consisted of silk, and 90 per cent of Japan's silk went to the United States. Unofficial estimates of unemployment in Japan ran as high as one quarter of all industrial workers. In *Japan Over Asia* William Henry Chamberlin summarized a conversation he had with a young Japanese weaver during the early 1930's: "He started work at six-thirty in the morning and continued until eight or nine at night, with intervals totaling about two hours for meals. He received two holidays a month and once every five days he could stop work after seven. On the other hand, he was obliged to remain at his loom until eleven-thirty at night in the busy seasons. His earnings varied with the orders he received but averaged from 28 to 45 yen a month [about fifteen to twenty-five dollars]. Like most of the weavers I saw at work in Kyoto, this young man was unnaturally sallow. It is not surprising that ill health is common among these handicraft workers, in view of the long hours of indoor work, the darkness of the sheds and rooms where most of the work is done, and the dampness which is a natural accompaniment of the process."

Nothing in their past history or present condition led the Japanese people to expect anything different. In Japan, as in all other Asiatic countries, the masses had always lived close to starvation, but the Japanese had never accepted their fate so stoically as the Chinese or so passively as the Indians. The warrior had always occupied a more honored place in Japan than in China or India, and the strenuous life remained the national ideal. Japanese of all classes found it difficult to take the depression lying down. Since their islands could not produce all the foodstuffs and raw materials they needed, they went down to the sea in ships, creating the greatest fishing industry in the world and building a merchant marine that threatened to monopolize the carrying trade of the Far East. But the white peoples from whom the Japanese had learned so much raised tariff barriers against Japanese goods and excluded all immigration from Japan.

The depression aggravated these grievances. The Japanese, with fewer resources than India and a much smaller population than either India or China, had nevertheless made themselves the mightiest of the Asiatic Powers. Yet the Anglo-Americans continued to patronize progressive Japan while making concessions to revolutionary China. The Anglo-Americans not only continued to discriminate against Japan; they would not let orderly Japan put disorderly China in its place. Bitterness against the white man increased; so did Japanese fears of Russian Communists, who had played so large and dangerous a part in the Chinese Revolution. But Japan did not dare turn openly against Britain or the United States, nor did an attack on Soviet Russia seem likely to be worth the cost. China offered the obvious target for Japan's pent-up aggressive impulses. If Japan's diplomats, soldiers, and businessmen could plan a co-ordinated offensive in that quarter, the Anglo-Americans might finally see the light.

Meanwhile dangerous symptoms of unrest appeared inside Japan. The threat did not come from the sweated proletariat but from the unemployed students, who showed themselves alarmingly receptive to dangerous ideas. Henry Hellsen, a German visitor to Japan in the spring of 1930, reported in the columns of the radical *Weltbühne:* "The fear of dangerous ideas hangs over Japan like a surplice. Out of politeness to Russia nothing is ever said against Bolshevism, just as one never mentions the murder of Chang Tso-lin, which is merely referred to as 'a certain serious episode in Manchuria.' The Japanese love this kind of circumlocution, yet they have reason to fear Bolshevism for Karl Marx has more readers in Japan than in any other country except Russia. Up to a few years ago, about sixty per cent of all university graduates could get good jobs immediately, but now barely twenty per cent can count on finding work. The result is a steadily growing academic proletariat, and as hunger and undigested learning form a chemical mixture in certain hotheads, explosions inevitably follow." The report concluded: "The country seems to have no soul. Everything is nervous, forced, exaggerated. Harmony is lacking. Neither Marxian theories nor exaggerated selfishness and hysterical patriotism indicate a steady pulse. Japan has fever. Its temperature is running high."

A French visitor, A. Féral, writing for the Roman Catholic *Corre-*

spondant of Paris, interpreted the same symptoms differently: "Mystic patriotism is one of the most exalted characteristics of the Japanese soul. It unites the dead and the living in an unbroken chain, each link of which is closely and indissolubly knit with the preceding and following link. The Japanese carries his patriotism within him like an impenetrable shield that we see him raise against every enemy of his country's grandeur, and in its shelter he often accepts the strangest traditional survivals in relation to his individual life as a citizen. Wherever he may be, he carries with him his family altar. He reserves for himself a certain hour and a certain corner in which he can always become himself again and remain in communion with the customs and ideals of his country."

The same observer summed up the Japanese character: "A religious patriotism based on a cult of heroes and ancestors who protect the family and the nation; a sentiment of honor carried to the extreme. Together with this primordial virtue, a profound comprehension of nature, joined to a keen artistic sense that manipulates even the laws of nature to create an imaginary countryside; a highly refined politeness in dealing with other nations; a spirit of adaptation unique in all the world; a marvelous diplomatic suppleness that never forgets the end in view."

Yet the younger generation had begun to turn against its parents. In 1931 a girls' high school in Tokyo asked the members of its graduating class: "Have you anything against your family? Do you wish that your mother behaved differently? Can you make any suggestions as to how your family life might be made happier?" One girl wrote: "I feel alone because Father is so much bound up in business that he has no time to give me and no interest in what I am doing." Many young people in Europe and the United States had talked that way before the depression, but nothing like this had ever been heard before in Japan, where the younger generation had always accepted the authority of the parents and where the mother always bowed down to the father. "Mother obeys Father too much," another young girl complained. "She does not understand me, and all that she knows about my life is what she sees before her eyes. She does not know the new ideas and purposes our school has awakened and established within us, or else she refuses to accept them because they do not coincide with her inherited ideals." Still another made this familiar point: "Parents should give us more freedom in our relations with young people."

Yet, in spite of these outbursts, tradition ran stronger than revolt in all classes. Every elementary school still had to rise in a body, stand at attention, and read with downcast eyes the Imperial Rescript on Education proclaimed by the Emperor Meiji. Two sentences summed up the essence of the official Japanese creed: "Ye, our subjects, be filial to your parents, affectionate to your brothers and sisters, be harmonious as husbands and wives and true as friends; bear yourselves in modesty and moderation; extend your benevolence to all; pursue learning and cultivate the arts and thereby develop intellectual faculties and perfect moral powers; furthermore advance public good and promote common interests, always respect the Constitution and obey the law. Should emergency arise, offer yourselves courageous to the State, and thus guard and maintain the prosperity of our Imperial Throne, coeval with Heaven and earth."

The rulers of Japan did not regard this oath as a form of spiritual opium, administered from on high to the lower orders. Every member of the Mitsui family, on coming of age, had to take a similar, more ancient vow that his ancestors had repeated for three centuries: "In obedience to the precepts of our forefathers and in order to strengthen the everlasting ancestral foundation of the families of our House and to expand the enterprises bequeathed by our forefathers, I solemnly vow in the presence of the August Spirits of our ancestors that, as a member of the House of Mitsui, I will observe and follow the regulations handed down in the Constitution of our House, and that I will not wantonly seek to alter them. In witness whereof I take the oath and affix my signature thereto in the presence of the August Spirits of our ancestors."

· VI ·

By 1931, the condition of Japan and the condition of the surrounding world gave the House of Mitsui its great opportunity. The depression cost the Minseito Party much of its popular support, as the opposition could now make out a strong case against the moderate policies that the country had followed during most of the 1920's. Reliance on foreign trade and international co-operation had ended in a world crash. How much better off Japan would have been if it had taken the advice of the Seiyukai leaders and done more to develop its own economic and military power. Surely it had at last become clear that the Chinese Revolution, in seeking to make China free and independent, threatened Japan's vital interests. During the 1920's China's textile mills and factories had more than doubled, and by 1927 Chiang Kai-shek looked as if he might, in another ten or fifteen years, unite the country. His two brothers-in-law, Dr. H. H. Kung and T. V. Soong, had excellent contacts in the United States. Nationalist China did not need Japan to act as intermediary with the West.

The Japanese Army which patrolled the tracks of the South Manchurian Railway went into action. In 1928 the Manchurian war lord, Marshal Chang Tso-lin, met his death when a bomb, presumably of Japanese origin, blew up his railway car while it was crossing a Japanese-patrolled bridge. His son, Chang Hsueh-liang, a profligate dope addict, chagrined the Japanese by coming to terms with the Chinese Nationalists and delighted Chiang Kai-shek by waging an undeclared war with Russia over the Chinese Eastern Railway. Chiang knew his Russians and thoroughly disliked them. The six months he had spent in Moscow during the early 1920's had given him a chance to learn the methods that he later turned against them before they could use them against him. But he feared the native Chinese Communists even more than he feared the Russian brand and regarded them as his chief enemies. "The Japanese are a disease of the skin," he once declared, "the Communists are a disease of the heart." But the Communists were not the only Chinese who rejected Chiang's leadership. In 1930 his authority did not extend over more than six of China's eighteen provinces. A rival faction in the Kuomintang, calling itself the South West Political Council, set up a separate government in Canton and local war lords controlled most of the interior.

In China as in India the peasants and workers lived so close to starvation that they saw little difference between prosperity and depression even in the best of times. One flood on the Yellow River in 1931 took 140,000 lives—almost as many as the Tokyo earthquake. "Millions have died of hunger in recent years," wrote Dr. L. von Ungern-Sternberg, Far Eastern correspondent of the *Berliner Tageblatt* in 1930. "Thousands of little girls have been sold for prices ranging between one and fifteen dollars in American money. Cannibalism presents a temptation that these famished people are not always able to resist." But a rising middle class demanded some taste of the better things of life: "The people want all kinds of novelties that a few dollars can buy and, in consequence, the traditional Chinese attitude of resignation no longer remains possible. For poverty and privation are no longer endured as they used to be. China's increasing consciousness of her misery has brought unexpected results and all the social structure of the country has changed. The big family is breaking up, for the father or son of the family can no longer support a great number of relatives, and hence they must depart to places where employment can be found. This change is not due to a new philosophy of life; it is the result of rising prices and the desire for new goods and new experiences, and particularly an eagerness for novelty which has become an outstanding phenomenon of modern China. And with the disappearance of the big family has come the end of the support it could lend to its members; there is nobody to help the unemployed during hard times."

China's growing pains plus the impact of the world slump on Japan led to the most serious act of aggression since German armies invaded Belgium. On September 15, 1931, a threatened mutiny on the British

© LOW, ALL COUNTRIES

"Uneasy Street." Cartoon by David Low

fleet led to a cancellation of the annual naval maneuvers. Five days later, perhaps by chance, perhaps by design, Japanese troops invaded Manchuria and routed a group of Chinese bandits who had blown up a stretch of railway track a few miles north of Mukden. More Japanese troops occupied the center of the city and took over the arsenal of young Chang Hsueh-liang. Within another three days, still more Japanese troops had seized all the key centers in south Manchuria and shifted their headquarters from Port Arthur to Mukden. Subsequent investigation showed that the length of the destroyed track measured thirty-one inches.

The whole affair caught Baron Shidehara's moderate government in Tokyo by surprise. The Japanese Foreign Office had just promised peace in Manchuria, but Shidehara had no authority over General Honjo, the commander in Manchuria, who committed an act of war on his own responsibility. "In order to be able to prevent the advance of American influence in the Orient," Honjo wrote to the War Ministry, "we must first consolidate our national defenses on land and attain a position of independence as far as material supplies are concerned. Therefore, before declaring war upon America we must strive to gain a superior position for our military strength in both China and Russia. We must aim to cripple China and Russia once and for all. . . . We should then be the sole master of the Pacific and nobody would be in a position to compete with us or make a protest." Knowing that the "Young Marshal," Chang Hsueh-liang, could not offer any real resistance, the Chinese national government protested to the League of Nations in the name of the Covenant and to the United States in the name of the Kellogg Pact. The League requested both parties to withdraw their troops and then resort to arbitration. Secretary Stimson reminded both Japan and China of their obligations under the Kellogg Pact and authorized Prentiss Gilbert, United States Consul General at Geneva, to attend the October meetings of the League Council as an unofficial observer.

The Japanese Army disregarded all these moves. Helpless Prime Minister Shidehara declared it was "of the utmost importance for us to concentrate our attention and energy on the promotion of foreign trade without unjust infringement upon the interests of any other nation." But the Japanese had tried that formula throughout the 1920's only to find themselves helpless and friendless when the world depression arrived. In the middle of December, the Shidehara Cabinet resigned. Within another three weeks, Japanese troops had occupied all of Manchuria. In February, the general election in Japan gave the Seiyukai Party a better than two-to-one majority in Parliament; in March, Japan announced the creation of the new State of Manchu, or Manchukuo, with young Henry Pu-yi, the last ruler of the Manchu dynasty, as Emperor.

Protests from abroad had no effect. In January Secretary Stimson proclaimed a doctrine that soon bore his name. The United States, Stimson told the world, would refuse to recognize "any situation, treaty, or agreement" brought about in violation of the Kellogg Pact. Sir John Simon, Liberal Foreign Secretary in MacDonald's national government, refused to make a parallel declaration, but in March he urged the League Assembly to apply the Stimson Doctrine to all future disputes. Britain's Tory die-hards took a different view, which the editor of the Conservative *Saturday Review* summarized: "Japan, not the United States, represents stability in the Far East, and it is natural to British interests to support the stable factor. Whatever may be the pros and cons of the rupture of the old Anglo-Japanese alliance, I hope that in the future Great Britain and Japan are going to work more harmoniously together than has been the case since the War. Japan was deliberately sacrificed on the altar of Anglo-American friendship, but the policy of playing second fiddle to the United States has not done this country much good anywhere."

George Bronson Rea, an American journalist whom the Japanese appointed as adviser to the Manchukuo government, agreed with the editor of the *Saturday Review*. When the League of Nations appointed an international commission, headed by Lord Lytton, a former Viceroy of India, to investigate and report on Manchuria, Mr. Rea let out a blast against the Chinese Nationalist government: "If the League Covenant is

UNITED PRESS PHOTO

Japanese Troops and Chinese Bandit Prisoners

interpreted as conceding to this group of irreconcilable warring factions the dignity of a self-governing state with the right to sit on the League Council and a vote in its deliberations; if the Nine-Power Treaty is to continue to recognize this saturnalia of lawlessness and ineptitude as something sacred that must not be interfered with; if, in other words, the war lords of China are to be permitted all the time necessary to fight out their differences and unify their rule of the sword (a policy that the American government declares it is prepared to uphold) while Japan is dragged down to economic ruin and exposed to certain attack through the inability of China to discharge her rudimentary obligations as a sovereign state, then the issue cannot be side-stepped. Treaties or no treaties, Japan will have to fight for her right to exist."

Other observers took a more friendly view of the Chinese. O. D. Rasmussen, a journalist with long experience in the Far East, told British radio listeners, via the B.B.C.: "As for bandits, I am afraid the term has been used rather loosely. A so-called 'bandit' might have been a farmer yesterday and a soldier the day before. The world has too many fixed ideas. It pays too much attention to war lords and bandits and not enough to the pluck and decency of the millions. One can marvel not at what the Chinese have not done, but that they have carried on despite drawbacks and done so much." The average Chinese soldier, reported Mr. Rasmussen, "looks sixteen but is probably nineteen. His uniform, faded blue homespun, sometimes khaki, is ragged and patchy. He has a peaked cap on. In Manchuria he would probably wear a fur-lined hat, the big ear-flaps sticking out like horns. His trousers are tucked inside his socks; garters, if he has any, being on the outside. His cartridge belt is also made of cloth, for leather costs too much. He is holding a long Chinese-made Mauser rifle with a long, thin bayonet affixed. The outside of the barrel is often brightly polished. If he is lucky his shoes are of leather; if not, they are made of cloth, or, in wet weather, of stiff rawhide with big hobnails. On his breast pocket is a dirty white tag covered with Chinese writing, giving his name, regiment and so forth. If he smiles, as he usually does, he reveals clean white teeth just as brightly polished as his rifle barrel."

In Manchuria, this soldier offered no real resistance to the Japanese: "The soldier feels it is his prime duty to scare his enemies away and fight them only in the last resort. He likes big guns for their big noise. Even the war lords used to brag and threaten one another by telegram." But in January, 1932, when the Japanese followed up their conquest of Manchuria with a bombardment of Chapei, the native quarter of Shanghai, they met with a different reception. The Chinese students called for an intensified boycott that cut Japanese exports to China 94 per cent, and when a Shanghai mob attacked five Japanese monks and killed one of them, a Japanese flotilla opened a bombardment of the Chinese quarter of the city. Japanese marines landed, but they found themselves faced with the Chinese Nineteenth Route Army, which took its orders from the

UNITED PRESS PHOTO

Chinese Traitor Confesses He Set Fires at Japanese Orders

Left Kuomintang government at Canton, not the Nationalists at Nan-king. A five-week battle began, costing twenty-three thousand lives, twenty thousand of them Chinese. But the Japanese finally had to with-draw.

A Chinese machine-gunner whom American correspondents nick-named Charlie Chan offered a description of the struggle in the *China Weekly Review:* "Our Big Sword Corps came. They were detailed to the front by headquarters on hearing that a hand-to-hand fight was in progress. I must explain about our Big Sword Corps because it is not found in the modern army. It is a medieval force employing primitive swords such as you find in Roman history. Stripped to the waist, bare-footed, these naked envoys of death swear never to return whenever they are sent forth. Armed with a huge sword, a pistol, and many hand grenades that hang around his waist, the Big Sword is a combination of the modern and the primitive soldier. His face is smeared with black grease, his hair is in disorder, and whenever he kills an enemy he puts the blood on his own face and body. His very sight is fearful even to his own men.

"These Big Swords came. To avoid gunfire they rolled on the ground. They distinguished their enemies by the white leg covers and by the simple method of feeling. They stretched their left hands to feel. When they felt tin caps, woolen uniforms, leather outfits, down went their swords. Sometimes they rolled on the ground to cut the white legs. The Japanese are infinitely well protected compared with the Chinese sol-diers, whose only armor is their love of fatherland."

"Charlie Chan" and the American newspaperman who wrote this de-scription for him drew a bow as long as any Big Sword. But in one respect they could not exaggerate. Never before had Chinese soldiers held their ground against a modern army, and the civilians whose fragile wooden houses went up in flames more than matched their heroism. Chapei belonged among the world's decisive battles because it marked the beginning of a new chapter in China's long history.

The Japanese also celebrated their warriors' feats. For weeks the whole populace sang "The Song of the Human Bombs" which told of three Japanese soldiers who blasted away a stretch of barbed wire by hurling themselves into it with bombs fastened to their bodies. Dozens of Japanese women attempted suicide when their men left for the front. As one of them wrote, before casting herself under the wheels of a troop train: "Though I cannot be a soldier, I can encourage them by dying." In taking her own life she hoped to make her husband more willing to give up his.

Although China's Nineteenth Route Army withdrew from Chapei after five weeks of fighting, the Japanese also pulled their forces out presently. Not only had the Chinese shown unexpected fight. The performance of the Japanese Army made the whole Japanese nation lose face. The Japanese Army, which organized itself along Prussian lines, drafted most of its soldiers from the peasantry. From its general officers down to its rear rank privates, it stood closer to the Japanese people than the smaller, more select Japanese Navy, which depended on volunteer enlistments and drew its inspiration from Britain. But the Japanese Army found itself in such trouble at Chapei that it had to summon the Navy to its aid.

Japan's attempt to drive all other influences, both Chinese and foreign, from the Shanghai area had failed, and the projected drive down the China coast had reached at least a temporary halt. Yet the expansionist pressures inside Japan remained as strong as ever. In spite of their military and political defeat at Shanghai, the Japanese had hung on economically, while conditions in other countries had gone from bad to worse. They had gone off the gold standard in December, 1931, letting the yen drop to one third of its original value, or twice as much as the British devalued the pound. With the value of their currency so drastically cut, Japanese exports increased. The Japanese had also rationalized their industries. They had better looms and textile machinery than the British, and during the depression years cheap Japanese textiles flooded the markets of the Far East.

Japan's economic progress stimulated the arrogance of the militarists. In May, 1932, several members of a secret patriotic society known as the Blood Brotherhood League assassinated Premier Inukai and Baron Dan, head of the house of Mitsui. A moderate faction in the Seiyukai Party, which had recently come to power, therefore got together with the Minseito Party leaders and set up a coalition government headed by Admiral Saito. As a Navy man, Saito deplored the belligerence and extravagance of the Army officers who had spent the equivalent of sixty-two million dollars on maneuvers in Manchuria and had forced two Japanese banks to lend Henry Pu-yi's puppet government two million dollars more. But Saito amounted to little more than a figurehead. The Army continued to dictate foreign policy as domestic affairs faded into the background.

The League of Nations Commission of Inquiry, headed by Lord Lytton, made little impression abroad and less in Japan. It reported in October, 1932, that the Japanese had no justification for their attack on Manchuria the year before. It described Henry Pu-yi's new state of Manchuria as a puppet regime and recommended the establishment of a Chinese government in its place. But Japan had already recognized the independence of Manchukuo and in March, 1933, quit the League of Nations. At the same time, Japanese troops invaded Jehol Province,

UNITED PRESS PHOTO

Buddhist Priests Carry Ashes of Japanese Dead Received in Tokyo
During Manchurian Incident

southwest of Manchuria, and advanced without opposition to the shadow of China's Great Wall.

General Sadao Araki, the Japanese War Minister and leader of the Japanese war party, developed a doctrine known as Kodo, the Way of the Emperor, which carried Shinto, the Way of the Gods, to a worldly conclusion. "It is a veritable measure of Providence," said Araki in March, 1933, "that the Manchurian trouble has arisen. It is an alarm bell for the awakening of the Japanese people. If the nation is rekindled with the same great spirit in which the country was founded, the time will come when all nations of the world will be made to look up to our Kodo. Kodo, the great ideal of the Japanese nation, is of such substance that it should be spread and expanded all over the world, and every impediment to it brushed aside—even by the sword. . . . The countries of the Far East are the objects of pressure on the part of the white races. But awakened Japan can no longer tolerate further tyranny and oppression at their hands. It is the duty of the Emperor's country to oppose, with determination, the actions of any Power, however strong, if they are not in accord with Kodo. Do not worry about deficiency of strength or material; everything depends on spirit."

Most Japanese had so few material possessions that they did not find Araki's appeal to the spirit either sentimental or hypocritical. Rather did it stir their noblest impulses. Kodo promised no rewards to its devotees, either in this world or the next. It summoned them to make every sacrifice for their emperor and their country. In the world of the twentieth century, the Japanese Empire had come rapidly to the top, as new ambitions gave rise to further progress until depression broke the cycle. The Japanese, having few resources on which to draw, sought escape from their troubles at someone else's expense. War offered the way out; China furnished the first victim. Moreover, the depression that caused Japan to turn against China caused other nations, with ampler resources, to turn in upon themselves. Britain, France, and the United States all had too much to do at home to take strong action in the Far East. So did the one European country that had the most to fear from Japan—Soviet Russia. But it was not the world depression that prevented Russia from moving against Japan. It was sheer physical inability to take effective action, aggravated by a domestic crisis that Stalin provoked when he forced the revolution into a new phase.

· VII ·

JAPAN's MILITARY leaders followed a schedule that called, first, for the subjugation of China and then for attack upon the Soviet Union. They looked back with pride on the victories their soldiers and sailors had won against the Russians in 1904 and 1905. They looked back with shame on the peace their diplomats had signed at Portsmouth. But they bided their time. In 1915 they had taken advantage of the war in Europe to present their Twenty-One Demands to China. In 1918 the Siberian Expedition offered the Japanese a brief opportunity to drive Russian influence from East Asia. But as soon as peace returned to Europe their diplomats could not resist Anglo-American pressure and had to sign the Washington treaties of 1922. The doctrine of the Open Door took a new lease on life; the Twenty-One Demands expired; the authority of the Bolsheviks replaced the authority of the Tsar. In 1925 Japan's liberal Minseito government followed the example of the leading European powers and established diplomatic relations with the Soviet Union, where Stalin's doctrine of socialism in one country had displaced Trotsky's doctrine of world revolution.

Having stabilized Russia's relations with the outside world, Stalin proceeded to stabilize his own position at home. Within three years' time, as already indicated, he wiped out all internal opposition, gaining power over the Communist Party, the Soviet government, the armed forces, and the secret police. And with this power in his hands he inaugurated, on October 1, 1928, a revolution hardly less momentous than that of 1917. "We must," said Stalin, "undertake the transformation of the U.S.S.R. from an agrarian and weak country, dependent upon the caprices of capitalist countries, into an industrial and powerful country quite independent of the caprices of world capitalism." Stalin's Five-

Year Plan replaced Lenin's New Economic Policy one year before the Wall Street crash. It called for doubling and trebling the production of coal, steel, oil, machinery, and electrical power. It demanded that at least one fifth of all the peasants in Russia join either state or collective farms.

Industrially, the Five-Year Plan meant that the Soviet Union diverted between one quarter and one third of its national income into building a new industrial plant. And about one third of this new construction went into heavy industry. Stalin named 1929, the year when the Plan first began to take hold, "the year of the great turn," and insisted upon "the liquidation of the kulaks as a class." In Tsarist Russia the word *kulak,* meaning "fist," described the one or two peasants in each community rich enough to lend money. Stalin, however, used the word *kulak* to describe the most successful 4 or 5 per cent of the entire peasantry. It was this group that had benefited most from the New Economic Policy and it was this group that refused to surrender most of its lands, livestock, and equipment to collectives or to state farms.

A period known as "civil war in the villages" followed. Soldiers and secret police deported between two and five million kulaks to Siberia and to forced-labor camps. The poorer peasants rushed to join the collectives. But all peasants—rich and poor—had so little faith in the future that they slaughtered and devoured their livestock. The collective farm program thus caused the liquidation of half the horses, half the cattle, two thirds of the sheep, and 40 per cent of the hogs in the Soviet Union. Grain production dropped from a prewar level of almost a hundred million tons a year to less than 70 millions in 1931. During the winter of 1931-32 an estimated five million people in the rich Ukrainian farming country starved to death. Instead of aiding the peasants in their time of need, the Soviet government sent troops and police into the Ukraine, where they collected the peasants' meager stores of grain by main force.

Both before and after this man-made famine, Maurice Hindus toured his native Russia talking to its people. His book *The Great Offensive,* published in 1933, reported what they told him during this critical period in Stalin's first Five-Year Plan. As a group of Ukrainian peasants were showing Hindus some of their pasture land, one of them spoke: "Now look. You can count the cows out here easily, can't you? That's all there are, I can assure you. But three years ago if you came here, you couldn't count the cows in that pasture, there were so many of them. Everybody had a cow then."

"What can we do?" one of them asked.

"There is nothing to be done, nothing," replied the first. "It is finished. Life is finished for our kind. Maybe our children will enjoy it—maybe. But as for us—goodby."

Some of the younger peasants emigrated to the cities and found jobs in the new factories built under the Five-Year Plan. Others joined the collective farms and gradually improved their condition. "In my judgment," wrote Maurice Hindus, "collectivization has been a most beneficial thing for Russian farming. It eliminates a multitude of crying wastes which are inherent in Russian individualist land-holding—wastes in seed, in labor, in human and animal energy. It wipes out at once the ancient and ruinous division of land into long and narrow strips with their adjacent weed-growing ridges. Under proper management it can at one stroke discard ancient methods of tillage. It can raise fertility of soil to a height unattainable under ordinary Russian conditions."

Most visitors to Russia at this time either damned Stalin and all his works or rhapsodized over the Gosplan's statistical reports. Hindus, one of the few visitors who came from the Russian people and knew their language, was also one of the few who reported both the bad and the good. Meanwhile, Stalin, more than any other man in the Soviet Union, had to appraise the Five-Year Plan's assets and liabilities and decide on a practical course. As early as March, 1930, with the Plan barely one year old, he recognized that he had made a frightful mistake, which he proceeded to correct in characteristic fashion. In an article entitled "Dizziness From Success," he pointed out that the collective farm program had gone forward too rapidly. Instead of collectivizing one fifth of Russian agriculture in five years, it had collectivized three fifths of it in one year. But the process had gone too far to be reversed and the best that Stalin could do was conceal the terrible results. The Soviet government therefore refused to let any foreign relief agencies send food to the famine areas and restricted all foreign correspondents to Moscow. Soviet city dwellers could not travel without obtaining passports from the secret police and could not leave their place of residence for more than twenty-four hours without police permission. Unemployed workers or peasants took the jobs assigned to them or lost their ration cards. Anyone convicted of stealing goods in transit or stealing crops from the fields suffered the death penalty. "Hoover has taught the Americans not to drink," one Russian is said to have told another at this time. "That's nothing," his friend replied, "Stalin has taught the Russians not to eat."

The socialist fatherland could not escape the effects of the crisis of capitalism. During the world depression, food prices dropped further than the prices of manufactured goods. This meant the Russians had to increase their food exports in order to purchase foreign machinery and in order to pay some ten thousand foreign specialists to help put through the Five-Year Plan. "When you miss your eggs and butter," the Moscow radio told its listeners, "you have the satisfaction of knowing that they are being sold abroad to France, Germany, or Great Britain and are returning to our country in the form of nuts and bolts." With the shortage of goods went a 90 per cent inflation of the currency. "We Russians are the richest people on earth," one saying went, "because we do not know what to do with our money." According to another humorist, "Soviet money is the jolliest with which to travel because the foreigner laughs when he sees it." Between 1929 and 1932 wages in Russia increased by two thirds, while prices doubled and trebled. Under the Tsar, eight hundred thousand Russians had jobs in the bureaucracy. This figure had risen to more than seven million by 1922; it dropped to less than four million in 1927. The Five-Year Plan brought it up to more than eight million. This new aristocracy did little productive work and received better housing, food, clothes, and education than the masses. A workman aboard a crowded streetcar is said to have remarked, as he pointed to several bureaucrats riding by in their shiny limousines, "I am the boss. Those people are just my clerks."

No such humor as this ever appeared in the Soviet press. And creative writers found the censorship ever more frustrating. Such poets and novelists as Essenin, Mayakovsky, Kusnietzov, Pyast, and Sobol committed suicide during the late 1920's or early 1930's. One essayist, bolder than most, spoofed the censor by including the following passage in a book entitled *Dialectics of the Myth:* "It is impossible for Communists to love art. Once there is art there is genius. Once there is genius there is inequality. Once there is inequality there is exploitation." But Stalin had the last laugh. When the authorities discovered the censor's oversight they shipped the offending humorist to an island in the Arctic and arrested and exiled his acquaintances who, unhappily, had ignored the six rules drawn up for the Russian intelligentsia under Stalin by a more discreet, anonymous writer: "If you must think, don't talk. If you must talk, don't talk to yourself. If you must talk to yourself, don't talk to others. If you must talk to others, don't write. If you must write, don't print. If you must print, deny it the next day." Then there was the mother of the three professional men who was reported to have said, "I have three sons. One is an agricultural expert. One is an engineer. The third is also in prison."

But none of this unofficial, underground humor surpassed the ludicrous, official glorification of Stalin. "Can anyone write on anything unless he knows his Stalin?" asked the editor of *Izvestia*. "Never. Without Stalin no one can understand anything of interest." Philosophers bracketed Stalin with Aristotle and Plato. Scientists rated him with Newton and Pasteur. Young writers aped his prose style. His name covered the map of Russia in such towns and cities as Stalingrad, Stalino, Stalinabad, Stalinsk, Stalinissi, Stalinir, Stalinogorsk, Stalin-Aoul, and just plain Stalin. It was not vanity; it was cold self-interest that led Stalin to sanction this kind of thing. The former religious pupil, turned atheist, tried to divert to his own person the religious impulses that once led so many Russians to worship God. Stalin's divine attributes did not, however, include the quality of mercy, which he never permitted to stand in the way of his ambition. When Lady Astor on a visit to Moscow in 1931 asked him, "How long will you go on killing people?" Stalin replied, "As long as it is necessary." Evidently he made an even rougher reply to his young second wife, Nadiejda Alliluyeva, when she meekly protested, in November, 1932, against all the starvation. The next morning the Moscow press laconically reported her death by suicide.

A year later, Stalin announced the completion of the Five-Year Plan in four years. His claim that it had come within 93.7 per cent of achieving all its goals hardly "corresponded with the facts"—to use a favorite Soviet expression. But even if the Plan did not achieve more than half its goals, it had made the Soviet Union second only to the United States as an industrial power. Since most of the effort had gone into the development of capital equipment, the standard of living remained pitifully low—lower even than in Tsarist times. Stalin therefore announced a second Five-Year Plan for the production of consumer goods, to begin at once.

Although the Russian people felt the weight of the world depression when they had to increase their food exports in order to buy machinery abroad, the rulers of Russia turned the crisis of capitalism to their advantage. They kept reminding the rest of the world that the socialist fatherland was going from strength to strength at a time when the capitalist world was going from bad to worse. In 1930 the Russians completed an important new railway, the Turksib, that enabled them to tap the wealth of central Asia and extended their influence to the vast Chinese province of Sinkiang. The drive against illiteracy also went well. Within four years, the great majority of the Russian people—especially the younger people—had learned to read and write. Under the Tsars, Russia had 859 newspapers with less than three million readers. Under Stalin, Russia had 9,700 newspapers and 36 million readers. A tighter censorship than any Romanov ever imposed kept the Russian mind unspotted by the capitalist or the Trotskyite world. Communist propaganda permeated every human activity. The organizer of a chess conference in Moscow proclaimed, in the controlled press: "We must finish once and for all with the neutrality of chess. We must condemn once and for all the formula 'chess for the sake of chess' like the formula 'art for art's sake.' We must organize shock brigades of chess players and begin the immediate realization of a Five-Year Plan of chess."

· VIII ·

Nowhere did the promoters of the Five-Year Plan work more effectively than in the schools. In November, 1930, Dr. George S. Counts, professor of education at Teachers College, Columbia University, in New York, came upon a newly published little Russian textbook entitled *The Story of the Great Plan,* written by a Soviet engineer, named M. Ilin, for Russian school children between the ages of twelve and fourteen. "Practically every page," wrote Dr. Counts in his preface to an English translation that was issued in the United States, "carries the mark of genius." He found much to admire in the way Ilin simplified a technical subject. "But perhaps most important of all," Dr. Counts added, "it reveals the temper of the revolutionary movement and the large human goals toward which it is consciously tending."

Although the starving peasants in the Ukraine did not reveal such Olympian optimism, Counts expressed a point of view shared by many young people in the Soviet Union and by still more foreign sympathizers with the "Soviet experiment." The opening pages of *New Russia's Primer,* as the American edition was called, compared the U.S.S.R. with the U.S.A. Ilin credited the United States with superior technique and equipment, but he found Russian socialism more productive and intelligent than American capitalism and expressed his views in free verse:

"We have a plan.
In America they work without a plan.
We have a seeding campaign.
In America they destroy crops.
We increase production.
In America they reduce production and increase unemployment.
We make what is essential.
In America hundreds of factories consume raw materials and
    energy in order to make what is altogether unnecessary."

New Russia's Primer contained pictures of tractors, dams, turbines, factories, lathes, oil wells, bulldozers. The accompanying text explained how some of them worked and how all of them ministered to human needs. Here was all the mystical faith of the young revolutionary who saw in modern machinery the sole instrument for salvation. But that machinery had to be harnessed to the Five-Year Plan of socialism to perform at peak efficiency, and Ilin's closing chapter, "New People," contained an eloquent statement of the higher aspirations of Soviet Communism: "We live badly. We change Nature, but as yet we have not changed our own selves. And this is the most essential thing. Why have we begun all this tremendous work which will last not five, but fifteen, twenty, and perhaps more years? Why do we mine millions of tons of coal and ore? Why do we build millions of machines? Do we do these things merely in order to change Nature?

"No, we change Nature in order that people may live better.

"We need machines in order that we may work less and accomplish more. By the end of the Five-Year Plan, the working day in a factory will be reduced fifty minutes. If we assume that the working year consists of 273 days (not counting rest days and holidays), the worker will labor 227 hours a year less than he did at the beginning of the plan. And 227 hours is almost 73 seven-hour working days.

"He will work less and yet accomplish more. During seven hours in the factory, he will do what now requires eleven and one half hours.

"In comparison with conditions before the Revolution, every worker will labor three hours less a day and yet will receive twice as much pay.

"But this is not all. Life will be made easier. No longer will there be bent backs, strained muscles, inflated veins on the forehead. Loads will travel, not on people's backs, but on conveyors. The heavy crowbar and hoe will give place to the pneumatic hammer and compressed air.

"Instead of dark gloomy shops with dim, yellow lamps there will be light, clean halls with great windows and beautiful tile floors. Not the lungs of men, but powerful ventilators will suck in and swallow the dirt, dust, and shavings of the factories. Workers will be less fatigued after a day's labor. There will be fewer 'occupational' diseases. Think of all the people who perish now from these ailments! Every metal worker has lungs eaten up by metal dust. You can at once recognize a blacksmith by his pale face, a stoker by his red, inflamed eyes.

"After we build socialism all will have healthy faces. Men will cease to regard work as a punishment, a heavy obligation. They will labor easily and cheerfully.

"But if work will be a joy, rest will be a double joy.

"Can one rest now in a crowded and noisy home amid the hissing of oil burners, the smoke of the kitchen, and drying of wet diapers, the filth of dim windows, dirty furniture, spittle covered floors, and unwashed dishes on the table?

"After all, man is not just muscles with which to work. He is not a machine. He has a mind that wants to know, eyes that want to see, ears that want to hear, a voice that wants to sing, feet that want to run and jump and dance, hands that want to row and swim and throw and catch. And we must organize life so that not merely certain lucky ones but all may be able to feel the joy of living.

"After socialism is built, there will no longer be dwarfs—people with exhausted, pale faces, people reared in basements without sunshine or air. Healthy, strong giants, red-cheeked and happy—such will be the new people."

Ilin belonged to the new generation of young Bolsheviks who brought to the Five-Year Plan the same aspirations that the old Bolsheviks brought to the revolution. Stalin exploited these aspirations but did not share them. After smashing the left opposition of Trotsky, Zinoviev, and Kamenev, Stalin smashed the right opposition of Bukharin, Rykov, and Tomsky. At home he moved to the left of the leftists. Abroad he moved to the right of the rightists. It was not that he planned it that way. The collective farm program had gone ahead much faster than he had contemplated—with disastrous, almost fatal, results. The world depression not only upset the calculations of the Five-Year Plan economists. It strengthened the Hitler movement in Germany and speeded the Japanese invasion of Manchuria. Under these conditions, propaganda for the Five-Year Plan became as important as the Plan itself. If the planners could not deliver the promised goods, the propagandists could administer a Soviet brand of opium to the people or a Communist slice of pie in the sky.

Faced with the threat of an aggressive Germany to the west and the reality of an aggressive Japan to the east, Stalin had to seek support from those capitalist countries which also feared Germany and Japan. And he had to seek this support at a time when his internal troubles forced him to order repressions that made Lenin look like a humanitarian by comparison. As President Masaryk of Czechoslovakia once said of Stalin and the men around him, "They have succeeded in suppressing the Tsar but they have not suppressed Tsarism. They still wear the Tsarist uniform, albeit inside out." To Stalin, in the later 1920's, the world revolution appeared a remote and perhaps unattainable goal. To Lenin, just before and just after the Armistice, world revolution seemed to lie just around the corner. To Lenin, the end justified the means. To Stalin, power became an end in itself. Lenin gave more weight to the doctrines of Marx and Engels, who had taught him that the proletarian revolution had to come first in one of the most highly developed bourgeois countries. Indeed, Engels said that anyone who argued that a proletarian revolution was possible in Russia "proves only that he has still to learn the A.B.C. of socialism." Marx expressed the same thing more pithily when he observed, "You cannot socialize poverty."

Lenin, before he died, saw the predictions of Marx and Engels fail to come true in both Germany and Russia. Germany, the most highly industrialized nation in Europe, rejected proletarian revolution whereas in Russia, the most backward of the major European nations, the proletarian revolution triumphed. Stalin inherited this condition and proceeded to develop the theories needed to explain and exploit it. He and the men around him addressed themselves to the purpose of preserving and extending their power, drawing here and there from the writings of Marx and Lenin to build up the new doctrine of Stalinism. The Russian proletariat, small as it might be as compared with the Russian peasantry, nevertheless constituted a mighty force and operated a vast and modern industrial plant. Inasmuch as the proletarian revolution was hanging fire everywhere else, the Russian proletariat and the Russian Communist Party faced the special responsibility of putting it through in a backward country. This entailed the rapid construction of new industries and the rapid industrialization of agriculture. The first Five-Year Plan made measurable progress toward both these goals, but at frightful cost. Whereupon the world depression which afflicted so many backward lands made difficulty for Russia, too.

SUMMING UP

SOUTH AMERICA, India, the Far East, and Russia: the world depression hit each of these regions hard. Many peaceful elections in the United States and Europe had led to greater changes than followed the five South American revolutions of 1930 and 1931. On the other hand, few violent revolutions accomplished so much as Gandhi achieved with his nonviolence campaign in India. The South Americans successfully asserted their independence of North America—and most North Americans applauded. Churchill and the die-hard Tories did not cheer the new Constitution that their country gave to India, but a large Parliamentary majority voted them down. Although India's Congress Party got much less than it wanted, the strength of India was clearly increasing while British power in Asia was entering an absolute as well as a relative decline.

Nationalistic ferment also stirred China and Japan, and there, too, the white man, whether British or non-British, had lost his old assurance. Militaristic Japan attacked Nationalist China before China had a chance to unite. The League of Nations and the United States showed themselves unwilling if not unable to intervene and people warned against a Second World War in the making. The depression began to look like the time when the postwar era ended and the prewar era began. In any case, it seemed unlikely to become that period of general revolution that some people feared and others hoped for. Under Stalin's leadership, the Russians continued to follow the road away from world revolution while building up the kind of heavy industry and large-scale farming that a country at war requires to survive. Depression had wrecked the 1919 settlement. Through peace or war, by revolution or evolution, the world had to seek a new balance of power to replace the lost world of Versailles.

13

Revolt of Europe's Masses

*How the impersonal, economic forces of world
depression brought the mass man to political
power in the heart of stricken Europe.*

B Y THE TIME Britain went off the gold standard in September, 1931,
all hope of restoring the pre-depression world went too. Even
President Hoover had to unbalance the American budget and set up a
federal dole for the benefit of needy corporations. He also made a last
effort to promote prosperity and peace through disarmament after Japan
had opened a localized, undeclared war on China and after the German
Nationalists and Nazis had opened a war of their own on the Weimar
Republic. The rise and triumph of the Nazi movement overshadowed
everything else that happened in Europe during the depression years.
Hitler not only exposed the weakness of all his rivals in Germany; the
example of Germany exposed the weakness of all the rest of Europe.
Ironically enough, the moderate Herriot came to power in France just
as the extremist Papen came to power in Germany. Britain, on the other
hand, had gone more nationalist without, however, borrowing any
Fascist or Nazi methods from abroad. Finally, the most convincing account of what had happened did not come from an economist or a politician. Nor did it come from Germany, France, or England. A Spanish
philosopher drew up a comprehensive indictment of Europe—and himself. His name: Ortega y Gasset; his book: *The Revolt of the Masses.*

· I ·

BY THE end of 1930, the world depression overshadowed the Wall Street
crash as the oak overshadows the acorn from which it springs. And before 1931 had run its course, the world depression had become a crisis of
world capitalism. As soon as the British pound went off the gold standard, the Scandinavian countries and the Dominions followed. By the
end of the year, only the United States, France, Italy, Switzerland,
Holland, and Belgium remained on gold. This put Hoover in strange
company. His British friends had gone off the gold standard which he
tried so hard to save. The French, on the other hand, whom he had an-

tagonized and ignored, now admired the gold standard even more than
he did. During 1930 their gold reserves had doubled and by the fall of
1931 France possessed twice as much gold per capita as the United
States.

Early in October, Lord Reading, Foreign Secretary in Britain's new
national government, went to Paris and proposed a redistribution of
gold. Premier Laval turned him down. Hoover then invited Laval to
Washington and urged him to give German private debts priority over
reparations so that American creditors could get their funds out of
Germany. Laval made no promises, but demanded cancellation of the
French war debt. The French economist Francis Delaisi described the
upshot of Laval's visit: "The development of the world crisis, by suddenly paralyzing the other two powers (England and America), had
placed the French government with its reserves intact at the strategic
point that dominated the field. It could, if it chose, give back monetary
supremacy to England or hand it over to America. It could also, since
Paris could not technically become the clearinghouse of the world, force
the two others to accept the institution of an international market of
exchange by making the Bank for International Settlements the controller
and independent regulator of the exchange market. Unfortunately, the
only point on which the three central banks could agree was precisely
not to create above themselves a superbank that would limit their superiority. M. Laval therefore did nothing. As he had said 'no' to Lord
Reading, he also said 'no' to Mr. Hoover. He returned having given nothing and obtained nothing. He had let the opportunity of France slip
by." Laval did, however, promise that France would stop draining gold
from the United States by converting paper dollars into hard metal, and
Hoover promised to reconsider war debts if Europe would make a new
reparations settlement. Both men agreed to maintain the gold standard,
not because either one felt the slightest regard for the other but because
neither one could think of anything else to do.

André François-Poncet, who became French Ambassador to Berlin
at this time, had many opportunities to study Laval in action. "Within
less than a decade, with ease and dispatch, he had built both his political
and his material fortune," wrote François-Poncet in his memoirs, *The
Fateful Years.* "He believed stoutly in himself and in his genius. He also
felt himself called upon to play a leading role as a French and European
statesman. He dreamed of appearing in Briand's old place as peacemaker
in a troubled and battered universe. At once bolder and more realistic
than Briand he would not rely upon the League of Nations. He was none
too fond of this assembly. He professed that the only prompt and fruitful method lay in direct conversations, in personal relations, man to man.
According to Laval a free exchange of ideas, *en tête à tête*, stripped of

BETTMANN ARCHIVE

Pierre Laval

elaborate terminologies and of such childish timidity as inspires professional diplomacy must surely lead to the solution of the most complex problems. Laval shared the mob's prejudices against diplomats. To be sure he was not hindered by knowledge of these problems or by the slightest inclination to study them carefully. He was smart, though less smart than he supposed and his smartness was vulgar. He was pleased to acknowledge what his countless flatterers and obligees reported daily to him, to wit, that his charm was irresistible."

The sterile meeting between Hoover and Laval left many questions—including this one: Why had Hoover failed to win for the United States the financial leadership that England had just lost and that France could not gain? The answer was that American production had dropped one third since 1929 and American prices had dropped one quarter. Between November, 1930, and August, 1931, 1,430 American banks with assets totaling a billion and a quarter dollars had closed down. At long last, just two years after the Wall Street crash, Hoover threw away the old weapons he had used in his vain fight against the depression and seized a couple of new ones. First, he put the federal government into the business of doling out relief and then he unbalanced the federal budget. On October 6, 1931, he announced the formation of the National Credit Corporation with assets of half a billion dollars to be spent on rediscounting frozen bank assets. In plain English, this meant that the federal government would spend good money of its own buying up depreciated paper from ruined banks. And the money did not come from taxes or current revenue. The government brought it into being by adding to the national debt.

The fact that the money went to the banks and not to the unemployed made no difference in so far as inflation was concerned. The President remained as convinced as ever that prosperity must be restored from the top, not from the bottom. And when the National Credit Corporation exhausted its resources by the end of 1931, Hoover sponsored the new two-billion-dollar Reconstruction Finance Corporation, which continued to try to save the masses by saving the big corporations first. His political enemies accused him of favoring the rich; they ignored the treason he committed to his own creed of "rugged individualism." Nor did his supporters acknowledge, even to themselves, that a Republican President had begun to commit the United States to the principle of a welfare state. Within five months one bank in every seven in the country had received RFC funds; so had innumerable railroads, insurance companies, and other financial institutions.

On one wide front, however, Hoover remained true to his deepest faith. In 1930 the nations of the world were spending more on armaments than they had in 1913. Although prices had dropped since 1925, spendings on armaments had risen one billion dollars. As a Quaker, Hoover wanted disarmament for moral reasons; he also favored it on economic grounds. But once again he tripped over his own feet. On February 2, 1932, delegates from sixty-one nations—including the United States, Germany, and the Soviet Union—assembled at Geneva for their long-prepared Disarmament Conference. The presiding officer, Arthur Henderson, had held the post of Foreign Minister in the British Labor government until the Tory sweep in the October elections robbed him even of his seat in the House of Commons. The Japanese added to the unreality of the whole affair. On January 28, five days before the Conference opened, Japanese troops began bombarding the native quarter of Shanghai. On January 30, the Japanese War Office announced that no action by the League of Nations could alter its policy and warned that meddling by the League could provoke a "world conflagration." Sir John Simon, Foreign Secretary in Britain's new national government, had already rebuffed Secretary Stimson when the latter called for collective economic action against Japan. As a good Republican, Stimson remained true to the "Large Policy" laid down at the turn of the century by Lodge, Roosevelt, and Beveridge and did his best to shake a modern version of T.R.'s "Big Stick" at Japan. Meanwhile, President Hoover and Ambassador Hugh Gibson, the chief American delegate at Geneva, did their best to whittle that big stick away.

Neither the aggressive Stimson nor the pacific Gibson got anywhere. Stimson tried to make common cause with England, France, and Italy by urging Japan and China to settle their dispute in the spirit of the Kellogg Pact. But neither Japan nor China had declared war. Technically, therefore, nobody had violated the Kellogg Pact because nobody had resorted to "war as an instrument of national policy." The United States, however, had resorted to naval disarmament as an instrument of national policy and Stimson's appeal to the spirit of the Kellogg Pact left the Japanese unafraid and the British unmoved. Maxim Litvinov, the Soviet spokesman, tried to make the delegates of the capitalist democracies look like hypocrites by continuing to plead, as he had since

© LOW, ALL COUNTRIES

"Better make it wide enough to hold yourself, too, big boy."
Cartoon by David Low

1928, for complete and universal abolition of armaments. André Tardieu, speaking for France, urged the League of Nations to create an international army to defend the postwar settlements everywhere and always.

After five months of argument, President Hoover made a supreme effort to break the deadlock. He had Ambassador Gibson propose the immediate reduction of all armies, navies, and air forces by one third and the abolition of all offensive weapons—tanks, bombing planes, mobile artillery, and chemical devices. When the French objected, Litvinov prepared a substitute resolution endorsing the Hoover plan as the only alternative to the international army that Tardieu wanted. Gibson, rather than support any motion proposed by Russia, voted against his own President's program, arguing that it violated the principle of "unanimity in international gatherings," which he defined as "not the point to which daring leaders had attained nor even the position occupied by perhaps the great majority of states, but rather that point which the last straggler seeking the same goal had passed."

As Hoover's disarmament proposals evaporated, Brüning offered a different formula, based on the extension of his abortive customs union with Austria. Having taken over the German Foreign Ministry, he persuaded Dr. Beneš of Czechoslovakia to approve a scheme to lower tariffs between their two countries. He then went to Geneva, where he conferred with MacDonald, Stimson, and Dino Grandi, the Italian Foreign Minister, on a general European customs union to promote European peace by promoting European trade. The British, Italians, and Americans agreed to permit Germany to buy abroad limited quantities of offensive weapons, forbidden by the Versailles Treaty, in exchange for the Germans' promise not to increase their arms output for the next five years. But an election campaign in France—complicated by a diplomatic attack of laryngitis—prevented Tardieu from attending the meeting, and Brüning had to go home empty-handed. Tardieu's Nationalists thereupon lost control of the Chamber of Deputies to Herriot's Radical-Socialists, and by the time Herriot took office in France, a small group of reactionary extremists had ousted Brüning in Germany.

· II ·

Brüning needed all the self-control he had learned as a machine-gun captain on the Western Front to last as long as he did. Between 1930 and 1932 unemployment in Germany rose from three to seven millions. When an underground explosion, caused by negligence, killed three hundred Silesian coal miners, three thousand survivors demonstrated against the government because it closed the mine. The Nazis won more and more support in local elections. "We are traveling the road prescribed in the Constitution toward the goals prescribed by us," said Hitler. "Certainly we fight with Marxist weapons," boasted Goebbels, "only we do it better than the Marxists." In October, 1931, Hitler reluctantly held a joint meeting at Harzburg with Hugenberg's Nationalists and the Steel Helmet veterans' organization to form the so-called "Harzburg Front." Hugenberg hoped to win over some of Hitler's mass support; Hitler hoped to tap some of Hugenberg's funds; both of them opposed Brüning and the Republic. At the end of 1931 Hitler proclaimed, "Let us march into this new year as fighters that we may leave it as victors."

The rapid growth of the Nazi Party led to divisions within the ranks. Ernst Röhm had made himself the leader of 800,000 brown-shirted Storm Troopers whom he hoped to have incorporated in the Reichswehr. The Storm Troopers wore cheap brown uniforms paid for from Party funds which the troopers themselves often collected. They policed Nazi meetings and fought Communists and Socialists for control of the streets. A few of them carried small arms, but most of them had only rubber truncheons as weapons. They engaged in military drill and submitted themselves to military discipline, swearing loyalty to Hitler and the Nazi Party. "When you are scared," Röhm told them, "always remember others are just as scared as you."

Röhm intrigued with General von Schleicher in the hope of getting his Storm Troopers incorporated in the Reichswehr. At the same time, Gregor Strasser, leader of the Nazi delegation in the Reichstag, tried to make headway among the working classes and their leaders. On May 10, 1932, he told the Reichstag: "The rise of National Socialism is the protest of a people against a state that denies the right to work and the revival of natural intercourse. If the machinery for distribution in the present economic system of the world is not capable of properly distributing the productive wealth of nature, then that system is false and must be altered. The important part of the present development is the anticapitalist sentiment that is permeating our people, that has by now laid hold of something like 95 per cent of our people, consciously or unconsciously. This anticapitalist sentiment is not in the least a refusal to recognize property acquired by personal labor and thrift as morally justifiable. Above all it has no connection with the senseless and destructive tendencies of the International. It is the protest of a people against a degenerate economic system; and it demands from the state that, in order to secure its own right to live, it shall break with the demons of Gold, World Economy, Materialism, and with the habit of thinking in export statistics and the bank rate, and shall be capable of restoring honest payment for honest labor. This anticapitalist sentiment is a proof that we are on the eve of a great change—the conquest of Liberalism and the rise of new ways of economic thought and of a new conception of the state."

Röhm and Strasser, each in his own way, went into the Nazi movement with a revolutionary purpose. Röhm aspired to re-create German military power on a new and wider mass base. Strasser aspired to project a social revolution. Both men tried to use the Nazi Party to achieve their aims. Hitler, on the other hand, had no purpose except to seize power for himself. Goebbels and Göring understood this far better than Röhm or Strasser did and therefore remained close to the Fuehrer. Nobody in the Party liked or trusted Goebbels, but nobody rivaled him as a journalist and orator. Everybody liked Göring, especially the aristocrats, the generals, and the big businessmen whose society he cultivated. During the winter of 1931-32 Hitler needed the money that Göring's friends contributed to keep his movement alive and for that reason he did not encourage Röhm's military ambitions or Strasser's revolutionary ones. But the desperate mood of the German people required Hitler to look like an extremist and he took out most of his venom on the Jews, the Socialists, the Communists, and the Weimar Republic.

Brüning knew as well as Hitler that the Weimar Republic could not last. He also knew, better than Hitler's wealthy backers, that Germany had more to fear from the Nazis than from the Communists. The Social Democrats still commanded, even in 1932, the support of a majority of the German working class, especially its more highly skilled and better organized members. But they had proved themselves, again and again, too timid, too cautious, too old, and too tired to defend the Republic they had created. The Communists, representing only a minority of the German workers, had plenty of zeal, but they had to keep changing their line on Moscow's orders. The Popular and Democratic Parties never attracted mass support and produced but one outstanding figure—the deceased Dr. Stresemann. Some of their members joined the Nationalists; some joined the Nazis. The rest supported Brüning, who also had the Center Party behind him. The Social Democrats—fearful of the Nazis and unable to produce a national leader of their own—also permitted Brüning to govern by decree.

Brüning respected many of the Socialist leaders and they respected him. But Brüning had no use for socialism and planned to scuttle the Weimar Republic before Hitler could beat him to it. Hitler hoped to take power within the framework of the Weimar Constitution. Brüning hoped to abolish the Constitution by making Hindenburg Regent—or *Reichsverweser*—for life, to be succeeded by one of the sons of the Crown Prince as constitutional monarch. But Hindenburg refused to regard himself as the trustee of anybody except the aging ex-Kaiser, who had no popular support, and the kind of constitutional monarchy that Brüning proposed horrified him. As Lord D'Abernon, the British Ambassador in Berlin, once said of Hindenburg: "The President—essentially a soldier —instinctively distrusts everything except force." The old Marshal did, however, let himself be persuaded to run again for the Presidency when his seven-year term expired in the spring of 1932.

John W. Wheeler-Bennett, drawing from personal observation, presented a vivid picture of Hindenburg as he recalled him the previous autumn: "A visitor to Berlin well remembers seeing him one brilliant morning in October, 1931. Some military ceremony was taking place and a guard of honor awaited the President's arrival. A large closed car drew up, an orderly opened the door, and out jumped two smart young staff officers. Then a pause, and slowly, very slowly, there emerged, backward and bare-headed, an enormous figure. Again a pause, though shorter this time, while one of the young officers extracted from the interior of the car a *Pickelhaube* [spiked helmet], which was ceremoniously placed upon the great square head with its hair *en brosse*. Then the figure turned about and one had the impression of a gigantic clockwork doll waiting for the spring to be released which galvanized it into movement. His eye caught the motionless line of soldiery. At once the absent glance changed—the spring had been released—and, one hand grasping his baton and the other resting on his sword hilt, Hindenburg moved stiffly and erect toward the guard of honor. The episode has always seemed to the writer symbolical of the Marshal's whole career. The moment of suspension while the mind was in a plastic state awaiting an impression, and then, once received, the immediate and vigorous action in the direction in which service and duty had pointed."

Germany's 1932 Presidential election presented so many contradictions that anything seemed possible. Hindenburg, the Prussian landowner who hoped to restore the Hohenzollern Empire, drew most of his popular support from the Social Democrats, the trade unionists, the Catholics, and the Jews. Hitler, born in Austria and brought up in the Catholic faith, did not become a German citizen until 1932. Yet Hitler drew his popular support from Protestant Prussian aristocrats, the Rhineland industrialists, and the young racial and nationalist fanatics. Hugenberg backed the official Nationalist candidate, Colonel Düsterberg, one of the Steel Helmet leaders. The Communists again put up Ernst Thälmann, who had represented them in 1925, and at least made the same kind of appeal to the same kind of voter he had tried to attract before, whereas Hindenburg sought the votes of those who opposed him in 1925, most of his 1925 backers having shifted their allegiance to Hitler. Hindenburg announced his candidacy in a characteristic manifesto: "In full consciousness of my great responsibility I have resolved to offer myself for re-election. As the request that I should do so does not come from any party but from the broad masses of the nation, I feel it my duty to do so. . . . If I am defeated I shall at least not have incurred the reproach that of my own accord I deserted my post in an hour of crisis."

Goebbels called Hindenburg "the candidate of the party of the deserters." Alfred Rosenberg, the leading Nazi theoretician, called him "the shield of black bishops and red pacifists." The *Deutsche Zeitung,* which had transferred its Nationalist allegiance from Hindenburg to Düsterberg, wrote: "The present issue at the polls is whether internationalist traitors and pacifist swine, with the approval of Hindenburg, are to bring about the final ruin of Germany." Brüning did most of Hindenburg's campaigning for him, and at the first balloting in March the old Marshal received 49.9 per cent of the popular vote. Because he just failed to win a majority a run-off was held, and Hindenburg had to go to the microphone and make a personal appeal for votes in the name of patriotism. According to Clark's *Fall of the German Republic,* "it was not an experience that commended itself to him and in that hour he was finished with the democratic system." But so many parties spent so much money on their candidates that some cynic suggested a permanent state of Presidential electioneering as the solution to the unemployment problem.

In the run-off election, Düsterberg dropped out and the Nationalists told his followers to vote as they pleased. Evidently they split their support between Hindenburg and Hitler. Hindenburg gained less than seven hundred thousand supporters, but he received 53 per cent of all the votes cast and six million more than Hitler, who, nevertheless, gained two million. Thälmann lost more than a million, most of them to Hitler. The man whom the Nationalists elected in 1925 because they believed he would destroy the Republic now drew his support from his former opponents, who regarded him as the Republic's keystone. The ex-Crown Prince announced that he was backing Hitler.

"Close the ranks," Hindenburg urged the German people. "In unity forward with God." Whereupon he proceeded to let down his new backers as he had let down his old ones. When Brüning, as a matter of form, presented his resignation as Chancellor, the President replied: "I have been expecting your resignation. You may issue a statement that I have asked you to remain temporarily in office. I have been considering the appointment of a government of the right." Even Oskar von Hindenburg and General von Schleicher cautioned the old gentleman. They pointed out that Brüning still might achieve something at Geneva and that he must remain Chancellor long enough to persuade the Reichstag to pass some crucial financial bills. He took their advice; moreover, three days after the election he accepted Brüning's suggestion and ordered the Nazis to disband their Storm Troopers as he had ordered the Communists to dissolve their Red Fighting Front some years before. It was Schleicher who played the trickiest game at this time. Having urged Hindenburg not to dismiss Brüning out of hand, he advised the President, as soon as Brüning left for Geneva, that a stronger man was needed to stop the Nazis. At the same time Schleicher also assured Röhm that Brüning would be out in a few weeks and that Germany would have a government with which the Nazis could deal. Schleicher was not trying to maneuver the Nazis into power. He was trying to split Röhm off from Hitler, to eliminate Brüning, and to set up an army dictatorship with the support of the Nazi Brown Shirts.

While Hindenburg and Schleicher prepared to dispose of Brüning, Hitler prepared to dispose of all who stood in the way of his march to absolute power. On April 24, exactly two weeks after the Presidential election, four fifths of Germany's voters again went to the polls to choose new state governments. The Nazis made huge gains everywhere, notably in Prussia, where they increased their seats in the State Diet from 9 to 162. For the first time, the Socialists lost the majority they had commanded since 1919. Now the combined forces of the Nazis and the Communists outnumbered them. On May 25 the Communists offered a motion proposing that the Prussian Diet vote Otto Braun's Socialist government out of power. The Nazis supported the motion, but the two groups could not agree on an alternative government and Braun remained in office.

While Braun governed Prussia against majority opposition, Brüning had to quit as German Chancellor, although a majority in the Reichstag supported him. On May 11 he told that body, "Don't think you can stop me now, a hundred yards from the goal." The Reichstag approved his financial program and he left for Geneva to score the personal triumph already described. Returning to Germany, he supported those members of his Cabinet who wanted to break up some of the larger, less efficient East Prussian estates into small holdings for destitute war veterans. The scandalous misuse of East Help (*Osthilfe*) funds brought the matter to a head, but Hindenburg, having accepted his Neudeck estate as a gift from certain East Prussian landowners and Rhineland industrialists, regarded Brüning's proposal as a form of Bolshevism. It also irked Hindenburg to have Schleicher constantly reminding him that he owed his re-election to Brüning. On May 29 Hindenburg summoned Brüning to Neudeck. "I am informed," the President declared, "that you have ministers with Bolshevist plans in your Cabinet. That cannot go on." When Brüning began to explain, Hindenburg protested against violations of his name and his honor. "I request you to give me no more emergency decrees to sign." The next day, Brüning formally turned in his resignation and when Hindenburg invited him to remain as Foreign Minister replied that he, too, had a name and honor to defend.

One night, shortly before the break, Brüning and Schleicher had it out together: Brüning, the civilian-soldier who had won the Iron Cross for service under fire, Schleicher, the professional military man, who had won the same decoration behind the lines. "The difference between us as soldiers," Brüning concluded, "was that I fought in the line and you served on the staff. In the line, with the machine-gun corps, we learned to control our nerves and hold our fire until the enemy were almost on us. At the end of the war, it was General Headquarters, not the Army, that lost its head in panic. *We* would have fought on; it was *you* who threw up your hands. And when the time comes, you, General Schleicher, will give up your battle and become lost in your own intrigues."

· III ·

THE fall of Brüning marked the end of constitutional government in Germany. In spite of all his shortcomings, he had always commanded the support, however reluctant, however negative, of a Reichstag majority. Franz von Papen, who succeeded him as Chancellor, did not even enjoy the support of the Center Party to which he nominally adhered. The new Chancellor belonged to a Roman Catholic family from the Rhineland. His wife, Martha von Boch, came from the Saar, where her people owned some of the richest coal mines. As Military Attaché in Washington during the war, von Papen got caught organizing acts of sabotage. After the war, he frequented the fashionable Herrenklub of Berlin and prided himself on his way with horses and with women. Hindenburg took to him at once. Schleicher, who joined the new Cabinet as War Minister, regarded Papen as a willing tool. According to Clark's *Fall of the German Republic*, Schleicher regarded Papen as the ideal man to put his policy through: "He was an aristocrat but not one of the detested East Elbean Junkers; he was a Catholic, but not a faithful Centrist; he was in touch with big business but not part of it. He could therefore probably rally at least three highly important sections of the community without being terribly obnoxious to the other sections, as many other Herrenklub members of much greater ability would have been. Dilettante, pleasure-loving, and always willing to experiment with a new sensation, he would, Schleicher thought, be easily managed."

Brüning's patient labors at Geneva helped get the new Chancellor off to a good start. A more liberal French government, headed by Édouard Herriot, had come to power and agreed, at a conference in Lausanne on July 10, to accept the offer Papen made to wipe the reparations slate clean and end the Young Plan by a single payment of three billion marks. But Papen still refused to accept any disarmament scheme that did not first grant Germany complete equality. Meanwhile, Hindenburg had dissolved the Reichstag on the ground that the results of recent local elections showed it no longer represented the opinion of the country. He set new elections for July 31 and gave Papen the power to govern by decree until late August, when the new Reichstag would meet. On July 20 Papen and Schleicher persuaded Hindenburg to proclaim a state of emergency throughout Prussia, to dismiss Otto Braun and all the other Socialist ministers, and to empower Papen to take over the government as Reich Commissioner. Karl Severing, the Prussian Minister of Police, declared that only force could make him yield. The appearance of two police officers in his offices did the trick. Severing left his office and walked home. The last bastion of the Weimar Republic had fallen.

In the Reichstag elections of July 31 the Nazis received 37 per cent of the popular vote and won the largest bloc of seats—230 out of 607. The Socialists won 133 seats, a slight loss, and the Centrists won 97, a slight gain. The Communist vote more than doubled and they won 87 seats. The Nationalists, the only party that backed Papen, gained no new support and won only 40 seats. Although the Nazi-Communist forces outnumbered the combined forces of all the other parties, they could not form a coalition since each promised to protect the German people against the other. Schleicher tried to bring the Nazis, Nationalists, and Centrists together, but Hitler demanded the same powers Mussolini received in 1922 when he headed his first Italian government, which in-

cluded some non-Fascists. Expecting to win Hitler's gratitude,
Schleicher persuaded Hindenburg to lift the ban on the Nazi Storm
Troopers and to place further restrictions on the Communists. Whereupon Hitler demanded that the Storm Troopers have the freedom of
the streets for three days and frankly predicted a death toll of five thousand victims.

Although Hitler's ranting horrified and terrified both Papen and
Schleicher, they arranged for him to meet Hindenburg. The old Marshal
went straight to the point: "Herr Hitler, I have only one question to address to you: Are you prepared to offer me your collaboration in the
Papen Cabinet?" Hitler mumbled that he had already named his terms.
"So you want the whole power?" asked Hindenburg. "Only as much as
Mussolini," Hitler replied. The interview, during which all present remained standing, lasted only ten minutes. "That man for Chancellor,"
exclaimed Hindenburg as Hitler left. "I'll make him a postmaster and
he can lick stamps with my head on them." The official communiqué
accused Hitler of having broken his word in failing to support the government that Hindenburg wanted. "Great hopelessness reigns among
the Party comrades," Goebbels wrote in his diary. "The S.A. is desperate."

Since the new Reichstag did not have to assemble until the end of
August, Papen had another month to continue governing by decree. He
permitted wage cuts, granted tax exemptions to employers who hired
new help, and set up a national labor force for unemployed young men.
His stern measures antagonized all the parties with any working-class
support—the Nazis and the Centrists no less than the Socialists and Communists. Even the Army felt he was going too far and an estrangement
between the Chancellor and his War Minister, General von Schleicher,
began. The new Reichstag met on August 30 and for the next two weeks
Papen, Göring, and other political leaders negotiated vainly behind the
scenes. On September 12 the Reichstag administered an unprecedented
vote of nonconfidence in Papen: 513 to 32. Papen retaliated by producing a piece of paper, signed by Hindenburg and declaring the Reichstag
dissolved. Göring, as Reichstag leader of the largest party, presided and
chose to ignore the decree Hindenburg had just signed. Papen, however,
insisted that the Presidential decree had already dissolved the Reichstag before it voted him down, and the courts later sustained him. As a
result, Papen continued to govern. Hindenburg set new elections for
November 6. The Nazis had nothing to fear from the parties of the right.
They worried mainly about the growing demand for revolution from
within their own ranks.

Hitler made the Nazi slogan "Against Reaction." When the Communists declared a wildcat streetcar strike in Berlin, the Nazis supported it.
But the strength of the Communists grew; the strength of the Nazis

BETTMANN ARCHIVE

Franz von Papen,
Chancellor of Germany

BETTMANN ARCHIVE

Göring Congratulated by Hitler on his
47th Birthday

dropped. "A somber mood prevails in the *Gau* of Berlin," wrote Goebbels on election night. "There is widespread despair among voters." The results justified his fears. The Nazis lost fifty-two Reichstag seats and more than two million votes. The Communists, on the other hand, gained eleven seats and now equaled the strength the Nazis had reached when they made their first big splash in 1930. But the Nazis and the Communists between them lost the Reichstag majority they had attained only two months before, and the Nationalists scored bigger gains than the Communists. General von Schleicher urged Papen to try to piece together a coalition government of Nazis, Centrists, and Nationalists. Papen replied that the day of majority governments had ended and on November 17 turned in his resignation. But it took Hindenburg several weeks to find a Chancellor to replace him, and even after Papen stepped down, his relations with the old Marshal remained close. The two men occupied adjoining offices and Papen treasured an inscribed photograph on which Hindenburg had written: *"Ich hat' einen Kameraden."*

On November 19 and 21 Hitler paid two more futile visits to Hindenburg. They lasted longer and passed off more pleasantly than the first one, but Hindenburg made it plain that Hitler did not inspire the "special confidence" he felt in Papen. Moreover, the election returns had made it plain that the Reichstag would repudiate any government Hitler might head. "You know that I prefer a Presidential Cabinet, one that is conducted not by a Party leader but by a man who is above Party, and that is the kind of man in whom I should have special confidence," Hindenburg told Hitler. "You have announced that you will place your movement only at the disposal of a Cabinet presided over by yourself as the Party leader. If I agree to this plan, I must request that such a Cabinet have a majority in the Reichstag." He also wrote to Hitler later: "I cannot give a leader of a Party my Presidential power, because such a Cabinet is bound to develop into a Party dictatorship and increase the state of tension prevailing among the German people. I cannot take responsibility for this before my oath and my conscience."

With Hitler out of the way, Hindenburg wanted to reappoint Papen. But Schleicher had other plans. He hoped to persuade Gregor Strasser to split a large Nazi bloc off from Hitler and head a coalition government. Schleicher also continued his intrigues with Röhm to bring the Nazi Storm Troops into the regular Army. On December 3 the Nazis lost 30 per cent of their vote in a local election in the province of Thuringia. Their future had not looked so dark in years. The desperate Hitler made contact with Schleicher through Göring, who asked to be appointed Prime Minister of Prussia. Schleicher, however, insisted on offering the job of Prussian Prime Minister to Strasser, and according to one story, Hitler set out by train from Munich to Berlin to approve the deal. But as soon as Göring and Goebbels got wind of this, they dashed after the train by automobile, intercepted it at Weimar, where they almost literally kidnaped Hitler, and took him back to Munich. In any event, Hitler vetoed the Prussian deal and Strasser quit the Party. This set off a crisis within the Nazi movement. Hitler, shaken with sobs, told the story of Strasser's treachery to a select group of leaders while Göring wept and Goebbels made mournful gestures with a large, white handkerchief. But they had more reason to cheer than to weep. They had won Hitler over to their point of view and Göring had become his right hand, Goebbels his left. The Nazis then put everything they had into another local election in the little province of Lippe, where they did well enough to hold their movement in line.

By this time, Schleicher's intrigues began to catch up with him. He had always enjoyed power without office; now he had to take office without power. Having persuaded Hindenburg that the Army had lost confidence in Papen, he put himself forward as Papen's only available successor. But Hindenburg did not share the Army's confidence in Schleicher. He still preferred Papen and refused to sign over to Schleicher the powers that Papen had always enjoyed. In the Reichstag, Schleicher could count only on the eleven votes of the German People's Party, but the leaders of the other parties had become so disgusted and alarmed by successive, futile elections that they offered to let him continue in office by the simple expedient of not demanding a showdown on a vote of nonconfidence.

Schleicher called himself "the social General." A week after he took office in December he told the German people, "My heretical view is that I am a supporter neither of capitalism nor of socialism. For me concepts like private economy or planned economy have lost their terrors." Having failed to split the Nazi Party by applying leverage on Strasser, Schleicher tried to win over the Social Democrats by gaining the support of a venerable, goateed trade-union leader named Theodor Leipart. "Schleicher is attempting to fill part of our demands," Leipart told the Reichstag in December. "This government will not bring us socialism; we are well aware of that. But can we, in this situation, reject the government's call to help in the task of providing employment?" The Socialist deputies ignored Leipart's appeal and Schleicher had to look elsewhere for support.

On December 14, 1932, Dr. Krupp von Bohlen und Halbach, chairman of the Reich Association of German Industry, had declared, "The world economic situation in the money market and above all in the raw-material market shows signs of improvement; the low point is definitely past." Schleicher, in early January, proposed a billion-dollar program of public works to help recovery along, but Krupp warned, "No government acting this way could escape moral responsibility if the present beginnings of improvement should be destroyed by a wave of distrust." Having antagonized the industrialists, Schleicher proceeded to antagonize the Junkers by threatening to reveal that many of them had bought expensive cars and blown themselves to costly vacations on the Mediterranean with funds that the government had given them to improve their land. Instead of submitting to Schleicher's blackmail, the Junkers rushed to Hindenburg, demanding the dismissal of this *Agrarbolschevik,* as they called him. Even the Army leaders who had never failed him in the past also turned against him.

With the end of January came the end of Schleicher. He had strangled himself with his own intrigues, which finally led Papen to bring Hitler to power. During the war Papen had made the acquaintance of a handsome young officer from the Rhineland named Joachim Ribbentrop who later became a champagne salesman, married his boss's daughter, and added a "von" to his name. Later, Ribbentrop joined the Nazi Party and made himself useful to Hitler translating articles for him from the British press. By the end of 1932, the Nazis faced complete bankruptcy—political as well as financial. Shivering Storm Troopers rattled collection boxes in the streets and cried, "Give something to the wicked Nazis." It fell to Ribbentrop to help save the day. He and Papen arranged for Hitler to meet several leaders of German industry on January 4, 1933, at Cologne in the castle of Baron von Schroeder, head of a large banking house in which Jewish capital was largely represented. Hitler left the

luncheon, which lasted an hour and a half, with promises of funds from
Fritz Thyssen, Otto Wolff, and other German industrialists. He also established direct contact with Papen and made the valuable discovery
that Hindenburg had refused to give Schleicher authority to dissolve the
Reichstag and govern by decree.

When Schleicher heard the news of the Hitler-Papen meeting he offered Strasser the Vice-Chancellorship and proposed that the Socialist
trade unions call a general strike with Army support. He toyed with the
idea of defying Hindenburg, but the Socialists and Centrists refused to
back him. The rumor spread that Schleicher had ordered Papen and
Hugenberg placed in protective custody. On January 28, Schleicher
appeared before Hindenburg and asked for power, in the event of an
adverse Reichstag vote, to dissolve that body, order new elections, and
govern by decree. Hindenburg cut him short before he had finished his
plea to let somebody—anybody—continue his policy: "Thank you, General, for what you have done for the country. Now let's see how the hare
runs from here." Hindenburg knew that Papen had already begun negotiating with Hitler to form a coalition government of Nationalists and
Nazis. Demands that the Reichstag investigate the *Osthilfe* scandals
had terrified the Nationalists into coming to terms with the Nazis. Hitler
became Chancellor, Frick Minister of the Interior, and Göring Minister
of Aviation in a new ten-man Cabinet. The other seven posts went to
Nationalists. Papen became Vice-Chancellor and it was also understood
that he should attend every meeting between Hitler and Hindenburg.
Hugenberg became Minister for Agriculture and Economics. General
von Blomberg inherited Schleicher's job as Defense Minister. The rest
of the Cabinet posts went to lifelong Nationalists.

On January 30, 1933, Hindenburg had told Hitler to form a Cabinet.
Two nights later, the old Marshal reviewed a torchlight procession of
cheering Storm Troopers who passed his palace with a shuffling gait,
followed by a much smaller body of disciplined Stahlhelm troops, clad
in the wartime field gray. "Ludendorff," Hindenburg is said to have
barked over his shoulder, "how well your men are marching, and what
a lot of Russian prisoners they've taken." The story may be true or false;
in any case it is understandable if not excusable. But there was no excuse
for the flippant Papen, who showed his own lack of understanding when
he assured his friends that the Nationalists now had the Nazis where
they wanted them: "We can always outvote them in the Cabinet."

Papen found it as difficult to outvote Hitler as to outsmart him. Within
twenty-four hours, he agreed to support the new Chancellor in an appeal
to Hindenburg for new elections. Hitler promised to keep the same
Cabinet even in the event of a Nazi victory, and his word seemed to
satisfy all the Nationalists except Hugenberg, who had just enough

imagination to foresee the result. "Now it is easy to carry on the fight," wrote the triumphant Goebbels, "for we can call on all the state's resources. The radio and press are at our disposal. We shall furnish a masterpiece of agitation. And this time of course there is no lack of money." On January 31 he defined the Nazi strategy in his diary: "In a conference with the Leader we establish the directives for the struggle against the Red terror. For the present we shall dispense with direct countermeasures. The Bolshevist attempt at revolution must first flare up. At the proper moment we shall strike."

Social Democratic and Centrist leaders expected Hitler's Cabinet to break up under the strain of its inner rivalries. Leipart said, "Messrs. Hugenberg and Papen have scarcely mentioned the name of their Leader in the Cabinet. Here are gaping contradictions which promise victory for our struggle." Adam Stegerwald, leader of the Catholic trade unions, wrote in the same vein: "Hitler will be the prisoner of Hugenberg, Papen, and the big agricultural interests." And when the Socialist mayor of a small city suggested a united Socialist-Communist front to Ernst Torgler, leader of the Communist faction in the Reichstag, Torgler replied, "It doesn't enter our heads. The Nazis must take power. Then in four weeks the whole working class will be united under the leadership of the Communist Party." But the Communists could not match the revolutionary audacity and initiative of the Nazis. Between January 30 and voting day on March 5 the Nazis killed fifty-one persons in street fights at an estimated loss of eighteen deaths in their own ranks. Röhm's Brown Shirts and Himmler's Black Shirts undertook police duties, and Göring ordered his Prussian police to "avoid so much as an appearance of hostility toward the S.A. and the Stahlhelm."

On the night of February 27, the Reichstag building in Berlin went up in flames. Göring appeared at the scene of the disaster suspiciously early, using the underground passage that connected his house with the shattered edifice. He blamed the Communists, and produced a half-witted, half-doped young Dutchman, Marinus van der Lubbe, who confessed to having committed the crime. But Göring never produced the documents that he claimed his police had discovered in Communist Party headquarters and none of the other evidence that other Nazi leaders described ever saw the light of day, either before or after the election held on March 5. Before the election the Nazis were too busy using the fire as an excuse to arrest most of the Communist deputies and some Socialists as well. Controlling the communication facilities, they also told the German people that the Communists had set the fire as a signal for a general uprising. After the election, the Nazis no longer needed to alibi themselves. They received more than 17 million votes, or 44 per cent of the votes cast, and, with the Nationalists, controlled a majority of

Reichstag seats. Hitler had come to power, and he proposed to hold it with the same weapons he had used to gain it.

· IV ·

THE triumph of Hitler meant that a new kind of revolution had come to power in the very heart of Europe. Defeat in war made Russia safe for Communism. The high cost of victory made Italy go Fascist. The first impact of the world depression on Spain overthrew Primo de Rivera's dictatorship and King Alfonso's monarchy. Germany escaped Communism in 1918 and 1919. The Weimar Republic even survived the inflation of 1923. Not until 1933 did all the accumulated frustrations of defeat, inflation, and depression set the stage for Hitler's New Order. And behind Hitler stood a ruined middle class, and an embittered younger generation led by ruthless gangsters and disillusioned idealists. The Nazis set emotion above reason; they glorified violence and reviled law and order. They subordinated the mass to the individual; they extolled dictatorship for its own sake and denounced democracy. In the person of Adolf Hitler millions of Germans found the incarnation of their repressed desires, hopes, and fears.

"The National Socialists had no program, still less a defined class interest," wrote A. J. P. Taylor of Oxford in *The Course of German History;* "they stood simply for destruction and action, not contradictory but complementary. They united in their ranks the disillusioned of every class: the army officer who had failed to find a place in civil life; the ruined capitalist; the unemployed worker; but, most of all, the 'white-collar' workers of the lower middle class on whom the greatest burden of the postwar years had fallen. The unemployed clerk; the university student who had failed in his examinations; the incompetent lawyer and the blundering doctor: all these could exchange their shabby threadbare suits for the smart uniforms of the National Socialist army and could find in Hitler's promise of action new hope for themselves. In England they would have been shipped off to the colonies as remittance men: their presence in Germany was the high price which the victors of 1918 paid for the worthless tracts of German colonial territory." The curtailment of emigration to the United States aggravated this condition still further.

Just as the war hit Germany harder than it hit any of the victorious Powers, so the depression hit Germany harder than it hit any other major country. Perhaps that explained why Erich Maria Remarque's *All Quiet on the Western Front* made an international sensation during the late 1920's and why Hans Fallada's *Little Man, What Now?* won a comparable success during the early 1930's. In the Remarque novel, an average German foot-soldier went through every experience of war only to perish in a minor skirmish of no consequence. The Fallada novel related the simple tragedy of an unemployed clerk and his wife and child. But both books presented universal characters in universal situations. Remarque dwelt on the comradeship as well as the cruelty of war, on the gulf that separated the front-line fighters from those who had not shared their hardships. Veterans of every nationality recognized themselves, just as unemployed white-collar workers all over the world understood the plight of Fallada's "little man."

When *All Quiet* first appeared in 1929 it sold enormously in Germany and abroad. By 1932, however, the Nazis attacked Remarque because he laid bare the inhumanity of war. Sometimes they denounced him for his French name. Sometimes they said he was a Jew who had changed his name from Kramer. When the American film version of his novel had its first Berlin showing, a few dozen Nazi Storm Troopers marched into the theater holding small boxes in their hands. At a prearranged signal, they opened the boxes, releasing swarms of white mice, and their leader threw in a snake for good measure. A panic ensued and the picture was never again shown in Germany. Fallada's book appeared before Hitler came to power, yet the victory of the Nazis made it plain that most of Germany's "little men" supported their program. Here was convincing, disturbing evidence of rottenness in the state of Europe.

Nothing quite like the world depression had ever before hit the nations that ruled the world or the classes that ruled those nations. The mass of the people in all the undeveloped regions always lived on the edge of starvation in good times and bad. During the war, victors and vanquished, the rulers and the ruled all bled and suffered. The depression, on the other hand, damaged the advanced countries more than it damaged the backward countries because the advanced countries had the most to lose. And, inside those countries, it affected the upper and middle classes more than it affected the working classes for the same reason: they were the classes that had accumulated some fat. Men did not kill each other during the depression as they killed each other in time of war; indeed, war preparations prevented conditions from becoming even worse. Nor did the depression spring from natural causes. Because the Germans garnered a record harvest in 1931, followed by a singularly mild winter, prices fell to new lows; unemployment rose higher than ever. A whole system had broken down and those who had benefited— or hoped to benefit—the most from that system suffered the most from its collapse.

Even by the time Hitler came to power in Germany, the people of France remained relatively unscathed by the depression. Back in 1926 the stabilization of the franc at one fifth of its prewar value had already cost the peasants and middle classes four fifths of their savings. They did

France: "They're trying to attack me." From 420, Florence

not come through the war as rich as the Americans, but they had avoided the total inflation that ravaged Germany, and their balanced economy protected them from the postwar woes that afflicted Great Britain. The depression did not hit France until 1932 and when it came, the parties of the left benefited. The Nationalists had not only failed to prevent Hitler from gaining power in Germany. Their rigid attitude toward his more moderate predecessors played into the hands of the extremists. Nor had French bankers done themselves or their country much good when they took a dog-in-the-manger attitude toward Great Britain. They had merely encouraged nationalism across the Channel as well as across the Rhine. French literature, in like manner, began to lose some of the cosmopolitan, international flavor it had cultivated during the 1920's. In 1931 the Goncourt Prize for fiction went to Jean Fayard's *Mal d'Amour*, a book which Edmund Jaloux, writing in *Les Nouvelles Littéraires*, placed in "the best tradition of the French novel, a tradition to which *Claire*, by M. Jacques Chardonne, and *Saint-Saturnin* by Jean Schlumberger also belong."

The depression had not only revived the traditional French novel. The spring of 1932 saw the first two volumes of *Men of Good Will* by Jules Romains appear. Here was the most ambitious and impressive work of French fiction since Proust's *Remembrance of Things Past*. Like Proust, Romains recalled the past, using a new technique with which he had begun to experiment in 1911. He called it "unanimism" and focused on an entire situation, culture, or period rather than on a single individual. "One of my oldest and most constant cares," he wrote in the preface to *Men of Good Will*, "has been to discover a method of composition that would permit us to escape our habit of focusing our attention upon the individual." And again: "The individual cannot prevail indefinitely against humanity. All that he can hope for is to be right sooner than humanity."

The opening volumes of *Men of Good Will* depicted many sections of Parisian society during the last four months of the year 1908. Romains planned, in the succeeding volumes, to write a social history of the Third Republic from the early years of the twentieth century, through the war, and on into the 1930's. He believed that his technique of unanimism had much in common with the art of the motion picture. But he had not borrowed anything from another medium. Rather had literature, in his hands, faithfully reflected contemporary reality: "The truth seems to be that in every epoch some art other than literature is particularly suited to satisfy the dominant tendencies in the sensibilities of that period. But since literature, because of its extreme suppleness and its great variety of methods, always remains in contact with every movement and every demand of the spirit, since, in a word, it is the 'art most coextensive with the human soul,' no spiritual need can be born without finding a response in literature and hence other arts become curiously preoccupied with analogous things and try to express themselves in parallel ways. Hence the deceptive notion that literature is influenced by some other art."

Romains had not devoted his entire life to writing novels. After the war he worked with blinded veterans on the theory that they could learn to see through their skins. He finally wrote a book on the subject, *Eyeless Sight*, which he signed with his real name, Louis Farigoule. Nor had Louis-Ferdinand Céline, whose *Journey to the End of the Night* also appeared in the spring of 1932, devoted himself exclusively to literature. Céline was a physician who ministered to the poorest people in Paris after having served in the war, suffered a nervous breakdown, and hoboed in the United States. The hero of Céline's book went through the same violent and tragic experiences that the author had known, experiences that Céline recorded not in the language of the street but of the gutter. "Do you remember," his hero inquires, "the names of any of the soldiers killed in the Thirty Years' War? Have you ever tried to discover even one of those names? You have never even looked. They are as unknown and as unimportant to you as the least scrap of paper under this paper weight in front of us or as the daily movement of your bowels. Therefore you see that they died for nothing, Lola, for absolutely nothing at all, those fools. I tell you. It's a fact. Only life counts. Ten thousand years from now I swear to you that this war, remarkable as it may appear to us, will be completely forgotten. . . . I do not believe in the future, Lola."

If Céline believed only in the present and Romains looked to the past, several of their literary colleagues pinned their hopes on the future and preferred Communism. Romain Rolland, André Gide, Henri Barbusse, and Jean-Richard Bloch all sympathized in varying degrees and for varying lengths of time with the so-called Soviet experiment. Rolland and Gide soon lost their faith. Barbusse died a devout member of the Communist Party. Bloch remained a sympathizer for many years. Céline had turned against the existing order more violently than any of them, but if his *Journey to the End of the Night* preached any lesson it was a lesson of solitary nihilism and of life for life's sake.

Although the depression caused more mass misery in Britain than in France, it produced no British Céline, much less any British Hitler. The chief victims of the depression in Great Britain belonged to the working class and bore the brunt of the sacrifices that the MacDonald-Baldwin national government imposed. The British middle classes, on the other hand, unlike the middle classes in Germany, came through the depression relatively well. After the pound went off the gold standard, the value of their savings dropped somewhere between 10 and 20 per cent—almost nothing at all compared with what happened in Germany, France, and other European lands. The national government did its expected duty. It defended the interests of the ruling class; it regained the support of the middle classes; it tempered the wind to the workers.

The depression also gave a measurable fillip to British nationalism and imperialism. Hoover had signed the Smoot-Hawley tariff in the United States; Hitler promised to make Germany more nearly self-sufficient. The Conservative Party which dominated Britain's national government moved in the same direction by slapping a 50 per cent protective tariff on twenty-three groups of manufactured goods in November, 1931, and then calling a great Imperial Conference at Ottawa the following summer. Here the Tory Chancellor of the Exchequer, Neville Chamberlain, second son of Joseph Chamberlain and younger half-brother of Sir Austen, felt he had completed his father's unfinished life-work when he persuaded the Dominions to buy and sell on a preferential basis with the mother country. How much real difference this might make remained to be seen. Psychologically, however, the Ottawa Conference marked a turning point in British history. The Tories welcomed it because the British family of nations seemed to be drawing closer together. The Liberals and Laborites could not see this as an unmixed blessing. They regarded the Ottawa Conference as the unhappy if inevitable equivalent of the Smoot-Hawley tariff in the United States—

inevitable because the whole world was moving in the same direction, unhappy because the trend threatened Britain and its Empire with ultimate disaster. The British and their Empire had prospered in a world of free trade. Now, in a world of rising tariff walls, the British Isles could not hope to hold their loosely organized Empire together in the face of German, Japanese, and American competition, and in the face of the political and social revolutions sweeping so much of Asia. The wonder, however, was not that the Tories carried the day. The wonder was that they adopted so moderate a program, and got away with it by appealing to national pride.

Early in the depression, a group of well-born and well-heeled young intellectuals who had joined the Labor Party set up what they called the New Party that offered the British people revolution from above. John Strachey, who soon preached Communism, belonged to this group. So did Sir Oswald Mosley, son of a well-to-do father and son-in-law of Lord Curzon. The New Party attracted little support, and Strachey edged over toward Communism while Mosley plumped for Fascism, with himself as leader of the British Union of Fascists. He borrowed Mussolini's symbol of the Roman fasces, and his followers wore, and called themselves, Blackshirts. Mosley preached the corporate state, the reform of Parliament, and "Britain First." Perhaps because his wife had a Jewish grandfather—Levi Leiter of Chicago—Mosley did not preach anti-Semitism until after her death some years later. But he did preach antisocialism, anticommunism, anti-internationalism: "Every party in the state is now internationalist," he wrote in 1934. "The only difference is that the headquarters of the Socialist International is Moscow and the headquarters of the Conservative International is Wall Street. It is only natural that these new Conservatives should adopt Mr. MacDonald as their leader. He is a very appropriate liaison between the two."

But Mosley's genteel Fascism made little popular appeal. Mussolini and Hitler both came from the common people and kept the common touch; Mosley's demagogy left the working class unmoved; the middle class found him too clever by half; the ruling class found him too brash. His movement aroused extravagant fears among Liberals and Laborites, who underrated both the intelligence and the integrity of the British people. It stirred some sympathy among the Conservative lunatic fringe and for a time Lord Rothermere's *Daily Mail* took him seriously. But no spokesman for the less privileged majority ever tried to succeed where Mosley failed, perhaps because his example produced such a discouraging effect.

Two short excerpts from the British press recall how the national scene looked during the summer of 1932 from the extreme Laborite and from the die-hard Tory point of view. The *New Leader,* weekly organ of the

Independent Labor Party, described Bilston in the Black Country, center of the British steel industry: "It is like a district devastated by war. There are huge waste stretches pocked with holes and ridges just as though they had suffered heavy bombardment. The grass grows thickly over black cinders. There are large patches of cinders with no grass at all. There are houses in ruins, with bricks scattered in confusion. . . . The only water supply is a tap in the back yard. The lavatories are also in the yard, primitive and filthy, shared by a row of houses. Bilston is capitalism in decay. Its industries have collapsed; its population is still unemployed and destitute. It is characteristic of a great part of Britain."

But not of the part that created the national government. In the time of Baldwin and MacDonald as in the time of Disraeli and Gladstone, England remained two nations—the rich and the poor, and the poor, it seemed, still knew their place or lacked the will or the power to change it. Compare this description of the annual horse race at Ascot, seen through the eyes of a reporter for the Conservative *Morning Post,* with the *New Leader's* account of Bilston: "Only one thing everywhere—lighthearted gaiety. Pounds, bank-notes, half crowns were thrown to the winds in a spirit that bespoke confidence in the future as much as revelry in the present. All the estates of the realm mingled together in happy unity. Red-coated bandsmen placed their bets cheek by jowl with owners. Above them all a smiling King inspired in his people a smiling spirit. Laughs, cheers, songs rose from end to end of the course and contested the obstreperous importunity of the layers. And the latter were for once satisfied. One after another was heard loudly protesting that he had never had a better day. Favorites lost and the concourse cheered. Hundreds of pounds left bag and purse and they cheered anew. And the sun shone with a hotter brightness than ever before; the flowers bloomed with a new freshness. Over all there was an atmosphere of elegance, reflected in the dresses, which savored almost of the Ascot of prewar days, its glory, its ease, its perfection."

One telltale phrase, however, betrayed an unconscious uneasiness on the part of the *Morning Post* reporter. It is that the atmosphere "savored almost of the Ascot of prewar days." The kind of world which the *Morning Post* wanted Britain to create lay in the nineteenth rather than the twentieth century. No wonder this outstanding mouthpiece of die-hard Toryism had earned itself the nickname of the *Moaning Past*. That was perhaps where Europe's future as well as Britain's lay.

· V ·

THE first European country in which the depression produced a revolution was also the first European country to produce a philosopher with a widely acceptable account of what had happened. The people of Spain had a long history and rich traditions. In the sixteenth century they built the first great overseas empire; in the seventeenth they gave birth to the Counter-Reformation. Although the nineteenth century saw Spain ousted from South America and the dawn of the twentieth saw the United States liberate Cuba and acquire the Philippines, the Spanish language, Spanish culture, and the Roman Catholic tradition remained strong in all the lands over which Spain had ever ruled. In some respects Spain anticipated the history of other European countries; in others it lagged behind. Primo de Rivera established one of the first postwar dictatorships. His was also the first of these dictatorships to collapse. And at a time when the moderate German parties were scheming to restore the Hohenzollerns, the moderate parties in Spain were demanding the abdication of King Alfonso. Situated on the fringe of Europe yet tied by blood, language, and religion to the New World, at once provincial and cosmopolitan, feudal and modern, Spain formed a bridge between past and present. At a time when the leading intellects of other countries devoted themselves to such specialized fields as relativity and psychoanalysis, two of the leading intellects of Spain remained philosophers of classic mold.

The Spaniards themselves regarded Miguel de Unamuno as their greatest man of letters since Cervantes. He taught philosophy and Greek; he wrote on religious and mystical themes. The twenty-first century may regard Unamuno as one of the titans of his time, but among his contemporaries—especially outside Spain—José Ortega y Gasset enjoyed a wider fame. A disciple of Plato, transplanted to the twentieth century, might have seen the modern world through Unamuno's eyes; a disciple of Aristotle might have seen the modern world as Ortega did. Unamuno wrote for himself—and for posterity. Ortega, in his popular book-length essay, *La Rebelión de las Masas*, wrote for his own time. The book appeared in Spain in 1930. Two years later, in English translation, *The Revolt of the Masses* experienced a combined popular success and a success of esteem, especially in England and the United States. Not since Spengler's *Decline of the West* had a frankly philosophic work commanded such wide interest and influence. The readers of Ortega, like the readers of Spengler, put their own interpretation on what he had to say, but Ortega became a cult for the same reason Spengler did: Spengler had thrown new light on the causes and results of the war; Ortega threw new light on the causes and results of the mass unrest that followed the war.

"The world today," wrote Ortega, "is suffering from a grave demoralization which, amongst other symptoms, manifests itself by an extraordinary rebellion of the masses, and has its origin in the demoralization of Europe. The causes of this latter are multiple. One of the main is the displacement of the power formerly exercised by our Continent over the rest of the world and over itself. Europe is no longer certain that it rules, nor the rest of the world that it is being ruled." From the sixth to the nineteenth century, Europe slowly built up a population of about 180 million. Then, between 1800 and 1914, Europe's population jumped to 460 millions. "I take it that the contrast between these two figures leaves no doubt as to the prolific qualities of the last century. In three generations it produces a gigantic mass of humanity which, launched like a torrent over the historic era, has inundated it. This fact, I repeat, should suffice to make us realize the triumph of the masses and all that is implied and announced by it."

The revolt of the masses, on the other hand, arose primarily from Europe's middle classes, whose numbers grew so rapidly that they could not saturate themselves in Europe's culture or understand the complicated system from which they benefited. A new kind of arrogance developed that had little in common with the revolutionary fervor of the workers and peasants or with the disciplined pride of the aristocrat: "The characteristic of the hour is that the commonplace mind, knowing itself to be commonplace, has the assurance to proclaim the rights of the commonplace and to impose them wherever it will. As they say in the United States, 'to be different is to be indecent.' The mass crushes beneath itself everything that is excellent, individual, qualified, and select."

Although the nineteenth century created the mass man, whom Ortega deplored, it also created the doctrine of Liberalism, which he admired: "that principle of political rights according to which public authority, in spite of being all-powerful, limits itself and attempts, even at its own expense, to leave room in the State over which it rules for those to live who neither think nor feel as it does, that is to say as do the stronger, the majority. Liberalism—it is well to recall this today—is the supreme form of generosity; it is the right which the majority concedes to minorities and hence it is the noblest cry that has ever resounded on this planet. It announces the determination to share existence with the enemy; more than that with an enemy which is weak."

Although the last years of the German Republic showed what happened when a divided majority made concessions to a united minority, Ortega anticipated Hitler's triumph three years before he took power: "A society divided into discordant groups, with their forces of opinion canceling one another out, leaves no room for a ruling power to be constituted. And as 'nature abhors a vacuum,' the empty space left by the absence of public opinion is filled by brute force. . . . There appears for the first time in Europe a type of man who does not want to give reasons or to be right, but simply shows himself resolved to impose his opinions. This is the new thing: the right not to be reasonable, the 'reason of unreason.'"

Ortega found nothing new in either Communism or Fascism. "Both Bolshevism and Fascism are two false dawns; they do not bring the morning of a new day, but of some archaic day, spent over and over again; they are mere primitivism. And such will be all movements which fall into the stupidity of starting a boxing-match with the past, instead of proceeding to digest it. No doubt an advance must be made on the liberalism of the nineteenth century. But this is precisely what cannot be done by any movement such as Fascism which declares itself anti-liberal. Because it was that fact—the being anti-liberal or non-liberal—which constituted man previous to liberalism. And as the latter triumphed over its opposite, it will either repeat its victory time and again, or else everything—liberalism and anti-liberalism—will be annihilated in the destruction of Europe."

Ortega had planned *The Revolt of the Masses* before the depression just as Spengler planned *The Decline of the West* before the war. But the events of the depression gave impressive endorsement to Ortega's analysis just as the events of the war confirmed much of Spengler. Ortega could not, however, transcend the provincialism of the European intellectual. He saw no glimmer of a new civilization in either Russia or the United States: "New York and Moscow represent nothing new, relatively to Europe. They are both of them two sections of the European order of things which, by dissociating from the rest, have lost their meaning. In sober truth, one is afraid to talk of New York and Moscow, because one does not know what they really are; the only thing one knows is that the decisive word has not been said by either of them."

For the word "one" in the last sentence, substitute the word "Europe" and Ortega's real meaning becomes more clear: "In sober truth, Europe is afraid to talk of New York and Moscow, because Europe does not know what they really are; the only thing Europe knows is that the decisive word has not been said by either of them." But only Europe itself could speak that word. Neither New York nor Moscow could speak for Europe, any more than Europe could speak for them. Indeed, Ortega himself had spoken the decisive word that Mussolini's Fascists and Hitler's Nazis obligingly confirmed: "The element of terror in the destiny of our time is furnished by the overwhelming and violent moral upheaval of the masses; imposing, invincible, and treacherous." He also predicted that "in the next few years, Europe may grow quite enthusiastic for Bolshevism," and continued: "It is simply a misunderstanding of the European to expect that he can hear unmoved that call to new *action* when he has no standard of a cause as great to unfurl in opposition. For the sake of serving something that will give a meaning to his existence, it is not impossible that the European may swallow his objections to Communism and feel himself carried away, not by the substance of the faith, but by the fervor of conduct it inspires."

Events in Germany soon confirmed his worst fears about Europe's desire of action for action's sake. But it was Hitler, not Stalin, who carried the "revolt of the masses" to its logical conclusion. Whereas Lenin and the men who made the Russian Revolution drew their inspiration from western Europe, Stalin turned against intellectuals in general and European intellectuals in particular. This justified his dropping the world revolution Lenin had preached and driving Trotsky into exile. And when he finally decided to cast Trotsky into oblivion, he pursued that course with characteristic determination. While foreign Communists and their fellow-traveling "friends of the Soviet Union" romanticized the Five-Year Plan, Stalin and the men around him recognized that they faced the colossal task of industrializing a backward country and they had no scruples about the means they used to achieve that end.

When Ortega admitted that he did not know what Soviet Russia had become, he could reach but one conclusion: that Russia could not speak the decisive word to Europe. Because the United States mystified him just as much he likewise closed his eyes to New York. And in 1930, his contention that the United States had nothing new or distinctive to offer the world seemed sound enough—to Americans as well as to Europeans. What Ortega wrote of Europe and the world at large in 1930 applied with special force to the United States in 1932: "We are in the presence of a style of living which cultivates sincerity and is at the same time a fraud. There is truth only in an existence which feels its acts as irrevocably necessary. There exists no politician who feels the inevitableness of his policy, and the more extreme his attitudes, the more frivolous, the less inspired by destiny they are." Even as Americans nodded with agreement while they read these words of wisdom from abroad, a new political leader had arisen among them to prove Ortega wrong.

SUMMING UP

NOTHING quite like the depression had ever before hit the world. From 1914 to 1918, the war had wrought unprecedented damage. The Russian Revolution that began in 1917 brought greater changes than any previous social convulsion. By 1929, however, the world had recovered from the war and Stalin had stabilized the revolution. Almost everywhere, the production of wealth broke all past records. Life in the twentieth century at last seemed to hold infinite promise for the common man. Then came the depression, cutting production and trade in half, throwing whole nations and classes out of work. World production and world trade had always oscillated, but never before had any slump seen them drop so low. And this at a time when the human race had made the greatest progress in its history toward abolishing poverty and bringing plenty to all.

The German Republic arose from the misery of defeat. It survived the rigors of inflation. But the world depression did it in. People who put up with the dreadful consequences of war refused to take the depression lying down. Hitler and his movement proved Ortega's case for him: the desperate middle class reacted more violently than the downtrodden workers. It was the middle class that had come to expect the good things of life, and when the senseless, inexorable, impersonal forces of the depression suddenly placed these good things beyond reach, the German middle class turned to Hitler. The Social Democrats and the trade unions stood by the Republic as the lesser evil; the Nationalists lost touch with the common man; the Communists cut their own throats. Hitler never attracted a majority of the German people, but the Nazis not only won the largest following of any single party; they took advantage of the general confusion in other parties and classes to seize all power for themselves.

In every country that permitted free elections, the outs came in and the ins went out. The Laborite MacDonald remained titular head of the British government by joining the Tories in a coalition. The rank and file of the trade-union movement still voted Labor, but the middle class swung back to the Conservatives. No revolt of the masses there. In France, on the other hand, Herriot's Radical Party ousted Tardieu's Nationalists. Although the depression had not hit France as hard as it had hit Britain and Germany, the people wanted a change. Spain had first ousted Primo and then replaced the Monarchy with a Republic, but Mussolini had established himself firmly in Italy and Stalin's position in Russia remained unassailable. His announcement that the Soviet Union had completed the first Five-Year Plan in four years made a world sensation. In 1928 the Soviet Union produced 5½ per cent of the world's industrial goods; by 1931 this proportion had increased to 11 per cent, and by 1932 the Soviet Union stood second only to the United States as an industrial power.

The Russian people already knew—if the outside world did not—what the success of the Five-Year plan had cost: at least five million persons dead of famine in the Ukraine and widespread hunger elsewhere. The Russians restricted all foreign correspondents to Moscow during the winter of 1932-33. When the *Manchester Guardian*'s man finally visited the northern Caucasus, the Ukraine, and the middle and lower Volga he found the people starving: "I mean starving in its absolute sense. There is not 5 per cent of the population whose standard of life is equal to or nearly equal to that of the unemployed in England who are on the lowest scale of relief." The depression had played its role in Russia too. The fall in raw-material prices cut down Russia's buying power on world markets by 50 per cent and more—and the whole program of industrialization suffered accordingly.

All these countries, however, could trace some of their troubles back to the war. The United States, on the other hand, had enriched and strengthened itself between 1914 and 1918, and during the 1920's American prosperity rose to record heights. Yet the depression began in Wall Street and hit the American people harder than the war did. Although the American people did not suffer in the depression the physical distress that racked so many Germans, their pride and assurance had never undergone such a shock. The German response to the depression boded ill for the future of Europe. A similar response in the United States could prove a world calamity.

14

Enter Roosevelt

The world depression hits bottom as the United
States prepares, under Franklin D. Roosevelt, to
pull itself up by its own bootstraps.

PREVIEW

FEW LIVING Americans could remember a blacker year than 1932. The
number of unemployed kept increasing. In February, the Lindbergh
kidnaping brought home the power of organized crime. In July, the rout
of the bonus marchers revealed the heartless bankruptcy of Hoover's
leadership. Although the sudden rise of Howard Scott's Technocracy
movement gave new hope to millions, its even more rapid collapse suggested that the social sciences still remained in a primitive condition.
Finally, the man of destiny appeared in the person of Franklin Delano
Roosevelt. The New Deal took power in Washington at the same moment the New Order took power in Berlin.

· I ·

THE DEPRESSION had shaken the United States like nothing since the
Civil War. Every day that passed since the Wall Street crash, more and
more Americans found themselves living, talking, thinking, and sleeping
depression all around the clock. Unemployment increased from a few,
floating millions in 1929 to five millions in 1930, ten millions in 1931,
twelve millions in 1932, fifteen millions, maybe seventeen millions by
1933. Out of every three Americans who had jobs in 1929, one had lost
that job in 1933 and the two who still had work lived in fear that they
would be the next to go, or join the growing army of "short-time" millions. And those few who did not fear for themselves worried about their
idle children, their bankrupt parents, their vanishing savings bank accounts, their lapsing life insurance policies, their overdue mortgage payments. Had the promise of American life betrayed them? Had Wall
Street liquidated the American dream?

Most Americans took spiraling prosperity for granted. Although few
of them expected to wind up millionaires, they hoped to do better than
their parents, and assumed that their children would go on from where

they left off. They knew that hard times follow good times, but never before had any slump in the United States seen business activity drop beneath the previous low. In 1931 and 1932 more people emigrated from the United States to Europe than came from Europe to the United States. Of course the immigration laws still kept many would-be immigrants out, but here was additional evidence that the period of endless expansion, the era of infinite possibilities had come, it seemed, to an end. In vain did Hoover, the product of publicity, try to exorcise the depression with the same wordy ritual that had created his own myth, invoking the spirit of rugged individualism during a period of rapid social change when group problems overshadowed individual problems.

A telltale incident occurred during the 1931 World Series at Philadelphia. Presidents at political rallies often have come in for rough treatment, but here a crowd of pleasure-seekers, attending their national game, burst into a chorus of boos and hisses when their chief of state walked across the field. President Hoover no longer symbolized the office that he held or the nation he represented. Instead, he had become identified with the people's shattered hopes and lost illusions. Indeed, many Americans came to hold Hoover personally responsible for the collective disaster that had overwhelmed them. After all, he had used every publicity trick, every technique of mass propaganda to stand before them as the supreme embodiment of the existing order. When that order collapsed, he found himself the obvious target of public fury.

The early 1930's dealt even more rudely with other heroes of the late 1920's. Albert H. Wiggin, chairman of the Chase National Bank, and Charles E. Mitchell, chairman of National City, quietly unloaded the stock they owned in their own banks, using their losses to escape income tax payments while urging the general public to buy what they refused to hold themselves. When a Senate investigating committee revealed the facts, both men resigned in disgrace. The British-born Samuel J. Insull fled to Greece to avoid standing trial for his manipulations of utility companies in the Midwest. Insull operated from Chicago, where his lavish bequests to the Civic Opera Company persuaded many leading citizens that not all Englishmen deserved the hard things that local politicians and newspaper publishers said about them. The Swedish match king, Ivar Kreuger, who had extended loans to half a dozen European governments and raised money through the gullible good offices of the Boston brokerage house of Lee, Higginson, committed suicide in his Paris apartment. Kreuger had found it as easy to raise money in the United States as to loan it in Europe, but his own lies and falsifications at last caught up with him.

Defiance of the Prohibition Amendment and the unrestricted spirit of free enterprise made it more and more difficult to draw any line between legal and illegal business. The question, "What's your racket?" addressed by one businessman to another expressed the cynicism of the time. Bootlegging helped to make crime big business. Law-abiding citizens bought liquor regularly from murderers, thugs, and degenerates. The New York Crime Commission estimated that in 1931, eighteen billion dollars went into enterprises that criminals and racketeers controlled or terrorized. Mitchell and Wiggin, the bankers, Insull, the utility magnate, Kreuger, the forger, Capone, the bootlegger, Chicago's Republican Mayor, Big Bill Thompson, and Boston's Democratic Mayor, James M. Curley, all seemed to the public to belong to a world of their own that made its own laws.

It may be doubted that the public got all the facts or reached sound conclusions on the basis of evidence presented. But it cannot be doubted that publicity, more publicity, and still more publicity, by newspaper and radio, through movies and magazines, created a widespread atmosphere of bitterness, cynicism, and disgust. Nobody in particular planned it that way. The men and women who catered to the mass audience gave that audience substantially what it wanted, paying little heed to what the publicity they released did to the human beings immediately involved. This callous disregard of the elementary decencies intensified the outstanding real-life tragedy of the depression era, bringing into clearer focus the dark forces that had grown so powerful during those years.

Colonel Charles A. Lindbergh had courted a hero's fame when he flew the Atlantic alone in 1927; he took that fame so modestly, he refused so consistently to exploit himself or his achievement for commercial purposes, that his stature grew and grew. He married Dwight Morrow's talented daughter Anne, and the young couple tried to make a secluded home for themselves and their baby, Charles, Jr., in Hopewell, New Jersey. But the publicity that made possible the fame Lindbergh had sought turned everything he had achieved to dust and ashes. Like Faust, who made his pact with the devil, Lindbergh had made a pact with the public. His failure to understand its nature added to his tragedy.

On the morning of March 2, 1932, the newspapers reported the kidnaping of the Lindberghs' infant son from their isolated, unprotected house. Within a few hours, the blundering New Jersey State Police obliterated all the obvious clues. The desperate parents promised cash and immunity to the unknown kidnaper. President Hoover issued a statement. Bishop Manning sent out a prayer for immediate use: "In a case like this we cannot wait until Sunday." William Green asked the American Federation of Labor to help. Evangeline Booth put the Salvation Army on the trail, invoking "the miraculous accomplishments with which God has honored our movement along these very lines through our lost and found bureau." The Lindberghs turned to two bootleggers, Spitale and Bitz, naming them as their ambassadors to the underworld. The snatch looked like the work of Detroit's "Purple Gang." Gaston B. Means, a lowly and smelly hanger-on of Harding's, wangled $100,000 from Mrs. Edward B. McLean of Washington—owner of the Hope diamond—on the false promise he could get the child back. A certain John Hughes Curtis of Norfolk, Virginia, persuaded Lindbergh to make contact with the kidnapers on a boat in Chesapeake Bay. But neither God nor man, neither criminals nor police turned up anything.

It remained for Dr. John F. Condon, a mildly eccentric social worker and lecturer who lived in the Bronx—"the most beautiful borough in the world"—to make headway. By inserting an advertisement in the personal columns of the *Bronx Home News,* Condon established contact by mail with a mysterious stranger to whom he sent $50,000 furnished by Lindbergh. But on May 12, before the date set for the baby's return, a truck-driver, stopping to relieve himself by the roadside half a dozen miles from the Lindbergh home, found the baby's half-buried remains. More than two years later, through tracing some of the $50,000 ransom money, the police caught up with the guilty man, Bruno Richard Hauptmann, a fugitive German felon who had entered the United States illegally. Hauptmann combined crime with his own desire to avenge the death of Germany's chief wartime ace, Captain von Richthofen. But almost two more years had to pass before Hauptmann, with the flash bulbs popping and the broadcasters chattering, went to the electric chair.

By this time, the Lindberghs found life in the United States insufferable. A Hearst reporter delivered the *coup de grâce* when, in his determination to photograph the "Lone Eagle," he forced Lindbergh's car against the curb. The Lindberghs decided to seek in England the privacy that they could not find in the United States. After they had gone their dignity in adversity brought a wholesome if belated reaction. The brutality of the criminal, the innocence of his victim, and the vulgarization af the whole affair through the press and radio dramatized the unholy power of organized crime. The price the Lindberghs had to pay for his fame and for his attempt to escape its consequences remains impossible to estimate. But it was only a part of the much larger price the whole American people were paying for the way their leaders divorced every kind of power from every kind of responsibility. Businessman and racketeer, politician and publicist, it was the same story with them all. The Lindbergh case told one chapter in that story in a language that none could fail to hear and few could fail to understand.

KEYSTONE

The Bonus Army in Washington

· II ·

THE Lindbergh tragedy showed, among other things, that neither wealth nor fame nor position nor achievement could withstand the power of publicity. Who, then, controlled the power of publicity? Not the lords of the press, not the movie magnates, not the radio tycoons. These men could make and break individuals; they drew great profits from their virtual monopoly of the channels of mass communication. But they all competed against one another for the widest audience. The last word therefore lay with the mass public whose preferences, during the depression years, often clashed with the interests of the diminishing well-to-do minority. As often as not the great news-gathering associations from which most newspapers and most radio stations got most of their news played down the demonstrations of the unemployed and the revolt in the farm belt. But their professional interests also clashed with their class interests and they could not afford, in their news-gathering capacity, to ignore the "Bonus Expeditionary Force" of fifteen or twenty thousand war veterans who, during the early summer of 1932, marched on Washington with their families, demanding immediate payment of the adjusted compensation certificates, or deferred bonus, that did not fall due until 1945. Soon, popular interest and popular sympathy forced the press, radio, and newsreels to cover the bonus marchers as exhaustively as they had covered the Lindbergh case.

For some weeks, scattered news items had reported a half-spontaneous, ha.f-organized movement of destitute veterans upon Washington. One or two hundred Communists played some part in the organization but it soon developed its own momentum, character, and leadership. Some of the veterans set up the usual Hooverville for themselves and their families on some vacant lots near the Capitol and on the Anacostia Flats across the Potomac River. The structures that made up a Hooverville consisted of broken-up packing-cases, rejected strips of corrugated metal, irregular shapes of tar-paper, and similar gleanings from city dumps, nailed or tied or piled together until they furnished some kind of shelter. Tramps and hoboes had built such shelters years before Charles Michelson and the Democratic National Committee coined the word "Hooverville" and gave it wide circulation. Not until the bonus marchers arrived in Washington had large numbers of women and children occupied Hoovervilles with their menfolk.

The veterans who built their Hoovervilles in Washington gave a new twist to an old tradition. They had gathered, in line with Constitutional procedure, to petition Congress for a redress of grievances. In other words, they were engaged in the ancient and honorable business of lobbying. Whereas busy men of affairs usually found money to pay other people to lobby for them, the veterans, with more time than money, lobbied in person. The lobbyist Washington knew best did not live in a Hooverville but in a hotel suite where he entertained members of Congress and government officials with bootleg liquor, girls, and other pleasures likely to appeal to weary public servants. The lobbyists appeared frequently in the corridors of the House and Senate, bearing carefully drafted pieces of legislation that obliging Congressmen incorporated in proposed bills.

At length the day came when the Senate voted on a bill incorporating the veterans' demands. Thousands of them, destitute, bedraggled, and forlorn, gathered on the Capitol steps, and when they received word that the Senate had rejected their program, their improvised band struck up "America" which the whole throng sang before trudging peacefully back to their shacks. Within the next few days, about half the Bonus Expeditionary Force left Washington, but several thousand, having no other place to go, stayed on. Although no sign of violence appeared, their continued presence in Washington caused embarrassment, shame, and fear. President Hoover had proved his physical courage under fire in China and his moral courage under pressure in Europe. Now, however, the prospect of civil war at the White House steps got on his nerves. Nor did Ogden L. Mills, the New York social leader and millionaire who had replaced Mellon as Secretary of the Treasury, administer the soothing syrup of which the sensitive President stood in such need. Instead, Mills gave vent to the arrogance of the ill-bred rich in the presence of an insolent rabble. The Treasury Department had charge of the Secret Service and bore responsibility for protecting the President and guarding the White House. Mills therefore ordered the White House gates closed and chained, he had the building itself put under guard, and instructed General Pelham D. Glassford, Washington chief of police, to clear the bonus marchers from all government property.

Until this new order came down from on high, General Glassford and his police had displayed patience, wisdom, and restraint. But when veterans began stoning a policeman who tried to drive them from their improvised homes, the man drew his gun and in the shooting that followed two veterans lost their lives. President Hoover ordered General Douglas MacArthur as Army Chief of Staff to drive all bonus marchers from the city. At first, the veterans cheered as four troops of cavalry, four infantry companies, and several tanks advanced toward them down Pennsylvania Avenue. Then, to the horror of the veterans and to the terror of their wives and children, American infantrymen assailed them with tear gas bombs, American cavalrymen rode them down. Milling spectators added to the confusion as the troops made their way to the veterans' hovels on Anacostia Flats and set them afire. The Army accomplished its mission, the bonus marchers scattered. And Hoover's popular reputation as the great humanitarian went up in the flames that set the sky over Washington aglow.

The Bonus Expeditionary Force had achieved two things. It goaded President Hoover into committing political suicide. In destroying Hoover politically, the Bonus Army also gave an impressive demonstration of what direct mass action could accomplish. Angry farmers in Hoover's native state of Iowa did him less harm and themselves more good by organizing a Farmers' Holiday Association, which refused to take food into Sioux City for thirty days "until the cost of production had been attained." They blockaded highways and dumped milk into ditches. When banks and insurance companies tried to auction off the properties of farmers who had failed to meet their mortgage payments, the neighbors took charge of the bidding, bought everything back for a few cents, and returned it all to the original owner. Judges in bankruptcy suits found it expedient to do nothing for fear of mob violence. Revolution had not come to the farm belt. Nothing like that. But the farmers, who had been excluded from the benefits of the boom, saw in 1932 their income drop from the nearly twelve billion dollars of 1929 to barely five billions, and the example set by Iowa proved contagious. "They say blocking the highway's illegal," an old Iowa farmer told Mary Heaton Vorse. "I says, 'Seems to me there was a tea party in Boston and that was illegal, too.'"

Many intellectuals, observing the scene from their crumbling ivory towers, mistook revolt for revolution. Norman Thomas persuaded thousands of college boys and girls of the case for democratic socialism, but his logic went over the heads of the masses and his ethics seemed old-fashioned to the intellectuals. The Communists, lacking both logic and ethics, depicted Norman Thomas as a Fascist. Their appeal transcended their meager numerical strength of some fifteen thousand zealous Party members who mechanically adapted to the United States the radical line that the Kremlin had fashioned to promote the welfare of the Soviet Union. In 1931, when the United Mine Workers of America withdrew their organizers from some of the more backward coal fields, the Communist National Miners' Union moved in. But the Communists made more headway among the unemployed, and they made the greatest headway of all among the intellectuals, who found such Communist slogans as "United Front from Below," "Self-Determination in the Black Belt," and "Organize the Unorganized" welcome substitutes for original and independent thought.

For the intellectuals, suffering more from the pangs of conscience than from the pangs of hunger, found it impossible to sit out the depression in their ivory towers. Those who had shared Mencken's cynicism discovered that it did not account for the disaster that had overwhelmed their country and the world. Those who had accepted Coolidge's new era awoke with a start. It was not that the American intellectuals had ever accepted the 1920's. Most of them had rejected the values of the decade, as the decade had rejected them. But the intellectuals, in their scorn of the businessman, had never bothered to study his problems and therefore had no firsthand knowledge either of his strength or of his weakness. The Wall Street crash seemed to mark the end of America's vaunted business civilization, and the Communists profited from the confusion of the intellectuals because the Communists, alone, seemed to have called the turn. The Communists also found Hitler a valuable ally because his anti-Communism enabled them to pass themselves off as the most militant of anti-Nazis and to denounce as Nazi sympathizers all who criticized anything they did. Like Hitler, the Communists foresaw themselves and the Nazis struggling for world mastery. Like Hitler, they despised the liberal as a coward and a compromiser. Like Hitler, they glorified action. Because the American intellectuals—especially those who considered themselves members of Gertrude Stein's lost generation—felt they had reached a dead end, the discipline, the authority, and the anti-intellectualism of the Communists appealed to them. They were the American equivalents of Hitler's armed Bohemians.

American intellectuals did not, however, flock to join the Communist Party as the German intellectuals joined the Nazis. Nor did the Communist Party seek to enlist them. The Communists soon learned that few intellectuals cared to submit themselves to the discipline and sacrifice that the Party required. They did, however, find that a large number of intellectuals were prepared to accept the Party's infallibility as an act of faith. Communism revived the atrophied religious impulses of the intellectuals, who found redemption for their sins and release for their energies by associating themselves with Communist causes, attending meetings of Communist-controlled committees, marching in parades and picket lines, and contributing money. Communism thus restored the intellectuals to fellowship with the human race, while appealing to the emotions rather than to the reason, to the bowels rather than to the brain.

The faith that sustained the Communist movement rested on an impressive body of dogma with which few American intellectuals had any previous acquaintance. Communists argued that the depression vindicated Marx and Lenin, who had predicted the inevitable collapse of capitalism. They pointed to the Soviet Union, which had advanced, under socialism, while the capitalist world had sunk into misery and despair. It was as publicists that the Communists proved most effective, and here the intellectuals made their distinctive contribution to the cause. Although at least 90 per cent of the American people remained uninfluenced, unmoved, and untouched by Communism, several outstanding men of letters came to the aid of the Party. Theodore Dreiser, John Dos Passos, and Edmund Wilson risked life and limb visiting the strike-bound coal fields of Kentucky's dark and bloody ground, where they succeeded in drawing public attention to what the depression had done to one of America's sickest industries. This was one of the earliest and most widely publicized excursions into "direct action" on the part of eminent intellectuals. Many others followed.

The American depression produced no Hitler, no Mussolini, not even an Oswald Mosley. It did produce a variety of regional demagogues, notably Huey P. Long, first Governor and then Senator from Louisiana, whose "Every Man a King" program appealed to the poor whites of the South as Hitler had appealed to the poor white-collar workers of Germany. But Long never attracted wealthy, reputable backers. They thought him too irresponsible. Perhaps more important, he had no Goebbels. Lawrence Dennis, author of *Is Capitalism Doomed?* and *The Coming American Fascism,* offered a program but he never attached himself to any demagogue and never got any important financial backing. In so far as some few wealthy, conservative Americans did lose confidence in the existing order and did seek some new solution, they probably felt as Republican Senator David A. Reed of Pennsylvania did when he remarked in May, 1932, "I do not often envy other countries their governments, but I say if this country ever needed a Mussolini, it needs one now." Reed himself, a rich and well-born Pennsylvanian, had nothing of the Mussolini in his own make-up. He merely fell into the same error the orthodox Communists committed of mistaking Fascism for capitalism with the gloves off. It was not because Reed had any acquaintance with Communist theory or practice that he fell into this error. Like almost all other members of his class, he scorned intellectuals, as they scorned him. It was here that American business leaders missed an important bet during the 1920's. Underestimating the potential contribution that American intellectuals could make to any cause, they developed no body of doctrine and no skill in presenting their case to the general public. If the Communists erred, they erred in the opposite direction and overestimated the prestige of the intellectuals and the power of propaganda. Thus, the chief strength of the Communist movement in the United States lay in its ability to exploit the intellectuals for political purposes, just as the chief weakness of the conservatives and reactionaries lay in their contempt for intellectuals. Fascism of the European type never took root in the United States. Nor did any American intellectual make converts to orthodox conservatism. The Communists were trying to corner most of the intellectuals available.

From the Bohemian heart of New York's Greenwich Village came the voice of the one American intellectual who stirred wide popular interest in a radical approach to the problem of the depression. Howard Scott had come to New York after the war, a gangling young man from Virginia, with some slight experience as an economic adviser to the I.W.W. He attached himself to a little group that clustered around Thorstein Veblen, the iconoclastic economist, who argued in *The Engineers and the Price System* and in other books that the scientist must save society from the rapacious stupidity of the businessman. After Veblen died in 1929 Scott continued to propound and develop the master's theories as the moving spirit of a research group that called itself Technocracy. Scott ran a small floor-wax business of his own but spent most of his time at Lee Chumley's restaurant and other Village hangouts predicting the imminent collapse of capitalism—or the price system, as Veblen had taught him to call it—and outlining a future society, based on the resources of the North American continent and able to provide every family with the equivalent of $20,000 a year in return for a four-day, twenty-hour work-week. The scientist, unhampered by the businessman and released from the price and profit system, could produce razor blades that would hold their edges for a year, men's suits that would wear ten years, automobiles that would last a lifetime.

During the 1920's, Scott appeared as eccentric as his master, Veblen. The arrival of the depression shortly after Veblen's death brought him into his own. Veblen's old admirers and associates respected Scott's persistence. Newcomers fell under the spell that his compelling personality cast upon a small group. As times went from bad to worse Scott persuaded himself and a small band of disciples that he possessed a unique capacity to interpret and apply the findings of science to modern life. He became the center of a cult, enlivening his discourses with yarns of personal adventure in the Baron Munchausen tradition. Even his closest adherents never praised him for his modesty. By temperament and choice, Scott belonged to the class he forever derided—the rootless intellectual for whom words take the

UNDERWOOD

Howard Scott

place of actions. Lashing himself with his own tail, he derided precisely the kind of bull session to which he devoted more and more of his waking hours.

He drew the material for these discourses from a project he directed known as Technocracy's Energy Survey of North America. Dr. Walter Rautenstrauch, professor of physics at Columbia University, Frederick W. Ackerman, a leading New York architect, and Bassett Jones, an engineering genius, sponsored the enterprise, which set out to measure the total energy output of the North American continent. Columbia University provided the space for Scott and his fellow researchers to collect and collate their data. Scott's flair for unorthodox publicity imparted an air of mystery and authority to his findings. Instead of courting newsreel and newspaper photographers, he refused to let them snap a single picture of his face. Instead of feeding the press and radio human-interest stories, he kept his personal affairs secret. Slowly he permitted some of Technocracy's data to leak out, in a tantalizing trickle, to the newspapers and magazines.

Through the fall of 1932 and on into the new year of 1933 Scott played an unexampled cat-and-mouse game with the American press and public, releasing just the right amount of the right kind of information to keep popular curiosity growing. Gradually the outlines of a technocratic utopia took shape in the mass mind, appealing to millions of Americans who rejected an avowedly radical program. Technocracy glorified the scientist over all other members of the community and the United States over all other nations of the earth. Technocracy also reviled the businessman and the politician, the foreigner and the stranger within the gates. In *The Living Age* of December, 1932, Scott's first signed pronouncement declared: "Technocracy proposes no solution, it merely poses the problem raised by the technological introduction of energy factors in a modern industrial social mechanism." Technocracy assumed that "the phenomena involved in the functional operation of a social mechanism are metrical" and that "value has no metrical equivalent." Scott estimated that the physical equipment of the United States had to carry a debt burden of two hundred and eighteen billion dollars, which always grew faster than production. Proclaiming that the price system could not operate a high-energy civilization at capacity, he described a new currency under which people would receive their income in the form of energy certificates. These certificates would purchase goods and services for a limited period and then a new set of certificates would be issued, based on the rate at which the country was producing energy. Price and value would not be measured in gold but in energy units, or "ergs."

A third of a century had passed since Bryan made a symbol of free silver. Scott did the same thing with energy. Bryan attacked the gold standard; Scott attacked the price system. But Bryan made his economic theories the tail of the Democratic Party's kite and put his oratorical genius in the service of his cause. Scott did not tie his economic theories to any political party or program, and he shunned conventional publicity as zealously as Bryan cultivated it. Yet Scott prepared a mystical blend of science and politics no less romantic and no less appealing than Bryan's mystical blend of religion and politics. "Europe discovered America in 1492," wrote Scott. "Today America is further from Europe than she was when Columbus sailed. The America of tomorrow will necessitate a rediscovery by Europe. European culture and traditions have nothing worthwhile to offer America in this twilight period preceding the dawn of a new era." Scott described Fascism as "the last ditch defense of the price system." Russian Communism "mistook the name tag of one phase of the price system for that system's entirety; it abandoned the tag, but retained the essential mechanics." Marx merely substituted Hegel for Aristotle and missed the secret of modern history—"the rate of growth of energy-consuming devices."

The Communists repaid Scott in his own coin. Recognizing his movement as a potential rival to their own, William Z. Foster and Earl Browder collaborated on a Communist pamphlet, published in January, 1933, which called Technocracy "a degenerate form of Veblenism." Technocracy, these two outstanding American Communists continued, "represents only the dreams and illusions of a baffled, unemployed mass of technicians who have been deprived of their functions by the decay of capitalism."

By 1933 Technocracy had become a favorite topic of discussion, both printed and spoken, in the United States. After several unauthorized versions of the new gospel appeared, Scott yielded to the popular demand for an authoritative report on Technocracy's findings and what they meant. He spoke over a national radio network from the dining room of the Hotel Pierre in New York, surrounded by many business and professional leaders of the country, most of them attired in evening dress. Scott, wearing his usual blue serge suit and soft, colored shirt, delivered a rambling mixture of scientific jargon and turgid abuse. When he rose to his feet, limitless possibilities lay open to him and his movement. By the time he sat down, the Technocracy bubble had burst, and within a week nearly all of his chief supporters abandoned him. Only the inner circle of a few dozen personal admirers remained and from them and a few thousand like them around the country, he set about rebuilding and reorganizing. Although Technocracy went down even faster than it went up, its trajectory left certain ineffaceable marks behind. Technocracy confirmed the tacit American assumption that modern science could assure plenty for all. It prepared the country for radical currency reform; it stimulated the nationalist spirit. But it remained for another man and another movement to reap what Scott and the Technocrats had sown.

· III ·

Technocracy boomed because it restored the American people's belief in their future. Technocracy bust because it failed to produce any program. Scott's scientific and social thinking belonged to the twentieth century; his political thinking belonged to the Stone Age. While he announced the doom of the price system and the dawn of a new era, the despised politicians went through the usual motions called for by a Presidential year. In June, 1932, the Republican National Convention renominated the Hoover-Curtis ticket, which never stood a chance of re-election. Perhaps the Old Guard, which had always distrusted Hoover, felt a somber sense of vindication. Certainly there was nothing somber about the Democrats, to whom Hoover seemed like a gift from on high. Just one fear haunted their leaders: that another dog-fight on the Convention floor might repeat the split of 1924 and prevent them from naming the next President of the United States.

For a while, the danger assumed considerable proportions. Although Governor Franklin D. Roosevelt of New York received a majority of votes on the first ballot, he needed a two-thirds majority to win. Fortunately for him, his enemies could not agree on an alternative candidate. Alfred E. Smith, embittered by his 1928 defeat, felt entitled to another chance, but religious bigotry ran as strong as ever. Smith had also drifted away from the progressive Democrats and had turned more and more to the conservative wing of the Party, which regarded Albert C. Ritchie, the "wet" Governor of Maryland, or Newton D. Baker, Wilson's former Secretary of War, as more acceptable. The balance of power, however, lay with William G. McAdoo and William Randolph Hearst, who controlled the California delegation and supported conservative John Nance Garner of Texas, Speaker of the House of Representatives. Hearst and McAdoo detested Al Smith; they had little use for Ritchie and less for Baker. They did not feel strongly about Roosevelt, one way or the other, and they made the best possible deal for themselves and their candidate when they permitted the California and the Texas delegations to switch from Garner to Roosevelt on the fourth ballot. In return for this support, which clinched the nomination, Roosevelt's managers agreed to give Garner second place on the ticket. As leader of the California delegation, McAdoo had buried the hatchet, as someone remarked at the time, in Al Smith's neck.

The Democrats had already produced a terse, conservative platform which pledged "a saving of not less than 25 per cent in the cost of the federal government," and a balanced budget derived from current revenue based "on the ability to pay." They favored reciprocal trade treaties and called for an international conference to restore international trade. Again, as in 1928, the Democrats demanded outright repeal of Prohibition. They urged the States to provide old age and unemployment insurance and they favored federal aid to States that could not care for their own unemployed. They promised to regulate certain holding companies and to consider "the rehabilitation of silver and related questions." Roosevelt lost no time in endorsing the platform. A few hours after receiving the news of his nomination, he flew from Albany to Chicago, where he addressed the Convention and promised "a new deal for the American people."

Two sharp observers at the Chicago Convention at once sold Roosevelt short. "Franklin D. Roosevelt is no crusader," wrote Walter Lippmann. "He is no tribune of the people. He is no enemy of entrenched privilege. He is a pleasant man, without any important qualifications for the office, who would like very much to be President." The personal charm that Roosevelt cultivated and exploited did not commend him to Heywood Broun, either, who described him as "the corkscrew candidate of a convoluting convention." Nor did Senator Morris Sheppard of Texas, author of the Eighteenth Amendment, believe that the wet plank in the Democratic platform would get votes. "There is as much chance," predicted

UNDERWOOD

John Nance Garner and James A. Farley Drink Andrew Jackson's Health

Sheppard, "of repealing the Eighteenth Amendment as there is for a hummingbird to fly to the planet Mars with the Washington Monument tied to his tail." But Will Rogers, observing the Democrats in conclave at Chicago, did not see how they could lose. "As soon as enough members of the committee get sober we probably will hear the Prohibition plank," he observed and then went on to predict: "I don't see how they could pick a weak enough man to lose. If he lives till November, he'll be in."

Roosevelt himself took nothing for granted. Under his governorship, New York had become the first State in the Union to provide direct relief to the unemployed, and he proposed applying to the whole nation the policies that had made him so popular in that nation's largest State. As the campaign went forward Hoover and his able Secretary of the Treasury, Ogden L. Mills, challenged Roosevelt's reform program head-on. The possibility of a Roosevelt victory led Hoover to predict: "The grass will grow in the streets of a hundred cities. Weeds will overrun the fields of millions of farms." Meanwhile Roosevelt continued to expound his reforms. "Every man has a right to life and this means he has also the right to make a comfortable living," he told the Commonwealth Club of San Francisco. "He may by sloth or crime decline to exercise that right; but it may not be denied him. We have no actual famine or dearth; our industrial and agricultural mechanism can produce enough and to spare. Our government, formal and informal, political and economic, owes to everyone an avenue to possess himself of a portion of that plenty sufficient for his needs through his own work.

"Every man has a right to his own property; which means a right to be assured, to the fullest extent attainable, in the safety of his savings. By no other means can men carry the burdens of those parts of life which, in the nature of things, afford no chance of labor: childhood, sickness, old age. In all thought of property this right is paramount; all other property rights must yield to it. If, in accordance with this principle, we must restrict the operations of the speculator, the manipulator, even the financier, I believe we must accept the restriction."

In November, Roosevelt swept the country as he had swept New York two years before, receiving more than 57 per cent of the popular vote: 22,800,000 to Hoover's 15,700,000. Outside New England, Hoover carried only two States—Pennsylvania and Delaware. The Republican Midwest as well as the Democratic South went solid for Roosevelt. Norman Thomas, stumping the country on the Socialist ticket at the bottom of the depression, received less than 900,000 votes, whereas Eugene Victor Debs, languishing in jail, had received more than a million votes on the Socialist ticket in 1920, when reaction rode high and half as many voters voted. But Thomas in 1932 got more than eight times as many votes as William Z. Foster, the Communist candidate. In short, the American voters rejected radical candidates and revolutionary parties far more heavily than they rejected Hoover and the Republicans. What most American voters wanted in 1932 was Franklin D. Roosevelt, who proved a better vote-getter on the Democratic ticket than Theodore Roosevelt had ever been, either as a Republican or as a Progressive. Indeed, not since the Civil War had the Democrats won a national election by anything like the majority Franklin D. Roosevelt piled up in 1932.

· IV ·

IF Hoover's morose frustration added to the margin of his defeat, Roosevelt's gay confidence added to the margin by which he won. When the Democrats made him their candidate, they chose a man with a progressive record and a magical name, but the tradition behind that name formed the core of his personality. Franklin Delano Roosevelt and his fifth cousin, Theodore, traced their descent to a common ancestor, Klas Martensen of Holland, who emigrated to New York in the mid-seventeenth century and assumed the name van Rosevelt soon after his arrival. The branch of the family that produced Theodore settled on Manhattan and at Oyster Bay on Long Island, nearby. Franklin's ancestors settled in the Hudson River Valley. James Roosevelt, the father of F.D.R., was born in 1828 and had another son, James Roosevelt Roosevelt, by his first marriage. "Rosey" Roosevelt married an Astor and they had no children. His widowed father married, in his early fifties, Sara Delano of

Fairhaven, Massachusetts, a handsome young woman of more distinguished ancestry than the Roosevelts. The Delanos—originally De la Noye—came to America twenty years before the Roosevelts did. They made a fortune in the China trade, which Sara Delano Roosevelt eventually inherited. With the death of her stepson, "Rosey," who left her some of the money his wife left him, the value of her estate totaled more than a million dollars.

James and Sara Roosevelt educated their only child, Franklin Delano Roosevelt, in the ways of self-reliance. They did not ignore him, after the fashion of the idle, nor spoil him, after the fashion of the newly rich. Ten years before his marriage to Sara Delano, James Roosevelt had bought a modest farm of about five hundred acres in Dutchess County and managed it with modest success. Here the son of his middle years hunted with his own gun and received his early instruction from private tutors. In summer he sailed his own boat on the Maine coast and visited Europe eight times before he reached the age of fourteen. James Roosevelt, who still wore the mutton-chop whiskers of an earlier day, spent much time with the boy, but the mother proudly wrote: "My son Franklin is a Delano, and not a Roosevelt at all." She did, however, sometimes criticize him for bossing his playmates around. Almost as a matter of course, the Roosevelts sent their boy to Groton, a boarding school recently founded by young Dr. Endicott Peabody, an Episcopal minister who had received most of his education in England, where the example of Eton, Rugby, and Harrow inspired him to establish a similar school in Massachusetts to train well-born young Americans for Christian leadership. Franklin Roosevelt put in only four years, instead of the conventional six, at Groton, where "the Rector" made an unforgettable impression upon him. The God of Endicott Peabody remained a real presence throughout Roosevelt's life, and his loyalty to the Protestant Episcopal Church never faltered.

Neither at Groton nor at Harvard, from which he was graduated four years later, did Roosevelt stand out as an athlete or scholar. At Harvard, however, he began to show qualities of leadership and a sympathy for those less fortunate than himself. He won the editorship of *The Crimson,* the college daily, and turned against the fashionable "final clubs" that had long dominated undergraduate politics. Yet Roosevelt belonged to a final club himself—not his cousin Theodore's ultra-fashionable Porcellian, but the no less esteemed if less pretentious Fly. He lost his father during his freshman year and, shortly after his graduation, fell in love with his distant cousin, Eleanor Roosevelt, President Theodore Roosevelt's favorite niece, and the beloved daughter of the President's tragic, alcoholic brother. Sara Delano Roosevelt tried without success to prevent or postpone the marriage, but nobody objected when the President insisted on attending the wedding ceremony and giving away the bride.

Eleanor Roosevelt regarded herself as a shy, plain girl and she accepted her cousin's offer of marriage in a kind of haze. Both her parents
had died before she reached the age of ten. She had lived in awe of her
beautiful mother; she had adored her father, who drank himself to death
to escape from a difficult domestic situation. Young Eleanor received her
education from tutors and at private schools in New York and abroad.
She read and learned with remarkable speed, but extreme shyness made
her misunderstood. She had known her future husband, off and on, from
early childhood, and neither one of them could have made a more conventional or suitable match. But marriage did not bring Eleanor either
freedom or independence. Sara Delano Roosevelt at once decreed where
they should live, how they should furnish their house, and whom they
should hire as servants. As they began to raise a family, she spoiled her
grandchildren as she had never spoiled her son. Having missed many
of the pleasures of childhood, Eleanor Roosevelt now missed many of
the pleasures of early married life as well. A dominating mother-in-law
at once usurped her place as head of her own household. A political
career soon competed for her place in her husband's heart.

The young Roosevelts spent the first years of their married life in
New York City. Here Franklin attended Columbia Law School, from
which he was never graduated, though he passed his bar examinations.
The respectable law firm of Carter, Ledyard, and Milburn gave him a
job and would certainly have made him a partner if the Democratic
politicians of Poughkeepsie had not offered him the chance to run for
the State Senate from his native Dutchess County district. In 1910 he
therefore quit the law to give his full time to politics. His family had
always voted Democratic; so had Roosevelt, except in the 1904 election,
when he voted for his cousin, whose example fired his own ambition.
Dutchess County had not elected a Democrat to the State Senate since
before the Civil War, and the professional politicians did not give the
twenty-eight-year-old candidate a chance. But Roosevelt hired a bright
red Maxwell car, toured every acre of Dutchess County, spoke at every
crossroads, chatted with farmers in their fields, and won his seat.

He continued to make his home at Hyde Park but shifted his winter
residence from New York to Albany. Here he led a successful revolt
against the Tammany machine and became one of the earliest and liveli-
est supporters of Woodrow Wilson. At the Baltimore Convention, he
seized the New York State standard to join the Wilson parade, while
the bulk of the Tammany-controlled delegation sat on its hands. As his
reward, young Franklin Delano Roosevelt received from Wilson the
same post as Assistant Secretary of the Navy that McKinley had given
to Theodore Roosevelt, and he acquitted himself as effectively as his

cousin. Josephus Daniels, his pacifist, Prohibitionist chief, kept on the good side of the politicians. Roosevelt cultivated the admirals and one of his proudest moments came when he represented the Navy Department at the funeral of Admiral Alfred Thayer Mahan, whose incendiary tracts on sea-power he greatly admired. Twice during the war Roosevelt tried to quit his desk job for active duty, but Wilson blocked his first attempt and influenza laid him low before he could complete his second.

Roosevelt put in his Washington years to good advantage. His ample private means enabled him to entertain on a large scale and he made the most of his opportunities. "Young Roosevelt is very promising," observed Newton D. Baker, "but I should think he'd wear himself out in the promiscuous and extended contacts he maintains with people. But as I have observed him he seems to clarify his ideas and teach himself as he goes along by that very conversational method." Franklin K. Lane, Wilson's Secretary of the Interior, offered a more caustic observation: "Young Roosevelt knows nothing about finance but he doesn't know he doesn't know." But it wasn't finance, it was politics that interested young Roosevelt, whose great chance came when he received the Democratic nomination for the Vice-Presidency in 1920. He showed himself a loyal Wilsonian and a reliable party man by campaigning on the League of Nations issue, although it spelled defeat. More important, he traveled and spoke everywhere, making friends for himself and spreading his name and fame.

Forced back into private life by the Republican sweep of 1920, Roosevelt resumed the practice of law, setting up a firm of his own in partnership with Basil O'Connor and serving as vice-president of the Fidelity Deposit Company of Maryland and head of its New York office at a salary of $25,000 a year. He spoke for naval disarmament and accepted the chairmanship of a peace endowment that became the Woodrow Wilson Foundation. Still on the sunny side of forty, Roosevelt had established himself with his party and the people as a man headed, in spite of his Harvard manner, for the very top. He had firmly subordinated his private, family life to his public, political ambitions. His wife had borne him one daughter and five sons, one of whom had died in infancy, but she still had not escaped the tyranny of her strong-willed mother-in-law. Then came the tragedy that Franklin and Eleanor Roosevelt, working together, transformed into triumph. In August, 1921, a swim in the cold water of the Bay of Fundy induced an attack of infantile paralysis that almost cost Roosevelt his life. For two years he concentrated his energies on trying to wiggle his toes, and by sheer grit and will power slowly regained some use of his wasted, lower limbs. His mother urged him to resign himself to lifelong invalidism; his wife knew better. Eleanor

Roosevelt at last defied her mother-in-law's authority, asserted herself, and put everything she had into helping her husband recover his health and resume his political career.

Frances Perkins, an old friend of the family and a devoted Roosevelt admirer, wrote in *The Roosevelt I Knew:* "Franklin Roosevelt underwent a spiritual transformation during the years of his illness. I noticed when he came back that the years of pain and suffering had purged the slightly arrogant attitude he had displayed upon occasion before he was stricken. The man emerged completely warmhearted, with humility of spirit and a deeper philosophy. Having been to the depths of trouble he understood the problems of people in trouble. Although he rarely, almost never, spoke of his illness in later years, he showed that he had developed faith in the capacity of troubled people to respond to help and encouragement. He learned in that period and began to express firm belief that 'the only thing to fear is fear itself.'

"He never displayed the slightest bitterness over his misfortune. In occasional asides he revealed that he had also a great strengthening of religious faith. He believed that Divine Providence had intervened to save him from total paralysis, despair, and death. His understanding of the spiritual laws of faith and of the association of man's feeble powers with God's great power must have come at this time. It was a basis for his future inner security in times of stress."

Roosevelt's paralysis wrought almost as great a transformation in his wife. She had long experience with her own kind of unhappiness and her energies more than matched his, especially after her long years of frustration. Now his adversity proved her opportunity; his confinement led to her release. "In the years of his illness," wrote Frances Perkins, "Mrs. Roosevelt developed a remarkable reportorial quality. She had always been an observant woman. She learned to be more observant and to be able to repeat to him what she saw and heard. This was of priceless help to him, handicapped as he was, longing to be in touch with people, and having to learn to take vicarious instead of direct personal experience." All Eleanor Roosevelt's immense, natural affections at last found their proper outlet. But she had something more than womanly, wifely qualities to put at his disposal. She had a strong social conscience and a lively political ambition of her own, and the task of furthering her husband's political career now gave her the wider scope of action she had always craved.

Before Roosevelt succumbed to polio, the gods seemed to have lavished so many gifts upon him as to set him apart from the common run of men. If his battle with illness made him human, his victory in that battle proved him almost superhuman. It was not that polio had changed Roosevelt's nature; rather did it serve to release more of his latent qualities. He had never lacked courage; now he had to develop humility as well. He remained the extroverted optimist. Adversity sharpened his ambition. His relations with all members of his family became, if possible, heartier and more affectionate than ever, yet he was never the kind of husband and father who probed deeply into the needs and natures of his wife and their offspring. His mother's personality still permeated the great house in which they all dwelt at Hyde Park.

Roosevelt drew heavily on the assets of a well-spent youth. A wise father and a fond mother had given him a happier start than he gave his children, wrapped up as he was in his political career. The first inspiration for that career came from Theodore Roosevelt, who also overcame adversity to rise to the top. The second strong influence came from Woodrow Wilson. Yet Franklin Roosevelt learned both from his cousin and from Wilson what to avoid. Theodore Roosevelt's last, bitter years taught Franklin Roosevelt never to trust the Old Guard Republicans. From Wilson he learned that righteousness alone is not enough and that self-righteousness spells suicide. Franklin Roosevelt also turned his wealth and family position to political advantage. He had none of the self-made man's awe of money, none of the social climber's reverence for family position. Long and intimate association with the rich and well-born convinced him that they produced more than their quota of boors and bores. After all, he had known from earliest childhood the spoiled children of millionaires and snobs. At the same time, he himself possessed the assurance of the born aristocrat, tempered by a sense of *noblesse oblige* and fortified by the purest courage.

His appearance as a young man suggested that the good things of life had come to him a little too easily. His close-set eyes and small mouth, the cocky tilt of his head, the set of his jaw, the lofty way he looked down on the world through his pince-nez glasses from his height of six feet two inches, gave him the appearance of a self-satisfied snob. "You know I was an awfully mean cuss when I first went into politics," he confided to Miss Perkins in later life. His pleasant speaking voice, his growing love of people, and his limitless energies broke down all barriers. He appeared at the Madison Square Garden in 1924, supported by iron braces, to nominate Al Smith as "the happy warrior." Had he not needed further treatments, he might even have received the nomination himself. But fortune had other plans: he emerged from the battle with the respect of both factions and spent the next four years building up his legs and his Warm Springs Foundation in Georgia. In 1928 he managed Al Smith's successful bid for the Democratic nomination.

Will Durant gave a vivid picture of Roosevelt as he addressed the convention at Houston, Texas: "A figure tall and proud, even in suffering; a face of classic profile, pale with years of struggle against paralysis; a frame nervous and yet self-controlled with that tense, taut unity of spirit which lifts the complex soul above those whose calmness is only a stolidity; most obviously a gentleman and a scholar. A man softened and cleansed and illuminated with pain." While Al Smith stumped the country, Roosevelt swam in the curative waters of Warm Springs, hoping in a few more years to regain his ability to walk without braces or crutches and to rise without help. But a personal plea from Smith to run for Governor of New York on the Democratic ticket persuaded him to give up his cure and return to politics full time—because he could do nothing by halves. The ironic result was that Hoover defeated Smith, carrying New York State by more than 100,000 votes, while Roosevelt won the governorship by 25,000. Two years later he won re-election with the record majority of 725,000, thereby establishing himself as the outstanding contender for the 1932 nomination. Smith's protégé had become Smith's nemesis.

"No one," Roosevelt once confessed while Governor of New York, "ever willingly gives up public life—no one who has once tasted it." Least of all a man with Roosevelt's background, experience, and temperament. His parents had impressed on him since earliest childhood that his natural gifts and inherited position laid special responsibilities and obligations upon him. Abundant health helped him to cultivate his interest in all sorts and conditions of men. A successful politician, like a successful actor, must possess enormous reserves of energy, and nature had endowed Roosevelt with the physical and nervous powers that his calling required. The people who had known Roosevelt longest and best had the greatest confidence in his capacity and his destiny. Louis McHenry Howe, the gnarled little newspaperman turned politician who had attached himself to Roosevelt back in the Wilson days, stayed close with him throughout his illness and seldom let him out of his sight thereafter.

It was as Governor that Roosevelt came into his own, widening his circle of intimates to include Samuel I. Rosenman, a bright young lawyer, Raymond Moley, professor of government at Columbia, James A. Farley, and Edward J. Flynn. Farley, a self-made product of New York's Rockland County, neither smoked nor drank and knew more political leaders by their first names than any man in the United States. He acted as Roosevelt's personal ambassador at large and spread the good word: "There's magic in the name of Roosevelt." Flynn, the astute boss of the Bronx, planned the finer points of political strategy. But Roosevelt divided power in such a way that he made himself singularly independent. He left Farley and Flynn free to make political deals and surrounded himself with a group of assorted experts, presently known as the brain trust, which advised him on policy.

Roosevelt's brain trust recalled T.R.'s tennis cabinet and the delegation of professors who followed Woodrow Wilson to Paris. Franklin
Roosevelt had few intellectual and fewer artistic interests. He enjoyed
collecting postage stamps more than he enjoyed reading; he preferred
politics to economics, naval history to philosophy or biography. But he
enjoyed the company of intelligent, articulate men and women, partly
because they interested him more than the members of New York's Four
Hundred, largely because they aided his political fortunes. As a student
of politics Roosevelt prized the contribution of the intellectual at its face
value. During his campaign two more Columbia University professors
joined the brain trust—Rexford Guy Tugwell, who taught economics,
and A. A. Berle, Jr., a former infant prodigy who taught and practiced
law. Tugwell may not have been the most learned, profound, or original
economist in the country; Berle may not have possessed the most brilliant mind or dazzling wit. But all the brain trusters stood high in their
diverse fields and they restored intelligence and conscience to American
public life.

The widening circle of advisers and sponsors who gathered around
Roosevelt before the Chicago Convention had seen his ambition, his
flair, his intelligence working for years with one increasing purpose: to
achieve the Presidency of the United States. And they shared his confidence in his ability to get and hold the job he wanted most in all the
world. The many qualities of his complicated character all seemed to
reinforce each other. By nature an extrovert, his years of illness had
turned him in upon himself. With the vitality of an athlete, his illness
chained him to his chair, and the physical energies that might have found
release in the exercise of his body went into the development of his mind
and spirit. He had always had a good mind; he had always worshiped
God devoutly. His infirmities forced him to cultivate his mind, but his
spirit flourished far more. Although he never regained all his bodily
powers, he attained a rare security of spirit and serenity of soul. Frances
Perkins, Louis Howe, and Eleanor Roosevelt knew where the secret of
his strength lay. Many of his supporters, however, mistook him for a
radical. So did some of his enemies. What neither his supporters nor his
enemies chose to recognize was the inner light that attracted some and
repelled others. In a time of general confusion and anxiety Roosevelt's
composure gave to some the confidence they themselves lacked though
to others it seemed smug and even hypocritical. But he did not fool himself and it is doubtful that he fooled the mass of the people who recognized in him the man who could master the depression, not with bloody
revolution, but with rational reform.

· V ·

ROOSEVELT'S PERFORMANCE between his election in November and his inauguration in March confirmed the hopes of his friends and the fears of his enemies. First he blocked a Republican project to liquidate all war debts and reparations. Secretary of State Stimson rightly recognized that the United States could expect no more war debt payments from Europe and that Europe could expect no more reparations from Germany. The Lausanne Conference in 1932 had cut Germany's reparations bill 90 per cent. That same December, the French defaulted on their war debt payment. The British reluctantly paid. Stimson wanted to gloss the whole thing over. But Stimson had not suggested that the United States might secure some concessions from Europe in exchange for saving Europe's face and sanctioning the inevitable. Roosevelt preferred to let the French default stand and have the American people draw their own conclusions. The French did not enjoy defaulting; the British did not look forward to following their example.

But Stimson, like his Wall Street friends and his Long Island neighbors, could not bring himself to turn Britain's difficulties to America's advantage. They had become accustomed to seeing the outside world through the eyes of the British banking fraternity and believed world prosperity, and consequently American prosperity, depended on the revival of Britain as a trading and manufacturing nation. Hoover took a somewhat different view. He had known the British long and worked with them intimately. He trusted them more than he trusted the continental Europeans. But he regarded his one-year moratorium on war debts and reparations as a temporary, emergency measure. He could not see that it must lead to cancellation any more than he could see that his decision to grant federal funds to needy banks must eventually lead to granting federal funds to needy human beings. Stimson described in his diary on July 11, 1932, one of his altercations with the President: "He told me that he entirely differed with me, in fundamentals, that we really had no common ground; that he thought the debts to us could and should be paid; and that the European nations were all in an iniquitous combine against us."

A majority of Republicans, inside and outside the Hoover administration, probably shared the President's views. But his moratorium had already committed his administration to a contrary policy, and it fell to Stimson, both as Secretary of State and as an adherent of this policy, to urge it upon Roosevelt. Few of the New Dealers—least of all the President-elect—had it in for the British. They did, however, have it in for the dominant New York bankers who instinctively looked to London for leadership. The New Dealers believed that the main, immediate task of the new administration lay at home and they fought to prevent Roosevelt from accepting Stimson's views. As the New Dealers saw it, outright cancellation of the war debts would give Europe something for nothing and open a new cycle of foreign loans, thus wrecking in advance the whole program of domestic reform. Raymond Moley, in *After Seven Years*, attached supreme importance to the strong stand that he and other New Dealers prevailed upon Roosevelt to take at this time. It was, he wrote: "the first spectacular step Roosevelt took to differentiate his foreign policy from that of the internationalists. It served notice on the League advocates, the pro-sanctionists, and those who desired a revival of foreign lending that Roosevelt was likely to be no Herbert Hoover or Henry Stimson on foreign affairs. It was a warning that the New Deal rejected the point of view of those who would make us parties to a political and economic alliance with England and France, policing the world, maintaining the international *status quo*, and seeking to impose peace through threats of war."

The man who entered national politics as a Wilsonian and went down to defeat in 1920 as the Democratic candidate for Vice-President on a League of Nations platform, never wholly accepted such views as Moley expressed. But Moley did set forth the views of most New Dealers at the time Roosevelt took office, and Roosevelt himself accepted those views in his war debt discussions with Hoover and Stimson. On another matter, however, Roosevelt went along with Hoover and Stimson and broke loose from the traditional foreign policy of the Democratic Party, which had always backed away from the responsibilities that the Republicans always wanted the United States to assume in the Far East. Perhaps because his Delano ancestors had engaged in the China trade, perhaps because he remembered Admiral Mahan's treatises on sea power, perhaps because he remained an internationalist at heart, Roosevelt endorsed the Hoover-Stimson decision not to recognize Japan's conquest of Manchuria. But on domestic matters, the Republicans got no cooperation whatever from the President-elect, who rejected, with positive delight, a proposal by Hoover and Mills to apply their methods to the banking crisis.

Ogden L. Mills belonged to New York's social and financial aristocracy. He and Roosevelt were Harvard classmates and Dutchess County neighbors who detested each other as only gentlemen can. On February 19, 1933, Hoover, in his exhausted haste, dispatched a hand-written letter asking that "Roosvelt" give the American people "prompt assurance that there will be no tampering or inflation with the currency; that the budget will be unquestionably balanced, even if further taxation is necessary; that the Government credit will be maintained by refusal to exhaust it in the issue of securities." Hoover had convinced himself that the world had passed the low point of the depression during the summer of 1932, that deflation had run its course, and that recovery would follow of its own accord if only the new administration would commit itself to follow his line. Roosevelt and the men around him, holding, with equal stubbornness, the opposite point of view, turned the proposal down. They believed that Hoover had pursued a radically mistaken policy and that any attempt to continue it would lead only to more disaster. Some even welcomed the prospect of a complete collapse of the American banking system—partly because such a collapse would discredit Hoover and the Republicans, partly because reconstruction from the ground up seemed to offer the country its best hope.

Having won his solitary battle against polio, Roosevelt had no doubt that he could lead the country to victory over the depression. The Hoover-Mills approach seemed to him negative, discredited, and timid, all the more so in the light of his own recent and narrow escape from death in Miami, Florida. He had just delivered a speech and was riding through the crowded, evening streets when a half-crazed assassin named Zangara tried to shoot him in his automobile, missed, but killed his companion, Mayor Anton Cermak of Chicago. Roosevelt carried himself with unflinching fortitude before the public and remained equally unperturbed in the presence of a few close friends soon afterward. A man who has escaped slow death from polio and sudden death at the hands of an assassin becomes so confident of his own destiny that he feels no need to accept the advice of a political opponent whom the voters have overwhelmingly rejected.

During the latter half of February and the first few days of March the American banking system disintegrated. In the middle of February when Hoover made his appeal to Roosevelt, Governor Comstock ordered all the banks in Michigan to close. By March 4, when Roosevelt delivered his inaugural address, Governor Lehman in New York and Governor Horner in Illinois had followed Governor Comstock's example. President Hoover saw his administration and the banking system of the United States go down together. Roosevelt, on the other hand, saw a new day dawning. From the opening words of his inaugural, "President Hoover, Mr. Chief Justice, my friends," Roosevelt's voice gave the country a lift: "This is a day of national consecration, and I am certain that my fellow Americans expect that on my induction into the Presidency I will address them with a candor and a decision which the present situation of the nation impels. This is pre-eminently a time to speak the truth, frankly and boldly. Nor need we shrink from honestly facing conditions in our country today. This great nation will endure as it has endured,

KEYSTONE

Franklin D. Roosevelt Inauguration, 1933

will revive and will prosper. So, first of all, let me assert my firm belief that the only thing we have to fear is fear itself—nameless, unreasoning, unjustified terror which paralyzes needed efforts to convert retreat into advance."

Roosevelt drew on his supreme virtue at this supreme moment. Courage had mended his stricken body and his stricken life. Now he lost no time communicating that same courage to a stricken people. He delivered his inaugural on Saturday, March 4, at noon. On Sunday he proclaimed a national banking holiday, forbade all exports of gold and dealings in foreign exchange, and summoned Congress to meet the following Thursday. Its members quickly approved everything Roosevelt had done and on Sunday, March 12, he delivered a radio fireside chat to the American people, explaining to them what he planned to do next. The next day the banks began to reopen and Roosevelt celebrated the occasion by suggesting that Congress legalize the manufacture of beer. Repeal of the Eighteenth Amendment had to take somewhat longer, but before he had spent ten nights in the White House, Roosevelt had laid the psychological groundwork for the new deal that he had promised the American people.

SUMMING UP

ROOSEVELT took his oath of office in the United States the day before the German people gave the Nazis enough votes to enable Hitler to rule Germany. Roosevelt's New Deal and Hitler's New Order thus began life together. In turning to Hitler the German people registered their opposition to both capitalism and democracy. Only a minority of them voted for parties that supported the Weimar Republic. A still smaller minority had any faith in capitalism. The defeat of 1918 and the subsequent inflation began a process of demoralization that the world depression completed, and many Germans turned to Hitler because his hatreds and neuroses reflected their own. Roosevelt represented everything that Hitler was not. He came from serene, aristocratic surroundings, received the conventional upper-class education, married within that class, raised a large family, made an easy success in law, politics, and business. Hitler, born unto trouble, went from failure to failure. He raged and revolted against adversity. When adversity came Roosevelt's way, he conquered it and went on to scale new heights.

To the Germans, Hitler stood for the destruction of everything they hated. To the Americans, Roosevelt stood for the recovery of everything they loved. The depression had shaken the American people severely, but it had not made them turn to any brand of Fascism or Communism, foreign or domestic. They wanted drastic and prompt reform, but they did not want to abandon democracy or destroy capitalism; both democracy and capitalism had served them too well and too long to be hastily discarded. The rise of Roosevelt also brought out certain contrasts between the United States and Europe. Germany suffered in more intense form from the same upheaval that shook so much of Europe; the upheaval that Ortega y Gasset described as a "revolt of the masses." Hitler in Germany, Mussolini in Italy, Stalin in Russia all came from the downtrodden masses and imposed themselves upon their followers. Even in the democracies, more and more men of the people had come to power—Lloyd George and MacDonald in England, Herriot in France, Masaryk in Czechoslovakia. The United States, originally an upstart among the nations, turned at this juncture to a member of the only aristocracy it had produced—the landed gentry of the Hudson River Valley. But the American people did not turn to Roosevelt as the British people turned to Baldwin. They did not want "safety first" under the old order. They wanted a new deal and they turned to Roosevelt to make that new deal at once exciting, effective, and respectable.

15

New Deal: New Order

The same crisis brings Roosevelt's New Deal and Hitler's New Order to power at the same time, but they use different methods to meet its challenge.

PREVIEW

ROOSEVELT'S EXUBERANT personality functioned at its best during the New Deal's fabulous first hundred days. Few of his countrymen dared oppose, most of them helped or cheered him as his program of domestic recovery got under way. While Roosevelt suffused the United States with hope and good will, Hitler suffused Germany with hate and fear. First, the Nazis resorted to terror and torture to consolidate the precarious majority they had won during the frenzy and alarm of the March elections. Two months later Hitler scored his first major triumph —not at home but abroad when he used a well-intentioned peace appeal by Roosevelt to pose as a peace-lover himself. Soon afterward, Roosevelt made a major move of his own in the foreign field when he wrecked the World Economic Conference in London in order to concentrate on his program of domestic reform. As for Hitler, he soon had to shoot down hundreds of his oldest friends and most fanatical followers to forestall a second revolution.

· I ·

GERMANY since 1924 had depended on the United States as a leukemia patient depends on a blood donor. The Dawes and Young Plans had encouraged American investors to finance Germany's revival until speculation in their own country's common stocks offered them such big, quick profits that the eastward flow of dollars began to dry up almost a year before the crash in Wall Street. By 1930 German production had dropped more than 40 per cent. America's difficulties intensified Germany's difficulties until the summer of 1932, when economic soothsayers announced that both countries had begun to turn the corner at last. But once again, human emotions refused to conform to the pattern of the experts' graphs. Millions of ordinary people—the "masses" of whom Ortega wrote—grew still more jittery. Nor did the "classes," the ruling groups in Germany and the United States, appear to have learned much from their ordeal. Soon the graphs of business activity plummeted to new lows, carrying the popular mood down with them. A rare touch of drama brought Roosevelt and Hitler to power at almost exactly the same moment.

Roosevelt's New Deal faced the task of restoring prosperity to a people who had recently enjoyed many of the good things of life and saw no reason why they should not enjoy still more. Hitler's New Order faced the more difficult task of restoring to the Germans a sense of self-respect that millions of them had already lost before they had experienced their few postwar years of relatively good times. On the surface the New Deal and the New Order seemed to have much in common. They both increased state power at the expense of the individual. Both concentrated that power in a single center. Both looked to one man for leadership. Both gave national recovery priority over world recovery. But they used different methods, and the contrasting characters of Roosevelt and Hitler symbolized the contrasting characters of the two movements they headed. Roosevelt came of a distinguished family who had trained him for leadership since childhood. He had made a good son, husband, and father. After happy school years and successful years at college, he won success in law and business, but found his greatest satisfaction in politics. His faith in Christianity, democracy, and himself sprang from the roots of his being and helped him triumph over a crippling illness. As a boy, Roosevelt loved his father; in maturity he loved to indulge a taste for benevolent paternalism.

Courage sustained Roosevelt; fear haunted Hitler who came of obscure, tainted stock, hated his father, and rejected the Roman Catholic faith in which he had been raised. He spent his early years among the insulted and injured, failing at everything he undertook, plagued by frustrations and self-pity. The war made him into a man, of sorts, bringing out latent qualities as polio did with Roosevelt. But no stream can rise higher than its source. Roosevelt, in his adversity, drew upon the simple virtues and values that his family, his church, his school, and his college had taught him. Hitler preached a cynical, revolutionary nihilism, based on his own warped and blighted life, exploiting the evil in human nature as effectively as Roosevelt exploited the good. Hitler also incorporated into the Nazi movement the violence, discipline, and even the uniforms of army life. But the secret of Hitler's strength lay in his weaknesses, which so many of his supporters recognized as their own. By the same token, Roosevelt's example appealed to the finest, not the basest, instincts of his people.

During his first hundred days in the White House, Roosevelt and a small group of helpers framed and put through Congress some fifteen pieces of new, major legislation. He named his program the New Deal and it fell into three phases: relief, recovery, and reform. Roosevelt himself provided the fourth "R," which included the other three and quite a lot besides. Relief came first—relief for the unemployed and relief for the shattered banking system. Although he announced in his inaugural address that "the money-changers have fled from their high seats in the temple of our civilization," Roosevelt appointed as his Secretary of the Treasury William O. Woodin, president of the American Car and Foundry Company. Until 1928, when he bolted to Smith, Woodin had voted Republican all his life. Four years later, he and two friends contributed $10,000 each to a "Friends of Franklin D. Roosevelt" fund shortly before the Democratic National Convention. The moment he entered the White House, Roosevelt gave Woodin a free hand to reopen the banks and restore confidence in the currency, whereupon Woodin sat down with Ogden L. Mills and within a few days they had all the major banks ready to resume operations. Raymond Moley lent a hand, but it was Woodin who devised the plan actually used, permitting the Federal Reserve Banks to issue their own notes in the event of a currency shortage. The job was done so well that after the moratorium ended and the banks reopened, deposits exceeded withdrawals.

Woodin had nothing of the grim reformer, nothing of the hardened reactionary about him. Wearing a silver-gray toupee, he acted more like a leprechaun than an industrialist, especially when he eased his nerves by playing the flute. As a young man he had composed poetry as well as music, and one of his early verses received a wide, if belated, fame:

> *"Oh, hear the happy blue-birds, singing in the rain.*
> *They're singing to the rainbow, shining there again.*
> *So let us be like blue-birds, happy all day long*
> *Forgetting all our troubles in a sunny song."*

Mellon had never played the flute at his Treasury desk; Mills had never written poetry in his spare time. Perhaps that helped explain why the sixty-four-year-old Woodin could work as long hours as any of the young New Dealers half his age. In addition, Woodin proved himself as practical as any Republican, as zealous as any New Dealer. He joined the administration, knowing that his health could not stand the strain, and quit after less than a year, on his doctor's orders. In May, 1934, he died, having given his life gaily—not for the New Deal, not for the old order, but for his country and for his peace of soul.

Other men reorganized the banking system and the currency on the foundation of confidence that Woodin laid. Conservative Senator Carter Glass of Virginia, author of the original Federal Reserve Act and Secretary of the Treasury under Wilson, put his name to a new banking act that increased the Reserve Board's powers, guaranteed deposits, and forbade banks to market securities. Senator Hugo L. Black of Alabama, who had seen the depression at its worst in the darkest South, drafted a bill, which the Senate promptly passed, fixing the normal work-week at thirty hours. In April, Roosevelt announced the suspension of the gold standard by the United States. A cry of "Foul!" at once went up from the British press, echoed by those Wall Streeters who looked to London for leadership in finance as well as in fashion. The Bank of England saw Roosevelt as a freebooter, deserving a pirate's doom. Of course, the British had also devalued the pound, but they had first exhausted all the devices of orthodox finance. No *force majeure* had compelled Roosevelt to follow their example. Rather had he committed the crime of *lèse-majesté* by lowering the prices of American exports on world markets and thus destroying the advantage that the devalued pound had given to the subjects of King George. But a substantial number of substantial property holders on both sides of the Atlantic thanked God for Roosevelt.

As well they might. For the New Deal, seen from any Main Street, U.S.A., looked like an attempt to channel the upsurge of radicalism that Hoover had vainly tried to dam. While Roosevelt, with his left hand, opened the floodgates of federal spending, with his right hand he signed the paper that installed Lewis W. Douglas, former Congressman from Arizona, as director of the budget. Douglas belonged to the conservative wing of the Democratic Party and quickly tried to make good the platform pledge to reduce government spending and pare government salaries by 25 per cent. At the same time, Roosevelt took advantage of the dazed condition of Congress to rush through a bill cutting veterans' benefits.

Hoover had permitted the government debt to increase by four billion dollars. Roosevelt used Douglas to bring the regular budget into balance. But having delegated that unpleasant business to Douglas, Roosevelt had the New Dealers work out an emergency budget to restore prosperity by deficit spending. They set up an Agricultural Adjustment Administration which paid farmers bounties for reducing output. Government funds financed a Civilian Conservation Corps to give young men work on reforestation projects. The Home Owners Loan Corporation helped hard-pressed home-owners pay off their mortgages—thus aiding both the mortgagor and the mortgagee. Congress created the Tennessee Valley Authority to build a huge power plant with federal funds. A National Industrial Recovery Act called upon the great trade associations to limit production, raise prices, sign codes of fair competition among themselves or with the government, and bargain collectively with union labor. Many businessmen called Roosevelt a Socialist or a Fascist. Radicals attacked him for failing to put through a drastic nationalization program. The money-changers may have fled the temple, but the New Dealers did not replace them. At most they could only try to put Humpty Dumpty together again.

Franklin D. Roosevelt did not read so widely nor write so well as his illustrious fifth cousin. His intellectual gifts did not begin to match Wilson's. He did not share Hoover's passion for blueprints and programs. Yet he surrounded himself, as few Presidents before him had ever done, with professional intellectuals—not because he had an ideology he wanted to impose on them nor because they had an ideology that he wanted to master. As Ernest K. Lindley wrote in *The Roosevelt Revolution: First Phase:* "Mr. Roosevelt did not recruit his professional advisers to provide him with a point of view, he drew them to him because their point of view was akin to his own." Raymond Moley, who later broke with Roosevelt, nevertheless wrote warmly of their early association in *After Seven Years.* Of his own "beliefs, decisions, judgments," Moley said they "were not arrived at by an orderly process of thought. They rose up willy-nilly out of a sea of feelings, senses, 'hunches,' to confront, grapple with, and finally take possession of me." And he recognized the same practical streak in Roosevelt: "I liked Franklin Roosevelt for the same elemental reasons that millions of other people were soon to like him—for his vibrant aliveness, his warmth, his sympathy, his activism. I had faith in him. The rest did not precede, it followed those bare facts."

First at Albany, then during the campaign, and finally in the White House, Roosevelt reached his political decisions by the pragmatic rather than the dogmatic route. Having put a conservative Republican industrialist in charge of the Treasury, he appointed a progressive Republican farm editor Secretary of Agriculture. Henry A. Wallace had inherited from his father and his grandfather before him the editorship of *Wallace's Farmer,* one of the most respected and widely read of the farm journals. Wallace's father had supported Theodore Roosevelt and served as Secretary of Agriculture under Harding. The plight of the American farmer throughout the 1920's and on into the depression years pushed both father and son to the left. Henry Wallace read widely, pondered earnestly, and established himself as one of the more responsible mouthpieces of the New Deal philosophy. But he had also run a million-dollar-a-year publishing enterprise and had found time to develop a new hybrid corn and to experiment with new strains of poultry. Rexford G. Tugwell, one of the original brain trust, worked under Wallace and the two men became good friends. Back in 1915, at the age of twenty-four, Tugwell had written verse:

"We begin to see richness and poorness; we begin to dignify toil.
I have dreamed my great dream of their passing,
I have gathered my tools and my charts;
My plans are fashioned and practical.
I shall roll up my sleeves—make America over."

Now past forty, Tugwell still nourished some of this youthful idealism. Moley, his teaching colleague at Columbia, compared him to a cocktail: "His conversation picked you up and made your brain race along." Roosevelt liked and needed this kind of stimulation partly because it had a therapeutic effect on him, partly because the energies of those who furnished it could be directed into practical channels.

For example, as his Secretary of the Interior Roosevelt chose Harold L. Ickes of Chicago, a one-man reform wave who had supported Theodore Roosevelt in 1912 and Robert M. LaFollette in 1924. Senator Hiram Johnson had recommended Ickes as an incorruptible conservationist, and Roosevelt took to him so much that he offered him the Secretaryship of the Interior at their first meeting, early in 1933. Ickes, a lawyer in his late fifties, had spent most of his life trying to reform American politics from the outside. Suffering from an almost pathological fear of grafters, he spent months double-checking every item on all the vast bids that came his way as head of the Public Works Administration. Younger men threw themselves into the relief and recovery phases of the Roosevelt program. Ickes preferred to concentrate on reform.

As ex-Republicans, Woodin, Wallace, and Ickes seemed more like political liabilities than political assets. As professors at Columbia, Moley and Tugwell controlled no votes. Frances Perkins, Roosevelt's Secretary of Labor and the first woman ever to hold a Cabinet post in the United States government, appealed neither to the politicians nor to the professional labor leaders. Born in Boston the same year as Roosevelt, Miss Perkins was graduated from Mount Holyoke College, and then received an M.A. degree from Columbia in 1910. Moving in the same social circles as both Franklin and Eleanor Roosevelt, Miss Perkins anticipated by many years the interest they later developed in improving working and living conditions among the great mass of the American people. But Frances Perkins did not remain either a settlement house worker or a spinster. In 1913 she married Paul Caldwell Wilson of New York, became the mother of a daughter, and went to work for New York State, specializing in factory legislation, women in industry, and the education of immigrants. She wrote books and lectured, served under Al Smith, and received from Roosevelt the post of Industrial Commissioner for the State of New York. Her surveys of unemployment conditions gave her a national reputation.

UNDERWOOD

Harry Hopkins and Harold Ickes

The man who later became Roosevelt's most intimate confidant arrived in Washington an almost complete unknown. Harry Hopkins, the son of an Iowa harness-maker, spent money as zealously as Ickes guarded it. Relief engaged all his passions. He cared little about recovery and still less about reform. He combined the conscience of a social worker with the tastes of a poker-player and race-track devotee. The combination made an irresistible appeal to Roosevelt's own complex nature. Roosevelt also felt a fatherly affection for Hopkins as a younger man whose zest for work and play triumphed over a delicate constitution. Hopkins had attended Grinnell College in Iowa, where his grades ran the whole gamut from A to E, and then had come to New York, where he worked with Lillian Wald's Henry Street Settlement. As he once told a friend, "I climbed tenement house stairs, listened to the talk of Morris Hillquit and William English Walling, went to Cooper Union meetings, and really got exposed to the whole business of how the working class lived and to their poverty and joviality. Many's the bottle fight I saw in those days. Real gangsters would walk into the settlement dances—Lefty Louie and others—just to bedevil us, and you'd try to throw them out. You know. Really tough. That's when I found out there was such a thing as a gangster. I got a dose of it, and not by the books." From his settlement house job, Hopkins went to work for Frances Perkins. Roosevelt met him in 1928, appointed him relief administrator for New York State, and in 1933 invited him down to Washington to take charge of the greatest make-work project since the Egyptian pyramids— the Works Progress Administration.

To such reformers, intellectuals, social workers, and public servants Roosevelt entrusted the development and execution of the New Deal. The New Dealers did not mesmerize Roosevelt into accepting their ideas. Those he liked best, those who accomplished most, had few ideas in the first place. Nor had they any previous experience in making policy. They had specialized either in talking and writing or in just getting things done, usually on orders from above. Ickes stood for nothing more radical than honesty in government and conservation of natural resources, the same principles for which Theodore Roosevelt had "stood at Armageddon and battled for the Lord." Wallace and Tugwell saw visions and dreamed dreams, but not on government time or in connection with the jobs Roosevelt assigned to them. At a time when the labor movement had blood in its eye and Communists in its blood stream, Roosevelt put the Department of Labor in the charge of a Boston gentlewoman whom no employer could bamboozle and for whom no labor leader could buy a glass of beer. But it was Hopkins who gained a unique place in Roosevelt's heart with his love of action for action's sake.

The use Roosevelt made of the New Deal and the New Dealers showed him at the top of his political form. Holding the real power in his own hands alone, he enlisted the New Dealers on his terms, never forgetting, however, that the wise ruler, especially in a democracy, uses his power sparingly. At the same time, the popular demand for the kind of reform that the New Dealers symbolized gave Roosevelt the whip hand over the professional politicians, who knew even less about the New Deal than the New Dealers knew about practical politics. John Franklin Carter, Jr., in *The New Dealers,* described the professional politicians Roosevelt enlisted:

"Not since Andrew Jackson won the Presidency has there been as ruthless and intelligent a riot-squad at the disposal of the Chief Executive. As Postmaster-General 'Big Jim' Farley, good-natured, bull-headed, and a fighter, handles the Party patronage. Suave Ed Flynn, the dynamic boss of the Bronx, is slowly wresting from Tammany the control of the biggest nugget of Democratic votes in the entire nation, as a preliminary to the 1936 showdown. Warm-hearted, cool-headed Frank Walker is co-ordinating the entire emergency apparatus of the New Deal and is directing it along the lines which will make votes for the Party, come November. Homer S. Cummings, as Attorney General, is able to supply Roosevelt with legal opinions which tell him he can go ahead and do whatever the President has decided to do. And Daniel Calhoun Roper, as Secretary of Commerce, is shrewdly and soft-spokenly holding in line the Democratic back-log in the rural South and West, in support of policies which are wildly at variance with all the traditional Democratic principles. It is a smooth-running, well-oiled machine: a couple of Irish

Catholics from New York, a Catholic lawyer from Montana, a Connecticut Yankee, and a dry Methodist from North Carolina."

What these men didn't know about practical politics, Roosevelt did. He knew that the American people wanted extensive changes made. He knew that the New Dealers could not put through these changes without the aid of a political machine, and he knew that the machine politicians could not put them through without the aid of the New Dealers. He alone had the support of both groups, based on the simple fact of their dependence upon him. The professional politicians would have preferred to staff the relief, recovery, and reform agencies with their own appointees, but they recognized that the New Dealers had caught the popular imagination and had gained popular confidence. The New Dealers, in their turn, welcomed any favors that came their way, and those who prided themselves on their realism recognized their limitations and respected the professional politician's sphere of influence. As for the specific New Deal policies, Roosevelt and his advisers played by ear, improvising on a day-to-day basis. Partly it was a matter of temperament. Mainly it was the result of a crisis that had taken everybody by surprise.

Long before Inauguration Day, Roosevelt had awarded the two top jobs in his administration to orthodox Democrats of long and proven loyalty to the Party. To appease the professional politicians and get the Democratic nomination, Roosevelt had accepted John Nance Garner of Texas, Speaker of the House of Representatives, as his running mate and next in line of succession. Perhaps Garner inherited some of his political acumen from his illustrious ancestor, Sir Robert Walpole, British Prime Minister during the eighteenth century; in any event he carried great prestige among both parties in Congress. So did Senator Cordell Hull of Tennessee, whom Roosevelt appointed Secretary of State and third in line of succession. Hull came of a moderately well-to-do family. As a boy he had rafted logs on the Cumberland River and, during the war with Spain, organized a company of volunteer infantry. He then became a lawyer, a judge, and a member of the Tennessee state legislature. Since 1906 he had served in Congress, never losing his simple faith in free trade as the sure cure for all ills in all times and all places. Hull regarded himself as a devoted Wilson man and on that score welcomed the nomination of Roosevelt. Nor had he forgotten that early in 1932 Roosevelt had called for a low tariff: "It is time for us to sit down with other nations and say to them: 'This tariff fence business, on our part and on yours, is preventing world trade. Let us see if we can work out reciprocal methods by which we can start the actual interchange of goods.'" Only the offer of the top job in Roosevelt's Cabinet persuaded Hull to give up his Senate seat. At last the chance of his lifetime had come to apply the free-trade theories he had always advocated. Almost alone among the leading members of Roosevelt's official family, Hull took office with a coherent body of fixed ideas and a program for making them come true.

Hull had reason to purr when Roosevelt's inaugural address pledged the United States to the "good neighbor policy," especially in reference to Latin America. One of Hoover's ghost-writers had coined the "good neighbor" phrase, and Hull's early enthusiasm for the cause of Cuban independence gave him an almost proprietary interest in better relations among all the American republics. But the Roosevelt inaugural contained one heretical passage that Hull preferred to ignore: "Our international trade relations, though vastly important, are in point of time and necessity secondary to the establishment of a sound national economy." Some weeks before Roosevelt spoke and some months before Hull awoke to what had happened, the British Foreign Office had already scented a change in the wind. Sir Ronald Lindsay, British Ambassador to the United States, knew that Roosevelt had rejected Hoover's plan to restore the international gold standard and write off the war debts. Before Inauguration Day, Lindsay therefore visited Roosevelt at Warm Springs, Georgia, and prepared the way for Prime Minister MacDonald to visit Washington in April to confer with the new President on the projected World Economic Conference. Roosevelt extended the necessary invitation, suggesting at the same time that France also send an official visitor to Washington in the person of Édouard Herriot, who had resigned the premiership in December because he stood out against war debt repudiation. But Roosevelt put an unexpected damper on his two visitors by taking the United States off the gold standard while they were on their way across the Atlantic. Their visits accomplished nothing except to remind Hull that Roosevelt planned to make his own arrangements with foreign countries. And these arrangements put domestic relief, domestic recovery, and domestic reform ahead of any kind of activity abroad.

During his first hundred days in the White House Roosevelt maneuvered more personal power into his hands than any other President had ever possessed in peacetime. While Hitler used his emergency powers under the Weimar Constitution to establish a one-party, one-man dictatorship, Roosevelt used his emergency powers under the Constitution of the United States to enlarge the authority of the President. Hitler suppressed all opposition, exterminated friends and enemies. Roosevelt did not shoot Republicans; he invited three of them to join his Cabinet. He did not throw anti-New Deal Democrats into jail; he appointed them to high office. As more and more newspapers opposed him, he did not imprison their editors and staffs but turned more and more to the radio, broadcasting ten fireside chats during his first hundred days in office. Theodore Roosevelt had made the White House into a glorified gymnasium and loved nothing better than to treat all his opponents like punching-bags. Woodrow Wilson turned the White House into an ivory tower from which he looked down lovingly, but from afar, on the masses. Franklin D. Roosevelt made the White House his home and the American people his friends.

Friendliness came naturally to the President. In 1934 Ernest K. Lindley, who knew him long and liked him well, wrote that Roosevelt "does not really rejoice in the hostility of anybody. It is true that he likes to be liked. He has exceptional talent for conciliation and compromise. He is happiest, I think, when he can be a benevolent arbiter." Mrs. Eleanor Roosevelt, in *This I Remember,* probed more deeply. Many people told her, she wrote, that her husband "misled" them and she admitted he often seemed to agree with them when actually he did not: "This misunderstanding not only arose from his dislike of being disagreeable, but from the interest he always had in somebody else's point of view and his willingness to listen to it. If he thought it was well expressed and clear, he nodded his head and frequently said, 'I see,' or something of the sort. This does not mean that he was convinced of the truth of the arguments or even that he entirely understood them, but only that he appreciated the way in which they were presented. I have never known anyone less really influenced by others."

Mrs. Roosevelt made no attempt to minimize the complexities of her husband's character. When Roosevelt nodded, he might or might not agree with the speaker. He might mean that he found the speaker's ideas "well expressed and clear." Or again he might mean that he had not "entirely understood them." Jim Farley's autobiography quotes Mrs. Roosevelt as having once told him: "Franklin finds it hard to relax with people who aren't his social equals." Farley assumed that this explained why he had been "left out of the infield." But Roosevelt never found a "social equal" so congenial as Louis Howe or Harry Hopkins, and Mike Reilly, chief of the White House Secret Service Detail, reported on the basis of long observation that Roosevelt never became "one of the boys," though not for want of trying. If Roosevelt was no introvert, like Wilson, he also lacked his cousin Theodore's gift for making scores of intimate friends. Crowds stimulated him; so did individuals. Yet he always held something of himself apart.

Roosevelt loved power even more than he loved people; indeed, he exploited his love of people to indulge his love of power. This did not entail any hypocrisy. It was a spontaneous process, a matter of second nature. Nobody relished more acutely than the President the conflicts and contradictions with which he surrounded himself. But these conflicts and contradictions mirrored the condition of the country as a whole. He therefore saw nothing inconsistent or underhanded about having Woodin and Wallace, Hull and Hopkins, Farley and Ickes, Garner and Tugwell all working together in the same administration. Indeed, he could see no other way to cope with the problems at hand. And behind it all lay his own supreme confidence. "Mr. President," one of Roosevelt's callers warned him in 1933, "if your program succeeds you will be the greatest President in American history. If it fails you will be the worst one." "If it fails," Roosevelt replied, "I shall be the last one." But Roosevelt never had any doubt he would succeed, and neither did the great mass of his fellow citizens. "The whole country is with him," wrote Will Rogers. "Even if what he does is wrong, they are with him. Just so he does something. If he burned down the Capitol, we would cheer and say, 'Well, we at least got a fire started anyway.'"

· II ·

IF Roosevelt's first hundred days seemed to many Americans the beginning of a new era of good feeling, Hitler's first hundred days seemed to many Germans the end of their world. Roosevelt and Hitler shared one important trait in common. Both wanted "action, and action now," as Roosevelt put it in his inaugural address. Both men also aspired to save their people—Roosevelt on the basis of courage and good will, Hitler on the basis of fear and hatred. Their methods differed even more than their purposes. Roosevelt had received close to three-fifths of the popular vote in the November election, and during the long wait before his inauguration, the remaining popular support for Hoover dwindled. Roosevelt's hopes on taking office matched the hopes of the American people. At the same time that Roosevelt won the American Presidency, Hitler's Nazis lost two million votes in the Reichstag elections. The following March, they received barely two-fifths of the total vote, and they got that only after they had set fire to the Reichstag building and muzzled the opposition. Having come to power by forming a coalition with the Nationalists, Hitler decided he had to move fast or lose everything.

On Monday, March 6, the day the results of the elections became known, Storm Troopers took control of most of the streets in most of the chief German cities. Göring, as Prime Minister of Prussia, ordered the regular police not to interfere as uniformed Nazis, in an area comprising more than half of Germany, broke into shops and homes, burned, destroyed, and stole property, beat up and arrested thousands of Communists, Socialists, and Jews. Even the more brutal German leaders, in the Kaiser's day, had made some attempt to apologize for the invasion

"Adolf Hitler Arrives at the Dictators' Club." Strube, Daily Express, *London*

of Belgium and the unrestricted campaign of submarine warfare, pleading that necessity knows no law. But Göring, the least disreputable of the top Nazis, coolly informed an audience in Essen: "I am in the habit of shooting from time to time, and if I sometimes make mistakes, at least I have shot." The Nazis also jailed all the newly elected Communist deputies they could lay their hands on, thereby assuring themselves a Reichstag majority, even without the Nationalists.

A few foreign reporters were able to inform the world that the Nazis had taken thousands of their enemies into "protective custody," beaten most of them, and shot them by the hundreds "while trying to escape." From a young Socialist worker, arrested with twenty other men by Nazi Storm Troopers, the Berlin correspondent of the *Manchester Guardian* got some gruesome details: "They were taken to the Hedemannstrasse and beaten with whips and rubber truncheons. They were then taken to another room, made to stand facing the wall, and beaten around the head, face, and eyes with whips, truncheons, and chair legs. Some of them fainted and fell to the ground, but were beaten until they got up again. They were made to do the double-knee bend with hands stretched forward, slowly and repeatedly." Many Nazis who inflicted these tortures on their victims found a sadistic pleasure in such acts of cruelty. But it was torture with a political as well as a psychopathic purpose. "The greatest of spirits can be liquidated," Hitler said, "if its bearer is beaten to death with a rubber truncheon." Terror and torture obsessed the rulers of the Third Reich. Fear of terror and fear of torture obsessed their victims.

The fortnight of terror with which Hitler ushered in his New Order culminated in an act of homage to the Old. On March 21, Hindenburg and the Junker aristocracy joined Hitler and the Nazi hoodlums in a ceremony at the Garrison Church of Potsdam, shrine of Prussian militarism. Almost the entire Reichstag, except the Communists and about twenty Social Democrats, attended, and Hitler's deferential attitude toward Hindenburg led some of the Hohenzollerns to hope that the Nazis might help them back to power. Two days later, at a formal session of the Reichstag in the Kroll Opera House, Hitler disillusioned them. In a speech outlining his plans for the Third Reich he declared: "In view of the distress now prevailing among the people, the national government regards the question of a monarchist restoration as indiscussable." He saved the heart of his speech for the close: "The government offers the parties an opportunity for a peaceful German development and for the future conciliation that can grow out of it. But it is equally determined and ready to take up any challenge of rejection and resistance. Now, gentlemen, you yourselves may make your decision: will it be peace or war?" Hitler had laid before the Reichstag an "enabling law," turning over absolute power for a period of four years to the government he headed. More than four hundred Reichstag members approved the enabling act. Only the Social Democrats, numbering less than one hundred, opposed it. Hitler had attained complete power within the framework of the Weimar Constitution.

While the Nazis fought the German Communists more savagely than ever, it was a different story abroad. As Göring put it: "It is no business of ours what happens in Russia and it is no business of Russia's what happens in Germany. German-Russian relations will remain as friendly as in the past years." In his Reichstag speech Hitler described the fight against Communism as "our domestic affair in which we shall never tolerate any interference," but "toward the Soviet government the Reich government is willing to travel friendly ways beneficial to both parties." On May 5, Hitler renewed the friendship pact with Russia that Brüning, Papen, and Schleicher had all permitted to lapse. It took Hitler, who had ridden to power on anti-Communist propaganda, to restore normal relations between the German fatherland and the fatherland of world Communism.

Nor did Hitler, the backsliding Roman Catholic, have any difficulty reaching an understanding with the Vatican. Early in April, 1933, Pope Pius XI gave Papen and Göring a private audience, and a concordat between the Roman Catholic Church and the Third Reich followed. The

Nazis agreed to tolerate many Catholic religious and social organizations. The Vatican forbade its clergy to engage in any political activity and promised to secure Nazi approval before appointing any new bishops and archbishops. The Protestant churches of Germany also pledged themselves to refrain from political activity, but they succeeded, with Hindenburg's help, in blocking Hitler's attempt to create a new Nazi-controlled German-Christian Church. Finally, Hitler came to terms with his fellow dictator—Marshal Pilsudski of Poland. In that case, however, it was not Hitler who took the initiative. Soon after the March 5 elections, Pilsudski ordered the Polish Army to hold a series of demonstrations on the German border. Then he asked Hitler to choose peace or war. The Polish and German governments issued a joint communiqué pledging themselves "to examine and treat the common interests of the two countries dispassionately," and a ten-year nonaggression pact followed. Treaties with the Kremlin, the Vatican, and Poland—National Socialism had lost no time in coming to terms with its chief enemies and rivals abroad.

National Socialism lost still less time liquidating its chief enemies and rivals at home. After crushing the Communists, the Nazis outlawed the Social Democrats, whereupon the Catholic Center Party and the Nationalists declared themselves dissolved. The government announced: "In Germany, the National Socialist German Workers' Party is the sole existing political party." By July, Hugenberg quit his Cabinet post as Minister of Economics and Agriculture, but Papen and a few other Nationalists lingered on. In the overcrowded professions of journalism, teaching, and law, Nazis replaced Jews, and they defined a Jew as anyone with a Jewish grandparent. This multiplied the number of Jews in Germany from some half million adherents of the Jewish faith to two million so-called "non-Aryans." "Thank God," an unknown humorist exclaimed, "my grandmother was illegitimate, and therefore I do not have to show her birth certificate." The story did not amuse the mother of General Milch, whom Göring had installed as head of the German Air Force. Because her husband was half Jewish, Milch's mother had to go to court and swear that her husband was not the father of her child, otherwise Milch would have lost his job. So many Germans dyed their hair to make themselves look like blond Aryans that a Nazi official exclaimed: "We must not tolerate this epidemic of blondness, which has already caused rivers of peroxide to flow. Not even the purest of blonds is necessarily a pure German, and in many a person with dark hair there is concealed an heroic soul."

As Minister of Propaganda and Enlightenment, Goebbels led the heresy hunt. He made and broke the careers of stage and screen stars and sanctioned, though with some misgivings, a burning of offensive books, most of them by Jewish writers. Goebbels saw to it that one of

Paradise Lost. The Emigrés: "Germany! What a beautiful garden. But how can we get back there now?"
Kladderadatsch, *Berlin*

his own unpublished novels and several of his unproduced plays found large audiences. He forced beautiful actresses to accept his attentions or lose their jobs. "All we National Socialists are convinced we are right," Goebbels announced, "and we cannot bear with anyone else who maintains he is right. For if he is right, he must be a National Socialist, and if he is not a National Socialist, then he is not right." Spoken like a Communist. For the Nazis, like the Communists, believed that the keys of the kingdom belonged to them and to them alone. Like the Communists, the Nazis also looked upon the Party as an end in itself, and that Party, in turn, consisted of an inner, ruling circle, bent on perpetuating their own power, and a fanatical rank and file who accepted the propaganda line handed down from above. But Communist propaganda stressed the class struggle and the role of the proletariat, whereas Nazi propaganda stressed racial factors and the role of the pure-blooded German. The Communists offered salvation to all who allied themselves with the proletarian cause; the Nazis offered salvation only to members of the chosen German people. The rest of humanity had to take orders from its racial betters.

On coming to power in Germany, the Nazis singled out the Jews as their chief victims. At first, Nazi anti-Semitism affected only those Jews whose jobs Nazis could fill. Jewish doctors and scientists, even Jewish department stores remained—for the while—relatively undisturbed. Ludendorff had once described Germany as a country occupied by Hitler's Storm Troopers. But by the time Hitler triumphed he no longer needed his shabby, undisciplined mass army of misfits. On their way to power, the Nazis had organized a state within a state and the more alert Storm Troopers at once usurped the duties of local officials whose jobs the Nazi revolution had liquidated. Hitler put a quick stop to this "second revolution," first appointing Dr. Schacht president of the Reichsbank, and then turning the Ministry of Economics over to Dr. Karl Schmitt, general director of the largest insurance company in Germany. "A businessman must not be deposed if he is a good businessman, but not yet a National Socialist," Hitler told a group of Nazi officials in July,

1933, "and especially not if the National Socialist who is put in his place understands nothing of economic affairs."

Few Nazi leaders, least of all Hitler himself, possessed this understanding. But Hitler, on his way to power, discovered that economics provided the slogans he needed to justify his national and racial obsessions. Nazi economists popularized the word *Autarkie,* meaning a self-sufficient economic system. They attacked "interest slavery." *Autarkie* justified nationalism; "interest slavery" justified anti-Semitism. Germany's prewar *Drang nach Osten* reappeared as anti-Communism. In spite of the formalities he had taken to improve the surface of German-Russian relations, Hitler had not abandoned the policy he outlined in *Mein Kampf:* "We stop the eternal German march to the south and west of Europe and turn our eyes toward the land in the East. We finally bring to a close the colonial and commercial policy of the prewar time and go over to the land policy of the future. If we speak of land in Europe today, we can only think, in the first instance, of Russia and her border states."

When Hitler looked to the east, he planned to bring more territory under German rule at the expense of the Russians and their neighbors. When he looked to the west, fear of attack caused him to warn: "The political testament of the German nation for its foreign dealing should and must read: Never to tolerate the existence of a second Continental Power in Europe. To see in every attempt at erecting a second military power on the German frontier, even if it be only in the form of a militarily capable state, an attack against Germany and to see therein not only the right but the duty with all means, up to the use of armed force, to hinder the rise of such a state, or if it has already arisen, to destroy it. To see to it that the strength of our nation shall have its foundations, not in colonies but in the territory of the homeland in Europe. To consider the Reich never secure if it is not able for centuries in the future to give every sprout of our own nation its own piece of ground and soil. To forget never that the holiest right in this world is the right to the land which oneself will cultivate, and that the holiest sacrifice is the blood which one pours out for this land."

In such outbursts as these, Hitler translated the strategic concepts of General Haushofer and the German General Staff into his own demagogic mysticism. His madness had a strategic method, and by the same token Germany's strategists suffered from a kind of madness. Because Hitler subordinated economics to propaganda he had to summon Dr. Schacht and Dr. Schmitt to his aid. Possessing the practical competence that the ignorant and fanatical Nazis lacked, Schacht and Schmitt devised an economic program that attempted to save German capitalism by pouring two billion marks from the public treasury into housing and highway construction. And Alfred Hugenberg, the conservative newspaper magnate, originated a scheme that turned another billion marks over to employers who created new jobs. The Germans, like the Americans, were pulling themselves up by their own economic bootstraps.

Roosevelt kept close tabs on the New Deal relief and recovery programs. Hitler paid less heed to the relief and recovery aspects of his New Order. For the moment, at any rate, he was content to let bankers, industrialists, and conservative politicians revive German capitalism while he devoted himself to liquidating his enemies—chiefly Socialists, Communists, and Jews. To establish himself firmly in power, he had to establish terror as the permanent way of life in the new Germany. Delegating the immediate problem of relief and the short-term problem of recovery to his conservative allies, he kept his long-term program of planned terror under his own control.

Hitler even bent Roosevelt's prestige to his own purposes. As soon as MacDonald and Herriot set the example for world statesmen to visit the White House, Dr. Hjalmar Schacht followed. On landing in New York he told the press that he was bringing "the heartiest greetings of Reich Chancellor Hitler to President Roosevelt, whose courage and astute conception of the world's economic problems has aroused the greatest admiration on the part of the Reich Chancellor." Hitler, Schacht continued, "admired the courageous and resolute American President; moreover, the situation of America is in many respects similar to that of Germany. The Reich Chancellor does not rule as a dictator; just as Roosevelt was elected by an immense majority and received extensive powers from Congress, so also was Hitler. This is the best kind of politics and democracy in its best form. You choose your leader and follow him. In this way you make it possible for him to carry out his plans."

The facts did not sustain the analogy Schacht drew. Hitler had not come to power with majority backing nor did he win his triumph in a free election. Although the same kind of internal crisis installed Hitler's New Order in Germany at the same moment the Roosevelt administration took office in the United States, Hitler sought national revival through force, fear, and hatred, while Roosevelt sought national revival through persuasion, courage, and good will. Hitler, despising mankind, released its basest passions by invoking terror. He staked the future of his country, his party, and himself on the exploitation of fear. Roosevelt staked everything on the proposition that the good in human nature outweighs the bad. He sought to banish the fears that Hitler sought to exploit. Morally, Roosevelt had everything, Hitler nothing. But the comparison does not appear so one-sided to those who view history as an unending and forever unresolved conflict between the closely matched forces of good and evil.

· III ·

THE MEN nearest to Hitler compared him, for propaganda purposes, to Roosevelt; only Roosevelt's bitterest enemies compared him to Hitler. Nor did Roosevelt relish the comparison: he shared the misgivings that Hitler's menacing talk and wild behavior had stirred abroad. The Disarmament Conference had reached a dead end; Japan had torn Manchuria loose from China and quit the League of Nations; Hitler's Germany looked like the worst news yet. When, therefore, Hitler summoned the Reichstag to a special meeting on May 17, Roosevelt spent several anxious days improvising a hasty countermaneuver. This took the form of a personal appeal for peace and disarmament addressed to the heads of fifty-four nations and issued on May 16, the day before Hitler was to speak. Roosevelt called for a reduction of offensive weapons, a new definition of aggression, and a universal, consultative nonaggression pact. But Hitler got in the last word. Although he devoted most of his speech to warning that Germany would quit the League of Nations unless given equal rights in the matter of armaments, he managed to turn the Roosevelt message to his advantage: "The proposal of the American President, of which I learned only yesterday, obligates the German government to warm thanks. Germany is ready to agree without further discussion to this method of relief for the international crisis." He continued: "Because of the boundless love and loyalty we feel for our own nationality, we respect the national rights of other people and desire to live with them in peace and friendship."

Roosevelt could not at one and the same time call Hitler a liar and plead effectively for peace and disarmament. Nor could the anti-Hitler majority of the German people call Hitler's bluff, and he thus emerged with new prestige. In the eyes of many, at home and abroad, Hitler had shown some disposition to reconcile his views with Roosevelt's, while at the same time winning his first diplomatic skirmish with the new President of the United States. Roosevelt himself had few regrets. He felt that he had scotched the war scare that followed Hitler's election victory and could now get along with the all-important job of domestic recovery.

But the World Economic Conference which assembled in London on June 12 put this job in jeopardy as Roosevelt and his top advisers shifted their attention from promoting recovery at home to promoting recovery abroad. And they found these two assignments irreconcilable. Secretary Hull and James M. Cox, head of the delegation to London, were conservative internationalists who believed that recovery in the United States depended on world recovery and that world recovery depended on a restoration of world trade. The New Deal nationalists, on the other hand, put American recovery first and suspected Hull and Cox of wanting to bring back the old order at home and abroad. For more than three weeks, the Americans in London battled the other delegations and one another, until Roosevelt suddenly dispatched Raymond Moley, a New Deal nationalist, to restore harmony. But so much confusion followed Moley's visit that Roosevelt finally sent a message that ended everything—except Cordell Hull's determination to continue his fight for lower tariffs.

"I would regard it as a catastrophe, amounting to a world tragedy," wrote the President in an opening sentence worthy of Henry James, "if the great conference of nations, called to bring about a more real and permanent financial stability and a greater prosperity to the masses of all nations, should, in advance of any serious effort to consider these broad problems, allow itself to be diverted by the proposal of a purely artificial and temporary experiment affecting the monetary exchange of a few nations only." He also lined himself up with the radical nationalists rather than the conservative internationalists when he predicted "old fetishes of so-called international bankers are being replaced by efforts to plan national economies with the objective of giving those currencies a continuing purchasing power which does not vary greatly in terms of the commodities and needs of modern civilization." He called, specifically, for "the kind of dollar which, a generation hence, will have the same purchasing and debt-paying power as the dollar value we hope to establish in the near future." This meant no stabilization of the dollar on gold and no return to any kind of international gold standard. The French delegation, whose currency remained on gold, had hoped to persuade Britain and America to stabilize on the same level as France. The British delegation, whose currency had gone off gold, had hoped to persuade the Americans to stabilize the dollar at a higher rate than the pound. As usual, the orthodox American bankers tended to accept the British view. But Roosevelt now sat at the controls and he had committed himself to a different approach.

The London Economic Conference forced Roosevelt to reveal himself as an unreconstructed nationalist and an unreconstructed currency reformer. "The present President is more truculent than President Wilson," wrote the Conservative *Saturday Review* of London. "He not only leaves the conference in the lurch, but he kicks it downstairs." John Maynard Keynes disagreed. He believed that in times of depression, governments must restore business activity by spending money on public works, even if they go into debt in the process. Keynes called Roosevelt

"magnificently right," leading Moley to quip, "Magnificently left."
Moley distrusted the President's plans for tinkering with the currency,
but he approved the decision to give national recovery priority over
world recovery.

Three days before Roosevelt sent the message that caused the conference to adjourn, Schacht announced the virtual repudiation of all Germany's foreign obligations. This action had respectable precedent.
Except for Finland, every country that owed a war debt to the United
States had either repudiated the debt or, as in the case of Britain, made
a negligible token payment. The main difference was that the Germans
violated an agreement with their former enemies whereas the former
Allies violated agreements with one another. Like the honorable British
before him, Schacht declared that Germany had to bow to the iron law
of economics. But he showed greater ingenuity than the British in devising methods of payment in kind instead of in cash. In the course of an
interview which welcomed the end of the conference as marking the end
of many illusions, he made shrewd use of Roosevelt's message. The
world, said Schacht, should give thanks to Roosevelt: "For Roosevelt
has in principle the same idea that Hitler and Mussolini have put into
action: take your economic fate into your own hands, and you will be
helping not only yourselves but the whole world."

True enough as far as it went. "In principle" Roosevelt agreed with
Hitler and Mussolini that domestic recovery came before world recovery. It was the way he put his program into effect that made the difference. Moreover, Roosevelt not only differed from Hitler and Mussolini
in the means he used to attain his ends; he differed from earlier American progressives in the ends he sought. Although Roosevelt regarded
himself as a disciple of Woodrow Wilson, New Deal economics broke
as sharply with the economics of the New Freedom as Roosevelt's
nationalism broke with Wilson's internationalism. Since the end of the
nineteenth century, American Populists and Progressives had singled out
the trusts and the monopolies as the chief enemies of the people, the
chief barriers to progress. Louis D. Brandeis had summed up the case
against big business in *Other People's Money*, which attacked "the curse
of bigness" and championed small business as the best hope for democracy. Wilson paid tribute to Brandeis by appointing him to the
Supreme Court, and the New Freedom tried to carry out Brandeis's
ideas.

But not Roosevelt, whose ignorance of economics proved an asset.
Knowing little about the evils of monopoly and the menace of the trusts,
he approached the problem of recovery with an open mind. Representatives of the United States Chamber of Commerce helped to draft the
National Industrial Recovery Act, which Congress passed and Roose-

velt signed on June 16, 1933, four days after the World Economic Conference opened. Henry I. Harriman, president of the U. S. Chamber of Commerce, at once exclaimed: "Today's passage of the NIRA constitutes the most important step in our progress toward business rehabilitation. . . . The Act will permit legitimate business enterprise to lift itself above the destructive competition which was threatening to bring about complete economic demoralization." Like many other business leaders, Harriman welcomed this attempt by the federal government to help business protect itself from the risks inherent in free enterprise. As J. S. Tritle of Westinghouse put it, Roosevelt had become "the great sponsor of a united front between industry and government."

"The idea," in the President's own words, "is simply for employers to hire more men to do the existing work by reducing the work-hours of each man's week and at the same time paying a living wage for the shorter week." Individual companies could sign a President's Recovery Agreement, pledging themselves to maintain certain minimum standards of wages, hours, and working conditions or entire industries could agree to accept a code, worked out with the National Recovery Administration. Wicked big business could usually afford to co-operate on the President's terms. Virtuous small business often could not. The kind of agreement that the NIRA urged businessmen to sign defied the Sherman Anti-Trust Act, which forbade combinations in restraint of interstate trade. But Roosevelt did not care; he wanted results, and his pro-labor supporters managed to give labor as well as business a break by inserting in the Recovery Act a section numbered 7a that required employers to agree to bargain collectively if their employees so desired. Only the force of public opinion, marshaled by the Roosevelt administration, compelled anybody to accept any code.

The President made an inspired choice when he appointed General Hugh Johnson to head the National Recovery Administration, or NRA. The American public knew little of Johnson when he took charge, but he became a national institution in record time. He had been born in Oklahoma in 1882 of fine pioneer stock. His mother recalled him at the age of four, defying his playmates with the words, "Everybody in the world is a rink-stink but Hughie Johnson and he's all right," words that he quoted on the fly-leaf of his autobiography fifty years later. At sixteen, Hughie ran away from home to serve in the war against Spain. He attended West Point, where he wound up at the foot of his class in deportment. He served with the cavalry until his energy and executive ability won him the job of applying the draft act in 1917, and when the war ended he was slated to command a brigade in France. In 1919 Johnson resigned his commission to enter the farm implement business with George Peek, who joined the early New Dealers, years later, as an official in the Department of Agriculture. Through Peek, Johnson became associated with Bernard Baruch, from whom he got the idea of self-regulated industry that he later applied to the NRA. In his spare time he wrote boys' stories.

Johnson came of a Democratic family and boiled with rage in 1932 because Hoover carried any states at all. Having entered the New Deal through Baruch, Johnson never belonged to the inside circle of brain trusters, although he formed warm friendships with many of them. Frances Perkins once said of him, "The trouble with Hugh is that he thinks a strike is something to settle." If Johnson shared the traditional army view of strikes and strikers, he also shared the traditional army view of businessmen and politicians. He stood in no awe of any vested interest and looked upon Roosevelt as his commander-in-chief, not as the leader of the Democratic Party. Baruch and Baruch only inspired his complete admiration, and he loved to quote the reply that Senator Glass once made to a man who called Baruch "too dogmatic." "Yes," Glass commented, "on a proposition like two and two make four, Bernie can be dogmatic as hell."

Johnson's comment on his appointment revealed a bluntness of mind and speech that gave the whole country a wholesome kick after twelve years of Harding, Coolidge, and Hoover: "It will be red fire at first and dead cats afterward. This is just like mounting the guillotine on the infinitesimal gamble that the ax won't work." NRA got off to a fine start when the Cotton Textile Institute, representing two thirds of the cotton textile industry, signed a code calling for a 40-hour week and minimum wages of $12 in the South and $13 in the North. "Men have died and worms have eaten them," commented Johnson, "but not from paying human labor thirty cents an hour." Within four months the NRA had 96 per cent of American business and industry displaying its Blue Eagle emblem, signifying the elimination of sweatshops and sweated labor, a shorter work-week, a minimum weekly wage scale of $12, and recognition of labor's right to collective bargaining. Best of all, two and three quarter million people had been put back to work.

Most of the press opposed the NRA and rightly described it as a triumph of ballyhoo. But had not ballyhoo first created and then destroyed Hoover? Had not ballyhoo persuaded the American public to accept most of the products of big business? The Roosevelt administration raised the art of ballyhoo to new heights. Every week or two the President delivered a radio fireside chat in which he took the people into his confidence concerning his plans. His clear, confident voice, his dignified yet informal delivery established a bond between him and the people and by-passed the attempts of the press to whittle away his prestige. By the time Roosevelt pulled Johnson from his hat he had established his own personality, with which Johnson's afforded an engaging contrast. Johnson spoke with the voice and language of a top-sergeant and his frequent radio addresses filled the clear American air with an aroma quite in keeping with the repeal of Prohibition. His expressions "chiselers" and "crack down" at once went into the language. Westbrook Pegler, the sports reporter turned columnist, dubbed him "Old Ironpants."

Johnson and his staff worked sixteen to eighteen hours a day as he flew all over the country in an Army plane which he transformed into an office. Like a man possessed, Johnson spread the word, "Buy now under the Blue Eagle." He compared the Blue Eagle crusaders with Richard Coeur de Lion, with Moses, even with Jesus Christ. He likened the chiselers to Judas Iscariot and Danny Deever: "As happened to Danny Deever, NRA will have to remove from him his badge of public faith and business honor and 'takin of his buttons off an' cut his stripes away' break the bright sword of his commercial honor in the eyes of his neighbors—and throw the fragments—in scorn—in the dust at his feet." Johnson described the revenge the American housewife would take on those businessmen who did not qualify to display the Blue Eagle: "When every American housewife understands that the Blue Eagle on everything that she permits to come into her home is a symbol of its restoration to security, may God have mercy on the men or group of men who attempt to trifle with this bird."

Henry Ford defied Providence. He refused to sign with the NRA solely because Section 7a of the Act gave employees the right to bargain collectively with their employers. But the public did not boycott Ford's products. Neither did his workers go on strike. Employers in at least one other part of the country did not get off so easily. During the summer of 1934 in the San Francisco Bay area Harry Bridges of Australia, the aggressive leader of a longshoremen's union who worked closely with the Communist Party, gave the American people first-hand experience with the kind of semipolitical general strike that frequently paralyzed European communities. It needed the personal intervention of General Johnson to put San Francisco back to work, and nothing quite like the Bridges demonstration ever happened again under the New Deal. But the attitude of Henry Ford on the one hand and of Harry Bridges on the other showed that the NRA lacked the sanction of both law and force to back up its decisions. It rested instead on the power of public opinion, which remained favorable enough to keep the Blue Eagle alive and flapping until the weary General Johnson bade his fellow workers a sentimental farewell and resigned his post on September 25, 1934.

The NRA spent most of its energies appealing to the minds and emotions of the American people, and it was on their minds and emotions that it left its chief effect. Conservative critics accused the NRA of nationalizing and socializing private enterprise. Radical critics accused it of turning the country over to the trade associations. The support that the NRA received from most Americans who once called themselves progressives suggested that they no longer regarded trusts as inherently evil or bigness as essentially bad. Just the opposite. The smaller the enterprise, the more it resisted NRA, and as big business came to terms with big government, the former progressives cheered.

· IV ·

While General Johnson used all the arts of ballyhoo to persuade business to support the New Deal program, other government agencies turned these same arts against the House of Morgan. Several months before Roosevelt took office, the Senate Committee on Banking and Currency had been investigating the conduct of the leading Wall Street bankers. Ferdinand Pecora, with a dozen years' experience in the District Attorney's office of New York City behind him, served as chief counsel and his questioning of Charles E. Mitchell of the National City Bank and of Albert H. Wiggin of the Chase National Bank, led both men to quit their jobs. Pecora's investigation also laid the groundwork for New Deal legislation forbidding banks to engage in the selling of securities.

Shortly after Roosevelt moved into the White House the Senate investigators decided to make their biggest splash by having Pecora summon J. P. Morgan and his partners to Washington for questioning. "Mr. Morgan," wrote Pecora in *Wall Street Under Oath*, "took the stand on May 23, 1933. Public interest in his appearance was almost hysterically intense. Not for a generation, not since the elder Morgan had been examined in the Pujo Committee investigation of 1912, had the public been permitted a clear view of the man whom everybody acknowledged as a world figure. His extreme aversion to photographers and interviewers alike was well known and unconquerable. His dry features, no less than his opinions and personality, were almost unknown to the millions of his fellow citizens over whose welfare his firm and its allies exerted so extraordinary an influence."

For more than fifty years, Americans had accepted the omnipotence of the House of Morgan as they accepted the omnipotence of God. The elder Morgan, a man of powerful intellect and will, had inspired this piece of folklore throughout the decades when private capital had financed the fabulous growth of American industry. The legend survived the man. When the elder Morgan died in 1914, just before the outbreak of war, his son inherited his position. From that time, the character of

KEYSTONE

KEYSTONE

General Hugh Johnson,
Head of NRA

J. P. Morgan with the Midget
on his Knee

the firm changed, along with the character of its chief, and the character of the problems with which he dealt. "Jack" Morgan, the modest son of arrogant "Pierpont," had cultivated the British aristocracy with such success that his social and business connections in that quarter gave his bank the inside track on wartime loans to the British and their allies. The Morgan firm under its new chief pioneered in the field of international banking as it had pioneered under the elder Morgan in the creation of great national monopolies and trusts. But the elder Morgan met and mastered the problems of his time. The more formidable problems of the 1920's proved too much for his less gifted son, whose firm ran into more and more competition at home and abroad, and had to descend to the high-pressure methods of its rivals.

That way lay disaster. Pecora revealed that the Morgan partners had avoided paying income taxes throughout the depression—sometimes by selling securities to their wives and claiming losses, sometimes by other more complicated devices. This was universal, standard practice at the time, and it never occurred to Morgan or any of the men around him that their position might demand of them a higher code than the one that every bucket-shop operator and racketeer in the land followed. Nor could the Morgan people see anything irregular in their practice of letting certain influential persons buy new securities at far lower prices than the general public had to pay. Most of the Morgan partners modeled their manners on those of the British ruling class, but the words *noblesse oblige* which the British aristocracy has always tried to apply went largely unhonored by their most fervent admirers in the United States.

The saving paradox of the Morgan investigation lay in the personality of Mr. Morgan himself. It is doubtful if more than one American in every ten knew that the original J. P. Morgan had died. Old John D. Rockefeller lived on; why shouldn't J. P. Morgan? Moreover, the younger Morgan had done little to distinguish himself—either from his father or in any other way. It was therefore generally assumed that he had inherited his father's ruthless will and powerful intellect along with his father's flourishing business and eminent station. It took some time for Mr. Morgan to make a clear impression in his own right. Asked why his firm lent money and did financial favors to a "preferred list" of influential persons, Mr. Morgan asserted: "We do make these loans, and we believe the people should have the money; that we should loan money if these gentlemen want it. They are friends of ours and we know they are good, sound, straight fellows."

To many these words sounded condescending, even arrogant. But at least they sounded real. They came from the heart of a human being, not from the multigraph machine of a public-relations counselor. To be sure, the human being who uttered them lived in a world apart and the public hardly knew whether to shake with rage or with laughter when the foremost private banker in the United States announced, during the fourth year of the depression, that the average American family maintained at least one domestic servant.

The climax of the Morgan investigation recalled Hans Christian Andersen's story of the emperor's new clothes. For weeks, everyone concerned with the investigation assumed, in the face of mounting evidence to the contrary, that Morgan himself must be either a superman or the fiend of hell. It took a professional ballyhoo artist in the person of a circus press agent to put the amateur ballyhoo artists of the New Deal in their places. During a lull at one of the hearings, this circus press agent slipped a little lady midget onto Mr. Morgan's lap and had their picture taken, with the great financier smiling kindly. The investigators raged against such cheap exploitation of a serious Senate hearing. Mr. Morgan's friends resented this new assault upon his dignity. Yet the appearance of the picture in the papers suddenly revealed what nobody up to that point had yet dared put into words. It showed the sinister J. P. Morgan as a kindly, almost bumbling old gentleman, incapable alike of doing the evil with which his enemies charged him or of wielding the power which his friends regarded as his by divine right.

Meanwhile the power of Roosevelt alarmed Wall Street as the power of Morgan had once alarmed Main Street. During the latter half of 1933, the President assumed that the government, by changing the price it would pay for gold from day to day, could make all prices move up and down. Every morning at breakfast, he and his advisers would set the gold price, but the theory did not seem to work and on January 15, 1934, he asked and received from Congress the authority to stabilize the dollar at between 50 and 60 cents. He chose to make it 59 cents, and the Treasury at once began paying $35 an ounce for gold. Roosevelt's political enemies accused him of ignorance, folly, and fraud, especially after one of his political supporters, Dean Gooderham Acheson, graduate of Groton, Yale, and the Harvard Law School, wrote a hot letter to the President, resigning the appointment he had recently received as Assistant Secretary of the Treasury. The press gave the incident quite a play and predicted the early defection of still more New Dealers.

What Roosevelt did to the budget came in for more abuse than what he did to the dollar. During the same month that he cut the gold value of the currency by more than 40 per cent he presented Congress with a budget more than twice as large as any President had ever before proposed in time of peace, calling as it did for the expenditure of ten and a half billion dollars and for a deficit of over three billions. Roosevelt, in his inaugural, had suggested Congress might have to grant him "broad executive power to wage a war against the emergency, as great as the power that would be given to me if we were in fact invaded by a foreign foe." Although the President never had to ask for this specific power, he fought the depression with the same financial weapons that governments use in time of war. That is to say, he asked Congress to increase the national debt and thereby burden future taxpayers with part of the costs of recovery. On this issue, however, no New Dealer chose to resign. Nor did any New Dealer define the essence of the New Deal so eloquently as the British economist, John Maynard Keynes, in an open letter to the President, written in December, 1933: "You have made yourself the trustee for those in every country who seek to mend the evils of our condition by reasoned experiment, within the framework of the existing social system. If you fail, rational change will be greatly prejudiced throughout the world, leaving orthodoxy and revolution to fight it out. But if you succeed, new and bolder methods will be tried everywhere and we may date the first chapter of a new economic era from your accession to office."

· V ·

ROOSEVELT'S POLICY of deficit spending compelled him to increase the power of the federal government. The Hitler dictatorship also led to an increased concentration of power, but that power was used for political rather than economic purposes. Because Hitler had never attracted a majority of the votes of the German people in any free election, he used terror and torture to break down opposition. The rank-and-file Nazis paid off some old scores and picked up some minor benefits during the spring of 1933, and by summer Hitler had eliminated the Socialists and Communists and tamed the Nationalists and Centrists.

Unlike Roosevelt, Hitler scored his first triumphs abroad. Having cleverly exploited Roosevelt's peace appeal of May, 1933, Hitler proceeded the following autumn to take Germany out of the League of Nations and the Disarmament Conference. The French, with British backing, refused to grant him the "equal rights" that he demanded, but when he held a plebiscite, soon afterward, 92 per cent of the German voters endorsed his double-barreled defiance of the outside world. Although many voted under pressure, most of them needed no coercion to vote as they did.

Nor did all the support for Hitler's foreign policy come from Germany and the Germans. As soon as Hitler withdrew from the Disarmament Conference, Mussolini took parallel action, announcing that only an observer would represent Italy at future sessions. Göring had paid the Duce two visits during 1933 and Mussolini rather enjoyed the flattery of Hitler's imitation. But their ideas on foreign policy did not coincide. Mussolini sought a four-power pact among Britain, France, Germany, and Italy. Hitler preferred a series of bilateral agreements. Mussolini wanted to act as middleman between Hitler on the one hand and the British and French on the other. He also wanted Russia excluded. Hitler sought the widest possible freedom of action: hence his pacts with Russia, Poland, and the Vatican. These he could make, or break, one at a time. He could also frame his promises to suit his own purposes, sometimes even making concessions. To Mussolini, for instance, he promised that Germany would respect Austria's independence, but he refused to do any business through the League of Nations for fear of having the whole world ranged against him. "This was the new German line," wrote Konrad Heiden in *Der Fuehrer,* "Peace with individual neighbors—yes; peace with the whole world as represented by the League—no!"

Yet even so thorough an anti-Nazi as Heiden recognized that a policy of collective security had no chance in 1933: "Actually this great peace of all with all was an impossible figment of the brain, unrealizable in the world of reality. To be true and possible it should have penetrated far deeper than the outer edges where the peoples touched one another; it presupposed a certain intimacy in the social relations between the nations; the London Economic Conference had tried to achieve such an intimacy, but with inadequate means. What was needed was a new form of life among the nations; what was offered was at best diplomatic agreements in which no two diplomats meant the same thing. To most of its

English proponents, for example, collective security meant a system in which England would not have to give much help, since her responsibility was shared with so many others. But for France collective security was a condition in which everyone would have to help her with all his forces."

Although Hitler went his own way, his departure from the League of Nations caused less alarm in London than in Paris. His anti-Communism also made him many influential British friends. In the summer of 1933, Sir Evelyn Wrench, president of the English-Speaking Union and editor of the Conservative *Spectator*, praised Hitler as "a man of austere habits" who "neither drinks nor smokes." He quoted "one prominent German, what we should call a progressive conservative, a landowner," who said, "I was skeptical as to whether Hitler had the qualities to make a national leader. Then I met him three years ago and have seen him several times since. He is really a wonderful man—a prophet without thought of self. He has an unfailing instinct for what to do at a moment of crisis. The only part of his policy I do not understand is his treatment of the Jews; but you must remember we have lived through a revolution. He has accomplished a rebirth of the German nation. We feel that we live again, that we hold our heads high once more, that we are not a subordinate nation in Europe. Hitler is not the fire-eater you in England seem to think; he does not want war, but he is determined that Germany shall have a fair deal."

While the Conservative *Spectator* tried to make Hitler acceptable to the British ruling classes, the Conservative *Daily Mail*, with the largest circulation of any British newspaper, tried to make Hitler acceptable to the masses. When Lord Northcliffe, who created the *Daily Mail*, died after the war, his uninspired brother, Lord Rothermere, inherited his properties and his position. He took up the quixotic cause of revision of the peace treaty with Hungary and sent one of his star correspondents, Ward Price, to Germany to establish friendly personal relations with Hitler. A few days after Hitler took Germany out of the League, Price told him, "There are signs that since last Saturday your popularity with the British public has risen amazingly." The Conservative *Morning Post*, of London, berated the French for rejecting Hitler's "outstretched hand." Lord Beaverbrook, the most aggressive newspaper publisher of the time, demanded that Britain renounce the Locarno Treaty because the French had already violated it by displaying hostility to Hitler. Lloyd George warned that only Hitler stood between Communism and the Rhine. Neville Chamberlain urged his fellow citizens to suspend judgment.

To the conservative European, Hitler embodied anti-Communism. To the radical European, Hitler embodied capitalism with the gloves off.

Neither the conventional conservative nor the orthodox radical saw in Hitler the embodiment of Europe's will to destroy itself. They both forgot that he had come to power by promising to give the destructive passions of his followers free play. Yet by the summer of 1933, he began to destroy the destroyers and to suppress the advocates of a second revolution. At first, he did not need to use much violence. The prestige of the Army, the threats of the secret police, and the truncheons of the elite, black-shirted Schutzstaffel men kept the rank-and-file Party members in line. But by the spring of 1934 the excitement of victory had worn off and Captain Ernst Röhm's two million brown-shirted Storm Troopers felt betrayed. They had expected the Nazi Party to become the new German state, the Third Reich, and many of them had counted on taking over soft, secure jobs. Instead, however, certain leading Nazis moved into high government posts and turned the machinery of government against their Party comrades. The Storm Troopers outnumbered the combined forces of their uniformed opponents by four or five to one, but their opponents had better arms, better discipline, better morale, better uniforms. The one concession Hitler made to the Storm Troopers was to give those who had suffered injuries in street fights the same pensions and benefits that wounded war veterans received.

Röhm, the Storm Troop commander, wanted much more. He wanted Reichswehr commissions for himself and his fellow Brown Shirt officers. He wanted the entire Brown Shirt Army incorporated in the Reichswehr intact. The regular Reichswehr officers rejected a plan that would have left them and their men outnumbered, twenty to one, by undisciplined upstarts. Hitler and Göring supported the Reichswehr; Goebbels also saw the light and dropped his revolutionary speechmaking—for a while.

Göring had many friends among the Reichswehr high command. He had also begun to organize, back in May, 1933, his own Secret State Police, the Geheime Staats Polizei, or Gestapo, for short, which took over administration of terror. A year later, Göring revealed that a new Nazi leader had joined the inner circle when he made Heinrich Himmler, who already commanded 200,000 young, black-shirted Schutzstaffel men, head of the Gestapo as well. "The career of Himmler is an epitome of Hitlerism," wrote the Australian historian Stephen H. Roberts in *The House That Hitler Built*, a book based on a firsthand study of Nazi Germany. "Nothing distinguished him in his youth. He studied agriculture at a technical high school in Munich and is said to have served in a Free Corps in that city against the Soviet government. He was with Hitler in the first *Putsch* and then retired from the public eye as an assistant in a Bavarian fertilizer factory. He lacks any distinction of appearance and is modest in manner. His very indefinite features and his glasses make him look rather insignificant, more of a student than an agitator; so that his fellow-Nazis made the mistake of underestimating him and thinking he could not stand up to the hearty manners of freebooters like Röhm and Heines. Hitler, however, had no illusions about Himmler's beaver-like capacity for quiet and effective work, and made him Party manager in sections of Bavaria and Swabia. In 1925 he joined the S.S. and within three years he had become commander of that organization throughout Germany. He is probably the best organizer the Nazi Party has produced and whenever a ticklish job presented itself, word was sent out for this young man."

While the success of the Nazi revolution intoxicated the rank and file, power corrupted their leaders. The old fighters, after years of privation and frustration, gave themselves over to orgies of vice and terror. It was quite typical that Röhm, the chief exponent of the second revolution, led a private life of exceptional depravity. On the other hand, his subordinate, Himmler, kept his political and personal passions in check or harnessed them to his career. Göring enriched himself with money and objects of art; Goebbels indulged himself with women. Like Hitler, both Göring and Goebbels remained opportunists at heart. Unlike Hitler, they frequently permitted themselves the luxury of relaxation. Göring's social contacts with the Army and the aristocracy led him to soft-pedal the socialist features of the Nazi program. Goebbels, the crippled, frustrated intellectual, talked the language of the left, but his cynicism inoculated him against his own propaganda. Both Göring and Goebbels also stuck close to Hitler, before whom they stood in awe. Göring, the man of action, and Goebbels, the man of intellect, recognized in Hitler an intuitive sense that they both lacked.

And Hitler's intuition told him, as soon as he gained complete power, to make haste slowly. Having come up from nowhere, he paused to take his bearings and appraise his situation. Would the men and the methods that had served him well in opposition still serve him well now that he had come to power? He had no problem about taking revenge on his enemies. He kept all his promises about persecuting Jews, suppressing Communists, outlawing Socialists, crushing political opposition generally. But he found it impossible to hand out all the rewards he had also promised. He turned, first of all, against the Storm Troopers: "Incapable of any real co-operation, ready to oppose any order, filled with hatred for any kind of authority, their excited and restless minds were appeased only by constant intellectual and conspiratory preoccupation with the destruction of existing institutions." That was the way, early in 1934, Hitler described the Storm Trooper leaders to their faces. By May, conditions inside Germany had become so critical that he opened a campaign against "bleaters, alarmists, and professional critics." In June

Göring admitted publicly: "The mood is deteriorating and dissatisfaction has broken out here and there." Hindenburg at eighty-seven could not live much longer and his death might set the stage for a Reichswehr coup d'état. Reichswehr officers had given Hitler his first postwar job back in 1919. Several generals had worked with him loyally through the years. Better make common cause with them than count any further on Röhm and his Storm Troopers, who threatened to wreck everything. Better yet, seek expert advice from the one man best qualified to give it —Benito Mussolini.

· VI ·

On June 14, the Fuehrer flew to Venice for a two-day meeting with the Duce. He arrived in a dark suit and a light, belted raincoat. Mussolini greeted him in a gold-braided uniform with a dagger at his side. As Hitler approached, Mussolini is reported to have whispered: *"Non mi pace."* ("I don't like the look of him.") There is also the story that Hitler hailed Mussolini with the words: *"Ave Imperator,"* and that Mussolini replied, *"Ave Imitator."* In any case, Hitler reassured his host that Germany would make no trouble in Austria; Mussolini warned his guest that Italian Fascists did not like Nazi anti-Semitism; Hitler explained his domestic difficulties. Mussolini had written in his autobiography: "At certain historical hours, the sacrifice of those who were the deserving lieutenants of yesterday might become indispensable for the supreme interest of tomorrow." He may not have quoted those exact words to Hitler, but he probably talked to that effect. The two men parted in friendly fashion and Hitler returned to find that conditions had taken a sudden turn for the worse.

As he landed at Munich he received the text of a speech that Papen delivered that day before the faculty and students of the University of Marburg. One of Papen's assistants, a brilliant young Jew named Edgar Jung, had helped him with the text, which read in part: "In the long run no propaganda and no organization, however good, can by itself maintain confidence. A sense of trust and willingness to serve can be fostered only by taking the people into confidence and not by working up high feelings, especially among youth, nor by threats against sections of the people who are helpless. The people know that heavy sacrifices are expected of them. They will make them and follow the Leader with implicit faith if they are allowed to have a voice in council and action; if every word of criticism is not at once interpreted as of evil intent; and if patriots in despair are not branded as enemies of the State."

The fact that Papen spoke as he did and, in so doing, stirred the German people forced Hitler's hand. Röhm and the Storm Troopers had

BETTMANN ARCHIVE

Captain Ernst Röhm

already renewed and redoubled their demands for a second revolution. By that they meant liquidating the old aristocracy and the old Army leaders as the Communists, Socialists, and Jews had already been liquidated. It was not enough for certain favored Nazis to take key positions in the state. The Nazi Party must become the state, and the old fighters must dominate that state. But physical exhaustion had forced Röhm on June 7 to go to a sanitarium at Weissee, in Upper Bavaria, for a rest cure. Before he left he wrote a message to his entire SA army announcing that they must disband for a month, beginning July 1, without uniforms, without arms, without pay. At the same time, he warned that those who predicted the break-up of the SA were lying and "would be given a suitable answer in due time and in whatever form is necessary." He concluded: "The SA is and remains Germany's destiny." Never once did Röhm mention Hitler's name and he even omitted the customary "Heil Hitler" at the end.

Röhm had not broken with Hitler. Röhm did not expect Hitler to break with him. But Röhm did feel it necessary to warn the man whom he had loyally served since 1919—and he dared to give that warning because he was the one member of the Nazi Party privileged to address the Fuehrer as "*du*." At just what point Hitler made up his mind to turn against Röhm may never be known. He spent the last few days of June flying from one corner of Germany to another on a frantic round of inspection trips. On the evening of June 29 Goebbels joined him at Godesberg on the Rhine and reported that the SA troops were preparing to flout the demobilization order. Hitler replied that he would go to Weissee and himself arrest Röhm. He telegraphed Röhm to expect him and Röhm believed it meant that Hitler had at last broken with the Reichswehr; that he was ditching Göring and Goebbels for his earlier friends. Röhm did not know that Hitler had also ordered the top Nazi officials in Munich to assemble for a meeting the next day.

Hitler arrived at Weissee just after midnight and stormed into Röhm's quarters. He found Röhm's friend Edmund Heines in bed with a boy and ordered him shot at once. He accused Röhm of treachery and gave him the chance to shoot himself. Röhm disdainfully refused and a firing squad executed him in the basement. The word went out from Munich that Hitler had discovered a plot by the SA to seize power and that he had ordered Röhm arrested and shot. During the next three days—Saturday, Sunday, and Monday—the Gestapo and the SS shot several hundred SA leaders and occasionally shot every tenth man in certain SA detachments.

The decimation of the SA took place in Gestapo cellars throughout Germany. "The victims were stood in a row against the wall," wrote Konrad Heiden in *Der Fuehrer*. "An SS man opened their shirts over their chests and drew a black circle around the left nipple with a piece of charcoal: this was the target. Five to six yards from the wall stood eight SS men with rifles. Four of the rifles were allegedly loaded with blank cartridges so that no one knew whether his bullet was the deadly one. . . . The shots from a distance of five to eight yards tore out the flesh of the victims. Especially the spot where the bullet left the body under the left shoulder was transformed into a gaping hole, and the bullets dragged out parts of the body. The observers in the cellar could see bloody pieces of flesh stuck to the wall after the victims had dropped and the darker heart fragments were clearly discernible. The wall was not cleaned in the intervals between the executions; hence, after a short time, it was completely covered with blood and human flesh."

As soon as Göring in Berlin received word that the purge of the SA had begun, he sent six assassins in civilian clothes to the house of General von Schleicher, where they shot the General and his wife in the presence of their sixteen-year-old niece. Two of Papen's aides were killed in gangster fashion—von Bose and Edgar Jung, co-author of the Marburg speech. Papen himself was placed under house arrest and only Hindenburg's friendship saved him. Erich Klausener, a leader in the Catholic Action movement, and several other eminent Catholics—including Gregor Strasser—were put out of the way. On July 13 Hitler told the Reichstag that he had discovered a plot against the regime; that he had also discovered immorality among

"The House Painter." Sennep in Candide, *Paris*

certain Nazi leaders; and that he had made himself "the supreme tribunal of the German nation" and had ordered the purge of seventy-nine persons. No evidence of a plot ever appeared; indeed, all the evidence pointed the other way, and the number of victims ran into the hundreds, at least. Nor had Hitler just discovered the abnormal behavior of Röhm and others. He had known and condoned it for years. Yet the doddering Hindenburg sent him a message of congratulation.

On August 2, one month to the day after Hindenburg had expressed his "profound thanks and sincere appreciation" to Hitler for having "saved the German nation from serious danger," the old Marshal died. Hitler's biographer, Konrad Heiden, advanced the theory that the men around Hitler forged a will in which the dying President expressed confidence in Hitler's ability to unify and reconstruct Germany. John Wheeler-Bennett, Hindenburg's biographer, has pointed out, however, that the will was dated May 11, 1934, and expressed Hindenburg's sentiments at the time. On August 19, Hitler held his second plebiscite—this time to ask the German people to approve the action his Cabinet had already taken in continuing him in office as Chancellor of the Reich and adding the new title of *Reichsfuehrer* as well. More than forty million Germans went to the polls, and more than 90 per cent of them voted to give Hitler the absolute power he demanded. The oath that Hess had composed and that millions of Germans had already taken at mass meetings now bound the whole nation: "By this oath we again bind ourselves to a man through whom—this is our belief—superior forces act in fulfillment of Destiny. Do not seek Adolf Hitler with your brains; all of you will find him with the strength of your hearts. Adolf Hitler is Germany and Germany is Adolf Hitler."

SUMMING UP

BEFORE the year 1933 had ended, New Dealers had already begun to speak of the "Roosevelt Revolution." At the same time, they could think of no more deadly epithet than "counterrevolutionary" to apply to Hitler and his New Order. Yet the New Deal was essentially a conservative movement; the New Order, essentially a radical one. It was not Roosevelt who destroyed the traditional American values. It was Roosevelt who restored these values from the big-shot plungers and the pipsqueak politicians who had disgraced American business and American government during the 1920's. The stock market boom had inflated such pygmies as Charles E. Mitchell, Albert H. Wiggin, and the younger J. P. Morgan to the dimensions of supermen. The elder Morgan and the whole generation of robber barons had ridden out the storms of their time.

They proved too strong for Bryan and the Populists. What pathetic figures, by contrast, the plungers of the 1920's cut by the time 1933 rolled around. They had abdicated their responsibility, if not their power, long before Roosevelt and his New Dealers arrived to clear up the wreckage. Nor did the New Deal apply radical remedies. Drawing its inspiration from the progressive tradition and spouting antimonopoly slogans that dated back to the 1890's, the New Deal started out as a salvage operation. Most New Dealers were professional men and women with their roots in the great middle class from which the older generation of Progressives and Populists also drew their support. But the antimonopoly slogans that the Populists coined in the 1890's and the reform programs that the Progressives drew up in the early 1900's had no place in the world of the 1930's. The Populists and Progressives of an earlier day championed small business against big. They had opposed every form of concentrated power, on practical as well as moral grounds. But big business proved more enlightened as well as more efficient than small business as labor-saving machinery and mass-production methods developed. Unable to prevent big business from getting bigger, the New Dealers concentrated such power in Washington as no monopolist ever held. And the New Dealers did this not to wreck big business but to save big business from its worst enemy—itself.

Hitler's New Order brought forth as many paradoxes as Roosevelt's New Deal. Because Hitler leaned, during his first year in office, on some of the bankers, industrialists, and generals who had helped him to power, he looked like their cat's-paw. His anti-Communist diatribes had won him the support of the orthodox conservatives and the opposition of the orthodox radicals. But Marxist dogma, which the conservatives had always feared and which the radicals had always accepted, could not account for Hitler. His purge of June 30 came down hardest on the most extreme Nazis, but it also mowed down scores of anti-Nazis, both to the left and to the right, with fine impartiality. Friends and foes, Nazis, non-Nazis, and anti-Nazis all tried to rationalize what had happened. But the realism of Bismarck and the dialectics of Marx proved as irrelevant in Hitler's Germany as the slogans of the Populists and the programs of the Progressives were proving in Roosevelt's America.

In 1936, Mark Sullivan spoke for many of his friends among professional Republican politicians when he wrote: "The New Deal is the American version of the new order that has been set up in three great European countries and some smaller ones. The term 'New Deal' is the American equivalent of the term 'Fascism' in Italy, 'Nazi' in Germany, and the term 'Soviet' in Russia." The comparison held water only in so far as Italy, Germany, Russia, and the United States all dealt with the same world depression at the same time on a national scale. But Roosevelt differed from Mussolini, Hitler, and Stalin in that he sought, by different means than they used, to restore the social and economic order they were attacking. And Hitler differed from Stalin in that the kind of revolution he led cut across class lines. But if Hitler's New Order could not be explained in the theology of Marx or Lenin neither could it be explained in any rational, logical terms. Some of his apologists deplored his hatred of the Jews and his love of violence, and tried to minimize these emotional obsessions. Actually, these obsessions lay at the root of his character and determined the nature of his revolution. Hitler showed himself as cynical as Lenin, but with Lenin the end justified the means; with Hitler the means became an end in itself.

In preaching racial hatred and practicing physical violence Hitler gave the German people what many of them wanted. True, he never won majority support in any free election. But he not only gained power against the wishes of the majority. What he gained he held. Many of the same Germans who failed to stop him while they still outnumbered his supporters came over to his side after he won control of the state. Nor was the Austrian-born Hitler made in Germany. He came from the very heart of Europe and the revolution he led transcended Germany. But it was a revolution for which certain Germans had prepared the ground. Before the turn of the century, Nietzsche had predicted Europe's doom. After the war, Spengler took up the same theme. Religious leaders turned to science. Scientists turned to mysticism. Painters and writers rejected the familiar, three-dimensional world of the five senses. They explored time, which Einstein called the fourth dimension, and psychiatry, which became a kind of sixth sense in the hands of Freud. The mind, they argued, derived its inspiration from emotion. Action, not thought; passion, not logic, ruled the world. In the Nazi movement, the dark impulses that the intellectuals had been describing for years finally reached the masses. In the person of Hitler, this movement came to power in Germany, and by the time Hindenburg died, Hitler and Germany had become one. And Hitler's Germany had taken as its motto: "First Germany; tomorrow the world."

16

The Axis Strikes

*Riots and assassinations in 1934 prepared the
ground for Italy and Germany to assault the peace
of Versailles in 1935 and 1936.*

PREVIEW

A MERICA'S RECOGNITION of Russia in 1933 and the establishment of
closer Franco-Soviet ties redressed the world balance of power
that the German and Japanese war lords were trying to upset. But the
new balance lacked firm underpinnings as riots in Paris and Vienna, a
blood purge in Germany, and assassinations in Austria, France, and
Russia warned Europe in 1934 of trouble ahead. Hitler and Mussolini
at once exploited the havoc that disastrous year had wrought. In 1935,
Hitler illegally rebuilt the German Air Force and restored conscription.
Mussolini flouted the League of Nations and invaded Ethiopia. In 1936
Hitler remilitarized the Rhineland and he and Mussolini backed General Franco's attempt to overthrow the Spanish Republic by civil war.
The resistance of the Spanish Loyalists proved unexpectedly strong, but
the British government tried to appease Hitler and Mussolini in Spain as
it tried to appease Mussolini in Ethiopia. The Versailles system had
crashed, but the victors in the last European war seemed impotent to
prevent another one.

· I ·

HAVING used the power of the federal government to save what he could
of the status quo at home, Roosevelt used the power of American diplomacy to save what he could of the status quo abroad. The same stand-
pat minority that denounced the New Deal as concealed socialism de-
nounced as concealed communism Roosevelt's decision to recognize the
government of the Soviet Union. The Bolsheviks had come to power
through violence and had retained power through terror. They had suppressed free speech, free elections, freedom of worship. They had refused to recognize the debts contracted by the Tsarist government or by
the temporary regime that followed. They had created the world-wide

547

Communist International to promote revolution everywhere. But the Soviet leaders had crushed all their domestic enemies by 1921, and in that same year they scrapped war communism in favor of their New Economic Policy. By 1925 they had won diplomatic recognition from most of the nations of western Europe and from all the major powers except the United States.

Secretary Hughes laid down the line that all the Republican administrations followed throughout the 1920's. The United States refused to recognize Communist Russia unless and until Communist Russia made amends for its violations of human rights in general and of American rights in particular. Although the Communist politicians in Moscow remained as adamant as the Republican politicians in Washington, economic relations between the two countries improved. The Soviet leaders sought the advice of American engineers, and American exporters gladly cultivated the Soviet market. Russian-American trade increased, and with the depression Communist ideas began to influence some sections of the American people. As soon as Roosevelt entered the White House, he decided that self-interest required the United States to put its relations with Russia on a normal basis. In July, 1933, the Reconstruction Finance Corporation lent four million dollars to American exporters to finance the sale of surplus cotton to the Soviet Union while at the same time Roosevelt saw to it that several hundred million dollars' worth of PWA funds went into the construction of new battleships. Hoover had tried to bluff the Japanese out of Manchuria by moving the bulk of the fleet to the Pacific. But he had let the Navy fall so far below treaty strength that he did not frighten the Japanese, and his refusal to recognize Russia made it impossible for him to work with Japan's chief enemy and rival in East Asia. Shunning the one ally who might have backed a strong stand against Japan, Hoover at the same time failed to build a navy adequate to perform the task singlehanded. To be sure, Secretary of State Stimson fretted and fumed. As a lifelong Republican, he knew that his Party had always stood for a strong policy in the Far East, and he had recently served as Governor General of the Philippines. Yet Hoover, who had supported the incendiary Teddy Roosevelt in 1912, Hoover who had much wider experience than Stimson in the Far East, refused to take the most elementary precautions.

It remained for Franklin D. Roosevelt, who considered himself a Wilson Democrat, to apply the sea-power politics of Admiral Mahan to East Asia. Having launched an impressive naval building program, Roosevelt invited President Kalinin of the Soviet Union to send a representative to Washington to discuss the establishment of normal diplomatic relations. No less a dignitary than Maxim Litvinov, Commissar for Foreign Affairs, made the trip, negotiated directly with Roosevelt, and committed the

Russian-American Relations. "*No, little mother, commercial relations will not be so close that we can export Communism itself. Unfortunately we'll have to keep that for ourselves.*" Simplicissimus, Munich

Soviet government "not to permit the formation or residence on its territory of any organization or group—and to prevent the activity on its territory of any organization or group—which has as an aim the overthrow or the preparation for the overthrow of, or bringing about by force a change in, the political or social order of the whole or any part of the United States, its territories or possessions." To Roosevelt and the men around him these words meant that the Russians had agreed to cut all ties between the Communist International in Moscow and the Communist Party, U.S.A. But the Soviet leaders proceeded as if no such ties had ever existed. The agreement said nothing about 86 million dollars' worth of American loans to the Tsarist regime or 187 million dollars' worth of loans to the Kerensky regime. The fact that most of the leading capitalist nations had already defaulted on the debts they incurred to the United States made the Bolsheviks' default on debts they had not incurred a matter of small importance. On the matter of religious liberty, Litvinov made one small concession and promised that his government would respect the civil and religious liberties of Americans on Soviet soil.

In his dealings with Japan, Roosevelt combined friendliness with firmness. Instead of following Hoover's example of threatening Tokyo with an empty gun, he ordered the Atlantic Fleet back to home waters before Litvinov arrived in Washington. Four months later, however, he signed the Vinson Act authorizing the construction of a full treaty-strength Navy and within another year he gave the required two-year notice that after 1936 the United States would no longer consider itself bound by any treaty limitations whatsoever. And on the same day that the President issued this warning to Japan, the United States Navy announced plans for fleet maneuvers in Far Eastern waters. It was not Russia, it was Japan that threatened the status quo in the Far East; in like fashion, it was not Stalin but Hitler who threatened the status quo in Europe. As a defender of the status quo abroad as well as at home, Roosevelt therefore lost no time in establishing closer ties with the Soviet Union.

A common interest in preserving the status quo brought Roosevelt and Stalin together. The same common interest also led to closer Franco-Russian relations. The depression which had brought Roosevelt and the Democrats to power in the United States had also brought Herriot and the Radicals to power in France, and Herriot at once paid a personal visit to Moscow which culminated on November 29, 1932, in the signing of a Franco-Soviet Nonaggression Pact. But it remained for Louis Barthou, who became Foreign Minister in 1934, to restore the prewar relations between France and Russia, long after Herriot, like so many French premiers before him, had fallen from office. Barthou, an eminent historian of conservative-nationalist views, felt about all Germans as Poincaré and Clemenceau had felt. As a devout Roman Catholic, he rejected Communism, but as a French patriot he remembered the contribution Tsarist Russia had made to the survival of the French Republic between 1914 and 1916, and he had no scruples about trying to establish as close relations with Stalin as Poincaré had established with the Tsar. The common interests of France and Russia, especially their common fear of Germany, seemed to Barthou more important than all their differences. He therefore made it his business to put new life into the various treaties France had made with the nations of eastern Europe and, finally, to bring the Soviet Union into a regional security system so strong and extensive that Hitler would not dare to attack it in any part.

· II ·

BY THE TIME Barthou's campaign to stabilize eastern Europe began, the French needed more help themselves than they could give to anybody else. Less than a month after Herriot returned from Moscow with his Franco-Soviet Nonaggression Pact, the Chamber voted him out of office because he wanted to pay the December 15 war debt instalment to the United States. Paul-Boncour, a sad-faced, long-haired orator, succeeded him and tried to balance the budget by refusing to hire any new civil servants for at least a year. The Chamber of Deputies, which could see no reason to pay the war debt to the United States, could see even less reason to crack down on its own people; it therefore overthrew Paul-Boncour, choosing instead the younger Édouard Daladier, the first war veteran to head a French government. Daladier was the self-made son of a small-town baker. Herriot had taught him in school and the pupil had moved somewhat to the left of the master. Energy rather than brilliance carried Daladier to the top, and he remained Premier for almost a year until the Socialists overthrew him because he demanded a cut in the salaries of government servants. The next Premier, Albert Sarraut, lasted three weeks. The next, Camille Chautemps, lasted two months. The Socialists preferred Chautemps, a slippery, elegant bourgeois, to the proletarian Daladier, and let him remain in office by refusing to vote against him on the same issue that caused Daladier's downfall. In January, 1934, Chautemps quit and Daladier came back, to face the worst crisis that had threatened the Third Republic since the days of Dreyfus.

In the United States, the Democrats did not come to power until after the depression had lasted so long and cut so deep that most of the people welcomed a bold reform program. In France, the Radicals came to power before the depression had run its course, and the measures they took to fight it created violent opposition. The Radicals needed Socialist votes to stay in power, but the Socialists refused to accept any office or any responsibility, much preferring the negative satisfaction of overthrowing Radical governments at will. The Nationalists, rebuffed by the voters and unable to command a majority in the Chamber, turned to direct action, but they did not produce any one leader like Hitler or Mussolini or any mass party like the German Nazis or the Italian Fascists. Léon Daudet and Charles Maurras stirred excitement in Paris with their Royalist newspaper, *L'Action Française*. The Clerical *Écho de Paris* attracted more readers and wielded more influence, but neither the French Royalists nor the French Clericals took the Nazi-Fascist path. It remained for Colonel de la Rocque, a war veteran, to organize his former comrades-in-arms into a private political army known as the Croix de Feu. The perfume manufacturer François Coty financed a semi-Bonapartist body known as the Solidarité Française, and another group who called themselves Francistes dressed up in uniforms like Hitler Storm Troopers.

The break for which they had been preparing came in December, 1933, when the *Écho de Paris* disclosed that the public prosecutor in Bayonne had issued a warrant against a certain Serge Alexandre Stavisky, the son of a Russian-Jewish dentist and a convert to Roman Catholicism. Stavisky operated a pawnshop and had issued a suspiciously large number of bonds which he sold to insurance companies. He also had a police record as a petty grafter, dating back to 1927, but

European Financier: "Please, gentlemen, don't end my life with a suicide!" Crocodile, *Moscow*

no record of any prosecutions. On January 3, 1934, *L'Action Française* had published facsimile copies of two letters written by the Colonial Minister in the Chautemps Cabinet, recommending Stavisky's bonds. *L'Action Française* charged that corrupt Radical politicians had protected Stavisky from arrest and profited from his crooked schemes. And no sooner did this charge appear than Stavisky committed suicide at Chamonix, where he had gone into hiding with the inevitable mistress.

It may be doubted that any important Radical politician acted as Stavisky's partner in crime. It cannot be doubted that Chautemps had blundered. His brother-in-law had charge of the bureau entrusted with prosecuting the Stavisky type of criminal. The brother-in-law did nothing. Chautemps did nothing. The Nationalists cried corruption and treason. Youthful Royalists and the private armies of de la Rocque and Coty rioted on the streets of Paris every night, short-circuiting power lines and tripping the horses of the police by rolling marbles on the pavements. Chautemps responded by trying to tighten the libel laws so that the press could not make the kind of charges that had appeared in connection with the Stavisky case. The leftist majority in the Chamber supported him, but the rioting became so serious that Chautemps quit and Daladier took his place. The rioters had won a political victory without precedent in the history of the Third Republic. Their illegal violence in the streets forced a government that commanded majority support in the Chamber of Deputies to resign. Similar symptoms had preceded Mussolini's seizure of power in Rome and Hitler's triumph in Berlin.

After failing to bring the Socialists and the Nationalists into a coalition government, Daladier reshuffled the same group of tired Radicals who had served with Chautemps. He removed Chautemps' brother-in-law from the prosecutor's office and made him a judge. He put the head of the detective bureau in charge of the Comédie Française, which had just outraged the Radicals by staging Shakespeare's *Coriolanus*, with its antidemocratic message. Daladier completed his self-destruction by firing Jean Chiappe, the efficient, anti-Communist Paris police chief, and then offering to make him Resident-General of Morocco, thereby setting off the explosion that wrecked the Radical government and threatened the foundations of the Republic. Chiappe spurned the Morocco appointment but ostentatiously asked members of his staff to show their "good citizenship and republican discipline" by staying at their posts, "no matter how keenly they feel the injustice done to their chief." Thirty deputies charged Daladier with having bowed to Socialist and Communist blackmail: "The head of the army of order has been sacrificed to the armies of disorder." On February 6, when Daladier went before the Chamber with his program, the "armies of disorder" marched on the Chamber. But most of the marchers belonged to the private armies of the extreme right, plus some Communists.

"The demonstration was soon a riot and soon again an *émeute*," wrote D. W. Brogan in *France Under the Republic*. "There were a few revolvers on the side of the rioters, but they were mostly equipped with weapons that recall the battles in the *Napoleon of Notting Hill*; they had as pikes the iron railings plucked up from around the trees, they had bottles and stones and, most formidable of all, razor blades on the end of sticks, very effective in use against horses. The police charged again and again; a bus was set on fire and the stink of burning rubber filled the air. The police were forced to fire—and all the time the debate went on, lifelessly, futilely; timid deputies slipped away, indignant deputies shouted that men were being killed outside; a wit among the newspapermen put a notice on the press gallery addressed to the rioters: 'Gentlemen, there are no deputies here.' At last the government got its majority, and the flight from the Chamber began."

Seventeen persons lost their lives in the riot. Hundreds suffered wounds. Daladier resigned the following day and ex-President Gaston Doumergue, a spry old Radical of seventy-two, of provincial, peasant descent, formed a coalition government excluding, however, the Socialists and Communists. He appointed one group of investigators, known as the "Committee of Thieves," to look into the Stavisky scandal and another, known as the "Committee of Murderers," to look into the riots of February 6. The first Committee failed to implicate the Radical Party in Stavisky's guilt; the second Committee failed to pin the riots on the parties of the right.

The so-called "Republic of Pals" which they tried to investigate and expose showed unexpected vitality. Personal friendships, cultivated over the years, saved many a wrongdoer. "The Republic of Pals," wrote

The Parliamentarians: "Have no fear, France, we are here."
France: "That is just what makes me afraid."
From Je Suis Partout, *Paris*

D. W. Brogan, "meant that rigorously honest men were on good terms with fairly honest men who were on good terms with shady men who were on good terms with despicable crooks."

Lucien Romier, a star reporter on *Le Temps*, quoted a typical French peasant, "a convinced Radical and anti-Clerical," at the time of the riots: "We favor a government with full power. Except for the priest, the notary, and a few property holders, you will not find anyone in favor of national union. National union means the right-wing parties. You know that perfectly well. We do not want them. Moreover, they would come in power too long after the damage had been done, and they would be able to accomplish nothing. They would let sleeping dogs lie and not correct any abuses. We want sweeping reforms carried out at once by sound Republicans."

"No doubt you mean radical economic and financial policies?" M. Romier inquired.

"Why not? We can do as well as Mussolini, Hitler, or Roosevelt but within the Republican framework." He did not want revolution. "No, not revolution, but the Republican fist, decision, justice, sanctions." Romier described this peasant as a man who "has some education, knows how to read his newspaper between the lines, and even does a little writing himself for a bulletin published by the group of wounded war veterans of which he is president. He loves the soil passionately and respects everything that has to do with his condition as peasant of which he is proud." If pride sustained the French peasant, hope sustained the French proletarian. Eugène Dabit, a resident of the Belleville quarter of Paris, depicted the typical French Communist in the *Nouvelle Revue Française:* "Somber men turn their eyes to new gods. They have nailed to the wall a photograph of Jaurès or Lenin, under which they pray during evenings of distress. If they go out it is to attend a meeting on the rue Mathurin-Moreau. Often they go even as far as the Maison des Syndicats on the rue de la Grange-aux-Belles, and on the first of May they try to parade through the grand boulevards. The comrades occupy a sixth of the earth's surface and their reign will be established here in time."

· III ·

THIS typical Paris Communist had halfheartedly taken part in the anti-Republican riots of February 6 that overthrew Daladier. He had thrown himself with more enthusiasm into the general strike called by the labor unions on February 12 as a gesture of defiance to all enemies of the Republic. Neither Premier Doumergue nor Foreign Minister Barthou enjoyed any support among the parties of the left, least of all among the rank-and-file French Communists. But the French and Russian leaders had begun to put some of their fears and suspicions to one side because they feared and suspected the Germans even more. What continued to make friction between Paris and Moscow was not their different ideologies; it was their clash of interests and loyalties in eastern Europe.

French statesmen devised and named the *cordon sanitaire* of small states, between the Baltic and the Black Sea, separating Soviet Russia from capitalist Europe. Most of Poland and all the Baltic states had belonged to Russia before the war; most of the remaining territory had belonged to Austria-Hungary. Conflicts between Slav and Teuton in eastern Europe, rivalry between the Austrian and Russian Empires had led to war in 1914. Few Frenchmen at that time wanted to fight a war of revenge against Germany to recover the lost provinces of Alsace-Lorraine. Twenty years later, few Germans wanted to fight France to bring these provinces back again into the Reich. But conditions in eastern Europe remained as menacing in 1934 as they had been in 1914.

If not more so. In 1914, the Austro-Hungarian Empire exchanged its raw materials and foodstuffs with western Europe and did a large volume of internal trade. Vienna served as the banking center not only for the Hapsburg lands but for most of the Balkan peninsula as well. The French had invested funds in Russia and Turkey. Germany served as the workshop of the Continent. The disintegration of the Austro-Hungarian Empire did far more harm to Europe than the Versailles Treaty, which left Germany's industrial power and political unity almost unimpaired. Moreover, the treaties that broke up the Austro-Hungarian Empire created nothing to take the place of what they destroyed. Half a dozen new or enlarged nations fenced themselves in behind tariff walls. Austria and Hungary, deprived of their former power and glory, became menaces to the peace of Europe—Austria by its weakness, Hungary by its resentment. Trade inside eastern Europe and trade between east and west stagnated. Russia remained in quarantine. Germany received sporadic help and contributed little to the prosperity of its neighbors to the east or south. Most of the money France lent to Poland and the Little Entente went into armaments.

The economic collapse that knocked the British pound off the gold standard in 1931 followed the failure of the Credit Anstalt bank in Austria. The social and political disturbances that brought Hitler to power in Germany shook Austria at the same time they shook the French Republic. On February 12, while the French Socialists demonstrated against Fascism, the Austrian Socialists began their four-day fight against it. When the Clerical government of Chancellor Dollfuss raided Socialist Party headquarters in Vienna and occupied the offices of the Socialist daily paper, rank-and-file Socialists went out on a spontaneous general strike. Dollfuss ordered the police and the Army to turn all their weapons, from pistols to heavy artillery, against the model workers' quarter of Vienna. This was no street fight *à la française;* this was full-scale civil war that lasted four days and cost two thousand lives before the Socialists surrendered.

The man who turned what armed force Austria possessed against the Socialist masses won the nickname of Millimetternich because he stood less than five feet high. Engelbert Dollfuss, the illegitimate offspring of peasant parents, had married a Protestant girl from Prussia, in spite of his own Roman Catholic faith. Great charm and still greater courage helped him to rise in the world. He entered politics as the protégé of that great Jesuit statesman, Monsignor Seipel, who led the Christian Socialist Party and served as Austrian Chancellor several times during the 1920's. Dollfuss never concealed his antidemocratic bias. After closing Parliament in September, 1933, he told a mass meeting: "The old Parliament with its leaders and members is gone, never to return. Socialist influence is dead, forever. I announce the death of Parliament." Dollfuss established a religious, not a racial, Fascism. He took as his slogan: "A truce to politics, a return to morality." He did not single out the Jews for special persecution. But he used many of Hitler's methods to set up his own brand of one-party state.

Hitler had his own private armies—first the SA and then the SS. Dollfuss always had the Austrian police and Army. In addition he had a private army, the Heimwehr, financed by Mussolini and commanded by

Prince von Starhemberg, a handsome, irresponsible playboy. Starhemberg amounted to no more
than a figurehead. Major Emil Fey,
the "Austrian Göring," provided
the real leadership and acted as
Dollfuss's adjutant. Fey was a sol-
dier-orator with an intelligent face,
a slit for a mouth, and a taste for
ruthlessness. Until Dollfuss and
Fey turned the Army, the police,
and the Heimwehr against the Vienna workers, the Socialists hoped
to form a common front with the
government against the Nazis. But
the militancy of the Socialists repelled Dollfuss and enraged Fey.

Berlin
"Chancellor Dollfuss on his Govern-
mental Seat." Garvens, Kladderadatsch,

Although both Dollfuss and Fey knew that the Austrian Nazis were
winning over many of their followers, they refused to have any truck
with the Socialists. The Communists never attracted mass support
in Austria, partly because of their antireligious views, mainly because
the Austrian Socialists showed so much more fight than their German
comrades. As for Dollfuss, he believed that he could wage a successful two-front war against both the Socialists and the Nazis. He won
the first battle of that war when he crushed the Socialists in February.
Five months later he lost his life trying to win the second.

For the first few months after Dollfuss smashed the Vienna Socialists,
the Austrian Nazis left Dollfuss in peace, and he reciprocated. The truce
ended in May when the Nazis began to set off infernal machines in railway stations, blow up small sections of track, and bomb the houses of
Dollfuss supporters. The official German radio told Austrian troops to
disobey their officers. German airplanes dropped leaflets urging the
Austrian people to start runs on banks and to pay no taxes. All these activities continued before and after Hitler paid his first visit to Mussolini
in June. Indeed, the month after Hitler took Mussolini's advice and
wiped out several hundred old-line Nazis, he ordered his Austrian supporters to assassinate Mussolini's Austrian protégé, Chancellor Dollfuss.

· IV ·

IT LOOKED like a sure thing. Dollfuss had already crushed the strongest
anti-Nazi force in Austria: the Socialist Party. At the same time, how-

"Divine power no longer has the last word. Today that lies with the state."
Simplicissimus, *Munich*

ever, the radical, racial propaganda of the Nazis attracted the same young middle-class desperadoes who had joined the Hitler movement in Germany. Dollfuss's own supporters also began to drift away. If they had to take orders from abroad, they preferred to take them from Hitler and Germany rather than from Mussolini and the Vatican. Government and police officials, eager to identify themselves with the winning side, made contact with the Nazis. Several dozen of them used to meet at cafés owned and patronized by Jews and there planned to seize power.

On July 25 they struck. Four truckloads of Nazis seized the Chancellery, and fourteen armed Nazis seized the government radio station. Another Nazi shot and wounded Dollfuss, who bled to death in three hours. At the same time, the government newscaster, with a Nazi gun against his ribs, announced that Dollfuss had resigned as Chancellor and had named Anton Rintelen, Austrian Ambassador to Italy, to replace him. Treacherous police officials had made it possible for the Nazis to enter the Chancellery and the radio station, but most of their colleagues remained loyal and opened a three-hour battle against the Nazis. They quickly halted the radio program, but the Nazis in the Chancellery were holding Major Fey as hostage and did not surrender for more than three hours.

Mussolini mobilized the Italian Army at the Brenner Pass and warned Hitler to call off his Nazi underlings. The Yugoslavs mobilized against the Italians. Hitler quickly obeyed Mussolini's orders. He withdrew his Ambassador in Vienna with a rebuke: "Dr. Rieth, by his actions, has involved the German Reich without any justification in an internal Austrian affair." Hitler then appointed von Papen to replace Rieth in Vienna, waking him at three in the morning to tell him to take the job. The same Clerical Fascist Party that ruled Austria under Dollfuss remained in office, with Dr. Kurt von Schuschnigg becoming Chancellor. Schuschnigg's grandfather came of Slovenian stock and did not earn the right to put the "von" before his name until he became a general in 1898. His father also followed a successful Army career, but the boy proved him-

self more a scholar than a soldier. "Schuschnigg took his studies too seriously," said one of his fellow pupils at the Jesuit academy where
Schuschnigg received his education until he went to war in 1914 at the
age of seventeen. He won four decorations and both he and his father
wound up as war prisoners in Italy. His release hung fire for more than
a year, and on his return to Austria he studied law and then entered politics as a protégé of Dollfuss's mentor, Monsignor Seipel. Schuschnigg
possessed as much personal courage as Dollfuss but less personal charm,
and he shared the political creed that both men had learned from Seipel,
who "always divined the right thing with absolute assurance and pursued it loyally and with all prudence."

Speaking before a Fatherland Front audience, Schuschnigg appealed
"not for the most votes but the best votes." He freed a number of Socialist prisoners from jail when he became Chancellor, but refused to form
a common, democratic front with them against the Nazis: "We consider
it impossible that parliamentary government should be restored in Austria." He also refused to work with the Nazis, calling instead for "Austria's rebirth in a Christian corporative state." The incorrigible humor of
the Viennese summed up Schuschnigg's personal plight in the legend
that his government had issued the following warning: "Any attempt on
the life of the Foreign Minister is punishable by a fine of 5,000 schillings.
Any attempt on the life of the Vice-Chancellor is punishable by a fine
of 10,000 schillings. Any attempt on the life of the Chancellor is absolutely forbidden."

The plight of Schuschnigg reflected his country's plight. The German
menace to western Europe obsessed France and immobilized Britain.
Unable to stand alone, Schuschnigg turned to Italy and the Vatican for
the outside support he needed. Prime Minister Baldwin felt he had
moved as far and as fast as the times permitted when he told the House
of Commons on the same day that Schuschnigg became Chancellor of
Austria: "Since the day of the air, the old frontiers are gone, and when
you think of the defense of England, you no longer think of the white
cliffs of Dover, but you think of the Rhine. That is where today our
frontier lies." Baldwin, like many of his compatriots, had not yet learned
that even before the air age the chief threats to Europe's peace lay well
to the east even of that frontier.

· V ·

LOOKING as far as the Rhine made Stanley Baldwin's eyeballs almost
burst. Mussolini, who prided himself on his eagle gaze, did not need to
see beyond neighboring Austria and Yugoslavia to find himself confronted by the shambles that the war, the peace treaties, and the depres-

Holland in Distress. Baldwin: "The frontiers of England are on the Rhine because I am big and you are small." Kladderadatsch, *Berlin*

sion had made of eastern Europe. The murder of Dollfuss caused Mussolini little distress and less surprise. He distrusted Hitler, but he also despised him. King Alexander of Yugoslavia gave him more serious concern. Alexander had suspended the Yugoslav Constitution and set up a personal dictatorship in 1929. He proved that an hereditary monarch could rule as efficiently, as ruthlessly as a self-made Duce—and in this case the monarch had scored some diplomatic victories at the Duce's expense. The very existence of Yugoslavia affronted Mussolini as a standing denial of Italy's right to divide and dominate the Balkan peninsula. Alexander not only challenged this arrogant assumption. He forced Italy's Fascist rulers to abandon their ambitions of eastward expansion and turn their attention to Abyssinia instead. But Mussolini could not give up all his hopes in the east without one final lunge at his principal adversary in that quarter.

Soon after Mussolini came to power he established close relations with Hungary—the first nation to set up a Fascist-type dictatorship. But it was not the character of Hungary's government that aroused Mussolini's sympathy so much as the character of Hungary's geography and history. Hungary lay at the center of eastern Europe and had a common frontier with the Yugoslav province of Croatia, which had formerly belonged to the Hungarian portion of the old Hapsburg Empire. Most Croats, before the war, wanted to break loose from Hungary and join their Serbian neighbors in some kind of South Slavic confederation. A minority, however, despised the uncouth Serbs and preferred their connection with Hungary and the Hapsburgs. They looked to Vienna and Budapest for their culture and to Rome for their religion.

In the prewar days, this minority included a clever young Croatian lawyer named Ante Pavelić who decided to make a career of working in behalf of Hungary among his fellow Croats. But when Croatia became a part of the South Slav Kingdom of Serbs, Croats, and Slovenes, Pavelić made common cause with the Croatian nationalists who resented the dominant position the Serbs occupied in the new state. Pavelić belonged to the Yugoslav Chamber of Deputies, but he left the country in 1928 to organize a Croatian army in Hungary and to raid Serbia from the north as the Macedonians were already raiding Serbia from their hideouts in Bulgaria. When the Yugoslav government sentenced Pavelić to death, *in absentia,* Italy began to subsidize him on a grand scale. Mussolini's agents put him on their payroll and gave him a comfortable villa near the Yugoslav frontier. Pavelić traveled on an Italian passport under the name of Antonio Serdar, visiting Budapest, Berlin, and Vienna. He established two camps for terrorists, one in Hungary, the other in Italy —both of them near the Yugoslav border. Here Croatian terrorists learned how to make bombs and conceal infernal machines, how to blow up railway tracks and sabotage factories, how to commit murder, forgery, and other crimes. But the popular response Pavelić counted on never materialized. The Croats continued to hate the Serbs, but they hated the Italians and Hungarians even more and refused to work for foreign paymasters. By 1930, Pavelić had only thirty Croats working for him, and he had to rely on the spectacular Internal Macedonian Revolutionary Organization for skilled instruction in terrorism.

Whereupon King Alexander, who had assumed dictatorial powers, went on to score an important diplomatic victory over Italy. In 1933 he visited Greece, Turkey, and Bulgaria and persuaded Greece and Turkey to sign a Balkan Pact which warned Italy to keep hands off the Balkans as the Little Entente warned Hungary to keep hands off central Europe. Since Yugoslavia already belonged to the Little Entente as well as to the Balkan Pact, it looked as if the small states of eastern Europe had at last begun to form a common front against any attempt by Germany, Italy, Austria, or Hungary to revise the peace treaties. But the Balkan Pact rested on an even weaker economic base than the Little Entente and neither of them could count on the complete support of any major power.

The fundamental weakness of the Little Entente encouraged Hitler to order the assassination of Dollfuss. The fundamental weakness of the Balkan Pact encouraged Mussolini to order the assassination of King Alexander. The Austrian Nazis got their man, but they failed to seize power afterward. In December, 1933, less than a month after the signing of the Balkan Pact, several of Pavelić's killers tried to murder King Alexander at Zagreb, the Croatian capital. When they failed, their chief assured his Italian sponsors that they would succeed the next time. Pavelić had to wait almost a year for that chance to come—a year of increasing tension among all the Great Powers of Europe. Hitler's withdrawal from the Disarmament Conference and the League of Nations brought Russia and France closer together. The attempted Nazi coup in Austria weakened the ties that had begun to form between Mussolini and Hitler. But the return of Russia to the councils of Europe doomed the Four-Power Western Pact, sponsored by Mussolini, and left him with nothing to do but make trouble further east. If he could not himself control a new European balance of power, at least he could prevent such a balance of power from being born.

The violent events of 1934—in Paris, Vienna, and Germany—knocked the last props out from under the Europe that the victorious Allies had tried to build after the war. The democratic Germany that Wilson once hoped to create had gone up in smoke. To counterbalance Hitler's Germany France sought the support of Stalin's Russia. Soviet Communism, once the chief menace to civilization, became its chief hope. After Foreign Minister Barthou of France had journeyed to Moscow and signed his mutual assistance pact with Litvinov, he made the rounds of the Little Entente capitals, winding up with a visit to King Alexander at Belgrade. Alexander had no objections to Barthou's plan for a grand anti-German coalition in which British Foreign Secretary Sir John Simon had expressed interest. Alexander wanted, therefore, to follow through with a visit to the British royal family and pay his respects to the Prime Minister and President of France en route. But he did not share Barthou's hopes that Mussolini could also be brought into the combination.

Nor did Barthou share Alexander's enthusiasm for the visit to France and England that the King insisted on making in October. The French delight in honoring visiting potentates at Paris; Alexander insisted on arriving at Marseilles aboard Yugoslavia's one-ship Navy, the destroyer *Dubrovnik*. Barthou put on the best face he could and agreed to meet Alexander at the dock and ride with him through the Marseilles streets. Nothing could have pleased Pavelić more. As a seaport near the Italian frontier, Marseilles afforded the ideal spot for a political assassination. Moreover, the fact that the French had to make themselves responsible for Alexander's safety in the unruly city put their country as well as

Yugoslavia on the spot. Pavelić had not forgotten the assassination of Crown Prince Franz Ferdinand at Sarajevo, and as a former subject of the Hapsburgs he saw his opportunity to repay Serbia for its complicity in that crime of twenty years ago. His Croatian patriotic society bore some resemblance to the Serbian Black Hand organization that had done Franz Ferdinand in. Its most formidable killer, however, was not a Croat but a Bulgarian of Macedonian origin—Vlada Georgiev Chernozemsky, a man of half a dozen aliases best known as Vlada, the Chauffeur. Vlada boasted that he had murdered thirty persons, more or less, sometimes using a revolver, sometimes a bomb. "Killing a man," he once remarked, "is nothing more to me than removing a tree."

Pavelić had many weeks to lay his plans because Alexander and Barthou announced theirs well in advance. Eight or ten accomplices, including Pavelić's mistress, got bombs, revolvers, and ammunition smuggled into the Hotel Nègre Coste in the resort town of Aix, near Marseilles, where Vlada and another professional killer, Mio Kral, picked them up the day before Alexander landed. Vlada accepted the assignment of shooting Alexander. Kral, a slow-witted Croatian peasant, promised to help him escape by throwing several bombs immediately after the shooting. Pavelić and the rest promised to help the two killers get safely across the Italian frontier. Vlada and Kral traveled from Aix to Marseilles by bus, arriving two hours ahead of time at the corner where they planned to assassinate Alexander. Vlada carried two revolvers—one of them a foot long—and his pockets bulged with bombs and ammunition. Kral carried almost as heavy and deadly a load. Yet these two desperadoes, dressed to kill, roamed the sidewalk freely and no police cordon, no escorts mounted on motorcycles or horses stood between them and their victim when he finally appeared.

King Alexander looked more like an English schoolteacher than a Balkan monarch. His weak eyesight compelled him to wear thick pince-nez glasses. He sported a small close-cropped mustache and carried himself rigidly. Although his personal tastes ran to rare editions of the masters of French literature, he did not shrink back from the rough-and-tumble of Balkan politics and he possessed more than his share of courage and self-confidence. He landed at Marseilles wearing an admiral's uniform with cocked hat and high, stiff collar. Airplanes roared overhead and newspaper and newsreel photographers kept rushing up to the ancient automobile that slowly bore the King, Barthou, and General Georges of the French General Staff up the Cannebière, chief boulevard of Marseilles. "This car is more like a hearse than an automobile," the driver complained to a policeman. "It won't go more than twenty miles an hour and it's very old. Wouldn't it be better to borrow the car of

UNDERWOOD

King Alexander and Foreign Minister Barthou Begin Their Fatal Ride

Monsieur the Mayor? After all—the King—it's not every day we have a King here."

"You are not entered in a race," the police officer replied. "You must not exceed the speed of five miles an hour. Keep her in first. Those are your orders."

The planes continued to roar and the photographers continued to snap their pictures during Alexander's slow progress up the Cannebière. Suddenly Vlada raced from the sidewalk to the running board of the car and fired two shots into Alexander's stomach. A third shot hit Barthou in the arm; a fourth shot killed a detective who tried to intervene; a fifth shot struck General Georges in the stomach. Other shots, fired by the police, killed two women spectators. If Mio Kral had kept his nerve and thrown his bombs, Vlada might have escaped in the confusion. But Kral fled in panic and a mounted policeman felled Vlada with a blow on the head and wounded him fatally with a revolver shot. Alexander died on the spot. Barthou bled to death in the hospital because the doctors and nurses in their excitement failed to apply a tourniquet in time. General Georges recovered.

Pavelić and the other instigators of the plot ran out on Mio Kral more shamelessly than Kral ran out on Vlada. Only one of them remained in Marseilles, watched Vlada commit the crime, and vanished. Pavelić had already fled to Italy. The French police finally caught up with Kral and two higher-ups so that when the Little Entente Foreign Ministers brought the whole case before the League of Nations, the part that Pavelić had played, with Italian backing, came to light. But Laval, who had replaced Barthou as French Foreign Minister, refused to countenance any action against Italy and when Bogoljub Yevtich, the Yugoslav Foreign Minister, threatened to quit the League of Nations, Laval agreed to back Yugoslavia if it brought charges against Hungary only. All that eventually happened was that the League censured the Hungarian government for the negligence of some of its frontier officials. A year later a French court at Aix-en-Provence condemned three of Pavelić's accomplices to life imprisonment and sentenced Pavelić and two of his closer associates to death. But Italy continued to give them sanctuary and refused to permit their extradition to France. They lived to fight—and kill—another day.

The assassination of Alexander and Barthou afforded an illuminating contrast with the assassination which inspired it. The Sarajevo assassination of 1914 set off a general European war; the Marseilles assassination of 1934 did not. Yet both sets of assassins risked a general war to get their men. The Serbian terrorists who killed Franz Ferdinand knew that they were defying Germany as well as Austria. They knew they had the support of France as well as Russia. To create a Greater Serbia they deliberately provoked a general European war. The Croatian terrorists who killed King Alexander also risked a general European war in order to break up Yugoslavia. They knew they had the support of Italy as well as Hungary. They knew they were defying France as well as Yugoslavia.

UNDERWOOD

King Alexander and Foreign Minister Barthou Murdered in Marseilles

But Europe had changed greatly in the two decades between the two assassinations. The Europe of 1914 was willing and ready to go to war. The Europe of 1934 was not. This state of affairs put a premium on aggression, and the discontented "have-not" powers, the losers in the last war, drew the logical conclusions. The events of 1934 proved that they could, quite literally, get away with murder. Dollfuss got away with mass murder in Austria until Hitler had him shot. Hitler got away with mass murder in Germany, but Mussolini checkmated him in Austria and then had King Alexander shot in Marseilles. But no general war followed. Instead, Mussolini turned his attention from eastern Europe to Ethiopia. The year 1934 ended with a political murder in Leningrad which attracted relatively little attention at the time, but presently led to more bloodshed than all the other killings of 1934 combined.

· VI ·

THE RIOTING, assassination, and civil war that convulsed Europe during 1934 did not destroy the postwar settlements. Both Hitler and Mussolini tried to undermine those settlements, but they worked at cross-purposes as often as they worked in concert. More important, Stalin suddenly joined the anti-German coalition. In 1930 he called Republican Germany "the most aggressive and militaristic country in the world," yet right up to the moment Hitler took power, Stalin vilified the Social Democrats and worked against them with the Nazis, whose strength he grossly underrated. By 1934 he recognized, though he never admitted, what a horrible miscalculation he had made. Treaties with France and recognition by the United States prepared the way for Russia to join the League of Nations, which Lenin had once described as "that thieves' kitchen at Geneva." In short, Stalin did his belated best to restore a balance of power that Hitler was trying to undermine by attacking the more vulnerable parts of eastern and central Europe.

The weakness of this part of the world distracted attention from the famine in the Ukraine and the failures of the Five-Year Plan. Moreover, the public had heard too many false predictions of Bolshevik collapse, especially at a time when a new menace was rising in Germany. The Nazis reserved their bitterest attacks for the Communists, and the Communists returned the compliment. Anyone who opposed the Nazis had to regard the Communists as no worse than the lesser evil, perhaps even as valuable allies. The anti-Communists, by the same token, played into Nazi hands. Demoralized liberals in western Europe, Britain, and France feared that democracy had outlived its usefulness and that the future belonged either to Communism or Fascism.

Individual statesmen, students, and correspondents knew about the dark side of Soviet Communism. They even tried to impart that knowledge to the public. But it suited the tastes and interests of other statesmen, other students, other correspondents to present Russia in a favorable light. If Stalin, on balance, seemed less of a menace than Hitler, why call attention to his weaknesses and shortcomings? It was difficult enough to rid the man in the street of his anti-Communist prejudices without having to admit that some of the Communist atrocity stories contained a grain of truth or that Hitler might have his uses as a stick with which to beat Stalin some day. Of course, the Rothermere press in Great Britain, the Hearst press in the United States, and assorted political and religious leaders in many countries preferred Hitler and Mussolini to Stalin, and made their views widely known. But fewer cried, "A plague on both your houses," or stressed the affinity between Germany's Brown Bolshevism and Russia's Red Nazism. It was so much easier to see the world picture in blacks and whites; it was so much more comforting to assume that the democratic world plus Hitler or the democratic world plus Stalin could stamp out sin.

Stalin, however, accepted his new role with some misgivings. In the fall of 1934, just after Russia joined the League of Nations, the Moscow *Izvestia* wrote: "The capitalist world is now divided into two camps: the powers that are not anxious for war at the present juncture because a war would endanger their winnings from the World War and the powers that are dissatisfied with the present state of affairs and are ready to take a chance to find a way out. The powers interested in the preservation of peace understand the futility of their struggle for peace without the collaboration of the Soviet Union. A League of Nations functioning without the participation of the nation that is the chief advocate of peace can evoke no confidence. The stronger the Soviet Union and the more staunchly its borders and its independence are guarded by the Red Army, the greater will be the fear of imperialist adventurers to carry out an aggressive policy." These words from the official organ of the Soviet government reassured millions who wanted to believe in Russia's willingness and ability to work with other countries to preserve peace. At the same time, however, Moscow *Pravda*, speaking for the Russian Communist Party, added this observation: "Lenin led the proletariat to socialist victory in one sixth of the world, established the Communist International, and headed the struggle during the first period of wars and revolution. In the second period of wars and revolution, Lenin's Communist International under Stalin's leadership will lead the proletariat of all countries to socialist revolution throughout the world."

The word *Pravda* means "Truth"; *Izvestia* means "News." Moscow correspondents used to say there was no truth in *Pravda* and no news in *Izvestia*. In this case, however, *Pravda* spoke the truth when it iden-

tified Russia with the anti-German coalition. And it may have been news
to some people outside Russia that Stalin still adhered to Lenin's policy
of world revolution. But *The Militant,* New York organ of the Trotsky
movement, denounced Stalin as a turncoat: "Under Stalinism, the
Comintern has degenerated into a border patrol of the Soviet Union.
It is not an instrument for revolution, and its fight against war degenerates into pacifism. The pacifist illusions that the Stalinists are sowing in
the ranks of the working class, both through the Comintern and the
Foreign Office of the Soviet Union, can be compared to the role of the
Second International on the eve of the World War. Now it is the Stalinist
Third International that competes with the Second International for
these reformist honors on the eve of a new world war."

Such outbursts suited Stalin's interests perfectly. Trotsky and his supporters could no longer inflict the slightest damage on the Soviet regime,
but Trotsky's continued agitation gave Stalin a whipping boy whom he
could hold responsible for all his own errors and troubles. In December,
1934, an obscure Communist named Nikolayev shot and killed Serge
Kirov, member of the Politburo, head of the Communist Party organization in Leningrad, and personal friend of Stalin. "It is difficult," Kirov
had written a few months before his death, "for one to imagine the figure
of such a giant as Stalin. During the last years, during the time when we
have worked without Lenin, we do not know of one change in our work,
of one big slogan, enterprise, or direction of our policy which was not
initiated by Stalin." This might have been taken two ways had not Kirov
gone on: "The powerful will and colossal organizing talent of this man
assure the Party the timely fulfillment of great historical changes, connected with the victorious building up of socialism."

Nobody, including Nikolayev, disputed the fact that he had killed
Kirov. But what were his motives, who were his accomplices? "There
is an unofficial theory," wrote William Henry Chamberlin in *The Russian Enigma,* "that Kirov's killing was personal, rather than political in
its inspiration. Kirov was a notorious Don Juan and Nikolayev's wife,
according to widespread rumor, was his secretary. Out of this could have
grown a familiar pattern of jealousy leading to murder." Stalin, however,
proceeded on quite a different theory. He acted as if Nikolayev belonged
to a world-wide network of conspirators, directed by Trotsky, who had
left Russia in 1929 to take up a life of exile abroad—moving from Turkey
to France to Norway. The authorities—meaning Stalin—not only had
Nikolayev jailed and executed. Fourteen Communists were seized and
put to death and another one hundred and three political prisoners, already in jail, were also shot for alleged complicity in the crime. Zinoviev
and Kamenev, who had apologized, recanted, and retracted themselves
out of prison as former leaders of the Left Opposition, were again jailed

along with ninety-five of their former associates, most of them Old Bolsheviks and disciples of Lenin. From these arrests and executions, Stalin's enemies deduced still another theory: that Stalin himself had engineered the murder of Kirov in order to justify the purges that followed.

Yet Stalin had not waited for Kirov's murder to order his purges or to stage the trials that accompanied them. In 1934, before Kirov met his death, three hundred thousand Russian Communists were expelled from the Party, and the secret police, or GPU, held the first of its public political trials back in 1930. At that time, Professor Ramsin and seven other outstanding professors and engineers confessed that they had sabotaged Soviet industry and taken orders and money from members of the British and French governments. Ramsin testified that he had plotted with P. P. Ryabushinsky, a wealthy prewar industrialist, who agreed to head a military dictatorship and oust Stalin. The Moscow radio put the whole trial on the air and the press carried most of the testimony. But the stage-managers of the trial overlooked one important detail. Ryabushinsky had died in Paris several years before. Ramsin also testified that he had conferred in London with T. E. Lawrence at a time when Lawrence was on the North-West Indian frontier. The Russian public never learned of these discrepancies in the government's case. By 1934, the foreign public had forgotten the whole thing. But the Soviet government steadily improved its technique. In 1933 it charged several British engineers, working for Vickers-Armstrong, with espionage and sabotage. Two of them confessed in court, one repudiated his confession, and the Russians finally permitted them all to leave the country. The British government, which interceded in behalf of the engineers, never questioned the verdict, but merely insisted on the release of the prisoners.

The Kirov murder marked a turning point in Soviet history in that Stalin for the first time used a single crime to implicate all his rivals and many of his subordinates. The indispensable Trotsky still played the role of chief villain and his hostility to Stalin, which he continued to express through every channel of mass communication, lent an ever-present if ever-fainter atmosphere of reality to the whole proceedings. The story of these trials belongs with the story of the years in which they occurred. But the complete story of 1934 must give the murder of Kirov a prominent place. For 1934 was more than a year of violence. It was a year that focused attention on eastern Europe. While Paris rioted, Vienna fought a civil war. The murders of Chancellor Dollfuss of Austria and King Alexander of Yugoslavia called attention to the disturbed condition of the former Hapsburg lands. And barely six months after Hitler's blood purge of June 30, Stalin seized upon the murder of Kirov to set in motion a far more comprehensive blood purge of his own.

· VII ·

THE DISTURBANCES that caused so much havoc in eastern Europe during 1934 made themselves more widely felt in the years that followed. Frustrated in the Balkans, Mussolini turned to Ethiopia, the one African nation that had never lost its independence. Ethiopia had abundant natural resources and a common frontier with the two Italian colonies of Eritrea and Somaliland. Many Italians remembered with shame that Ethiopian troops had defeated one of their armies back in 1896 at the famous Battle of Adua, and Mussolini jogged the memories of those who had forgotten. If he could not dominate the Balkans he could build a new empire in Africa and make the Mediterranean once again *Mare Nostrum* —"Our Sea."

Hitler welcomed the prospect of Italian expansion into Africa. Mussolini had blocked the Nazi conquest of Austria; an adventure in Africa would divert him from Germany's European *Lebensraum* and set him at odds with the British and French. The guardians of the British and French colonial empires resented further Italian intrusion upon Africa. The mass of the British and French people resented the methods Mussolini used to gain his ends. Yet the British people feared war; the French people feared Germany. Their leaders therefore sought to appease Mussolini, lest their opposition throw him into Hitler's arms.

The death of Barthou eliminated one of the few French statesmen capable of pursuing a wider policy. He recognized that his country must re-establish its prewar alliance with Russia in order to restrain Germany and keep the peace. Barthou also hoped to improve relations with Italy, but he gave the Russian alliance priority. Pierre Laval, who succeeded Barthou as Foreign Minister, gave priority to good relations with Italy. He even hoped to come to terms with Hitler and had little sympathy for Barthou's partiality for the Soviet Union. Laval came of peasant stock and had flirted briefly with Communism just after the war. But his acquisitive instincts proved stronger than his revolutionary passion, and the more money and power he acquired the more he turned against the idealism of his youth. Barthou, never having gone through Laval's revolutionary phase, coolly appraised the Soviet Union in terms of its potential value to France.

Early in January Laval went to Rome, where he signed a series of agreements with Mussolini covering Austria, central Europe, and Africa. Italian troops had already attacked Ethiopian troops at the border town of Wal Wal, and the day before Laval reached Rome Ethiopia asked the League of Nations to arbitrate the dispute. But Laval, like most Frenchmen, felt less concerned about the future of Ethiopia than he did about the future of the Saar Valley, where on January 13, 1935, in a plebiscite held under the auspices of the League of Nations, in accordance with the terms of the Versailles Treaty, more than 90 per cent of the voters cast their ballots in favor of joining Nazi Germany. If the German-speaking people of the Saar Valley did not prefer dictatorship to democracy, at any rate they preferred dictatorship under the German swastika to democracy under the tricolor of France or the administration of the League.

Two months after the Saarlanders followed the advice of Nazi propagandists and "came home to the Reich," Hitler made two more moves that deepened the alarms of the French. On March 9 he announced the reconstitution of the German Air Force. On March 16 he restored universal compulsory military service. Both these moves violated the Versailles Treaty, but a Cabinet crisis prevented the French from taking any action. The conservative Pierre-Etienne Flandin became Premier, with Laval as Foreign Minister, but both men had lost the confidence of the people, who were turning, under the continued pressure of deflation, to the parties of the left. Hitler then took shrewd advantage of the deadlock in France to invite Sir John Simon, British Foreign Secretary, and Anthony Eden, Lord Privy Seal, to visit Berlin and to inform them that Germany had already attained air equality with Britain. They returned to London sadder and wiser men. Eden quickly took off for Moscow, where he held useful conversations with Stalin and Litvinov. But a rough airplane ride back put him out of commission for a month and prevented him from accompanying Simon to a vital conference with the heads of the Italian and French governments at Stresa.

Eden, like Barthou, believed in trying to work with the Russians toward a system of collective security. Simon took a more cautious view and made it clear at Stresa that Britain would not take sanctions against violations of the Versailles Treaty. Mussolini persuaded the three powers to come out against "any unilateral repudiation of treaties which may endanger the peace of Europe." This left Africa out of account and gave Italy a virtually free hand to continue preparations for an attack on Ethiopia. Shortly afterward, Laval went through the motions of signing a mutual assistance pact with Russia, but it contained so many provisions calling for consultation with the League and the signers of the Locarno Pact that it had little practical value. And he completed his sabotage of collective security with Russia by failing to push the new Franco-Soviet treaty rapidly through the Chamber of Deputies.

Laval fancied himself as a slick operator. Baldwin preferred to pose as the embodiment of bluff honesty. But the clever Laval could not match the bumbling Baldwin in winning the confidence of his fellow countrymen. Back in November, 1934, Baldwin had assured the House of Commons that Britain's margin of air superiority over Germany amounted to considerably more than 50 per cent. Four months later, when Simon and Eden returned from Germany and reported Hitler's boast that Germany had already attained air equality with Britain, Baldwin kept silent. Not until late May did he speak and then he made this stunned confession: "I was completely wrong. . . . We were completely misled. . . . It is the responsibility of the government as a whole and we are all responsible; we are all to blame."

· VIII ·

FAR from destroying Stanley Baldwin's authority in the House of Commons, this frank confession of total failure added to his stature, and in June he swapped jobs with the ailing Ramsay MacDonald, thereby becoming Prime Minister in name as well as in fact. At the same time he replaced the Liberal Sir John Simon as Foreign Secretary with the Conservative Sir Samuel Hoare. Within less than two weeks—on June 16, the anniversary of the Battle of Waterloo—Hoare took off his gloves and signed a naval treaty with Ribbentrop, Hitler's ambassador-at-large, granting Germany the right to build a navy 35 per cent as large as Britain's. Hoare, with Baldwin's consent, had not only connived with Ribbentrop to violate the Versailles Treaty; he did not inform either the French or the League of Nations. He simply had the First Lord of the Admiralty announce the Anglo-German Naval Treaty as an accomplished fact. It meant that for the next ten years the Germans could build all the warships, including submarines, that their yards could produce. The French considered themselves betrayed. They knew, even though Baldwin and Hoare apparently did not, that Hitler's *Mein Kampf* called for a deal with Britain as the necessary preliminary to an attack upon France. By the same token Mussolini took heart and concluded that his conquest of Ethiopia could proceed without interference from England. "We will imitate to the letter those who are lecturing us," Mussolini informed his foreign critics. "They have shown us that when it was a question of creating an empire or of defending it, they never took any account at all of the opinion of the world."

Baldwin and Hoare prepared to improve even on Mussolini and to flout the opinion of their own countrymen. During the summer of 1935 eleven million persons in Great Britain had participated in a "Peace Ballot" prepared by the League of Nations Union and sponsored by the Liberal and Labor Parties. On this informal, unofficial "ballot," more than eleven million Britons registered their approval of continued British membership in the League, all-around reduction of armaments, abolition of all air warfare, prohibition of the private sale and manu-

© LOW, ALL COUNTRIES

"Progress of man, 1935 A.D." Cartoon by David Low

facture of arms and munitions—four points that appealed to the pacific temper of the British public at the time. But the fifth and last point read: "Do you consider that if a nation insists on attacking another, the other nations should combine to stop it by (*a*) economic and non-military measures, (*b*) if necessary military measures." If the eleven million "voters" on the Peace Ballot read and approved these words, they obviously believed that Britain should first use every means short of war to enforce collective security and should finally resort to war itself after all other means had failed. But it was a big, big if.

A still bigger if arose in connection with a statement made by Sir Samuel Hoare before the League Assembly at Geneva on September 11. If Sir Samuel Hoare meant what he said on that occasion, he had obviously committed himself to the same proposition that the signers of the Peace Ballot had also endorsed. But this assumes that men and women, in high station and low, always use words to commit themselves to courses of action and never to release noble emotions or to gain some other purpose to which the words do not refer. "It is to the principles of the League and not to any particular manifestation that the British nation has demonstrated its adherence," declared Hoare. "Any other view is at once an underestimation of our good faith and an imputation upon our sincerity. In conformity with its precise and explicit obligations the League stands, and my country stands with it, for the collective maintenance of the Covenant in its entirety, and particularly for steady and

UNITED PRESS PHOTO

Ethiopian Natives Salute Mussolini's Picture

collective resistance to all acts of unprovoked aggression." Baldwin endorsed Hoare's speech, not only as British Prime Minister but as leader of the Conservative Party in the approaching general election. While Hoare's speech made some eleven million British voters glow with the same sense of righteousness that they felt when they voted for collective security on the Peace Ballot, this same speech meant something quite different to its author and to Stanley Baldwin. It meant that the Conservatives had stolen the election thunder of the Liberals and the Laborites. And to clinch matters Baldwin back in June had created a new Cabinet post, Minister of League of Nations Affairs, to which he appointed the popular, handsome Anthony Eden.

Everything worked out according to plan. The Conservatives swept the general election, winning the enormous majority of 247 seats over the combined Liberal and Labor forces in the House of Commons. The government remained a coalition, at least in name, for its supporters included two splinter groups that called themselves National Laborites and National Liberals. One important piece of unfinished business clamored for immediate attention. Mussolini had just sent his modern Roman legions marching into Ethiopia—a League member in good standing since 1923. For several years both the British and the French governments had known that Mussolini planned to conquer Ethiopia. At the last minute they even tried to buy him off by offering through the League Council to back any claims he might make to annex some of the largest, poorest, and least populous Ethiopian provinces. "Italy's need for expansion in East Africa is not to be satisfied by the cession of a couple of deserts, one of salt, one of stone," Mussolini replied. "The League Council seems to think I am a collector of deserts."

Having failed to buy off Mussolini, the British and French governments did the next best thing. They embargoed arms exports to both Ethiopia and Italy. This prevented the Ethiopians from securing any arms at all but did not prevent the Italians from using the Suez Canal to ship their own arms and their own troops to make war in Ethiopia. Less than a month after Hoare's Geneva speech, Italian troops crossed the Ethiopian border, near Adua, without any declaration of war. Yet as recently as 1928 Italy and Ethiopia had signed a treaty of friendship and arbitration. No serious military action ensued. The Italians had some 200,000 of their own troops ready for combat plus some 60,000 native troops. Twenty thousand more Italian soldiers arrived during October, another 38,000 followed in November, all of them passing

Ethiopia and Neighbors, 1935

through the British-controlled Suez Canal. One of the native chiefs made a feeble attempt to start a civil war against Emperor Haile Selassie, the tiny, spidery, bearded intellectual who personally financed and directed his country's resistance. He had 35,000 troops with some light modern arms and some slight training in their use. Another million untrained tribesmen, armed with primitive muskets, swords, and spears, made up the rest of his fighting forces.

The British journalist, Geoffrey T. Garratt wrote this description of the average Ethiopian soldier in *Mussolini's Roman Empire:* "Many had no rifle but only a sword or spear. They were decent men, with an elementary courage, believers in a simple form of Christianity, tough, superstitious, frugal, and unambitious. Those Europeans who watched them hastening to their death knew what our civilization had prepared for them. Perhaps it was as well that the Ethiopians themselves did not know, for their minds would have been totally unable to understand the subtle intrigues, the mixture of feeble humanitarianism and cynical egotism which so brought it about that when they reached their chieftain's camp there were no modern rifles and modern ammunition waiting for distribution. Wood would have to go out against steel, the sling against the tank, and overhead would be the Italians' four hundred bombers, and the 'pursuit planes' which had nothing to pursue." The pilot of one of these pursuit planes, Vittorio Mussolini, son of the Duce, found "wonderful sport" bombing Ethiopian cavalry: "One group of horsemen gave me the impression of a budding rose unfolding as the bomb fell in their midst and blew them up. It was exceptionally good fun."

During the first two months of the war the Italian commanders did not try or expect to fight any battles. They assumed that the appearance of their armies, in the north and south, would cause the Ethiopians to capitulate. In addition, Mussolini had reason to hope that the French and British governments might come forward in accordance with long-laid plans and propose an acceptable settlement. He already had Laval in his pocket. He had only to wait for the British Conservatives to win the general election for Baldwin and Hoare to break the pledges they made to their own people and come to his aid. For Italy's action in Ethiopia clearly and frankly violated the League Covenant that Baldwin, Hoare, and all the eleven million British signers of the Peace Ballot pledged themselves, in their various ways, to uphold. And, sure enough, as soon as Mussolini gave his marching orders, all members of the League Council and fifty of the fifty-four League members agreed that Italy, by making war on Ethiopia, had violated the League Covenant and then went on to organize a co-ordinating committee to consider what kind of sanctions to apply. But Laval, who had become Premier

UNITED PRESS PHOTO

Ethiopian Slave

UNITED PRESS PHOTO

Ethiopian Warrior

as well as Foreign Minister of France, managed to delay action. For a month, even those nations that voted to apply sanctions sent arms and munitions to uncommitted nations for transshipment to Italy. In November, however, they finally stopped all loans, all arms shipments, and most exports of raw materials to Italy. If Laval had not seen to it that oil continued to flow, Mussolini's mechanized forces might have ground to a halt.

Nor was Laval Mussolini's only foreign friend. Sir Samuel Hoare proved no less helpful when he left England in November for a short vacation of ice-skating in Switzerland. For months, experts in the British and French foreign offices had been working on a scheme to partition Ethiopia, and Paul van Zeeland, chairman of the League's Co-ordination Committee, had accepted the suggestion of Hoare and Laval that England and France be "entrusted with the mission of seeking, under its auspices and control and in the spirit of the Covenant, the elements of a solution which the three parties at issue—the League, Italy, and Ethiopia—might find it possible to accept."

By the time Hoare arrived in Paris, the British and French foreign offices had agreed on a plan to award Italy most of the rich, populous northern province of Tigré and the extensive southeast province of Ogaden. Ethiopia, in return, was to receive a narrow stretch of desert country in Eritrea, including an outlet on the Red Sea. Hoare and Laval put the finishing touches on the plan, gave it their names and their blessings, and went their separate ways—Hoare to enjoy his vacation, Laval to give the story to the Paris newspapers.

A loud explosion followed at once. On December 9, the British Cabinet quietly approved the Hoare-Laval Pact which the French press noisily and simultaneously released. The League of Nations did not get the text until four days later. The British press and public denounced the whole business with virtually one voice, and on December 18, Prime Minister Baldwin described the Hoare-Laval Pact as "absolutely and completely dead." As in his candid admission of error concerning German rearmament, Baldwin once again made a virtue of stupidity: "If there arose a storm and I knew I was in the right, I would let it break on me, and I would either survive it or break. If I felt after examination of myself that there was in that storm something which showed me that I had done something that was not wise or right, then I would bow to it." Mr. Baldwin bowed. Hoare resigned as Foreign Secretary and Anthony Eden replaced him. Laval survived a milder storm but had to step down a month later on a domestic issue.

Hoare and Laval had tried to do three things: save Haile Selassie some of his country, stop further bloodshed, and prevent a complete breach between their two countries and Italy. And the worst that could be said against them was not that they betrayed Ethiopia, scuttled the League, or rewarded aggression. Mussolini had the will and the power to crush Ethiopia, to defy the League, and to get what he wanted. But Hoare and Laval, in their ignorance of eastern Europe and their anti-Soviet prejudice, underrated and antagonized the one country that might have swung the balance of power against Hitler. Perhaps Litvinov was bluffing when he preached collective security at Geneva. Certainly Stalin had other strings to his bow. Russian relations with Germany remained formally correct, and the Soviet trading organization had no more scruples about shipping oil to Mussolini than he had about buying it. Stalin had always done business with anyone who wanted to do business with him. He never permitted sentiment or ideology to stand in the way of his country's national interest. But Laval, for all his cynicism, and Hoare, for all his realism, could not bring themselves to deal rationally with the Soviet leaders. Barthou and Eden, on the other hand, had always wanted to bring both Russia and Italy into a broad anti-German coalition, but now that Barthou had died, Eden did not choose to continue the fight alone.

Nobody can prove that a majority of the British people wanted to oppose Mussolini's African adventure at the risk of war. Nor can anyone prove that the majority of the British people wanted peace at any price. Baldwin apparently gauged public opinion accurately when he made

UNITED PRESS PHOTO

Italian Troops Enter the Ethiopian Town of Makale

Hoare the villain of the piece and Eden the hero. But the promotion of
Eden to the post of British Foreign Secretary did Ethiopia no good and
Mussolini no harm. As soon as the Hoare-Laval Pact blew up, Mussolini
ordered all-out war. He replaced General de Bono, an ineffective Fascist,
with Marshal Badoglio, an effective soldier, who decided on December
22 to hurry the campaign along by releasing mustard gas. G. L. Steer's
Caesar in Abyssinia gives an eyewitness account of what happened to
the forces of Ras Imru on whom this attack fell: "Some were blinded.
When others saw the burns spread upon their arms and legs and felt
the increasing pain, whose source and end they could not understand
and for whose cure they had no medicine, Imru's men broke and fled.
The moral effect was more terrible than the material. From their easy
perches in high heaven the Italians could see with their own eyes, and
with a feeling of rich treasure trove, an Ethiopian force, jerked suddenly
backward, horrified and scattered. Bombing had never shown such fine
aesthetic results. Total dispersion."

The Italian progress continued. On May 2 Emperor Haile Selassie
left Ethiopia and traveled to Europe aboard a British warship. At Geneva he and Maxim Litvinov made an incongruous pair, but no one
seconded the appeals of this absolute monarch so eloquently as the
spokesman for the revolutionary proletariat. Perhaps it was a case of
extremes meeting. Perhaps Litvinov proved himself an even greater
cynic than Eden because throughout the Ethiopian war Russian-Italian
trade boomed whereas Anglo-Italian trade stagnated. On May 5 Marshal

UNDERWOOD

Emperor Haile Selassie

Badoglio entered the Ethiopian capital of Addis Ababa; on May 9 King Victor Emmanuel of Italy proclaimed himself Emperor of Ethiopia as well. One month later Baldwin received Hoare back in his Cabinet as First Lord of the Admiralty. The following month the League of Nations called off the sanctions against Italy. "It cannot be expected by anyone," Eden told the House of Commons, "that continuance of existing sanctions will restore in Abyssinia the position that has been destroyed. So far as I am aware no other government, certainly not this government, is prepared to take military action." But before the curtain went down on Ethiopia, it went up on events of greater moment in Germany and France, in Russia and Spain.

· IX ·

No SOONER did Hoare's attempted deal with Laval drive him temporarily from office than the danger both men tried to avert materialized. If the British and French governments did little to save Ethiopia from Mussolini, they did still less to save themselves from Hitler. The Hoare-Laval Plan had two merits: it avoided war and it left Emperor Haile Selassie a small fragment of his native country. If the deal had gone through, it might also have delayed or even prevented the formation of the Rome-Berlin Axis. But the collapse of the Hoare-Laval Plan, the war in Ethiopia, and the breach between Mussolini and the western democracies gave Hitler his opportunity. On March 7, defying the advice of his generals, he ordered thirty-five thousand German troops to violate the Versailles Treaty and the Locarno Pact with a "symbolic" occupation of the Rhineland.

Hitler gave as his excuse the impending ratification of the Franco-Soviet mutual assistance treaty. The Chamber of Deputies had at last taken favorable action, but Hitler chose to regard the arrangement as a breach of the Locarno Treaty although the French Senate had not yet confirmed the Chamber's vote. Hitler announced his action two hours after his Foreign Minister, Baron von Neurath, had summoned the British, French, Italian, and Belgian Ambassadors to his office and proposed to them a twenty-five-year peace pact, covering both eastern and western Europe. Utter confusion followed at once. A stopgap government had just come to power in France, with the Radical Albert Sarraut as Premier and Flandin as Foreign Minister. It hoped to remain in office until the results of the forthcoming elections became known and had its hands full trying to decide what to do about embargoing oil shipments to Italy. But Hitler's occupation of the Rhineland pushed the war in Ethiopia off the front pages of the papers. Sarraut and Flandin wanted to mobilize immediately, as they had every right to do. France had the biggest and best army in Europe and could have crushed the Germans in no time. In fact, the German officers marching into the Rhineland carried sealed orders to withdraw in the event of French mobilization. But Sarraut and Flandin did not dare to mobilize without previous British approval, and when Flandin hastened to London he received divided counsels. Lloyd George told him that Hitler had "provocation" for breaking the Versailles and Locarno Treaties. He urged "keeping our heads." Neville Chamberlain, Chancellor of the Exchequer and strongest man in the Baldwin government, disagreed with Flandin's judgment that Hitler would back down before a show of force: "We cannot accept this as a reliable estimate of a mad Dictator's reaction." Flandin quoted Baldwin as having told him, "If there is even one chance in a hundred that war would follow from your police operation, I have not the right to commit England. England is not in a state to go to war." Eden told the German Ambassador that he found Germany's action "deplorable."

Flandin argued that England, by strong action, could lead Europe. Winston Churchill concurred. But Churchill also pointed out that a Clemenceau or a Poincaré would not have waited, as Sarraut and Flandin did, for England to take the lead. If the French had mobilized, England would have had to back them up. But Sarraut and Flandin, remembering the casualties at Verdun just twenty years ago, dared not take the risk. Hitler dared not refuse the gamble, and promptly won his greatest and cheapest victory. The German occupation of the Rhineland produced tension inside France and Britain and friction between them. It destroyed what little authority the League of Nations still enjoyed, and what little hope it still inspired. It put Hitler in position to menace more than western Europe. Baron von Neurath put it this way to William C. Bullitt, United States Ambassador to Russia: "As soon as our fortifications are constructed and the countries of central Europe realize that France cannot enter German territory, all these countries will begin to feel very differently about their foreign policies, and a new constellation will develop." Mussolini, recognizing that he could no longer expect to beat Hitler, did the next best thing and joined him.

BETTMANN ARCHIVE

Hitler in Rome, Flanked by Mussolini and King Victor Emmanuel II.
Standing in the rear are, left to right, Ribbentrop, Ciano, and Hess

· X ·

AT THE SAME TIME that Mussolini completed his conquest of Ethiopia
he reopened negotiations with Hitler. Two months later, on July 11, 1936,
Hitler signed a treaty with Chancellor Schuschnigg of Austria, recognizing that country's sovereignty while Austria "acknowledged herself
to be a German state." Mussolini approved of everything, and in October, Count Galeazzo Ciano, his son-in-law and Foreign Minister,
visited Hitler and returned with an agreement that Mussolini later
dubbed the Rome-Berlin Axis. Of Hitler, Ciano remarked to his father-
in-law: "The man believes his own atrocity stories." Ciano told the press
that the treaty called for peace and security in western Europe, co-operation in the Danube basin, and reconstruction in Spain.

The clause about Spain drew attention to the most menacing condition that had developed in western Europe since the end of the war.
During 1932 and 1933 the Spanish parties of the left and center governed
the newly formed Republic. They opened ten thousand sorely needed
new schools, but their land reform program moved slowly. "We have
made our Republic, let us now make our Revolution," the extremists
exclaimed. Two years after the abdication of King Alfonso, ten thousand
families still owned more than half the farming land in Spain. A million
and a quarter peasants owned only 2 per cent; another two million peasants owned no land at all. Many large estates still lay uncultivated. Spain

remained a country of "men without land and land without men." It also remained a battleground of religious strife. In March, 1933, the Pope issued an encyclical protesting the continued persecution of Roman Catholics. The newsstands carried anti-Catholic literature and Marxist tracts that the monarchy and the dictatorship had both forbidden. Pornographic publications also boomed. *"No era so"* ("It wasn't this we expected"), commented Ortega y Gasset, a good Republican, and in November, 1933, the parties of the right won 207 seats in the Cortes, the center parties won 167, and the parties of the left won only 99.

At the head of the government stood the veteran Radical politician, Alexander Lerroux. At the head of the War Ministry stood the strongest man in the Cortes, young José María Gil Robles, whose Catholic Action Party had won more seats than any other. Gil Robles, an ex-Monarchist in his middle thirties, still sought Monarchist votes but worked with Republicans to get himself in power. Within another two years, the right and center coalition proved as ineffective as the left and center coalition that preceded it. Discontent increased. General strikes broke out in many cities. In the Asturias mining region, miners and civil guards fought pitched battles. Mobs again set fire to churches and monasteries and exchanged shots with armed priests and monks. The Basques and Catalans resented the efforts of Madrid to deprive them of the greater autonomy they had gained under the Republic. Finally, President Zamora called for new elections. Within the space of less than five years the Spanish Republic had seen twenty-eight governments rise and fall—an average of almost one every two months. In December, 1935, General Molero left his post as commander of the Seventh Division at Valladolid to assume the post of War Minister. By the time he arrived in Madrid, a new Premier had formed a new government which clapped him into jail for deserting his post. Twenty-four hours later, this government fell in its turn and he was released from jail to become War Minister after all. On December 31, 1935, the *A.B.C.* of Madrid commented, "Yesterday came the seventh and last political crisis of the year—we say the last as we presume there will hardly be a fresh one before nightfall."

The elections that President Za-

Gil Robles: *"How well I could govern if there were no workers." Bagaría in* Luz, *Madrid*

mora ordered to take place on February 16 gave the parties of the left
a majority of seats in the new Cortes. The center parties suffered the
heaviest losses. Gil Robles's Catholic Actionists remained the largest
single bloc, but the right and center coalition could no longer form a
government although the parties of the right and center had won a
slightly larger popular vote than the parties of the left. The politicians
of the right and center made the mistake of campaigning against each
other. The politicians of the left closed ranks and after the elections
formed a *Frente Popular,* or Popular Front, government headed by
Manuel Azaña of the Left Republicans. But Azaña presently quit the
Premiership to take over the Presidency from Zamora, who had resigned
under pressure from the left.

Just as the parties of the left resorted to direct action while the left
and center tried to govern Spain, so the parties of the right now resorted
to violence in their turn. But first they turned abroad for aid. Calvo
Sotelo, who had served as Finance Minister under Primo de Rivera, and
Juan March, who had laid the foundations of one of the biggest fortunes
in Spain by smuggling fuel to German submarines during the war, made
contact with Mussolini and Hitler. As far back as the spring of 1934,
Mussolini had received a deputation of Spanish Monarchists to whom he
promised to deliver 20,000 rifles, 20,000 hand grenades, 200 machine
guns, and a million and a half pesetas. At the same time, the German
Embassy in Madrid and German consulates throughout Spain established contact with Spanish generals and placed Nazi officers in the
Spanish Foreign Legion.

Four months of Popular Front government gave the plotters their
opening. Between early March and early July Spain went through 113
general strikes and twice as many other strikes. Crowds burned 170
churches and set fire to 251 more. They wrecked 69 political clubs and
ten newspaper offices. The opposition parties in the Cortes asked the
government to end the disorders: "A country can perfectly well live
under a Monarchy or under a Republic, under parliamentary rule, Soviet
rule, or the rule of a dictatorship. But a country cannot live in a state of
anarchy, and Spain is in a state of anarchy today." The logic of this
statement contained at least one flaw. Both the Popular Front and the
opposition had proved they could not establish parliamentary rule. The
Popular Front could not restrain its supporters outside the Cortes.
The opposition proved as ineffective inside the Cortes. Unable to gain its
ends by parliamentary means, the opposition took the offensive in another area. And the Popular Front leaders, bewildered by the violence
of the left, showed the same bewilderment in the face of much greater
violence from the right.

UNITED PRESS PHOTO

Madrid Church Wrecked by Republican Rioters

· XI ·

VIOLENCE did not bewilder the opposition. Violence inspired the opposition to redouble its zeal. In April a prominent labor leader, José Castillo, murdered the organizer of one of the Fascist bands that had begun to spring up all over Spain. Three months later, on July 11, the Fascists retaliated by murdering Castillo, whose friends struck back, within twenty-four hours, murdering Calvo Sotelo, a leading anti-Republican conspirator. The parties of the right, convinced that the moment had come to overthrow the Republic, set in motion a strategy that they had begun devising back in 1934. At the center of their plan stood General Sanjurjo, "Lion of the Riff," and former commander of the Civil Guard. As Salvador de Madariaga had once said, "The ambition of every Spanish general is to save his country by becoming her ruler," and that ambition had possessed Sanjurjo since 1932, when he tried to overthrow the Republic, which, however, jailed him before he could establish his projected "republican dictatorship." Two years later, the victorious conservatives released him from jail, and in another two years, after the Popular Front victory of 1936, Sanjurjo fled to Lisbon. But he did not stay there long. After the murders of Castillo and Sotelo, General Sanjurjo took off in a plane from Lisbon to Seville, where he planned to summon the army to overthrow the Republic. But the plane crashed, for reasons unknown, and Sanjurjo perished.

Another General at once jumped into his shoes. Short, pudgy Francisco Franco, still on the sunny side of fifty, had served as Chief of the General Staff between 1934 and 1936, when Gil Robles held the post of War Minister. When the Popular Front came to power, it virtually exiled Franco by appointing him Military Governor of the Canary Islands. On the death of Sanjurjo, Franco disguised himself as an Arab and flew from the Canaries to Morocco, where he assumed command of 55,000 Moors and Foreign Legionnaires and called himself "Commander-in-Chief of the Fighting Forces in Morocco." On July 17 he ordered the Army to rise and overthrow the Republic. This Army, in 1936, numbered about 100,000 men, of whom 15,000 held commissions. It had 195 generals on its active list and another 437 in reserve. The officers supported the rebellion and the enlisted men obeyed the orders of their superiors. Most of the Navy, on the other hand, supported the Republic. So did the bulk of the Air Force, including General Franco's younger and more celebrated brother, Ramón, who had led a group of Spanish planes in a transatlantic flight.

But Ramón Franco's fame dwindled and Francisco Franco's grew as Army garrisons throughout Spain rebelled against the Republican government in Madrid. When a government plane dropped bombs on one of these rebellious garrisons at Tetuan, General Franco accused the Republic of shooting civilians. "It will not be long before the movement for the restoration of Spain will be victorious," he warned the officials of the Republic. "The reprisals that we shall take will be in proportion to the resistance you offer." On July 19 a cruiser from Spanish Morocco shelled Algeciras so that Moorish troops could land. The Foreign Legion, organized by Nazis along German lines, had already made Spanish Morocco safe for Franco. Military insurrections broke out in most of the principal Spanish cities, and the rebels, who called themselves Nationalists, gained control of Seville, Toledo, Valladolid, and Burgos, where they established a provisional government on July 25. Workers' organizations kept the Republic in power in Madrid, Barcelona, Valencia, and most of the northern and eastern parts of the country. The rebels controlled the Portuguese border and most of southwestern Spain.

"The Left did not know how to win. The Right did not know how to lose," wrote Professor Alfredo Mendizabal of the University of Oviedo in *The Martyrdom of Spain*. Back in October, 1935—"Red October," as the Spaniards called it—revolutionary Asturian miners had occupied his house at Oviedo and burned all his books and papers. The following summer, as soon as Franco ordered the revolt to begin, the same kind of struggle broke out again all over Spain, and nobody has written a more vivid, authentic account of what happened than this Spanish professor whose devout Roman Catholicism did not alienate him from the most militant members of the Popular Front; indeed, his religious faith and national pride sharpened his insight:

"Fifteen of us, after our home had been occupied by revolutionaries, were taking refuge in a building which had been abandoned by its inhabitants when it was bombarded by the Red Army. A permanent guard of well-armed Communists lived with us and shared the little food we had and also the trials of our very anxious lives. In this town, first captured by the Red Army and then by Government Troops (who, on the 14th of October entered the streets held by the rebels since the 5th), during nine interminable days and their terrible nights we heard nothing but the sound of machine guns, rifles, and cannon, and the constant detonations of dynamite skillfully handled by the miners. Every street was the scene of a battle without truce or mercy, and the sky became red from the flames of burning buildings. But in each man of the little revolutionary patrol who sheltered in our house there was a truly Spanish chivalry. For several days we were at their mercy; they could have done what they liked, even killed us, for in their eyes we were *bourgeois* and enemies. Nevertheless we have nothing but praise for them: in the rough miner, inflamed by revolutionary propaganda, we found a nobility of heart, a chivalry and respect for women, which it was hard to suspect behind the red cockade of the soldiers of the social revolution.

"Through a hail of bullets these men stormed a confectioner's shop as soon as they learned that we had not eaten for some time—'they could not bear this because there were women with us.' When they came back carrying three large trays of cakes, covered with broken glass from the windows on account of the fusillade, they, who also had not eaten all day, refused to take anything before we did. They did not search us because 'our word of honor was enough' to assure them that we were not armed. And when they had to fight, they crossed the road, at the risk of their lives—'so as not to drag us into it'—drawing the fire from our house which might have sheltered them.

"The plain facts are that kindness and sympathy awoke in them such deeply human and brotherly Christian feelings (unconsciously Christian, since they thought they were opposed to this), that these two groups, *bourgeois* and 'Communist,' were welded into one community, closer than a brotherhood. On the day that the leader of the party received permission to return on leave to his native village, he refused, although needing rest, 'because his successor might treat us badly.' So he chose to say. He fell ill—and we nursed him like a brother, watching over his sleep. Every time we entered his room he was overcome by emotion, and embraced us. During one of our long conversations, he said,

UNITED PRESS PHOTO

*Dead Spanish Loyalists in the Streets
of Lérida*

'Do you see how we have got to
know one another? You had not
a very high opinion of us, nor
we of you. But now, everything is
changed.'

"It was true; everything was
changed for us who had passed
through that crucible of suffering.
We thought a great deal and we
modified many of our opinions.
Everything was changed at the
bottom of some souls, blinded by
hate, who found a little charity in
their path. But it was necessary
that the attitude of the powerful
toward the weak should also
change."

The hopes inspired by this first
taste of civil war never came true.
The Popular Front victory a few months later did not mean that the pendulum had swung again to the left and that the Republic was stabilizing
itself. It meant that the moderates had lost out to the extremists. Azaña,
the creator of the Popular Front, made no attempt to come to terms with
the anti-Monarchist Army officers who had helped to set up the Republic in 1931. As a result, they had to turn to Gil Robles, Sanjurjo, and
Franco. Nor did Azaña try to moderate the revolutionary zeal of the
extreme left. In the Cortes he welcomed the support of Socialists, Communists, and Anarchists while the rank and file of these same parties,
outside the Cortes, continued the same violent tactics they had used
when Lerroux and Gil Robles ruled. Under pressure from the left,
Azaña's government redistributed nearly two million acres of land to
poor peasants, or four times as much as all previous Spanish governments had distributed since the establishment of the Republic. But he
could not bring the parties of the left which had forced him to grant
these reforms to accept the responsibilities of power. Events in Spain
thus conformed to the individualist passion that possessed members of
all parties. The Spanish Socialists did not abdicate, like the German Socialists; they did not wait, as the Austrian Socialists waited, to be attacked. They carried the attack to the enemy. So did the Anarchists, but in
their own way. Only the Spanish Communists proved themselves more
Communist than Spanish. They followed the new Popular Front line
laid down by Moscow and called for defense of the Republic, not revolu-

tion. Which made them closer to Azaña than to the other parties that made revolutionary appeals to the workers and peasants.

Nor did the Franco movement follow the Mussolini or the Hitler pattern. Franco himself was a professional soldier, not a professional agitator. He came from the propertied classes, not from the great unwashed. He made few demagogic promises and therefore needed foreign soldiers, as well as foreign money and supplies, to start his rebellion and keep it going. Franco summoned Moorish Moslems to make Spain safe for Christianity. He enlisted Foreign Legionnaires to revive Spanish nationalism. Franco had no disciplined party, no private army. The bulk of his followers did not represent those "masses" whose revolt Ortega y Gasset had described. They were spirited young men of means or position behind whom stood the power and prestige of the Roman Catholic Church. Like these young men, Franco identified himself with the restoration of the old order in Spain—minus the person of King Alfonso XIII. The wall of the Pyrenees had helped to keep Spain neutral throughout the war. Its lack of industry and resources kept it poor afterward. Spain suffered from a general backwardness comparable to Tsarist Russia's. But events had moved faster in war-torn Russia than in peaceful Spain, which gave promise, for several years, of evolving into a democratic Republic. The forces released by the world depression ended this hope. Internal troubles, aggravated by external pressure from Germany and Italy, finally resulted in civil war. As Trotsky declared, from his latest place of exile in Norway, "Europe is turning red at both ends."

· XII ·

SPAIN certainly turned red with blood. During the first two weeks of the rebellion, the insurgents killed at least fifty thousand civilians. "When the troops occupy a place," Franco instructed his Moors and his Foreign Legionnaires, "the local authorities must first be taught a lesson in respect; if they have escaped, the same lesson must be adopted towards members of their families. In every case, the methods resorted to must be of a clearly spectacular and impressive character, and must indicate clearly that the leaders of the troops are determined to proceed with like severity against anyone who offers resistance." Franco counted upon a swift and complete coup d'état. As J. Alvarez Del Vayo, later Foreign Minister of Republican Spain, wrote in *Freedom's Battle:* "The military uprising, planned with the complete agreement and promise of support of Germany and Italy, and carefully organized from the moment the Popular Front came to power at the February elections, spread like wildfire. Its leaders were convinced that within a few hours, or at the most a couple of days, they would be masters of the country. Everything had been carefully arranged. But these generals, who had never been distinguished for their political acumen or knowledge of mass psychology, had overlooked one small detail when they drew up their plans with so much care. They had forgotten the Spanish people."

Miners and artists, students and metalworkers, musicians and peasants, engineers, schoolteachers, clerks, factory hands, and lawyers formed themselves spontaneously into a Republican Militia. "A belt and a pair of cartridge pouches were fastened over the mechanic's overalls, which thus acquired the status of a uniform," wrote Del Vayo. "The great thing was to get hold of a rifle and as much ammunition as possible, even if it had to be kept in pockets for lack of cartridge belts. Sandals took the place of army boots. The question of food was of secondary importance; a few tins of sardines and a good-sized piece of bread go a long way when the mind is set on higher things. Every man fought with the weapons at his disposal. In the mountains the shepherds used their slings against the rebels, hurling sticks of dynamite instead of stones. Behind the military columns would march reservists, unarmed, ready to take the place of the men who fell, or hoping that a good haul of prisoners would give them not only something to shoot with, but also the satisfaction of being able to arm themselves at the Fascists' expense. In the rear guard, women did the work of men. Many of them, however, were not willing to resign themselves to this relatively passive role, and the more determined among them—in particular those belonging to Youth organizations—went off to the front as soon as they could get hold of a mechanic's overall."

More than a month passed, however, before any real front materialized to which they could go. The Spanish Civil War, during its opening weeks, consisted of local struggles in some of which the Republic crushed the rebellion while in others the insurgents set up military governments that soon acknowledged the authority of General Franco in Burgos. The popular support for the Republic took the rebels by surprise, forcing them to change their plans and increasing their dependence on Mussolini and Hitler. Franco started with about a hundred Italian and German planes, ten or twenty thousand Italian troops, and a few thousand German technicians. But he lost his first major battle when he failed to take Madrid in November. "This afternoon," the Burgos radio announced on the morning of November 7, "we shall have coffee in Madrid." The citizens and militiamen of Madrid had other ideas and made good their slogan, "No Pasarán" (They Shall Not Pass). The rebels had five to fifteen times as many planes, tanks, and artillery pieces as the Republicans, and by 1937 Franco had 50,000 Italian troops, 12,000 Germans, and several hundred German and Italian planes. Barely five hundred of the 15,000 officers in the Spanish Army stood by the Republic, which had to improvise its war effort from the ground up.

Decisions reached in London and Paris prevented the Republic from crushing the rebellion in a matter of weeks. Decisions reached in Moscow prevented Franco from crushing the Republic in a matter of months. Decisions reached in Rome and Berlin kept the fighting going for years. Italy and Germany intervened in the Spanish Civil War from the start and recognized the Franco regime on November 18, 1936. It took the British less than two months to organize in London "The International Supervisory Committee for Non-Intervention." Margret Boveri, correspondent for the *Berliner Tageblatt,* and author of *Mediterranean Cross-Currents,* offered this appraisal of British policy at the time: "The first conflict between Italy and England took place in Abyssinia; the second in Spain. In Spain, as in Abyssinia, Italy knows what she wants, England what she does not want. England does not want a Franco victory, but she does not want a Government victory either, nor does she want to take part in the struggle. That is the decisive factor. As long as England's will for peace is greater than her will to dominate, the prospects for Italy—whatever risks she may run—will continue to be favorable."

The same will for peace, the same reluctance to dominate, also possessed France, where a coalition of Radicals, Socialists, and Communists won a majority of seats in the Chamber of Deputies and set up a Popular Front government shortly after the Popular Front victory in Spain. Léon Blum, the first Jew and the first Socialist ever to head a French government, became Premier. The Communists received no Cabinet posts, but agreed to support the Popular Front program of domestic reform, including a forty-hour week. Frightened millionaires sold francs and bought dollars or moved their hoarded gold, bodily, to New York. One of Blum's more savage, reactionary critics said his very name sounded like a bullet hitting the body of a traitor. Another remarked, "Better Hitler marching under the Arc de Triomphe than Blum in power." Blum himself was more a scholar than a statesman, more a man of letters than a politician. Like the German Social Democrats, he and his French Socialist comrades felt they had to lean over backward to prove their respectability. Knowing also the fear of war that ran through almost all Frenchmen of every party, he yielded to the pressure of his British friends and allies on the matter of Spain.

Only the Italians and the Germans joined the Non-Intervention Committee with real enthusiasm. They had no thought of keeping out of Spain; they had no fear that Britain or France would try to thwart their plans. If the Russians took any countermeasures, so much the better: that would make the Spanish Republic appear Communistic. Not that the Russians wanted revolution in Spain. Like the British and French, they sought for peace at almost any price. But their new strategy of the Popular Front forced them to join the Non-Interventionists—distrustfully, unwillingly, and with the words of Talleyrand perhaps ringing in their ears: "Non-intervention? Between ourselves, it's the same thing as profitable intervention, but profitable only for the other side."

While the Non-Intervention Committee took shape in London, a new Republican Cabinet took office in Madrid, headed by sixty-nine-year-old Largo Caballero. The new Premier, known as the Spanish Lenin, led the left wing of the Socialist Party and enjoyed his widest support among the labor unions. His fifteen-man Cabinet included members of all parties that supported the Republic—Basque and Catalonian Nationalists, Left Republicans, Socialists, and two Communists. Only the Anarchists held aloof. They joined the struggle against Franco but refused to subordinate themselves to any state authority. Their chief strength lay in the labor unions of Barcelona, where the civil war threatened on several occasions to turn into social revolution. Leon Trotsky also had some influence in Barcelona—more, at any rate, than Stalin or even Caballero. The Partito Obrero de Unificación Marxista, known as the POUM, for short, had more members in the city than the Socialists and Communists put together and its leader, Andres Nin, got much of his inspiration from Trotsky, who argued that the time had come for the Spanish workers to organize a revolution based on the Russian, 1917, model.

The Communists had no more use for Trotsky in Spain than they had in Russia. Having dropped the strategy and tactics of world revolution, Stalin found himself forced to play balance-of-power politics. At home he tried to strengthen his own regime by whipping a recalcitrant peasantry into line. At the same time his Communist agents abroad used no less ruthless means to achieve no less moderate ends. Thus Vicente Uribe, the Communist Minister of Agriculture, carefully refrained from putting through a radical program of land reform. Spain had only a few thousand card-carrying Communist Party members when the civil war started, but their numbers increased ten times over and their influence multiplied a hundredfold as the fighting continued. Within a month after Franco started his rebellion, foreign Communists and fellow travelers began to stream into Madrid, where they organized an International Brigade that numbered more than a thousand men during the crucial battle of November. More important, in October the Soviet government announced its refusal to "consider itself bound by the agreement for non-intervention to any greater extent than any of the remaining participants of the agreement." By the end of the month, Russian planes, artillery, tanks, and ammunition began to arrive in Spain, along with a few hundred technical advisers. Not more than five hundred

UNITED PRESS PHOTO

General Franco and General Wilhelm Faupel, German Ambassador to Nationalist Spain

UNITED PRESS PHOTO

Madrid Crowds Cheer Loyalist Troops Departing for Valencia

Soviet citizens ever took part in the Spanish Civil War at any one time, but the Soviet secret police and the Comintern always kept special agents in Spain to maintain discipline among Communists of every nationality. The International Brigade, which the Republic armed and equipped, never had more than fifteen thousand men in the field.

The Anarchists and the POUM accused the Communists of sabotaging the revolution. Franco's supporters habitually referred to the Republic as "Red Spain." The British Foreign Office, knowing the real facts, also knew how to exploit for its own purposes the confusion that this fear of Communism aroused. The British Foreign Office had never questioned the legality of the Spanish Republic nor of the 1936 election which brought the Popular Front to power. But when civil war broke out in Spain, the risk of bucking Franco openly seemed, to Anthony Eden and his advisers, greater than the risk of backing him tacitly. The Spanish Popular Front looked shaky. Less than half the Spanish voters had cast their ballots for its candidates, and the victorious supporters of the new government included a disorganized and divided assortment of adventurers and idealists, of Communists and Catholics, of Anarchists and Republicans who often hated one another more than they hated Franco.

Nor could the Spanish Republic expect much help from abroad. The Russians had shown more enterprise than the French, but what motives inspired them? The Soviet leaders welcomed the Spanish Civil War be-

cause it promised to set the democratic and the Fascist powers at logger-
heads and to make them less eager and less strong to form a common
anti-Soviet front. The Russians and their Communist dupes in western
Europe and the United States therefore gave the Loyalists enough aid to
keep them in the fighting but not enough to assure a Loyalist victory.
The British and French wanted the Spanish Civil War to end as soon as
possible for the same reasons that the Russians wanted it to continue as
long as possible. For the British and French wanted peace at almost any
price, including the price of a Franco victory. Mussolini had a greater
stake than any other foreign statesman in Franco's cause. Even a victorious Franco would continue to depend on Italian support, and a
Rome-Madrid Axis would certainly weaken the British position in the
Mediterranean and might even take Hitler down a peg. Some of the
Italian legions that fought in Spain received the Pope's blessing before
they departed, and the Pope, as Churchill remarked in another connection, had a number of legions of his own in Spain "not always visible on
parade."

Hitler felt little more enthusiasm for Franco than Stalin felt for the
Loyalists. Like Stalin, Hitler welcomed a long-drawn-out struggle in
Spain because it promised to divide and weaken his potential enemies.
Like Stalin, Hitler limited his own commitments. In a conference with
his generals and admirals Hitler declared, "A one hundred per cent
victory for Franco was not desirable from a German point of view."
Hitler expressed more enthusiasm for a "continuance of war," since that
would lead to friction between France and Italy and give him a free
hand to make his own arrangements in Czechoslovakia, Austria, and
points east. Anthony Eden expressed no enthusiasm whatever for anything to do with the Spanish Civil War. "I am fully aware there are
Italian volunteers in Majorca," he wearily informed a questioner in the
House of Commons, "as there are other foreign volunteers in other parts
of Spain. I deprecate it, but I cannot deal with this question alone."
When pressed on the futility of nonintervention, he replied: "As far as
concerns nonintervention, I wish to say categorically that there are other
governments more to blame than those of Germany and Italy." The die-
hard Tories accepted this statement at its face value; a much larger
section of British public opinion may have deplored Eden's hypocrisy,
but his constant emphasis on the shortcomings of both groups in the
Spanish struggle made him appear neutral and fair-minded. Actually,
his neutrality played into Franco's hands.

Eden operated under no illusions. He felt no personal enthusiasm for
Franco. He did not look forward to the prospect of an Axis victory in
Spain. But he regarded such an outcome as a lesser evil. The supporters
of the Spanish Republic presented the struggle as one between democ-

racy and Fascism; Franco's supporters called it a struggle between order and Communism. The Republicans of the left who governed Spain in 1932 and 1933 and the Popular Front that took office in 1936 had shown themselves no more competent or honest than the Monarchists and right Republicans who held office in 1934 and 1935. A Republic needs more than majority support to endure. Unless its institutions command the loyalty of a preponderant number of its people, a determined minority can always upset the government of the day. It was Franco's purpose to prove that such a minority could also seize power and hold it. The pragmatic British and the realistic French dared not oppose Franco and back the Republic; they feared that a Republican victory would result in the ultimate triumph of Communism and that a Franco defeat would result in a general European war. The Russians viewed such prospects with somewhat less alarm, but they had too much unfinished business to attend to at home to intervene as actively as the Italians. Domestic affairs also monopolized the attention of Roosevelt's New Dealers in the United States. And the British monarchy, in 1936, faced a crisis that threatened the one symbol that held the whole Empire and Commonwealth together.

SUMMING UP

During 1934, the peace settlements of 1919 began to collapse at their weakest points—in eastern Europe. During 1935 and 1936 Mussolini and Hitler exploited and extended this collapse. At first the British and French tried to split the dictators by coming to terms separately with Mussolini, but the opposition of the British public killed the Hoare-Laval Plan to buy off Mussolini at Ethiopia's expense and hastened the formation of the Rome-Berlin Axis. The equivocal attitude of certain British and French leaders strengthened the Axis still further. Most Frenchmen feared Germany more than they feared Russia, but Laval regarded Communism as a greater menace than Nazism and sabotaged the Franco-Soviet Pact that Barthou had originated. The British were less anti-German and more anti-Russian than the French. They also voted Conservative six months before the French voters gave the Popular Front a majority in the Chamber of Deputies. Both peoples dreaded the prospect of another war. Both had lost one generation of young men. Neither could afford to lose another. The Germans had lost a generation; but they had also lost a war and even Hitler still hesitated to risk the loss of another generation in the hope of having better luck, next time, on the battlefield.

Spain was the largest, most populous European nation to remain neutral from 1914 to 1918. More, perhaps, than any other nation in western Europe, Spain had also escaped the industrial revolution of the nineteenth century and the social revolution of the twentieth. With the abdication of King Alfonso in 1931, Spain tried to catch up with the times, but it could not jump from the eighteenth to the twentieth century overnight. The same sharp contrasts between old and new, the same fierce conflict between religion and revolution that had convulsed backward Russia appeared in backward Spain. During the spring and summer of 1936, the Republic that had replaced the Monarchy moved to the left. Civil war tore the country in two, as Mussolini and Hitler threw their weight on the side of General Franco's rebellion. This time Britain tacitly backed the Axis; France timidly followed Britain's lead. Communists and fellow travelers from all over the world swarmed to Spain, but the soldiers from the Axis Powers far outnumbered them. The Russians sent some help to the Republic; they could not afford to stay out; they dared not go all the way in. Only the United States, among the Great Powers, kept hands off Spain. The New Deal still took precedence over events abroad.

17

Western Europe Goes to ⅃

Internal weakness in Britain and France, inte
tensions in Russia, Germany, and Italy prolo
Spain's Civil War and promote anarchy throug̣
out western Europe.

PREVIEW

T̲HE A̲BDICATION of King Edward VIII called the world's attention t̲
unsuspected points of weakness—and strength—in the British Empire. The pacifist Oxford Oath and the radical Left Book Club stirred
mixed emotions—and so did the Moscow purge trials. The Spanish Civil
War split Europe into two hostile camps as Hitler and Mussolini kept
Franco in the fighting while Britain and France had adopted a policy
of nonintervention and Stalin sent limited aid to the beleaguered Republic. By the end of 1937 Franco looked like a sure winner as the
chances of a general European war steadily increased.

· I ·

T̲HE S̲AME internal pressures that thrust Mussolini and Hitler to power
in Italy and Germany sent their Fascist and Nazi legions marching into
Spain. The Fascist Corporative State had failed to solve Italy's domestic
problems, and Mussolini at first sought diversion and compensation in
the Balkans. His plot to break up Yugoslavia missed fire, but his invasion
of Ethiopia proved more successful. Hitler's New Order did not solve
Germany's domestic problems, but when the Nazis failed to win the
quick, cheap victory they had hoped for in Austria, they turned west
and proceeded to remilitarize the Rhineland. Then Spain offered the
two dictators wider scope for their pent-up energies. Mussolini needed
bases on Spain's Mediterranean islands. Hitler welcomed the chance to
put France in a squeeze by establishing German influence beyond the
Pyrenees. And Franco needed Italian and German support to overthrow
the Republic.

Domestic considerations also influenced the policies that Britain,
Russia, and the United States pursued throughout the Spanish Civil

598

War. It took the 19...
war had cost the...
young men trai...
taken their...
rulers in la...
Hardly ...ler...
lacke...ther
Ba...

...ring home to the British people what the
...t wiped out virtually a whole generation of
...dership. The British upper classes had always
...riously. Educated from childhood to become
...ad been the first to sacrifice themselves in 1914.
...vived unhurt, and if Anthony Eden stood out he
...flair, Winston Churchill's brilliance, and Stanley
...nse. It was perhaps no wonder that Eden did not
...ers' stature. What did him most credit was that his
...ther stunted nor warped his growth. He had seen
...poraries killed in action on the Western Front and the
...rn broken in body and spirit. Providence had spared
...e resolved to make the most of it. But how lonely he
...henever he thought of his prewar friends and wartime
...n he would see no more.

...urden lay on the shoulders of Eden's most illustrious con-
...he man who bore three different titles during the year 1936:
...ales, King Edward VIII, and Duke of Windsor. With the
...ing George V on January 20, 1936, almost everyone in the
...s felt that an era had ended. The rigid limitations of George's
...had come to symbolize permanence during a quarter century
..., revolution, depression, and now threatening war again. His
...dest son, long known as the Prince of Wales, who now began to reign
as Edward VIII, had received a long and thorough training for kingship.

In his perceptive autobiography, *A King's Story*, Edward modestly acknowledged that "however hard I tried, my capacity was somehow not appreciably above the standards demanded by the fiercely competitive world outside palace walls." He found himself "without quite understanding why . . . in unconscious rebellion against my position. That is what comes, perhaps, of sending an impressionable Prince to school and war." He also felt weighed down by a life of "duty without decision, service without responsibility, pomp without power."

Although Edward's intelligence and ability did not set him apart from the common run of men, he possessed exceptional spirit and charm. He loved steeplechasing better than studies, but he had always tried to live up to the motto of the Prince of Wales—*Ich dien*, "I serve." His old-fashioned father disapproved of dangerous sports; he disapproved still more of Edward's still more dangerous friends, the bright young people of London's cosmopolitan Mayfair Set who talked in cockney accents, danced to American jazz, and adopted Continental morals. Like most other fathers of the prewar generation, George V could not understand that the Mayfair Set released his son's frustrations and lulled his ambitions.

"His habits, tastes, and view reflected the era when his grandmother ruled over the British Empire, and the British aristocracy stood admired and envied throughout the world," Edward wrote of his father in *A King's Story*. "It would not be correct to say that he rejected the twentieth century. It was only that he determined to resist as much of it as he could." Of himself he wrote: "Mine is a story of the life of a man brought up in a special way, as a Prince trained in the manners and maxims of the nineteenth century for a life that had all but disappeared by the end of his youth." Edward's determination to identify himself with his own century made him peculiarly responsive to the United States and its people. There, too, his restless spirit felt itself at home. Many of his younger subjects shared this enthusiasm, finding, for instance, the crisp humor of *The New Yorker* more to their taste than the stodgy pages of *Punch*. For the war which had left the British weary unto death gave the Americans a new lease on life. At the same time, certain Americans, finding Old World ways more to their liking than New, took precarious root abroad. They consorted with London's bright young people, who introduced them to glamorous foreigners, the suave and intelligent Ambassador Dino Grandi from Fascist Italy and the crude, cocky Ribbentrop, Hitler's special adviser on foreign affairs. Edward's association with these people led him to conclude that he was witnessing "the birth of a new era" in which "high office or ancient lineage were no longer the sole criteria of status. Beauty, wit, sophistication—these had now become the valid passports to the Sovereign's intimate circle."

It was with the Mayfair Set, in 1933, that the Prince of Wales first made the acquaintance of Mrs. Wallis Warfield Simpson, the Baltimore-born wife of a London stockbroker. Mrs. Simpson had already divorced one husband, an American naval officer named Spencer, and by 1936 when she filed divorce proceedings against Ernest Simpson, she and the King had fallen deeply in love. The British press steadfastly ignored their affair even during the summer of 1936 when American newspapers publicized Mrs. Simpson's presence as Edward's companion on a private yacht cruising the Mediterranean. Both Edward and Wally, as the American journalists now called them, had not only reached the age of consent, they had passed the age of forty, and he found in her such understanding, such assurance, such responsiveness that nothing else could do: she must become his wife. In mid-October, Prime Minister Baldwin sought an interview with the King and warned him that the rumors of his romance with Mrs. Simpson, then appearing in the American press, threatened to compromise the prestige of the throne. A week later, Mrs. Simpson received her uncontested divorce, but she could not remarry for another six months. On November 25, the King sent for

Baldwin and asked if Parliament could pass legislation permitting him to contract a morganatic marriage with Mrs. Simpson, making her his wife but not his Queen. Baldwin expressed strong personal doubt that such a plan could go through but promised to consult his Cabinet and the Dominion Prime Ministers. Before he had time to keep this promise, the Bishop of Bradford on December 1 publicly expressed the hope that the King was aware of his dependence on God's grace—adding: "Some of us wish he gave more positive signs of his awareness." That tore it, and the curtain went up on what H. L. Mencken called "the greatest story since the Resurrection."

· II ·

SEX, religion, politics: the drama of Edward's abdication had everything. The young King symbolized something more than the British Empire; he represented the whole war generation. And he had to endure more than the loneliness of kingship; he had to endure the loneliness that assailed all those sad young men whom the war had spared. His own personality enhanced his pathos. During his thirties he looked and acted like a man in his twenties. At forty, he still kept the smile, the figure, and the manners of youth. As Baldwin said at the time of Edward's accession: "He has the secret of youth in the prime of age." Baldwin also called attention to Edward's singular fitness for the job at hand: "He has a wider and more intimate knowledge of all classes of his subjects not only at home but throughout the Dominions and India, than any of his predecessors."

To the world, Edward presented a youthful face, but the eyes through which he viewed the world wore an anxious look. He had rebelled against the puritanical teachings of his father as the grandfather whose name he bore had rebelled against the equally puritanical teachings of Queen Victoria. Nor did the "managed irregularities of Edward VII" appeal to the grandson. In the democratic twentieth century, publicity had become the price of fame and romantic love the basis for marriage. Neither the royal mistress nor the arranged alliance appealed to so thoroughly modern a monarch as Edward VIII. But Mrs. Simpson with her American assurance, her Baltimore charm, and her natural intelligence bowled Edward over. Her two childless marriages may have left her maternal instincts unsatisfied. In any case, it was to those instincts that Edward chiefly appealed. To some he may once have seemed a Prince Charming, but he never grew up into a lady's man or a man's man either. Instead he remained a perennial little boy lost.

Edward's political immaturity matched his emotional immaturity.

The plight of the unemployed stirred his sentimental heart. After attending a ceremony on board the recently completed transatlantic liner, *Queen Mary*, at Glasgow, he insisted on visiting the worst of the local slums and then exclaimed: "Strange, isn't it? We can afford money to build this beautiful toy, but we cannot afford money to eliminate slums." And after he had seen the miners of South Wales in their wretched homes, he surveyed a dead blast furnace from the top of a slagheap, bit his lip, and muttered: "Something must be done." His concern for his least fortunate subjects and his outspoken sympathy for their plight led some of his admirers to call him a "people's King," but the most he could do was throw light into dark places.

UNDERWOOD

King Edward VIII and Prime Minister Baldwin

The field of foreign affairs offered wider scope. More than once he had risked his life on inspection tours of the Western Front, where he acquired some firsthand understanding of what modern war meant to the common soldier. The prospect of another war filled him with revulsion, and the only way out he could see was to come to terms, almost any terms, with the defeated Germans and the disgruntled Italians. One of the few convictions he shared with his father was a hatred of Russian Communism, based on what the Communists had done to their relatives in the Russian imperial family. During his summer cruise in 1936, Edward took time out to hold meetings with King George of Greece, Prince Regent Paul of Yugoslavia, President Kemal Ataturk of Turkey, and Chancellor Schuschnigg of Austria. In themselves these visits seemed harmless enough, but the responsible heads of the British government saw in them further signs of instability. They knew that the King frequented the Mayfair Set in a casual way; they knew that Mrs. Simpson, who cultivated the society of Ribbentrop, belonged to it completely. They probably did not know that Ribbentrop also assured Hitler that the lax morals of the British aristocracy proved that the country had gone to pot.

Winston Churchill's quixotic streak never revealed itself so clearly as when he championed Edward during the abdication crisis. For years,

Churchill had taken the unpopular course of warning against German rearmament. He attacked Laborite pacifism, Liberal disarmament, and Tory appeasement with fine impartiality. But Churchill had known and admired Edward for twenty-five years. He also felt a romantic loyalty toward whoever occupied the throne. George V deplored his son's partiality for ill-bred, newly rich Americans. The half-American Churchill not only felt a sentimental affinity toward his mother's native land. Churchill, like Edward, never ceased stressing the priceless value of American good will to the British Empire, and the fact that Baldwin wanted the King to abdicate clinched matters as Churchill stood almost alone in the House of Commons pleading Edward's lost cause. The small group of "King's Men" also enjoyed, ironically enough, the support of the British Communists and of Sir Oswald Mosley's Union of British Fascists. But all to no avail. Within ten days after the Bishop of Bradford had brought Edward's romance with Mrs. Simpson into the open, the King had quit.

A curious little book, *Why Edward Went,* by the British journalist Warre Bradley Wells brought together many items of rumor and gossip that circulated during the abdication crisis. Wells represented Edward as the victim of a "clique" whose perverse devotion to collective security and the League of Nations brought the British Empire "within an ace of war" with Italy. Wells praised King Edward for having refused to receive the exiled Emperor Haile Selassie: "If he did so it would be a direct slap in the face for Signor Mussolini from the King of England in person. . . . It might even provoke Signor Mussolini, flushed with victory, to cast discretion to the winds and declare war on England." Wells also wrote, ironically, "King Edward had paid informal, friendly calls on the Heads of State of Austria and Turkey, Germany's allies in the Great War! What would the man do next? Why, he might even take it into his head to spend his next vacation in Bavaria, and go and pay a similar, informal friendly call in his holiday home on Herr Hitler himself!"

Wells praised Edward for his partiality toward Hitler and Mussolini. He attacked the hypocrisy of the Church of England for its refusal to sanction the King's marriage to a twice-divorced American. But if Edward possessed the courage, the generosity, and the zest of a boy, he also suffered from a boyish ignorance of his own, special world. His determination to marry Mrs. Simpson violated the ancient, rigid code of the Established Church of England. True, Henry VIII violated that code, flagrantly and repeatedly; so did all the four Georges who lived openly in sin with their mistresses. What Edward failed to understand was that a democratic, twentieth-century King must subject himself to stricter personal disciplines than the more powerful monarchs of earlier times. Yet Lloyd George's Liberal voice, the Socialist voice of Bernard Shaw, and the cockney accents of H. G. Wells all backed the King. Lloyd George attacked "the mean and shabby treatment" that Edward had suffered. Shaw, when the crisis had passed, announced: "The King had all the cards in his hand. Nothing could have shaken him off his throne if he had stuck to it." And H. G. Wells expressed sympathy for Mrs. Simpson for having been subjected to "the most outrageous attack upon a woman that has ever been made in England."

Edward's defiance of the Church of England won him some sympathy, but the Archbishop of Canterbury probably spoke for the majority of the British people when he commented, two days after the abdication: "Strange and sad it is that he should have sought his happiness in a manner inconsistent with the Christian principles of marriage and within a social circle whose standards and ways of life are alien to all the best instincts and traditions of his people." As for nonbelievers, many of them had reason to censure Edward for putting personal happiness before public duty, and there was many a commoner in the land who had given up the woman he loved for something less than the British throne.

Two memorable oratorical efforts brought the abdication crisis to a close. First Stanley Baldwin gave a masterly outline of the events leading up to the King's decision to leave the throne. Never did his contrived candor appear so sincere: "This House today is a theater which is being watched by the whole world. Let us conduct ourselves with that dignity which His Majesty is showing in this hour of his trial. Whatever be our regrets at the contents of the message, let us fulfill his wishes to do what he asks and do it with speed. Let no word be spoken today that the utterer will regret in days to come. Let no word be spoken that causes pain to any soul." The House of Commons accepted the King's message of abdication during the morning of Friday, December 11. It took effect that afternoon. That evening Edward, now Duke of Windsor, delivered what Lowell Thomas called "the greatest broadcast of all time." He began poignantly: "At long last I am able to say a few words of my own." He continued frankly: "I have found it impossible to carry the heavy burden of responsibility and to discharge my duties as King, as I wish to do, without the help and support of the woman I love." He closed on a crescendo note: "And now we all have a new King. I wish Him and you, His people, happiness and prosperity with all my heart. God bless you all. God save the King!"

The second son of King George and Queen Mary seemed to need the divine assistance Edward invoked. George VI, as he called himself, took the same name as his father, whom he resembled and tried to emulate. He had seen active service in the Royal Navy during the war, and afterward learned to pilot his own plane. His Scottish wife had borne him

© LOW, ALL COUNTRIES

"Cooked tour." Cartoon by David Low

two attractive daughters and had helped him make some progress over-
coming a painful, serious speech impediment. They were crowned King
and Queen on May 12; two weeks later Baldwin resigned as Prime
Minister to enter the House of Lords. His retirement marked as decisive
a break in British history as the coronation of King George VI. Baldwin
and MacDonald, either separately or together, had dominated every
British government since the postwar era got under way during the
early 1920's, and their partnership wound up with Baldwin dominating
MacDonald. The story went around that Baldwin proudly compared
himself to Sir Robert Walpole, the British Prime Minister who kept his
country at peace during two troubled decades of the eighteenth century
when most of Europe was at war. And when someone to whom Baldwin
expounded this comparison pointed out that Britain's prestige and power
had steadily declined during the more recent lotus years of "safety first,"
and asked what was to be done about Hitler, Mussolini, Stalin, Franco,
and other contemporary scourges, the Prime Minister was said to have
replied, "That is a problem for my successor."

That successor had all of Baldwin's confidence and ten times Baldwin's
energy. Neville Chamberlain regarded it as a compliment when Churchill referred to him before a Birmingham audience as "pack-horse in our
great affairs." Chamberlain cared less for Lloyd George's caustic phrase
—"a good Lord Mayor of Birmingham in a lean year." During the abdication crisis Baldwin had told the Cabinet that the matter must be

settled by Christmas. The practical and energetic Chamberlain warned that the country could not afford to wait so long. Continued uncertainty was hurting holiday trade.

Two quotations from the semiofficial London *Times*, the first written the day of Edward's abdication, the second a few days later, complete the story. The first denied that Edward was a "people's King" whom "a hidebound set of aristocrats and ecclesiastics" deliberately destroyed. "It would be far more accurate to say that His Majesty's circle was too largely composed of men and women, some of them of high birth and all of them remote from 'the people' who cared less for his welfare than for their own amusement. The real clash was between the thoughtlessness of an exotic society and the hard core of a British tradition of conduct which is common to all classes of the country; but it must also in fairness be said that none of us can realize how hard is the path of a King in choosing good friends. That, amid all his great qualities, there was also something lacking in himself is sufficiently shown by the unprecedented decision announced this morning: for it is proof of obstinacy rather than of strength that it must have been reached in the face of a very human

UNDERWOOD

After the Wedding: The Duke and Duchess of Windsor, Flanked by Herman Rogers and Major Metcalfe

reluctance to abandon a position which afforded him so many proofs of success."

The second editorial became still more specific when it congratulated the British people on having rejected certain "reckless and authoritative hints that a substitute for democratic government, based upon the exploitation of a popular King, might provide a way of escape. These hints have themselves served a purpose. The response to them was instant, unanimous, and exemplary. All the world knows now that Fascism has neither past, present, nor future amongst us."

· III ·

AN INFLUENTIAL, intellectual minority did not share these views about the past, present, or future of Fascism in Britain or anywhere else. While Edward found stimulation with the bright young people of the Mayfair Set, the more serious-minded members of his generation looked either to the left or to the east, either toward the Labor Party and Socialism or toward Russia and Communism. During the 1920's and 1930's, the London School of Economics instructed hundreds of bright young people in a new and radical approach to the social "sciences." Professor Harold J. Laski, sometime Fellow of Magdalen College, Oxford, former special lecturer at Harvard, Yale, and McGill Universities, active member of the British Labor Party, had helped to make the London School of Economics a renowned and influential place of light and learning. Laski admired the Russian Revolution and the men who made it, but never argued that Britain needed a revolution of the same kind. He had faith that the Labor Party, working through peaceful, evolutionary, democratic methods could achieve the same ultimate objective of complete socialism.

Although Laski stimulated hundreds of young people through his teaching and thousands through his writing, many of these pupils came to regard their master as almost a back number. When the depression first struck, they attributed it to capitalism and its wars. As conditions grew worse they held the depression responsible for Hitler's success in Germany. And as Hitler's power increased, they came to believe that only Communism could defeat Fascism. The Labor Party had twice tried and failed to give the country a new lead. The Liberal Party never recovered from the wartime split between Asquith and Lloyd George and ceased to attract the young intellectuals destined for future political leadership. In 1933, students at the Oxford Union, where generations of Parliamentary leaders had received their training, voted approval of a resolution "That this House refuses to fight for King and Country." These young men did not speak for the entire British ruling class; neither did their resolution reflect majority opinion in the British Isles. But they seized upon this pacifistic resolution to protest against the kind of leadership that had taken Britain to war in 1914, that had failed to establish peace afterward, and that had finally brought the country into a great depression that seemed to have no end.

By the time the Oxford Union gave pacifism this vote of confidence, the Tories had returned to power in the guise of a national government that cut the dole, raised tariffs, and sought to develop trade within the Empire. The Labor Party still held its mass support in the trade union movement but failed, in 1935, to win back the middle-class vote it had attracted in 1929. During the early 1930's a group of young Laborite intellectuals therefore tried to form a new organization, within the Party ranks, in behalf of new, radical reforms. This group included Sir Oswald Mosley, who had married Lord Curzon's daughter, and John Strachey, cousin of the biographer and son of J. St. Loe Strachey, editor of the Conservative *Spectator* and president of the English branch of the English-Speaking Union. But the program had no support among the Labor rank and file and never got off the ground. Mosley cut loose and proceeded to organize his own Union of British Fascists, while Strachey became a persuasive pamphleteer for Communism. Never a card-carrying Party member, Strachey shared some of Laski's hopes that Britain might make the transition from capitalism to socialism without violence, just as Laski shared some of Strachey's confidence in Soviet Communism. The two men, separated by about ten years in age, came together in a new semipolitical, semiliterary enterprise—the Left Book Club. Victor Gollancz, son of the great Shakespearean scholar, Israel Gollancz, had made a considerable splash publishing and publicizing best-selling books of nonfiction. He wanted to do more than make a commercial success. He believed in the ideas that Laski and Strachey expounded and he persuaded them to help him launch a popular, low-priced book club that would declare intellectual war on Fascism with a program of mass education.

Laski, who still belonged to the Labor Party, had made many converts addressing middle-class audiences. Although primarily a great teacher, he had considerable experience as a Labor Party spokesman and his ambitions and interests were shifting from academic to political fields. Strachey owed his prestige to a single book, *The Coming Struggle for Power,* which appeared in 1932 and presently became a standard handbook of young radicals on both sides of the Atlantic. Strachey not only commanded a fluent prose style. His analysis of capitalism in decay included much shrewd comment on the whole contemporary scene—its culture, its personalities, its religion. Just too young to go to war, he had attended Eton and Oxford, where he received every educational benefit the English aristocracy had to offer. Standing in no awe of the class to which he belonged, he saw its shortcomings as clearly as he saw the failure of the Liberal and Labor Parties. Intellectual communism became his substitute for religious faith: "The ebb of religious belief brings man face to face with his environment; but it also brings him face to face with the necessity of remodeling that environment. For unmodified by man, the world is intolerable. It must be re-created, if not in fancy by the comforts of religion, then in fact by the hand of man himself. Fortunately, by the inevitable interweavings of historical cause and effect, that very growth of knowledge which has robbed man of his protective cloak of religious illusion gives him in compensation the power to refashion the earth. It is precisely because man is at last in sight of being able to control nature himself that he now can neither maintain, nor should he need, the illusion that nature is controlled by God."

In abjuring faith in God and all forms of organized religion, Strachey affirmed a no less absolute faith in the working class as the instrument and the Communist Party as the guiding hand of human salvation. In like manner, he regarded capitalism as the prime enemy and Fascism as the mass movement the capitalists created to save themselves and their privileges. Strachey therefore called on all classes to support the working class and on all countries to rally around the Soviet Union: "Not only the working class, but every man, woman, and child who has any sense of reality must surely begin to realize that we cannot retain both capitalism and civilization. Fascism and war are today the inescapable fruits of leaving modern instruments of production in private hands. . . . There is only one thing which can avert the prospect of destruction and secure broad, secure, and plentiful civilization. And that is the workers' power: the destruction of every vestige of this hateful system and the construction in its place of a planned socialist economy as the one possible basis for modern civilization."

This passage appeared in the original, 1932 edition of his book. But a new introduction written for a 1935 edition paid tribute to the Communist who "is, and always must be, the champion of civilization against all and every form of barbarism. He actively works for the banishment of all forms of force and violence from human affairs. He must desire, above everything, the establishment of a form of society in which social and international peace becomes, for the first time, possible. But he knows that such a harmonious society is not possible till the factories, the fields, and the mines have been taken out of the ownership of a numerically small class and made the common heritage of man. Hence, in working for the abolition of capitalism, he is convinced that he is attempting to achieve the one thing that can make peace possible."

Although the introduction to the original edition did not mention

Communism, Strachey did praise the Soviet Union: "Even today in the Soviet Union, during the very brunt of the initial struggles of a working-class dictatorship, before a classless society has fully emerged, there is perceptible an exhilaration of living that finds no parallel in the world. To travel from the capitalist world into Soviet territory is to pass from death to birth. Certainly death, until the final agony ensues, is the more peaceful, quieter, and tidier process." This extraordinary passage, written at the very moment when Stalin was starving five million Russian peasants to death, continued to appear in later editions long after the outside world had learned the full story: "For those who cannot support the sight of a continent in labor, of the vast, baffling, contradictory stirrings of a young giant, still half conceived in the womb, the Soviet Union is an alarming place. We may leave such people to enjoy their tiny pleasures and comforts, for these will not long remain to them. They will find that in shrinking from the agony of birth they have chosen the agony of death."

In forswearing the old-time religion, Strachey accepted the new Communist faith, which he preached with the single-minded fervor of a Seventh-Day Adventist: "The coming of communism can alone render our problems soluble. A working-class dictatorship can alone open the way to communism. A working-class dictatorship can be successful only if the workers as a whole achieve a clear understanding of the historic destiny of their class. And this understanding, in turn, cannot be developed unless the working class succeeds in organizing its most conscious and clear-sighted members into that indispensable instrument of the workers' will, a Communist party." And the same logic that assigned this unique and essential role of revolutionary leadership to the Communist movement identified the Socialists with the capitalists and the Fascists.

From 1932 through 1935, Strachey followed Stalin's lead and referred to all Socialists as "Social Fascists." But when Stalin suddenly ordered all Communists to organize and join "Popular Fronts" to "fight war and Fascism," Strachey bowed to the superior wisdom of the man in the Kremlin, as a matter of discipline if not of faith. Strachey made the Communist Party line appear rational by avoiding some of the more obvious clichés in which the true believers expressed themselves. His gift, almost his genius, for clarifying other people's ideas more than compensated for his inability to think for himself—or even, at times, to think at all. "Intellectuals of the world, unite: you have nothing to lose but your brains," John Dos Passos commented as his contemporaries on both sides of the Atlantic accepted the Communist analysis of world politics while refusing to submit themselves to the discipline that Party membership required. Strachey converted few of his readers to accept a discipline that he himself rejected, but the fact that he wrote and spoke as a free agent impressed many of the indifferent or hostile majority.

And during the later 1930's that majority began to lessen as the Left
Book Club became the nearest British equivalent of the Popular Front
movements in France and Spain. The Left Book Club organized meetings, published pamphlets, persuaded members of Parliament to its
point of view, thereby reaching indirectly the same mass audience that
signed the Peace Ballot of the League of Nations Union. The influence
of the Left Book Club so permeated the literary and intellectual life of
Great Britain that it became a formidable political force. Sir Oswald
Mosley's intellectual Fascism never attracted one tenth so wide or influential a following.

The Left Book Club and the Union of British Fascists, the supporters
and opponents of King Edward all revealed symptoms of unrest and
anxiety. Britain during the 1930's split up into numerous energetic minorities, some large, some small, all driven toward action for action's
sake. In Russia, Italy, and Germany, larger, better-disciplined minorities
had gained control of the entire machinery of national government.
Britain's ruling class, on the other hand, faced no single challenge and
imposed no single solution. It made compromises and played one minority off against another, permitting to all the unrestricted right of free
speech and assembly. As usual Spain presented a unique spectacle.
There, irreconcilable conflicts among rival minorities led to civil war.
Italian Fascists and German Nazis backed Franco's rebellion from the
start and to the limit. The British government, as cautious at home as
abroad, improvised a policy of nonintervention, more favorable to
Franco than to the Republic. Then and not till then did Communist
Russia begin sending limited aid to the Republic. But Communist Russia suffered from internal troubles of its own.

· IV ·

FROM the death of Lenin in 1924 until the murder of Kirov ten years
later Stalin's limitations served him well. He knew enough Marxist
phrases to sound like Lenin's successor, but he never permitted general
ideas to distract him from his drive for personal power. During the relative stability of the later 1920's, Stalin built up his own political machine
inside the Soviet Union. During the world depression, he completed
the first Five-Year Plan, liquidating five million peasants and hastening
industrialization. His ignorance of other countries led him to subordinate
world revolution to the Five-Year Plan. But the rise of Hitler confounded
him. His limited experience and meager philosophy made no allowance
for anything like that.

All that Stalin knew about revolution he had learned in Russia in

1917. Because Kerensky and his predecessors had lasted only a few months and because General Kornilov had collapsed even more rapidly, Stalin assumed that events would take a similar course everywhere else. He expected the German Social Democrats to go the way of Kerensky and Hitler to go the way of Kornilov. But Stalin was not the only national leader to underrate Hitler. What distinguished Stalin from other national leaders was his stubborn adherence to a dogmatic interpretation of history and a stubborn insistence that the revolution in Germany must follow the same course it had followed in Russia. It took him until 1936 to adjust himself to reality and work out a new line to meet the new situation. First, Stalin put the Soviet Union in the League of Nations, endorsed collective security, and urged foreign Communists to join Popular Front governments with Socialists, Liberals, Radicals, Conservatives, and Anarchists—with any party, in fact, that opposed Fascism. Second, he announced a new Soviet Constitution. Third, he exterminated all his political rivals, especially the Old Bolsheviks and the heirs of Lenin.

Stalin's conversion to the League of Nations, to collective security, and to the Popular Front made little difference to the daily life of the average Soviet citizen. It did, however, divide the capitalist world into democratic sheep and Fascist goats and began to align the Soviet Union with the democracies. As collective security became the order of the day, the Russian people experienced a welcome sense of kinship with other countries. They no longer felt quite so alone in a world that they had almost forgotten and that had almost forgotten them.

Stalin therefore addressed himself to wooing this world outside as cynically as he had formerly abused it. In 1936 he promulgated a new Constitution that granted freedom of speech, press, assembly, and religion—on paper. In practice, everything remained as it had been except that the Soviet government moderated its persecution of religion. The population of Russia's cities now almost equaled the rural population and every citizen had the right to cast his ballot in secret. In 1937, when the Russian people voted for the first time under the new dispensation and chose all the candidates that the Party had listed, Stalin proudly commented: "The world has never seen elections so really free, so truly democratic. Never. History knows no other example of this nature." But the economic rather than the political features of the Stalin Constitution evoked the most comment and admiration. They guaranteed, among other things, the right to work, the right to an education, the right to a seven-hour working day and to an annual paid vacation of two weeks. Certain clauses attracted ridicule abroad, notably the one giving the Republics of the Soviet Union "the right freely to secede." But Stalin also won many friends among those who wanted to believe the best of

Russia. They took his word for his deed and resolved all doubts in his favor.

Yet what Stalin did inside Russia violated his own Constitution and made a mockery of the Popular Front aspect he wore abroad. In 1936, 1937, and 1938, the Soviet government staged three public trials at which former high officials confessed to treason, sabotage, murder, and every kind of conspiracy against the regime. Zinoviev and Kamenev, the closest surviving friends of Lenin, starred at the first trial. Piatakov, industrial director of the Five-Year Plan, and Radek, foreign editor of *Pravda*, starred at the second. Bukharin, editor of *Izvestia*, and Rykhov, former Soviet Premier, starred at the third. Marshal Tukhachevsky, Chief of Staff of the Red Army, and eight of his leading generals were shot after a secret trial in 1937. Yagoda, the chief prosecutor at the 1936 and 1937 trials, was himself liquidated in 1938, and Yezhov, his successor, also vanished in his turn along with most of the generals who court-martialed Tukhachevsky.

Nearly all the confessions followed the same pattern. The accused admitted that they had conspired with Trotsky to murder Stalin, to wreck Soviet industry, to turn the Ukraine over to Germany and the maritime provinces to Japan. One of the prisoners withdrew his confession on the witness stand, but returned at a later session and confessed to even more than he originally admitted. The government prosecutors based most of their cases on the detailed confessions of the accused, which the radio carried from the courtroom and which the press reproduced in full. Later the People's Commissariat of Justice issued full transcripts of the court records in book form and in many languages. The English version of one of the volumes, *The Case of the Anti-Soviet "Bloc of Rights and Trotsky-ites,"* includes the testimony and confession of Nikolai I. Bukharin, the outstanding theoretician of Bolshevism, who had curried favor with Stalin by attacking the extreme radicalism of Trotsky's views only to come into disfavor as leader of the "Right Opposition" when Stalin drove Trotsky into exile. After three months in prison, Bukharin confessed to having plotted with Trotsky against Stalin, but "a peculiar duality of mind, an incomplete faith in this counterrevolutionary cause," doomed him and his renegade accomplices to futility: "I will not say that the consciousness of this was absent but it was incomplete. Hence a certain semiparalysis of the will, a retardation of reflexes. And this was not due to the absence of consistent thought, but to the objective grandeur of socialist construction. The contradiction that arose between the acceleration of our degeneration and those retarded reflexes expressed the position of a counterrevolutionary, under the conditions of developing socialist construction. A dual psychology arose. Each one of us can

discern this in his own soul, although I will not engage in a far-
reaching psychological analysis."

Why did Bukharin confess? "Because while in prison I made a
revaluation of my entire past. For
when you ask yourself: 'If you
must die, what are you dying
for?'—an absolutely blank vacuity
arises before you with startling viv-
idness. There is nothing to die for,
if one wanted to die unrepented.
And, on the contrary, everything
positive that glistens in the Soviet
Union acquires new dimensions in
a man's mind. This in the end disarmed me completely and led me
to bend my knees before the Party
and the country. And when you

KEYSTONE

Nikolai Bukharin

ask yourself, 'Very well, suppose you do not die; suppose by some miracle you remain alive, again what for? Isolated from everybody, an
enemy of the people, in an inhuman position, completely isolated from
everything that constitutes the essence of life. . . .' And at once the
same reply arises. And at such moments, Citizen Judges, everything
personal, all personal incrustation, all the rancor, pride, and a number of
other things fall away, disappear. And, in addition, when the reverbera-
tions of the broad international struggle reach your ear, all this in its
entirety does its work, and the result is the complete internal moral
victory of the U.S.S.R. over its kneeling opponents."

Bukharin's trial inspired the Hungarian ex-Communist, Arthur
Koestler, to write a novel, *Darkness at Noon*, that sought to re-create
the whole story. Here Koestler put into the mouth of his character,
Rubashov, almost exactly the same words Bukharin spoke in court. But
Koestler went further. Drawing on his own personal experience inside
the Communist movement, he showed how a typical young inquisitor,
Gletkin, persuaded Rubashov to abase himself by expounding the Stalinist line: "When our Revolution had succeeded in one country, we believed that the rest of the earth would follow suit. Instead, came a wave
of reaction, which threatened to swamp us. There were two currents in
the Party. One consisted of adventurers who wanted to risk what we had
won to promote revolution abroad. You belonged to them. We recognized this current to be dangerous and have liquidated it." But Gletkin

made one last appeal to Rubashov's loyalty to the Party: "The policy of the opposition is wrong. Your task is therefore to make the opposition contemptible; to make the masses understand that opposition is a crime and that the leaders of the opposition are criminals. That is the simple language which the masses understand. If you begin to talk of your complicated motives, you will only create confusion amongst them. Your task, Comrade Rubashov, is to avoid awakening sympathy and pity. Sympathy and pity for the opposition are a danger to the country. Comrade Rubashov, I hope you have understood the task which the Party has set you."

Rubashov replies, "I understand," and Gletkin reiterates that the Party must demand the death penalty. He concludes: "You were wrong and you will pay, Comrade Rubashov. The Party promises only one thing: after the victory, one day when it can do no more harm, the material of the secret archives will be published. Then the world will learn what was in the background of this Punch and Judy show—as you called it— which we had to act to them according to history's textbook." He paused: "And then you and some of your friends of the older generation will be given the sympathy and pity which are denied you today."

Louis Fischer, who spent twenty years as a Moscow correspondent, used the word "superpropaganda" to describe the Moscow trials. "They serve to rewrite history." In his autobiography, *Men and Politics*, Fischer also compared the atmosphere at the Moscow trials with the atmosphere of everyday Russian life. He called them "merely the sensational highly silhouetted shape of an everyday Soviet phenomenon and it is only against the background of this phenomenon that the confessions can be understood. Millions of Soviet citizens live lies every day to save their lives and their jobs. They make false confessions day in and day out. They write lies, speak lies. They lie to one another and know it. They lie to themselves and get accustomed to it. They lose their illusions and succumb to the sole cynical goal of self-preservation until a better day. The assassination of character and the annihilation of personality is the dictatorship's chief weapon which it never forgets."

In another passage Fischer probed more deeply into Russia's recent past: "1916 to 1937—twenty-one years of hardships, turmoil, and spiritual travail. Oh, for some quiet and solace! Women I knew, fine intellectual women with government jobs, would meet after hours and just drink themselves into a stupor. Citizens who always followed politics at home and abroad with keen interest escaped into apathy. Suicides multiplied. Youth took refuge in cynicism. Everybody played for Safety First. Lying, hypocrisy, humiliating obeisances, violence toward one's deepest convictions, and disloyalty to friends were a small price to pay for keeping out of prison. To divert suspicion from yourself you accused the other fellow. You yelled loudest at meetings when resolutions were voted calling on the government to execute Piatakov, Radek, and their accomplices. When Stalin's name was mentioned you applauded, and you did not dare to stop even though it might go on for ten minutes."

The Moscow trials gave rise to two mysteries—one of Russian, the other of foreign origin. Why, in the first place, did the Soviet government lend itself to such a palpable and damaging fraud? And why, in the second place, did anyone abroad believe it? According to the official story, every surviving Old Bolshevik of any consequence had turned against Stalin. All of Lenin's closest associates had tried to do away with Lenin's self-proclaimed heir. Yet the Stalin regime survived the liquidation of nearly all the top military leaders, most of the top diplomats and Foreign Office officials, the most talented and influential journalists, and forty-nine of the seventy-one members of the Central Committee of the Communist Party. Of the seven members of the Politburo at the time of Lenin's death only Stalin and Trotsky survived. Four had confessed to treason; a fifth, Tomsky, had killed himself. But for every Old Bolshevik who confessed, ten refused to lend themselves to Stalin's purposes, and for every ten big shots who disappeared, a hundred minor victims vanished. The Soviet press listed no less than five thousand victims of the purge.

How could any dictatorship survive such wholesale treason? Or, if the confessions were all staged, how could any dictatorship conceal such wholesale fraud? The answer to both questions was the same. The Stalin dictatorship wielded absolute power over the lives of the Russian people because it controlled all jobs and housing, all factories and farms, all food and clothing. Through its control of all forms of expression, all channels of communication, it controlled the minds and emotions of its subjects. But the Stracheys and the Laskis, the Popular Frontists and the Left Book Clubbers did not work for the Politburo. They did not confine their reading to the Soviet press or their listening to the Moscow radio. They bore no resemblance to Dostoevsky characters; they had never subjected themselves to Communist discipline. Nevertheless, they accepted the Stalin version of the trials as meekly as the most subservient Soviet citizen. They had access to information that never reached Russia; they enjoyed the freedom to write, speak, and think for themselves.

Sidney and Beatrice Webb, who inspired Britain's evolutionary Fabian Socialism, spent months in Russia collecting information for *Soviet Communism: A New Civilization?*, which admitted certain injustices and evils, but concluded that the virtues of Stalin's Russia far outweighed its vices. Neither of the Webbs knew a word of Russian. Now in their sixties, they had devoted their lives to studying and organizing the British trade union movement. But their unfamiliarity with their subject attracted more readers than it repelled because neither the Webbs nor their readers wanted an objective report on the facts; they wanted subjective reassurance. They wanted to believe the best of the new Russia, partly because it symbolized some of their own aspirations, partly because their political enemies at home wanted to believe the opposite. Many of the Webbs' older readers harbored guilty recollections of their antagonism or skepticism toward Lenin and Trotsky during the bloodiest and cruelest period of the Russian Revolution. Most of the Webbs' younger readers looked upon Stalin, twenty years later, as Hitler's surest and strongest enemy. Finally, the aid that the Russians began sending to the Spanish Republic in 1936 blinded the eyes of many observers to conditions inside Russia itself, not to mention the terms on which the Russians supplied that aid.

· V ·

THE Spanish Civil War quickly revealed how much vitality Europe's clashing national impulses could generate. The Italian Fascists and German Nazis committed themselves to Franco from the start, and when they ran into unexpected difficulties they committed themselves still further. Both Mussolini and Hitler assumed they had to choose between expansion and explosion. Britain's abdication crisis revealed a different national mood. Stanley Baldwin, having failed miserably to grapple with Hitler, rose magnificently to a crisis nearer home and shunted the equivocal figure of King Edward VIII off the throne whereas Churchill, whose warnings against Hitler went unheeded, persisted in his quixotic loyalty toward a sovereign who did not know how to put duty before pleasure. Fearful of friction anywhere and determined to avoid war everywhere, Britain's rulers practiced a neutrality benevolent to Franco. The French, weak and divided, followed Britain's lead.

The same mystery that surrounded the Moscow trials permeated Russian policy toward Spain. While Hitler and Mussolini intervened violently during the summer of 1936, Stalin did nothing. At first he joined the Non-Intervention Committee; then, in October, some weeks after the Committee's pro-Franco bias had become clear, the Russians began sending supplies to the Republic. But they sent limited amounts, by fits and starts; they received payment in gold; they dispatched no volunteers. Never did the Russians have more than five hundred of their nationals in Spain, and they served as technical experts. It was a different story with non-Russian Communists and fellow travelers from all over the world who enlisted with the International Brigade to fight for the Republic, while Communist agents, notably agents of the Soviet Secret Police, played an ever-increasing part in every phase of the Spanish Civil War.

Back in 1931, when the Spaniards drove King Alfonso off the throne and established their Republic, Walter Duranty put his finger on the true inwardness of Soviet policy in Spain. As Moscow correspondent for *The New York Times,* Duranty wrote with considerable sympathy and considerable knowledge of the Soviet regime, and few other correspondents ever chose, during the heat of the Spanish conflict, to express themselves quite so bluntly. *Pravda,* so Duranty wrote from Moscow, took an "unexpectedly pessimistic tone" in its comments on the fall of Alfonso, and he attributed this to "Soviet anxiety lest events in Spain disturb European peace during the present critical period of the Five-Year Plan. Rightly or wrongly, it is believed here that the peace of Europe hangs literally on a thread, that the accumulation of armaments and national hatreds are much greater than before the war and make the present situation no less dangerous than the spring of 1914, and that Spanish fireworks might easily provoke a general conflagration. Paradoxically enough, it appears that Moscow is not over-delighted by this circumstance—in fact it may almost be said that if the Spanish revolution 'swings left' as Moscow now expects, Moscow will be more embarrassed than pleased."

Five years later, the outbreak of the Spanish Civil War saw Duranty's prediction come true. With Azaña and the Republic offering democracy, with Franco and the Army offering dictatorship, and with most of the Anarchists and some of the Socialists offering revolution, Stalin and the Communists backed the Republic. Trotsky, quoting Lenin, urged his little band of followers to turn the civil war into revolution. He compared Azaña to Kerensky and Franco to Kornilov. Although Stalin did not challenge the comparison, he dreaded its practical application. To turn the Spanish Civil War into another Russian Revolution would either lead to a new world war or create a four-power anti-Communist coalition of Britain, France, Germany, and Italy. Stalin therefore gave the Spanish Republic enough help to keep it in the fight, but not enough to encourage revolution or to incite Italy and Germany into declaring full-scale war.

As members of the first government set up by Largo Caballero, the Communists put the brakes on land reform and stressed the importance of fighting a conventional war with the widest support from all classes, especially the well-to-do. Most of the Socialists took the same line, and when Franco failed to capture Madrid in November, 1936, their moderation appeared justified. But while the central government in the Republican capital of Madrid worked smoothly with the Communists, revolutionary currents ran stronger in Barcelona, Spain's largest city and chief industrial center. The Barcelona workers, like the workers in the other Spanish cities, had prevented Franco from seizing full power back in

July when they threw up barricades, seized communication centers, and even disarmed the regular soldiery. But they did not follow through as the Russian Bolsheviks had followed through by setting up soviets of soldiers and workers. The Barcelona workers made no attempt to interest the soldiers in revolution; having prevented Franco from seizing power in the surrounding province of Catalonia, they refused to submit themselves to the authority of Madrid, where Communist influence rapidly increased. As early as December 17, 1936, *Pravda* declared, "As for Catalonia, the purging of the Trotskyists and the Anarcho-Syndicalists has begun; it will be conducted with the same energy with which it was conducted in the U.S.S.R."

That time *Pravda* spoke the truth. While Communists fought Fascists with their left hands, they fought the Anarchists and the POUM with their right. In May, 1937, a group of Anarchist, POUM, and Trotskyist leaders in Barcelona called for a revolution against the Republic. "No compromise," read a Trotskyist leaflet. "Disarmament of the National Republican Guard and the reactionary Assault Guards. This is the decisive moment. Next time it will be too late. General strike in all the industries excepting those connected with the prosecution of the war, until the resignation of the reactionary government. Only proletarian power can ensure military victory." From the morning of Monday, May 3, until the morning of Thursday, May 6, the revolutionary workers of Barcelona controlled the city and its vital centers. But the Barcelona uprising had caused so much destruction, confusion, and distress that its leaders came to terms with the Republic.

The Communists took advantage of the opportunity to crush the POUM and to strengthen their position at Madrid. When Caballero refused to suppress the POUM, they engineered his overthrow and backed his Finance Minister, Dr. Juan Negrín, a younger and more moderate Socialist, as the new Premier. Negrín agreed to dissolve the POUM, but the strong man in the new Cabinet was Indalecio Prieto, leader of the Right Socialists and Caballero's great rival. Negrín remained Finance Minister; he put Prieto in charge of defense. The Communists still held the Ministries of Agriculture and of Education. Otherwise, the Negrín Cabinet represented a measurable step to the right. La Pasionara, one of the most popular of the Communist orators, called it "the government of victory." She continued: "We have made up our minds to win the war quickly, though that victory cost us an argument with our dearest comrades."

While the Communists preached war first and revolution afterward, their dear ex-comrade Trotsky urged a different course: "It is necessary to proclaim that from now on the land, the factories, and shops will pass from the capitalists into the hands of the people. It is necessary at once

UNITED PRESS PHOTO

Barcelona Air Raid

to move toward the realization of this program in those provinces where the workers are in power. The Fascist Army could not resist the influence of such a program: the soldiers would tie their officers hand and foot and hand them over to the nearest headquarters of the workers' militia. But the bourgeois ministers cannot accept such a program. Curbing the social revolution, they compel the workers and peasants to spill ten times as much of their own blood in the civil war."

Felix Morrow, an American supporter of Trotsky, continued this line of thought in his little book, *Revolution and Counter-Revolution in Spain:* "In the face of an alert proletariat, what would the bourgeoisie do? The French bourgeoisie would open its borders to Spain, not for intervention but for trade enabling the new regime to secure supplies— or face immediately a revolution at home. The Spanish Workers Republic would not, like Caballero and Negrín, aid and abet 'non-intervention!' England, irrevocably tied to the fate of France, would be held back from intervention both by the whole weight of France and by her own working class for whom the Iberian Revolution would open a new epoch. Portugal would face an immediate revolution at home. Germany and Italy would, of course, increase their aid to Franco. But Anglo-French policy must continue to be: neither a socialist Spain nor a Hitler-Mussolini Spain. Hoping to whittle down both sides eventually, Anglo-French imperialism would be forced to keep Italo-German intervention within such bounds as to prevent the Rome-Berlin Axis from dominating the Mediterranean."

Such counsels of perfection maddened the Loyalists and their supporters as much as Communist tactics maddened the POUM. It may be doubted that the high purposes of most Loyalists justified the crude, devious means the Communists used to achieve these purposes. It cannot be doubted that the Republic needed the widest and strongest kind of Popular Front to survive and conquer. No mass basis existed in Spain, or anywhere else, to put through the kind of revolution Trotsky and his supporters preached. Nowhere did popular discontent reach such proportions as it reached in Russia in 1917. Nowhere had all forms of authority disintegrated so completely. Nowhere did the discontented element produce the kind of leadership Lenin and the Bolsheviks supplied. For the struggle in Spain was a military struggle, not a revolutionary one, a clash of nations, not a clash of classes. As a result, the so-called Civil War became more and more a miniature world war that all the belligerents confined, by a sort of non-gentlemen's agreement, to the Iberian peninsula. The battles fought on that peninsula never involved such masses of men as fought on the Western Front, but they did witness the first use of new weapons in actual combat. The tanks went five times as fast as the tanks of 1918; the planes flew four times faster; they dropped ten times as many bombs. But the Republic fought on. Air power did not prove the absolute weapon; the morale of civilians proved as strong, and as important, as the morale of soldiers at the front.

More often than not, indeed, civilians put the soldiers to shame. Early in 1937, poor leadership and lack of fighting spirit lost the city of Málaga, in southern Spain, to the rebels. It remained, however, for some ten thousand Italian "volunteers" to put on the most craven exhibition. In early March, a sudden surprise attack by a small number of lightly armed militiamen in the mountains near Guadalajara north of Madrid produced an immediate rout. At the same time, Glasgow Communists of the International Brigade broke up another rebel offensive on the Jarama River to the south. Having failed once again to take Madrid and win the war, Franco shifted his chief attacks to the northern end of the thousand-mile front and during the summer subdued the Basque and Asturian provinces. Here the Germans distinguished themselves on the ground and in the air. Nowhere else did the Loyalist troops have less equipment; nowhere else did Franco have such an advantage in weapons. Yet in spite of the brutal German bombing of the ancient Basque capital of Guernica and the devastating German artillery fire, most Spaniards hated the Italians even more than they hated the Germans. They resented Mussolini's arrogance in seeking to dominate the whole Mediterranean and in claiming the leadership of all Latin peoples. German brutality they took for granted.

The war at sea also went badly for the Republic. The Non-Intervention Committee set up a naval patrol of Spanish waters, and when Loyalist planes bombed the German pocket battleship *Deutschland,* the Germans retaliated by subjecting the unprotected coastal city of Almería to several hours of heavy shellfire. This incident caused the Germans and Italians to withdraw from the Non-Intervention Committee's naval patrol, and presently Italian submarines began sinking British, French, and Russian vessels carrying supplies to the Republic. The British responded swiftly and vigorously to this direct assault on their control of the seas, and summoned a conference at Noyon where all members of the Non-Intervention Committee, except the absent Germans and Italians, agreed to establish a rigid antisubmarine patrol. The sinkings at once ended, and the Italians and Germans promptly returned to the Committee and took over some of the patrolling duties. The incident proved two things: none of the major Powers wanted to start a major war, but Anglo-French fear of such a war gave the Germans and Italians freedom to continue aiding Franco.

The military balance sheet for 1937 showed substantial but inconclusive gains for the rebels. The Republic had won no victories; no hope of victory lay in sight. The whole trend of world events worked for Franco and against the Republic. Neville Chamberlain, who succeeded Baldwin as British Prime Minister, in June felt he had no choice but to gain time for the inevitable showdown by appeasing the Axis. The purge trials in Moscow, culminating in the execution of Marshal Tukhachevsky, made the Soviet Union look like a bad risk. Stalin, for his part, suspected Chamberlain of scheming to steer Hitler eastward. Léon Blum was losing his grip on France, and his Popular Front government seemed unable to organize the country either for prosperity and peace or for austerity and war. In July, 1937, Japanese troops crossed the Marco Polo Bridge and within a few weeks had forced the ancient Chinese city of Peiping to surrender. The threat of full-scale war in the Far East ended the last hope of increased aid for Republican Spain. Ever since 1936 when Hitler had signed the Anti-Comintern Pact with Japan, Stalin had felt himself menaced by a two-front war. It now became necessary for Russia to send help to China as well as to Spain and at the same time to build up its own defenses.

In Washington, Japan's invasion of China caused as great a stir as it did in Moscow. Under the New Deal, the United States had repudiated the horse-and-buggy economics of the McKinley era. Abroad, however, most Americans wanted to wipe out almost every commitment their country had undertaken since McKinley's time. Throughout his first term and on into the first few months of his second, Roosevelt did little to disturb this mood. He had broken up the London Economic Conference in 1933. He had remained passive throughout Italy's invasion of Ethiopia. The Spanish Civil War seemed to stir him less than it stirred the majority of his fellow citizens. By instinct and inheritance, Roosevelt tended to see Europe through British eyes. In addition, he had his own, private corollary to the Monroe Doctrine and assumed that when Europe pledged itself not to intervene in Western Hemisphere affairs, the United States by the same token pledged itself not to intervene in European affairs, except at Europe's bidding. And because British sea power underwrote the Monroe Doctrine, Roosevelt followed Britain's lead in Europe.

But Roosevelt's tacit acceptance of the Non-Intervention Committee in Spain did not mean that he accepted Britain's lead in Asia. Like Stalin, he saw developing in the Far East a situation that might expose the United States, no less than Russia, to the danger of a two-front war. Between his election in November, 1932, and his inauguration the following March, Roosevelt had backed the Hoover administration on just one front. He endorsed the firm stand Secretary of State Stimson took against Japan in Manchuria. Five years later, when Japanese troops entered Peiping, Roosevelt lost little time in going Stimson one better. Without consulting any other country, without revealing his final text either to his own State Department or to Secretary Hull, Roosevelt on October 5, 1937, outlined an entirely new American foreign policy, both in theory and in practice. And the fact that he made this declaration at Chicago, the capital of American isolationism, served only to stress the importance he attached to his words:

"The high aspirations expressed in the Kellogg-Briand Pact and the hopes for peace thus raised have of late given way to a haunting fear of calamity. The present reign of terror and international lawlessness began a few years ago. It began through an unjustified interference in the internal affairs of other nations or the invasion of alien territory in violation of treaties and has now reached a stage where the very foundations of civilization are seriously threatened." To remedy this condition, Roosevelt declared that "the peace-loving nations must make a concerted effort in opposition to those violations of treaties and those ignorings of humane instincts which today are creating a state of international anarchy and instability from which there is no escape through mere isolation or neutrality." Dividing the world into the "ten per cent who are threatening a breakdown of all international order and law" and "the ninety per cent who want to live in peace under law and in accordance with moral standards that have received almost universal sanction through the centuries," he drew this analogy: "When an epidemic of physical disease starts to spread, the community approves and joins in a quarantine of the patients in order to protect the health of the community against the spread of the disease." Describing war as a "contagion," he concluded: "Most important of all, the will for peace on the part of the peace-loving nations must express itself to the end that nations that may be tempted to violate their agreements and the rights of others will desist from such a course."

The contrast between Roosevelt's precise diagnosis and vague proposals aroused immediate suspicion throughout the United States. Anyone who could follow up such a devastating and accurate description of the ills of the world with such a hazy program must be trying to fool either the public or himself. In Britain, Churchill and Eden welcomed the quarantine idea. So did some of the more conservative newspapers along the Eastern seaboard of the United States. But no speech Roosevelt had made since he became President received such a cold and hostile reception from his own people. As the hostile mail and editorial comment piled up, he confided to his friend and adviser, Judge Samuel Rosenman, "It is a terrible thing to look over your shoulder when you are trying to lead—and to find no one there." Within a week the President therefore sought to reassure his fellow citizens. "Remember," he told them in a radio talk, "that from 1913 to 1921 I personally was fairly close to world events and in that period while I learned much of what to do I also learned much of what *not* to do." The man who had vainly campaigned for the Vice-Presidency in 1920 on a League of Nations platform endorsed by Woodrow Wilson did not yet dare to risk once again walking in his master's steps.

SUMMING UP

By the end of 1937 Europe had relapsed into a condition of international anarchy that recalled 1914, when soaring national ambitions, unconstrained national sovereignties, and rising war budgets finally led to war. A quarter of a century later, social unrest threatened Europe with a new catastrophe. Mussolini and Hitler harnessed some of this unrest to their own purposes and crushed all opposition by main force. Stalin encouraged what they scorned, and scorned what they encouraged. The Western democracies, equally fearful of Communism and Fascism, of revolution and war, did as little as possible. But the Spanish Civil War gave all these movements wider scope, and the Spanish earth became a battlefield on which the Axis Powers and the Russians engaged in a limited test of strength.

The one nation that had the power and prestige to ensure a victory for the Spanish Republic did nothing. Since Roosevelt's inauguration, the American people had devoted most of their energies toward promoting recovery at home. The New Deal domestic policy gave rise to an isolationist foreign policy. To secure the Democratic nomination in 1932, Roosevelt had accepted the support of William Randolph Hearst and granted second place on the ticket to John Nance Garner. Roosevelt came out against American membership in the League of Nations, for which he had campaigned in 1920. The responsibilities of office heightened his sense of the expedient. He saw nothing to be gained by challenging British policy on Spain. He saw much to be lost by refusing to take a strong stand in the Far East. He knew—he always had known—that the kind of isolation and neutrality that the American people craved had no place in the twentieth century. But pride in this superior knowledge in one direction made it easy for him to disregard his ignorance of another, equally stubborn fact of twentieth-century life. His arbitrary division of the world into a "peace-loving ninety per cent" and a "war-making ten per cent" had no more reality than the isolation he scorned.

18

War in China

*The Second World War began on July 7, 1937, as
Japanese troops crossed the Marco Polo Bridge
and took Peiping as their first step in the conquest
of China.*

PREVIEW

MASS PRESSURES inside Japan and China made war inevitable. Fear of
expanding democracy inspired a group of military extremists to
murder their way to power in Japan. They killed several outstanding
moderate leaders but failed in their immediate objective. Nevertheless,
their long-range plans prevailed. A new Cabinet, dominated by the
Army, adopted a "positive" policy in China, and the Chinese, in their
turn, prepared to fight back. Generalissimo Chiang Kai-shek's recurrent
anti-Communist campaigns and his recurrent capitulation to Japan
turned the younger generation against him. But Chiang remained the
only man capable of uniting China. Chang Hsueh-liang, the "Young
Marshal," son of the late Chang Tso-lin, therefore had the Generalissimo
kidnaped and persuaded him to drop his anti-Communist campaign and
fight Japan. The Chinese Communists, following the new Popular Front
line laid down by Moscow, agreed to submit themselves to their former
enemy, but before the Chinese could organize effective resistance the
Japanese launched full-scale war.

· I ·

IN Spain the revolt of the masses gave rise to civil war. In Asia the revolt
of the masses led to a wider, bloodier conflict between Japan and China.
The Spaniards who fought for the Republic wanted to make their country over, but they could not agree on any common, constructive program. General Franco's attempt to destroy the Republic gave them the
unity they lacked. But it was a defensive, negative unity not unlike the
unity Franco instilled among the rebels, who agreed only in their hatred
of the Republic. Some of them wanted to preserve and restore Spain's
traditional beliefs and practices. Others, however, looked on Franco as

the Spanish equivalent of Mussolini and Hitler, the man who must succeed where Primo de Rivera had failed.

Having led popular revolts in their own countries, Mussolini and Hitler hoped to extend their power by intervening on Franco's side in Spain. In him they recognized a kindred spirit; in his revolt, a rebellion somewhat similar to those that had brought the Fascists to power in Italy and the Nazis in Germany. The dangers that filled Mussolini and Hitler with excitement filled the British and French politicians with fear—chiefly fear of a new war, partly fear of change. The policy of nonintervention allayed this fear in that it seemed to establish a kind of quarantine, as President Roosevelt might have called it. Stalin, on the other hand, saw the Spanish Civil War in quite a different context. He regarded Mussolini and Hitler as counterrevolutionaries, bent on destroying the socialist fatherland that he and Lenin had begun to build in Russia; Italian and German intervention in Spain threatened both Russia and its revolution. But Stalin had to consider home affairs as well as events abroad; he had to watch Asia as well as Europe. The trials and purges of 1935 and 1936 extirpated any possible revolt of the classes—not to mention the masses—in the Soviet Union. In 1937 another danger threatened Russia from another quarter when Japan attacked China with such force as to raise in Stalin's mind the specter of a two-front war.

Mass discontent inside both China and Japan aggravated the conditions that resulted in war. In China, the revolution that had overthrown the Manchus back in 1911 and established a Republic in the place of the Empire had not yet run its course. While western Europe and the United States struggled back toward normalcy during the 1920's, Chiang Kai-shek struggled on toward full power in China, setting himself up as head of a one-party state and devoting much of his time to suppressing Communism. Chiang had learned something about the theory of revolution in Moscow, where he had spent six months and where one of his sons by an early marriage had remained and married a Russian wife. Chiang learned still more about the practice of revolution from the Russian advisers who surrounded him during the mid-1920's. Ironically enough, his Communist enemies devised their own revolutionary tactics, without benefit of advice from Moscow. Chiang liquidated most of the founding fathers of Chinese Communism during the later 1920's by the simple expedient of turning their own weapons against them. But he found himself more and more helpless against the younger group of Chinese Communist leaders who rallied around Mao Tse-tung and Chou En-lai and the rebellious peasants they organized.

The Japanese enjoyed some of the prosperity of the 1920's, but the world depression hit them as hard as it hit the Germans. Whereupon Japan's military leaders acted with a resolution that the German Junkers

UNITED PRESS PHOTO

Japanese Troops Bow Respects to Ashes of Dead Comrade

had never regained after their country went down to defeat in 1918. First, the Japanese militarists engineered the invasion of Manchuria and then its incorporation in the Japanese Empire as the puppet kingdom of Manchukuo. Every Japanese knew the glowing record of his country's undefeated Army, which had humbled backward China in 1894 and mighty Russia in 1905. And Japanese bankers and industrialists did not dare oppose a military caste that had won such impressive victories. Indeed, many Japanese bankers and industrialists found that they could profit mightily by co-operating with the Army's program of expansion. Nor did the depression breed a younger generation of armed intellectuals such as swarmed around Hitler. Japan had no embittered veterans of a lost war, and the younger men still looked on the Army with respect and on the Emperor with reverence.

The spirit of revolt among the young people of Japan who came of age during the depression did not run to Russian-style Communism or to German-style Fascism. It ran to a violent, even a radical nationalism. During the first few months of 1932 several young Army officers who belonged to various secret patriotic societies assassinated four outstanding civilian leaders of moderate views. As a result, control of foreign and military policy shifted from civilian to military hands. Japan quit the League of Nations in 1933 and announced a year later that it would let the naval limitation treaty with Britain and the United States lapse in 1936. During 1934 the Japanese proclaimed their version of a "Monroe

Doctrine" for East Asia. Eiji Amau, an obscure spokesman for the Japanese Foreign Office, made himself an international celebrity overnight by announcing: "This country considers it only natural that to keep peace and order in East Asia, it must act single-handed and upon its own responsibility. In order to be able to fulfill this obligation, Japan must expect its neighbor countries to share the responsibility of maintaining peace in East Asia, but Japan does not consider any country, except China, to be in a position to share that responsibility with Japan."

Amau had not proposed a Chinese-Japanese partnership. He had proposed that Japan give orders to a puppet Chinese regime with no more independence than the government of Manchukuo. Chiang Kai-shek's government did not fill the bill, but the steady advance of Japanese troops into North China foreshadowed the time when Chiang might have to choose between capitulation and full-scale war. He had chosen capitulation in 1933, when Japan's Kwantung Army overran Manchuria and Jehol Province. He chose capitulation again when the Japanese entered Chahar in 1935 and Chiang agreed to the establishment of an "autonomous" government in five of China's northern provinces. Japan's repudiation of the Open Door in China went down worse in Washington and London than in Nanking. It went down worst of all among the Chinese students, who protested against each new capitulation and kept demanding that Chiang take a stronger stand against Japan, even at the risk of war. Nowhere did these demonstrations stir such hope and sympathy as in Moscow, where fear of encirclement and a two-front war obsessed the men in the Kremlin. Nor did the Foreign Office in Tokyo entirely approve the adventurous policy of the Japanese Army leaders.

Anti-Japanese demonstrations in China and symptoms of nonconfidence at home stirred the Japanese militarists to direct action. On February 20, 1936, the Japanese voters elected a huge majority of liberals to the new Parliament. The militarists reacted to this display of mass moderation with the utmost speed, resolution, and violence. Early in the morning of February 26, fourteen hundred young Japanese officers and enlisted men occupied several government buildings in Tokyo, scattered guards about the grounds of the imperial palace, and tried to murder the leading moderates in the government and the Imperial Household. They succeeded in killing Admiral Saito, Lord Keeper of the Privy Seal and former Prime Minister; General Watanabe, Inspector General of Military Education; and Finance Minister Takahashi. They wounded Admiral Suzuki, the Grand Chamberlain, and thought they had also done in Prime Minister Okada when his brother-in-law heroically attracted their fire, thus saving Okada's life. Count Makino, a trusted member of the Imperial Household who had represented Japan at the Paris Peace Conference, had a lucky escape when his granddaughter shielded him with her kimono and persuaded the awe-struck, ignorant young soldiers to hold their fire. It was Makino who had told the editor of the Paris *Temps* in 1935: "When you return to Paris and make your report or write your editorials on the domestic situation in Japan, eliminate the word 'danger' from your vocabulary. We have a safeguard in Japan which other countries do not possess in the same degree, namely the Imperial Household. There will never be 'danger' from military Fascism or Communism or from any other kind of 'ism' simply because the Emperor is supreme and will *always* have the last word."

Admiral and Viscountess Saito spent their last evening at a party given in their honor by United States Ambassador Joseph C. Grew, who reported some poignant details in his book, *Ten Years in Japan:* "Gradually, from the accounts of friends, we can reconstruct the way the assassinations took place, and not only do the stories redound to the credit of the men, but they show the true stuff of Japanese womanhood—how Viscountess Saito placed herself in front of her husband, said, 'Kill me instead; my husband cannot be spared by the country,' and actually put her hand on the mouth of the machine gun until her wounds forced her aside, and how Mrs. Watanabe embraced her husband so firmly that the assassins had to force the gun underneath her body."

The frustrated coup d'état had not, perhaps, established a new order in Japan but it had certainly shaken the old one. The rebels held part of Tokyo for four days and slowly surrendered without any further bloodshed or shooting. The government gave the officers who led the revolt two hours to themselves in which to commit hara-kiri, but the officers, hoping for a civil trial at which they could make speeches, refused to oblige, only to face a secret court-martial and a firing squad. Ambassador Grew wrote in his diary at the time: "The period of the insurrection lasted only four days, and yet we in the Embassy feel as if an era had passed since that happy evening when we had the Saitos and Suzukis under our roof last Tuesday. If time is measured by events, certainly an age has gone by since then." Premier Okada did not lose his life but he lost his job to Foreign Minister Koki Hirota, whom the Emperor invited to form a new government. But when Hirota tried to put Admiral Yoshida, a son-in-law of Makino's, in charge of the Foreign Office, the Army leaders objected and Hirota withdrew his appointment. General Terauchi, the War Minister, became the real power in the new Cabinet, and it was he who announced that Japan would now follow a new and "positive" foreign policy, which he launched by demanding "autonomy" for five more provinces in North China. Chiang Kai-shek, as already related, felt he had no choice but to yield. As a result of trade concessions already granted in 1935, the Japanese were smuggling so much merchandise into one of these provinces that they dried up its principal source of local revenue and ruined its principal local industries by price-cutting.

Having quit the League of Nations in 1933, Japan took the next logical step and joined Germany in signing the Anti-Comintern Pact. After lengthy negotiations in Berlin the Hirota Cabinet pledged itself in vague, bombastic language to stand with Germany against the spread of Communism. The Russians at once charged that the agreement contained secret military clauses, calling for joint action against themselves. Some non-Russian diplomats accepted the charge, but Constantin Yurenev, the Soviet Ambassador to Tokyo, told Grew that though "Soviet-Japanese relations had suffered a severe setback" the real purpose of the Anti-Comintern Pact was to partition the British and Dutch colonial empires with Germany in the event of war.

Japan's military fanatics and Germany's fanatical Nazis had less in common than met the eye. On the surface, their traits and purposes appeared the same. In both countries disciplined minorities imposed their will by force on divided majorities and used war and threats of war against their weaker neighbors. But the Nazis had more revolutionary attributes. Hitler came to power by stages, first working behind the scenes with Papen and the generals while fighting on the streets against the Communists, then extending the terror against all other groups, one by one, until no opposition remained. The young Japanese Army officers, on the other hand, revered the Emperor as Hitler never revered the Kaiser. They did not regard themselves as the forerunners of a new era but as the restorers of an old one. "It is easier," wrote Ambassador Grew, "to understand how such things as the incident of February 26 can occur in Japan if one stops to think that the history books upon which the Japanese youth is brought up are full of the records of just such deeds from the earliest times—assassinations or suicides for motives of revenge or loyalty to one's chief or the assumption of responsibility for a given situation. Paradoxically—and Japan is a country of paradoxes—the young officers held that they were acting in the interests of the Emperor, ridding him of the alleged nefarious influences around the Throne, men whom the Emperor himself had chosen. And there was no personal animosity involved. When they killed Saito and Watanabe and Matsuo (mistaken for his brother-in-law, the Prime Minister), they called for incense to burn beside the bodies; in the Takahashi house, no incense could be found, so they insisted on putting lighted candles beside the murdered statesman." What a contrast with Hitler's "night of the long knives."

The Nazis rode to power on a mass party drawn chiefly from the dispossessed and desperate middle classes, at whom Hitler aimed his racial and revolutionary propaganda. The Japanese militarists relied on the Army, which drew most of its recruits from the peasantry. The young officers in this Army did not regard themselves or their men as revolutionaries. They regarded themselves as patriots and the rank-and-file soldiers accepted them as such. They did not form a new party or follow a new leader. They lavished all their attentions on their comrades in arms, whom they tried to forge into a more perfect instrument of the Emperor's will. The Nazis, on the other hand, tried to infiltrate and subvert the German Army into a more perfect instrument of the will of Hitler.

In spite of these differences, common interests, common purposes, and common fears brought Nazi Germany and militarist Japan together. The new candidates for leadership in both countries wanted to expand at the expense of China, Russia, and the Western democracies. They advertised themselves as anti-Communist—partly to shake down money from the frightened rich, partly to mislead the democracies, partly because they meant it. Both Nazi Germany and militarist Japan planned to use war as an instrument of national policy. Both feared democracy at home and abroad. During the summer of 1936, the Nazis began to intervene cautiously but decisively in Spain's Civil War. A year later the Japanese militarists went them one better and launched a large-scale invasion of China, thus risking if not initiating a second world war.

· II ·

CHIANG KAI-SHEK'S PROBLEMS in China paralleled Stalin's problems in Russia about as closely as the rise of Japan's militarists paralleled the rise of Germany's Nazis. Chiang posed as the heir of Sun Yat-sen as Stalin posed as the heir of Lenin; Chiang liquidated the founders of Chinese Communism as Stalin liquidated the Old Bolsheviks. This did not, however, depress Stalin unduly because the early Chinese Communists and their Russian advisers leaned toward Trotsky's doctrine of world revolution rather than toward Stalin's doctrine of socialism in one country. But Chiang proved less successful than Stalin in consolidating his own and his government's power. China had far less natural wealth than Russia, fewer factories and railways, poorer farms and roads—and several times as many people living on less than half as much land. Nevertheless, both countries excited the fear and envy of the outside world. Both had gone through revolutions from which they emerged stronger and more unified.

By the mid-1930's, the Western democracies had reconciled themselves to the Russian and Chinese Revolutions and stabilized their relations with Stalin and Chiang Kai-shek, who had also decided to get along with each other. Chiang had broken with Russia in 1927 when he turned against the Chinese Communists, but the two countries resumed relations in 1932 after their delegates at Geneva had held friendly con-

UNITED PRESS PHOTO

Chinese Communist Cavalryman

versations on Manchuria, together with the Americans. This discussion also led to American recognition of the Soviet Union a year later. All this went down badly in Berlin and Tokyo. Hitler had tried to sell himself abroad as the number one enemy of the Kremlin, and the Kremlin as the number one enemy of mankind. The Japanese had tried to convince the world that they and they alone knew how to open up China to foreign trade and investment.

Hitler's propaganda proved more convincing abroad than Japan's. Chiang Kai-shek's proved more convincing than either. Until 1936 the Generalissimo represented himself as a fighting Nationalist whose recurrent military expeditions into Communist-held territories unfortunately kept boomeranging. The Communists routed, looted, or converted the Kuomintang troops and kept Chiang so occupied that he did not fight the Japanese. In 1933 he turned over five northern provinces to Japanese control; in 1935 the Japanese demanded five more. The early Bolsheviks had made comparable surrenders of territory to Poland, Finland, and the Baltic States, but they ruled the lands they held with a firmer hand than the Generalissimo could show in China. It was hard to say which of his own policies turned more students and intellectuals against him—his repeated concessions to the Japanese or his repeated offensives against the Communists.

Chiang launched his first big offensive in 1930, attacking the chief Communist stronghold in Kiangsi Province in the southeast. Ninety thousand Communist guerrillas, with less than ten thousand rifles, set out on their celebrated "Long March" of six thousand miles to Shensi Province in the northwest. Less than half of them completed the journey, carrying factory machinery as well as their personal effects on their backs and in hand-drawn carts. In Szechuan they made contact with other Communists who had already set up their own local administration. Though Moscow provided no help and few instructions, the native Communist program of land reform and industrial co-operatives won ever wider support. By 1936, the Communists were doing so well that Chiang ordered a sixth expedition to take the field and wipe them out, once and for all.

At the head of this expedition stood Chang Hsueh-liang, known as the "Young Marshal," whose father, Chang Tso-lin, the "Old Marshal," the Japanese had blown up, along with his private railway car, in 1928. Chang Tso-lin had once controlled Manchuria; his son inherited a large fortune and the Tungkei Army of 135,000 men, one of the best in China. The son had received a good education but acquired the opium habit as a young man. In trying to cure himself he became a morphine addict until 1934, when an American missionary for the Seventh-Day Adventists got him back to normal ways. His reputation as a playboy prevented him from becoming a powerful figure in his own right, but he nourished two passions: to avenge his father's death and to make China a great power in fact as well as name. Chang concluded that he could not achieve either purpose unless and until China had a strong central government. Convinced that only Chiang Kai-shek could head such a government, the Young Marshal put himself at the orders of the Generalissimo, who saw a chance to kill two birds with one stone and ordered the Young Marshal to head the new anti-Communist drive.

The subsequent campaign in North Shensi Province opened the Young Marshal's eyes to some of the more important facts of Chinese life. He had proved himself an able military leader. He got on well with people. He believed in his country's destiny. But he had never believed in Chiang's policy of appeasing the Japanese and now he questioned Chiang's wisdom in fighting native Communists rather than foreign invaders. He found his own troops more interested in fraternizing with the Communists than in exterminating them, especially after the Comintern had ordered its affiliates all over the world to adopt the new policy of the Popular Front. During the 1920's the local Communists had tried and failed to make a Chinese revolution on the Russian model. Now, Chiang Kai-shek was devoting most of his energies to fighting them while Japan's inroads on the Asiatic mainland steadily increased. It all might end with Chiang coming to terms with Japan and planning common action against Russia. Chiang Kai-shek had imported a number of military advisers from Germany, notably General von Seeckt, creator of the postwar Reichswehr. The Japanese and the Germans signed the Anti-Comintern Pact late in 1936. Stalin, fearful of falling victim to a squeeze play from east and west, limited his intervention in Spain and told the Chinese Communists to subordinate themselves to Chiang Kai-shek in a common war effort against Japan.

As chairman of the Chinese Soviets, Mao Tse-tung obeyed Stalin's orders and called for a Chinese version of the Popular Front. The Young Marshal, welcoming any policy that gave priority to fighting the Japanese who had murdered his father, tried to convert the Generalissimo. But the Generalissimo rebuffed his young subordinate, who turned, in

his despair, to the man who had inspired him to break the drug habit—
W. H. Donald, Chiang Kai-shek's blunt Australian adviser. "My men
won't fight the Communists," the Young Marshal told Donald. "It isn't
Communist bullets they're afraid of. They listen to what the Communists say to them, and the Communists say, 'We are Chinese and you are
Chinese. Why do you fight with us? Your officers get rich. They don't
pay you your wages. They have their motorcars, their concubines, their
silk gowns, and you get nothing.' Everything they say, of course, is quite
true. But what am I to do? Old man Chiang says we've got to fight the
Communists."

"Old man Chiang," inspired by the courage of his convictions, flew to
the Young Marshal's headquarters at Sian on an upper tributary of the
Yellow River, seven hundred miles west of Nanking and almost a thousand miles from the coast. He had heard about the Young Marshal's
flirtation with the Communists and warned him, face to face, at the risk
of his life, against working with them. When the Young Marshal asked
him why he had not yet begun to fight the Japanese, Chiang called him
a Bolshevik, and said the time to fight the Japanese had not yet come. "I
do not say you are wrong," the Young Marshal replied—according to his
own version as related in E. A. Selle's *Donald of China,* "but at the time
of the Manchurian trouble, you declared that we must prepare and in
two years we could drive the Japs from China. Five years have elapsed.
We cannot go on saying to the people that we are still preparing, for the
enemy is digging deeper into the country. Now, the government is like
a bank. If it defaults, confidence is lost. We only talk, and, therefore, we
default. Sir, there are only three choices—we fight the Japanese, we retreat, or we submit." At this point the Generalissimo turned livid and
screamed that he would never surrender. The Young Marshal left in
despair and wrote a long letter requesting that he be permitted to lead
his troops against the Japanese since they would fight no one else.
Chiang insisted that he continue to fight the Reds.

When the students in Sian learned of the Generalissimo's attitude,
they demonstrated against him in the streets. This served only to make
him angrier than ever and to accuse the Young Marshal of having inspired the demonstrators. One of the Young Marshal's generals suggested arresting Chiang, and some of the other officers urged executing
him then and there. But the Young Marshal agreed with the Communists that only Chiang could rally a united China against Japan, and he
appeased some of the hotheads around him by ordering his personal
bodyguard to arrest the Generalissimo but on no account to do him any
harm. Early in the morning of December 12, at almost the same moment
when Edward VIII was abdicating the British throne, a drama of comparable moment unfolded deep inside Asia. Members of the Young

Marshal's bodyguard broke into the Generalissimo's temporary head-quarters in a local temple at Sian, seized several of his companions and, in their excitement, shot one of his nephews. Chiang, clad only in under-wear, jumped out a rear window, climbed over a ten-foot wall, fell into a deep moat, wrenched his back getting out, and ran until he tripped in a bramble patch on a nearby mountainside. Here he was discovered be-hind a rock, trembling with cold, his hands and bare feet cut and bleeding. "If you are my comrades," he croaked, "kill me and finish it all." The officer who made the capture replied: "We do not want to shoot you. You are the Generalissimo," and escorted him back to the local temple, where he shut himself up in his room with a copy of the Bible. Later, they brought him to the headquarters of one of the generals in Sian, where the Young Marshal told him: "Your bad temper is always the cause of trouble." Again he urged Chiang to call off his anti-Commu-nist campaigns and fight the Japanese. "I never change my ideas," Chiang replied. "My ideas are all right. Anyway you talk too much. You always talk too much. All I will say to you is: Either kill me or send me back to Nanking. I don't care which."

For almost two weeks the rebellious troops at Sian held Chiang prisoner while a group of generals at Nanking organized an expedition to attack Sian and effect his rescue. Finally, on Christmas Day, the Sian rebels let the Generalissimo fly back to Nanking. The man who broke the deadlock was neither a supporter of Chiang nor a member of the rebel garrison at Sian. He was Chou En-lai, the Communist commander of a Communist army outside Sian. Chou had studied in Germany and France and had joined the Communist Party in Paris. He returned to China during the 1920's when all good Chinese Communists were taking orders from the Kuomintang. It was Chou En-lai who organized the working-class uprising in Shanghai that turned the city over to Chiang Kai-shek, and it was Chiang Kai-shek who promptly suppressed the uprising and killed its leaders. Chou was lucky to escape, but he lived to organize the Long March and to lead Communist troops against all of Chiang's anti-Communist campaigns. Yet this same Communist leader, ever obedient to Moscow's orders, appeared at Sian shortly before Christmas Day, 1936, to plead and argue, more passionately and more convincingly than anyone else, for unity against Japan. Such matters as face and consistency did not trouble him at all. If Chou En-lai acted the part of the good Communist, Chang Hsueh-liang acted the part of the good soldier, taking the whole blame for the kidnaping and putting himself at the Generalissimo's mercy. At one point, however, the Young Marshal could not restrain himself from shouting at the officers in charge of his court-martial: "The only one of you all who is worth a damn is the Generalissimo! None of the rest of you would be any loss to China. If I

get out of this I'll start a revolution!" The Young Marshal did not get out.
The court sentenced him to ten years in prison, which Chiang commuted
to ten years under surveillance. Chou En-lai, with everything to gain
and nothing to lose, came out on top. His appeals and concessions persuaded Chiang to call off the anti-Communist campaign without loss of
face while at the same time the Communists pledged themselves to work
and fight under Chiang's leadership for a united China and against
Japan.

· III ·

THE Sian kidnaping had taken place on "double twelve," as the Chinese
call the twelfth of December. Seven months later, on "double seven," the
seventh of July, Japan struck. China's civil war had ended and Chiang
now headed China's strongest central government since the time of the
Manchus. The young Japanese Army officers who had organized the killings of February, 1936, could wait no longer. Abroad, they feared the
power of a unified, militant China, where the student movement kept
pressing Chiang to fight any further Japanese encroachments; at home,
they feared the continuing growth of liberal, antimilitarist opinion. The
time had come to transform the localized China Incident into full-scale
war.

Before the summer of 1937, only the people of North China had any
direct experience with the Japanese military. Within another year most
of the China coast and most of China's great cities had come under Japanese attack and occupation. Thanks to Japan, the Chinese people thus
achieved a sense of national unity that they had never attained on their
own. But at what a cost. The Japanese attack on China proper began on
the evening of July 7, 1937, near the village of Lukouchiao, twenty miles
west of Peiping, where Japanese troops were maneuvering near a railway intersection. Their commander claimed that Chinese troops of General Sung Cheh-yuan's 29th Army had attacked them, and the Japanese
authorities demanded that the Chinese withdraw from all strategic
points outside Peiping and permit Japanese troops to search all villages
near the famous Marco Polo Bridge, leading to Peiping. The Japanese
also demanded that the Chinese join them in a common anti-Communist
crusade. The Chinese agreed to appoint members of a joint investigation
committee, but they could not prevent some local fighting between
Japanese and Chinese units. Both sides brought up reinforcements. General Sung, the governor of Peiping, proclaimed martial law. The Japanese set up barricades and machine guns around the Legation while
more troops from Manchuria massed outside the city. Japan had 160,000
men and 200 military planes in North China. General Sung had 10,000
troops inside Peiping, but no tanks or planes and only a few pieces of

UNITED PRESS PHOTO

Japanese Troops Entering Nanking

light artillery. On July 25, the Japanese gave Sung forty-eight hours to withdraw from the city with his troops. With the approval of the national government at Nanking, Sung chose to stand and fight. Three thousand of his men made a last-ditch stand in which two thirds of them perished. Japan's conquest of China had begun.

The American correspondent Edgar Snow witnessed the opening stages of the fighting and some days later talked with a number of Japanese soldiers. His *Battle for Asia* quotes some of their comments: "We Japanese are peaceful, but the Chinese keep making trouble." "The dirty Chinese murdered our people at Tungchow." "We came to save China from the Communists. Italy and Germany understand Japan, but America and England do not." One peasant boy admitted he did not understand the cause of the war, but added, "Chiang Kai-shek is always hurting our people, and we are fighting him, not the good Chinese." An old-timer from the Manchurian front spoke more frankly: "We came to teach the Chinese a lesson. They were getting too bold."

The Japanese themselves did not lack boldness, and it was a barbaric lesson they taught. Having taken Peiping and Tientsin, about one hundred miles to the southeast, the Japanese prepared to attack the larger, more important cities of Nanking and Shanghai to the south and eventually to occupy Canton and Hankow as well. As early as July 17, Chiang Kai-shek laid down certain "minimum conditions" for negotiation. These required the Japanese not to infringe upon China's territorial integrity and sovereign rights, to make no more demands upon North China, and to seize no more positions from General Sung's 29th Army. Chiang recog-

UNITED PRESS PHOTO

*Japanese Soldiers Force Aged Chinese
to Display Their Flag*

nized that these conditions meant war. "Let our people now realize," he
warned, "the full meaning of the phrase 'the last extremity' and the extent of sacrifice thereby involved, for once that stage is reached we have
to fight to the bitter end. Should we hesitate, however, and vainly hope
for temporary safety, then indeed we should be lost forever." General
Sugiyama, Japanese War Minister, replied on August 2 that China
"must be chastised for her insincerity" and that Japan's nonaggression
policy had come to an end. But no declaration of war ever followed on
either side.

Which was quite as it should have been. For Japan's soldiers disgraced
their country and their calling. They did not fight a war; it takes two to
do that, and the Chinese had no means of defending their great cities,
which fell, most of them without resistance, to Japanese attack. The port
of Shanghai, the capital of Nanking, and four cities lying between them,
on the Yangtze and its delta, all fell to Japanese troops who killed three
hundred thousand Chinese soldiers and another three hundred thousand
Chinese civilians during the latter months of 1937. In 1900 the disciplined behavior of the Japanese troops who took part in the international expedition to liberate the Peiping legations from the Boxer rebels
put the looting Europeans to shame. Thirty-seven years later, fifty thousand Japanese troops at Nanking, from the highest officers to the least of

UNITED PRESS PHOTO

Japanese Flower Arrangement as Practised by Japanese Troops
Advancing upon Shanghai

the rear-rank privates, wallowed in an orgy of murder, rape, torture, loot, and ruin, killing forty-two thousand Chinese civilians in less than a month. "Anything female between the ages of ten and seventy was raped," wrote Edgar Snow in *The Battle for Asia.* "Discards were often bayoneted by drunken soldiers. Frequenty mothers had to watch their babies beheaded and then submit to raping." The Japanese looted twelve thousand stores and houses and then set them on fire. As War Minister Sugiyama put it, "Some force even greater than God has inspired our men." A student of abnormal psychology might well have defined that force as the release of long-suppressed passions which seethed beneath the surface composure of so many Japanese.

J. B. Powell, American editor of the *China Weekly Review* of Shanghai, supplied some more details in his autobiography, *My Twenty-Five Years in China:*

"I inspected numerous photographs snapped in mission hospitals showing Chinese with deep gashes in their heads, necks, shoulders, and arms caused by Japanese soldiers who were putting into practice the ancient and popular Japanese military exercise in which soldiers, wearing heavy leather headgear, wire masks, and shoulder guards, beat each other over the heads until they drop from exhaustion. I had frequently watched these exercises at Japanese barracks in Manchuria and in Japan and marveled at the ability of the soldiers to stand such brutality. I did not realize that the exercise would ultimately be put to practical use with real swords against unarmed civilians."

Mr. Powell also culled from the pages of the Tokyo *Nichi Nichi Shimbun* an account of the meeting in Nanking of two young Japanese officers, former schoolmates at the Tokyo Military Academy—Sublieutenants Tashiaki Mukai and Iwao Noda: "After two formal bows the two Japanese officers drew their swords and pointed with pride to the badly nicked edges of the long blades. Said Lieutenant Noda, 'I have killed 105—how many have you killed?' Lieutenant Mukai replied, 'Aha-ha, I have killed 106—so sorry.' " Since they could not decide who had first killed one hundred Chinese, they agreed to call it a tie and to continue the competition with 150 Chinese as their new goal.

H. J. Timperley, China correspondent for the *Manchester Guardian*, wrote at the time: "Should anyone believe that the Japanese Army is in this country to make life better and happier for the Chinese, then let him travel over the area between Shanghai and Nanking, a distance of some two hundred miles, and witness the unbelievable devastation and destruction. This area, six months ago, was the most densely populated portion of the earth's surface, and the most prosperous section of China. Today the traveler will see only cities bombed and pillaged; towns and villages reduced to shambles; farms desolated, and only an old man or woman here and there digging in the once 'good earth.' The livestock has been either killed or stolen, and every sort of destruction that a brutal army equipped with all the modern implements of war can inflict has been done here."

Although China had a standing Army nominally amounting to 1,800,-000 men, only 600,000 of them had received modern training and carried some modern equipment. Half of these consisted of Chiang's German-trained troops, around whom he had grouped eighty partially trained, partially equipped divisions. Another 300,000 troops were concentrated in Kwangsi Province to the southeast. The Japanese who attacked Nanking and Shanghai outnumbered the Chinese and had far better equipment. J. B. Powell's autobiography describes what happened when a Chinese pilot, trying to jettison two heavy bombs over a race-track, dropped them amid more than five thousand refugees who had gathered at a street intersection in Shanghai to receive free rice. Nearly two thousand persons were killed; another twenty-five hundred were injured. Burnt, mangled bodies of men, women, and children were piled against the walls of buildings to a height of five feet. "The explosion," wrote Powell, "shook the entire city. I hurried to the scene and for the first time in my extensive coverage of battles, I actually saw human blood running in the gutters. When I got home late that night after covering the story, my shoes, socks, and trousers were caked with blood."

A Chinese pilot inadvertently killing his own people symbolized the tragedy of his country's war effort. But the Japanese inflicted most of the casualties. A correspondent of Reuters, the official British news agency, described the damage that Japanese bombing planes inflicted on the slum section of Hankow: "The streets in the district, only six feet wide, were fringed with poor hovels which collapsed like a pack of cards, burying their occupants as well as passers-by. Parts of bodies were strewn everywhere, which were gathered and piled in heaps by rescue parties. More ghastly, however, was the occasional sight of an arm or leg waving feebly from beneath masonry which was too heavy to move without adequate apparatus. Standing at a street corner for ten minutes, the Reuters correspondent saw over 120 bodies carried past, some moaning terribly, others completely lifeless. Particularly pathetic was the sight of stretchers bearing infant victims. . . . Tiny bodies seemed to outnumber those of adults."

The carnage in China surpassed the carnage in Spain as the importance of China overshadowed the importance of Spain. China embraced more territory and contained more people than all of Europe. And as Europe on the map amounted to no more than an Asiatic peninsula, so Spain, on the map, amounted to no more than a peninsula of Europe. To Japan, China counted for infinitely more than Europe did. To Russia, both Japan and China meant as much as any countries in the world. Back in 1930, before the Japanese attacked Manchuria, their imports from Russia exceeded their total imports from Siam, French Indo-China, British Borneo, and the Philippines. After 1932, the Russians cut this trade down to almost nothing. Japanese purchases from the United States, on the other hand, came to more than a thousand times as much as Japanese purchases from the Soviet Union. This contrast did not signify superior virtue on the part of the Russians. All it meant was that the Russians considered themselves directly threatened by Japanese expansion and directly interested in strengthening China. After all, the better a fight the Chinese could put up against Japan, the better a chance the Russians would have of either defeating or preventing a Japanese attack on themselves. In the long run, the German menace from the west overshadowed the Japanese menace from the east. Over the short pull, however, Japan posed the more immediate threat. Hence the curtailment of Russian aid to Spain and the increase of Russian aid to China.

While Russia sent limited aid to Spain and China, the democracies did next to nothing. In Spain, the United States followed Britain's lead. As Roosevelt interpreted the Monroe Doctrine and as he understood

UNITED PRESS PHOTO

Survivors of the Panay

the interests of the United States, he had little choice in the matter. But Japan's attack on China defied the principle of the Open Door, as proclaimed by John Hay back in 1900. The Japanese had also violated the more specific pledges they had undertaken under the Nine-Power Washington Treaties of 1922. But Roosevelt's quarantine speech of October 5, 1937, produced no more effect among the "peace-loving ninety per cent" of mankind than it did among "the war-making ten per cent." Secretary of State Hull appointed Norman Davis to represent the United States at a meeting summoned in Brussels the day after Roosevelt's quarantine appeal to consider the status of the Nine-Power Treaty on the Far East. "Was it a bust?" a New York reporter asked Davis on his return. The best Davis could say was that it had given the peace-loving nations a chance to go on record against Japanese aggression. But that was all they did. The European democracies were devoting all their attention to Hitler, Mussolini, and the Spanish Civil War. Polls of public opinion in the United States showed 55 per cent of the people in favor of withdrawing all American civilians and troops from China.

On December 12, Japanese planes bombed and sank the American gunboat *Panay* on the Yangtze River, below Nanking, where it was convoying a group of Standard Oil tankers. The planes machine-gunned the boats in which the survivors tried to escape, and Norman Alley, a daring American newsreel cameraman, photographed the whole episode. The seventeen victims included, ironically enough, Sandro Sandri, special correspondent for *La Stampa* of Turin and one of the organizers of the Shanghai branch of the Italian Fascist Party. Other Japanese planes also attacked two British gunboats and five British river steamers. But it was the attack on the *Panay* that caused the greatest consternation in Tokyo. The local Japanese commanders had gone beyond their orders, and the Japanese Ambassador in Washington was apologizing to Secretary Hull before the State Department had received the full story, while in Tokyo Prime Minister Hirota dropped everything to convey similar apologies to Ambassador Grew. President Roosevelt asked the American motion picture industry to show the films of the attack on the *Panay* as widely and rapidly as possible, with the result that popular support for American withdrawal from the Far East jumped from 55 per cent to 70 per cent. In the field of domestic policy Roosevelt satisfied the aspirations of the average American more successfully than any President in living memory. On matters of foreign policy a great and widening gulf separated him from his fellow citizens.

SUMMING UP

JAPAN'S INVASION of China continued a shift in the world balance of power that began with the turn of the century. When Japan checked Russia in 1905 it marked the first time in five hundred years that an Asiatic people had defeated a European people in war. Japan's attack on China, thirty years later, marked another step in the same direction. The ensuing clash between two Asiatic nations shook the world. Before invading China, the Japanese signed the Anti-Comintern Pact with the Germans. A month later, Chiang called off his campaign against the Chinese Communists and improved his relations with Moscow. Three months after Japanese troops crossed the Marco Polo Bridge, President Roosevelt summoned the peace-loving 90 per cent of mankind to quarantine the war-making 10 per cent. The League of Nations seconded the motion. The point was not that Roosevelt's quarantine speech fell flat. The point was that a war in Asia hit the vital interests of Europe and the United States. The fate of China caused so much concern in Moscow that the Russians curtailed their aid to the Spanish Republic, thereby assuring Franco's victory.

Believers in collective security, in the League of Nations, in quarantining aggressors could see no more in Japan's attack on China than a blow to their hopes and theories. Looked at from another point of view, the warfare in China meant that Asia had come up still more in the world and that Europe had slipped still further back. No major European Power wanted war in the Far East, but none could stop or even control the war that had blown up in their faces—or, rather, behind their backs. The Japanese in China showed no more mercy to Italians than they showed to the English, no more consideration to Americans than to Germans. Nor did the Chinese have any illusions about the white men who posed as their friends. Chiang Kai-shek always suspected the Russians. Roosevelt talked big, but his words meant little. American businessmen sold munitions of war to the Japanese. The majority of the American people wanted to pull out of the Far East entirely. Nevertheless the United States possessed immense reserves of untapped strength. What it chose to do with this strength could certainly change the course of history in the short run; possibly in the long run, too.

19

From Country Squire to World Messiah

*How a series of setbacks to the New Deal followed
by Japan's invasion of China forced Roosevelt to
revert to Wilson's role of world messiah.*

PREVIEW

ROOSEVELT'S FIRST TERM ended with an overwhelming election victory.
His second term started with a political defeat. The Supreme Court
declared many New Deal laws unconstitutional, and Roosevelt retaliated
by sponsoring a bill to enlarge the Court with his appointees. He lost his
fight to reform the Court, although the Court reversed itself on the New
Deal. Then came a sharper slump than 1929. The New Deal had failed
to solve the major problems that plagued Hoover, and the literature of
dissent and social protest grew. The cultural level of the mass communications industries rose, but few new practitioners of the lively arts
appeared. In the latter half of 1937, Japan's attack upon China led Roosevelt to call for collective action against aggression, but even the sinking
of the gunboat *Panay* failed to arouse the martial spirit. Belief in neutrality, desire for isolation ran too strong. But Roosevelt had stepped
upon the world stage as a world messiah and had not yet spoken his
last word.

· I ·

ROOSEVELT liked the White House as much as the American people liked
to have him there. No President since T.R. had enjoyed the job as much
as his fifth cousin enjoyed it. No President since Andrew Jackson had
commanded such popular support. Never since the Civil War had the
party in power won increased majorities at the midterm Congressional
elections as the Democrats did in 1934. Two years later, Roosevelt scored
a still more striking personal victory. He defeated Governor Alf M. Landon, "the Kansas Coolidge," by a popular vote of twenty-seven to sixteen
millions. The Republicans carried only two states, Maine and Vermont,
and their representation in Congress continued to dwindle. Nevertheless,

they still had wide mass support: Landon got more votes in 1936 than Smith got in 1928.

The Republicans during the 1930's reaped the harvest of their bigotry, folly, and stubbornness in the previous decade. Nor did Roosevelt's cocky personality sweeten the taste of defeat after defeat. Perhaps the President overcame enough when he won his fight against polio. Perhaps he had a long run of easy political triumphs coming to him. But it was a minor personal tragedy and a major national one that the Republican Party did not produce a leader or an issue dramatic enough to force Roosevelt to extend himself.

The phrase "happy warrior" that he once applied to Al Smith fitted Roosevelt himself still better. His gaiety, energy, courage, and confidence infected all his official family and spread throughout the land. The New Deal, during its first two years, concentrated on relief and recovery. During its next two years, especially in the 1936 election, the accent shifted to reform, and Roosevelt wound up his campaign in a Madison Square Garden speech with his most radical appeal to date: "I should like to have it said of my first administration that in it the forces of selfishness and of lust for power met their match. I should like to have it said of my second administration that in it these forces have met their master." And again: "We know now that government by organized money is just as dangerous as government by organized mob. Never before in all our history have these forces been so united against one candidate as they stand today. They are unanimous in their hate for me —and I welcome their hatred."

Roosevelt welcomed the hatred of his enemies not because he hated back but because it helped him put on a better political show. Only in the final speech of his campaign did he give the "hate Roosevelt" Republicans a whiff of their own medicine. More serious matters needed attention. He and his aides had created the National Industrial Recovery Act, the Agricultural Adjustment Administration, the Securities and Exchange Commission, the Social Security Act, the Tennessee Valley Authority, and other long-range plans designed to stabilize industry and agriculture, to establish a minimum wage scale, to provide some protection to small investors, some help to the aged and the unemployed, and some low-cost power to underdeveloped areas. But this program began to crumble in 1935 when the Supreme Court ruled one New Deal reform after another unconstitutional. The heaviest blow fell when the Court unanimously joined in the decision written by Chief Justice Hughes outlawing the National Industrial Recovery Act. The case, which involved the marketing by a man called Schechter of some allegedly ill poultry, led Farley to comment: "The Blue Eagle was literally replaced by a sick chicken."

Hughes had once declared, "The Constitution is what the judges say it is," and the judges proceeded to say that almost every New Deal reform, except some features of TVA, violated the Constitution. The Court made three main points: first, that the New Deal had attempted to transfer the lawmaking powers of Congress to the President and to various new executive agencies; second, that the federal government had usurped certain powers reserved to the states; third, that no government, state or federal, had the power to fix wages and otherwise interfere in the workings of a free economy. Roosevelt, on the other hand, compared the outlawing of the NIRA with the Dred Scott decision. "The big issue is this: Does this decision mean that the United States government has no control over any economic problem?" He gave his own answer when he added: "We have been relegated to the horse-and-buggy definition of interstate commerce."

But the Supreme Court had not voted unanimously against the New Deal on every issue. It was only on the Schechter Case, outlawing the Blue Eagle, that all the Justices agreed. And on that case, many Roosevelt supporters, fearing the President's tolerance of monopoly, wondered if the Supreme Court were not saving the New Deal from some of the New Dealers. Moreover, Roosevelt had not mentioned the Supreme Court's anti-New Deal decisions during the 1936 campaign. If they rankled, he kept his rancor to himself. Nor did Landon urge scrapping a single New Deal reform; he even tried to outbid Roosevelt in appealing for the farmer's vote. Owing his nomination to the Hearst press and to the conservative Republican politicians of the Central and Midwestern states, Landon stressed economy and efficiency. His name meant nothing on either the West or the East coast, and his platform and personality meant little more. Farley let himself in for some ribbing when he referred to Landon's native Kansas as "a typical prairie state," but many other Americans knew no better and sympathized with genial Jim's embarrassment.

Few Republicans held Landon responsible for the debacle of 1936. As one profane politico remarked, the Republicans could not have won with Jesus Christ Himself. Most voters liked the New Deal and wanted the same witch doctors to serve more of the same brew. When Roosevelt told his Madison Square Garden crowd at the close of the campaign, "We have just begun to fight," millions of voters throughout the country took heart, and his second inaugural spelled out his hopes for the next four years in more grim and solemn detail: "I see a great nation, upon a great continent, blessed with a great wealth of natural resources. Its hundred and thirty million people are at peace among themselves; they are making their country a good neighbor among the nations." But he also saw a challenge to its democracy:

"I see millions of families trying to live on incomes so meager that the pall of family disaster hangs over them day by day.

"I see millions whose daily lives in city and on farm continue under conditions labeled indecent by so-called polite society half a century ago.

"I see millions denied education, recreation, and the opportunity to better their lot and the lot of their children.

"I see millions lacking the means to buy the products of farm and factory and by their poverty denying work and productiveness to many other millions.

"I see one third of a nation ill-housed, ill-clad, ill-nourished."

Two weeks later Roosevelt showed the fight he had promised during the campaign. Having disposed of the Republicans, he decided to take on the Supreme Court and invited the Democratic leaders in Congress to attend a Cabinet meeting at which Attorney General Homer Cummings outlined the administration's plan. It came as a complete surprise to those present when Cummings proposed expanding the Supreme Court from nine to as many as fifteen Justices if those members of the bench who had passed the age of seventy did not retire and let the President appoint their successors. Roosevelt and Cummings had worked out the details together, taking as their model a scheme that Justice McReynolds, the bitterest anti-New Dealer on the Supreme Bench, had devised as Attorney General, back in 1913, when he wanted to force older judges to retire from the lower federal courts. "That's the one, Homer!" Roosevelt had cried when Cummings suggested applying the same principle to the Supreme Court. It required no Constitutional Amendment and the joke on McReynolds appealed to the President's boyish sense of humor. His legal sense being equally juvenile, he made no use of the fine legal talent his administration had at its command, preferring to turn, as he had turned in creating the ill-fated NIRA, to his stodgier experts, who served him no better than they had served him before.

The good joke Roosevelt thought he had played on McReynolds presently became a bad joke on the New Deal. For four years, members of Congress had accepted White House leadership with growing reluctance. During the first hundred days, Republicans and Democrats welcomed any sort of action, but the initiative had passed so completely from the legislative to the executive branch of government that even Democratic Congressmen became resentful. The personal triumph that Roosevelt won in the 1936 election intensified the Congressional inferiority complex, and when the President, two weeks after his second inaugural, revealed his plan for reforming the Supreme Court as a finished product, a revolt at once developed within his own Party. The Republicans welcomed their first break since 1928 and shrewdly let Senator Burton K. Wheeler of Montana lead the opposition. Wheeler, who came originally from Massachusetts, got his political start through Senator Thomas J. Walsh, also of Montana, with whom he helped expose the Teapot Dome scandals. In 1924, Wheeler ran for the Vice-Presidency with LaFollette on the Progressive ticket. Thus Wheeler entered the fight against the "Supreme Court Packing Bill," as the opposition called it, with a longer and cleaner progressive record than many of its defenders. Nor was he the only man with such a record to take such a stand. Justice Brandeis opposed the President.

The press had a field day. Bar associations, business groups, and newly organized committees passed resolutions and issued statements denouncing the bill. To judge from the front pages and editorial columns of most newspapers, Roosevelt's proposal to reform the Supreme Court had given rise to the greatest demonstration of mass protest since the fight against Prohibition, but few evidences of this fight could be discovered in the daily lives of the American people. Not one American in a hundred tried to grasp the legal and constitutional issues. The opposition put on a better show than the defense, partly because Roosevelt picked colorless, conservative Senator Joe T. Robinson of Arkansas, Smith's running mate in 1928, to lead the fight; partly because the supporters of the bill hardly knew what they were backing whereas the attackers knew exactly what they were fighting.

The fight helped kill Robinson, who died of a heart attack before the bill could come to a vote. Yet Roosevelt finally got what he wanted, and perhaps he chose the only practical course. Finley Peter Dunne's "Mr. Dooley" had coined the memorable phrase, "The Supreme Court follows the election returns," and once again the Supreme Court did just that. In March, 1937, the Court suddenly began reversing itself on the New Deal. Justice Roberts and Chief Justice Hughes found merits they had not discerned before in New Deal legislation. The same Supreme Court that had forbidden the State of New York to pass a minimum wage law permitted the State of Washington to do so. The same Supreme Court that had voided the NIRA approved the Wagner Labor Relations Act, which not only authorized collective bargaining but set up a National Labor Relations Board to enforce it. It may be that the Supreme Court would have reversed itself anyway in the light of the election returns. But, in the opinion of many, Roosevelt's "packing bill" forced the issue.

It was Roosevelt, not his enemies, who paid the highest price in the end. For the Supreme Court battle created a permanent breach in the Democratic Party and forced the President to make more than one decision that weakened his leadership still further. Justice Van Devanter, one of the New Deal's chief enemies on the bench, resigned shortly after the death of Senator Robinson. Vice-President Garner then scuttled the whole Roosevelt plan as far as Congress was concerned, and the President showed his displeasure by naming Senator Hugo L. Black of Alabama, a devoted New Dealer with little legal training, to fill Van Devanter's shoes. Die-hard lawyers compared Roosevelt to the Roman Emperor Caligula, who once made his horse a consul, but the Senate followed its usual practice and automatically confirmed the appointment of one of its own members. Not until after the Senate had acted did the storm break, when a Pittsburgh newspaper published documentary proof that Black had once belonged to the Ku Klux Klan. For weeks Black kept silent, and when he did speak it was not through the newspapers but in a fifteen-minute radio broadcast. Here he cited his liberal record in both Houses of Congress and finally admitted that he had belonged to the Klan years ago, but had withdrawn soon afterward and no longer maintained any contact with it. Roosevelt's Supreme Court fight thus ended as it had begun in an atmosphere of mystery, misgiving, and mistrust.

· II ·

THE ECONOMIC as well as the political tide also turned against the President during the first year of his second term. The index of industrial production had dropped from 126 in 1929 to 58 in 1932. It stood at 59 when Roosevelt entered the White House and did not reach 100 until December, 1935. A year later it hit 121 and the brain trusters decided that they could stop financing prosperity by running an annual budget deficit of between three and four billion dollars. When the New Deal economist Leon Henderson asked what they would do to prevent the depression that would ensue, they called him a defeatist. "We planned it that way," President Roosevelt had boasted during the 1936 campaign, but during the summer of 1937 something went wrong with the plans and the planners.

Without more than half knowing what they were doing, the New Dealers had applied the theories of John Maynard Keynes, who advocated deficit spending during periods of depression, followed by high taxes to wipe out the deficit during times of prosperity. When Keynes visited the White House in 1934, Roosevelt's ignorance of economics shocked him. Nor did Henry Morgenthau, Jr., who had replaced the late William O. Woodin as Secretary of the Treasury, know much more. Morgenthau's father had served as Ambassador to Turkey under Wilson and had bought an estate at Hyde Park, near the Roosevelts. His son became a friend of the future President, studied farming at Cornell, and got in on the ground floor of the New Deal with a job in the Agriculture Department. He had no other ambition than to serve Roosevelt loyally, and he craved no higher honor than he received when the President made him Secretary of the Treasury to succeed Woodin. As crotchety Jack Garner saw it, "Wallace has crazy ideas and Morgenthau none." A conservative by temperament and training, Morgenthau distrusted deficit financing and helped to convince Roosevelt that the budget for the fiscal year ending June 30, 1938, should be balanced.

The decision proved instantly disastrous. Most of the recovery that the United States had enjoyed since 1933 came from government spending, and the moment the government began to balance intake and outgo a Roosevelt depression even sharper than the Hoover depression set in. In nine months, from August, 1937, to May, 1938, industrial production lost two thirds of all the gains it had built up in five years. Prices of common stocks plunged faster than they had plunged in 1929. United States Steel dropped from 121 to 38; General Motors from 60 to 25. Yet the steel industry had been operating close to capacity during the summer of 1937, and automobile sales in 1936 had approached the levels of 1928 and 1929. During the 1920's, competition for the consumer's dollar had forced American industry to increase its efficiency by replacing men with machines. During the 1930's, the depression intensified the competition and speeded up the rate of technological advance—and of technological unemployment. That was why, even at the height of Roosevelt's deficit spending, unemployment never dropped below ten millions. That was why most high school and college graduates had to spend months and even years finding jobs.

New Deal promises more than New Deal performance accounted for the great Democratic sweeps in the 1934 and the 1936 elections. The New Deal had not yet given security to the white-collar worker or to the laboring man. It had not yet given prosperity to the farmers, opportunity to the young people, or jobs to the unemployed. But it had given hope to millions and better living conditions to millions more. No one saw more clearly than Roosevelt how much unfinished business remained. That was why he boasted in his campaign speeches, "We have just begun to fight." That was why his second inaugural called attention to "one third of a nation ill-housed, ill-clad, ill-nourished." But could he do more than talk? Had he anything more than a new line of ballyhoo to offer? The first four years of the New Deal had done little for one third of the nation—by the President's own admission. His bill to reform the Supreme Court never even came to a vote, and meant nothing to the mass of his supporters in the first place. The first year of his second term then saw two thirds of the gains the country had made during his first term evaporate.

Attacks on the New Deal from the left proved more effective, at all levels, than attacks from the right. Senator Huey Long had backed

KEYSTONE

Huey Long

Roosevelt at Chicago in 1932, but after one conversation with him in Washington a year later, Long told Farley: "What the hell is the use in my coming down to see this fellow? I can't win any decisions over him." Long therefore extended his Share-Our-Wealth Clubs beyond Louisiana and won millions of followers among the poor whites of the South with his slogan: "Every man a King." In March, 1934, he boasted, "Two hundred and fifty-four thousand earnest men and women are now dedicated to an unrelenting fight to divide up the wealth of this Land of Plenty so that children will not starve and their parents beg for crusts." Long demanded that the federal government guarantee every American family an income of five thousand dollars a year and represented the New Dealers as tools of Wall Street:

> "*Black Sheep, Wall Street, have you any gold?*
> *Yes, sir; yes, sir; all I can hold.*
> *Thanks to the New Deal I've made a billion more*
> *And I've stuck it all away in my little chain store.*"

Long established a personal dictatorship in Louisiana based on a one-man political machine. Accused of establishing Fascism in America, Long predicted that if Fascism ever did come to the United States, it would come disguised as anti-Fascism. His movement combined political corruption, economic extortion, and social reform. He shook down private industry and used some of the proceeds to build roads, schools, and hospitals. During the summer of 1935 he also completed a book, *My First Hundred Days in the White House,* which he planned to use to promote himself into the Presidency in 1936. But before the book appeared in print, the son of one of his political opponents shot him down in public before Long's henchmen mowed down the assassin in his turn. The bad aim of Zangara spared Roosevelt's life in 1933; the good aim of Huey Long's assassin removed the one man who might well have cost Roosevelt enough votes in 1936 to assure the election of Landon.

The kind of support that Long was attracting at the time of his death suggested that Roosevelt no longer spoke for the bulk of America's forgotten millions. Early in 1933 Roosevelt had called for plans "that put their faith once more in the forgotten man at the bottom of the economic pyramid." In 1935 Louis Hacker's *Short History of the New Deal* reported: "Class antagonisms were to be charmed away by the use of the magic device of the just price, that is to say a higher price level all around." Hacker also predicted that the New Deal would have to look abroad for foreign markets and new investment opportunities, thus risking a foreign war. *The Economic Consequences of the New Deal,* by Stolberg and Vinton, concluded that the New Deal had done nothing that an earthquake could not have done more efficiently. On the other hand, James P. Warburg's *Hell Bent for Election* charged that the New Deal had slyly abandoned the Democratic Party's 1932 platform and substituted the platform of the Socialist Party instead. The Republican National Committee helped make the Warburg book a best seller, but when Election Day came around, its author voted for Roosevelt because he liked the New Deal's foreign policy.

The most engaging and persuasive piece of New Deal propaganda did not come from the idealistic left or the indignant right. It came from a lawyer-professor-politician named Thurman Arnold, whose *Folklore of Capitalism* represented most of the current theories of law, politics, and business as expressions of religious faith and described most formal discussions of such matters as religious ceremonials. Arnold repudiated the Marxian assumption that economic interest determined human behavior, preferring the view of Freud, who sought for human motives within the individual. In 1937 Arnold pointed out: "The legislative branches of the government were under constant supervision and their acts were presumed to be malevolent. The incompetency of Congress was an assumed fact everywhere. The great trouble with the legislative branches was that they were influenced by an unlearned, untheoretical, illogical, and often corrupt force called 'politics.' Politics was continually putting unworthy persons in power as opposed to business where, because of economic law, only worthy persons rose to the top. A body influenced by political considerations could not give any disinterested judgment as to the soundness of any economic theory. Hence Congress was constantly picking unsound theories, listening to unsound economists, and letting the practical convenience of the moment overweigh the needs of posterity. Politicians were the kind of people who would not care if a thing called bureaucracy were established so long as it gave them jobs."

Arnold got his inspiration from William James: whatever worked was right. The NRA and the bill to reform the Supreme Court had perhaps not "worked," in a narrow sense, but they had brought results, and their enemies had not prevailed. As a true New Dealer, Arnold offered no theory, no ideology of any kind. He tried to observe, record, and explain what people actually did, and he suspected that giving names to different kinds of human behavior added nothing to the sum of human wisdom, especially when the name became more important than the fact it described. A master of Socratic dialogue might have made Arnold look ridiculous, but not so ridiculous as he made the New Deal's orthodox and respectable critics appear. Arnold justified the New Deal with a pragmatism, even a cynicism, worthy of a successful man of business. But even Arnold remained an intellectual whose theories, however realistically presented, sometimes appeared remote from the reality they sought to describe.

Arnold made hearty fun of the arguments used against the President's Supreme Court Packing Bill, but that was one fight the President lost. Nor did the world of Thurman Arnold allow for the Roosevelt Recession, as the New Dealers called it, or for the strike crisis that came to a head as the President's second term began. Arnold ridiculed conservative businessmen when they put religious devotion to economic dogma ahead of their own self-interest. But the picket lines that labor unions threw around some of the biggest industrial plants in the country and the sit-down strikes they held inside had more than a ritualistic significance. And the employers took no less practical countermeasures.

Until the mid-1930's most labor unions in the United States had affiliated themselves with the American Federation of Labor, which organized its membership on a craft-by-craft basis. Only the coal miners, the garment workers, and the railwaymen had organized themselves by industries, and the railwaymen did not belong to the A. F. of L. but to an independent group of brotherhoods. In 1935 John L. Lewis of the United Mine Workers, Sidney Hillman of the Amalgamated Clothing Workers, and David Dubinsky of the International Ladies Garment Workers set up a group inside the A. F. of L. and called it the Committee for Industrial Organization. The following year they brought forward a plan to organize the mass-production industries, and when their colleagues voted it down, they quit the Federation, took their unions with them, and transformed the Committee for Industrial Organization into the Congress of Industrial Organizations, which proceeded to organize the unorganized and to take over some A. F. of L. unions. Lewis headed the new C.I.O., as everybody called it, and welcomed all comers to membership. When warned against Communist infiltration, Lewis inquired: "Who gets the bird, the hunter or the dog?" Nevertheless, he took care not to admit Communists to his own United Mine Workers.

The A. F. of L. lost a million members to the C.I.O. Within another year, however, it had more than made good this loss and claimed a total membership of 3,272,000 while the ranks of the C.I.O. increased to 3,750,000. Between them, the two organizations had brought more than four million American workers into labor unions—an increase of more than 100 per cent in the space of two years. The New Dealers wrote most of the history of Roosevelt's first term in the legislation they drafted and in the speeches they helped the President and others to frame. Then organized labor took over. The United Mine Workers contributed half a million dollars to the Democratic Party's campaign fund in 1936, but Lewis considered himself betrayed when the President commented, "A plague on both their houses," during the strike wave that swept the country from the close of 1936 into the first half of 1937. For forty days, from December, 1936, until the following February, 126,000 employees of the General Motors Corporation in twenty-five cities struck for recognition of their union—the C.I.O.'s United Automobile Workers of America—and for higher pay and better working conditions. In some plants they used the sit-down technique, enraging their employers by remaining at their places of work for days and even weeks on end. In Michigan, Governor Frank Murphy refused to use troops to drive strikers from General Motors property and the management finally capitulated. The intellectuals had written the New Deal laws; workers wrote strikers' songs:

> *The boss is shaking at the knees,*
> > *Parlez-vous.*
> *The boss is shaking at the knees,*
> > *Parlez-vous.*
> *The boss is shaking at the knees,*
> *He's shaking in his BVD's,*
> > *Hinky-dinky parlez-vous.*

The favorite song of the sit-down strikers ran:

> *When they tie a can to a union man,*
> > *Sit-down! Sit-down!*
> *When they give him the sack, they'll take him back,*
> > *Sit-down! Sit-down!*

> *When the speed-up comes, just twiddle your thumbs,*
> > *Sit-down! Sit-down!*
> *When the boss won't talk, don't take a walk,*
> > *Sit-down! Sit-down!*

General Motors came to terms with the strikers; Ford did not. Myron C. Taylor, chairman of the Board of United States Steel, talked quietly with John L. Lewis and agreed to recognize the C.I.O. Steel Workers Union. Tom Girdler, chairman of the board of Republic Steel, took a tougher attitude: "I won't have a contract, verbal or written, with an irresponsible, racketeering, violent Communistic body like the C.I.O.,

UNITED PRESS PHOTO

Republic Steel Strike

and until they pass a law making me do it, I'm not going to do it." The showdown took place outside Republic's South Chicago plant on Memorial Day, 1937, when police shot down and killed ten C.I.O. pickets. That was one of the few strikes the C.I.O. lost.

· III ·

IN *Since Yesterday*, Frederick Lewis Allen picked 1933 as the year when the American people finally sloughed off the twenties and moved into the new decade: "It is almost as if the people of the United States had walked backward into the depression, holding for dear life to the customs and ideals and assumptions of the time that was gone, even while these were one by one slipping out of reach; and then, in 1933, had given up their vain effort, turned about, and walked face-forward into the new world of the nineteen-thirties." If the first year of Roosevelt's first term in the White House saw the American people looking forward rather than backward, the first year of his second term witnessed the first great division among his followers. The Supreme Court crisis, the 1937 recession, and the rise of the C.I.O. led many Democrats to turn against the New Deal—and caused the New Dealers, for their part, to turn to more drastic measures. Not entirely by chance, the New Deal turned to the left at the same time that Stalin's Politburo in Moscow ordered the world-wide Communist movement to turn to the right and co-operate in Popular Fronts with liberal and progressive movements all over the world.

In the United States this meant, among other things, that Communists rode the C.I.O. wave. It did not mean that they created or directed it. They and their more numerous fellow-traveling friends did, however, insinuate themselves into important positions. No job was too dirty, too dangerous, or too dull for them. They formed factions and caucuses at union meetings, prolonged the discussions until most of their opponents had gone wearily home. They sought no private gain. They handled union funds with scrupulous honesty. But they used violence, lies, threats, blackmail against all who stood in their way. In times past, they had followed rule-or-ruin tactics. Now, however, they were content to work with other groups for the reformist objectives of the New Deal. Two issues always made them see red. They would tolerate no discrimination, no attacks against Communists. They also agitated, in season and out, for support of the foreign policy of the Soviet Union, raising funds at union meetings to aid the Spanish Loyalists, and demanding an American boycott of silk from Japan. They called Communism "Twentieth-Century Americanism."

During the first half of the 1930's when it suited Stalin's interests to follow a revolutionary line, the American Communists talked a different language, especially in the manifestoes denouncing the New Deal: "The policies of the government in Washington have one purpose, to make the workers and farmers and middle classes pay the costs of the crisis, to preserve the profits of the big capitalists at all costs, to establish Fascism, and to wage imperialist war abroad." That was the official line of the Communist Party, U.S.A., in February, 1935. Six months later, Moscow called for a Popular Front, American style, and the same Party hacks who had called Roosevelt a Fascist during most of his first term praised him as an anti-Fascist before and after his re-election.

The Communists, during the New Deal years, had little mass support. They carried some weight in the labor movement because they knew how to manipulate it. They carried more weight among young people, especially the students. They carried the most weight of all among the intellectuals. Here Earl Browder, Stalin's personal choice for Secretary of the Party, proved invaluable. John McCarten, writing in the *New Yorker*, described Browder as "a haggard little man with grizzling hair and a stubby mustache who looks as though he had just eaten something that didn't agree with him. His pinched, gray face is creased with troubled lines. His restless red-lidded eyes are set in worried pouches. There is a trace of distress in his quick, uneasy smile." Eugene Lyons, former Moscow correspondent of the United Press who had fellow-traveled with the Communists in the 1920's but broke with them in the early thirties, compiled the record on what he called "the Stalinist penetration of America" and entitled it *The Red Decade*. "In Browder," wrote

Lyons, "Stalin had found the perfect resident sales manager for one of his lesser foreign branches—too meek and ineffectual ever to set up in business on his own."

The type of American intellectual who embraced Communism during the later 1930's recognized, in the mediocre Browder, a kindred spirit. During the first half of the decade several writers of talent had turned toward Communism—hopefully, earnestly—only to discover that it did not measure up either to its professed ideals or to their own. But during the second half of the 1930's Communism, in its Popular Front phase, exercised a more potent spell over a greater number of men and women of lesser talent. Edmund Wilson and John Dos Passos had broken with the Communists before Roosevelt's first term had begun. Later, Waldo Frank and Archibald MacLeish denounced the Moscow purge trials. John Dewey headed an inquiry into the charges that the Stalin regime brought against Trotsky. But a larger number of lesser lights refused to take any public stand against any action of the Soviet government and joined United Fronts with Communists against Franco in Spain, Hitler in Germany, and Japanese aggression in China. Heywood Broun, who renounced Communism to become a Roman Catholic shortly before his death in 1940, expressed the feelings of many when he confessed in one of his syndicated columns that he did not care to argue about Russia; he simply "believed" it was going places. Lincoln Steffens, when asked to write a rational defense of the Stalin dictatorship, replied that he had given up trying to think the thing out. He just "felt" the Communists had the right idea. Dorothy Parker found in Communism the equivalent of a new religion: "There is no longer 'I,' there is 'We.' The day of the individual is dead."

A few young "proletarian" novelists enjoyed brief periods of fame among the limited company of fellow travelers. But the writers of established reputation who came at least partway to Communism during the middle-1930's did not seek fame. They had already attained that. They sought expiation. Most of them had gone through at least one divorce. Most of them had found that commercial, worldly success had not brought them the satisfaction they once anticipated. None of them accepted any religious faith—until Broun quit Communism for Catholicism. In short, American intellectuals did not accept Communism for intellectual reasons. They turned to Communism to satisfy personal emotions and to release private frustrations. In redeeming others, they hoped to save themselves.

Those who sought redemption in public knowingly joined organizations controlled or infiltrated by Communists—the American League Against War and Fascism, the National Committee for the Defense of Political Prisoners, the League of American Writers, and innumerable committees to aid Spain and China. They read the *Daily Worker* and contributed to the *New Masses*. Some took out Communist Party membership, but few cared to submit themselves to its discipline. A zealous minority operated in secret. Sometimes as Party members, sometimes as fellow travelers, they found jobs in government agencies, new and old, where they concealed their affiliations if not their sympathies, all the while taking orders from one or another small cell or apparatus, dominated by Soviet espionage agents. Years later, their methods and achievements received world-wide publicity in the trials of Alger Hiss, former State Department official, and in the autobiography of Whittaker Chambers, who served briefly as an editor of the *New Masses* before being transferred to the Communist underground in Washington. If Chambers in retrospect exaggerated the importance of his activities, few people at the time, even such bitter anti-Communists as Eugene Lyons, knew the detailed workings of the Communist conspiracy. Nor could Chambers or anyone else exaggerate the condition of mental bewilderment and moral decay on which this conspiracy thrived.

Given the atmosphere of the time, the Communists had little difficulty exploiting certain outstanding New Dealers. Eleanor Roosevelt, Harold Ickes, Leon Henderson, and Frances Perkins either spoke at meetings organized by Communists or lent their names to Communist Party fronts. Then and later, their political opponents accused them of favoring Communism, even of deliberately betraying their country. Such attacks missed the mark. Some New Dealers worked with Communists in order to show their own good faith and tolerance, while putting Communist good faith and tolerance to the test. Others learned Communist techniques of infiltration in order to fight fire with fire.

Eugene Lyons explained why, in his opinion, Mrs. Roosevelt devoted so much time to the Communist-controlled American Youth Congress: "Repeatedly the First Lady explained she was defending the right of young people to think and act for themselves, even if they were Communists. And she meant it from the bottom of her capacious heart. Unfortunately she was defending the exact opposite. In allowing herself to be used as respectable window-dressing for the organization, she was really helping the Youth bureaucracy to *prevent* the young people from thinking and acting for themselves. She was in effect lined up with the canny leaders and their secret caucuses against the mass of the members; with the political machine against the more naïve and unsuspecting religious and liberal and social affiliates. In a larger sense she was siding with the tiny organized lobby against the vast unorganized mass of young people."

Mrs. Roosevelt may have erred through excessive kindness of heart. Nobody ever accused Harold Ickes of sentimentality, yet he gave aid and comfort to the Kremlin when he wrote: "So far as the present is concerned, Fascism is the deadly and insidious foe that we must prepare to combat without loss of time. For this reason, I suspect either the motives or the intelligence of those who would have us marshal our forces against a barely imaginary danger of Communism while Fascism thunders at the gates of our citadel of liberty." The clear and present dangers of German Nazism, Italian Fascism, and Japanese militarism made Russian Communism look like the least of all possible evils, and Professor Frederick L. Schuman of Williams College expressed what many Americans, unversed in the mysteries of foreign policy, wanted to believe when he described the League of Nations as "a grand alliance of liberalism and Communism for mutual defense against Fascism." But Eugene Lyons spoke for the anti-Communist minority when he pointed out, in *The Red Decade:* "Basically it is Moscow's strategy to involve the rest of the world in a war from which it would then, itself, withdraw in high-handed and hypocritical disdain for 'imperialist squabbles.' . . . The Soviet hope, quite justifiable from the angle of Russia's own *Realpolitik,* was to set Japan and the United States at each other's throats on one side; to get Germany and the Western nations fighting on the other. But literally millions of Americans refused to see the obvious Soviet self-interest behind the thin pretense of anti-Fascist posturing."

The intellectuals did not wish to see this possibility because it shattered a neat and gratifying world image that they carried in their minds. They did not dare to see this possibility because those who questioned the wisdom and virtue of "a grand alliance of liberalism and Communism for mutual defense against Fascism" more often than not found themselves friendless and jobless. This is not to suggest that anti-Communism did not pay. The Hearst and Scripps-Howard newspapers and mass-circulation magazines always had space and funds for Red-baiters, for violent diatribes against the New Deal, and for vicious abuse of the Roosevelt family. But the fellow travelers on the left and the professional patriots on the right formed a common front against the independent leftists who attacked both Hitler and Stalin and warned against the possibility of a Nazi-Soviet pact.

Willi Schlamm, editor of the Berlin *Weltbühne,* whose Jewish ancestry and anti-Nazi opinions forced him to flee to Prague when Hitler came to power, made this prediction in 1936, a prediction that went unnoticed by American liberals and conservatives alike: "The Third Reich is marching against Europe. When and as long as Stalin's Russia opposes its march, it will be attacked. When Stalin withdraws from France and the European democracies, he can count on Hitler's tolerance. The anti-Bolshevik crusade of the Third Reich is designed to obtain not the Ukraine, but parts of western and central Europe and colonies; it is designed to break not Stalin's regime, but the Franco-Soviet military alliance. It won't take long, and the Führers will conclude a realistic nonaggression pact. The one will guarantee Stalin's nationalistic states, the other will leave Europe to a Hitler fate." The next year General Walter G. Krivitsky, former Soviet chief of West European espionage, quoted Stalin as having said, "We must come to an understanding with the Germans." Krivitsky himself added: "The *rapprochement* with France was viewed by Stalin as a means of strengthening his position in the expected negotiations with Hitler, who was given to understand, officially and unofficially, that Stalin is very much in earnest about a Nazi-Soviet deal."

Thanks to "the Stalinist penetration of America," General Krivitsky's views counted for least with those New Dealers who regarded themselves as experts in his field. Nor could those who took Krivitsky seriously hope to make any headway. For Krivitsky dealt with facts and ideas; the fellow travelers dealt with fears and hopes. Those who questioned the wisdom of "a grand alliance of liberalism and Communism for mutual defense against Fascism" rested their case on reason and logic. The fellow travelers appealed to emotion and interest. It was an appeal that only an intellectual of the first order could resist.

· IV ·

YET Eugene Lyons overstated his case when he spoke of the treason of the intellectuals—*le trahison des clercs,* as the French philosopher Julien Benda once called it. Actually, few if any American intellectuals of the first rank worked long or closely with the Communist movement. America produced no outstanding Communist pamphleteer, like England's John Strachey; no outstanding Communist novelist, like André Malraux in France. The half-dozen or so outstanding American writers who had affiliated themselves with Communism during the early 1930's soon fell away. The most talented and influential men and women of letters steered clear of Communism and Communists throughout the decade.

They did not steer clear of the material that the Communists entreated their fellow travelers to exploit. American literature in the thirties mirrored American life no less accurately than it had in the twenties. Realism gave way to journalism. John Dos Passos, in *Manhattan Transfer,* had experimented with the stream-of-consciousness technique made famous by James Joyce. In his massive trilogy, *U.S.A.,* Dos Passos used the skills he had developed during the 1920's to present a novelist's interpretation of twentieth-century America from the turn of the century to the Wall Street crash. "U.S.A. is the slice of a continent," he wrote. "U.S.A. is a group of holding companies, some aggregations of trade unions, a set of laws bound in calf, a radio network, a chain of moving picture theaters, a column of stock quotations rubbed out and written in by a Western Union boy on a blackboard, a public library full of old newspapers and dog-eared history books with protests scrawled on the margins in pencil. U.S.A. is the world's greatest river valley fringed with mountains and hills. U.S.A. is a set of big-mouthed officials with too many bank accounts. U.S.A. is a lot of men buried in their uniforms in Arlington cemetery. U.S.A. is the letters from the end of an address when you are away from home. But mostly U.S.A. is the speech of the people."

James T. Farrell wrote another trilogy, *Studs Lonigan,* dealing with the partial rise and complete decline of an Irish-American family on Chicago's South Side. Like Dos Passos, Farrell established brief contact with the Communist movement during the early 1930's. He broke more sharply than Dos Passos and showed some sympathy for Trotsky's views. Dos Passos, ten years Farrell's senior, later turned more and more toward Jeffersonian liberalism and became increasingly skeptical of the New Deal. Farrell could never regard the New Deal as anything more than a mildly reformed capitalism, and his novels, which tended to repeat themselves, gave a consistently critical and radical interpretation of lower-middle-class American life. Throughout the thirties, Farrell played a lone, courageous hand. His occasional critical essays and his conversation contained more wit and humor than his novels, which never broke away from the prewar naturalist tradition.

Erskine Caldwell plumbed lower depths than Farrell and made a much greater financial and popular success. *God's Little Acre* and *Tobacco Road* depicted the poorest whites of Caldwell's native Georgia. On the stage, *Tobacco Road* became the hit of the decade, but its appeal rested on the humorous obscenities of its hero, Jeeter Lester, rather than on its author's social philosophy. Caldwell stressed the impact of industrialization on Georgia and the Carolinas, and a strong current of sex ran through all his work: "The men who worked in the mill looked tired and worn, but the girls were in love with the looms and the spindles and the flying lint. The wild-eyed girls on the inside of the ivy-walled mill looked like potted plants in bloom. Up and down the Valley lay the company towns and the ivy-walled cotton mills and the firm-bodied girls with eyes like morning glories, and the men stood on the hot streets looking at each other while they spat their lungs into the deep yellow dust of Carolina."

The South produced more than its share of the literature of the 1930's, and neither of its two outstanding writers cultivated the journalistic realism of social protest that characterized most American writing during the period. Thomas Wolfe, like Walt Whitman, celebrated himself.

Look Homeward, Angel appeared in 1929. *Of Time and the River* and *The Web and the Rock* followed, but Wolfe himself did not outlive the decade of the thirties, dying of a brain tumor. It seemed as though even his vast six-foot-six frame could not contain the passions that possessed it. His writing followed his own laws and necessities: "For what are we, my brother? We are a phantom flare of grieved desire, the ghostling and phosphoric flickers of immortal time, a brevity of days haunted by the eternity of the earth. We are an unspeakable utterance, an insatiable hunger, an unquenchable thirst; a lust that bursts our sinews, explodes our brains, sickens and rots our guts, and rips our hearts asunder. We are a twist of passion, a moment's flare of love and ecstasy, a sinew of bright blood and agony, a lost cry, a music of pain and joy, a haunting of brief, sharp hours, an almost captured beauty, a demon's whisper of unbodied memory. We are the dupes of time."

William Faulkner of Mississippi, a few years older than Wolfe, had flown in the war for Britain's Royal Air Force and written an unremarked bitter novel during the 1920's, *Soldier's Pay*. Then in 1930 came *As I Lay Dying*, followed by *Sanctuary, Light in August, Pylon, The Unvanquished*. "The themes look unbelievable stated in bald summary," wrote Halford E. Luccock in *American Mirror*, a study of American literature during the 1930's. "*As I Lay Dying* tells the story of hauling a corpse for nine days in midsummer heat; *Sanctuary* chronicles the journey of a young girl and her escort, searching for liquor, with the rape of the girl by a pervert named Popeye as the central figure, and the addition of a lynching and an execution, and a devil's chorus of prostitutes and imbeciles. *Light in August* features a murder and a lynching. *Pylon* is a little lighter, its high spot being a group of aviators with a common wife and a child of uncertain parentage. *The Unvanquished* has some variety by way of nailing up the corpse of a murderer on a door, and setting up his amputated hand on the victim's grave." Faulkner explained that he "invented the most horrific tales I could imagine" as "the right answer to current trends."

In 1938 all of Faulkner's books had not sold sixty thousand copies. By that same year, the sales of a single book by another Southern novelist sold three million copies. Margaret Mitchell's *Gone With the Wind* was the most popular novel of the decade and became one of the greatest motion picture hits as well. Faulkner and Caldwell presented the seamiest sides and the grisliest insides of the modern South. Margaret Mitchell went back to the Civil War and Reconstruction period and wrote a romantic novel of universal appeal. She never wrote another book before or since, and there is every reason to believe that *Gone With the Wind* would have proved a best seller in any decade and will remain a classic of sorts. It did not, however, tell so much about the thirties and the tastes of the time as several other best sellers: *Anthony Adverse,* by Hervey Allen, *Northwest Passage,* by Kenneth Roberts, and a slew of nonfiction, self-help books, led by Dale Carnegie's *How to Win Friends and Influence People,* the second best-selling book of the period. Allen and Roberts offered their readers escape into the past. Dale Carnegie, Walter Pitkin, Dorothea Brande, Marjorie Hillis, offered them solutions of their personal problems. The steady sale of books that told their readers that "life begins at forty," to "wake up and live," and to "live alone and like it" indicated widespread bewilderment and anxiety.

But all the self-help best sellers did not minister only to practical needs. Lin Yutang's *Importance of Living* showed that Americans in the thirties responded to China's philosophic wisdom. Nor did all the best-selling fiction offer romantic escape. George Santayana turned from philosophy to fiction and *The Last Puritan: A Memoir in the Form of a Novel* made a surprising success. John Marquand turned from his popular "Mr. Moto" series to social satire in *The Late George Apley: A Novel in the Form of a Memoir.* Both Santayana and Marquand dealt with Boston, the only American city with a distinctive culture and an established set of values. They wrote with irony, affection, and maturity, thereby suggesting that the American reading public may have been ready for more adult ideas and emotions than many American authors offered.

Nevertheless, it was journalism that distinguished American literature of the 1930's from the literature of other decades. Lincoln Steffens' two-volume autobiography started the vogue. Here the leading prewar muck-raker explained why reform was not enough; why "the system," as he called it, had to be rebuilt from the ground up. Steffens never lost the faith that he found in Russia during two visits there, but the American Communists never quite regarded him as one of their own. Vincent Sheean spoke for a new generation in *Personal History,* written while still in his mid-thirties and recounting his experiences as a foreign correspondent, especially during the Chinese Revolution. Later, in *Not Peace But the Sword,* he continued the story through the Spanish Civil War. Other newspapermen won comparable successes: Negley Farson in *The Way of a Transgressor,* Webb Miller in *I Found No Peace,* Frazier Hunt in *One American.* John Gunther turned fifteen years of personal experience to account in *Inside Europe,* which he followed up with *Inside Asia.* He emphasized personalities and went along with most of his colleagues, who shared his faith in the possibilities of collaboration between the Soviet Union and the democracies.

The thirties ended with the appearance of two significant works of journalistic fiction: Ernest Hemingway's *For Whom the Bell Tolls* and

John Steinbeck's *Grapes of Wrath.* Hemingway won acclaim during the
1920's with *In Our Time,* a book of short stories; *The Sun Also Rises,* an
autobiographical picture of the lost generation of American expatriates
in Europe; and *A Farewell to Arms,* a romantic novel of love and war.
During the early thirties, however, he suffered even more than most of
his literary compatriots from arrested development. While Sinclair Lewis
wrote and rewrote the same satirical comedy of American middle-class
manners, Hemingway lavished his rarer gifts on the narrower field of
his own search for pure sensation.

Most Americans during the 1930's were long on ideology and short
on style. With Hemingway it was the other way around. He had no
ideology except action for its own sake and the kind of action he esteemed most highly was writing. He therefore made few ideological
enemies in the literary world while inspiring a host of eager imitators.
He continued to produce admirable if monotonous short stories of the
hard-boiled school, but it was not until he quit literature for journalism
and covered the Spanish Civil War for a newspaper syndicate that he
found inspiration to write a panoramic war novel in the grand manner.
For Whom the Bell Tolls had an American hero, and the story concerns
the last few days of his life. First, he discovers love in the arms of the
Spanish girl, Maria; then he goes to his death for a cause in which he
believes.

Hemingway dealt with Spain at war; Steinbeck dealt with the United
States at peace. The New Deal had not driven the money-changers from
the temple or rescued the forgotten man, and during the mid-1930's a
succession of dust storms in the Southwest sent three hundred thousand
farmers from the State of Oklahoma to California. Steinbeck had already
written several novels—notably *In Dubious Battle,* the best account anyone turned in of a Communist-led strike. The dust-bowl tragedy stirred
his sympathy and he spent months among its victims. *Grapes of Wrath*
tells their story. Hollywood made it into an honest movie and the Joad
family whose adventures Steinbeck related became so celebrated that
Roosevelt referred to them in one of his radio fireside talks, and Hitler accepted Steinbeck's "Okies" as typical Americans. "You never been called
'Okie' yet?" a returning wanderer asks the Joads. " 'Okie' used to mean
you was from Oklahoma. Now it means you're scum. Don't mean nothin'
itself; it's the way they say it. But I can't tell you nothin'. You got to go
there. I hear there's three hundred thousan' of our people there—an' livin'
like hogs 'cause ever'thing in California is owned. They ain't nothing left.
And them people that owns it is gonna hang on to it if they got to kill
ever'body in the worl' to do it. An' they're scairt an' that makes 'em mad.
You got to see it. You got to hear it. Purtiest goddam country you ever

seen, but they ain't nice to you, them folks. They're so scairt an' worried they ain't even nice to each other."

Only a camp for transients, operated by the federal government, showed the Joads any humanity. Otherwise, the New Deal had done little about their plight: "Burn coffee for fuel in the ships. Burn corn to keep warm, it makes a hot fire. Dump potatoes in the river and place guards along the bank to keep the hungry people from fishing them out. Slaughter the pigs and bury them and let the putrescence drop down into the earth.

"There is a crime here that goes beyond denunciation. There is a sorrow here that weeping cannot symbolize. There is a failure here that topples all our success. The fertile earth, the straight tree rows, the sturdy trunks, and the ripe fruit. And children dying of pellagra must die because a profit cannot be taken from an orange. And coroners must fill in the certificates—died of malnutrition—because the food must rot, must be forced to rot.

"The people come with nets to fish for potatoes in the river and the guards hold them back; they come in rattling cars to get the dumped oranges but the kerosene is sprayed. And they stand still and watch the potatoes float by, listen to the screaming pigs being killed in a ditch and covered with quicklime, watch the mountains of oranges slop down to a putrefying ooze; and in the eyes of the people there is a failure, and in the eyes of the hungry there is a growing wrath. In the souls of the people the grapes of wrath are filling and growing heavy, growing heavy for the vintage."

The journalism of Steinbeck and Hemingway sometimes turned into poetry. The poets of the time turned to journalism. The thirties produced no new talent as striking as that of E. E. Cummings, but Kenneth Patchen and Kenneth Fearing used the same trick of writing free verse in slang that Cummings originated. But where Cummings made ironic commentaries on life, these younger men offered a more political message. Kenneth Patchen's *Before the Brave* contains this "Letter to a Politician in Kansas City":

> *"I'm not too starved to want food*
> *not too homeless to want a home not*
> *   too dumb*
> *to answer questions come to think of it*
> *   it'll take a hell*
> *of a lot more than you've got to stop*
> *   what's*
> *going on deep inside of us when it starts*
> *   out*

when it starts wheels going worlds
growing
and any man can live on earth when
we're through with it."

Archibald MacLeish, the most popular and representative poet of the thirties, had played on the Yale football team, fought as an officer in the war, attended Harvard Law School, and begun what promised to become a lucrative and distinguished career at the Boston bar. But in the middle 1920's he put conventional success behind him and went to Paris with his wife and family to write poetry. He began with derivative, experimental verse that appeared in little magazines, but soon found himself more at home with more conventional forms. He returned to the United States and in the early 1930's joined the staff of *Fortune*, which Henry Luce had founded in 1929 to serve as the mouthpiece for enlightened big business. Having quit the slavery of the law for the freedom of the poet's life, MacLeish turned once more against himself and denounced the futility of the ivory tower poet. "Unless," he wrote in 1931, "we can not only perceive, but also feel, the race of men to be more important than any one man, we are merely fighting back against the water." His early volumes of verse bore such titles as *Streets of the Moon, The Hamlet of A. MacLeish.* In 1935 he wrote *Public Speech,* which contained these representative lines:

"Brotherhood! No word said can make you brothers!
Brotherhood only the brave earn and by danger or
By harm or by being hurt and by no other.

Brotherhood here in the strange world is the rich and
Rarest giving of life and the most valued:
Not to be had for a word or a week's wishing."

Neither books nor magazines reached the mass audience for whom MacLeish believed he had a message. He therefore turned to the radio, for which he wrote two plays—*The Fall of the City* and *Air Raid.* "Politics," MacLeish decided, "is a subject for poetry because with us the public world has become the private world. The single individual, whether he wishes so or not, has become part of a world that contains also Austria and Czechoslovakia and China and Spain." The significance of MacLeish's discovery was not that the individual, prior to 1935, could "live alone and like it"—as the title of Marjorie Hillis's best seller assured worried spinsters. The significance of MacLeish's discovery was his conviction that he had come upon a new truth—or at least found himself in an unprecedented condition. John Donne's lines from which

Hemingway drew the title of his novel about the Spanish Civil War should have reminded MacLeish and other members of his generation that the gregarious instinct in human nature manifested itself before Roosevelt's time, or even Wilson's: "No man is an *Iland,* intire of it selfe; every man is a peece of the Continent, a part of the *maine;* if a *Clod* bee washed away by the *Sea, Europe* is the lesse, as well as if a *Promintorie* were, as well as if a *Mannor* of thy *friends* or of *thine owne* were; any mans *death* diminishes *me,* because I am involved in *Mankinde;* And therefore never send to know for whom the *bell* tolls; It tolls for *thee.*"

· V ·

FEW Americans needed to read John Donne to discover their involvement with mankind. The radio and the movies told them that. The automobile brought the city dweller to the country and the country dweller to the city. The radio brought the whole world into every American home. When the Duke of Windsor broadcast his abdication message at the end of an American business day, millions of office workers stayed overtime to hear him speak. A still larger audience heard the same message rebroadcast later that same evening. Roosevelt was the first President to discover and exploit the full possibilities of radio in his fireside chats. Father Coughlin, the radio priest, attracted listeners by the millions where Bryan had numbered his largest audiences in the tens of thousands. During the 1930's the radio made its greatest advance in its coverage of news and special events, its programs of good music and serious discussion and debate.

While railroads purchased bus lines, newspapers purchased radio stations. Radio advertising steadily increased throughout the 1930's, and while the number of radio stations increased, the number of newspapers declined. But the newspapers that survived owned more than one quarter of all the radio stations in the country. An irresistible trend toward monopoly ran through all the mass-communication industries, and in radio the larger networks almost invariably provided superior service. They had the money to buy the best talents and the facilities to broadcast their programs to the widest audiences. It was the same story in the newspaper, the magazine, and the motion picture field. The growth of the mass-communication industries steadily raised the intellectual and aesthetic standards of the American people. The phonograph did not eliminate the piano any more than the radio eliminated the phonograph. The number of symphony orchestras in the United States increased from seventeen in 1915 to over two hundred in the thirties. More than ten million Americans listened to radio symphonies every weekend.

The weakness of the mass-communication industries lay in their refusal to experiment, their tendency to play everything safe. They at-- tracted large audiences—and of course Bing Crosby attracted more listeners than Toscanini; Jack Benny was more popular than America's Town Meeting of the Air. But all the mass-communication industries ignored large potential audiences; they appealed to certain known sec- tors of the entire public—high-brow, low-brow, middle-brow; they did little to encourage new talent. As a result the lively arts that Gilbert Seldes praised in the early 1920's languished. In 1950 he wrote *The Great Audience,* a sad sequel to his earlier book, concluding that the movies and the radio had become so conventionalized that they could not hope to produce the kind of talent that appeared in such profusion during the first three decades of the century. The audiences of the 1930's saw no new Al Jolson, Ed Wynn, Charlie Chaplin, Fannie Brice, W. C. Fields, Fred Allen, or Will Rogers. Most of the great comedians who still domi- nated the radio and the movies got their start in old-time vaudeville and burlesque, which the movies had driven out of business. But the new fields of entertainment cultivated little new talent. Nor did the 1930's produce any new popular song writer comparable to Irving Berlin, George Gershwin, Jerome Kern, Cole Porter, and Richard Rodgers.

Developments in the movies paralleled developments in radio. The explorer Robert J. Flaherty fathered the documentary film when he photographed *Nanook of the North* in northern Canada in the early 1920's. But it remained for the *Time* organization to develop a style and find an audience when it pioneered the "March of Time" newsreel. Pare Lorentz, former movie critic for *Judge,* also made two outstanding con- tributions in *The Plow That Broke the Plains* and *The River,* both pro- duced under the auspices of the Federal Resettlement Administration. But most Americans went to the movies for entertainment and the in- dustry made little effort to give them anything else. Sound pictures raised the standards of writing and acting far above the level of the twenties, but the motion picture industry set its sights more and more on the adolescent audience and the great hopes of D. W. Griffith never came true. The flame of Charlie Chaplin's genius still burned. *City Lights,* in 1931, told the story of a blind flower-girl whose sight Chaplin saves only to lose her love when she sees her comical benefactor. *Modern Times,* in 1936, satirized mass production. Chaplin still played the same character he had made famous in the silent picture days, and still con- fined himself to pantomime. The sound track gave forth only music and sound effects. Walt Disney made the most original new contribu- tion to the art of the motion picture with his animated cartoons. The *Three Little Pigs* with their song of the big, bad wolf exactly suited the popular mood in the year of its release—1933.

Each in its own way, the radio and the motion picture broke down the rugged individualism that Hoover had tried to glorify and restore. Throughout the 1930's the American people drew closer together, losing in the process their old-fashioned spirit of independence and self-reliance. But it was not the New Deal that made for uniformity. Neither was it big business. The size of the United States, the number of its inhabitants, the speed of its transport system, the economies of mass production, mass consumption, and mass distribution all stimulated a standardized, uniform way of life. The radio and motion picture industries produced entertainment and instruction for the masses as other industries produced automobiles and chewing gum. A few large movie companies owned or controlled most of the theaters that displayed their products. Four radio networks owned or controlled most of the best radio stations. Competition existed among the few large motion picture companies and the four big radio networks. The motion picture and radio industries also competed against each other for the public's time. And, like the leaders of other competitive industries, radio and motion picture men tried to give the largest possible number of people the best possible product at the lowest possible price.

The bigger the radio and motion picture industries grew, the more careful they had to be not to offend any substantial part of the mass public to which they catered. Fewer and bigger newspapers presented increasingly innocuous editorials, except on the subject of Roosevelt. The radio, more responsive to public taste, gave the New Deal a better break. But radio had no ideology. Neither did the motion picture industry, the press, or big business generally. During the 1936 campaign most big businessmen backed the Liberty League in order to save American freedom from New Deal tyranny. But these same businessmen had praised the NRA because it promised to save them from "cutthroat" competition. It was not government intervention that big business feared. It was government intervention by New Dealers.

Russia had a Five-Year Plan. The New Dealers said the United States also needed a plan. In the eyes of certain businessmen, this made the New Dealers indistinguishable from Communists. But the New Dealers had no more ideology than the businessmen. The New Deal had no more in common with Communism than big business had with Fascism. All that either the New Deal or big business ever wanted to do was make the American system function more efficiently, and the New Dealers did not make quite such a mess of things during the 1930's as big business did during the 1920's. And many of the mistakes big business made during the 1920's went back to the contempt and fear that men of intellect and talent inspired in the business community. By the same token, the New Deal gave the United States new leadership because it enlisted precisely those men of intellect and talent whom big business had spurned.

Here lay the secret of the New Deal's strength and its essential difference from the Harding-Coolidge-Hoover era. Under the Republicans, most of the ablest young Americans sought careers in private business. Under the New Deal, the power of the bureaucrat began to rival the power of the businessman. The bureaucrat had not displaced the businessman. The bureaucrat had moved into a new kind of job that the depression created. In certain directions, Roosevelt allowed these bureaucrats the widest latitude, and nothing he did reflected greater credit on his imagination and sympathy than the help that the Works Progress Administration gave to unemployed writers, artists, actors, and musicians. Roosevelt did not share Wilson's bookish tastes; he cared even less for the arts. Nevertheless he tried to conserve America's intellectual and artistic resources as he tried to conserve its natural resources and made it possible for government funds to finance a great variety of literary, musical, theatrical, and artistic projects. A Federal Writers' Project produced a series of regional guidebooks that filled a need no commercial publisher could afford to meet. The WPA also produced plays and concerts in dozens of cities, bringing the theater to audiences of moderate means and music to localities that had not heard a live orchestra in half a dozen years. Painters and sculptors contributed to the beauty of the new public buildings that the WPA was financing throughout the country. The beneficiaries of the WPA's cultural projects included few geniuses but they worked under intelligent direction and their contributions more than measured up to professional, commercial standards.

· VI ·

From the advertising industry, in the heart of the enemy camp, came a technique that guided Roosevelt throughout his White House years. Young Dr. George Gallup of the University of Iowa persuaded the Young and Rubicam advertising agency in New York to poll carefully chosen cross-sections of the public concerning their opinions of certain advertised products. The results proved so successful that Dr. Gallup presently set up the American Institute of Public Opinion to apply the same sampling technique to matters of public interest. By polling cross-sections of the American people, Dr. Gallup announced, weeks before the 1936 Presidential election, that Roosevelt would carry every state except Maine, Vermont, and New Hampshire. At the same time the *Literary Digest* polled millions of telephone subscribers and automobile owners and predicted a Landon landslide. Gallup's prediction not only came close to the mark. He took time out to poll a small cross-section of the group on which the *Digest* concentrated and correctly predicted the *Digest*'s prediction. A few months after the election, the *Literary Digest* suspended publication.

Having called the turn on many elections, local as well as national, Gallup went on to poll public opinion on other matters that never came to a popular vote. Alarmists warned against government by Gallup poll. It was bad enough having Gallup predict election returns and thus perhaps swell the band-wagon vote. It was still worse having Gallup influence day-by-day decisions of Congress and the President by conducting polls on so many subjects. For Roosevelt always followed Gallup carefully. How could he lead the people if he did not know where they wanted to go? In the domestic field, the polls showed that the people wanted to go where Roosevelt was going, but in the foreign field they told a different story. During the Spanish Civil War, for instance, a growing majority favored the Loyalists and wanted to sell them arms. But Roosevelt knew that the anti-Loyalist minority packed a heavier political punch because most of them supported Franco for religious reasons. He not only kept hands off the conflict but sponsored a bill passed by Congress banning munitions shipments to both sides.

Roosevelt's Far Eastern policy and his quarantine speech stirred even wider opposition. Although Japan's attack on China violated America's historic Open Door policy as well as the more specific and more recent Nine-Power Treaties, the Gallup poll showed a majority of Americans favoring complete withdrawal from China. Roosevelt never questioned Gallup's figures, even when he disagreed with the views that the majority held. Nor did he expect his speech of October 5, 1937, calling for a quarantine of aggressor nations to change the popular mind overnight. But he did feel let down, two months later, when the sinking of the *Panay* led even more Americans to favor pulling out of the Far East.

In 1937 Gallup polls repeatedly showed more than 70 per cent of the American people expressing the view that the United States had made a mistake in declaring war on Germany in 1917. In 1935 the Book-of-the-Month Club had distributed Walter Millis's *Road to War* to more than a hundred thousand members, followed by H. C. Engelbrecht's and F. C. Hanighen's *Merchants of Death*. The Millis book gave an ironical, witty account of America's involvement in the war, representing Bryan as the defeated hero of the piece and Wilson as the duped villain. The Engelbrecht-Hanighen book stressed the part that munitions makers had played in fomenting war in 1914 and trying to make more trouble in later years.

These books and others told the American people what they wanted to hear. It was part of the truth, a new part, but not the whole truth.

The war propagandists between 1914 and 1917 had oversold the American people so heavily that a reaction set in. Revisionist historians indicated that Serbia, Austria, and Russia bore a greater responsibility than Germany for the outbreak of hostilities. They stressed the illegal British blockade of Germany as well as the illegal German blockade of Britain. Roosevelt had to fight this trend. In spite of his personal popularity and the support that the New Deal commanded, the decisions he made in foreign policy excited suspicion. Unhappy memories of the way Wilson used his broad, wartime powers made Roosevelt suspect when he attempted to regain those powers himself.

Roosevelt stilled these suspicions by promoting a foreign policy that seemed, at first, to have little in common with Wilson's. His sabotage of the World Economic Conference at London during the summer of 1933 dazed the internationalists, but his quick adoption of the Good Neighbor policy in Latin America won general support. Under Roosevelt's leadership, the United States abrogated the Platt Amendment, which sanctioned intervention in Cuba's internal affairs. The last United States troops left Haiti; the last United States Marines left Nicaragua. After the 1936 election Roosevelt and Hull journeyed by battleship to Buenos Aires to attend an Inter-American Conference for the Maintenance of Peace. It resulted in a declaration of solidarity by all the American republics. The prestige of the United States stood as high in Latin America as Roosevelt's prestige stood in the United States. Throughout the American republics, Roosevelt became the embodiment of the Good Neighbor who had superseded the Colossus of the North.

The Republicans endorsed the Good Neighbor policy. Many of them also voted for the bill that provided for Philippine independence, having already passed an earlier measure of the same kind over a Hoover veto. In 1934 Hull's cup of happiness overflowed when Congress approved his reciprocal tariff program under which the United States agreed to cut its tariff rates as much as 50 per cent to those nations that extended similar treatment. From the days of McKinley and Taft and on into the Harding-Coolidge-Hoover era, lowering the tariff seemed to many Republicans like lowering the flag. To Hull, on the other hand, high tariffs seemed a dangerous anachronism in twentieth-century America. But Cordell Hull's free-trade world had little more reality than the Old Guard Republican's world of the protective tariff. The Germans were staking out a self-contained living space for themselves in eastern and central Europe. The British were attempting to make their Empire self-sufficient. Russia had set out to build socialism in one country. Yet Hull still hoped for freer trade in all directions. The Old Guard assumed that American manufacturers could flood the world with their goods as long as American tariffs remained high enough to prevent any foreigners

from selling their wares to the United States. Most Americans preferred
Hull's approach to the approach of the Old Guard.

Roosevelt's friendliness toward Latin America, his generosity toward
the Philippines, and Hull's high-minded devotion to free trade enlisted
wide popular support. But the good will Roosevelt and Hull built up in
these directions did not always overbalance the suspicions that their
attitude toward neutrality aroused. Under the Hoover administration,
a former night-club proprietor named William B. Shearer had caused
an international commotion when he sued a group of American shipbuilding companies for the services he had rendered them at the Geneva
Arms Limitation Conference of 1927. Shearer had delivered speeches,
written pamphlets, and issued news releases attacking naval disarmament. Summoned before the Senate Naval Affairs Committee, he proudly
admitted to having beaten his "big bass drum" for a big Navy. The more
reputable Navy League issued more reputable propaganda, but Hoover's support of disarmament and Roosevelt's enthusiasm for sea power
led some of the shipbuilders to contribute to the 1932 Democratic campaign chest. And, during his first year in the White House, Roosevelt
began allocating WPA funds to naval construction and having the Navy
built up to treaty strength as fast as possible.

It was under these conditions that an exceptionally strong Senate
committee, headed by Gerald P. Nye, Progressive Republican from
North Dakota, and including Arthur H. Vandenberg of Michigan, Bennett C. Clark of Missouri, and Walter F. George of Georgia started an investigation of the munitions industry in April, 1934. They brought out a
great amount of miscellaneous information, revealing connections between bankers, industrialists, and politicians in wartime. Actually, the
Nye Committee revealed little that Millis, Engelbrecht, and Hanighen
had not already published in book form, but the investigation made a
powerful public impact. In January, 1935, the Senate voted once again
not to join the World Court and later that year Congress passed a stopgap Neutrality Act banning all loans and arms shipments to belligerents
in case of war and replacing the old concept of freedom of the seas with
the new concept of neutrality at any price.

Admiral William S. Sims, who had directed American sea power in
the war against Germany, lent the weight of his name to the neutrality
cause. "The whole point of the business is this," he declared in a broadcast in May, 1935. "We cannot keep out of war and at the same time
enforce the freedom of the sea—that is, the freedom to make profits out
of countries engaged in a death struggle. If a war arises we must therefore choose between two courses: between great profits with grave risks
of war, on the one hand; or smaller profits and less risk on the other.
When I say 'we' I mean not only the traders themselves but all of us,

for practically our whole population benefited by this wartime trade— though we did not understand we were inviting disaster for ourselves and for the world." These views won wide support, and because the Nye investigation had shown Wilson and the men around him bowing to British and Wall Street pressure, Congress required the President to enforce its kind of neutrality in all war situations automatically and at once.

By 1937, however, Roosevelt maneuvered Congress into reversing itself. He and the State Department had already cut some ground out from under the Nye Committee by denying its investigators all the information they wanted in connection with Anglo-American wartime relations. And all the while Roosevelt was making statements that reassured the advocates of peace by neutrality. In October, 1935, he told a San Diego audience: "Despite what happens in continents overseas, the United States of America shall and must remain as the Father of our Country prayed that it might remain—unentangled and free. . . . We not only earnestly desire peace, but we are moved by a stern determination to avoid those perils that will endanger our peace with the world." A year later, at William J. Bryan's beloved Chautauqua, the President committed himself more clearly and specifically: "We shun political commitments which might entangle us in foreign wars; we avoid connection with the political activities of the League of Nations; but I am glad to say we have co-operated wholeheartedly in the social and humanitarian work at Geneva." He warned that if war should break out "we would find in this country thousands of Americans who, seeking immediate riches—fool's gold—would attempt to evade and break down our neutrality." He followed this virtual endorsement of the Merchants of Death theory of war with a combined plea and pledge in behalf of neutrality: "We can keep out of war if those who watch and decide have a sufficiently detached understanding of international affairs to make certain that the small decisions of each day do not lead toward war and if, at the same time, they possess the courage to say 'no' to those who selfishly or unwisely would let us go to war."

The Senators who had worked on the munitions investigation feared that the President's actions might not entirely square with his words, but the general public and most of the rest of the Senate took his assurances at face value, choosing to ignore certain qualifying statements: "We are not isolationists except in so far as we seek to isolate ourselves completely from war. Yet we must remember that so long as war exists on earth, there will be some danger that even the nation which most ardently desires peace may be drawn into war."

Roosevelt had promised and performed so much at home that his reassurances on matters of foreign policy carried weight. No organized public pressure materialized in behalf of any specific neutrality program, and Roosevelt asked Bernard M. Baruch for expert advice. The man who headed America's industrial mobilization under Wilson proposed what he called a "cash-and-carry" system under which nations at war could buy munitions in the United States provided they paid cash on the line and transported them in their own vessels at their own risk. Congress then wrote the cash-and-carry procedure into a new and permanent Neutrality Act, passed in May, 1937, and signed with casual misgiving by the President. The heart of the permanent Neutrality Act, the feature that distinguished it from the earlier stopgap measures, was that it gave the President sole power to decide when a state of war existed anywhere in the world and sole power to determine which belligerents could take advantage of the cash-and-carry system and which could not.

John Bassett Moore, who knew as much about international law as any living American, wrote at the time: "No one who asked unlimited power to make war could ask for more than the authority, in his own discretion, to impose and revoke, and to modify and adjust embargoes on our foreign commerce. . . . To commit to the executive the power in his discretion to adopt and prosecute measures that naturally lead to war, is virtually to transfer to him the power to make war, so that the formal declaration by Congress of the existence of a state of war would be an essentially perfunctory act."

Most of Roosevelt's detractors agreed with Judge Moore that sinister motives inspired the President. Most of his supporters argued that he had merely tried to recapture control over foreign policy, as vested in his office by the Constitution. His detractors accused him of flouting the popular demand for total neutrality; his admirers praised his determination to seek peace through preparedness and victory through collective action.

· VII ·

BOTH interpretations contained an element of truth. Frances Perkins, one of Roosevelt's oldest and most observant friends, described him as the most complex personality she had ever met. Yet she attributed his conquest of polio—and of his own pride—to a simple act of religious faith. Eleanor Roosevelt in *This I Remember* also stressed the part religion played in her husband's life: "I always felt that my husband's religion had something to do with his confidence in himself. As I have said, it was a very simple religion. He believed in God and in His guidance. He felt that human beings were given tasks to perform and with those tasks the ability and strength to put them through. He could pray for faith and guidance and have faith in his own judgment as a result." Roosevelt got his religion from his father and mother and from the Reverend Endicott

UNITED PRESS PHOTO

President Roosevelt Opens the Washington Baseball Season, 1938. Left to right: Harry Hopkins; the President; Connie Mack, manager of the Philadelphia Athletics; and Bucky Harris, manager of the Washington Senators

Peabody, headmaster of Groton School. They also taught him lessons in courage that served him at times of crisis. Roosevelt appeared complex because he liked to use devious tactics against his enemies and hated to hurt his friends. But a few simple principles, learned at an early age, guided all his great decisions.

Roosevelt got his start in politics by attaching himself to Woodrow Wilson. He suffered his first major defeat when he campaigned for the Vice-Presidency on a platform that endorsed American membership in the League of Nations. Although, as he himself once said, he learned from Wilson what not to do, he also learned from Wilson certain principles that he never abandoned. On his road to the White House and during his first term there, Roosevelt took care not to talk or act like another Wilson. He faced a different kind of situation than Wilson confronted and therefore resorted to different methods. But by 1937, the international anarchy that Wilson had warned against reappeared in new and violent forms, and Roosevelt reverted to his Wilsonian past. His quarantine speech, however, fell measurably short of Wilson's greatest utterances which always glowed with more moral fervor and intellectual passion than the genial Roosevelt could generate.

"Those who cherish their freedom and recognize and respect the equal right of their neighbors to be free and live in peace, must work together for the triumph of law and moral principles in order that peace, justice, and confidence may prevail in the world. . . . There must be a recognition of the fact that national morality is as vital as private morality. . . .

"It is, therefore, a matter of vital interest and concern to the people of the United States that the sanctity of international treaties and the maintenance of international morality be restored. . . .

"The situation is definitely of universal concern. The questions involved relate not merely to violations of specific provisions of particular treaties; they are questions of war and of peace, of international law and especially of principles of humanity. . . .

"The triumph of law and moral principles . . . National morality is as vital as private morality. . . . Maintenance of international morality must be restored. . . . The situation is definitely of universal concern." There spoke the disciple of Woodrow Wilson, responding to the foreign crisis that coincided with the beginning of his second term as he had responded to the domestic crisis that coincided with the beginning of his first. And when the people did not respond either to the crisis or to the leadership Roosevelt offered, he opened the same kind of indirect attack he used against the Supreme Court. Unable to prevent Congress from passing some kind of neutrality legislation, he saw to it that the final bill left his freedom of action unimpaired. Unable to persuade Congress to do anything about quarantining aggressors, he called for a "Super-Navy." On January 21, 1938, the House passed the largest peacetime naval program in American history. A week later, Roosevelt called for further increases and Congress gave him what he wanted—overwhelmingly.

When Roosevelt called for a quarantine of aggressors in October, 1937, his political enemies accused him of trying to distract attention from the defeat of his plan to reform the Supreme Court. Raymond Moley disapproved of Roosevelt's plan for the Supreme Court; he disagreed with the quarantine speech; he had broken politically and personally with the President. But he devoted an eloquent passage in *After Seven Years* to a defense of Roosevelt's integrity and idealism in his conduct of foreign affairs: "Those who charge that Roosevelt threw himself into foreign affairs in 1938 because of a calculated desire to swing the attention of the country away from the unsolved economic problems at home do not know their man. There was nothing of conscious cynicism in Roosevelt's psychology. He had none of that hard-bought realism that made it possible for a Clemenceau to talk of permanent peace in 1919 while he privately admitted that the Treaty of Versailles was a way of hamstringing France's enemies before the next war. In this sense, Roosevelt was never an actor, creating illusions for others which he did not share himself. On the contrary, he had an almost Wilsonian need to justify himself to himself, for assuring himself that there was always 'good' reason for his acts. The intuitive pranks of his mind, the deep-rooted principles, the variations occasioned by circumstances, and the steps toward long-time objectives—all had to be explained in the same terms. Roosevelt was no cold-blooded, moral opportunist. In fact, he felt so intensely the need to do right that he had to believe he did right. He was incapable of sustaining a planned duplicity. His exoterics almost automatically became his esoterics.

"In this case, the shift was the more easily made because the play of forces in Europe had so long been described in moral terms by our internationalists. There was no need to see in preoccupation with foreign affairs a political vehicle, if one could visualize it as a crusade to provide for the common defense of international laws and principles."

Born and bred a Christian gentleman, Roosevelt held Hitler, Mussolini, and the Japanese militarists responsible for the danger of another war as he held the American money-changers and economic royalists responsible for the danger of another crash. In Manchuria, in Ethiopia, in Spain, the peace-loving 90 per cent of mankind had failed to halt the war-making 10 per cent. The situation brought the memory of Woodrow Wilson vividly to mind. "You know," Roosevelt once told Frances Perkins, "Wilson had an uncanny understanding of the European problem. He understood the moral drives of modern man. He was a Presbyterian, you know, and a tough one, and he was perfectly sure that all men are born sinful by nature. He figured it out that Western civilization would attempt to destroy itself through the natural, sinful activities of modern man unless by the grace of God the decent people of Western civilization resolved to support the Golden Rule." Again, as in Wilson's time, the democratic world needed a new messiah to lead it against the false messiahs who threatened war.

What if Wilson had failed? So had his rival messiah, Lenin. Roosevelt, the genial Episcopalian, did not entirely share Wilson's tough Presbyterian outlook. Nor did Stalin share Lenin's messianic vision. Stalin had repudiated world revolution for socialism in one country. He threatened nobody with war. His Foreign Minister, Maxim Litvinov, had coined the phrase "peace is indivisible." Although Roosevelt included Russia in his appeal to the "peace-loving" 90 per cent of mankind, he did not mistake Stalin for a Jeffersonian Democrat. He knew how Stalin had come to power and his religious faith made him wonder whether the means that Stalin used to remain in power could ever lead to harmony at home or peace abroad. But optimism played as large a part as courage or religion in Roosevelt's nature and he wanted to believe better of Stalin than he could of Hitler. Bullitt, the first United States Ambassador to Moscow, turned against Stalin when Stalin turned against the Old Bolsheviks whom Bullitt had admired in his salad days. In 1936 Roosevelt chose as his next envoy to Russia an old friend whom he met in the 1912 campaign—Joseph E. Davies of Wisconsin, one of the most successful lawyers in Washington and husband of one of the great American heiresses, the former Marjorie Post Hutton. As a self-made Midwesterner who belonged both to the world of big business and to the progressive group within the Democratic Party, Davies could report realistically and objectively. His appointment assured Stalin of Roosevelt's desire to establish closer relations between Washington and Moscow. It also assured the American people that they would be represented in Moscow by a capitalist of unquestioned solvency.

Roosevelt's pride, which polio had deepened, reasserted itself. While his wife, in an excess of humility, let Communists exploit her name and position, Roosevelt, in an excess of pride, put the full weight of his name and position behind a new American foreign policy that called upon the peace-loving 90 per cent of mankind, including the Russians, to pool their united strength and prevent war. Yet even so sympathetic an observer as Ernest K. Lindley, author of several admiring Roosevelt biographies, could write in 1936: "It was reasonably clear before the Italo-Ethiopian crisis, and it should be doubly clear now, that concerted action to check a determined aggressor means war." Roosevelt had not become a warmonger. Roosevelt had followed Woodrow Wilson's example and had begun to proclaim a series of absolute propositions that he laid down, not only in behalf of the American people but in behalf of all humanity. Roosevelt differed from Wilson in that he rarely spoke to the German, Japanese, or Italian peoples over the heads of their rulers. On Roosevelt's books the war-making 10 per cent of mankind included the masses as well as their leaders just as the peace-loving 90 per cent included Chamberlain and Stalin as well as the British and Russian peoples.

In August, 1914, when war broke out in Europe, Wilson urged the American people to remain neutral in mind and thought. As late as December, 1916, he called for peace without victory. And the fighting in Europe had lasted two years before Wilson joined the preparedness parade. Franklin D. Roosevelt never called for neutrality as between aggressor and victim. He championed preparedness from the moment he entered the White House. The Gallup poll showed wide popular backing on the preparedness issue, but opposition to his appeals for collective action. Many Republicans questioned Stalin's good faith and his will to peace. Many Democrats suspected that Chamberlain wanted to turn Hitler east against Russia. And the handful of American Communists were not the only people in the country who deplored that prospect. No authentic New Dealer called for a Nazi-Soviet war.

Although no authentic New Dealer accepted the Communist slogan, "Communism is twentieth-century Americanism," plenty of New Dealers believed that the Communists believed it. Communists opposed war. Communists befriended the common man, the Negro, the Jew. Communists and New Dealers sought the same ends, differing only in the means they used to reach them. Priding themselves on their realism, the New Dealers worked with anyone who opposed Fascism at home and abroad. That was the acid test. What if the Communists took the view that the Soviet Union was always right, that its interests took precedence over the interests of any nation, class, group, or individual? Roosevelt had divided the world into two camps—the peace-loving sheep and the war-making goats—and there was no doubt which camp included the Soviet Union.

Roosevelt's new foreign policy for the United States and his new program for the whole world rested on two assumptions. The world program assumed that the leaders and the people of the peace-loving 90 per cent of mankind accepted the propositions laid down by the President of the United States. The new American foreign policy he proposed assumed similar acceptance by his own people. Unfortunately for Roosevelt, millions of people in Britain and France wanted peace at any price, and certain political leaders in both countries hoped to turn Hitler against Stalin. As for Stalin, he regarded the whole Popular Front, collective security line as nothing more than a temporary maneuver. Foreign Commissar Maxim Litvinov, who preached this line, did not belong to the inside circle of Soviet rulers. Most Americans knew little about these cross-currents abroad, but peace-at-any-price sentiment ran even stronger in the United States than in Britain or France. Roosevelt's words therefore aroused little response abroad and less support at home. Nevertheless, the delivery of the quarantine speech on October 5, 1937, marked a turning point in the history of Franklin D. Roosevelt and his times. He spoke out loud and clear—more loudly, more clearly than any other chief of state—in warning against war. He also spoke, as Wilson had spoken, in behalf of all mankind, warning the whole world of certain clear and present dangers. Early in his second White House term, Roosevelt thus discovered that destiny had thrust the role of world messiah upon him.

SUMMING UP

DURING the first year of his second term, Roosevelt confronted the same problem that faced Wilson during the second year of his first term. In 1937 the threat of a general war menaced Roosevelt's New Deal as the outbreak of a general war menaced Wilson's New Freedom in 1914. For more than two years after war had broken out in Europe, Wilson tried to keep the United States neutral. But Wilson never suggested that the

United States isolate itself from the rest of the world. On the contrary. The kind of neutrality Wilson preached led him, in 1916, to call for peace without victory and finally, in 1917, to announce that only by declaring war on Germany could the United States achieve the purpose he had always sought—to make the world safe for democracy.

Roosevelt began where Wilson left off. He never regarded neutrality as an end in itself. He did not even regard neutrality as a means that the United States might adopt to attain an end he considered worth while. As a series of local aggressions broke out, in Manchuria, Ethiopia, Spain, and China, Roosevelt adopted the same slogans that Wilson began to proclaim in 1917. But the introverted Wilson loved humanity only in the abstract. His austere religious faith separated him from the common run of men. The extroverted Roosevelt enjoyed human beings and tolerated, in his friends and family, foibles that Wilson could never have excused. Roosevelt's religion made him charitable toward others and filled him with courage and optimism. Wilson's religion made him judge others harshly and drive himself hard.

Wilson believed that the American people had a mission to save the world and that he, as their President, had a mission to lead them to salvation. Roosevelt also believed in the American mission and in the high obligations of his office: "There is a mysterious cycle in human events," Roosevelt told a Philadelphia audience in June, 1936. "To some generations much is given. Of others much is expected. This generation of Americans has a rendezvous with destiny." Although Frances Perkins called Roosevelt the most complex human being she had ever met, he defined himself, quite simply, as a Christian and a democrat. As a Christian, he considered himself his brother's keeper. As a democrat, he hated tyranny. Drawing upon the same resources that had pulled him through his personal crisis with polio and the national crisis of 1933, he spoke up for the peace-loving 90 per cent of mankind with whom he identified both himself and the American people. He did not have to wait long for Hitler and Mussolini, Stalin and Chamberlain to put his courage and his optimism to the test.

20

Peace for Our Time

Hitler destroys the last vestiges of the Versailles system and Neville Chamberlain seeks at the Munich Conference what the world had sought for more than twenty years—peace for our time.

PREVIEW

B**Y February, 1938, Hitler had completed the conquest from within of his adopted country, Germany, and proceeded to conquer his native country, Austria, from without. His own movement had worked out a philosophy and strategy of sorts, but he owed much of his success to a general condition of European decadence. Less than two years after the Popular Front parties had won a majority of seats in the French Chamber of Deputies, their power had disintegrated—and their country's power with it. In Britain, Prime Minister Chamberlain sought peace at almost any price, rejecting the co-operation of Roosevelt and losing the services of Eden in the process. Hitler, having forced Austria to capitulate by a show of force, tried the same tactics on Czechoslovakia. Failing in May, Hitler decided to turn from threats of war to war itself. Chamberlain took the lead in staving off what looked like certain war and sat down with Hitler, Mussolini, and Daladier at Munich, where they agreed to dismember Czechoslovakia and swing the European balance of power in Hitler's favor without war. Returning to London, Chamberlain announced to his cheering compatriots that he had brought them "peace for our time."

· I ·

D**URING the 1930's Hitler transformed Roosevelt's public personality as polio had transformed Roosevelt's private personality during the 1920's. It had taken a crippling illness to bring out in Roosevelt personal qualities which early good fortune had never required him to develop. In like fashion, Hitler forced Roosevelt to develop the qualities of world leadership. Roosevelt and Hitler both came to power early in 1933, and their ambitions did not clash directly during the next three years. By 1936, however, Hitler had put Germany on a war economy, thereby creating a threat to world peace, a threat that Roosevelt challenged in his 1937 quarantine speech. Roosevelt's memorable phrase, in his first inaugural, "We have nothing to fear but fear itself," had broken the spell of the depression, but his quarantine speech failed to exorcise the threat of war. For the whole world faced a more ominous crisis in the latter 1930's than the United States had faced during the early years of that same decade. It was all very well to proclaim: "When an epidemic of physical disease starts to spread, the community approves and joins in a quarantine of the patients in order to protect the health of the community against the spread of the disease." Just what did these words mean? What commitments did they entail? Were not some victims of aggression as diseased as the aggressors? The failure of Roosevelt's quarantine appeal, both at home and abroad, did not, however, prevent him, in January, 1938, from persuading Congress to vote record naval appropriations.

By this time Hitler had placed Germany on a virtual war footing. The purge of June 30, 1934, had established his authority over the Nazi Party. A month later, as a result of Hindenburg's death, he found himself the unchallenged ruler of Germany. February 4, 1938, marked the final triumph of the Nazis over the Junkers. On that day Hitler forced General von Blomberg to quit as War Minister, General von Fritsch to quit as Chief of the General Staff, and Baron von Neurath to quit as Foreign Minister. Nevile Henderson, British Ambassador to Germany at this time, wrote of Blomberg in *Failure of a Mission:* "He was a fervent admirer of Hitler whose praises he never tired of singing. He once said to me that if Hitler ordered him and his army to march the next day to the North Pole, they would do it without a moment's hesitation." Yet Hitler distrusted Blomberg, whose Junker friends, ironically enough, urged his dismissal because he married "a lady with a past." General Keitel, who had no "von" before his name, became Hitler's personal Chief of Staff. Ribbentrop, who added a "von" to which he had no right, became Foreign Minister.

Behind this shift lay Hitler's decision to seize Austria and Czechoslovakia—with Austria coming first on the timetable. There Hitler had to avenge a defeat he had suffered at Mussolini's hands back in 1934 when the Nazis failed to seize power after they had murdered Dollfuss. Like Monsignor Seipel before him, Dollfuss had aspired to transform Austria from a socialistic federal republic into a clerical corporative state, and Dr. Kurt von Schuschnigg continued the good work. With the backing of Mussolini and the Vatican, he organized a Fatherland Front and got rid of his two chief rivals—Major Emil Fey and Prince von Starhemberg. Both men had commanded a private Fascist army known as the Heimwehr; both had held the post of Vice-Chancellor; both gave way before the Fatherland Front. But the Fatherland Front never made its peace with the Socialists, who comprised more than 40 per cent of the population, nor with the Nazis, who comprised almost 20 per cent. Schuschnigg therefore never had the backing of a majority of the Austrian people. And the Fatherland Front fought the Socialists harder than it fought the Nazis.

Of the new Constitution he had established in 1934 Schuschnigg said: "It deliberately turns its back on formal, democratic principles and universal, equal direct suffrage. It lays weight on independent and strong leadership; hence the providing of emergency powers and the right to alter laws by decree." He did, however, admit that "we do not regard dictatorial government as ideal. We shall be glad later to consult the people and hear their advice, within the framework of the Corporative State." For democracy he had still less use: "We consider it impossible that parliamentary democracy should be restored in Austria."

This attitude alarmed the Nazis far less than it antagonized the Social Democrats, described by Schuschnigg as Austro-Bolsheviks. He himself remained in power only by virtue of the support he received from Mussolini, who, since his invasion of Ethiopia, had become largely dependent upon Hitler. In 1936 the two dictators launched their joint attack upon Spain, and before the end of the year they formed the Rome-Berlin Axis. During that summer Schuschnigg had to sign an agreement with Germany recognizing "the mutual interests of the two Germanic states." Germany also recognized Austrian sovereignty and pledged "that she would not interfere in Austrian internal affairs." But before Hitler signed this treaty, he insisted that Schuschnigg admit two camouflaged Nazis to the Austrian Cabinet—Dr. Guido Schmidt as Foreign Minister and General Glaise von Horstenau as Minister of the Interior. In 1938 these two men revealed their true purposes.

The British correspondent G. E. R. Gedye wrote an eyewitness history of these years, *Betrayal in Central Europe*, in which he summed up the views of his Nazi acquaintances as they expressed themselves to him early in 1938: "We have pretty well got Schuschnigg where we want him. Mussolini is now completely tied to Hitler. Chamberlain is scared stiff of him and sends Halifax to beg for terms, trying to buy him off in Central Europe by offering him colonies. Chamberlain has got the reply that Central Europe is Germany's business, not his, and that Germany will talk colonies to England when she is ready to take them, a little later— not yet. And anyway, Chamberlain has made it obvious enough to us that his guiding principle is to back Nazism against all its internal enemies. We have the easy game of threatening him alternately with our strength and our weakness. The Front Populaire in France is breaking up, and soon France—thanks to Chamberlain's ingenious 'nonintervention' swin-

dle—is going to be immobilized by a Fascist dictatorship of Franco . . .
Thanks to February, 1934, the workers won't go with Schuschnigg. The
game is ours! Of all silly things, the idiotic English are now trying to
find out Mussolini's price for betraying Hitler. Of course Mussolini will
name the price—and betray the British."

Hitler broke with the Junker generals when they warned that this
program meant immediate war and ultimate disaster. But the double-
dealing Franz von Papen remained as German Ambassador in Vienna,
where his aristocratic birth and Roman Catholic faith gave him a standing that he exploited without limit and without shame. For instance,
early in 1938 Papen had little difficulty persuading Schuschnigg to visit
Hitler in Berchtesgaden and to bring Dr. Schmidt along too. Both
Schmidt and Papen assured Schuschnigg that Hitler wanted to give
Austria further reassurances of German good will. "You will then have
the protection of Adolf Hitler's glittering and immaculate word of
honor," Papen told him, "behind which everyone who obtains it feels
secure." Schuschnigg accepted the invitation only to have Hitler refuse
to rise when he entered his room, refuse to shake him by the hand, refuse
even to call him by his correct name and proper title. "How have you
dared all these years to suppress and torture *my* people—*my* German
people in Austria?" Hitler yelled. "Now your hour has come. God has
made me Führer and ruler of every man and woman of German blood
in every country on earth. You shall bow to my will as all the rest of the
world shall bow, or I will break you. I demand obedience from you and
shall enforce it, if necessary with my armies. You have played your last
card, Herr Schuschnigg, and you will accept and sign here at once before
you leave this house the terms I have prepared for you, or I give the
order to march into Austria immediately."

Even Keitel, Hitler's hand-picked Chief of Staff, warned him shortly
before the Schuschnigg interview not to precipitate a general war:
"*Mein Führer,* if you require the Army to add military support to a
bluff, we await your orders. But we are not yet ready for serious action,
and so I could not place the Army at your disposal for war in its present
condition." But Hitler used a combination of bluff and psychological
warfare on the Austrian Chancellor, whom he kept waiting in an anteroom where he had his mobilization plans for the invasion of Austria
spread out on the table. And Hitler's diatribe included a reference to
Mussolini, designed to complete the destruction of Schuschnigg's morale: "I know you are thinking of Mussolini. I am filled with admiration
for him and his work, and I stand for a far-reaching, firmly based solidarity between Fascism and National Socialism. But the military efficiency of the Italians is quite another question. Don't be under any
illusions in that respect. If Mussolini wants to help you, which inciden-

tally he certainly will not, then one hundred thousand German troops will be sufficient not only to push Italy back from the Brenner but to chase the Italian Army as far as Naples."

After ten hours with Hitler and his military and political advisers Schuschnigg agreed to hand over the Ministry of the Interior to Dr. Arthur Seyss-Inquart, an out-and-out Nazi, to release all Nazi prisoners from jail, and to permit Nazis to join his Fatherland Front. He refused to grant eight more of Hitler's demands, but agreed to recommend them to President Miklas for favorable action. Hitler reciprocated by promising once again to guarantee Austria's independence in a speech before the Reichstag and to forbid German Nazis to intervene in Austria's internal affairs. But Hitler also told Schuschnigg he would keep the German Army mobilized on the Austrian frontier, pending full acceptance of all his demands. Returning to Vienna, Schuschnigg released no publicity about Hitler's brutal tactics, preferring to give the impression that he and the Führer had established a "happy peace" between their two countries. For several days even the Nazis felt let down until German troop maneuvers forced more Austrian capitulations. And when Schuschnigg and Miklas announced the admission of Seyss-Inquart to the Cabinet, the Nazis knew that complete victory lay close ahead.

Schuschnigg had visited Hitler at Berchtesgaden on Saturday, February 12. A week from the following Sunday Hitler violated the pledge he had made to renew his guarantee of Austrian independence. Although Schuschnigg and Miklas, faced by German troop movements, had given way to Hitler's demands, the Führer nevertheless delivered a broadcast declaring that ten million Germans living on the borders of the Reich must no longer be denied "the general right of self-determination simply because they are Germans." He called it "intolerable for a self-conscious world power to know that at its side are racial co-equals who are subjected to continuous suffering because of their sympathy and unity with the whole German race and its ideology." On Thursday Schuschnigg told the Austrian Parliament: "We have gone to the very limit of concessions, where we must call a halt and say, 'Thus far but no further.'" The ovation Schuschnigg received at first dazed and then inspired him. For two years he had called Austria a Christian, German, corporative state, an attitude that hardly commended him to the cosmopolitan Viennese. Nevertheless, they overlooked his recent past when he prepared to take a last-minute, last-ditch stand against the far greater evil of Hitler. Crowds in the galleries of Parliament shouted his name. Larger crowds, outside the building, chanted *"Oesterreich, Oesterreich!"* over and over again. Leaders of the illegal underground Socialists visited him in his office and hammered out an agreement under which Schuschnigg restored their civil rights and the Socialists promised to support his government. Meanwhile, the Nazis violated the rest of the Berchtesgaden agreement by seizing power in the provinces. *"Heil Hitler! Heil Seyss-Inquart! Heil Deutschland! Ein Volk, ein Reich, ein Führer!"* they shouted. Seyss-Inquart visited the cities of Graz and Linz, where he gave the forbidden Nazi salute and announced, "Austria is German and only German. The only guarantee for Austria's independence can be one given by the German people. The spiritual Great German Reich is already a fact."

The temporal Great German Reich was not far behind. As Schuschnigg saw the Nazis seizing power in the provinces, as he recognized that Dr. Seyss-Inquart, Dr. Guido Schmidt, and General Glaise von Horstenau were betraying their country and the government in which they served, he attempted one last, desperate expedient. On a Wednesday night, three and a half weeks after his return from Berchtesgaden, he announced that the government would hold a plebiscite the following Sunday when the voters would pass on the question: "Are you for an independent and social, a Christian, German, and united Austria?" At least one of these adjectives appealed to every major group of organized Austrians, but at least two of them—"independent" and "united"—stuck in the craws of the Nazis, who paraded in Vienna and, in the provinces, attacked members of the Fatherland Front, without interference from the local police or from the federal authorities.

Not until Saturday, with the plebiscite only twenty-four hours away, did Schuschnigg's supporters at last appear with red and white Austrian flags. Government planes dropped pamphlets urging the people to vote *"Ja."* Socialist workmen distributed leaflets backing Schuschnigg. The Nazis suddenly made themselves scarce. But at ten o'clock that same Saturday morning, Seyss-Inquart handed Schuschnigg an ultimatum that General Glaise von Horstenau had just brought from the German authorities in Berlin threatening immediate invasion if the Sunday plebiscite were not canceled. With these two members of his own Cabinet acting as agents for Hitler, Schuschnigg agreed to call off the plebiscite, whereupon Hitler increased his demands and called for Schuschnigg's resignation as well. Schuschnigg complied; President Miklas refused to accept the resignation; Hitler demanded the appointment of a new Cabinet headed by Seyss-Inquart. By seven o'clock Saturday evening, Miklas withdrew his objection to Schuschnigg's resignation and asked Seyss-Inquart to form a new government.

Schuschnigg, surrounded by all his Cabinet members, including Seyss-Inquart and Horstenau, broadcast a brief farewell message that he had scrawled in pencil on a scrap of paper. "President Miklas asks me to tell the people of Austria that we have yielded to force," he concluded, "since we are not prepared even in this terrible situation to shed blood.

We decided to order the troops to offer no serious"—here his voice broke
—"to offer no resistance. So I take my leave of the Austrian people, with
the German word of farewell, uttered from the depths of my heart—
'God protect Austria.' " For a few minutes the speaker collapsed in sobs,
then pulled himself together, refused to leave the Chancellery by a side
door, refused to let his friends rush him to an airport and escape to safety
abroad. "No, no—I do not run away. My place is here in Austria. Please
let me give the orders—to my own chauffeur at least. Home, Franzl,
please." Had Schuschnigg, in power, shown the same qualities he displayed in defeat, how different his fate and his country's fate might have
been. But he failed to make common cause with the best elements among
the Austrian masses until Hitler had already defeated him by organizing
the worst.

Hitler had an old score to settle with Vienna, the city that had humili-
ated and rejected him during his early years of failure and obscurity.
The prospect of gaining revenge intoxicated him. As usual, he ignored
the precepts of Bismarck, who once spoke of revenge as "a delicacy that
should be served cold," and who asked himself in 1874, "What should
I do with Vienna? Personally if the Austrian provinces desired to unite
with us by force, I should be prepared to go to war about it—*against*
them." Bismarck wanted no part of the Balkans, with which Austria
maintained so many ties, but Hitler regarded himself as much greater
than Bismarck and considered Ribbentrop Bismarck's peer. And if Hitler
remembered the statement Mussolini had made in May, 1925, he did not
let it disturb him: "Italy will never permit such a gross breach of the
treaties as the union of Austria with Germany. In my opinion that union
would destroy the whole fruits of Italy's victory. It would add to Germany's power in respect both of population and territory and would
create a paradox whereby Germany would, of all the nations, be the
only one to have increased her territory and added to her population."
By 1938 Mussolini, on whom the hapless Schuschnigg had staked everything, could not even protect himself.

Less than an hour after Schuschnigg's farewell broadcast, the victorious Hitlerites had taken over Vienna. "As I crossed the Graben to my
office," wrote Gedye in *Betrayal in Central Europe*, "the brown flood
was sweeping through the streets. It was an indescribable witches' sabbath—storm troopers, lots of them barely out of the schoolroom, with
cartridge belts and carbines, the only other evidence of authority being
Swastika brassards, were marching side by side with police turncoats,
men and women shrieking or crying hysterically the name of their leader,
embracing the police and dragging them along in the swirling stream of
humanity, motor-lorries filled with storm troopers clutching their long-
concealed weapons, hooting furiously, trying to make themselves heard

INTERNATIONAL NEWS PHOTOS

Nazis Taking Over Vienna

above the din, men and women leaping, shouting, and dancing in the
light of the smoking torches which soon began to make their appearance,
the air filled with a pandemonium of sound in which intermingled
screams of 'Down with the Jews! Heil Hitler! Sieg Heil! Perish the Jews!
Hang Schuschnigg! Heil Seyss-Inquart! Heil Planetta [the murderer of
Dollfuss]! Down with the Catholics! Ein Volk, ein Reich, ein Führer!' to
which was now added a fourth ready-learned slogan 'Ein Sieg!' making
the whole incantation 'one People, one Reich, one Leader, and one Victory!' Fragments of the Horst Wessel song struggled above one's head
for survival against the strains of 'Today we have all Germany, tomorrow
we have the world' and 'Deutschland Über Alles.' "

Late Saturday night the Nazis ran up the swastika flag over the Chancellery. At one o'clock Sunday morning Miklas announced the appointment of the new Nazi Cabinet, headed by Seyss-Inquart, whose first act
was to telegraph Hitler inviting him to help prevent bloodshed. But if
Hitler did march his Army into Austria, how would the menaced Czechoslovaks react? Three times that night, the German Minister at Prague
sought and received assurances from the Czechoslovak government that
it was not mobilizing its Army, and finally at 3 A.M. Hitler gave the word
for German troops to occupy Austria. The warnings of the General Staff
proved only too well founded. Hundreds of tanks and armored cars
broke down, clogging the roads and setting the German advance so far
behind schedule that Hitler did not cross the frontier until four in the
afternoon. Seyss-Inquart met him at Linz and demanded Miklas's resignation and all of Miklas's powers. Miklas complied, and Seyss-Inquart

signed a decree making Austria a "land of the German Reich." Hitler ordered a new plebiscite, to be held on April 10 in both Austria and Germany, when the peoples of both countries would have a chance to vote "yes" or "no" on the union that Hitler had already enforced upon their two countries. Of the Austrians 99.75 per cent voted "yes"; of the Germans 99.08 per cent approved.

The railroads and the highways told a different story as thousands of Viennese of all classes jammed the trains and crowded the roads, seeking to escape to Czechoslovakia only to be turned back at the border. The Jews received the most brutal treatment. "Day after day," wrote Gedye, "Nazi storm troopers, surrounded by jostling, jeering, and laughing mobs of 'golden Viennese hearts,' dragged Jews from shops, offices, and homes, men and women, put scrubbing brushes in their hands, splashed them well with acid, and made them go down on their knees and scrub away for hours at the hopeless task of removing Schuschnigg propaganda. 'Work for the Jews at last, work for the Jews!' the mob howled. 'We thank our Führer for finding work for the Jews.' "

The Nazis seized Jewish property, dismissed Jews from jobs, sent Jews to concentration camps. "You will shrug your comfortable shoulders," wrote Gedye at the time, "and say 'bogey tales' when I tell you of women whose husbands had been arrested a week before without any charge, receiving a small parcel from the Viennese post-office with the curt intimation—'To pay, 150 marks, for the cremation of your husband—ashes enclosed from Dachau.' " Every day for weeks, hundreds of Viennese Jews committed suicide until, as Gedye wrote, it became accepted "as a perfectly normal and natural incident of every Jewish household. It is quite impossible to convey to anyone outside Austria in how matter-of-fact a way the Jews of Austria refer to this way out of their agony. When I say one's Jewish friends spoke to one of their intention to commit suicide with no more emotion than they had formerly talked of making an hour's journey by train, I cannot expect to be believed. Nevertheless, the fact must be recorded. It is not your fault that you cannot believe me, because it is impossible for you to conceive of the diseased and degenerate mentality which lies behind the pathological anti-Semitism of the Nazis." In Germany, Julius Streicher's *Der Stürmer* headlined the accounts of Jewish suicides in Vienna with the line: "Recommended as Example to Others."

· II ·

THE Nazi seizure of power in Austria vindicated Hitler's strategy of terror. Anti-Semitism proved as popular in gay Vienna as in grim Berlin. The atrocities Hitler inspired did not take place in darkest Africa or

© LOW, ALL COUNTRIES

"Not only the Austrians voted." Cartoon by David Low

poorest Asia, but in the heart of enlightened Europe. Individual Germans, and individual Austrians, too, quietly aided individual Jews. Jewish and non-Jewish citizens of other countries contributed funds to care for refugees and to spread propaganda against the Nazis. But no concerted movement took shape in Germany to overthrow Hitler; no concerted movement took shape in Europe to restore Germany to civilization. If responsibility for Hitler lay with the German people, responsibility for Germany lay with the people of Europe. And the people of Germany showed themselves as helpless against Hitler as the people of Europe showed themselves against Germany.

By 1938 the Nazis had built enough concentration camps in Germany to hold several hundred thousand persons, and the stories told by released inmates did not encourage opposition to the regime. A survivor of the camp at Dachau described his arrival on February 4, 1938: "We had an eighteen-hour night journey behind us during which no one had slept, and now we had to stand from 9 A.M. to 6 P.M. with no food at all. From the first day we were constantly beaten at Dachau. The Jewish prisoners worked in special detachments and received the hardest tasks. They were beaten at every opportunity, overwhelmed with abusive epithets such as 'Sow Jew,' 'Filth Jew,' and 'Stink Jew.' During the working period the non-Jewish prisoners were issued one piece of bread at breakfast—the Jews nothing. But the Jews were always paraded with the others to see the bread ration issued. On May 16th the Standard Leader informed us all that from now onwards all Jews would be isolated as retaliation for the articles describing concentration camp life which had appeared abroad. The windows of the 'Jew huts' were nailed up and painted over, and the doors locked. They had to lie inside on their plank beds all day and all night except for one hour mornings and evenings, when they were brought out for 'sport' under the supervision of the Block Leader." But why go on? The story of the Nazi persecution of the Jews seemed to have no limit and no end.

But it had a purpose. The Christian communities which had persecuted Jews for more than a thousand years before Hitler came into the world always held out conversion and salvation as alternatives. Hitler, on the other hand, offered the Jews no alternative to extermination. His program and his personality demanded an atmosphere of terror. Exposés by his victims and denunciations by his enemies never quite explained the phenomenon of Hitler. Disillusioned supporters threw more light on the subject—men like Hermann Rauschning, for instance, a former Nationalist who joined the Nazis, got to know Hitler well, and served as president of the Danzig Senate on Hitler's orders. Late, strangely late in the day, Rauschning broke with Hitler and set down his impressions in the widely read *Revolution of Nihilism*. Rauschning placed Hitler among the great destroyers of history: "Men of this type are inventive in destruction, they have a flair for the weak points at which they can apply pressure in order to bring down the old order. And it is their destiny to do this until a really creative will opposes them or until their environment is exhausted. These are the men of great tactical gifts. They are also the men possessed of demons, of second sight, dreamers urged on by visions, who regard themselves as men like unto gods, and who live in an unreal world in spite of all the realism they attain upon occasion."

Rauschning also recalled that Hitler bore out Ortega y Gasset's observation: "Civilization is the endeavor to reduce violence to the *ultima ratio*. This is now becoming all too clear to us for direct action reverses the order and proclaims violence as the *prima ratio*, or rather the *unica ratio*. It is the standard that dispenses with all others." Rauschning quoted Sorel that "violence is the basic force in life," and continued: "When all other standards have been unmasked by skepticism of all doctrines, reason is robbed of all its force. The anti-intellectual 'dynamism' is not mere chance but the necessary outcome of an entire absence of standards. Man, it holds, is not a logical being, not a creature guided by reason or intelligence, but a creature following his instincts and impulses like any other animal. Consequently reason cannot provide a basis for a social order or a political system. That is why revolutionary direct action has won the day against the responsible, nonrevolutionary socialism of the working class, just as it has violently eliminated the middle class itself as the ruling class."

Rauschning had never written a book before *The Revolution of Nihilism* and he did not write that until after he emigrated from Germany.
Nearly all the outstanding men of letters in pre-Nazi Germany and Austria had preceded him—some because they came under Hitler's racial
ban, the rest as a sign of protest. Hans Fallada, author of *Little Man,
What Now?*, remained and wrote concealed anti-Nazi allegories. Heinrich Hauser, a rugged reporter built on Ernest Hemingway lines, stuck
it out, but his Jewish wife emigrated to the United States. Only one
writer of any stature made a serious effort to come to terms with the
regime and to express, in universal terms, the kind of aspiration, idealism,
and experience that went into the making of the Nazi attitude toward
life. Ernst Jünger, born in 1895, had served on the Western Front
throughout the war, fighting at Verdun and on the Somme, and winning
the Pour le Mérite medal, rarely awarded to any infantryman. Before
the war he had sought adventure in African exploration. Afterward he
spoke for those veterans who did not share the utter disillusionment expressed by Remarque in *All Quiet on the Western Front.* "The war,"
Jünger discovered, "transformed me." Of his generation he wrote: "War,
mother of all things, is our mother. It hammered, forged, hardened us
into what we are. As always, as long as the wheel of life within us turns,
this war will be the axis around which it revolves."

Jünger first earned fame and fortune with two war novels, published
in the 1920's, but his best work came ten years later in the form of epi-
grammatic essays, some of which suggested an extroverted Nietzsche.
"Death gives birth to life." "War is not the end but the beginning of violence." "We want no peaceful and refined world; we want a world with
all its possibilities." "In the dazzling, deathly war of matter, we witnessed the collapse of a hopelessly lost era." "We are entering a strange
period in which one lives at once more naturally and more artificially
and in any case more dangerously." "Work is the movement of the hand,
the mind, the heart; it is life by day and night; it is knowledge, love, belief, superstition, war; work is the vibration of atoms, it is the force that
moves the stars and the solar system." Jünger ignored the technical
points of Nazi Party doctrine as expounded by Hitler, Goebbels, and
Rosenberg. He probed deeper. What he wrote about death, war, action,
and violence summed up the aspiration and experience that had made
millions of Germans ready converts to the Nazi creed.

Like Nietzsche, Jünger lived dangerously. Like Bergson, he gave the
élan vital its head. Like Spengler, he made efficiency an end in itself:
"Whatever works is legitimate." His cult of the emotions recalled D. H.
Lawrence. In short, Jünger, like other Nazi intellectuals, derived the
content of his faith from his own country and points west. But the form
this faith took bore a Russian trade-mark. From their long experience in

war and revolution, the Russian Communists had learned the supreme importance of a disciplined, infallible party to which every member gives absolute, unquestioning allegiance. From comparable experience, and with the Russian example ever before them, the Nazis drew similar conclusions. Lenin assumed that the Communist Party could establish a proletarian paradise on earth. Hitler, less sanguine, never had any illusions about means and ends. He created the Nazi Party to establish a gangster state, dressed up to look like a restoration of Germany's tribal, Teutonic past.

In so far as madness possessed Hitler, the same madness possessed millions of his followers. In so far as he followed a rational plan, he owed a certain debt to General Karl Haushofer's Institute for Geopolitics at Munich. During the 1920's, Rudolf Hess had become a disciple of General Haushofer, who had served as Military Attaché with the German Embassy in Tokyo before the war and as the chief promoter of the new science of geopolitics afterward. Geopolitics might be defined as the politics of geography; Admiral Mahan might be described as the geopolitician of sea power because he preached that the nation that controlled the seas controlled the world. Haushofer, on the other hand, preached the importance of land power and owed his fundamental doctrine to the British geographer, Sir Halford Mackinder, who warned the peace-makers at Versailles: "Who rules East Europe commands the Heartland; who rules the Heartland commands the World Island; who rules the World Island commands the world."

In November, 1934, Haushofer's magazine, *Die Zeitschrift für Geopolitik,* warned that "the military weakness of the Austrian space" involved a risk of war "which can be avoided only if a great power again takes on the protection of Austrian territory." Haushofer did not foresee a localized war among the Succession States of the former Hapsburg Empire. He foresaw a war between Slav and Teuton, between Russia and Germany, perhaps between Asia and Europe. To avoid that war he urged that Germany take Austria under its protection and bring Czechoslovakia under its control. He also hoped for Russian-German collaboration and warned the Russians and Germans not to "fight each other to the death," as they had between 1914 and 1917, when they "pulled the chestnuts out of the fire for the imperialistic purposes of the neighboring Western powers, burning their flesh and crippling their souls in the process." While Nazi propagandists denounced Communism and Communist propagandists denounced Nazism, the rulers of the German and Russian states maintained entirely correct relations even after Hitler came to power. They suspected one another; they plotted against one another. But neither group wanted trouble in the near future. Each aspired to world leadership, based on control of the Eurasian land mass.

Meanwhile dissident Communists charged that Stalin had purged the Party and the Army in order to free himself for a direct deal with Hitler —a deal that certain factions in the Nazi Party and the German Army would have welcomed, not as a permanent solution but as a temporary arrangement that would give them freedom of action elsewhere.

Hitler's timetable called first for the absorption of Austria, then the elimination of Czechoslovakia and Poland, and after that the annihilation of France. While this series of attacks against his immediate neighbors went forward, Hitler needed to insure himself against trouble further east. Austria, Czechoslovakia, Poland, and France all had to be assimilated, neutralized, or destroyed before he could take his final gamble in the east and fight Russia. He planned to destroy France not for destruction's sake but in order to remove any threat of trouble from France when the time came for him to wrest control of the Eurasian land mass from Russian hands. In *Mein Kampf* Hitler berated the Kaiser for having allied himself to the "mummy" state of Austria-Hungary and to the moribund Turkish Empire and for having antagonized both Britain and Italy. "The greatest world power of the earth," meaning Britain, "and a youthful national state," meaning Italy, "would constitute different premises for a struggle in Europe than did the putrid corpses with which Germany had allied herself in the last war," wrote Hitler in *Mein Kampf*. And he called for nothing short of the total destruction of France: "Only when this is fully understood in Germany, so that the German nation's will to live is no longer allowed to waste itself in purely passive defensiveness, but is drawn together for a decisive, active settlement with France, and is thrown into a final, decisive battle for the vastest German goals: only then will it be possible to bring to a conclusion our eternal struggle with France, in itself so fruitless; on condition, of course, that Germany really sees in France's destruction a means of subsequently and finally giving our nation a chance to expand elsewhere."

Professor Friedrich Ratzel of Munich, the grandfather of all the geopoliticians, had written before the turn of the century: "Every people has to be educated up from smaller to larger space conceptions; and the process has to be repeated again and again to prevent people from falling back into the old, small space conceptions. The decay of every state is the result of a declining space conception." Half a century later, Hitler incorporated Ratzel's general proposition in his specific program of military conquest. And in doing so Hitler gave Germany the kind of leadership that Haushofer had praised—before Hitler came to power: "It should not be forgotten that the geopolitical world view requires the supplement of the heroic part of men, of hero worship. Only about one fourth of the problems of human development can be derived from earth-conditioned factors which lead to the geopolitical explanation of men's destinies through their environment. The other three quarters of the complex problems of human development should be derived from man's racial qualities and his ethical will."

Haushofer respected Hitler more than Hitler respected Haushofer. For Haushofer acknowledged, as Hitler did, the dominating part that passions and personalities played in Germany's political affairs, whereas Hitler never fully grasped Haushofer's principles of geopolitics, preferring to follow his instincts and intuition. Haushofer knew how to popularize the theories of others. Hitler had little interest in theories except in so far as he could use them to further his ambitions. His genius lay in his ability to fuse shoddy ideas and base passions into a dynamic political program. His program of eastward expansion entailed so many risks of war in so many directions that the most experienced soldiers and statesmen in Germany believed it could spell nothing but doom for their country. In like fashion, Hitler's distorted passions led trained psychiatrists to pronounce him certifiably insane. Yet through sheer force of will, Hitler subjected all Germany to his personality and his program.

· III ·

ABROAD Hitler produced an even more bewildering effect. At first, foreign opinion dismissed him as a joke. Then the belief spread that such evil and folly must soon destroy itself. But as Hitler went from triumph to triumph, foreign opinion tried to believe that he must possess virtues which his enemies had misrepresented. After all, the German people were backing Hitler for some of the same reasons that the American people were backing Roosevelt. Both men gave the bread, the work, the hope that they had promised. Indeed, Germany enjoyed a bigger boom under Hitler than the United States enjoyed under Roosevelt. While the New Deal cut government spending and courted a new depression, the Third Reich stepped up its armament program and abolished unemployment. In 1938 Germany's national income hit an all-time high of 88 billion marks, though 40 per cent of it went back to the government in taxes. Germany's public debt had mounted from less than 24 billion marks in 1933 to between 80 and 100 billions. Industrial production had more than doubled. Employment increased from twelve and a half to twenty-two million. The Nazis abolished the considerable powers that the various states, large and small, had enjoyed. Mighty Prussia, proud Bavaria, little Württemberg all became provinces, ruled by Nazi governors who took their orders from Hitler in Berlin. Two thirds of German industry came under the control of the central government, which plowed back half the taxes it collected into building new factories to produce war goods. But Germany still had to import seventeen of the nineteen basic raw materials its industries required. It could make only half its oil and one third of its rubber by costly synthetic processes. The income of the German farmer had shown a 40 per cent increase—from 10 to 14 billion marks. In 1933 the Germans produced 75 per cent of all the food they ate. By 1938 they were producing 82 per cent. But the German people owned only a million and a half private automobiles, one to every fifty persons. In the United States, one person in every five owned a car.

Although the German standard of living still lagged far behind the American, the Germans led the world in another field that the United States had once claimed for its own. In 1936 the Olympic Games took place in Germany, and the Germans won. The Nazis turned the whole affair into one long propaganda show, marred only by the victories of several non-Aryan American Negroes who defeated the best sprinters and middle-distance runners that the Third Reich, or any other part of the world, could produce. No such rude disturbances marred the placid and uniform pattern of German cultural life under the Third Reich. A Reich Culture Chamber and a Reich Senate co-ordinated all the arts, and every writer, painter, musician, and actor had to belong to the Chamber in his special field. The Third Reich outlawed abstract art and forbade the publication of the works of Jewish authors. It could not suppress the text of Heine's "Lorelei," but it did place beneath the title the words "Author Unknown." Nor did the Nazis suppress most of the classical dramas and operas. They preferred to make certain that no new work of any originality appeared. The most popular play under the Third Reich had as its star a live pig.

The more the power of the new Germany increased, the more the culture of the old Germany declined. The people of western Europe could not doubt that Hitler's brutality carried within itself the seeds of its own destruction, and by the same token their own superior virtues assured their survival. The further the balance of military power swung in Hitler's favor, the further the balance of moral power swung in theirs. But those same Europeans who denounced Hitler most fiercely also insisted that all Europe, indeed the whole world, had become a single community. They liked Roosevelt's analogy between disease and aggression and commended his proposed quarantine. But they did not choose to push the quarantine analogy to its logical conclusion and to study some of their own symptoms as critically as they studied Hitler's. What if Hitlerism were the German symptom of a primarily European disease that took other forms in other countries?

Again and again in Europe's history, certain creative artists have expressed the character of their times in painting, music, and literature. The outbreak of war in 1914 coincided with a period of exceptional creative activity, culminating in the Diaghilev ballet. After the war, Oswald

Spengler gave utterance to a spirit of gloom, by no means peculiar to his native Germany. The Dada movement released the impulse to anarchy that extended from Rumania to France, from the Italian to the Scandinavian peninsula. After Dada came another movement that swept all Europe, surrealism. All the arts became more esoteric as more and more artists flew off on individual tangents. Prewar literature had dealt with social themes; postwar literature delved into the subconscious mind of the individual. Finally, the outstanding painter of the postwar years completed the circle of modern art and translated the most recondite of all cults into forms that the mass public could accept.

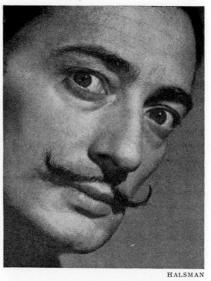

HALSMAN

Salvador Dali

If the career of Hitler epitomized the degeneration of European politics during the 1930's, the career of Salvador Dali epitomized the degeneration of European culture. His autobiography, *The Secret Life of Salvador Dali*, begins: "At the age of six I wanted to be a cook. At seven I wanted to be Napoleon. And my ambition has been growing ever since." He was born in 1903, the spoiled and talented child of prosperous, middle-class Catalonian parents. While still in his teens, Dali boasted that he could win admission to the Academy of Fine Arts at Madrid without touching a brush to canvas, and proceeded to make good by flicking small gobs of paint into a striking design. With brush in hand, he developed a technical mastery that combined the precision of Memling, the shading of Vermeer, and the brilliance of Ingres. But Dali used this proficiency to depict the "surrealist object," which he described as "one that is absolutely useless from the practical and rational point of view, created wholly for the purpose of materializing in a fetishistic way, with a maximum of tangible reality, ideas and fantasies having a delirious character." By the middle and later 1930's, his paintings acquired such notoriety that they fetched high prices on both sides of the Atlantic. Dali went in for blindingly realistic hand telephones, loaves of bread, watches turned to treacle, marsupial centaurs, "Mysterious Mouth Appearing in the Back of my Nurse," "The Specter of Sex Appeal," "Sodomy Committed by a Skull with a Grand Piano." He painted a precise and lovely likeness of his Russian wife, Gala, with olive branches sprouting

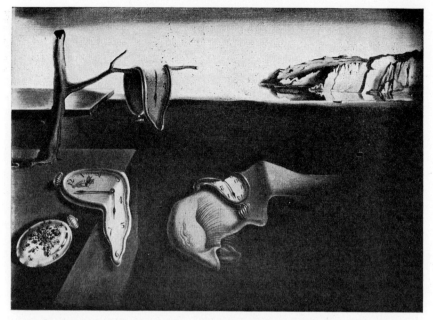

Salvador Dali: "The Persistence of Memory." Collection, The Museum of Modern Art, New York

from her head. His treatment of seashore scenes, of light, shadow, and perspective on the sand, set a style that advertising artists soon imitated. Indeed, Dali found his own spiritual home in New York creating a surrealist window-display for a Fifth Avenue department store.

Cézanne, Gauguin, and Van Gogh, the leading painters of the previous generation, painted what they believed without thought of worldly success and without ever gaining in the course of their whole lives such fame and fortune as Dali won before he reached the age of forty. Although Sargent and De Laszlo painted what the public wanted, they did not prostitute their talents to win contemporary recognition any more than Cézanne, Van Gogh, or Gauguin chose rebellion for its own sake. All of them lived out their various potentialities in their separate ways. Dali, on the other hand, never lost sight of the main chance. He made revolt a paying proposition and used his fabulous technical skill to shock the bourgeois into paying fabulous sums for paintings that had no other purpose than to stun the senses of the beholder. The old masters used their proficiency to depict the surface of the world around them. The development of photography forced the modern painter to depict a reality of his own—a superreality. But to Dali surrealism did not mean, primarily, a new and higher form of artistic expression. Lacking creative imagination, he could do nothing but represent familiar objects in new and fantastic combinations. Dali described his own technique as "hand-made photography" and said that surrealism presented three images of life—"excrement, blood, putrefaction." Art critics therefore "need expect nothing from the surrealist images but disappointment, distaste, and repulsion." Mencken once said that America's outstanding philosopher devoted himself to justifying the popular saying, "I don't know anything about art, but I know what I like." Dali carried the pragmatism of William James one step further. He did know about art—just enough to make it yield him the money and the publicity that he craved.

Of himself Dali wrote: "I am the most representative incarnation of postwar Europe: I have lived all its adventures, all its experiments, all its dramas." Dali incarnated postwar Europe, all right, but not in quite the way he imagined. "Postwar Europe," he observed in his autobiography, "was about to croak of the anarchy of isms, of the absence of ethical, aesthetic, ideological, and moral vigor. Europe was about to croak of skepticism, arbitrariness, drabness, lack of form, lack of synthesis, lack of cosmogony. Postwar Europe was about to croak from lack of faith. It thought it knew everything from having tasted the forbidden fruit of specialization. But it believed in nothing and trusted in everything, in an anonymous flaccidity of the 'Collective.' "

The personal and political philosophy with which Dali responded to this challenge suffered from the same disease that he sought to cure: "My position was that happiness or unhappiness is an ultra-individual matter having nothing to do with the structure of society, the standard of living, or the political rights of the people. The thing to do was to increase the collective danger and insecurity by total, systematic disorganization in order to enhance the possibilities of anguish which, according to psychoanalysis, condition the very principle of pleasure." Dali's aesthetic ideas paralleled Hitler's political ideas: "to increase the collective danger and insecurity by total, systematic disorganization." Yet Dali opposed Fascist politics—as Hitler opposed surrealist art. Dali sup-

Salvador Dali: "Portrait of Gala." Collection, The Museum of Modern Art, New York

ported Republican Spain—at a safe distance. During the summer of
1938 he predicted the immediate outbreak of general war in Europe,
ending in the collapse of both Communism and Fascism. Ultimately,
he foresaw the dawn of a new age of faith, with himself the first prophet
of the new renaissance. In his megalomania Dali spoke for Europe as
well as for himself, for that Europe whose doom, degeneration, and
death his paintings had depicted and his career had symbolized.

Dali cashed in on decadent aesthetics; Hitler cashed in on decadent
politics. They resembled those profiteers of inflation and war who flourish on crisis and misery, drawing their sustenance, like noxious weeds,
from the surrounding decay. In Europe, during the 1930's, this was a
decay that spread beyond Germany, beyond aesthetics, beyond politics.
The French, with the best Army in Europe, had not dared to move in
March, 1936, when Hitler bluffed his way into the Rhineland. Within
another two years the Germans had militarized the whole area and built
up their Army and Air Force to such a point that they had the French
at their mercy. The Popular Front of Radicals, Socialists, and Communists that had won a majority of seats in the French Chamber of Deputies
a few months after Hitler began militarizing the Rhineland pledged
itself to "defend democratic freedom, give bread to the workers, work
to the young, and a great human peace to the world." Yet Léon Blum,
a year before he took office as head of the Popular Front government,
said of himself: "My real vocation was to write books." Two years after
he came to power, French industrial production had dropped 20 per
cent while German industrial production had increased 30 per cent. The
France of the Popular Front built fifty military planes a year, while Nazi
Germany built five hundred.

Of the sixty-seven-year-old Blum, Proust once said: "He knows nothing of the mysteries of the human heart." Blum knew little more of the
mysteries of economics. To stimulate production he devalued the franc,
thereby cutting costs. But he more than canceled off the increased production that a cheaper currency might have yielded by cutting the
working week and encouraging a rise in wages. A stronger leader—a
Clemenceau, a Poincaré—might have bent the stubborn factions in the
Popular Front to his will; a more skilled maneuverer, like Briand, might
have played these factions off against one another. But not the doctrinaire Socialist, Léon Blum. He considered himself a disciple of Jean
Jaurès, who had once declared, "It is not war but peace which is revolutionary." Distrusting professional soldiers on principle, Blum saw no
need to increase the size of the French Army. He distrusted even more
the "two hundred families" who dominated the Bank of France through
its self-perpetuating Board of Regents. The Popular Front could not,
however, nationalize the Bank of France or expropriate the two hundred

families. It could only subordinate military preparedness to social reform.

As a Socialist, Blum favored more drastic measures than he could adopt as the leader of the Popular Front coalition. Five million voters had supported the Popular Front at the polls. Four million had opposed it. The Radicals, who received two million of the Popular Front's five million votes, wanted a somewhat milder French equivalent of the Roosevelt New Deal. The Communists, who received a million and a half votes, shouted anti-Fascist slogans, pressed for more help to the Spanish Republic and more concessions to French workers, but refused to accept any Cabinet posts. Their purposes and their methods remained equally suspect. The Moscow purges and confessions of 1936, 1937, and 1938 gave evidence of panic at the top of the Communist hierarchy and of treason in every rank.

Supporters of the Popular Front smugly referred to themselves as "men of good will," and Jules Romains was writing an epic novel with that title—*Les Hommes de bonne Volonté*. Such men had rejected Poincaré's policy of revenge in 1924. Ten years later, they thwarted the conspiracy against the Republic. They triumphed in the 1936 elections when the Communists increased their representation in the Chamber from ten to seventy-two seats, picking up most of these gains at the expense of the Radicals, in whose eyes any advocate of militant anti-Fascism thereby established his virtue. No man of good will dared mention the recent past when Communists called Socialists Social Fascists and when Moscow prosecutors charged that Léon Blum had conspired with Trotskyites, White Russians, the British Secret Service, and the French General Staff to dismember the Soviet Union.

The Popular Front soon succumbed to the same galloping paralysis that had destroyed so many other left coalitions in France. During the summer of 1937 Camille Chautemps of the Radical Party replaced Blum as head of the government. Chautemps kept the Popular Front label, retained Blum as Vice-Premier, but added Georges Bonnet, French Ambassador to the United States, as Finance Minister. Bonnet had a long nose, sharp profile, and shifty eye. He belonged to the Radical Party but followed his own line—the line of least resistance. André Géraud, who wrote for the conservative, Clerical *Echo de Paris* under the name of Pertinax, attributed the decline of France during the middle and latter 1930's to three men—the rapacious Laval, the conceited Flandin, and the incompetent Bonnet. As the decade of the 1930's drew toward its close Laval played the Fascist, even the Nazi, side of the street and opposed the Popular Front. He frankly preferred Mussolini and even Hitler to Stalin. Flandin had fewer convictions and less courage. He got himself up to look like an Englishman and impressed

Churchill as intelligent rather than forceful. Flandin had done his fatal work back in the spring of 1936 when as Foreign Minister he permitted Hitler to militarize the Rhineland. Bonnet completed what Flandin had begun when he became Foreign Minister in still another Popular Front Cabinet organized by Édouard Daladier in April, 1938. Daladier's bungling of the riots in February, 1934, had pushed him into the background, but he came to the top again by taking as his motto: "When one is out of office the way back starts at the extreme left."

As a Radical, Daladier boasted that he had no enemies on the left. The rank and file of his Party consisted—as Pertinax put it in *The Grave-diggers of France*—"of peasants who are small landowners, of the lower middle class in the cities, second-rate doctors and lawyers, the personnel of the government services, and most of the retail shopkeepers." The Radicals had ruled France since the turn of the century, yet they mistrusted the power of the state. "This explains," wrote Pertinax, "why participation in the government meant to them, above all, protection against the state. Protection from the state through participation in the state. They wanted material advantage, various favors from the administration, all that the word patronage implies. Social jealousy, but not hatred, is the mainspring of the Radicals." Or, as Jules Ferry wrote a generation earlier: "What France needs is a weak government." Such strong leaders as Millerand, Poincaré, and Briand did not belong to the Radical Party, which talked the language of nineteenth-century liberalism and believed that the best government governs least. Daladier, the baker's son who had served bravely on the Western Front, had more stubbornness than intellect. Ambition overrode all other emotions. Although he had little knowledge of foreign affairs, he had an instinctive sense of his country's interest and his country's peril. Bonnet, his sophisticated Foreign Minister, understood clearly enough that the fall of Austria put Czechoslovakia next on Hitler's list, but his blind determination to follow the course of least resistance prevented him from seeing what came after Czechoslovakia. Daladier did not have to go through any complicated mental process before he could make up his mind. But his affinity with the common man made him no less susceptible than Bonnet to any proposal that seemed to promise peace.

· IV ·

NEITHER the leaders nor the people of France minimized the German danger during the spring of 1938 when the Popular Front played its last card and the Chamber of Deputies voted Daladier dictatorial powers for a limited period. The new Premier did not doubt that grim decisions lay ahead, and he dreaded the inevitable outcome. Across the Channel,

Prime Minister Chamberlain also foresaw a dark future. Like Daladier, he inherited the mistakes of his predecessors. Unlike Daladier, he neither received nor required any special grant of power. The rank-and-file Conservatives, in the House of Commons and out, had confidence in Chamberlain, whose refusal to take for granted the inevitability of war commended him to a wider public. At the age of sixty-eight, he had at last gained the office that had eluded his abler father and his more popular half-brother. With the vigor of a man in his forties, he worked for what Foreign Secretary Eden called "Not peace at *any* price, but peace at *almost any* price." Or, in two words, "settlement and appeasement."

On July 10, 1938, Herbert von Dirksen, the German Ambassador in London, wrote his Foreign Office that the British government had made up its mind "to oppose—even at the price of war—any further attempts to shift the balance of power on the Continent without a previous understanding with England." But Dirksen also explained that the Chamberlain Cabinet "shows the greatest understanding for Germany that is possible for any group of British political leaders of Cabinet caliber. The present Cabinet possesses sufficient strength at home to carry out this task. In essential points it has approached the guiding principles represented by Germany: elimination of the Soviet Union from decisions on the fate of Europe; elimination of the League of Nations from the same task; advisability of bilateral negotiations and treaties. It is showing growing understanding for the demands of Germany in the Sudeten question. It would be willing to make great sacrifices to satisfy Germany's other legitimate demands—on the one condition that these objectives are sought by peaceful means. If Germany should resort to military means to reach these objectives, then England would without any doubt resort to war at the side of France."

Ribbentrop, who had preceded Dirksen in London and now occupied the post of German Foreign Minister, took a more belligerent view and held Britain in greater contempt. Early in January, 1938, Ribbentrop had reported confidentially to Hitler: "With the realization that Germany does not want to be bound by the *status quo* in Central Europe, and that war in Europe is possible sooner or later, the hope for an understanding among the British politicians favorable to Germany—if they do not for that matter at present simply play a role that has been assigned to them—will gradually come to an end. The fateful question is thus raised whether in the long run Germany and England will of necessity be driven into separate camps and march against each other someday. To answer this question the following must be realized: A change in the eastern *status quo* to Germany's advantage can be accomplished only by force."

Ribbentrop did not express these views with the thought of persuading Hitler to share them. He expressed these views because he knew they were what Hitler wanted to hear. Early in November, 1937, Hitler had told a secret conclave of high Army and Party officials in his office that "Germany's problem could be solved only by means of force" and that "it was his unalterable resolve to solve Germany's problem of space at the latest by 1943-5." Hitler had never pretended that he expected to get what he wanted for Germany without war. But he had always talked and acted as if he believed what he had written in *Mein Kampf* about the importance of good relations with England. Not until this secret meeting on November 5, 1937, did he reveal that he had changed his mind: "England does not desire in close proximity a paramount Germany, which would be a constant menace to the British Isles. On this she will fight. . . . England is our most dangerous enemy."

Nobody in England, not Chamberlain nor Churchill, not Baldwin nor Eden, knew that Hitler had spoken in this fashion at this time. Nor did Roosevelt, in the United States, know that one month to the day after he delivered his quarantine speech, Hitler had resolved upon war by 1945 at the latest. Chamberlain, like Baldwin, hoped that appeasement of Hitler could prevent war. Eden went reluctantly along. Churchill considered war almost inevitable and urged his fellow countrymen to prepare for the worst and build a wider, tighter network of alliances. Roosevelt took the more hopeful view that preparedness plus collective security might still keep the peace. But this hope rested on two gambles— first, that a strong and united anti-Axis coalition could be formed and, second, that such a coalition would scare Hitler into behaving himself. The events leading up to Hitler's seizure of Austria did not make the first gamble look attractive. Subsequent events did not encourage the second.

On February 21, 1938, Anthony Eden resigned as British Foreign Secretary, apparently as a protest against Prime Minister Chamberlain's efforts to reach an understanding with Mussolini. Actually, however, Chamberlain had declared, "If only we could get on terms with the Germans, I would not care a rap for Musso." As for Eden, what finally decided him to quit was not Chamberlain's long and patient campaign to appease Mussolini and Hitler; it was Chamberlain's more recent refusal to do business with Roosevelt. Eden had never objected to appeasement as a temporary expedient and he had gladly accepted office from both Baldwin and Chamberlain. Indeed, it was as private secretary to Neville Chamberlain's pro-French half-brother, Sir Austen, that Eden got his start back in the 1920's. During the 1930's, as Minister for League of Nations Affairs under Baldwin, Eden came to symbolize the principle of collective security to which the Conservatives were paying belated and reluctant lip service, and he saved the day for the Conservatives by accepting the post of Foreign Secretary in December, 1935, when

© LOW, ALL COUNTRIES

"Would you oblige me with a match, please?" Cartoon by David Low

Sir Samuel Hoare's abortive deal with Laval over Ethiopia almost wrecked the newly installed Baldwin government. Eden then went on to create and apply the nonintervention policy in Spain on the theory that aid to the Republic would have been "bad humanity and bad politics." Even Winston Churchill, who warned against appeasing Hitler and Mussolini, supported nonintervention in Spain and urged his countrymen to keep out of "that dismal welter."

As long as Baldwin remained Prime Minister, he gave Eden a relatively free hand at the Foreign Office. Baldwin, as Churchill had said, was "largely detached from foreign and military affairs. He knew little of Europe, and disliked what he knew." Chamberlain, on the other hand, "conceived himself able to comprehend the whole field of Europe, and indeed the world." Chamberlain and Eden belonged to different generations; they possessed different temperaments; they held different convictions. The wonder was not that Eden quit after less than a year in office. The wonder was that he lasted so long. And, if we are to believe Chamberlain's admiring and conscientious biographer, Keith Feiling, President Roosevelt unwittingly hastened the showdown.

Whereas Eden praised Roosevelt's quarantine speech, Chamberlain read it "with mixed feelings." He felt "something lacking" in the President's analogy between aggression and disease, "seeing that patients suffering from epidemic diseases do not usually go about fully armed."

Of Roosevelt's attitude toward the Far East he commented, "It is always best and safest to count on nothing from the Americans but words." But Roosevelt believed he was offering the British something more than words on January 13, 1938, when he dispatched what he called "a bomb" to Chamberlain. In Keith Feiling's words: "President Roosevelt suggested that he might make a world appeal for an agreement on disarmament, keeping of treaties, and access to raw material, which, if well received, might be followed up by a meeting of American and other neutral states, as a preliminary to a world conference. This thrust the wedge between the Prime Minister and the Foreign Minister a little deeper. For while Chamberlain feared the dictators would pay no heed, or else use this 'line-up of the democracies' as a pretext for a break, it was found on Eden's return [from a brief vacation] that he would rather risk that calamity than the loss of American good will. There was a first breath of resignation."

Chamberlain dreaded and opposed any attempt to form a wide, democratic front against the Axis. That meant, he believed, immediate war. The one path to peace that Chamberlain could see in 1938 lay in an agreement with Hitler, and he regarded Roosevelt's intervention as a piece of inadvertent warmongering. When Sir Ronald Lindsey, British Ambassador in Washington, urged acceptance of the Roosevelt proposal, Chamberlain made the counterproposal that the United States recognize Italy's conquest of Ethiopia. Chamberlain, moreover, took these decisions and actions in Eden's absence and without consulting or even informing him. When Eden returned to the Foreign Office, he at once cabled Lindsey to undo the damage, but the message arrived too late. Cordell Hull had already seen Chamberlain's counterproposal, which he and Roosevelt rejected because they believed it would "rouse a feeling of disgust and would revive and multiply all fears of pulling chestnuts out of the fire." Churchill, in *The Gathering Storm*, written ten years after the accident happened, appended this further observation: "That Mr. Chamberlain, with his limited outlook and experience of the European scene, should have possessed the self-sufficiency to wave away the proffered hand stretched out across the Atlantic leaves one, even at this date, breathless with amazement. The lack of all sense of proportion, and even of self-preservation, which this episode reveals in an upright, competent, well-meaning man, charged with the destinies of our country and all who depended upon it, is appalling."

The man who conceived the plan that Roosevelt tried to put through did not place all the blame on Neville Chamberlain. Sumner Welles, as Under Secretary of State, held his chief, Cordell Hull, equally responsible. According to Welles's book, *Seven Decisions That Shaped History*, he and Roosevelt wanted to announce the plan from the White House on Armistice Day, 1937. Hull, however, disapproved. He described the projected White House affair as "pyrotechnics," and the plan itself seemed to him "thoroughly unrealistic." Some weeks later he agreed to a more cautious procedure which called, first, for consultation with Britain and then with Italy, France, and Germany. Welles protested in vain: "For the United States to make its move dependent upon Mr. Chamberlain's consent, and contingently upon a green light from Berlin and Rome, was to court disaster if we wanted any practical results. To this argument I added that with the moral and emotional impact of the move already lost, if we were now to have any chance whatever for success the project must be launched without prior warning." Chamberlain reacted as Welles had feared—and as Hull perhaps had hoped—and within a month Eden quit.

Lord Halifax, who replaced him, shared Chamberlain's passion for peace. He had shown his tolerance for the Nazis by attending a boar hunt in Germany as Göring's guest, but he drew the line when it came to meeting the Russians halfway. Chamberlain regarded the Russians as "half Asiatic" and hence beyond the pale. Halifax had no prejudice against Asiatics; his applied Christianity had won Gandhi's heart. But atheistic Communism affronted his religious nature. Halifax's service as Foreign Secretary began inauspiciously. The news of Hitler's seizure of Austria hit him in the same way and in the same place that the news of the German invasion of Belgium hit Sir Edward Grey when he saw the lights going out all over Europe in 1914. "Horrible, horrible," Halifax exclaimed as he paced the floor of the same Foreign Office in which Grey had broken down and wept when England declared war on Germany. "I never thought they would do it."

· V ·

THE matter-of-fact Chamberlain responded more coolly. The League of Nations, declared Chamberlain, "as constituted today cannot provide collective security for anybody." As he saw it, "The peace of Europe must depend on the attitude of the four major powers—Germany, Italy, France, and ourselves. . . . If we can bring these four nations into friendly discussion, into a settling of their differences, we shall have saved the peace of Europe for a generation." But what caused Chamberlain the most acute concern after Austria fell was Czechoslovakia: "If we can avoid another violent coup in Czechoslovakia, which ought to be feasible, it may be possible for Europe to settle down again and someday for us to start peace talks with the Germans." On March 20, however, he told the House of Commons that he had "abandoned any idea of giving guarantees to Czechoslovakia or the French in connection with her obligations to that country."

Chamberlain referred here to the mutual assistance treaty that bound France to aid Czechoslovakia against any act of external aggression. Another treaty bound Russia to aid Czechoslovakia, on condition that the French moved first. But neither France nor Russia had a common frontier with Czechoslovakia. The French could aid Czechoslovakia only by attacking Germany; the Russians could aid Czechoslovakia only by sending troops across Poland or Rumania—and both Poland and Rumania warned that they would resist any such move with force. At the same time Chamberlain was making it clear that Britain would not underwrite the French treaty with Czechoslovakia, the British Ambassador in Prague informed him that Russia would also keep hands off. The treason trials in Moscow and the purge of the Red Army's High Command seemed to confirm this report.

Winston Churchill took a different view. On March 14, the day after Chamberlain called for "peace talks with the Germans," Churchill treated the House of Commons to a characteristic blend of irony, humor, and moral indignation on the subject of Czechoslovakia: "To English ears, the name of Czechoslovakia sounds outlandish. No doubt they are only a small democratic state, no doubt they have an army only two or three times as large as ours, no doubt they have a munitions supply only three times as great as that of Italy, but still they are a virile people, they have their rights, they have their treaty rights, they have a line of fortresses, and they have a strongly manifested will to live, a will to live freely." Churchill did not argue that British support for Czechoslovakia would mean peace. He did argue that it would spell Hitler's doom, whereas further appeasement of Hitler would spell the doom of western Europe.

Chamberlain believed that support for Czechoslovakia would spell war, defeat, and the end of all things: "You have only to look at the map to see that nothing we or France could do could possibly save Czechoslovakia from being overrun by the Germans if they wanted to do it." And plenty of British politicians agreed with Chamberlain. Lloyd George had declared, after a visit to Nazi Germany, that its leaders wanted British friendship. Sir Archibald Sinclair, leader of the Liberal Party in the House of Commons, described Hitlerism as a revolt against humiliation. Nor did any Labor Party pacifist denounce war more sweepingly than Neville Chamberlain, who said that war "wins nothing, cures nothing, ends nothing." The loss of seven million young men "cut off in their prime" and the thirteen million "maimed and mutilated" convinced Chamberlain that "in war there are no winners, but all are losers."

On May 21 the Germans massed eleven divisions at war strength along the Czechoslovak border. The war that Chamberlain feared seemed about to explode. Within five hours the Czechs replied with a counter-mobilization of four hundred thousand men. Another million and a half armed reservists stood by. The Russians praised the Czech stand. The French declared their loyalty to their ally. Even the British government warned Germany not to count on its standing aside if war came, and Hitler called off his mobilization. Had he planned to attack? According to the detailed and authoritative *Crisis Over Czechoslovakia,* published by the Royal Institute for International Affairs, and edited by R. G. D. Laffan, "What was certain was that a most dangerous situation existed and continued to exist. In such circumstances it was most unfortunate that many newspapers in France and Britain indulged in complacent talk about vigorous diplomacy having saved the peace. Instead of saying as little as possible, they rubbed it in that Hitler had recoiled before the determined front presented to him and had abandoned, at any rate for a time, his projected attack on the Czechs."

But not for long. On May 30, nine days after the fiasco of his mobilization against Czechoslovakia, Hitler issued a new directive, entitled "Operation Green," to the commanders of the Army, Navy, and Air Force. A covering letter to Keitel, Chief of the General Staff, gave October 1, 1938, as the latest possible date for carrying the plan through. "It is my unalterable decision to smash Czechoslovakia by military action in the near future," wrote Hitler. "It is the business of the political leadership to await or bring about a suitable moment from a political and military point of view. An unavoidable development of events within Czechoslovakia, or other political events in Europe providing a suddenly favorable opportunity which may never recur, may cause me to take early action. The proper choice and determined exploitation of a favorable moment is the surest guarantee of success. To this end preparations are to be made immediately."

During the summer months of 1938 Hitler waged the same war of nerves against Czechoslovakia that he had waged during the previous winter against Austria. But with this difference. Hitler used his leadership of the German people to justify his conquest of Austria. Although the majority of the Austrian people opposed Nazi rule to the end, they commanded little support abroad and Hitler's claim to represent all Germans gave the outside world the excuse it needed to look the other way. Czechoslovakia not only had the protection of its treaties with France and Russia. Barely 20 per cent of its people came of German ancestry. More than half the population was Czech; another quarter was Slovak. But the substantial German minority lived close to the German frontier. A small, no less compact Hungarian minority lived on the Hungarian

UNITED PRESS PHOTO

Konrad Henlein, Leader of the Sudeten Germans, Presents His Party's Flag to Rudolf Hess, Representing Hitler

border, and some eighty thousand Poles inhabited the Teschen district near Poland. The peacemakers who drew the frontiers of Czechoslovakia followed the line laid down by geography, history, and economics. They paid rather less heed to Wilson's new doctrine of self-determination. Indeed, President Masaryk complained that Lloyd George had forced him, against his will, to include in the Czechoslovak Republic more than three million Sudeten Germans. Czechoslovakia thus took shape as a strategic unit rather than a national one. Its frontiers did not follow the new principle of national self-determination promulgated by Wilson but the older principle of economic and political interest that had governed the conduct of the Hapsburgs and their neighbors for so many centuries.

Some of the subject nationalities that gained independence as a result of the war persecuted their former persecutors or found new and weaker victims. Not so the Czechs. Recognizing their own vulnerability, within and without, they gave Czechoslovakia's various national minorities more freedom than any other minorities enjoyed in any other part of eastern Europe. But the Sudeten Germans, in their dependence upon industry rather than farming, suffered acutely during the depression, and when Hitler came to power he quickly won over most of the younger generation. These young people had joined a chain of sports clubs organized by a veteran of the Austrian Army named Konrad Henlein, who gave up his first postwar job as a bank clerk to become a gymnastics instructor. These clubs assumed more and more of a political character, especially after 1933, when Henlein founded the Sudeten German Party. Two years later, when Czechoslovakia signed its treaty with Russia, the Henleinists received 70 per cent of all the German votes and became the largest single political party in the country. But not until the summer of 1938, when Henlein's party received 90 per cent of the German vote in local elections, did he identify himself with the Nazis. Until that time he asked only for greater autonomy within the Czechoslovak Republic, and even his eight-point "Karlsbad Program" called only for full liberty to "demonstrate Germanism," including support for the Nazi program.

Actually, Henlein had taken orders from Hitler for years, and Hitler in his turn had planned for years to crush Czechoslovakia by disrupting it from the inside. He set about this business not by stressing his own racial doctrines but by appealing to Wilson's principle of national self-determination. Czechoslovakia held the late American President in singularly high esteem, and the founders of the young Republic had honored him by giving the chief square and the chief railway station in Prague his name. They also tried to apply his principles to their own national minorities, as the Austrians had never applied these same principles to them. Although the Nazis spurned and violated Wilson's doctrines in their relations with non-Germans, they invoked these same doctrines in behalf of German minorities outside the Reich. In like manner, the same people who deplored agitation in behalf of Hitler's Jewish victims in Germany expressed sympathy for the plight of the Sudeten Germans in Czechoslovakia. It was the old question of whose ox was being gored.

By late July, Chamberlain finally descried in Czechoslovakia a threat to the roast beef of old England. He therefore turned to Lord Runciman, formerly Sir Walter Runciman of the Liberal Party, and asked him to head a mission to study the Sudeten problem on the spot and to recommend a solution. "I quite understand," said Runciman to Halifax before he left. "You are setting me adrift in a small boat in mid-Atlantic," and Halifax replied, "That is exactly the position." The Sudeten Germans met Runciman on his arrival and kept close beside him during the month he spent in Czechoslovakia. "This is granting belligerent rights to our Franco before he has even started the open rebellion," one Czech editor remarked. "I have much sympathy for the Sudeten case," said Runciman, who spent little time getting the point of view of the leaders of the Czechoslovak Republic. "It is a hard thing," he added, "to be ruled by an alien race." He admitted that Czechoslovak rule was "not actively oppressive and certainly not 'terroristic,'" but he did find it marked by "tactlessness, lack of understanding, petty intolerance, and discrimination." He foresaw inevitable revolt, referred to the Czechs as "invaders," opposed any plebiscite as a "sheer formality," and recommended the transfer of the frontier districts to Germany plus local autonomy for German minorities remaining inside the Czechoslovak Republic. Chamberlain concurred: "My personal opinion was that on principle I did not care two hoots whether the Sudetens were in the Reich or out of it, according to their own wishes, but I saw immense practical difficulties in a plebiscite."

Whatever personal prejudices may have driven Chamberlain and Runciman to these conclusions, they rationalized the fears and hopes of millions. Mackenzie King, Canada's Liberal Prime Minister and Roosevelt's old friend and admirer, wrote to a member of the British Cabinet in April: "I hope you will tell Mr. Chamberlain that I cannot begin to express the admiration for the manner in which he has performed a task, more difficult than any with which any Prime Minister of Britain has ever before been faced. I approve wholeheartedly of the course he has adopted, particularly of his determination to get in touch with Germany and Italy, to seek to restore good will between these countries and the United Kingdom, instead of permitting ill will to develop to the point of another world war, and his exposure of the unreality and worse of the situation at Geneva." Mackenzie King spoke for the majority of the Canadian people, and the Prime Ministers of all the other British Dominions echoed his views. Support for Chamberlain cut across party, class, and even national lines. Most of the peoples of the world hoped that Europe could avoid a second war at any cost. Although the French nicknamed Chamberlain *"J'aime Berlin,"* the prospect of another war less than twenty years after more than a million of their young men had lost their lives in the last one froze their blood. The British, who had suffered almost as heavy losses, did not entirely share the French fear and suspicion of Germany. Most Conservatives regarded Churchill as a dangerous alarmist; most Laborites and Liberals considered him a warmonger. Only the Russian leaders and their Communist supporters and fellow travelers throughout the world called for a wide, strong anti-Fascist front. However, their own inconsistencies and weaknesses made them suspect. Too often before, their support for any cause except their own had proved the kiss of death.

· VI ·

You cannot beat something with nothing. Hitler offered the German people a program that promised to make their country the leading power in Europe. The prospective victims of this program offered no alternative. The League of Nations did not exist as an independent force. "Peace is indivisible," announced Litvinov as one localized war after another broke out all around the world—in Manchuria, the Chaco, Abyssinia, Spain, China. The words "collective security" proved equally meaningless. Roosevelt's quarantine appeal fell flat. His popular domestic policies failed to allay the suspicion that his policies abroad might drag America into war. In Britain, Churchill carried a heavy burden of popular distrust. In 1915 and 1916 he had identified himself with the Dardanelles disaster. In 1918 and 1919 he had backed the futile intervention in Russia's civil war. He had led the fight against the general strike in 1926 and had opposed any concessions to the Indian Nationalists. He had expressed admiration for Mussolini and had endorsed non-intervention in Spain and Edward VIII in England. This record of backing wrong or reactionary horses made his warnings against Hitler almost as suspect as Stalin's belated conversion to anti-Fascism.

Neville Chamberlain appealed to a wider public when he preached peace for its own sake. He dismissed the possibility that a wide and solid anti-Nazi front might cause Hitler to back down without war or that continued concessions to Hitler might lead to war under still worse conditions. The immorality of the Hitler regime influenced him no more than the righteousness of Czechoslovakia's cause. Immediately after Hitler seized Austria Chamberlain commented: "It is perfectly evident now, surely, that force is the only argument Germany understands and that collective security cannot offer any prospect of preventing such events until it can show a visible overwhelming strength, backed by determination to use it." In May, 1938, he went further than any British statesman had dared to go in July, 1914. He warned Germany that in the event of a general European war, Britain probably could not stand aside. But in the months that followed Chamberlain reversed himself while Hitler made it ever plainer that further warnings of this kind would be more likely to provoke than to prevent war. Reliable reports of Hitler's plan to smash Czechoslovakia reached Chamberlain, who could see but one hope of peace: appeasement.

This strategy suited Hitler, who kept in the background during the summer of 1938 while Konrad Henlein pressed Premier Hodža of Czechoslovakia to grant the Sudeten Germans more autonomy. In July, Henlein quietly visited Hitler at Munich and soon afterward his followers demanded the breakup of Czechoslovakia into several self-governing national states. Chamberlain had no illusions about German methods and intentions: "The Germans who are bullies by nature are too conscious of their strength and our weakness and until we are as strong as they are, we shall always be kept in this state of chronic anxiety." Arthur Robinson of the British Supply Board had just told him that it would be a year before England could fight Germany on more or less equal terms. "The government of which I am at present the head," Chamberlain told a Birmingham audience in late July, "intends to hold on its course which is set for appeasement of the world." At the same time, Halifax told Premier Daladier in Paris: "The French alliance with Czechoslovakia is at present the greatest menace to European peace."

In August, while the Runciman mission to Czechoslovakia stalled for time, plane production in France dropped almost to zero. French metalworkers, taking advantage of the social legislation just passed by the Popular Front government, all went off on paid vacations that extended from August 5 to August 29. Yet the Germans had at least four thousand

UNITED PRESS PHOTO

Hitler Addresses a Nazi Rally at Nuremberg

military planes of the latest design, the French only about twelve hundred earlier models. The Germans, working full time at war production, had fortified their Siegfried Line to such a point that French ground troops could not hope to break through except after weeks and probably months of slaughter.

On September 7, the semiofficial London *Times* gave Hitler the opening he had waited for all summer. "If the Sudetens," wrote the *Times*, "now ask for more than the Czech government are apparently ready to give in their latest set of proposals, it can only be inferred that the Germans are going beyond the mere removal of disabilities and do not find themselves at ease within the Czechoslovak Republic. In that case it might be worth while for the Czechoslovak government to consider whether they should exclude altogether the project, which has found favor in some quarters, of making Czechoslovakia a more homogeneous state by the secession of that fringe of alien populations who are contiguous to the nation with which they are united by race. In any case the wishes of the population concerned would seem to be a decisively important element in any solution that can hope to be regarded as permanent, and the advantages to Czechoslovakia of becoming a homogeneous state might conceivably outweigh the obvious disadvantages of losing the Sudeten German districts of the borderland."

The British government, replying to protests from Prague, announced that it did not endorse the *Times* editorial. The *Times* itself denied that it spoke officially. But the break for which Hitler had been waiting had come at last. On September 12 at Nuremberg he opened the climax of his

UNITED PRESS PHOTO

War Scare Drives Sudeten Germans across Boundary to German Soil

final speech before the annual Nazi Party rally with the expectoration: *"Ich spreche von der Tschechoslovakei,"* and went on to charge the Beneš regime at Prague with having terrorized the Sudeten Germans: "This may be a matter of indifference to the leaders of the democracies, but to us it is not. If these tortured creatures cannot find justice and help from themselves, they will obtain it from us. To believe that such a regime can continue its sins shows incredible blindness." He called Beneš a *Verbrecher*, a criminal, and Henlein broke off his talks with Hodža in Prague. The distraught Czechs found bitter satisfaction in circulating the story that Henlein had demanded the post of Minister of the Interior. Hodža supposedly refused the request but was alleged to have offered to create a new post for Henlein—Minister for Colonies. "How come?" asked Henlein. "That's impossible. Czechoslovakia has no colonies." "What of it?" Hodža retorted. "Has not Italy a Minister of Finance and Germany a Minister of Justice?"

"Grace under pressure"—Ernest Hemingway's definition of courage— summed up Czechoslovakia's response to Hitler's incitement that the German radio kept repeating. The sporadic riots that had broken out in the Sudetenland in early September subsided. The Czechs quietly established martial law, many Sudeten Germans assured the Prague authorities of their loyalty to the Republic, and the pro-Nazi leaders fled or went into hiding. Most of the violence in the Sudetenland came from the same kind of armed intellectual who had supported Hitler in Germany. These armed intellectuals had powerful friends across the German border and submissive if reluctant helpers in Paris and London.

The day before Hitler demanded the dismemberment of Czechoslovakia Chamberlain committed this line of thought to paper: "I fully
realize that if eventually things go wrong and the aggression takes place,
there will be many, including Winston, who will say that the British
government must bear the responsibility, and if only they had the courage to tell Hitler now that, if he used force, we should at once declare
war, that would have stopped him. By that time it will be impossible to
prove the contrary, but I am satisfied that we should be wrong to allow
the most vital decision that any country could take, the decision as to
peace or war, to pass out of our hands into those of the ruler of another
country, and a lunatic at that." The day after Hitler made his Nuremberg
speech, Chamberlain cabled him: "In view of increasing critical situation, I propose to come over at once to see you with a view to trying to
find a peaceful solution. I propose to come across by air and am ready to
start tomorrow. Please indicate earliest time at which you can see me,
and suggest place of meeting. Should be grateful for very early reply."

This message wafted Hitler, as he himself put it, into the realms of
bliss. He had expected and prepared for war; now the British Prime
Minister gave him reason to hope for his most spectacular peaceful victory to date. Everything seemed to be going Germany's way. On September 9, Roosevelt had told his weekly news conference that it was
"100 per cent incorrect" to associate the United States with Britain and
France in a common front of resistance to Hitler. The Polish government, eager to wrest the border city of Teschen from Czechoslovakia,
was backing Germany. Litvinov had announced that Russian troops
would come to the aid of Czechoslovakia only if the League of Nations
could persuade the Rumanians to let those troops cross their soil. The
Rumanian Foreign Minister at once repudiated the suggestion and
added that if the Russians tried to move across Rumania, Polish as well
as Rumanian troops would block their way.

With all these cards in his hands, Hitler invited Chamberlain to his
Berchtesgaden retreat. At first, according to Chamberlain, Hitler exclaimed, "I can't possibly let a man of his age come all this way; I must
go to London." But Chamberlain continued: "Of course, when he considered it further, he saw that wouldn't do, and indeed it would not have
suited me, for it would have deprived my coup of much of its dramatic
force. But it shows a side of Hitler that would surprise many people in
this country." When the two men sat down together on the evening of
September 16 and talked for three hours through an interpreter, Hitler
impressed his British visitor more favorably than not. "We sat down,"
wrote Chamberlain immediately afterward, "I next to Hitler, with the
interpreter on his other side. He seemed very shy, and his features did
not relax while I endeavored to find small talk. I: 'I have often heard of

this room, but it's much bigger than I expected.' H: 'It is you who have big rooms in England.' I: 'You must come and see them sometime.' H: 'I should be received with expressions of disapproval.' I: 'Well, perhaps it would be wise to choose the moment.' At this point H. permitted himself the shadow of a smile." Hitler did most of the talking, mostly in low tones, and promised, after stating his case, not to give any order to march until Chamberlain had consulted with his government and with the French. "I had established a certain confidence, which was my aim," Chamberlain wrote three days later, "and on my side, in spite of the hardness and ruthlessness I thought I saw in his face, I got the impression that here was a man who could be relied upon when he had given his word."

It was a grudging and qualified word that Hitler finally gave. He assured Chamberlain that he wanted no Czechs inside the Third Reich, but he did want those parts of the Sudetenland where Germans predominated. He suggested an eventual exchange of minorities, but when Chamberlain finally pressed him on ways and means he exclaimed: "I am determined to settle it and to settle it soon and I am prepared to risk a world war rather than allow this to drag on." Chamberlain, weary, disgusted, and angry, asked if Hitler had any further suggestion to make and received the mild reply that if the British government would accept the principle of "the secession of the Sudeten German region by virtue of the right of self-determination," some solution might be arranged. It was left that Chamberlain should consult his Cabinet colleagues in London, exchange views with the French, and return in a few days' time for a second meeting at or near Cologne.

· VII ·

THE INTERVIEW at Berchtesgaden and the discussions that followed among British, French, and Czech leaders set off demonstrations of mass hysteria heard around the world. The radio, especially in the United States, carried a steady flow of bulletins, interpretations, arguments, discussions, reports. H. V. Kaltenborn's round-the-clock commentaries over the Columbia Broadcasting System's network made him almost as celebrated, among his fellow Americans, as Hitler himself. But while the American public followed the Czechoslovak crisis as if it were a new and more exciting spectator sport, the people of Europe felt themselves directly involved. Having charged the Czechs with committing atrocities against the Sudeten Germans, Hitler told Chamberlain at Berchtesgaden that he could not guarantee to keep the peace unless the Czechs ceased their endless provocations. Inasmuch as the Czechs had shown exemplary restraint and all the provocation had come from the German

UNITED PRESS PHOTO

H. V. Kaltenborn Covers the Crisis with CBS News Director Paul White

side, Hitler's attitude was not calculated to convince the Czechs that forbearance paid. Nor did Hitler's own record encourage the belief that he would refrain from further provocations. Yet the Czechs continued to restrain themselves, while preparing for the worst. On September 22 a general strike in Prague forced the Hodža government, which had become the symbol of capitulation, to resign. In its place President Beneš appointed a nonpolitical coalition of National Defense, headed by General Syrovy, the one-eyed leader of the Czech Legion's legendary march across Bolshevik Russia in 1918. Only the Henleinists and the Slovak Agrarian Party had no representation in the new regime, which ordered a general mobilization on September 23. "I guarantee," Syrovy told the Czechoslovak people, "that the Army stands and will stand on our frontiers and defend our liberty to the last. I may soon have to call upon you here to take an active part in the defense of our country in which we all long to join." Beneš spoke in the same vein: "If it is necessary to fight, we shall do so to our last breath. If we have to negotiate, we shall do so. But our beloved Czechoslovakia shall not perish."

Sentiment for Czechoslovakia grew ever stronger abroad. But it was sentiment only. Determination to back this sentiment with force, if need be, failed to materialize. Clement Attlee as leader of the Labor Opposition in the British House of Commons vainly asked Chamberlain to summon Parliament into session and give it "an opportunity of confirming or rejecting" his decisions. Receiving no reply, he accused Chamberlain of having committed "a grave departure from declared British policy" in that he had accepted "the dismemberment of a sovereign state at the dictation of the ruler of Germany." For Chamberlain and Halifax had persuaded Daladier and Bonnet to join them in urging the Czechs to cede certain Sudeten German areas to Germany at once and to permit plebiscites in other disputed areas. At first the Czechs refused to capitulate, but gave way when they were informed that France would not aid them if they persisted in their refusal. No demonstrators appeared in the streets of London and Paris protesting against Chamberlain and Daladier as the people of Prague protested against Hodža. Indeed, the French government warned its Czech allies that if they refused to accept the Anglo-French proposals unconditionally and war broke out, the Czechs would be responsible and could expect no help.

"There it was at last," wrote R. G. D. Laffan in *The Crisis Over Czechoslovakia*. "The British government covered their meaning in the decent phrases of diplomacy, but that meaning was plain. Great Britain would not fight. And France was repudiating her treaty obligations, so often publicly declared to be sacrosanct. Czechoslovakia not only stood alone and unsupported, but was to be held responsible for the outbreak of hostilities, should she be attacked." Yet what else could France, or Britain either, have done? In both countries there were those who urged support for Czechoslovakia at all costs. In both countries there were those who called for peace at any price. But most Britons and Frenchmen, most West Europeans and Americans watched the events of September with agonized and mixed emotions. They sympathized with Czechoslovakia. They detested Hitler. They yearned for peace. They hated war. Bewildered Parisians began setting up first-aid stations to treat the victims of air attacks; uncomprehending Londoners dug trenches in their parks. The people of Czechoslovakia were at first staggered. For a few days in mid-September, the Sudeten Nazis demonstrated in the streets, kidnaped Czech and German democrats, and shipped them across the border to Germany. But soon the Czech people responded more sharply as workers and soldiers demonstrated in the streets of Prague and the Nazis ran for cover.

The Czech press argued that enlightened self-interest should persuade the British and the French to stand firm against Hitler, even at the risk of war. "One thing must be clear," wrote Colonel Moravec in *Lidove Noviny*. "If there should be a conflict between the Third Reich and the West, the West will be far weaker without Czechoslovakia on its side. Another thing must be clear. The crippling of Czechoslovakia cannot avert the clash between the Third Reich and the West but will rather

UNITED PRESS PHOTO

Czech Soldiers Mobilize

hurry it forward, because it will increase the power of the Third
Reich. . . . The question at issue is who shall dominate Europe." Dr.
Hubert Ripka wrote in the same paper in the same vein: "It is incredible
that anyone should imagine such a surrender would preserve peace. It
could at the best merely postpone the explosion. We are horrified at the
blindness of the Western Powers if they really imagine that Germany is
concerned about the Sudeten Germans. She is using them because she
sees very rightly that if she succeeds here and breaks up Czechoslovakia,
she will be master of the entire Danube basin right down to the Black
Sea." And the British correspondent G. E. R. Gedye quoted a Czech official who watched the Czech soldiers preparing to go to the frontier, still
unaware of the fact that their government had finally capitulated to the
Anglo-French demands: "Such fine boys—such gallant, gallant boys—
only asking for the chance to save their country at the cost of their own
lives. Our children—ours and France's. France told us how to arm them,
France built our forts, France sent her officers here to train our boys to
fight her battles and ours at her side. And now France has strangled
them, before they could strike a blow for all we believe in—for liberty,
for democracy, for decency."

The French, no longer strong enough to stand up to the Germans,
had to turn to the British, and in due course the Socialist Léon Blum
found himself praising the "noble initiative" of the Tory Neville Chamberlain, who, at the age of sixty-nine, took his first airplane trip and
humbled his own and his country's pride for the sake of peace. The

worst remained to come. Having persuaded the French and the Czechs to accept the dismemberment of Czechoslovakia that Hitler had demanded, Chamberlain flew to Cologne for a second meeting at the little town of Godesberg on the other side of the Rhine. He opened their first conversation with a progress report on the agreement that the British, French, and Czech governments had reached concerning the peaceful and gradual transfer of the German-populated areas of the Sudetenland to Germany. Hitler, however, rejected the terms that he himself had outlined at Berchtesgaden the previous week, and insisted that Poland and Hungary also receive some portions of Czechoslovakia. Worse yet, he demanded a definite and complete settlement by October first at the latest. "A frontier line must be drawn at once," Hitler told Chamberlain, "from which the Czechs must withdraw the Army, police, and all state organs; this area would be at once occupied by Germany." If this "peaceful solution" were not accepted, Hitler threatened a "military solution," which meant a frontier "not on a national but a strategic basis."

Chamberlain went back to Cologne from this first conversation sick at heart. Fearing the interpreter had translated incorrectly, he opened an exchange of letters with Hitler and requested a memorandum. But Hitler still threatened to invade Czechoslovakia if the evacuation of the Sudetenland did not begin by September 28. Forty-eight hours after their first conversation, Chamberlain and Hitler conferred at Godesberg again, late on the evening of Friday, September 24, when Hitler produced a map and a memorandum which read more like an ultimatum. Chamberlain agreed to pass this on to the Prague authorities without endorsement and then expressed such indignation at the whole performance that Hitler agreed to postpone his deadline for the evacuation of the Sudetenland from September 28 to October 1. "You are the only man," he assured his visitor, "to whom I have ever made a concession." Then came another tirade, followed by a quiet, private conversation during the small hours of the morning. Hitler assured the British Prime Minister that he had made his "last territorial demand in Europe," and almost pleaded for an Anglo-German agreement: "You take the sea and we take the land."

Did Hitler put on the air of earnestness that so impressed Chamberlain or did he mean exactly what he said? Was he deliberately lying or did he hope to revert to the policy of friendship with England that he had outlined in *Mein Kampf*? Was Hitler still set on starting a general war or did he hope to gain his ends by threats and bluff? A peasant cunning accounted for many of Hitler's actions, but he also relied heavily on his intuition, and at critical moments the peasant and the mystic in his split personality struggled for mastery. Confronted by Chamberlain,

UNITED PRESS PHOTO

Hitler Defies Czechoslovakia. The Sign above the Speaker's Rostrum Reads: "The Germans in Czechoslovakia are Neither Unprotected Nor Abandoned. Let That Be Noted."

the peasant and the mystic found themselves in accord. The peasant in him lied; the mystic in him believed the lie. And Chamberlain's will to peace led him to put the most favorable possible construction on Hitler's words.

Snatching a few hours' sleep in Cologne, Chamberlain flew back to London the next morning. Already Hitler had wrecked the institution of the British weekend: on Sunday the Cabinet met three times. Chamberlain permitted himself a characteristic outburst of understatement: "I must say I find Herr Hitler's conduct unreasonable." The British and the French governments told the Czechs that they could no longer advise them to do anything but mobilize. Syrovy needed no encouragement to take the hint. Daladier and Bonnet came to London and let it be known that France would fulfill its treaty obligations and fight Germany if Hitler invaded the Sudetenland. The British government, without consulting the Soviet authorities, announced that both Britain and Russia would stand by France. On September 26, President Roosevelt sent identical messages to Hitler, Beneš, Chamberlain, and Daladier urging continued negotiation: "I earnestly repeat that so long as negotiations continue, differences may be reconciled. Once they are broken off, reason is banished and force asserts itself. And force produces no solution for the future good of humanity."

That same evening Hitler addressed a mass meeting in the Berlin Sportspalast: "The existence of Czechoslovakia is based on a lie, and the

father of that lie is Beneš. When Beneš's lies had created this state, he
began a rule of terror. He was determined to exterminate the Germans.
And up to a point he has succeeded." Near the end, however, Hitler expressed gratitude to Chamberlain: "I have assured him that the German
people desire nothing else than peace, but I have also told him that I
cannot go back behind the limits set to our patience. I have further assured him, and I repeat it here, that when this problem is solved, there
is no further territorial problem in Europe. And I have further assured
him that at the moment when Czechoslovakia solves her problems, that
means when the Czechs have come to terms with their other minorities,
and that peaceably and not through oppression, then I have no further
interest in the Czech state. And that is guaranteed to him! We want no
Czechs!" He wound up with the statement that the decision, peace or
war, lay with Beneš alone.

At noon the next day Chamberlain's personal friend and emissary, Sir
Horace Wilson, called on Hitler in Berlin to express the hope that he had
not spoken his last word at the Sportspalast. Again Hitler insisted that
the Czechoslovak government must accept the Godesberg memorandum.
"Ich werde die Tschechen zerschlagen!" he shouted more than once.
Wilson pointed out that if Hitler tried to smash the Czechs, both France
and England would fight. "If France and England strike, let them do
so," Hitler replied. "It is a matter of complete indifference to me.
I am prepared for every eventuality. I can only take note of the position.
It is Tuesday today and by next Monday we shall all be at war." A second message had just arrived from President Roosevelt, addressed to
Hitler alone, again urging negotiation: "Should you agree to a solution
in this peaceful manner, I am convinced that hundreds of millions
throughout the world would recognize your action as an outstanding
service to all humanity." Roosevelt suggested a conference of "all the nations directly interested in the present controversy," at the same time
making it clear that the United States could "assume no obligations" in
this connection. Roosevelt also sent messages to Mussolini, Stalin, and
the heads of other interested governments suggesting they make personal appeals to both Hitler and Beneš. The possibility of a general
European conference to deal with existing tensions began to receive
serious attention in several quarters.

Chamberlain, however, feared that time was running out. The German ultimatum to Czechoslovakia expired the following day. Chamberlain summoned Parliament to hear a report on his efforts to keep the
peace, and at eight o'clock in the evening of September 27 he broadcast
a message to the people of Britain and the Empire: "How horrible, fantastic, incredible it is that we should be digging trenches and trying on
gas masks here because of a quarrel in a faraway country between

people of whom we know nothing. It seems still more impossible that a quarrel which has been settled in principle should be the subject of war." He then discussed the Sudeten German problem and described Hitler's attitude as "unreasonable." He offered to pay a third visit to Germany, but could see little hope for success. And then he struck quite a different note. "However much we may sympathize with a small nation confronted by a big and powerful neighbor, we cannot in all circumstances undertake to involve the whole British Empire in war simply on her account. If we have to fight, it must be on larger issues than that. I am myself a man of peace to the depths of my soul. Armed conflict between nations is a nightmare to me; but if I were convinced that any nation had made up its mind to dominate the world by fear of its force, I should feel that it must be resisted. Under such a domination life for people who believe in liberty would not be worth living; but war is a fearful thing, and we must be very clear before we embark on it that it is really the great issues that are at stake, and that the call to risk everything in their defense is irresistible. For the present I ask you to await as calmly as you can the events of the next few days. As long as war has not begun, there is always hope that it may be prevented, and you know that I am going to work for peace until the last moment. Good night."

· VIII ·

Two HOURS later Chamberlain's flickering hopes revived. He was working on his report to the House of Commons when a letter arrived from Hitler, replying to the letter that Sir Horace Wilson had presented at the Reichschancellery the day before. Hitler's letter did not modify the Godesberg memorandum or his remarks to Wilson. But the fact that he had committed himself in writing led Chamberlain to conclude that he had narrowed down the differences "to a point where it was inconceivable that they could not be settled by negotiations." At any rate, that was what Chamberlain told the House of Commons the next afternoon. He also told the House that he had sent "one more last letter" to Hitler along with a letter to Mussolini thanking the Italian dictator for having persuaded Hitler to postpone his mobilization order for another twenty-four hours. Chamberlain had just paid tribute to Mussolini when Sir John Simon called his attention to two sheets of paper that Lord Halifax had rushed in to him a few moments before. Chamberlain glanced at them briefly and then whispered to Simon: "Shall I tell them now?" Simon nodded and the Prime Minister went on: "That is not all. I have something further to say to the House yet. I have now been informed by Herr Hitler that he invites me to meet him at Munich tomorrow morning. He has also invited Signor Mussolini and M. Daladier. Signor Mussolini

UNITED PRESS PHOTO

British Children Receiving Gas Masks

has accepted and I have no doubt that M. Daladier will also accept. I need not say what my answer will be." Liberals and Laborites joined in congratulations and good wishes as the House adjourned for a few days, when, in Chamberlain's words, "we perhaps may meet again in happier circumstances."

The combined talents of D. W. Griffith and Max Reinhardt could not have staged a more effective performance. But the confusion that had prevailed throughout the morning in Rome, Berlin, and Paris gave no hint of the dramatic climax witnessed by the House of Commons that same afternoon. Both Roosevelt and Chamberlain had urged Mussolini to put all possible pressure on Hitler not to go to war—and Mussolini needed no urging. He dreaded as much as anyone the prospect of war; he also saw a great role for himself as the keystone of European peace. Early in the morning of September 27, he ordered his Ambassador at Berlin to get through as soon as possible to Hitler in person, and while the British and French Ambassadors stood by, the Italian Ambassador made a special appeal, direct from the Duce. Göring and Neurath had been giving the same kind of advice, but Hitler hated to accept it. His intuition told him that the time for the showdown had come. An irrational passion for a bloody reckoning possessed him. But an equally powerful instinct held him back. Caution and cunning finally prevailed.

The Czechs had mobilized their Army. The British had mobilized their Navy. The French were summoning their reservists to the colors,

© LOW, ALL COUNTRIES

"What, no chair for me?"
Cartoon by David Low

"reluctantly and dourly," as Laffan wrote in *The Crisis Over Czechoslovakia.* "Hardly one, however, felt that France was plunging into war to defend her honor or her life. In so far as the public could understand what was going on, it seemed that Europe had become entangled in an argument from which all the contestants desired to escape without a loss of dignity." Daladier, equally fearful of French pacifists and German Nazis, saw the invitation to Munich as a way out of his dilemma, yet he went about muttering, "I shall not yield at Munich."

It was with a heavy heart that Daladier flew to Munich accompanied by Alexis Léger, permanent secretary at the French Foreign Office. Neville Chamberlain, accompanied by his friend Sir Horace Wilson, left London in a more buoyant frame of mind. "Out of this nettle, danger, we pluck the flower, safety," he told the crowd that gathered at the Croydon airport. Daladier and Chamberlain did not confer before they joined the two dictators and their two foreign ministers for a light noonday luncheon at the Munich Führerhaus. But Hitler had met Mussolini's train at the Italian border and had ridden with him in his private car. A Nazi official told Foreign Minister Ciano: "The Führer is half satisfied." This proved an overstatement. To Mussolini's horror, Hitler unfolded an enormous military map on which he outlined his plans for the quick conquest of Czechoslovakia and for his subsequent campaign against France. He fussed over the twenty-four-hour delay in mobilization as Mussolini sat nodding, in silent despair, until he remembered that his

UNITED PRESS PHOTO

The Munich Conference.
Left to Right: Chamberlain, Daladier, Hitler, Mussolini, Ciano

Ambassador at Berlin had sent him the gist of the demands Hitler was going to make at Munich. Mussolini believed Chamberlain and Daladier would accept these demands, but feared that Ribbentrop might urge Hitler to ask for more. Mussolini therefore let Hitler go on talking, but planned to do some talking himself at the conference table in behalf of the demands that he knew Hitler had already formulated.

The conference began at quarter of one. Three of the four chiefs of state had one adviser, and Hitler had two—Ribbentrop and the professional diplomat Baron Weiszäcker. Schmidt, who served as Hitler's personal translator, also attended as translator for all those present. Only Mussolini did not need his services because he alone spoke English, French, and German. Hitler spoke no language but German; Daladier no language but French. Chamberlain knew a little French and less German. The business of translation therefore slowed down the proceedings. Chamberlain started the ball rolling by urging the inclusion of a representative of Czechoslovakia. Daladier supported him, but Hitler insisted that the heads of the four powers must take responsibility for all decisions. Mussolini then surprised the Germans by using their proposals as the basis for discussion. To the British they seemed "a reasonable restatement of much that had been discussed in the Anglo-French and Anglo-German conversations." Hitler indulged in one brief tirade against the Czechs. Daladier asked if the conference had met to destroy Czechoslovakia or to assure its continued, if diminished, existence. Mussolini calmed them both down.

At seven in the evening, as the conference was entering its seventh hour, two representatives of the Czechoslovak Foreign Office who had spent more than two and a half hours waiting in an anteroom were given some details of the Four-Power plan to partition their country. Three hours later, they were handed a map and told by a member of the British delegation: "If you do not accept this, you will have to settle your affairs with the Germans absolutely alone. Perhaps the French may tell you this more gently, but you can believe me that they share our views. They are disinterested." At 1:30 A.M., after the four chiefs of state had signed the final agreement, the Czechs were permitted to enter the conference chamber and told they had until five o'clock that afternoon to go to Berlin and accept the settlement. It called for German troops to occupy a few German-speaking areas of Czechoslovakia on October 1, and to complete the occupation within ten days. Polish and Hungarian claims were to be considered within ninety days. The British and French governments guaranteed the new frontiers of the diminished Czechoslovakia.

On the afternoon of Friday, September 30, the Prague government announced the acceptance of the Munich Agreement because "any other decision today is impossible." But it added: "The Government of the Czechoslovak Republic, in announcing this acceptance, declares also before the whole world its protests against the decisions which were taken unilaterally and without our participation." A few hours later General Syrovy announced over the radio: "We have had to choose between making a desperate and hopeless defense, which would have meant the sacrifice of an entire generation of our adult young men, as well as of our women and children, and accepting without a struggle, and under pressure, terms which are without parallel in history for their ruthlessness. We have been anxious to make our contribution toward peace and we have been willing to make it, but not in the way which we are now constrained to do. We were deserted. We stood alone."

Mussolini's attitude at Munich seemed to Chamberlain "quiet and reserved." The Italian dictator appeared cowed by his German imitator, but showed himself "more than friendly" to the British Prime Minister, whom Hitler greeted with "the double handshake he reserves for specially friendly demonstration." At one in the morning, half groggy after twelve hours of negotiation and translation, Chamberlain proposed that he and Hitler hold a private conversation. Hitler, according to Chamberlain, "jumped at the idea and asked me to come to his private flat." They met, later that morning, Chamberlain bringing with him a brief statement which Hitler gladly and promptly signed: "We regard the Agreement signed last night, and the Anglo-German Naval Agreement, as symbolic of the desire of our two peoples never to go to war with one

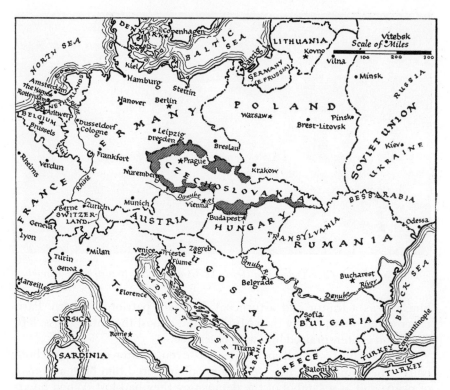

Europe After Munich, 1938. Shaded areas show territories acquired by Germany in March, 1938, after Hitler seized Austria, and in October, 1938, after transfer of Sudetenland from Czechoslovakia at Munich.

another again. We are resolved that the method of consultation shall be the method adopted to deal with any other questions that may concern our two countries, and we are determined to continue our efforts to remove possible sources of difference, and thus to contribute to assure the peace of Europe."

Meanwhile, the exhausted and despondent Daladier flew back to Paris. At Munich he dared not face the Czechs and tell them the decisions that he had endorsed at the conference table. He also refused to talk to journalists. The cheers he received from the sidewalks of Munich made him perk up a little, but the Germans had good reason to cheer. They were receiving the fruits of victory without having to pay the costs of war. The French people had less reason to celebrate. Indeed, as Daladier's plane approached Paris his gloom and fear increased. Spying a large crowd at the airport, he ordered the pilot to circle the field a few times as he steeled himself for the lynching that he expected—and thought he deserved. But when the throng rushed forward, they hailed

UNITED PRESS PHOTO

Parisian Crowds Give Daladier a Hero's Welcome on His Return from Munich

him, not as a traitor and a turncoat, but as a patriot and hero. Paris cheered him more loudly than Munich, and almost the entire press, left, right, and center, praised him with one voice.

Chamberlain received—and expected—even greater ovations at both ends of his return trip. The German people cheered him both as a man of peace and as a symbol of the democracy they had lost. When he arrived, in the afternoon, outside London, he drove at the invitation of King George from the airport to the palace and from the palace to Downing Street. The streets, he wrote, "were lined from one end to the other with people of every class, shouting themselves hoarse, leaping on the running board, banging on the windows, and thrusting their hands into the car to be shaken. The scenes culminated in Downing Street when I spoke to the multitudes below from the same window, I believe, as that from which Dizzy announced peace with honor sixty years ago." The peace and prosperity that the British, like all other peoples, had sought since the 1918 Armistice had not materialized, yet London celebrated as it had not celebrated in twenty years. Nobody expected to live in a new world any more. That Chamberlain had won at Munich reprieve from immediate war seemed cause enough to rejoice. "This is the second time there has come back from Germany peace with honor," he told the crowd that packed Downing Street. "I believe it is peace for our time."

SUMMING UP

THE FOUR STATESMEN who met at Munich attempted to set up a new balance of power in Europe without either American or Russian participation. Russian armies had saved Paris by invading East Prussia in August, 1914. American armies on the Western Front had turned the tide against Germany in March, 1918. Since then, the industrial power of both Russia and the United States had more than doubled. Europe, on the other hand, had gone into a relative decline. Nevertheless, Chamberlain snubbed Roosevelt eight months before the Munich meeting from which Hitler insisted that Stalin be barred. Mussolini and Daladier concurred with both decisions.

On almost every other major issue, the four chief participants at Munich split various ways. Chamberlain distrusted the weak and demoralized French, respected Germany's strength, and acted as if he could do business with Hitler. Mussolini and Daladier suffered from fewer illusions. Mussolini knew that he had to take orders from Hitler and that Hitler already planned to attack France. Daladier knew that Munich finished France as a great power. Chamberlain, Mussolini, and Daladier all dreaded the possibility of war. Hitler did not. Hitler signed the Munich Agreement because he believed it would demoralize his enemies and strengthen his hand in the ultimate, inevitable conflict. Chamberlain, on the other hand, convinced himself that Munich offered Hitler a preferable alternative to war. When Chamberlain described Munich as "peace for our time," he assumed that he and Hitler at last saw the world through the same eyes. And if Hitler should ever again spoil for a fight, the Munich Agreement left him free to move eastward against Russia.

Chamberlain's wishful assumptions ignored the warnings that Hitler had already given in *Mein Kampf*, where he explained that he planned to annihilate France

We, the German Führer and Chancellor and the British Prime Minister, have had a further meeting today and are agreed in recognising that the question of Anglo-German relations is of the first importance for the two countries and for Europe.

We regard the agreement signed last night and the Anglo-German Naval Agreement as symbolic of the desire of our two peoples never to go to war with one another again.

We are resolved that the method of consultation shall be the method adopted to deal with any other questions that may concern our two countries, and we are determined to continue our efforts to remove possible sources of difference and thus to contribute to assure the peace of Europe.

September 30. 1938.

UNITED PRESS PHOTO

The Chamberlain-Hitler Peace Pact

before turning against Russia. Nor did any of the men who persuaded Hitler to sign the Munich Agreement see how much he and Stalin had in common, at least over the short run. Both Hitler and Stalin regarded war as not only inevitable but desirable. Hitler assumed that only through war could Germany win control of Europe. Stalin assumed that only through war would the world revolution that failed to come off in Lenin's lifetime at last materialize. Stalin had no illusions about Hitler's ultimate plans. He expected little sympathy and no help from the Western democracies. But he doubted that Hitler could count on quick and complete victory in that quarter. Stalin foresaw Hitler and the Western democracies fighting a long and bloody war from which he would hold aloof. Roosevelt, on the other hand, in his new role as world messiah, had committed himself in advance to throw what influence he could on the side of Britain and France. His quarantine speech and his abortive efforts to interest Chamberlain in a collective security approach to peace made his sympathies quite apparent.

The Munich Agreement led a despised but growing minority in many countries to predict a Hitler-Stalin pact. It was more comforting and popular to assert that before the worst happened and war came, the Western democracies and the Russian Communists would form a common front against the Nazi-Fascist Axis, thereby preventing war or at least ensuring immediate victory. And the invincible democratic coalition would of course include China, just as Japan would surely join the Axis.

Near the end of his life, Woodrow Wilson predicted that if the League of Nations did not establish universal peace, another world war would have to be fought to achieve that purpose. In 1938, few of Wilson's countrymen believed that they could not have world peace unless and until they fought another world war. Still fewer Europeans entertained any such notions. Although Hitler had persuaded many Germans that they could win control of Europe through force and threats of force, most Europeans doubted that their civilization could survive another war. In any case, no democratic statesman at the time of the Munich Conference, least of all Roosevelt, advocated war as a means of establishing peace on earth. Most of them still preached peace for its own sake, although some had begun to urge military preparations and military alliances as safeguards of peace. Only Hitler and Stalin saw anything to be gained from war.

The world of 1938 made little sense to the citizen of the world of 1900 who had assumed that enlightened self-interest dictated human behavior and that material progress would therefore continue indefinitely. Four years of war had destroyed the world of 1900. During the twenty years between 1918 and 1938 a succession of world messiahs established a succession of secular religions based on the hopes for universal peace and plenty to which the achievements of modern science and industry had given rise. The world depression finished off these hopes and brought forth Adolf Hitler, the end human product of the twentieth century's first great war and its ten-year aftermath. At Munich Hitler gained his greatest victory, winning virtual mastery of Europe without war. Nevertheless, of the four chief participants at Munich, Hitler appeared the least satisfied. Germany's armed forces had gained such a lead over the rest of the world that he had wanted to display that superiority in battle. Hitler did not at this time want or expect to unleash a general war. He wanted only to unleash a lightning war of annihilation against Czechoslovakia alone, and he did not expect France and Britain to intervene effectively, if at all. Nor did he propose to attack the West until he had built up Germany's strength still more. Chamberlain of course talked nonsense when he spoke of "peace for our time." For the question was not peace, which had already gone by the board, but time. How much remained and who would use it best?

BIBLIOGRAPHY

ABEND, HALLET. *My Life in China. 1926–1941.* New York: Harcourt, Brace, 1943.

ADAMS, SAMUEL HOPKINS. *The Incredible Era.* Boston: Houghton, Mifflin, 1939.

ALDINTON, RICHARD. *D. H. Lawrence.* New York: Duell, Sloan, and Pearce, 1950.

ALLEN, DEVERE, editor. *Adventurous Americans.* New York: Farrar and Rinehart, 1932.

ALLEN, FREDERICK LEWIS. *Only Yesteraay.* New York: Harper, 1931.

ALLEN, FREDERICK LEWIS. *Since Yesterday.* New York: Harper, 1940.

ANDERSON, SHERWOOD. *A Story Teller's Story.* New York: B. W. Huebsch, 1924.

ARENDT, HANNAH. *The Origins of Totalitarianism.* New York: Harcourt, Brace, 1951.

ARMSTRONG, H. C. *Gray Wolf: Mustapha Kemal.* New York: Minton, Balch, 1933.

ARMSTRONG, HAMILTON FISH. *The New Balkans.* New York: Harper, 1926.

ARMSTRONG, HAMILTON FISH. *Where the East Begins.* New York: Harper, 1929.

ARNOLD, THURMOND. *The Folklore of Capitalism.* New Haven: Yale University Press, 1938.

BAGGER, EUGENE S. *Eminent Europeans.* New York: Putnam, 1922.

BAILEY, THOMAS A. *Woodrow Wilson and the Great Betrayal.* New York: Macmillan, 1945.

BAILEY, THOMAS A. *Woodrow Wilson and the Lost Peace.* New York: Macmillan, 1944.

BAKER, RAY STANNARD. *American Chronicle.* New York: Scribner, 1945.

BAKER, RAY STANNARD. *Woodrow Wilson and the World Settlement.* Two vols. Doubleday, Page, 1923.

BALABANOFF, ANGELICA. *My Life as a Rebel.* New York: Harper, 1938.

BALFOUR, LORD. *Retrospect.* Boston: Houghton, Mifflin, 1930.

BALTZLY, ALEXANDER, and SALOMONE, A. WILLIAM. *Readings in Twentieth Century European History.* New York: Appleton-Century-Crofts, 1950.

BARCH, OTIS T., and BLAKE, NELSON M. *Since 1900: A History of the United States in Our Times.* New York: Macmillan, 1947.

BARZUN, JACQUES. *Darwin, Marx, Wagner.* Boston: Little, Brown, 1941.

BASCH, ANTONIN. *The Danube Basin and the German Economic Sphere.* New York: Columbia University Press, 1943.

BEALS, CARLETON. *Pan America.* Boston: Houghton, Mifflin, 1940.

BECKER, CARL L. *Modern History.* New York: Silver, Burdett, 1931.

BELOFF, MAX. *The Foreign Policy of Soviet Russia: 1929–1941.* Two vols. London: Oxford University Press, 1949.

BEMIS, SAMUEL F. *A Diplomatic History of the United States.* New York: Holt, 1942.

BEN-HORIN, ELIAHU. *The Middle East.* New York: Norton, 1943.

BENNS, F. LEE. *Europe Since 1914.* New York: Crofts, 1930.

BERTRAM, JAMES M. *First Act in China*. New York: Viking Press, 1938.

BIRCHALL, FREDERICK T. *The Storm Breaks*. New York: Viking Press, 1940.

BIRDSALL, PAUL. *Versailles Twenty Years After*. New York: Reynal and Hitchcock, 1941.

BISHOP, JOSEPH BUCKLIN. *Theodore Roosevelt and His Time*. Two vols. New York: Scribner, 1920.

BITHELL, JETHRO. *Modern German Literature: 1880–1938*. London: Methuen, 1938.

BLAND, J. O. P. *China: The Pity of It*. New York: Doubleday, Doran, 1932.

BONSAL, STEPHEN. *Unfinished Business*. New York: Doubleday, 1944.

BORCHARD, EDWIN, and LAGE, WILLIAM POTTER. *Neutrality for the United States*. New Haven: Yale University Press, 1937.

BOSE, SUBHAS CHANDRA. *The Indian Struggle: 1920–1934*. London: Wishart and Co., 1935.

BRADY, ROBERT A. *The Spirit and Structure of German Fascism*. New York: Viking Press, 1938.

BRENNER, ANITA. *The Wind That Swept Mexico*. New York: Harper, 1943.

BROGAN, D. W. *France under the Republic*. New York: Harper, 1940.

BRUCK, MOELLER VAN DEN. *Germany's Third Empire*. New York: Norton, 1934.

BRUUN, GEOFFREY. *The World in the Twentieth Century*. Boston: D. C. Heath, 1948.

BUELL, RAYMOND LESLIE. *Europe: A History of Ten Years*. New York: Macmillan, 1928.

BUELL, RAYMOND LESLIE. *Poland: Key to Europe*. New York: Knopf, 1939.

BULLITT, WILLIAM C. *The Bullitt Mission to Russia*. New York: B. W. Huebsch, 1919.

BUSS, CLAUDE A. *War and Diplomacy in Eastern Asia*. New York: Macmillan, 1941.

BYAS, HUGH. *Government by Assassination*. New York: Knopf, 1942.

CARLSON, OLIVER, and BATES, ERNEST SUTHERLAND. *Hearst: Lord of San Simeon*. New York: Viking Press, 1936.

CARTER, JOHN FRANKLIN, JR. ("The Unofficial Observer"). *The New Dealers*. New York: Simon and Schuster, 1934.

CARTER, JOHN FRANKLIN, JR. ("The Unofficial Observer"). *Our Lords and Masters*. New York: Simon and Schuster, 1935.

CHAMBERLAIN, JOHN. *Farewell to Reform*. New York: Liveright, 1932.

CHAMBERLIN, W. H. *The Russian Enigma*. New York: Scribner, 1943.

CHAMBERLIN, W. H. *Russia's Iron Age*. Boston: Little, Brown, 1934.

CHAMBERLIN, W. H. *Soviet Russia*. Boston: Little, Brown, 1930.

CHAMBERLIN, WILLIAM HENRY. *The World's Iron Age*. New York: Macmillan, 1941.

CHAMBERS, FRANK P., HARRIS, CHRISTINA PHELPS, and BAYLEY, CHARLES C. *This Age of Conflict*. New York: Harcourt, Brace, 1943.

CHEN, STEPHEN, and PAYNE, ROBERT. *Sun Yat-sen: A Portrait*. New York: John Day, 1946.

CLARK, R. T. *The Fall of the German Republic*. London: Allen and Unwin, 1935.

CHURCHILL, WINSTON S. *The Aftermath: 1918–1928*. New York: Scribner, 1929.

CHURCHILL, WINSTON S. *The Gathering Storm*. Boston: Houghton, Mifflin, 1948.

CHURCHILL, WINSTON S. *Great Contemporaries*. New York: Putnam, 1937.

CLYDE, PAUL H. *A History of the Modern and Contemporary Far East*. New York: Prentice-Hall, 1937.

COHEN-PORTHEIM, PAUL. *The Discovery of Europe*. New York: Dutton, 1932.

CRANE, MILTON. *The Roosevelt Era*. New York: Boni and Gaer, 1947.

CRANSTON, RUTH. *The Story of Woodrow Wilson*. New York: Simon and Schuster, 1945.

CRAVEN, THOMAS. *Modern Art*. New York: Simon and Schuster, 1934.

CUMMINGS, E. E. *Collected Poems*. New York: Harcourt, Brace, 1940.

D'ABERNON, VISCOUNT. *The Diary of an Ambassador*. Three vols. New York: Doubleday, Doran, 1929.

DALI, SALVADOR. *The Secret Life of Salvador Dali.* New York: Dial Press, 1942.

DAMPIER, W. C. D. *A History of Science and Its Relations With Philosophy and Religion.* New York: Macmillan, 1932.

DANIELS, JOSEPHUS. *The Wilson Era.* Chapel Hill: University of North Carolina Press, 1944.

DAVIES, JOSEPH E. *Mission to Moscow.* New York: Simon and Schuster, 1941.

DAVIS, FORREST. *The Atlantic System.* New York: Reynal and Hitchcock, 1941.

DAY, J. P. *Introduction to World Economic History since the Great War.* New York: Macmillan, 1937.

DEAN, VERA MICHELES. *Europe in Retreat.* New York: Knopf, 1939.

DECOMBIS, MARCEL. *Ernst Jünger.* Paris: Editions Montaigne, 1943.

DEL VAYO, J. ALVAREZ. *Freedom's Battle.* New York: Viking Press, 1949.

DESMOND, SHAW. *The Drama of Sinn Fein.* New York: Scribner, 1923.

DEUEL, WALLACE R. *People under Hitler.* New York: Harcourt, Brace, 1942.

DEUTSCHER, ISAAC. *Stalin: A Political Biography.* New York: Oxford University Press, 1949.

DILLON, E. J. *The Inside Story of the Peace Conference.* New York: Harper, 1920.

DUGDALE, BLANCHE E. C. *Arthur James Balfour.* Two vols. New York: Putnam, 1937.

DUMOND, D. L. *America in Our Time: 1896–1946.* New York: Holt, 1947.

DUNLAP, ORRIN E., JR. *Marconi, the Man and His Wireless.* New York: Macmillan, 1938.

DURANT, WILL. *The Case for India.* New York: Simon and Schuster, 1930.

DUTT, R. PALME. *World Politics: 1918–1936.* New York: Random House, 1936.

EASTMAN, MAX. *Stalin's Russia and the Crisis in Socialism.* New York: Norton, 1940.

EASTMAN, MAX. *Since Lenin Died.* New York: Boni and Liveright, 1925.

EDSCHMID, KASIMIR. *South America, Light and Shadows.* New York: Viking Press, 1932.

EDWARD VIII, DUKE OF WINDSOR. *A King's Story.* New York: Putnam, 1951.

EINSTEIN, ALBERT. *Out of My Later Years.* New York: Philosophical Library, 1950.

EINSTEIN, ALBERT. *The World As I See It.* New York: Philosophical Library, 1949.

"EPHESIAN" (Carl Eric Bechhofer Roberts). *Lord Birkenhead.* London: Mills and Boon, 1926.

"EPHESIAN" (Carl Eric Bechhofer Roberts). *Winston Churchill.* London: Mills and Boon, 1927.

FAIRBANK, J. K. *The United States and China.* Cambridge: Harvard University Press, 1948.

FARLEY, JAMES A. *Jim Farley's Story: The Roosevelt Years.* New York: Whittlesey House, 1948.

FEILING, KEITH. *Neville Chamberlain.* London: Macmillan, 1946.

FISCHER, LOUIS. *The Life of Mahatma Gandhi.* New York: Harper, 1950.

FISCHER, LOUIS. *Men and Politics.* New York: Duell, Sloan, and Pearce, 1941.

FISCHER, LOUIS. *The Soviets in World Affairs.* New York: Cape and Smith, 1930.

FISCHER, RUTH. *Stalin and German Communism.* Cambridge: Harvard University Press, 1948.

FLOYD, ARVA C. *White Man, Yellow Man.* New York: Abingdon-Cokesberry Press, 1946.

FLYNN, JOHN T. *Country Squire in the White House.* New York: Doubleday, Doran, 1940.

FODOR, M. W. *Plot and Counterplot in Central Europe.* Boston: Houghton, Mifflin, 1937.

FOERSTER, F. W. *Europe and the German Question.* New York: Sheed and Ward, 1940.

FORD, HENRY, and CROWTHER, SAMUEL. *My Life and Work.* New York: Doubleday, Page, 1926.

FORD, HENRY, and CROWTHER, SAMUEL. *Today and Tomorrow.* New York: Doubleday, Doran, 1926.

FRANÇOIS-PONCET, ANDRÉ. *The Fate-*

ful Years. New York: Reynal and Hitchcock, 1949.

FRANK, PHILIPP. *Einstein. His Life and Times.* New York: Knopf, 1947.

FROMM, BELLA. *Blood and Banquets.* New York: Harper, 1942.

FUESS, CLAUDE M. *Calvin Coolidge, the Man From Vermont.* Boston: Little, Brown, 1940.

FÜLÖP-MILLER, RENÉ. *Lenin and Gandhi.* New York: Putnam, 1927.

FÜLÖP-MILLER, RENÉ. *The Mind and Face of Bolshevism.* New York: Knopf, 1929.

GALLUP, GEORGE. *The Pulse of Democracy.* New York: Simon and Schuster, 1940.

GANDHI, M. K. *The Story of My Experiments with Truth.* Ahmedabad: Navajivan Publishing Co., 1945.

GARRATT, GEOFFREY T. *Mussolini's Roman Empire.* Indianapolis: Bobbs Merrill, 1938.

GARRETT, GARET. *The American Omen.* New York: Dutton, 1928.

GEDYE, G. E. R. *Betrayal in Central Europe.* New York: Harper, 1939.

"Gentleman with a Duster" (HAROLD BEGBIE). *Windows of Westminster.* New York: Putnam, 1924.

GIDE, ANDRÉ. *Return from U.S.S.R.* New York: Knopf, 1937.

GOOCH, G. P. *History of Modern Europe: 1878–1919.* New York: Holt, 1923.

GORDON, JAN. *Modern French Painters.* London: John Lane, 1923.

GOULD, RANDALL. *China in the Sun.* New York: Doubleday, 1946.

GRAHAM, STEPHEN, *Alexander of Yugoslavia.* New Haven: Yale University Press, 1939.

GRATTAN, C. HARTLEY. *Introducing Australia.* New York: John Day, 1942.

GRAVES, GENERAL WILLIAM S. *America's Siberian Adventure.* New York: Cape and Smith, 1931.

GREW, JOSEPH C. *My Ten Years in Japan.* New York: Simon and Schuster, 1944.

GRISWOLD, A. WHITNEY. *The Far Eastern Policy of the United States.* New York: Harcourt, Brace, 1938.

GUEDALLA, PHILIP. *The Hundred Years.* New York: Doubleday, Doran, 1937.

GUEDALLA, PHILIP. *The Hundredth Year.* New York: Doubleday, 1939.

GUÉRARD, ALBERT J. *André Gide.* Cambridge: Harvard University Press, 1951.

GUNTHER, JOHN. *Inside Europe.* New York: Harper, 1936.

HACKER, LOUIS. *American Problems Today.* New York: F.S.Crofts, 1934.

HACKER, LOUIS. *A Short History of the New Deal.* New York: F. S. Crofts, 1934.

HAHN, EMILY. *The Soong Sisters.* New York: Doubleday, Doran, 1943.

HAINES, C. GROVE, and HOFFMAN, ROSS, J. S. *The Origins and Backgrounds of the Second World War.* New York: Oxford University Press, 1943.

HALE, RICHARD WALDEN. *Democratic France.* New York: Coward-McCann, 1941.

HALL, WALTER PHELPS, and DAVIS, WILLIAM STEARNS. *The Course of Europe since Waterloo.* New York: Appleton-Century, 1941.

HALLGREN, MAURITZ A. *The Gay Reformer.* New York: Knopf, 1935.

HALLGREN, MAURITZ A. *Seeds of Revolt.* New York: Knopf, 1933.

HEARD, GERALD. *These Hurrying Years.* New York: Oxford University Press, 1934.

HEIDEN, KONRAD. *Der Führer.* Boston: Houghton, Mifflin, 1944.

HEIDEN, KONRAD. *A History of National Socialism.* New York: Alfred A. Knopf, 1935.

HERRING, HUBERT. *Good Neighbors.* New Haven: Yale University Press, 1941.

HIBBEN, PAXTON. *The Peerless Leader: William Jennings Bryan.* New York: Farrar and Rinehart, 1929.

HINDUS, MAURICE. *Broken Earth.* New York: Cape and Smith, 1931.

HINDUS, MAURICE. *The Great Offensive.* New York: Smith and Haas, 1933.

HINDUS, MAURICE. *Humanity Uprooted.* New York: Cape and Smith, 1929.

HINDUS, MAURICE. *Red Bread.* New York: Cape and Smith, 1931.

HINSHAW, DAVID. *Herbert Hoover: American Quaker.* New York: Farrar and Strauss, 1950.

HITLER, ADOLF. *My New Order*. New York: Reynal and Hitchcock, 1941.

HOOVER, CALVIN B. *The Economic Life of Soviet Russia*. New York: Macmillan, 1931.

HOOVER, HERBERT. *The Memoirs of Herbert Hoover: The Cabinet and the Presidency, 1920–1933*. New York: Macmillan, 1952.

HOOVER, IRWIN HOOD. *Forty-Two Years in the White House*. Boston: Houghton, Mifflin, 1934.

HORRABIN, J. F. *An Atlas of Current Affairs*. New York: Knopf, 1935.

HORRABIN, J. F. *An Atlas of Empire*. New York, 1937.

HOUSE, E. M., and SEYMOUR, CHARLES. *What Really Happened at Paris*. New York: Scribner, 1921.

HUDDLESTON, SISLEY. *Europe in Zigzags*. Philadelphia: J. B. Lippincott, 1929.

HUGHES, E. R. *The Invasion of China by the Western World*, New York: Macmillan, 1938.

HUGHES, H. STUART. *Oswald Spengler: A Critical Estimate*. New York: Scribner, 1952.

HUGNET, GEORGE. *Fantastic Art, Dada, and Surrealism*. New York: Museum of Modern Art, 1949.

HULL, CORDELL, *The Memoirs of Cordell Hull*. New York: Macmillan, 1948.

HU SHIH. *The Chinese Renaissance*. Chicago: University of Chicago Press, 1933.

HUTCHISON, KEITH. *The Decline and Fall of British Capitalism*. New York: Scribner, 1950.

HUXLEY, ALDOUS. *Eyeless in Gaza*. New York: Harper, 1936.

ILIN, M. *New Russia's Primer*. New York: Harcourt, Brace, 1931.

INDIA LEAGUE DELEGATION. *The Condition of India*. London: Essential News, 1933.

INMAN, SAMUEL GUY. *Latin America. Its Place in World Life*. New York: Harcourt, Brace, 1942.

ISAACS, HAROLD. *The Tragedy of the Chinese Revolution*. Stanford: Stanford University Press, 1951.

JACKH, ERNEST. *The Rising Crescent, Turkey*. New York: Farrar and Rinehart, 1944.

JACKSON, J. HAMPDEN. *The Post-War World: 1918–1934*. Boston: Little, Brown, 1935.

JEANS, JAMES. *The Mysterious Universe*. New York: Macmillan, 1930.

JESSUP, PHILIP C. *Elihu Root*. Two vols. New York: Dodd, Mead, 1938.

JOAD, C. E. M. *Guide to Modern Thought*. New York: Stokes, 1933.

JOHNSON, GERALD W. *Roosevelt: Dictator or Democrat?* New York: Harper, 1941.

JOHNSON, HUGH S. *The Blue Eagle. From Egg to Earth*. New York: Doubleday, Doran, 1935.

JONES, TOM B., and BEATTY, W. DONALD. *An Introduction to Hispanic-American History*. New York: Harper, 1950.

KAZIN, ALFRED. *On Native Grounds*. New York: Reynal and Hitchcock, 1942.

KESSLER, COUNT HARRY. *Walther Rathenau*. New York: Harcourt, Brace, 1930.

KEYSERLING, COUNT HERMANN. *Europe*. New York: Harcourt, Brace, 1928.

KLUCKHOHN, FRANK L. *The Mexican Challenge*. New York: Doubleday, Doran, 1939.

KOESTLER, ARTHUR. *Darkness at Noon*. New York: Macmillan, 1941.

KOHLSAAT, H. H. *From McKinley to Harding*. New York: Scribner, 1923.

KOHN, HANS. *The Twentieth Century*. New York: Macmillan, 1950.

KRAUS, RENÉ. *Old Master: The Life of Jan Christian Smuts*. New York: Dutton, 1944.

KRUPSKAYA, NADEZHDA K. *Memoirs of Lenin*. New York: International Publishers, 1930.

LAFFAN, R. G. D. *The Crisis over Czechoslovakia*. New York: Oxford University Press, 1951.

LANDAU-ALDANOV, M. A. *Lenin*. New York: Dutton, 1922.

LANG, OLGA. *Chinese Family and Society*. New Haven: Yale University Press, 1946.

LANSING, ROBERT. *The Peace Negotiations: A Personal Narrative*. Boston: Houghton, Mifflin, 1921.

LATOURETTE, KENNETH S. *The Chinese: Their History and Their Culture*. Two vols. New York: Macmillan, 1934.

LATOURETTE, KENNETH S. *A Short History of the Far East*. New York: Macmillan, 1946.

LATTIMORE, OWEN. *Manchuria, Cradle of Conflict*. New York: Macmillan, 1932.

LEVINE, ISAAC DON. *The Man Lenin*. New York: Seltzer, 1924.

LIN YU-TANG. *My Country and My People*. New York: Reynal and Hitchcock, 1935.

LINDLEY, ERNEST K. *Half Way with Roosevelt*. New York: Viking Press, 1936.

LINDLEY, ERNEST K. *The Roosevelt Revolution*. New York: Viking Press, 1933.

LINEBARGER, PAUL. *Sun Yat-sen and the Chinese Republic*. New York: Century, 1925.

LLOYD GEORGE, DAVID. *Memoirs of the Peace Conference*. Two vols. New Haven: Yale University Press, 1939.

LOCKHART, R. H. BRUCE. *British Agent*. New York: Putnam, 1933.

LODGE, HENRY CABOT. *The Senate and the League of Nations*. New York: Scribner, 1925.

LUCCOCK, HALFORD E. *American Mirror*. New York: Macmillan, 1941.

LYND, ROBERT S. AND HELEN M. *Middletown*. New York: Harcourt, Brace, 1929.

LYND, ROBERT S. AND HELEN M. *Middletown in Transition*. New York: Harcourt, Brace, 1937.

LYONS, EUGENE. *Our Unknown Ex-President*. New York: Doubleday, 1948.

LYONS, EUGENE. *The Red Decade*. Indianapolis: Bobbs-Merrill, 1941.

MACKINDER, SIR HALFORD G. *Democratic Ideals and Reality*. New York: Holt, 1942.

MACLEISH, ARCHIBALD. *Public Speech*. New York: Farrar and Rinehart, 1936.

MADARIAGA, SALVADOR DE. *Spain*. New York: Creative Age Press, 1943.

MAKI, JOHN M. *Japanese Militarism*. New York: Knopf, 1945.

MALLORY, WALTER H. *China: Land of Famine*. New York: American Geographical Society, 1926.

MARCOSSON, ISAAC F. *Turbulent Years*. New York: Dodd, Mead, 1938.

MASSIS, HENRI. *Defense of the West*. New York: Harcourt, Brace, 1928.

MATTHEWS, HERBERT L. *Two Wars and More to Come*. New York: Carrick and Evans, 1938.

MAUROIS, ANDRÉ. *The Miracle of France*. New York: Harper, 1948.

MAXTON, JAMES. *Lenin*. New York: Appleton, 1932.

MAY, ARTHUR JAMES. *Europe and Two World Wars*. New York: Scribner, 1947.

MAYNARD, SIR JOHN. *Russia in Flux*. New York: Macmillan, 1948.

MAYO, KATHERINE. *Mother India*. New York: Harcourt, Brace, 1927.

McGOVERN, WILLIAM MONTGOMERY. *From Luther to Hitler*. London: Harrap, 1944.

MENCKEN, H. L. *Prejudices. First through Sixth Series*. New York: Knopf, 1919–1927.

MENDIZABAL, ALFREDO. *The Martyrdom of Spain*. New York: Scribner, 1938.

MICHELSON, CHARLES. *The Ghost Talks*. New York: Putnam, 1944.

MISHIMA, SUMIE SEO. *My Narrow Isle*. New York: John Day, 1941.

MITRANY, DAVID. *The Effect of the War in Southeastern Europe*. New Haven: Yale University Press, 1936.

MOLEY, RAYMOND. *After Seven Years*. New York: Harper, 1939.

MOON, PARKER T. *Imperialism and World Politics*. New York: Macmillan, 1926.

MOORE, DAVID R. *A History of Latin America*. New York: Prentice-Hall, 1941.

MORRIS, LLOYD. *Not So Long Ago*. New York: Random House, 1949.

MOWAT, R. B. *European Diplomacy: 1914–1925*. New York: Longmans, Green, 1926.

MOWAT, R. B. *The History of European Diplomacy*. New York: Longmans, Green, 1931.

MOWRER, EDGAR ANSELL. *The Dragon Wakes*. New York: Morrow, 1939.

MUNRO, DANA G. *The Latin American Republics*. New York: Appleton-Century, 1942.

MYERS, WILLIAM STARR, and NEWTON, WALTER H. *The Hoover Administration. A Documented Narrative*. New York: Scribner, 1936.

NAMIER, L. B. *Diplomatic Prelude: 1938–1939*. London: Macmillan, 1948.

NEHRU, JAWAHARLAL. *The Discovery of India*. New York: John Day, 1946.

NEUMANN, FRANZ. *Behemoth*. New York: Oxford University Press, 1942.

NEVINS, ALLAN. *John D. Rockefeller*. Two vols. New York: Scribner, 1940.

NEVINS, ALLAN, and HACKER, LOUIS H. *The United States and Its Place in World Affairs*. Boston: Heath, 1943.

NEVINSON, H. W. *More Changes, More Chances*. New York: Harcourt, Brace, 1926.

NICOLSON, HAROLD. *Curzon: The Last Phase*. Boston: Houghton, Mifflin, 1934.

NICOLSON, HAROLD. *Dwight Morrow*. New York: Harcourt, Brace, 1935.

NICOLSON, HAROLD. *Peacemaking 1919*. Boston: Houghton, Mifflin, 1933.

NICOLSON, HAROLD. *Portrait of a Diplomatist*. Two vols. Boston: Houghton, Mifflin, 1930.

NOWAK, KARL FRIEDRICH. *Versailles*. New York: Payson, Clark, 1929.

ORTEGA Y GASSET, JOSÉ. *Invertebrate Spain*. New York: Norton, 1937.

ORTEGA Y GASSET, JOSÉ. *The Revolt of the Masses*. New York: Norton, 1933.

PARKES, HENRY B. *A History of Mexico*. Boston: Houghton, Mifflin, 1938.

PARKES, HENRY B. *Recent America*. New York: Thomas Y. Crowell, 1941.

PATCHEN, KENNETH. *Selected Poems*. Norfolk, Connecticut: New Directions, 1946.

PECORA, FERDINAND. *Wall Street under Oath*. New York: Simon and Schuster, 1938.

PEERS, E. A. *The Spanish Tragedy: 1930–1936*. New York: Oxford University Press, 1936.

PEFFER, NATHANIEL. *China: The Collapse of a Civilization*. New York: John Day, 1930.

PEFFER, NATHANIEL. *Basis for Peace in the Far East*. New York: Harper, 1942.

PERKINS, DEXTER. *America and Two World Wars*. Boston: Little, Brown, 1944.

PERKINS, FRANCES. *The Roosevelt I Knew*. New York: Viking Press, 1946.

PERTINAX. *The Grave-Diggers of France*. New York: Doubleday, 1944.

PETERSON, H. C. *Propaganda for War: The Campaign against American Neutrality: 1914–1917*. Norman: University of Oklahoma Press, 1939.

POWELL, E. ALEXANDER. *The Struggle for Power in Moslem Asia*. New York: Century, 1923.

POWELL, J. B. *My Twenty-five Years in China*. New York: Macmillan, 1942.

POWERS, JAMES H. *Years of Tumult*. New York: Norton, 1932.

PRICE, WILLARD. *Children of the Rising Sun*. New York: John Day, 1938.

PRINGLE, HENRY. *The Life and Times of William Howard Taft*. Two vols. New York: Farrar and Rinehart, 1939.

PRITCHETT, V. S. *The Living Novel*. New York: Reynal and Hitchcock, 1947.

PUNER, HELEN WALKER. *Freud. His Life and His Mind*. New York: Howell, Soskin, 1947.

RAMAN, T. A. *Report on India*. New York: Oxford University Press, 1943.

RAPPARD, WILLIAM E. *The Quest for Peace since the World War*. Cambridge: Harvard University Press, 1940.

RAUSCHNING, HERMAN. *The Revolution of Nihilism*. New York: Alliance Book Corporation, 1939.

REISCHAUER, EDWIN O. *Japan Past and Present*. New York: Knopf, 1946.

RIPLEY, WILLIAM Z. *Main Street and Wall Street*. Boston: Little, Brown, 1927.

RIPPY, J. FRED. *The Historic Evolution of Hispanic America*. New York: Crofts, 1932.

ROBBINS, LIONEL C. *The Great Depression*. New York: Macmillan, 1934.

ROBERTS, STEPHEN H. *The House That Hitler Built*. New York: Harper, 1938.

ROBINSON, HENRY MORTON. *Fantastic Interim*. New York: Harcourt, Brace, 1943.

RODELL, KATHERINE CARR. *South American Primer*. New York: Reynal and Hitchcock, 1941.

ROOSEVELT, ELEANOR. *This I Remember*. New York: Harper, 1949.

ROSENBERG, ARTHUR. *A History of the German Republic*. London: Methuen, 1936.

ROSINGER, LAWRENCE K. *China's Crisis*. New York: Knopf, 1945.

ROWE, DAVID NELSON. *China among the Powers*. New York: Harcourt, Brace, 1945.

SANSOM, G. B. *The Western World and Japan*. New York: Knopf, 1950.

SAUNDERS, KENNETH JAMES. *A Pageant of Asia*. London: Oxford University Press, 1934.

SCHACHT, HJALMAR. *The End of Reparations*. New York: Cape and Smith, 1931.

SCHEIDEMANN, PHILIPP. *The Making of New Germany*. Two vols. New York: Appleton, 1929.

SCHOENBERNER, FRANZ. *Confessions of a European Intellectual*. New York: Macmillan, 1946.

SCHRIFTGIESSER, KARL. *The Gentleman from Massachusetts*. Boston: Little, Brown, 1944.

SCHRIFTGIESSER, KARL. *This Was Normalcy*. Boston: Little, Brown, 1948.

SCHWARTZ, BERNARD I. *Chinese Communism and the Rise of Mao*. Cambridge: Harvard University Press, 1951.

SCOTT, JONATHAN F., and BALTZLY, ALEXANDER. *Readings in European History since 1814*. New York: Crofts, 1931.

SELDES, GEORGE. *Sawdust Caesar*. New York: Harper, 1935.

SELDES, GILBERT. *The Great Audience*. New York: Viking Press, 1950.

SELDES, GILBERT. *The Seven Lively Arts*. New York: Harper, 1924.

SELDES, GILBERT. *Years of the Locust*. Boston: Little, Brown, 1933.

SELLE, EARL ALBERT. *Donald of China*. New York: Harper, 1948.

SENDER, RAMON. *Counter-Attack in Spain*. Boston: Houghton, Mifflin, 1937.

SERGE, VICTOR. *Russia Twenty Years After*. New York: Hillman Curl, 1937.

SETON-WATSON, HUGH. *Eastern Europe between Two Wars, 1918–41*. New York: Macmillan, 1945.

SEYMOUR, CHARLES. *The Intimate Papers of Colonel House*. Four vols. Boston: Houghton, Mifflin, 1926–28.

SFORZA, COUNT CARLO. *Contemporary Italy*. New York: Dutton, 1944.

SFORZA, COUNT CARLO. *Europe and Europeans*. Indianapolis: Bobbs-Merrill, 1936.

SHARMAN, LYON. *Sun Yat-sen*. New York: John Day, 1934.

SHEEAN, VINCENT. *Lead, Kindly Light*. New York: Random House, 1949.

SHEEAN, VINCENT. *Personal History*. New York: Doubleday, 1935.

SHEEAN, VINCENT. *Not Peace but a Sword*. New York: Doubleday, 1939.

SHERWOOD, ROBERT E. *Roosevelt and Hopkins*. New York: Harper, 1948.

SIMONDS, FRANK. *Can America Stay at Home?* New York: Harper, 1932.

SIMONDS, FRANK. *Can Europe Keep the Peace?* New York: Harper, 1931.

SIMONDS, FRANK. *How Europe Made Peace without America*. New York: Doubleday, Page, 1927.

SLOCOMBE, GEORGE. *A Mirror to Geneva*. New York: Holt, 1938.

SLOSSON, PRESTON WILLIAM. *The Great Crusade and After*. New York: Macmillan, 1930.

SNOW, EDGAR. *The Battle for Asia*. New York: Random House, 1941.

SNOW, EDGAR. *Red Star over China*. New York: Random House, 1938.

SOKOLSKY, GEORGE E. *The Tinder-Box of Asia*. New York: Doubleday, Doran, 1932.

SOUVARINE, BORIS. *Stalin*. New York: Longmans, Green, 1939.

SPENDER, J. A. *Life, Journalism and Politics*. New York: Stokes, 1928.

SPENGLER, OSWALD. *Decline of the West*. Two vols. New York: Knopf, 1926 and 1928.

SPENGLER, OSWALD. *The Hour of Decision*. New York: Knopf, 1934.

STEED, H. WICKMAN. *Through Thirty Years*. New York: Doubleday, Page, 1924.

STEER, GEORGE. *Caesar in Abyssinia.* Boston: Little, Brown, 1937.

STEFFENS, LINCOLN. *Autobiography.* Two vols. New York: Harcourt, Brace, 1931.

STIMSON, HENRY L. *The Far Eastern Crisis.* New York: Harper, 1936.

STIMSON, HENRY L., and BUNDY, MCGEORGE. *On Active Service.* New York: Harper, 1948.

STOLBERG, BENJAMIN, and VINTON, W. J. *The Economic Consequences of the New Deal.* New York: Harcourt, Brace, 1935.

STRACHEY, JOHN. *The Coming Struggle for Power.* New York: Modern Library, 1935.

STRASSER, OTTO. *Hitler and I.* Boston: Houghton, Mifflin, 1940.

STRODE, HUDSON. *Timeless Mexico.* New York: Harcourt, Brace, 1944.

SULLIVAN, MARK. *Our Times: The Twenties.* New York: Scribner, 1935.

TAGORE, RABINDRANATH. *Letters to a Friend.* New York: Macmillan, 1929.

TAKEUCHI, TATSUJI. *War and Diplomacy in the Japanese Empire.* New York: Doubleday, Doran, 1935.

TANG LEANG-LI. *The Inner History of the Chinese Revolution.* New York: Dutton, 1930.

TARDIEU, ANDRÉ. *The Truth About the Treaty.* Indianapolis: Bobbs, Merrill, 1921.

TAWNEY, R. H. *Land and Labour in China.* London: Allen and Unwin, 1932.

TAYLOR, A. J. P. *The Course of German History.* New York: Coward-McCann, 1946.

THOMPSON, DOROTHY. *I Saw Hitler!* New York: Farrar and Rinehart, 1932.

THOMSON, VALENTINE. *Briand, Man of Peace.* New York: Covici Friede, 1930.

TIMPERLEY, H. J. *Japanese Terror in China.* New York: Modern Age Books, 1938.

TOYNBEE, A. J. *A Study of History.* New York: Oxford University Press, 1947.

TOYNBEE, A. J. *The Western Question in Greece and Turkey.* Boston: Houghton, Mifflin, 1922.

TROTSKY, LEON. *The History of the Russian Revolution.* Three vols. New York: Simon and Schuster, 1932.

TROTSKY, LEON. *Lenin.* New York: Minton, Balch, 1925.

TROTSKY, LEON. *Problems of the Chinese Revolution.* New York: Pioneer Publishers, 1932.

TROTSKY, LEON. *The Revolution Betrayed.* New York: Doubleday, Doran, 1937.

UGARTE, MANUEL. *The Destiny of a Continent.* New York: Knopf, 1925.

VOIGT, F. A. *Unto Caesar.* New York: Putnam, 1938.

WEBB, SIDNEY and BEATRICE. *Soviet Communism: A New Civilization?* Two vols. New York: Scribner, 1936.

WECTER, DIXON. *The Age of the Great Depression.* New York: Macmillan, 1948.

WEIGERT, HANS W. *Generals and Geographers.* New York: Oxford University Press, 1942.

WEIL, FELIX J. *Argentine Riddle.* New York: John Day, 1944.

WELLS, WARRE BRADLEY. *Why Edward Went.* New York: McBride, 1937.

WERTH, ALEXANDER. *France in Ferment.* London: Harper, 1935.

WHEELER, POST. *India against the Storm.* New York: Dutton, 1944.

WHEELER-BENNETT, JOHN W. *The Forgotten Peace: Brest-Litovsk.* New York: Morrow, 1939.

WHEELER-BENNETT, JOHN W. *Munich: Prologue to Tragedy.* New York: Duell, Sloan and Pierce, 1948.

WHEELER-BENNETT, JOHN W. *Wooden Titan.* New York: Morrow, 1936.

WHITE, WILLIAM ALLEN. *The Autobiography of William Allen White.* New York: Macmillan, 1946.

WHITE, WILLIAM ALLEN. *Masks in a Pageant.* New York: Macmillan, 1928.

WHITE, WILLIAM ALLEN. *A Puritan in Babylon.* New York: Macmillan, 1938.

WHITEHEAD, ALFRED NORTH. *Science and the Modern World.* New York: Macmillan, 1925.

WILSON, EDMUND. *The American Jitters.* New York: Scribner, 1932.

WINTER, ELLA. *Red Virtue.* New York: Harcourt, Brace, 1933.

WISH, HARVEY. *Contemporary America.* New York: Harper, 1945.

WOLFERS, ARNOLD. *Britain and France between Two Wars.* New York: Harcourt, Brace, 1940.

WRONG, GEORGE McKINNON. *The Canadians: The Story of a People.* New York: Macmillan, 1938.

YAKHONTOFF, VICTOR A. *The Chinese Soviets.* New York: Coward, McCann, 1934.

YOUNG, A. MORGAN. *Imperial Japan.* New York: William Morrow, 1938.

YOUNG, EUGENE J. *Powerful America.* New York: Stokes, 1936.

ZIFF, WILLIAM B. *The Rape of Palestine.* New York: Longmans, Green, 1938.

ACKNOWLEDGMENTS

MOST OF the personal and professional acknowledgments listed in connection with the first volume of this work apply to the second. One major additional acknowledgment must, however, precede all others. It is to the University of Illinois, especially to certain officials and departments of that University, where I have spent the past three years as an Associate Professor of Journalism and Communications and as news analyst with its radio station, WILL. Although I still owe a debt to the New York Society Library for work done during 1949, 1950, and the summers of several succeeding years, my debt to the Library of the University of Illinois and especially to Miss Eleanor Blum, now head of the Journalism Library there, takes precedence. For bringing me to Illinois and helping to make it possible for me to combine teaching, broadcasting, and writing, I owe special acknowledgment to Dean Wilbur Schramm of the Division of Communications, to Director Fredrick S. Siebert of the School of Journalism and Communications, and to Professor Robert B. Hudson, director of University broadcasting.

The copyright page lists those authors and publishers from whose books I have obtained permission to quote at some length. From some of them, however, I have done much more than quote. For instance, Konrad Heiden's analysis of Hitler's character in *Der Führer* contains insights that only a profound and gifted scholar could achieve. Raymond Moley's *After Seven Years* gives a unique interpretation of the first phases of the New Deal. Frances Perkins's *The Roosevelt I Knew* probes the personality of its subject with deep understanding. Certain books listed in the Bibliography (pages 737 ff.) also call for more than passing mention. G. E. R. Gedye's *Betrayal in Central Europe*, published by Harper's and now out of print, gives a vivid eyewitness account of Hitler's seizure of Austria and of the events leading up to the Munich Conference. Not only have I quoted from this book; future historians will always have to draw from its interpretations. This also applies to R. G. D. Laffan's *The Crisis Over Czechoslovakia* and, indeed, to all other volumes in the Royal Institute for International Affairs publications that A. J. Toynbee edited during most of the years between the two world wars. Thomas A. Bailey's *Woodrow Wilson and the Great Betrayal* and his *Woodrow Wilson and the Lost Peace,* now available in one volume, offer a convincing version of the great Wilson-Lodge battle. Isaac Deutscher and Boris Souvarine both have written valuable lives of Stalin. Max Beloff's two volumes on *The Foreign Policy of Soviet Russia: 1929–1941* are equally essential. Keith Feiling's life of Neville Chamberlain provides a useful balance to Winston Churchill's *The Gathering Storm.* Ruth Fischer's *Stalin and German Communism* embodies a vast amount of original research and reflection. Lloyd Morris's *Not So Long Ago* proves that Americans can write "cultural history" with as much scholarship as any German and more readability. Herman Rauschning's *The Revolution of Nihilism* furnishes many unique closeups of Hitler. Bernard I. Schwartz has written the first authentic account of Mao Tse-tung's early and middle years in *Chinese Communism and the Rise of Mao.* Two of Albert Einstein's books, *The World As I See It* and *Out of My Later Years* bring together many of his philosophic reflections; so does Philipp Frank's *Einstein. His Life and Times.*

If this volume shows any improvement over the one that went before, the credit goes to Dr. Samuel J. Hurwitz, Professor of History at Brooklyn College, who checked both manuscript and galley proofs, saving me from more errors of fact and judgment than I have the space or inclination to list. He bears no responsibility for any defects or shortcomings that remain. Margaret Bevans and the Immerman Studios again executed the maps. Three members of the staff of Simon and Schuster, in addition to those listed in the first volume, worked efficiently on this one—Charlotte Seitlin, Elizabeth Farrar, and Bennett Glazer. And my wife, adaptable as ever to academic ways, worked long hours at no pay on the index.

QUINCY HOWE

Champaign, Illinois
April, 1953

Index

ABOUT THE AUTHOR

QUINCY HOWE *was born in Boston, Massachusetts, in 1900, attended St. George's School at Newport, Rhode Island, and received his A.B. degree from Harvard in 1921. The next year he spent abroad studying at Christ's College, Cambridge, and traveling in Europe. Returning to the United States in 1922, he worked until 1929 with the Atlantic Monthly Company. Here he devoted most of his time to translating and reprinting articles from the foreign press for* The Living Age, *of which he became one of the editors in 1926. Two years later, the magazine was sold to a new owner in New York and Mr. Howe remained for six months as assistant to the editor of the* Atlantic Monthly. *After a few months with the advertising agency of Pedlar and Ryan in New York, he rejoined* The Living Age *as editor, a post he held until 1935. His first book,* World Diary: 1929-1934, *appeared in 1934.*

From 1935 to 1942 Mr. Howe worked as head of the editorial department for Simon and Schuster and wrote three more books: England Expects Every American to Do His Duty, Blood Is Cheaper Than Water, *and* The News and How to Understand It. *From 1939 to 1942 he also served as news commentator for radio station WQXR in New York. In 1942 he went to the Columbia Broadcasting System as news analyst, moving into television in 1949. In September, 1950, he resigned from CBS to become Associate Professor of Journalism and Communications at the University of Illinois and news analyst for the University's radio station, WILL. He has also filled a number of news assignments for the American Broadcasting Company.*

Mr. Howe began work on his World History of Our Own Times *in 1944. The first volume,* The World We Lost, *appeared in 1949. He hopes to complete the third and final volume,* The World We Made, *in 1955. He is the son of the biographer and historian M. A. DeWolfe Howe, and the brother of the novelist Helen Howe and of Professor Mark DeWolfe Howe of the Harvard Law School. He married Mary L. Post of Boston in 1932 and they are the parents of a son and a daughter.*

Also by ANTHONY F. C. WALLACE

The Death and Rebirth of the Seneca (1970)

Religion: An Anthropological View (1966)

Culture and Personality (1961, 1970)

King of the Delawares: Teedyuscung, 1700–1763 (1949)

ROCKDALE

ROCKDALE

*The growth of an American village
in the early Industrial Revolution*

*An account of the coming of the machines, the
making of a new way of life in the mill hamlets,
the triumph of evangelical capitalists over
socialists and infidels, and the transformation of
the workers into Christian soldiers in a cotton-
manufacturing district in Pennsylvania in the
years before and during the Civil War* ✠

ANTHONY F. C. WALLACE

TECHNICAL DRAWINGS BY ROBERT HOWARD

Alfred A. Knopf, New York, 1978

HD
9878
.R6
W34
1978

THIS IS A BORZOI BOOK
PUBLISHED BY ALFRED A. KNOPF, INC.

Copyright © 1972, 1978 by Anthony F. C. Wallace
All rights reserved under International and Pan-American Copyright Conventions.
Published in the United States by Alfred A. Knopf, Inc., New York, and simultane-
ously in Canada by Random House of Canada Limited, Toronto. Distributed by
Random House, Inc., New York.

The appendix, "Paradigmatic Processes in Culture Change," was originally
published, in slightly different form, in the American Anthropologist,
74: 467–478, 1972.

Permissions to reproduce photographs and other illustrations are given on pages
xi–xiii.

Library of Congress Cataloging in Publication Data
Wallace, Anthony F   C [date]   Rockdale.
Bibliography: p.   Includes index.
1. Cotton trade—Pennsylvania—Rockdale—History.
2. Rockdale, Pa.—Industries—History.
3. Rockdale, Pa.—Social conditions.
4. Rockdale, Pa.—Religious life and customs—History.   I. Title.
HD9878.R6W34   1978   974.8'14   77–20346
ISBN 0–394–42120–5

Manufactured in the United States of America

First Edition

97351

ROCKDALE

The growth of an American village in the early Industrial Revolution

An account of the coming of the machines, the making of a new way of life in the mill hamlets, the triumph of evangelical capitalists over socialists and infidels, and the transformation of the workers into Christian soldiers in a cotton-manufacturing district in Pennsylvania in the years before and during the Civil War ✗

ANTHONY F. C. WALLACE

TECHNICAL DRAWINGS BY ROBERT HOWARD

Alfred A. Knopf, New York, 1978

HD
9878
.R6
W34
1978

THIS IS A BORZOI BOOK
PUBLISHED BY ALFRED A. KNOPF, INC.

Copyright © 1972, 1978 by Anthony F. C. Wallace
All rights reserved under International and Pan-American Copyright Conventions.
Published in the United States by Alfred A. Knopf, Inc., New York, and simultane-
ously in Canada by Random House of Canada Limited, Toronto. Distributed by
Random House, Inc., New York.

The appendix, "Paradigmatic Processes in Culture Change," was originally
published, in slightly different form, in the American Anthropologist,
74: 467–478, 1972.

Permissions to reproduce photographs and other illustrations are given on pages
xi–xiii.

Library of Congress Cataloging in Publication Data
Wallace, Anthony F C [date]   Rockdale.
Bibliography: p.   Includes index.
1. Cotton trade—Pennsylvania—Rockdale—History.
2. Rockdale, Pa.—Industries—History.
3. Rockdale, Pa.—Social conditions.
4. Rockdale, Pa.—Religious life and customs—History.   I. Title.
HD9878.R6W34   1978   974.8'14   77–20346
ISBN 0–394–42120–5

Manufactured in the United States of America

First Edition

97351

To Monty, Dan, Sun Ai, and Sammy,
who explored the mills and streams with me

CONTENTS

Contents

Contents

PART FOUR

ROCKDALE FROM 1850 TO 1865 ·
THE TRANSCENDING OF A WAY OF LIFE

ILLUSTRATIONS

Illustrations

PREFACE

This book tells the story of a small American community, with a population of about two thousand souls, between the years 1825 and 1865. It is not a community with a conspicuous history; none of its residents achieved national prominence during those forty years. No famous battles were fought there; it was not particularly unique in its industry or its society. It initially attracted my interest because I lived there and was curious about the old mills and tenements that lined the creek at the bottom of the hill. But as I came to know the sources and personalities and events, this piece of local, grass-roots history became, for me, a fascinating journey into the past.

No historical or ethnographic writing can be done as a piece of "pure" description; there is always a set of more or less articulate assumptions, theories, hypotheses, methodological principles that guide the selection of sources, determine the points of emphasis, and decide the experience of closure. In this case, the requisite theoretical framework turned out to be more complex than I had expected. Minimally, I was anxious to see to what extent the concepts of the cultural anthropologist, who is used to conducting fieldwork with living informants in a small community over a one- or two-year period, could be applied to the documentary remains of a community of about the same size during a generation. At first I attempted to supplement the documentary sources with "oral history" interviews but found that, by and large, the distance into the past was too great to enable me to recover much verifiable information. This study therefore is based on written documents and drawings and on the personal observation of mill seats and buildings.

But small communities, no matter how primitive, are never really isolated, and in the case of a nineteenth-century cotton-manufacturing town, its significant environment was, literally, the entire world, for the manufacturers, and through them the workers, responded directly to economic and political events occurring in the lower Delaware Valley, in the United

States as a whole, and even in India, China, Africa, Latin America, and of course Europe. In order to understand Rockdale, it is necessary to have some grasp of the social processes going on around it—in other words, to have a theory of American, if not world, history. In this case, the significant processes were the course of the Industrial Revolution, the transformation of Enlightenment liberalism into early Utopian socialism, and the evangelical millennialist enthusiasm which, allied with Western economic and military power, was driving the industrial nations toward the conquest of the world.

And beyond this, there is an even more general theoretical frame—the notion of the way in which self-contained developments in science and technology affect the host society. The general theory of paradigmatic processes in culture change guided my initial formulation of the historiographic problem and the structure of the book. My technical paper on this topic is included as an Appendix to this book.

But what I did not really expect, and found to my considerable surprise, was the presence of "plot"—that is to say, an organized structure of conflict among the main participants in the story that required a period of time before the strategies of the sides combined toward resolution. It is this structure of conflict, among named persons about whom considerable information remains, that has made the work a poignant chronicle of struggles between well-intentioned men and women all striving toward a better age. From the diaries, memoirs, personal correspondence, letters to newspaper editors, and even business ledgers emerges a world of motives, of hopes and fears, of loves and hates, which lies just beyond our lives, but from which much of the character of our lives has been drawn.

My initial concern was whether the sources would be adequate, whether it would be possible to find enough information about one small manufacturing district to put together anything of any interest at all about its experience in the Industrial Revolution. The sources available in standard repositories turned out to be adequate for useful study, even in this microhistorical scale; in some respects, they are embarrassingly rich. For instance, concerning the major manufacturers, there exist both a published autobiography (privately printed) of the leading manufacturer, John P. Crozer, and a competent biography, based on his lost diary and containing liberal quotations from it, plus miscellaneous letters and business correspondence of his own and of his family. There is a semi-autobiographical history of Chester and vicinity by John Hill Martin, the son of William Martin, another early manufacturer, filled with local anecdote and genealogy; John Hill Martin was a devoted local family historian who joined the Historical Society of Pennsylvania and left it his own memoirs and various family papers, including his father's receipt book during the years he operated a cotton mill. There are apparently no collections of personal papers of Samuel Riddle the elder, but by some miracle business papers survive, including a daybook of 1832–35, a rent book for the tenements, and a paybook for one of the mills from 1846 to 1850. The Peale-Sellers Papers at the American Philosophical Society Library include some of the papers of Peter Hill, William Martin's partner, who married Nathan Sellers' daughter Hannah and thus acquired control of the two Chester Creek mills that Nathan bought shortly before his death. There are extensive papers of two cotton mill families preserved among the Du Pont papers at Eleutherian Mills Historical Library because of the affinal and friendship relationships among the Du Ponts, the Lammots, and the Richard S. Smiths. Some of these collections are voluminous: the correspondence of Clementina Smith, who lived in Rockdale off and on from 1832 to her death in the 1880's, includes about two thousand letters. There is a Du Pont family diary—the Tancopanican Chronicle—which records the unsuccessful courtship of Sophie du Pont by a free-thinking young cotton manufacturer, John S. Phillips. There are genealogies of the leading families. There are two local newspapers with extensive runs throughout the period preserved by the Delaware County Historical Society. There are letter-series from families of working people employed in the mills. And there are the expected standard official records: county and state archives, including tax records, wills, probate inventories; birth, baptismal, and burial records in local churches; U.S. decennial census schedules in the National Archives. And finally, there is an excellent county history by Henry Ashmead, a local resident, and several good maps from about 1810 on, including a fine real estate map of Delaware County by Joshua Ash made in 1848.

My gratitude goes out to many people and institutions who have helped me in this study. My principal debt is owing to Mr. Richmond D. Williams, Mrs. Betty-Bright Low, Mr. Robert Howard, Dr. Eugene Ferguson, Dr. Norman B. Wilkinson, Mrs. Carol B. Hallman, Mrs. Susan Danko, and other members of the staff of the Eleutherian Mills Historical Library, where many of the most valuable manuscript holdings and technological works were drawn to my attention and made available to me. I am also particularly grateful to Mr. Samuel Newsome, former president of the Delaware County Historical Society, and the staff at the library of Widener College in Chester, Pennsylvania; to Mr. J. W. Vitty of the Belfast Library and Society for Promoting Knowledge, Ireland; to Mr. Peter Parker, at the Manuscript Room of the Historical Society of Pennsylvania; to Ms. Martha Simonetti and Ms. Barbara Philpott of the Pennsylvania State Archives; to Ms. Miriam Reynolds of the Delaware County Institute of Science; to Ms.

Mary Patterson of Historic Delaware County Society; to Mr. Robert Montgomery of the Tyler Arboretum; to Dr. Whitfield Bell and Dr. Murphy Smith of the Library of the American Philosophical Society; to Ms. Helena Wright of the Merrimack Valley Textile Museum; and to Ms. Aline Bradley of the Library of the Workingmen's Institute, New Harmony, Indiana. Mr. Harold Rackley kindly showed me through the Halifax Cotton Mill of South Boston, Virginia, where cotton is still processed from the bale to finished cloth. Valued institutional support was given by the University of Pennsylvania, which provided a sabbatical year in 1972–73, by the National Science Foundation for research grant SOC 72–05293 during the years 1972–77, and by the Haas Community Fund Foundation of Philadelphia for a grant in 1970–71.

I owe special thanks to a group of research assistants and student seminar participants who contributed greatly to the project over the years, particularly Dr. Christine Lemieux, Dr. David Kasserman, Dr. Janet Robison, Mr. Robert King, Ms. Pam Crabtree, Mr. Michael Replogle, Mr. Douglas Dinsmore, Mr. Gary Dunn, Ms. Wendy Pollock, Dr. Richard Horowitz, Dr. Marshall Becker, Ms. Diane Walters, Ms. Jean Lesnick, Mr. Bertrand Masquelier, Ms. Marilyn Crill Auchincloss, Ms. Sandra Marks, Ms. JoAnn Bromberg, Dr. David Gilmore, Mr. Steven Lott, Ms. Jean Smithe, Mr. Stephen Del Sordo, and Mr. Steven Ostrakh, all of whom contributed data and ideas. Readers of chapters of the manuscript who helped the writer avoid unnecessary errors and clichés include Ms. Betty-Bright Low, Mr. Robert Howard and his father Mr. George Howard of Taylor Instrument Company, Dr. Hilda Greenwald, Dr. Eugene Ferguson, Dr. Bruce Sinclair, and Dr. Norman B. Wilkinson. Dr. Regina Flesch helped me in identifying and characterizing the fabrics produced. Mr. Walter M. Phillips of Philadelphia, Mr. Clifford Lewis III of Media, Mr. Mark Wilcox, Jr., of Ivy Mills, and Dr. Peter Sellers of Philadelphia very generously shared family records of ancestors who were residents and owners or manufacturers in early Rockdale. The Reverend Mr. David A. McQueen of Upland Baptist Church, the Reverend Mr. James F. McKendrick of Calvary Episcopal Church, the Reverend Mr. George W. Eppeheimer, Jr., of Mount Hope Methodist Church, the Reverend Mr. John W. Gilbert and Mr. George Felton of Lima Methodist Church, and the Reverend Mr. Ray Pinch of the Middletown Presbyterian Church all very kindly made available to me or to my assistant Christine Lemieux valuable materials from their church records. Mr. J. E. Rhoads of Wilmington, Delaware, provided an illuminating discussion of the philosophy of manufacturing in the older American corporation. To the present-day community of the Rockdale manufacturing district, I owe a general debt of gratitude for their patience in allowing me to wander through the various properties, taking photographs and asking questions.

Today the seven mill hamlets still remain and still bear their old names. Descendants of the first immigrant weavers from Lancashire still occupy old stone houses on English Hill, above West Branch; other working families, heirs of nineteenth-century operatives whose names appear in the old day-books and paybooks, live in houses scattered up and down the hills. Knowlton Mill was long ago washed away again, not to be rebuilt, and its place is only a grassy meadow; but the old mansion house still looms on the cliff above the stream, and a few of the stone tenements still stand in a row along the road that runs steeply up the hill to Village Green. All of the other mill structures house active businesses, although the early stone factory is often today embedded in accretions of sheds, extensions, and other improvements. At Rockdale, the old brick nail mill was torn down a few years ago, but the cotton mill still stands, now occupied by a lumber yard. The factory at Glen Riddle is used by the Sunroc Corporation, which manufactures water coolers, and when this study was begun, the old dam and race and part of the gateway system were intact. Some of these structures have been destroyed in recent years for reasons of public safety, but one of the Riddle mansions survives, still in use as a company office. West Branch, Lenni, and Parkmount were until 1972 used by the Aldon Rug Company; turbines were still in place in the wheelpits when this study commenced; all three suffered severe damage in the great flood of 1972 and the old stone factory at Parkmount was gutted by a fire in the following year. West Branch and Lenni are now occupied by, among other firms, the Westlake Plastics Corporation. Crozerville factory is intact but almost entirely surrounded by new structures of the Container Research Corporation.

Although in some cases their members have moved away, the presence of the great families is still felt in the district. All of the churches created during the evangelical movement are in good repair, with active congregations. The Willcoxes continue to occupy the tract about the grassy ruins of Ivy Mills; Darlingtons still live at Darlington Station, just north of the district. The son of Samuel Riddle, Samuel D. Riddle, maintained a home at Glen Riddle until his death in 1951; he was widely known for a breed of extraordinary thoroughbred racehorses, sired by the most famous of them all, Man O'War; and the Riddle estate has in recent years provided the community with funds for the new Riddle Memorial Hospital. John P. Crozer's family, after his death, endowed the Crozer Theological Seminary in Upland (recently removed to Baptist headquarters in Rochester, N.Y.), where generations of Baptist clergymen were trained, the most famous of course being Martin Luther King, Jr.; and further Crozer funds have gone for the support of Bucknell University, Crozer Hospital and its School of Nursing, and other institutions in the Chester area and elsewhere. The Sellers family continued to hold the lands of Parkmount and Lenni until 1908. Thus in a general way the Rockdale community continues to be affected by estates created from the profits earned by the cotton manufacturers of a century ago.

Among the many residents of Aston and Middletown who have, directly or indirectly, helped me in the course of the study, I want to acknowledge several in particular: Mr. Orville C. Morrison, president of the Sunroc Corporation, who let me wander through the ruins of the Riddles' old house and water power system; Mr. and Mrs. Robert Cropper of Lenni, Mrs. Florence Hibbert, formerly of West Branch, Mr. Merrill Fisher of Concord Road, and Mr. William Gorman of Glen Riddle, descendant of the miller of Rockdale, and his wife Nellie, all of whom gave me interesting information about life in the mill towns in the nineteenth century; Mr. E. B. Westlake, Jr., who let me see a late nineteenth-century Riddle paybook; Mr. Lou Esaph, of Middletown, who arranged for me to tour and photograph the Aldon Rug Company properties at Parkmount, West Branch, and Lenni; Mr. Thomas Ahearn, of Rockdale, who allowed me to go through the old mill at Rockdale; and my wife Betty and my sons and daughters Anthony, Daniel, Sun Ai, Samuel, Cheryl, and Joseph, who know today's town better than I. My thanks go to Mr. Angus Cameron, Ms. Bobbie Bristol, Mr. Neal Jones, Mrs. Ann Adelman, and others of the staff at Knopf for thoughtful and helpful collaboration in producing the book. Finally, I want to thank Ms. Ellen Troxler, who over the years has been able to decipher my hand and type a clean manuscript, and Ms. Vanessa Fogler and Ms. Jeanne Gallagher, who together prepared the final draft.

Anthony F. C. Wallace
Rockdale
December 1977

Part One

ROCKDALE IN 1850 ✗
THE CLIMAX
OF A WAY OF LIFE

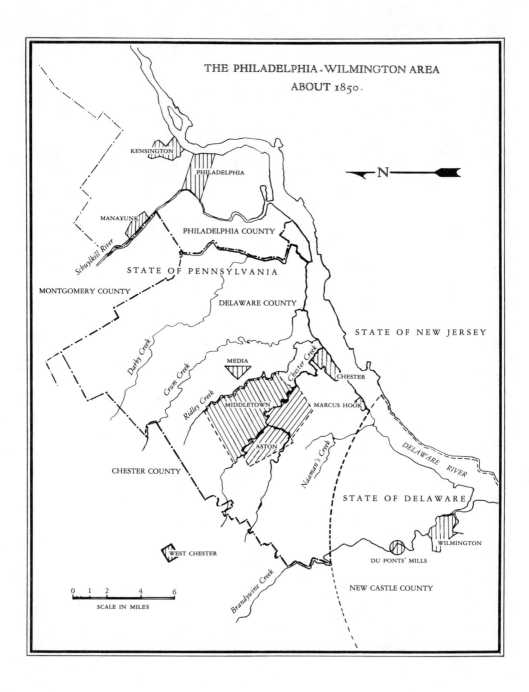

THE PHILADELPHIA-WILMINGTON AREA
ABOUT 1850.

N

KENSINGTON

PHILADELPHIA

MANAYUNK

Schuylkill River

PHILADELPHIA COUNTY

STATE OF PENNSYLVANIA

MONTGOMERY COUNTY

DELAWARE COUNTY

STATE OF NEW JERSEY

Darby Creek

Crum Creek

MEDIA

Chester Creek

CHESTER

Ridley Creek

MIDDLETOWN

MARCUS HOOK

ASTON

Naaman's Creek

DELAWARE RIVER

CHESTER COUNTY

STATE OF DELAWARE

WILMINGTON

WEST CHESTER

DU PONTS' MILLS

Brandywine Creek

NEW CASTLE COUNTY

0 1 2 4 6
SCALE IN MILES

Chapter I ✗

SWEET, QUIET
ROCKDALE

There is a village in America called Rockdale where the people used to manufacture cotton cloth. It lies along the banks of Chester Creek in Delaware County, in southeastern Pennsylvania, between Philadelphia and Wilmington. None of the people who worked in the first cotton mills is alive anymore, but some of their children's children still live there, and the ruins of stone factories, as well as stone tenements and fine stone mansions, are yet standing. Nearby are remains of the other hamlets that made up the Rockdale manufacturing district—Lenni, Parkmount, West Branch, Crozerville, Glen Riddle, and Knowlton—where cotton yarn was spun on mules and throstles and cloth was woven on looms powered by water wheels. In the first part of the last century, in fact, all along the east coast, from Maine to the Carolinas, and inland to the Mississippi, there were manufacturing districts more or less like Rockdale, nestled along the millstreams in the hinterland of coastal and riverine ports. Now all the machines are broken up for scrap, and the northern mills are empty, and spinners and weavers work only in the great factories of the south.

As I leave my house on the outskirts of the village, drive the car along the roads twisting among the mills, tramp in the weeds by the old dams and races, stroll along the paths in the cemetery at Calvary Church, I sometimes feel that I can almost reach out and touch the people I have come to know from their letters and diaries and ledgers, that they are near, behind a thin veil of time. It was just yesterday, just down the road. And it was so far away, so long ago . . . In a certain mood of elegiacal sentimentality I can see old Rockdale glimmering through a golden haze, where the spinster Sunday School teacher Clementina Smith and her sister Harriet are still sweetly instructing the mill hands in the elements of Christian faith, and the nervous manufacturer John P. Crozer still sweats over preparing a report to the Board of Directors of the Delaware County National Bank, and John

S. Phillips, that clever mechanician, still drives his horse Mazeppa in a Byronic fury down the hills and over the bridges to court the Du Pont girls on the Brandywine, fifteen miles away.

So let us first look at Rockdale with a sentimental, even romantic eye, in the age when it had reached a kind of climax of its way of life, in the years around 1850. Later we can look more closely into the furnace of technological and social change that also was Rockdale. Rockdale at this point was enjoying the few brief years of relative equilibrium that came after decades of growth and economic uncertainty and social unrest, and just before the disaster of the Civil War.

When Sophie du Pont wrote to her friend Clementina Smith in October 1841, she mentioned with favor the contrast between "sweet quiet Rockdale" and the bustling city.[1] The quality of life in Rockdale, day by day, had a naturalness that appealed to romantic sensibility. Rocky hillsides and beech woods, farms and mills, combined wildness with cultivation in a pastoral landscape. The town was still a part of that antebellum rural north that is evoked partly by Currier and Ives pictures of cozy farms and little country mills, and partly by the Hudson River School's wilder landscapes. In both images, the elements of technology are often visible, but they are not obtrusive. Rockdale was in truth a pastoral community not far from wilderness. There was as yet no jarring sound of locomotive engines and shrieking whistles (the railroad that was to connect the Rockdale district with West Chester and Philadelphia would not be completed until 1856).[2] The mills themselves, powered only by water, whispered and grunted softly; the looms clattered behind windows closed to keep moisture in the air; even when the workers were summoned, it was by the bell in the cupola and not by a steam whistle. The machine was in the garden, to be sure, but it was a machine that had grown almost organically in its niche, like a mutant flower that was finding a congenial place among the rocks, displacing no one else and in fact contributing to the welfare of the whole.[3]

In economic matters the decade 1844–54 was for the Rockdale district an era of calm prosperity for almost everyone there. It came after nearly a generation of struggle; and it ended in an almost explosive expansion of manufacturing. But in that brief period the dream of an "American System" of manufactures, a harmony of rural and industrial interests and lifeways, nearly became reality. Industry was not harnessing power out of proportion to local resources; the falling water that turned water wheels and turbines was a non-polluting, self-renewing source of energy. The mills themselves were small, scattered along the creek at the several mill seats, and each one employed dozens rather than hundreds of workers. The system of spinning and weaving machines, and of the machine tools needed to build them and keep them in repair, after three-quarters of a century of development, was now virtually complete. And the local farmers were not incommoded by the mills; rather, the proximity of a mill enhanced the value of a farm. Advertisements of nearby farms for sale emphasized the advantage of their closeness to the mills, which were a source of alternative employment for the farmer and his family, a reservoir of laborers during slack times, and a market for produce.[4] Even the conflicts between the capitalists and the workers had been resolved in the nearly complete ascendancy of the values of evangelical reform capitalism.

Rockdale, indeed, can serve as a symbol of the early phase of the Industrial Revolution in America. Unlike England where, because of the almost universal use of steam engines for power, manufacturing was concentrated in sooty cities like Manchester, the American manufacturing districts were rural and depended upon the new country's as yet unexploited resources of water power. The Rockdale manufacturing district was almost a self-sufficient rural community, like a plantation or a commune, tied economically to world markets and financial centers by the buying of raw cotton and the selling of yarn and cloth, and linked intellectually and spiritually to the wider culture by the participation of its citizens in migration, travel, and reading. Its social structure of caste and class, its style of family life, were for the moment not seriously in question, and the deeper dilemmas inherent in its way of life were not yet fully realized by its citizens.

A TYPICAL MILL HAMLET ABOUT 1850: A SYNTHETIC RECONSTRUCTION.

Above Left: MAN IN GIG.

Above Right: A HOT JULY DAY.

Below: FARMER WITH COWS.

Above: SWIMMING IN CHESTER CREEK.

Below: PICNIC ON NUT ROCK.

SLEEPY HOLLOW DAYS

In July and August of 1845, a young man from Lenni named Richard Griffith took his sketchbook in hand and wandered about the Rockdale district, drawing the buildings and landscapes familiar to him from youth (along with caricatures of his neighbors disguised as dogs, cats, pigs, and other assorted livestock). The sketchbook was also adorned with quotations from Shakespeare and comical illustrations of actors dressed in elaborate costume; these conceits mark him as a man of some education and worldly sophistication, perhaps now on a summer vacation at his boyhood home. (Later he was to become a cotton manufacturer on the Brandywine, but in 1845, aged twenty-six, he was apparently not yet engaged in the industry.) His views show an almost classically pastoral world: boys swimming in the creek, their clothes piled on a flat rock high above the water; a horse panting as it draws the shaded carriage up a steep hill, the driver in the seat urging "Bob" to greater effort, the ladies, on foot, heads shaded with parasols, plodding along behind to lighten the horse's burden; a picnic on top of "Nut Rock," with three bare-headed, long-haired young women and two swains, one of them on his knees before his girl (who is on her knees, too), all beneath a canopy of lofty trees; a horse (probably Bob again) trotting along the road beside a post-and-rail fence, with the same wagon behind him, captioned: "The Journey to 'Sleepy Hollow.'" (Sleepy Hollow was —and is—the name of the valley around the forks in the creek.) He even shows, in a carefully drawn sketch labeled "July 15th Lenni," made from the west side of the race, the newly reconstructed mill of Daniel Lammot. The drawing reveals a wagon pulled by three horses in line (urged on by a driver with a whip) just leaving the picker house, which is filled with unbroken cotton bales; looming above them is the typical two-story-plus-clerestory mill, with long lines of black windows, and a cupola in the middle of the roof. The mood of the drawings, where it is not simply documentary, is mildly condescending, picking out the antic foibles and rustic habits of the remote rural mill town to which he is perhaps returning after college and travels in the outside world.

But there is also an aura of prosperity about the landscape and of self-satisfaction, even of smugness, in the postures and faces of the uniden-tified people whom he shows. A man drives a gig, his legs encased in tight-fitting, loudly checquered pants, his chest swelling beneath a sharply cut jacket, a figure of stiff pride from the footboard up to his jutting jaw and stovepipe hat cocked forward on his brow. Huntsmen, coattails aflying, race their steeds past a farmer's well-fenced field. Ladies with parasols parade, heads demurely covered in bonnets and veiled in lace, bodies protected from neck to ankle by dresses and shawls. Four young gentlemen, one of them in a military cap, practice archery, shooting at a tripod-mounted bull's-eye target in a field. Picket-fenced stone houses with latticed porches and overarching trees stretch out along country lanes; a small barn, surmounted by weathervane, is evidently the home of pigeons returning to a pair of carefully made roosts. A bath house is seen beneath a weeping willow, sitting out in the creek at the end of a wooden quay. Workingmen, wearing low-crowned, flat-brimmed hats, perch on a wagon emerging from a covered bridge; a farmer, puffing on cigar, brings his two cows in to be milked. Even the sketch of Lenni Mill has a feeling of summer calm: in the foreground flows the smooth water in the race flanked by graceful grasses, and a large bullfrog sits on the bank, contentedly observing activities at the factory. It is all very easy, very prosperous, very pastoral; there is only one note of distress, and that is a rather stiff sketch of the great flood, captioned merely: "August 5th 1843." It shows a small tenement house inundated by swirling water, with a human figure beckoning desperately from the attic window. Clearly the world of man keeps its order; it is nature that sometimes gets out of hand. And the bath house, a very model of serenity, lies on the same page, as if it were a sequel.[1]

The leaders of the community were mostly inclined to preserve the pastoral character of the Rockdale scene and resented efforts to change it. Manufacturer Samuel Riddle was severely criticized when he cut down a beautiful grove of linden trees in front of his mansion in order to have a better view of the road.[2] Clementina Smith's mother, in describing to a friend the "view from Clemma's chamber," became almost lyrical; she was deeply moved:

> Sometimes I cannot take my eyes away—it fascinates even more than ocean scenery—there is no thought of loneliness in looking at these hills and vallies and the blue shores of Jersey, so far in the distance. This scene from Rockdale Parsonage fills me sometimes, with inexpressible enjoyment I never did enjoy any scene more, for it seems to be heavenly to me.[3]

These attitudes are, perhaps, understandable in terms of the romantic appreciation for scenes of natural beauty of the time; but even today, after much has been done to destroy the views that charmed educated residents in the 1840's, the steep forested hills, and twisting stream with grassy meadows bordering it, still conceal factories only a few hundred yards away, and allow the eye uninterrupted enjoyment of rural landscape.

There were no noisy taverns and only a small inn in the Rockdale

CHESTER CREEK.

district; the public houses were a mile or more off, the Black Bear on the Baltimore Pike and the Seven Stars at Village Green. The nights were still and dark, except when the sounds of hymn-singing at Calvary broke the stillness; the air was clear and the stars shone brightly. People were peaceful, and respectable young ladies like Clementina and Harriet walked freely, unescorted, along the dusty lanes among the fields, and in the woods in spring, gathering the wildflowers. As Clemma wrote Sophie from busy Philadelphia one May, after a brief visit to Rockdale:

> I languish now for the green fields and country quiet, and enjoyment—
> I do not know when I have felt so happy as I did last Sunday in a walk
> in the woods, to renew my acquaintance with my little friends the violets
> and anemonies.[4]

THE LORDS OF THE VALLEY

Rockdale undoubtedly drew its name from the rounded fieldstones that lie about on the surface of the ground, tumble down the steep hillsides after rain, and pave the channel of the stream. Rocky was the ground; rock was the material used for construction; and, in some sense, the men who ruled the valley were rocklike too, hard-minded competitors in business, and stern in Christian faith.

The Valley of Chester Creek

The part of the creek chosen for the business of cotton manufacturing was the three-mile stretch that descended through the most precipitous part of the fall line, where the height of the streambed above sea level dropped from about 120 feet at the upper end to no more than 30 at the lower. This steep fall of 90 feet in about three miles permitted the construction of mills at frequent intervals. By 1850, there were seven cotton mills in the three-mile stretch, with sundry machine shops and saw- and gristmills associated with them. The steepness of the gradient enabled miller and manufacturer to obtain the necessary head of water—from 10 to 20 feet—with a relatively short race and thus permitted them to economize not only on construction and maintenance costs for race and gates, but also on the cost of acquiring and maintaining the necessary acreage to contain the water right and the adjacent banks.

Chester Creek was not much different from other streams that cut their way through the fall line which runs southward like a long scar, parallel to and about ten miles inland from the Delaware River below Philadelphia. Some, like the Schuylkill, were broader; others—Cobbs Creek, Crum Creek, Darby Creek, and Ridley Creek—were perhaps smaller streams; and the Brandywine, to the south and west, ran through a less narrowly dissected terrain, which yielded a softer, more rolling landscape, and a more comfortable mixture of mill and farm.

The upper and lower reaches of the two branches of the creek were less well suited to cotton manufacturing. The only cotton mill higher up, at Trimble's on the West Branch, had reverted to the grist- and sawmill business after the failure of a cotton manufacturer in 1816. There were of course a number of grist- and sawmills, but the only other sites suitable for major manufactories were already occupied by two very old and very different enterprises—the paper mills of the Willcoxes, at Ivy Mills on the West Branch, and Old Sarum Forge, on the main branch. Both of these plantations lay at the upper edge of the fall line; the Forge in particular required the extensive forests in its surrounding area for its charcoal-fired furnaces. The fall of water above this region became much less rapid, however, and the volume slighter, as one pursued the stream across the plateau toward its headwaters near West Chester. Below the cotton district, similarly, the creek was less suitable for manufacturing. The stream completed its cut through the fall line a half-mile or so below Knowlton Mill, and thereafter flowed slowly, a broad stream wandering through widening meadows, reaching Chester four miles farther down at approximately 10 feet above sea level, after a further fall of only 20 feet.

Within the cotton district itself the landscape was craggy, not suitable for farming or grazing. The hillsides, between which the creek had for millions of years been cutting its path, dropped steeply, in some places precipitously, to the narrow floodplain through which, from mountain wall to wall, the creek meandered. The tops of the hills stood at elevations of about 200 feet above the creek, and their flanks sloped down at angles of from 30 to 45 degrees, so that across the valley from rounded crest to rounded crest stretched a space of no more than a quarter of a mile, with the creek winding a couple of hundred feet below. The flat plains, only 3 or 4 feet above the water, were made of a rich, loamy soil; being left uncultivated because of frequent flooding, they were covered with few trees, mostly with long long grasses, softly brown in winter and a rich, waving green in summer. In swampy places there were stands of cattails. The bed of the stream, except in the ponds behind the dams, was filled with sand and round pebbles of various sizes. The stream itself was most of the time no more than 50 feet wide, and a foot or two deep; clear and cold, it rushed quickly with a soft rustle over its uneven bed.

The hillsides fell so steeply that the valley had nearly the character of a rocky gorge or ravine here and there, with boulders tumbled in profusion and rough outcroppings of granite; the southern slopes remained almost perpetually in shade. The soil over the hills was filled with large rounded pebbles—fieldstones—of various weights, from the size of an egg to heavy boulders. These stones were almost universally used for construction of houses, walls, dams, and races, for they could be dug out of shallow pits by the side of the roads that clung to the hillsides and used without dressing.

In winter the hardwood forests on the hills shone with a bronze and silver sheen, as the silvery trunks of the beech and the lingering reddish brown leaves of the oaks stood out from the gray background of maple, tulip, and ash and the softer brown of the leaves on the forest floor. But in summer the gorge became a monotonous green jungle of trees and grass and weedy underbrush. The climate lay in the middle range, summer temperatures reaching the nineties, and in winter falling sometimes to zero, with rain and snow both moderately heavy. The creek thus varied in fullness not so much seasonally as occasionally in response to irregular fluctuations in rainfall and snow-melt.

It was, then, a place too rugged in terrain for farming but naturally pre-adapted for the early manufacture of cotton, with plenty of water power and an abundance of quarry and fieldstone for dams, races, houses, mills, and bridges. It was a niche prepared by time for the harmonious combination of men, machines, and nature in the pastoral phase of American manufacturing.

The Mills and the Mill Hamlets

The sites chosen by the cotton manufacturers on Chester Creek all lay within a short distance of one another. The farthest upstream, Lenni and West Branch, were only two miles as the crow flies from the lowest, Knowlton Mill; but because of the meanderings of the stream, the distance by water was about three miles. Rockdale was at the midpoint. Half a mile above Rockdale the creek forked, with the northernmost branch suffering no change of name, and the narrower and more southerly fork being called West Branch. Because the hills rose steeply from the banks, except where a narrow floodplain intervened—at most 100 yards in width—the total area of the cotton-manufacturing district was about one and a half square miles. Within this arena were concentrated the mill villages—the dams, races, mills, roads, stores, and housing—all complete and neatly separate from the farms on the plateau above.

The boundaries of the manufacturing district, the location of the mills, and the layout of the hamlets were all determined by specific limitations of terrain and technology. As we have seen, the boundaries of the district itself were set by the combined requirements that there be sufficient water power to operate the machines and that the race need not be so long that it demanded an excessively large tract of land along the stream. Within the district, the location of each mill was again decided by a combination of topographic and mechanical considerations. Each mill seat required a suitable place for a dam, a suitable stretch for a race, and a suitable spot for a mill. The ideal place for a dam was either at a natural fall or rapids or at a natural narrowing of the valley to form a gorge. At Knowlton, there was a gorge which permitted a short but relatively high dam; at the other sites, there were natural rapids which allowed shallow dams. In all cases, the

"ENGLISH HILL": TENEMENTS AT WEST BRANCH.

races were relatively short, sometimes (as at West Branch) as brief as 50
yards. Every one of the mill seats except Parkmount had been identified
and used for other purposes before cotton manufacturing came in, in three
cases for paper mills, in two for forges, in one as a grist- and sawmill.

The nexus of dam, headrace, wheelpit, mill, and tailrace thus
defined the mill seat itself. Around the mill, other considerations determined the settlement pattern of the hamlet. First, a road had to pass by
the mill in order to bring in machinery, cotton, and other supplies, and
take out the mill's products. This road had to run roughly parallel to
the stream as it neared the mill. The housing of the mill workers was,
of necessity, in tenements constructed by the mill owner or manufacturer and located on his land, for the most part along the road that led
to the mill, and as close as possible to it, for the workers had to walk
back and forth to work in all kinds of weather. Neighboring farmers
might board a few hands, but they simply did not have enough space
for all. On the hillside above the tenements, at successively higher levels as the status of the occupant increased, were the houses and mansions of the managerial personnel, the capitalists who owned the machines, and the mill owners who owned the land. Everything was made

TENEMENTS AT PARKMOUNT.

of stone. The mills, tenements, and many of the houses were constructed of fieldstone laid in lime-and-clay mortar, reinforced with
horsehair, and stuccoed yellow-brown or white. The bridges and some
of the mansions, however, were made of a gray quarried stone, cut in
rectangular blocks, and these houses were not stuccoed.

Looking down from the hillsides in winter (for foliage in summer
concealed almost the entire scene), each hamlet across the valley presented much the same image: a road, a palisaded mill of three stories
including a clerestory on the third and a bell cupola in the center, a
race, a dam; on the hillside immediately behind the mill and along the
road, several rows of neat stone tenements, and a few separate houses,
where workers and tradesmen lived; and ascending the hill, the larger
houses of the supervisory staff, with the mansions at the top, surrounded by gardens. Plumes of smoke would be ascending from the
stoves in the mill and from the fireplaces and cookstoves of the houses;
if one were watching at lunchtime, one might hear the bell ring the
hour, and see the workers—men, women, and children—trooping home
in family groups for the midday meal.

The Cotton Lords

Each hamlet was administered as almost a patriarchal domain by a mill owner or a manufacturer (often one and the same person). In the Rockdale district, only one of the mills had an absentee landlord; for all the rest, the owners and manufacturers either resided in the mansion or were represented there day by day by members of the family. In the case of the one exception, at Old Sable in Rockdale, the owner and manufacturer was a wealthy and aged Irishman who owned mills in nearby towns; he was represented locally by an English mill superintendent who lived near the mill. Thus, although there might be a considerable difference in life style and standard of living between workers and capitalists, in the normal course of events they lived next door to each other, knew the insides of one another's houses, were familiar with members of each other's family, and worked, albeit at different jobs, in the same mill.

The manufacturers were sometimes jibingly referred to by their employees, at times of labor unrest, as "cotton lords," in uncomplimentary allusion to the legendary Manchester millionaires. These English capitalists, who were often enough unfavorably described in the American press, were understood to be bloated, lecherous tyrants who brutalized their employees, worked juvenile apprentices to death, and made their money by grinding the faces of the poor. This image did not really fit the capitalists and landowners along Chester Creek, however. They were eager enough to make money. But they were not, in this generation at least, really alienated from the people who worked in their mills. Their feelings were truly hurt when, on rare occasions of labor trouble, they were accused of exploiting their employees; they believed that capitalists and factory operatives were in principle a cooperating team.

Among the eight mill owners and manufacturers, there were four men who might be called, if not the lords, at least the oligarchy of the Rockdale manufacturing district: John P. Crozer, Daniel Lammot, Jr., Richard S. Smith, and Samuel Riddle. They owned much of the land, operated the major mills, had most of the money, and—perhaps more important than anything else—controlled access to the sources of money, information, and political influence outside Rockdale itself. The most prominent of these by far was John Price Crozer, who owned two of the mills, West Branch and Crozerville. Crozer was a man of English and Huguenot descent, in his mid-fifties, and extremely wealthy. He had recently expanded his enterprises to include a new mill at Upland, downstream on the outskirts of Chester, and now lived there in a new mansion with his family and servants.

His son Samuel was in immediate charge of operations in the Rockdale district and Crozer himself took charge of the Upland development. Crozer was proud of being a self-made and largely self-educated man, a local farmboy from the county who had by toil and inflexible determination made his fortune. Crozer was a Baptist and had recently become intensely religious; he devoted much of his time to religious causes and he regarded himself as God's steward, managing his mills and mill hands and his wealth for the advancement of the community. He kept a diary in which he carefully recorded the spiritual transformation he was experiencing as the love of victory and the desire for gold were transmuted into a longing to be of service to his Savior.

Across the forks of the creek lay Lenni Mill, so named by an earlier manufacturer who associated the wild charm of the spot with its original Indian inhabitants, the Lenni Lenape, or Delaware, Indians. Lenni (and also the mill seat below it at the forks, Parkmount) was owned by Hannah, the second wife of the gentleman farmer Peter Hill. Peter Hill was a former merchant whose reputation for shady business practice and succession of bankruptcies had persuaded Hannah's father to leave his daughter the two mill seats in trust, so that Peter Hill could not sell them to cover his debts. He administered the properties for her, and the family lived in a substantial mansion from the rentals of the mill seats. Hill came of an old Quaker family in the county; his wife was a Sellers, of the famous mechanicians' clan in Philadelphia, whose members and connections included such poor but celebrated geniuses as Charles Willson Peale and whole generations of inventors, engineers, and mechanicians. But they were socially marginal in the Rockdale district, visiting little with the manufacturing families. Lenni was leased by the aging Daniel Lammot, Jr., a man of French descent in his late sixties who was connected by business and marriage to the Du Ponts along the Brandywine. The Lammots were, with their friends the Richard S. Smiths of Crozerville, the society people of the Rockdale district, the ladies spending part of the winter social season in Philadelphia and part of the summer at fashionable resorts like Cape May and Saratoga. The Lammots were very active in the religious affairs of the Church of the New Jerusalem. Peter Hill, like his father-in-law Nathan Sellers, was also a Swedenborgian, and his wife Hannah had some sympathy for her father's faith.

The Smiths were only summer residents in the Rockdale district but they were nonetheless extremely powerful in the community. Smith himself was a man of sixty, who boasted Swedish ancestry and spoke the language well (he had even served as U.S. consul in Sweden during the War of 1812). Years ago he had owned the cotton mill at the site of Old Sable Forge, and had been principally responsible for the establishment of Calvary Episcopal Church, the religious center of the community. He and his family throughout the year managed the affairs of the church, teaching in its Sunday School and parish school, selecting and providing housing for the rector, and promoting the interests of the congregation in the larger councils of the diocese, in which he was one of the leading low church evangelical laymen. His wife Elizabeth and his unmarried daughters Clementina and Harriet were constantly moving back and forth between Philadelphia, where they had a house on fashionable Clinton Street, and the old Crozer mansion which they were renting. Smith was the president of the Union Insurance Company, a post he had held since 1837, when he lost the mill during the panic; and, like their close friends the Lammots, the Smiths were connected by business and marriage with the Du Ponts.

The other major figure in the community was Samuel Riddle, who owned and operated the old Penn's Grove factory. Riddle, now in his fifties, was an Irishman who had come over from Belfast in the 1820's with only a few dollars in his pocket and had worked his way to wealth. Riddle was a nominal Presbyterian; his brother and former partner James was a "forcible," and successful, Methodist preacher who now ran his own cotton mill on the Brandywine. Samuel served as postmaster at Penn's Grove and was later to marry the daughter of a postmistress in Chester. Samuel Riddle had a salty tongue, was a genial raconteur, a cantankerous neighbor with a propensity for quarreling over fences, a conspicuous member of the Hibernian Society; having been brought up as a lad in a spinning mill on the other side of the water, he could identify with his workers. Although he was not a frequent guest in the more religious households of the community, such as the Smiths' and the Lammots', there was far less labor trouble in his mills than in those of his more religious peers.

So diverse a group would not, superficially, seem capable of much mutual understanding; yet they cooperated successfully for decades in business, politics, and local social reform and improvement. In denomination and degree of religious devotion, in social manners, in ethnic origin, in level of education, in acceptability to polite society, they were very different from one another. But they shared certain basic features which were, in their eyes, so fundamental to civilized society that they could also be regarded as necessary to a fully human identity. Foremost in this regard was fidelity-to-contract. It is difficult to overestimate the importance of this virtue in the eyes of these men. In his autobiography, written a decade later for the edification of his children—and of other people's children too, one may infer, inasmuch as he published it as a book—John P. Crozer testified in two remarkable paragraphs to the centrality of the notion of fidelity-to-contract in his scheme of things. Simple commercial honesty was, as he saw it, the moral axis around which all his human relationships 'were formed.

But a kind Heavenly Father had endowed me with some elements of power which saved me from ruin. Indomitable perseverance, and unwavering integrity, a firm resolution to do justly to others, ever ruled in my mind; and I may now, in the maturity of age and in the possession of a large fortune, recall what, in review of a long life, I believe to be strictly true—that I never knowingly or intentionally wronged any one in business. It has been the uniform tenor of my life to be upright and honest in my dealings. I may perhaps have driven hard bargains; I know I have been pretty close in my dealings; but a bargain or promise once made by me has ever been regarded sacred, and to be kept inviolable; no waver, no temptation to dishonesty, has ever assailed me, or ever crossed my mind as a suggestion.

I wish that I could make the same record as to my character and conduct, especially the thoughts of my heart in every other matter; but alas I cannot; I can think of innumerable cases, when I would be compelled to write bitter things against myself. My industry and integrity were recognized, I believe, by all with whom I had intercourse; and being careful to fulfil every pecuniary obligation or promise, I early inspired confidence. I was often much straitened for money; but, with a full knowledge of my business resources, I was careful never to make a promise to pay, without assurance in my own mind that I could comply. The people with whom I dealt early learned that I was reliable in my promises to pay, and, as a consequence, running bills were often not called for by my creditors for months after they were actually due. This was a benefit to me, and I may here recommend a similar course to every young man commencing business. Be careful never to disappoint when you promise to pay; and, if you have not the money to pay bills when due and called for, say so frankly, and at the same time say *when* you will pay, and never suffer the creditor to call beyond the second time. If it be practicable, pay a little earlier (by sending the money to him) than you had engaged to do. You will soon find your account in this course. Nothing is of so much importance to a young man commencing business as a character for integrity, industry, and promptness. The community around him will early recognize these qualities, and duly appreciate them; and they will secure a credit and willingness to do business with him, thus making amends for any want of cash capital he may be deficient in. I speak with confidence on this subject. I have witnessed it in my own case and in that of others.[1]

CROZER'S MANSION AT WEST BRANCH.

In an even more extraordinary piece of dialogue (whose alleged occurrence is significant whether or not the story is apocryphal), a Rockdale businessman once defined commercial probity as a virtue inherent in masculinity. The owner of a small coalyard, so the story goes, went to Philadelphia, all dressed up in clean overalls, to order coal. At the supplier's office the clerks paid no attention to him, a mere workingman in overalls. When at last they discovered that he wanted to buy coal, they told him that they didn't sell small lots. He explained that he wanted two or three carloads. At that they perked up, asked him his name, sat him down, and requested references. He pointed to his loins and said, "My references are here."[2]

The point of these hyperbolic testimonials on the importance of, and qualifications for, a good credit rating is that a *real man* keeps his promises, that the cornerstone of manhood is fidelity-to-contract. It was not just a Protestant ethic of hard work, punctuality, cleanliness, and other displays of godliness. And it was not an individualistic virtue; on the contrary, it was by definition a social virtue, and its significance lay in its assumption that contracts make society work and that mutual trust makes *contracts* work. These were men who really believed that social contract was the basis of human society, that manhood was a state of social responsibility, that to be a man was not just to be a virile adult male but a male credited by a community of other males with being honest in their ceaseless mutual business dealings. Thus the contract principle was at once an ego ideal and a theory of society.

But, in addition to being honest, these were men, as Crozer said of himself, of "indomitable perseverance." They wanted increase: increase in wealth, in power, in prestige; they expanded their factories, they added to their number. Bound by the rule of fidelity-to-contract once made, they were free to drive hard bargains in the negotiations leading to agreement. The contract defined the limit of mutual obligation; the participants in the game were, within bounds of legality, free to engage in shrewd practice. Thus the system was a paradox: a community of mutually trustful men, each one trying desperately to accumulate wealth and power at the possible expense of others, even as the others' sharpness, and the fluctuations of the market, constantly threatened to wash away his own accumulation. And the possibility of disaster was ever in mind, too. Only Samuel Riddle, so far as is known, had never known failure in business. A businessman's life was not conceived to be normally a smooth and steady ascent, but a perilous traversal of uneven terrain, with great peaks and valleys to be crossed before arriving at last on the green plateau of great wealth. But in this early phase of industrial capitalism, the manufacturers did not view themselves so much as competitors as colleagues, all engaged in the same profession, all matching wits against the impersonal market, with success ultimately possible for all who worked hard and made wise choices. And they were all believers in hierarchy. All had been poor and dependent upon others in their adult lives. Even in republican America, where no nobility or rigid system of classes arrogated to itself a monopoly of rank, there was visibly an order based on the exercise of power by men of capital, of political position, of judicial authority, of religious eminence. With power came the responsibility to use that position as God's steward on earth: to punish those who made mistakes or behaved wrongly, as parents punished children, and to reward the virtuous and competent. Indeed, the image of the sinner punished in his lifetime by an almighty but unpredictable Father was inscribed on the conscience of every one of these Christian leaders. At any moment the Heavenly Father might visit disaster upon any man, depriving him, in the interest of awakening in him an awareness of his ultimate need for salvation, of money, property, even family. Only at the last might the iron law of punishment be relaxed, if the Savior were willing to pardon the penitent sinner trusting in his Lord for mercy. The days of a person's dying were thus the culmination of life, for in them man and woman gave evidence of their moral condition. In his last hour, man settled his affairs on earth, providing for the payment of his debts and testifying to his hope of salvation.[3]

The psychodynamic problem, then, was to balance arrogance and trust. Intensely ambitious, striving constantly to excel others, to climb in the hierarchy, to become *more* wealthy, *more* powerful, *more* respected than other men, each believed at the same time that the world was built on trust.

A man had to trust others and be trustworthy himself, and so earn the trust of others, or he could never excel them or become a steward over them, for they would not admit him into commerce with them; and if he failed their trust, they would punish him for violating the rules. But while he strove to make others trust him, he also labored to trust in God's mercy, even though he knew that God could never have trust in him, being so miserable a sinner. One can see the structure of these capitalists' religious faith as almost a mirror image, reversed in directions, of the structure of their conception of the social contract. In the commercial world, man could rise to glory; in relation to God, he was already fallen. In the commercial world, punishment for violating the rules was certain, and trust must be mutual. In man's relation to God, the just punishment for man's untrustworthiness was ultimately withheld and man was saved from Hell if only he had trust in God and accepted Jesus as his Savior. Thus the drama of death and salvation formed, as it were, a negative image of the commercial world.

But despite the reverse symmetry in the relation between values necessary to the stability of the natural world and to the salvation of the soul, a latent dilemma remained. Can, in principle, *every* man achieve economic success? Can, in principle, *every* man's soul be saved? The noisy rhetoric of Jacksonian oratory did not answer these questions, for they fundamentally challenged not only the orthodox Protestant interpretation of Christian doctrine but also the orthodox economic assumption that there was an unredeemable class of immoral or incompetent persons who could not be trusted and whose poverty thus was made certain by the fact that they could not be admitted to the society of businessmen who were eligible for economic success.

THE SISTERHOOD

But the businessmen wrote mostly of themselves. It is in the quiet correspondence of women that the quality of life among the ruling families in Rockdale is most clearly recalled, in brief vignettes of their encounters with each other, and with their menfolk, and with the working people of the neighborhood, and in intense discussions of books and ideas and people that interested them. Out of this correspondence, and particularly the correspondence between the Smiths and the Du Ponts, emerges the outline of a network of cultivated women who constituted an intellectual society along Chester Creek and the Brandywine that played a powerful role in the polite social life of the twin communities.

If we take Clementina ("Clemma"), the daughter of Richard S. Smith, as the center, the network of women who were her constant friends and associates—with whom she talked and visited and regularly and frequently worked and corresponded—numbered fourteen. In her own family, they included her mother Elizabeth Smith, her sister Harriet ("Hattie"), and her cousin Joanna Smith. A mile up the creek, there were Anna Lammot and her stepdaughters Eleanora ("Nora") and Mary; and on the Brandywine was Mrs. Lammot's other stepdaughter Margaretta ("Meta"). Still farther up the creek above Lenni was Mrs. Willcox at Ivy Mills. On the Brandywine were the three Du Pont sisters, Sophie (Clemma's best friend), Eleuthera ("Eleu"), and Victorine ("Vic") Bauduy (Mrs. Smith's best friend). And also on the Brandywine at Kentmere were little Mary Gilpin and her sister Sarah, who had no nicknames. It was a tightly coupled network in the sense that each member knew most of the others personally and all by reputation.

They were women of parts, with one or two exceptions trained in one or another of the fashionable female academies in Philadelphia (the exceptions were educated at home by tutors and relatives), and thereafter continuously active in literary or artistic pursuits. Their education differed from the men's in paying less attention to mathematics and practically none to such disciplined fields as physics and chemistry; but the training was thorough in botany and natural history, English literature, classical and modern languages, and political and religious history; and the girls learned not merely to appreciate music and art but to play, draw, and write passable verse and essays. Furthermore, this learning was seriously valued and laid the basis for a lifelong regard for the intellectual and artistic work not only of men but of women as well. Elizabeth Smith, writing ruefully to her friend Victorine Bauduy, expressed the values clearly in praising her sister-in-law Eliza Smith:

> There are few who know the worth of [her]. The capacities of her mind are really great. . . . [Has read much, was once] the best musician I have known . . . excellent French and Italien schollar. She had a great talent for painting and is ingeneous in all the tasteful employments of our sex. Everything however has been given up for the duties of the nursery & housewife.[1]

And if to a person's intellectual accomplishments were added a sincere religious concern, the possibilities of social intercourse with her were especially promising. As Clementina put it, "What is there dear Sophie more delightful than intellectual Christian society?"[2]

Ten of the members of the sisterhood were married; of these ten, two were childless; and some of the mothers employed wet-nurses for their infants at birth, or shortly after, thus freeing themselves to move about, to work, and to travel. This practice entailed the occasional inconvenience of losing some of the intimacies of motherhood; but the mothers took a practical view of the matter. Anna Lammot, on returning home from a trip, discovered that her son did not remember her at all. Although "his old associations" soon restored her to his recollection, he could not remember her name (and he evidently never did learn the name of the wet-nurse). As she put it in her usual down-to-earth style, "My title of Mamma is forgotten & he calls me nothing but 'titt-tee.' "[3] Nor were the children, boys or girls, allowed to disrupt their mothers' lives at older ages, being kept to a strict household discipline, with obedience emphasized and enforced. Boarding school at ten or eleven ended the child's residential connection for several years during the teens, except for summer vacations; after the school years, the mother was confronted with an adult child who remained pretty much under parental control as long as he or she remained in the house. It was a no-nonsense system, which functioned (and no doubt was designed) to protect the mother's role as hostess and household administrator and, increasingly, her continued intellectual development and participation in evangelical and reform activities in the community.

Like a host of others in America at this time, many of the sisterhood were ambivalent about marriage as an institution, not merely the spinsters but those already married as well. The attitude was not expressed—at least in their written correspondence—in open criticism of their own or each other's husbands. Rather, it took the form of complaints about the restrictions which the duties of housewifery and motherhood had placed (or would place) on some woman's ability to fulfill herself in an intellectual or artistic or even religious career. In writing to his daughter Margaretta shortly after her marriage to Alfred du Pont, her father simply advised her to be diligent and attentive "in the discharge of all your duties" in order to gain happiness in this world and the next. Anna was more candid. She believed strongly in the necessity of marriage, but she tended to regard the male as the dependent partner. In a series of letters to her stepdaughter, she conveyed in more or less subtle fashion this view of the potentially dominant role of the female in the marital relation. Thus in commenting on a recently announced union, she remarked in high spirits:

There is a trifling advantage on the lady's side of 10 or a dozen years—but you know your father's old maxim in choosing chickens may apply equally to all *paired* animals—"Put an old one with a young one & it will be better taken care of."

Her analysis of the character of a young clergyman was even more emphatic:

As to Mr. Ives if he does not get married soon, the best thing his friends in particular & his congregation in general can do for him is to hire him a tall strapping dry nurse—who will souse him in cold water three times a day & rub him dry with a good hard towel—He is the biggest baby extant & ought not to be tolerated in the society of even half grown ladies & gentlemen—I may venture to class myself among this last mentioned number. At least I would be glad to do so to have a writ of expulsion on him in my favour.

After Mr. Ives's marriage, he visited Anna's father's house, and she met him again there. In her opinion, marriage had not improved him:

Mr & Mrs Ives are at Papa's—They came round to spend the day about week ago, she had a relapse & was obliged to remain—He is too great a Baby to be endured among grown up people—& I have been obliged almost to make him absolutely angry before I could make him listen to reason in the management of his Wife's indisposition—The girls & Mamma can do nothing with him—but Rebecca coinciding with me, rendered him in some measure tractable—The poor girl—with a little baby to *come* & a big one *never away,* she has a poor prospect—'Tis a comfort however that the first will grow every day less of a baby, while the last is becoming more & more of one—

But as to the choice between romantic marriage and attachments to parents and siblings, she conceded—with some difficulty—that marriage probably should come first, in some cases. She discussed with her step-daughter the case of a young wife forced to choose between husband and family:

Sally Hodge goes the first of next month to Havre to meet her husband & expects to settle in France. Her youngest child was seized with convulsions in consequence of violent screaming a few weeks ago & died in a few hours—This is shocking!—And now she goes away from all her friends & family to the end of the world for her husbands sake—This is right—but hard—He ought to be the best of husbands for she sacrifices much to him—Yet a woman would scarce feel that she sacrificed any thing if her only choice was *husband* or *family*—particularly if they were truly united & have young bonds to bind them closer—[4]

Clearly, in Anna Lammot's view, not only was marriage itself a choice, but how to conduct it was a matter of choice as well. In a marital dilemma, where divorce was not in prospect (and in most circumstances it was unthinkable), the woman might still choose to return quietly to the family in which she was born rather than remain with or join her husband. Such a possibility was no doubt vividly apparent to married women whose husbands, being forced to travel on business for prolonged periods, left them to stay with their "own" families of birth.

Within the group, Anna Lammot was regarded as the most intellectual and most accomplished. She came of a distinguished family, her father being a well-to-do merchant, and her mother the sister of the prominent Episcopal theologian John Hobart, then Bishop of New York.[5] She had been introduced to the widowed Daniel Lammot by her school friend Victorine because both enjoyed German literature and found few companions with whom to share this interest. (Anna was particularly fond of Goethe and wrote a love poem in the style of his "Ich Denke Dein.") Anna was a practiced versifier by the age of eleven, and when the young ladies from Mme Rivardi's school put together their little manuscript booklet of poetic remembrances to a departing friend, Miss Antoinette Brevost, Anna Smith's lines were more numerous than all the rest.[6] She continued to write throughout her life, in early years offering sonnets to her beloved Victorine, and later turning to verse on occasions of sorrow, as at the sickness or death of a friend or of her own children.

She took a strong interest in political affairs. On reading Mme de Staël (who like Anna appreciated German literature), she was moved to write to Victorine (who "hate[d] German") her view of what the famous writer might do for America and for her own understanding:

I wish Made de Stael would come to our country & be so good as to convince the literary world that we have some national character—It requires some helping hand as powerful as hers to raise & exhibit the genius of the Americans. She might find something here which she finds not in other countries—blessed Liberty—and the effect of this liberty on the happiness of the people would be a fine subject for her. She would indeed find no literary heroes here but we could point out to her view the Father of our country more worthy of panegyric than many whom her pen has immortalized—she would find his name entombed in the hearts of his countrymen—& behold his monument in the felicity of the people he has freed—[7]

A few years later (after eight years of marriage and the birth of three of her nine children), she launched on a public literary career, "consenting" to the printing of two pieces in a short-lived Philadelphia literary paper called *The Souvenir,* which appeared from 1827 to 1830; other contributions were published by Carey.[8] Of particular interest is an elegy on the death of George Canning, the British prime minister, published in the summer of 1828 after the statesman's sudden death, for it reveals much about Mrs. Lammot's political awareness.

The Grave of Canning

How still the scene around. Not e'en a cloud
Curtains the abbey with a passing shroud.
All, all is still, and Cynthia's silver falls
With mellow'd softness on the sacred walls.
No marble marks the spot where Canning sleeps,
A living statue pauses here, and weeps:
Affliction's semblance bends not o'er his tomb;
Affliction's self deplores his early doom.
Yes, name to England dear, the pilgrim feels,
Who trembling reads it, grief, no verse reveals;
His bosom heaves, his aching heart is dim,
The tablet quivers and the letters swim.
Farewell Freedom's martyr'd friend! Lament him, Greece!

His star arose, and in excess of light
Itself outshining, vanish'd at its height.
The dazzled world was gazing, which the spell
Broke with his broken heart, and darkness fell.
To idolize his fame, alike combine
Rank, wealth, and beauty; and with skill divine
The sculptor's chisel consecrates his fate,
To comfort England left disconsolate.
Pale widow'd Isle, methinks, she lingers lone,
While Chantry's genius bids him live in stone.
Alas! that all his mighty mind is wreck'd;
His glancing eye, and flashing intellect.

And oh! his tongue, his magic tongue, that still'd
The sound of strife, and blending, as it will'd,
The Whig and Tory with an honest zeal,
Together marshall'd for his country's weal.
Relentless Faction's pestilential breath
Can breathe no dimness over Canning's death.
With glory flush'd, and in the pride of power,

Cut off, too sensitive, ephemeral flower!
The canker care, a feverish summer cherish'd,
Just indignation nurtur'd and he perished.
Fond hope be ours, when Mercy's hallow'd breath
Winnows the seed of life, from chaff of death.
That God may bless him, and his waking eyes
Open an angel's and in Paradise.[9]

Anna Lammot was farsighted in her recognition of the importance to Americans of George Canning's career in British politics. He had been an associate of William Pitt in the House of Commons from 1793 and had taken an active part in the literary counterattack against writers of republican sentiment, contributing pieces to *The Anti-Jacobin;* later, during a stormy career as a Tory member of Parliament and public official, he served for a time as foreign secretary during the Napoleonic wars. The orphaned son of a penniless Irishman who died a year after his birth, his mother an actress of soiled reputation, he was not acknowledged as a gentleman by many of his Tory associates. He possessed a sharp and merciless tongue, which he used freely in political debate; he made many enemies, and his relations with his political rival Viscount Castlereagh led the two of them to the highly publicized duel in which Canning was wounded. After Castlereagh's suicide, Canning assumed the post of foreign secretary and leader in the House of Commons, and in this capacity managed to move England into a moderate or even liberal position among the European powers. Great Britain in effect abandoned the "holy alliance" of despotic monarchies that had been organized by Metternich and Castlereagh in the "Concert of Europe," gave diplomatic support to Greece in her struggle for independence from Turkey, and—most importantly for the United States—opposed pending Spanish efforts to reclaim her lost colonies in North and South America by recognizing the new republics and tacitly interposing the British fleet. These British actions gave powerful support to the newly enunciated American doctrine (asserted in 1823 by President Monroe) that also disallowed any Spanish effort to regain her colonies and recognized the new sister republics to the south.

Canning thus was a symbol of both liberty and conservatism in a sense not unlike Washington, whom Mrs. Lammot had lauded earlier; he represented a principle of national self-determination coupled with popular freedom from monarchical despotism. ("Popular" of course meant, for Canning—and presumably Mrs. Lammot—the middle class, the manufacturers, merchants, and professional people.) And when he died, under the stress of trying to form a Tory cabinet while his Tory political enemies refused their cooperation and resigned in droves and he was forced to derive support from the Whigs, he could be seen as a fallen hero, a martyr in the cause of liberty, without being in the least tainted by any expression of sympathy for freethinkers, Jacobins, and other radicals of the Enlightenment camp.

Anna Lammot thus was acutely responsive to the need for, and contributed her talents to the formation of, a type of social ideal that could combine patriotic American nationalism (which Canning's foreign policy then encouraged), the notion of an open class system (of which the ill-born Canning himself was a prime exemplar), and a pro-middle-class political and economic policy (which Canning, as the ally of William Pitt, and later as a member from Liverpool, had fought to preserve both from revolutionary assault and from aristocratic reaction). And Canning's were perhaps the "deeds of fame," "strange adventures," and "glorious actions" which in her premature epitaph (she lived to be eighty-two) she had lamented that her "simple life" denied her.

None of the other women in the group achieved the degree of public recognition—as well as in-group admiration—for intellectual and artistic achievement that was accorded Anna Lammot. The only one who aspired to a similar level was Mary Gilpin; but she, unfortunately for her, chose to do so not along the conventionally acceptable lines of Anna Lammot, but in a sphere that required competition with men: natural history. Intellectual interests were Mary's birthright, for her father Joshua and uncle Thomas Gilpin—papermakers and cotton manufacturers of Brandywine—were active in writing on technological and economic subjects, and Joshua was a versifier himself, particularly prolific in poems about shepherds and shepherdesses in imitation of Virgil, and a writer of works on natural history. Mary, during a walk one autumn day along the Brandywine with Sophie, revealed to her a plan to carry out research and eventually to publish a book on the natural history of the Brandywine Valley. Sophie was interested enough in natural history herself to write Clemma detailed accounts of the transformation of grubs into winged locusts. But publication was something else, and she recorded in her diary her amazement at Mary's idea:

[She] proposed to me to assist her in writing a work like the journal of a naturalist about this country. The plan was, we should each keep a journal, & read & obtain scientific information, & afterward condense our observations, lumbrations & informations, into a work like the above cited. She hinted that if we found it worthy afterwards, we might anonymously publish it! Oh dear! I was shocked at the bare idea of any words of *mine* in any way appearing in print!

Sophie politely agreed to help in secret but confided to her diary that, although she admired Mary, she could not imagine ever loving her.[10]

There are no remains to indicate that Mary ever did go on to bring together her natural history of the Brandywine. She took a long trip to England and Ireland to visit English relatives and the ancestral estate at "Kentmere." After her father's death in 1841, her home at Kentmere on the Brandywine was broken up, her mother and sister Sarah going to England, and Mary herself moving away to teach in a new school. Mary, in the opinion of Sophie, was very well qualified for a school, reading freely in Latin, French, and Italian, speaking French, and being very thoroughly educated in English literature. She was also becoming increasingly religious, residing in Bishop Lee's house and enthusiastically attending the Episcopal conventions in Philadelphia (unconventional as usual, she climbed in through a window when the entrance way was crowded). But the new teaching position ended and, without work, she fell into a depression. She recovered in the course of developing a plan for a religious school, to be conducted under Bishop Lee's auspices in Wilmington. Then this plan too fell through, despite the Lees' encouragement, because "others could not make allowances for Mary's eccentricities." Mary, in Clementina's opinion in the fall of 1845, was "not well" and ought in fact to give up teaching and go to live with her mother. Attempting next to teach Sunday School in cooperation with Sophie, Mary fell into difficulties with her former friend and began to accuse Sophie of conspiring against her.[11] Sophie blamed Mary's "unfortunate want of tact and practical knowledge of the world" for the fact that the size of her school was so far below what her "superior teaching" deserved.[12] Clementina, less closely involved, saw Mary more to be pitied than blamed. "Poor Mary!" she exlaimed in a letter to Sophie, "I do feel for her the deepest pity—her nervous state of mind makes every thing in her life sad."[13] By 1851, Mary Gilpin was accusing Bishop Lee of "persecution" because he would not let her run the parish school herself; she threatened to set up a competing school, and finally succeeded, but it, too, quickly failed.

By the spring of 1852, Mary was confined in Philadelphia in the insane asylum of the Pennsylvania Hospital, under the care of the renowned Dr. Kirkbride. For a time she was not even allowed visitors.[14] She profited from the kindness, regular discipline, good food, and physical exercise this institution (like others of the period) provided, and she was released in a few months. She then made the pilgrimage to the fashionable resort at Cape May, "so hopeful of the effect of salt air and bathing upon her health . . . poor child."[15] Thereafter she virtually disappears from the correspondence of Clementina and Sophie, except for a brief allusion in 1857 to "Mary" as a living-in patient of a Dr. Linn in New York.[16]

During the Civil War, Mary moved to the southern states, where she lived with her sister Elizabeth and brother-in-law, Matthew Maury, the eminent naval engineer and oceanographer; there she became an ardent defender of the south. After the war, she briefly adopted a pretty child from Wilmington whom she took to live in Naples; the American consul put the girl in an orphanage. Then she wandered from continent to continent and finally vanished from view. She was rediscovered in Alaska by an English-woman of rank who happened to visit a little Indian village where she found a gray-haired, wild-eyed Mary Gilpin, lying on a couch in a dilapidated hut, surrounded by a library of Greek and Latin books, all showing signs of repeated reading.[17] She eventually left Alaska for California and then took residence in Denver with her brother William Gilpin, the Governor of Colorado. But she soon departed from his house too, claiming that he held her prisoner for her money, he "contending that she had been insane for forty years and that a clergyman had written him to take her into his home because she had been living on an Indian reservation." A few months later, Mary died.[18]

The intellectual and artistic lives of the other members of the group were less public but just as serious. The correspondence of Clementina Smith and Sophie du Pont, extending over nearly half a century, from its inception was devoted in considerable part to exchanging comments and recommendations on the books the two women were reading and accounts of intellectual conversation with their mutual friends. The Smith family like others of their class (including the Crozers) was in the habit of spending an hour or two in the evening, around the fire, reading aloud to one another from the Bible, Shakespeare, and such popular writers of the day as Sir Walter Scott, Robert Browning, Washington Irving, Bayard Taylor, Hugh Walpole, Isaak Walton, and Macaulay ("he is quite beyond me . . . but . . . makes me think"). Much of Clementina's private reading—accomplished late at night or during the free hours of morning before the daily routine of housekeeping, visiting, shopping, and sewing began—was in serious religious literature and moral philosophy, such as Bishop Wilberforce's *Practical Christianity* (supplemented by a biography of Wilberforce), Abercrombie on the moral feelings, St. Thomas à Kempis's *Imitation of Christ,* various works of Matthew Arnold, Huntington's *Christian Believing and Living,* and Mrs. Jamieson and Mme Necker on the characteristics of women. She attended the lectures of Professor Agassiz on the Animal Kingdom and took a close interest in the controversy over the new Smithsonian Institution. She wrote constantly to Sophie about her reading and other intellectual and artistic experiences, particularly her music (she played the organ, piano, and harp) and painting.

And all of the women circulated their books amongst each other, or copied out long extracts for their friends' information and delectation. "Our little society," as Clementina called it, was before all else a society of people who talked about intellectual and artistic things that they had read and heard and seen and thought, whether face to face or on paper, tête-à-tête or at formally organized teas, for they planned to meet at least weekly at one or another of their houses.[19]

A TOWN OF
MULES AND WIDOWS

For a social survey of Rockdale that includes all components of the population, one must turn to the federal census. In August of 1850, exactly five years after Richard Griffith made his sketches, enumerators trudged from door to door in the Rockdale district, interviewing the people and recording the information in the schedules sent from Washington. These schedules reveal in detail the composition of Rockdale's society at the zenith of its development.

ROCKDALE IN THE 1850 CENSUS

The 1850 census was much more thorough than those of earlier decades.[1] The enumerator was instructed to record the names of all individuals enumerated; in addition, he was to note various other facts of interest about each person: age, sex, race, country or state of birth, occupation (of adult males only); the value of real estate owned; whether the individual could read, had attended school in the past year, or had been married in the past year; and whether he was crippled or handicapped in any way, and if so, how. The information was arranged by household, with the head of the household at the top, and others below him or her (there was no reluctance to recognize females as household heads) in general order of age or status. Where two complete families occupied the same dwelling, that fact was noted, but the general assumption was that each house (for there were no apartment dwellings) was occupied by one family; other arrangements, such as the inclusion of other families or individuals as boarders, were viewed as modifications of this plan.

The enumerators—there were several for each township, each with his

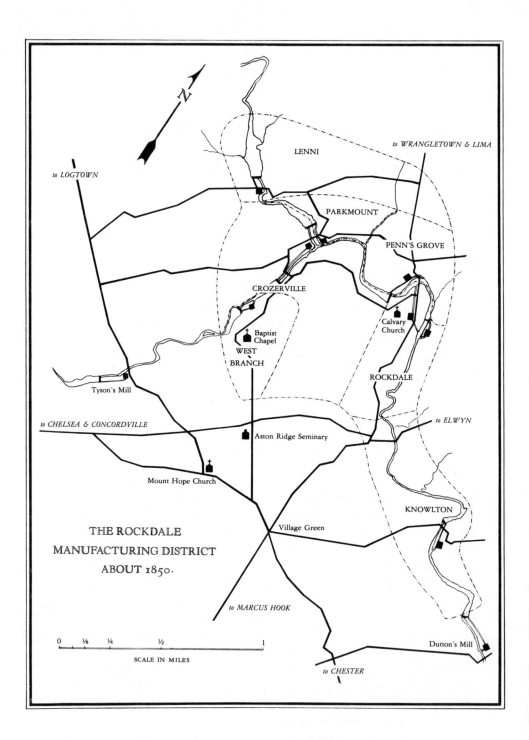

to LOGTOWN

to WRANGLETOWN & LIMA

LENNI

PARKMOUNT

PENN'S GROVE

CROZERVILLE

Baptist
Chapel

WEST
BRANCH

Calvary
Church

ROCKDALE

Tyson's Mill

to CHELSEA & CONCORDVILLE

to ELWYN

Aston Ridge Seminary

Mount Hope Church

KNOWLTON

Village Green

THE ROCKDALE
MANUFACTURING DISTRICT
ABOUT 1850.

to MARCUS HOOK

Dutton's Mill

0   ⅛   ¼   ½   1

SCALE IN MILES

to CHESTER

own jargon for occupational titles and his own ear for foreign-sounding names—did not record the addresses or even general location of the households. The final lists as they were sent to Washington consequently seemed, superficially, to present merely a random succession of the households in each township. But in fact each township schedule had a structure, for each enumerator's list remained intact as a section on the schedule. Each township list thus was a sort of collage, in which every piece represented a single field enumerator's data recorded for a particular day. This feature makes it possible to know where in the township the enumerator was at any point in the schedule. There is enough information in the property map published by Dr. Ash in 1848, in the county tax assessments, and in Samuel Riddle's paybook for Penn's Grove Mill to pinpoint the mill villages. When mill owner Peter Hill and his rentor-manufacturer Daniel Lammot were listed as neighbors, surrounded by operatives of various kinds, the enumerator was evidently in Lenni; when dozens of operative families surround Samuel Riddle's name in the list—families whose members worked for Riddle and whose names appeared in his paybook for that year—the enumerator was certainly at Penn's Grove; when the names of operatives clustered together in the census are also found together in the tax assessments as rentors from John P. Crozer at West Branch, the enumerator was obviously at West Branch. And similarly at the other mill hamlets.

From the 1850 census, therefore, emerges a reasonably complete survey of the population of the seven mill hamlets that made up the Rockdale district.

TABLE 1: *The Population of the Rockdale District by Age and Sex (1850)*

	MALE	FEMALE
80–89	2	3
70–79	8	9
60–69	27	18
50–59	70	52
40–49	84	89
30–39	102	127
20–29	161	193
10–19	277	265
0–9	281	238
	1,012	994

2,006

General Facts About the Manufacturing District

The total population of the Rockdale manufacturing district in 1850 was 2,006 persons (it thus accounted for 57 percent of the total population of the two predominantly rural townships in which it was located). These 2,006 persons were distributed among 7 hamlets whose average population was 287. There were 351 houses in the district; the average number of houses per hamlet was 50; the average number of persons per house 6. The total area of the district was almost exactly one and one-half square miles; thus the population density within the district was 1,302 per square mile. The breakdown of this population by age and sex is shown in the population pyramid in Table 1, which indicates that there were several interesting anomalies in sex and age ratios.

The most easily explained anomaly is the apparent underrepresentation of female as compared to male children under ten years of age. It is likely that, in this somewhat patriarchal society, parents and older siblings who talked to the enumerators sometimes simply failed to mention the smaller children and infants, particularly female infants, in their own or their neighbors' households.

Also readily explained is the second anomaly: the overrepresentation of both boys and girls between ten and twenty. This is almost certainly the result of a process of selective migration into the manufacturing district by families (both complete families and fatherless families) with teen-age children who could be put to work in the mills full or part time to help supplement family incomes.

More mysterious is the third anomaly: the overrepresentation of women in their twenties and thirties. There were 20 percent more women than men in their twenties, and 25 percent more women than men in their thirties: a total of fifty-seven more individual women than men in these age groups. Several factors seem to have been responsible. One was a greater tendency for unmarried adult females to remain with their families; in fact, there were thirty-seven more unmarried females than males in this age group living with parents or siblings. Another factor was a selective in-migration of broken families consisting of husbandless women and their children. Widows (as the manufacturers were wont to claim in defense of their practice of employing children) often moved into cotton-manufacturing districts for the express purpose of supporting themselves by putting their children out to work in the mills. There were fourteen such fatherless families in the Rockdale district with mothers in the twenty to thirty-nine age group. There were, on the other hand, more unattached male boarders than female of these ages. The excess of young women would seem largely to be the product of two things: a tendency for unmarried women to stay at home while their unmarried brothers moved out to seek their fortunes; and a tendency for the manufacturing district to attract widows with children of working age.

The fourth anomaly, the excess of males in their fifties and sixties, is less easy still to understand. There were far fewer unmarried widowers than widows in this age group, and even fewer old bachelors. The explanation seems to be a tendency for males to marry younger wives and, when widowed, to remarry even younger wives (this would also help to account for the slight female excess in the forty to forty-nine group and part of the female excess in the twenty to thirty-nine group).

About a quarter of the population were foreign-born: 9 percent were English, 15 percent Irish (mostly from Northern Ireland, to judge from the frequency of Scottish surnames), and 1 percent from various other countries. Although the mill owners, managers, and operatives were the core of the population, both among native- and foreign-born, there was a considerable variety of other occupational types. A number of farmers resided in the district (and the mill owners themselves usually operated a farm in connection with the mill site); there were physicians, public school teachers, clergymen, and even a musician; craftsmen plied their various trades; there were a number of shopkeepers; and there were unskilled laborers and domestic servants. Racially, the district was almost entirely white; a black man and woman worked in the inn at Lenni, and a six-person black family (the father a laborer), a single black woman, and two black teenagers lived at Knowlton, the latter in the house of mill owner Phineas Lownes (one of them—Jane Lownes—bearing his name).

But the Rockdale manufacturing district was not really a town. Administratively divided between Aston and Middletown townships, it was even more fundamentally divided among its seven constituent hamlets: West Branch, Crozerville, and Knowlton (all owned by John P. Crozer), Rockdale (owned by absentee manufacturer Bernard McCready), Lenni and Parkmount (owned by the Hills), and Penn's Grove (owned by Samuel Riddle). So let us turn to a consideration of these hamlets.

General Facts About the Mill Hamlets

The seven hamlets were in many respects very similar to one another. Each was a cluster of houses nestled around a mill, or strung out along the road that passed the mill, with a few extra structures to serve as community centers: Calvary Church at Rockdale, the Baptist chapel at West Branch, the inn at Lenni, the schoolhouses, the blacksmiths' shops (but most of the craftsmen and shopkeepers plied their trade in a room or two of their residences). The population of the hamlets ranged from 186 at Parkmount to 411 at Crozerville; the number of houses varied accordingly, from 32 to 77. The house—whether the usual two-rooms-plus-attic-plus-half-cellar stone tenement, constructed in blocks of two to four units, or the much larger farmhouses and mansions—was the natural enumeration unit, because it partitioned the population neatly into a finite number of households.

But the household was not conceived—even by the census enumerator —to be the fundamental social unit. The fundamental social unit was the simple nuclear family, composed of a mother and a father (who were assumed to be legally married, of course) and their natural children. Of the 351 houses in the district, 156 were occupied by such families living by themselves; another 96 were occupied by simple nuclear families who had taken in other people, sometimes relatives (like an aging parent or the sibling of one of the spouses or the orphaned child of a kinsman) and sometimes boarders (from individuals to whole families). If one includes all those households where the central unit was a simple nuclear family, then fully 72 percent of all the houses were occupied and headed by simple nuclear families. Most other households were composed of anticipations or remnants of the simple nuclear family: recently married couples who had not yet had children, older married couples whose children had moved away, a set of unmarried adult siblings whose parents had died, and—more common than any of the rest—one-parent families.

Most of the one-parent families were headed by women. It is not possible, in most cases, to know whether the woman was widowed, deserted, temporarily separated, or divorced. Forty-nine households in the district contained a family consisting of a woman and a child or children bearing her name. Often such female-headed families also contained several unmarried adults who remained with their mother and supported her by working in the mill. Most of the female-headed families either lived alone or helped to support themselves by taking in boarders. These forty-nine independent female-headed households amounted to 14 percent of the households in the district. Nine other independent male-headed households with motherless children, amounting to 3 percent of the total households, bring the number of households headed by a parent or parents with children to 89 percent of the total in the district. The remainder consisted largely of married couples living together (sometimes with boarders) without children. There were only six people (five white men and one black woman) listed as living alone; these, along with two female landladies and a male innkeeper, constitute the only persons in the entire district who were not living as members of a family or as boarders with a family.

The social organization of the mill hamlet was clearly based upon the nuclear family and its various modifications, no doubt in large part because, in these hamlets, most of the housing consisted of tenements rented from the mill owner, who usually let out the houses at a nominal rental to heads of households on condition that the family supply two or three hands to the mill. But this economically determined familistic structure among the mill workers was mirrored in all other segments of the community, from the mill owners down to the poorest laborers. Furthermore, in view of the tendency for adult siblings to migrate together, and for many families to remain, to acquire land in the district, and to see their children marry and move from one hamlet to another as work and housing opportunities changed, the family system involved many households in extensive sibling and affinal networks that helped to tie the whole district together into a loose consortium of related nuclear families.

If the family system was uniform and pervasive throughout the seven hamlets, so was the structure of occupation. Each hamlet had as its core the two contracting parties: the manufacturers and the operatives. The operatives were by far the most numerous occupational category in each hamlet; there were on an average thirty-six male operatives per hamlet (and about fifty women and children whose work status was not specified in the census). But there were also, on an average, ten tradesmen per hamlet—perhaps a couple of shoemakers and a tailor, a stonemason or bricklayer, a couple of carpenters, a cabinetmaker, a wheelwright or millwright, a plasterer, a watchmaker. There were about eight common laborers. And there would be about six farmers whose residences lay within the hamlet itself and who might take in as boarders an operative or a tradesman or two. In addition, there were likely to be a few educated residents as well as the mill owner's and manufacturer's family: a physician, a schoolteacher, a shopkeeper, a clerk from the mill, a musician, a colporteur (a lay missionary and distributor of religious tracts), and a clergyman. Thus in each hamlet, within the space of a few hundred yards along the road, there would be an impressive variety of social and occupational types.

This variety allowed each hamlet to a considerable extent, and the district to an even larger extent, to be a self-reliant community insofar as specialized personal services were concerned. People grew up and lived in intimate awareness of the nature of the lives and work of others; they performed services for the benefit of persons whom they knew; each was aware of his dependence upon and his responsibility for other people.

TABLE 2: *Social Composition of Mill Hamlets in the Rockdale District* (1850)

	Population	Number of Households	Households Containing a Fatherless Family	English-born	Irish-born	Mill Workers	Tradesmen	Farmers	Laborers
WEST BRANCH	192	32	2 6%	48 25%	25 13%	40 21%	0	2 1%	6 3%
CROZERVILLE	411	77	17 22%	13 3%	28 7%	36 9%	20 5%	6 1%	14 3%
LENNI	328	56	4 7%	12 4%	35 11%	30 9%	15 5%	14 4%	4 1%
PARKMOUNT	186	33	4 12%	16 9%	31 17%	26 15%	7 4%	1 1%	15 8%
PENN'S GROVE	360	62	6 10%	18 5%	93 26%	53 15%	8 2%	8 2%	13 4%
ROCKDALE	250	43	9 21%	16 6%	88 35%	28 11%	12 5%	5 2%	6 2%
KNOWLTON	279	48	7 15%	59 21%	7 3%	42 15%	6 2%	7 3%	5 2%

The Uniqueness of Each Mill Hamlet

Each hamlet took its name from the name the manufacturer gave to his mill; each also took its particular and distinguishing social characteristics from the size and composition of the work force that the mill's technology demanded. Each hamlet was unique and the sense of place was strong, so strong that even to this day, long after the spinning and weaving have ended, the people who live there will say such things as that they were born in Rockdale and grew up in Lenni, or that they married someone from West Branch, not Crozerville.

Some of the grosser statistical dimensions in which the hamlets differed were size of population, number of houses, percentage of households containing a fatherless family, percentage of population Irish-born, percentage English-born, and number of mill workers, tradesmen, farmers, and laborers. These data, arranged by hamlet, may be seen in Table 2. They show clearly that each hamlet was a unique mix of social constituents. West Branch, for instance, was small, had a disproportionately large share of English-born residents (six of the surviving tenements still stand on a bluff called "English Hill"), and was almost exclusively industrial, with no tradespeople at all, no farmers except the two that worked the mill estate itself, and very few unskilled laborers. West Branch Mill, with its two hundred looms, was specialized as a weaving mill; its yarns were made at nearby Crozerville. At West Branch, as a result of this fact, there was little call for the services of children, who were most useful as unskilled piecers and scavengers around the spinning mules and in the departments concerned with the preparation of the yarns. And the dearth of positions for children meant that few fatherless families settled there.

Crozerville, by contrast, had a high proportion of households—22 percent—containing fatherless families. This high percentage is probably related to the fact that Crozerville Mill was the spinning mill whose 7,032 spindles on mules and throstles supplied West Branch with warp and filling for its looms. Thus it provided employment opportunities for the children of widows and wives separated from their husbands, as well as children in intact families. Crozerville, the largest of the hamlets, was in a sense also the most cosmopolitan. It was the summer residence of the wealthy Smith family from Philadelphia, who rented the former Crozer mansion, and the year-round home of their friend the Reverend Mr. Charles Breck, rector of Calvary Church, and his family.[2] Crozerville also had three stores and a "huckster," two physicians, a schoolteacher in residence, ten shoemakers and a tailor (who no doubt were patronized also by the people from West

Branch), a number of small farmers, and various masons, carpenters, black-smiths, wheelwrights, drovers, and common laborers. With a high propor-tion of families of American-born farmers and tradesmen, Crozerville had a relatively low percentage of foreign-born mill operatives; and a number of its Irish were domestic servants.

Knowlton, the third of the Crozer enterprises, combined both spinning and weaving processes (60 looms, 1,548 spindles) in one factory and, accordingly, attracted a middling large number of fatherless families. Like West Branch, it was somewhat isolated and held few tradesmen, and like West Branch it seems to have favored English immigrants. Formerly managed for Crozer by an English-born weaver, Abraham Blakeley, it was now operated by Blakeley and a partner, while Crozer retained title to the land. Crozer's three hamlets together contained only sixty persons born in Ireland, amounting to only 7 percent of their total population, the lowest ratio for any set of mills owned by one person.

Lenni, owned by the Hills, who of course were large landowners in the neighborhood, and operated by Daniel Lammot, who maintained a more elegant style of living than anyone else in the district, was like Crozerville something of a social center. It boasted the mansions of the Lammots and the Hills, which were well kept and tended by professional gardeners, and a small hotel with black hostler and maid. There were numerous tradesmen. The tenements for the Lenni workers were mostly constructed across the creek some distance from the mansions, and a number of the workers boarded at the farms scattered along Lenni Road that ran through the hamlet, connecting the Rockdale district with Concordville to the west. The Lammots seem to have been slightly more nativistic than any other of the manufacturers, recruiting only 11 percent Irish- and a mere 4 percent English-born people for their settlement. Many of the Irish were domestic servants and farm workers, and one elderly Irish-born family, the McCrack-ens, were well-to-do landowners who had come over from Ireland before the War of 1812. In fact, only four Irishmen actually worked in Lammot's mill. This mill, a spinning and weaving mill, had about 2,000 mule and 2,000 throstle spindles. The number of fatherless families was low. Lenni, indeed, seems to have been designed to minimize the visibility of social problems and to maximize the charms of the pastoral life for the sophis-ticated Lammots and Hills.

The remaining three mills were all owned or operated by Irishmen and it is probably no accident that the proportion of Irish immigrants in the three hamlets associated with them was the highest in the Rockdale district. The population of Rockdale proper was 35 percent Irish-born, of Park-mount 17 percent, and of Penn's Grove 26 percent (the English-born in these hamlets amounted to only 6 percent, 9 percent, and 5 percent, respectively).

Rockdale proper, like Crozerville and Lenni, was more nearly a general village than some of the other hamlets. For more than a century it had been the site of industry, first as the home of Old Sable Forge and the nail manufactory, then of Phillips' weaving mill. The mill was now owned by Irish-born Bernard McCready and managed by English-born Thomas Blackburn. Rockdale provided housing for a number of workers at Penn's Grove factory, which was situated only a few hundred yards up Rockdale road on the other side of the covered bridge. And it served also to some degree as village center for both the Penn's Grove and Rockdale population, being the site of Calvary Church, which overlooked both hamlets from its commanding position on the hill above, and also the residence of a considerable number of tradespeople. Rockdale had a relatively large number of older males (there were fourteen men in their fifties as contrasted with only six in their thirties) and a high proportion of fatherless families (21 percent of the houses contained such a family). Both kinds of families, as at Crozerville, had no doubt been attracted by the nearby employment opportunities for children, and perhaps also by the proximity of the church, stores, and tradespeople generally. The colporteur, a twenty-six-year-old native of Ireland, was a member of one of these fatherless families; his illiterate mother, bereft of husband, was supported by him and his twenty-four-year-old brother, who worked in McCready's mill, and their sister, nineteen, who probably worked there also.

If Rockdale shone as the spiritual center of the manufacturing district, Riddle's mill at Penn's Grove was its industrial heart, with 160 looms and 4,980 spindles (both mules and throstles) in one factory. More than fifty male workers above the age of sixteen lived there, according to the census enumerators, and the payroll actually included an additional seventy women, many of them part-time workers whose occupation the enumerators did not record. Although Penn's Grove had a relatively large population—360, the largest after Crozerville—and boasted a general store and a post office, it was home to fewer tradesmen, and most of these worked for the Riddles as carpenters, plasterers, and millwrights, keeping the mill and the tenement houses in repair. Penn's Grove mostly depended on Rockdale, Lenni, and Crozerville for its shoemakers, watchmakers, tailors, seamstresses, and other practitioners of domestic crafts; it was solidly committed to work of the factory.

Parkmount was the smallest hamlet. The mill there in 1850 was being operated by an Irish carpet weaver, George Callaghan, and his son George Jr. George and Mary Callaghan were forty-four years old, had nine of their children living in their house, and provided room and board to two weavers. The Callaghans had lived for a time in Scotland, the birthplace of Mrs. Callaghan. They had emigrated to Connecticut and thence moved to Pennsylvania. They had leased Parkmount only two years before and were still working hard to make a go of it, employing their own children as piecers and scavengers at the mules. Their mill was a small one, vacated by Samuel Riddle a few years before; it housed four mules, eighteen power looms and hand looms, and worked both cotton and wool. The Callaghans wove cotton counterpanes and figured tablecloths on their power looms and woolen carpets on draw looms, which were big, complex, pre-Jacquard hand looms that required the use of drawboys to help the weaver.[3] Callaghan was making fancy goods and his mill required older, highly skilled male operatives. This may explain the curious fact that seventeen males in their thirties lived at Parkmount and only eleven in their twenties.

THE SOCIAL STATIONS

Among the residents of the Rockdale district it was recognized that there were four social levels: a highly solidified managerial class, composed of the manufacturers, mill owners, merchants, and gentlemen farmers, and their wives and children; an amorphous and embryonic middle level, probably with little clear awareness of itself as a group, composed of people who performed skilled services on a contractual basis for all classes—ministers and physicians, innkeepers, schoolteachers, small farmers, and the various mechanics, such as masons, blacksmiths, carpenters, and machinists; a large and reasonably self-conscious working class, made up predominantly of people who worked by the day for the managerial class as operatives in mills, as manual laborers, and as domestic servants; and a bottom level of indigent and degraded poor. Members of this last class of people were not visible in Rockdale, however, because, being unable to take care of themselves, they were for the most part housed in the "House of Employment" at Media, several miles away. This lowest group, physically extruded from the community and supported at public expense (with some supplemental funds from their own work in the poorhouse industries), included the insane, the mentally retarded, the chronically ill and handicapped, young orphans, some deserted wives or widows with children too young to work, and no doubt one or two who simply could not seem to manage without constant supervision. A few other members of the class of degraded poor were housed in the county prison or the Eastern State Penitentiary in Philadelphia.

The Managerial Class

Insofar as one can judge from the correspondence, property maps, and tax assessments, the families who constituted the managerial class in the Rockdale district in the 1840's were about twelve in number. Four of these households have already been mentioned as lords of the valley: the Smiths, the Lammots, the Crozers, and the Riddles. There were others, more briefly noted: Peter and Hannah Sellers Hill, who owned the mills at Lenni and Parkmount and farmed a considerable tract; George W. Hill, Peter's brother, who before his death owned Penn's Grove and farmed and operated the store there; the Willcoxes of Ivy Mills; the Sharpless family, at the iron plantation of Old Sarum Forge; the Tysons, who owned Aston Mills and other land in the township. There was Davis B. Stacey, a retired importer turned gentleman farmer, and an old and dear friend of Richard S. Smith and William Martin; the Pennells, an old and well-established family of local landowners; and the Duttons, mill owners, tanners, and inventors. This ruling group seems to have divided socially (not economically or politically) into cliques along several lines of cleavage. The Smith-Lammot-Willcox-Stacey network included "society" people, originally from the Boston, New York, and Philadelphia areas, who shared an interest in evangelical Protestant religion and came from the same general background of urban commercial families. The indigenous Quaker clans—Sharplesses, Pennells, and Duttons—kept apart socially, probably on religious grounds, and their ladies do not appear in the Smith and Lammot correspondence as participants in the sisterhood. The Hills, Crozers, and Riddles seem to have been socially alone, perhaps in part because their churches were distant (Peter Hill was a Swedenborgian and went to church at Upper Darby, the Crozers Baptists who worshipped at Marcus Hook, and the Riddles Presbyterians whose church also was located some distance away), but probably more because of personal feelings. Crozer was shy and suffered from feelings of inadequacy in social situations where he was expected to speak. Peter Hill was regarded as an unscrupulous rascal in money matters. Samuel Riddle had just lost his wife Martha, who died after giving birth to their first son, Henry, in the spring of 1850. He did not marry again until 1860, when he took as his second wife the twenty-three-year-old Lydia C. Doyle of Chester, who bore him four children, the last in 1868 (when Samuel was sixty-eight years old).[1] Riddle had a reputation, among some of the working people at least, for using broad language and telling earthy stories. In Riddle's case, too, some prejudice may conceivably have been based on the relative recency of his arrival from Ireland, but that seems unlikely to have been a major factor. The Willcox family was of Irish extraction (albeit a century and a half before), and Catholic to boot, but they were freely included in the social affairs of the Smiths and the Lammots.

The stratification of Rockdale society was physical as well as mental. The upper class lived in substantial stone houses, locally referred to as mansions, with ten or twelve rooms, always near the top of a hill overlooking the family property; the lesser classes occupied dwellings below, with the workers' tenements often almost on the edge of the stream, and immediately adjacent to the mill. (Altitude was symbolic of social elevation and thus was often invoked in names of prestigious institutions. The churches were "Calvary" and "Mount Gilead" and "Mount Hope"; Riddle's mill was "Parkmount"; the hill above Rockdale was "the Mount" and the road below it "Mount Road"; and the cluster of new tenements at West Branch, occupied by English immigrants, was dubbed "English Hill.") Each mansion had outbuildings where the horses and carriages were kept, and there might be a detached summer kitchen and a greenhouse (Phillips at least kept a

OLD MANSIONS AT LENNI HEIGHTS.

greenhouse and raised flowers through the winter, which he gave to his friends). In the 1840's, some of the mansions were being equipped with indoor toilets and had indoor pumps and facilities for bathing, and they were heated less often by open fireplaces than by iron stoves. Furnishings were comfortable: carpeted floors, upholstered chairs, beds with mattresses stuffed with cotton waste; there were pianos and harps, and tables for books and prints. Portraits and daguerreotypes ornamented walls and mantels.

One of the most distinctive features of the managerial class's culture was its cosmopolitan quality. Both men and women were accustomed to travel, or at least to the idea of travel. The women summered at the fashionable resorts at Cape May or Saratoga (the men, if they attended, suffered agonies of boredom), and in the winter they often spent part of the social season in Philadelphia or visited with friends and relatives in Boston, New York, Washington, and cities of the south. Some of the men had lived abroad (the Riddles) or had traveled abroad on business (like Richard S. Smith and Davis B. Stacey). And everyone was constantly conscious of living, not just in Rockdale, but in a nation and a world with all regions of which he or she had a concern. Every businessman followed national, international,

THE LUNGREN MANSION AT LENNI.

financial, and commercial affairs because they affected his enterprises directly, as the prices of raw cotton and cotton goods fluctuated, discount rates changed, or wars and threats of wars opened and closed markets. Every wife and daughter read books from England and France and thrilled to missionary adventures in India, China, and Africa.

Theirs was a world in which intellectual and artistic interests were part of a normal gentle life. These gentlemen farmers, merchants, and manufacturers and their ladies did not feel that they had to acquire intensive technical training in college in order to be liberally educated, well informed, and capable of managing large affairs. In fact, evangelical religion led some of them to a kind of genteel anti-scientism. In a letter "to a young man who thought that God can be better known through science than Revelation," Smith somewhat patronizingly explained that the *important* knowledge was knowledge of Scripture:

It is evident that you understand the ground of my faith and hope to be the *Scriptures,* which I believe fully to be a revelation from God, and *without* which there is good reason to believe that man, with all the helps of science, would have a very inadequate idea of God . . . the humblest Christian can better attain through the Scriptures to a knowledge of God, and a confident hope of eternal life through Jesus Christ, than can the most learned philosopher and man of science, by any other means than through the same Scriptures. . . . When vain man attempts, as is sometimes the case, to set aside revelation by setting forth what is called some new discovery, either in natural science, or in some new system of philosophy, I remember the warning of the apostle Paul—"Beware lest any man spoil you, through philosophy or vain deceit." In reading over what I have written, it seems to me a rambling sketch of my own convictions, and I am not sure that I make myself understood; but I will sum up what I have written by saying that I hold in respect and admiration every advance in science and learning, and among Christ's most faithful followers, recognize many of the most scientific and learned men that have lived on the earth; yet I contend that God, in his revelation of himself, through the Scriptures, has given us sufficient light to *know* and serve him, and has furthermore revealed that "Eye hath not seen, nor ear heard, neither hath it entered into the heart of man to conceive the things which God hath prepared for those who love him."[2]

The members of the managerial class had a much stronger feeling of solidarity than did the members of the other classes. In addition to the women's networks, and the common commitment to an ecumenical evangelism, the group was united by a remarkable sense of economic loyalty.

Although in some abstract sense the cotton manufacturers on Chester Creek were in competition with one another, it was not the sort of competition where one man's gain was understood to require his neighbor's loss. The maxim was not "Every man for himself" in a pursuit of scarce values; to the contrary, the maxim was closer to "Sink or swim together." Everyone was expected to act in concert politically with respect to tariffs, labor relations, and the government's financial policies. Everyone was expected to be strictly honest in business dealings involving such matters as loans and discounted notes (Peter Hill's failure to abide by these norms rendered him subject to severe criticism). Everyone was expected to—and did—bring men and equipment at once to help put out a fire in anyone's mill. The contest was not so much with other manufacturers; rather, it was with a capricious environment that frequently threatened everyone with adverse economic conditions, unfriendly legislation, or hostile administrative action. This sentiment of solidarity among the members of the managerial class was not a parochial, district-by-district thing, either. It included managerial people throughout the whole region in and around Philadelphia.

Perhaps the most dramatic evidence of the strength of this feeling of mutual obligation and responsibility was the way in which the industrial and commercial insurance companies were operated. They were mutual companies in which the members bought stock and subscribed funds to be called upon when operating expenses and casualty losses required additional money. The commercial and industrial community in effect insured itself as a whole; and this meant that each manufacturer and merchant insured his "competitors" as well as himself. The boards of directors of these companies were elected from the major stockholders and subscribers. The two senior officers—the president and the secretary—were drawn from the same class. These two staff positions, which were salaried, were regarded as a kind of rotating unemployment insurance fund for failed members of the group. Among the Chester Creek managers, no less than three were at one time or another beneficiaries of the system and one other tried unsuccessfully to secure its benefits. Daniel Lammot, after his commercial failure in Philadelphia, tried (unsuccessfully) to secure appointment to the vacant post of secretary of the American Fire Insurance Company.[3] William Martin, a few difficult years after his failure in 1829, became the secretary of the Delaware County Mutual Safety Insurance Company, of which Crozer and other manufacturers were directors, and later its president.[4] John S. Phillips, after his cotton mill at Fairmount failed during the depression of the early 1840's, for a few years held the post of secretary of the Columbia Insurance Company.[5] And in 1837 Richard S. Smith, after the collapse of his merchant house in 1833, accepted the position of president of a marine insurance firm, the Union Mutual Insurance Company—and held the office until his death.[6] In assuming these positions, the officer was certain to find on the Board of Directors a number of old cronies and business associates (who had in fact been responsible for his appointment). Thus Martin's board included John P. Crozer and other Delaware County businessmen with whom he had formerly dealt as merchant, attorney, manufacturer, or state representative; Richard Smith's board included John R. Neff, the cotton importer; and John S. Phillips' board included a number of old cotton business associates and family friends: Charles du Pont, Daniel Lammot, Joseph Ripka, William Young, and Francis Gurney Smith.

The most explicit explanation of how the system worked is contained in a memorandum of Charles du Pont concerning Charles N. Buck, the president of the Columbia Insurance Company. The company was formed in 1840 shortly after Mr. Buck, a Wilmington merchant, failed in business. The early major subscribers were the Du Ponts, Lammot, and Ripka. Du Pont was very explicit in his statement in favor of continuing Mr. Buck in the presidency: "The Col. Insce. Co. was got up with the view of giving Mr. C.N. Buck the means of living."[7]

It is evident, from their use of the mutual insurance company as not only an underwriting mechanism but also a source of employment for their financially embarrassed associates, that the businessmen who made up the core of the managerial class were not simply intent on maximizing personal profit by competitive or monopolistic methods. Quite the contrary: they were committed to preserving the standard of living of all the members of a social class, often at the risk of considerable financial loss to themselves as individuals. They acted on the assumption that if they did not support one another against economic competition from outside the region, capriciously fluctuating markets, and governmental bodies apparently indifferent to their needs, they would *all* suffer. The failure of a fellow merchant or manufacturer was like the wounding of a fellow officer in combat or the illness of a fellow missionary in a heathen land—everyone rallied around to give whatever support and assistance was possible; to let him sink in adversity would only weaken, not strengthen, the survivors.

The attitudes of members of the managerial class toward the other classes, particularly the working class, can be discerned in their correspondence and memoirs. (The reciprocal attitudes of other classes are not so easy to elucidate, because their members were less often literate and less likely to leave papers to historical societies.) The managerial class was in constant and intimate contact with the other classes, employing their members to work on their farms and in their factories and to provide services of all kinds. There was a marked ambivalence evident in the expressions of class attitude. On the one hand, the managerial person definitely looked down on the members of other classes as inferior to him not merely in education, power, and wealth but also in moral strength and emotional sensibility. Even the poorer clergymen, like Mr. Huntington and Mr. Murphy, and their families, were patronizingly referred to by Clementina as "the class of people who will suffer" during hard times.[8] On the other hand, the managers were committed to the principle that individual members of the lower classes could rise and approach, even achieve, equality with their betters, not merely in the fellowship of Christ but in the pursuit of Mammon as well (and some of the managerial families were living examples of this achievement). The classes were thus fixed and permanent institutions, but individuals were not permanently fixed in any class.

The most severe expressions of class prejudice came from the pens of Clementina and Sophie and were directed at female servants and female mill hands. Sophie, for instance, once confided in her diary her surprise at seeing a working-class woman show grief over a sick child. Sophie had come on a visit of charity and found the child in the care of its Aunt Rebecca, a young woman who regularly cared for the child while the mother worked. The mother was unable to help much during the child's illness; "she did sit up once or twice—but its of no use—she only loses her rest—& she has to work." The neighbors were kind but the child would only take medicine from Aunt Rebecca, to whom fell all responsibility for its fate. When Sophie called, Rebecca was overcome with emotion; as Sophie put it, "The poor girl hid her face in her apron in an agony of tears." This seemed remarkable to Sophie, who declared in her diary, "I never saw so much feeling evinced in that class of life."[9]

Clementina too believed that women of the lower class were deficient in the finer feelings, as well as lacking in moral strength (and, if they were Irish, a prey to "Hibernianisms" and "superstitious terrors" as well). In 1857, during the illness from scarlet fever of her little nephew, which came at the time of a great snowstorm that piled drifts up against the window 5 feet deep and was followed by temperatures of twenty degrees below zero, she and Harriet had trouble with the wet-nurses. The first nurse ("Irish," for Clementina always noted the ethnic membership of servants, whether Irish, Welsh, German, or black) came down with infected breasts. The baby, after he vomited blood several times, was taken from her. The baby then lost weight and Clementina feared he would starve, for he threw up the cow's milk offered as a substitute. So he was given to a second nurse ("Welsh"), who placed her own baby with another family. Clementina nursed the Irish wet-nurse, poulticing and massaging her breasts, but regarded it as "the hardest nursing I ever did," for the nurse was "refractory" and "as you know that class of people have little self-control or patience in sickness." But now the Irish nurse, without a baby to suckle, suffered in addition from engorged breasts, and, the artificial breast pumps failing, her own baby was sent for to give her relief. After this baby had performed its service, it was sent back to *its* wet-nurse while the mother's breasts healed and she began to lose her milk. Then suddenly the Irish baby became ill and the woman and her husband rushed it back to the Smith house early in the morning through cold and muddy streets. On the doorstep the baby went into convulsions; the Smiths put it into a bath of warm water, but within a few minutes it was dead, without having reached its mother. Clementina had to tell the poor woman. The experience, she confessed to Sophie, was trying, and not least the absence of true grief:

> The passionate expression of what at first seemed like grief but proved to be rather disappointment not to have relief, mixed up with a sort of maternal instinct of pain in not having been with the child, the interment in catholic ground & endless difficulties—Marys strange and trying course, not to be entered into here, the difficulty of getting at the truth about her thro' the protestant bitterness against her among some [of] the domestics including the little new wet nurse—all these things we have had to contend with till yesterday when Mary left for another place—[10]

To what extent the conception of the lower-class person as deficient in the finer sensibilities may have been grounded in fact is difficult to judge. Certainly the view was a literary convention of the day. Clementina and Sophie read, and approved, a novel about a factory girl by the well-known English authoress Charlotte Elizabeth, whose collected evangelical fiction and poetry (with an introduction by Harriet Beecher Stowe) had been published in New York in 1847. *Helen Fleetwood* concerns an orphaned country girl who, when her foster mother is evicted by the landlord, is forced to go to the city of Manchester at the age of sixteen. Helen takes employment in the carding room of a great factory, perseveres in Christian virtue despite the coarseness of her companions and the hostility of the irreligious, and then returns to her village to die, still a maiden, of over-work, an unjust beating by a supervisor armed with an iron bar, and consumption. The work aimed to expose the hypocrisy and sham of the administration of the laws that supposedly regulated working conditions in the English factories, and to make ladies and gentlemen aware of the harsh reality that condemned the children of the poor to a living death, chained to the ceaseless machines. But the effectiveness of the plot depended upon the contrast between the pure, if simple, country girl and her evil urban proletarian fellow workers; it was almost as if the sympathy for the poor which the author sought to arouse in the reader was reserved only for the exceptional Christian poor. In a matronly and condescending way, the author described the advantages that made Helen Fleetwood more deserving of a literary memorial than most of the members of her class:

Helen Fleetwood was a girl of delicate mind, such as is often found in our sequestered villages, under the guardianship of watchful prudence, more especially when influenced by early, simple piety. There was nothing in her character unusually elevated above the class to which she belonged; but it owed something of its finer texture to the scenery of her native place, and its association with a tale of infant bereavement, of parental sorrow, that she indeed could scarcely remember, but which had often been related to her with touching pathos, though in homely phrase, by the fishermen's families around. By brooding on these, as she marked the rolling of the billows that had once ingulfed her father, she acquired a more contemplative, and perhaps a more imaginative turn of thought than most of her young companions, while a modest reluctance to make her own concerns more prominent than was suitable for so humble a person habituated her to what Mary [her friend] termed keeping her own counsel.[11]

Like Charlotte, Clemma and Sophie were willing to admit of exceptions —particularly if the exceptional person were humble and respectful. As we shall see later, Sophie once made a protégée of a little weaver named Maria Miles, who married Abraham Blakeley and eventually became a lady. Clementina also spoke highly of a young woman, Mary Elliot, who with her husband Robert was a regular member of the Calvary congregation. They were English-born, lived at Parkmount; Robert worked in one of the mills and Mary worked as a "waitress" in the Smith household and "took her meals with our girls." Mary Elliot had been a Sunday School scholar of Clementina's and in the winter of 1851, at the age of twenty-eight, became one of the teachers in the school. She wrote to Clementina in Philadelphia asking for sympathy and counsel. She also wanted advice on how to proceed with a special course of instruction for her class of girls in the proper use of the Book of Common Prayer, for she had observed that many of the girls made no use of the prayer book during services, "whether from indolence or from ignorance of its usefulness I cannot tell." She asked Sophie to recommend a book to assist her. Clementina's father at once sent Miss Elliot a copy of such a book and Clementina wrote to Sophie, who had been giving a course in the subject at the Brandywine Manufacturers' Sunday School, asking her to send a list of the lesson topics. Sophie did better than this, proceeding to copy out all of her lesson notes. On hearing of this, Mary Elliot wrote back in haste to Clementina (addressing her as "My Dear Friend"), urging her to ask Sophie not to go through with "the labor of copying her notes in order to assist me in my class." In a style both familiar and slightly stilted, she went on:

> Give my love to her as a fellow Christian and co-worker in the cause of Christ and tell her that with the very excellent books with which you have so kindly furnished me I shall be able to get along I think very well always relying on the help of God through prayer to assist me. I feel it would be imposing an unnecessary and laborious task upon her kindness to allow her to persist in her kind intentions. I shall probably be in the city next week if I am I shall come to see you.[12]

Some years later Clementina wrote Sophie praising a Mrs. Elliot, now a widow living on the Brandywine, and recommending her as the housekeeper for Victorine Bauduy.

> She is refined, and pleasant in temper and I am sure her experience and trials in life must have all tended to improve & to elevate a naturally fine character which grace has sanctified too—*All* I know of Mary Elliott is very much in her favour—and I feel sure the position must be very congenial to her feelings unless she is changed since I knew her—I dont know much of her as a housekeeper but she will certainly (after keeping house herself) know enough to be a dependance for Sister & Eleu, and she is what they most wish I believe a very nice seamstress—How glad I will be to know she is with her Sister for I do think she will be a comfort to her—She is in mind & manners much above her station too, but only shows this to her superiors by a gentle & respectful demeanour—[13]

Clearly, the members of the managerial class expected men and women of the working class to employ a style of address in their conversation and correspondence that evoked the image of equality in Christian fellowship. Clementina and Sophie expected their ex-Sunday School scholars to salute them as friends, despite the vast difference in their social positions, and dozens of letters to Sophie (and the few to Clementina that survive) from former students show an uncomfortable balance in the effort to use the language of equality while the poor grammar, uncertain handwriting, effusive politeness, and supplicant messages convey extreme dependence and fear of giving offense. No letters from workers to their employers seem to have survived; but during the 1842 strike the expressions of resentment by manufacturers against striking employees who would not take up their grievances in man-to-man discourse betray a similar standard. The managers wanted to maintain social control over the workers and at the same time they wanted to maintain the doctrine of equality before God and the law; they wanted intimacy and trust in their relationship with them and also a recognition of hierarchy.

Managerial people felt a strong sense of responsibility for the personal welfare of those workers whom they personally employed or who had been personally associated with them in church affairs. Clementina and Sophie's letters are filled with accounts of obligatory care for servants in difficulty (who are almost invariably referred to by first name with "poor" as a prefix). Thus, referring to a servant girl who died in the house of her employer, Sophie observed that it had been a difficult time for the Grimshaws, for the girl had been ill for several weeks, during which she was "entirely out of her mind." She added, "As the poor girl had no relatives in this country all the trouble & responsibility fell on them."[14] The Smiths sent a servant girl home to her family when they thought she was about to marry unwisely.[15] When "our poor little Jane" became an invalid, they kept her with them ("she has a home with us") and hired someone to do her work.[16] When the local scrap man fell ill, they arranged to get "our old friend the scrap man into the Hospital" through the help of a physician who was a cousin of Clementina's. "The poor old man builds all his hope of recovery on this, the medical treatment he will have the benefit of there."[17] The responsibility did not end with death; when "my poor Rosie" died in the almshouse in Philadelphia, Clementina tried (in vain) to persuade her minister to bury her in the churchyard instead of in the common grave ("that shocking wholesale manner practiced in those places").[18] With the Sunday School scholars, the initial assumption of managerial responsibility for a poor person's religious welfare automatically involved a mutually recognized general economic responsibility as well. Former scholars felt no compunction in writing to Sophie asking for favors: money to finance the setting up of a store, assistance to a mother in getting a letter delivered to her son who was a seaman aboard one of Commodore Du Pont's ships, advice on how to handle a difficult husband.

The concept of responsibility for those one employed or instructed might, if the person had special qualities of intelligence or character that set him apart from the mass of working people, lead to the establishment of a patron-client relationship that could endure for life. Having a patron could mean, for the workingman or woman, an opportunity to rise into the ranks of the middle class or even the managerial class. From the perspective of the managerial class, the acceptance of a working-class person as a client was a declaration that class boundaries were not impermeable; it was a means of recruiting virtuous and talented people into the society of those who ran things, and testified to the reality of America's claim to be the land of equality and opportunity for all. But we shall examine these patron-client relationships in more detail later when we look at the whole question of the social aspirations and successful careers of men and women who started out poor.

The notion of managerial responsibility for the poor—particularly the deserving poor—was also an ingredient in the ideology of the manufacturers. Crozer, writing to the liberally inclined Minshall Painter about the time that he joined the Delaware County Institute of Science, observed that he had read some articles in the *Lowell Offering* that Painter had lent him, and "if they are as they profess to be, from the pens of the female operatives it is clearly indicative of considerable intelligence amongst the females of Lowell." He went on expansively about the implications of this evidence of intellect among members of the working class (and females at that):

> I have long been sensible that there is an unjustifiable prejudice prevailing against females employed in factories—our operatives in Penn[a] are in education much below that of Eastern Factories, but in virtue morality our factory girls, with here & there an exception, are unimpeachable. As an Employer my mind has often been exercised on the moral & religious improvement of the employees, we have done a little in this vicinity; yet but very little compared with what ought to be, and probably could be done.[19]

Evidently the idea of stewardship, as well as the general belief in the importance of evangelical missions among the workers, was based in part in Crozer's mind on the more general notion that the manager was in some ways responsible for the welfare of his employees, especially if they were virtuous and intelligent.

The Level of Poor Professionals, Small Farmers, Storekeepers, and Master Craftsmen

Next to the managers in the social hierarchy was a group that is difficult to characterize as a class except by exclusion from the other classes. There were a number of people, some of them living in the Rockdale district and some in the nearby crossroads centers at Village Green, Corner Ketch, and Lima, who considered themselves (and were considered by others) to be lower in rank than the managers but higher than the working people. They probably did not think of themselves as a group with common interests; it is difficult to use the term "middle-class" to denote them, for that label suggests a stable and more or less uniform life style and a considerable degree of self-awareness. Many members of this "class" were only temporarily there, being either on the way up to join the managers, or on their way down into the lower orders.

Not all professional people were of this station in life. Many were the scions of well-established families, who had chosen the ministry, the law, medicine, or the military as a respectable alternative to commerce or manufacturing or farming. Not all the brothers in a managerial family were needed to manage the family's capital ventures in the new generation. Crozer's sons, to be sure, all did go into the cotton business. But Smith's son Richard went to West Point, became an engineer, and for a time served as president of Girard College; John S. Phillips's brother was a physician; Francis Gurney Smith's son, the Thomas Mackie who married Eleuthera, was a physician; of the sons of E. I. and Victor du Pont, one—Samuel Francis—entered the Navy, and another, Henry, went to West Point. William Martin's son, John Hill Martin, also attended West Point but dropped out to become a lawyer. And Alfred Lee was the son of a well-to-do New England merchant and had independent means. These people, while remaining members of the managerial class, found careers in the professions.

But there were also poor professional people. In Rockdale, after the Reverend Mr. Lee left to become Bishop of Delaware, the rectors at Calvary Church were generally men with education but without means, who depended for their living upon the skimpy salary paid by the congregation. The situation was similar with Rockdale's physicians. Until 1841, when he left to become customs officer in the Philadelphia harbor's quarantine station (the "Lazaretto"), Rockdale was the home of the managerial-class Dr. Samuel Anderson, who lived a varied career as Navy surgeon, Army captain, sheriff, state representative, congressman, justice of the peace, president of the Delaware County Bible Society, and—incidentally—private physician. Far less conspicuous, and definitely not of the upper class, were the lesser physicians, such as Dr. Gregg of Wrangletown, Dr. Marsh of Concord, and Dr. Humphrey, the homeopathic physician of Aston. The physicians in Crozerville in 1850 were young men who boarded with the local storekeepers. And the "teachers" appear in the census as boarders and renters. There were, so far as the record shows, no military men or lawyers resident in the Rockdale district.

Apart from the professional people, there were a number of other occupational categories that fell into the level between the managing and the working class. The self-employed master craftsmen in the district whom one might wish to include in this intermediate class were quite numerous: a few tailors, a dozen shoemakers, a dressmaker, a few highly skilled masons and builders, some wheelwrights and millwrights, carpenters, plasterers, blacksmiths. There was the miller who leased and operated the gristmill at Old Sable Forge. There were several storekeepers. There were mill managers. And there were the five or six practical farmers, like the McCrackens (who were rich) and the Eachus family (who were poor), who worked for the Riddles now and then as carters and operatives, and the ten or twelve householders with half a dozen acres or so, whose properties lay within the district itself. All together, the class of poor professionals, master craftsmen, storekeepers, and farmers amounted to about 150 households.

With a few exceptions, the members of this group were self-employed. The exceptions were the ministers and the public school teachers (and probably the mill managers too), who were hired on a contract which called for an annual cycle of services in return for an annual salary; and these individuals, being better educated than the workers, certainly had a higher social status. The self-employed persons—the physicians, the storekeepers, the craftsmen, the seamstress, the miller, the farmers—sold either a service or a product to anyone with the money to buy. Cash incomes, in many cases, were probably no higher than the better paid operatives'. A few—storekeepers and farmers—had substantial real estate or other capital; the rest had only a few tools or some books and an education.

There is nothing to suggest that the members of this class, when they looked horizontally, as it were, at the others on their level who differed from them in occupation, would have thought of them all as sharing a common set of interests. The only feature they did in fact share was a view of themselves as standing below the managerial class and above the working class.[20]

The Working Class

Most of the people who lived in Rockdale belonged to the working class. They were mainly mill hands and their families; but there were three other kinds of working people: farm hands and gardeners, common laborers, and domestic servants. With only a few exceptions, working people were employed by members of the managerial class, either as hands in their mills and about their estates or as servants in their houses.

The fundamental social unit for workers, as for managers and middle-level people, was the simple nuclear family residing in its own house. To be sure, working-class families were more likely to have been broken by death or separation, and there were many unmarried men and women who had jobs in the mills and boarded with other working-class households or who were servants and lived in with well-to-do families. But the basic unit was the simple family and almost all working people lived as members of, or boarders or servants with, such a family or one of its transformations.

Economic conditions in the district made it possible for working people, and particularly the employees of the mills, to live well and save money. The functioning of the system for mill workers can best be seen by looking at circumstances of particular households for whom records have survived. Take, for instance, the family of John Blair. In August 1850, John Blair and his family were living in Rockdale in a house which they rented from Archibald McDowell (Samuel Riddle's son-in-law and the manager of Penn's Grove factory). Blair was fifty and his wife Jane forty-eight; they had five children: Ann, thirteen, Isabella, twelve, Sarah, nine, Matthew, six, and William, five; and they took in as boarders James Garrett, twenty-two, the clerk at the mill, and a young woman of twenty-four, Sarah Barlow, who was a weaver at the same mill. Sarah Barlow was English; all the rest were Irish-born. The Blairs had arrived at Penn's Grove in 1847, fresh from Ireland. During 1847, 1848, and 1849, the Blairs supplied three hands to the mill. The father, John, worked in the card room, six days a week, at $2.50 per week; in 1849 his wages were raised to $3.50 per week. The mother, Jane, worked in the card room at $2.50 per week. Their ten-year-old daughter Ann worked in the throstle room at $1 per week; her wages were raised to $2 per week after about a year. In 1849 the family could have earned, in the fifty-two weeks of the year, a maximum of $364 at the factory, but this amount was reduced by temporary layoffs and sickness to a total of $257.46 earned by the three of them during the year.

At the year's end, the father was able to obtain employment as a stonemason, which had probably been his original employment in Ireland, and his place in the mill was taken by the next daughter, Isabella, aged twelve. Young Matthew and William thus were left in the house in the care of their older sister Sarah. About 1855, the Blairs moved to Crozerville, where John worked in his trade as a stonemason; probably his family worked in the mill there. In 1860 they moved again, to a house they rented from the Riddles on "Church Hill" in Crozerville, and resumed working at Penn's Grove.

In 1850, John Blair's wife Jane worked in the card room as before. It may be worth while to look more closely at the social composition of this department of the factory. The employees who were listed in the payroll under the rubric "card room" were responsible not merely for the operation of the carding machines, which produced slivers for the spreaders, stretchers, and spinning frames in the throstle room, but also for the initial preparation of the cotton for feeding into the cards. This included the picker room, where the bales were opened and the contents mixed and beaten to remove dust and dirt, and the spreading machines, where laps (sheets of cotton wool of uniform thickness, width, and length) were carefully prepared. Proper mixing, picking, lapping, and carding were essential for the production of good-quality yarn. In March 1850, twenty-nine people worked in the card room—eight males and twenty-one females. For four of these no information remains except the presence of their names on the payroll. Of the twenty-five others, twenty had other members of their own households working in the mill, and twelve had housemates working in the card room itself (two households supplied three workers each; three supplied two).

Men dominated the card room in technical authority and were highest in pay. The boss carder, John Thompson, was paid at a rate of $48 per month (four weeks of six days each). He had held this job for six years. The four carders received from $14 to $18 per month. Three males served as laborers, probably in the picker room; one of these, the boss's fourteen-year-old son, received $6 per month, the others $8 and $10. All twenty-one of the women received $10 per month except for five, who made only $6; two of these were fourteen, one was sixteen, and there is no information about the ages of the other two.

Families, however, determined the informal social network of the department. Two of the men—the boss and one of the carders—had two other members of their households in the card room, Thompson's son and a twenty-two-year-old female boarder in his house, and the two daughters (nineteen and twenty-two) of the carder. Thompson had a daughter (fifteen) working in the throstle room as well. There were three pairs of sisters: the McDowell girls, twenty-three and twenty (they had a brother and a sister in the throstle room); the Ferguson sisters, twenty and fourteen, who came from Knowlton, where their father worked in a mill; and Hannah Massey, eighteen, and her recently married sister Ann Powell (a third sister worked as a weaver). Hannah's father owned a small farm on the hill above Crozerville.

The web of kinship was probably even more complex than the available data indicate, for census records and ledger numbers do not reveal most of the affinal connections and fail to show whether male heads of different families with the same surname were consanguineally related. Thus there were certainly brothers, sisters, cousins, and in-laws of close degree working together in the same department or in the same mill whom we cannot identify now. The statement that four out of five workers in the card room had relatives working in the same mill, or that nearly half of them had a housemate in the card room itself, is simply an understatement of the pervasiveness of kin relationships. And, of course, the workers in the card room, in addition to being tied together by kinship, were many of them close neighbors. Of the twenty-three for whom residential information is available, fifteen lived near to one another as residents of ten houses rented from among Riddle's forty-three tenements at Penn's Grove; others came from Rockdale, Knowlton, and Crozerville.

The other large departments of the factory—the throstle room and the weaving room—were similarly organized. There was a throstle-room boss who earned $24 per month and two loom bosses who earned $36 per month. Their departments were similarly composed of both males and females, with a preponderance of women: twenty to twelve in the throstle room, and twenty-nine to twenty-two in the weaving room. But there were differences in the social character of the two rooms. The throstle room was mostly occupied by young people between twelve and twenty, supervised by a few mature adults. The weavers, by contrast, were mostly men and women in their twenties and thirties, with only a few teenagers. Fifteen of the thirty-two throstle-room workers came from six households; eighteen of the fifty-one weavers came from eight households. Throstle-room workers were paid by the day and earned from $6 to $10 per month; the weavers, who were on piecework, usually producing some combination of the mill's final products (tickings, stripes, denims, and calicoes), could earn as much as $30 per month or even more, depending on skill and the time put in. The most highly specialized workers—the five mule spinners and the three warpers—earned more than any other employees except the bosses, the warpers all earning over $29 per month, and the mule spinners between $40 and $50 per month. Two of the spinners earned over $49 in the month ending March 2, 1850, making them the highest paid employees in the mill (but they, of course, had to pay their piecers and scavengers out of these earnings).

Wages were, in fact, substantial in comparison with subsistence expenses. Food cost about 15 cents per day for an active adult male requiring 3,500 calories per day; women and children required proportionately less. Rent in particular was extremely low—about 5 percent of earnings. Riddle for instance rented out to his workers a block of five stone tenements on Mount Road in Crozerville, part of an unsettled estate being administered by Edward Darlington. The block was 90 feet long, with a piazza running the entire length, and was constructed along the steep slope of Church Hill, next to where the Crozerville Methodist Church would in a few years be constructed. There was a palisade fence around the block and a dug well for the use of the families. If the houses were characteristic of the time, they were four-story structures, including a half-dug dirt-floored cellar, two main stories, and a slope-roofed attic, one room above the other, with a column of semicircular staircases rising from floor to floor on one side of the small fireplaces, and closets on the other. Cooking was probably usually done in a kitchen outside so that three rooms could serve as bedrooms. The rooms were about 15 by 15 feet in floor area and were plastered (they had been replastered a year ago, in fact).

The rental for the better of the houses was $25 per year, which amounted to $1.93 every four weeks; the other two went for $1.16 per month. Other Riddle tenements in Crozerville and Rockdale rented for about the same amount. Most of the houses and tenements in Penn's Grove itself were more expensive, generally between $2 and $4 per month, depending on size. The "old mansion," for instance, was rented out to two families who shared the $5.38 per month rental. Thompson, the card-room boss, paid $3.46 per month for a house containing himself, a wife eight months pregnant, seven children, a mother-in-law, and a boarder. House rentals ranged, to be precise, from a low of $1.15 per month to a high of $3.46 per month per household.

Rent thus claimed a very small proportion of subsistence expenses for even the lowest paid mill-working family, far less than the cost of food, which was the main expense. The Blairs, for instance, as we noted earlier, in 1849 earned $257.46 from the mill, plus about $2 per week from their male boarder and $1.25 per week from the girl, for a total of $169 in board money. This added up to a family income of $426.46 for the year. They paid in rent that year a total of $15.75; firewood for a house of that kind was about $16 per year; and food for the entire household (including the boarders) would have amounted to about $272.22. Thus the family would have had subsistence expenses of about $303.97, leaving a "profit" of $122.49. Some of this would of course be spent on shoes, clothing, household articles, and other incidentals, but it would be possible for the family to end the year with a small amount of cash savings. The card-room boss, John Thompson, paid $45 per year for his house. He himself earned $603.50 from the mill; with two of his children working, the family income from the factory was $744.24. In addition, a female weaver boarded with them; at $1.25 per week, they would take in from her another $65 for a grand total of $809.24. Samuel Duncan, the carder, and his daughters earned $430.95 from the mill, and $104 from a male boarder, for a year's income of $534.95; their rent was $30.

Boarders were somewhat less secure. Sarah Barlow, the weaver who was staying with the Blairs, earned $198.38 in 1849. Paying about $65 for board and lodging would leave her $133.38 for clothing and incidentals; she was probably able to save money. Her earnings were a little below the annual average of $198.64 for all weavers at Penn's Grove; males earned on the average slightly more than women (although at the same piece rates), averaging $237.10. A male weaver paying $104 per year for room and board would, in effect, be spending nearly half his income for bare subsistence; a woman weaver would be paying between a third and a half. But employees in the throstle room, earning $6 to $10 per month (or at most $130 per year), would have had trouble making ends meet as boarders. And, in fact, we find that there was only one person who worked in the throstle room who may have been a boarder—a fifteen-year-old girl who lived with her sister, who was eighteen, in a household whose nuclear family actually may have been relatives. Indeed, the average age of the twenty-five throstle-room employees for whom we have ages was twenty; and if one excludes from this group the five adults over thirty, the average age of the throstle-room employees drops to fifteen. Clearly, then, only an industrious weaver, spinner, warper, senior carder, or foreman could support himself or herself as a boarder; throstle-room workers and others had to be members of nuclear families.

Obviously it would be a gross error to think of the mill hands at Penn's Grove, as stereotyped views of mid-nineteenth-century cotton factory workers would have it, as an undifferentiated mass of exhausted, sick, and starving women and children pushed about by cruel male overseers. There was a wide range of ages, of types and degrees of skill, and of income; and the women and children, being the members of families who lived in the villages around the mills and went to local churches, were not likely to be beaten and abused with impunity. Furthermore, the working people were extraordinarily mobile, and this mobility is an indication of financial ability to escape from unfavorable circumstances. Many had just recently arrived from England or Ireland and regarded places like Rockdale as temporary residences, where they consolidated their means and prepared themselves to move on to better jobs or even to homesteads in the west.

The mobility of Riddle's employees is revealed in his rent books, which show that families seldom stayed much more than a year or two in the same house. On one of the properties, for instance, which contained three houses, the average length of stay was exactly eleven months and three weeks. Some workers, of course, remained for many years and eventually bought small farms. But many more simply passed through Rockdale on their way to better (or worse) situations somewhere else.

The Riddle account books show that of the first cohort of twenty families employed at Parkmount in September 1832, eight were still employed there in January 1835 (that is to say, the attrition rate was 60 percent in two and a half years). Of the seventy-two employees listed at Penn's Grove in January 1844, only sixteen were still working there in March 1850 (an attrition rate of 78 percent in six years). Of the original twenty families working for the Riddles in 1832, members of only one were still working for Samuel Riddle in 1844 (an attrition rate of 95 percent in twelve years). Evidently there was a very high turnover—about 50 percent—in the first two years of employment, and a steady attrition at a rate of about 4 percent or 5 percent per year after that.

Not all of the workers who left Parkmount left the Rockdale district, however. Some took employment in another factory. Again looking at the 1832 cohort, it appears that in addition to the eight families who remained at Parkmount from 1832 to 1835, at least three others found work elsewhere in the Rockdale district; the attrition rate for the district as a whole was only 45 percent in these two and a half years. If we attempt to locate the 1844 cohort in the 1850 census, we find that the attrition rate for the district as a whole has gone up to 63 percent for six years. Of the 120 workers at Penn's Grove in 1850, at least 14 can be identified ten years later in the 1860 census as living in the Rockdale district; the rate now is 88 percent. These figures show that a similar, but lesser, rate of loss applied to the district as a whole; a working family had about a 10 percent chance of remaining in the Rockdale district for more than ten years.[21]

A typical case is the Morris family. Between 1829 and 1832, four brothers from Lancashire, their father, two of their brothers-in-law, and all their wives and children emigrated to America, along with a friend named John Smith. The Morris brothers were hand-loom weavers who, although still profitably employed, were discouraged about their prospects for economic and social advancement in England. The father was a carpenter and the brothers-in-law were a blacksmith and a farmer. Thomas, one of the brothers, immediately moved to Ohio with his wife and children and bought a farm; the others remained in the Philadelphia area, working at their trades. For a time they lived in the city itself; then they all moved to the Brandywine to operate power looms (except for the blacksmith, who was doing well in Philadelphia). In 1833 two of the remaining brothers, Andrew and William, and their friend John Smith moved from Brandywine to Rockdale to work at Phillips' mill as power-loom weavers. Andrew, the married brother, rented a house with a small cellar and three bedrooms for $25 per year. He worked in the mill while his wife Jane took care of the two children, one a newborn son, and also the four boarders (the unmarried brother, their friend John Smith, and two other men). Andrew and William each earned between $16 and $24 per month, and the married couple charged the boarders $2 per week. Once when the mill was stopped for five weeks to put in a new water wheel, William went to work in Manayunk; Andrew found work with a neighboring farmer at 50 cents a day and meals. In 1835, their father died at Brandywine and their mother went to live with her son-in-law the blacksmith and her daughter in Philadelphia. In 1836 brother John, his wife Ann, and their son Thomas moved from Brandywine to West Branch and all three went to work "on the power looms at mr Crosher's Mill." In October 1836, Phillips closed his mill and Andrew was thrown out of work. "He could have got plenty of work in the neighborhood but they thought it best to go to the western country. So they had a publick sale and then packed up for their jurney."

Their plan was to move out to Ohio, near brother Thomas, to buy land and set up a farm. They hired a wagon to take them to Philadelphia, where they stayed a few days visiting with mother and sister. Then they took passage by railroad and canal to Pittsburgh; this cost $21 for a family of four. Another $6.50 got them to Thomas. Andrew paid a neighbor $2 for a couple of days' looking for farmland; finding what he liked, he bought 120 acres for $150, a pig and two sows for $11.50, and hired some men to help him build a log house. The cost of the entire operation (except for food), including transporting the whole family and buying a farm, was on the order of $200. All of this had been saved out of the rent money and the earnings of one man, Andrew, a skilled power-loom weaver, in three years of work at Phillips' mill in Rockdale (he had no capital on arrival in America, for he had had to borrow money to leave England, and had not gotten himself established before settling on Chester Creek).

Next year, brother John and his wife Ann bought a $400 farm adjoining Thomas and also moved out to Ohio. The remaining components of the Morris family straggled out over the next several years. Eventually, all of them were established as farmers in eastern Ohio, except for brother William, who had become a manufacturer of jeans, which he sold from farm to farm in the summer from a peddler's wagon. The power looms on Chester Creek now were far behind them; they had been merely a means of acquiring the cash with which to buy land in the west.[22]

THE FORMS OF THE FAMILY
IN A COTTON-MANUFACTURING DISTRICT

The American doctrine of family, sanctioned in religion, morality, and law, and almost universally accepted in the 1850's, held that the married pair and their children constituted the natural basis of human society. From this fundamental unit, the simple nuclear family, radiated lines of ascent and descent and affinal connection that bound each nuclear family together with others in loose aggregations of kinship. The nuclear family itself might also exist in several more or less incipient or modified forms: as a married couple whose children had not yet been born or who had died or moved away; as a surviving spouse with children; as surviving children whose parents had died. Such a family, however modified, lived together in a house. There might, however, be others who shared the house with its proprietary family: individual grandparents, uncles and aunts, cousins, nephews and nieces, grandchildren, or even more remotely connected relatives; domestic servants; and boarders who paid rent. A household thus consisted of at least one nuclear family (simple or modified) and, usually, various kinsmen, servants, or boarders.

Within the outlines of this basic pattern, several different styles of family organization were possible. In the Rockdale manufacturing district (and in other, similar manufacturing districts nearby, as on the Brandywine), two of these different styles—the workers' and the managers'—must be noted, because they functioned very differently in the economic life of the community.

Among the workers, the nuclear family was vitally necessary to the economic welfare of most adult individuals. An unmarried working-class adult of either sex could not live alone. There were no small apartments or dormitories, and even if there had been, and the person could have afforded to pay the rent, there was not enough time in view of the long working hours to keep house and cook for oneself. Thus the unmarried adult either lived with his parents and siblings (in which case he either paid rent or put his earnings into the common fund) or moved out to live as a paying boarder in the household of another nuclear family. He or she could not live indefinitely as a boarder, however. The single person was expected to marry; there was little opportunity for sexual activity outside marriage, and much risk attached to it; and, if one were eager to improve one's situation in life, it was clear that the quickest way for the working-class person to do so was to form a nuclear family partnership.

Such partnership was fundamental to the survival-and-advancement strategy of the people of the working class. Among the mill workers, the members of a nuclear family (simple or modified) constituted an effective economic partnership. Each person above infancy contributed either work or money to the unit; cash was saved and pooled as a capital fund for future travel and investment, usually in land or tools and equipment for a trade (or even manufacturing). Any combination of members might work in the factory, including husband, wife, or children, so long as there was a female at home to cook, mind the children, and take care of boarders.

The boarders were a crucially important factor in the financial plans of many working-class households, for they paid good money—$2 per week if male, $1.25 per week if female. The wife, who cooked for the boarders and did their housekeeping (which probably included laundry services), could bring in as much as $24 per month by caring for three male boarders —very likely more than the rest of the family earned at the mill. At the time of the 1850 census, between a quarter and a half of all mill workers' households were keeping boarders. The nuclear family partnership thus used the house which it rented from the mill owner as capital with which to make money.

In this working-class system it is difficult to see marriage as a means of establishing an alliance between groups. Although an extended family might—as in the case of the Morrises—travel together, it was essentially traveling as a large, dispersed nuclear family, consisting of aged parents and their married children. The in-laws came along as spouses rather than as representatives of the families of their parents. Marriage and procreation established a partnership among individuals; the nuclear family partnership was the necessary condition for the renting of capital equipment (a house) and the pooling of factory income.

The implications of the partnership family system for social attitudes within the working class at this time are interesting. A hardworking and well-disciplined family could in a few years, if not impeded by illness or unemployment, save enough money to travel west, buy land, and become farmers (where the family partnership concept was equally applicable)—or, alternatively (and far less frequently), establish credit, borrow money, and become merchants or manufacturers. The mother and teen-age children evidently were almost as productive financially as the father; and, since the partnership could remain even if the father (or mother) died or moved away, many working-class widows and widowers were heads of families and of households. As on the farm, the labor of children, even small children, was essential in household and baby-minding chores. The system did tend to reduce the amount of schooling the children received (only about half of the eligible working-class children in 1850 were listed as having attended school in the previous year). But it also probably tended to minimize the patriarchal quality of family life—a quality that only the wealthy manufacturer or merchant was able to support. In many families the wife, in addition to being a wage or rent earner, was also the partnership's business manager, collecting the family paycheck directly from the manufacturer, or from her husband and children, and formulating and administering the family budget. This situation should, theoretically, have been conducive to tension between a working father whose contribution to the partnership was not worth much more than, if as much as, that of his wife and children. And such tension in turn should have contributed to a centrifugal tendency that would, as it were, spin off discontented young unmarried men and women, to live as boarders with other working-class families, thus perpetuating that most necessary aspect of the whole system.

In the managerial class, where income was the profit of a business or a large farm owned and administered by the father, the nuclear family partnership was not economically necessary for the survival and progress of the individual. The father—the businessman—could take care of himself and his wife and children. Bachelors could live comfortably on their fathers' profits and spinsters remain at home happily with their parents and sisters. Sons might go into the family business or they might turn to one of the professions or to benevolent and charitable activities. And instead of paying boarders, the nonfamily members of the household were paid servants. Indeed, the nonpartnership aspect of the marital relationship might be most emphatically demonstrated, as in the care with which the Sellers family kept the estate of their sister, Peter Hill's wife, separate from his estate by putting it in trust.

In contrast to the working-class concept of the marital economic partnership, the managerial class thought in terms of the potential alliance implications of marriage. Nathan Sellers and James Knowles objected to their daughters' marriages to men with whom a family connection seemed economically perilous. When Sallie Knowles married John P. Crozer without her father's consent, he made it plain that no financial claims could be made on him by her new family. And when Hannah Sellers finally did receive permission to marry Peter Hill, there was thereafter a continuing financial alliance (an irritating one to the Sellers') between the two families. The Lammots and Du Ponts were intimately joined by the marriage of Lammot's daughter to E. I. du Pont's son; the business connections and friendships of the Smiths and the Du Ponts were cemented by no less than two marriages. And we shall later note the importance of affinal connections to Henry Moore, John S. Phillips, and John P. Crozer in acquiring the capital to carry out their plans for manufacturing.

Among the managerial class, furthermore, the patronymic descent group was far more important than among the workers. Such a group was formed of the successive generations of persons patrilineally descended from and bearing the name of an original male ancestor or ancestors (if they were a group of brothers) who had become established in America many years before. Living members of such patronymic descent groups considered them to be in some sense great families, and marriages were sometimes actually recognized as alliances between patronymic groups (as in the case of the Lammots and Du Ponts). One of the members would keep the genealogical records and be able to trace the family's ancestry back deep into European history. Great families often maintained contact with kinsmen in Europe and exchanged visits occasionally. To the list of such old great family names as Sharpless, Phillips, Smith, Lewis, Sellers, Gilpin, Du Pont, Dutton, and Darlington would in the next generation be added those of the managers who had become successful in this—Crozer, Lammot, Riddle. This emphasis upon a descent group identity, represented by a name and a genealogy, no doubt contributed to the members of the group a sense of being a meaningful member in an immortal corporate entity— an estimate of self far different from the identity gained as a member of a nuclear family partnership, which eventually would be dissolved by the death of its members. And it had different implications for social attitudes, too: it emphasized the value of age and of the male line, and treated women as peripheral (the daughters' children, bearing another patronym, were forever lost); indeed, in this class they were peripheral in an economic sense, being engaged in financially nonproductive tasks. Women served as the links that joined men in systems of descent and alliance, which were of course economically significant relations; but their own primary work was neither heavy housework nor factory production but rather the administration of servants, church activity, and the cultivation of artistic and literary interests.

But the working-class family style and the managerial-class family style, however different in some ways, were precise complements to one another. The managers, in order to make the profits required to support their own extended family alliances, needed a stable and contented work force, composed of nuclear family partnerships and unmarried boarders in households that provided the proper mix of males and females of various ages. They attracted such a work force by paying relatively high wages, by providing houses at very low rents, by allowing workers to raise vegetables on company land and even keep a cow or some chickens, by reducing the rents during hard times, and by helping them in many small ways with credit, banking services, and transportation. The workers, in order to save the cash needed to buy land in the west, worked hard and for the most part without complaint in the managers' mills, enduring periods of unemployment, partial employment, and reduced wages, foregoing the prospect of education for many of their children, and even allowing the evangelical women of the managerial class to find respectable and interesting work in saving their souls.

Part Two

ROCKDALE FROM 1825 TO 1835

THE CREATING OF A WAY OF LIFE

Chapter III

THE ASSEMBLING OF
THE INDUSTRIALISTS

The lives of the manufacturers who came to the Rockdale district in the 1820's were, in the beginning, guided by the simple dream of wealth. Their careers had all in one way or another reached an impasse and the new venture of the day, cotton manufacturing, offered them a chance of making the fortune, and the reputation, denied them in other spheres. Despite the newness of their machines, these industrialists were conservative people who sought to preserve the gentleman's way of life in a world of shifting privilege.[1] They were not, as yet, reformers and evangelists. They were not trying to effect an industrial revolution. They were not, most of them, even very well informed about their own machinery.

But their actions were transformative. They bought up cheap the old merchant mills and common gristmills, the sawmills, paper mills, and forges that now languished along the banks of the creek, victims of economic decline. Gradual soil exhaustion, excessive lumbering, the depredations of the Hessian fly, and competition from the more efficient automated flour mills of the Brandywine were bringing ruin to the formerly prosperous wheat-producing country of southeastern Pennsylvania. The little mill hamlets that suddenly sprang up, as if conjured out of the rocky hillsides by a magician's spell, were not so much modifications of old rural communities as newly created towns. And the immigrant Irish and English operatives imported to work in the mills were to live a way of life that was still new on the earth.

It was already a region with memories of change. A hundred and forty years before, only Indians and a few Swedes lived in the valley; a trio of aboriginal survivors, an elderly man and his brother and sister, were still waiting to die in a rock shelter along Dismal Run.[2] The log cabins of the early settlers still dotted the hillsides. There were old sodden races and the ruins of dams and abutments built and abandoned so long ago that no one today knows how they began. But the importance of the new mills seemed, at first, to consist more in their contribution to national self-sufficiency than in industrial transformation. Memories and mementoes of the Battle of the Brandywine and of the War of 1812 were common reminders of the national need for independence. The British Crown was still the enemy and the Indians to the west were still the enemy within. And the new tariff of 1824, protecting the infant American industries from unfair British competition, seemed to give patriotic sanction to the daring American manufacturer.

THE FIRST ARRIVALS

In 1825, only a small group of businessmen were manufacturing cotton along Chester Creek. They were William Martin, merchant of Philadelphia, who had bought an old paper mill a few years before and had converted it to cotton spinning; John S. Phillips, a wealthy Philadelphia bachelor of uncommon mechanical aptitude, who that year took a ten-year lease on a new stone mill and installed two hundred new power looms—an extraordinary number for that day; John P. Crozer, the farmer's son, who had just acquired another old paper mill and was also converting it to cotton spinning; and the Englishman John D. Carter, who had long been a cotton spinner in the neighborhood. There were a couple of smaller cotton enterprises, soon to be replaced, of which little record remains. And several other merchants and manufacturers were on their way: James Houghton, a power-loom weaver, and John Garsed, machinist and manufacturer of power looms; the Riddle brothers, Samuel and James, cotton spinners en route from the mills of Northern Ireland; and Richard S. Smith and Daniel Lammot, prosperous Philadelphia merchants seeking fresh air and investment opportunities in the countryside close to their friends the Du Ponts along the Brandywine, the next creek over.

Some of these people would become casualties in the economic and ideological struggles of the era and would move away. The survivors—the Crozers, the Riddles, the Smiths, and the Lammots—would go on to form the nucleus of the Chester Creek manufacturing community.

It was the families of these successful evangelical industrialists who, after installing the new machines, and after defeating the freethinkers and associationists, would determine the moral character of the community. They would lead their workers through the strikes and tariff battles of the 1830's and 1840's, on into the free soil movement of the 1850's. At the last they would urge them to the carnage of the war between the states, which simultaneously—if temporarily—destroyed both the slave-labor cotton plantations of the south and the free-labor cotton-manufacturing villages of the north. And in that holocaust the struggle between the old radicalism of the Enlightenment and the newer tradition of evangelical Protestantism for control of the Industrial Revolution would for a time be resolved in a reformist, millenarian Christian capitalism.

William Martin, Jr.

William Martin was a young commission merchant in Philadelphia in 1822 to whom the Lungren family, owners of the old Lungren paper and cotton mills on Chester Creek, owed money. When the Lungrens ran into financial difficulty, Martin became one of the assignees (or receivers). In 1823 at a sheriff's sale he bought the mills, and he and his brother-in-law, Joseph W. Smith, formed a company to operate them. The Martins moved out of the city a couple of years later to live in the Lungren mansion, a new and elegant stone house, built in 1815, while William Lungren moved to the Sellers' shops at Cardington, in Upper Darby, to work as a millwright.[1] The house stood on a slope facing down the green valley, with a long prospect of the winding stream and the little clusters of houses, mills, dams, and races that sat here and there along the banks. They christened the hamlet Lenni (pronounced "Len-eye"), after the tribe of Indians—the Lenni Lenape, or Delaware—who only a century before had occupied southeastern Pennsylvania.

In 1823, just before the move, their son, John Hill Martin, was born, and it is owing to his love of his father, and his nostalgic attachment to the towns along Chester Creek where he spent his early years, that so much information remains about William Martin. John never married; during his long life as an insurance lawyer, he developed a passion for preserving records of all kinds. He made lists of the attorneys admitted to the bar of Philadelphia from the earliest times; he collected genealogical notes; he kept a diary and wrote memoirs; he finally published a semi-autobiographical history—*Chester (and its Vicinity,) Delaware County, in Pennsylvania* (Philadelphia, 1877). And he gave to the Historical Society of Pennsylvania, of which he was a member, all his historical papers, including his father's receipt book during the time when he owned the mill at Lenni.[2]

William Martin had been born in 1797 of old Delaware County families. His father, who died in the yellow fever epidemic of that year, had been a physician, trained at the University of Pennsylvania by the renowned Benjamin Rush, who it is said came to Chester to attend his former student when he learned of his illness. His mother was a daughter of old Judge Crosby, famous as a Revolutionary War hero and the last slaveowner in Delaware County. William studied law and was admitted to the bar in Chester, the county seat, in 1821. But a legal career did not appear to be as promising as a career in business, and later that year he formed a partnership with his stepuncle Peter Hill (the brother of his mother's second husband) as commission merchants in Philadelphia. Commission merchants received consignments of goods of various kinds—such as paper and cotton yarn and cloth—and held them in their warehouses for sale at the consignee's asking price. When the goods were sold, the merchant remitted the sale price minus his percentage commission; if they could not be sold, they were returned or transferred.[3] The 1822 partnership with Joseph W. Smith in the cotton mill was also a family affair. Martin had married his partner's sister, Sarah Ann, in that same year, and the partner in turn had married Martin's younger sister Ann Crosby, in a sibling exchange not unusual in those times.

The young William Martin was a fine-looking man, it was said, about 6 feet tall, with fair hair, blue eyes, and rosy cheeks, and like his father he liked to live well. He was a fancy dresser and something of a gourmet. He was a patron of Peale's natural history museum and seems to have had literary pretensions too, for he wrote poetry, of a sort, in a clear, precise, rounded hand, unusually legible in an era of spiky penmanship. The following effusion, celebrating his passion for oysters, is the only sample of verse ascribed to him that survives:

The Oyster Supper

Gently stir and rake the fire,
  Put the oysters on to roast,
"Duck Creek planted," I desire,
  They're the kind that please me most.
As the odor strikes my nose,
  My appetite much keener grows.

On the plate now see them lie,
  In the gravy plump and fat,
Finer "fish" ne'er met my eye,
  Nor "An opening rich as that";
Let me season to the taste,
  With pepper, salt, etc.,—haste.

> *The cloth upon the table spread,*
>   *Now knife and fork as quickly get,*
> *With butter fresh and toasted bread*
>   *I'll have a feast unheard of yet,*
> *While* poney *brandy and segars*
>   *Will set me up beyond the stars.*[4]

As 1825 unfolded, the young Martins of Lenni appeared to be in a very prosperous condition. William's ambitions soared; he aspired to a political career, and in the fall of the next year entered the race for the state assembly on the federal Republican ticket—and won. In 1826 and 1827 he represented the county in Harrisburg, the state capital, leaving the conduct of the mill business to his brother-in-law. In the legislature he associated himself with those who were interested in the promotion of the state's system of internal improvements, particularly the canals.[5] All in all, he was a glowing young man.

John S. Phillips

Another young gentleman of promise, twenty-five-year-old John Smith Phillips, joined the ranks of the Chester Creek manufacturers in the summer of 1825. His father was a Philadelphia merchant who kept his office in the commercial quarters facing the wharves along Front Street; he also served on the Board of Directors of the Phoenix Insurance Company. The family lived alternately in a town house on Front Street and at a summer place along the Delaware above the city. John S. Phillips, the eldest of the children, had already entered the business world, as a sugar refiner in the city in partnership with Joseph S. Lovering, formerly of Wilmington, and as the partner of David Lewis, Jr., in a cotton-weaving mill in Holmesburg, an industrial suburb in north Philadelphia.[6] He was a youth with an intense interest in and aptitude for science and mechanics. In 1824 he became one of the founding members of the new Franklin Institute, along with a glittering array of the Philadelphia region's leading merchants and manufacturers —Charles and Victor du Pont, clothmakers, and Thomas Gilpin, paper manufacturer, from the Brandywine; Oliver Evans, the famous inventor and iron founder, proprietor of the Mars Iron Works; Paul Beck, Jr., the merchant and shot manufacturer; Nicholas Biddle, president of the Second Bank of the United States; George Escol Sellers, the engineer; and Joseph Siddall, manufacturer of cotton. In the same year he joined another illustrious band, the members of the older, and politically somewhat more radical,

Academy of Natural Sciences of Philadelphia. He was proposed by George Ord, famous foe of Audubon, ornithologist and editor of Alexander Wilson's *Ornithology,* and wealthy retired ropemaker, and by Benjamin Coates, a physician. Phillips' special interest, even at this early date, was conchology—a field in which he was later to publish scientific papers (and eventually to become the Academy's Curator of Conchology). From October 1824 to February 1825, Phillips attended the meetings conscientiously, along with the other regulars, Charles Lucien Bonaparte (naturalist son of Napoleon's elder brother the exiled King of Spain), John Speakman (chemist), Charles Lesueur (scientific illustrator), Thomas Say (conchologist and entomologist), Gerard Troost (chemist and geologist), and three or four others.[7]

The Academy was the scene of considerable excitement in 1824 and 1825, for these were the years of the first visits to Philadelphia of Robert Owen, the British cotton manufacturer-turned-social reformer, on his way to establish an associationist community at New Harmony, Indiana. The wealthy patron of the Academy, geologist and educator William Maclure, and his friends and fellow naturalists in that institution—particularly the conchologist and entomologist Thomas Say and Say's partner in the drug business John Speakman, the wandering botanist Rafinesque, the geologist Gerard Troost, and the artist Charles Lesueur—were captivated by Owen's visions of a new moral world. Along with hundreds of others, they were persuaded in January 1826 to make the move to the western Utopia.[8]

Phillips, despite his close association with the academicians in scientific and perhaps philosophical matters, remained behind, to emulate Owen's illustrious career in another aspect—cotton manufacturing. He was already in partnership in the cotton-weaving business in Holmesburg with his new brother-in-law, David Lewis, Jr., who had married Camilla Phillips.[9] In August 1825 the two men entered into contract with Henry Moore, the owner and manager of Old Sable Forge and Nail Works, along Chester Creek, agreeing to lease a cotton-weaving mill for ten years. Moore was to construct the mill at his own expense; it would be of stone, four stories high, 40 by 60 feet; and he was to erect tenements for the workers.[10] The mill would soon house two hundred power looms.

Phillips' motive in the move to Chester Creek was to recover the family fortunes. The firm of Phillips and Lovering had recently encountered financial trouble, and Phillips' father had endorsed his son's notes in the amount of $90,000; the father was eventually forced to pay when sometime in 1826 or 1827 the firm was unable to meet its obligations. The failure caused the entire family embarrassment; the elegant summer house, so fondly described in the memoirs of John's sister, had to be sold, and the family retired to the house on busy Front Street, only a couple of blocks from the office. Joseph, John's partner, would spend a couple of unhappy months in debtor's prison in Philadelphia.[11] At this juncture in family and partnership affairs, it was to be Lewis money and Phillips practical management that would, hopefully, recoup the loss. But to Phillips, the move out to Chester Creek was to be only a temporary exile; about 1835 he and his partner closed down operations at Old Sable Forge, removed the machinery, and set up again at Fairmount along the Schuylkill in Philadelphia.[12]

The Phillips family were principal members of Philadelphia society at a time when the city still claimed to be the greatest metropolis of the New World; they were a proud, closely knit group, who preserved family tradition. According to that tradition, the paternal grandfather, John Phillips, had settled in Philadelphia after profitably selling a cargo of slaves in the West Indies. With his profits he established a successful rope-making business and, when the Revolution came, was a staunch and prominent patriot. His son William, John's father, in later years recalled giving a drubbing to the son of General Howe when the British occupied the city and the commander chose to live in the Phillips house. William was successful in the French trade during the French Revolution; in later years, the family remained devoted admirers of Lafayette and of the refugee king, Joseph Bonaparte, who lived at that time near Philadelphia. The house at Front Street—a cavernous mansion, inhabited by the ghost of the first occupant, who fell down the grand circular stairwell in a moment of inebriation—was the scene of tea parties and balls in the early 1820's, when the Phillipses entertained their friends and their daughters made their débuts.[13]

A favored scion of distinguished stock, a youth who had never known anything but comfort and position until his recent débâcle, gangling, awkward young John S. Phillips—6 feet 3 inches tall, and thin—in 1825 was still searching for a career in which to make his mark.

John P. Crozer

Unlike William Martin and John S. Phillips, John Price Crozer was a man of little standing when he entered the cotton-manufacturing scene on Chester Creek in 1825. He came from a respectable but impecunious family of Delaware County farmers; he himself, a robustly built man of middle height, had worked the family farm unsuccessfully for ten years until 1820, when he lost the property. Since 1821 he had been struggling to maintain a sorry little cotton manufactory on Crum Creek, equipped with broken-down machines, and housed in an old mill rented from George G. Leiper, the man who had bought the farm and with whom he had briefly been partners in an unsuccessful merchant and sawmill enterprise. In 1825 at the age of thirty-two John P. Crozer had known little but hard work and failure.

But, despite the inadequacy of his machinery, Crozer had recently had some momentary success in cotton. Encouraged, in the autumn of 1824 with borrowed money he had bought the dilapidated old Mattson paper mill at West Branch, just across the forks from William Martin's place. And then, with homestead in possession, despite her father's objections he had in March 1825 married his sweetheart of five years, Sallie Knowles.

The paper mill and associated real estate cost $7,330 at sheriff's auction. Of this, $4,000 was accounted for by a mortgage (probably obtained with Leiper's help from the Delaware County National Bank, of which Leiper was a director); the balance was obtained in notes secured by his brother-in-law John Lewis's signature. (John Lewis, a prosperous gentleman farmer, had married Crozer's sister Elizabeth several years before and his mansion on the old Lewis estate at Castle Rock on the West Chester Pike had been a second home for John and his other sister Sarah.) Most of the 183 acres was rocky, wooded hillside. The mill, crowded between a steep slope and the stream, perpetually in shadow, was large enough for only two vats (for soaking the rags); nearby were a few tenements for workmen, and the two-story stone mansion house overlooking the mill, with four rooms on each floor, and various outbuildings: kitchen, barn, stable, wagon-and-gig house, smokehouse, stone springhouse, and a two-story tenant house with two rooms on each floor.

The newly married couple began housekeeping in mean circumstances. His wife brought only her clothing from home and presents from a few friends worth perhaps $50; Crozer had a few articles of furniture taken from his bachelor quarters, including bed, bedding, and some silver spoons. They spent $300 to furnish the house, with a rag carpet and windsor chairs and a mirror for the parlor, a second-hand mahogany dining table, an $8 bed, and a $5 breakfast table. They kept one female servant and boarded a number of mechanics and laborers. Mrs. Crozer did much of the housework herself while her husband worked at the mill every day till dark, and afterward at the house doing the mill's clerical and accounting work. As Crozer somewhat sharply noted in his autobiography, "The improvement in our style of living was very gradual; indeed scarcely perceptible for perhaps eight years of marriage."[14]

The objection of Sallie Crozer's father, James Knowles, was based on a parent's concern lest his daughter enter into lifelong contract with a poor man who, in Knowles's opinion, had little prospect for success. Mr. Knowles's unfavorable judgment of Crozer's prospects was not without grounds. Crozer himself, five years before, in a letter to Sallie had formally

JOHN PRICE CROZER (1793–1866).

relinquished his claims to her affection, not wishing to reduce his bride's standard of living to the level of a poor farmer. With heavy heart he had then set forth on the back of a faithful nag to seek his fortune, and a bride, in the western country. But after a tour of western Pennsylvania, Ohio, Indiana, Illinois, and Kentucky, he had returned.

The association between the Crozer and the Knowles families was an old one. Before the Revolution, Crozer's father had been a carpenter and builder; with the decline in construction brought on by the war, he had rented the Delaware County estate of the older James Knowles of Wilmington, a farm of over 150 acres. When Knowles died, it was Crozer—not the son John, Sallie's father—who was named executor, perhaps because Crozer was a principal creditor. It was no doubt in his capacity as executor that the elder Crozer collected a debt of nearly £300 on behalf of his wife's stepmother from the Knowles estate. Farming was then profitable and the elder Crozer was able to buy a farm of 173 acres in Springfield. And it was on this farm, in the fine old stone house where the celebrated painter Benjamin West had been born and first learned to draw, that John P. Crozer was born.

But the Crozer family fortunes declined drastically thereafter. The father was afflicted with rheumatoid arthritis and increasingly neglected the farm's management; the work was done by one tenant and by the sons, particularly John. The father did not believe in fertilizing the fields with either lime or manure and they grew less and less productive. At the last only the apple orchard and the small dairy of eight or nine cows were earning money. Crozer's mother was in poor health, with a sensitive stomach and a tendency to sick headaches which lasted for days. She suffered and moaned loudly and John Crozer recalled vividly, in later years, that he "would sit by the foot of the bed and weep, sometimes gushing tears and sobs, so as to excite my mother's sympathy amidst her own intense suffering."[15]

Trying to keep the farm going, and to care for an austere but increasingly inactive father and a sickly and complaining mother, Crozer as a boy had little opportunity for formal education, and attended school only up to his thirteenth year. His elder brother James, a weakly youth, was of little help on the farm and at the age of seventeen—when John was nine—he went to Philadelphia as an apprentice in a wholesale grocery house. When the father died in 1816, Crozer, now twenty-three, tried to keep the farm going. But it belonged equally to the three brothers and Crozer alone could not afford to buy it. So the family decided to sell. Even this move was a disaster. The brothers held out for $100 an acre; the only likely prospect was willing to pay $95, but they refused to lower the price, and he would not go higher. Next year (1820) they were forced to sell for $55 an acre.

In that year too another tragedy struck. The younger brother Samuel —the brilliant, talented youth of the family, who had studied medicine in Philadelphia, worked as a machinist, entertained his friends with experiments in chemistry and electricity, and studied night and day—was smitten by a religious concern. In short order he was sent by the American Colonization Society as its agent in the establishment of the first colony of repatriated slaves and free persons of color on the West Coast of Africa. The nation of Liberia was eventually to be the fruit of this venture. But young Samuel Crozer, then only twenty-three years old, died of a tropical fever, along with most of the expedition, a few weeks after arriving in Africa.

Thus to an anxious parent, the Crozers did not present the image of a family well prepared to care for a young bride of gentle birth. The couple at West Branch were not welcome at the Knowles mansion and her father did not visit them. Apart from some of Sallie's brothers and sisters, and his own sister Elizabeth and her husband John Lewis, the only friends whom the newlyweds had outside the community were—surprisingly—the family of George Gray Leiper. This was the man who had purchased the Crozer farm (at bargain price) to add to the Leiper holdings on Crum Creek, where lay the great quarries and mills of Leiperville and the family mansion "Lapidea." It was the same Leiper who had gone into partnership with Crozer in their short-lived saw- and gristmill enterprise, and it was from the same man that Crozer had rented the mill to house his rickety cotton machines. Something about Crozer must have inspired Leiper's interest, for he, his wife, and his sister Jane are remembered affectionately in Crozer's autobiography as having been among the few who stood up with them at their wedding at the Lewis house (none of the Knowleses was present). Jane Leiper's interest was particularly well remembered, as well it might be, for she was a celebrated beauty and the wife of fashionable lawyer John J. Kane of Philadelphia. Just last year she had achieved the social triumph of the season in Philadelphia, leading the ball, held in his honor, on the arm of the visiting Revolutionary hero, the Marquis de Lafayette.[16]

What Leiper, unlike Knowles, saw in Crozer was not the harassed scion of a falling family. Rather, he perceived certain moral qualities which Crozer brought into his business dealings. Poorly financed, ill-educated, and possessed of little mechanical aptitude, Crozer nevertheless (by his own confession) was a man of "untiring industry and indomitable perseverance."[17] He worked hard with his hands and in later years recalled the little, low-ceilinged card room "where I had spent so many weary and tedious hours at the cards—where I had toiled through long, anxious days and evenings—where I had figured and calculated until both mind and body were so absorbed that I could neither talk nor think of anything else."[18]

Furthermore, he insisted upon maintaining an "unwavering integrity, a firm intention to do justly to others." This, in business, meant, as he put it, that he was "careful never to make a promise to pay, without assurance in my own mind that I could comply." It was in this spirit that Crozer had acted in the summer of 1821, when he realized that the lumber business was failing, and had asked Leiper to buy him out ("I lose my summer's labor, and he to repay me, without interest, the capital I put in"). Leiper was impressed by the straightforward conduct of his partner, and the business was closed "in strict harmony and by mutual consent."[19]

Thus it must have been on the grounds of character alone (certainly not of wealth or industrial success, for the mill had barely started) and on George G. Leiper's recommendation, that in November 1825 the stockholders of the Bank of Delaware County (of which Leiper had been one of the founders, ten years before) elected John P. Crozer to the Board of Directors.[20]

John D. Carter

John D. Carter, the fourth of the cotton manufacturers who were at work on Chester Creek in 1825, was the only one of the group with extensive experience in cotton manufacturing. He was an Englishman who, having emigrated to America about 1812, shortly after his arrival took charge of an old paper mill owned by the Trimbles of Concord Township and converted it to a small cotton factory.[21] He had probably been a mill manager in England brought over for the purpose.

The Trimble cotton manufactory, as operated by Carter and his partner McKenzie, was short-lived. British manufacturers, in an almost-successful effort to destroy the American industry after the end of the war, dumped enormous quantities of cotton goods on the American auction market, driving prices for domestic products too low for any but the most resourceful to compete. Carter and McKenzie failed in 1816 in the general collapse of the American cotton-manufacturing business and their machinery was disposed of at sheriff's sale.[22]

But Carter was quickly able to recoup his fortunes. In the same year as the failure of the Trimble factory, he leased the substantial mill called Rokeby along the Brandywine,[23] and became one of the charter subscribers of the Brandywine Manufacturers' Sunday School, founded in November 1816.[24] Carter installed new spinning machinery and power looms. He was listed in the 1820 Census of Manufacturers as the proprietor of what, for that time and place, was a substantial establishment. His equipment consisted of about 2,300 spindles, 10 hand looms, and 20 power looms; he employed 79 men, women, and children, in both an old mill and a new stone one. Many, if not all, of the workers lived in the eleven tenant houses on the twenty-acre property.

In February 1822, however, Rokeby—along with all the other mills along the Brandywine—was seriously damaged by a sudden freshet. The river, choked with ice and melted snow, rose about 16 feet, and the machinery on the lower story was damaged.[25] Carter struggled on with the business but finally was forced to sell the machinery in August 1825.[26] It is a temptation to suggest that Phillips and Lewis bought Carter's power looms, for they signed their lease with Moore only five days before the publicly announced date of the Rokeby sale. But before selling Rokeby's machinery, the resourceful Mr. Carter had already acquired at sheriff's sale the Sharon Mill on nearby Squirrel Run.[27] He had difficulty, however, with his neighbor, E. I. du Pont, who had rented some of the tenant houses from the former owner to house his own workers, displaced by the freshet, and Carter was delayed in starting up his spindles.[28] Perhaps in response to the frustrations resulting from trying to re-establish the cotton business at Rokeby and Sharon after the flood, in February 1825 Carter bought the old copper-rolling mill on Chester Creek a mile below Old Sable Forge. This estate, of eight acres, with its stone mansion house, stone furnace, frame rolling mill, and thirteen tenement houses, he proceeded to convert to the cotton manufacture.[29]

A former owner of this mill was one John Hart;[30] and a Richard Hart, who was "engaged in the cotton spinning business," lived with the Carter family after the sale. The year ended for Carter and Hart on a melancholy note: the suicide of Mr. Hart. The *Upland Union*—the only local newspaper, published in Chester—rarely offered much in the way of local news. But on December 27 it published a sad account:

SUICIDE OF COTTON SPINNER

A melancholy event. On Thursday morning the 22d inst. a person by the name of *Richard Hart,* shot himself at the dwelling house of John D. Carter, Esq., in Middletown Township, Delaware County. What led to the cause of this rash deed, is not known. The following are a few of the particulars which have been stated to us. It appears that Mr. H. previous to taking his life, stated to the family that he was going to Baltimore, and between the hours of eight and nine o'clock a servant girl heard the report of a pistol, she went upstairs and found Mr. Hart, sitting on a chair and his clothes on fire, she asked him what was the matter, when he gave a groan and expired; she immediately went for Mr. Carter, and upon examination it was discovered that he had shot himself, the ball passing through his breast.

Mr. Hart had no family; he was engaged in the Cotton Spinning business and had become very much in debt.[31]

THE FIRST CASUALTIES AND REPLACEMENTS

During the six years from 1826 to 1831, the remainder of the principal manufacturers in the story, except for a few who appeared toward the end, entered the scene: Edward Darlington, lawyer and politician, who briefly owned Carter's Mill; the Garsed family, who manufactured power looms, and James Houghton, who had a weaving mill; Nathan Sellers, Peter Hill, and Daniel Lammot, who took over from William Martin at Lenni; and the Riddle brothers from Ireland. These industrial figures and their families and associates in politics and religion, and the Smith family, whom we shall look at separately, complete the cast of characters on the industrialists' side. Each of them will appear and reappear as the process of cultural transformation unfolds.

Edward Darlington

The first economic casualty among the early arrivals was the oft-bankrupted John D. Carter, whose manufactory did not long survive the suicide of his associate Richard Hart. In April 1826, the Farm Bank of Delaware issued a summons against Carter demanding payment of $250.76.[1] In June, the cotton mill was sold at sheriff's auction.[2] In August 1826, all his goods and chattels, lands and tenements, along the Brandywine, including such machinery at Rokeby as still remained unsold, were attached by the Bank of Wilmington and Brandywine, and he was summoned to appear before the Supreme Court at Newcastle.[3] On November 14, 1826, he published a notice in the *Upland Union,* notifying them that he had applied to the court of common pleas "for the benefit of the acts of assembly . . . for the relief of insolvent debtors." A hearing was appointed for him and his creditors.[4] The consequence of this unrelenting series of financial disasters was to be his departure from the county and the state. He ultimately came to Elkton, Maryland, where in 1860 he was still in the trade of millwright.[5]

The purchasers of Carter's Mill were Edward Darlington and Thomas Clyde of Chester. Darlington was a thirty-year-old practicing attorney and Thomas Clyde was the keeper of a general store on Market Square. Neither moved out of Chester. It is not unlikely, in fact, that they kept on John D. Carter as manager of the mill until they themselves sold the place in 1829.[6] Darlington and Clyde, however, are of importance in Chester Creek affairs because of the significant role Darlington was soon to play in the legal and political system of the county as a defender of law and order and a spokesman in Congress for Anti-Masonic and industrial interests.

Edward Darlington was born in 1795 and grew up on a farm that lies along the creek just about a mile above Lenni. (The farm is still there, and occupied by the Darlington family; a small railway station has been added, and a post office named Darling which mails out, every year, thousands of Valentine cards postmarked "Darling, Pa.") His father was a member of the large Darlington clan of Chester County, and both his father and mother were devout Quakers.[7] After he graduated from the West Chester Academy,[8] Darlington taught school for a time and read law with Samuel Edwards, a prominent attorney of Chester, with whom he practiced in the county seat after he was admitted to the bar in 1821 (the same year as William Martin).[9] He was appointed deputy district attorney in 1824 and immediately achieved acclaim for his successful prosecution of a case then arousing intense public indignation. As a result of his efforts, the murderer of a defenseless Quaker shopkeeper was publicly hanged in Chester.[10] A partnership with Samuel Edwards was a passport to success in Delaware County law practice. Edwards was a Democrat, a personal friend of James Buchanan, with whom he had served in Congress, and had been one of the committee appointed to receive General Lafayette in 1824; he was a director of the Bank of Delaware County and of the Delaware County Mutual Insurance Company.[11] As his protégé, Darlington prospered rapidly and soon was looking for investment opportunities (in 1825, for instance, he was advertising in the *Upland Union* that he had $2,500 to lend).[12]

Thomas Clyde in 1826 lived at his store in Chester with his family, having just moved there from Philadelphia. His wife Henrietta's sister Arabella had married Preston Eyre, also a prosperous shopkeeper of Chester. Young Darlington was then courting Arabella Eyre's daughter Ann and they were married in April of next year.[13] Thus Darlington's partner was the husband of Ann's maternal aunt and no doubt he was addressed as "Uncle" by them both.

Peter Hill and the Sellers Family

The next of the early cohort to fail was William Martin. Martin was vulnerable because he had lost his partners. He had been bought out of the commission merchant business about 1825 (probably when Martin went to

Harrisburg) by his uncle Peter Hill. Hill applied to his father-in-law, Nathan Sellers, for a loan with which to buy out Martin's share of their partnership. Nathan approved the idea, saying to his favorite son Coleman, "Peter wishes to pay off his partner and be done with him, and it appears to me the sooner the better, if he can be wise enough to avoid other flattering connections."[14] Perhaps the elderly, plainspoken engineer was not eager to see a son-in-law associated in business with an Episcopalian gentleman-barrister; the tone is reminiscent of Mrs. Lovering's prejudicial remarks about the Phillipses—"those fine folks." And in 1827 Martin in turn bought out his brother-in-law Joseph's half share of the paper and cotton manufactory at Lenni. Thus he was left financially isolated when the panic of 1829 ruined the cotton business.

His financial needs were extensive. It was a large estate which he had bought in 1823, embracing about 206 acres on the two sides of the creek, and improved—in addition to the two stone mills and a countinghouse—by three mansions, five stone tenements, five log tenements, a barn, and a stable; livestock included six horses, fifteen cows, and a dog. All this had cost him $17,800. In addition, he had bought cotton machinery worth about $11,000. In order to obtain these sums, he had borrowed at least $8,000 from his uncle Peter Hill and $9,000 from the Contributors to the Pennsylvania Hospital. The hospital secured the loan by a mortgage on the property and Martin agreed to endorse some of Hill's notes, in effect mortgaging the rest of the property. Martin did not pay off his loans; to the hospital he simply continued to pay the 6 percent annual interest, in semi-annual installments.

Martin's ability to pay even the smallest bills ended abruptly in January 1829 when the price of cotton fell; he was unable to pay even the semi-annual interest charges on the sum owed to the hospital fund. He had no other recourse than to appeal to the Delaware County Court, who put his properties in the hands of receivers.[15]

For a businessman in such a situation, there were now several possible outcomes. If he could convince the assignees, and through them his various creditors (including the assignees), that he would in a reasonable time be able to satisfy their claims, he might be able to recover. Creditors were apt to be sympathetic if prospects were good and their own creditors not pressing, for everyone might lose if the debtor's assets were disposed of at a public auction. All that might be required, in such a case, would be a sound reputation, patient creditors, and a little time—time for the market to go up, time for the debtor to collect the sums owed him, time for friends and relations to endorse his notes or lend him money. Martin estimated that the mill property was worth about $34,500 by now; $8,000 for the two mills, $11,000 for the cotton machinery, and the rest in houses and other improvements.

But time was what one of the creditors did not have. Peter Hill had borrowed money on the security of Martin's property. With the news of Martin's failure, Hill's creditors demanded their money. Hill, unable to pay, and unable to use Martin's credit, applied to the court and demanded that sufficient of "the goods and chattels, lands and tenements" of William Martin be sold to recover the loan. Martin prepared a list of his cotton machinery, worth by his estimate $11,050, and attempted to sell it privately, but was unable to do so.[16]

Hill now turned in desperation to his wife Hannah's family, the Sellers of Upper Darby, for aid. Coleman Sellers, as the acting head of the clan, helped Hill financially "as far as [he] could afford and prudence will allow." But Hill continued importunate, and Coleman now turned to his father, the aging and unwell Nathan Sellers, for advice on how to deal with their hapless in-law. The letter is revealing:

Dear father   Apr. 2. 1829—
In consequence of the failure of William Martin Hannah and Peter requested my advice, as it has got Peter into some difficulty. if I could have given assistance, I would not have suffered this present difficulty to have come before thee—I am not willing to make any important move without thy concurance—& have advised Peter to lay the case before thee before he proceeds any further. As far as I can understand the whole business, the difficulties arise from the want of him in getting in his debts —which are no doubt greatly abundant for the purpose, he has secured himself on Martin's property but cannot get the money until June—I have assisted them as far as I could afford, and prudence will allow and am not doubting in his ability to meet all his engagements as an honest man ought to do, I told them they should be content with a less and more sure business—which they have been indeavouring to do and I have every reason to believe they would have done but for this unfortunate failure of Martin's, with much sorrow for the necessity of given thee one moments uneasiness—

                              I remain affectionately thy Son
                              C Sellers
I am willing to do any thing for them that thee may sanction and advise[17]

This was not the first time that Peter Hill had given his father-in-law, Nathan Sellers, cause for alarm. Nathan had, in fact, refused to permit his daughter to marry Peter Hill when he first asked for her hand in 1822. Hill had been married before; both his wife and daughter had died, and Hill himself, failing in business, had been forced to sell his interest in his wife's home, in which he held a life estate. (His wife was a granddaughter of John Morton, a signer of the Declaration of Independence; the house is now a historic landmark.) The father based the refusal on his concern that Peter Hill's "circumstances" might not enable him to support her in comfort and happiness (or in what Hill, somewhat tartly, described as "the easy affluent Style she had been accustomed to").[18] But Hill continued to court Hannah, and in July 1824 he overcame parental objections and married her. Nathan Sellers, no doubt recalling his earlier worries, now seems to have advised Hill to press the matter in court, for on Hill's application the court ordered the sale of the Martin property by the sheriff at public auction, in July.

The records do not indicate how much the machinery, the two factories, and the two hundred-acre plantation brought; but it was not enough to save either William Martin or Peter Hill. Martin lost everything, even (temporarily) his son John, who went to live with his grandfather John F. Hill (the brother of Peter Hill) in Ridley Township, where the boy remained until years later. Martin and his wife and the younger children moved to Chester, where Joseph W. Smith also resided, and made a home in a house rented for $6 per month. There Martin resumed the practice of law.[19] The Martin family tradition, as recorded years later by Martin's son John, retained a permanent sense of bitterness at the duplicity which, Martin told his son, Peter Hill had shown in the matter. John's personal journal for 1856 charged that his father failed

by *endorsing* for his *intimate* friend Peter Hill, a brother of my decd. Grandfather Jno. F. Hill. Peter Hill was, and is a rascal. And though he pretended to have failed and thus obliged father to take up the paper endorsed by him which ruined him, Peter Hill had still money enough to purchase in his wife's name the Mills & property, when they were sold, Money enough in reality to pay his debts—and what is more he ownes them now and rents them to Robt. L. Martin Esq. agent of Gen. Robt Patterson, manufacturer of Philadelphia. There is an old Mortgage debt due on this place held by an Aunt of this Peter Hill's, and Judgment now over 22 years old entered on the Bond against father—it is in reality barred by the statute, but Peter Hill with that inherent rascality of his nature, asks Father to give him $200 to satisfy it, thus admitting he really owns the Mortgage on his own property. This prevented Father from taking the Title to the Land referred to in his own name—though in reality every just debt that he ever owed has been paid in full.

John F., William and George W. Hill, his brothers, also, endorsed Peter, and were all ruined by having to pay the notes they endorsed.[20]

Apparently the Martins were not aware of the financial involvement of the Sellers family in the affair. Nor was John Hill Martin correct in his claim that Peter Hill's brothers were all "ruined," for young Martin himself lived with and was supported by one of these brothers for about seven years, and, as we shall see, George W. Hill was a well-to-do landowner in Middletown already and so remained for many years.

Peter Hill himself did not long survive Martin financially; he failed in May 1829.[21] His estate too passed into receivership, one of the assignees being his wife's brother, Coleman Sellers.[22] Nathan Sellers in the meantime moved to protect his daughter Hannah. It was he (not Peter Hill, as Martin believed) who purchased the Martin estate. He then deeded it over to his son Coleman in trust for Hannah; and Coleman gave Peter Hill his power of attorney to lease the farm and mills. Nathan died in 1830, leaving Hannah $12,000 in cash and the Lenni property safely in trust. Hannah's mother died in 1832 and Coleman in 1834; thereafter the trustee was Peter's own brother, George W. Hill. Peter Hill (fortunately for Hannah, as we shall see) never did get his hands on the property, although he realized a profit from leasing it and a few years later moved onto it as a farmer.[23]

George W. Hill was a natural choice for trustee. He and Peter in 1827 had bought the old Sharpless estate, just downstream from Lenni, which contained a variety of mills and mill seats, as well as good farms and a country store. George bought out his brother in 1829, when Peter failed, and thereafter lived happily as landlord, storekeeper, and country gentleman. This meant that the Hills and the Sellers together now controlled the mill sites along the entire stretch of creek on the Middletown side, from Lenni to Rockdale, and much of the land on the Aston side as well.[24] They proceeded to settle cotton manufacturers upon their mill seats. The first of these was Daniel Lammot.

Daniel Lammot, Jr.

In May of 1831 Coleman Sellers leased to Daniel Lammot the Lenni Cotton Factory, "the large mansion house" (the old Lungren place) with its gardens and lot, the various tenements, stables, machine shop, and so forth immediately associated with the mill, occupying in all about ten acres. The Lammot family was already in residence at the mansion and Lammot had already purchased Martin's spinning machinery and was successfully

ANNA POTTS LAMMOT (1819–75) IN 1850.

DANIEL LAMMOT, JR. (1782–1877) IN 1829.

operating the mill. The five-year lease (at an annual rent of $1,200) thus was the formalization of an existing arrangement; indeed, the lease was so precise about the exact amount of water to be drawn from the race, and the improvements needed on the water wheel, that both Lammot and Sellers were evidently writing specifications based on a year or more of actual experience.[25]

Daniel Lammot, at the age of forty-nine, was an older man than the other Chester Creek manufacturers. Like Peter Hill, he had already had a career as a merchant, first in Baltimore and then in Philadelphia; and he too had been married before and had remarried. Before moving to Lenni he had lived in the Kensington district of Philadelphia with his new wife, their little boy Daniel (age seven), and the son and three daughters of the previous marriage.

Lammot was a man with interesting connections. He had been in earlier years a partner of Paul Beck, Jr. (until 1814, when Beck retired from the firm, leaving the business to Lammot),[26] and had married Beck's daughter Susanna. Beck was a shot manufacturer and one of the most eminent of the Philadelphia importing merchants; his principal rival was Stephen Girard. The son of a young apprentice of Nuremberg who had emigrated from Germany in 1752, Beck amassed a fortune estimated at his death in 1844 to be in the neighborhood of $1.25 million. In the course of this successful financial career, however, he devoted much of his time to the improvement of Philadelphia's port facilities, serving as Warden of the Port for many years, and he was active in many philanthropies and religious causes, particularly in the support of the Episcopal Church and of the American Sunday School Union.[27]

Lammot was also connected by marriage with the Du Pont family along the Brandywine nearby, his daughter Margaretta having married Alfred Victor du Pont, the son of Eleuthère Irénée du Pont, in 1824. Lammot had been friends with the E. I. du Ponts for many years. The firm of Beck and Lammot had traded with the Du Ponts ever since the early days of their powder business, and Lammot was accustomed to visiting on the Brandywine both on business and as a family friend. After his first wife died in 1817, he met his second wife, Anna Potts Smith, through the good offices of the Du Pont family. It seems, as one of the Du Pont ladies recalled years later, that Daniel Lammot was a "grand amateur" of the German language (perhaps having acquired that taste from his association with the Becks). Victorine Bauduy had a friend from schoolgirl days who, unlike Victorine (who "hated" German), "was very much occupied at this time in reading German literature." Victorine brought them together, and Daniel and Anna were married in 1819.[28]

Lammot failed in business in 1823. For the next four years he supported himself and his family entirely from the rent of a piece of property in Baltimore which his father had purchased thirty-eight years before and which had been the subject of litigation for the past twenty.[29] His mind was "beclouded and disturbed by anxieties"; no longer actively "engaged in business,"[30] he devoted his time to the affairs of the Swedenborgian Church in Philadelphia (of which he was one of the pillars) and to vainly forming "many projects of business"—none of which amounted to anything. But in March 1825 an opportunity came to hand. The plan was for Lammot to organize a company of Philadelphia financiers, who would buy the now empty cotton-spinning mill of his friend E. I. du Pont and install Lammot as partner and superintendent. He would move himself and family to the Brandywine.[31] After some months of awkward negotiating, the plan fell through; but in the course of it, Lammot immersed himself in conversation with cotton manufacturers, sought books on the subject, and indulged in calculations of profits to be gained. What seemed at first to be "a pleasing dream" gradually began to acquire the solid shape of possibility, although, as he cautiously admitted to Du Pont, "my dear Sir, is there anything easier than to make money—on paper." In April he confided that while the plan might fall through, "I have spent several weeks in reading and thinking of mill seats and spindles, so that in any event I shall be a gainer by the amount of knowledge acquired by my reading and thinking." In June he was still studying the cotton business: "since I first began to think seriously of becoming a manufacturer, I have permitted no day to escape without gaining some knowledge."

The scheme eventually came to nothing, for the gentlemen of Philadelphia would not make Du Pont an offer for his mill that was satisfactory in his or Lammot's eyes. But Lammot was not dismayed, writing cheerfully, "Well, now I am in the market—at the disposal of the highest bidder—ready for the newest fashion, and care not how soon the change takes place."[32]

It is not clear how the finances were arranged, but in March 1828 Lammot went into business as a cotton spinner with a Mr. Robinson (perhaps the Philadelphia Swedenborgian of that name) in Kensington, the industrial suburb of Philadelphia just north of the old city, along the Delaware River. Kensington was the site of several of the textile machinery manufacturers. The family moved out in April, complaining because Kensington was "neither in the city nor out of it."[33] Daniel Lammot, however, was just happy to "get into active life again."

The competition in cotton manufacturing was intense, and, he told his daughter, "I was compelled to improve my machinery, and from my limited capital these improvements were made out of the daily produce of the Mill." He had barely gotten under way, and had accumulated little in the way of profits, when a decline in the market for cotton yarn took place in the winter of 1828–29. He went down in the same general ruin as had William Martin and Peter Hill; in fact, he was involved in the collapse of Peter Hill. Writing to his daughter on the Brandywine at the end of May, he advised her, "It is true that Peter Hill has failed." He explained that this left him in an awkward situation. Hill had borrowed about $3,000 from him, giving notes in return; in order to get cash, Lammot had had the notes discounted. But now, if the purchasers of these notes were unable to collect from Hill when they shortly fell due, they could then come back to Lammot, "and I shall be protested." Hill told Lammot that he stood "on a different footing with him from all his other creditors; and if he get time to settle his affairs, all my notes shall be paid with punctuality, and if he be compelled to make an assignment, I shall be protected." As Lammot remarked, "such may be his feelings and wishes; but in the settlement of every estate difficulties arise which had not been dreamt of."

Lammot feared having to pay off Hill's notes at that moment because his cotton business was in trouble. As he explained to his daughter,

Now, there are so many Spinners embarrassed with old debts, who from the general stagnation in trade are compelled to sacrifice their yarn to meet their engagements, that to sell at the present prices would be certain ruin to me; but to stop the mill until an improvement in business takes place, renders it necessary that I should have the means to pay my notes issued for Cotton as they fall due between this and the month of August. I had a free and confidential communication with Mr DuPont, who agreed fully with my views, and with a degree of kindness and magnanimity altogether unexpected, he made an offer of assistance which I feel most sensibly. Your Grandfather [Paul Beck, Jr.], however, is persuaded that all manufacturers must fail, and therefore refuses to give any assistance. If I cannot compass my object, but be compelled to sell my Machinery at this time, it will not command the one third of its value—indeed I do not believe any one would give much more than the price of old iron for it—such is the depressed state of Cotton spinning at this time. If I could have foreseen the present state of things, you will readily believe I would not have engaged in manufacturing. But who foresaw it, or who ever witnessed such universal commercial & manufacturing distress? It is not confined to this Country, but, from intelligence, it appears to pervade Europe, especially England & France. Such is the case and *such* is my situation. *How* it may eventuate I know not; but of this I am confident that my present embarrassment and difficulty do not arise from idleness or neglect on my part. A few days will determine the business, and whatever may be the issue, I shall have the consolation of having used my best exertions.[34]

The catastrophe happened as feared. The machinery was sold; the cotton manufactory ended its operations; and the Lammots descended into genteel poverty. Minor embarrassments followed major ones. They had to discharge the cook; and the cook, in leaving, stole half of Mrs. Lammot's favorite printed recipes. Lammot searched desperately and unsuccessfully in Philadelphia for another position. As his wife Anna described the situation to Margaretta,

Your father is occupied every day in making interest for himself among the directors & stockholders of the American Fire Insurance Company in order to obtain the office of Secretary, which Jones vacates—The salary is 2500 dollars, with a house & fuel found—His chance is *among the best* He has been told this by the President Mr. Price—It is so long since we have known such *great prosperity* as this office would secure to us that we seem to distrust the possibility of realizing it. The prospect of it however occupies *all* your father's thoughts, sleeping & waking. I remember well when I used to think all these offices were held by persons certainly not above mediocrity. They are now sought after by some of the first men of our city. But the fashion of the times passeth away & those who were highest are now prostrated.[35]

With some grumbling, the family moved again in the summer or fall of 1829, this time to Lenni.[36] Evidently Peter Hill had lived up to his word by promptly paying off enough of what he owed him to enable Lammot to buy Martin's machinery. Mrs. Lammot, who was pregnant and expecting to deliver in about three weeks, was anxious to get the transfer over before her baby was born. She did not want to travel in the fall with a young infant, even if it were only "a cold ride from Chester." And besides, she wanted to see her husband settled. As she explained it to her daughter,

I think the change elligible & every way desirable as a matter of expediency—The first wish of my heart is to see your dear & excellent father relieved of part of that anxiety which is consuming the tranquility of his life—& if by the severest economy or any other deprivation so desirable an end can be obtained, the reward would be far beyond the self-denial it would require.[37]

Unfortunately the baby was stillborn, and by the time they arrived at Lenni, the roads were so bad as to preclude a visit from their friends either in Philadelphia or on the Brandywine.[38]

So Daniel Lammot, fully separated from the familiar merchant's world of Philadelphia, isolated with his family in the little mill town of Lenni, began his second try at success in cotton spinning.

Samuel and James Riddle

The next move in the Hill and Sellers mill-seat development venture was the construction, about 1830, of a new stone factory on the main branch of the creek, just opposite the forks, on the lands held in trust for Hannah Hill. It was named Parkmount, in honor of the Irish home of the tenants, Samuel and James Riddle, and was about a quarter of a mile downstream from Lammot's mill at Lenni.

The Riddle brothers were part of a family of Scots-Irish Presbyterians from the area of Belfast. The Riddles had established themselves on Irish soil in the seventeenth century, when one of their ancestors received substantial estates as a reward for his military services in the Irish wars. Samuel and James's father, Leander, had served in the British Navy and on his retirement had become a successful cotton manufacturer. The eldest son, Samuel, born in 1800, went to school until he was fourteen, acquiring in the process what was later described, somewhat doubtfully, as "a fair English education."[39] (Samuel Riddle was not remembered, in later years, for correctness of diction so much as for his skill as a raconteur.) After quitting school, he worked for nine years in a cotton factory in Belfast, there learning the practical details of cotton manufacture. His brother James, three years his junior, followed the same course.

In 1823 Samuel, seeking "a more profitable field," set sail for the United States as an emigrant on the bark *Hope.* The *Hope* sank on the shoals off Sable Island, the famous destroyer of ships, but crew and passengers evidently were able to get ashore, and Samuel even saved his sea chest. They were picked up after a three-month stay on the island and taken to Halifax, and from there to Philadelphia, where Samuel landed with his sea chest on his back and a total of $5 Spanish in his pocket. He walked to a boarding house and immediately obtained employment in a spinning mill in Manayunk, the cotton-manufacturing district at the Falls of Schuylkill. There he became rapidly sick with "fever and ague" and had to quit. He then moved to Pleasant Mills, New Jersey, where he was able to work steadily for three years.

Evidently his letters home to Ireland were encouraging, for in 1826 the

SAMUEL RIDDLE (1800–88).

rest of the family came over: his father Leander, then about sixty, and retired from business; his brother James; and his three sisters Elizabeth, Mary Ann, and Jane (the latter two were to marry cotton spinners Archibald McDowell and Hamilton Maxwell in the Riddles' employ). In 1827, with the money they had saved, Samuel and James rented a small mill owned by George G. Leiper of Avondale, in Delaware County, Pennsylvania, and installed 2 mules of 240 spindles each. (This may have been the same mill earlier vacated by John P. Crozer.) The family moved with them and probably they all worked in the mill, which employed only ten hands.[40] When the Riddles moved in 1831 to Parkmount Mill on Chester Creek, they left Archibald McDowell behind to manage the mill at Springfield.[41]

The Riddles borrowed some of the money to purchase machinery from their neighbor in Springfield G. B. Lownes. Their financial arrangement with Coleman Sellers was apparently the same as Daniel Lammot's. They paid (directly to Peter Hill) $1,000 annual rent for the mill and the associated houses, tenements, and other structures; and they were expected to reimburse Hill for the township real estate taxes on the estate. In addition, they did business with Peter Hill for a time in his capacity as a merchant, sending him boxes of shuttle cops (yarn wound on bobbins ready for use as filling by weavers) and accepting his notes in payment for yarn sold. These transactions ended in March 1834, when one of his notes, passed on by the Riddles for cash, was protested by the next holder.[42]

The final action of the Hill brothers in locating cotton manufactories on their lands was the leasing of the old mills at Penn's Grove to new and more efficient occupants. They had leased the old woolen factory to James Houghton about 1827 shortly after they purchased the Penn's Grove tract. Houghton converted it to a cotton-weaving mill. In 1830 or 1831 John Garsed, an English machinist and weaver lately of Yorkshire, and more recently from Philadelphia, leased the old fulling mill and converted it to a manufactory of power looms. With him was his twelve-year-old son Richard, who already had four years' experience working in a cotton mill in New Hope, Bucks County, and who was later to become one of the principal manufacturers of textile machinery in the United States.[43]

With these accessions, there were now six cotton factories in the Rockdale area. Beginning downstream, the owners and managers were: Edward Darlington and Thomas Clyde, owning the spinning mill at Knowlton, and probably employing John D. Carter as manager; John S. Phillips, operating a power-loom weaving mill at Rockdale on lands owned by Henry Moore; James Houghton and John Garsed at Penn's Grove, operating a power-loom weaving mill and a manufactory of power looms, on land owned by George W. Hill; Samuel and James Riddle, running a spinning mill at

Parkmount on the Hannah S. Hill estate; Daniel Lammot, running another spinning mill at Lenni, also on the Hannah S. Hill estate; and, on the southerly branch of the creek, the spinning mill at West Branch, owned and operated by John P. Crozer.

Now came the Smith family, catalysts of community improvement, to complete the roll of major industrialists.

THE SMITH FAMILY

Richard S. Smith was a well-established Philadelphia commission merchant when at forty-four he almost inadvertently acquired ownership of Old Sable Forge, including the nail mill and Phillips and Lewis' cotton factory. Smith and his partner Joseph Haven had acted as agents for Captain Moore in the sale of his nails and had loaned him a considerable sum of money when in 1832 he became financially embarrassed. Smith and Haven took a bill of sale to his property as security, "with the condition that we should re-convey the property to him when his indebtedness should be liquidated, giving us the right of absolute possession if the debt was not paid by a time fixed." Moore then leased his own mill back from Smith and Haven for seven years. But Moore failed in business the very next year, and in May 1833 Smith (Haven having died) called in the debt and became full owner.[1]

Smith continued to rent Phillips the weaving mill and the little stone farmhouse, with its attached greenhouse, where Phillips was now cultivating rare and exotic flowers. There was some social exchange between Phillips and the Smith family living in the big frame house on the road 50 feet below him, for both families moved in the same circles of Philadelphia society. But the association was not close, and amounted mostly to an exchange of Phillips' flowers for occasional dinners; of intellectual concourse there was little, for the Smiths, although well read and well informed, were extremely devout Episcopalians, and Phillips was indifferent to organized religion. Clementina Smith's friend Sophie du Pont went so far as to refer to him as an "open Infidel," whose mill was a morally unfit environment for young Christian female operatives.

Richard and Elizabeth

The Smiths had long been uncomfortable living in Philadelphia in the summer and, believing that children were especially likely to get sick in the city in warm weather, usually sent them to friends in the country. The summer and fall of 1832—the year of the great cholera epidemic—were particularly alarming: one of their younger daughters, Eleuthera (namesake of the family's friend on the Brandywine), fell gravely ill.[2] They already knew the Rockdale community, having spent a summer there a year or so before. Now, in the spring of 1833, probably motivated in part by the desire to find safe summer quarters in the country, and in part by the prospect of being near their friends the Lammots at Lenni and the Du Ponts on the Brandywine, Richard Smith moved his family and the servants out to Rockdale. They retained, of course, their residence at 1010 Clinton Street in Philadelphia, where the family generally resided in winter, the women enjoying the social season, music and opera, and church activities, and Mr. Smith, in addition to working his usual long hours at the office, indulging his hobby of painting in oils.

Richard S. Smith was a Philadelphia gentleman. His Swedish and English forebears had played a respectable role in the life of the city and had served with distinction in the armed forces during the Revolution. He himself had played a public part during the War of 1812. Having gone to Gothenburg in Sweden as supercargo on a merchant vessel, he found himself unexpectedly advised by a pilot-boat captain of the U.S. Congress's declaration of war against England. As he received the news before the officers of British cruisers lying in harbor heard it, he hastily assembled the captains of forty American merchant vessels lying in the roads and gave them the information. Thirty-two quickly ran up the river to safety under the guns of the Swedish fortress. For saving a part of the American merchant fleet the energetic young Smith was promptly appointed vice-consul, in which capacity he busied himself trying to save other vessels and providing for the sailors discharged from the blockaded ships.[3] After the war, being fluent in Swedish and French, and having friends in England and other parts of Europe, he was successful in the commission business and became acquainted with the Du Ponts—the firm of Smith and Haven acting as Philadelphia agent for the Brandywine powder makers. His brother Francis Gurney also served as an agent of the Du Ponts. In 1824 Richard entered the insurance business, and in 1830 he was elected one of the directors, and in 1837 the president, of the Union Mutual Insurance Company; by January 1833, he had become a director of the Bank of North America.[4]

While they lived in Philadelphia, the Smiths were family friends with the Lammots. The Smith women were particularly fond of Anna, the second Mrs. Lammot, and exchanged long visits with her; they lamented the distance out to Kensington when the Lammots moved there in 1827 during Daniel Lammot's first, ill-fated foray into cotton manufacturing. They were also very good friends of the family of E. I. du Pont, with whom Smith was constantly involved in business matters. Smith greatly respected the elderly powder manufacturer and declared to Sophie, years later after her father's death, "I never loved a friend more."[5] He delighted in the stories E. I. du Pont told of his adventures during the French Revolution, particularly of the nights he spent in hiding, soaked with rain and looking "like a drowned chicken," in the Bois de Boulogne "during Robespierre's dreadful reign."[6] Members of the two families regularly exchanged house visits. And Du Pont's widowed daughter Victorine Bauduy, who managed her father's house after her mother's death, was on intimate terms with Elizabeth Smith, who referred to theirs as a "friendship which has now become necessary to my happiness."[7]

At the time of his purchase of the Rockdale property, Smith was a church-going man but not yet enthusiastic in his religious sentiments. He had been brought up in a religious way by a widowed father, who had promised his wife on her deathbed to send the children to church twice every Sunday. On his return from Sweden in 1813 he was confirmed and thereafter dutifully attended St. Peter's Episcopal Church in Philadelphia.[8] But it was the women of the family who were most warmly interested in religion. By 1829 Clementina, only fifteen years old, was teaching Sunday School at St. Peter's in the winter and at the Brandywine Manufacturers' Sunday School during her visits with the Du Ponts in the summer.[9] And it appears that the establishment of the church at Rockdale "was in large measure due to the active and untiring efforts of Mrs. Smith."[10]

Elizabeth Beach, who had married Richard Smith in 1813, had been born on Cape Ann and brought up in a palatial old house in Gloucester, Massachusetts. After her marriage she enjoyed frequent summer vacations in the northern resort. On these occasions she visited busily with old friends and relations, saw to it that the children learned to swim in the chilly water off Gloucester, and kept up her correspondence with Victorine. From wherever she was, throughout the year, she sent her friend news of illnesses and family accidents, plied her with recipes for pumpkin pudding and children's cough syrup (a heroic mixture, half paregoric, one-quarter antimony wine, and one-quarter nitre), and passed on gossip about the Lammots and other mutual friends. But mixed with the domestic information were religious bulletins, such as the latest word on the Episcopal convention in Philadelphia, and remarks about her aspirations for Clementina's spiritual growth ("pray heaven to continue her in the paths of religion and virtue"). Indeed, she was perhaps a bit possessive of Clementina's morality, reporting from New York, where they had gone for a winter round of parties, that her daughter was being very good, avoiding gaiety and display. Clementina had an admirer, a gentleman from Marseilles, with whom she talked French, but, reported her mother proudly, she was "indifferent to all his politeness."11

On their arrival in Rockdale in the summer of 1833, Elizabeth Smith and her daughter Clementina urged the paterfamilias to commence a Sunday School. As he described the event later on:

> . . . the nearest Episcopal church being at Concord, five miles distant, we, when the weather permitted, rode over there. Being frequently prevented by the weather, we were many Sundays deprived of usual public worship, and my wife and daughter, having been previously connected with the Sunday-school at St. Peter's, Philadelphia, proposed to me to open a Sunday-school in the vacant room of a factory building on my property. This was commenced with an attendance of twenty children, which soon increased to one hundred.12

The building chosen was actually Moore's old nail mill, now vacant, and the Sunday School met on the upper floor, sitting on benches bought at an auction. The organization of the school was simple: Richard S. Smith served as superintendent, and his wife and daughters were the teachers; the children were largely from the families of mill operatives in the district. The Smiths also wanted formal Episcopal church services in addition to the Sunday School, and they persuaded the rector of St. Paul's—the venerable Protestant Episcopal church in Chester—who was also the lay preacher at the Baptist church in Chester, to officiate occasionally. These services in the nail mill were so well attended that in the summer of 1834 the bishop licensed a young divinity student to serve as lay reader to the congregation. Several Philadelphia clergymen also came out from time to time to conduct services. By the fall of 1834, when the Sunday School had "the names of 140 children . . . inscribed on its roll-book," and the Sunday services were being regularly attended, "it finally became evident that the Church had many friends in the neighborhood and many anxious desires and prayers were [being] offered for her prosperity and establishment therein." The time had come to attempt the regular organization of the congregation.13 Later we shall look closely into the growth of Calvary Church and its evangelical role in the Rockdale district.

Clementina and Sophie

The Smiths were actively encouraged in their missionary course by the Du Pont women, and particularly by Sophie, Eleuthera, and Victorine. Clementina and Sophie, of course, were best friends. When Sophie in the summer of 1833, just after the Smiths moved out to Rockdale, married a

SOPHIE DU PONT (1810–88) IN 1831.

naval officer, her cousin Samuel Francis (Frank) from across the creek, she confessed to her dear Clemma that she had committed "treason against the Sisterhood."[14] But the marriage barely interrupted her intimacy with Clementina and actually soon was thrusting the two women closer together. For Sophie discovered herself to be in a surprisingly difficult marital situation and Clemma was her confidante.

Sophie and her husband had known and liked each other from childhood, having been brought up in the nearby mansions of their fathers, the brothers Eleuthère and Victor du Pont. Their courtship was romantic, with Sophie shyly recording in her diary a growing attachment to her handsome and amiable cousin. Usually she wrote in plain English, but on these occasions she used a simple cypher to conceal her sentiments from prying eyes. In November, after five months of marriage, she and her husband moved the few hundred yards across the creek to his family home at Louviers; the separation from Eleutherian Mills and her family there filled her with dread beforehand and regret afterward, and reminded her of the death of her mother five years before (and perhaps also of her homesickness when she was sent to school in Philadelphia ten years before, a homesickness so acute she was brought back to be educated at home). She herself expressed some bewilderment at the intensity of her distress. "Who could understand," she wrote in her diary at the time, "that my heart would be so wrung at going so little a way from my old home, & going too with such a husband, & such kind relations?"[15] A month later she was suffering such severe chest pain that she was unable to write. By February, now pregnant, she was feeling debilitated. In March she took to her bed, suffering from pain and weakness in her back, and eventually the child she carried was aborted or born dead.[16]

Sophie remained virtually bedridden, except for occasional remissions, for the next fifteen years. Her illness was diagnosed and rediagnosed as a "disease of the spine." The endless blisterings and cuppings did little to improve her condition. She became addicted to morphine, which she took regularly in order to sleep, and suffered from a generalized depression (which in later years she attributed to the fact that she "had been taking morphine a great deal & my nervous system, was greatly affected by it").[17] This depression manifested itself in part in worrying guiltily over the "wasted years" during which she should have been performing useful Christian service to others. In 1845, after a discouraging medical consultation which included a prescription of "abstinence from exercise," she concluded, "I may consider myself an invalid for life . . . unless God gives me aid I know not how to bear the burthen of life—pray for me—it is all any of my friends can now do for me."[18]

SOPHIE DU PONT CIRCA 1850.

The "contention between languor of body & energy of spirit" which Sophie recognized within herself seems to have been exacerbated at the times when she was worrying about her husband Frank's imminent departure on a new voyage. He was a naval officer when she married him, but was not ordered to sea until three years later. In the meantime she lived in dread of his leaving. In May 1834, only a couple of months after she had taken to her bed, she wrote to her friend:

> Dearest Clementina, never marry a Navy officer! That is my advice to you, when you leave the Society of *Tabbies*—'Tis too dreadful to have to look forward to such long separations from one's nearest & dearest friend—[19]

She had been haunted by the thought that their first parting would be final (since the age of fourteen she had had a superstitious presentiment that she would die in 1838). Her husband's absences were, indeed, prolonged ones, and some of her acquaintances thought he should resign his commission for the sake of Sophie's health. His sea duty ran on a roughly two-year cycle, with a tour of a year to eighteen months at sea alternating with six months to a year at home. When Frank was home he was kindness itself, carrying his wife up and down stairs in his arms, on and off boats, and even into the ocean at Cape May for "sea bathing." But he was ambitious for advancement and could not linger with his wife too long. Six months after his return from his first voyage, despite his wife's presentiments of doom (or perhaps because of them), he himself applied to the department for orders to sea. Sophie deeply resented these departures and on one occasion exclaimed to Clementina, in a martyred tone, "I do not repine—I acquiesce—it is all right—but I do feel it. . . ."[20]

Actually, a few years after this, Sophie's health improved substantially and by 1850 she was again able to walk, to travel, and to visit Clementina and her other friends in Rockdale and Philadelphia, sometimes with her husband and sometimes not. She never again bore a child, however, and one may look in vain in her diary and correspondence of later years for any expression of surprise or dismay at her failure to give birth. It is as if, until some moment of acceptance of her fate, a taut body was rendered incapable of marital happiness, housewifery, and motherhood under conditions of repeated and prolonged abandonment by her beloved friend. And even after the body relaxed and the pain eased, the scars of the ordeal remained in the contours of a grim and ravaged countenance.

Clementina avoided the marital trap into which Sophie had fallen. Her sustained correspondence with Sophie began in 1834, after her friend's marriage, when she herself was nineteen years old. She had already made her appearance in society, at balls and teas and public entertainments in Philadelphia, New York, and Boston, and would continue to grace the winter social season for many years. She was used to the attentions of young swains but was already expressing disillusionment with the male part of mankind. In her first letter of the year 1834, she exclaimed: "I must really say I have given up all faith in friendships between gentlemen and ladies."[21] Although she continued to be courted by hopeful suitors for several years more, she paid little attention to their addresses. A few years later, she was claiming to have "a reputation as a member" of the society of "old maids," and by 1841—at twenty-seven—she was able to assure Sophie that she was firmly committed to a life of single blessedness.

> I think I was never so safe in my life, as I am now, against all invasion. I think the *territory* proof against every attack (were there any) and [you] may believe me when I tell you, your friend *Clementina Smith* will to all appearances be *always* the same C.B.S.[22]

Clementina was correct in her opinion of herself: she never married.

Her letters do not reveal from what personal experiences and private observations Clementina derived her set aversion to marriage. But her choice of spinsterhood was explained publicly by the readily stated conviction that the marital state was, for the wife, a condition of bondage, and that only as a single woman could she have the independence she wanted. Her comments to Sophie were very blunt:

> Ah Sophy well may you mourn your dependence and sigh for the unshaded state of single blessedness, when even health is so materially influenced by it. You are among the number of those infatuated beings however, who though they talk very reasonably upon those matters, would not for the world give up that state of bondage to which they have subjected themselves.[23]

She complained of her own "housewifery" in her parents' home as drudgery which interfered with reading, and labeled the ladylike activity of mantua-making a "penance" for previous enjoyments. Not for her was Sophie's "perfect resignation to circumstances." While Sophie dramatized her fate by suffering in eloquent silence, Clementina took care to protect herself by busy, even aggressive, commitment to Sunday School and missionary society duties.

There were, to be sure, disadvantages even in this course. She was subject, as long as she resided in their home, to the beck and call of both her parents. She was not allowed to visit Sophie whenever she liked but only when the complex schedule of the Smith household permitted it. Their plans had to be delayed time and again because of the necessities of waiting until after a parental vacation, or a fit of house-cleaning, or the completion of one of the semi-annual migrations between Philadelphia and Rockdale, or the need to nurse ailing relatives and to mind infant nephews and nieces, or because her parents were worried about *her* health. The frequency of these restrictions led her to occasional outbursts. Once, when she had been refused permission to visit the Brandywine because she had a cough, she complained: "indeed dearest if I could do just as I pleased, I should not be long away from you, but you see that even in a state of single *blessedness* when ladies are supposed to have their own way they are not always without restraint."[24] Her disillusionment with spinsterhood once—but only once—made her question the wisdom of her choice: "Spinsters are no more independent, than married people, if they are as much so indeed, I cannot pretend to say, what may be the effects of such a conclusion."[25]

Clementina, like the somewhat older Anna Lammot, whom she regarded as "fascinating," wanted to involve herself somehow in the real affairs of a real world. She regretted from time to time the triviality of her efforts and felt that she was not "acting a part in the busy scene" and could only "peep at the world from out the loop hole of retreat."[26] One of the women whom she knew in the city, single like herself, desired to engage in the work of foreign missions on her own, without first marrying a male missionary; Clementina encouraged her and tried to arrange for her training. But her greatest admiration was reserved for a lady missionary who had been "rescued" from her brutal husband in China by Bishop Boone and his wife, and sent back home, where she resumed her maiden name. Miss Harries (the ex-Mrs. Innes), who had a school in New York and did "missionary work" in the city, spoke before missionary groups about her adventures. Clementina heard her, met her, and was deeply impressed. "She is I think one of the most wonderful persons I ever met," she confided to Sophie.[27]

Sophie was the central person in Clementina's life; and it would be difficult to say whether her husband Frank or her friend Clemma was more important to Sophie. Theirs was a special friendship, like those of other women in the sisterhood. Friendship was a relationship that might, as Clementina observed, be difficult to maintain between men and women; but in this age of romanticism, friendships between women and women, and men and men, were perhaps more freely contracted than at later times in American history. These were intense relationships, entitling the partners to exchange intimate secrets in an atmosphere of trust and the expectation of moral support. The partners thus entered into an almost romantic commingling of identities; indeed, among the women, the language of romance was used freely and a considerable degree of physical intimacy—embracing, kissing, sharing the same bed—was regarded as normal. In the case of women, such unions were frankly considered to compete with marriage for the partners' time, and although marital duties came first, there was recognition of the legitimacy of jealousy.

Yet there is little to suggest, in most of these friendships, that the partners engaged in any form of overt, mutually recognized, sexual congress. It is as if the friendships satisfied another need, at least among the managerial class, a need no other institution was prepared adequately to meet. To be sure, society allowed male-female friendship—but, with rare exceptions, only in the context of legitimate and fulfilled, or soon to be fulfilled, sexuality (i.e., in the affianced and marital relationship). In the correspondence and diaries of the sisterhood, husbands and wives referred to each other as friends (Sophie dubbed her husband "my dearest friend on earth"); it would seem that they did, in fact, do their best to treat each other in the warm, intimate, understanding, and respectful fashion that could properly be called friendship.

Friendship between men and women was manifestly dangerous outside courtship and marriage because it might lead to sexual relations (although marriage itself did not necessarily lead to perfect friendship). But, although it might be possible to restrict sexuality to monogamy or even deny it altogether, the need for friendship was less easily confined. This need the same-sex friendship was able to satisfy. Friendships between persons of the same sex could be cultivated with such intensity precisely because they were formally defined as (and most probably were) sexually safe. Female partners might thus innocently engage in the most extravagantly romantic rhetoric with each other, exchange intimate communications denied to their spouses, offer sonnets to each other celebrating their love, and freely fondle and caress one another both privately and in public, without either they or their friends being allowed to question the propriety of the relationship.

From the beginning of their correspondence, while they were teen-age summer visitors at each other's house, Clementina and Sophie addressed one another in terms of dearest friendship, and over the years the relationship became steadily more close. By 1835—after Sophie's marriage and the beginning of her illness—Clementina was dreaming of Sophie. Thereafter they included each other in their dreams with fair regularity and of course confided the contents to one another. At least by 1837 they were sufficiently close for Clemma to tease her friend by reporting that she had received three letters from a young gentleman in New York. "Are you not alarmed?" she inquired playfully, but quickly added the reassurance that "these were letters of business."[28] Sophie did in fact worry lest Clementina marry and be thereafter "still more beyond my reach." As Sophie confessed in her diary, a few months later,

> We took a short walk in the wood together on Friday—when we returned, she played for me & sung, "Hail to the Lord's annointed." When I listen to her singing hymns; when I hear her converse, to look on her angelic countenance, I feel an admiration I cannot express. Pure & lovely being! & might *I* too, *once,* have become even such?[29]

The friendship had reached its high plateau of intimacy by the beginning of 1844, when Clementina, alluding to herself and Sophie, wrote of "the hope of an eternal union with the one ['you love' crossed out] dearest to you on earth," and urged Sophie to visit Clinton Street so that "we shall be able to be together in a room in the second story." At the end of that summer of 1844, Clementina spent some time with her friend on the Brandywine. On her return to Philadelphia she wrote Sophie a glowing letter that, in its easy transitions from romantic sentiment to religious piety to shared plans to care in a quasi-maternal way for young children of friends and relatives to news of housekeeping, testifies clearly to Clementina's sense of the fitness of their friendship in the context of church and home. The letter began:

> Phil^a September 18th /44
>
> My dearest Sophie
> This day I must tell thee how many thoughts I have of thee though ever so briefly—May it be a day of blessing to your heart, beloved, and the beginning of increased and holy hopes, and joys, for the coming year. It is a day of rejoicing to my heart that God has *so blessed me,* with so precious a treasure in giving me your love and affection—so long tried and enduring—May this love and affection be more & more sanctified dearest Sophie, until the imperfect sympathy of earth shall be exchanged for heavenly intercourse—If there is one wish I would offer more fervently than another dear Sophie for your happiness it is that this year might realise to you the wish of your heart for your Husband. How much I wished for you both on Sunday that you could have listened with me to our good Bishop in the morn^g at St Andrews afternoon at old Trinity The morn^g sermon on the text "what shall it profit a man if he gain the whole world" &c in the afternoon "those who by patient contuance in well doing obtain glory, honour, immortality & eternal life"—The morn^g sermon was to unconverted, afternoon more especially to careless professors—I wish I c^d say all I w^d of them. . . .[30]

Clementina carried her identification with Sophie's household so far that, in a sense, she identified with Sophie's marriage. She reported to her friend that she dreamed of her husband, then at sea ("he was before me so vividly & looking so well"). And, expecting Frank's imminent return a few months later, she wrote that when she thought of them together, "in that dear home, a sort of ecstasy takes possession of me in the very anticipation."[31]

The substance of their friendship was communication: they found that they could talk to each other face to face, and write to each other, and even think themselves into a state of spiritual communion when apart. Physical closeness was important because it made the communication that much more intimate. Thus Clemma could say that she wished for "a few days with you, in comfortable converse beside that *dear brown sofa—dear,* for the sake of its occupant."[32] And Sophie could make plans for a joint visit with Clemma at her sister Eleuthera's house, where "I will have a double bed in my room there so that we can occupy it together & have some cozey talks."[33] What they talked about, of course, apart from their friendship itself, was mostly conventional things (insofar as the correspondence reveals it), mainly religion, books, parties and vacations, births, marriages, illnesses, and deaths among family and friends, fancy needlework, and household chores. But it was not so much the overt informational content that mattered. The recognition of the shared attitudes, the mutual endorsement of identities, the knowledge of the other's empathy for one's own pleasures and pains were the important parts of these communications. As a result, neither could really feel alone in the world.

THE MECHANICAL KNOWLEDGE
OF THE INDUSTRIALISTS

In the early years, while their women dealt in spiritual matters, the men thought about machinery and sought out knowledgeable friends. There were important differences in the levels of mechanical information wanted by different kinds of management specialists. The mill owner and the manufacturer needed information at a relatively general level; the technical supervisor in the mill itself needed more precise data. None required the intimate knowledge of the mechanic, machinist, inventor, and practical engineer, who had to have extremely detailed tactile and visual experience, only to be acquired by working in a machine shop.

The Owner and Manufacturer:
Books, Articles, Conversation, and Travel

Many men went into the cotton manufacture after failing in another line
of work or after coming into the ownership of an unfamiliar enterprise
through the accidents of inheritance and financial settlement, without any
prior knowledge or experience. Daniel Lammot is the best example. In an
earlier section we have seen how, after he decided in 1825 to go into cotton
spinning, he began a desperate search for information. A similar problem
beset John P. Crozer, who had committed himself to the cotton manufacture in 1821 in an almost equally offhanded way ("I was anxious to do
something, and my mind took hold of cotton spinning"). Technical ignorance nearly ruined Crozer, for he depended on others who had little more
knowledge than he; "it seems to me," he observed years later,

almost a miracle that I was not crushed at the very outset. It was difficult
to get any one that understood the business. There were but few in this
country, at that time, who did understand it. I engaged a man named
Johnson, who came well recommended, but, though industrious and
honest, was incompetent. My machinery . . . was very inferior; and I an
entire novice; and, what made the matter worse, yarns had become plenty
in the market, and rather unsaleable, unless of very good quality. "Fearful odds" were against my success, and I now became distressingly anxious. My little all was involved, and a great deal of my brother-in-law's
money. I early made up my mind that he should be protected, and every
one else; that when I believed my own capital was sunk, I would go no
farther; and I felt that impending ruin hung over me. My yarns would
not command the full market price, while they cost me more to produce
them than if the machinery had been of better construction. My mind was
so thoroughly engrossed that for months and years no other subject than
my business could engage or at least hold my attention. I feel, in review,
that this was very sinful.[1]

What both men needed at the outset was printed literature, but there
was very little available in 1821 and that little was inadequate. Lammot's
principal reliance (in 1825) was on an English work, published in 1816, by
a mechanician named John Sutcliffe. Sutcliffe was a millwright, a draftsman,
a builder of cotton mills, a designer of atmospheric engines, and a hydraulic
engineer. To his *Treatise on Canals and Reservoirs* Sutcliffe had added two
sections containing "Instructions for Designing and Building a Corn Mill"
and "Observations on the best Mode of Carding, Roving, Drawing, and

Spinning, all Kinds of Cotton Twist." The account of cotton manufacture occupied about 120 pages, was not illustrated, and was less a straightforward description of the machinery and its operation than a miscellany of administrative advice to a person who already understood the cards, roving frames, throstles, and mules themselves.[2]

Also available to Lammot (and to Crozer) was Abraham Rees's excellent and authoritative *Cyclopaedia,* published in London from 1802 to 1820 and republished in Philadelphia from 1810 to 1822 in forty-one volumes. The fifteen-page article on "Manufacture of Cotton" first appeared in 1812. It concentrated, however, largely on the history and economics of the industry; the actual descriptions of the several processes took up altogether only a page and a half and thus were necessarily too brief to do much more than introduce the subject. The *Cyclopaedia* also contained an eighteen-page technical article on the varieties of cotton and a history of its production; a thirty-page article on the mechanical principles involved in machinery of various kinds; and fourteen plates of excellent engravings of the machinery used in cotton manufacture, including cards, draw frames, roving cam frames, the double speeder, water-spinning frame, throstle, mule, rolling, doubling, and twisting machines, and a calico-printing machine.[3] In 1823 Richard Guest's *Compendious History of the Cotton-Manufacture* appeared in England, with its engravings (later to become famous) of eighteenth-century spinning machinery of Hargreave's, Arkwright's, and Crompton's era; Baines's history of the industry, with good illustrations of newer machinery, appeared in 1835.[4] And in 1825 John Nicholson's *Operative Mechanic and British Machinist* appeared in London; the Carey and Lea edition came out in Philadelphia in 1826. It contained a clear and concise eleven-page outline of the machine processes of cotton manufacturing, along with several excellent schematic drawings.[5] But it appeared too late to give initial guidance to either Lammot or Crozer.

The situation began to improve in the 1830's, with the anonymous publication in Glasgow of *The Theory and Practice of Cotton Spinning: or the Carding and Spinning Master's Assistant.* The first edition was published in 1832; a second edition appeared the following year, and included an account of Roberts' self-actor. The author was James Montgomery, an experienced mill manager who had not only visited many English mills but also mills in America. In his preface, he noted that

it is much to be regretted, that nothing has ever appeared on the art of cotton spinning, fitted to assist the master, manager, or artisan, in acquiring a correct and systematical knowledge of the *real* principles of the business. Almost every other important art or manufacture has its periodi-

cal, or other publication, wherein its principles are elucidated, its improvements recorded, and its difficulties explained, and to which the
artisan can apply in cases of difficulty; but the manager of a Cotton
Spinning Factory can only acquire a proper knowledge of his business,
by long experience and application in the practical department of the
manufacture, and it will depend upon the situation in which he is placed,
and the advantages he enjoys, if he ever obtain that correct knowledge
of all its details, which is essentially necessary to render him fully qualified
for managing a large establishment with satisfaction or profit to the
proprietors. Hence a treatise on this subject, in which the principles of
the art may be *unfolded,* and its details *explained* and *exemplified,* has long
been felt and acknowledged as a desideratum by the trade; to supply
which the following treatise is respectfully presented to their notice.[6]

Montgomery presented both "theory and practice combined," in a
systematic, well-illustrated work of 332 pages and 10 plates. He described
each machine, explaining its principles of operation and its function in the
total process; gave instructions on how to adjust it; and demonstrated how
to perform "the various Calculations connected with the different departments of Cotton Spinning." In 1840 Scott's *Practical Cotton Spinner and
Manufacturer* appeared; Joseph Bancroft on the Brandywine acquired a
copy of the English edition. This work went farther than Montgomery in
giving the detailed mathematical instructions of the sort Bancroft had hitherto kept in his manuscript journals. A Philadelphia edition appeared in
1851, edited by Oliver Byrne, with new material on American machines.[7]
Montgomery, Scott, and the incomparably lucid science writer Andrew Ure
with his *Philosophy of Manufactures,*[8] dominated the scene until the 1850's,
when American managers began to publish too, with Connecticut's Daniel
Snell putting out *The Manager's Assistant* in 1850 and Boston's Robert Baird
publishing (posthumously) *The American Cotton Spinner* in 1851.[9] Comparable manuals by various writers, usually experienced managers, continued to
appear year after year thereafter.

The literature available to the aspiring business manager on how to
operate a machine shop in connection with his mill was even less adequate.
The earliest general publication was the article published in Rees's *Cyclopaedia* in London in 1819, entitled "Manufacture of Ships' Blocks." It
described in some detail the system of advanced woodworking machinery
devised by Sir Samuel Bentham and Marc Isambard Brunel to manufacture
the hundred thousand pulley blocks required by the Royal Navy each year.
These machines, installed by 1808, were regarded as one of the "mechanical marvels of the time"; some of them were still in use 145 years later![10]

But the *Cyclopaedia*'s account did not address itself to the metalworking tools. In 1826 Nicholson's *Operative Mechanic and British Machinist* devoted 19 pages out of 350 to metalworking machine tools, including an account of the lathes built by the Sellers' old friends in Philadelphia, Isaiah Lukens and William Mason.[11] Not until 1841 did a general account of metalworking machine tools appear in England in the third, revised edition of Buchanan's *Practical Essays on Mill-Work and other Machinery.*[12] In the 1850's the American Oliver Byrne published a series of handbooks for the machinist and mechanic; as with the technical literature on cotton machinery, the American machine tool industry seems to have felt itself to be on a par with England's in the sixth decade of the nineteenth century.[13]

The Managers: Experience in England

At the beginning, Daniel Lammot sought an experienced technical manager for the projected mill on the Brandywine. Writing to E. I. du Pont in 1825, he touted two candidates: a "Mr. Sutton, the young man on whose judgment Mr. Beck relies," who was reputed to be well qualified as to "talents, management and economy"; and "young Bancroft," newly arrived from England and not yet established in his own mill on the Brandywine.[14] (It was this same Joseph Bancroft who eventually acquired the mill property for which Lammot was scheming.) And Crozer likewise had to turn to a supposed practical expert, the incompetent Mr. Johnson, for assistance in the technical management of his early venture in 1821. The Riddles, the Garseds, and John D. Carter—all of them British-born and bred up in cotton mills—could manage their own mills. But the less experienced Chester Creek manufacturers—Phillips, Crozer, Martin, Lammot, Darlington, and the rest—were radically dependent at the outset upon technical managers.

The manager of a cotton mill trained and supervised workers in the practical operation of their machines; he knew how to set up the machines, that is, adjust the various settings in order to have the machines produce the right weight and dimensions of lap, sliver, roving, yarn, and cloth; and he could diagnose mechanical trouble and send for the mechanic when necessary. These skills could not be acquired solely by reading even an excellent manual; they required experience in actually operating and setting the machines, experience acquired over the course of years in a number of different mills. In the early 1820's, such experience could be had in only a few places in America; for the most part, at this date, such men had to come from England. In 1821, in Delaware County, the only mill mentioned by Crozer as still operating at a profit was managed by Hugh Wagstaff—

"a practical cotton spinner from England."[15] It was a small mill, along Ridley Creek, with only 1,272 spindles (600 throstle and 672 mule) and 16 power looms; it employed 13 men, 6 women, and 40 boys and girls. Perhaps the mill's margin of success was owing to the employment primarily of children. But in 1825 the mill was purchased by James Ronaldson, who in 1827 placed Joseph Bancroft's father, John Bancroft, in charge of it.[16]

What made these English technicians so valuable, particularly in the 1820's and 1830's, was their possession of precise numerical information about machine settings and a knowledge of how to calculate such esoteric quantities as the several radii which described the form of the cam controlling the motion of the flyer on a fly frame. (The method of this calculation was copied by Joseph Bancroft from the papers of Josiah Woods. The algorithm involved six variables: the number of turns of the flyer for each turn of the front roller, the diameter of the front roller, the shrinkage of the yarn for each turn of the front roller, the diameter of the bobbin barrel, the diameter of the full bobbin, and the sum of the diameters of the cones.) Bancroft copied other machinery-setting recipes from the papers of another of his mule spinners, Evan Davies. Davies had made notes on the machine settings in the mills he had observed in England; for instance:

20's Throstle twist. Roller 55 revolutions pr minute. 1 In. diam. Rim runs 139 1/4 pr min. spindle 3920 & puts 21 1/2 turns to the Inch.[17]

Bancroft kept notes and sample calculations of his own, as well as extracts from his readings, from about 1827 to 1830, while he was getting started in his business.

Until the repeal of the laws in 1824 and 1825, England, of course, officially prohibited the emigration of persons bearing this kind of technical information; but the laws were not effectively enforced. From the 1790's onward, a constant stream of experienced supervisory personnel left England for responsible positions in American factories. By 1812, there were at least 314 alien British textile workers in the lower Delaware Valley.[18] After the repeal of the emigration laws, the stream became virtually a flood, including operatives of all levels of experience as well as managerial personnel.

Chester Creek received its share of these English immigrant technicians. Perhaps the most successful of the immigrant managers on Chester Creek was Abraham Blakeley, whom Crozer hired in 1833 to become foreman of the newly established weaving department at West Branch. Blakeley was the Lancashire weaver who had come to this country in 1828, at the age of twenty-two; thus he was twenty-seven when he was hired by Crozer. As we shall see, he married, prospered, and eventually became a prominent cotton manufacturer in Chester himself.[19] Another successful pair of manufacturers in the area (not mentioned by Crozer) were the unrelated Irishmen Dennis and Charles Kelly, who had a cotton and woolen factory in Haverford. Charles Kelly managed Penn's Grove briefly in the late 1820's.[20] And members of the British Bottomley family had been operating cotton and woolen mills along the Creek ever since 1810.[21] In fact, of the six cotton factories in the Rockdale district in 1832, three were certainly managed in whole or in part by British immigrants (the Garseds at Penn's Grove, the Riddles at Parkmount, and Blakeley in the weaving department at West Branch). Carter may have been still managing Knowlton. For the situation at Phillips' mill and at Lenni, no information is available.

ENTERING THE COTTON MANUFACTURE IN THE 1820's

In Pennsylvania, and in particular along Chester Creek, the cotton manufacture was not solidly established upon a firm basis until the 1820's. Earlier efforts did not survive the resumption of the imports of British cotton goods after the War of 1812. The enterprises along the Merrimac River in Massachusetts, established about 1815, had survived the British assault, and were already flourishing mightily, because they were founded on a somewhat different plan from those to the south: they employed a different technology, a different work force, and (of relevance to the immediate discussion) a different method of financing.

The Chester Creek system of financing cotton manufacture (and, apparently, the system in the Delaware Valley generally) had four characteristic features: (1) the mill owners and the cotton manufacturers were not normally the same people; (2) in almost every case, both owners and manufacturers assembled capital and secured themselves against failure by drawing much of their funds and assurances of support from an assemblage of both in-laws and blood kinsmen; (3) the capital committed to manufacturing was surplus money—savings and profits from other businesses—borrowed by impecunious entrepreneurs directly from individuals rather than (for the most part) from banks; (4) when the manufacturing firm was owned by more than one person, the parties were always in partnership (none of the firms was incorporated) and were usually kinsmen.

Let us look at the pattern more closely, reviewing the evidence for the nine owner/manufacturer pairs from the six mill sites (two from Knowlton, one from Rockdale, two from Penn's Grove, one from Parkmount, two from Lenni, and one from West Branch). At two of the mill seats, the mill owner and the manufacturer were the same person or persons: John D. Carter during his time at Knowlton, and after him Thomas Clyde and Edward Darlington; and John P. Crozer at West Branch. In the other six cases, the mill owner and the manufacturer were different people. (In one case, that of Peter Hill and William Martin, the parties were related by marriage, Peter Hill being the brother of Martin's stepfather.) The roles of owner and manufacturer were clearly distinct. The owner leased to the manufacturer a tract of about ten or fifteen acres, containing a mill and associated buildings for auxiliary purposes, such as machine shop, drying house, tenement houses for workers, and a mansion for the manufacturer himself. Along with the land and buildings, the owner agreed to provide power for the mill, which meant that he was responsible for the expense of maintaining a dam, head- and tailraces, gates, sluices, a water wheel and wheelpit, and shafting and gearing. The manufacturer owned the textile machinery, which he connected to the shafting in the mill, and he was responsible for buying raw cotton and selling the yarn and woven cloth; sometimes he maintained an office in Philadelphia to manage these exchange activities. The value of new machinery for a small mill like Lenni would be on the order of $10,000; when used, it might bring a third of that. The value of the mill seat and its improvements would be roughly equal to the value of the machinery, and would rent for about $100 per month.

The importance of his kindred to the manufacturer in providing the capital to acquire machinery and the mill property cannot be overemphasized. With the exception of John D. Carter, James Houghton, and John Garsed, whose financial connections are not known, every single owner and manufacturer was able to turn to nearby kinsmen for aid in assembling capital, and in every case there is evidence that he did so. At Knowlton, we have seen that in the partnership of Edward Darlington and Thomas Clyde, Darlington was the nephew. At Rockdale, the manufacturing partners Phillips and Lewis were brothers-in-law; and the owner, Henry Moore, had bought the property from *his* brother-in-law George Odiorne of Massachusetts, who was in turn related by marriage to the Willcox family of Ivy Mills, above Lenni.[1] At Penn's Grove, the owners were brothers, George and Peter Hill. At Parkmount, the owners were the Hill-and-Sellers trust, and the manufacturers were the Riddle brothers. At Lenni, the first owner-manufacturer, William Martin, had gone into business with his brother-in-law. The next owner was, again, the Hill-and-Sellers trust, and the next manufacturer was Daniel Lammot, who was backed financially by his daughter's father-in-law, E. I. du Pont. On the West Branch, owner-manufacturer

John P. Crozer had gone into business with a loan from his brother-in-law, John Lewis.

Local banks and insurance companies became important in a few years in providing capital and security against loss; but at the beginning they seem to have played little part except possibly in the case of Crozer, who became a director of the Bank of Delaware County in 1825. The Bank of Delaware County was undersubscribed, held about as much specie as it would take to build one mill, and mostly invested its funds in farms and taverns.[2] The Philadelphia banks and other lending institutions were more useful. The Riddles, and no doubt others, wrote checks on the Girard and other banks for small amounts such as workmen's wages and grocery store accounts, but the banks apparently rarely lent money to finance the ventures of the Chester Creek mill owners and manufacturers. The $10,000 or so needed to build a small mill and its associated structures, or to buy the machinery, were assembled as a patchwork of personal savings, profits from other businesses, and loans, in amounts from a couple of thousand to nine or ten thousand, secured on the property or by the endorsement of still other relatives.

There were no corporations after the model of the great, heavily financed enterprises at Waltham and Lowell in Massachusetts. These northern organizations were able to amass a starting capital of hundreds of thousands of dollars, to buy up miles of stream bank, to construct whole towns, and to engineer large systems of raceways years before the mill sites were ever leased to manufacturers. The only suggestion of such an enterprise was an ill-fated scheme of Daniel Lammot's to form a company to buy a tract on both sides of the Brandywine and to use that river's whole water power for manufacturing cotton. The gentlemen whom Lammot tried to interest in that matter included his father-in-law Paul Beck, Jr., one of the wealthiest men of Philadelphia, and his son Harvey; Guy Bryan, another wealthy merchant (as Lammot advised Du Pont, he "has *lots of money*") and president of the first fire insurance company in Philadelphia, and his son William; Joshua Lippincott (who consulted with *his* father-in-law); and a Commodore Stewart. Lammot wanted to put together a capital of $150,000 or more, buy Du Pont's vacant cotton mill (the one recently abandoned by Carter), and also the vacant mill seat across the Brandywine, and create a "large establishment." He would be the manufacturer and would hire as technical manager either young Joseph Bancroft, the cotton spinner newly arrived from England, or a protégé of Paul Beck's from New Orleans. The firm would have as many as 10,000 spindles; by contrast, Martin's single mill at Lenni at that date had only 1,584 spindles. The investors would realize 6 percent on their investments; and, according to his own hopeful calculations, Lammot would gain, even if only five thousand spindles were operating, a solid $40,000 per year after all expenses.

The plan fell through. Du Pont wanted $37,000 for his own mill, with the company to buy the seat across the Brandywine at the forthcoming sheriff's sale. But Lippincott, the central figure in the negotiations, insisted that Du Pont buy the vacant mill seat first and give it to the company along with the existing mill for the same price. When Du Pont refused this suggestion, Lippincott countered with an offer of $25,000 and the company to buy the other property. When Du Pont refused this offer too, denying that he had ever suggested such a ridiculous price, Lippincott withdrew in a huff.

Lammot next urged a corporation. A Mr. Andrews was interested in purchasing the Du Pont cotton mill and visited the Brandywine to discuss the matter. Lammot, rather casually, warned his friend:

> As to Mr. A, I presume he is fickle, and would not be a pleasant partner except under an act of Incorporation. *Entre nous,* it is said that he is an excellent judge of Cognac, and preserves his skill by constant practice. This however would not be important to a concern of 5 or more Directors; for if he but contribute his money, there will be no difficulty in employing it.[3]

Nothing came of this idea either.

In effect, it would appear that the Philadelphia area was not the place to form a corporation or even a large investment company to finance cotton manufacturing on a scale comparable to Lowell. Wealthy merchants like Beck and Bryan were not interested in putting up large sums of money on their own behalf; they were seeking safe places to invest such monies on behalf of their children, sons-in-law, and other protégés. Cotton manufacturing was only one of a number of investment possibilities for idle capital, and most of the other alternatives were probably looked upon as safer unless the associated real estate could be bought at a bargain price.[4]

Thus the mills along Chester Creek remained small, at first only amounting to one or two thousand spindles. According to Lammot's calculations, even a small one thousand-spindle mill, spinning No. 16 yarn, should make a net profit for the manufacturer of between $8,000 and $9,000 per year —a very respectable income for the period. But paper profits are only paper profits. Even Lammot, as he said (partly in humor) to Du Pont, would have been willing to give up the possibility of $40,000 per year from cotton spinning for a guarantee of $5,000 as agent. For there were many risks in the cotton manufacture: a financial panic, like the one in 1829, which set loose a chain reaction of protested notes, lawsuits, assignments, sheriff's sales, and even condemnations to debtor's prison; the inexperience of the new manufacturers, who might have trouble at first in getting and maintaining decent machinery and in hiring and retaining competent and reliable workers; and fire and flood, which could destroy only partially insured machinery, buildings, and hydraulic systems. Of the nine manufacturers, three had been involved in business failures before they came to Chester Creek, two of them (Carter and Lammot) in cotton manufacturing; and two failed within a few years of their arrival (Carter again, and Martin).

It is difficult to escape the conclusion that the pattern of low capital investment, much of it derived from private loans, including notes of indebtedness even to his cotton suppliers, made the cotton manufacturer extremely vulnerable in the early years of his venture. His loans and other financial obligations might be suddenly called in; his own creditors might suddenly be unable to pay him; the price of cotton might go up, or that of yarn and cloth down. Without much in the way of assets beyond his machinery and the notes of merchants to whom he sold or consigned cloth, he could not ride out even a brief period of business reversal. Even an experienced cotton spinner like Carter might go under, while a technically inexperienced novice like Crozer survived, because the saving factor in a financial panic was not technical expertise but a sound credit rating and loyal kinsmen.

Yet the system, in a sense, had a virtue. It selected for economic survival those manufacturers rigorously honest in business practice, sufficiently patient to start small and grow slowly, intellectually capable of recognizing (or even of inventing) useful innovations, and pragmatic enough in human relationships to be able to assemble and keep together a network of kinsmen, business associates, operatives, and representatives in the political community.

THE MACHINES, THEIR OPERATIVES, AND THE FABRICS

In the spring of the auspicious year 1826 a number of manufacturers and other interested citizens met at the courthouse in Chester. Their purpose was to organize a survey of the mill seats in Delaware County. George G. Leiper, Crozer's friend, who owned the mills and quarries on Crum and Ridley creeks; William Martin, the cotton manufacturer from Lenni; and John Willcox, papermaker from Ivy Mills, were elected the survey committee. Young Willcox (he was only thirty-seven) died shortly afterward and at a second public meeting in August John P. Crozer was elected to fill his place.

The committee report was presented to the public at the second public meeting in August and was thereafter printed as a pamphlet in five hundred copies.[1] In its twenty-seven pages it described in detail the state of manufactures in the county, giving information on the water supply at each mill seat, the size and construction of buildings, the machinery in use, the number of workmen, and the productivity of the enterprise. It proceeded, from east to west, stream by stream, to list all gristmills, sawmills, oil mills (for the making of linseed oil), paper mills, iron forges, cotton and woolen "manufactories," and unimproved sites available for development. By its account, there were in the county fifty-three sawmills, thirty-eight flour mills, eleven paper mills, two powder mills, five rolling and slitting mills, fourteen woolen factories and thirteen cotton factories, and a sprinkling of other enterprises. All in all, the committee found two hundred mills and mill seats, forty-two of them as yet unimproved.

According to the survey, the five Chester Creek cotton manufacturers evidently had installed conventional equipment and were following traditional methods of operation. Their machines had been invented, in their fundamentals, in England a generation or more before. In the organization of these machines, these early manufacturers followed the principle that in the previous century the English cotton industry had followed. This principle was the physical separation of the two parts of the cotton-manufacturing process. All the machinery necessary to the *spinning* of cotton, from bale to yarn, was assembled in one manufactory. The *weaving,* whether by hand or power looms, and the finishing operations were conducted under different roofs by different entrepreneurs. Such division of the total process into two parts made it possible for an individual manufacturer to commence work with less capital and in a smaller building than if (as in the more modern fashion of Lowell) all the processes from bale to finished cloth were conducted by one manufacturer. This smallness of scale was almost a necessity, also, in a situation where the owners of mill seats were making available a dam, race, water wheel, and building which had been constructed originally for other and more limited purposes, such as papermaking or grinding grain.

THE MILLS AND MILL SEATS

Five of the mills were located on mill seats long in use. Knowlton had been a copper-rolling mill.[1] Rockdale had been developed early in the eighteenth century by the Pennell family as an iron forge—Old Sable Forge —and was still the site of a gristmill, a rolling and slitting mill, and a nail factory when Henry Moore built a cotton mill for his new tenants in 1825.[2] Penn's Grove had been the site of a grist- and sawmill and a fulling mill (to serve local hand-loom weavers of woolens) since the late eighteenth century at least, and probably (to judge from the presence of very old ruins of dams and races) from even early in that century too. Lenni had been the site of the Lungren paper factory. And West Branch had been the site of Mattson's paper factory.[3]

The Water Power:
Dams, Races, and Water Wheels

The effective machinery of the water system was a wooden wheel. These water wheels which, in their slow and ponderous revolutions, turned the gears that communicated power to the machinery in the mill, were themselves driven by the weight of water delivered to them by a more or less elaborate hydraulic system. Some were "overshot" wheels: that is to say, the water was brought over the top of the wheel in a wooden sluice, to pour down the front into wooden buckets built into the outer rim of the wheel;

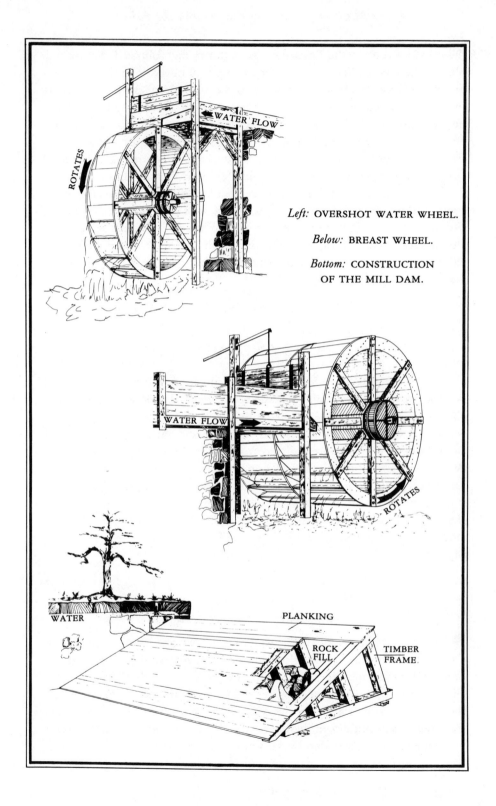

ROTATES

WATER FLOW

Left: OVERSHOT WATER WHEEL.

Below: BREAST WHEEL.

Bottom: CONSTRUCTION
OF THE MILL DAM.

WATER FLOW

ROTATES

WATER

PLANKING

ROCK
FILL

TIMBER
FRAME

others were "breast" wheels, revolving in the opposite direction, moved by water delivered to the back of the wheel at about middle height. It was the weight of the water that turned the wheel, not its impact. At the bottom, the water fell out of the buckets into the wheelpit and thence flowed out into the tailrace and so back into the stream. The wheels typically were 10 to 15 feet in diameter and 3 to 4 feet in width, and were left exposed or shielded only by flimsy sheds.

In order to drive a wheel, it was necessary to secure a vertical head of water of 10 to 15 feet, somewhere between an upstream point where the headrace cut in from the creek, and the downstream point where the tailrace returned the "used" water to the stream. The maximum theoretical horsepower derivable from the system was a function of the head and the quantity of water delivered per unit of time. An adequate head could be secured at, or beside, a waterfall, and in fact such opportunities were exploited where they occurred (as they did at Waltham, Massachusetts, for instance, or at the falls of the Passaic at Patterson, New Jersey). But along Chester Creek, and in most other situations in the Delaware Valley, the necessary head could best be obtained by digging a canal along the bank parallel to the stream, descending at a shallower angle than the stream itself. After a few hundred yards, the surface of the water in the race would be a number of feet above the surface of the water in the stream. When that vertical difference—the head—was sufficiently large to accommodate a water wheel, the wheelpit could be constructed and a mill located. The five mills cited in the 1826 survey had the following "head and fall": Knowlton, 16 feet; Rockdale, 16 feet; Penn's Grove, 21 feet; Lenni, 16 feet; and West Branch, 13 feet.[4]

The head ideally approximated (but obviously could not be greater than) the actual fall in the stream between intake of the headrace and exit of the tailrace. In order to shorten the race, and thus to reduce both the labor needed for its construction and the amount of land required for a mill seat, the universal practice was to dam the stream. The dam ensured a more constant level of water in the race because, except in flood or drought, the water would always run off at the height of the crest of the dam. Also, by the extent to which the dam raised the water level, it increased the head and provided an important reserve supply of water. Most of the dams were relatively shallow, rising no more than 4 or 5 feet above the streambed; often (as at Penn's Grove) the effective height was increased by setting heavy wooden planks into deep slots running across the crest of the dam. These shallow dams, at West Branch and Penn's Grove and perhaps at other sites, appear to have been constructed simply by piling up stones and boulders in the streambed, used wood for facing instead of concrete, and, presumably, could be built without the trouble of diverting the water into other channels. They were butted against large rocks or steep banks where a flood was least likely to carve out a new course around the dam. In cross section they generally had a relatively steep downstream side and a gently sloping upstream one. In some sites the downstream side of the dam was vertical, and constructed of cut and carefully fitted stone, sometimes with the breast coated with a smoothly rounded cement shield. The dams at Lenni and Rockdale were of this kind, and were higher, too, than any of the others. No record remains of the dam at Knowlton.

When new, the race was about 10 or 12 feet wide and nearly as deep (but silting might reduce the depth to 3 or 4 feet), with movable gates at the dam and at the pit to control the level and quantity of water being delivered to the wheel. Sometimes, if the terrain crowded the race onto a steep hillside, it would have to be constructed in part of masonry. Close to the wheelpit, wooden or metal booms and a wooden trash rack were set in the race before the final water gate, to prevent floating debris from getting into the pit to foul the wheel and clog the tailrace. The headrace might be as short as 50 yards (as at West Branch) or as long as a quarter of a mile (as at Penn's Grove).[5]

The construction of the water system, of course, required an initial outlay of considerable money, to pay a millwright to design and construct a water wheel and the auxiliary equipment in the pit, race, and dam; to pay a master mason to design and supervise the building of the race and dam;

LENNI MILL.

KNOWLTON MILL CIRCA 1920.

and to hire pick-and-shovel laborers to dig the race, quarry or find the stone, and raise the dam. Once constructed, the system could last almost indefinitely, provided breaks in the dam and race were repaired promptly, silt was removed periodically, and rotten or worn parts of the wheel and its setting were repaired. Such tasks were generally performed by local millwrights, masons, and laborers hired by the day as occasion demanded, with some help from the hired hands of the landowner, who was apt to be running a farm on the land around the mill, and from operatives, who were unemployed whenever the water wheel stopped. In any case, the water system was the financial responsibility of the landowner rather than of the manufacturer, although a manufacturer or mill manager might write the specifications, make arrangements for repair, and supervise the work.[6]

The Buildings

The arts of building dams, races, and water wheels were old and well established; but they were not standardized, nor could they be. Each water system, from dam to wheel, was a unique product, tailored to fit as well as possible the special requirements of the user and the particular potentialities and limitations of the site. Each had a special quality of its own, special problems, special possibilities for improvement.

But the early buildings were relatively standardized. They were rectangular, on an average about 40 feet wide and 55 feet long, two to four stories high, and were constructed of fieldstone laid in mortar and covered inside and out with whitewashed stucco. (The actual dimensions of the "typical" mills were: Rockdale, 41 by 61 feet, four stories; Penn's Grove, 45 by 50, two stories; Lenni, 35 by 55, three stories; and West Branch, 45 by 60, three stories. Knowlton was larger, 40 by 90.)[7] Along all walls on each floor except the top were rows of large, glass-covered windows, 5 or 6 feet high, and (because of the nature of the construction) set in softly rounded embrasures. The floor beams were massive, spanning the width of the building, set into the walls, and each supported on two posts; the floors were 3-inch-thick oak planks. The clearance from floor to beams was anywhere from 10 to 14 feet. The pitched roof was lined by a clerestory, which provided fairly even lighting to the top floor—the only room in the mill that did not require the dual lines of posts down its length. At night the rooms were lighted by oil lamps. In the original design of the buildings (except perhaps for the new building constructed for Phillips and later in the Riddles' new mill) there was no provision for heating; but Martin, and probably the other manufacturers, provided a stove for each floor.

At one end of the building was a square stairwell; all movement of personnel and small supplies had to be up and down these steps. At a place along the edge of the building where it stood next to the road a block and tackle hung from a beam near the roof, for hoisting heavy gear and bulk supplies, like bales of cotton, from carts below. Surmounting the whole, in the center of the roof, stood a cupola containing the bell that called the workers to the mill and signaled the hours of work, and also sounded the alarm in case of fire.

Well-run mills were surrounded by wooden panel fences, which enclosed the mill yard with its main mill, the mill office building, and various auxiliary frame buildings, sluices, and gates, and protected the mill from the depredations of livestock, little boys, and importunate visitors.

A system of roads and bridges was also needed for horse-drawn wagons to haul in the bales of cotton to the mill and take finished products away. The creek was too small for navigation, even if it had not been interrupted by dams, and the local Chester Creek railroad would not arrive for another thirty years. The roads were not paved, so far as we know, and they crowded in close by the mills—or the mills were built close by them—in order to facilitate the loading and unloading process. Where the mills remain today, it is evident that they were originally located at the very edge of the highway.

The Power Train:
Gears, Shafts, Pulleys, and Belts

Power was delivered into the mill by shafting geared to the water wheel. The wheel initially drove a horizontal shaft which, intersecting inside the mill with a bevel gear, transmitted its power to an upright shaft that rose the height of the building; from this, line shafts extended along under the ceiling on each floor. At this date much of the shafting was still being made of wood. From the line shafts, leather belts running on wooden pulleys transmitted power down to the machines below.[8]

There were innumerable mechanical arrangements by which this could be accomplished, but all of them required lubrication. The gudgeoned (provided with an iron-tipped bearing) wooden axle of the water wheel could be geared to the upright shaft; but the wheel could also drive, by gears, a horizontal shaft intersecting the wheel along its circumference. The upright shaft itself was apt to be made of iron; its lower tip rested in a seat lubricated by oil. The line shafting running off the gearing on the upright shaft extended along the length of the rooms, high up under the ceilings, and had to be supported in lubricated boxes or journals. The proper lubrication of all gearing and bearings was essential, not only in order to preserve as much of the power of the water wheel as possible for running the machinery, but also to protect the moving parts from wear, breakage, and overheating, which might lead to fire. Petroleum-based lubricants had not yet been invented; the lubricants available had to be compounded from animal fats and vegetable oils (such as the tallow and tar used on metal gears).

Another requirement for the power train was the coupling of sections of shafts. This had to be done by placing square-flanged collars around the ends of the shafts to be coupled, keyed to prevent slippage, and screwed or bolted together so that the axes of rotation of the two parts were in the same line. Usually the shafting, whether wooden or the increasingly common metallic, was square or octagonal in cross section. In the case of wooden shafting, there must have been a considerable degree of flexibility in the whole assembly. Nonetheless, shafting in the mills was regularly constructed to run horizontally as much as 100 feet from the upright shaft.

Leather belts were used to transmit power from the primary line shaft under the ceiling to parallel line shafts above the rows of machines, and thence to the machines on the floor below. These belts were manufactured on special order from local tanneries, particularly the Duttons' a few hundred yards away. Each belt would be 20 to 30 feet long and had to be

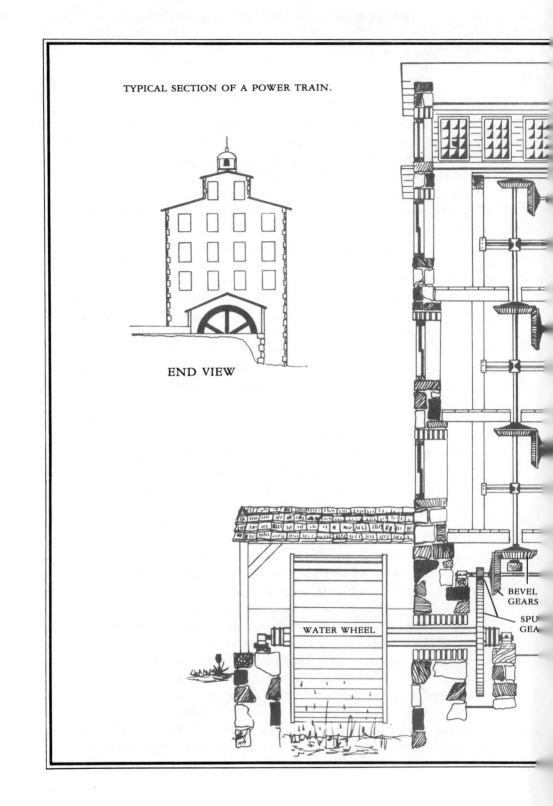

TYPICAL SECTION OF A POWER TRAIN.

END VIEW

WATER WHEEL

BEVEL
GEARS

SPU
GEA

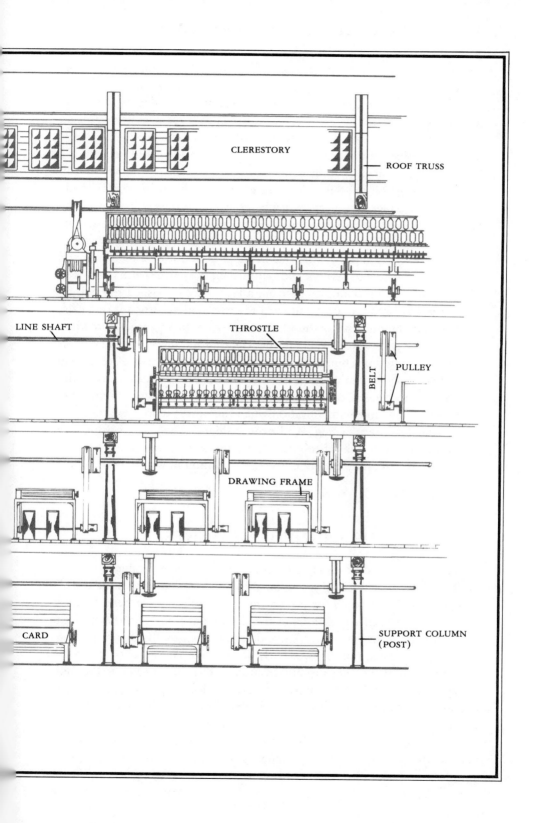

CLERESTORY

ROOF TRUSS

LINE SHAFT

THROSTLE

BELT

PULLEY

DRAWING FRAME

CARD

SUPPORT COLUMN
(POST)

constructed from 5-foot-long sections of cowhide; depending on the horse-power applied, they were from 2 inches to 2 feet in width. The sections were stitched, hooked, clamped, or glued together and the ends eventually joined so as to form an endless loop. Stretched over a pulley or drum fastened to the line shaft above, the belt ran down around a pulley fastened to the drive shaft of the machine. The effect of gearing could be achieved by varying the diameters of the connected pulleys. Once in motion, the belt resisted slippage off the pulley because to slip it would have to tilt slightly and the tilting met resistance. An ingenious clutch device known as the fast-and-loose pulley system permitted the operative to turn his own machines individually on and off. The machine drive shaft was fitted with two pulleys, closely set side by side, one of them bolted fast to the shaft, and the other loose, able to revolve without turning the drive shaft. The operative turned off his machine by shoving a lever, which pushed the belt off the fast pulley onto the loose pulley; a reverse motion turned it on again.

The mill in motion was a shuddering, creaking, hissing mass of shafting turned by the great water wheel outside. Gearing and the varying diameters of pulleys brought machine speeds up to velocities hundreds of times that of the six to twelve revolutions per minute of the wheel. Belts whirred and hummed; gears clicked; cams and cranks clanked. The whole mill must have seemed to come alive with vibration when the power train was connected at the wheel in the morning. And even at night, when the shafting and machines were still, the wheel was allowed to run at idle lest it become uneven in its motion by resting in the same position in water every night.[9]

THE SPINNING MACHINERY

The spinning mills consumed bales of raw cotton and produced, for the most part, boxes of cotton yarn—spun, dyed, and wound on "shuttle cops," or wound in warps ready for placement in power looms or hand looms.

The cotton itself all came from the slave plantations of the American south; for the most part it was Upland cotton from the piedmont plateau of Georgia and the Carolinas, a fairly short-staple cotton, eked out with small amounts of the finer product from New Orleans. It came to the mill wrapped and tied in large burlap-covered bales weighing 300 to 350 pounds. The bales were picked up at the wharf in Philadelphia or Marcus Hook by large wagons owned or hired by the manufacturer; a wagonload of cotton was ten to fifteen bales. No two bales weighed exactly the same because the cotton, after being cleaned of its seeds by the cotton gin, was

TABLE 5: *Productivity of the Mills in the Rockdale District (1826–1850)*

	Number of Hands	Mule Spindles	Throstle Spindles	Yarn Counts	Power Looms	Raw Cotton Consumption per Week	Cloth Production per Year in Yards
WEST BRANCH							
1826	30	648	588	15–20	none	1,100 lbs.	
1832	52	3,000 (both)		15–33	none	2,500 lbs.	
1850*	179	7,032 (both)		not given	200	not given	1,425,000
LENNI							
1826	45	936	648	18–25	none	1,200 lbs.	
1850	113	1,956	2,044	not given	not given	not given	1,000,000
PARKMOUNT							
1832	50	c. 2,500	none	8–20	none	3,400 lbs.	
1850	23	4	none	none	18	none	102,000 (diaper cloth only)
PENN'S GROVE							
1826	32	570	492	6–24	160	1,140 lbs.	
1850	114	4,980 (both)		not given	not given	not given	1,460,000
KNOWLTON							
1826	46	616	808	20	none	1,278 lbs.	
1850	46	1,548 (both)		not given	60	not given	470,000
ROCKDALE	Data too fragmentary to warrant inclusion.						

*1850 data combines West Branch and Crozerville. The 1826 data are from Leiper and Martin, 1826, p. 1821. The 1832 data (West Branch and Parkmount only) are from McLane, 1833, pp. 210–12 and 224–6, and (for Parkmount only) DCHS, Parkmount Pay Book. The 1850 data are from the NA, 1850 Census of Manufactures.

squeezed in large presses into a standard size and shape; the quality of the cotton, the design, condition, and operation of the press, and the level of humidity would cause each bale's weight to be slightly different. Each bale had to be separately weighed and numbered as soon as it was received at the mill in order to verify the weight claimed by the merchant in Philadelphia from whom it had been bought.

A series of specific operations had now to be performed on the raw cotton; each had its own location, its own machine, and its own operatives. After the bales were opened, the cotton was blended to produce a uniform staple length and was run through the picker room; then it was transferred to the carding engine; then to several preparatory spinning devices, including the double speeder, the drawing frame, the roving frame, and the stretcher; then either to the mule or to the throstle for the final spinning of usable yarn; then, for some of the yarn, to the dyehouse; and finally to the warping machine or to the machine for spooling yarn on bobbins or cops specially prepared for insertion into shuttles.[1] The number of machines of various types and the number of operatives in the Chester Creek spinning mills in the period 1826–32 and again in 1850 are summarized in Table 3.

The Picker House

In some of the mills, as a protection against fire, a separate shed attached to the main mill was used for the dust-producing initial preparation of the cotton; in others, a special room protected by iron doors and fire-resistant walls and ceiling was set aside on the ground floor. Here the bales were deposited from the wagon onto the scale, weighed, and then opened; released from the intense pressure of the packing, the loose cotton spilled out in an expanding mass of tufts and clumps. The packing rope and burlap were laid aside for sale to the nearby paper mills. The cotton from several bales (if the operation was properly done) was mixed in a large bin to form a synthetic bale or "bing." This was done in order to homogenize the raw material. Cuts from the bing were then fed into the picker (or other machines for cleaning cotton such as the willow), which clawed apart the lumps, agitated the fleece, and, by circulating air through the mass, cleaned out a large quantity of debris. Dirt, sand, grit, bits of leaves, twine, insects, seeds that had been missed by the gin, all dropped through a perforated cylinder to the bottom of the machine while the fleece moved on in the teeth of meshing gears. This machine also produced a quantity of flying dust —a highly flammable mixture of fragments of cotton and impurities—which filled the air in the picker room with itching particles. Hence work in the picker room was sometimes compared to labor in Satan's domain. After the picker, the fleece was run through the blower, which produced a long smooth sheet or "lap" of clean white cotton fleece, 2 or 3 feet wide and 1 inch thick, which could be wound on wooden drums or placed on an endless belt, for delivery to the carding engine.

The two or three male operatives who worked in the picker room, opening bales, mixing the bings, and feeding and regulating the picker, were generally young, strong, and relatively unskilled, and were paid about 40 or 50 cents per day.[2] A frequent visitor at the picker room—and perhaps this was a discouragement to those working there—was the mill manager, or a clerk representing him, who supervised and recorded the weighing of the bales of raw cotton.

The Card Room

It was universally agreed, at least by the English authorities, that the crucial stage in the preparation of cotton for spinning was the process of carding. The cotton as it left the picker room was in the form of sheets of clean batting. In this state, the individual fibers lay higgledy-piggledy in a twisted and loosely tangled mass; it was the task of the carding engine to sort them out so as to lie more or less parallel to one another. The task had to be done without breaking the fibers and had to produce a uniform, regular product; and this requirement laid upon the carding room a heavy responsibility, for cotton fibers were delicate. The finest American cotton, Sea Island cotton, had a long average fiber-length or staple, from 1 1/2 inches to 1 5/8 inches, and a very fine diameter, down to 1/2,500 of an inch; coarser cottons, of the kind used in the Chester Creek mills, were shorter by half an inch or so and could be as coarse as 1/250.

A carding engine was essentially a set of rotating, wire-toothed cylinders waist to chest high and 2 to 3 feet wide. The main cylinder seized the cotton lap, pulled it over or under other cylinders stationary or rotating at a slower pace, and delivered it to a drawing head, which transformed the thin sheet of carded cotton continuously emerging from the rollers into a loosely cohering rope or sliver (pronounced "sly-ver"). The sliver dropped in a spiral into a large tin can about 3 feet high and 18 inches in diameter.

Generally the carding machines worked in pairs, the first one to receive the lap being called the breaker card; it delivered only a carded lap to the second, or finisher, card, which produced the sliver. Each carding engine had to be of the right size and specifically adjusted to produce a sliver suitable for spinning a certain type of yarn. Usually the five or six workers in the card room, both male and female, were paid by the day; and the supervisor of the card room could earn substantial wages, on the order of

$40 to $50 per month. Each mill contained about ten cards; Martin's mill had eleven carding engines worth, by his estimate, $3,200 (nearly a third of the value of all his machinery).

The Frames for Preparing the Roving

The cotton as it issued from the carding engine looked like an endless, loosely twisted rope about as thick as one's thumb. In this form it was not ready for spinning into yarn, and it was therefore passed in sections through one or more machines that stretched and twisted it into a roving ready for one of the spinning machines. The first of these intermediate processes was "doubling," which meant the combining of slivers from two or more cans into one filament, while it was lightly twisted and considerably stretched. This operation was performed on machines called double speeders and could be repeated again and again. Doubling might commence with (as in the Riddles' mill) running twelve ends into one in the first frame, twelve into one in the second frame, and three into one in the third, yielding a doubling by a factor of 432. It then moved to a drawing frame, where the doubled and redoubled sliver was further twisted and attenuated; and thence to a roving frame, which produced a filament called a roving, wound on bobbins ready for the spinning process. For particularly careful spinners, a fourth type of machine, the stretcher, took the roving and further twisted and drew it, in a final preparation for the mule.

Essentially, all these machines were variations on a basic model, the "water frame," by which a coarse filament was made longer, stronger, and more tightly twisted. The speeders took slivers from a larger number of cans and deposited their product into a smaller number of cans; the others moved from can to can, always drawing the filament out and giving it more twist. (The number of cans required to supply the carding room and preparatory frames in a typical mill like Martin's was about two hundred.) The drawing was accomplished by passing the filament from one pair of rollers to another revolving at a higher rate of speed. From the rollers of the roving frame the sliver went down to a bobbin, on which it was wound by a flyer (whose revolutions around the bobbin imparted the necessary twist).

These preparatory doublings, drawings, and twistings took place on machines which long experience had rendered highly reliable and almost completely automatic. The room in which they functioned was serviced largely by half a dozen or so semi-skilled boys, girls, and young women. The workers carried the cans filled with slivers from the carding engines to the first of the speeders and transferred cans thereafter from machine to machine. They removed filled roving bobbins; fastened on the slivers to start a new run; pieced broken slivers; and tried to keep the floors and machinery reasonably clean. They did not regulate the speed of the machines, the pressure of the rollers and their relative speed, or do other technical manipulations; these settings were the responsibility of the overseer, probably the overseer of the carding room. They received on the order of $7 for a "month" of twenty-four days.

The Throstle

The spinning process produced "yarn"—the strong, uniform, twisted filament of hundreds of microscopically fine fibers that was the main consumer product of the mill. There were two kinds of machine used for the final spinning of cotton: the throstle and the mule. The two machines operated on different principles to accomplish the three motions of drawing (i.e., stretching), twisting, and winding onto bobbin or spindle, which are necessary in any spinning procedure. The throstle performed continuous spinning; the mule, intermittent spinning. The throstle was used largely for the manufacture of warp threads for power looms, because it made a hard, strong, coarse yarn very cheaply. The mule was the machine of choice for weft, or filling, of power looms and for all fine cotton yarn (although some of the mills used the advanced Danforth throstle, which made a relatively soft yarn).[3]

In practice, continuous spinning meant that the operations of drawing, twisting, and winding were conducted successively on a continuously moving length of roving. The roving was supplied on a large bobbin mounted

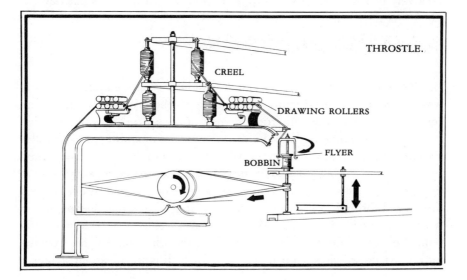

on the head of the throstle. It was drawn down through two pairs of metal rollers revolving under power. The first pair of rollers simply pulled the roving off the bobbin at a certain speed. The second pair of rollers pulled the roving out of the first pair; and because it turned at a faster speed, it pulled and stretched the roving as it passed between the two pairs. From the roller head, the thinner, attenuated roving passed down to the eye of a flyer mounted on a spindle which rotated continuously, again under power from the train, around a fixed bobbin. In order to distribute the yarn evenly on the bobbin, the flyer was made to rise and fall regularly.

A throstle was then simply a long wooden frame in which were mounted a series of such spinning units, all operating off shafts powered from the line shafting. A single throstle, like the ones in Martin's mill at Lenni, would contain about a hundred spindles and be about 50 feet long; but there was really no limit to the number of spindles which could comprise a throstle beyond the mechanical convenience of space and power supply, for each spinning unit, from supply bobbin to take-up bobbin, was a self-contained spinning entity that operated independently of the rest.

The task of the throstle operative was simple. She (for most throstle operatives were female) had simply to watch one or two throstles, stopping the machine occasionally to repair broken roving, doff the spindles of their filled bobbins, and replace the supply bobbins. This required some walking back and forth, and up and down stairs, with arms full of bobbins, some piecing of ends, and some wiping of oily parts and sweeping of cotton dust from around the machine. But basically the machine ran itself. Operatives in the throstle room therefore did not receive much more pay than the relatively unskilled labor of the picker room, about 40 cents per day.

The Mule

The supreme machine of the spinning industry was the mule. The mule was said to spin intermittently because the machinery had to be stopped regularly in order to change from one part of the process to another. What made the mule different from the throstle was the mounting of its spindles on a moving carriage which, in the 1830's, still had to be physically pushed by the spinner during parts of its movement. The roving, unwinding as in the throstle from a bobbin mounted on a creel in the main frame, passed downward through rollers which, by revolving at different speeds, somewhat attenuated it. From the rollers, the drawn roving was fed horizontally onto the tips of the spindles mounted on the carriage. As this carriage moved backward slowly on metal rails for a distance of about 4 feet 6

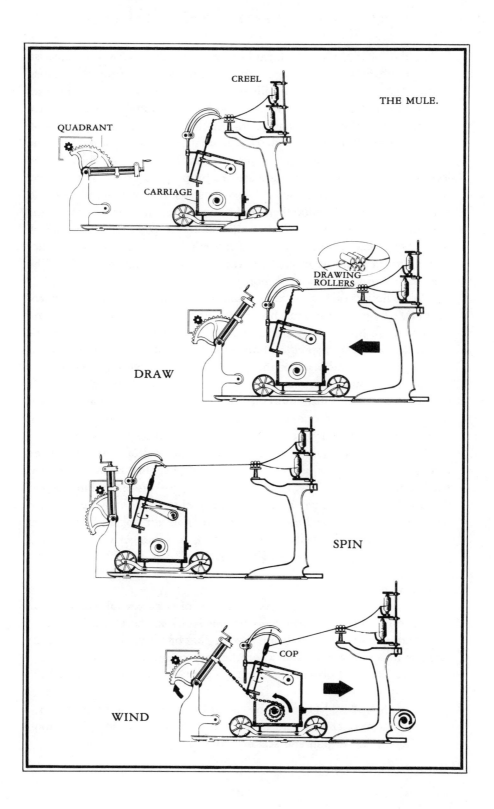

inches, the spindles rotated a fixed number of revolutions, imparting twist, while simultaneously the moving of the carriage away from the rollers, slightly faster than the rollers delivered roving, drew it out an inch or so. It was the simultaneity of the motions of drawing and twisting which gave the mule its distinctive advantage in spinning the finer yarns, for cotton roving is so constituted that if there is an unevenness in the strength of the roving, the twist will first go to the weakest (in effect the thickest and loosest) part. The mule thus made use of a property of the cotton to correct automatically any developing flaws or weak spots. A skilled operative could make finer yarns on a mule than could be made on the throstle. After the twisting terminated (automatically), the spinner tripped a faller wire, which pressed the yarn down to the base of the spindle, and started the spindles moving again while he pushed the carriage back toward the frame. The spun yarn during this forward motion was wound onto the spindle.

The mule was one of the largest and most complex mechanical devices ever made by man; larger machines, like locomotives and stationary steam engines, were power generators. The maximum size of the mules of this period was about 280 spindles. Such mules were about 60 feet long, and the size limitation was based on the physical strength required of the spinner to push, and control, the massive carriage on its inward course. The mule spinner—invariably a man—was the highest paid operative in the mill. Each spinner was assisted in operating his mule by a small team of two or even three lower paid boy or girl operatives: a piecer, whose job it was to repair the broken threads (five or six a minute) at the end of a run, when the carriage was briefly motionless; a creel attender, keeping the mule supplied with bobbins of roving (which meant carrying baskets of bobbins up and down stairs); and the scavenger, who scurried about under the sheet of yarn between the carriage and the frame, sweeping up dirt, picking up broken ends, and picking fuzzballs off the yarn. The scavenger's situation was graphically described by the English novelist Charlotte Elizabeth:

"And what is scavenging?"

"Oh, that made me laugh. You see, bits of cotton wool will stick to the thread, and they mustn't go on the reels; so there is a little girl huddled up under the frame and she snatches off all the loose wool, and throws it down so fast! and when the machine runs back, if the little scavenger did not bob and duck, and get very low, she would have a fine knock on the head."

"Poor thing!" said Helen, "she can never stretch herself out, hardly; and she is almost choked and smothered in the dust of the light cotton bits that she has to pull and scatter about her."[4]

All of the workers in the mule room were barefoot. In advanced British mills the spinner managed a pair of mules which stood parallel, back to back, so geared that while one was running out on automatic power, the spinner was free to push in the carriage of the other. But in many American mills at this date, the spinner's own muscular effort pushed the carriage in and pulled it out, and the spinner operated only one mule.

The work of the spinner required not only strength but also great skill. He had to know how to set the draw and twist adjustments on the machine so as to produce the desired thickness of yarn; he had to be able to ease the machine delicately into position during the putting-up motion. The mule spinner was not subject to an overseer; he was his own man and in charge of others; indeed, he usually was held responsible for hiring and paying his own helpers. He was paid by the piece—by the number of hanks which he produced (a hank equaled 840 yards). A good mule spinner might produce 35,000 hanks of yarn and earn $50 per month—five times as much as even the best paid operatives in the throstle room.

Warping, Balling, Spooling, and Dyeing

The final production process in the typical spinning mill was the packaging of the yarn doffed from the mule or throstle. The throstle-spun yarn, destined to be wound on the beams of power looms, was processed in a large device called a warping mill. This bulky device was essentially composed of two parts: a creel, where dozens of bobbins of yarn were mounted, enough to supply the number of threads required for the warp of a particular kind of cloth; and a large winding apparatus. The threads were assembled, before being wound on the slats of the warping mill, in a kind of gate, where they were alternately passed above and below a cord, or a rod, called a lease. This kept the warp threads in an order that could be readily reestablished when the time came for the weaver to wind them onto the supply beam of his loom. After being assembled, leased, and wound, the warp was usually packaged for transport to the weaver.

The mule-spun yarn was prepared on the mule itself in the form of cops —carefully assembled conical spirals of yarn, wound on a specially shaped spindle and removable therefrom without loss of shape. The cop was specifically designed, in shape and size, to fit into the shuttles of the weavers to whom it would be sold, and to unwind easily with the passage of the shuttle back and forth across the loom.

In addition to the warps and shuttle cops, however, the mill might have some call for yarns wound in balls or (after about 1828) on spools for household thread or for weavers who wished to make their own warps.

Such yarns were transferred to appropriate bobbins or spools on balling and spooling machines, which simply transferred the yarn from one type of bobbin to another without changing its physical quality.

Commonly, yarn was sent out to be chlorine-bleached or dyed; but some simple vegetable dyes—black from logwood, blue from indigo, yellow from sumac—were used at the mills to dye the raw stock. Indigo dye made fast color without a mordant; but most of the other dyes required a mordant and for this purpose copperas (blue-green ferrous sulfate) was used.[5]

THE WEAVING MACHINERY

The only weaving mill was that of John S. Phillips. Into his and his partner's newly constructed building, containing four stories, and measuring 41 by 60 feet in outside dimension, he had packed a total of two hundred power looms, thus creating at one stroke the largest power-loom cotton manufactory in Delaware County and perhaps in the Philadelphia area. As late as 1832, when Secretary of the Treasury Louis McLane made his famous survey of manufactures for the Congress, the nearest listed power-loom weaver in point of size was Joseph Ripka[1] of Kensington (later of Manayunk).

The weaving process was simpler so far as factory organization was concerned. There was only one basic machine to consider: the power loom itself. Undoubtedly those used by Phillips were of the so-called Scotch loom type. These looms differed from the patented Lowell looms largely in the fact that the reed or batten, which "beat up" the filling (i.e., pressed the yarn evenly against the edge of already-woven cloth after the shuttle had passed it across the warp), was actuated by a crank rather than by a combination of cam and springs. The power loom had four motions to carry out, which essentially duplicated the actions of the hand-loom weaver. First, the warp—which stretched horizontally from the beam at the back of the machine, on which the ends of yarn were wound, to the beam at the front, on which the woven cloth was taken up—had to be advanced regularly by winding the finished cloth while the warp ends were kept taut. Second, at least two heddles had to be alternately raised and lowered from a frame arching above the warp. A heddle was composed of a row of strings or wires, each with an eye through which a warp end passed. When one heddle was raised, the other was lowered, thus forming a shed or open path within the warp through which the filling was passed; after an end passed, the heddles alternated in position, enclosing the passed yarn and forming a new shed. Third, the filling had to be carried through the shed by a shuttle, a little box about a foot long with steel points at both ends. The shuttle was not so much moved by any positive control comparable to (in the days before the flying shuttle) the weaver's arm; rather, it was thrown, hard. This action was called picking; and the speed of the loom was measured in number of picks per minute. Finally, the line of yarn lying in the shed had to be pressed evenly, and as tightly as the design of the cloth required, against the line of the already-woven cloth.

The power loom was an extremely noisy machine. The shuttle was thrown through the shed by the action of a rocker arm called a picker stick, which propelled it with high velocity. It slammed hard against the side of the carriage, stopped, and as soon as the heddles shifted, was hurled back in the opposite direction. The force was sufficient to make the shuttle a dangerous projectile if it escaped from the carriage; and it was a noisy one under the best of circumstances. A room filled with power looms, in sharp contrast to spinning apartments, was so filled with the clacking of shuttles that it was impossible to hear a person speak.

Phillips crammed as many power looms as possible into his mill. Each loom measured approximately 4 feet from front to back, 6 feet from side to side, and 5 feet in height. Many of his looms were described by one of his weavers as being "double looms." This presumably meant that two looms were joined by sharing the same pulley system; they could stand closer together than two looms each separately connected to the line shafting, and thus save floor space. Record of the precise geometry of the

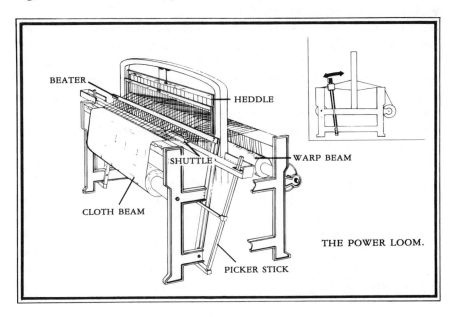

THE POWER LOOM.

arrangement of single and double looms in Phillips' mill has not survived, however.

Power looms were often served by experienced hand-loom weavers who found that they could make more money in this work than at the hand looms on which they were trained. Some of the weavers in the Rockdale mill were experienced English weavers who came to Rockdale for the money (one of whom described it, in a letter back home to England, as "an old established mill caled Philipses Mill").[2] Each weaver would handle either a pair of single looms or a pair of double looms, earning $4 to $5 per week on the former, and $5 to $6 on the latter—substantial wages, perhaps not competing with those of the mule spinners but by no means poor. Presumably there was at least one overseer, perhaps one to each floor.

The mill employed, in 1826, about 120 hands, who earned as a whole about $500 per week. This amounts to an average of a little more than $4 per week per worker. No doubt most of these operatives worked at the looms, but there were auxiliary jobs to be done: receiving and uncrating the yarn; sizing the warps (in a turbid solution of starch and tallow in water); mounting the warps on beams; setting the beams in the looms, and threading each warp end through the eye of its proper string in the proper heddle, according to the prescribed weave pattern; putting each warp end through its proper slot in the reed. After a loom had woven the completed cut (about 64 yards) of cloth, the remaining warp and the beamed cloth had to be removed; the cloth had to be taken off the beam; it might then be bleached, dyed, further sized, or treated in other ways; and at last, it had to be packaged for shipment to Philadelphia.

While the loom was weaving, the weaver was necessary for only one regularly recurring task. When the cop of filling in the shuttle was exhausted, the weaver had to replace it with a new cop. Apart from this, he had to make sure that the machinery was operating satisfactorily and producing cloth of the desired pattern and quality. And if an end of warp or filling should break (an event which automatically stopped the machine), he had to tie the warp ends or twist together the ends of filling before weaving could continue.

It is not possible to say, from the data available on Phillips' mill, what proportion of his "hands" were male and what female. Evidently, however, the pattern here was not the same as at Lowell, with its legendary legions of young female operatives. A letter written by an English weaver named John Morris from Rockdale in 1834 identified five men who were all working in "Philipses' Mill"; his sister Jane stayed home and took care of the children and boarders. Later he noted that two male relatives and one female were "working on the power looms at Mr Croshers Mill."[3] Later on still, in the 1840's, the Riddles' paybook indicates that in the weaving department, females outnumbered males on the pay list two to one, but evidently many of the women worked only part time, so that the number of males and females actually attending looms on any one day may have been about equal. The piecework rates, 15 cents per piece (about 30 yards) of cloth, were the same for all weavers, male and female alike.[4]

Phillips' mill was a productive one. In 1826 he was weaving 30,000 yards of cotton cloth per week, worth $3,000.[5] This would represent, if the mill operated continuously throughout the year, an annual gross income on the order of $150,000.

THE MACHINE SHOPS

A typical American machine shop in the 1830's was a room containing a lathe, a workbench on which were mounted a vise and a grindstone, and a tool chest full of assorted hammers, chisels, files, and wrenches. The machinist used these tools to fashion the wood and metal parts for machinery, from the bolts and screws all the way to the massive frames, out of cast or wrought iron or steel and, sometimes, to assemble the parts. In this shop he made his own benches and lathes. Such small shops were regularly associated with textile factories. Journeymen mechanics also sometimes set up small personal shops attached to their rooms in the cities.[1]

But the independent machine shop was not really a viable business. Unlike the traditional "turner" (as the elder John Garsed had called himself in England), who used the woodworking lathe to fashion such objects as table and chair legs and who thus could serve a variety of neighborhood household needs, the machinist who worked in metal was necessarily connected not so much with households as with industries. He had to take castings, rods, or sheet metal made in a foundry, work on it in his shop, and then send the parts—or the machine—to a factory for use. This work was time-consuming and expensive. Thus, apart from the shops associated with particular factories, the bulk of machine shop practice was carried on in larger "works" employing from ten to twenty hands—and in the largest, fifty or more. These works, like the Sellers' shops in Upper Darby, Oliver Evans' Mars Works in Philadelphia, Horatio Allen's Novelty Works in New York, and the Matteawan Manufacturing Company and the West Point Foundry on the Hudson River, contained several departments: a machine shop proper, with an assemblage of lathes and other tools; a blacksmith shop, where welds could be made; a foundry, where castings were poured, and where if necessary other iron and steel products could be rolled or slit; a pattern room, where the wooden patterns for the castings were catalogued and kept; a drafting room, where plans and specifications were put on paper; and an assembly area, where the parts of large machines such as locomotives, marine and stationary steam engines were put together.

Working in a Machine Shop in the 1830's

The tools of the machinist were, in most places, very primitive. The lathe was often operated as it had been for hundreds of years, by a treadle and springpole apparatus; sometimes a hand crank was employed; in the larger shops, the lathe was belt-driven. The work was held fast in a horizontal position between the two mandrels and was rotated by a cord wrapped around one end; the cutting tool was held by the operator, with one end resting on his shoulder and the other, supported by a fixed rest, pressed against the work. Power-operated slide rests which moved along a track were still a rarity. Most of the actual finishing of metal parts other than cylindrical rollers and rods was done with a hammer, cold chisel, and a set of files, and this involved not merely the routine task of smoothing off the snags and rough edges on a casting, but also the difficult task of producing plane surfaces. (Yet incredibly accurate test planes could be achieved, always made in threes to preclude parallel concave/convex pairs, so near perfect that one surface floated on a film of air above the other and could only be removed by sliding rather than by lifting.) Milling machines were still relatively rare. It was not until 1832 in England that a really effective metal-planing machine was patented. In 1834, the Sellers brothers at Cardington Works made their own planing machine—the first such machine in Pennsylvania and the third in America.[2]

The external forms of the old guild organization were followed in a loose sort of way in the organization of these larger works. The person in charge (who might or might not be an owner) often was referred to as a "master mechanic." He might earn a substantial income, anywhere up from $100 per month. The journeyman—who owned his own chest of hand tools but not the lathes—might earn $2 to $3 per day. And the apprentice, on a three-year contract, received about 50 cents a day the first year, 66 2/3 cents the second year, and 83 1/3 the last. Apprentices usually were not legally bound, as in the old days, to a single master, but could and did move from one job to another to gain experience in the various branches of work. For instance, the artist John Rogers—later to achieve fame as the creator of "Rogers Groups," the popular table statuary of the latter half of the century—in his early years followed the machinist's trade. He served his three years apprenticeship at the Amoskeag Mills in Manchester, New Hampshire, and at Horatio Allen's Novelty Works in New York, from 1850 to 1853, learning first the use of the hand tools, then the use of powered tools, then drafting, and finally the pattern room (which housed 12,000 patterns). He served for three more years as a journeyman at Amoskeag, studying both locomotives and textile machinery; and finally went out in 1856 for a year to Hannibal, Missouri, as the master mechanic in the machine shop of the Hannibal and St. Joseph Railroad. His career as a mechanician was terminated by the panic of 1857 and he turned his talents fully to art thereafter.[3]

The work was hard and dangerous. As in the cotton mills, machinists got to work at dawn (or before) and left at dark (or after), putting in a twelve- to fourteen-hour day standing at bench or lathe. The constant handling of oily tools and iron filings quickly blackened the hands; as John Rogers complained to his father, after four days of work,

> In the first place the bells are rung at about 4 1/2 in the morning—that is to get up—at seven minutes before five they ring a second time and then we have to go into the shop and commence work. At seven we wash and go to breakfast and come back a quarter before eight—At half past twelve to dinner and back quarter past one and to tea at seven when I have felt so tired I have been to bed soon after. . . . My hands get almost black before I have been in the shop five minutes but they keep growing blacker and blacker till at last they get a regular shining polish like a new air tight stove and you may imagine what a job it is to wash them three times a day before eating. I wonder if that famous washing mixture wouldn't be good. I wish mother would try it and give her opinion. I have almost used my nail brush up for I am bound to have them clean once a day.[4]

The rooms were large, noisy with the sound of clanging hammers and scraping files, hot in the summer and cold in the winter, being poorly heated. Men arrived in relatively formal dress, with street pants, shirt, neckpiece, waistcoat, and jacket; but they stripped down to pants and shirt before standing up to the bench, where after a day's work the neophyte's ankles swelled from standing and the neck ached from bending over.

Industrial accidents were common. There was little or no personal protective equipment like goggles, and fast-moving machinery and belts were largely unshielded. George Escol Sellers recalled the time when one of the machinists at Cardington, turning a shaft in an engine lathe powered by belting, leaned over and allowed his long black silk cravat to become entangled in the carrying clog. He was nearly choked to death. A foreman of John Rogers "got his hand caught in a belt & pulled under a drum & badly hurt." Eyes were particularly vulnerable to the hot metal chips turned off by lathe and chisel: Isaiah Lukens, one of the Sellers' circle, lost an eye in this way; John Rogers got his tongue badly burned when a hot chip flew into it while he was whistling at his work, and some of his friends had permanently scarred eyeballs.[5] The most spectacular accident which Rogers recorded happened in the foundry; he reported it to his father in some awe:

> We have had several accidents at the shop today. First, the main shaft in our room broke & as all speed was on it made a great disturbance. It was close to where I was at work. This afternoon the chain to the large derrick, in the foundry, broke by the weight of a tub of melted iron containing five tons of the metal & went completely over one man from head to foot & strange to say though he is pretty badly burnt yet he is not dangerously. It went over another man's face & burnt his whiskers off & that was all. They say that when iron is so hot it runs off before it burns & the reason this man was burnt so was because of his clothes.[6]

Despite the arduous nature of the work, the machinist's trade attracted in general an extremely intelligent group of young men. They were aware of the vast industrial expansion under way in the textile and transportation industries, and looked forward to educating themselves widely and generally in manual skills, technical, and even scientific knowledge as preparation for the administrative role of master mechanic or engineer, where the earnings could be substantial and the work constantly called for a creative intelligence.[7]

Machine Shops in the Rockdale District

Because of their size and weight and the consequent difficulty of transporting them (and of calling in a distant mechanic), the machines were for the most part serviced and repaired by local people. Each factory had two or three male employees who specialized in this work. The Riddles, for instance, employed a carpenter, a blacksmith, a tinsmith, and a machinist—and must have provided them with a shop of sorts. The carpenter was employed to repair the wooden parts of machines, to screw, pin, or bolt together and to varnish wooden parts of the carding engines, to cover rollers with deerskins and sheepskins, to install card clothing and fillets (wire-studded leather strips) on the cards. The tinsmith made the large cans in which the slivers were accumulated and carried in the preparation rooms. The Parkmount machine shop in the early 1830's included, at least, a small blacksmith's forge, a lathe on which the machinists could turn their own rollers for machines, a "grinder," a "cutting engine" (i.e., a milling machine), workbenches, and a supply of chisels, files, saws, and other hand tools. Other, more generalized carpenter's tools may have been kept in the barn.[8]

The Riddles' facilities were small compared with those at Penn's Grove, where the Garseds maintained a water-powered machine shop in the old woolen factory.[9] The Garsed equipment was more extensive and to them the Riddles sent some of their more difficult repairs, such as welding a broken iron shaft. Another substantial machine shop was part of the establishment at Lenni bought by William Martin in 1823. The advertisement in the *Post Boy* for December 3, 1822, contained the following specification of equipment:

> Three slide lathe and fluteing engine, turning lathes, top and fluted rollers unfinished, one cutting engine, one roving frame, seven vices, four anvils, three pairs blacksmith's bellows, stocks, dies, and taps, a quantity of cut brass wheels with blocks, spindles unfinished, fliers, lumber, iron, cast steel, a number of cast iron wheels for machinery, and a great variety of tools for machine making.[10]

No details are available on the shops at West Branch beyond Crozer's noting that his mechanics were paid almost as much in wages as the operatives for "building machinery."[11]

It is evident that each manufactory in the Rockdale district had a larger or smaller machine shop from which tools could be borrowed, repairs made to the machinery, new replacement items like card clothing be installed, and where breakable wooden items like spindles and wooden shafts could be manufactured for use in the mill. These shops also built, in part, the machines used in the mill. The manufacturer hired mechanics full or part time to operate these shops. If a particular mill did not happen to have the tools, or the skilled personnel, to handle a service-and-repair problem, the manufacturer turned first to his neighbors within the district to hire the job done. It is also noteworthy that the Garsed and Riddle shops contained machine tools of advanced design for the times: slide lathes and milling machines, both just recently invented.

Even with new machinery purchased from outside the Rockdale area, a dependence on local resources was necessary for much of the work. Mules and spinning frames purchased from distant suppliers were too large to be shipped assembled. Instead, they had to be crated in sections and put together in the factory. This reassembly could take some time. At Parkmount, the "tenth mule" arrived from Philadelphia on May 17, 1832. It was not until October that the Day Book noted that Alexander Cochrane was beginning to get the new mule ready, and in November it was recorded that it was nearly "ready for starting."[12]

The Garsed Manufactory of Power Looms

The only machines completely manufactured in the Rockdale district were the power looms produced by the Garseds. The Garseds had taken over the old woolen factory at Penn's Grove in 1830 or 1831. The history of the site, as it developed through the period up to their acquisition, is illustrative of the interplay between economic change and technological development and may be worth reviewing in some detail. A Quaker farmer, Nathan Sharpless, owned a twelve-acre tract including the old mill seat at Penn's Grove from 1791 on through 1818. (It probably had been the site of a mill from the late seventeenth century, to judge from the presence of old abandoned and forgotten dams and races in the area.) Up to 1815, the mill seat contained a three-story gristmill, sawmill, frame barn, and two houses, one of stone and the other frame. The gristmill was three stories high, in ground plan 45 by 50 feet, and contained two burr mill stones and bolting cloths for merchant work (i.e., for making the fine flours exported by Philadelphia merchants). In 1815 Sharpless constructed a "commodious" woolen spinning factory and fulling mill "with machinery complete." The property was advertised for sale in 1817 in the West Chester newspapers and was duly purchased by Isaac Sharpless and Gideon Hatton, who leased the factory and sawmill to John Hastings and the gristmill to Joseph Mancill. Sharpless, Hatton, and Hastings converted the woolen mill to a cotton factory and the associated fulling mill into a "weaver and machine maker shop." In the cotton factory they installed new machinery of the kind standard in the spinning mills of the locality: a picker, a blower, and a willowing machine for use in the picker room; 10 carding engines, with a grinding machine for the teeth; 12 drawing frames, 12 roving frames, and 1 stretcher; 4 throstles of 123 spindles each; 2 mules of 204 spindles each; 4 reels; 3 winding blocks; a yarn press; and a banding machine (for fastening crates of yarn). Becoming financially embarrassed, Hastings in 1823 sold the cotton machinery and the lease to Dennis Kelly, the Irish cotton manufacturer of Cobbs Creek; John Turner and Company seems to have taken over the machine shop.

In 1829, George W. Hill and Peter Hill jointly purchased the Penn's Grove farm and mill seat, and immediately proceeded to improve it. The old stone-and-frame building, which had been originally constructed in 1815 as a woolen factory and fulling mill, and more lately had been a cotton-spinning and -weaving factory, and "machine maker shop," they leased to John Garsed, who probably purchased the machine tools still there. This building was 60 by 30 feet, and two stories in height. Probably in view of the decline in the prosperity of the flour-milling trade (as a result of soil exhaustion and the incursions of the Hessian fly), they converted the stone gristmill into a cotton-spinning factory. This too they leased to Garsed. Garsed at first rented a house for his large family (in 1830 he had three sons and three daughters under twenty years of age; his wife died about 1835 after bearing two more children). As his profits amassed, however, he was enabled to buy first a couple of houses in Middletown, where he lived, and then a twenty-acre farm in Aston, with the necessary barn and springhouse, and a large mansion. The Hill brothers also constructed a new stone cotton-weaving mill, 96 by 42 feet, four stories high, with an attic, which they leased to James Houghton. Houghton bought a small farm with nineteen acres of land across the creek in Aston Township. He installed power looms, probably made in Garsed's shop a few yards away. The Hills quickly began to acquire more land around the site, in order to house the employees, and to add more factory buildings: a stone "drying house" (28 by 18 feet), a blacksmith shop, and a store which also housed a post office. They constructed stone and frame tenements. By 1835 the Penn's Grove site had expanded to fifty-six acres and housed twenty-two tenant families, seventeen of them in rows or "blocks" of two or four houses; by 1836 the number of families at Penn's Grove, both on and off the Hill property, was nearly forty. Garsed's three-story cotton mill had been expanded by a two-story extension 42 by 34 feet.

The Garseds probably made and sold power looms to Houghton (he installed about 150 such looms). They certainly sold power looms to the Riddles: in November 1833 the Riddles bought ten at $70 apiece; they received ten more in May 1834. They also bought eight surplus looms from John S. Phillips in the same year which may have been produced by the Garseds. Whether the Garseds had constructed the original power looms for Phillips in 1825 is doubtful; perhaps John Turner and Company, or John Hastings after his removal in 1823, had made them. Who made the looms which Crozer installed, about the same time as the Riddles, is not known.

The Garsed power-loom factory by 1840 was producing both cotton and woolen looms, probably of the "Scotch" cam-operated type, and of several qualities.[13] In that year the son Richard succeeded to his father's business, and in 1842 he began to manufacture looms which produced, in his own factory, cotton and worsted damask table and piano covers. These received a silver medal award in the exhibition of the Franklin Institute that same year for "novelty and excellence." It has been claimed that "this was probably the beginning of the manufacture of articles of this description in Pennsylvania, if not in America."[14]

In the meantime the other machine maker from Penn's Grove, John Hastings, was not far away. He and David Trainer established a weaving mill on Naaman's Creek, just above Marcus Hook in Lower Chichester Township, and there installed some sixty power looms, no doubt of Hastings's own manufacture.[15] They went out of business in 1840.[16]

John Hyde's Contract for Making Four Mules

Most of the spinning machinery used on Chester Creek had to be made by people from outside the valley. Many of them were machinists and founders in the immediate area (within a day's hauling distance), in Philadelphia, Chester, Wilmington, and along the Brandywine. Sometimes these people could be hired to take up temporary residence at the mill while they built the machinery. There is no clear example of this at Parkmount. But the records of Joseph Bancroft, who was setting up a cotton-spinning mill at Rockford on the Brandywine, fifteen miles away, simultaneously with the Riddles at Parkmount, describe the practice. A mechanic named John Hyde, of the partnership "J. and J. Hyde," agreed to make four mules of three hundred spindles each at a cost of $1.15 per spindle (i.e., $345 per mule). It was estimated that it would take Hyde and the four hands working with him six months to complete the job. Hyde would be paid $1.50 per day for each man employed at the work and $2 per day for himself while he was working. With advice from Bancroft, Hyde was to find all the materials and secure or fabricate all the patterns for the castings; the Rockford Manufacturing Company would reimburse him for the cost. He was to supply his own hand tools; the company would provide a shop equipped with certain specified pieces of water-powered equipment—three lathes, one upright drill (presumably a drill press), two grindstones, three vises, one circular saw; and various hand tools—glazers, hammers, drills, reamers, arbours, turning tools, taps, and dies. The company would also provide the services of a blacksmith. The payment was to be in installments as the work progressed, $200 by the end of the first month of work, and $140 per month thereafter, with the balance being paid in quarters at the starting of each mule. Hyde would be allowed to keep any tools not needed in the company shop when the job was over.[17]

Local Assembly of Imported Parts

The Riddles, as we have seen, bought some at least of their mules from a supplier in Philadelphia but had to assemble them in their own factory using their own mechanics. This was not the case with the spooling machine ($120) and warping mill ($50) that they bought in November 1833 from Samuel Jackson, a Philadelphia machinist. A week after they had hauled the machines to Parkmount in farmer McCracken's wagon, Jackson himself came out to set up the machinery.

In the case of some of the preparation machinery (the cards, draw frames, and so forth), the Riddles seem to have followed a third procedure: to order the necessary cast-iron sections from machinery makers in the region, to make the wooden parts in their own shop, to purchase the card clothing and other special working pieces from various Philadelphia and Wilmington suppliers, and then put together the whole machine themselves. Some of the cards they managed in this way (and some they bought complete). In October and November 1832, for instance, they bought about 1,000 lbs. of iron castings for the cards from James Flint (now a partner of the John Hyde who made the mules for Bancroft). They also paid for the use of patent patterns belonging to Parke and Tiers of Philadelphia (Parke being a "brass founder" and Tiers a "manufacturer"). Castings cost only 5 cents per pound. At the same time the Parkmount mechanics were making some of the patterns for the card parts themselves. The wire-covered card clothing and fillets they bought from Cunningham and Crawley, card clothing manufacturers of Philadelphia.

The draw frames were made in the same way. A month later they bought two cast-iron drawing frame heads from Flint, presumably making the major wooden structural parts themselves, and buying special moving parts like spindles, rollers, bobbins, and flyers from still other suppliers. The rollers for the draw frames were purchased from George Hodgson, the well-known Brandywine machinist. Each frame required two pairs of long rollers; the Riddles bought four pairs, weighing a total of nearly 150 lbs., at 35 cents per pound. The lower roller of each pair had to be fluted; the upper was covered with a soft skin. The roller coverings were bought from George Moore, a Philadelphia skin dresser. The fluting was done by Wood and Reeves. (The Hodgson firm had also earlier made rollers for two throstles for William Martin but the Martin machine shop did their own fluting.) The bobbins (634 of them) were purchased from John Crowther, a Philadelphia "turner," at a price of $6 per 100.

Exactly the same procedure was followed after they bought their twenty power looms from the Garseds in 1833. The shuttles were purchased from Jackson and Snyder. The reeds and heddles were secured from William Higham.

The Riddles, in fact, dealt with a considerable number of suppliers of machine parts and supplies, within the Philadelphia-to-Wilmington area. They bought surplus parts from other cotton manufacturers, such as Daniel Lammot, just up the stream, G. B. Lownes, near the McDowell Mill in Springfield, and William Almond, of Blockley in Philadelphia. They ordered castings from James Flint and Jonathan Bonney and Company, both probably from the Brandywine area; from Parke and Tiers of Philadelphia; and from Alfred Jenks, the former employee of the Slater enterprises who had set himself up as a cotton spinner and machine maker in Kensington. (Jenks made most of the machinery in Houghton's and Garsed's mills, except for the looms, which were Garsed's.) Their rollers they bought from Hodgson on the Brandywine. Copper steampipes for the sizing trough were installed by Benjamin O'Bryan, Philadelphia coppersmith. Carding machines and supplies were purchased from the Sellers firm of Upper Darby (the same family that had purchased Parkmount and Lenni). Chain cables and iron of various kinds came from Washington Jackson and J. S. Riddle, a firm of merchants and machinists on Front Street in Philadelphia.

The general pattern of machinery procurement followed by the Riddles is thus fairly clear. The structural frame of the machinery was made of iron, cast from patterns made by the Riddles or provided by the manufacturer, in foundries and machine shops in Wilmington, in Philadelphia, and (in the case of power looms) on Chester Creek. The card clothing, brass gears, steel rollers, bobbins and spindles, and other finely machined parts were also made in outside shops but were ordered separately by the Riddles. Many wooden parts, and parts that could be put together by the local tinsmith and blacksmith, were made on the site; and the whole machine was then assembled, tested, and adjusted by the factory's own mechanics. There were some exceptions, as in the case of the warping mill, which was set up by the supplier, but the general rule seems to have been one of local assembly.[18]

Patent Machinery from Distant Manufacturers

The Riddle Day Book for the period 1832 to 1835 reveals no instance of the purchase of machinery or parts from outside the Philadelphia-to-Wilmington area. But records from the area show that other manufacturers, at least, did turn to famous outside textile machinery manufacturers for some of their equipment. These items were shipped by water to Philadelphia, Chester, Marcus Hook, or Wilmington, and carted from there.

One of these outside manufactories which was well thought of in the Philadelphia-Wilmington area was the Savage Manufacturing Company near Baltimore. In 1825, when Daniel Lammot was making his first unsuccessful attempt to launch himself in the cotton business, he was told that it would be a good place to buy machinery. Perhaps being partial to Baltimore, his birth place, he wrote to E. I. du Pont about the matter.

If you can obtain any information respecting the "Savage Manufactory" (belonging to the Williams family of Baltimore, and situated on the Patuxent, on the Washington road, about 15 miles from Baltimore) I will thank you. I wish to know whether they manufacture Cotton machinery, and whether they have any Spindles in operation in their mills. I heard yesterday that it would be the best and largest establishment in the Country. Do not put yourself out of the way to gain the information.[19]

Joseph Bancroft bought machinery from Savage in 1832 when he was setting up his mill.[20]

Another famous machine-making locality was Patterson, New Jersey. Located in the old industrial park below the Falls of the Passaic, developed in the 1790's by Alexander Hamilton and his associates in the Society for Useful Manufactures, the Patterson mills had led a checkered career. The early ventures in textile manufacture had not been successful, but under the management of Roswell Colt, the site had attracted a considerable number of machinists, including the famous brothers George and Charles Danforth. The Patterson works produced a famous "double speeder" and William Martin's list of machinery for the mill at Lenni includes a "Patterson speeder—$100.00."[21] At a sale of machinery along Ridley Creek in 1841, also two "Patterson ring speeders" were advertised.[22]

There is no reference in Delaware County sources to machinery from the great New England manufacturers of textile machinery (although Joseph Bancroft bought some equipment from the Lowell shops and other suppliers in Massachusetts). The other great machinery supplier, however, was the Matteawan Manufacturing Company. Bancroft bought extensively from them; and in the Ridley Creek machinery sale of 1841, a "Matteawan double speeder" is mentioned.[23] Evidently, Matteawan products were being used in the area. It would appear likely that these products of distant manufactories, undoubtedly more expensive because of the shipping costs, were selected because they included patented improvements that made them essential for increased efficiency.

The famous machine-making establishments in Kensington, Patterson, Matteawan, Taunton, and Lowell represented an important and recent development on the American industrial scene: the factory which, in effect, manufactured factories, by specializing not in the production of a consumer product but in the production of machinery to make that product. These factories had an interest in making their competitors' machinery obsolete and thus added a new intensity to the pressure for technological improvement.

COMMERCIAL ASPECTS OF COTTON MANUFACTURING

Within the mill, activities were largely confined to production, to the care of the machinery, and to the training and disciplining of the labor force. The commercial aspects of the business were conducted elsewhere. These included the keeping of records, the payment of workers and other creditors, the making of decisions about the nature of the product and about expansion or curtailment of activities, the buying of raw materials and machinery, and the selling of the product.

The Mill Office

The records of the company were preserved in a small building—sometimes a house—near to but detached from the mill. These records included a daybook (or journal) and various ledgers. The daybook was simply a large bound volume of blank paper in which, day by day, important transactions were recorded informally, in order of occurrence, by the manufacturer himself or by a clerk. Such transactions included the payment of employees and other creditors; the assumption of debts; the receipt of cotton bales; and the shipping out of boxes of yarn or cloth. But the daybook also served as a kind of business diary in which significant events of all sorts were written down: the breaking of a shaft, the repair of a gudgeon, a flood, a fire, the arrival of new families, the dismissal of an unsatisfactory operative, the construction of tenements, and so forth.

In well-kept journals prepared by clerks who knew double-entry bookkeeping, each notation carried instructions to the clerical staff as to the debit/credit status of the transaction, the account in which it was to be formally recorded (Machinery, Cotton, Employees), and the ledger number of the entry (each employee's wage record, for instance, would be recorded under his or her family's personal number). At least annually the company went through the books and prepared a statement of financial position, summarizing credits and debits.

The mill office served also as a place where petty cash business was transacted. Operatives, or members of their families, often borrowed small sums of money to buy groceries; local suppliers—general storekeepers like George Hill, millers, carters, masons—would show up requesting payment for goods and services. Although payday came around every four weeks, individual operatives might be dismissed, or leave, at any time, and they had to be paid off by cash or check. (Checks were drawn on the Delaware County Bank in Chester, on the Girard Bank in Philadelphia, and occasionally even on banks as far away as New York.)

The mill office no doubt also served as a location for discussing business; but much of the business conversations of concern to the firm were conducted elsewhere, in Philadelphia particularly, either at the offices of the firm's suppliers and customers or in the firm's own office. From the beginning, Phillips and Lewis traded in cotton cloth at their own office on Front Street; Crozer, the Riddles, and Lammot established Philadelphia offices later on.[1]

The Quality of the Product

The four spinning mills listed in the 1826 survey produced for the most part coarse yarns: "coarse," by Crozer's definition, being "No. 20, and under."[2] Cotton yarn was, and is, measured with respect to the dimension of coarseness-to-fineness by the ratio of weight to length. Although schemes differed in various parts of the world, in England and in most parts of America a standard system was employed: the "count" was given by the number of hanks which made up a pound of yarn.[3] The hank was a unit of 840 yards. Thus a pound of No. 1 yarn—a very coarse yarn—would, if laid out in a line, stretch 840 yards. Very fine yarns could be spun with counts of 300 or more; a pound of No. 300 would unwind into a single strand nearly 144 miles long!

The market determined the manufacturer's decision about yarn count. The fine mule-spun British yarns, with counts up to 300 (at least as spun by the "prince of cotton spinners," Robert Owen of New Lanark in Scotland), pre-empted the American market for fine yarns; only at the low counts could American yarns be competitive. Thus in 1826 Knowlton Mill was producing about 1,100 lbs. of No. 20 yarn per week; Penn's Grove, about 1,000 lbs. of Nos. 6 to 24; Lenni, about 1,100 lbs. of Nos. 18 to 25; and West Branch, about 1,000 lbs. of Nos. 17 to 20.[4] Yarns in this count range were suitable for the manufacture of cloths like cotton flannel, jeans, and bed tickings.

Although for economic (not technical) reasons only coarse yarns were made, this did not mean that such yarns necessarily were of poor quality. Some American manufacturers, in fact, prided themselves on the high quality of their "coarse" yarns. Quality was expressed in the strength and evenness of the strand. The better, long-stapled cottons of course produced better yarn. The common practice of spinning the waste—broken filaments with very short staple—would weaken the yarn. British mills often did this, reintroducing the sweepings into the carding process and thus into the finished product, thereby reducing the strength as well as the price of the yarn. Since about 10 percent by weight of baled cotton received in the mill was eventually lost as waste, and since the cost of raw materials was about half the manufacturer's cost, this practice could be economically significant. Other processes, too, affected the quality of the product: the efficiency of the carding, the adjustment of the drawing and twisting frames, the skill of the mule operator, the frequency of breaks in the yarn, and the deftness of the piecers. In order to be competitive with British low-count yarns, which often in periods of overproduction were dumped on the American market to be sold *below* cost, the American product had to have a reputation for quality.[5]

Buying and Selling

Much of the manufacturer's time was spent traveling between his mill on Chester Creek and the offices of the merchants from whom he bought his cotton and of the weavers to whom he sold his yarn. These people were usually located in Philadelphia. From the mill to Chester or Marcus Hook, the only means of transportation was by carriage or on horseback. From Chester or "the Hook" to Philadelphia there was, in addition to the same modes of private travel, the option of public conveyance, on water by the steam packet or on land by stagecoach (the railroad between Philadelphia and Wilmington was not completed until 1838).

There were merchants in Philadelphia who specialized in importing cotton from the south, some of it no doubt transshipped from New York but much coming directly from southern ports. Such Philadelphia firms included J. R. Neff and Company, E. N. Bridges and Company, Samuel Comley, James G. Crozier (no relative of John P. Crozer), Jackson and Riddle, Richard Pettit, W. D. Prescott, and Sloan and Relf.[6] Buying cotton involved shopping for both quality and price; purchasers would shift from one merchant to another, depending on the availability of cotton, its price and quality, and the state of the credit relationship between buyer and seller. Cotton was bought on credit, the manufacturer generally giving a note for three or four months and paying within the time period, either by check or by passing on a note (minus discount) the buyer had received from one of his customers. Cotton was sold by the name (and reputation) of the region that produced it—Upland Georgia, Mississippi, Louisiana and New Orleans, Roanoke. All of the above types, which were of middling quality, were used on Chester Creek, but Upland Georgia seems to have been preferred. The price of the cotton in Philadelphia fluctuated constantly, and over the period from 1825 to 1835 showed a gradual rise. In 1832 the price was fluctuating between 11 and 13 cents per pound; next year it rose to between 16 and 18 cents per pound. Cotton was often bought sight unseen and delivered weeks later, by ship, at Philadelphia or the Hook. When notified of its arrival, the manufacturer had to send a driver with a wagon and a team of horses to bring it from dockside to the mill. A wagonload would average about ten to fifteen bales, or 1 1/2 to 2 tons.

On his journeys to Chester, the Hook, and Philadelphia, the manufacturer also had occasion to order other materials, which similarly he had to haul in his own or a hired wagon—oil for lubrication and for the lamps that lighted the mill on winter mornings and evenings; coal to burn in the stoves; mordants and dyestuffs; sheet iron and tin; leather belts for the shafting; and, of course, the machinery.

The products of the mill were sold to three kinds of market. In the case of spinning mills, yarn was sold to power-loom factories; to merchant houses who took goods on commission, or bought them outright; and to a miscellany of small local buyers—storekeepers, individual employees, and neighbors. The weaving mill, of course, produced gray goods ready for bleaching, dyeing, or printing. The spinning mills produced several types of product. Shuttle cops, in the count range of No. 8 to No. 24, were sold primarily to other manufacturers who operated weaving mills. They were packed in numbered wooden boxes, weighing when full anywhere from 150 to 200 lbs. each, and were carted in the company's wagon to the purchaser. The yarn in cops was sold by the pound: "Angola" cops (about No. 8) in 1832 sold for 45 cents per pound; lower-quality "Canton Flannel" cops (about No. 15) brought only 20 to 22 cents. In general, the higher counts of yarn, within the 8 to 24 range, might bring a few cents more in price but the major variable was quality. Some boxes of cops (in the same count range) were sold to commission merchants, who retailed them to hand-loom weavers in Philadelphia. A very small quantity of "balled yarn" was also produced for retail sale.

Finished cloth from the weaving mills was counted by the "piece." A piece of cloth (i.e., the quantity woven from a single warp) would be about 28 to 30 yards in length. The cloth was packed either in cases, about thirty pieces per case, or in bales of about forty pieces. The cloth was sold by the yard, however, not by the piece. In 1834 "printing cloth" from the Riddles sold for 6 cents per yard; Canton flannel for 13 cents per yard.

The third major product was cotton laps. The cotton lap was a sheet of thick cotton batting, perhaps a yard wide and several yards long. It was an intermediate product of a spinning mill, being initially produced by the machine called the spreader, immediately after the raw cotton had come through the picker, and then refined at the special card called the lap card. Laps were originally designed as a standardized, carefully weighed quantity of cotton—usually 8 ounces—which could be fed evenly into the carding machine to yield a more uniform sliver. But there was a considerable domestic market for laps, which could be used as the filling for patchwork, and for other purposes as "cotton wool." Laps sold for about 10 cents a piece and a spinning mill would consign hundreds of them per month to commission merchants, local general stores, employees and neighbors.

Even the by-products of the mill were sold. Some clean waste was sold off to employees and neighbors; but most of the waste (much of it very dirty waste from the picker room and some of it oily floor sweepings) was sold to nearby paper mills, along with the ropes and bales in which the raw cotton was delivered, to be used in the manufacture of rag paper (wood pulp was not yet used to make paper). Some was sold to manufacturers of carpet filling. And some was also sold to nearby machine shops, for use as wipers for oily parts and to clean up metal filings, and later to fill up journal boxes on railroad cars. The bagging sold at about 1 1/2 cents per pound; ropes brought 1 1/4 cents; waste brought 1/2 to 1 cent per pound. The quantities were considerable: the Riddles sold at least 5 tons of waste per year to two nearby paper mills, and smaller quantities to a variety of local enterprises and individuals.

The various commercial transactions were handled for the most part by an exchange of four-month notes: the manufacturer would take personal three- to six-month notes in exchange for his wares, and would give notes in payment for his raw materials. Because the manufacturer's debtors and creditors were in turn buying and selling by exchanging notes, the system was one of intricate financial interdependence. James Houghton sold much of his cloth to Henry Farnum and Company. He accepted their notes, and when he bought yarn from the Riddles, he passed them on (allowing a discount of about 2 or 3 percent) to the Riddles, who either turned them in to the local bank for cash (minus the bank's discount) or passed them on to a cotton merchant. If they got into the hands of a bank, the bank collected from the original debtor. A typical example of note passing occurred in January 1834, when the Riddles paid Henry Sloan $378.96 on their bill for a load of cotton with a note they had accepted from Peter Hill, to whom they had consigned yarn. Peter Hill had received the note from Moses Redpath, who had originally received it from Robert Cumming. Inasmuch as Peter Hill was not commonly looked upon as a good risk in financial matters, the Riddles had secured an endorsement from Peter's brother George, the local storekeeper, with whom they kept an account for groceries.

Thus the note-exchange process permitted complicated financial transactions to be completed "in the city" with a minimum use of cash (paper money or specie). Complementing the use of commercial paper, some bills were also paid by checks on the Delaware County Bank in Chester and the Girard Bank in Philadelphia. And in the local community, a barter system operated on a small scale to supplement the exchange of paper. The paper mills, for instance, to whom waste was sold, paid part of their bills with reams of paper.

The principal outlay of cash, in fact, was in the payment of the workers. On payday every fourth week, the mills brought in a few hundred dollars in cash from the Delaware County Bank. Petty cash was also available in the mill office at all times to lend to employees or their families as an advance on wages. But some of the workers preferred to leave some part of their money on the books, uncollected, until such time as the family moved, or some substantial new expense required its use.[7]

The Shift to Complete Process Factories

The first generation of factories—those built before 1832—were modeled after the English practice, in that each mill conducted *either* spinning or weaving; none did both. And the Riddles even excluded throstle spinning, concentrating exclusively on their ten mules to produce filling (and small quantities of warp).

This procedure was perhaps efficient in its simplicity, but it minimized the potential profit of both the spinning mills and the power-loom factories by introducing a packaging and transportation cost, a discount cost, and a profit margin between the spinner and the weaver. A spinner, if he added power looms, could sell to himself the necessary yarn cheaper than he could sell it to a weaver; consequently, he could sell the cloth cheaper than the specialized weaver could. Furthermore, if the spinner had both throstles and mules, he could manufacture all the kinds of warp and filling he required.

The first major shift in the manufacturing process along Chester Creek was more an economic or managerial than a technological one. It was the installation of power looms in mills hitherto exclusively devoted to spinning, and the elimination of businesses exclusively devoted to weaving.

The Riddles began the shift in November 1833 when they bought their first ten power looms from John Garsed. It is not entirely clear when John P. Crozer came to the same decision. When he answered Secretary of the Treasury Louis McLane's questionnaire in April 1832, he made it clear that all he made was "Cotton yarn, No. 15 to 33. . . . There are power looms in the neighborhood which consume part of the yarn; the balance is sold in Philadelphia to hand loom weavers."[8] But by March 1834, the English weaver William Morris who worked in Phillips' mill wrote home, "There is 4 powerloom mills in this neighborhood, 2 more starting, 2 of them containing about 150 looms each."[9] The two large ones were Phillips's and Houghton's. One already in motion, on a small scale, was at Parkmount. This leaves three other sites for the introduction of power looms in 1834; and the only possible locations were Lenni, West Branch, and Knowlton. Evidently by the end of 1834 *all* of the spinning mills had added power looms. By 1836 three members of the Morris family were "worcking on the power looms at Mr Crosher's Mill."[10] By May 1837, when Crozer testified to the Senate Committee, he had looms in his main mill and had added "a small weaving factory, employing twenty-seven persons; only three or four young children employed in the latter."[11]

The exclusive power-loom factories lingered for a few years. But Lewis and Phillips' lease was not renewed in 1835 (in part, as we shall see, for reasons other than economic) and their place at Rockdale was taken by a complete process manufacturer, Bernard McCready. And both James Houghton and the Garseds were displaced in 1842 when the Hills sold Penn's Grove to Samuel Riddle. Thus in the decade between 1832 and 1842, the old system of partial process mills was entirely replaced by complete process mills, which took baled cotton in and sent out cloth.

WORKING IN PARKMOUNT MILL IN 1832

Construction of the factory on the Hills' unimproved mill seat at the forks was begun in 1831. The work was done to the specifications of the brothers Samuel and James Riddle. The Hills invested $7,000 in the dam, race, and water wheel, and $10,000 more in the mill building.[1] The building was made of a local green stone (serpentine), 132 feet long and 58 feet wide, two stories and an attic, and was set along a sloping hillside on the north side of the main branch of the creek, just above the forks.[2] The dam was about 5 feet high, and a relatively short race, perhaps 100 yards long,

Top: COTTON PLANTATION

Bottom: WILLOWING

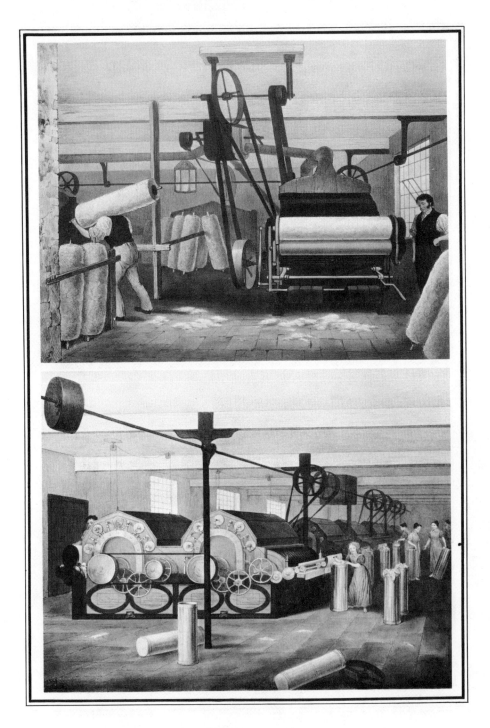

Top: LAP FRAME

Bottom: CARDING

(166)

Top: BOBBIN AND DRAWING FRAMES

Bottom: SPINNING

Top: BLEACHING

Bottom: WARPING AND WINDING

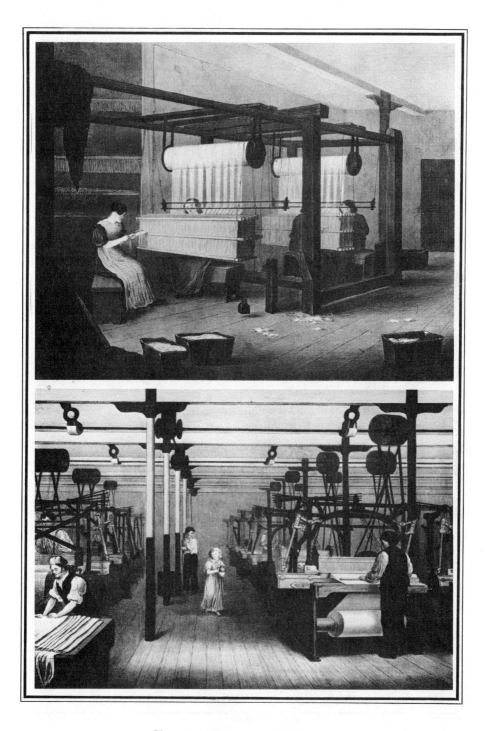

Top: REEDING, OR DRAWING IN

Bottom: WEAVING

(169)

Top: DYEING

Bottom: PRINTING

ran along the hillside to the water wheel. The wheel was a breast wheel, at the upstream end of the mill, and was roofed over with boards. The road curved around the mill and crossed over the race by the picker house to the covered bridge that led across the creek to John B. Ducket's paper mill.

The Riddles owned the machinery, which cost them about $16,000. They started out with a highly specialized operation, buying no throstles at all, investing instead in ten mules, a larger number than the other local mills. This gave them between 2,500 and 3,000 spindles. The mules were probably located in the attic, which provided a large floor space, well lighted by the conventional clerestory windows, and unencumbered by the lines of supporting pillars needed on the floors below. The floor below probably housed the card room, containing a spreader and at least two large carding engines—a breaker, or lap, card and a finisher card. In the adjoining room on the same floor were probably located the double speeder and the six drawing frames. The warping mill was probably on the same well-lighted floor. The machine shop, the packing and shipping room, and the storage areas for machinery, lumber, metal, cotton bales, and dyestuffs were probably on the ground floor. The picker room and the dyehouse very likely were in attached buildings. Nearby were the barn and the mill office.[3]

The Riddles' mill was unique among the local spinning mills in its exclusive use of mules for spinning and in its roomy floors. Although they put the wheel in operation late in 1831, the business of manufacturing began a few months later. The journal of "Parkmount factory" opens with the notation: "Day Book commenced on the first of February one thousand eight [hundred] and thirty two." But the Riddles were not content to leave their manufacturing methods constant. From that first day on, the daybook records a constant sequence of modifications and improvements: the building of new tenements, the purchase and setting up of new machinery, the adjusting of the old machines to make better yarn, the covering of the water wheel, eventually the purchase of power looms (in 1834). Later we shall discuss in detail the nature and implications of these technological changes.

The December 12, 1832, Cohort of Workers

The first regular payday was December 12, 1832. Before that time— no doubt because the mill was still establishing itself and the Riddles were spending almost all their cash on the purchase of machinery and materials —the workers were paid only small sums "on account" and were buying their groceries on the mill's credit. They were living, of course, in tenement houses owned by the mill and credit was also being extended for their rent.

Let us look at this first cohort of workers at Parkmount—the workers present on December 12, 1832—in some detail. The first observation, one whose importance cannot be overemphasized, is that the factory treated the domestic household, not the individual, as the unit of production. Usually the household consisted of a nuclear family, including husband, wife, their children, and perhaps attached relatives. But it might also consist of a one-parent family, or a man and his sisters, or various other household combinations. Occasionally, the "household" consisted of only a single male boarding with a worker family or at a nearby farm. Such situations often were temporary, occurring when a man took a job, leaving his wife and children behind to catch up with him later when circumstances (including the availability of a house near the factory) permitted. These household units were treated as economic units. The wages of all the workers in the household were paid to the effective head of the household (male or female), and all the members were assigned the same ledger number. When a new head of household rented one of the mill houses, he sometimes even signed an agreement to make available for work in the mill a specified number of "hands." The rent book contains seven such contracts in 1853 and 1854. For example, the following is the agreement signed by Joseph Wright:

Octr 1—1853   I have rented to Joseph Wright the house lately occupied by Alexander Crozier on the following Conditions. Joseph Wright Agrees to keep 2 Hands working in the factory at all times While he occupies the House, (sickness of the Hands excepting) and that he will give 2 weeks notice of his intentions to leave the house and of the hands to quit work (under all Circumstances) if required and at the expiration of the 2 weeks notice to give up peaceable possession of the House or forfeit the lying times of the hands or in case of removal the hands will forfeit without a regular notice being given. [signed] Joseph Wright[4]

At the time of the first payday on December 12, 1832, there were twenty household units providing hands to the mill. It is worth introducing them by name:

JESSE ALEXANDER and family, consisting at least of Alexander, his wife Margaret, and his two sisters. Jesse Alexander began work as a carder in April; his family joined him and moved into "the new house" in May 1832. His two sisters also worked in the mill and they had as a boarder still another worker, Neill Cairns. The Alexanders left the regular employ of the Riddles in April 1833 but remained in the neighborhood at least until November, when Jesse Alexander was paid $40 "for repairing the Dearborn" (a type of light wagon). For work in the mill during this period they received at least $189.32.

RICHARD BATES and family, including Bates and his wife, both in their twenties, and their three sons, two of them infants and one between seven and twelve. The nature of his work in the mill is not disclosed in the daybook. His son, from his age, must have been a piecer or scavenger. Presumably Bates occupied a house, for he paid road taxes and owned a cow. The Bates family arrived from Lower Darby (a township adjacent to Philadelphia) in the summer of 1832 and left in May 1833. During this period they earned at least $253.23. The Bates seem to have been a troublesome household, for the daybook notes in October that Bates's cow "went out of the pasture" and in December the son was fired "for smoking a Cigar in the mill."

FRANCIS BONNER and family, including at least himself and his wife; whether or not they had children is not known. Bonner arrived in September and worked briefly in the mule room as a creel attender; before the month was out he had his own mule and was spinning flannel. His family joined him late in November. They remained at least until January 1835, when the daybook closed, but were no longer in the neighborhood when the decennial census was taken in 1840. From September 1832 to September 1833 the Bonners earned at least $250.24.

NEILL CAIRNS, single, boarded with the Alexanders. It is not clear what he did in the mill. He remained from May 1832 to April 1833 and during these eleven months earned at least $160.88. He could read and subscribed to a newspaper.

ALEXANDER COCHRANE, a man in his sixties, and his family, consisting of his wife (in her fifties) and three grown children (ages seventeen to thirty-two, the youngest a son John, and two girls) arrived from Chester in October 1832, in the wagon usually used for hauling cotton bales. He was an experienced mule spinner and was initially assigned to getting the new mule ready. In the first year of work, the family earned at least $180.65. They remained through 1834.

WILLIAM COCHRANE, age about thirty and probably a son of Alexander, and his family, consisting of his wife, a brother of working age, a working sister named Sarah, plus another sister or sister-in-law and three male children under five years of age. William Cochrane was a mechanic who specialized in fine carpentry, such as making wooden patterns for the castings of carding engine parts. He also did general carpentry, making the boxes for shipping shuttle cops, and maintaining and repairing the barn, the sluice gates, and the mill building itself. At least two of his family also worked in the mill. The William Cochranes earned, from November 1832 through October 1833, at least $414.95.

JAMES CROOKS arrived in December 1832. His wife Mary, and their son James Jr., who was about five years old, came on in the following summer, occupying one of the tenement houses. Crooks, who was between twenty-two and thirty-two years of age, was a warper and his wife sometimes worked at balling yarn. They were a stable family who worked steadily for the Riddles until 1849. They bought books, purchased a cow from the Riddles (at a cost of $19), and produced babies. By 1840 the household consisted of eight persons, three of them engaged in "manufacturing": James and his wife Mary, his teen-age son James, another son under five, three daughters, one under five, and two (Jane and Isabella) in their teens. One of the grandmothers, a woman in her sixties, also lived with them. During the first year, December 1832 through November 1833, the family earned at least $217.32.

RUTH ANN FREDD, a widow (or abandoned wife) of about fifty, and her five children arrived in February 1832 and occupied one of the tenement houses. The children included little Mary, aged somewhere between seven and twelve; Elizabeth, between twelve and seventeen; William, between seventeen and twenty-two; James, in his twenties; and John, age unknown. All of the children worked in the mill, as did Mrs. Fredd; James, apparently, was also a hand-loom weaver who manufactured cloth at home. But Mrs. Fredd collected the wages for the whole family and carried out the various little financial negotiations with the mill that included borrowing petty cash, purchasing firewood, and securing orders on local millers and storekeepers for barrels of flour and other foodstuffs. Between February 1832 and February 1833 the family earned at least $148.33 in wages plus unknown amounts from boarders. They remained in the area into the 1840's and worked for the Riddles at least through January 1835.

JOHN GAUN worked for the Riddles only occasionally in the period May 1832 to February 1833. There is no information about what work he did or about his household. He earned only $3.50 and disappeared from the record after February 1833. By 1835 a "Jno. Gawny" was working in Bancroft's spinning mill on the Brandywine.

JOHN McDADE was apparently a single man of about thirty who arrived from Marcus Hook in July 1832. His mother Rachel was at the time the only McDade in Delaware County. She seems to have been a widow between fifty and sixty years of age, and had three sons between seventeen and thirty-two, of whom John was probably one. John learned about mules by working his way up from a piecer to creel attender; he began operating a mule in September. His sisters joined him in January or February. But in March he was "turned off" for fighting with Neill

Cairns; the Riddles evidently considered him to be at fault. He did not leave the area immediately, however, for he reappears in the 1840 census with a wife and three children, the eldest younger than ten. The McDades earned at least $184.20 during their time of employment.

ARCHIBALD McDOWELL, age twenty-four, was if not already, then soon to become, a brother-in-law of the Riddles, marrying their sister Mary, age twenty-two. He arrived in the United States about 1831 and may have been living and working at the factory in Springfield before moving to Parkmount. McDowell worked as a mule spinner for the Riddles from September through January. By next March 1833, Mc-Dowell had entered into a partnership with Joseph Gibbons, the owner of the land on which the Springfield factory was located, and the family moved back to Springfield. The Riddles continued to keep an account with them, ordering their cotton and selling their yarn. The McDowells eventually moved back into the area, and McDowell worked again for the Riddles as a highly paid spinner; by 1850 he had become the superintendent of the Glen Riddle factory.

SAMUEL McMULLEN was a mule spinner who began to work in July 1832 and continued through January 1835. There is no mention of his having a wife and children; he may have been one of the sons of a well-established local family across the creek in Aston Township headed by James McMullen. James McMullen first appeared as a head of household in the census lists in 1810; in 1830 he was between forty and fifty years old and had a son between fifteen and twenty. James was mentioned in the daybook as a purchaser of a piece of Canton flannel. The last mention of James McMullen in the census records was in 1840; he then still had in his household a son aged between twenty and thirty. From July 23, 1832, to July 28, 1833, Samuel McMullen earned at least $281.28.

HUGH McMUNN, age twenty-five, mule spinner and later carding superintendent, arrived at Parkmount directly from Ireland in December 1832; his family, including wife Elizabeth (also twenty-five) and four children (Mary, five; Eliza, three; John, one; and Archibald, a newborn infant), emigrated in the spring of the following year, no doubt after the birth of the new baby, and moved into one of the company houses. He worked for the Riddles until 1844, and returned to Penn's Grove in 1850, along with wife and children. He purchased books and subscribed to a newspaper. From December 1832 to December 1833 he earned at least $191.33.

JOHN McNAMEE, age twenty-five, was a blacksmith who worked full time for the Riddles from November 1832 until about January 1834. He was unmarried. From December 1832 through November 1833 he earned at least $160.94. In 1850 he was practicing his trade in the industrial suburb of Kensington and was married.

HENRY McNEILL, mule spinner, arrived with his family at Parkmount about November 1832 and left on May 27, 1833. He did not move far, only to Lenni, where he entered the employment of Daniel Lammot. Based on the information contained in the 1840 census, he was in his middle twenties to early thirties in 1832, with a wife in her twenties, a son between seven and twelve; an older man, between fifty-two and sixty-two, lived in the household. At least three of the family worked. Later on, the McNeills returned to work for the Riddles at Penn's Grove. Between December 1832 and June 1833, at their final reckoning, the family earned $220.74—a substantial income for six months.

HENRY McVEY arrived in August 1832 and in September began to operate a mule. His family seems to have joined him in December, when they began to rent one of the tenement houses. They left in January 1834. From August 1832 through July 1833 McVey earned $208.31.

HAMILTON MAXWELL, in his twenties, was another of the Riddles' brothers-in-law. A Scots-Irishman too, from the Belfast area, he was soon to be married to Jane Riddle, twenty-five, and came over to the Springfield factory from Ireland in 1829 or 1830 with his mother Mary Maxwell. They seem to have had no children. Hamilton Maxwell was an expert carder and on occasion the Riddles lent his services to the McDowell and Gibbons factory for a day or two. He worked at Parkmount from August 1832 at least until January 1835 but disappears from the local records after that. His wife Jane died in 1836. From August 1832 through July 1833 he earned (from the Riddles) at least $156.

ISABELLA MOORE was the daughter of a Mrs. Moore who collected her child's petty wages. Apparently she worked only occasionally from April 1832 to May 1833. This may have been the family identified in the Middletown census of 1830 headed by Mary Moore, a woman then in her fifties, who lived with two males, fifteen to twenty and twenty to thirty, and two females, fifteen to twenty and twenty to thirty, presumably sons and daughters and perhaps sons and daughters-in-law.

WILLIAM SHAW, originally from Baltimore, began to work as a mule spinner for the Riddles in July 1832 at the age of twenty-one. There was a Mrs. Shaw who worked as a weaver at Houghton's; and "William Shaw and girl" were paid together on two occasions. The composition of the Shaw household is not clear; there was a house (road taxes were paid); perhaps Mrs. Shaw was his mother, and presumably the "girl" was a member of the household, for joint payment of wages invariably implied household unity. Shaw left the Riddles in May 1833 to go to work for

John P. Crozer. His wages for the eleven months amounted to at least $176.38. He later moved to Manayunk, and in 1837 testified on working conditions in cotton mills during the Pennsylvania Senate's investigation of child labor.

JAMES WIER was a man in his early forties who already lived in Aston Township, with three of his children—a daughter Maria (aged twelve to fifteen), a son (seven to twelve), and another son (under seven). His wife, in her early thirties, in 1830 resided with the rest of the children (William, aged ten to fifteen, Lydia, aged five to ten, and a son under five) in Christiana Hundred along the Brandywine. In September 1833 the family was reunited, moving into "the Log House," and they remained at least through January 1835.[5]

It is clear, from the characteristics of the households just described, that they mostly were simple nuclear families composed of husband, wife, and children. The married couples were usually young, in their twenties or early thirties. Occasionally the household consisted of a woman (or a man) supporting herself (or himself) and children without the aid of a spouse through the collective labor of parent and children. Bachelor males tended to be boarders in other households. Usually the husband was the principal wage earner, with additional smaller sums being earned by the children and sometimes also by the wife.

The Organization of Work in the Factory

Ten of the male wage earners were mule spinners. With the exception of John McDade and William Shaw, they were all married men. Each of them operated a single mule. Each had at least two and probably three helpers: a creel attender, who replaced exhausted bobbins of roving and probably doffed filled cops; a piecer, who mended broken threads and cleaned up around the mule; and a scavenger under the sheet of yarn. These helpers could be either boys or girls and were often the children of the spinners themselves or of their co-workers. The spinner was treated as a subcontractor (and in census returns, even as late as 1850, might be referred to as a "cotton manufacturer"), paying his creel attender and piecer out of his own wages. As Samuel Riddle said, "The mule spinners are paid by the quantity they do, and they employ their own help."[6] Although the spinners did not own their own mules, they traditionally took a proprietary interest in them. A mule spinner seems to have learned his skills at first by serving as a creel attender on someone else's mule for a month or so; at least the Parkmount Day Book shows several spinners beginning work as spinners' helpers. The spinner was theoretically paid by the number of hanks he produced. But the number of hanks was not measured directly; rather, it was calculated by taking the product of the number of pounds of cotton spun and the yarn count. Thus 700 lbs. of No. 15 was calculated to produce 10,580 hanks of yarn. The spinner was paid between 2 1/2 and 3 cents per pound of cotton spun, getting more for the finer counts. Using the equipment installed in 1832, an average spinner could spin something like four bales of cotton (at 350 lbs. per bale) into No. 15 yarn per month.[7]

The other identifiable male job specifications were the carding master, the mechanic, the blacksmith, and the carpenter. The mill office clerk, not identified, probably was also male. There may have been a man in charge of the drawing and stretching frames. The mill superintendent was probably one of the Riddle brothers. These positions (not counting a superintendent) would account for the "16 men, from 8 to 10 dollars per week," that the Riddles reported employing in the questionnaire printed in the McLane report in 1832. They also reported employing "20 young women, 2 dollars per week, and fourteen at 4 to 5 dollars per month." The young women worked for the most part in the carding room and around the draw frames; but some worked as helpers at the mules. The "fourteen at 4 to 5 dollars per month" would be the creel attenders and piecers at the mules, who might be children of twelve or less, and workers in the picker room.

Because of the smallness and intimacy of the group, who not only worked but also lived cheek by jowl, the participants in the system probably thought of its organization less in terms of a "table of organization" than as a system of rules, enforced by discipline, that would ensure the continuous, uninterrupted performance of the various interdependent parts of the manufacturing process. In the Riddles' mill, these rules were not printed and posted (although Samuel Riddle, in his testimony to a Pennsylvania Senate investigating subcommittee, averred that they should be) but were normally told to an employee when he was hired, and thereafter communicated by example and by informal word-of-mouth transmission among the workers. From Riddle's testimony, and from the Parkmount Day Book, the Parkmount factory "rules" can be readily deduced. It may be worth noting that Riddle and other manufacturers used the word "rule" to indicate both a standard operating procedure in a descriptive sense ("This is a pretty general rule," "It is not a regular rule") and also as a requirement enforced by discipline, having the nature of a contract ("We have not required the hands to sign the rules; at some they do; I believe it the best way").

1 A week's work is seventy-two hours. The mill starts at five o'clock in the morning in the summer, stops half an hour for breakfast and three-quarters of an hour for dinner (both eaten at home), and closes at seven. In winter, the mill starts at six-thirty and ends at eight-thirty, with the same time off for meals. Time is signaled by the bell.

2 Workers are paid every four weeks in cash money.

3 Two weeks' notice is required of intention to leave employment and to vacate rented housing; workers will continue to work as usual during this period.

4 Fighting, swearing, obscene language, and undue familiarity between the sexes are not allowed.

5 Workers will be clean and suitably dressed for their work.

6 Two weeks' wages will be kept back until the worker's account is settled at the termination of employment.

7 There will be no tobacco smoking or possession of alcoholic beverages within the mill.

8 Work shall meet standards of quality set by the manufacturer.

These rules were enforced by threats of dismissal or suspension, of docking and withholding wages, and of blacklisting—punishments that were imposed on non-complying workers. Thus the Riddles fired John McDade for fighting with Neill Cairns, and the Bates boy for smoking a cigar in the mill. They also "turned off" Robert McMullen in August 1832 "for making bad work." John P. Crozer testified to the standards of sexual morality required, saying of his young women weavers, "departures from chastity are not common. Females of loose character, if known, or *even suspected* as such, would be immediately dismissed from my factory, and I think could not get employment in any of the neighboring factories."[8]

Actual records of docking wages for tardiness, or of permanently withholding the two weeks (or more) back wages as punishment for tardiness or for not giving notice, do not appear in the Riddle Day Book. Samuel Riddle testified:

We have no punishment, but putting persons who offend away. We keep two weeks' wages back. We have always paid back wages when persons left us without giving two weeks' notice, after holding it a little while; a great many, in such cases, retain it. It is a rule that those employed shall give two weeks' notice of their intention to quit. Very often, this is notified to persons employed; sometimes it is not; it is generally mentioned when an engagement is made.[9]

Blacklisting also is not mentioned in the Riddles' account books but it was implied in Crozer's remarks about unchaste female employees.

Perhaps the most difficult and controversial aspect of discipline had to do with children. In the first place, the young piecers, creel attenders, and scavengers were not technically the manufacturer's employees at all; their discipline was the responsibility of the mule spinner who hired them. Riddle, in recalling his youth in Ireland ("I have been working in a cotton factory since I can recollect. . . . I was not more than nine years old when I was put into a factory, and have been raised in one"), observed, "There was a great deal of whipping there, we have not here." Crozer, speaking in a similar vein in 1837, said, "when factories were first established in this vicinity, severe whipping was often practised, but it was found not to be the best mode of management, and has been, in a great degree, abandoned." Riddle even claimed that if the children who worked for the mule spinners "were oppressed in any way, they would tell me, of course." Certainly the children not working for spinners were disciplined by foremen and carding masters. But probably the most effective measure in maintaining both the general level of efficiency, cleanliness, and propriety and a not-too-severe mode of discipline for "the little ones" (as Riddle called them) was the informal culture of the workers. It must be remembered that all of the people who worked in the mill lived within easy walking distance, and most in the sixteen tenement houses located within 100 yards of the mill. The spinner's team, the carding masters' assistants, the young hands in the preparation room, were, if not their own children, then the children of neighbors who also worked in the same mill. Real brutality, made visible by bruises, welts, tears, and headaches, would not only offend the abused child's parents but also interfere with the work, for an injured or panic-stricken child would not be able to do good work. And a large proportion of the piecers were, the daybook makes plain, not the children of the spinners. The record shows, for instance, that Joseph Pedrick pieced for Francis Bonner, Mary Fredd pieced for Richard Bates and later for Sarah Cochrane (in the card room), Sarah McDade pieced for James McBride, Lydia Wier and later Joseph Pedrick for Hugh McMunn, Charles McNamee for David Crummer, and so on. One may suspect that, at least by the 1830's, the manufacturer and his agents must have avoided, as much as possible, involving themselves in any direct way with the physical discipline of "the little ones," leaving that arena to the community of workers. This meant, as other witnesses in the Philadelphia area testified, discipline by ridicule and "taunting," occasionally supplemented as required by cuffs, slaps, kicks, and ear-boxings.

Physical Working Conditions

As Crozer testified, many of the mills had not been designed as cotton factories. The ceilings were too low, the rooms were too small, and as a result the operatives were crowded together in narrow quarters with inadequate ventilation. None of the mills on Chester Creek employed exhaust fans, although they were known in the Philadelphia area, and on cool or windy days the windows were kept shut. In two places, the picker room and the card room, the problem of ventilation was particularly severe. The air was filled so thick with "flyings" that breathing was difficult and workers developed a constant cough. In an effort to prevent the escape of the dust the machines were boxed in, but this was not particularly effective. Furthermore, windows in these rooms could not be opened because the breeze would blow around even more of the fibers. As Crozer remarked,

> In the extreme heat of summer, the spinning mills, particularly the card rooms, are rather oppressive, when a free passage of air cannot be admitted, which is the case, if there is any wind—but in modern built factories, with high stories, a free circulation is always preserved; no other means employed to ventilate, but by the windows.[10]

Even in winter the room temperature was kept reasonably high (in the seventies if possible) by using stoves, because the cotton required warmth.

The language used by Crozer to describe the mill in the summer was mild compared with the vivid rhetoric of a Pittsburgh physician. He testified:

> The factories are ill ventilated; their atmosphere is constantly impregnated, and highly surcharged with the most offensive effluvia—arising from the persons of the inmates, and the rancid oils applied to the machinery.
>
> The temperature of their atmosphere is generally high, approaching a medium of from sixty to seventy degrees in winter, and rising to eighty and even ninety degrees in summer. Their atmosphere is constantly filled with floating particles of cotton; the finer the yarns to be spun, the higher the temperature must be. Cotton yarns cannot be spun in any atmosphere other than this. The cotton wool, when impregnated with the oil used to diminish friction in the machinery, and in the usual temperature of the rooms, emits a most offensive fetor. This fetor, acted on by the azote and hydrogen abounding in the rooms, gives an atmosphere which none but those accustomed to it can respire without nausea.
>
> In the rooms where the cotton wool undergoes the first process of

carding and breaking, the atmosphere is one floating mass of cotton particles, which none but those accustomed to it, can breathe, for an hour together, without being nearly suffocated.

No doubt this odoriferous effect was intensified in some mills (not the Riddles') by the provision of loosely partitioned water closets on the working floors (usually but not always separate for males and females). Other observers noted that new employees experienced "a little nausea at first and their appetite for food is lessened."[11]

Another factor significantly affecting the comfort and ease of the work was the quality of the early stages of preparation. American factories generally devoted less attention to the carding and preparation of the roving than did English factories. The result was an inordinately high frequency of breakage, starting with the sliver emanating from the finisher card, continuing with the various drawing and stretching frames, and culminating in the throstle and mule rooms. An experienced spinner reported that in English factories, where one piecer attended two mules, the child walked twenty-five miles per day. With only one mule to attend in America, the distance theoretically would be halved; but this advantage was more than overbalanced by the effects of poor quality in the preparation of the rovings. An experienced English carder, employed by Joseph Ripka of Manayunk, testified: "I consider the work of piecers, here, at the mule, greater than in England, although here the children attend but one mule; the reason is, that the work in England is much better prepared, and requires less piecing."[12] Thus, ideally, a child might sit a large part of the day, if the work were well prepared; but in general it was not possible, and the child, like the other workers, had to stand and walk for the full twelve to fourteen hours per day.

The effect of the long hours of constant physical labor, attending the continuously operating machines, was fatiguing enough for adults. Some spinners, being piece workers, preferred to work less. A Scottish spinner, for instance, testified, "I consider a great evil in the business the length of time we have to labor; I consider eight hours labor per day, as much as I can bear, in justice to myself; I work by the piece." The effect on children was striking, particularly upon first entering the mill. The ankles tended to swell, the appetite to decline. William Shaw, erstwhile Parkmount employee and afterward one of Crozer's workers, testified succinctly in 1837 about the effect on children of conditions in the factories he had known:

The children are tired when they leave the factory; has known them to sleep in corners and other places, before leaving the factory from fatigue.

The younger children are generally very much fatigued, particularly those under twelve years of age; has not heard frequent complaints of pain; more of being worried; has known the children to go to sleep on arriving home, *before* taking supper; has known great difficulty in keeping children awake at their work; has known them to be struck, to keep them awake.[13]

THE PRODUCT: THE FABRICS OF CHESTER CREEK

The final product of the mills on Chester Creek was woven cloth, packed in wooden boxes and shipped to Philadelphia for sale by commission merchants. All of this cloth, with the exception of a small amount of carpeting woven on draw looms (later replaced by Jacquards), was made on power looms, most of them Garsed's. These looms had an approximately 40-inch beam and produced "cuts" of cloth approximately 64 yards long. It was all relatively "coarse" stuff, made from the short-staple Upland cotton, which could only be spun in the lower counts (up to 42), and woven in plain and twill weaves. The yarns commonly used were 10 to 20 count, and the closeness of the weaves was on the order of forty-five to sixty warp ends and forty-five to sixty picks to the inch. Whatever the technical capabilities of the machines and the workers, they were only able to compete profitably with British manufacturers in the coarse lines (fabrics made from yarns of

PRINTED CALICO FROM BUSTLETON MILL, PHILADELPHIA, CIRCA 1825.

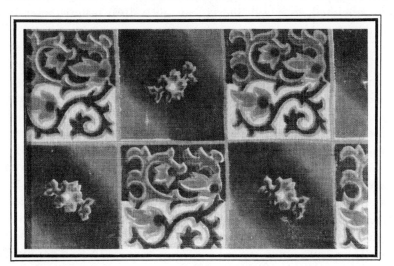

count 20 and below). In 1832, the Riddles complained: "We have to spin and weave the coarse and less profitable article."[1] In 1845, when John P. Crozer was asked whether it would be practicable to get up an exhibition of Delaware County cotton manufactures, he replied in an almost apologetic way:

> The manufacture of cottons & woolens in this county though considerable in amount does not comprise any great variety of styles nor of a kind fitted to make much display but I presume most of the manufacturers might be induced to exhibit samples, and some of them would take some care in getting up these samples or specimens,—[2]

The only relatively fancy cloths of which record remains were a quantity of soft but finely woven "diaper" cloth, manufactured by the Callaghans, who took over Parkmount in the 1840's, and Garsed's "damask" tablecloth, woven on his own special patent power loom—but the Garseds moved to Philadelphia in the 1840's, and the Callaghans' output was relatively small (about 100,000 yards of diaper cloth per year, selling at 16 cents per yard).

The fabrics produced by the other six mills were destined to be tailored into workclothes, flannel underwear and night clothes, ticking, and tablecloths. Of the over 5 million yards of goods produced on Chester Creek in 1850, about 1 million were plain-woven gray goods or printing cloths, mostly called calicoes and muslins. They were undoubtedly gray goods as they left the mill (i.e., neither bleached, dyed, or otherwise finished), and in construction ranged from about forty-five by forty-five up to sixty by sixty threads per square inch. Their ultimate use could range from grain bags, if left unfinished, to muslin sheets and calico dress material after being finished by bleaching, dyeing, or calendering in a Philadelphia factory. The rest of the fabrics were mill-finished, with some mill-dyed yarns used in the warp or filling, and in the case of some fabrics like the Chambray used for workshirts, sized in a solution of starch. Chambray was a plain weave; but by far the majority of the approximately 4 million yards of mill-finished goods were twills. Twills, with their fine herringbone construction, were the preferred weave for the ticking, Canton flannel, drills, denims, and stripes, for they could be compacted more easily into a strong, heavy-duty fabric, with construction on the order of sixty-five by sixty-five, than could the square-woven printing cloths. Although twill weaves required looms fitted with more than the two harnesses sufficient for plain weave, the number of harnesses (usually only three, four, or five) was well within the lobe-number capacity of the cam shafts that raised and lowered the harnesses. The manufacturer's price for tickings was 9 or 10 cents per yard; for

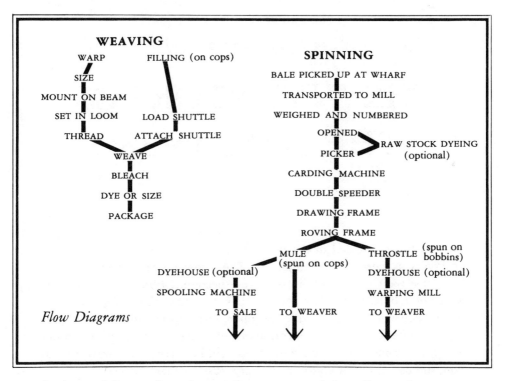

WEAVING

WARP   FILLING (on cops)

SPINNING

SIZE

BALE PICKED UP AT WHARF

MOUNT ON BEAM

TRANSPORTED TO MILL

SET IN LOOM   LOAD SHUTTLE

WEIGHED AND NUMBERED

THREAD   ATTACH SHUTTLE

OPENED

RAW STOCK DYEING (optional)

WEAVE

PICKER

BLEACH

CARDING MACHINE

DYE OR SIZE

DOUBLE SPEEDER

PACKAGE

DRAWING FRAME

ROVING FRAME

MULE (spun on cops)   THROSTLE (spun on bobbins)

DYEHOUSE (optional)

DYEHOUSE (optional)

SPOOLING MACHINE

WARPING MILL

Flow Diagrams

TO SALE   TO WEAVER   TO WEAVER

denims and Canton flannels, 7 or 8 cents per yard; for calico, only 3 cents.

Although the fabrics were "coarse," in the technical sense, this did not mean that they were of poor quality in their lines. From the 1840's on, the Chester Creek manufacturers exhibited at the annual fall fair at the Franklin Institute, at the Delaware County Institute of Science's fair, and on occasion at the national fairs in Washington, D.C., and were not unsuccessful. Daniel Lammot, who produced mostly fine-quality ticking, in 1846 exhibited at the National Fair in Washington, D.C., and his ticking earned special mention; in 1851 he won a gold medal for bed ticking at the Franklin Institute. In 1856 Samuel Riddle received mention at the Franklin Institute's fair for his Canton flannel—"fair merchantable goods." Crozer and others of the Rockdale district's manufacturers exhibited at the Delaware County autumn fair and their goods received favorable notice.

The fabrics were plain, serviceable goods, which passed into the market to be finished and cut up into workclothes, uniforms, underwear, bedding, tablecloths, and other humble articles. Gray, or striped in blue and brown (the dyes were indigo and logwood, bay, and sumac, with copperas as mordant), they were used and no doubt when worn out were for the most part sold as rags for the paper mills. No identifiable fragments have survived into the twentieth century.[3]

THE INVENTORS OF
THE MACHINES

The machines installed in the mills in the 1820's were regarded by few observers as permanent equipment. The knowledgeable manufacturers knew that their mules and throstles were becoming obsolete even as they were being bolted into place and that they would have to be replaced long before they wore out. For textile machinery was still evolving at a rapid rate. In 1837, after their surveys of cotton manufacturing in the state, a committee of the Pennsylvania Senate reported that, because of continual innovation, the useful life of cotton machinery was less than a decade.

> Ten years ago, it was generally supposed, that few improvements in machinery could take place. The machinery of that day, is now useless; and another period of ten years, may make the same difference; manufacturers are subject, in this particular, to a heavy tax. He who advances with the times, must incur the cost of continual improvement; he who lags behind, must lose in the cost of his productions.[1]

It was not until the 1850's that spinning machinery reached a relatively stable plateau in the curve of progress so that, once installed, a card, a throstle, or a mule could be expected, with decent care and minor improvements, to continue working at a profitable level of efficiency for thirty or forty years. And it was not until the 1890's that the power loom reached a comparable degree of completeness.

Each major improvement in the technology, wherever made, eventually put pressure on virtually every textile manufacturer in the world, because each improvement made it possible to make a product more cheaply, or of better quality, or both. Many innovations were, of course, found to be far less important than their sponsors claimed; but some of the minor inventions were effective in special applications, and even the inventions that were to prove useless contributed to a general climate of technological drivenness. The awareness of a constant progress of technology forced every manufacturer to be alert at all times to the degree of obsolescence of his machinery and to be prepared to buy new equipment in order to stay in the technological race.

Crozer was acutely conscious of the significance of technological advances for his own business. He complained in his autobiography that the poor quality of his first machinery—bought used from "a little mill on the Brandywine" for $4,000—was nearly fatal to his enterprise at the start. Not only was it badly made, it was also "badly planned."[2] But he and his mechanics worked with it and he added newer and better machines as well. By 1832 he reported that the cost to him of spinning yarn had decreased over the past seven years entirely as a result of technological progress. "The improvements continually making in machinery has lessened, in a greater or less degree, the cost of spinning in each successive year." But he noted, too, that each year about two-fifths of his profits were spent in buying new machinery.[3] Daniel Lammot remarked also, in connection with his short-lived cotton-spinning venture in Kensington in 1829, the imperative nature of technological change: "In order to work to advantage, I was compelled to improve my machinery, and from my limited capital these improvements were made out of the daily produce of the mill."[4] These necessary expenses for mechanical improvements contributed to his financial embarrassment in that year. Although the Riddles did not explicitly note in their daybook the need for continual upgrading of machinery, there are frequent entries indicating that they were aware of, and keeping up with, technological progress. By October 1832 they had had a spreader installed, and were having trouble with it, finding it difficult to weigh the laps in a reliable way. The spreading machine was described in Montgomery's 1833 Glasgow edition of *The Theory and Practice of Cotton Spinning* as "a recent invention," which had become so popular in Scotland that "there are few Spinning factories in this country where it has not been adopted."[5] Montgomery also discussed the very same difficulty in its use that the Riddles had met with —an irregularity in the weight of the laps if great care were not taken. And concern about the quality of the machinery was expressed by the working people, no doubt because it affected the ease of the work, the productivity of the mill, and the mill's competitive position in the market; the last would in turn affect earnings and job stability. Thus, in writing home to his brother in England a series of answers to questions about prospects for immigration, William Morris reported, among other good features of Phillips' mill, "Our machinery is good. . . ."[6]

Everyone, in fact, in the Chester Creek manufacturing district was thinking about machinery: how to operate it, how to arrange it, how to adjust it, how to maintain and repair it, how to improve it, how to construct it. There were local inventors, local machinists and mechanics, local machinery manufacturers. And outside was an immediately significant American and European industrial community, filled with people manufacturing and improving textile machinery, not only in nearby centers like Wilmington and Philadelphia, but in Patterson, New Jersey; at Matteawan along the Hudson River; in New England; and, of course, in the great textile districts of England, Scotland, and France. What was happening in these places, in the way of invention, affected Chester Creek directly and almost immediately because it affected the price and quality of competing yarns and fabrics.

THE MAIN SEQUENCE OF INVENTIONS

The stream of inventions transforming the cotton manufacture were made almost exclusively in the three countries of England, France, and the United States; and by the 1830's, these inventions were no longer likely to be the work of talented amateurs. In the eighteenth century, a motley group of English and American inventors had produced the great initial inventions: a clergyman, a barber, a vacationing college graduate, and a cottage weaver, among others. Now the situation was different. By the 1820's the significant improvements for the most part were being made in the great machine shops, by professional engineer-machinists whose attention was directed to the solution of classic problems in textile machinery and to the perfection of machine types according to well-established principles. Invention had become a competitive activity in research and development, requiring considerable capital for the support of the inventor, the production of prototypes, the patenting of the product (if possible) in at least three countries, and its marketing and installation in an actual factory.

In America there were seven great centers of innovation in textile machinery: the shops at Saco, Maine; the Lowell machine shops in Lowell, Massachusetts; the Mason and the Whitin machine shops in Taunton, Massachusetts; the various shops in and around Providence, Rhode Island; the shops of the Amoskeag Manufacturing Company in Manchester, New Hampshire; the Matteawan Manufacturing Company, along the Hudson; and the complex of shops at Patterson, New Jersey. The important inventors, men like Paul Moody, the Danforth brothers, John Thorpe, Gilbert Brewster, William B. Leonard, and William Mason, allowed themselves to be employed in these centers because only here could be found the money, the machine tools, the machinists, and the ambition needed to support successful major inventions. But many individual contributions also came from more isolated inventors in machine shops in places like Wilmington, Philadelphia, and even Rockdale.

Although the intensity of work toward particular inventions was determined in large part by the inventors' perceptions of what the market demanded, the possibility of success and the nature of the solutions were determined by a more abstract principle: the implications inherent in the technological paradigm itself. In a sense, the inventor's improvements were prefigured in the possibilities inherent in the machine or in the form of interaction between the machine and the operative. The goal of invention was to increase productivity and decrease cost. The means were three: first, to replicate, in wood and metal and leather, some action of a human operative; second, to perform this action faster than the operative (or than another machine); third, to render the machine less subject to failure and easier to readjust, repair, or replace if and when it did fail. The main principles along which a solution could be sought often were well known and even traditional. Typically, many efforts would be made before one or two successful solutions cast other partial solutions into obsolescence and swept the field. But once such successful solutions were found, it became necessary for virtually all manufacturers to acquire them in order to remain in the price competition.

Hence came the sense of technological pressure even in small places like the Chester Creek manufacturing district. There were no great machine shops there to produce major innovations (although, as we shall see, there were inventors on a smaller scale). Technological progress appeared to the manufacturer, no less than to the operative, as a continuous threat to his economic survival. The manufacturer had to improve his old machines or buy new machines in order to increase productivity and reduce labor cost per unit of production; the operative had to prepare himself for the day when a less skilled person (a young woman, or a child perhaps) could take over his job at an improved machine, or even to see the machine operate by itself, almost like an automaton.

The Self-Acting Mule

A classic example of—and a major event in—the innovative process was the development of the self-acting mule, which was adopted in the Chester Creek area in the early 1840's. Because of the economic importance of this invention, and the social consequences resulting from the changes it made in the role of the mule spinner, we shall go into the history of this invention in some detail.[1]

The mule in its simplest form had been invented in England in the previous century by a young weaver named Samuel Crompton. Crompton was unmarried and lived with his mother and crippled father in an ancient manor house, Hall i' th' Wood, near Bolton in Lancashire. Bolton was a major textile district and Crompton had worked in the area since childhood, first at the spinning wheel, then at the jenny, and finally at the hand loom. He had acquired some formal education by going to school at night and was aware of the development of Arkwright's water frame.

As a hand-loom weaver, Crompton was acutely conscious of a serious shortcoming of both the jenny and the water frame: neither could produce the fine yarn (from the 40's on up) in the quantity that was needed to make the more expensive cloths like muslin. These yarns had still to be imported from India. The limitation of the water frame was the dragging action of the flyer which, as it pulled the attenuated roving around the bobbin, tended to break all but the coarse hard yarns suitable for warp. The jenny, although it could spin fine soft yarns for the filling, was relatively slow and laborious. Crompton's goal was to invent a machine that could quickly and easily manufacture soft yarns in the high numbers. Beginning at age twenty-one, he spent the years from 1774 to 1779 perfecting the device to accomplish this task. He worked entirely alone and made all the parts himself except for some brass gearing.

The mule jenny, or mule, as a concept was a combination of certain parts of Arkwright's water frame (patented in 1769) and Hargreave's spinning jenny (invented in 1767 and patented later). There are three essential actions which any spinning machine must perform: the draw, by which the loose roving is attenuated or drawn out (usually 1 inch of roving being stretched to between 9 and 10 inches of yarn); the twist, by which the attenuated roving is twisted, the amount of twist determining in part the fineness and the hardness of the yarn (for No. 20, made from No. 2 roving, for example, the twist would be on the order of twenty-three turns to the inch); and the winding on, by which the spun yarn is wound onto a spindle or bobbin to form a removable yarn package. The simultaneity of twisting and stretching was the great virtue of the mule. It is a mechanical property of cotton yarn that, when stretched and twisted simultaneously, the stretch goes first to the loose, fat, weak sections. Drawing out these loose spots allowed more twist to be added to them and produced a finer, more even, and stronger yarn.

For the draw, the mule employed pairs of drafting rollers, as did the water frame. The roving ran from a bobbin, entered the first pair of metal rollers, where it was pinched between the leather-covered top roller and the fluted, polished bottom roller, and passed on to the second, similar pair of rollers. But the second rollers were rotating more rapidly than the first, and this drew the roving out lengthwise. From the front rollers, the roving passed to spindles, rotating rapidly (in the early mules, at about 1,700 revolutions per minute). The spindles were slanted, as in the spinning wheel and jenny, so that the yarn ran off the continuously rotating rounded end, thus acquiring twist as on the spinning wheel. As the drawn roving issued from the front rollers, the carriage bearing the spindles retreated for anywhere from 54 to 60 inches, gaining slightly—1 or 2 inches—on the rate of supply from the rollers, and thus further stretching the yarn. At the end of the draw the rollers stopped, clamping the roving tightly. The spindles however continued to rotate, now at double speed, imparting more twist up to the number of revolutions required by the count being made. The carriage might next retreat another 6 inches or so, the spindles still spinning. This slow second stretch, supplemental to the draw, was of great importance to the quality of the finer yarns (but was not necessary to the low counts). The movement of the carriage then stopped and the spindles were rotated briefly backward to free the yarn from the tips (the "backing-off" motion). Next, the yarn was pushed into position for winding by dropping a wire onto the yarn, thus pressing it down onto the cop being formed. Finally, the winding on was accomplished by the spinner pushing the carriage with his knee back toward the rollers while the yarn wound on the rotating spindles. The winding on was the critical operation for the spinner; the best contemporary description of how the spinner accomplished this task is that of Andrew Ure in 1835:

The spinner having seized the faller-rod with his left hand, gives the faller-wire such a depression as to bear down all the threads before it to a level with the bottom of the cop, or conical coil, of yarn formed, or to be formed, round the spindles. While his left hand is thus nicely applied, under the control of an experienced eye, his right hand slowly turns the handle of the pulley in communication with the spindles, so as to give them a forwards rotation, and his knee pushes the carriage before it at the precise rate requisite to supply yarn as the spindles wind it on. Three simultaneous movements must be here very delicately and dexterously performed by the mule-spinner; first, the regulation of the faller, or guide-wire, continually varying in obliquity; secondly, the rotation of the spindles, perhaps 1,000 in number, at a measured speed; and thirdly, the pushing in of the carriage at such a rate precisely as to supply yarn no faster than the spindles take it up. In fine spinning upon a mule . . . where nearly 1,000 threads were spun at once of almost invisible tenuity; the skill and tact required in the operator deserve no little admiration, and are well entitled to a most liberal recompense. In the process of winding-on, so as not to break the threads, and in coiling them into the shapely conoid, called a cop, the talents of the spinner are peculiarly displayed. As the carriage approaches to its primary position, near to the roller-beam, he allows the faller-wire to rise slowly to its natural elevation, whereby the threads once more coil slantingly up to the tip of the spindle, and are thus ready to co-operate in the twisting and extension of another stretch of the mule. Having pushed the carriage home, the spinner immediately sets the mule again in gear with the driving-shaft, by transferring the strap from the loose to the fast steam-pulley, and thus commences the same beautiful train of operations. It is during the few instants after the carriage starts that the lively little piecers are seen skipping from point to point to mend the broken threads. Whenever it has receded a foot or two from the delivering rollers, the possibility of piecing the yarn being at an end, the children have an interval for repose or recreation, which, in fine spinning at least, is three times longer than the period of employment. The spinner likewise has nothing to do till after the completion of the fresh range of threads, when he once more *backs off* the slanting coil, and winds on the "stretch."[2]

The mechanical structure that Crompton built to perform these actions involved three main parts: a fixed frame or head, which included the creel (the rack of roving bobbins) and the drafting rollers; a movable carriage, bearing the spindles, which rolled back and forth on wheels in tracks laid on the floor; and a power train, which as Crompton developed it amounted to a man turning a handle on a fly wheel (the "fly") mounted at one end of the machine, thereby turning a combination of belts, gears, and drums that ultimately turned the rollers and spindles and moved the carriage back and forth. The number of spindles in Crompton's first mule was only forty-eight; but there was no limit in principle, since any number of segments of bobbin-rollers-and-spindle could be set up side by side on a longer or shorter frame and carriage. The limit on size was imposed partly by the need for a completely rigid, correctly aligned machine and partly—and just as importantly—by the limitations of the mule spinner's strength and skill.

Crompton at first used his mule to make fine yarns to weave on his own loom. He did not have enough money to patent his idea (and in fact the principle of the mule was never patented). As his skill increased, Crompton was able to make and sell his fine yarns at enormous prices, ranging from 14 shillings per pound for No. 40 to £2.10s. per pound for No. 80. But he was unable for long to keep his machine a secret and was finally induced to reveal it for the small sum of £70. Mules were soon being produced in great numbers. By 1780 the British cotton trade had increased fivefold, in considerable part because British weavers could now produce fine muslins cheaper than imported Indian fabrics. The machine so swept the British spinning industry that thirty years later there were 4.5 million mule spindles at work in England and Scotland and only 500,000 spindles in jennies and water frames combined.

Improvements were made quickly and for the most part were, like the mule itself, not patentable. By the 1790's, water and steam power were being applied to the movement of the carriage and of the spindles during the draw. The size was increased to several hundred spindles. The limit, however, was about three hundred spindles, because one strong man could turn no more than about three hundred spindles during the winding-on motion, and the winding-on motion still remained manual. The fly was moved from the end to near the center of the machine because that position gave better balance to the movement, and (in England) the machines were operated in pairs facing each other so that one spinner could manage the winding alternately on each machine while the draw (being a simple but slower operation) proceeded mechanically. By 1800, however, the course of improvement of the mule had reached a plateau, for the winding-on action remained a task for the spinner himself to control.

At this plateau, the mule as it was managed in England was an extremely productive device. The cycle time, from the first wind on a bare spindle to the last on the completed cop of No. 80, was about twenty hours; for No. 20, it would be nearer ten hours. During this time, the machine performed about 2,400 draws—roughly 2 draws per minute, for the high English counts, and 4 to 5 per minute for the coarser yarns being spun in America.[3] (This difference accounts for the fact that in American mule rooms the spinner could mind only one mule, the draw being too quick to permit him to turn around and wind on another machine.) The completed cop was a package of yarn about 5 inches in length and 1 1/2 inches in width, with a conical shape at both ends. A cop of No. 20 contained about three hanks, weighed a couple of ounces, and took a day to make; but inasmuch as each machine had on the order of three hundred spindles, its production per day was about three hundred cops, weighing about 45 lbs. in all.

The goal of inventors, from Crompton's time on, was to make the mule completely automatic so as to reduce to a minimum the manufacturer's dependence on the highly skilled, highly paid, and often independent-minded adult male spinners. A number of unsuccessful automatic mules were introduced, one as early as 1790; but it was not until the brilliant English mechanician Richard Roberts, of the firm of Sharp and Roberts of Manchester, turned his attention to the problem that a fully effective solution came. The story is told that Roberts was solicited to undertake the task of developing an effective self-actor by a delegation of manufacturers intent on breaking the spinners' strike in 1824. However that may be, Roberts did solve the problem. It took him five years, two patents, and an outlay of £12,000 by his firm.

The problem in completing the automation of the mule lay in the winding-on action; and the solution was, in a sense, predetermined by the requirement that the mule produce the coreless yarn package which slipped off the spindle when it was complete, called a cop, rather than a spool wound on a bobbin which had to be removed with the yarn. The cop was the most ancient of the package forms, going back to the earliest spinning wheels and before that to the distaff and spindle. It was perfectly adapted to installation in a shuttle, for it unwound without snarling in either direction at high speeds. But its changing size and geometry during the ten to twenty hours of its formation precluded any simple mechanical coupling of spindles to a source of power so as to draw in the carriage and wind on at a constant speed. A substitute had to be developed for the spinner's left hand on the faller wire guiding the yarn up and down the spindle, and for his knee and right hand varying the speed of the spindles, the tension in the yarn, and the distance that the carriage ran in, so that the carriage arrived at its stopping point after winding on exactly the amount of the draw. If it arrived too soon, the yarn remaining in front of the rollers would snarl into lumps that would not stretch out on the next draw. If it arrived too late, all the ends would break at once in the spinning disaster called the "sawney."

Roberts first solved the guide wire problem in his 1825 patent by adding a counter-faller to press the yarn up from the bottom a few inches in from where the faller pressed it down, and by attaching the faller itself by rods to a doubly inclined plane or "copping rail," which moved the wire and thus the yarn up and down on the winding surface of the cop. The whole rail also moved slowly downward on inclined planes as the cycle continued, to move the whole winding action farther and farther up the spindle (see the illustrations on pages 141 and 167).

The other problem was to vary the winding speed of the spindles in direct proportion to the inward speed of the carriage and in inverse proportion to the diameter of the cop at the point of winding on. Roberts solution was so ingenious, and so perfect, that it excited universal admiration in his day and enjoys continued acclaim even in this. It was to drive the spindles during the run in by the unwinding of a chain wrapped around a drum geared to the shaft that drove the spindles. One end of the chain was fixed to the drum, the other to a movable nut mounted on a screw shaft that was attached to a "quadrant arm." The quadrant arm was a quarter wheel, which rotated a fixed distance during the run in of the carriage and at a speed exactly proportional to the speed of the carriage. As the arm moved through its quarter rotation, it pulled the chain off the drum at a varying speed directly communicated to the spindles. Further variation was accomplished by setting the nut so as to be closer or farther from the drum, thus also varying the speed of the spindles by varying the length of chain drawn during the run in. The nut had to be reset frequently during the first part of the cycle while the base of the cop was being built up.

Roberts' achievement provided the breakthrough to real automation of the mule at a level comparable to that of the throstle. Although the spinner at first was required to remain in attendance to reset the quadrant nut as required, this job could be taught simply and even itself be made automatic —so automatic that eventually, in British factories, the spinner could be transformed into an overseer of a dozen or more mules, supervising the work of piecers and creel attenders and making sure that the machinery was operating correctly. Only three years after its introduction, the experienced Scottish manufacturer James Montgomery, in a book widely read in America, enthused:

> The self-acting mule described above, is necessarily complex; but, perhaps, it is one of the most beautiful specimens of mechanical combination that is to be found; exhibiting a rare degree of original invention, highly creditable to the ingenuity and perseverance of the inventor; whilst, at the same time, it furnishes an illustrious example of the wonderful perfection to which machinery has attained in our manufacturing processes.[4]

By 1865, as a result of the continuing success of the self-acting mule, there were 44 million spindles in operation in Great Britain.

Although the patent was announced and the English machines came into production in the early 1830's, Americans do not seem to have hastened to secure them. It was not until 1840 that the self-actor came to America. In 1838 Sharp and Roberts sold one of their self-actors, and the American patent rights, to a partnership including the owner of the Globe Mills of Fall River, Massachusetts. The mule itself was delivered in the spring of 1840. Davol & Durfee immediately began manufacturing the Roberts self-actor, and (in the opinion of the cotton historian William Bagness) "soon revolutionized cotton spinning in America." The labor cost of spinning low-count yarns went down from about 11 cents to (eventually) 3 1/2 cents per hundred hanks. About the same time the experienced American mechanic William Mason—a counterpart of England's Roberts—patented his own self-acting mule and began producing it in his own machine works. It was similar in design to Roberts' but lacked the quadrant arm, replacing that action by other devices. About 1841 the strenuous, if illegal, efforts of Mr. Leonard of Matteawan to secure a model of a third type of self-actor, the Scottish mule, were crowned with success and a few shops produced some of Mr. Smith's self-actors. Mason and Davol & Durfee both produced excellent machinery and shared the American market for years, although other manufacturers later entered the mule-manufacturing business. But the Roberts and Mason mules manifestly outperformed the less effective Scottish mule and its production was discontinued.[5]

The self-acting mule was adopted on Chester Creek and in the Brandywine area about 1842. It was an expensive machine. John Bancroft purchased a "self act[8] Mule" on December 31, 1842, at a cost of $4,439.09.[6] It would appear that this represented the total cost of a new mule fitted with the self-actor mechanism; but the mechanism could be purchased separately, along with a new head-stock, for about a fifth of the cost of a new machine. Riddle seems to have been using self-actors in his new mill at Penn's Grove in 1844, for in January of that year he was paying only five mule spinners (out of a total work force of seventy-four). They were producing from 35,000 to 45,000 hanks every four weeks, at a piece rate of 10 cents per 100 hanks. Ten years before, his ten mule spinners working ten mules at Parkmount were producing 10,000 to 20,000 hanks in the same period at a piece rate (for No. 15) of 11 cents per 100 hanks. It seems likely that Riddle simply moved his mules, replaced the head-stocks with the self-actor mechanism, and got along with half as many spinners (each minding two mules) at 10 percent lower piece rates. This is assuming the yarn counts remained the same; if the counts were raised, the piece rates would be more than 10 percent lower.[7]

Improvements in the Throstle

The economic goal in introducing the self-acting mule was to reduce production costs by increasing the speed and reliability of the machine, thereby allowing a reduction in the piece rates; because the machines worked so nearly automatically, the number of skilled spinners necessary to mind a given number of spindles was simultaneously reduced. The case of the throstle was different. It had already been perfected to the point where relatively unskilled hands, usually young women, could mind these highly automatic machines. The reduction of cost in the throstle room was to be sought principally by improvements in its most vulnerable part: the bobbin and flyer. The traditional flyer, as introduced by the Arkwright generation of water frames, was little different from that invented by Leonardo da Vinci and still commonly used on household spinning wheels. Operating at the high speeds made possible by water power, the flyer tended to wobble and vibrate; minor imbalances, presenting no problem at speeds below four thousand rpm, at higher speeds caused injury and breakage to the yarn and even damage to the flyer itself. The higher speeds were necessary to the spinning of finer yarns.

The throstle inventions were made in America because in England the mule had virtually absorbed the spinning industry. The traditional practice was to fix the flyer to the top of the spindle; flyer and spindle rotated together, pulling the yarn around a more slowly rotating bobbin. The first improvement was the "dead spindle," used at Waltham and Lowell from about 1813. Here the spindle was fixed and was used merely as a pivot on which the flyer turned, the flyer itself being welded to a power pulley that rotated around the spindle. Speeds up to nearly five thousand rpm could be reached with the dead spindle. The next major improvement was the invention of cap and ring spinning about 1828. Both inventions proposed to solve the problem of flyer vibration by making the bobbin the actively rotating, twist-imparting element. In the cap frame (which ultimately proved to be less successful in cotton spinning), the yarn was guided onto the bobbin by the edge of a fixed cap, around which it was dragged by the rotation of the bobbin. The ring frame employed a similar principle, but less cumbersomely, the rotating bobbin pulling the yarn through a guide or eyelet ("traveler"), which also was pulled around the bobbin on a ring —or, in some models, with the ring itself moving.

Ring spinning made possible speeds in the neighborhood of seven thousand rpm, and eventually, after the 1850's, it replaced all other forms on the spinning frame; but initially the "Danforth throstle" was very popular. It was probably in widespread use on Chester Creek by 1850 when the Delaware County Institute of Science awarded a prize to Lownes and Blakely, of Knowlton, for "one box of Danforth throstle bobbins, filled with yarn."[8] Samuel Crozer was one of the judges, and Abraham Blakeley was one of the Crozers' former employees. Alfred Jenks of Bridesburg, in Philadelphia, was manufacturing "ring frame throstles" in 1853.[9] Some time after he left Rockdale, Richard Garsed invented an improved spindle and bobbin arrangement for the ring frame. He did this at a time when concerted efforts were being made to improve the ring spindle, by a number of inventors, so as to enable it to be run at high speeds with less power. The purpose of these efforts was to make it possible to spin a soft filling yarn at as low a cost as on the mule.[10] The problem was eventually solved and the mule thereby doomed to ultimate extinction in the twentieth century. By 1905, the ring frame had nearly taken over the field in America, there being then 17.9 million ring spindles to only 5.2 million mule spindles.[11]

Richard Garsed and Improvements
in the Power Loom

Rockdale's only contributor to the main sequence of inventions was Richard Garsed, the young son of John Garsed, manufacturer of power looms.[12] He had been thoroughly steeped in a family tradition of mechanical arts. His father had been a joiner by trade in England before emigrating to the United States. He himself began to work as an operative in a mill in New Hope, Bucks County, in 1827 at the age of eight, and after the family moved to Chester Creek, he continued to work in his father's power-loom factory. In 1837, at the age of eighteen, he began to experiment with increasing the speed of the Garsed looms. At first they ran slowly, at 80 picks (i.e., crossings of the shuttle) per minute; by 1840, when he took over the management of the business, they were running at 140 picks per minute. The means by which this was accomplished have not been recorded and he took out no patent for these improvements.

Garsed also set himself to solve one of the main problems with power looms as they existed in the 1830's: their inability to weave figured fabrics, like damask, automatically. The difficulty had to do with the fact that, for anything except simple weaves, a relatively large number of heddle harnesses was required. Each harness was attached to a rod (called a treadle), which rode on a cam attached to a rotating shaft under the loom. This system of revolving cams replaced the foot treadles of the old hand loom. Because the warps could not be raised more than 6 or 7 inches high to make the shed (the space between the warp ends through which the shuttle passed), the lobes of the cams could not be more than 6 or 7 inches in their maximum extension, and had to be rounded gradually enough to give a reasonably smooth action to the heddles. This posed no problem for the plain, over-and-under weaves used for muslins and calicoes, for which the shed was formed by two harnesses only. Nor did simple twills—such as Canton flannels, denims, and tickings—require an elaborate harness system, three or four being sufficient. Very simple satins could also be made with four harnesses. But, because of the geometry of the cams, four or five harnesses was the limit. Shedding required that only one cam—and thereby one harness—be raised at a time; and, with the necessary dimensions, there was space for only three or at the most four cam lobes to be introduced before a given lobe came into raised position again. Adding more cams would simply mean that the shed would become too narrow for safe passage of the shuttle.

By 1842, Richard Garsed had solved the problem and exhibited at the annual fair at the Franklin Institute a sample of "cotton and worsted damask table covers." The judges were impressed by the "novelty and excellence" of the Garsed damask, "a new article in our manufactures, which promises successful competition with the imported." The Garseds were awarded a silver medal. They exhibited "marseilles toilet covers" (a heavily figured fabric with an embossed effect) in 1844 and received an honorable mention, and in fact continued to receive awards for various fabrics up until 1850.[13]

The contribution of Richard Garsed to the development of the power loom thus lies in that part of the power-loom paradigm which may be called the "cam-and-harness" action. But the cam-and-harness action is only one way of forming a shed; there is also a type of action in which a harness containing a fixed set of heddles is not used at all, each heddle being pulled by a separate cord or wire, as in the old hand-operated draw and Jacquard looms and the newer dobby loom. Eventually the dobby and Jacquard principles proved to be the most practical for complex weaves, because they could be used not only for relatively simple damasks but also for elaborate tapestries. Dobby looms could manage fifty or more harnesses; the Jacquard program of punched cards could manage thousands of combinations of warp threads. Garsed's inventions, and others in the cam-and-harness tradition, thus were an interim solution, to become obsolete when the dobby and Jacquard-programmed looms came into extensive use in American weaving mills.

The patent for his first cam-and-harness invention Garsed received in July 1846. His solution to the multiple cam problem was to take an old mechanical principle—the production of a reciprocating action by means of a grooved cylinder—and combine it with the motion of a rotating cam. Instead of requiring as many cams as there were harnesses, Garsed's device used only one cam. On either side of the cam extended a cylindrical hub. The cam and cylinder were both carefully grooved around the circumference and each circumferential groove connected with the adjacent groove by a diagonal. There was one less groove than the total number of harnesses on the hubs plus one on the cam. As many treadles as there were harnesses rode in the grooves, one riding at all times on the cam lobe. As the cam shaft rotated, the cam and cylinder slid back and forth on the shaft, the lobe of the cam raising each harness in order as its treadle passed over the cam. In principle, half a dozen or more harnesses could be easily controlled in this way, because the treadle of inactive harnesses simply rode out the rotation of the shaft on the cylindrical hub.

Garsed claimed that this shedding process worked at a higher speed than those relying on an ordinary cam system (and certainly it worked faster than shifting cams by hand or using the hand loom).[14] Garsed's biographer maintains that the scroll-cam, patented in 1846, "greatly simplified the power loom, and was almost universally adopted on the sliding cam loom."[15] Garsed went on (after leaving Rockdale) to invent an even more complex shedding system, for which he received a patent in 1849.[16]

In other ways the power loom was being improved during this period. The Draper self-acting rotary temple (to keep the selvage of the finished cloth from pulling in as it was wound on the beam) was in common use by the 1830's, effecting an increase of loom productivity of about 15 percent. (The saving lay in eliminating the labor time required for the weaver to adjust the old temples by hand.) Automatic stop actions, which detected faults such as broken warp or filling yarn, or a shuttle being caught in the shed as the harness changed, were developed in the 1830's and 1840's, greatly reducing the amount of time required to supervise the looms and permitting economies on labor. One major desideratum was not achieved, however, until the Northrop loom was perfected in the 1890's. This was a fully automatic cop-and-bobbin changing action, which would permit filling in the shuttle without stopping the loom. In the 1830's, a weaver had to put new cops into shuttles anywhere from five hundred to a thousand times per day. In order to save time, the weaver pulled the leader of filling through the eyelet near the end of the shuttle by "sucking in." In the process, he inevitably inhaled a certain amount of dust and lint. Improvements in shuttle design, and eventually the fully automatic Northrop loom, saved both time and the weaver's health.[17]

THE LESSER INVENTORS OF CHESTER CREEK

Although Richard Garsed was the only member of the Chester Creek community in this period to contribute to the main sequence of inventions, he was not the only inventor. The lower Delaware Valley—like most other parts of the country—was buzzing with news of mechanical progress. Much was being done, particularly in nearby Chester County, in the way of improvements in agriculture: new methods of fertilizing the fields, new crops, new breeds of livestock, new plows, mowing machines, threshers, and reapers. Interest in machinery was almost universal; mechanical progress appeared almost as an agency of millennium. Invention was usually a matter of making a small improvement on a machine already in widespread use. Some such improvements were patented; but often they were not patented at all because they were regarded, by their originators, as processes for use in their own shops or factories rather than as new objects for sale or lease. Some improvements involved no new gadgetry at all and were simply a rearrangement or recombination of the old (as in the shift to complete process manufacturing), or an alteration of a procedure (as by repeating a step), or an experiment in changing the conditions of the process (such as temperature, time, pressure, or tension). Thus the history of patents is less than the history of invention and far less than the history of mechanical progress. What is significant is the constant and intense concern with improving mechanical processes at all levels, from the unpatentable empirical discovery of a better schedule for oiling spindles to the highly patentable main sequence invention of the self-acting mule.

Of particular interest to us are five figures: John S. Phillips, who invented and patented an industrial filter; the Riddle brothers, who seem to have devised a new method for sizing warps; J. Dutton, cousin or brother of Thomas Dutton the tanner, who made the industrial belts for the Riddles' (and probably for other manufacturers') machinery; the family of Henry Moore, who held a patent on a nail-making machine; and Nathan Sellers, manufacturer of wire card teeth.

John S. Phillips and His Filter for Turbid Liquors

In 1828 Phillips received a patent for "an improvement in the construction of filters, for separating the impurities from turbid liquors." The invention was noticed in the *Journal* of the Franklin Institute, but unfortunately Phillips had advised the editor that he was planning to make some additions which would be the subject of a future patent; further description was deferred until the future patent should be granted, "when the whole shall be particularly noticed."[1] Apparently he never took out another patent on his filter, and so the *Journal of the Franklin Institute* never printed an account of the whole thing as was its custom. With the Patent Office fire in 1836, the official record was destroyed. Phillips never bothered to reconstruct the patent and no other record seems to have survived.

Although it is conceivable that the Phillips filter was intended to remove lumps and other impurities from the thick starch solution (a "turbid liquor") used for sizing warp yarn, it is more likely that it applied to sugar manufacturing, in which he was still engaged in 1828 with Joseph S. Lovering. He probably did not bother to perfect the device after the business—and the friendship—ended. As described in 1833 in Benjamin Silliman's *Manual on the Cultivation of the Sugar Cane, and the Fabrication and Refinement of Sugar,* the new method of refining by steam, then being practiced by

Joseph Lovering and his new partner Merritt Canby in their Philadelphia factory, depended critically upon the filtering process. The filter, noted Silliman, had been patented in 1828, and its construction and function were described in general terms:

> The syrup . . . is raised to a slight simmer and the first scum removed; when it is let into the filter, which is situated in the next story below and directly under the clearing cistern. The external part of the filter is a strong box; it contains a great number of filtering frames, which are covered with a kind of Russia duck, or cotton cloth. The frames are arranged vertically; they are made of tinned copper, crimped, so as to present vertical grooves on each side against the canvass, which is made into flat bags, with a hem about an inch broad and one-eighth of an inch thick, all around the mouth of each bag, and a frame is put into each bag to distend it. The distended bags being put into the filtering box, with their mouths downwards, and all the hems pressed tightly together, the fluid percolates from the outside of the bag to the inside, trickles down the grooves, and runs off by a cock. The pans prevent the turbid liquor from running down outside of the frames, and, at the same time, serve to keep the bags at a small distance from each other. . . . The syrup, at an elevated temperature, and aided by hydrostatic pressure, traverses the filter, whence it flows perfectly clear and bright to the receiving cistern.[2]

It would seem that after the dissolution of the partnership, Lovering continued to use the process he and Phillips had developed together. At that time, only three other sugar refineries were using this process, one in Philadelphia, one in New York, and the third in New Orleans. All the rest employed blood and eggs—in large quantities—to precipitate impurities, a process less effective than the steam, filter, and vacuum system, and possessing the added disadvantage of filling the neighborhood with the stench of rotten eggs and putrefying blood. In all likelihood, at least in the beginning, Phillips also manufactured the cotton cloth used in the filters.

Lovering's refinery was given high praise by Silliman, who was one of the most eminent American chemists of the day. Lovering, of course, went on to wealth as a maker of superior sugar in his anthracite-fired steam refinery in Philadelphia, and to fame as the practical chemist who, by devising a method of processing it, made sorghum a major source of refined sugar.

The Riddles and Their Sizing Trough

One of the classic problems of the weaving process was presented by the need to "size" or "dress" the warp threads in order to lubricate and toughen them. The old-fashioned method, used by hand-loom weavers for centuries, was to brush a soupy mixture of oil and starch made from flour onto the warp after it had been wound onto the take-up beam. This operation required halting the actual weaving while the size was applied by hand; and, worse than that, the weaver had to wait for the warp to dry before he could pass the shuttle again. With the advent of power looms early in the nineteenth century, both in England and America, the demand for increased productivity led to the invention of devices to spin the warp yarn on a special warping frame (a variety of throstle), which built it upon a beam rather than a bobbin, in order to eliminate the time spent on the warping mill. The need to reduce the time the weaver spent dressing the warp led to the development of mechanical dressers that automatically applied sizing before the warp went into the loom. Radcliffe's dresser of 1803, for instance, applied sizing to a temporary beam as it came from the warping frame, dried it by fans or (after 1832) on hot cylinders, and wound it on a back beam ready to be inserted into the loom. Warping frames and dressers, however, were expensive (the Lowell products, for instance, sold for about $600 and $1,000 respectively).

When the Riddles set up their weaving operation in 1833 and 1834, they could not take advantage of all this new technology. Their mules could not spin warp yarn onto beams, only onto cops, which then had to be rewound onto beams. Nor did they invest in one of the expensive dressers. Instead, they employed a method of their own which was never patented but which anticipated by several years the English invention of the tape-sizing machine or slasher. The Riddles assembled the system themselves; like so many of the "improvements" of the period, it was an unpatentable new process rather than a patentable new gadget.[3]

The Riddle system was to rewind their warp yarn from mule-spun cops onto a beam by use of a warping mill. The ends were then drawn, in parallel, through a trough filled with hot size, heated by steam-filled copper pipes in the bottom. The steam was produced in a copper boiler over a furnace burning anthracite coal (hauled from Norristown, on the Schuylkill River). The boiler arrived in November 1833 (purchased from James Houghton); not until July of next year were the copper pipes installed in the trough. It is not clear how the sized warp was dried; very likely it was put through rollers to squeeze out excess size and then passed over steam-heated plates or cylinders as it was wound on the loom back beam.

Whether the Riddles themselves developed the system or found it in use, perhaps in Houghton's and Garsed's mills, is not likely to be known. But it doubtless was effective in accomplishing its purpose—to size the warp in a particularly smooth and effective way, by drawing warp yarn through hot size (which was much less lumpy than cold size), and then packaging the warp so that it reached the weaver completely sized and dry, ready for uninterrupted use.[4]

The Duttons and the "New Planet"

The Duttons were an old Quaker family. They had arrived with William Penn in 1682 and, according to tradition, had trudged up the Indian trail from Chester to occupy their five hundred-acre farm along the creek. Their tract now lay just over the hill from Rockdale and was the site of the tannery, operated by Thomas Dutton, which made the leather driving belts for the mills in the neighborhood. A generation before, a branch of the family had purchased the Forest Dale mills, just below Knowlton, where the road (now known as Dutton's Mill Road) crossed the creek. This branch of the family were country millers, operating a grist- and sawmill for local people.

In the 1830's, the proprietors of these two establishments were, respectively, Thomas Dutton at the tannery and Jonathan Dutton at Forest Dale mills. Thomas Dutton, born in 1769, was already an elderly man, thrice-married, corpulent, with an interesting history. He told tales of the time when the British Army under Lord Cornwallis camped at Village Green after defeating the Americans at the Battle of Brandywine. He described how the British hung two of their own soldiers who had plundered local houses and molested young women; they remained hanging from the limbs of an apple tree on a farm in Aston after the Army moved away. Dutton even remembered hearing the cannon salute at the signing of the Declaration of Independence in Philadelphia when he was seven years old. Young Dutton built the tannery in 1790 and followed the trade until 1808, when he moved with his family to the Quaker mission of the Seneca Indians at Tunessassa, at the edge of the Seneca reservation, just across the Pennsylvania line in New York State. There he remained as manager for four years, during the time when the Quakers and the prophet Handsome Lake and his half brother, the old Chief Cornplanter, revitalized the decaying Indian culture by introducing a new religion and modern agricultural methods. After that, for four years he directed the Delaware County Poorhouse. On returning to Aston after the death of his first wife and his remarriage, he took up his tanning business again. He achieved some local notoriety as an innovator for establishing a stationary steam engine at his works, made by William Parrish in Philadelphia—the first, it is alleged, in Delaware County.

Jonathan Dutton was a cousin of Thomas and at this time the miller of Forest Dale. This Dutton was an inventor—one might almost say an indiscriminate inventor, for he experimented constantly with all sorts of new processes and machines, and sometimes even patented his devices. Of immediate relevance, for instance, to the needs of his cousin and the local industries was his "Clasp to Unite Belting." A problem with leather industrial belts was, and is, that they have to be made up of sections of cowhide. The usable portion of a hide is only about 5 feet long and 4 or 5 feet wide, from the back and sides of the animal. Any belt longer than 5 feet therefore has to be made up of 5-foot (or less) sections; and the sections must be firmly joined. Dutton's description of his clasp gives some insight into the methods then in use:

This clasp, for uniting any kind of belting, on wheels or pulleys, for propelling different kinds of machinery, is a very economical plan for tightening the slack of belts, &c. as it is strong, durable, and makes a smooth splice, and is done in one-tenth of the time that a thong splice can be made, and is also 50 per cent. better than that or a buckle. It consists of two plates of iron or brass, 1/2 or 3/4 of an inch wide, with their edges made circular, so as to fit the face of the pulleys, and connected together with three or four screws or whatever number is necessary; the taped plate which the screws connect in should be rather thicker than that under their heads, to allow a sufficiency of thread in it for strength.

To make the connection, the belt being the right length, lay the flesh sides of the ends together, as a shoemaker holds his work to close it,—lay a plate on, mark and make the holes through,—then put both plates on and screw them together,—then open it and hammer the seam inside. . . .[5]

In 1848, Dutton gathered together the accounts of his various inventions, both patented and unpatented, and published a description of them in a twenty-eight-page pamphlet entitled *The New Planet, Containing a Degree of Novelty: Being an Effort Toward the Pleasure, Comfort and Convenience of all Citizens.* He introduced the work with a little philosophical essay which breathes, in simple language, the climate of enthusiasm for invention of the time:

The subject of this small treatise is interesting, directly, to almost every person, as it is calculated to cast some reflection on new theory, or lead to new ideas, in this rapid progressing age of improvement,—when the apparel with which we are clad, the vehicles in which we ride, the seats on which we repose, the publications which we read, the music which soothes and delights us, the articles which furnish our dwellings, the implements of husbandry, the vessels which float upon the ocean, the artificial channels for the transportation of the productions of the soil from one part of the country to supply the wants of another, all have incorporated within them the inventor's skill, and have attained their present degree of perfection through his labor; and man, whatever may be his occupation, scarcely moves during the livelong day, or performs a single act during the whole of his routine of business or pleasure, without having constant occasion to thank departed inventors for the convenience, facilities, and comfort afforded by their mechanism.

With respect to our primary and most elegant pieces of mechanism, however incomprehensible they may appear to the inexperienced, they are, in the eye of the practical man, mere elegant modifications and combinations of a few simple principles.[6]

The body of the work gave descriptions and drawings of no less than sixteen novelties: an ornamental fountain (covered by a design patent); a patented method for cooling and freezing water by means of the alternate compression and expansion of air; a plan for cutting ice by means of a steam-powered rotary saw mounted on a steam-powered sled; a machine for kneading dough ("This is meant to do away with the practice among bakers of kneading the dough with their hands—even the bare feet have been represented to have been used"); a portable chain pump; a pressure fountain pump; a method of preventing ice from forming on sidewalks by means of steampipes under the pavement; a sportsman's boat with secret (underwater) oars ("a very successful contrivance for getting within shooting distance of wild geese, black duck, or any kind of water fowl"); the belting clasp noticed earlier; a machine for shelling corn; a mincing machine for the sausage maker; a system for manufacturing ice in an icehouse by spraying water in fine drops against the walls; a similar method for making ice in the open field; a substitute for the water wheel, in the form of an endless chain carrying buckets; a vertically shafted windmill with collapsing vanes (a re-invention of the old Persian windmill); and a proposal to provide locomotive engines with boxes of sand to scatter on the rails and so prevent the wheels from slipping in snow or ice.

Of all these devices, the refrigeration equipment and the endless-chain water power would seem to have been potentially the most significant. The cooler and ice-making machine, while perhaps not widely used, was based on the same thermodynamic principles as the refrigerators of a century later; the hydraulically efficient chain wheel, being designed to make possible the use of small streams as well as large, and obviating the need for big, expensive wheels and large wheelpits to accommodate them, probably was never widely used. The idea had been current for years, however (in fact, patents for overshot strap or chain water wheels dated back to 1809), and the 1831 edition of Jacob Bigelow's *Elements of Technology* contained a description of the chain wheel and a drawing virtually identical with Dutton's.[7] Furthermore, the hydraulic turbine—compact, cheap, easy to install, and efficient for applications, like driving cotton machinery, where horsepower requirements were known and constant—was being introduced from France during the 1840's and would soon be installed in the mills on Chester Creek.[8]

Thomas Odiorne, Henry Moore, and Their Old Sable Works

The Henry Moore from whom Phillips and Lewis leased their cotton factory in 1825 was the owner of an old forge built in the previous century by the Pennells. Moore had acquired it from one Thomas Odiorne of New Hampshire. It was Odiorne who had bought it from the Pennells and named it Old Sable Forge, after the family foundry of the same name in New England. The Moores and the Odiornes were intricately connected by a maze of cousinships and marriages, and were further related by marriage to the Willcox brothers of Ivy Mills, who had wedded a pair of sisters whose mother was an Odiorne.

The Odiorne family had a variety of industrial interests. Thomas had gone into cotton manufacturing as early as 1791 in Exeter, New Hampshire.[9] Later, in 1814, he owned the Old Sable Forge which supplied the nails used in building the Boston Manufacturing Company's factory at Waltham;[10] about the same time, he had an interest in a foundry on French Creek in Pennsylvania (not far from West Chester).[11] The acquisition of a foundry on Chester Creek was therefore only one chapter in the history of an expanding family business. Thomas Odiorne bought the mill in 1808 and sold it to his cousin and brother-in-law (Captain Moore had married Thomas's sister Ann) in 1815. Moore held it until 1832.

The Odiornes were an educated family—"Boston people of that cultured kind," as Mary Willcox's biographer put it.[12] The brothers George (1764–1846) and Thomas (1769–1851) were the active leaders of the clan in the early 1800's. George left school at the age of eighteen and began his career as a merchant in Exeter; in 1799 he moved to Boston with his brothers to establish a dry-goods importing firm and spent two years in England as the company's agent; between 1805 and 1809 he was the cashier of a Boston bank. Thomas acquired a more extensive formal education, graduating from Dartmouth in 1791 and going into the book business. He took advantage of this connection to publish some volumes of his own poetry that celebrated the progress of mankind. In 1792, for instance, he produced *The Progress of Refinement,* which asserted a divinely planned coordination of man's development in science, in the fine arts, and in virtue.[13]

In 1806, the three brothers bought a mill seat at Malden, Massachusetts, and erected a nail factory. Shortly thereafter they bought, for $10,000, the rights to the patented nail-cutting and -heading machine of one Jesse Read, and began to manufacture cut nails automatically. As Read patented successive improvements on his nail-making apparatus over the next twenty years, the brothers bought them up one by one; finally, in 1829, Thomas Odiorne himself took a patent on "nail machine feeding machinery."[14] Although there was some temporary sales resistance from conservative carpenters, and the nail mill at first lost money, it eventually became successful.[15] It was probably in order to control their supply of nail rods, which were generally made from Pennsylvania iron, that the Odiornes acquired the forges on Chester Creek and French Creek. By 1815, the manufacture of machine-made "cut-nails" was an "enormous industry," for the manufacturers could make such nails far faster and far cheaper than the old wrought-iron nails, which had to be individually hand-fashioned.[16]

Jesse Read and the Odiornes were not the first Americans in the cut-nail business. One of the oldest patents had been taken by Jacob Perkins in 1795; and he and others before and after, both in England and America, were busy making improvements from 1790 on into the 1850's. Perkins was forced out of his partnership in the nail factory at Amesbury, Massachusetts; his place was taken by Paul Moody, later to become famous as the mechanical genius of Waltham and Lowell. The Odiornes and their nail factory at Malden, and Moody and the Amesbury works, eventually came into conflict over the issue of patent infringement. Thomas Odiorne sued Amesbury in 1819, alleging infringement of Read's patent; the suit was dismissed on the grounds that Jacob Perkins' patent already covered the process.[17]

By 1820, when the census takers recorded American manufactures, the Old Sable Works on Chester Creek—a rolling and slitting mill and nail factory—was consuming 150 to 200 tons of bar iron per year and employing ten men. The principal product was nails, with some hoop and sheet iron, sold in part to neighboring enterprises (the Riddles would buy their nails from Moore). The nails were made on five "patent Saving-Labour nail machines . . . which cut & head nails at one operation."[18]

Old Sable probably bought bar iron from Sharpless's Old Sarum Forge, up the creek a few miles, or from the ironworks on French Creek. The Old Sable Forge reheated the iron, rolled it out into broad sheets 1/2 to 1/4 inch thick, and then slit these sheets into long strips as wide as the nails were long. The nail machine received the red-hot strips, cut them into the roughly tapering form of the finished nail, and formed a flattened head. Some human skill was still required, as an early description of a nail factory near Patterson, New Jersey, reveals:

> The human portion of the machine holds in his hands a staff or stick, one end of which rests in a prop behind him for the sake of steadiness, and upon the other end is a clamp with which the plate is held. As the action of the cutter is not reciprocal, it is necessary that the plate should be turned at each cut; and as the machine moves rather rapidly, this is a delicate operation which the feeder only acquires after considerable practice. The end of the plate being square the first clip from each is an abortion, and this accounts for the fact of so many of these misshapen nails being found in each cask.
>
> When the plate is cut up the feeder throws his clamp over a spur which projects from the side of the machine, pries it open, throws the remnant aside to be reheated with the rest of the scraps, seizes another plate with a pair of pincers, fixes it in his clamp, and goes on as before.
>
> The machines are gauged to cut different-sized nails, and their speed decreases in the same ratio as the size of the nail increases. Thus the machine which cuts a "twenty-penny" moves at about one-eighth the speed of another which is cutting "eight-pennies."[19]

Although the Odiornes' nail patents were based on the work of others, Thomas Odiorne did take out two unrelated patents of his own, both in 1835, one for a ship's pump, and the other for a steam whistle to signal the alarm "when the water is low and perilous in a steam boiler."[20] The boiler alarm could conceivably have been of value in his own enterprises, if any of them made use of stationary steam engines to power the forge machinery. But the main power was still water in 1832 when, before the date of the invention, Henry Moore sold the forge on Chester Creek to Richard S. Smith and Old Sable's fires went out forever.

Nathan Sellers and the Making of Card Teeth

Nathan Sellers, even before the Revolution, is said to have been the first American to enter the business of wire drawing and wire working; during the war he was released from military service because these skills were needed in the making of paper currency and other essential paper products. He used fine brass wire to make flat woven molds, which he supplied to the Willcoxes at Ivy Mills and the Gilpins on the Brandywine. These molds were employed to scoop up a film of rag pulp from the surface of the vat; the water would drain out through the spaces in the molds. Later he went into the business of making card teeth for carding cloths and fillets. Card teeth were made of fine iron wire about 3/32 of an inch in diameter. The Sellers firm would make the wire teeth, bend them, and then send them out to a veritable army of thousands of women and children who set them in leather. (Later he took on as partner John Brandt, the Lancaster mechanic, who had invented a machine for setting card teeth automatically.)

Sellers' wire came from the Old Sable Forge as a secondary product of the earlier, pre-Odiorne nail-making process. In the old process, the slitting rollers produced long, thin rods, which could be cut into wire nails, or slit rods reworked into wire. The first task in making wire from slit rods was to transform the cross section from square to circular; next, the wire was drawn through a die to reduce the cross section and elongate it; and finally the drawn wire was coiled by hand and annealed (reheated in an oxygen-free container).

Before the Revolution, Sellers attempted unsuccessfully to mechanize the first part of the process at Pennell's forge on Chester Creek (which then produced old-fashioned wrought-iron hand-finished spike nails). As his grandson recalled:

Grandfather induced the proprietor of this slitting mill to erect a furnace for reheating these rods and to have some grooves turned in his plate rolls, thinking that by passing two or three times through these grooves would give a good round wire rod; but it was not a success, the slit rods were rough and irregular on their corners; on passing through the rolls corner pins were driven into the rods not perfectly welded, so that the wire drawn from them was full of flaws.[21]

So they reverted to the older blacksmith's process of pounding the repeatedly heated rods into cylindrical form with a water-powered triphammer, using a semicircular die as a bedplate, and cracking off the scale by hand. The hot wire was then drawn through a die with the desired cross section, lengthening it as well as making it finer. And finally, the coils of wire were annealed in a special process developed by Sellers. The annealing, which was necessary to make the wire more malleable and ductile (and thus less subject to breakage while being formed and set as teeth in card clothing), required heating to a high temperature and then gradual cooling. Annealing in the open furnace permitted extensive oxidation of the surface of the wire; the resulting scale was conventionally removed in a bath of sulfuric acid. But this damaged the wire and made it brittle again. Sellers' solution was to heat and gradually cool the coils of wire in sealed earthenware or iron pots, so tightly packed with wire and wet clay that all air was excluded. The wire thus annealed came out of the pots as bright and shiny as when first drawn. Sellers invented the annealing process before 1780. He never patented it and he even communicated it to an English firm which, after the unsuccessful experiment at Pennell's forge, was supplying him with wire for card teeth. The English firm successfully kept the secret until the turn of the century when the retort method of annealing was reinvented in France and reintroduced into England.

Sellers also devised other improvements for his wire business, such as a machine for weaving the faces of wire molds. But for the most part the improvements were intended not as patentable inventions, a source of income in themselves, but—as in the case of Crompton and his mule—as labor-saving devices for use in Nathan Sellers' own business.[22]

THE INTERNATIONAL FRATERNITY OF MECHANICIANS

The production machines—the machines that transformed raw materials into consumer products, that generated power, that propelled bullets— were made by a small group of highly skilled men then termed "mechanicians." They designed these machines and often themselves worked with forge and lathe, and hammer, cold chisel, and file, to make the mules and looms, the steam engines, the firearms parts, and all the other machinery that made up the Industrial Revolution. These men were also the inventors and users of machine tools—the machines that made machines.

The presence of a substantial cadre of mechanicians in England, France, and the United States was probably a main reason for the rapidity of the spread of manufacturing in those countries. The production machines themselves did not move easily across oceans until the latter part of the nineteenth century. Thus, although Great Britain was the source of most of the basic *ideas* for textile machinery, few if any of her machines were actually being imported into America. Whether English or American in concept, American machines were made in America in American machine shops, largely by American-born machinists. To be sure, there were emigrant English machinists and they were an important source of mechanical information as well as manpower. Such men as the Hodgson brothers, the Brandywine machinists who made throstle rollers for the Chester Creek manufacturers, and James Wagstaff (probably a relative of Hugh Wagstaff, the cotton spinner), also of Brandywine, who made spindles, were however probably not bringing over uniquely British machine tool designs.[1] For America already had a well-established machinists' trade, which was attracting many extremely talented men and even young gentlemen.

The machinist's practice in the early nineteenth century merged imperceptibly into that of the blacksmith, the iron master, the machine maker, the engineer, the draftsman, the artist, the inventor, and the natural scientist. Established and successful manufacturers and merchants—men of good family—were quite willing to commit their sons as apprentices in machine shops. The trade was an old one and had a sense of community, which encouraged the transmission of technological information by methods of demonstration and practice, as well as by the immigration of experienced operatives and the travel of American machinists abroad.

Although some successful mechanicians were manufacturers, the culture of the machinist was fundamentally different from that of the manufacturer: the machinist thought with his hands and eyes, and when he wished to learn or communicate he made a drawing or a model; the manufacturer and manager thought with his larynx, as it were, and when he wished to learn or communicate, did so with words, in conversation or in writing. The machinist had dirty hands from working with tools; the manager had cramped hands from writing.

In contrast to the British machine shops, where the workers, "according to the English plan of division of labor, were only perfect on a single branch," the American shops emphasized the acquisition of general technical skills and the perfection of machinery. George Escol Sellers, in his visit to England in 1832, was constantly amazed at the technological backwardness of the British machinist trades (even in their most advanced forms, as in the famous Maudslay Works). In England there was a strict specialization of labor, some "men working a lifetime with hammer and cold chisel," others devoting themselves to the lathe, and all (with the exception of planers) working with relatively clumsy tools. Observed Sellers:

As a boy I had worked on a Maudslay single mandrel ungeared lathe, with one of his slide rests that had been imported as something extraordinary, the lathe being driven by a great wheel with a man at [a] handcrank. I have the impression that this slide rest started both Tyler and Lukens to designing their improved one, which, for solidity and firmness, so increased the amount of work that the Maudslay rest was laid aside and the lathe transferred to the pattern shop as a light-running wood lathe long before I went to England. Therefore I was much surprised at finding that class of tools without any improvement in daily use.

I had been accustomed to see in our American shops, although many of their lathes had wooden shears with light cast-iron guide shears bolted on them, the rests or tool carriers traversed by chain or pinion in rack, with heavy suspended weight to hold them firm on the guide shears, turning off shavings of more than double the depth and feed of anything I saw in the Maudslay Works. It did appear to me that tools were not keeping up with the requirements of the times, but I noticed under construction a heavy double shear lathe, and two planers in use. This was evidence that the proprietors were looking towards saving manual labor. I thought if they could see the festoons of great wrought-iron shavings from the lathes of Rush and Muhlenburg, of Bush Hill, Philadelphia, or of Kemble's West Point Works, New York, as hung in their offices, it would spur them on in that direction. . . .

When I took in my hand their heavy, short, stubby cold chisels, their short, clumsy, broad-faced, short handled hand hammers, I felt it would be impossible for me to handle such tools with any prospect of approximating their results; I would as soon expect to reach them with the stone cutter's round wooden mallet. The evolution in form and make of such tools had in America far outstripped England.[2]

Another notable feature of the American shops was the heterogeneity of workers. In the Sellers' shops one might meet, work side by side with, and learn from, a veritable social potpourri: German princes traveling incognito to learn the mechanician's art, gentlemen's sons, college professors, professional artists, English artisans with literary tastes, third-generation American mechanics. American workmen tended to be respectable, literate, independent, jealous of seniority and privilege, and ready to fight foreigners: John Morton Poole at Matteawan recounted how an English master mechanic was beaten up by the man he replaced, and the youthful George Escol Sellers learned with dismay of the plot to abuse his friend Henri Mogeme, the wandering German mechanic of noble blood.[3]

The career of George Escol Sellers' young drafting teacher, John

Henry Hopkins, illustrates the quality of men who entered the mechanicians' fraternity in this period. Born in Dublin in 1792, he had emigrated to America with his parents and lived for a while in Bordentown, New Jersey, with the French émigrés who concentrated there. He was taught by his mother, a professional teacher, to paint and draw and play the cello; he colored the engraved plates for Wilson's *Birds of America*.[4] On his arrival in Philadelphia, he supported himself in part by teaching mechanical drawing to a class of young, aspiring machinists, including the five-year-old George Escol, and by playing the cello. He also served a mechanic's apprenticeship in the Mars Works of Oliver Evans and for a time lived with the Evans family, studying broadly in mineralogy and chemistry. In 1813 he moved from Philadelphia to manage an iron furnace in the Ligonier Valley. Then he moved to Pittsburgh, studied law, and became one of that city's leading attorneys. But, now converted from deism to Christianity, he abandoned law for the Episcopal ministry, and eventually became the first Bishop of Vermont. In this post he gained notoriety as a defender of slavery although his actual position on the subject, articulately presented in sermons, tracts, and books, was merely that the Bible did not explicitly prohibit slavery.[5]

The Philadelphia Mechanicians

The master mechanics who made the production machines for other men to use in England and America were, in the early decades of the nineteenth century, a small group of a few hundred men, all of whom knew each other by sight or reputation. As a recent mechanician remarked in his *History of Machine Tools*, "over the years those interested formed a closely knit federation."[6] Each locality had its own network, but the networks overlapped as apprentices traveled to gain experience and the journeymen and masters to gain fame and fortune.

In the Philadelphia area, in the 1820's and 1830's, there were a number of well-known machine makers who employed others in their shops and gave leadership to the trade; there were also plenty of lesser figures. In general, even the more prominent proprietors of the specialized machine shops did not make the great fortunes of the successful merchants, nor were they or their families usually members of "society." As the son of Coleman Sellers—one of the most famous mechanicians of the day—said of his father:

As to Fathers social position in Phila. it was all he wanted. Neither he nor Mother made any pretentions to the St. Peter's set or the codfish aristocracy that had better been called. High wines sugar rum and molasses with a spice of African blood.[7]

They were respected by the gentlemen merchants but were not part of their social world.

In Philadelphia, and its surburban industrial suburbs to the north, some names were long distinguished. In Bridesburg, Alfred Jenks maintained his great shops for making textile machines; later, Richard Garsed would be prominent there also. Oliver Evans, the early inventor of automatic flour-milling machinery and of high-pressure steam engines for river steamboats, had his foundry and shops, the Mars Works, on Spring Garden Street; after his death in 1819, it was continued by his sons-in-law, James Rush and John P. D. Muhlenberg. On Market Street between Fifth and Sixth was the store and paper mold and card manufactory of Nathan Sellers; his son Coleman, and John Brandt of Lancaster, built the shops at Cardington, on the Sellers estate in Upper Darby, where they manufactured machine-set card clothing and built locomotives. Matthias Baldwin's locomotive shops were also downtown near the Sellers' Market Street factory. Patrick Lyon manufactured his famous line of fire engines; and Jacob Perkins worked in partnership with Thomas Gilpin to develop an automatic watermark-impressing roller before his departure for London in 1819. Joseph Saxton—later to work for Alexander Dallas Bache, first president of the American Association for the Advancement of Science, in the Coastal Survey, and to become an associate of Joseph Henry, of the Smithsonian Institution—was then working for Isaiah Lukens. Franklin Peale was employed by the U.S. Mint, designing improvements in the machines used for coinage,[8] and collaborating with Matthias Baldwin in the development of steam locomotives.

After the death of Benjamin Franklin, the public relations manager and in a sense the public symbol of the fraternity, until his own death in 1827, was undoubtedly the aged Charles Willson Peale. Peale as a youth had studied in London under Benjamin West. Remembered by later generations as the principal portrait artist of the Revolution, he painted one of the most popular likenesses of George Washington. Peale was the very prototype of the eighteenth-century intellectual. He operated, for a time, a small cotton factory at Belfield, in north Philadelphia; he made numerous mechanical inventions; and he established his famous Museum of Natural History, for many years located in Independence Hall, as a kind of public educational institute. There he displayed such interesting objects as stuffed animals and birds, shown in their natural habitat in well-painted and appropriately furnished settings, and the newest mechanical inventions (such as Oliver Evans' steam engine and Baldwin's locomotive). There distinguished mechanician-scientists gave lectures on chemistry and electricity, aided by laboratory demonstrations and illustrated by lantern slides. Peale represented to the full the Enlightenment's profound faith in man's ability to solve his problems, and to secure happiness for himself and others, by the observation of nature and the application of reason alike to mechanics, to husbandry, and to social relations.[9]

The interconnections of this technological community were multifarious, for the men were intimately involved with one another in business, and the women were related by marriage and by the business associations of their husbands. Coleman Sellers—Hannah Hill's brother—had married Charles Willson Peale's daughter Sophonisba in 1805 and had been (briefly) a partner with Jacob Perkins in the manufacture of fire engines. Sellers and Perkins dissolved their partnership when Sellers objected to Perkins' unsuccessful effort to outdo Pat Lyon's celebrated fire engine — an effort that impaled a child onlooker's foot on a steel spike. Perkins then teamed up with Thomas P. Jones, a lecturer at the Franklin Institute and editor of its *Journal* from 1826 until his death in 1848, and Commissioner of Patents in 1828 and 1829. Some institutions were magnets for mechanically inclined people because of their need for advanced technology. The U.S. Mint, for example, was a center of collaborative enterprise. The directors included the Drs. Robert Patterson, *père et fils,* of the University of Pennsylvania; among the first coiners were Adam Eckfeldt, the inventor of Pat Lyon's fire engine design, and Franklin Peale, erstwhile manager of his father's Museum.

The kaleidoscopic quality of this flux of business relationships was simplified by the intimacy of the men in their personal contacts. They visited each other's shop constantly to exchange information, to stand silently watching a new machine or a new process, to speculate about the future of mechanism. By and large, they knew each other's business and did not hesitate to show each other inventions in embryo, trusting their peers to honor their priority and the economic advantage it might mean. Their patents were often not taken out until years after the invention had become widely known in the fraternity; patents once taken were sometimes not announced or enforced, the patentee trusting his customers to honor his interest without reminder. To be sure, there were patent-infringement suits, like those levied by the embittered Oliver Evans, yet many of these were directed not against fellow mechanicians but rather against exploitive manufacturers.

The Network Outside Philadelphia

The mechanicians traveled frequently, partly on business to discuss new construction and partly just to gain information. Travel was a mode of education for mechanicians as well as merchants. The mechanicians of the Brandywine Valley, which was in its own right a center of machine shops of all kinds, were in constant contact with their brethren in Philadelphia. Charles Willson Peale sent his sons Titian and Franklin to serve apprenticeships with the Hodgson brothers. George Escol Sellers recalled in his later years riding out to Delaware County about 1818 (when he was a boy of ten) with his father Coleman Sellers and Oliver Evans. Evans was then sixty-four and within a year or two of his death; but he talked vigorously about the future course of technological progress. On another occasion about the same time, George Escol and his father visited Thomas Gilpin and Lawrence Greatrake, Gilpin's technical manager, and spent the evening with them and E. I. du Pont from the powder mills.

The pattern of traveling to learn is also illustrated by the peregrinations of John Morton Poole and his brother-in-law Edward Bancroft of Wilmington. Initially financed by a loan of $100 from Charles du Pont, they wandered in a leisurely way through the 1830's from one machine shop to another, stopping for a couple of years to work at Matteawan, returning to the Brandywine, then spending two or three more years in the shops at Providence, Rhode Island, and finally going on to Boston and Lowell (where letters of introduction provided by Du Pont made possible their first commissions). Poole returned to work as a foreman (at $60 per month) in the locomotive shop of Charles and George Escol Sellers at Cardington in Upper Darby, before finally going on to establish the Poole machine shops in Wilmington.[10]

The mechanicians also often made a pilgrimage to England, still the fountainhead of mechanical innovation, in order to acquire technical sophistication (and, sometimes, to steal industrial secrets and entice away English mechanics). The visits to England of Francis Lowell, who there gained knowledge of the working principle of the power loom, and of Joshua and Thomas Gilpin, who studied textile and papermaking machinery, were well known in their day. Lowell's trip resulted in the patent Waltham loom and the great industrial growth at Lowell; Gilpin patented his imitation of John Dickinson's endless papermaking machine (the first introduction of continuous papermaking in America).

But many trips were undertaken less in the spirit of espionage than of a genuine desire to learn about English machines and processes that were not regarded as secret and to tell the Englishmen about American progress. These visits seem to have been understood in that light and were carried on even during the War of 1812 (Joshua Gilpin was in England and traveled freely gathering technical information all during the conflict). Many of the Philadelphia mechanicians who worked as civil engineers during the period of canal and railroad construction before 1840 visited England, including Erskine Hazard, Samuel Kneass, Solomon Roberts, and William Strickland. In the winter of 1832–33 George Escol Sellers traveled in England to learn about English papermaking machinery from Bryan Donkin and John Dickinson; but he also visited the shops of the late Henry Maudslay—celebrated as the inventor of the first workable slide rest for the engine-powered lathe; Sharp and Roberts' shops at Manchester; the Royal Mint; and the tunnel under the Thames then being constructed by Marc Isambard Brunel. And he found time to visit his old friend Jacob Perkins' "Adelaide Gallery" (or "National Gallery of Practical Science"), where he found a display of remarkable machinery invented by Perkins and his old Philadelphia friend Joseph Saxton. Saxton had in fact just invented the first practical commutator for an "electric magnetic motor" and an electric generator. Soon after Sellers' return, Isaiah Lukens built an electric generator for Peale's Museum.[11]

The inter-state and international character of the mechanicians' fraternity was also maintained by migration in search of opportunity. After the lifting of British restrictions in the 1820's, a steady stream of English and French mechanicians of greater or lesser degree came to America; of the hundreds of these immigrants in the Philadelphia area, among the best known were the Hodgson brothers and the Greatrake family on the Brandywine. The Du Ponts imported French mechanics while they were setting up their cotton and powder mills. And within the country, as opportunities opened one after the other in the growing frontier cities in the west and burgeoning south, mechanics from the east coast traveled to construct railroads, locomotives, steamboats, mints, and textile factories.

The mechanicians' fraternity, then, was consciously international, indifferent (insofar as technology was concerned) to national boundaries and to international conflict, committed to facilitating technological progress by a continuous, free exchange of information among themselves. They talked constantly to one another of ideas for improving processes and were eager to show the uninformed the value of a more advanced procedure.[12]

The Size of the Fraternity

It would be interesting to develop a census of the fraternity in order to measure its size and other social characteristics. Although this task would go far beyond the needs of the present study, some notion of an order-of-magnitude kind is worth having. The materials provided by the mechanicians of the Sellers family, who were among the leaders in the group, give an intimation of the number of mechanicians—the creative, innovative master mechanics working in metal—in the English-speaking world. In the period 1820 to 1840, something like three to four hundred such men were working. The whole group, including journeymen and apprentices, totaled probably no more than six thousand persons, if one estimates (generously) an average of twenty journeymen and apprentices for every master.[13]

The memoirs and recollections of George Escol Sellers even provide a minimal list of names for the members of the network whom the Sellers family of this period counted as kin, as teachers, as business associates, or as friendly acquaintances. Although the Sellers network included some people from the worlds of politics and commerce, its male members were primarily people who worked with their hands as mechanicians, artists, scientists, and naturalists. Taken all together they made up a substantial portion of the leadership of the technological community of the lower Delaware in the early nineteenth century; as the century wore on, many of them contributed largely to America's industrial and scientific development. Many names in the fraternity are missing, but their absence does not necessarily imply lack of acquaintance, for George Escol Sellers was writing in his eighties and was being deliberately selective. His roll call is impressive, nonetheless, numbering perhaps 100 men in America and England whose names are well enough known even 150 years later to justify inclusion in the national biographical dictionaries, and another 50 who were at least significant figures in their own communities during their lifetimes. Sellers' description makes it plain that nearly all the several hundred master mechanicians of the English-speaking world knew each other by name and reputation, and that each man probably had met and talked with most of his peers on one occasion or another or had corresponded in writing. The mechanicians' fraternity of England and America was a tightly woven network of men, who shared a common awareness of the state of the art, the problems to be solved, and the progress each man was making. The fraternity can only be compared to the practitioners of a discipline like physics or mathematics, or of a school of art or a theological tradition. It was, in Thomas Kuhn's sense, a paradigmatic community.[14]

THE SELLERS FAMILY

One way to understand how the fraternity of mechanicians was organized and how it functioned is to study its families. We have already observed how, for the small beginning cotton manufacturer, an assemblage of kinfolk was indispensable as a source of capital. A similar importance must be attached to the role of kinship in the organization of the mechanicians, at least on a local level. In addition to family's importance in capital formation, when and if the mechanic expanded his enterprise from the level of a craftsman's shop to a machine manufactory, family also served to recruit young people into the trade, to provide a setting for education even more effective than the apprentice system (which in itself was a quasi-kinship system anyway, even in a legal sense), to channel new technical information, and generally to reinforce the solidarity of the class of mechanicians by binding them together in loosely overlapping networks of marriage and descent.

The Sellers family, already met in various capacities in the Rockdale district, provides a classic example of this reinforcing and uniting role. Geographically centered in Upper Darby, their kin network extended throughout the lower Delaware Valley; their business connections extended throughout the United States and Great Britain; and their technical contributions to mechanics, engineering, and science, both during and after this period, were widely recognized as important. In this discussion, however, we shall be concerned not so much with recording their triumphs of invention as with delineating the way in which the Sellers family connection interpenetrated a large sector of the mechanical community.

The Network of Blood Relations

Inasmuch as the mechanicians were exclusively men, it is best to look at the Sellers family first as a system of descent in the male line. The patronymic descent group provided the structure of educational opportunity and career identification that was basic to the role of the family.

Samuel (1655–1732), the first of the Sellers family to come to Pennsylvania, arrived in 1682 along with the earliest Quaker settlers and acquired the original Sellers estate on Cobbs Creek in Darby. He was a weaver and so was his son Samuel Jr. (1690–1773), who invented a machine for twisting worsted yarn (a mixture of cotton and wool) and built Sellers Hall. His son John (1728–1804) was the first of the great Sellers mechanicians. He developed the water power of the Sellers estate to run a complex of sawmill, gristmill, and tilt mill. He developed a method of weaving, not the traditional worsteds, but wire, to make sieves for sifting grain. He was a friend of Franklin and along with him one of the original members of the American Philosophical Society. He was also a surveyor, and in 1769 contributed his skills to the Society's celebrated observations on the transit of Venus, which established Philadelphia as a place of learning in the eyes of many European *savants*. He represented the growing radicalism of the intellectuals of Philadelphia: a revolutionary patriot, he was disowned by the Friends.

Among John Sellers' children, Nathan, David, and John are of particular interest in this connection. John remained on the Sellers place as the miller. Nathan (1751–1830) and David (1757–1813) teamed up as partners in 1798 and on Cobbs Creek started the first cotton mill in Delaware County (it burned in 1815). The brothers meantime had moved to Philadelphia, where they established their shop to make wire for card teeth and paper molds, and where they made the cards and the paper molds, and did other kinds of machine shop work.

Nathan's children included Hannah, who married Peter Hill and moved to Chester Creek, and on whose behalf Nathan purchased Lenni Mill and the mill seat at Parkmount. One of Nathan's sons was Coleman (1781–1834). After David died in 1813, and Nathan retired to Millbourne in 1817, Coleman and his cousins James and David carried on the business in Philadelphia. James invented a new kind of riveted leather hose for fire engines. In 1828 Coleman and his cousins divided the family machinery business. James and David maintained the old Philadelphia wire works. Coleman took as partners his own sons George Escol (1808–1897) and Coleman Jr. (1827–1907), and moved out to a new factory site that they called Cardington, in Upper Darby, where they manufactured everything from carding and papermaking machinery to locomotives. George Escol, who later published an intimate and revealing memoir, *Early Engineering Reminiscences (1815–1840)*, went on after his father's death in 1834 to become a machinery manufacturer in the western states; the young Coleman became a famous engineer who, among other things, in 1860 invented the first stereoscopic movie camera and in the 1890's designed and installed the Niagara Falls hydroelectric plant.

But perhaps the most famous Sellers mechanician of them all was descended from Nathan and David's brother John, the miller at Upper Darby. This John's son, also named John (1789–1878), built up the establishment at Millbourne into one of the most productive merchant flour mills in the country by constantly adding new machinery. And *his* son William became one of the pre-eminent mechanical engineers of the nineteenth century. In 1853 he organized, with his brother John, a factory that manufactured machine tools, thus moving effectively the mechanician's practice to a second level. (During the earlier period, the machine shops that turned out the parts for production machines made their own lathes and other machine tools. A few machinists in England and America in the 1820's and 1830's were building small numbers of lathes for the trade. Sellers' factory manufactured machine tools of many kinds, in large numbers, for other machine shops.) He was granted over ninety U.S. patents for various inventions. He organized the plant which supplied—at no profit—most of the structural steel for the Roeblings' Brooklyn Bridge. He proposed a system of screw threads which became the U.S. standard. He became president of the Franklin Institute, a trustee of the University of Pennsylvania, and a member of the National Academy of Sciences.[1]

Even so brief a review as this suggests that more was at work in the Sellers mechanical tradition than the simple inheritance of talent. There is an evident accumulation of expertise, an intensification of focus in the four generations from John (of transit-of-Venus fame) to Coleman Jr. and William. The process by which this trans-generational growth was accomplished was one of careful personal tutoring of the young sons of each generation by their grandfathers, fathers, uncles, and older brothers. The clearest account of the practical combination of family identification and education is afforded by the George Escol Sellers memoirs of his own, his brother Coleman's, and his father's boyhoods in Philadelphia in the late eighteenth and early nineteenth centuries. George Escol was not bound out as an apprentice but was with his father almost constantly, in the shop and on other occasions of interest:

I was standing with my father on the curb looking at the fire, when Philip Garrett rushed up in a great state of excitement, seized my father by his arm, and said: "Coleman, if thee can dam the stairways and hatchways of the upper floors of those two warehouses (pointing), and I can get a foot of water on the floors, we can stop the fire at that fire wall, but if we let it work down the walls will fall, the whole block will go, and there is no knowing how much more." My father turned me over to some one to see me safe home, and left with Mr. Garrett. I learned afterward that my father, with board partitions that he tore down, succeeded with them and gunny bags in damming both stair and hatchways, making small crevices tight by having large quantities of bran thrown on the floors. The roofs were on fire and would soon fall in. Lines were formed for carrying up water by the bucketfull.

Instead of going home as directed, I for hours had my place in the empty bucket line. While this was going on Garrett was having section after section of hose attached to both the Philadelphia and the Diligent engines, only to burst before the water reached the upper floors. Fortunately the Resolution Company had a number of new sections of hose which were pressed into the service, and were attached next the engines where the pressure would be greatest. The floors were flooded, the attics and roofs fell into the water, and spreading fire was stayed. The success of this expedient was so complete that it turned the attention of all firemen in the direction of securing more reliable hose. . . .[2]

Young George Escol, and presumably Coleman Jr. as well, were present in the shop on occasions when the famous and near-famous mechanics of the day stopped in to talk and tinker, and as we have seen, he went along with his father to meet the aged Oliver Evans, the Gilpin brothers, and the Du Ponts along the Brandywine. He watched inventions being made, was present at their trial, and saw them discarded when they failed. He heard the mechanicians who visited his father's shop converse about machinery. "Old Blind Hawkins," for instance, who had lost his sight during an epidemic while he was serving as supercargo on a slave-ship in his youth, would visit and expound his ideas for the use of high-pressure steam to operate steam engines and rapid-firing steam guns. These ideas were later developed by another of the visitors, Jacob Perkins, when he went to London. A list of the men whom George met and listened to in conversation with his father would include all the famous mechanics of Philadelphia and many others from towns all up and down the east coast.

But it was not only a father and son relationship. He spent summers in the country with his paternal grandfather Nathan at Cardington, and with his maternal grandfather Charles Willson Peale near Germantown, absorbing a sense of the traditions of both family and the trade. George Escol's father Coleman had likewise spent summers with *his* grandfather John Sellers, the first of the great inventors of the clan.

George had the highest esteem for his father and his grandfather. He wrote in his later years of his intense youthful admiration of his father, who was

a very fine horse man, and I recollect when I thought him the best rider with a single exception, that I had ever seen. He sat as if he and his horse was of one flesh. . . .

My earliest recollection of Father was that I thought him the most wonderful man that ever lived. He had the knack of explaining everything to a boy's comprehension and often in very few words. He was free with his pencil in making clear and accurate sketches of what he wanted to illustrate. When what puzzled us at school and we were called stupid by the teacher all we had to do was to go to Father with our troubles to be set right. He went to the bottom of everything left nothing to chance.[3]

In the old house in Philadelphia, his father had a small machine shop in the garret which he shared with his sons and in which he gave them their initial instructions in machine tools.

> The garret [was] all in one, had dormers front and rear and one window in the centre in the west wall. It was by this window that Father had his file bench and turning lathe. On the front side of the great chimney stack was our boys carpenter bench. Father's bench was on the other side the chimney, both sitting crossway of the garret. It was in this garret that both Charles and myself got our first lessons in handling tools. We were always encouraged to try, no matter what failures we met with. One day father came up and found me with my little jack plaine trying to plaine a pine board about 6 or more feet long. He stood a moment looking at me, then said, "Escol if you would begin at the stop end it would be easier and make smoother work. It is easier to plane down than up hill," but said I, "Father the board is dirty and would dull my plane, I am trying to get under the dirt. What do you mean by planing down hill?" He said, "The front end of your plane is held up by the rough board and you have to set the bit deeper than if you take a short shaving off of the stop end, then the front of the plaine is below what you want to cut and the bit need not be set so deep and the work will be smoother. Try it." And I did, and I tell this as evidence of his always giving a reason and his reasoning and illustrations a lesson.[4]

George was also proud of his grandfather Nathan, of whom he wrote (although slightly patronizingly):

> We all know that he was a skillful worker in wood and wire and not bad in metal for the time in which he lived and with the poor tools and appliances at his command. When I think of what he accomplished he appears to me to be as great if not greater inventive mechanic, everything considered, as the grandest of the present time.[5]

These recollections, written in 1894, three-quarters of a century after the events, were warmed perhaps by nostalgia. But they show clearly enough a pattern of family training which was based on the assumption that the father's craft was good enough for his sons to follow and that the son should become, in effect, his father's apprentice in very early childhood. This meant a close, personal association in which the father deliberately included the child in his work, showing him how to use the tools, keeping him around the shop, and carrying him along on business travels. In this way was laid the basis for a deep, if somewhat competitive, identification, as the son sought first to become like his father and then to excel him if possible in their shared and chosen craft.

The Network of In-Laws

Connections by marriage were as important as descent for economic purposes, for they provided added sources of partnership and capital, opportunities for education and recommendation, and a forum for the exchange of ideas. After children were born, of course, they were the source of consanguineal alliances as well. They offered an additional set of connections to tie together the loose fraternal assemblage of mechanicians.

One important affinal connection of this kind was formed between the John Sellers line of Millbourne and the Pooles of Wilmington, Delaware. John Sellers was a successful miller but he did not contribute much personally to the family's tradition of mechanical invention. In 1817, at the age of twenty-seven, shortly after undertaking the management of the new mill his father had built for him, he married Elizabeth Poole, the eldest daughter of William Poole, a Brandywine miller (and friend of Oliver Evans). Elizabeth Poole was a strong and intelligent woman, who "had been the congenial companion of a very intellectual father," and (in the opinion of the county historian, who knew them well) "brought into her husband's home a wisdom beyond her years."[6] One of their eleven children, William, born in 1824, was apprenticed at the age of fourteen to John Morton Poole, his maternal uncle, when Poole started up a machine shop in the basement at Joseph Bancroft's mill. This John Morton Poole, who had been born in 1812, had served his mechanical apprenticeship at the Matteawan Manufacturing Company and had studied science and mechanical drawing at the Franklin Institute in Philadelphia. He had been partners briefly with Edward Bancroft (the brother of Joseph), who had worked at Cardington for several years for Coleman Sellers and Sons, and his sister Sarah was married to Joseph Bancroft.

William Sellers stayed with his uncle for seven years as a machinist's apprentice. He then took charge of the machine shop at Edward Bancroft's mill on Ridley Creek. In a few years he moved to Philadelphia to set up his own plant for the manufacture of machine tools; there he was joined in partnership by Bancroft. In 1853 William's brother John joined the firm as partner. The firm of William Sellers and Company, as indicated earlier, pioneered the design and manufacture of machine tools.[7]

An affinal connection of equal importance was formed with the Pooles in 1805 when Nathan Sellers' son Coleman married Charles Willson Peale's daughter Sophonisba. This alliance brought the two families into a close consortium. Charles Willson Peale was then principally devoted to the development of his famous Museum, which he hoped would become a "School of Nature" at the heart of a national university. To the Museum, as lecturers and laboratory workers, he attracted most of the scientists, artists, and mechanicians of Philadelphia. Of Peale's numerous progeny, two—Franklin and Titian—had at the suggestion of E. I. du Pont been apprenticed in 1813 to the Hodgson brothers in their machine shop on the Brandywine.[8] After a year, with an introduction from Coleman Sellers, Franklin went for another year's experience to work at William Young's cotton mill at Rockland. This was to be their preparation for taking part in managing the Peale family's little cotton factory at Belfield near Germantown. But, like so many others, the Peales' cotton factory did not survive the renewal of British imports after the end of the War of 1812, and the three mechanically trained brothers—Franklin, Titian, and Charles Linnaeus—went on to other things. Franklin, however, returned to mechanics, working for Coleman Sellers for a time, and later serving as an employee of the U.S. Mint, where he invented a steam press and eventually (in 1840) became Chief Coiner. It was Franklin also who, a temporary victim of religious enthusiasm, married the daughter of the Gilpins' mechanical expert, Thomas Greatrake. The Greatrakes were Quakers and the young woman was a "Quaker Preacher" of extreme religious zeal. After their daughter was born, Eliza became psychotic, running away from home and threatening to kill the child. She was placed in the Philadelphia Hospital for a time and the marriage was annulled; eventually she was returned to her parents.[9] Another of the Peales, Raphaelle's son Edmund, lived with the family of Coleman Sellers and worked for a time in his factory.[10] And George Escol remembered in later years his own summer visits to Belfield, to stay with his grandfather Charles Willson Peale, where he recalled hearing a discussion of Redheffer's famous—and fraudulent—perpetual motion machine.[11]

Evidently, then, the Sellers' connections by marriage with both the Pooles and the Peales were routes by which young people were recruited into mechanical pursuits, trained, and placed in positions of employment. They bound together three important mechanicians' families of Philadelphia and Wilmington.

THE FRANKLIN INSTITUTE

Although the mechanicians' work in its informal organization and its function was not unlike a scientific field, in other important respects it differed markedly from any of the academic disciplines. For one thing, they lacked a publication in which issues of importance to the profession could be debated and new information of general concern be communicated. They also lacked a formal method of proof that went beyond the claims of experience and authority to be comparable to the experimental method of science or the logical methods of mathematics or theology. They had no way of conclusively demonstrating the validity of a technical proposition, such as "Overshot wheels are more efficient than breast wheels." And, finally, they did not have a system of formal education, which could standardize mechanical training and relate it to useful information in the sciences; all that remained of formality in the mechanics' education was the lingering remnant of the apprentice system.

Up to this time, mechanicians had perhaps not felt such a disciplinary apparatus to be necessary. It was notoriously difficult anyway to talk or write about machinery without recourse to drawings or even three-dimensional demonstration. "Proof" of correctness or error often seemed self-evident to the eye—a thing either worked or it didn't. The apprentice system—limited, in America, by the need for generalization—was an effective one in a largely nonliterary field of knowledge; and the physical sciences had little to offer the mechanician beyond the opportunity for training and employment as instrument maker. Indeed, up to this point in history, science probably owed more to technology than technology did to science.

But technological problems were beginning to arise that required a more "scientific"—that is, methodical and systematic—approach. The increasing demand for power was stimulating a deluge of improvements and inventions in water wheels, turbines, and steam engines. Questions about the relative efficiency of the many different designs were not easily answered; and the increasingly obvious dangers of imperfectly understood mechanisms, such as steam engine boilers, which had a distressing propensity for explosion, particularly on passenger-carrying steamboats, could no longer be dismissed. Mechanicians themselves were realizing, furthermore, that they were wasting a lot of time reinventing each other's discoveries and —worse yet—rediscovering each other's mistakes. Oliver Evans, for instance, in 1818 complained to Coleman Sellers, while they were on their way to install some flour-milling equipment in Delaware County, about the need for published records in technology:

Mr. Evans had much to say on the difficulties inventive mechanics labored under for want of published records of what had preceded them, and for works of reference to help the beginner. In speaking of his own experience, he said that everything he had undertaken he had been obliged to start at the very foundation; often going over ground that others had exhausted and abandoned, leaving no record. He considered the greatest difficulty beginners had to encounter was want of reliable knowledge of what had been done.

Even at that early day Mr. Evans suggested and urged the formation of a Mechanical Bureau that should collect and publish all new inventions, combined with reliable treatises on sound mechanical principles, as the greatest help to beginners. He did not believe it could at that time be made self-sustaining, but it would be to the interest of mechanics, manufacturers and merchants to subscribe to its support.[1]

Evans on the same occasion also remarked on the need for a school to teach mechanical drawing. This was not felt only as a technical requirement. It was believed by some that "theory" (i.e., science) and "practice" (i.e., mechanics) should be taught together in order to render practice more consistent and theory more realistic. Furthermore, both in England and in the United States there was a widespread feeling that mechanicians, who were assuming an increasing importance in the economic life of their countries, ought to be more broadly educated so that they could assume a role of nearer social equality with the liberally educated merchants and financiers who dominated society.[2] In England and Scotland, institutes for the education of young mechanics and operatives had been popular from the turn of the century and libraries already existed there; in Philadelphia and Boston, where young mechanics could read, clubs were often formed (and as often dissolved) where books were discussed and issues of the day debated.

And then, overshadowing all of this, there was the problem of proof. Every profession needs to have conventional standards for judging the merit of the productions of its practitioners. Sometimes the citation of authority will do, but this was not the tradition among the mechanicians, who tended to be more or less irreverent toward the pretensions of the great. The elegant proofs of mathematics, based on the laws of logic, hardly seemed applicable. The prevailing criterion for the merit of a mechanical "statement" was experience: whether the thing worked, whether it created more problems than it solved, how much trouble it was to manufacture, how prone to break down, and so forth. These criteria, however, were difficult to apply systematically and were liable to provoke unresolvable arguments, like the acrimonious contention between Oliver Evans and Benjamin Latrobe over the potential usefulness of high-pressure steam engines in propelling boats and wagons. Furthermore, the criteria were crudely empirical and not based on an analysis of the significant variables at work in the system. When such variables became too numerous, the complexity of the problem exceeded intuitive comprehension and required recourse to some system of experiment, some protocol for recording results, some means of publishing the findings.

The Founding of the Franklin Institute

The Franklin Institute of Philadelphia was organized in 1824 for the purpose of solving, or at least contributing to the resolution of, all these problems.[3] The "leading spirits" in organizing it were the master mechanicians of Philadelphia, the mechanic-manufacturers: Matthias Baldwin, then running "a general jobbing machine shop"; Samuel V. Merrick and John Agnew, who were partners in a foundry in Southwark and manufactured fire engines; Henry and Steven P. Morris, makers of iron and brass forgings, particularly umbrella frames; James Sellers and Abraham Pennock, inventors and manufacturers of riveted leather fire engine hose; James Rush and John P. D. Muhlenburg, sons-in-law of Oliver Evans, and owners of the Bush Hill ironworks; Professor Robert M. Patterson, Professor of Mathematics at the University of Pennsylvania, and later director of the U.S. Mint; and Franklin Peale, then working for Coleman Sellers.

Bestirring themselves with vigor, these gentlemen succeeded in mobilizing the support of the entire mechanical community of the Philadelphia-to-Wilmington region, gaining subscriptions for membership from the Du Ponts and the Gilpins along the Brandywine, from James Ronaldson the cotton manufacturer of Darby, from Philadelphians Charles and George Escol Sellers, Oliver Evans the iron founder's son, himself an iron founder, William Lippincott, the cotton manufacturer with whom Daniel Lammot would be involved next year, John S. Phillips the sugar refiner, and many others, including even some men who were principally merchants and financiers like Nicholas Biddle and Paul Beck, Jr., Lammot's first father-in-law.[4]

The Board of Managers went to work at once to implement solutions to the problems of the mechanical community. Ad hoc committees were appointed to examine and evaluate new inventions; John S. Phillips, selected for his knowledge of chemistry, was a member of the first committee, along with the well-known mechanicians David N. Mason and Isaiah Lukens. After careful tests at Frankford Arsenal, they published a report recommending the new percussion caps for use in firing rifles and cannon.[5] A mechanics' high school was begun, with a well-qualified academic faculty, to teach philosophy, mechanics, chemistry, mathematics, and architectural and mechanical drawing. A standing committee was formed to examine and report on newly patented inventions and an exhibit was held for domestic manufactures, with prizes for quality and novelty; both of these activities continued for many years. And a new hall was constructed to house the growing organization. In 1826, the *Franklin Journal and American Mechanics' Magazine* was launched under the editorship of Thomas P. Jones. (In 1828 the name was changed to *Journal of the Franklin Institute.*) Jones, an Englishman by birth, had been editor of the *American Mechanics' Magazine,* founded in New York the year before. Jones moved to Washington in 1828 to become the superintendent of the U.S. Patent Office, but he continued to edit the *Journal* from Washington until his death in 1848.

The mechanics' school slowly foundered; the committee structure and the *Journal* gradually became the principal agencies by which the purposes of the Franklin Institute were carried out. The problem with the school, apparently, was the difficulty of actually joining the technological and scientific subjects. To be sure, the mechanical and thermodynamic principles by which machines moved and bridges stayed in one place were those expounded in Newton's physics; the geometry of mechanism was no different from that of Euclid. But many of these principles were, in simplified language, matters of common knowledge; it was not always clear to the mechanic what advantage the more abstruse theoretical formulations of science gave him in solving practical problems. Take, for instance, the highly publicized claim of the Edinburgh mathematician and physicist Dr. John Robison that James Watt had based his improvement of the steam engine upon the doctrine of "latent heat" expounded in courses of lectures he had attended at the University of Edinburgh. Although Robison and Watt were indeed close friends, Watt was obliged to deny the connection (although he politely conceded the general value of science). The knowledge on which he depended in making the improved steam engine with external condenser was in large part folk knowledge; thus, said Watt, "It was known very long before my time, that steam was condensed by coming into contact with cold bodies and that it communicated heat to them. Witness the common still, &c. &c." Furthermore, he had conducted a series of experiments of his own on the Newcomen engine which led to the practical improvements. Dr. Joseph Black and his theory of latent heat had been useful only in explaining "how so much cold water could be heated so much by so small a quantity in the form of steam." Watt went on to explain:

But this theory, though useful in determining the quantity of injection necessary where the quantity of water evaporated by the boiler, and used by the cylinder, was known, and in determining, by the quantity and heat of the hot water emitted by Newcomen's engines, the quantity of steam required to work them, did not lead to the improvements I afterwards made in the engine. These improvements proceeded upon the old-established fact, that steam was condensed by the contact of cold bodies, and the later known one, that water boiled in vacuo at heats below 100°, and consequently that a vacuum could not be obtained unless the cylinder and its contents were cooled every stroke to below that heat. These, and the degree of knowledge I possessed of the elasticities of steam at various heats, were the principal things it was *necessary* for me to consider in contriving the new engine.[6]

Ignorance of such elementary principles could of course be crippling to a mechanic's program of invention, as George Escol Sellers remarked in discussing his friends John Brandt and Jacob Perkins. Brandt had had no formal education in geometry; "he did not understand the simplest drawings. He said he was often mortified by not being able to understand sketches." All his drawings had to be made full size; he could not understand them reduced to scale. As Sellers recalled it,

It was by mere accident that I discovered his mental difficulty. All his thinking was, if I may so express it, *full size.* The trouble was in reducing to a given scale and carrying both in his mind at the same time. Up to the point of this discovery it would take pages to describe the various devices I resorted to, but now all was plain sailing. By working with him on full-size drawings, it was not long before he understood them and became quite proficient.[7]

But the real question was not whether all mechanics needed to know how to read scale drawings and to calculate proportions, or to have an elementary knowledge of the condensing power of cold water and the expanding power of steam; it was rather whether this level of need required a long series of abstract academic lectures on the major branches of science and mathematics.

The standing committee on exhibitions, from the fall of 1824 onward for half a century, annually organized a public exhibit where American manufacturers could display their products, particularly those notable for novelty and quality. Premiums, advertised in advance throughout the country, were awarded in the fall and the names of the winners were published in the *Journal.* Among the categories of prominence, of course, were cotton yarns and cloth and the machines used in manufacturing them. Entries were submitted from all parts of the United States, and the Philadelphian, Chester Creek, and Brandywine manufacturers submitted their samples. In 1825, for instance, the firm of Lewis, Phillips, and Company, then of Holmesburg, won the silver medal for "the best piece of blue Nankeen made in the United States, in imitation of the Chinese."[8] J. Garsed and Company, then of Frankford, submitted eighteen rolls of gray shoe thread; although it did not receive a medal, it was commended for being "well made and strong." In 1827, Robert Beatty, a toolmaker of Village Green (and briefly later the lessee of Knowlton Mill), received a silver medal for his edged tools, which "sustained the high character they have always borne" as superior to foreign. The Garsed brothers received awards through the 1840's for their power-loom-woven "cotton and worsted damask table covers," their "Marseilles . . . toilet covers," and other fabrics. It was not until the 1850's that Daniel Lammot and Samuel Riddle began to exhibit; Lammot received a gold medal in 1851 for bed tickings, and Samuel Riddle honorable mention in 1856 for his Canton flannels, rated as "fair merchantable goods." Crozer never seems to have exhibited at the Franklin Institute.[9]

Another regular feature of the *Journal* was its report of British and American inventions. This was undoubtedly a great boon to inventors and manufacturers alike. The Patent Office issued annual lists of inventions, giving the name assigned to the device by the inventor, but neither describing nor evaluating it. The *Journal* published a description of what its committee on inventions considered to be the most significant, often quoting directly from the patent specifications, and sometimes essaying an evaluation of an invention's utility compared with others in its class.

And there were formal articles: summary descriptions of the state of the art in some branch of technology; outlines of the principles of a discipline of science; exhortations to mechanicians to make use of the accumulating contributions of science.

The Franklin Institute undoubtedly had an important effect upon the mechanicians' practice. By stimulating national pride in American manufactures, by providing the mechanicians themselves with news of the state of the mechanical arts and the sciences, by communicating in the pages of its *Journal* an awareness of the need for scientific method, the Institute facilitated the pace of mechanical progress. But the failure of the mechanics' schools, which were patronized more by the general public than by young mechanics, was perhaps an omen of an effect its own success was slowly helping to bring about: the splitting of the mechanicians' fraternity into two, unequal, classes—the class of the practical artisan-mechanic, with limited education; and the class of the engineer and the architect, who employed scientific knowledge to solve fundamental problems of design.

The Committee on Water Power

Five years after its birth, the Institute began to function as a research organization, carrying out applied scientific investigations on behalf of the industrial community. The first of these enterprises was launched in 1829, when a "committee of inquiry" was formed to "fix by actual experiments ... the value of water, as a moving power, and the relative effects produced by it upon wheels of different construction."[10] Within a few years, two more committees were formed: a Committee on Weights and Measures, and a Committee on the Explosion of Steam Boilers. The last was also the most highly publicized and its work resulted in federal safety legislation as early as 1838—the first such federal regulatory action, in fact, in the national experience.[11] But of more immediate relevance to the cotton manufacturers on Chester Creek was the work of the Committee on Water Power.

The Committee was composed of many of the leading mechanicians of Philadelphia, including some of the men who had founded the Institute a few years before. The chairman was Samuel V. Merrick, the iron founder; the first members were Benjamin Reeves, nail manufacturer; Isaiah Lukens, machinist; Rufus Tyler, machinist; and Andrew Young, brass founder. They were soon joined by Matthias Baldwin, machinery manufacturer; John Agnew, Merrick's partner; James Espy, mathematics instructor at the Franklin Institute; James Rush, iron founder; Frederick Graff, superintendent of the Philadelphia Water Works; William H. Keating, chemist; and at the last moment Alexander Dallas Bache, the professional scientist who was to head the scientific activities of the Institute for many years. This blue-ribbon panel announced their plan and solicited subscriptions, and letters with reports and suggestions, from all over the United States. Money and information came from local manufacturers, of course, but also from such other interested concerns as the Schuylkill Navigation Company, the Society for Useful Manufactures at Patterson, the New England Society for Promoting Mechanical Arts, and Warren Colburn, engineer at Lowell. The City Council of Philadelphia granted the Committee the right to use the water power at the dam connected with the Fairmount Water Works; the firm of Rush and Muhlenburg constructed the building to contain the experimental apparatus.

The Committee first analyzed the nature of the problem. Their approach was essentially a Baconian, inductive one, depending less upon *a priori* theory than upon systematic collection and tabulation of quantitative data. They described this empiricist approach succinctly in their report:

There is perhaps no subject connected with the extensive branch of mechanics, for which theory has done so little as for that which considers the effect of water upon wheels; the different theories advanced are at variance with each other, and with practice, so that the candid theorist confesses that the circumstances, attending the action, are of so complicated a nature as to baffle his powers of investigation. Experiment, then, can alone guide to results worthy of confidence.

The experimental inquiries in relation to water-wheels which have, deservedly, attracted most attention, are those of Smeaton. The means of a single individual could not be competent to prosecute such a subject upon the scale required to make the results entirely practical, and we find the ingenuity of Smeaton labouring against the difficulties incident to the contracted dimensions of the apparatus which he was obliged to employ, and arranging with great skill and resource the best means to render serviceable the working models which were used in his experiments.

The experiments of Bossut, which rank next in extent to those of Smeaton, were comparatively few, and were principally made upon the undershot wheel.

It would not be profitable to enumerate the isolated experiments made in different countries upon this subject, since the sum of the information which they convey is extremely small. Of late years this branch of inquiry has been but little prosecuted, and the committee are not aware that any experiments, except a few in France, having in view a particular form of wheel, have been made, which tend to throw light upon the subject of their labours.

Such was the progress made in this subject when the Institute undertook it, with a view to obtain such results as should afford to the millwright a sure and safe guide in his practice, and thus contribute essentially to the promotion of one of the most important of the Mechanic Arts.[12]

The problem was indeed a complex one, in view of the number of variables that could have an effect on the usable power produced by water wheels. These variables included the volume of water turning the wheel; the head (the distance from the mouth of the sluice above the wheel to the floor of the wheelpit); the size and shape of the gate releasing the water; the type of wheel (overshot, pitchback, breast, or undershot), the diameter of the wheel, the number of buckets, its mass and angular velocity; the materials of which it was made; friction, lubrication, and so on. Apparatus had to be designed so that these variables could either be kept constant (so as to simplify the analysis) or be carefully and precisely varied according to plan. The Committee's analysis of the problem was pragmatic but in its way elegant too; the central problem of measurement, of course, was to compare power applied (energy expended) with work accomplished by any particular wheel arrangement.

One of the most important questions which arose for the discussion of the committee, was the measure of power expended, and of effect produced, to be adopted in their investigations. They finally determined upon one which, while strictly correct in principle, was at the same time, from its simplicity and ease of application, well adapted to their purposes, viz. for the measure of the power applied, the weight of water expended multiplied by the height of the head, (kept invariable,) above the bottom of the wheel; and for that of the effect, the weight raised multiplied by the distance through which it was raised. In order that this measure of effect may be accurate, the friction and inertia of the machine must be considered. The friction was carefully ascertained by experiment and the proper allowance made for it, as will appear in the course of this report. Any resistance from inertia was avoided by causing the wheel, and of course the weight raised by it, to move, before beginning an experiment, with a velocity which would remain constant during its progress.[13]

The apparatus, consisting essentially of a variable water-delivery system, a work-measuring device, and a set of water wheels, was built by the fine machinist Phillip Garrett and completed by the spring of 1830. The 123 planned experiments, involving 1,381 trials, each one repeated at least once to ensure reliability, were immediately begun. The research had to be interrupted in December 1830, with a few of the experiments still to be done; these were probably completed in the spring of 1831.

The result of these labors was a massive body of tabulations which, in effect, rated each combination for its efficiency. Efficiency was measured as the ratio of power expended to effect produced. Power expended was measured simply by the weight of the water, multiplied by the distance (head) through which it moved, necessary to lift a constant mass a certain distance. The "effect" was the sum of the weight of this mass, and the quantity of friction overcome in raising it, multiplied by the distance it was raised. Efficiencies ranged from lows of about 60 percent, for some combinations, to highs of nearly 90 percent for others.

By July 1831 the Committee was ready to give practical answers to practical questions of the kind hundreds of millers and manufacturers were asking.[14] Questions and answers were drafted to give a quick response to standard letters of inquiry. They may be summarized as follows:

Q: What is the advantage of the overshot over the breast wheel?
A: About 4 to 3.

Q: What is the optimum ratio of the diameter of the wheel to the head of water in the pit?
A: The power of the water comes from gravity not from impulse; hence the diameter of the wheel should be the maximum possible fraction of the head.

Q: What is the proper head?
A: Take care to ensure an adequate supply at all seasons.

Q: What is the optimum number of revolutions per minute?
A: It varies directly with the head.

Q: Where is the best working point for gearing, belts, etc.?
A: There is no rule; it depends on convenience at the particular installation.

Q: What is the optimum depth of the back water under the wheel?
A: No clear answer can be made but the committee recommends low heads and the "pitchback overshot" wheel, whose direction of rotation tends to free the wheel of water.

Q: What is the optimum depth of shrouding on the buckets?
A: That which minimizes the loss of fall.

But, having completed their research, and having publicly promised to publish the results, the Committee on Water Power now faced a frustrating problem of communication. The results were crudely empirical, in the sense that they could not be expressed in a concise set of mathematical equations. The whole mass of data would have to be presented so that the practical millwright could find the optimum type of wheel for his particular setting somewhere in the tables reporting the 123 experiments. The report never was published in a single volume; instead (an unfortunate decision), it was published in installments in the *Journal of the Franklin Institute*. The first installment appeared in March 1831; additional parts came out in 1832 and 1841. The early chapters created an international sensation. The British Association for the Advancement of Science was told by a distinguished speaker, the engineer George Rennie, that the Committee's researches "eclipse everything that has yet been effected on this subject," and the London *Mechanics Magazine* praised it as an example of the value of "organized and cooperative" inquiry.[15] But the last sections, apparently, never were published. By the 1850's, the new and more efficient turbines, and the versatile steam engines, were combining to drive out the water wheel from just those sophisticated establishments whose managers would earlier have wanted to read the Franklin Institute's study. The water wheel research was a landmark in the application of scientific method to technology. But its value to the community of mechanicians was drastically reduced by the difficulty the researchers had in communicating their findings to an eagerly waiting public.

THINKING ABOUT MACHINERY

The work of the mechanician was, in large part, intellectual work. This was true in spite of the fact that he dealt with tangible objects and physical processes, not with symbols, and that some of what he did was done with dirty hands. The thinking of the mechanician in designing, building, and repairing tools and machinery had to be primarily visual and tactile, however, and this set it apart from those intellectual traditions that depended upon language, whether spoken or written. The product of the mechanician's thinking was a physical object, which virtually had to be seen to be understood; descriptions of machines, even in technical language, are notoriously ambiguous and extremely difficult to write, even with the aid of drawings and models.

As with the work of those who think in words, schools of thought or traditions flourished among the mechanicians too, embracing a preference for a particular kind of solution to a type of mechanical problem, or a devotion to a particular expertise. Some of these traditions could be subsumed under the relics of the ancient craft guild system. There were turners, tinsmiths, masons, millwrights, brass founders, and so forth. The master in each of these crafts was the custodian of highly specialized skills, which he passed on to the coming generation of apprentices, teaching largely by demonstration and example. But the other kind of tradition depended upon the collaborative working out, by generations of mechanics, of the potentialities hidden yet implicit in a certain principle of mechanism, and the solving of the problems each successive improvement called forth. Their situation was not unlike that of scientists in the normal development of what has been called a paradigm.[1] When a basic innovation was introduced, it was embodied in an actual machine; the machine, and copies of it, rather than verbal descriptions, communicated the paradigm. But with each machine came problems to eliminate and improvements to add, all within the ambit of the original conception. Thus the mule of Crompton—a synthesis of the jenny and the water frame—constituted a paradigm for mechanicians to work on for the next 150 years. Machines were not "invented" in complete and finished form; rather, they were the product of generations of collective effort. The paradigms themselves often were never patented, and if they were, the patent was rarely left valid and uninfringed for long; what was patentable was not the paradigm but an improvement.

The kind of thinking involved in designing machine systems was unlike that of linguistic or mathematical thinking in its emphasis on sequence as opposed to classification. To the linguistic and mathematical thinker (for mathematics is merely very formal language), the grammar that embodies the rules of sequence is a given; what is crucial is the choice of the correct word or phrase, denoting a class of concepts, and the collection of attributes appropriate to describe the thing in mind. To the mechanical thinker, the grammar of the machine or mechanical system is the successive transformations of power—in quantity, kind, and direction—as it is transmitted from the power source (such as falling water or expanding steam), through the revolutions of the wheel, along shafts, through gears and belts, into the intricate little moving parts, the rollers and spindles and whirling threads, of the machine itself. The shapes and movements of all these hundreds of parts, sequentially understood, are a long yet elegantly simple moving image in three-dimensional space. In this mode of cognition, language is auxiliary—often so lagging an auxiliary that the parts and positions of a machine have no specific name, only a generic one, and if referred to in words, have to be described by such circumlocutions as "the 137th spindle from the left," "the lowest step of the cam," or "the upper right hand bolt on the governor housing."

The complexity of thought required to understand mechanical systems would seem in no way inferior to what is required for the trains of reasoning in mathematics or the common language. Thinking visually and tactilely has an inherent disadvantage, however, in comparison with thinking in language. Those who think in words—on subjects which are thought about effectively in words—can think a sentence and then utter it for others to hear. If one visualizes a piece of machinery, however, and wishes to communicate that vision to others, there is an immediate problem. Speech (and writing) will provide only a garbled and incomplete translation of the visual image. One must make the thing—or a model, or at the least a drawing—in order to ensure that one's companion has approximately the same visual experience as oneself.

In the Western world, an effect of this special problem in communicating technological information has tended to be the growing isolation of those who think in mental pictures. Theologians, humanists, even scientists can converse freely because the thinking is done with the same system of symbols as those used in communication. Indeed, it has become conventional to assume that thought itself is merely a kind of internal speech and to disregard almost completely those kinds of cognitive processes that are conducted without language, as though they were somehow more primitive, and less worthy of intellectual attention. Those who think about machinery have tended to undervalue their own accomplishments, or to deny that the process is intellectual at all, and to belittle "intellectuals" in turn.

This process was already evident, and efforts were under way to combat it, in the 1830's. The flourishing of mechanics' institutes, mechanics' literary associations, mechanics' magazines and newspapers, all filled with traditional humanistic verbiage, must be seen as efforts to bridge the gap between the two cognitive styles. Daniel Lammot could and did write fluent pages on the problem of determining the relation between the truth of good and the good of truth in Swedenborgian theology; but he had difficulty finding out how cotton machinery worked. The mechanics who founded the Franklin Institute understood the working of machinery; they had little patience with philosophical arguments that could not be settled by recourse to experiment. Science appealed to both sides as a suitable means for closing the gap, for it was couched in some of the most elegant linguistic formulations developed by man—the symbol system of mathematics—and yet referred itself to nature by means of experiments which required tangible apparatus and visible measurements. The result of bringing together the mechanician and the scientist was productive: it produced scientific engineers and clever experimental scientists. But it also split off the lower range of the mechanicians, to remain as mere "mechanics," artisans, and craftsmen fundamentally alienated from the engineer and the architect, who design machines but leave it to the mechanics to build and maintain them.

The problem of the relationship between science and technology has remained. In the 1830's, the inventive mechanician needed to have some knowledge of basic physical principles and, increasingly, an awareness of the rigorous requirements of the experimental method of proof. Yet, although he thus profited from some scientific training, his improvements in machines and industrial process seem to have been suggested less by new scientific discoveries calling for application than by interesting old technological problems calling more urgently for solution because of economic pressures. And as often as not—perhaps more often than not—the solution was suggested by other innovations within the mechanicians' tradition rather than by advances in science. The problem is still being argued 150 years later.

Part Three

ROCKDALE FROM 1835 TO 1850 ✗ THE STRUGGLE FOR CONTROL OF A WAY OF LIFE

Chapter VI

THE ENLIGHTENMENT'S LAST CAMPAIGN

The way of life in Rockdale at any given time, as in any cotton-manufacturing district, was in some respects imposed on everyone, from mill owner to operative, by the technology itself. Location, settlement pattern, work organization, and household structure were at the beginning not so much forced by a selfish managerial class upon an unwilling working class as developed as the most immediate mutually convenient solutions to the problem of powering and operating the machines.

But other aspects of the quality of life were usually determined unilaterally by the manufacturer, and this was the case in Rockdale too. Because he controlled the machinery, the manufacturer could set wages and hours for the operatives on a take-it-or-leave-it basis, could decide whether to operate his factory full time, part time, or not at all, and could freely exercise his right to replace workers with new labor-saving machinery. Some manufacturers, like John P. Crozer, claimed these privileges as a moral right. The manufacturer's goal was to employ his machinery to make as much money as possible for himself and his partners, or for his corporation; the operatives were incidental to this process, and their financial profit, or even general welfare, was not conceived to be a primary economic purpose of the enterprise.

A clear conflict of interest between operatives and manufacturers was thus built into the whole system of cotton manufacturing from the beginning. But not only were the operatives in the mills themselves in economic competition with the factory enterprise. Traditional craftsmen—hand-loom weavers, carders, spinners, and other artisans who worked in the cottage textile trades—were threatened with unemployment; and, as the factories spread, thousands were in fact left to choose between the poorhouse and the cotton mill. Furthermore, some of the early urban industrial centers, the most conspicuous of which was Manchester, grew helter-skelter and as a consequence of the private decisions of dozens of industrial capitalists and landowners. These urban conglomerations of mills and tenements, far more than planned company towns like Lowell and New Lanark, displayed social pathologies plain for all to see, in the shape of high rates of industrial accidents and industrial diseases, squalid housing, smoke-filled air and polluted rivers, inadequate sanitation, malnutrition and starvation, drunkenness and prostitution. These conditions were, of course, deplored by all observers. But who was responsible? The more self-righteous manufacturers, and their clerical apologists like Bishop Potter of Chester, were prone to blame the poor for their own poverty, claiming it to be a result of immorality and neglect of Christian principle. Angry workmen blamed the manufacturers for throwing people out of work by bringing in new machines, for reducing wages and closing the mills when the market fell, and for forcing the workers, particularly women and children, to spend long hours under poor conditions. But behind the question of immediate blame was the larger issue: Who *should* control the machines of the Industrial Revolution?

The manufacturers, and economists generally, were not in a position to give much more of an answer to this question than to point out that the person who owns the machine obviously has the right to turn it on and off and determine the conditions of its use. The employment of semi-automatic machinery on this large scale had not really been conceptualized as yet in philosophical or economic terms. Classical economic treatises, like Adam Smith's *Wealth of Nations* (1776), could not foresee the new social and economic problems soon to be posed by industrialization. The problems of concern had to do with wages and rents and commerce, not industrial production; and the theoretical task was conceived to be the forging of a rational alternative to a state-controlled mercantilism. The traditional European capitalist was a merchant, not a manufacturer, anyway. He might be a landowner, an owner of buildings, an owner of money, an owner of raw materials, commodities, and manufactured goods. But he was not a manufacturer himself. Manufacturers were traditionally people who made things by hand—artisans, tradesmen, craftsmen, mechanicians—and many of them owned their own tools and machines. The traditional spinners and weavers, in the slowly dying cottage textile industries, owned their own spinning wheels and looms and were manufacturers; in relation to them, the role of the merchant-capitalist was to distribute raw materials, collect finished products, and place goods upon the market.

It was, furthermore, common in this period for certain large, technologically sophisticated enterprises to be the monopoly of the state. In the United States, the federal government operated a postal service, mint, navy yards, and arsenals; the states built and managed turnpikes, canals, railroads, harbors, icebreakers, towboats, and breakwaters and, in the case of Pennsylvania, proposed to use the profits to support government without taxes. Religious communities, practicing a kind of primitive communism, successfully operated factories employing the most modern machines. Crozer himself had visited Father Rapp's establishment at New Harmony. Public enterprise was accepted as being in the public interest.

Thus, despite the rapid investment of private capital in the new machines in England and in America, it was by no means a settled economic principle in either country that large-scale manufacturing, and other technological enterprises that exceeded the capacities of handicraft industries, should necessarily be regarded as exclusively the province of private capital, along with banks and merchant houses and great estates. By hindsight, it may appear that because large-scale manufacturing required great capital investment, far beyond the capacities of inventors and mechanicians, the existing sources of private capital would necessarily take control. But in the late eighteenth and early nineteenth centuries, before industrial capitalism became the dominant economic institution, there were many thoughtful people who still saw alternative ways of using the new machinery. Much of the social conflict in England and America in the early nineteenth century can be regarded as a struggle—a brief struggle, to be sure—for control of the machinery of the Industrial Revolution.

The most immediately available line of answers to the question of who should control the machinery was provided by articulate men and women who had been brought up in the intellectual tradition of the Enlightenment. The common principles of that extensive intellectual movement had been laid down in the late seventeenth century and the first three quarters of the eighteenth; by 1825, these principles had been proclaimed for so long, and by spokesmen with such varying degrees of talent, that to some they seemed archaic intellectual conventions when they were not self-evident truths; to others they appeared as a tattered collation of infidel abominations. It was a complex tradition, with its own national and theoretical varieties, and it is not possible here to do more than summarize those commonly accepted ideas that were most relevant to the social issues raised by the rise of industry. In brief, the Enlightenment taught an orderly universe, the adequacy of reason to solve man's problems, the necessity of learning from nature and experience rather than from books, the innate goodness of man, the essential equality of man, a universal natural religion devoid of priests, revelation, and superstition, and the progressive improvement of civilization without divine intervention. In America the creed was given various theological phrasings by the left-leaning religious sects and factions, such as the Hicksite Quakers, the Unitarians, and the Universalists, and by nonsectarian Deists; it was articulated in the economic and political theses of the more radical members of the mechanicians' community, who as craftsmen supported the Workingmen's movement, and by a number of philosophical economists.

The application of these general principles to the problems posed by industrialization was to be the work of a generation of romantic, freethinking radicals who tried—and failed—to wrest control of the machines away from the private owner and place it in the hands of the community. This radical movement had its adherents in Rockdale.

THE FREETHINKERS OF CHESTER CREEK

To play with the ideas of the Enlightenment, and particularly to practice free thought—that is, to question the established wisdom openly—was one of the traditional perquisites of the educated. It did not imply abandonment of one's place in society. On Chester Creek, it was the literate people— gentlemen farmers, merchants, manufacturers, lawyers, doctors, clergymen, mechanics—who in the 1820's were reading and debating the ideas of the early Utopian socialists. At the county seat itself, the infant Chester Debating Society in January 1826 considered the subject: "Will Robert Owen's system as explained by himself contribute to the happiness of mankind?" The secretary of that Society, John K. Zeilin, who announced the topic, was hardly a radical freethinker. He was twenty-three years old, deputy prothonotary, and clerk of the town council. At the moment he was reading law under Edward Darlington, and would later become well known in the county as an attorney, occupant of various appointive offices, and colonel of the militia. In politics he, like his mentor Darlington, moved from the Democratic Republican side in the 1820's to the Whigs in the 1840's.[1] But right now, free thought was still respectable, and at the jubilee celebration of the Fourth of July in Chester in 1826, toasts were raised to such symbols of liberty as the Marquis de Lafayette, Simon Bolivar, and— by John K. Zeilin—to Missolonghi and the grave of Byron.[2]

The Democratic Republican newspaper, the *Upland Union,* similarly, while in no sense an organ of free thought, gave space and consideration to more or less liberal positions, printing bulletins on the progress of the New Harmony settlement, publishing Robert Southey's "Complaints of the Poor" in the poetry column and notices of feminist Mary Wollstonecraft Shelley's new book, *The Last Man.* All this, of course, was to be found amidst material of very different tenor: editorials on the female virtues and on the need to be ever aware of approaching death, reports of the activities of the major political parties, church announcements. Perhaps the *Upland Union's* policy might be summarized as one of attempting to appeal to the full spectrum of respectable educated opinion and interest—and this, in 1826, included the freethinkers.

Among the owners and manufacturers in the Rockdale district, however, there seems to have been at this period only one man who could be regarded as a freethinker in any sense. This was John S. Phillips, the manager of the power-loom factory by Old Sable Forge. And among the nearby gentry, the best-known free enquirer was the gentleman farmer Minshall Painter.

John S. Phillips, the "open Infidel"

There is no evidence to suggest that Phillips was an active follower of Robert Owen or Fanny Wright, or that he had any interest in the Valley Forge Commune (of which more later), which was founded on Owenite principles. It would seem that he was a freethinker in the generic sense: an adherent of no creed, whether religious or political, but dedicated rather to the application of intellect—and particularly his own very considerable powers—to the answering of questions of interest to mankind. Before his removal to Rockdale, it will be recalled, he had joined both the Franklin Institute and the Academy of Natural Sciences. He had a particular interest in one of the specialties of Thomas Say—conchology, or the study of molluscs by the collection and examination of their shells—and after he returned to the city he continued this interest as the Curator of Conchology at the Academy. During his early membership in the Academy, he regularly attended the weekly meetings, where he met and conversed with both the liberal naturalists Say, Bonaparte, Troost, and Lesueur, and also the more conservative faction, including his own sponsor George Ord, who was strongly opposed to the political tendencies of his colleagues. Phillips' attendance temporarily ceased, however, early in 1825, about the time when his plans for the Rockdale cotton factory were getting under way.

Upon his arrival at Rockdale, Phillips rented a small stone house from Moore, on the hill overlooking the forge and factory. He lived alone, except perhaps for a housekeeper, and seems to have devoted himself intensively to mechanical interests, including the new sugar-liquor filter which he patented, and to the problems of power-loom machinery. There were not, in 1825, many intellectual companions for him in the neighborhood. Crozer, who lived a couple of miles down the road, was preoccupied with the problems of his own machinery. He had some interest in communal experiments, having visited New Harmony on his western tour, during Father Rapp's occupancy, before he sold it to Owen. But Crozer was a shy man, country-educated, and not comfortable with worldly intellectuals from Philadelphia.

Phillips' prospects for intellectual companionship improved in 1829 when the Lammots arrived at Lenni. One of the family was a young man of about twenty-one, Ferdinand Fairfax Lammot, and despite the difference in age (Phillips was nine years older) they became fast friends, riding about the countryside together and oftentimes spending the night with Ferdinand's sister Meta, now Mrs. Alfred du Pont, at Nemours on the Brandywine. Although the Lammots were Swedenborgians, and thus adherents of a complex theology designed to counteract deism, they too challen d conventional religious wisdom. In any case, the young men seem to have been able to understand one another well.

By the fall of 1830, Phillips was becoming a frequent visitor to the Brandywine, sometimes with Ferdinand, sometimes with his brother Clifford or his sisters Camilla, Eveline, or Elizabeth, but most often alone on a gig drawn by his horse Wildfire. His visits were all the more frequent because he was often in Wilmington on business and spent many weekends at the spa at Yellow Springs to the north. An overbearingly talkative man, insistent on expressing his own thoughts, he was not sensitive to the needs of others for food, rest, and privacy, and he drove the Brandywine ladies to distraction by his attentions. He was, furthermore, looking for a wife, now that his cotton business was successful, and had his eye most particularly on the twenty-year-old Sophie Madeleine du Pont (although his eccentricities kept everyone in doubt as to his actual intention). The Du Pont girls kept a sardonic diary of the visitors to the house, often including a disparaging quip about any male who displeased them. John S. Phillips for three years occupied a conspicuous place in this diary and its entries reveal a good deal about his interests. He liked to read the Romantic poets, reciting Burns's poetry aloud from memory, and naming his new horse (after Wildfire went blind) Mazeppa, no doubt in honor of Lord Byron. He adored the opera, especially *The Hunchback.* His favorite song was "How Shall He His Pain Discover?" and he liked to entertain the ladies with ghost stories on cold winter evenings. He grew quantities of exotic flowers—*Datura,* roses, *Thunbergia alatta,* heliotrope, dahlias—in his greenhouse and presented them to the ladies in arrangements of his own design. He invented mechanical devices for smoking and watering his plants, and new procedures for curing them when ill. He planned to grow grapes by the thousands under glass. He designed and manufactured fireworks; he lec-

JOHN S. PHILLIPS (1799–1876).

tured people on phrenology and the mechanical principles of power looms. He made outlandish clothing for himself: huge India rubber boots, a woven nose-mask for the cold, a gray suit that looked like a coat of armor. And, of course, he was forever advising the ladies on their own proper skills: knitting, sewing, and cooking.

The image provided by the diary, thus, is of an awkward "giant" (as Eleuthera described him), a big bearish man, enthusiastic and overbearing in manner, indiscriminate in his interests. They called him "the Knight of Rockdale" and (in allusion to another tilter after windmills) "Val de Peñas." Indifferent to religion and no attender of churches, he nonetheless tried to please a group of highly evangelical young ladies by bringing them tracts for their Sunday School. Little is recorded of his social views from the diary, except for what can be inferred from his taste for Romantic poetry. He talked, as one of them said, of everything: "Of dogs & horses, love & marriage, death & heaven, politics & domestic economy &c &c &c." It is only in the correspondence of Sophie du Pont that an intimation of a more sinister kind appears—the allusion to the "mill of an open Infidel" who can only have been Phillips. Phillips himself seems to have had a wry awareness of the awkward contrast in his character between the manufacturer and the intellectual. Among his favorite works was *Warreniana,* a mildly satirical volume that celebrated the poetic advertisements written by a fictitious manufacturer, Robert Warren, for his "immortal" brand of boot blacking. Warren, "egotistical" and "unfortunate in love," was saluted in this memorial by a series of poems in the style of the English poets, particularly Byron and the Lake poets, that invariably concluded with a request that the reader buy Warren's shoe polish. Phillips thought it very funny.

Phillips was a bore to the ladies in his social group—and, as it turned out, he never married. But, as we have already seen, the fault lay not entirely in his character. Really to interest the Smith sisters, the Brandywine ladies, and the Lammot girls would have required more than light conversation and considerate manners. They were looking for men whom they could convert to evangelical Christianity; men like Phillips "the Knight of Rockdale," freethinkers with a loudly romantic flair, would-be Byronic heroes, were not good candidates for Heaven.[3]

Minshall and Jacob Painter
and the Delaware County Institute of Science

About a mile north of Wrangletown lay the farm of the bachelor brothers Minshall and Jacob Painter, the last scions of a Quaker family long resident in the area. Although they still kept to the use of "thee" and "thou" in family correspondence, they were Deists—avowed infidels and rationalists. Their faith was that science—the study of nature in the largest sense—would lead both to personal serenity and to human progress. They approached the world of learning with a kind of innocent, wide-eyed eclecticism. In the style of the early naturalists, they imported live exotic plants and built up a botanical collection which became known, after the estate passed into the hands of a brother-in-law, as the Tyler Arboretum. They kept a cabinet of minerals, observed the heavens through a large telescope, set up their own printing press, tinkered with early photography. They subscribed to horticultural and technological journals and put together a library that makes a fair sampling of early nineteenth-century titles in geography and natural history. They were interested in the cause of women's rights (and particularly in Fanny Wright), in Utopian socialism, and in the workingmen's movement. And for a time they were involved in political anti-Masonry, taking the populist interpretation that Freemasonry was nothing but a cloak for nepotism.

They had no use for religion. Minshall, the more articulate of the two brothers, once wrote to his sister:

I will not permit myself to be chatechised but openly profess to be infidel to the popular religions they being neither what nature inculcates nor good sense allows. . . . If we knew when a man was born we might almost unerringly foretell his religious faith, but infidelity is that peaceable state where dogmatical nonsense is preached no more tho' the leprous taint of slander is on the name. Credulity is great and ignorance is her prophet. . . . Modern orthodox religion [is viewed by the infidel] as picture gallerys and fossil museums dug out of ancient literature and now strangely associated.[4]

And Jacob Painter was equally critical of organized religion:

Old forms of religion like old forms of government must submit to the revolutionary effects of time. Antiquated views and rites yield slowly and obstinately. It has been concluded that there must be a creed, terrible in its effects to the disobedient—laws must be cruel—religion must be stern —and ceremonies must be strict, and instead of promoting a good feeling, the whole becomes a thing of formulas.[5]

Despite their unorthodox religious views, the Painters were fully accepted as members of the Philadelphia area's community of mechanicians and natural philosophers. In the gatherings of this group, disputation about religion and politics was regarded as bad manners, and infidel and evangelical cooperated comfortably in projects for the advancement of systematic knowledge. Out of the informal gatherings of Delaware County's intellectuals there grew, in 1833, the organization known as the Delaware County Institute of Science. One of the five founding members was Minshall Painter, who acted as secretary for thirty-six years; among the others were George Smith, M.D., who served as president until 1882, and who as a Pennsylvania legislator was in the 1830's working with Thaddeus Stevens for the passage of the public school law (actually passed in 1834); and John Cassin, who would become internationally renowned as an authority on ornithology. Within a few years William Martin, Edward Darlington, and John P. Crozer had joined; Daniel Lammot, the Riddles, the Hills, John Garsed, and James Houghton did not join but did subscribe to the building fund for the hall, which was constructed near the future site of Media, the new county seat, in 1837, on a lot donated by Minshall Painter.

The Institute was consciously modeled after the Franklin Institute (minus that Institute's initial concern with mechanics' education). It attracted the attention of the leading mechanicians of the area. One of its sponsors was James Ronaldson, the cotton manufacturer who had been a prime mover in the founding of the Franklin Institute; and Dr. Robert Patterson, then director of the U.S. Mint, gave the address at the opening ceremonies for the Institute's building. Its program of monthly lectures attracted much attention, for controversial topics were confronted, such as the question of an alleged native inferiority of the African race. Its library included works on all sides of important subjects: in the field of education, for instance, it contained both Pestalozzian Joseph Neef's progressive *Sketch of a Plan and Method of Education* (1808) and Joseph Lancaster's popular rote-learning program *The British System of Education* (1812). In the natural sciences it had *The Bridgewater Treatises on the Power, Wisdom, and Goodness of God as Manifested in the Creation* (a series of texts in popular science) and also technical journals like Silliman's *Annals of Science* and the *Journal of the Franklin Institute*.

Further, the Institute undertook significant research and development activities. It inaugurated an agricultural development program, distributing seeds and cuttings of "all the most important grains, plants, and fruits suitable to our soil and climate." One of the members, Dr. Joshua Ash, produced a detailed property map of the county in 1848, showing natural features, roads, all major towns, factories, and township and property lines; the president, Dr. Smith, prepared a geological survey and went on to complete a history of the county (although its publication was delayed until after the onset of the Civil War). In 1846, and for ten years thereafter, the Institute held a competitive fair in the autumn, awarding prizes to Delaware County producers in various fields of endeavor: to cotton manufacturers for their cloths, to mechanicians for edge tools and machinery, to ladies for their needlework and painting, to farmers for their corn and vegetables and livestock, even to professional men for improvements in medical and scientific equipment.[6]

In all of this, the Institute served as an open marketplace for ideas, not only on technical and scientific subjects but on controversial social issues as well. In such a setting, criteria of religious orthodoxy were out of place and the only goal was knowledge. As Minshall Painter put it, "Truth we want be it ever so terrible . . ."

Such a point of view was a legacy of the Enlightenment that was difficult for even the most hardened evangelical professors to put aside. John P. Crozer was an increasingly zealous Christian, but he found the Institute's scientific positivism compatible with his own Christian understanding. He was closely involved with the Institute's affairs until he moved to Upland, and in the 1840's was for a time its corresponding secretary. After reading Buckland's *Bridgewater Treatise* on geology and paleontology, which contained much evidence from the fossil record about the antiquity of Creation and the succession of life forms leading up to man, he was moved to write in his diary a liberal testimonial of mingled scientific and religious faith:

The yet not fully understood science of geology may interfere with the literal sense of the first chapter of Genesis, but can never overthrow the Christian theory; and it is satisfactory to find eminent geologists—those who have adopted the opinion that the world has existed many thousand ages—fully and unequivocally believing in the truths of revelation.

When I was a child, and first learned the philosophy of the rainbow in the heavens, I was disappointed, grieved, and wished I might be misinformed. I had always been struck with the beautiful sublimity of the Scripture account of the rainbow, and had received the impression that it was sent as a special messenger from God on each occasion of its appearance; and when I saw it accounted for as an ordinary arrangement of nature, it seemed to detract from the high dictation, "I do set my bow in the clouds." Thus it was with me when geologists assumed the position that the world, instead of being the Almighty's work in six of our days, was clearly many thousands or millions of years in becoming what it now is. I felt confounded, but further reflection makes me think differently; and if geologists establish their position, and agree among themselves— which as yet they are far from doing—I shall find no difficulty in the least with my religious sentiments. God is yet the Creator of all, and Moses was his prophet; man is a fallen creature, and Jesus Christ came into the world to save sinners. These truths remain unaffected by geological discoveries, and will ever remain amid the wreck of matter and the crash of worlds.[7]

It was Minshall Painter who nominated Crozer for membership in the Institute. The two men had had a brief prior correspondence, on the subjects of the need for savings banks for working-class people and the intelligence of the mill girls of Lowell. After Crozer joined, the correspondence continued on Institute subjects for at least several years. Crozer addressed his infidel colleague as "Esteemed Friend," and was almost certainly influenced in a liberal direction by Minshall Painter's evident good will and by his exposure to the positivistic philosophy of the English naturalists. Whether Crozer ever influenced Painter is less sure. Some years later, still an unreconstructed and even dogmatic infidel who had no use for the idea of God and afterlife, he expressed his irritation at the patronizing attitude of some evangelicals he knew:

> go where you will the *presumptious man of god* is flaunting his religion and asking a part of your substance to support it, lauding those who side with him and hurling damnation on his opposers. It is common to hear it said infidels who are honest and intelligent, are Christians at heart and it is no consequence they deny it religious professors will have it so.[8]

The Workers

Little information remains about the political views of the workers in the Rockdale district in the period from 1825 to about 1832. There were no strikes and no local chapter of a Workingmen's Party. There were, however, many freethinkers among the working people. Writing in retrospect, the mill owner Richard S. Smith, who came to Rockdale in 1833, recorded:

> Infidelity stalked boldly among the people; the disciples of Paine held public meetings to inculcate his doctrines, and on one occasion when a Presbyterian clergyman gave notice that he should preach on the evidences of Christianity, he was interrupted by some of those who attended for the purpose with a volume of Paine's works in their hands.[9]

Yet there survives no direct evidence of informed political interest in early Utopian socialism among the workers of the Rockdale district. One weaver, a member of an English immigrant family, the Morrises, who worked at Phillips' and Crozer's mills from 1832 to 1834, expressed fervent satisfaction in one of his letters home: ". . . to think that we are in a free country, free from the oppressive tyrants of King, Priests and Lords." And the same man, writing in 1841 after he had moved to Ohio, wrote to his brother in

England: "I have been informed that you have gained some steps of reform in England and also that there is a new society there called Sochilestes [socialists] which have increased very fast and got very numerous. Please to let us know if there is many of them about you. . . ."[10] But the evident unfamiliarity of weaver Morris with the word "Socialists," and his failure to mention any analogous society in America, suggests that Fanny Wright, Robert Owen, and the Utopian socialists generally had not been a common topic of conversation among the operatives in the Rockdale mills during his sojourn there in the early 1830's.

One is left with the impression that despite the presence among the workers of some anti-clerical freethinkers who read Thomas Paine and liked to heckle preachers, there was little organized radical political thought among the rank-and-file operatives. There would be a number of reasons for the confinement of such views to a few literate mechanics and ex-perienced mule spinners (of whom altogether there cannot have been more than about fifty at this date). One was the illiteracy of many of the popula-tion; a number had come from England, Scotland, and Ireland, where schooling was not yet universal, and the state of Pennsylvania did not provide free public schools until late in the 1830's. Many of the workers who put their receipts for wages in William Martin's receipt book in the 1820's could not sign their names and had to make their mark.[11] Women and children, who constituted about half the work force, could not vote and were expected to be politically passive. A few men were conservative Catholics, Methodists, Baptists, Presbyterians, Episcopalians, and Quakers, and would be unlikely to identify with disciples of Paine and Volney. And some of those who might have been interested were probably intimidated by the general opposition to such views on the part of their employers (Phillips, who had hired William Morris, perhaps excepted). Furthermore, because the roles of mule and throstle spinners were new and did not have behind them an ancient, medieval guild, the spinners on Chester Creek, as in Philadelphia, had no union which could join, or be inspired by the example of, the Mechanics' Union of Trade Associations and its socialist leader William Heighton.

The workingmen (other than mechanics) on Chester Creek were in an ideological limbo, as it were, separated by barriers of geography, illiteracy, sex, age, and novelty of profession from the sources of radical thought in the cities.

The Hecklers

And finally, there were local rowdies who made up a kind of infidel rabble. The best example of their anti-religious terrorism is preserved in the history of the Lima Methodist Church (as later recorded by William Fox, an early member of the congregation), at the time when James Riddle was preaching in the early 1830's. The house in which devotional services were held stood near the Porcupine Tavern and not far from the Black Horse Tavern; the neighborhood, about a mile north of Rockdale, was called Wrangletown. The tavern people, as Fox recalled later, were "very wicked, drinking, swearing & dancing," and did not take kindly to the presence of evangelists turning their "world upside down." The confrontation between evangelical Christianity and its enemies was sometimes violent:

the rabble would come and swear we should not hold Meeting that they would tear the house down upon us, and would try to pull out the Logs and throw stones at the door and burst it open; and hold dogs by the ears to make them howl and [illegible] to throw brimstone down the chimney and smoke us to death, often fasten us in, when we would have to put one out of the window to open the door.

One man came and took the Bible from the preacher and said it was not the word of God and broke up the Meeting; We tried to hold Class Meeting at nights but this they would not allow for they would come with such force that they would break the Meeting up for that night. One night they struck Wm Fox on the head 3 or 4 times and cut his head, we then applied to the Law for that man and put him to jail and he had to pay 100 dols so that put a stop to their carrying on and the little church had peace for some time.[12]

THE CONTEXT OF POST-REVOLUTIONARY RADICALISM IN THE LOWER DELAWARE VALLEY

The few freethinkers of Chester Creek were by no means isolated from sympathetic colleagues, however, and the educated class, whether religious or infidel, were constantly exposed to radical social doctrines. The Philadelphia-Wilmington area which surrounded Chester Creek was, during the years of the American Revolution and in the two generations that followed, the center of radical social thought in America. As the commercial, industrial, and (for a time) political center of the state and the country, Philadelphia in particular attracted to itself all varieties of opinion. Here, in the citadel of freedom, the home of the religiously tolerant Quakers and the forum of the great radical mechanicians Benjamin Franklin and Thomas Paine, belief in the principles of the Enlightenment survived in public life long after it had been politically eclipsed in both France and England. The European Enlightenment never really took intellectual root in New England, preoccupied from the first by the challenge of establishing (or disestablishing) a rigorously Calvinist commonwealth. It flourished in Virginia, despite the presence of slavery (repugnant to men of advanced mind), but as the northern cotton-manufacturing industry stimulated the plantation economy, the need to justify slavery increasingly diverted the attention of southern intellectuals. It was in the City of Brotherly Love, and in the lower Delaware Valley region of which that city was the center, from Wilmington to Trenton—and increasingly during the 1820's in New York City—that the goals of the Enlightenment continued to motivate a significant body of citizens.

Because the Philadelphia area provided the intellectual environment of the educated members of the Chester Creek community, we shall now look carefully at the radical tradition of thought in the region in the early nineteenth century. Both Christians and infidels among them had friends among the freethinkers, read newspapers reporting and editorializing on free thought and Utopian socialism, knew cousins and nephews who attended progressive schools, listened to political speeches extolling the communal way of life. The families of conservative manufacturers and mill owners in the Rockdale district might indeed feel themselves to be besieged by a surrounding army of infidels.

The Pennsylvania Constitution of 1776

The Commonwealth of Pennsylvania itself had been created in a kind of radical *coup d'état* by the left-wing Patriotic movement, which in 1776 produced a revolution within a revolution. Led mostly by mechanicians—Benjamin Franklin, printer; David Rittenhouse, surveyor; Thomas Paine, bridge-builder; Christopher Marshall, druggist; and George Clymer, merchant—the radicals seized the opportunity provided by a widely based popular clamor for separation from England to press for leveling social reforms. At a hastily assembled constitutional convention in 1776, a state constitution was framed which fundamentally challenged the old economic and social structure of the commonwealth; it was put into effect before the promised referendum could be held. It has been termed the most radical charter for government yet adopted in the English-speaking world, being more egalitarian in its franchise provisions than anything produced in even the most extremely republican stages of the French Revolution. Coleman Sellers's father-in-law, Charles Willson Peale, was an ardent partisan of this constitution.

The constitution began with a preamble on the nature of man, following in general the precepts of John Locke, to the effect that man was a creature of his experience and thus of his society. It went on to a declaration of rights. This bill of rights established almost complete religious liberty by making all free persons who professed belief in God and the Bible eligible to vote and hold office. This meant that all Protestant sects were on an equal footing; beyond that, that Roman Catholics could vote and hold office; some believed it even opened the franchise and officeholding to Jews (for the Jewish bible was, in effect, the Christian Old Testament). The constitution also eliminated all property qualifications, not only for the right to vote but for the right to hold office as well; the franchise was extended to all free men who had reached their twenty-first year, had resided in the state for one year, and had paid some tax (or—a concession to the wealthy—who were the sons of freeholders). Thus not only were the white working poor enfranchised; even free blacks were eligible to vote and hold office. Judges were to be elected for a fixed period on fixed salaries; there was to be a unicameral legislature (reducing the power of the wealthy class, which traditionally was exercised in the upper house) with broad administrative as well as legislative powers; the traditional high authority of a usually conservative president and council were greatly weakened; and a Council of Censors was appointed to protect and amend the constitution. Various specific reforms were incorporated, too, to meet popular complaints, such as a prohibition on the imprisonment of bankrupt persons for debt, and a provision for universal education at county expense.

This constitution was so revolutionary in its implications that the social conflict it aroused seriously hampered the commonwealth's ability to wage war against the British. Conservative religious leaders, like Henry Melchior Muhlenberg, voiced fears of a government by "Jews, Turks, Spinozists, Deists, perverted naturalists."[1] And on the economic front, as one constitutional historian has summarized it, it was a class struggle between an incipient middle class of tradesmen and mechanicians and a well-established aristocracy of landowners and bankers.[2]

The political forces supporting the constitution of 1776 centered in the cities of Philadelphia and to a lesser extent in Lancaster and Pittsburgh; it had the support of the "New Light" Presbyterians, and thus of many of the Scots-Irish in the western counties. The well-to-do rural agricultural areas, particularly in Delaware and Chester counties, were staunchly in favor of replacing it by a less restrictive document, and at length the anti-constitutionalists were able to assemble a new convention, which in 1790 produced a new charter for the state. This document turned the state back to a system of government that maintained more nearly the traditional separation of powers among the executive, legislative, and judicial branches. The executive was restored to strength, the legislature returned to bicameral form, and the judiciary were virtually tenured for life; their removal required impeachment. In many ways it was a copy of the federal Constitution of the same year; and not coincidentally, for Pennsylvania's experience was debated in the federal convention. But the 1790 constitution could hardly be called reactionary: there was still universal manhood suffrage for tax-paying freemen; the right to the franchise and office was open to all who believed in one God and a future state of rewards and punishments; and all children were to be educated, if necessary in public schools.

The disillusioned adherents of the earlier constitution, as the years of Federalist power slipped by, coalesced as "Republicans" around the figure of that arch symbol of Enlightenment man, Thomas Jefferson; hard-line patriots, they cherished an enduring sympathy for France, a festering suspicion of England, and a fear of any step toward a system of centralized federal power as being merely a means for gradually returning the people to the monarchical and mercantilist shackles from which the Revolution had freed them.[3]

Revolution's Legacy: Jeffersonian Republicans, Freethinkers, and New Lights

The spectrum of post-revolutionary ideology, ranging from the most conservative Federalists at one end to the most radical Democratic Republicans at the other, included more shades of opinion than could be represented in party politics. Parties, indeed, were apt to be condemned as mere instruments of political expediency, and after the temporary triumph of the Federalists in the 1790's in establishing workable organs of state and national government, a single Republican "party" seemed to accommodate most shades of social thought. Under the aegis of Thomas Jefferson, a leftward-leaning rhetoric returned increasingly to favor in the first two decades of the new century.

The principles commended by this rhetoric, which have been called Jeffersonian, were most popularly expressed in the writings of Thomas Paine and Constantin François de Volney. Paine had been the literary firebrand of the American Revolution; his calls to revolt had been predicated upon the notion, enshrined in the Declaration of Independence, that all men are created equal, that all have certain inalienable rights, and that governmental interference with these rights justified—indeed, required— a people's rebellion. Paine was condemned to death *in absentia* in England; moving to Paris in support of the French Revolution, he was imprisoned there. In 1797 he wrote *The Age of Reason,* an Enlightenment tract heavy with anti-clerical sentiments. When Jefferson entered the White House in 1801, he wrote cordially to Paine in France, inviting him to return to the United States on an American warship as the guest of the nation. Although he was constantly harassed by the Federalist and religious press, Paine lived out his life in New Jersey and New York, promoting deism as the "Republican Religion" and conversing with his friends (including men like Charles Willson Peale and Robert Fulton) among the Republican mechanicians of the new country.

Volney, a scholarly Frenchman, for a time the administrator of an experimental agricultural community in Corsica, and an actor in the French Revolution also, in 1791 had published his *Les ruines; ou, méditation sur les révolutions des empires,* and in 1793 a popular little "catechism" deriving morality from the laws of nature. Volney's *Les ruines* was quickly translated into English and in that language became widely known as *Volney's Ruins.* It was a popularization of common eighteenth-century theories of cultural evolution and historical criticisms of religion. Acknowledging only an otiose deity, Volney roundly condemned all existing religions as priestly impostures motivated by greed and facilitated by ignorance. He saw the origin of civilization as an event that had occurred in Egypt, where, he asserted, "A race of men now rejected from society for their *sable skin and frizzled hair,* founded on the study of the laws of nature, those civil and religious systems which still govern the universe."[4] In effect, Volney argued that the social contract, potentially so ennobling to all when founded on natural law, had been broken by greedy men who had used, and still used, palaces and temples to take the riches of the earth to themselves and plunge the balance of mankind into misery and despair by means of their false superstitions and despicable religious justifications.

In the 1790's, Volney was as impressive to the young freethinkers as was Paine. Jefferson was very much pleased with *Les ruines* and corresponded with Volney; and when in 1798 the aging Pierre du Pont de Nemours came to New York as the appointed French consul, Volney accompanied him. Du Pont was rejected, however, and Volney returned to France. But Jefferson, reading Volney's *Les ruines,* translated the first twenty of its twenty-four chapters and sent them to Volney, by hand of a mutual friend, William Maclure, for his approval. (Eventually the American poet Joel

Barlow completed the translation, and Jefferson's draft was burned at his request.) Paine made use of Volney's book in writing his own tract, *The Age of Reason.*[5]

The "Jeffersonian" position (if it can be treated in such typological terms) was essentially a middle ground between the extremes. "Jeffersonians" believed in a God but not in ritualistic, priestly, theologically involved religions, and were apt to be Unitarians, Universalists, or Quakers, denying both the bureaucracy of Catholicism and the cosmic élitism of the Calvinist tradition. They believed (rhetorically) in freedom and equality, but in fact were apt to be slaveowners and to regard Negroes and American Indians as inferior races doomed to extinction if they remained in contact with the more advanced European stocks. They conceived of an America (to use Leo Marx's felicitous phrase) "of the middle landscape," comfortably enjoying the virtues and delights of the rural life, yet taking up the advantages of the mechanician's ingenuity; they would exchange American (and especially southern and western) farm products for European (and to some extent northeastern U.S.) manufactured goods.[6] They indulged themselves in literature, natural history, and mechanical experiments, and were apt to sympathize more easily with the philosophy of the French Revolution than with that of the pragmatic English constitutional monarchy.

But pervading the Jeffersonian tradition was a position on the matter of civil government. The Jeffersonians disapproved of, feared, and saw no need for a strong, centralized, hierarchical administrative apparatus. They sought minimal expenditures, minimal debts, minimal taxes, minimal tariffs, minimal governmental regulation, minimal banking, minimal chartered monopolies. In an America of plantations and hamlets, diversified in economy and only lightly dependent on a few seaports for foreign trade, there would be no need for standing armies, legions of depraved urban poor, swollen bureaucracies. The people would rule directly. Everyone would be a kind of country gentleman, on some level on the scale from yeoman to master of Monticello; and even if he were much of the time occupied by commerce, by a profession, or by a mechanic's trade, he would still be able to retire to his house and garden, to read and write pastoral odes, or papers in natural history, or letters to a circle of thoughtful friends.

In an America for a generation, from 1800 to 1824, presided over (one can hardly say administered) by Jeffersonians, free thought in the Enlightenment style flourished. There was a large segment of the press that served as a forum for Republican freethinkers. Some of the newspapers, like the Philadelphia *Aurora,* were in effect party organs, which translated into immediate political application the general principles of republicanism. The *Aurora* had been edited at first by Benjamin Franklin Bache—a grandson of the American philosopher—and then, after his death, by a fiery immigrant Irishman, William Duane, who married his widow. Duane, a friend of Tom Paine, quickly became one of the leading political figures in the party and, as editor of the *Aurora,* one of the principal propagandists of Republican principles. Another Republican editor was John Binns, a pro-Irish Englishman who had been a close associate of William Godwin and other English radicals. He was tried in England for treason in 1798, but acquitted; he came to America in 1801, to live in Northumberland County near Thomas Cooper, the English radical, and Joseph Priestley, the exiled chemist and fellow Unitarian, who also had been a victim of the repressive English reaction to the French attempt to translate Enlightenment principles into political realities.

Until his death in 1809, Paine tried heroically to make Reason the "Republican Religion." Most Enlightenment intellectuals would find nothing offensive in the bland contention that man could know God by the use of reason, and know by the same means the duties that God expected of him, and thereby be able to live happily in this world and the next. But such a generalized belief, coupled with an antipathy toward organized religions, would not entirely satisfy those who valued the ceremonial fellowship of co-religionists or the leadership of a recognized ministry. For such liberals as these, the three plain creeds—the Society of Friends, the Unitarians, and the Universalists—offered the congregational structure of religious denomination without demanding much more than simple Reason in the way of ritual or theology. The Quakers, and particularly the followers of Elias Hicks, were devoted to social equality (including the abolition of slavery); the Unitarians, who had grown out of the liberal movement in the Congregational and Presbyterian churches, denied the doctrine of the Trinity and even the divinity of Christ; the Universalists asserted that all men were eligible for salvation. In these denominations, as in all of the period, there was a wide range of political and social beliefs; the most radical of them all, politically, were probably the "New Light" or "Blue Light" Quakers, who advocated immediate emancipation of slaves, and equal rights for women, and regarded the grave and respectable officers of the conventional Friends' meetings as a stiff, authoritarian, repressive lay priesthood.

The ideological ambience of Jeffersonian post-revolutionary Pennsylvania was thus one in which many of the beliefs and values of the previous century's Enlightenment were widely held by respectable people in all social classes. Even the more conventionally devout, and more aristocratic, Federalists were for the most part accustomed to recognizing all but the more extreme exponents of these views as respectable colleagues and fellow citizens. Deists were no longer impelled to write anti-clerical literature and were willing to accept quiet church-goers as practitioners of natural religion. In these matters, for many Pennsylvanians, a live-and-let-live philosophy would seem to have been the most comfortable. And in political matters, too, the issues were (in regard to the national offices) less and less a struggle of Federalists and Republicans, and more and more a matter of factional dispute among adherents to an all-embracing, inchoate populism.

The superficial vulnerability of the Jeffersonian Republicans lay in their indifference, if not antipathy, to the traditional religious organizations. The more orthodox Protestant groups, from the days of the Revolution onward, maintained a kind of guerrilla warfare, characterized chiefly by intermittent hit-and-run tactics against infidels and freethinkers like Tom Paine. This guerrilla warfare, as we shall see, eventually in the 1820's turned into an organized onslaught of awesome proportions. But the Jeffersonians had an inner weakness which would only become crucial as the pressure of increasing population and technological improvement mounted. They believed, fundamentally, that men were accountable not to their superiors but to their peers; they could not tolerate a principle of subordination. They placed a kind of blind faith in the reasonableness of men; they expected that cooperation would occur naturally, without constraint, as soon as artificial restraints of property, class, government, and religion were removed, and spontaneous associations could arise. And thus they did not think very seriously about the problems of designing efficient bureaucratic management; they rejected the very concept of one "managing" another as unmoral.

French Educators in the Enlightenment Tradition

The "rich Scotchman" William Maclure who had been Jefferson's messenger to Volney was at the center of a rather specialized contingent of émigré French naturalists and educators in the Philadelphia area (including one who taught school for a time in the Rockdale district), whose pedagogy was founded on the theories of Jean Jacques Rousseau and the practice of Pestalozzi and Von Fellenberg. Maclure himself had been born in Scotland in 1763; he came to America on commercial business frequently after the Revolution, and in 1796 he was naturalized as a United States citizen. He was a tall, heavy-set man, quiet and polite in conversation, a bit shy, and inflexible in his opinions. Having accumulated a private fortune by the age of thirty, he was retired from business and was devoting himself to the intellectual interests and the philanthropies which his great wealth allowed him to indulge. He was elected to the American Philosophical Society in 1799 and in 1812 helped to found the Academy of Natural Sciences, of which he was president from 1817 until his death in 1840. He personally carried out the first geological survey of the United States and became president of the American Geological Society; he came to be known as the "Father of American geology." He knew France from his mercantile days, was a devotee of the rational principles of the early Revolution, and traveled extensively on the continent attempting to settle American claims against the new régimes. In the course of these activities, he acquired a collection of some 25,000 books and pamphlets on the French Revolution, which he presented to the Academy of Natural Sciences in 1821 (and which is now kept as a special collection by the University of Pennsylvania). In politics he was a Jeffersonian Republican-turned-socialist, who believed that the salvation of the world depended upon improving the education of youth. In 1821 he had founded an experimental educational community near Alicante in Spain; the community had been disbanded and the lands returned to a monastery as a result of the conservative revolution in 1823, and he was now back in Philadelphia.[7]

Maclure had first encountered the Pestalozzian system of education in 1805 when, in the company of Napoleon Bonaparte, Minister Talleyrand, and the American ambassador, he visited the experimental school of Joseph Neef in Paris, where Neef was attempting to demonstrate the value of the Swiss innovator's new method of education in an asylum devoted to war orphans. Although a committee of inquiry eventually reported favorably to the First Consul on the Pestalozzian method as an effective means for educating the poor, the immediate reaction of Napoleon and Talleyrand was cool. Maclure took advantage of the educator's disappointment to invite him to bring Pestalozzi's method to America, promising to pay his and his bride's expenses and guaranteeing him three years' salary at $500 per year. Neef, disillusioned by the circumstances of the orphanage and the inflexibility of the French bureaucracy, agreed.

Joseph Neef was an Alsatian, a big, burly, bearded ex-soldier of Napoleon's, with a *basso profundo* voice and a penchant for loading his language with military oaths. He had been wounded in battle in 1796 and still carried a musket ball lodged in his skull above the palate (where it was to remain for the rest of his life, the cause of constant headaches). He was an independent-minded and ingenious man, now thirty-six, who had acquired a good Jesuit education and was familiar with the philosophical works of the Enlightenment, including the writings of Condillac—the purveyor of a Lockean philosophy of learning not ill adapted to rationalizing the Pestalozzian point of view. During his convalescence he read the early works of Pestalozzi. Inspired, he went to meet Johann Pestalozzi in Switzerland and was at once employed by him as a teacher of gymnastics and various elementary subjects.

The Pestalozzian theory of education could not have been more dramatically at odds with conventional theories of education in the Western world. Pestalozzi had been inspired by reading Rousseau's old pedagogical fantasies, *La Nouvelle Héloïse* and *Émile,* and he had resolved to implement the principles which they—and the whole thrust of Enlightenment humanism—implied. Rote-learning from books, and the kinds of false conceits that books taught, were eschewed as an inadequate, indeed a perilous base, on which to set the early education of a healthy, courageous, happy, and creative human being. Men should live according to the laws of nature, and nature herself should be the teacher, both the extrinsic nature that surrounded the child and the child's own nature within. The teacher was not to be an authority but rather a kind of friendly Socratic elucidator, who put the child in the way of knowledge and, depending on his natural curiosity and enjoyment of learning, encouraged him to *discover,* in himself and the world, the elementary principles on which all knowledge was based. The child learned the mental reckoning of numbers, arithmetic, and geometry by manipulating objects; morality and ethics from inner contemplation; geography, geology, biology, astronomy, and the other natural sciences in excursions and observations. The child was never to be punished; but his natural sociability would readily inspire him to follow his teacher in the disciplined marches, gymnastic exercises, use of firearms, and military drill which Pestalozzian educators believed were necessary to a free people.

Neef came to Philadelphia in 1806 and first set himself to learn English. No doubt as an exercise in the language, as well as for the sake of advertising the method and the new school, he began shortly to write a book in English—*Sketch of a Plan and Method of Education*—which he published at his own expense (or more likely Maclure's) in Philadelphia in 1808. This work was remarkable not only for its value as a pedagogical treatise but also for its simplicity and clarity. In the preface, Neef set forth the philosophy of his plan for saving America from the fate of Europe by means of education:

There lives in Europe, beneath the foot of the Alps, an old man whose name is Pestalozzi, a man as respectable for the goodness of his heart as for the soundness of his head. This man, endowed by nature, or rather nature's god, with the felicity of an observing mind, was forcibly struck by the vices, follies, and extravagancies of the superior ranks, and the ignorance, superstition, and debasement of the inferior ranks of society. He perceived that from these impure sources flowed all the miseries that afflicted his unhappy fellow creatures. Being no disciple of Zeno, the woes of his brethren naturally imparted their anguish to his sensitive heart. The host of calamities, under which he saw his fellow men groaning, deeply grieved his feeling soul, and the gulf of evils, into which he viewed mankind plunged, called forth the most cordial and sincere compassion. Tears fell from his mourning eyes but they were manly tears. Far from being disheartened by such a sad spectacle, he had the courage to enquire into the causes of human misery; he went even a step farther and endeavored to find out a wholesome remedy, calculated to destroy at their very source those evils which inundate the world.

Considering that man is born neither good nor bad, but that the disposition to become either good or bad is intimately interwoven with his organization, he became soon convinced that our education is the only cause of our becoming either good, useful, intelligent, rational, moral and virtuous beings, or wicked, noxious, ignorant, senseless, superstitious, and therefore miserable creatures. His mind was necessarily directed toward investigating the established systems of education; and after a mature examination thereof, he conceived that, without a radical reformation of the prevailing methods, it would be perfectly useless to expect any better results. This reformation became now the subject of his meditations. After having sufficiently digested these most important ideas, he began to communicate his thoughts to the world. In a plain but striking way he unfolded his plan of reformation and displayed the happy consequences to which it would lead. His book was read; his sagacity was admired; his benevolent counsels were applauded—and forgotten: But he did not despond. The same object was exposed to view over and over again, in all the forms and shapes of which it was susceptible; and yet was the desired reformation still to be begun and executed. Determined not to depart this life without at least seeing his theory tried, he resolved, in his old age, of making a full experiment of it himself. He therefore established a school. Other men, animated by his philanthropical enthusiasm, joined him; and thus began a work which will render Pestalozzi's name as dear and venerable to posterity as the deeds of many of his contemporaries will render them execrable to future generations.[8]

In 1809 Neef opened his boys' school on a hill above the Falls of Schuylkill, in the old mansion on the estate of the late Reverend William Smith, first provost of the University of Pennsylvania. The school rapidly acquired both pupils and reputation. His neighbor at the Falls, Oliver Evans, sent his son Oliver Jr. to Neef; other prominent Philadelphia families sent their young scions, including the son and stepson of William Duane, leading Republican politician and editor of the *Aurora,* and still other children were sent from places as far away as Savannah, Louisville, and Boston; in all, he taught about a hundred boys during the four years the school remained at the Falls. Visitors described in vivid terms the boys on excursions into the surrounding woods, which they were allowed to penetrate to the distance of half a mile, and Neef's whistle to bring them back:

Mr. Neef had a method of putting his two fingers in his mouth and producing a tremendous loud whistle. The boys would be scattered around the neighborhood, but when they heard the whistle, you could see them running from all directions to a common center.

It was his custom when roaming around the country with his boys to encourage them to hunt for anything singular or curious in the way of a plant, flower, mineral, etc. When they found anything that excited their curiosity, they would take it to him, and he would on the spot make it the subject of a lecture with his boys gathered around him. . . . 9

And politician William Duane was still sufficiently impressed, fifteen years later, to write an enthusiastic testimonial for his sons' former teacher, whom he recommended as the man to direct the public school system of the State of Kentucky:

There is only one system of Education in existence fit for a country that is free, or for a people to whom intellectual knowledge is essential in an age where knowledge is power and ignorance is weakness. And perhaps you may be surprised to learn, that there is only one man in this country, and that one man is in Kentucky, who is powerfully qualified to teach and to enable others to teach it. But such is the fact, and I shall not hesitate to name him to you, and to give you my ideas of his system; as I know it; I can warrant the perfection of its practice. There is living near Frankfort, a German of the name of Joseph Neef. He was a coadjutor of Pestalozzi of Switzerland. He was offered very rich temptations to go to Russia; he preferred coming to the United States, and he was mistaken. He is the most disinterested man I ever saw, and most capable. No science to him difficult or strange, because his method is such that he can analyze them all. In short, his system is expressed by the word analytic; for as all knowledge consists of the comprehension of facts, and the ideas of which that knowledge is composed, he is a teacher of facts. . . .

Locke and Condillac have given the outline; but it was Pestalozzi of Switzerland who realized it (the system) in modern times; and it is now spreading silently over Germany, and has been introduced into France, Spain, Russia, and England. There are, and were, of the schools, in England and in Ireland, eleven. I am possessed of several of the elementary books, translated into English, from the German, published in Dublin, and have 20 volumes in German published in those countries. But Mr. Neef requires no book; nor does any one who acquires his method.[10]

Maclure in the meantime had brought over as an assistant teacher a frenetic, arrogant, half-trained physician and experimenter with Pestalozzian methods whom he had met in Paris, one Phiquepal d'Arusmont. Phiquepal's vanity left an indelible impression on anyone who knew him. Maclure, later on, was to say, "He is a dangerous man who can influence so many men. . . . He is, I think, the vainest man I ever knew and when the Vanity is disappointed, he will go to bedlam." Robert Dale Owen was of a similar opinion: "A wrongheaded genius whose extravagance, willfulness, and inordinate self conceit destroyed his usefulness." But Neef, dependent upon Maclure for support, was unable to get rid of Phiquepal. In 1813 the two men left Philadelphia to set up their school in Village Green, just half a mile from Chester Creek; Maclure apparently had hopes of adding a farm to the school, for he believed in combining manual education with the Pestalozzian method, after the manner of Von Fellenberg at Hofwyl. Some of the pupils accompanied Neef and Phiquepal in the move; and others were added, notably David Farragut, later admiral and Civil War hero. Farragut, then under the guardianship of Commodore Porter of Chester (a controversial sailor who surrendered his ship to the British during the War of 1812 and was, with Midshipman Farragut, released on parole), remembered Neef warmly all his life:

I accompanied my friend Captain Porter to Chester, where I was put to school at a queer old individual named Neif [sic]. His method of instruction was simple to the extreme; he had no books, but taught orally on such subjects as he desired us to understand. The scholars took notes, and were afterward examined on these lectures. In the afternoon it was customary for us to take long walks, accompanied by our instructor. On these occasions Mr. Neif would make collections of minerals and plants, and talk to us about mineralogy and botany. The course of studies was not very regular, but we certainly had an opportunity of gaining a great deal of useful information and worldly knowledge. We were taught to swim and climb and were drilled like soldiers, branches of instruction to be accounted for probably by the fact that the old gentleman had been one of Napoleon's celebrated guards. I do not regret the time passed at his school, for it has been of service to me all my life.[11]

But the school at Village Green gradually dwindled, fewer and fewer boys attending (perhaps on account of the financial exigencies of the war) until Neef and Phiquepal had only twelve pupils. At this point, in 1815, Neef abandoned Village Green and moved—with Josiah Warren, one of his pupils, as his assistant—to a new school in Kentucky, which also failed, and then out to a backwoods farm. Phiquepal went back to Paris in disgust.[12]

But Maclure was not disheartened. He successfully established his manual labor schools in Georgia and tried to reopen the Pestalozzian school in Philadelphia with a new teacher from France. This venture also failing in 1820, he persuaded Phiquepal to open a Pestalozzian school in Maclure's house in Paris. Here Phiquepal trained the remarkable Mme Marie Duclos Fretageot, who was soon to found Maclure's second Pestalozzian school in Philadelphia.

Mme Fretageot was a vivacious woman of thirty-seven who needed to work. She was the sole support of a young son and of an invalid husband, a French officer who had managed to survive the long retreat from Moscow but who had been both mentally and physically ruined. In 1821 Maclure sent Mme Fretageot and her son to Philadelphia, with money to pay for school supplies; accompanying her as teaching assistant, also at Maclure's expense, came the young naturalist and artist Charles Lesueur. In the fall she opened a boarding school for girls in a rented house on Filbert Street. The physician to the school was Dr. William Price, next-door neighbor to Coleman Sellers, and a successful Philadelphia physician. The son of the superintendent of the Friends' School at West Town, not far from Chester Creek, Price had a close interest in educational reform, and was enchanted by the enthusiastic French schoolmistress. She taught him about the new methods of education and gave him books about Robert Owen's new views of society. Gradually they came to share romantic plans for a life in the same household, devoted to Pestalozzian educational projects and the realization of Robert Owen's new moral world.[13]

Among the pupils who attended Mme Fretageot's school was a young lady named Gabrielle ("Ella") du Pont. Gabrielle was the offspring of an unfortunate marriage between Amelie, daughter of Victor du Pont, and a rascally Englishman who had been recommended to Victor as an experienced woolen mill manager, alias William Clifford. Clifford, to the great if temporary satisfaction of Amelie's parents, married the plain-looking but virtuous and intelligent young woman after he had been managing the mill for a year. But a year and a half after the wedding, with Gabrielle already born, the family learned from an English workman that Clifford had a wife, a child, and another name in England. Clifford left the banks of the Brandywine and Victor arranged for both Amelie and her daughter to use her maiden name of Du Pont.[14] The ten-year-old Gabrielle was sent to Mme Fretageot's school in the fall of 1823; from her letters, it is clear that she formed a strong attachment to the place. Mme Fretageot was a strict headmistress, who provided an education that seems to have emphasized more the sciences and practical arts than the classics. The girls studied drawing (with M. Lesueur, who became a summer visitor to the Brandywine), music, English composition, French, arithmetic (with Phiquepal), botany, and geography; they were taken on excursions to Peale's Museum and to the zoo, where they were allowed to ride on a real live elephant's trunk. Also they all were taken to Quaker religious services on Sundays, probably at the Hicksite meetinghouse; Ella, unimpressed, alluded in her casual spelling style to "the foolish Rediscules quacer Meeting I am allways tierd when I am there."[15] She formed some friendships which survived the break-up of the school two years later, particularly with the Sistaire sisters, Frances, Lucy, and Sarah. After two years with Mme Fretageot, Ella wrote her cousin Sophie, who was attending Mrs. Grimshaw's establishment, that Mme Fretageot's school was "as good as all the Mrs. Grimshaws in the world."[16]

All in all, it would appear that the Maclure-sponsored Pestalozzian schools of Philadelphia, by the quality of the education they offered, were able to attract substantial respect and patronage. They were to become one of the channels through which Owenite news and propaganda were fed into the city.

The Academy of Natural Sciences of Philadelphia

At the meeting of September 28, 1824, John S. Phillips—not yet removed to Rockdale—was nominated to the Academy of Natural Sciences of Philadelphia by Dr. Benjamin Coates, a physician, and George Ord, a wealthy ropemaker. He was immediately elected—and also allowed a continuation of the loan of two books on conchology which he had borrowed from the Academy Library. For several months thereafter Phillips was one of the most active of the eighty or so members of the Academy, attending the weekly meetings with the eight to ten regulars, borrowing books, and conversing with the eminent naturalists and mechanicians who belonged to the institution.

The Academy had been formed in 1812 by seven idealistic young professional men who believed in science and the "rational disposal of leisure moments." Their founding minutes observed that

In this large city young gentlemen generally have few modes of social recreation when their daily business is over except frequenting theaters at considerable expense, taverns, gaming houses, dancing rooms or places of a more degrading atmosphere, where they can gain no improvement but are sure to acquire habits injurious to the spirit of a good citizen.

The Academy's rooms were to provide "a literary lounge and points of reunion . . . where younger men may improve in company with men of travel and information, and where every respectable individual . . . may read the American and foreign journals . . . without exposure to the intrusion of improper elements." Banned from the conversation of these young gentlemen would be the disturbing topics of religion or partisan politics; instead, science, which like natural religion "allows and promotes the good of all without limitations of Sect, Party, or of Nation," would be their sole topic; they would devote their attention to "the progress of science, the facts discovered, the efforts, the developments, the expansion, the illucidation, the lightening penetrations, the gleanings, the irradiations of the human mind throughout the world."[17] The kind of science the founders had in mind was what might best be called descriptive natural history: a mixture of botany and zoology (emphasizing the Linnaean classification of new species), geology and mineralogy, and chemistry. Thus their interests were more specific than those of the already aged and prestigious American Philosophical Society and less practical than those of the yet-to-be-created Franklin Institute.

After its founding, the Academy proceeded to add new members, one of the first being William Maclure. Among the early recruits were the leading mechanicians of the city, including John S. Phillips, Titian Peale, Stephen Long, William H. Keating, Robert M. Patterson, Thomas P. Jones, Isaiah Lukens, and William Kneass, all of whom would in 1824 help to found the Franklin Institute. Many eminent and highly respected Philadelphia businessmen were also added in the early years, including Nicholas Biddle, soon to be president of the Second Bank of the United States; Roberts Vaux, the Quaker philanthropist and educational reformer; John Vaughan, wealthy merchant and long-time secretary of the American Philosophical Society; and John P. Wetherill, successful chemist and one-time pupil of Joseph Neef's at the Falls of Schuylkill. The institution also took on more extensive functions as its membership grew. A technical *Journal* was begun in 1817, the library was expanded, and the collections of specimens for study—thousands of minerals, fossils, insects, shells, fish, reptiles, birds, and plants—were rapidly expanded. The Academy became an internationally known center for scientific research and publication.

In this development, among the most aggressive intellectual entre-preneurs were a small set of Enlightenment radicals, mostly Pennsylvania Hicksite Quakers and Bonapartist exiles from Europe. Four of the seven founders were of this group. Their president from 1812 until 1817 (when he moved temporarily to Baltimore and Maclure took over the office) was Dr. Gerard Troost, the Dutch geologist and pharmacist from Amsterdam who in 1807 had volunteered to serve Napoleon. Louis Bonaparte, King of Holland, sent him to Java as a mineralogist; the expedition was inter-cepted by the British and Troost eventually found himself in Philadelphia. Troost was a noted Freemason and in religion a promulgator of the anti-Calvinist Arminian heresy. Dr. Camillus Macmahon Mann, a physician, was a pro-French refugee from the Irish rebellion of 1798 (which had been instigated and supported, albeit ineffectually, by the French Revolutionary régime). John Speakman and Thomas Say were deistic Quakers and part-ners in an apothecary shop that failed. Speakman moved, temporarily, to Pittsburgh, where he became a principal figure in the notorious "Pittsburgh Society of Deists" (whose fate will be considered in a later section); he claimed that "lack of knowledge of the laws of nature is the source of all social evils." Thomas Say was a nephew of the well-known naturalist Wil-liam Bartram. After his father set him up in business with Speakman, the young apothecary endorsed the notes of a brother who was soon afterward bankrupted by *his* partner's embezzlement. Say lost everything he owned and turned his face away from business, devoting himself to science, living in poverty, and depending on the patronage of wealthy friends, particularly Joseph Gilliams, dentist and co-founder of the Academy, and William Mac-lure. Despite the technical inadequacy of his education in the Friends' School at West Town, Say carried on an astonishing program of scientific studies. He taught himself to read in Latin, German, and French. He collected specimens of insects and molluscs with Maclure, George Ord, and Titian Peale in Florida in 1816 and in the west in 1819 when he accom-panied Stephen Long's exploring expedition. Back in Philadelphia, as a curator of the Academy he lived with his collections in the hall of the institution, allegedly subsisting on 6 cents per day for food and sleeping under the skeleton of a horse.[18] Say lived up to the hoary myth of "mad scientist in his laboratory"; but he also published forty-four scientific papers by 1825.

Later recruits on the radical side included Charles Lucien Bonaparte, son of Napoleon's brother the ex-King of Spain, who lived with his famous $10,000 mistress on an estate in New Jersey nearby and, with Say's help, was writing papers and a book on ornithology; Charles Lesueur, artist-naturalist, protégé of Maclure and Mme Fretageot, and one of the few surviving members of the disastrous French scientific expedition to Australia of 1800 (with François Peron he brought back 100,000 specimens, including 2,500 new species), who was now writing with Ord's help some forty-one papers for the Academy's *Journal;* and Reuben Haines, Hicksite Quaker, brew-master and farmer of Germantown, who was for twenty years the recording secretary of the Academy.

Although in 1824 the truly radical group within the Academy's membership probably amounted to no more than a dozen persons, they were among the most active in the institution's affairs, publishing most of the scientific papers and occupying many of the offices (including the presidency and the secretaryship). They maintained close working ties with the faculty of Peale's Museum, with the American Philosophical Society, and with the Franklin Institute. They had access to many of the leading merchants, mechanicians, and professional men of the city. They were in a position to keep alive and vigorous, and in favorable public view, the Enlightenment tradition of social criticism and Utopian rationalism.[19]

The Associationists in Philadelphia and Wilmington

Word of exciting new English speculations on the means of curing the evils of society began to reach the lower Delaware Valley and the Rockdale district early in the 1820's. In the year 1820, a friend was writing to Coleman Sellers about "Robert Owen's plan laid before the Parliament of Great Britain for employing the poor and the labouring classes who have no employment and improving their morals, also for educating and training their children to virtue and usefulness."[20] Mme Fretageot possessed a French translation of Macnab's description of Robert Owen's new views of society and lent it to her friend Dr. Price in 1822. In the next year, a New York chemist and schoolteacher, John Griscom, published an account of his visit to Owen's community at New Lanark.[21] And William Maclure, who visited New Lanark in 1824 and said that the three or four days he spent there were "the most pleasant of my life," in a letter to Mme Fretageot (perhaps unconscious of the irony) compared New Lanark to the admirable new Philadelphia jail:

I never saw so many men, women and children with happy contented countenances, nor so orderly, cheerful and sober a society without any coercion or physical constraint. It is on a par with the moral experiment in the new jail of Philadelphia, with the advantage of being executed by one philanthropic individual free from the caprice of municipal regulations.[22]

Owen's own major works were already before the public in English editions and were being discussed in the widely read English and Scottish reviews. The first—*A New View of Society; or, Essays on the American Principle of the Formation of the Human Character, and the Application of the Principle to Practice* —was opened for sale in 1817, after private circulation by the author to the principal men and governments on earth; and the second—*Report to the County of Lanark of a plan for relieving public distress, and removing discontent, by giving permanent, productive employment to the poor and working classes, under arrangements which will essentially improve their character and ameliorate their condition, diminish the expences of production and consumption, and create markets co-extensive with production*—appeared in 1821. The Philadelphia *Aurora*, the Republican party organ, had been publishing pieces of Owen's writing from 1818 on. And numerous visitors from England, the continent, and America had for years been making the pilgrimage to New Lanark to observe the remarkably efficient and productive factories of "The Prince of Cotton Spinners," surrounded by the neat tenements of pleasant, orderly workers and their families, and the remarkable schools; almost to a man, they returned praising Owen's solution to the problem of humane industrial management and his proposals to reform society by means of "association."

Owen's arguments were well timed. The notion of "association" as an alternative to the traditional capitalistic order of society was being made respectable in the revivals of Christian communalism, currently practiced with visible economic success in America at New Harmony, Indiana, where the followers of Father Rapp had gathered, and in the several Shaker communities. In England several small experimental communities were already forming, inspired by Owen's writings and by economist John Gray's *Lecture on Human Happiness* (itself influenced by Owen); in Spain, Maclure was launching his ill-fated educational commune.

The first communal plan in Pennsylvania was probably the one revealed by John Speakman of the Academy of Natural Sciences. Temporarily residing in Pittsburgh, and a member of the Society of Deists there, in about 1823 he wrote to his friend Thomas Say in Philadelphia about his experiences, and concluded the letter with the unveiling of a truly Utopian scheme for the creation of an associationist community, which would be a "heaven" for scientists:

it is the intention of some of us as soon as we can acquire the necessary funds to purchase and improve some insolated spot, and there form a community something like the Harmonites and Shakers, who we see have arrived at the height of prosperity although governed by phantoms, and would it be slandering common sense to suppose, that a number of rational beings could not do as well, in a community so organized that the interest of each individual depended upon the prosperity of the whole. But our object is not riches, rather a school for ourselves and children as it is particularly intended that the knowledge of nature shall be the polar star or grand object to which all our exertions shall tend. A combination of talents (unrestricted) we hope will be as productive as the combination of labours and our happyness will be necessarily in proportion as we acquire knowledge, for man cannot err but from ignorance or disease. Their is no learned or scientific men among us; but as I said before our grand object will be to make our community a heaven for men of that description. We also hope to give our fellow plebians a practical proof that the whole train of parasites who are sucking their best blood are not only not necessary but that they are in reality the principal cause of all the disorders in society.[23]

The plan went forward during 1823 under the unfortunate title of "the community of wealth." Thomas Say wrote to Maclure about the project and Maclure wrote back casting cold water on the idea. Mme Fretageot heard of the plan in March 1824 and, as she said, "laughed much" when she learned where it stood. There had been at first a "great number" but now only two or three remained interested. Mme Fretageot, ever mindful of the power of sex to prompt association, merrily advised Mr. Say that "they would never put such project in execution if they cannot have some ladies among them."[24] (Mme Fretageot's flirtatious ways were something of a disadvantage in certain quarters of the Academy, however. Say's friend and biographer George Ord was later to refer to her, on the news of her death in Mexico during the cholera epidemic of 1832, in unusually uncharitable terms as a "brazen strumpet." But he took a dim view of the "whims and follies" of associationists generally.)[25]

PREACHING THE NEW MORAL WORLD

The high-water mark of post-revolutionary efforts to improve the world by the earnest application of Enlightenment principles came in the years 1824 and 1825, when an aged hero, the Marquis de Lafayette, and two young reformers, Fanny Wright and Robert Owen, landed almost simultaneously on America's shores. The associationists of the lower Delaware Valley were galvanized into action; the people generally were caught up in the dialogue of social reform.

Lafayette and Fanny Wright

The Marquis de Lafayette was, of course, revered by all as a comrade-in-arms of the American soldiers who had fought for America's freedom. But he was also known as a political activist in the cause of liberal social ideals that flowed generally out of the French Enlightenment tradition. Fanny Wright was a popular British writer, an admirer of America, which she saw as the land of freedom, equality, and progress, where the rights of women, of slaves, of the working poor, could be advanced by legislation and educational reform and by the establishment of Utopian communities. Robert Owen had developed his ideas for social reform out of practical considerations involved in the planning of New Lanark, the optimal company town. He believed that man was, for good or ill, the product of social institutions, and that these institutions could be rationally designed so as to produce a healthy, happy, wholesome, creative people. The key was the establishment of rural communes similar to New Lanark.

The Marquis de Lafayette arrived first, in August of 1824, as the guest of a grateful nation. He was popularly remembered as the young warrior who had come to Washington's aid in the dark days of the American Revolution; he was almost continuously fêted, wined, dined, interviewed, waited upon, paraded, and otherwise celebrated by Americans of all parties for a solid year. He was entertained lavishly in Philadelphia in September and October, and his hostess at the grand ball was, as we noted earlier, the Crozers' friend Jane Leiper Kane. He took the time to visit Mme Fretageot and Phiquepal's school. From Philadelphia he descended to Chester, where after a midnight celebration in the brightly illuminated village, he was entertained at the house of Colonel Joseph Anderson, an old companion-in-arms (also recently a Republican congressman and a friend of William Martin). The Marquis had visited Chester once before, nearly fifty years ago, having stayed there the night before the Battle of Brandywine, and returning there to have the wound in his leg dressed after the defeat. From Chester, the Marquis went on to Wilmington, staying with another old friend, Victor du Pont, and taking time to attend his son's wedding.[1]

On and on the Marquis's tour went, endlessly triumphal, crisscrossing the country back and forth from his headquarters in Washington. He visited Philadelphia again, in July of next year, and again stayed with Victor du Pont on the Brandywine, where he had a private business matter to settle between the Du Ponts and their relatives in France. It was a time of celebration, almost the half-centennial of the Revolution, in which everyone joined to honor the plainly dressed, slightly gruff old soldier for deeds of glory in the country's dawn.

There were those, however, who were less than pleased with the Marquis's concurrent political conduct. A believer in Enlightenment values, and an ardent Freemason, he had been one of the movers in the early days of the French Revolution. And after the Revolution's demise, during the Bonapartist and Bourbon accessions, he remained a conspirator on behalf of all sorts of liberal, even revolutionary causes in France (including the bomb-planting Carbonari, a terrorist group), and a personal patron of the new generation of radical believers in liberty, equality, and paternity. In 1821 he read a book praising America as the land of freedom, written by a young Scotswoman, Frances Wright, and at once wrote to her, inviting her to visit him in his medieval château at La Grange, forty miles from Paris. Fanny Wright, fresh from her visit to utilitarian philosopher Jeremy Bentham, visited the Marquis with her sister Camilla in the summer of 1821, and they in turn were frequently visited by him in their apartment in Paris. There Fanny took as her lover one of the Carbonari conspirators, General Pepe, who was soon to fight in Spain and Greece, and finally in Italy, against the resurgent despotisms in Europe. After Pepe's removal from the scene, Fanny's companionship with the aging and widowed Marquis became so close that scandalous stories began to circulate. They talked of marriage and of adoption, but his sisters intervened.

It was in the midst of this platonic liaison, uncertainly and by turns romantic and respectfully filial in its content, that the Marquis's voyage to America was planned. Fanny and her sister hoped to make the trip as members of the official party, but they were persuaded to travel separately. And so, mile after mile, the Wright sisters followed the official procession, sometimes waiting in rented rooms for secret midnight visits from the general after the day's speechmaking and dining were ended, and sometimes, in congenial company, joining the party of Fanny's "Paternal Friend." Such an occasion was afforded by the Marquis's visit to the aged Jefferson at Monticello, where the two women were invited to spend some time—"the invitation which they value most in both hemispheres."[2]

The Advance on New Harmony

It was in the midst of this atmosphere of revolutionary nostalgia and reformist anticipation that Robert Owen descended on the United States in November 1825, literally like a god from a machine, to recruit associationists to form his first Utopian socialist community—the "Community of Equality"—at New Harmony, Indiana. With his son William and his aide-de-camp Captain Duncan MacDonald, he made a triumphal social tour of New York, Philadelphia, and Washington, D.C., lecturing on his new view of society and displaying his scale model of the Utopian community of the future (eventually to be deposited in the U.S. Patent Office). In Philadelphia he visited the Franklin Institute, the Athenaeum, the American Philosophical Society; an affable and chatty man, on numerous social occasions he met and charmed the mechanicians, the scientists, the intellectuals, and their wives and daughters. He visited Mme Fretageot at her school and captivated her at once. She described their meeting in an enthusiastic letter to her old friend William Maclure:

> . . . I have had the visit of Mr. Owen. When he entered in my house I took his hands saying: there is the man I desired so much to converse with! And you are, said he, the woman that I wish to see. We are old acquaintances and in the mean time he gave me a kiss of friendship that I returned heartily. We talked about one hour and half, but we could not talk freely. I was surrounded by some visitors and our conversation was but on general subjects. He told me he will in his return have a private conversation with me. He thinks it will be in April next.
>
> You have no idea what pleasure I felt when I was talking by the side of a man whose actions and principles are so much in harmony with mine. When he said that children must be taken just when born in order to write in those blanck paper but what is correct, I felt an encrease of desire to arrive at that periode of my life where as much by my economy and the help of some friends I shall be able to put in practice that project of taking little babies who will be absolutely mine. Next Spring I will be in company with those two me[n] for whom I have the greatest esteem: You and Him . . .[3]

Owen bore an introduction to, among others, Coleman Sellers from the Sellers' London correspondent, and Sellers in turn introduced Owen to his friends at a gathering which young George Escol (who was not especially taken by Owen) recalled somewhat wryly in his reminiscences:

Father to introduce Owen who he felt bound to show some attention to, gave a party mostly to gentlemen in the old square parlour. If I could recall and name all the male guests it would give a good idea of Fathers social standing, but I shall only name those who were *roped in by Owens silver* tongue, it could not have been by his personal[ity], to a Phrenologist or Physiognomist his narrow high back sloping forehead would give no indication of his great brain power.

Dr. Wm. Price and wife
P. M. Price
Thomas Say, the Naturalist
Dr. Fraist—chemist then head of Farr & Kenzies afterward Powers &
Whiteman
Charles Longstreth
Sarah Turner
Mr. McCluer, a rich Scotchman

. . . It was in the square parlor that I first became acquainted with Rob.
Dale Owen, David Dale [Owen] and the sister afterwards Mrs. Fontleroy
wife of the Civil Engineer. David [*sic*—Sellers undoubtedly meant Richard Owen], the youngest son, I did not become acquainted with, but with
Robert and David a life long friendship existed.[4]

The affinity between the Owen party and the intelligentsia of the Philadelphia area was grounded in part in a common interest in machinery of
all kinds. But it went beyond this. They were all products of a British social
system that encouraged men of unusual mechanical aptitude to rise above
the traditional restraints of class and guild. Free to accumulate capital, to
patent useful inventions and to reap the profits, to acquire manners and
education, and if sufficiently successful even to mingle in gentle company,
the English and American mechanicians formed an élite cadre dedicated to
the rule of reason and the improvement of mankind. England and America
owed their accelerating industrial pre-eminence over other nations in large
part to the freedom of innovation they granted their mechanicians. But
freedom to think rationally about technological improvements could not
easily be separated from freedom to think rationally (more or less) about
social improvements also. Thus the fraternity of mechanicians included a
vital part of what remained of the radicalism of the Enlightenment.

Sweeping on with an entourage of followers to New Harmony, Indiana
(accompanied part of the way by the notorious John Dunn Hunter, the
"white savage," on his way to set up a Utopian interracial Indian-white
community in Texas), Owen concluded the purchase of the ten-year-old
religious community of the Rappites, who were moving back to Pennsylvania. The town and surrounding plantations, including some buildings
located on a little over thirty square miles, cost him $150,000. Leaving one
son and Captain MacDonald to receive the quickly assembling mélange of
would-be members of the new community, Owen returned to the east and
began again, in a somewhat more leisurely manner, to propagandize among
the élite of America. He visited Jefferson, Madison, Monroe, and Jackson.
He was received by President Adams and delivered two discourses "on a

New System of Society" in the hall of the House of Representatives, before the President, the cabinet, and the members of Congress. These speeches received wide public attention. He ceaselessly endeavored to mobilize all of the disparate enlightened reformers around his standard, arguing that "the more good means are reunited the effects are powerful, but when scattered they do little or no effect."[5] He served, indeed, as a kind of seed-crystal, around whom arranged themselves in regular form a remarkable number of Enlightenment Utopians, for in each of the towns that he visited he was received by the local Free Thinker's Society, converted a number of the local radicals to his plan, and encouraged a few families to pull up stakes and move west.

It was not, however, until a year later that Owen was able to bring together his great Philadelphia contingent in the "Boatload of Knowledge" that floated unsteadily down the ice-filled Ohio River in January 1826. The forty persons who made up the party included Owen, MacDonald, and Robert Dale Owen; William Maclure and his scientific library; a contingent from the Academy of Natural Sciences: Dr. Gerard Troost, Thomas Say, John Speakman, and Charles Lesueur; the two Pestalozzian teachers from Philadelphia, Mme Fretageot and Phiquepal d'Arusmont, along with a number of their pupils, including the son of one of Lafayette's Carbonari associates, and several of the girls from Mme Fretageot's school, among them the Sistaire sisters, favorite friends of Gabrielle du Pont; and Dr. Price and his family, who were planning to join in the teaching experiments. On the way they visited Joseph Neef near Louisville and contracted with him to come to New Harmony in the spring to teach in the schools. And by summer, Fanny Wright was there on a visit from her experimental plantation at Nashoba, Tennessee, where she and her sister planned to educate and eventually to free a small group of Negro slaves. With the arrival of Fanny Wright, it appeared that Owen had managed to put together the best library, the best school, the best institute of natural science, and the best assembly of liberal intellectuals in the United States. In that same summer of 1826 on the Fourth of July—the fiftieth anniversary of the United States —Owen was encouraged to proclaim his "Declaration of Mental Independence." As, fifty years before, the American colonies had emancipated themselves from political tyranny, so now the New Harmonites declared themselves free of the principal social evils that afflicted mankind: "PRIVATE, OR INDIVIDUAL PROPERTY—absurd and irrational SYSTEMS OF RELIGION—and MARRIAGE, founded on individual property combined with some one of these irrational systems of religion."[6]

But even at the hour of celebration, disaster was fast overtaking the Enlightenment's last campaign. Within a year John Dunn Hunter, who had been inspired by Owen to create his Red and White Republic of Fredonia, would be lying dead in a shallow creek in Texas, shot in the back by hired Indian assassins.[7] Fanny Wright, prostrated with fever, would be on her way back to England with her new friend Robert Dale Owen to recuperate from the frustrations of Nashoba, now being characterized in the public press as "one great brothel."[8] And in the spring of 1827 Maclure and Owen would have parted on ill terms, Owen selling his interest to Maclure and returning to England, and Maclure making preparations to move forever to Mexico. Although there remained at New Harmony, under the leadership of Owen's sons, many of the original settlers in a loose federation of communities, and although in after years the town nourished a remarkable concentration of natural science research, the great communitarian Utopia, which was to serve as the model for reforming the world, had failed.[9]

News of the trouble at New Harmony was on its way back to the Philadelphia area long before the public collapse of 1827. The people of the Brandywine received word from a quixotic, impecunious Parisian friend of Victor du Pont's, one Gabriel Rey, who was visiting America to recoup his fortunes, and who had walked and floated out to New Harmony in the spring of 1826, hoping to become a member of the Society there. He carried with him friendly letters of introduction to her old teacher Mme Fretageot from Gabrielle du Pont and her grandfather. Gabrielle expressed a wish to see her "dear Madame" and the Sistaire sisters, and wished "that Harmony is not so far from here for I would love to have the pleasure of going there to see you. And we have heard tell so much good of the settlement of Mr. Owen that we have a great curiousity to see it."[10] Victor was equally cordial, asking to be remembered to his acquaintances Phiquepal and Lesueur, and recommending Rey warmly as one who had been recommended from France by members of a family closely connected with Lafayette:

M. Rey whose first goal was to betake himself to Arkansas to establish there, having [read] all the publications of Mr. Owen has become enthusiastic about a plan which tends so evidently to ameliorate and to realize the great goal of all societies, and which should, under a government free and exempt from prejudices like ours, succeed better than anywhere else. The object of M. Rey in visiting the establishement at Harmony is to settle there and become a member of it, if they judge that his knowledge and talents of several kinds can be useful.[11]

Mme Fretageot wrote back in a letter to be delivered by William Owen, who wanted to visit the Du Pont powder factory and the Gilpin paper mill, and who would bring the Du Ponts up on events at New Harmony. But she conveyed some doubt about the acceptability of M. Rey, who was keeping everyone in the dark about the nature of the skills he could bring to the service of the community.

Rey for his part was extremely critical. In a long letter completed on April 14, after he had left, he described in picaresque detail his ten days in New Harmony. He arrived in a broken-down steamboat at supper time on April 5 and went at once to Mme Fretageot's house to present himself and his letters from the Du Ponts. Seeking to please, he addressed her as

the patroness of the Society. She replies to me that she was not even a member of it, that she would be whenever she wished, but that up to now she had not had any reason to want it . . . that what it is that is responsible for the fact, she tells me whispering as if for fear of being indiscreet, that the Society is not getting along very well at this moment, is that there are more heads than arms. . . .

Rey went to bed supperless, spent a sleepless night on a hard, short, creaking bed, and got up at dawn to walk around New Harmony. On his peregrination he came upon a mired horse, groaning and apparently in extremis; the horse was still lying there helpless when he left nine days later. Eventually M. Rey was admitted as a probationer but he left anyway, disillusioned by what he had seen.

As Mme Fretageot had said, there were too many heads and not enough arms. No one seemed to be really in charge. Rey spoke to Robert Owen and his son, to William Maclure, to Phiquepal, to Mme Fretageot, and found that they were not even members of the Society (perhaps not wishing to risk all their capital in so uncertain a venture). And certain community services, like laundry and shoemaking, were not being performed at all because they were considered degrading. "The great equality which they publicise, has the result that if no one wants to take up certain jobs, no one dares or is able to require anyone to do them." Phiquepal made his own shoes and did his own washing; Mme Fretageot was able to persuade her schoolgirls to wash her linen but had to do her own ironing. A new constitution was just being announced but already two groups had separated themselves from the main body

because, being workers, they did not care any longer to take responsibility for a large number of women and children and parasites, or to support various expenses of which they did not appreciate the utility, such as the $30 in candles per month to enable the pantalooners to dance, or for the daily reports made in the evening at the Chancellery, on the conduct and work of everyone, and on the plans for the administration in general;

(282)

divided into 8 departments presided over by 8 prefects or chiefs: 1st science, 2nd teaching . . . agriculture, commerce, etc.

The farms were not producing enough even to feed the population, let alone produce a salable surplus. And, although full membership required a substantial endowment of the community, no profits were promised (these being devoted to founding new societies) and the individual could not sell his interest if he decided to leave. Indeed, Rey now regarded himself as a dupe, along with the rest, for having entered the community at all:

> There is perhaps not one who does not regret having come: but when they find themselves without money enough to leave, are not even with their family, and there are some who have even taken children from their parents, since it does not cost more at New-Hny. Thus they stay only because they cannot do anything else (without the obliging, the persuasive foresight of Mme. Du P. I would find myself in the same situation) but some pray that things worsen to the point they will be forced to clear out.[12]

New Harmony was only a small town of 750 people; but among the principalities of mind it was an empire, and the crash of its falling was heard throughout the Western world. By the nascent evangelical Christians, in particular, the New Harmony experiment was seen as "designed to revolutionize, not to improve, but to break up, the existing condition of society." Its failure was to be hailed happily by John P. Crozer: "This is another instance of the folly of men in their efforts to establish communities repudiating or failing to recognize the Christian religion as the basis of society and good government."[13]

But the failure of New Harmony did not discourage the prophets of associationism. Even before the model communes at New Harmony and Nashoba collapsed, their founders had taken to the road to preach the Utopian socialist gospel to the American people. The *New Harmony Gazette* (and its sequel, the New York *Free Inquirer*) and other free-thought presses circulated news, theoretical essays, and propaganda. Owenite clubs were founded in many cities and fledgling communes formed in country places. For about a decade Fanny Wright, Robert Owen and his sons, and the anarchist Josiah Warren kept America in a stir, from St. Louis to New York, and from Niagara Falls to New Orleans.

Robert Dale Owen and Fanny Wright made public addresses repeatedly in both Philadelphia and Wilmington in the later 1820's and early 1830's. In Philadelphia a newspaper was established in 1828, the *Mechanic's Free Press,* which, along with the usual miscellany of news, sentimental poetry, and advertisements, published extensive political and economic discussion on cooperative and socialist lines. In Wilmington, the *Delaware Free Press* appeared in 1830, dedicated to providing a forum for the Hicksite Friends of the Brandywine area and for the views of Robert Owen, Frances Wright, Thomas Paine, William Maclure, Johann Pestalozzi, and their colleagues. The effect of all this talking and writing on the people of the lower Delaware Valley was complex: it mobilized some to defend received religion; it inspired others to question, to experiment with "association," and to organize the first workingmen's political movement. These social developments were perhaps more important, even if relatively inconspicuous, than the glamorous disaster on the Wabash.

The Valley Forge Commune

There were many people who listened with enthusiasm to Robert Owen during his Philadelphia visits in 1824 and 1825 but for one reason or another were not free to follow him to New Harmony.

Thomas Gilpin, for instance, the paper and cotton manufacturer from the Brandywine, and uncle of Sophie's friend Mary Gilpin, met Owen in Philadelphia in 1824 and "expressed a great desire to see Mr. Owen's plans introduced."[14] In a small way, Gilpin was already emulating Owen, for he had built around the paper mill a very pretty little industrial community which, like New Lanark, excited admiring comment from its many visitors. A bachelor, he lived part of the year in Philadelphia and part in a cottage adjoining the mill, where he had a greenhouse, an icehouse, and a garden with lemon trees and various fruits and vegetables; his elder brother Joshua lived nearby with his family in the mansion of Kentmere. Gilpin's cottage and the greenhouse and icehouse were always open for the refreshment of the many summer visitors who walked out from Wilmington to admire the Brandywine scenery and the Gilpins' endless papermaking machine; the workers and their families were allowed to keep their produce cool in the icehouse. "As a manufacturing district," recalled a literary commentator of the day who had been brought up in Wilmington, "it was long proverbial for the neatness and orderly conduct of its population." The paper mills themselves were said to be a marvel of neatness and order. The various departments were located in different structures. In the mote-picking room, for instance, thirty women sat at high stools at a long table set along the wall below the windows, each wearing a clean, ironed apron, picking flaws out of the wet paper. "Not a cobweb marred these white walls, nor was dust allowed to soil the floors." Outside, the thirty or so families who supplied the ninety hands employed in the mill lived in model industrial housing:

"Tier upon tier of stone cottages, yellow-dashed and well ventilated, rise up before you on these hills, shaded by forest trees, each having a yard nicely paled and ornamented with shrubs and vines, climbing to the roofs, mingling taste with comfort."[15] Like Owen, Gilpin went to great pains to educate the workers' children, building a schoolhouse for sixty pupils and employing a full-time schoolmaster; in the winter there was a night school for adults.[16]

Another friend and admirer of Owen was the secretary of the Academy of Natural Sciences, Reuben Haines of Germantown. Like Gilpin (who was an old school mate) an anti-slavery Quaker of the Hicksite faction, he was a gentleman farmer and brewer of Germantown. He was a particular friend of the émigré Bonapartes, of the Peales, of the Sellers, of Audubon, and of the radical members of the Academy who joined Owen in New Harmony. His special concern was education and he was in the midst of planning an infant school in Germantown when Owen arrived in 1824.[17] Haines first met Owen, however, on his second visit to Philadelphia, in the fall of 1825, had him out to Wyck, the family mansion, for dinner, and accompanied him on a recruiting trip to New York a few days later.[18]

Haines was to be the prime mover in the formation of the Delaware Valley's first and only experiment with Owenite socialism. But apparently the earliest stirrings were made in Wilmington. The day after dining with Haines, Owen went off to Wilmington with Dr. Price and a Mr. Gause "to see the society formed there."[19] This was very likely the same group who in 1824 had "formed themselves into a sort of society for the purpose of promoting his plan of association." They had invited Owen to meet with them but he had been unable to find time then.[20] Now seemingly inspired by Owen's presence, the group consolidated its plans. On December 22, 1825, fifteen members of the Friendly Association for Mutual Interests met and subscribed $28,000 to get things started.[21] On January 19, 1826, they formulated a constitution, which in March was printed as an appendix to the Philadelphia edition of Owenite economist John Gray's *Lecture on Human Happiness.*

The preamble to the constitution, after first declaring that the great first principles of human action should be love for "The Great First Cause and Creator of All Things" and for "our fellow-creatures," went on to condemn the present unhappy condition of mankind. Man today was "the enemy of man"; only "a new and *entirely different* plan" could give hope for a better state, in which man's natural rights, "which have been taken from us by human policy," could be realized again. The new plan, as laid out in the constitution, envisaged the accumulation, by the subscription of $10 shares and the donation to the common fund of all of the members' private property except furniture, of a capital stock of up to half a million dollars. With this fund the Association would purchase real estate and establish buildings for the community at Valley Forge on the Schuylkill River. There, the constitution declared,

. . . we will commence erecting a commodious establishment for the accommodation of visitors and travellers; also, permanent buildings for commercial, manufacturing, mechanical, scientific, religious, and other purposes; and, as soon as necessary arrangements can be made, we will commence and complete the building of a village for the permanent and *equal* accommodation of all the Members, on a plan similar to that presented by *Robert Owen.*

The actual organization of the community, however, was left rather vague, except for the specification of the shareholders' financial rights and obligations. There was to be initially a board of twelve town managers, including both men and women, plus a clerk and treasurer, "to transact the affairs of the Company." The distilling, vending, and excessive use of ardent spirits was discouraged, and all members must be "MORAL, SOBER, and INDUSTRIOUS." Free medical and nursing care would be available to the sick and injured; a communal kitchen, laundry, clothing and furniture warehouse, and heating plant, all built and operated on "scientific principles," would relieve the female part of the Company "of domestic labor and permit them equally to enjoy the pleasures of social intercourse, and the acquisition of knowledge." All children, including children of deceased members, would be educated by a method combining practice and theory. All members were expected to engage in useful work "according to their age, experience, and capacity." But the solution of the problem of *ensuring* the adequate performance of technically and economically necessary tasks was left rather vague. Members, "if inexperienced in that which is requisite," were expected to "apply diligently to acquire the knowledge of some useful occupation or employment." Even this might not ensure the success of business enterprises, so the hiring of specialized labor was authorized: "If at any time there should not be a sufficient number of persons in the Company, fully competent to the management of the different branches of industry, the Company shall engage the assistance of skilful practical men from general society." And if enough funds were not subscribed at the outset, the Company was authorized to go into debt in the purchase of the Valley Forge estate.[22]

The names of the organizers were not printed with the constitution which they signed, but it is clear that Reuben Haines of Germantown was one and John T. Gause of Wilmington another. John Rogers, Philadelphia hardware merchant and the owner of some mills at Valley Forge near the Association's property, was the president; one James Jones, "the only wealthy person among them" and the principal shareholder, was the treasurer. William Maclure subscribed $5,000 (but his subscription was never taken up). And in the summer of 1826 the Prices, discontented with New Harmony, returned at Haines's urging to join the Valley Forge community.[23] Other members are said to have included the Philadelphia Hicksite Quaker Abel Knight; Constantin Rafinesque, the widely traveled botanist; and the eccentric "high priest" of the associationists, E. Postlethwaite Page, who dressed himself entirely in green "as a rebuke to the devotees of fashion."[24] (Duncan MacDonald with Robert Dale Owen met Page first in New York where, preceded by a green calling card, he announced himself as "the page of Nature." After listening to Page claim that he was in constant receipt of revelations from nature, and that he had in olden times been King David's page, MacDonald asked Owen uncomfortably, "Are we *all* crazy, do you think, Robert? Have we been poking into great subjects and thinking of a world's reform, until our brains are addled, and we are fit inmates of a lunatic asylum?")[25] All in all, about three hundred people (perhaps fifty families) settled at Valley Forge—only about a quarter of the number anticipated by the organizers.[26]

The estate upon which the community was established was a pair of old iron-manufacturing plantations about fifteen miles above Philadelphia. It was a well-chosen site, strategically located on the semi-navigable Schuylkill River and canal down which anthracite was being carried to Philadelphia, and already established as an industrial and farming community. One part of the estate, including Washington's old headquarters, the forge itself, and a rolling and slitting mill, was purchased from a private owner in Germantown for $17,000. The other, of several thousand acres, including a rifle armory and the old cotton mill of Hugh Wagstaff, who had recently died, was contributed by John Rogers in return for stock scrip with a face value of $65,000. Thus the community possessed a valuable industrial establishment which should, under its own operation or by lease, have been able to earn a substantial profit. It had been inspected the year before by Haines, Troost, Lesueur, Thomas Say, and William Maclure, and Maclure had recorded in his diary the active state of the enterprises:

stoped at the Phenix Iron works passed Mr. Rogers cotton mill 1500 spindles & 24 power looms spins to No 30 all iron frames and well made the Iron works welding scraps made up into bundles which they rais to a white heat in a reverbatory furnace with Virginia coal and after it has passed thro the Cylinders brings it to a red heat in a furnace with anthracite have not yet applied with success the anthracite to smelting iron or making bars supposed that they have not yet applied a sufficient blast nothing but the common bellows. . . .[27]

The farmland, laid out among softly rolling hills, was fertile and well watered. The Valley Forge community probably had, economically, more prospects of success than New Harmony and was commensurate in scale.[28]

The community was launched in the spring with a fanfare of publicity even in newspapers of generally conservative editorial sympathies. It was the subject of a long and friendly notice in the *Gazette of the United States,* which saw it as affording full evidence "for judging of the adaptation of Mr. Owen's system to the views, policy, habits and education of our citizens." This account was republished in the Federalist *Village Record* of West Chester.[29] Of course the *New Harmony Gazette* and other associationist papers gave it their congratulations. And at Kendall, Ohio, a copy of the Valley Forge Constitution was used as the basis for the formation of still another Owenite community under the same name: "The Friendly Association for Mutual Interests." The Kendall community's constitution, dated March 17, 1826, copied the Valley Forge community's preamble verbatim, with a few added phrases condemning economic competition. The text itself followed the Valley Forge version very closely, although there was less careful specification of financial arrangements, and the other articles were somewhat reordered. There is no indication of any overlap in membership.[30]

But despite good will and extensive resources, the Valley Forge commune failed, almost simultaneously with New Harmony. (The Kendall community survived until 1828.) The course of events is not clear but by July 1826—which cannot have been more than three or four months after families moved to the site in substantial numbers—William Maclure was writing in alarm to Mme Fretageot. He had received a copy of the Valley Forge Constitution and was appalled; it "seems to retain no feature of the cooperative system but the money making. . . . I do not know what to think of it." His financial agent in Philadelphia advised him "that he is afraid they will not succeed." By September, he reported, "The Valley Forge is broken up into separate communities and many of the old number in whom I had confidence when I subscribed to their community left it and the whole tottally changed so that Im exhonerated from all claims to my subscription."[31]

The break-up evidently was precipitated by the withdrawal from membership of the principal stockholders and their demand that they be paid in cash for their contributions. This was impossible, so John Rogers and James Jones took their reimbursement in kind, Rogers receiving all the combined estate except Washington's headquarters, which fell to Jones, who moved out from Germantown and lived there until his death about 1840.[32]

It was later to be claimed that Presbyterian religious opposition in the community drove the Friendly Association out; but this is unlikely. Many, if not most, of the associationists were members of the Society of Friends, albeit of the more radical Hicksite persuasion, and were not likely to be persecuted by Presbyterian vigilantes. The reason for the collapse of the community, in Maclure's opinion, was a faulty perception of the principles of cooperation. The doom of the Valley Forge community, he felt, was written into its constitution:

> an article gives no interest for 5 years to any of the members that may put in money but 5 p c to all thus a trifle that will induce all the members to put anything they hold in a false name. Beginning with [illegible] all the profits are to be divided equally the 5th year and every year afterward ... the division of profits puts all into the individual scramble I fear there is not a sufficient number of adults on the continent who comprehend the system to form a community we must take time and not give money without securing the end we wish to accomplish for the only means we have of forwarding the system is by our money preaching goes to the wind and is lost in the forests I'm convinced that a few thousand dollars some years hence will do 10 times more good than at present of all the spurs to industry money is the most inaffectual[33]

The disillusioned associationists, however, blamed John Rogers—"a deceitful, speculative person," wrote the daughter of Abel Knight—rather than any deficiency in the constitution or the principle of "communism," as she called it. The community sent out a "Macedonian cry for help" in the persons of Abel Knight and his wife, who visited the Shaker settlement at New Lebanon, New York, in the summer of 1827. The Shakers sent down missionaries in the fall and the upshot of it all was that a good many of the dispossessed Valley Forge families were converted to Shakerism and removed to New Lebanon, about ten families joining in the summer of 1828 and a number of others later.[34] Still others no doubt found homes in various religious communities and some must have remained in the area. By 1828 the Valley Forge commune was no more.

Craft Unions and the Workingmen's Party

The ideas of Owen and of the socialist followers of the English economist David Ricardo were brought forcefully to the attention of the skilled workers of Philadelphia by a number of articulate social philosophers in the workingmen's movement. One of the most influential was a young English-born shoemaker named William Heighton of Southwark, who signed his writings "Unlettered Mechanic." Heighton had, in point of fact, acquired sufficient learning to read John Gray's *Lecture on Human Happiness* (which had earlier been an inspiration to the Valley Forge associationists) and he was a forceful writer himself. Some of Gray's ideas in turn came from Robert Owen, but he had been most deeply impressed by William Thompson (an erstwhile secretary of the utilitarian Jeremy Bentham), who had written a book entitled *Distribution of Wealth* (published in London in 1824) about inequalities in society. Both Gray and Thompson, and Heighton after them, argued for the Ricardian socialist view that it was labor that gave value to commodities and manufactured products and that the laborer was entitled to receive *all* the value of his labor. The inequalities and miseries of society stemmed from the fact that in actual practice the producer received only a fraction of the value he added to the product by his labor, the balance being usurped by the capitalist, who charged rent and interest and paid minimal wages, keeping the difference to himself as "profit." A more equitable system would require purchase by the exchange of labor time alone.

Heighton in 1827, in his initial "Address to the Members of Trade Societies, and to the Working Classes Generally," suggested a plan by which laborers could improve their condition and ultimately effect this end. He proposed to secure new legislation to restrict the introduction of new "labor-saving machinery" (which was used by manufacturers to get rid of dissatisfied workers) and to curtail bank charters, corporations, and monopolies. This new legislation was to be secured by the workingmen themselves *nominating and electing their own candidates.* He was not proposing, then, the creation of new exemplary communities, like New Harmony and Valley Forge (both, he probably knew, already failed); rather, he was proposing a seizure of legislative power in existing communities by organized political action. Owen, who read Heighton's address during a visit to Philadelphia in June 1827, commended it in his lecture at the Franklin Institute as important reading for "every producer in America" and as containing more wisdom than "all the writings on political economy I have met with." He had it republished in England in 1827 and again in 1833.

But Heighton's "Address" was only the starting point. He went on to found three preparatory organizations: a Mechanics' Union of Trade Associations, to provide economic and legal aid to strikers; a Mechanics' Free Library; and a newspaper, published by the library, of which he served as editor—the *Mechanic's Free Press.* With these tools, Heighton was prepared to create a political party. The Mechanics' Union was a source of funds, an organizational structure, and rallying point; and the newspaper was a medium of communication, not only of socialist philosophy but also of news of local economic conditions, strikes, meetings, petitions, and political information.

In format, the four-page *Mechanic's Free Press* was similar to other weekly newspapers of the time. It provided bits of poetry, fiction, editorials, foreign news, local news, announcements, and advertisements. It reprinted Gray's *Lecture on Human Happiness* and regularly ran news of Robert Owen, William Maclure, and Frances Wright. It announced that Neef's book on the Pestalozzian system of education was for sale (agent Reuben Haines), and reprinted essays by Robert Burns and poetry by Lord Byron. It gave space to Hicksite Quakers, advertised the *Universalist Review,* and ran announcements of Masonic publications. It opposed the enforcement of the Christian Sabbath blue laws, particularly those closing taverns on Sunday. And it called for subscribers to new communalistic ventures, including a housing cooperative entitled "The Associated Friends for Mutual Interest," which proposed to buy houses for subscribers at 50 cents per week; a successful "Labor for Labor Association," which modeled itself after Josiah Warren's "time store" in Cincinnati, where labor time was exchanged for goods; and several producers' cooperatives which dispensed with the services of the wholesaler.

But all this was preparatory to the major political effort. In the summer of 1828, public political meetings were held (regularly interrupted by hecklers from the pro-Jackson organization), which led eventually to the nomination of candidates on the ticket of the Workingmen's Party for all thirty-nine of the municipal and county offices. Most of the candidates were also on either the Adams or Jackson tickets, but eight were put up exclusively by the Workingmen's Party. None of the Workingmen's exclusive candidates won in 1828, for they polled on the order of 300 to 500 votes each, as against 3,500 for the typical Adams candidate and 4,500 for the Jacksonite. In 1830 the Workingmen did better, however, actually electing six of their own exclusive candidates to city and county offices. But the party's strength declined in 1831 and it never fielded candidates again. The Mechanics Union itself had already met for the last time, in 1829, and the *Mechanic's Free Press* ceased publication in 1831.

The reasons for the quick demise of the Workingmen's Party are complex. It was inspired by a social philosophy that required, not just local improvements in wages, hours, and working conditions, but fundamental changes in major social institutions. Its platform called for universal free public education, limitation of the powers of banks, a mechanics lien law, restriction of monopolies, abolition of imprisonment for debt, repeal of the militia laws, and curtailment of the introduction of labor-saving machinery. Some of these positions, to be sure, were already being, or were soon to be, seized by the Democrats or by the nascent conservative parties like Clay's National Republicans and the Anti-Masons; but others were condemned as abominations of infidel "workeyism." Furthermore, it was a third party challenging the local remnants of the old Federalists as well as the ascendant Democrats under Jackson; a political nuisance, threatening to take the balance of power in closely contested elections, it was harassed from all sides.

But the workingmen's movement, as it was being organized by Heighton and his associates, had an internal vulnerability as well. It was essentially a federation of the old skilled trade organizations, which in an earlier age had functioned as guilds, admitting masters as well as journeymen, and serving as much or more to regulate the quality of work and to provide death benefits as to control prices and wages. In this newer age, these ancient associations were being called upon not only to continue their functions but to add more: to serve as an efficient mechanism of economic conflict over wages and hours by the use of the strike; to raise the social level of the mechanic by means of education; and to transform society as a whole in accordance with a radical (conventionally radical, to be sure) secular social philosophy. Thus oriented, the movement could only call upon the resources of the *nonreligious* members of the traditional handicrafts unions —the carpenters, cordwainers, hand-loom weavers, housepainters, printers, pharmacists, and so on. Most of these craftsmen were middle class in aspiration and, with their religious fellows, eschewed the thousands of unskilled Irish and black laborers; they had no use either for the women and children employed in the mills. The mule spinners, who might have been recognized as practitioners of a skilled trade, had not organized themselves into a handicraft union that would fit into the overall trade union structure.

With the demise of the Workingmen's Party in Philadelphia, and of its associated organs, the craft unions restricted themselves to the narrower issues of wages and hours. In this arena they were successful. In 1835 a general strike by the handicraft unions brought masters to recognize the ten-hour day generally for the skilled trades in Philadelphia. But the political price was high. The craft unions abandoned the political field to the representatives of capital. And they failed to establish effective ties with the textile mill workers, who therefore remained unorganized and whose employers were still able to impose the twelve- to fourteen-hour day.[35]

THE THEORY OF COMMUNAL INDUSTRIALISM

The various political and intellectual traditions which have been brought together here under the banner of the Enlightenment were, of course, diverse. But they did share certain general beliefs that can be understood as applications of the principles of Enlightenment philosophy to societies undergoing industrialization. The Enlightenment proper, clearly, while it included an avid interest in mechanism on the part of its philosophers, and while it foresaw continuing improvements in the condition of mankind as the result of advances in science and technology, was not aware of any "Industrial Revolution." Diderot's *Encyclopédie,* for instance, devoted much space to technology but the English inventions in cotton manufacturing came too late to be represented. Thus what is labeled the "theory of communal industrialism" was derived from, but was not part of, the classic Enlightenment tradition, and had other roots as well, particularly that aspect which emphasized the small rural commune as the primary economic institution.

The idea that a balanced agricultural-industrial economy was possible in a nation of small rural communes was reasonable at this time in American history. Southern cotton plantations and northern iron plantations, both raising much of their own food, providing for the educational and spiritual needs of their residents, and producing a crop or product for exchange, showed the economic feasibility of the arrangement. So also did the well-established tradition of Christian Utopian communities like the Shakers and the Economists, which successfully combined industry, agriculture, and trade. Company towns like New Lanark and Lowell, with their carefully planned integration of technology, social structure, and education, developed as corporate communities in rural areas. The social and ideological innovations proposed in the theory of communal industrialism would, the idealistic reformers argued, simply improve on these models, leading to greater material prosperity and to a more wholesome social life. It was not until relatively inexpensive and efficient steam engines were available in quantity in the 1850's that the idea of the rural commune lost its manifest reasonableness. No longer dependent on the water wheel and turbine, the reliable steam-driven factory could now be placed along a railroad beside a harbor, within a great city, with associated savings in transportation costs, and with such accessibility to the seat of commerce that the wilderness lost its plausibility as a site for industry.

The essential tenets of the theory of communal industrialism would seem to be contained in eight points:

1 Mutual agreement and cooperation, rather than selfish competition, are the basic principles upon which to found the institutions of a good human society.

2 Man is a product of learning in a physical and social environment; the community can produce good, or depraved, men and women, depending upon the education of children and the social conditions of adults.

3 Reason and experiment, not revealed religion, are man's only proper guide.

4 Rank, social class, and the bonds of matrimony are unimportant as a principle of social organization and in a good society can be dispensed with.

5 Local economic decisions, as well as political decisions at all levels, should be made by democratic procedures.

6 Real estate and machines should be owned and controlled by the community, not by individual proprietors.

7 Small rural communities, combining in a balanced way both agricultural and industrial pursuits, are the natural context of human economic, educational, and social institutions.

8 Such communities can be largely self-supporting insofar as food, fuel, and other necessities are concerned, but should also engage in specialized production and trade in a national and international system of exchange.

But it was not only the triumph of steam over water power that doomed the rural industrial commune (as it did also the privately owned country cotton mills). There was a kind of romanticism in the attitudes of the radical reformers. In their passage through the wars of liberation, the ideals of the Enlightenment had gradually assumed a heroic posture. The American Revolution, the French Revolution, the struggles for freedom in Spain, Italy, and Greece, and the Romantic movement in art and literature had given the cool wisdom of illuminism a ruddy, dawn-streaked, romantic fervor. It seemed that the transformation of the world was now about to happen. Their eyes fixed on new horizons, the romantic radicals failed to perceive certain fundamental contradictions in their position. Great rationalists, they failed, like Robert Owen at New Harmony, to recognize that the organization of work in a free Utopian community must be at least as rationally designed as in a capitalist's factory or plantation, and that the efficiency of workers must be ensured by an equally effective system of inducements and discipline. Great proponents of equality, they assumed that an intellectual élite, standing above the democratic process, should make the fundamental decisions. Great opponents of concentrated wealth, they allowed their social experiments to depend upon private fortunes not merely for their capital but their operating budgets. Severe critics of the institution of marriage, they chose to overlook the importance of the nuclear family to the financial plans of working people. Thus, although some of their opponents might concede them to be right in certain particulars, such as their demands for free public education, for freedom for slaves, for increased rights for women, for the reform of the militia, and for a mechanics lien law, these opponents could also point to the fact that not one secular communal society had been able to succeed. And the failures could be attributed, not to specific reform sentiments that looked reasonable to almost anyone, not even to the advocacy of communal as opposed to private property, but to the two major social positions of romantic radicalism: its opposition to marriage and—worst of all—to organized religion.

Religion, in fact, was the wheel on which the theory of communal industrialism would be broken.

Chapter VII

THE EVANGELICAL COUNTERATTACK

In the 1790's, as the new republic was settling down to a national life, some of its Christian citizens, alarmed by the progress of "infidelity," began to seek a revival of religion. They believed that the violent excesses of the French Revolution were a direct result of the infidel philosophy of the Enlightenment. And they began to realize that many of their comrades-in-arms, in their own American Revolution, had been infidels and devotees of the same Enlightenment, and that thousands of their friends and neighbors, personally respectable and patriotic though they might be, were tainted by these beliefs.

The first phase of this second Great Awakening was not as spectacularly successful in converting infidel artisans and merchants in the cities, and gentlemen on plantations, as it was in exciting religious hysteria in remote and lonely settlements along the western frontier. But during the second decade of the century the evangelical movement began to reformulate its ideology. The harsher dogmas of Calvinism, codified in the Hopkinsian doctrine that the damned should be converted and taught to take pleasure in the prospect of eternal suffering at the hands of God, were being softened to offer a likelihood of salvation to all who would be saved. Large organizations, ecumenical in spirit, drew upon the vast financial resources of successful businessmen; the American Bible Society, the American Tract Society, the American Sunday School Union, and many other Christian and benevolent societies applied sound business methods to the task of reforming America.

Prominent in these affairs, and an extreme example of the evangelical type, was Philadelphia's young, wealthy Presbyterian evangelist, the Reverend Dr. Ezra Stiles Ely. Born in New England in 1786, he had graduated from Yale and early in the century had spent a year saving souls in New York City's hospital and almshouse. As a product of that year's work he published a remarkable book on his evangelical experiences with prostitutes, the destitute and dying, and the insane. After publishing also a refutation of Hopkinsism, he was called to the Pine Street Church in Philadelphia, where he quickly became a leader in the evangelical movement. Handsome, curly-haired, and aggressive, he was a charismatic leader. He was one of the founders of the American Sunday School Union; he launched the campaign to stop the federal government from breaking the Sabbath by transporting the mails on Sunday; he was the secretary of the Board of Trustees of new Jefferson University and personally paid the cost of the first building.[1] On the Fourth of July, 1827, Dr. Ely delivered a sermon (later published) in the Seventh Presbyterian Church in Philadelphia which signaled to the wise that the evangelical movement had entered a new phase: a counterattack against the infidels by direct political action. It was to stir violent controversy and, in its literal sense, was neither correctly understood by his opponents nor implemented by his followers. Under the title "The Duty of Christian Freemen to Elect Christian Rulers," the sermon declared that the United States was a Christian nation and that "all our rulers ought in their official stations to serve the Lord Jesus Christ." God did not want "Deists." "I propose, fellow-citizens, a new sort of union, or, if you please, *a Christian party in politics,*" cried Dr. Ely. Christians should be politically active and should go to the polls, using their franchise to exclude infidels and immoralists (such as slanderers, seducers, and drunkards) from public office. His spirit was ecumenical: he admitted Presbyterians, Congregationalists, Baptists, Methodists, and Episcopalians to the fold; Catholics were not mentioned, and Jews and Mohammedans were excluded.

Although he stated explicitly that he did not wish any religious test to be prescribed by the Constitution for the inauguration of public officials, he was at once accused—and not only by infidels—of advocating a union of Church and State. His American Sunday School Union, currently applying for articles of incorporation from the State of Pennsylvania, was condemned as part of a scheme to fill the nation with Sunday School scholars, who would in ten or twenty years elect one another to fill every public office in the land. The Sunday Schools were seen by worried liberals as "dictators to the consciences" of millions, as exercising a power of censorship over the reading matter of the people, as a secret Christian army preparing to conquer the republic from within.[2]

Although Ely's call was shouted down, it expressed a widely felt mood of evangelical determination to go on the offensive against infidelity and to convert America into a truly Christian commonwealth. The lot of the publicly avowed unbeliever would be a hard one, for he was obstructing God's work. And the true Christian would have to do more than preoccupy himself with the evidences of his own salvation; he would have to work hard to save the unbeliever.

CALVARY CHURCH IN ROCKDALE

In the Rockdale district the leaders of the evangelical response to the threat of infidelity were Richard Somers Smith, his wife Elizabeth Beach Smith, and their daughters Clementina and Harriet. As their young friend John Hill Martin said of them later in his history, the story of their Christian work shows "what good one man and three women can accomplish in a country neighborhood."[1] The Smiths guided the revival of religion in the little cotton hamlets and inspired other community leaders to make substantial contributions to the evangelical cause. The Lammots, the Crozers, the Willcoxes, the Darlingtons, and the Riddles were influenced by their example; each in his own way served the cause of Christ among the working people, whether directly by way of religion, or indirectly through politics or knowledge of political economy. And ultimately as a group they were able to impose a Christian moral dominion over the Rockdale district.

The Organizing of Calvary Church

The decision to organize the parish was made during a time of growing economic distress both for the Smiths and for the operatives in the Rockdale district. A brief economic recession swept the country in early 1834, caused (so the Smiths and the Du Ponts believed) by an inevitable tightening of credit as the Second Bank of the United States fought bravely back against the tyrant Andrew Jackson's veto of its charter and his reckless removal of the federal deposits. Discount rates on new loans were as high as 19 percent; the value of cotton yarn was falling.[2] Clementina wrote to Sophie from Philadelphia in January complaining of the depression and reporting that there was "a great deal of misery among the lower classes in this city."[3] And by February Sophie was responding with exclamations of dismay at "the dreadful consequences of distress that fill every part of our land . . . this change over its once flourishing and happy population!"[4] In March the Riddles' Parkmount Mill was closed for a week "owing to the business being so dull," and the price of yarn was down, No. 15 from 24 to 22 1/2 cents per pound and No. 20 from 26 to 23.[5] But John Phillips' mill apparently was unaffected by the general decline in commerce, for in March

RICHARD S. SMITH (1789–1884).

one of his weavers, William Morris, wrote home to England reporting cheerfully that he and three other men were boarding with his brother Andrew and "all working" in "an old established mill called Philipses Mill."[6] And Crozer was not affected by the decline until 1835, when the death and total insolvency of his chief customer for yarns cost him nearly $6,500, about half of his assets in finished goods.[7]

Merchants, perhaps, were more sensitive to the shrinking of credit than were the manufacturers. In any case, in January 1834 Smith's commission house failed, and in April he lost his membership on the Board of Directors of the Bank of North America.[8] Although he "bore it perfectly . . . the Christian in adversity,"[9] he must have been profoundly distressed. His financial difficulties continued to deepen and soon the Rockdale property itself was in jeopardy. In February 1836 it was put up for sale by the sheriff. No doubt by prearrangement, it was purchased by a nephew (his brother's son), who reconveyed it to his uncle five months later, after the difficulty was settled.[10]

Despite these distractions, the Smith family proceeded resolutely with their evangelical plans. In November 1834 a meeting was held in the nail mill for the purpose of organizing a congregation. A constitution was adopted as prescribed by the Episcopal canons and the name Calvary (suggested by the then Bishop Onderdonk) was given to the new church. Smith became one of the two wardens and young Ferdinand Lammot served as a vestryman. Soon after, the Reverend Mr. Marmaduke Hirst, the rector at nearby St. John's in Concord, was appointed "missionary" by the Society for the Advancement of Christianity in Pennsylvania. The designation of this church as a mission—meaning that it was not financially self-supporting —survived for more than a hundred years.

The next step was to construct a church building. Now for the first time substantial sums of money were required; and at this juncture Smith was in no position to make a large contribution. Nevertheless, in July 1836—just about the time when he resumed possession of his own property—the vestry met and decided to purchase a lot offered to the church by a neighbor for $100. At this same meeting, a building committee was elected, including Smith. Five days later the committee reported that they had agreed with a local man to do the carpenter's work for $250 on the building, which was to be 45 by 30 feet, two stories in height, with a tower 10 feet square, and a basement with two finished rooms. It had been designed "in the Gothic style" by Smith's friend, the architect—now Bishop of Vermont—John Henry Hopkins. In August, the cornerstone was laid by Bishop Onderdonk; at the end of the service an offering was taken amounting to $27.78. By winter the shell was completed and a basement school room, with accommodations for 250, was plastered and furnished; and in this school room, on Christmas Eve in 1836, the first service was held in Calvary Church before a crowded congregation. Thereafter divine service was held in the basement at least once every Sunday. As Smith proudly reported (in partial justification of a request for more funds): "The attendance is seldom less than 100 persons, and although accommodations are prepared for 250 persons, it sometimes happens that there are not seats for all who attend."[11]

It is plain in the records that the young church constantly suffered from want of money. Many of the parishioners were hard-pressed mill workers, and the Smiths, the principal organizers, were able to provide more in the way of time and influence than hard cash. Even in 1838 the upper part of the building, intended for divine worship, was still unfinished; thus, no pew-rents, the normal source of an Episcopal church's income, could be collected. As Smith put it in his request:

> ... it is now the anxious desire of the Congregation to raise the necessary funds to complete it; and by means of the pew-rents to offer a more adequate compensation to their Rector; the mode of raising funds by voluntary contributions being too uncertain. . . .
>
> The embarassments which have affected every branch of industry, having borne peculiarly hard upon the operatives of the manufacturing districts, the Congregation of Calvary Church are not able to raise among themselves the means necessary to complete the building, for which purpose about $1000 will be required. They appeal therefore to the pious members of the Episcopal Church for aid to enable them to establish the good work which has been commenced.[12]

The problems in completing the building were matched by the difficulties of providing adequately for a rector. For a year, the Reverend Mr. Hirst survived on a salary of $200 per annum, "which was raised by contribution in sums averaging $3.00 each." He resigned, however, in June 1838, and was replaced in September by the Reverend Mr. Alfred Lee, who fortunately for Calvary Church was a man with a private income from stocks and bonds. Lee, his salary advanced to $300 per annum, donated the entire amount over the next three years to pay for putting in the pews and generally completing the church edifice (although a bell was not installed in the tower until 1859).[13]

In all of his activities on behalf of Calvary Church, Smith had the backing and support of important figures in the Protestant Episcopal Church. His elder brother James was a prominent Philadelphia attorney and a zealous evangelical layman—counsel for the Bank of North America, a member of the Common Council of Philadelphia, a trustee of the University of Pennsylvania, a vestryman at St. Peter's Church (of which the Richard S. Smiths were communicants), and founder of the Society for the Advancement of Christianity in Pennsylvania. He was a prominent committee man in state and national Episcopal organizations, and thus was in a position to give his brother Richard advice and support in his efforts to establish Calvary Church.

But probably the most important of Richard Smith's advisers was John Henry Hopkins, Bishop of Vermont. He was in the habit of staying with the Smiths, in Philadelphia or at Rockdale, whenever business brought him to the Philadelphia area. A former architect who specialized in churches in the Gothic style, Hopkins provided without charge the plans for Calvary Church. He preached from the pulpit of the church and no doubt his many books and pamphlets, presenting a high church approach to evangelical religion, were read and circulated among the congregation.

Hopkins could present forceful advice on the danger of foreign and domestic radicalism to a working-class congregation. As we noted earlier, he had been brought to America at an early age by parents fleeing from Dublin about the time of the pro-French Irish rebellion of 1798. He had been an apprentice to free-thinking Oliver Evans at the Mars Works and had lived with the Evans family. He had taught George Escol Sellers mechanical drawing.[14] He had managed an ironworks in western Pennsylvania. He grew up among the French émigrés who congregated around Bordentown, New Jersey, and after moving to Philadelphia he got to know a crowd of refugee foreigners—French, Scottish, Irish, Spanish, German. They were "irreligious, infidel, and loose on many subjects of morality." His youthful reading was "Paine, Volney, Hume, Mirabeau, Voltaire, and Rousseau," and it was only gradually that he was weaned away from deism by reading tracts attacking Tom Paine and his ilk by Hannah More and other early evangelical authors. He was at first attracted by the Quakers and the Swedenborgians; after he moved to Pittsburgh in his twenties he joined the Episcopal Church.[15]

Thus Hopkins could stand before the working people of Rockdale not only as the bishop who was Smith's houseguest and as the architect who had designed their church, but also as a former workingman himself—a former Deist, a draftsman, an iron master's apprentice, and for a time an iron master himself. A vigorous defender of Christianity against infidelity, he also was a living example of spiritual growth in a man of working-class origins who had moved from youthful skepticism to mature Christian faith. As Smith and Hopkins walked side by side along the winding roads of Rockdale, they demonstrated for all to see the Christian fellowship of the worker and the capitalist.

The Congregation

By 1841, when Lee was called away to Wilmington to serve as the first Bishop of Delaware, the organization of Calvary Church was complete, with a rector and a vestry (even though this was technically a mission), two wardens (one of them Smith), and a loyal congregation.

The congregation in the initial period from 1834 through 1844 included on the average members of at least seventy-five or eighty households. There were nineteen contributors from fifteen families to the original building fund at Easter in 1838. They paid amounts ranging from $2 from working people to $10 from Richard S. Smith. This fee entitled the donor to the right to worship and "all of the privileges of the Church & of the burial ground." Bishop Onderdonk, at the time of the dedication of the new church in July 1838, confirmed a class of twenty-five new members, and he confirmed two more classes in 1839, together amounting to thirty-four persons. Some of those confirmed had already contributed to the building fund; and there were several families with more than one member undergoing confirmation. There were a number of baptisms and marriages in this early period too, many of them involving persons who neither contributed nor were confirmed in Rockdale; and among the first wardens and vestrymen were some persons who were not mentioned as contributors and who were not confirmed at Rockdale. By the end of Lee's ministry, he and his predecessor had confirmed a total of 135 new members of the church and he listed 77 communicants.

Clearly the congregation included a core of persons who were already confirmed Episcopalians. Some of these, like the Smiths, were well-established members of the Church when they moved to the Rockdale district; others were old residents of Aston and Middletown townships, who had been accustomed to worship (weather and the roads permitting) at St. John's in Concord and St. Paul's in Chester, both five miles or so away, and now found it more convenient to attend Calvary. This old-resident group certainly included Isaac C. Derrick, Smith's co-warden, a prosperous farmer and head of a large family who lived at Village Green. The already confirmed Episcopalians, both new residents (about eighteen families) and old (about seven families), would be entitled to present their children for baptism, to be married in the church, and to be buried in the churchyard without further ado. Thus some of the new confirmations were simply young adults from families in which the parents were already confirmed. Parents in about twenty-five families joined confirmation classes and were brought into the church in 1838 and 1839. And there were certainly a considerable number of other families—one might estimate about twenty-five—who had a connection with the church that did not include full membership, such as attending Sunday services, sending children to the Sunday School, presenting children for baptism with a regular member as sponsor, being married to a regular member, and perhaps even being buried in the church cemetery. Some of these persons were members of other denominations who found it difficult to travel the distances required to worship elsewhere. Many of the unaffiliated, as time went on, no doubt were confirmed, and probably the size of the confirmed congregation grew to include members of as many as a hundred families. But the population's mobility was so high that as one family joined, another left the district, and an accurate measure of the congregation's size would have been difficult to accomplish even then.

The social composition of the congregation seems essentially to have involved two classes: a group whom one can call the local gentry and a group of mill operatives and domestic servants. There seem to have been relatively few ordinary farmers and mechanics. The gentry were the substantial farmers, like Warden Derrick, and a set of mill owners and manufacturers: the Richard S. Smith family; the families of Joshua and John Garsed of Penn's Grove; the family of James Houghton, also of Penn's Grove; and young Daniel, Ferdinand, Eleanora, and Eugenia Lammot (who did not follow closely their parents' Swedenborgian preferences). The working people included the Pattersons, who worked as domestic servants for the Smiths, and a large number of operatives' families. Many of these were English- or Irish-born and a number were widows' households.

Let us take for example Elizabeth Standring (age sixty-two years in 1840) as head of a fatherless household that included a boy fifteen to twenty, a woman twenty to thirty, and a girl fifteen to twenty. From 1844 to 1846, Riddle's mill employed an Elizabeth Standring (probably a daughter) as a weaver; the same mill also employed a James Standring (listed under the same ledger number and probably her son) until December 1844. James Standring and his sisters moved out of the Rockdale district before 1850, for no one by the name of Standring was listed there in the census of that year.

Another case of a Christian widow's household is that of English-born Elizabeth Taylor. In 1836, when she was fifty-one, she and her husband Joshua presented their six-year-old son Joseph for baptism by Rector Hirst. Joshua died (or left) in the next year or two. In 1838 Elizabeth contributed in her own name to the building fund; she was confirmed in 1839; and her teen-age daughters Mary and Hannah were baptized the next year. In 1850, at sixty-five, she was living with Hannah, a weaver, and her son James, also

CALVARY CHURCH.

a weaver, in Middletown. Evidently James and Elizabeth both moved, for neither was buried in Calvary churchyard.

And still another instance is presented by John and Rachel Cardwell, aged thirty-two and twenty-three, both of them Irish-born and recently married, who in 1840 presented their newborn daughter, Sarah, for baptism. Ten years later, John Cardwell was working as a weaver at Penn's Grove and his family had expanded by the addition of four more children. None of this family of Cardwells was buried at Calvary; they probably moved out of the district in the 1850's.

Because of the frequency of removals from the district, the uncertain vicissitudes of records, and the ambiguities of names, it is not possible to learn much about most of the other working-class families who were associated with Calvary Church in the early years. But from these few examples, and others about whom census or employment data survive, it is clear that most of the people in the congregation were from working-class households, with the mother living and working at home and husband or children working as operatives in the local cotton mills. It was these people who filled the pews at worship service and whose children came to the Sunday School in the basement, who made up the bulk of the confirmation classes, and who called upon the rector for the sacraments. It was the manufacturers and landowners who served as wardens, as vestrymen, and as representatives to the diocesan convention in Philadelphia.[16]

The Message from Calvary

In addition to performing the sacraments, a Protestant Episcopal rector had another duty: he was expected to deliver at least one sermon every Sunday, or to arrange for a "supply." The balance of his emphasis between ritual and preaching determined whether the minister was high church or low church. The Reverend Mr. Lee was a low church man. A slender, scholarly young man of thirty-one, he had graduated from Harvard Phi Beta Kappa and was near the top of his class. He had practiced law for several years before entering a theological seminary, and had been ordained only a few months before. He had been recommended to the Smiths by the Reverend Dr. Clemson, the rector of the church in Chester, who had met him while Lee was traveling for his health, and in September 1838 Lee had visited the Smiths in Rockdale. There he met and was approved by Bishop Hopkins. Upon accepting the ministry at Rockdale, the young rector, with his wife, two children, and two domestics, being unable to find a comfortable house in the neighborhood, was invited to live with the Smiths. As Smith expressed it in later years, the two households made "a most happy family circle," and "the love and affection then commenced" continued for the rest of their lives.

In the years after he left Rockdale to become the Bishop of Delaware, Lee became a prolific author of works on Christian subjects; well versed in Greek and Hebrew, he assisted in the preparation of the revised version of the New Testament which was issued in 1881. He prepared his sermons carefully—a severe trial for him, for his eyes were weak and sore, and he depended upon Mrs. Lee to read to him and act as his amanuensis. Many were to be printed later, some by his former congregation at Rockdale. But, although they were elegant in composition and erudite in their allusions to scientific knowledge and to classical literature, their rhetoric was evangelical. He was at all times conscious that his duty was preaching sinners to repentance and salvation. He held before the congregation the nature of sin—infidelity, the envy of others' prosperity, the frequenting of taverns, gambling houses, and haunts of vice—and its awful consequences—eternal torment. He pictured the satisfaction of repentance, of placing one's faith not in the world but in the love of God, and of confidently awaiting, at life's end, translation into a realm of eternal and peaceful joy. And not only this; God would reward His servants in this life as well:

The Lord honors his young servants by giving them favor in the sight of men, attracting them to love, confidence and esteem.

. . . They who seek first the honor that cometh from God, who act upon convictions of right and duty, who pursue the straight-forward course of virtue and obedience to God, inspire the confidence and command the respect of society. They are trusted and beloved. They are honored in prosperity. They are befriended and assisted in adversity. Even those who oppose and dislike religion are constrained to admire it when fairly and consistently presented in the daily life.[17]

Lee was ever aware that he was actively opposed by enemies of religion. In his "Farewell Discourse" to the Calvary congregation in September 1841, he not only adjured his flock to be consistent in Christian conduct, as he had taught them "publicly, and from house to house." He also warned them not to believe "the slanders so often spread abroad by the enemies of religion." He deplored the fact that "these who call themselves Christians [are] broken into sects and parties almost innumerable," and noted that "the infidel and scoffer seize upon the inconsistencies of Christians, as a matter of railing accusation against the gospel."[18]

The new rector was, in fact, attempting to launch a revival of religion in the Rockdale district by a type of preaching and personal counsel which created intense anxiety. It was very effective. One Sunday afternoon Mr. Lee preached from the text to be found in Acts, Chapter XVI, verses 30 and 31: "Sirs, what must I do to be saved? And they said, Believe on the Lord Jesus Christ and thou shalt be saved, and thy house." Lee went on in a solemn way to represent "the unwillingness of the human heart to receive this doctrine and rely upon it." After church the people sang "Jesus Saviour of my Soul," and "many of the congregation appeared to be much impressed." Next Sunday, Clementina reported to Sophie, "Mr. Lee preached the most admirable discourse I have heard from him." She went on to describe with pious satisfaction the spreading of religious fervor in the congregation:

Coming out of church I saw a young person very much affected so much so she could not repress her tears, she told me the cause of her grief was that she was so great a sinner she did not know what would become of her. There are many in this frame of mind among the congregation. I know how much you will rejoice with holy joy to hear of repenting sinners.[19]

By the spring of 1841, Clementina and Sophie were congratulating one another on the success of the Rockdale mission. Clementina exulted:

The state of things & the spiritual state of the people at Rockdale, is most encouraging—I never heard anything like it, except in Baxter's charge at Kidderminster where I believe he preached to a congregation of renewed people.[20]

And Sophie confided to Clementina that Ferdinand Lammot had told her "that the congregation was already too large for the church, & that they spoke of adding to the building."[21] It was, indeed, in large part because of Lee's reputation for evangelical success in a difficult working-class mission that he was, in 1841, elected Bishop of Delaware, with headquarters in Wilmington.[22]

After Lee's departure, his successors were supervised by Bishop Alonzo Potter of Chester, a learned clergyman who had a close interest in congregations of laboring people. Potter had been Professor of Moral Philosophy at Union College in New York and was the author of *The Principles of Science*, a popular book first published in 1841, aimed at tradesmen and apprentices. In this work he celebrated the recent progress of industry and the dignity of labor; he compared the hierarchical organization of the cotton mill to the Great Chain of Being. Potter was a perennial favorite speaker at mechanics' institutes and had lectured to the operatives at Lowell.[23]

But Lee's zealous ministry and Potter's interest in the spiritual advancement of workers were only half the story of the revival at Rockdale. The other half was the Sunday School which the Smith ladies administered and taught. Clementina and Harriet, and their mother, launched the operation on a Saturday afternoon in October 1833 with a magic lantern exhibition in the old nail factory; "the children & parents were highly gratified." Clementina busied herself with the administrative problems of collecting books and tracts and arranging for teachers. The school gained about twenty regular attenders during the summer but it lapsed during the winter when the Smiths went back to the city. They returned in the spring, redoubling their efforts, and by 1836 the school seems to have been fully established, with about 120 scholars; in 1838, there were 150 scholars, 15 teachers, and a library of 300 volumes.[24] Clementina complained to Sophie that forty-two of them "were commited to my attention in the Infant School, which I concluded was no desirable undertaking." Indeed, with major responsibility for the Sunday School falling to her, and with her duties as church organist requiring her to practice as well as perform, Clementina felt herself to be overworked.

The school was organized into three classes: an infant school, a boys' school, and a girls' school. Later on there would be classes for young adults as well, but of that more later. The general model for the school was, of course, the Brandywine Manufacturers' Sunday School, which had been organized and led by Victorine Bauduy since 1816. Clementina during her summers with Sophie along the Brandywine had served as a teacher in this school. It was nonsectarian, accepting children whose parents were Catholics, Episcopalians, Presbyterians, or in fact of any religious persuasion (including outright indifference). There the ladies instructed the young in the elementary skills of reading, writing, and arithmetic, and taught them some of the basic principles of Christian belief and practice.[25] Although the Calvary Sunday School was conducted under the auspices of the Protestant Episcopal Church, there is every reason to think that it too was relatively nonsectarian in its approach, in accordance with the ecumenical nature of Lee's views and the anti-sectarian philosophy of the community's leadership. Probably, however, it was more openly religious in its style than the Brandywine, for the Pennsylvania law of 1836 providing free public education for all children enabled the Sunday Schools to concentrate on religious subjects.

Some of the children who attended the Calvary School were former scholars from the Brandywine. This was so with the Miles family; it is worth recording their case in some detail, for it illustrates the profound moral impact which the intimate relationship between the Du Pont and the Smith ladies and their charges had on some of the growing young people in the community.

Mrs. Sarah Miles, a widow and a Methodist, appears in the record book of the Brandywine Manufacturers' Sunday School in 1829, when she is recorded as having entered her three children, Maria, age fifteen; Sarah, age ten; and William Sampler, age seven. In October 1831 the family removed to the Rockdale district. Mrs. Miles was in very poor health, suffering from consumption, and Maria worked in a mill to support the family. One of the Du Ponts, on visiting the Lammots at Lenni in preparation for a wedding, looked up the Miles family and found that Maria wanted to talk to her former teacher Sophie. So a meeting was arranged for nine o'clock in the morning a few weeks later. Sophie put a very careful account of the occasion in her diary:

Accordingly after breakfast I was called out of the parlour, & told a girl wanted me—I found my poor Maria, seated in the kitchen, terrified & shrinking from the noisy bustling assembly of servants. To talk to her there was impossible. I first asked her to come upstairs. Her timidity made her fear to do so, which instantly perceiving, I led her out into the yard, where we conversed some time. Maria's humility, the piety she evinced, her tearful eyes, & simple expressions of affection for me, touched me deeply. I could not help contrasting the scene, the conversation, the *feelings* it inspired, with those of the gay houses the night before, & I deeply felt that for my self, happiness was more to be found in the humble hope of having directed or encouraged a fellow being in the way of peace; than in all the laughter, & dresses & noise & folly the world calls gaiety. . . . Maria was sad—she said her mothers health was bad—she said she wished extremely I would have come to see her mother—I wished it too—I gave her my little hymn book, she was much gratified—she opened her bag to put it in, observing at the same time "This is the bag you gave me, I have kept as well as I could" & in truth, she has kept it as well as I could, it looks like new—I spoke to her of our eternal interests, I reminded her, tho' here we might meet no more, yet we had the same Home in view, where we would be in a little while—She wept so much she could scarcely say goodbye, but pressed my hand warmly, & so we parted—I love to think of this visit.[26]

A year later, after spending a day in Rockdale, Clementina told Sophie that Mrs. Miles was now gravely ill, and so the two women went to visit. Again Sophie, deeply moved by the experience, recorded the event in detail in her diary:

She is evidently in a consumption, & was confined to her bed since many weeks—she spoke of her illness & its probably fatal result with the calm resignation & hope of a Christian. But one thing troubled her, she said: it was, to leave her girls in a place so unsuitable to their moral welfare, without guide or protector—She said she had greatly desired to see me that she might request me to be a friend to her Maria, after death had removed her last parent. She thought that she should leave them in such easy circumstances, that they being industrious girls, could get their own living very well. She hoped that they would have saved enough to be able to learn a trade & be set up in it. But then, who would give them advice? Who would direct their minds beyond this world's gain, to the attainment of treasures for eternity. Who would counsel them to follow in the narrow way that leadeth to everlasting life?—She said that she knew I had been a true friend to Maria & given her the best of advice when she was my scholar—All she asked was, that if Maria came to me when she was gone, I would give her the same counsel & instructions I gave then. I promised her that I would, as far as it might be in my power—And I gave Maria *then* such advice as my brief time allowed—I was much touched &, I trust, benefitted, by the mother's converse—I thanked my God who had made me the instrument of giving some comfort to her last hours by the knowledge there was *one* who would care for her Maria's *soul*—& I prayed that I might be of use to the poor Girl. But I found *her* changed from the meek, drooping, yet frank & affectionate girl I used to instruct. There was a certain carelessness about her, & sometimes a smile rather sneering altho' she appeared really rejoiced to see me, & tho' she wept much when I spoke of her Mother's illness—still, when I dwelt on religious subjects, the aspect of her face was changed from that reverential interest it used to wear—This pained me, for I knew she worked in the mill of one who was an open Infidel & whose workmen were very worthless! Poor Girl, I trust she may yet be saved from the dangers that surround her, & be a true disciple of our blessed Lord—[27]

The "open Infidel" in whose mill Maria worked was, as we noted earlier, John S. Phillips.

In order to save Maria, after her mother's death a year or so later, Sophie decided that she and her sister Sarah should learn the milliner's trade. She was able, "after a good deal of difficulty," to get them a good situation in Wilmington, with board and room with a respectable family. But after learning the trade they went back to Rockdale to work in the mills anyway, "as they made more money." Although Maria was not listed as being connected with Calvary Church, Sophie reported with satisfaction that her conduct remained "always highly satisfactory" and "she continued pious." Sarah, however, "attended long the Sunday School at Rockdale," where she gave evidence of being really interested in religion.[28]

Another family of Brandywine scholars who moved to Rockdale were the Millers. In 1830 Henry Miller, a forty-five-year-old German-born Presbyterian, a weaver by trade, and his thirty-five-year-old wife Margery entered their daughter Sarah, age eight, in the Brandywine Manufacturers' Sunday School. Eight years later the family moved to Rockdale and Sarah carried with her a card of recommendation to Calvary Sunday School. In 1839 the Millers had their new son Bartholomew baptized and in the same year Sarah and another daughter, Hannah, were confirmed. Hannah and Sarah worked as weavers at Penn's Grove in the 1840's. In 1850 the family was still residing in the neighborhood, the father now retired and living with his wife and five of his children, including Sarah, who was thirty-four and still unmarried. They seem to have been supported by their twenty-six-year-old wheelwright son.[29]

The school had its ups and downs, for Elizabeth Smith, Clementina, and Harriet were frequently away, spending the winter in the city and part of the summer vacationing. Sometimes it was not possible to recruit sufficient teachers and for a while the boys' department was closed for want of an instructor. But nonetheless the operation was a great success, and Clementina and Harriet continued to help the school until their deaths in 1884 and 1905.

Calvary Sunday School's importance to the community was made conspicuous in its triumphant management of the Rockdale district's Fourth of July celebration in 1837. Ordinarily, in this period, the Fourth of July was a day of disorderly political picnics; innumerable long-winded toasts were drunk to the heroes of the Revolution and of subsequent transactions, including such figures of infidelity as Byron, the martyr of Missolonghi; the saloons were open and the roads were crowded with rowdy men and women. The Smiths and the rest of Calvary's congregation made the Fourth of July of 1837 an occasion of a different sort. No less than six hundred Sunday School scholars and their teachers assembled for a religious celebration; about the same number of spectators were present.

In fact, virtually the entire population of the district must have gathered together in the open air to honor the nation's birthday. Clementina, writing to Sophie a month later, was still ecstatic over the sight of the community "uniting in a rational and proper celebration of the day." She said, "It was the happiest day I ever passed."[30]

Evangelical Womanhood

Clementina and Sophie were not the only members of the Rockdale sisterhood to take an active interest in religion; religion became almost a profession for some of them. The sisterhood were not feminists; their correspondence is bare of favorable mention of Fanny Wright and other early advocates of women's liberation. They did not, at least in writing, advocate female suffrage, or liberalization of the divorce laws, or restrictions of a husband's right to administer his wife's property, or female entry into the all-male professions. But they did press enthusiastically into the one niche in the occupational structure that was opening its doors wide to women. This niche was Christian evangelism, an enormous business which not merely permitted, but actively encouraged, the participation of women. The evangelical movement across the nation recruited thousands of women to work as Sunday School teachers, benevolent association organizers and fund raisers, musicians, tract distributors, visitors to prisons and almshouses, and home visitors in the domestic missionary field; as fund raisers for foreign missionary societies; and even as co-workers with their husbands in accessible foreign areas (which by the 1840's included parts of Europe, India, China, and Oceania). Although men generally directed all of these operations, they were genuine team efforts in which the female members played specialized and therefore indispensable roles. Nowhere else in American society (except in the mills themselves) could women be accepted by male associates as intellectual and moral equals.

The reasons for this acceptance of women in the evangelical movement were complex. It was not that in these settings men stood aside and turned "morality" over to the women, on the ground that by some constitutional predisposition women were the proper custodians of social virtue. The evangelical clergy claimed moral authority not only over the male laity but over women as well; the lay leaders at least conceded no superiority to women. It was rather that middle-class women were an indispensable source of educated hands to the work. Largely excluded from the professional and commercial worlds, bored by "housewifery" and "the nursery" (where most of the chores were done by servants and nurses anyway), they could dedicate twenty or so hours per week to the day-to-day work of evangelism, freeing the clergy for the more special tasks—administration, preaching, administering the sacraments, writing sermons and books, counseling—for which they had been trained. The work of conversion and reform yielded immediate rewards. It was done with real people in real communities and it had visible consequences in social change. It was done in company with real colleagues, male and female, with whom strategy and tactics, triumphs and defeats could be discussed face to face. In the evangelical movement, women were making a commitment to change the world.

There was, inevitably, a certain sexual tension inherent in this situation. Infidels and heathen men might not respect the female visitor's claim of chastity; how she would protect her virtue, without driving away the object of her benevolence, was a topic of considerable interest to the evangelical woman. The story which Clementina's ideal, Miss Harries, told in Boston, and which Clementina wrote out for Sophie's edification, revolved around precisely this dilemma, and is worth quoting here because Clementina regarded Miss Harries as an avatar of womanly perfection in the Lord's work, and her life's history as a kind of female *Pilgrim's Progress:*

Her ac't of the visit of a chief of the island of Balet where she was in the house alone, at midnight (for no earthly friend was near to care for her protection) was evidence how our Heavenly Father provides for the care of his weakest ones—in the tact and ability she displayed. She heard a knock at the door in the middle of the night, a night she said of deep depression and hardly knew what to do, in her loneliness but she felt as the knocking continued she must open the door, and instantly a rough grissly looking native, with only a girdle to cover his nakedness sprang in—She received him with a smile and apparent pleasure and much

formal politeness addressing him in his own language—He had a bowl
of buffaloe milk he said he had brought to the white woman hearing they
were fond of it, but the evident motive was curiousity to see her—She
then set herself to work to entertain him, though all the time very much
alarmed particularly when he asked if all her skin was as white as her face
—she put a bold face on the matter & instantly drew up her sleeve to
assure him it was, and in some of the accounts she gave him of our country
customs, that of churning with sheep he rolled over & over on the floor
& roared with laughter—I can give you but a trifling idea of all that lovely
lady said & hope I shall remember much to tell you, when we meet
dearest. (When we meet!!!) What a privilege it is on our earthly pilgrimage to meet such persons so highly gifted, so humble and so tried.[31]

Temptation presented itself also in the interactions between male and
female workers in the movement, particularly as they involved the clergyman and his female congregation and staff. Scandalous rumors were constantly afloat, implicating this or that minister and a female member of his
flock. Bishop Onderdonk of New York was publicly convicted of adultery
with one of his parishioners by an ecclesiastical court; and the Reverend Dr.
Tyng advised all young men in the ministry to be as circumspect as possible
and never to enter into even the most spiritual of discussions with a woman
alone. Perhaps tensions of this kind were among those that Clementina
meant when she replied, in a long and emotional letter, to Sophie's an-
guished report that she had been condemned to abstinence and invalidism
by a new physician's diagnosis in 1845:

My portion as you know has not been without trial of its kind and it is
only each individual heart that knoweth its own bitterness. I have had
trials of sin and temptation which you have never known (I believe) and
no words could express the gulf of my heart as I find myself yielding to
them—It almost overthrows my hope of adoption many times and makes
me fear that mine is only the hypocrite—My many privileges rise up as
fearful witnesses against me, and I cannot say that I have "My heart
sprinkled from an evil conscience"—I cannot say this to any but you
beloved or my dear Hattie, but do pray very earnestly for me dear Sophie
not for comfort, but that I may be enabled to overcome and inherit a
portion in Christ at last. I only want a steady single eye and a heart filled
with the *one* purpose to do God's will—You told me to tell you of myself
& I did not mean to do so when I began but you see that I have, instead
of comforting you, (which I so long to do) poured out the sorrows of my
own heart—[32]

The problem posed for the evangelical layman by the practical need to work in intimate comradeship with attractive women was perhaps more difficult than that of the clergyman, who was expected to maintain a certain reserve in the conduct of his religious duties. Those members of the male population who considered themselves to be by birth, breeding, and occupation "gentlemen" (and who were so considered by others) were often still guided, in their relations with women, by a moral standard and a set of beliefs about sexuality that had prevailed in England during the seventeenth and eighteenth centuries. In this view, women were not the inherently pure, gentle, but fragile vessels that a later generation believed them to be. To the contrary, they were as apt as men to be lusty, deceitful, and even violent; a good and intelligent woman was to be admired and respected for having achieved her character by much the same application of energy and determination as it required in a man. A gentleman, in turn, was expected to honor his female relations and women of character; but he was allowed, or even expected, to indulge his natural appetites with women of a lower category, whose status did not require respect for their sexual virtue. Such accessible females might be ostensibly virtuous but lonely wives and widows, or intelligent and educated courtesans, or servant girls, or whores, and the escalations of male gallantry and female response provided a more or less standardized gambit for distinguishing between the truly virtuous women and the ones who in varying degrees of readiness would surrender to temptation. The traditional gentleman thus could legitimately be something of a sexual sportsman in his spare time; womanizing was a kind of recreation, sharply distinct from the man's work, but taken seriously to the extent that here, as in other sports, the pursuit, and evidences of success in the hunt, involved masculine vanity and honor.

Although America was supposedly a simpler and more virtuous nation, where the amatory adventures of decadent aristocrats did not characterize the republican gentleman's life ("gentleman" here ideally being defined by such meritorious qualities as fairness, hospitality, and generosity rather than by birth, breeding, and occupation), the traditional sportsman's ideal was in fact very much alive. And, inevitably enough, it was more alive among infidels and populist politicians than among Christians and sober manufacturers. (The failure of the Enlightenment tradition to rationalize any real equality of the sexes was perhaps one of its major weaknesses in the ideological combat of the early nineteenth century.) A classic illustration of the public survival of the sporting gentleman image during this period is the widely rumored career of the beautiful Italian courtesan Amerigo Vespucci. This "black-eyed, well-formed Italian lady," allegedly a descendant of the Amerigo Vespucci for whom the continent was named, had come to the

United States in 1838 in hope of a congressional grant of public lands in appreciation of her ancestor's role in the country's history. She circulated interesting accounts of herself: that she (like Fanny Wright) had been the mistress of a revolutionary officer who fell in one of the battles to free Europe in the 1830's, that she had dressed as a man, that she had even fought in the same engagements. She bore a saber scar on her hand to prove it all true. The Biddle family introduced her to Philadelphia society and she was escorted about the city by the great Whig banker Nicholas Biddle. But Biddle's interest was friendly, fascinated—and platonic. Vespucci soon tired of Philadelphia and went on to Washington, where she met the Democratic President's son, "Prince" John Van Buren, one of the leaders of the more radical wing of the New York Democrats, and became his mistress. John Van Buren was a gentleman of the sporting type. Putting her up in the final hand of a high-stakes poker game, he lost her to a wealthy upstate New Yorker, who took her off as his "fancy woman" and kept her in "utter loneliness," so it was said, in his remote mansion at Ogdensburg, New York, along the St. Lawrence River.[33]

Against the model of the sporting gentleman, the evangelicals were in the process of creating a new image: that of the "Christian gentleman." Both sexes contributed to the formulation of this ideal. The Christian gentleman would be, of course, a *converted* Christian, fully sensible of his need for salvation and for justification by faith. But he would also be vigorous, hardworking, and successful in a professional, commercial, or manufacturing career; a contributor to missionary and reform causes; intelligent, well informed, and articulate. In his personal relations he would be trustworthy, humble, sincere, lively and amusing on social occasions yet fundamentally serious and concerned. In his dealings with women, he would regard the fair sex as man's complement, of a softer constitution but one of equal value, deserving always of respect, even in the case of those whom lowly birth, or financial disaster, or seduction by a philanderer had brought low. He would avoid consorting with prostitutes and other loose women before marriage and would be faithful to his wife after.

Evangelical women placed great pressure on their male friends and relatives to conform to this ideal. Sophie and Clementina pressed Samuel Francis Du Pont mercilessly, during the 1840's, until early in 1844 Sophie reported that he was having a religious awakening. Clemma responded (in italics): *"It is unmingled joy."*[34] After one visit to the Brandywine, Clementina said of her departure that it would be a relief to Sophie's husband to be able to "smoke his segar in peace."[35] But she dismissed their fears of offending him; a higher duty stood before them: "Our conduct and our conversations *ought* to condemn the worldly minded around us, and if it *does,* we cannot hold the place we desire in their estimation, we want to make our religion amiable, forgetting the impossibility of this."[36]

At last he surrendered and in April 1849 was confirmed by Bishop Lee in Wilmington. Although Sophie was not present, at the bishop's command ("the excitement might have disabled her for the whole summer"), her victory was an enduring one. Samuel Francis Du Pont became an evangelical worker, too, supporting foreign missions and requiring Christian services on board his ships.

The women of the Chester Creek-Brandywine sisterhood pressed Christianity on others as well, sometimes with success and sometimes without. Sophie's sister Eleuthera contributed to the conversion of their brother Alexis. Alexis became an ardent evangelical, and he and Victorine nearly precipitated a family feud by insisting on the construction of a church on Du Pont company grounds. (Alfred du Pont, a nonsectarian of deistical leanings, clung angrily to the old family policy that forbade the promulgation of *sectarian* religion on their business property.) Those who persistently refused to submit to conversion, and who defied the ideal of the Christian gentleman in other ways, were subjected to heavy sanctions indeed: they were silently excluded from the list of men eligible to marry members of the group (and thus excluded from reproductive and educational participation as well). Clementina, for instance, dismissed a potential male admirer airily as "a Unitarian, and apparently indifferent to religion, not a man of cultivated mind."[37]

But the courtships of John S. Phillips provide the best case in point. At first, in their view, arrogant and inconsiderate, boastful and excessively gallant (unlike the *"good* humble Mr. Lee"), then sickly, depressed, and contrite, he was made a figure of fun in the private communications of the sisterhood, as "Val de Peñas," the Knight of Rockdale. As word of his rejections spread, his addresses, already deemed painfully boring, became demeaning as well, and one after another the objects of his attention—Sophie, Eleanora Lammot, Joanna Smith, Clementina, and Harriet—turned him away with pity. The fate of Phillips testifies to the power of evangelical womanhood, in the 1830's and 1840's, to control the system of marriage in well-to-do Christian families. Phillips was a gentleman; but he was not, in their opinion, a truly *Christian* gentleman.

THE BENEVOLENT WORK
OF OTHER MANUFACTURERS

Although Calvary Church was the leading religious institution in the Rockdale district, ministering to Protestants generally, members of other denominations contributed along their own lines to the evangelical effort. There were Baptists, Methodists, Presbyterians, Swedenborgians, and Catholics in the district, and the manufacturers attempted, in one way or another, to provide for their needs.

John P. Crozer and the Baptist Sunday School

John P. Crozer was a Baptist who had been converted in his youth by the Reverend Dr. William Staughton. Staughton was, like so many of the influential evangelical leaders, a man of education and intellectual accomplishment as well as a spellbinding preacher. He had been a minor published poet in his early years; he had earned his Doctor of Divinity at Princeton; he edited an edition of Virgil and prepared a Greek dictionary. From 1823 to 1827 he was Chaplain of the U.S. Senate; before he died in 1829 he had been president of two colleges. It was an image of the *educated* Christian that Staughton projected; and Crozer, who was not well schooled himself, believed profoundly in a Christian education.[1]

So also did his wife. She had been brought up along Ridley Creek, not far from the mill, and although nominally an Episcopalian had for several years before her marriage been a member of a small informal congregation of Baptists there. She "often raised the hymns in public worship" and taught in the Sunday School, which, as she told her sons, "was under the Robert Raikes plan, that is, it was intended to teach the ignorant to read and write, with a religious influence." (It was Raikes's ideas that also had inspired the Du Ponts to found the Brandywine Manufacturers' Sunday School and thus indirectly the school at Rockdale.)[2]

When the Crozers arrived at West Branch in 1825, there was no school closer than Village Green and all schools were private "pay-schools." In order to induce his workers to remain during periods of unemployment, Crozer found that an effective tactic was to pay out of his own pocket their children's school fees. But these schools provided a purely secular education. Nor were there frequent opportunities for religious worship in the neighborhood, either for the mill workers or the Crozers. As Crozer recalled it years later: "We went to places of worship irregularly. There was no stated preaching near except at Mount Hope (Methodist), one and a half miles distant; and alas! we were not under a strong religious influence. I look back on this part of our life with grief."[3] It was not until some years had gone by, and the cotton factory was beginning to bring them a more comfortable income, that the Crozers began to think seriously again of church and school.

The first renewed conscientious church attendance by the Crozers was at the tiny Baptist church in Marcus Hook, five or six miles away on the banks of the Delaware. This church was only 25 feet square. Crozer's son Samuel recalled the place with mixed feelings:

It was old and dried up, as it appeared to me. There were few young people in attendance, and the singing was execrable, but there were some very good old people in the congregation, which was small. . . . Rev. Joseph Walker preached there for many years and without salary. He had, I think, no theological training, but received a collegiate education. Perhaps no man ever lived who felt more strongly "woe is me if I preach not the gospel." Originally a country merchant, he conducted his business with success, and then felt called on to preach, continuing the two employments. Finally he abandoned the store, and devoted his life to God's service. He would preach morning and evening at Marcus Hook, and ride five miles to West Branch in the afternoon, and preach in the building erected by my father. I also remember that Mr. Richard S. Smith, an Episcopal gentleman, had a room cleaned up in an old nail factory at Rockdale, and Mr. Walker preached there. This grew into the Episcopal church at that place. He had an intimate acquaintance with the Bible, and was one of the salt of the earth.[4]

By about 1832, the Crozers began to think of establishing a Sunday School. They encouraged a young Presbyterian clergyman, then located in the neighborhood as an assistant to the aging pastor, to stay in the area and revitalize an old and decaying Presbyterian church called Mount Gilead or the Blue Church, which had originally been constructed to serve the needs of the Scots-Irish workmen at Old Sarum Forge a few miles to the north. It was located in a neighborhood called Logtown, not far from West Branch, and its Irish-born pastor was famous for his strong sermons on the subject of temperance. The Crozers, as nominal Baptists, were committed to temperance by church doctrine anyway, and Crozer found himself drawn to Presbyterianism. He took an interest in denominational politics in Philadelphia and became active in the affairs of the Middletown Presbyterian Church, of which Mount Gilead was an outpost. Middletown Presbyterian was one of the oldest churches in the countryside, having been founded in 1720, and its present building dated back to 1766. In 1842

Crozer gave an address at Middletown Presbyterian and spoke warmly of the ancient edifice and its builders:

This ancient edifice, truly venerable in appearance, was erected by godly men, who have for three-quarters of a century slept in death. This is one of the oldest places of worship in the whole country and its substantial and venerable walls testify that the yeomanry by whom they were erected were willing to honor God with their substance, and in that day when farm-houses were of the plainest and simplest kind, they were willing to pay for a large and commodious edifice, and dedicate it to the worship of Almighty God.[5]

Crozer's remarks were made at a time when the Presbytery of Philadelphia was (in his words) making "some attempt to impress life into these decaying churches." And, in truth, both churches were sadly in need of inspiration, for in 1835 the Crozers' friends the Landises left Mount Gilead, and in 1839 its pastor was trampled to death by his horse. "Mount Gilead," Crozer wrote his friend, "looks very desolate I fear that it is destined to remain in its present forlorn state." Early in 1842 Middletown Presbyterian lost its minister too and for the next four years was to be dependent upon "supplies."[6]

With the departure of the Landises, Crozer seems to have determined to take matters into his own hands at West Branch. In 1836 he built a commodious chapel, 60 by 40 feet in plan, to house a Sunday School and to provide a place where visiting clergymen, such as the pastor from Marcus Hook, could occasionally preach. The Smiths were delighted to hear of the new school at West Branch, "where it is very much needed," and they responded gladly when Crozer invited them to march their scholars the two miles along Mount Road to West Branch for a ceremonial opening in February 1837. The core of the occasion was a lecture on the subject of Sunday Schools. As Clementina described it:

. . . we assembled 90 children and walked over in procession to the chapel. The children sang the 110th hymn very sweetly & were very suitably addressed by a Mr. Chaugis from Delaware. I trust the example of our school will induce some to follow it and Mr. Crozer will succeed in his undertaking.[7]

Crozer assumed the responsibility of superintendent of the new Sunday School, and probably Mrs. Crozer, already experienced in Sunday School work, served as one of the teachers. It used the standard publications of the American Sunday School Union (of which Crozer was later to become a member of the board), which started the children off with a primer and spelling book, carried them forward with first-, second-, and third-class readers, and gradually exposed them to readings from the testaments. Samuel Crozer years after recalled the method of teaching Bible verses to little children:

Tickets were likewise given us for committal to memory of God's word. When I was a child, we received one ticket for each seven verses recited, and when they accumulated to three hundred and sixty, a Bible was presented. I remember also I received my Bible. I am of the opinion that memorizing God's word was more prevalent in olden times than at present.[8]

It is difficult to estimate the success of Crozer's school. A few months after its opening, in testifying before a Pennsylvania Senate committee investigating the employment of children in manufactories, he strongly emphasized the value of the combination of religious and secular instruction, and (although modestly omitting his own name) drew attention to the usefulness of his own enterprise at West Branch:

Considerable attention is now given to Sabbath School instruction, at the factories of Chester creek, and its influence promises to be extensive upon the whole; the religious, moral, and social condition of the factories there, is advancing, particularly amongst the young women and children, including the boys under fifteen years of age.

The common school system is adopted in our township, and the school directors are desirous to make it efficient; two of the schools are located near the factories. An owner of one of the factories, built at his own expense, a house for Sabbath schools, and occasionally, a place of worship, or lecture room, the basement story of which, he has given free of rent to the school directors of the district, in order to give the children in his employ, increased opportunity of education, by bringing the school to their residence.[9]

When the Crozers moved in 1839 to a house near a new factory at Crozerville, they apparently brought their Sunday School with them, conducting it in their own home. The original chapel became in effect one of the public schools and its religious functions were eclipsed; certainly no regularly organized Baptist congregation developed in West Branch, although as late as 1848 "West Branch Chapel" still was to be found in Ash's map of Delaware County, at the site of the Crozer's former mansion. After the closing of West Branch Chapel, the Crozers rented pews and worshipped at Calvary Church.

Crozer's other contributions to the religious and moral development of the district consisted of serving on committees of the local chapters of larger benevolent societies. He was, as early as 1829, a member of the Board of Managers of the Delaware County Bible Society, whose goal it was to place a copy of the Scriptures in every dwelling in the county. In this work he was associated with the various clergymen and county court officers who were active in evangelical and reform causes. The Bible Society, finding only about three hundred families destitute of the Bible, placed a copy in each household and went out of business in 1830. But the same men now organized themselves into the Delaware County Tract Society, which distributed the nonsectarian Christian classics published by the American Tract Society. In 1838, when the Aston Township Committee of the Temperance Reform Association of Delaware County was organized with two hundred members, Crozer and Alfred Lee were two of the founders. The Society met on occasion at Calvary Church, to hear addresses on missionary topics and to collect money (at a meeting in June 1841, for instance, the collection at Calvary amounted to $63.36).[10]

James Riddle and the Methodists

The Riddle brothers were not united in their religious affiliations. Samuel was a nominal Presbyterian, as befitted a Scots-Irishman; but he was not noted for zealousness in the faith at this period of his life, and the Presbyterian churches at Middletown and Mount Gilead were in a languishing condition anyway. His younger brother James, however, had been converted to Methodism as a young man before leaving Ireland, and on his arrival on Chester Creek he associated himself with old Mount Hope Church. He was the more scholarly of the two, devoting his spare time in his early years to "reading and religious exercises," and amassing a substantial library.[11]

Mount Hope was one of the oldest congregations in Delaware County, dating back to 1807, when Aaron Mattson, the paper manufacturer, donated land on Aston Ridge for a cemetery and a strictly Methodist meetinghouse. Before this, the local Methodists had met at Mattson's house on the hill overlooking West Branch (the same house later to be the Crozers' home). The congregation had been formed when the district was primarily agricultural; thus it included, in addition to the patron Mattson, the McCrackens (a prosperous English farming family who among other things did hauling for the Riddles) and a number of local millers, lumber dealers, and substantial farmers.[12]

Shortly after the Riddles arrived in 1832, the church at Mount Hope was the scene of a revival led by the itinerant English revivalist James

Caughey. As a result of his inspirational sermon, Methodism enjoyed a marked revival in the Rockdale district.[13] The congregation at Mount Hope expanded so much that a new church, across the creek in Middletown, was organized, and in 1838 Mount Hope itself was enlarged. James Riddle became the lay preacher of the new Lima Methodist Church, although he retained his original membership at Mount Hope. He was relieved by ordained ministers from the Chester Circuit in 1835.[14]

About 1839 James married a Quaker lady and at the same time moved to the Leiper estate at Avondale, on Crum Creek, where he operated a cotton mill in partnership. In 1844 he purchased the old Gilpin estates on the Brandywine and the family removed to Kentmere. But, until he built a Methodist chapel along the Brandywine, he retained his membership at Mount Hope Methodist Church, and served on the board of the Delaware County Tract Society. He apparently was ordained after the removal and bore the title "Reverend." The family genealogist recorded:

> He has been heard to say he had two calls: one to preach the gospel, and the other to manufacture cotton goods; and he was one of the few who proved successful in both. He occupied a very leading position among the local preachers of his denomination, and was president of their National Convention in 1864. Being a natural and forcible speaker, his pulpit and platform efforts were received with great favor. Not forgetting in the tide of business the calls of duty, he provided well for the moral and religious welfare of his tenants.[15]

The Society of Friends

The mill owners and manufacturers who were members of evangelical denominations—Smith, Garsed, Houghton, Crozer, and James Riddle— were the leaders in building new religious institutions in the community. Those who belonged to denominations that were not evangelical—at least not at this point in their history—were less active.

There were numbers of Quakers in the district, for many of the original settlers had been members of the Society of Friends, and their descendants still lived on the large farms and plantations in the area. There were monthly meetings at Chichester, to the south, and at Concord and Middletown, to the north. But few if any of the workers in the mills were Quakers, either local or migrant. And anyway the Society of Friends was rent by the bitter internal struggles of the Hicksite schism, which left little energy for missionary efforts. Indeed, perhaps the last Quaker missions from Delaware County had been to the Seneca Indians in northwestern New York and

Pennsylvania, where in a little settlement called Tunessassa Quaker families had lived since 1798, teaching the Indians the practical arts of agriculture, raising cattle, and keeping up a family farm in the white man's style.[16] Thomas Dutton, the tanner who supplied the belts for the local cotton factories, had managed the farm at Tunessassa from 1808 to 1813; after that he took charge of the county poorhouse for four years before returning to his tanning business.[17] Edward Darlington, the owner of the mill at Knowlton from 1829 to 1832, was a Quaker, but he was more concerned with law and politics than religious enthusiasm.

Daniel Lammot, the New Church, and Fourierism

Daniel Lammot, Jr., at Lenni, was still a Swedenborgian, although he and his family worshipped at Calvary Church, as well as at the newly built Church of the New Jerusalem on Darby Creek, near the Sellers estates.[18] Probably so also was Dr. Gideon Humphrey, the homeopathic practitioner of Village Green whom the Lammots and occasionally the Smiths called upon (and who sometimes treated the Riddles' employees when they were sick or injured).[19] The Swedenborgian faith, which had so excited Lammot when he lived in Philadelphia, was millennialist in philosophy, holding that the millennial age had already begun. But it was not evangelical in practice. It was very much an élitist religion, offering experimental church services and promulgating new and unusual Christian doctrines of a generally Unitarian character, which required extensive study and which were difficult for simple Bible-reading working-class people to understand. Furthermore the "New Church," still establishing itself in America and in the throes of angry factional disputes over church governance, was in danger of being subverted by the socialist doctrines of Robert Owen and Fanny Wright. Thus the immediate task for conservative Swedenborgians like Lammot was not to bring the working people to Christ but to keep the radicals from taking over the New Church while its bickering factions looked away from the Temple.

Lammot had been especially busy in 1824 and 1825 when radical propagandists swept through Philadelphia. "New Light" Quakers had preached before his congregation, denying the divinity of Christ. His minister, the Reverend Mr. Maskell W. Carl, and another, the Reverend Mr. Roche, listened to Owen lecture in 1824. Roche was so much impressed that he tried to start a community in Bucks County. Lammot regarded Roche's enthusiasm for socialist experiments as naïve and confided to a friend:

I fear Mr. Roches plan of establishing a New Church commonwealth will lead to the injury of his friends. Knowing but little I shall not say much on the subject: yet it is not difficult to see that with $50,000 very little could be done in the establishment of the different manufactures contemplated—the erection of the necessary dwellings & other improvements & the purchase of land whereon to commence the Commonwealth. I understand that Mr. Owen expended 10,000 pounds sterling on his New Lanark establishment.[20]

This same friend, speaking of another vulnerable Swedenborgian, said that "a Mr. S." worshipped an idol—and that idol was Fanny Wright. Lammot approved of the evaluation.[21] The Mr. S. in question was David Simmons, a gentleman farmer of Bucks County, who actually offered his farm as the site for the community, claiming $10,000 thereby as his investment. But Roche and Simmons could not recruit enough people to complete the capital fund and the plan was abandoned.

Once out on Chester Creek, Lammot's concern over the state of the New Church continued. In 1840 he brought out the Philadelphia minister Robert de Charms to christen the infants and to administer the New Jerusalem sacraments to the grown-up children, including "even Ferdinand."[22] In 1843 he felt obliged to take a stand against Fourierism (though he had not read any of the works of Fourier) because so many in the New Church, particularly in New York City, were discussing the possibility of establishing Fourierist phalanxes. (New York was a center of dissemination of Fourierist doctrines, largely purged of their free-love content, through the writings of Charles Brisbane in Horace Greeley's New York *Tribune.*) The dalliance of Swedenborgians with the idea of religious community was not new. In England in the 1790's, as Lammot recalled, there had been a plan to establish a Utopian settlement on the West Coast of Africa, at Cape Masurado, close to where the Colonization Society had later attempted to plant its colony. But the plan fell through.

Lammot gave the subject of associations careful thought and concluded that, Owenite or Fourierist, they were neither practical nor spiritually desirable. His position was clear and articulate and, coming from a leading layman, no doubt influential. A few of the phalanxes that were organized on Fourierist lines had a substantial number of New Church adherents; but the movement within the church never fully matured as an official commitment:

The question presented to my mind on this subject has been what is the object of association? Is it to supply our wants our comforts or indulgences with less labour and more certainty or is it to help us forward in our regeneration? If it be for temporal purposes it must be viewed in that light, and its feasibility considered. What capitalist would place his money out of his reach and control without the prospect of gain commensurate with the risk of thus placing his funds? Out of church, I apprehend the scheme would not receive much favor, and in the church there are but few capitalists, and these few so far as I can judge would not submit their judgement and means to the management of persons who have not given evidence of capacity to ensure equal or greater success in the accumulation of capital. Success is the criterion by which capacity for business is judged.

That greater economy can be observed by a well regulated association than by families generally I admit; but why? because families have some love to gratify such as handsome habitations, furniture and clothing or luxurious indulgences and display in society, and to obtain this, every opposing consideration is forced to yield. All this is human nature, and for a season it may remain latent in an association, but will in time manifest itself and then the supposed grievance will be magnified by the consideration that restraints are imposed and liberty curtailed for in addition to the laws of the country, the laws of the association must be observed. All this will beget discontent, and will work out the distruction of the association. Very few of us consider any expenditure extravagant which lends to our gratification and any restraint upon such gratification will be felt as oppressive. . . . I may yet add that there are and ever will be grades in society and every parent desires to select associates for himself and family. Such selection cannot be made in an association and hence will arise dissatisfaction.[23]

MORAL ORDER IN THE MILLS

The ambience of religious revivalism in the manufacturing district did not suffuse the factories themselves with the spirit of Christian love. To be sure, in the mills certain realistic requirements of factory discipline, such as punctuality, subordination, and sobriety, could be rationalized in terms of traditional Protestant ethical conceptions. But they could also be rationalized in terms of technological necessity. The relationship between the evangelical propaganda to which the manufacturers subjected the workers on Sundays, and the actual regimen of work during the rest of the week, was complex, for the manufacturers were moved to maximize profit and minimize the expense of management as well as to promote Christian conduct.

A curious customary mixture of moralities in the factories was developing, with some management actions and attitudes clearly aiming at the moral improvement of workers and others indicating indifference. These mixed messages pertained to the presence—and sometimes the absence—of work rules.

Work Rules in Cotton Factories

Beyond those rules of thumb that operatives had to learn and practice in order to run the machines efficiently and safely, every factory had a set of rules of a more general kind, some of them vaguely moral and some explicitly so. Sometimes these rules were printed; often, printed or in long hand, they were posted in the factories; frequently (although not at Riddle's mill) new hands were required to sign them.[1] Violation of these rules was enforced by a system of punishments.

Some of the rules were safety regulations of an obviously necessary kind. At Parkmount—and no doubt in every establishment in the industry—there was a fixed rule against smoking inside the mill. Oil and cotton dust were all about; in some places they made an explosive mixture, which could be ignited by sparks from a pipe or cigar. Violation of this rule was grounds for discharge. Fighting in the mill could also lead to discharge, for it could result in lost time, inattention, and damage to machinery and goods. Coming to work drunk would be grounds for dismissal.[2]

Other rules dealt with the organization of work. Punctuality had a peculiar importance in these early mills, far beyond what has become customary in later times when each machine is moved by its own electric motor, and this importance had nothing really to do with the Protestant ethic (although that ethic could be used to rationalize it). As we showed earlier, in mills of this era, whether powered by water or steam, each machine in the plant was driven by a belt attached to a line shaft running off the main shaft which was connected to the water wheel. Once the main shaft was connected to the prime mover, every shaft and every belt in the building began to turn. Although each machine could be disconnected from the shafting by moving a hand clutch, which shifted the belt to the loose pulley, the entire factory was designed mechanically to run under a full load of machinery. Furthermore, at the big mules and carding engines, where several people were required to service one machine, the absence of one little boy or girl piecer might immobilize not only the machine but also the mule spinner and another helper. And, since the machines were designed to run in line, so that cotton was moving continuously through the plant from one machine to another, the absence of workers to tend any machine could stop the entire factory by interrupting the supply of materials at one point and piling up excessive quantities at the next.

Rules about punctuality therefore were rigid. Tardiness was punished by docking wages or, if repeated, by dismissal—even in the case of the small children. Working conditions in the mills of two of the Chester Creek manufacturers were described in the 1837 Pennsylvania Senate investigation, and the witnesses (including Riddle and Crozer and William Shaw, one of their past employees) all agreed on the severity of the punctuality requirements. William Shaw, who worked two years for the Riddles and then for Crozer, reported:

> I have known work to commence as early as twenty minutes past four o'clock, in the summer season, and to work as late as half an hour before eight, P.M.; an hour and a-half allowed for breakfast and dinner, when the hands all leave to go to dinner—children and all; the ringing of the bell was the notice to begin, and docking wages the penalty; the foreman rings the bell and stops the machinery. In the cities, the engineer rings the bell and stops the machinery.
>
> The period of labor is not uniform; in some cases, from sun to sun. It is most common to work as long as they can see; in the winter they work until eight o'clock, receiving an hour and a-half for meals; an hour and a-half is the entire time allowed for going, eating and returning; and that time is often shortened by the ringing of the bell too soon.
>
> Punishment, by whipping, is frequent; they are sometimes sent home and docked for not attending punctually; never knew both punishments to be inflicted; generally the children are attentive, and punishments are not frequent.

Riddle felt that the factory regimen in Northern Ireland, when he worked there as a youth, was more strict than in the Chester Creek factories: "Children suffered very much under that system. They got to adhere to their regular hours, pretty much. The time was still severe on them. There was a great deal of whipping there, we have not here." And Crozer noted that the children, if they were to be employed at all, had to work under the same discipline as adults: ". . . the work of children cannot be shortened, without also abridging that of adults, as the labor of one is connected with that of the other, being part of a system, which, if broken in upon, destroys a connecting link in the chain of operations.[3]

A related work rule mentioned by the Chester Creek witnesses was that children should be constantly attentive and not sleep in the mill (even if not at the moment actively employed). Violations of such rules were punished in a variety of ways: notifying the parent, sending home, docking wages, pulling ears, slapping, whipping, and outright dismissal.

Not even mentioned, but implicit throughout the testimony, was the assumption that the orders of managers to overseers, overseers to spinners and weavers, spinners to piecers and scavengers, and in general orders from bosses to operatives, were to be obeyed promptly and efficiently. Also unmentioned was the assumption that there were some limits to the power of the manager to discipline workers. In 1833 there had been a precedent-setting case in the nearby Montgomery County's Court of Quarter Sessions. An overseer in the cotton factory of Bernard McCready had been indicted on the charge of beating one of the young operatives under his direction, a lad of fourteen. The jury found him guilty, fined him $1, and assessed him the costs of prosecution. *Hazard's Register* intoned:

> By this trial a principle has been established for the government of those "clock-work institutions," which will deprive certain petty tyrants of much of their usurped authority, and secure to the operatives a degree of protection under the laws of our country, which will tend to render their situation less onerous, because they will feel themselves more secure from oppression. The march of free principles is onward, and the time is fast approaching when the rights of the working-man shall be respected, and his person be protected from wrong and outrage.[4]

But for less obviously work-related moralities, the practice differed from factory to factory. Thus, speaking of cleanliness, one of the traditional Protestant virtues, William Shaw declared that "no attention is paid by the manufacturer, or others in the factory, to the personal cleanliness of the children." Robert Craig, the manager at John S. Phillips' mill at Fairmount in Philadelphia, reported, "No attention is bestowed by the managers or proprietors, to the personal or bodily cleanliness of the children." But Crozer said that the children in his mill were "generally cleanly." Another object of varying concern on the part of manufacturers was the possibility of undue intimacy between the sexes. No manufacturer attempted to segregate the sexes by room or even by type of machine, except for putting males at the more strenuous or more skilled jobs. But there was concern about the provision of water closets. The Senate committee regularly asked about sanitary conveniences. Shaw observed: "No particular attention is paid to morals; the boys and girls are not kept separate in the factories; they have different water closets, generally separated only by a partition. . . ." Craig also noted that "the water closets of the boys and girls are separate." The Riddles went a little further, separating workers by age as well as sex: "The boys and girls at our mill have different water closets; the boys and girls in different parts of the yard; the men and women the same house, but a partition between them." Crozer did not mention the subject of toilets in his testimony.

Still more various was the attitude toward profane and obscene language. Although the one was deemed wrong because blasphemous, and the other because it implied—or might lead to—loose sexual conduct, the mills varied in their concern. Crozer was emphatic: "no improper conduct or conversation is allowed in well conducted factories—at least there is not in mine." But Samuel Riddle was indifferent to the whole question, putting it on a "Boys will be boys" level: "I do not think that boys in factories are more in the habit of using profane and obscene language, than those out of doors; when a number of boys get together out of doors, they always do these things. I think that the girls do not use such language." Shaw's experience was that the typical manufacturer did not care: "No particular attention is paid to morals . . . obscene language is frequently used, not often by females; profane language is frequently used; care is seldom taken to prevent these things; if their work is done, it is all that is required. . . ." And Craig contradicted himself, declaring in one passage that "no attention is paid to the morals of the children in the factory; they are neither advised nor reprimanded, unless they neglect their work," yet in another place testifying that children were dismissed for using bad language: "Profane and obscene language is too frequent in the absence of the superintendent, and happens between boys and girls, and is injurious to the morals in a great degree; no other means to prevent it is resorted to other than dismissal when the superintendent hears them at it."[5]

Crozer, indeed, as might have been expected, was the most moralistic of the local manufacturers whose factories were the subject of testimony. He had, he said, a policy of dismissing any female employee who had a doubtful reputation:

> The young women employed, are possessed of a proper self-respect, and departures from chastity are not common. Females of loose character, if known, or *even suspected* as such, would be immediately dismissed from my factory, and I think could not get employment in any of the neighboring factories.[6]

None of the written regulations survive from any of the Rockdale mills, but the "Rules and Regulations of the Matteawan Company" in 1846 have been preserved. Matteawan, as we noted earlier, was one of the most successful of the cotton manufactories, and a center of machine-making. When it was visited by Robert Owen in 1824, the proprietor had made a point of his high moral expectations, informing Owen's party, when they praised the appearance of the workers, "that when a girl did not shew a disposition to be clean & neat in her dress they turned her off."[7] The rules in 1846 had not been relaxed; their severity certainly exceeded that of the Rockdale district (perhaps as a result of the hard Calvinist convictions of the proprietors, who were members of the Dutch Reform Church):

No person will be admitted into the yard during working hours, except on business, without permission of an agent. At all other times, the watchmen will be invested with full control.

The work bell will be rung three minutes, and tolled five minutes; at the expiration of which, every person is expected to be at their work, and every entrance closed, except through the office, which will at all times be open during the working hours of the factory.

No person employed in the manufacturing departments can be permitted to leave their work without permission from their overseer. All others employed in and about the factory are requested to give notice to the agent or superintendent, if they wish to be absent from their work.

No talking can be permitted among the hands in any of the working departments, except on subjects relating to their work.

No spirituous liquors, smoking, or any kind of amusements, will be allowed in the workshops or yards.

Those who take jobs will be considered as overseers of the persons employed by them, and subject to these rules.

Should there exist among any of the persons employed, an idea of oppression on the part of the company, they are requested to make the same known in honorable manner, that such grievances, if really existing, may be promptly considered.

To convince the enemies of domestic manufactures that such establishments are not "sinks of vice and immorality," but, on the contrary, nurseries of morality, industry, and intelligence, a strictly moral conduct is required of every one. Self-respect, it is presumed, will induce every one to be as constant in attendance on some place of divine worship as circumstances will permit. Intemperance, or any gross impropriety of conduct, will cause an immediate discharge of the individual.

The agent and other members of the company are desirous of cultivating the most friendly feeling with the workmen in the establishment, believing they are to rise or fall together. Therefore, to promote the interest and harmony of all, it is necessary there should be a strict observance of these rules and regulations.[8]

Creating an Ethical System for the Workers

It is clear, from the consideration of work rules, that the manufacturers, whether ardent evangelicals or stubborn infidels, all gave to the requirements of technology and economics the first priority in designing factory discipline. They were willing, in fact, to require the workers to behave in ways, and to labor under conditions, that they themselves, and the community generally, conventionally regarded as conducive to immorality. They recognized that the system of long hours prevented the children who worked in factories from getting any education at all—even though the spirit of the Revolution, and the rhetoric of Jacksonian democracy, favored educating all the young people of the commonwealth. Illiteracy, by rendering religious instruction more difficult and Bible-reading impossible, was in itself an obstacle to the moral improvement of the working class. Both Riddle and Crozer therefore testified in favor of prohibiting the labor of children under twelve in cotton factories, in order to free the early years for basic education and to protect the very young from the immoral influences of factory life. And both Riddle and Crozer favored an overall reduction in hours of labor. But they were not willing to introduce these reforms into their own factories, and opposed unilateral legislation by the Pennsylvania legislature on the subject, because, they said, they feared that manufacturers in other states, lacking such laws, would have a competitive advantage and would drive the Pennsylvania manufactories out of business. The demands of conventional morality, when they conflicted with the iron laws of technology and economics, regularly were accorded second place.

Samuel Riddle was eloquent and direct on the problem of balancing economic interest against child welfare:

I think that it would be better to prohibit the employment of children under twelve years of age; the children under that age, would then have a better chance of going to school. I don't think it would increase the wages of labor; I don't think it would make any difference in this respect. The parents of children employed in factories, would be generally opposed to it, I think. A great many widow women have no other way of support, and they would want to get their children into factories at an earlier age. There are too many fathers who are themselves idle, and live by the work of their little children; they would be opposed to it. If children over twelve only, went into factories, the time of labor as now practised, would not make any odds. No system could be established about factories by which children could be required to be schooled a portion of time; when children are employed, the men could not do the work the little ones does; we can't dispense with the work of children in factories. I believe the manufacturer would be better if the hours were shortened—if they were shortened all over the U. States; otherwise I would fear the competition of other States. The children might be instructed under such a system, by night schools.

I should think that it would be good, that boys should not be employed until they were twelve, and until they can read and write. I think it would be better all round; it would not increase the wages of labor; it would be good for the rising generation, and better for the factory. Generally, the children in factories are not able to read and write; they would be inclined to learn, if they had the opportunity. It would be preferable to have girls put on the same footing, but as to age of employment we do not consider it so important.

A system, such as I suggest, would operate very hardly on the poor people, unless you gave it time, by providing that it should commence a year or two as the public schools have been commenced.

. . . I think that a length of labor of sixty-six hours a week in Pennsylvania alone, would effect us so that we could not compete with other States. We pay higher for wages here than they do at the Eastward, and when times are bad, they can under-sell us, so that we have to stop.[9]

Crozer was also eloquent, but somewhat more defensive than Riddle, blaming the resistance to reform even more explicitly on the parents:

The adults employed in manufactories, have, within the last few years, expressed much anxiety to shorten the hours of labor, and have made application for this purpose, to their employers; no direct grant has been made, but the time has been somewhat shortened generally; the parents of children employed, have not, I think, taken an active part on this subject, probably from the fear, that a corresponding reduction of wages would follow; I think many employers might oppose abridging the hours of work, because it would then be necessary to increase the fixed capital of buildings and machinery, to obtain the same amount of work—but the strongest objections arise from the apprehension that a change in the time of work, unless it was of general application throughout the United States, would give other States an advantage over us.

Education is much neglected about manufactories; a large portion of the families employed, are those of indigent widows, who require the work of their children for support, or of idle, intemperate fathers, who do little or nothing themselves towards supporting their families: and these, especially the latter, have but little inclination to school their children, and it is frequently the case, when employers encourage the schooling of the children, the parents object and postpone, with the complaint of being "unable, *for the present,* to lose the labor of the child"; employers have not always encouraged education; small operatives have often been scarce, and employers were therefore, desirous to retain the children in the factories; this difficulty has mostly disappeared on Chester creek, and perhaps in other places as small children have become more abundant.

I think legislative action, for the protection and education of factory children, desirable—yet, I am constrained to say, the necessity of the case arises more from the conduct of parents, than that of employers.[10]

The manufacturers evidently were experiencing a moral dilemma. They were committed, at least as responsible citizens if not also as evangelical religionists, to the moral and mental improvement of the people, and especially of the children, who were connected with their mills. But successful management of a factory in a competitive market economy in their opinion required them to tolerate, or even create, noxious working conditions for their employees: denial of educational opportunity, exposure to profane and obscene language, promiscuous association of the sexes and of different age groups in intimate working arrangements.

The solution was to urge reform, not in the mill but in the institutions of the community, and particularly in the educational system. The Pennsylvania Senate investigating committee in 1838 reported a bill which provided that no children under ten would be permitted to work in factories; that children over ten who did work in factories, but could not read, write, or keep accounts, should be sent to school three months in every year of employment; and that children under sixteen should not be allowed to work more than ten hours per day.[11] But the bill did not pass; in fact it was never brought to a vote.

The manufacturers relied on the community to resolve the problem: on the parents to bring up their children properly; on the Sunday School to educate them and give them elementary religious instruction and moral guidance; on the newly created system of public schools (instituted in 1836 as a result of the Commonwealth law of that year) to provide free education to all children; and on the Sunday School teachers and clergy to instruct both children and adults in Christian duty.

The clergy responded to this charge in a complementary way. Instead of demanding of the manufacturers that they reform their factories, they demanded of the workers that they recast their own thinking along lines that would render factory reform unnecessary. Ministers across the land prepared tracts for presentation to working-class people that would detach them from any lingering remnants of infidel philosophy and provide them instead with a set of Christian ethical principles. These would enable them, among other things, to cooperate successfully with the existing capitalist economic system and with the factory system that was growing up within it.

Alonzo Potter, the Smiths' friend and after 1841 the Bishop of Pennsylvania, wrote such a tract. It was first published about 1838 as a review in one of the periodicals, when Potter was Professor of Moral Philosophy at Union College, and republished in 1841 as an appendix to a book entitled *Political Economy* which bore Potter's name on the title page. The basic treatise on political economy contained in this book was actually an acknowledged republication of the first ten chapters of Scrope's *Political Economy* (published in England in 1833), with fairly extensive editorial changes by Potter. Potter's appended seventy-page essay, entitled "The Condition of Labouring Men in the United States," is however worthy of close attention not only because Potter was to become an influential Church leader, but because as the Smiths' friend, and as the bishop personally responsible for the Rockdale mission, he visited the community on many occasions, spending at least one day annually to confirm new members, and on these and other occasions he addressed the people from the pulpit of Calvary Church. We can be sure that the view of the workers expressed in this essay was communicated to the people of the Rockdale district both directly by the bishop and indirectly by the rectors and Sunday School teachers.

Potter's essay was a warning to the nation against what he regarded as the wave of political demagoguery, feeding on working-class disaffection, that in his view was associated with the party of Andrew Jackson. He explicitly compared the present age to turbulent periods of the past, from the French Revolution back to classical times, and repeatedly associated trade unions with such labels as Jacobinism and Terrorism and such names as Marat and Robespierre. He painstakingly exposed the shallowness of the "something for nothing" philosophy of the workingmen who clamored against the unequal distribution of property. He compared them to the "champions of equality" in Revolutionary France and demonstrated that, although *extreme* distinctions of wealth and property were politically undesirable, a degree of inequality was unavoidable. A "community of goods," as proposed by Robert Owen and Saint-Simon, would merely produce an "equality of servitude" under a dictatorial master like Owen himself at New Lanark. Only a society based firmly on the principle of private property would permit both true liberty and a reasonable distribution of wealth.

Having established the moral principles on which a good society must be based, he went on in more detail—and this discussion was the major part of the work—to show that "combinations of working men," with their fearful power to strike against employers and to coerce into obedience their own members and other workers as well, were inherently undesirable. Although not referring to the Masonic order in so many words, he compared the evils of trade unionism to the evils of Freemasonry:

> We hold that the power lodged with associations is safe from great and dangerous abuse only when their objects are clearly avowed and their proceedings substantially public; when their composition is so far promiscuous as to secure them from a clannish spirit and an anti-social policy; and when the influence on which they rely is of a purely moral nature, appealing to something higher than fear. Allow them the use of violence, or even of intimidation, and they will soon usurp the place of law, and erect themselves into the most intolerable of all tyrannies. Suffer them to imbody but the members of one profession or class, and those but of one sex, and they will evince an exclusiveness and identity of feeling, and be liable to ebullitions of passion, which will render them always troublesome, finally, permit them to proceed in secret, and for purposes not fully known or explained, and the temptation to convert them into instruments of oppression for political or religious ends will be nearly irresistable.

And he flatly accused the trades union movement of being foreign in origin and tending to socialism, atheism, and sedition:

> However desirable it may be to ameliorate the outward condition of men and to enlighten their understandings, it must be admitted to be inconceivably more desirable to raise the tone of their deportment and moral sentiments. In increasing their physical and intellectual resources merely, we may but increase their misery, and the mischief which they will inflict on their families of the public. No body of men is more dangerous than one raised in influence above the mass of those engaged in similar pursuits, and constantly busied in inspiring jealousy and promoting agitation. That such is the case with these Unions we do not affirm. But it is worthy of notice, that their leaders are generally from abroad, and that their doctrines respecting labour and capital are often propagated in close connexion with tenets by Mr. Owen respecting Politics and Religion. Now we know something of the style and spirit of the literature which thrives amid such tenets. The Halls of Science established under the auspices of Mr. Owen push their researches into the realms of atheism and sedition. They have little taste for anything farther. So with Trades' Unions. They convene their members to hear of "equal rights," "rapacious capitalists," "grinding employers." But we are informed of no

libraries that they have established; of no lectures that they have instituted; nor, indeed, of any measures for the diffusion of useful knowledge, which were not already prevalent and of easy access.[12]

Potter's views on unions were extreme. Probably not even the Rockdale manufacturers were prepared to go as far as he in condemning unionism. But in his intellectual polarization of Enlightenment and evangelical approaches to problems of economics, he correctly formulated the dialectic out of which the synthesis of the next decades would evolve.

THE RISE OF POLITICAL ANTI-MASONRY

Ever since the 1790's, there had been chronic harassment of political radicals in America on the grounds of religion. Sometimes, within a community, the harassment was subtle and covert, amounting to no more than some degree of social isolation (as in Phillips' case) or a refusal to take a "good and intelligent" infidel as more than a crypto-Christian (as with Minshall Painter). But often the harassment involved was more harsh. Personal attack, both physical and literary, was a technique used more or less openly by the more militant Christians throughout the first two decades of the century to suppress the freethinkers and Deists who questioned fundamental Christian beliefs and touted radical social doctrines. Sometimes the violence involved prominent freethinkers: Tom Paine, formerly hailed as the heroic pamphleteer of American freedom, was now made a symbol of degraded atheism in the torrents of abuse that flowed over him from the religious press; mobs hurled rocks and imprecations at Fanny Wright and forced her to cancel appearances when she passed through Pennsylvania; Abner Kneeland, erstwhile Philadelphia Universalist clergyman and chaplain to the Masonic lodge, was convicted of blasphemy in New England and served sixty days in jail. But usually the violence was more discreetly managed and was applied to more vulnerable targets. In either manner, it created—or continued—a tradition of Christian terrorism against followers of the Enlightenment tradition that must be recognized as part of the ambience in which the ideological conflict of the age was being fought.[1] Two cases, involving persons on the edge of the network that centered in Rockdale, are worth citing as illustrations of the phenomenon: the harassment of John Speakman, John S. Phillips' associate at the Academy of Natural Sciences of Philadelphia, when Speakman was a member of the "Pittsburgh Society of Deists"; and the brutal treatment of the widely read and outspoken journalistic critic of evangelical Christianity, Anne Royall.

It was in the midst of this feverish Christian response to the threat of infidelity that a political movement arose, quasi-terrorist in some of its aspects, dedicated to the exclusion of members of the Masonic order from the public life of the nation. This movement must indeed be regarded, as Lee Benson and others have suggested, as the political shock force of the Protestant evangelical movement, responsive to the call of the Reverend Ezra Stiles Ely of Philadelphia for "a Christian party in politics." The Anti-Masonic members of the legislature in Albany stated defensively in 1829:

> Anti-masons proscribe and persecute no man. The charge is founded upon the fact that anti-masons resolve *not to elevate to office* those who ADHERE to the masonic fraternity. This is neither proscription nor persecution. No individual has a right to demand the suffrage of another. The bestowment of it is exclusively the right of him who possesses it. To withhold from an individual what he has no right to demand and no claim to possess until it is freely given, is no *persecution.* To annihilate the institution of Freemasonry, or render it harmless, anti-masons have formed the resolution to *withhold* their suffrages from those who adhere to the order.[2]

But the apparatus of terrorism was still there: spectacular trials, legislative investigations, and pressuring of witnesses to testify under the threat of being jailed for contempt of court.

John Speakman
and the Pittsburgh Society of Deists

During his brief sojourn in Pittsburgh in the early 1820's, John Speakman was a member of a group known as the Pittsburgh Society of Deists. It was an informally organized colloquium, which met in the home of a tradesman. Upwards of two hundred people would assemble on Sunday evenings to hear religionists and freethinkers debate such issues as the authenticity of the Scriptures and the divinity of Jesus. Writing to his friend Thomas Say later on, Speakman described how one after another the zealous defenders of the faith, Methodist and Presbyterian, were laid low by the powerful arguments of their free-thinking opponents. At last the ministers of Pittsburgh laid aside "all their petty broils of rivalship, and united as a band of brothers, prophesying and doling out the dreadful consequences to all those who undertook to judge the scriptures according to the dictates of their fallen natures." Six of the principal participants were accused before a magistrate of "speaking loosely of Jesus Christ and of the scriptures of truth," and one was charged with conspiracy. At jury trials in the mayor's court, conducted with questionable fairness and relying upon perjured witnesses, the man at whose house the meetings were held was convicted (although an appeal to the State Supreme Court later reversed the conviction)[3] and fined $10 and costs. Another victim, although found not guilty, was assessed court costs; he went to jail rather than pay. The leader's shop, next to his house, was mysteriously set afire and burned down. The Deists' meetings ceased.

It was in response to this sequence of events that Speakman developed his early plan for a Utopian community of scientists, to be founded in some remote place, far from the clutches of the Holy Alliance—"that all devouring monster whose voracity increases in proportion to the number of its victims."[4]

Anne Royall and the "blue-skinned Presbyterians"

The aging widow of long-dead Major Royall, a Virginia gentleman of deistical views who had served the republic during the Revolution, Anne Royall in the 1820's and 1830's was a traveling newspaper woman who wrote "black books" about her travels, full of personal anecdote and social criticism. She repeatedly passed through the Philadelphia-Wilmington area. In a material sense, she lived poorly on her subscriptions and fees; her delight came from exposing corruption in high places and from cutting through the pretensions of popular fads, such as anti-Masonry and the evangelical crusade, to reveal the hypocrisy within. Although she was not a follower of Owen, she wrote up a friendly interview with him, and published a favorable notice of Joseph Neef and his Pestalozzian School ("I should rejoice to see a school of this description in every county, town, and city of the Union"). She chose to defend the Masonic order, which had helped her financially during the writing of her "black books," at the very time when the tide of anti-Masonic feeling was running high. And she tilted constantly at the "blue-skinned Presbyterians" ("May all their throats be cut") and other fanatical religionists who were creating the evangelical alliance. The American Sunday School Union, the American Bible Society, the American Tract Society all came under her displeasure. She labeled as "treason" Ely's proposal for a Christian party in politics.

But the response was brutal and effective. She was accused in print of having been a prostitute. She was regularly snubbed by the pious. When she sought an interview and a subscription from the Reverend Dr. Ezra

Stiles Ely, she was refused; she memorialized the moment in her usual mocking way:

> I was informed that his house stood back from the street, in a square, and on his gate I would see a silver plate with "Rev. Dr. Stiles Ely" on it in large letters. I found the gate, and the silver plate—the big letters—the big house—and the BIG man. The big door was open. The doctor appeared, but I briefly repeated my business. He turned off short and said he was engaged.

She was horsewhipped in Pittsburgh and run out of town by a mob of students in Virginia. In 1827 she visited Burlington, Vermont, and was thrown out of a store and down a 10-foot flight of steps by a zealously religious storekeeper. She suffered a broken leg, a dislocated ankle, and a sprained knee, and was for a time severely hampered in her movements. In 1829, living in Washington, D.C., her house was stoned and windows broken by a Sunday School class meeting in an engine house next door; the parents, led by an elder of the First Presbyterian Church, kept her awake at night, praying beneath her broken windows for her salvation. The parents were succeeded by mobs of children, black and white, employed "to shower the house with stones, yell, and blow horns." A few weeks later she was accused before a grand jury by the same elder and his son, his daughter, and his daughter-in-law, and by several federal officials, including the recently dismissed Librarian of Congress (to whom she had complained about the presence of the books and pamphlets of the American Sunday School Union scattered over the reading tables), the House Sergeant-at-arms, and the Senate office clerk. There were three charges: that she was "an evil-disposed person"; a common scold and slanderer; and a disturber of the peace and happiness of her peaceful and honest neighbors. At a nationally celebrated trial she was convicted, fined $10 (which she did not have), and required to post a $100 bond to guarantee that she would keep the peace for a year (i.e., that she would not write). Two newspaper reporters, concerned over the freedom of the press, paid the fine and put up security for her good conduct.

Anne Royall was not silenced; she went on attacking the evangelicals in her "black books" and giving favorable notices of liberals and even radicals. But there were fewer and fewer journalists and local free enquirers who were willing to risk poverty, beatings, insults, and harassment by the courts in following her example.[5]

Edward Darlington and the Anti-Masonic Party

The seed around which political Anti-Masonry crystallized, in the supersaturated solution of ideological controversy that was filling the nation in the 1820's, was the reported murder in 1826 of William Morgan of Batavia, New York. Allegedly, he had been abducted and executed by the Masons for having, contrary to his oath, planned to reveal the secrets of the order in a published book. Allegedly, also, a conspiracy of Masons in the courts and legislature was protecting the murderers and impeding the investigation. By 1828 mass meetings were being organized in New York, Massachusetts, Pennsylvania, and other northern states; petitions were being drafted and forwarded to legislatures; newspapers were being established (one, *The Anti-Masonic Register,* on Chester Creek) to promulgate Anti-Masonic doctrine and to serve as the vehicle for ticket formation and party organization. Eventually, Pennsylvania elected an Anti-Masonic governor and legislature; the former governor, and other witnesses, were subpoenaed to testify before a legislative committee to reveal the crimes of Masonry. It was not until the Buckshot War of 1838 (when rioting Democrats drove the Anti-Masons out of the Assembly) that the tide of Anti-Masonic fervor really began to subside from the commonwealth.

One of the manufacturers of Chester Creek was prominently involved in political Anti-Masonry: Edward Darlington. In politics he had begun his career as a Democrat in a part of Pennsylvania traditionally dominated by one of the few surviving Federalist constituencies in the nation. In 1830, running for Congress as an Anti-Mason from Delaware County, he was defeated by the candidate of the Chester County Anti-Masons. In 1832 and 1834, however, he was elected to Congress on the Anti-Masonic ticket itself and in 1836 was returned as a Whig. Thus the Chester Creek manufacturing district was, from 1833 to 1839, represented in the House of Representatives in Washington by an anti-Jackson man who, for the first four years, was actively affiliated with the Anti-Masonic Party. Although there is no reason to suppose that Darlington was not genuinely opposed to the Masonic order, his political activity and his correspondence do not actually concern themselves with the issue of Freemasonry. He was the close friend, legal representative, and partner of the Chester Creek manufacturers and he represented their interests in Congress. He was a friend of Henry Carey, the leading American economist. He opposed Jackson's veto of the recharter bill for the Second Bank of the United States; he opposed the withdrawal of funds; he supported the tariff to protect the cotton industry; he opposed the expansion of slavery into the new states and territories of the Union; he opposed slavery in the District of Columbia and favored the plan of the American Colonization Society to ship freed blacks back to Africa; in his most vehement political stand, he opposed prohibiting the introduction of anti-slavery petitions to the House of Representatives. He was, in short, the very epitome of the proto-Republican as he appeared in the days before that party was able to mobilize the numerous but scattered proponents of the protective tariff, benevolent Christian capitalism, and free soil into a national political consensus.[6]

The Odiornes and the Meaning of Anti-Masonry

The conduct in office of such respectable Anti-Masons as Edward Darlington (and there were many like him) does not suggest in any way a paranoid, fanatical, extremist type of politics. There were, to be sure, political inquisitions on the state level of suspected or admitted Masonic evil-doers; many lodges closed temporarily. But it would appear that, fundamentally, the Anti-Masonic activities of the decade 1828–38 simply provided an organizational mold within which to form a party composed of many of those who—whether they considered themselves to be former Federalists, anti-Jackson Democrats, pro-Clay National Republicans, or Whigs—shared a belief in America as a Christian capitalist nation, dedicated to manufacturing and progress and populated by free men, all of whom would have sufficient education, religious training, and income for personal success, and who would therefore be able to view the social classes as complementary rather than antagonistic.

But this ideological position was being *consciously* formed as an answer to the very popular deistic and atheistic socialist doctrines of Robert and Robert Dale Owen, Fanny Wright, Thomas Paine, and in general the deistic *philosophes* who had rationalized the Revolution in France. The Anti-Masons also opposed the Democrats, including not only the liberal "loco-foco" faction but also Jackson and Van Buren and their bank and tariff policies. Furthermore, the Anti-Masonic Party developed very shortly after —and in obvious opposition to—the Workingmen's parties of Philadelphia, New York (the Owen-Wright faction), and Boston. One might indeed suggest that it was Anti-Masonic rhetoric which forced upon "The Democracy"—an old, entrenched, and in its own way very conservative political machine—the image of liberalism. The Enlightenment policies of Thomas Jefferson lived on, in reality, more fully in the Workingmen's Party than in the Jacksonian Democratic Party, despite the presence in that party of some old-line liberal politicians.

From the perspective of ideological combat, then, let us look more closely at the doctrines of anti-Masonry. They were, to begin with, not new but already a generation old and were formed, not in western New York in response to the murder of William Morgan, but in England, France, and Germany in response to the French Revolution. The doctrines of anti-Masonry were expounded in some detail in a little work compiled by James C. Odiorne (who was the cousin and brother-in-law of George Moore, nail-maker of Chester Creek until 1832, and cousin also of the Odiorne sisters of Ivy Mills who had married the wealthy, politically active, and conservative Willcox brothers).

Odiorne's *Opinions on Speculative Masonry* was published in Boston in 1830. Much of the content was conventional rhetoric, condemning the order as an élitist group held together by secret oaths and obscene and blasphemous rituals requiring the Mason to give higher loyalty to his order than to God, Church, or State. This was the superficial populist objection to Freemasonry, the first level of analysis of the institution. It appealed to a wide body of public opinion.

But there was a second level, and this harked back to the hue and cry against Freemasonry which had developed in England during the 1790's, when the British establishment was undertaking to discredit the French Revolution. The argument on this level was formulated by Dr. William Robison, the distinguished physicist of the University of Edinburgh, in 1794. Robison claimed that an ancient conspiracy existed, which aimed to overthrow all organized religion and to destroy all legitimate governments; in recent years it had worked through a peculiar secret organization, the Illuminati of Bavaria, which had infiltrated the Masonic order to infect French public opinion with the infidel views of the *philosophes.* The Masonic order thus was held to be directly responsible for launching the Revolution in France and for fomenting popular disaffection in England, Ireland, and even the United States. Robison was the supreme authority for Anti-Masonic intellectuals. The organizational aspect of his view was expressed succinctly in Albany on May 5, 1829, in an address by the "Republican Anti-Masonic Members of the Legislature of New York, to their Constituents":

The institution in this country receives with passive obedience, whatever is transmitted from the *foreign* seat of its empire. Here it has formed a confederacy embracing the whole extent of our republic. All our territory is parcelled out, and a branch of the institution established in every section. It has its meetings in the darkness of night and security of secrecy, for towns, counties, states, and the whole Union. The institution is prepared to act throughout the land, with concert, energy and decision, and to receive its impulse from *foreign command.* Its immense resources enable it to attempt the greatest objects. Nothing is too lofty for its ambition or beyond its means of accomplishment. In Europe the institution has been made the cloak of innumerable crimes. In its dark conclaves plots, stratagems, and treason have been designed against governments and religion, and the institutions of civil society, and put in a train of successful execution, while its infatuated votaries were unconscious of the object of the master spirits that impelled them to action. What has been attempted in other countries *may* be expected in our own. The organization of the institution here, fits it for the purposes of treason. Its extended confederacy furnishes the opportunity for the widest communication. The masonic cipher gives the instrument of safe correspondence, and its secrecy enforced by horrid obligations and appalling penalties, affords the assurance of security. The question then is presented to the American people whether they will sacrifice DEMOCRACY or annihilate the institution of *Freemasonry,* which threatens its existence.[7]

The Reverend Moses Tacher of Massachusetts expressed the ideological issues in another succinct discussion in Odiorne's volume of illuminism as a kind of acephalous social movement:

You inquire "what evidence I have, that masonry leads directly to infidelity?" and, if "it is pretended that masonry and the system of illuminism are mutually coupled together?" If you had said *systems* of illuminism, I think you would have given a more just representation of the subject. Illuminism, I conceive to be *one;* but its *systems* are many. Illuminism is a popular name for infidel Philosophy, comprising all its doctrines, and shades of doctrine, from Deism, to Atheism and complete skepticism. The *systems* of this philosophy are exceedingly various, and so artfully either contrived or *adopted,* as to "deceive, if it were possible, the very elect." I speak of systems belonging to illuminism, as either contrived or *adopted;* because this infidel philosophy has indeed contrived some, and *adopted* others, already fitted for its reception. Of some of these systems you have given the names: as, the "Society of Carbonari" in Germany, the "United Irishmen," and the "Ribbon-men," in Ireland, &c. You justly observe, that "distinctions like these are of little consequence where one grand object is in view." Yet I think, you have fallen into a mistake, and confounded the *systems* of illuminism with illuminism itself. Illuminism, I grant, is the same, in every place, and in every country; whether it is called "Philosophy," "Reason," "Liberty and Equality," or "infidelity." Its systems, however, are not only as various, but as *distinct* as its *names;* and exactly adapted to answer its own purposes, though suited to the different nations. By systems, I here mean, those different combinations and societies, organized and governed in very different ways, professing to promote entirely different objects; but whose grand and ultimate design *has always centred* in infidelity. Now, I ask, What system was adopted by the illuminees of France in order to "crush the Wretch," and to accomplish their designs against religion and government? To trace all their plans, and develop all their schemes of wickedness, would require more time, talents and learning, than can be commanded by me, or perhaps by *you*. The following, however, are among some of the measures which they adopted: To hold secret correspondence, to circulate infidel tracts, control and corrupt the press, and to superintend the instruction of children and youth. Some of their bolder steps, were, to publish their Encyclopedia, seize upon the Royal Academy, and bring it entirely under their corrupting influence. . . .[8]

It is clear enough, then, that Anti-Masonry attacked precisely the views of the liberal-to-radical range being so energetically promulgated in the 1820's by the Marquis de Lafayette, Robert Owen, Fanny Wright, and the Workingmen's Party of Philadelphia. These views, based in considerable part on the philosophy of the Enlightenment (illuminism), proposed, in effect, to take control of the Industrial Revolution away from capital and put it in the hands of workers. Anti-Masonry now defined them as the corrupt doctrine of an ancient, worldwide conspiracy, which aimed to annihilate Christianity, topple existing governments, abolish private property, and violate the sanctity of marriage.

But there is an even deeper level of analysis than this. Anti-Masonry appealed to the dormant yet by no means forgotten tradition of witch-fear in European culture. The testimony at English trials of accused witches, and the records of the Inquisition, clearly show that their accusers believed witches to be members of an ancient, secret, and powerful organization, with its own hierarchy, its own mythology, and its own orgiastic rituals. This tradition was invoked by the Anti-Masonic scholars Dr. Robison and the abbé Barruel, upon whom the Anti-Masonic agitators who chose the second level of analysis all depended for their information. Dr. Robison virtually accused the Bavarian Illuminati (the corruptors of French Masonic lodges) of practicing old-fashioned witchcraft (although he himself did not believe that witches had supernatural powers). Thus, in revealing the contents of the papers found during a police raid on the house of one of the Illuminati, he noted plans to organize a sisterhood of sacred prostitutes (to "procure us both much information and money") and a series of infernal recipes or secret poisons, aphrodisiacs, and abortifacients:

There are, in the same hand-writing, Description of a strong box, which if forced open, shall blow up and destroy its contents—Several receipts for procuring abortions—A composition which blinds or kills when spurted in the face—A sheet, containing a receipt for sympathetic ink—Tea for procuring abortion—A method for filling a bed-chamber with pestilential vapours—How to take off impressions of seals, so as to use them afterwards as seals—A collection of some hundreds of such impressions, with a list of their owners, princes, nobles, clergymen, merchants, &c. —A receipt *ad excitandum furorem uterinum,*—A manuscript intitled, "Better than Horus." It was afterwards printed and distributed at Leipzig fair, and is an attack and bitter satire on all religion.[9]

And the abbé Barruel charged that the Masons were the perpetuators of the ancient Manichaean heresy.[10] In effect, they raised the specter of an ancient pagan cult, its members despising God and the Christian virtues, dedicated to the use of love magic and abortion medicine in its pursuit of sexual license, and prepared to murder its enemies if threatened. This is indeed the image of the witch cult of Western Europe, cast upon the screen of political events in the Atlantic community less than a hundred years after the last witchcraft execution in England, and not much longer in America.

The conclusion is inescapable that political Anti-Masonry in America in the decade 1828–38 must be understood, ideologically, as an aspect of the evangelical Protestant crusade against infidelity. It singled out, as the symbol of the hated tradition of the Enlightenment, the institution of Freemasonry, and cast itself in the role of savior of the republic from an international conspiracy. It was, in effect, the "Christian party in politics" for which the more zealous evangelicals were calling. Its intellectual origins in the immediate past lay in the conservative polemical literature that opposed the French Revolution, particularly Dr. Robison's book *Proofs of a Conspiracy;* but more deeply it drew emotional form from the traditional European fear of a pagan underground of witches and worshippers of Satan.

Although the movement passed quickly as an organized political force, it was able to gather together a variety of respectable men dissatisfied with the policies of the Democratic Party of the day. These men—inconspicuous men like Chester Creek's Edward Darlington and also conspicuous figures like the redoubtable Thaddeus Stevens—worked together to hammer out an economic and political policy that emphasized capitalist industrialization, free soil, universal free education, and the complementary rather than competing interests of the social classes. They thus contributed importantly to the development of an articulate Christian capitalist philosophical alternative to the still influential spokesmen of illuminism. And they contributed to the branding of an indelible impression in one part of the American political consciousness that somewhere, somehow, beyond America's shores there exists a Satanic empire whose minions are ever at work to destroy the republic and take over the world.

DEFEATING THE INFIDELS ON CHESTER CREEK

Despite the rhetoric of Jacksonian democracy and its apparent benevolence toward the common man, America in the 1820's and 1830's was drifting to the right. The thousands, perhaps hundreds of thousands, of respectable Deists and social liberals were less and less free to express their views publicly. A tighter order in society was in the making, and its signs —the rise of machine politics and modern party organization; the expansion of slavery in the south and the progressive denial to free blacks in the north of access to former economic and political privileges; the growth of powerful evangelical religious organizations and benevolent societies—were visible everywhere. On Chester Creek, the mill owners chose an Anti-Mason to represent their views in Congress. Calvary Church hammered the few infidels and radicals among the manufacturers, mechanics, and operatives into silence. Pennsylvania's new constitution of 1837 *withdrew* the franchise from free blacks.

Smith's assessment of the success of Calvary Church in changing the moral tone of the Rockdale district was enthusiastic as early as April 1838:

. . . much of good has been done and the cause of religion and piety advanced by the establishment of the Church and School in the neighborhood. The population being Manufacturers and a large proportion of them young persons, no one who is not familiar with the privations that neighborhood suffered for want of religious instruction, can imagine the change that has been effected by the opportunities thus offered and by the establishment of the means of grace among them. The nearest place of worship heretofore was two miles distant. The children roamed at large on the Lord's Day trespassing on their neighbors, and that sacred day was more than any other marked by noise and turbulence, intemperance and profanity. Infidelity stalked boldly among the people; the disciples of Paine held public meetings to inculcate his doctrines, and on one occasion when a Presbyterian clergyman gave notice that he should preach on the evidences of Christianity, he was interrupted by some of those who attended for the purpose with a volume of Paine's works in their hands. These persons, no longer finding countenance for such opinions, have either left the neighborhood, or no longer advance them, and the improvement in the morals and deportment of the people is so evident to persons who, altho' themselves indifferent to religious truths, are yet interested in the establishment of order, that a voluntary testimony has been given in favor of the Church as the means by which this great change has been produced.[1]

Clementina's friend Sophie, who when she first heard of plans for a Sunday School wrote to say, "from what you have told me of the people in your neighborhood, I know of no place where the benefits of a Sabbath School instruction are more needed," by 1839 was congratulating her friend that "the cause of the Lord [was] thus prospering." And in 1842 she was reporting to "Clemma" the "most cheering account of Rockdale" she had heard from another friend.[2]

The leaders of Calvary Church clearly had in mind the link between infidelity—the lack of faith in Christ—and the social philosophy of the Enlightenment. In inviting Lee to accept the call to Calvary Church, Smith drew explicit attention to the peculiar spiritual needs of the locality. "Rockdale," he said, "is not a regular village but a manufacturing establishment . . ." And he went on to explain:

A large proportion of the congregation consists of operatives in the Factories many of whom are young persons of 17 to 25 years of age brought up in the Sunday School—& of the impression made among these you may judge by the fact that 25 persons chiefly of this class were confirmed in the Church by the Bishop at his annual visitation on Sunday last—[3]

And again, reporting a few years later in the wake of the turnout of 1842, he pointedly noted the incompatibility between striking and Christian conduct:

And should some of those to whom their beloved pastor dispensed the visible signs and tokens in the Holy Sacrament have violated the covenant of which they were the pledges; should they during the season of angry strife and excitement which a year after convulsed our manufacturing establishments, have forgotten the commandment delivered unto them, and departed from "that conversation which becometh the Gospel of Christ," we are not without hope that some even of these have discovered the "root of bitterness" which lay undiscovered in their hearts until this temptation caused it to spring up; and having by God's grace succeeded in eradicating it, may hereafter produce good fruit, as evidence of the sincerity of the profession made at our altar.[4]

There is no reason to accuse Smith or Lee of consciously conspiring to use the Church as a tool to control the workers in order to increase or protect their own personal financial profit. Smith probably suffered a loss by the departure of the "Infidel" Phillips, who maintained a large establishment and must have paid substantial rent; for a number of years, Smith was able to rent Old Sable Works only as a grist- and sawmill. Neither Smith nor Lee personally managed or owned, even in part, any of the mills that were struck. The issue was a much larger one and involved competing world views—views of the nature of man and the cosmos that challenged at every point the doctrines of the Enlightenment. Where the Enlightenment taught a vague deism and an assured afterlife, the evangelicals taught a Christian Trinity and the risk of hellfire. Where the Enlightenment taught the adequacy of reason, the evangelicals taught the need for faith and revelation. Where the Enlightenment taught that man is by nature good and that flawed societies have made him bad, the evangelicals taught that he is by nature sinful and the faults of society cannot be cured until he accepts his need for salvation. Where the Enlightenment taught that children should learn from the school of nature, the evangelicals taught that they should study from the Bible. Where the Enlightenment taught that all men were equal, the evangelicals taught that there were mutually dependent social classes. Where the Enlightenment taught that social life is based on negotiable contract, the evangelicals taught that it is based on government and law.

On an ideological level, then, the conflict was dialectical—a stable, structured system of opposites. The initial strategy of the evangelicals was not to produce an intellectual synthesis but to deny categorically any validity to the "infidel" position and to convert or suppress the infidel himself. In this campaign they were moderately successful: few dared to assert an infidel, Enlightenment philosophy on Chester Creek after 1838; and only the more militant, nationally famous freethinkers were likely to be heard at public lectures or to be read. But on Chester Creek and elsewhere, private opinion was more varied than public behavior would indicate, and even the silenced infidels subtly contributed to the eventual formation of a synthetic social strategy in the next decades.

Chapter VIII ✠

THE EMERGENCE OF CHRISTIAN INDUSTRIALISM

The conflicting ideological systems of illuminism and evangelism were, like systems of theology or science, pure paradigms that admitted little in the way of compromise. They could be cherished or abandoned but they could not in their main arguments be changed: the number of their proponents might wax or wane but the basic propositions were immutable.

Yet the attention of ideological disputants may wander, may turn to the practical issues of the day, to the realities of technological and economic change. This is what happened to Chester Creek, and to other American communities, in the ideological struggle between the free enquirers and the evangelicals. Even as Bishop Potter was fulminating against combinations, and the aging Robert Owen was still roundly condemning priestcraft, the lawyers and judges and practical politicians, the manufacturers and economists, were putting together the outlines of a creed that was neither illuminism nor evangelism but a little bit of both, with ad hoc principles thrown in as needed solutions to practical problems.

The proffered solution was ingeniously simple: it offered the promise of earthly prosperity to all who worked, and spiritual prosperity to all who had faith. To be sure, the infidel would have to accept his need for Christian salvation, and the manufacturer would have to concede the right of a union of workers to improve their economic condition. But a smooth "Harmony of Interests" (as the economist Henry Carey put it), rather than conflict, was really the natural state of society; and if everyone realized it and cooperated, everyone's interests would prosper.

But the full working out of this scheme of salvation was not realized on Chester Creek until after a period of hard times, of depression, and of labor conflict, culminating in an appalling natural catastrophe: the great flood of 1843.

THE RECESSION OF 1834 TO 1842

Hard times came to the capitalists and workers in the cotton industry well in advance of the national panic of 1837; but the panic never was for them the economic disaster it became to other segments of the economy. There was a brief drop in yarn prices in the winter and spring of 1834, as the nation's economy sagged after Jackson vetoed the bill to recharter the Second Bank of the United States and withdrew the federal deposits from the embattled institution. Parkmount Mill closed for a week because business was slow and other mills closed temporarily or went on part-time schedules. In April, Crozer, writing to his congressman, Edward Darlington, enclosed a census of underemployment and unemployment in the Rockdale mills which vividly displayed the uncertainty of the cotton business in this period:[1]

Lewis and Phillips	130 hands	half-time
James Houghton	120 hands	less than half-time
S. and J. Riddle	30 hands	two-thirds time
J. P. Crozer	90 hands	one-third time
Daniel Lammot		full time

But within a few weeks the Riddles were back to normal in yarn and in addition had commenced their weaving operation, making chambray, twill, and Canton flannel. By the end of the year 1834, an inflationary process was under way, the price of raw cotton rising and the price of yarn going up correspondingly; No. 20, for instance, recovering from its low of 23 cents per pound in the spring to 29 cents by Christmas.[2]

Crozer's only difficulty during this period of general economic uncertainty came early in 1835, when his chief customer for yarn, John Steel of Frankford, died insolvent owing Crozer $6,500—"nearly half of what I was worth," as he recorded in his autobiography. "The shock was tremendous and nearly drove me distracted." But Crozer, with his usual ability to rebound from "ruinous loss," went to work harder than ever:

For some days I felt so cast down that I could not attend to my factory business, could not stay in the factory; but in a week or ten days my native energy triumphed. I had much ado to meet my engagements, to "keep my head above water"; but all went right and I redoubled my diligence. Hitherto I had spun yarn only; I now decided to weave also. Power-looms had now become general. I borrowed money to buy twenty looms. All subsequent extensions, in both weaving and spinning, were out of profits. I was very successful in weaving, and in all my business from this date.[3]

Indeed, Crozer profited from the difficulties of others. In the very year of Steel's insolvency, he was able to purchase Knowlton Mill from the man who had acquired it from Darlington. In 1837 John B. Ducket, the paper-maker who operated a small mill in the forks of the creek, opposite Park-mount, fell into financial difficulty, and in 1838 the Bank of Delaware County foreclosed the mortgage and took title to the property.[4] Crozer was a stockholder and, as the bank's official history declared, "a director of the Bank of Delaware County from 1825 to 1862, except with intermissions as required by the laws of those times . . . a dominant figure in the history of the institution."[5] Although he did not take title from the bank until 1843, Crozer took physical possession of Ducket's property in the fall of 1839. As he recorded the event in his autobiography:

> Our residence was at West Branch until the year 1839. All our children but the two youngest were born there. We had purchased Crozerville property and built a factory there, tearing away the old paper-mill, and putting up some tenements, but had not decided to remove. The dwelling-house there was better than that at West Branch, but there were some objections which made us hesitate. In the month of November, 1839, however, we removed, with the expectation of this being our permanent home. We had often thought of a city life in the future, but had made no definite plan about it.[6]

Evidently one of the economic functions of the panic was to facilitate a kind of economic selection, stronger enterprises gobbling up defaulting ones cheaply with the assistance of sheriff's sales and bank foreclo-sures.

Although no financial records of the Riddles remain for the period 1835–43, there is no reason to suppose that they were in serious difficulty during the recession. In 1837, Samuel Riddle declared, "We are now working but three days in the week, some have stopped altogether."[7] But he was sufficiently solvent in 1843, after his brother James split the partner-ship, to purchase the entire George W. Hill estate.

Among the mills which did stop was Phillips'. But his decision to end his enterprise at Old Sable was not the result of financial reverses, for business was generally good in 1836. Perhaps he was prompted by his disappointments in love; perhaps by the pressure of opinion in the Calvary congregation (the church's front door opened almost directly onto his front yard, 50 feet away) against his "Infidel" views. In any case, he left, and with his brother-in-law invested instead in a mill at Fairmount. The workers left unemployed were quickly taken up at other factories in the neighborhood. As the brother of one of his former employees succinctly put it, "It seems that his employer was a wealthy man and thought he could make more by some other kind of speculation. So he stopped the greater part of his machinery. B[rother] Andrew was thrown out of employment." But by the next year things were different. Writing in June to his brother in England, William Morris gave an account of the recession on Chester Creek and its causes:

> . . . times have been very dull for six or seven weeks past. Some cotton mills have stopped, some runing half time and some full time and their is a great many manufactorers and mechanicks out of employment. This pressure of the times is oweing to the bad regulations of the currency for since the United States Bank has been put down from being a national bank, it gave rise to many petty banks. These encouraged a high run of speculation and everything demanded high price but the foreign merchants demanded payment in hard money which [strained?] the banks and then the merchants and speculaters began to fail which [led to a] great stagnation. . . .[8]

Actually, only two of the factories in the Rockdale district remained "standing" during most of the recession. One of these was the Knowlton cotton factory. This factory had burned to the ground in 1834 before Crozer purchased it. Crozer continued to rent the tilt mill to the manufacturer of edge tools from whom he bought it and a year or two later rebuilt the stone cotton mill; but this probably did not get into operation at once, given the general dullness of business. The only cotton manufacturer who seems to have failed outright was James Houghton, who closed his weaving mill about 1837 or 1838. Houghton died a few years later owing a sum to commission merchant Henry Farnum sufficiently large for Farnum to be appointed by the court as administrator of his estate.[9] Burt and Kerlin, who leased the Phillips mill from Richard S. Smith, failed in the spring of 1843, but their failure may have been in part the result of labor trouble.[10]

Daniel Lammot is the one manufacturer whose experience in the depression is recorded in any detail. In his correspondence with his son-in-law Alfred du Pont for the period 1836 through 1842 there is a clear record of his difficulties and of the expedients by which he managed to survive. He entered the period of recession under the handicap of a large loan from his other son-in-law Thomas Hounsfield, on the order of $30,000, which he had spent enlarging his works to accommodate a weaving department. Hounsfield decided to leave the area and, despite his prior verbal assurances that it was a "permanent loan" for seven years, now demanded his money. With some difficulty, Lammot managed to get his friends to make credit arrangements to satisfy Hounsfield with notes for shorter periods—up to eighteen months.

Lammot had labor trouble in 1836 and was forced to raise wages. And he was never able to count on the "tricky" Peter Hill, his landlord, to be cooperative in emergencies like breaches in the race or broken headgates. By May 1837 he was under the necessity of borrowing still more money, "on the ground that sales cannot now be effected, but that it is still desirable to keep the mill running." He turned repeatedly to the better capitalized Du Ponts, who were customers for some of his yarns, for aid in the form of direct loans and credit assurances. The crisis for Lammot and Son was reached in July 1837, at a time of year when sales were low anyway. Waln and Leaming, the commission merchants to whom they consigned most of their principal product (fine printing cloths), told Lammot (and other customers) that henceforth they would "refuse to advance on any goods until sales are made." Since the Lammots depended on these cash advances to pay off their notes as they came due, and thereby to renew their credit for the purchase of more bales of cotton (paid for with still other short-term notes), they were on the brink of having to stop their mill for want of cotton. It was little comfort to be told by commission merchants to hold on to the printing cloths until January, when the "low prices of Goods at auction" would rise again, as they always did, as the printers began to make new goods for spring and the ice-choked harbors kept out competing supplies from New England.

The Du Ponts came to the rescue, working out a deal with Lammot to manufacture fine cloth for them, at so much per pound, out of raw cotton furnished for the purpose. The house of Francis Gurney Smith in Philadelphia, the agents of the Du Ponts, forwarded the cotton bales to Marcus Hook and Chester, whence the Lammots had them hauled to Lenni, re-weighed them (saving the Du Ponts from 5 to 15 lbs. per bale), and worked them into printing cloth. The cloth was then baled and sent back to Smith's for sale at Du Pont's risk. (A bale of fine printing cloth contained on an average 1,235 yards, weighed about 195 lbs., and sold for about 8 to 8 1/2 cents per yard.) Between August, when the arrangements began, and November, when the job was completed, Lammot's mill had received thirty-five bales of cotton and sent out sixty-five bales of finished cloth. The total cost to E. I. du Pont de Nemours and Company was estimated by Lammot at about 7 1/4 cents per yard of printed cloth; for a total of 80,122 3/4 yards, this amounted to about $5,800. Of this, Lammot charged $3,640 (most of which no doubt was manufacturing cost). The rest of the cost to the Du Ponts was for buying the cotton and commission fees. At a price of 8 cents per yard, the Du Ponts would make a net profit of about $600.

Lammot's enterprise limped along through the depression and he never did extricate himself from the maze of notes in which he was enmeshed. In 1838 he shifted to the manufacture of coarser cloths, after hearing that the Boston firms were unable to sell their fine cloths but could not meet the demand for coarse. By 1842 he was in trouble again, the mill stopped, and Peter Hill (himself as usual in financial distress) demanded payment of rent. Once again he turned to Alfred:

> Remington still urges us to start, promis^d to advance as formerly, and stating his conviction that Tickings must rise in the spring as the stock is not heavy and many manufacturers of them have failed. Common prints are said to be scarce in the market, and printing cloth must advance next month. But we are not yet started and not entitled to advance, and know not where to apply for relief but to yourself and we do it reluctantly because you have already advanced us so largely. Yet if you can advance or lend us your note at 4 ms, for about $900 we can have it discounted at the Bank of N. America.[11]

THE STRIKES OF 1836 AND 1842

The workers in the Rockdale district had been quiet during the labor disturbances that agitated Philadelphia in the late 1820's and early 1830's, probably because there were few members of trades unions in the Rockdale district (except for the mechanics). Cotton mill operatives, even though they might be termed "spinners" and "weavers" in tax and census lists, did not proceed from formal apprenticeship to the status of journeyman; often they were merely called "laborers," and mostly did not belong to the unions of cotton spinners and weavers. There was not even any vigorous opposition when mills closed or went on part-time work in 1834. But in 1836, as prices rose again and the mills' business quickened, there were turnouts, the strikers demanding raises in pay or shorter hours at the same pay. They were acting in unison, if not in concert, with striking craftsmen in Philadelphia.

The Strike in 1836

The confrontation began in February, when operatives employed in the Chester Creek manufactories met at the Seven Stars Tavern in Village Green to organize a "Trades Union" (also referred to as the "Chester Creek Trade Association") in opposition to "the long-hour system enforced by employers on hands in cotton mills against their will." One of the organizers was William Shaw, who worked at West Branch. Crozer fired him at once; and immediately Crozer's hands turned out briefly in protest.[1] Shaw was a young but experienced mule spinner (he was twenty-five), who had been born in Baltimore and had come north eight years before to work in the mills. He had spent two years with Samuel Riddle (he and "his girl" were one of the cohort of families who started out with Riddle in the new mill at Parkmount) and the last three years with Crozer. His particular objection was the overworking of children in the mills. After being discharged, he went to Philadelphia to work in a mill in Fairmount, and while there he helped to organize the petition to the Pennsylvania legislature that resulted in the Senate investigation of 1837. Shaw was the first witness interviewed by the committee and we reviewed some of his testimony in the last chapter; we shall look at his testimony in detail again later.[2]

Negotiations between the workers and the employers continued without result until May, then the disturbances began. The dispute dragged on all through the summer. The rhetoric used by the operatives was radical (as the Smiths painfully observed during their efforts to establish Calvary Church); the methods may have been violent. In January, the mill at West Branch burned out; at the end of June, Crozer's barn burned down.[3] Lammot's factory was struck in May and June, and his surviving account provides most of the detail of the tactics of the two sides. On May 18, writing to Alfred, he reported that the anticipated turnout had occurred after he fired two of the troublemakers and was preparing to replace them with new hands:

> As I apprehended, I found the mill in an uproar on my return home. My spinners were out and the other hands ready to rebel. Ferdinand will start immediately for Norristown, where there is a suitable family anxious for a place. I have now two spinners at work, but the discharged hands are prowling about, doing nothing the law can lay hold on, but keeping the hands so uneasy, that I am confident, if I were to leave home for one hour, there would be another uproar and turn out. The hands that are threatened and driven from their work dare not tell me, for they believe

their lives would be endangered by giving testimony against each other. The matter is a manifest conspiracy, but I have not testimony to pursue it, otherwise I would have the Sheriff at work very quickly.[4]

Two weeks later, the mule spinners were still out on strike and the ringleaders were still fomenting trouble. Lammot attempted to appease the weavers by raising their piece rates; the rest of the factory then turned out, demanding that their wages be raised too.

I have been extremely anxious to get over to see you all, but for the last two weeks, I have had a very anxious and perplexing time. My Mule spinners turned out 2 weeks ago, and when they found I had discharged the two ring leaders, they became turbulent, and excited almost an insurrection amongst the other hands. The morning I started to town, the hands were quiet. I had not been absent an hour before the weavers turned out. Ferd. remonstrated with them for waiting until I had left home, and then turning out. They returned to work and continued until I returned, and then turned out again. I advanced the price of their weaving, and then the rest of the hands turned out. These had to turn in as they came out, and the discharged spinners kept up the fomentation by geering them for returning to work, calling them nobs. Until to day I have not felt easy for half an hour; but how it will be on Monday I cannot say, but expect further excitement. At this time the disturbance is peculiarly unfortunate for we are short of hands in every department. This long story will account for my not visiting you sooner.[5]

The strike, coming at a well-chosen time when the demand for cotton yarn and cloths was high, seems to have been at least partially successful. And although the "Trades Union" itself did not survive the strike for long, hostility toward the manufacturers remained. Writing to Minshall Painter a few years later, Crozer deplored the suspicions that workers still entertained against their employers:

The work people cannot be convinced that employers have not some interested & selfish motive in view in all their plans. This prejudice had its origin in the unfortunate "Trades Union" which embodied, a few years ago, all our work people nearby—and although the Society is, I believe, quite broken up its injurious influence exists, and is likely to exist for a long time to come in a greater or less degree.[6]

A reciprocal prejudice, of course, was held by the employers. Crozer's and Lammot's language was guarded, but their attitude of perplexity and resentment at the distrust in which they were held, and their readiness to take punitive action against ringleaders, were plain.

The whole matter came in for a public airing next year in the Senate's abortive investigation of the working conditions of children employed in cotton mills. Crozer and Riddle both testified, more or less blandly, that they would like to see the hours of child labor reduced nationally, not just in Pennsylvania. The more extreme positions were taken by William Shaw, the discharged ringleader from West Branch, on the operatives' side, who testified first, and by Joseph Ripka, the principal manufacturer in Manayunk, who testified last. Shaw was forthright in condemning the manufacturers for the overworking of children and the neglect of their educational needs:

> The greatest evils known are, first, the number of hours of labor, and the number of children employed. . . . The proportion of children varies in different establishments; has known more than one-fourth to be children under twelve years of age: under twenty years, would include in many cases, three-fourths; not many are apprenticed; they are usually hired to employers by parents and guardians. The hours vary in different establishments; in some I have worked fourteen and a-half hours. . . . The labor of the children is in some cases excessive—in others it is not. The children are employed at spinning and carding. The question of excessive labor is more upon the kind of work; carding is the hardest work; their work is regulated by the operation of the machinery, at carding; and they must stand during the whole time; considers twelve or fourteen hours labor excessive at either branch for a child. I have known children of nine years of age to be employed at spinning; at carding, as young as ten years. . . . I think no attention is paid to education during the time they are employed in factories, except what they receive from Sabbath schools, and some few at night schools, when they are in an unfit condition to learn; the children attend Sabbath school with great reluctance; many will not attend in consequence of the confinement of the week.

But Joseph Ripka saw the matter in a completely different light, claiming that the only reason for labor strife was the evil "Trades' Union" and that he employed children mostly as an act of charity:

> If any evil exists in the factory system, it is the principles of the Trades' Union, which has been introduced amongst the laboring classes in general; it has been imparted to this country by English and Irish men within a few years, and has the tendency to destroy the good feeling which has, heretofore, existed between the employer and the workman in this coun-

try, and the leaders are men, either of low character or designing politicians. To show that the principle is a bad one, the leaders are always trying to keep the working people in an excitement, to have them always ready for a turn-out, they lay contribution on the working classes, and expend the money amongst themselves, by going about from place to place to make speeches, and encourage them to turn out. When labor is plenty, the workingmen will get good wages and find plenty employment without the aid of the Trades' Union, and in hard times, the Trades' Union cannot keep up wages or find employment for the working classes. If they could do it, why don't they do it at the present time. . . .

I employ twenty-five children under twelve years of age, and they are pressed on me by widows, or by mothers of dissipated husbands; and when I do employ them, it is for mere charity than any thing else. Children, under twelve years of age, are of no profit to the employers in cotton factories, it is the age when they ought to be educated, and I have always been against to employ them. . . .

The labor for children is not excessive.

The children do not appear tired when they leave work.[7]

The general economic decline, beginning with the financial panic of 1837, placed the unions in a poor position to call for strike actions against employers who reduced wages or otherwise failed to meet the expectations of operatives. Some of the manufacturers kept their mills operating more to provide wages than to produce cotton goods, for although the yarn and cloth might be unsalable now, it would probably be sold later, and if starving operatives left the district to find work elsewhere, the manufacturer would be hard-pressed to find new, trained operatives at a time when all the mills would again be seeking them. Besides, providing work was a matter of Christian charity in an age when there was no source of public relief but the poorhouse, which separated husbands and wives and children, and exposed the respectable poor to the influence of the immoral, the improvident, and the insane.

The Strike in 1842

The mills on Chester Creek kept limping along in an off-again on-again fashion through the depression; but a nadir of some sort was reached in the spring of 1842, when, in an effort to keep their mills running and their books showing some sort of profit (or at least a lesser rate of loss), the manufacturers imposed a third 15 percent reduction in wages. The blow was softened, in Crozer's case at least, by a reduction in the rent charged for company houses; but since rents were already very low, amounting to only about 5 percent of a family's earnings, such an economy was not significantly compensatory at all. And so the workers struck again. This time the outcome was less favorable for them.

The precipitating event was the announced intention of the manufacturers to reduce the piece rates for weavers a further 10 to 15 percent depending on the employer's circumstances, beginning Monday March 21. This reduction had been agreed upon by all the manufacturers as a result of a meeting amongst themselves. It was the third such percentage reduction since the relatively prosperous year of 1840 and meant, in effect, that the rates had gone down almost 50 percent in two years. But the reduction itself might not have been enough to precipitate a strike. Some of the manufacturers went to the trouble of talking the matter over with their employees in advance, explaining that the fall in the selling price of the cloths required this temporary measure and that rates would go up again as soon as economic conditions justified it. Samuel Riddle specifically showed his employees this courtesy; in the ensuing disturbance his mill was not struck; and he did not testify as a witness against the strikers at the trial. Other manufacturers were prevented in part by circumstance: Lammot's mill was idle for repairs but scheduled to open on Monday the 28th, and he posted the new rates on the gates in the workers' absence. Crozer posted his "military notice" as he always did. Garsed and Pierce never made any announcement at all; they simply deducted 12 1/2 percent from the paychecks on the payday at the middle of April. Whether Burt and Kerlin announced the reduction is not clear, but as a precaution against trouble they had erected a watchtower. With their mill at Old Sable already surrounded (as was typical of the day) by a wooden panel fence, the addition of a watchtower must have made the place look like a fortress. Some of the manufacturers —notably Garsed and Pierce—also were already in the practice of paying in orders on the local store (which might be the company store) and in notes due, which could only be redeemed (if at all) at banks in town. Crozer, by contrast, always paid in cash.

The first meeting of the strikers was held after work on Saturday afternoon, March 19, at Brown's general store, which was located on Mount Road in Crozerville. Mark Wild, a young foreign-born weaver at Lammot's Lenni Mill, spoke to a crowd of disgruntled male weavers from the porch of the store, introducing the main speaker, and urging the group not to commit violence and to act only in ways that were within the law. The main speaker was Hiram McConnell, also an immigrant (probably from Northern Ireland), a retired worker from outside Delaware County who was living on his savings "earned long ago"[8] and devoting his time to organizing cotton mill operatives in Delaware County, New Jersey, and perhaps elsewhere. He was, in fact, a professional labor organizer who expected trouble and carried a pistol for self-defense. (While he was serving as chairman of the Chester Creek committee, McConnell also served as a delegate to a committee of strikers in New Jersey and even organized a march of armed men from Rockdale to Darby to protest conditions at Charles Kelly's mill there.) The business of the meeting at Brown's store was to make plans for a turnout at Burt and Kerlin's weaving mill.

The turnout at Burt and Kerlin's took place as planned on Monday about nine o'clock when the mill stopped to allow the hands to take breakfast. A core of strikers left the mill. Then a crowd of men, as many as one hundred, surrounded the gates of the mill and called to those remaining inside to come out. Some of the leaders entered the mill and terrorized the female operatives, seizing them by the arms and attempting to drag them out. The mill resumed working, with a reduced number of operatives, while the strikers outside kept up their shouting, and small groups of frightened workers gradually trickled out through the gates. Threats were made to duck or drown in Chester Creek any "nobstick" (one who continued to work—in later jargon, a scab). The mill closed at dinnertime. And next day a burly striker did in fact duck a "nobstick," one James Broadbent, in full view of an assembled crowd. Broadbent was thrown into the millpond from the breast of the dam and his head was held under water for a while; then as he made his escape, he was beaten and knocked into the race. His persecutor laughed and said, "That'll wash the bugger's sins away." It was these events at Burt and Kerlin's—the plan to duck nobsticks, the shouted threats, the actual ducking—which formed the basis for the later trial of the strike organizers on charges of conspiracy and riot.

At the end of the week, on Saturday afternoon again, the strikers held another meeting, this time to formalize their organization and to turn the force of the strike against the next manufacturer. This meeting was attended by women as well as men, and again Wild and McConnell, the principal organizers, spoke first, followed by others. At this meeting, the usual parliamentary procedure at public meetings was employed: a chairman and other officers were chosen, resolutions were passed, and a committee was then elected to conduct the business resolved upon at the meeting. The resolutions were reduced to writing. Although no copy has survived, the testimony of witnesses who were present shows that there were demands that the manufacturers reverse the piece rate reduction for weavers and that they cease the despised practice of paying wages in the form of orders on storekeepers. Hiram McConnell, as experienced labor leader, became chairman of the committee. McConnell then turned the crowd's attention to the issues concerning Lammot's mill at Lenni. It was to be struck on Monday morning, when it was scheduled to be reopened; nobsticks were as usual threatened with ducking or worse. On Monday morning, in due course, the strikers presented themselves at Lammot's mill. The mill's operatives streamed out and the machinery stopped.

The next mill to be closed was Garsed and Pierce's weaving mill at Penn's Grove. In addition to the main general charges, Garsed and Pierce were accused of paying their workers less per piece than Crozer paid. By now, McConnell had at his disposal a small army of striking men and women, whom he kept busy at meetings every day or so where he and others harangued them. On Thursday March 31, the workers formed themselves on Church Hill and marched across the Rockdale bridge toward Garsed's mill. The workers ran to the windows and the aged Joshua Garsed and his sons personally guarded the gates as the column of strikers, two abreast, approached up the hill. The men marched in front, some of them banging on kettles; then came a small fife-and-drum corps; a squad of women took the rear. The usual process occurred: the sympathizers quit at once and the rest of the operatives, their resolve to stay gradually worn down by anxiety, straggled out after them.

Crozer's mills were struck about three weeks later. Crozer, of course, was operating three mills by this time: the original factory at West Branch and the two new mills at Crozerville and Knowlton, the latter specialized as a weaving mill. This case was complicated by the fact that while his weavers were on strike demanding merely a return to former rates, his mule spinners were out demanding an increase. Crozer's factories were infested by columns of marching, shouting, fife-and-drum-playing men and women.

By the end of the month of April, all the mills along the creek were at a standstill except Samuel Riddle's at Parkmount. Efforts to persuade the strikers to return to work had been unavailing, for the 20 to 30 percent who wished to return at the former rates were intimidated by their more violent fellows. But the employers had no intention of giving in. John P. Crozer's views were probably representative of the rest. He had recently begun to keep a diary, and in it he recorded his feelings about the strike. Comparing it to the events of 1836, he said:

In the present disagreement there is more of deep determination and greater indications of violence than formerly. But as the issue is fairly joined, I cannot for a moment think of yielding. . . . I do not know if all the employers will be firm, but for myself I have not the most remote idea of yielding, and shall rather never start than be compelled to yield.

After forty days had gone by, some of his mule spinners requested an interview with him, which he granted. He was unbending:

> I had a good deal of conversation with them, perfectly calm on both sides, and we parted in a friendly manner. I am inclined to think that the interview was sought under the hope or expectation that I would propose some compromise. I, however, thought best, in reply to a question asked me as to the probability of the mill starting, to say, positively, that the mill would never start except upon my terms.

His resolution was fortified by his awareness that the strike was in fact a benefit to the employers, permitting them to stop the mills entirely at a time when continued operation would merely take money out of the employer's pocket and put it in the hands of the operatives. As he noted in his diary: "In a pecuniary view the cessation of work will not, I think, be any injury to me or to any of the employers. With all of us, goods, if sold now, must be sold at a sacrifice, and none of us could continue working without making sales. We are therefore prepared for a long suspension."[9]

But Burt and Kerlin seem to have panicked. Perhaps they feared damage to their persons and property; perhaps they took a moralistic view. In any case, unable to open their mill on Monday April 25, five weeks after they had been struck, they summoned the sheriff "to quell the riot and violence, which was said to exist in this place." Mark Wild and Hiram McConnell were not arrested at this time. As McConnell described it: "Myself and a few others endeavored to explain the matter to the Sheriff and those with him, and it is due to the Sheriff to say, his conduct and the conduct of those with him was highly commendable, and instead of taking us prisoners, they went away our friends." Failing to persuade the sheriff that a riot was in progress, John Burt made a written offer to the strikers the same day. The committee rejected it and Hiram McConnell now took his case to the people at large, publishing a long exposition of the issues in the *Upland Union* for May 3. Burt and Kerlin's curious offer is worth quoting:

> The proposition is, that if the hands will agree to work and take goods at the price they brought last fall, they shall be paid the old price, after deducting the price of fall cotton; otherwise, if the hands agree to work at the deduction and work up the stock now on hand, and if goods will not allow the advanced price, stop the mill entirely.

The strike dragged on. There were now roughly four hundred people out of work in the Rockdale district. In order to provide food for the strikers and their families, the committee set up a store which accepted the provisions donated in substantial quantity by sympathetic neighbors and farmers; these, and other supplies purchased by the committee, were distributed to those who needed assistance.[10] But such expedients were hardly adequate. Crozer's diary makes it plain that he was prepared to see hunger motivate the workers to return on his terms: "Some of the families around us are beginning to need the necessaries of life, which we would, under different circumstances, supply with a liberal hand. We have to do something for a few of them, but feel it due to ourselves to be sparing, in consequence of the cause of their distress."[11]

Toward the middle of May, the employers resolved to act firmly to end the struggle in such a way as to discourage a repetition. Eighteen of the strikers, including Hiram McConnell and Mark Wild, were arrested on charges of conspiracy and riot. The case was brought to trial very quickly —within a couple of weeks of the arrest—in Chester in the Delaware County Court of Sessions, Judge Thomas S. Bell presiding. Judge Bell, now in his forty-third year, had been an attorney in West Chester and a delegate to the State Constitutional Convention. He bore a reputation for learning, for courtesy, and for severity. As a local historian later put it, "on one occasion . . . he aroused considerable feeling in sentencing a child ten years of age to a protracted term of imprisonment for stealing a small sum of money."[12] The public prosecutor was the prominent Chester attorney and politician Samuel Edwards under whom Edward Darlington had read law. Edwards had served in Congress and was a close friend of James Buchanan; he was reported to be one of the most influential background advisers in the Democratic national machine. He held the sinecure of Inspector of Customs at the port of Chester, was a director of the Delaware County National Bank (as were both Kerlin and Crozer), and counsel for the Philadelphia, Wilmington, and Baltimore Railroad. The attorneys for the defendants, Joseph S. Lewis of West Chester and William D. Kelly of Philadelphia, were competent lawyers but were from outside the community that supplied both prosecutor and the jury. The issues involved were sufficiently important for Philadelphia readers to take an interest. And so the *Public Ledger* sent a correspondent to cover the trial, who dutifully recorded a partial transcript of the testimony in the five-day hearing.

It was a colorful trial. Some, but not all, of the manufacturers testified against the strikers: John P. Crozer, John Pierce, John and Richard Garsed, and John Burt. Daniel Lammot and Samuel Riddle did not testify, nor did any of the accused testify in their own defense. Most of the witnesses were workers, some of whom had been opposed to the strike (including the man who had been ducked in the creek) and some of whom had taken part. Five of the witnesses were women.

After five days of testimony, the jury was charged by Judge Bell. They retired briefly and returned with a verdict of not guilty of both charges for fifteen of the defendants. Hiram McConnell, Mark Wild, and Major Rowe were found innocent of riot but guilty of conspiracy, and sentenced to pay fines of $35, $30, and $30, respectively. Hiram McConnell was in addition required to pay the cost of prosecution on the charge of riot, which amounted to more than $1,000. Unwilling (and perhaps unable) to pay, they were committed to the old Chester jail, where they were visited by the friendly editor of the *Upland Union.* He said he found them

> now living with our Sheriff, happy as the King in his princely palace, and declare their present situation a kingdom compared with the prison of cotton tyrants. They have been prepared with feather beds, chairs, table and stationary, and our good citizens are constantly loading them with the comforts of human bliss. The former companions and friends of these benevolent men are still holding meetings on Church Hill, in the vicinity of Rockdale, and I understand that several factory ladies are delivering public addresses to hundreds in attendence.[13]

But the conviction really did signal the end of the strike. One by one, the mills reopened as the weavers agreed to work at the reduced rates; Crozer's mule spinners came back on Crozer's terms. Governor Porter, hearing of the hard feelings being engendered by the protracted dispute, remitted the fines, and the sheriff released Wild and Rowe; shortly after that, a subscription paid for the costs of prosecution, and Hiram McConnell was freed. He left the district. By the Fourth of July the mills were limping along again, at reduced rates, operating part time, sometimes stopped for extended periods.[14]

The Meaning of the Strikes

Throughout the decade from 1828 to 1837, while the craft unions were successfully organizing, the workers in the mechanized textile factories lagged behind. During the boom year of 1835, after a series of strikes, most of the craft unions of Philadelphia even won the ten-hour day for their journeymen, including Kensington's thousands of hand-loom weavers. But the ten-hour day did not apply, even in a legal sense, to the operatives in the city's cotton mills. The men and women who tended the power looms in Manayunk, Blockley, and Fairmount still put in their twelve to fourteen hours, and so did the weavers on Chester Creek. So too did the mule spinners, with their piecers and scavengers, as did the young women who tended the throstles and drawing frames, and the lads who worked in the card and picker rooms.

The cotton mill workers had no craft unions in America (in contrast to England, where the mule spinners at least were organized in a trade union). The traditional crafts themselves were old, hundreds or even thousands of years old; and their trade associations, formed in medieval times to control standards of training (through the apprentice-journeyman-master system) and quality, and to provide benefits for unfortunate members and their families, were also old. The journeymen usually hired out at daily wages or on piecework to a master craftsman, but often they owned their own hand tools and sometimes even worked in their own homes; thus they could be, in a sense, small capitalists. When the hand-loom weavers struck, the master weavers (who were really capitalist cloth merchants and manufacturers, some of them employing hundreds of weavers) could not replace them with strikebreakers because the strikers owned much of the machinery. A clear career line was laid out in the trades, from an apprenticeship unpaid (or even paying) of three to seven years in the shop of a master tradesman, to a journeyman working for daily wages or at piecework, in his own home or a master's shop, to the master tradesman, who might become in effect a wealthy merchant-contractor.

Among the factory skills, mule spinning came closest, perhaps, to a craft but it was a craft learned informally, and often quickly, by a youth who first familiarized himself with the machine by working for a few weeks as a piecer, and then, under the instruction of the experienced spinner, by trying out the machine himself. The mule spinner was the employer of his piecers and scavengers; but they were certainly not apprentices. And he did not own the mule he operated; the mule, which was far too large ever to be accommodated in an ordinary private dwelling, was the property of the manufacturer, who paid the spinner by the hank of yarn. Similarly with the power looms: they were the property of the manufacturer and were assembled in a factory, where men and women supervised them. Experienced hand-loom weavers, like the Morrises, sometimes took jobs operating "the power looms," in order to make more money, but their craft skill was not needed and inexperienced young women (ineligible by sex for membership in the weavers' union) could be, and were, taught to operate them successfully. Still less could the skills involved in tending the throstles and draw frames and carding machines and pickers and blowers be compared to traditional crafts. All of these jobs were new, less than a hundred years old in England, and less than fifty years old in America, and they were jobs, not occupations. Although they required some skill (as does even "unskilled" labor), they could not be defined as crafts because the entire social context in which the job was done was different from the craft context.

Thus from the first in the cotton districts, not only on Chester Creek but in the Philadelphia mill neighborhoods as well, the problem of labor organization differed from that in the already organized urban-based trade districts. The organization was an ad hoc strikers' group rather than a union that endured between strikes. Furthermore, the cotton weavers' approach, both in 1836 and 1842, was to organize factory by factory (or district by district) rather than by craft, and the organizations were named after the district rather than after a skill. One job specialty (invariably either mule spinners or weavers) might take the lead; but the action was against the factory as a whole (or a group of factories) and the technique was to turn out *all* the workers, not just the mule spinners or weavers. The strategy of organization was more comparable to what later came to be called "industrial" unions than to "craft" unions. These differences explain in part why the operatives in cotton mills seem to have been marching to a different drummer. During the flurry of strikes by the painters, trimmers, glass cutters, white smiths, saddlers, cordwainers, and other crafts in Philadelphia in 1835 demanding the ten-hour day, the operatives on Chester Creek were quiet. In 1836, the same trade unions in Philadelphia struck for higher wages; this time the operatives on Chester Creek struck too, for higher pay or shorter hours. But the strike in 1842, although not an isolated one, and led by a professional outside organizer, seems to have been fought out on strictly local issues at a time when some trades organizations were turning their attention to national unions and Fourierist socialism.[15]

An examination of the records of the 1842 strike (the names of only a few strikers survive from 1836) shows that it was led by substantial members of the community.[16] Of the eighteen men brought to trial, thirteen (including a "boss weaver" and a beamer) were weavers or connected with the weaving department; one was a machinist; the occupations of four cannot be determined. Most (ten) were single but there were about five married men in the group. Their incomes ranged from $100 to $200 per year (according to tax assessments, which were apt to underestimate). At least seven were church members, and probably more, because the early membership records of the Methodist and Presbyterian churches have not survived. And eleven continued to live in the Rockdale district for at least two years after the strike.

Mark Wild—the local co-leader with McConnell, and the advocate of law and order—was perhaps typical of the better established leadership. His name does not appear in the 1840 census, which means that he and his wife Sarah probably arrived in Rockdale in 1841. He was an English-born weaver who in 1842, according to the tax assessor, was earning at the rate of about $200 per year. He and his wife were baptized at Calvary by Bishop Onderdonk in the same year. He remained in the district after the strike, still working as a weaver—and saving money. In 1847, when he was employed by Samuel Riddle at Penn's Grove, he purchased a residential building lot from the Houghton estate. As late as 1856 he was still working as a weaver for Crozer.

Other members of the trial group were established members of the community. John Radcliff, the machinist, had been a resident of Aston Township before the 1840 census. In 1840 he was a man of between forty and fifty, with a wife about the same age; four children lived with them, the eldest a girl between fifteen and twenty. He owned his own house and two and a half acres of land. He and his wife were members of Calvary Church and like Wild remained in the area after the strike. John Gore, one of the men who ducked Broadbent, was more representative perhaps of the younger men. He was a weaver, twenty-three years old, and he remained after the strike—in fact, he lived in Aston Township all his life and was buried in Mount Hope Cemetery in 1895. Joseph Talbot, the other man who helped to duck Broadbent, was also a weaver and single. He had paid taxes in Aston since 1829; he left in 1842 after the strike.

The leaders of the 1842 strike were evidently for the most part a nontransient group, interested in putting down roots in the community. Their demands were essentially conservative: they objected to a pay cut and to certain practices, specifically the failure to consult with them beforehand about the reduction, and the payment of wages not in cash but in store orders.

The public rhetoric, both verbal and dramatic, seems to have been commanded by Hiram McConnell. But even McConnell's rhetoric was curiously unradical. Although he roundly condemned the despotic manufacturers, he threatened only to bring the people's wrath down upon them by supporting the political fortunes of the Democratic Party and by opposing the Whig tariff: ". . . if after the pains the whigs have taken to show their real character, the people ever trust them again, it shall not be till my humble voice had been heard by every ear and resounded in every grove throughout this union." And his invective, while colorful, was not radical in the Paine sense. He did not condemn the clergy; he did not attack the institutions of society; he did not even attack the class system, but only the injustices perpetuated by those who exploited it:

While ambition, jealously [*sic*], cupidity and the blind love of innovation keep up a deplorable struggle among the people—some misguided by false promises of an expiring faction that has been laboring to overthrow the sovereignty of the people and establish an aristocracy; others influenced by needy circumstances and dependent on the few for employment, to gain the necessaries of life, the majority of the citizens of these free states are miserably brutalized, to languish out their days in incessant drudgery, by those of opulence and tyranny. The lordly manufacturer, speculator and adventurer dispise the people and believe themselves born to reign over them and drive them to and fro over the land as beasts of the field. They seek to decieve the ignorant by night and by day, mentally, moral [*sic*] and politically, when myself and others having suffered from their faithlessness, dared to withstand their tyrannical and oppressive measures, and expose their craft, they combinedly entered into a malicious prosecution, raked up all their tools and menials who had to swear at their bidding against a number of humble and industrious operatives, and were wanton enough, so far as regards myself, to try to villify [*sic*] my character. . . .

The public organs of the two political parties of Delaware County responded, of course, very differently to the strike and to the populist declamations of Hiram McConnell. The *Upland Union,* ever-watchful sentinel of the locally outnumbered Democrats, at first took the strike as an opportunity to vilify the opposite party. In March and April the *Union* attempted to portray the strike as the working people's revenge against the Whigs for having misled them into voting for William Henry Harrison in 1840:

The Tippecanoe and Tyler too editor of the Delaware County Republican stated in his last paper, that there had been a strike among the workmen on Chester Creek, and that he was not aware of the cause. So far as we have been informed on the subject it appears, that the deluded operatives, misled by log cabin parades, the idle display of flags and banners, inscribed with a reduction of wages, and the direct and positive declarations of their Tip & Ty leaders, that their wages were at that time too low and that rather than reduce them, they would quit business and that a change of administration only, was wanting, to ensure higher wages and better times. The change has been had and the golden dreams of the deceived workmen have resulted in two reductions of their wages each time 15 per cent, and in the unholy attempt to reduce them 15 per cent more. Under this gross violation of promises and professions the present strike has been produced, and the sympathy of the whole community is on the side of the workmen, who have been deluded by political knavery and humbug. Another political crusade is about commencing and instead of log cabin and hard cider, protective tariff home league, American Industry, etc. are the political catchwords of the same party, let the producers guard against the election of wooden whiggery in all time to come.

But the paper eventually withdrew this charge, inviting as it did the countercharge of the *Delaware County Republican* that the Democrats were trying to take partisan advantage from a community misfortune.

The *Republican*'s editor fancied himself a master of political satire and he took the turnout as an opportunity to portray the striking operatives as a passel of silly revolutionary followers of the outmoded associationist creed of Robert Owen. In May the *Republican* ran a letter to the editor describing a visit to "the Thermopylae of America, where the few resist the many and where oppression such as was never before heard of had driven hundreds of half-starved operatives to collect en masse and demand their natural rights." He went on (tongue in cheek) to describe the resolutions which were, he alleged, "unanimously adopted" at a meeting of the striking workers:

RESOLVED, That a great revolution is about to take place of which we are the thrice honored instruments, a revolution that will teach men the strength of weakness, the riches of poverty, and the omnipotence of despair.

RESOLVED, That the eyes of the world are upon us; that the starving millions of Europe are at this moment urging us onward.

RESOLVED, That our names and the name of Alexander M'Keever [editor of the *Upland Union*], our great, talented, and immaculate mouthpiece will descend to posterity adorned with such honors as the heroes of the paltry revolution of 76 never dreamed of.[17]

And on July 8, long after the strikers had been convicted, the *Republican* still was harping on the same theme. On that date it published a hoax in the form of another letter to the editor from "A Hater of Oppression" (the style suggests the author was the same as before). The letter proposed the establishment of a "Chester Benevolent Factory," a cooperative enterprise to be owned by the workers, and to be housed in the courthouses and jails of Chester—"the hateful establishment of a bygone and barbarous age." The factory's "Rules and Regulations" were to be as follows:

RULE 1 No stockholder shall be permitted to hold more than _____ shares of stock at fifty dollars per share.

RULE 2 Every operative employed shall have the privilege of subscribing for five shares of stock without obligation to pay for the same. The fact of his being a workman is to be considered equivalent to money paid.

RULE 3. No person shall be employed in this factory who cannot bring satisfactory evidence that he or she has been distinguished either in *this* or some other country, by opposition to the employer; or, in other words, to tyranny and oppression.

RULE 4. The workmen shall always have the privilege of keeping one or more persons to regulate matters with the foreman or manager, whose business it shall be to dictate to said foreman how and where the hands are to be placed in the factory—what new workmen shall be employed; what amount and kind of work shall be done, and all other things conducive to the comfort of the work people.

RULE 5. No person shall be discharged from this factory without his or her consent. A contrary course evidently conflicts with proper liberty, and is one of the greatest evils in factories generally.

RULE 6. No reduction of wages shall at any time take place, without the workmen themselves request it to be done; they are certainly the best judges as to what is reasonable and proper.[18]

But the windy political rhetoric of Hiram McConnell, the *Upland Union,* and the *Delaware County Republican* fails to convey the more visceral sentiments of the local participants in the conflict. The manufacturers expressed resentment at the operatives' lack of trust; the clergymen deplored their falling away from grace. In his diary, Crozer recorded some personal discomfort at the alienation of his employees:

It would be gratifying to me to see the laboring classes have plenty of work at a fair compensation, but this can never be unless employers are prosperous. This is so plain that it is to me a subject of surprise that work people so generally rejoice in the embarrassments and downfall of their employers.[19]

But in a public letter to the *Republican* he was even more defensive than in his privately recorded thoughts. In the open forum, Crozer went to some pains to defend his "right to conduct my own business in accordance with my own judgment," and to justify his actions:

The unfortunate Chester creek excitement has for some time past occupied a full share of interest in the county. The tendency of these disturbances to destroy peace and good order in a community is so evident, that whatever difference of opinion may exist as to the cause from which they originated, all good citizens must unite in deploring such occurrences. But it is gratifying that quiet is again restored, and though there may be remains of disaffection—a rankling and smothered feeling of resentment in the breasts of some—it is hoped that such feelings will subside without unnecessary proscription on the part of employers, or deep rooted hatred on the part of the employed. . . .

Much has also been said of the lordly and aristocratic conduct of the employers, and especially as applied to myself; particular charges have not been made I believe, and therefore I can only reply in general terms —nearly the whole of a life, not now short, has been spent in the bosom of this my native country. I am consequently, known to very many of its inhabitants; they are therefore competent to judge how far the epithets, aristocrat, lordly oppressor and tyrant will apply.[20]

Probably Crozer felt more pain at the rupture with his working people than did some of the other manufacturers. A man at once shy, ambitious, and devout, he repeatedly acknowledged—to his diary—that he had trouble balancing his intense drive toward worldly success with his need for assurances of salvation. His general solution of the dilemma was to believe, and claim, that he acted as God's steward, responsibly administering his profits for the general welfare. Public accusations by his own employees that he was doing no such thing, that he was a "cotton lord" motivated solely by self-interest, were disturbing and spurred him to vigorous efforts to convince others that he was indeed righteous as well as successful.

The professional evangelicals of the district—and particularly the clergymen and the Sunday School teachers—saw the strike as a setback in the battle against the infidels. Church and Sunday School attendance fell away (no doubt because strikers did not like to be told that they were morally wrong in striking). Even pillars of the congregation, like Mark Wild, had lamentably assumed roles of leadership in the turnout. Clementina, when she came out to Rockdale after the strike, found "much that is saddening in this place now." Among the saddening things was the bitterness of some of the working people, and particularly of strikers against nobsticks. Sarah Miles, the sister of Maria, had joined the turnout (Maria, now married to Crozer's foreman, "took no part in the 'turnout' or the improper conduct"). Sarah would not even speak to the members of other families who did not join the strike. Clementina, on visiting one family on some errand of mercy, asked if they knew the Mileses. "The Mother of the family said they did,

with much emotion, that since the 'turn out' Sarah . . . whom she loved as a daughter would not speak to them, because this poor woman's daughter had persisted in going to the mill." Clementina went on to generalize about the disregard of religion among the striking workers:

There is much to grieve and distress the heart of christians here, in the thought that many have made shipwreck of their faith and have gone far astray from the promises they professed to love—It would seem as if the Spirit of Evil had been abroad among this people, and the evil speaking lying, and slandering we hear of is really heart sickening—But I hope and believe there are some who are returning to a sense of their duty, some who mourn bitterly, who have been insensibly led into a course for which their hearts now condemn them, and to such I believe their experience in error will be a salutary lesson. I feel assured dear Sophie these poor deluded people have had an interest in your sympathy, and prayers, remember them still dearest, and him who ministers in the midst of them —The Sunday School, was really desolate the first Sunday we were here, but the children as well as the people are returning to their former habits, and have Many of them appeared in the school again.[21]

But perhaps in the end the most significant public appraisal of the strike was contained in Judge Bell's widely published charge to the jury (which in effect gave the rationale for the jury's subsequent conviction of the three conspirators). Judge Bell carefully reviewed the English common law, and British and American precedents, bearing on the nature of the crime of conspiracy. He pointed out that it was not criminal for two or more persons to combine or confederate to perform a lawful act. But if the combination sought an unlawful end, or planned and encouraged the use of unlawful means—such as violence against persons, destruction of property, or the threat of such acts—to attain even a lawful end, then it was a criminal conspiracy within the meaning of the law. Certainly it was a lawful act to refuse to work at certain wages, or to combine to request or attempt to persuade an employer to raise wages or to restore them after they had been reduced. But if the evidence showed that the combination of strikers advocated or planned the use of force (such as ducking nobsticks) in the pursuit of such legal aims, then, whether or not the force was ever used, they, or some of them, were guilty of conspiracy. If force was in fact used, then conviction on the charge of riot was also justified. The jury decided that the evidence against the defendants for their actual use of illegal force (i.e., the ducking of James Broadbent) was in some manner inadequate, but that the threats constituted a conspiracy. And thus the three men were convicted.[22]

The significance of the judge's charge lay in the fact that it declared that a combination of workers *peacefully* turning out on a wage-and-working conditions issue, and *peacefully* attempting to persuade fellow workers, and employers, of the justness of their cause, was not illegal. The jury's verdict might be argued with on the grounds of evidence; the conviction of the three leaders might leave a residuum of gall. Yet the judge's charge represented a moral victory not for the manufacturers but for the workers.

THE GREAT FLOOD

No sooner had the strike been settled than workers and capitalists were assailed by a disaster affecting both: the great flood in 1843. The problem of flash floods (or "freshets," as they were called in that day) was a perennial one along millstreams. Every now and then, high water would damage dams, races, headgates, and the machinery and materials in the lower stories in the mills. But with the increasing industrialization of the county, freshets were becoming an ever more serious threat, partly because of the increasing magnitude of capital investment, and partly because the environment itself was changing as a result of human action. The progressive denuding of once forest-covered hills, the building of drains and culverts, and the construction of roads and covered areas all helped rain and melt-water to flow more rapidly into the streams. And the dozens of dams and bridges added a special danger. Always built *above* the mill and most of its associated housing, when a dam broke it released a sudden burst of water upon the structures below it, structures already weakened by the rising stream. Bridges had the same effect because, as floodwaters rose, they created artificial dams by trapping large and small trees, floating debris, and silt and stones. Eventually, when the bridge fell, the effect upon structures below it was much the same as in the breaking of a dam. The potentiality was building for a catastrophe of unanticipated proportions along Chester Creek.

There had been some warning. In January 1839, there was an unusual warm spell accompanied by rain. The streams rose fairly rapidly and eventually reached a high-water mark as much as 18 feet above normal. Clogged with floating ice, in addition to the usual wooden debris, this freshet destroyed a number of bridges and swept away the breasts of many dams. The stone spans at Rockdale and Penn's Grove were demolished and many factories were damaged. At Knowlton, newly acquired by Crozer, the loss amounted to $5,000.[1]

On August 5, 1843—a Saturday, the day before Lammas, the ancient harvest festival, when St. Peter's imprisonment and release were to be celebrated at Calvary—there occurred the greatest flood in the memory of the inhabitants of Delaware County.[2] It was preceded by a northeasterly storm that deposited up to an inch of rain over all of the lower Delaware Valley. Late in the afternoon, primarily over northern Delaware County, the northeaster was followed by three hours of wildly stormy weather. The sky was so dark that it was difficult to read a newspaper; observers thought that the irregular movement of low-flying clouds must be the result of some extraordinary atmospheric commotion like the collision of two separate storm systems. A tornado tore down a swath of fences and trees in Concord and Bethel. Small gales struck from varying quarters. There was heavy and continuous thunder and lightning; barns were burning on the horizon. And rain fell in great sheets and lines and gobs of translucent water, sometimes reducing visibility to 50 yards or so, sometimes strangely permitting distant scenes to be perceived unobscured. Within three hours, on the upper waters of Chester Creek, there fell approximately 16 inches of rain. Crozer, immobilized (he was still recuperating from the midwinter spill from a sleigh in which his thigh had been broken), observed the scene from three to six o'clock in the afternoon from his residence on the hill above Crozerville factory:

About 3 o'clock under an unusually dark sky, rain commenced falling in torrents, accompanied with vivid lightning, and almost continuous peals of thunder. The lightning was more vivid than ever before witnessed by him in the day time, nor had he ever before heard so much loud thunder at one time. The heavy rain terminated a few minutes before 6 o'clock. Crozerville lies in a basin surrounded by steep acclivities. In every direction from these hills, sheets of water poured down, and mingling with the swollen current below, presented, together with the rapid succession of forked lightning, a scene of awful sublimity.[3]

By about 4:30, long before the end of the cloudburst, the creek had escaped its banks. At about 4:45 the creek began suddenly to rise at a rate of approximately 1 foot per minute, to an added height of about 8 feet as it moved downstream during the next hour. This sudden rise would take the form of a sloping wall of water 5 to 10 feet high, thundering along at about twenty miles per hour, carrying with it as battering rams a tumbling mass of trees, furniture, and parts of buildings. Between six and seven o'clock the waters reached their maximum height: at West Branch factory, they were 23 feet above normal; at Lenni Mill, 18 feet; and at Knowlton, where the flats narrowed and the stream flowed be-

tween two high, steep banks, the flood reached its highest level at 33 feet.

All of the dams and bridges in the Rockdale district were severely damaged and most of them were washed out. At West Branch, the dam gave way at 4:45 P.M. and its ten acres of impounded water descended suddenly upon the stone warehouse; by five o'clock, the warehouse began to disintegrate and soon fell, sending up clouds of dust from the crushed mortar. Soon after that the water wheel, mill gearing, dyehouse, and size house floated off. Then the northern wing of the factory collapsed into the torrent, with its eighty power looms and other machinery; the center building lost a corner. At Knowlton, Crozer's newly constructed weaving factory, three stories high, 76 by 36 feet—"beautiful . . . and filled with power looms, all new, and of the best construction"—was swept away to its foundations. The onlookers were romantically impressed by a peculiar circumstance of the disaster: "When the large factory went down, the roof remained entire while in view of those who witnessed its fall, the undulations of the current being sufficient to cause the factory bell in the cupola to toll the knell of its own sad catastrophe."[4]

At Lenni on the East Branch, the damage was less severe than at West Branch or at Knowlton, but even here the loss was considerable: the dam, race, stone office building, smith shop, and log tenement swept away, the county bridge just below the mill almost totally destroyed, a large quantity of cotton and finished goods and yarns ruined. Recalling the episode years later, Lammot's memory of the freshet was that "it washed away my office and all its contents—all my books, papers &c, including all my N[ew] C[hurch] correspondence, &c."[5] Crozer's office was also destroyed. The loss of an office was particularly serious because duplicate sets of books, receipts, orders, and other papers were not kept, so the amount owed by the mill owner's debtors, and his debts to his creditors, could not be positively determined; the manufacturer had to depend on the good faith of those with whom he did business.

Along with the collapse of the mill structures, the operatives' tenements on low ground were also washed away; it was in these structures that all the loss of life occurred in the Rockdale district. Most occupants were able to escape before their houses were destroyed, but some waited until their homes were surrounded by the flood. Six persons were killed when a set of four stone tenement houses near Penn's Grove factory collapsed. Their owner was an elderly, retired English cotton worker, John Rhodes, who lived in one of the houses and rented out the others. He refused to leave the safety of his dwelling until the suddenly rising waters made escape impossible. He was drowned, along with his two unmarried daughters and a granddaughter who was visiting with them at the time. An adjacent house,

occupied by a young married woman with a nursing child, also collapsed and the mother and daughter disappeared; their bodies were not found for some time. In addition to the six who died, there were dozens of homeless people in the Rockdale district whose houses were washed away or so damaged and filled with mud as to be unfit for habitation. And all the workers lost the vegetable gardens which they were accustomed to plant on the fertile bottom lands by the edge of the stream. Most of the ten or twelve ruined houses had been occupied by workers, the owners and managers ordinarily placing their mansions on higher ground; the only mill owner whose residence suffered was Samuel Riddle, and that building did not collapse.

One of the first things done after the flood was the organization of a county-wide relief committee, which collected over $3,000 and made cash grants to 131 families (including 404 children). In addition to this, well-to-do local families extended aid on a personal basis to individuals whom they knew. Inasmuch as most of the houses were rented from employers at rates of $1.25 to $2.50 per month, and the average grant per family was about $25, it seems that the committee was able to grant money sufficient to provide rent and food for several months for each family. Much furniture, clothing, and household utensils were lost in addition. But there was plenty of work in reconstruction for households with able-bodied adult males. And though the twenty-one households headed by widow women were likely to suffer because they included no one able to take part in the heavy work of reconstruction, this social category was so explicitly an object of special recognition in the factory towns, and so emphatically singled out for iden-tification in the report of the flood written by Crozer and his colleagues, that the special needs of widows and their children were probably met by charitable neighbors.

The damages and financial losses in the Rockdale district were listed in contemporary records as follows:

LENNI MILL (owned by Hannah Hill and occupied by
Daniel Lammot and Son)—$3,000 for Lammot,
$2,000 for Hill

Dam and race swept away
Office destroyed
Goods and yarns swept away
County bridge ruined

WEST BRANCH MILL (John P. Crozer)—about $20,000
Dam and race swept away
Road between West Branch and Crozerville washed away

Warehouse, containing goods and yarns, swept away
Stone dry house and office swept away
Size house swept away
North wing of factory, containing 80 power looms, swept away
Center building damaged and machinery injured
Water wheel and mill gearing swept away

CROZERVILLE MILL (John P. Crozer)—about $5,000
Dam and race nearly destroyed
Cotton house with 30 bales of cotton swept away
Spinning machinery on lower story injured
Bridge carried away

PARKMOUNT MILL (owned by Hannah Hill but unoccupied)—$1500
Dam injured
Forebay of mill swept out
Water-wheel thrown out of position

PENN'S GROVE MILL (Samuel Riddle)—$3,000
Dam and race swept away
"Old Mill" carried away
Machinery in cotton factory much damaged
Riddle residence damaged
2 houses (owned by George Peterson) destroyed $700
4 houses (owned by John Rhodes) destroyed $1200
1 house (owned by E. Churchman) destroyed
County bridge destroyed

OLD SABLE MILL and Estate (owned by Richard S. Smith)—$3,000
2 dams destroyed
4 stone dwellings (unoccupied) destroyed

KNOWLTON MILL (John P. Crozer)—about $20,000
New stone mill, 76 × 36, filled with new power looms,
with much stock in woven goods, swept away
Old frame mill occupied by James Dixon swept away $1,000

Crozer's factories suffered so much more than those of his fellow manufacturers because of their particular sites. West Branch and Knowlton were both located on very low ground, below very short races, at points in the stream where there were natural rapids and where the hillsides were steep and very close together (at Knowlton the gorge was only about 100 feet wide). Crozer noted that "other mills suffered much less than ours," and for a while seems to have regarded his calamity as a divine dispensation to which he must resign himself. As he set down his thoughts in a letter to his sister, a few days after the flood (while still "water-locked" in his residence):

My loss of property is very great, probably little, if any, short of fifty thousand dollars; and I feel, of course, and feel deeply, for this is human nature; but I trust and believe I meet it with the resignation of a Christian and the firmness of a man somewhat accustomed to vicissitudes; and, moreover, though I have witnessed the result of years of diligent application to business pass away in a few hours, yet I have a considerable fortune left, sufficient with the economy which we have hitherto practised, to maintain my family genteelly.

But even as he was resigning himself to a lowered standard of living and a less extensive business, Crozer was taking steps to restore his enterprises to their former state of prosperity. Three days after the flood he had more than eighty people at work, "cleaning machinery, hunting for goods, washing and drying them, and a part digging a channel for the creek" (its old channel being filled with rocks, the stream had taken over the tailrace of Crozerville Mill as its new course). A month later, Crozerville Mill was in full operation, and his men were at work rebuilding West Branch—a complex operation, involving cutting a new road into the hillside, reconstructing the dam and race, relocating the creek, and constructing new buildings. Thirty looms had been salvaged from the waters of Chester Creek, some of them as far as a mile downstream, and he had ordered forty new ones. Crozer expected to see West Branch back at work in October. But as for Knowlton, Crozer gave up; and this meant that all the workers' families left the hamlet. In his diary he recorded, in his typically defensive way, his sorrow at the abandonment of the village:

There is something impressive in the sudden breaking-up, like that of Knowlton; and the scattering for ever of a little community of workpeople, with whom I had pleasant intercourse, saddened my heart almost or quite as much as the loss of so valuable an estate. I really feel an interest in my people, an affectionate interest, but I suppose few or none of them think so, or are aware of it.

Within about a year, all of the factories were re-equipped and at work again with the exception of Knowlton and still-unoccupied Parkmount. The unsightly mud deposits on the flats at Crozerville and at other points in the stream were covered with green grass and weeds; the bits and pieces of machinery still lying scattered about in the underbrush were rusting and rotting; the eye was becoming accustomed to the new course of the stream. The ruin of the first construction work on the Chester Creek Railroad to connect Rockdale with Chester and West Chester was abandoned. (The railroad was not actually put through until a decade later, although it had been incorporated in 1836, with Crozer, Smith, Lammot, and Samuel Riddle as commissioners.) Crozer's valedictory summation was almost casual:

My loss was greater than I supposed when I wrote to you last. But great as it is, I am not a poor man by any means. And though it was trying, extremely so, to have the earnings of years pass away in a few hours, I feel now pretty much the same as though it were not gone. The loss need occasion no change in our mode of living, not even in our little deeds of charity, and can only be felt in the amount we might have to leave our children. Your sister bears this, as indeed she does every sudden visitation, with becoming firmness and resignation.

And he added later in his diary: "by-and-by all will no doubt appear right and easy."[6]

THE REDEFINITION OF THE COTTON MILL OPERATIVE

The 1842 strike won for the cotton mill operatives a clear recognition from the court that, like the workers in traditional trades, they had a right to organize a union and to strike (just as the employers had the right to fire them and hire strikebreakers). But the changing position of the operative was in fact, as a result of the working of three other processes, moving him even further away from the status of the skilled craftsman. These three processes may be called leveling, depoliticizing, and the favoring of managerial over manual skills.

Leveling: The Self-Acting Mule
and the Decline of Labor Specialization

In the earlier years, the cotton mill typically contained a highly diversified group of people doing a variety of tasks requiring different degrees and kinds of skill: males and females; children, youths, and adults; the small and dexterous and the big and burly; the unskilled laborer, the highly skilled carder, mule spinner, and weaver, and the inventive mechanician; part-timers and full-timers; the low-paid scavengers and piecers, earning $1 or $1.50 for a full six-day week, and the well-paid mule spinner, earning $30 or $40 per month. But a number of technological and social processes were at work to reduce the amount of variation in some of these categories. To be sure, the conscious goal of the manufacturers and the operatives was not to homogenize the work force; yet this was an effect of their actions.

One of the leveling factors was the introduction of new machinery that was more nearly automatic, or faster, or less prone to break yarn, or less likely to break down and require repair. A most significant innovation of this sort was the self-acting mule, which (as we saw in Chapter V) was introduced into his mills by Samuel Riddle prior to 1844, probably at the time when he moved from Parkmount to Penn's Grove. Bancroft on the Brandywine bought a self-actor about the same time and almost certainly Riddle's fellow manufacturers in Rockdale were also investing in self-actors. The self-actor worked faster, broke fewer threads, held more spindles, self-cleaned much of the fly, and did not need a spinner to push in the carriage during winding on. Although a spinner had to mind the self-actor, tuning it and repairing the bands, and although it still needed the service of piecing, a single spinner could now manage two mules back to back, each of which was substantially larger than the single mule he operated before, and do it with only two piecers to take care of both piecing and cleaning. In Riddle's case, between 1834 and 1844 the number of mule spinners was reduced from ten to five but the number of hanks produced per month quadrupled. Thus he was able to reduce the piece rate, and increase the total monthly wage for the mule spinner without increasing the amount of labor the spinner had to perform.

The effect, however, was a leveling. The mule spinner did not have to be as skilled as he once was; he approximated more closely the passive machine-minders who worked in the spinning and weaving rooms. And in terms of potential labor organization, it reduced the number of mule spinners to so small (but so highly paid) a fraction that their potential utility as strike leaders was probably actually reduced. There is a tradition, in fact, that the self-acting mule was deliberately perfected by Richard Roberts in the 1820's in England for manufacturers aiming to break the power of the mule spinners' union, which was constantly inconveniencing the manufacturers by turnouts for higher wages. When in 1835 the *Journal of the Franklin Institute* brought Roberts' mule to the attention of American mechanicians, the editor listed its advantages:

It produces a considerably greater quantity of yarn, of more uniform twist, and less liable to break, and it winds on the cop more evenly and closely, so that the yarn is more desirable for the weaver. . . . One of the recommendations of this machine to the spinners, is, that it renders them independent of the working spinners, whose combinations and stoppages of work have often been extremely annoying to the masters.[1]

But even the self-actor required a spinner to supervise it; and strikes were factory-wide turnouts, anyway, so it is doubtful that the new mules were introduced in America with anti-union sentiments as the principal motive. The primary effect was to reduce the cost per hank of spun yarn to the manufacturer; and, by improving quality, to increase the value of the product. The reduction in number of mule spinners was a secondary consequence. But halving the number of mule spinners was not all; the self-actor was so clean and broke so few ends that the scavengers, who were the youngest children working in the mill, could be dispensed with. Thus even without any laws against child labor, the advance of technology reduced the need for it. The self-acting mule, in sum, cut in half the number of most highly skilled adult operatives and least skilled child helpers in any mill into which it was introduced.

By 1835 the Scottish mathematician and popularizer of technological development, Andrew Ure, was able to generalize about this leveling process. The situation now, he declared, was far different from what it had been when Adam Smith wrote his "immortal elements of economics." At that time, automatic machinery being little known, Smith was led to regard "the division of labour as the grand principle of manufacturing improvement." But now, as a result of the continuing improvements in machinery, the differentiation of labor by skill and strength was outmoded:

In fact, the division, or rather adaptation of labour to the different talents of men, is little thought of in factory employment. On the contrary, wherever a process requires peculiar dexterity and steadiness of hand, it is withdrawn as soon as possible from the *cunning* workman, who is prone to irregularities of many kinds, and it is placed in charge of a peculiar mechanism, so self-regulating, that a child may superintend it. . . .

The grand object therefore of the modern manufacturer is, through the union of capital and science, to reduce the task of his work-people to the exercise of vigilance and dexterity,—faculties, when concentrated to one process, speedily brought to perfection in the young. In the infancy of mechanical engineering, a machine-factory displayed the division of labour in manifold gradations—the file, the drill, the lathe, having each its different workmen in the order of skill: but the dexterous hands of the filer and driller are now superseded by the planing, the key-groove cutting [i.e., milling], and the drilling-machines; and those of the iron and brass turners, by the self-acting slide-lathe. . . .

An eminent mechanician in Manchester told me that he does not choose to make any steam-engines at present, because with his existing means, he would need to resort to the old principle of the division of labour, so fruitful of jealousies and strikes among workmen; but he intends to prosecute that branch of business whenever he has prepared suitable arrangements on the equalization of labour, or automatic plan.[2]

The tendency in the 1830's and 1840's, then, was for the cotton mill machinery to become progressively more specialized and intricate, while the cotton mill operative became progressively more standardized and indifferently skilled.

The Depoliticizing of Labor

Another process that was tending to alienate the operative from the artisan was the general depoliticizing of labor. Political activity provided a basis for association among trades and specialties that transcended differences in the particulars of each group's economic problems. Driving labor from the political arena would reduce solidarity among the groups. This end had already been achieved in part by the conservative press's successful association of the "workeyism" of the 1828–32 period with Robert Owen, Fanny Wright, and Tom Paine. Although there had been indeed many radicals in the Workingmen's Party then, there had also been many who were essentially middle class in aspiration—not only mechanicians, physicians, and other professionals, but many ordinary craftsmen as well. The workingmen's popular front had proposed to achieve certain broad social reforms by sending liberal representatives to Congress and the state legislatures. The charge of "infidelity" split the workingmen's movement and silenced many of its advocates of reform.

Into this breach the evangelicals and conservatives moved with alacrity, simply taking over from the radicals certain of their own issues, particularly the establishment of a free public school system, the dismantling of the militia system, the abolition of imprisonment for debt, and the passage of a mechanics lien law. Again, it is not likely that many of the capitalists consciously plotted to eviscerate the labor movement politically by stealing its best reform issues and pursuing them piecemeal. (This degree of Machiavellian foresight might have been possible for an iron founder like Thaddeus Stevens, who was able so adroitly to develop popular political issues which coincided with the pursuit of private interest that despite his economic conduct he became known as "The Great Commoner." But not many manufacturers were as ruthless as Stevens in the pursuit of power.) Rather, these reforms, long advocated by workingmen's groups, were simply swept up in the swelling tide of the Christian social reform movement, along with temperance, prison reform, the rehabilitation of prostitutes, and the building of special hospitals for the insane. Thus the liberal newspapers and workingmen's organizations were deprived of exclusive advocacy, as it were, of their most readily salable issues, and were left in an exposed position to argue the most controversial ones: religion, the licensed monopolies (such as the Second Bank of the United States), tax reform, electoral reform.

Working together, the evangelicals, capitalists, and workers managed to put through the Pennsylvania legislature in the period from 1831 to 1854 a series of reform bills. In 1831, 1834, and 1836, a series of laws was passed which created a system of free (but not compulsory) public schools. In 1833, imprisonment for small debts was abolished. The old law establishing the compulsory militia system was repealed in 1849. And in 1854, a mechanics lien law was passed after a generation of earnest pleading. Each of these legislative reforms was of primary benefit to poor working people, and each benefited them twofold: in relieving them of some aspect of the social stigma of economic inadequacy, and in providing practical economic aid.

Before the public school laws were passed, there had indeed been a provision, written into the state constitution in 1790 and implemented by appropriate legislation (the so-called Pauper Law) in 1809, that children whose parents could not afford to send them to the private schools in their neighborhood were entitled to public aid. This aid took the form of tuition payments by the county directly to the teachers. But in order to determine eligibility, applicant parents had to declare their indigence to the township tax assessor; the name was recorded in the tax records; and the children going to school at the expense of local taxpayers were branded with the stigma of poverty among their peers. The Sunday Schools were a less invidious alternative but they operated irregularly and required submission to some sort of religious discipline.

Let us look at the system in Aston Township in 1829. In that year a total of nineteen children from ten households were listed as applying and being eligible for schooling at county expense. Two of the households were headed by widows (one of them was the Hannah Lower who with her family joined Calvary Church when it was founded). Three of the poor parents were weavers who later came to work power looms for Samuel Riddle. The children, eight boys and eleven girls, ranged in age from five to eleven. Of these only one boy and seven girls actually attended school in that year. These "parents of poor children" eligible for county aid were by no means poor in the sense of the poorhouse poor. The families were headed either by respectable widows or by men who worked in trades; they earned at a rate (if regularly employed) of up to $250 a year and one man even owned a cow. But the children's tuition was just too much. Furthermore, if working-class people earning up to $250 per year were eligible, it is certain that many working-class families who were eligible were not applying, some of them no doubt wanting their children to earn money in the mills rather than go to school at their parents' or the county's expense, and some also presumably not wanting the social stigma of a public disclosure of poverty.[3]

The new laws of 1831–36 proposed to change all this, and a number of the manufacturers were active in their support of the reform. William Martin—now a prosperous attorney and secretary of an insurance company—took the lead in organizing a petition in favor of the act of 1834 (which its opponents threatened to repeal). In Aston, Richard S. Smith was in 1836 elected a member of the first school board of Aston Township, and he offered the Rockdale school (which stood on his property) to the board rent-free. Crozer offered his chapel as a schoolhouse. John Garsed became a school director in 1840. In Middletown, Peter Hill sold the board a half-acre lot near Parkmount Mill and a schoolhouse was erected on it in 1837. In 1844 Samuel Riddle was elected a school director.[4]

Another emotionally freighted reform—but one that all classes joined in demanding—was the abolition of imprisonment for debt. Both rich and poor were vulnerable to the archaic procedures which permitted the court, on petition of a creditor, to incarcerate a debtor under noxious prison conditions for an indefinite period, until the debt was paid or the creditor satisfied. Patrick Lyon, the eminent mechanician, had been unjustly imprisoned for debt years before in Philadelphia and had written an impassioned account of his experience; for years petitioners had bombarded the legislature demanding an end to the practice, especially as it bore so harshly on the poor, who did not have wealthy relatives and friends to buy their freedom and who consequently might languish for months for want of a few dollars. Shocking accounts were printed in the liberal press of the abuses to which the poor, particularly moneyless widows, were subjected in debtors' prisons. At last in 1833 the state legislature passed an act "to abolish imprisonment for small debts." Other legislative enactments followed.

The next of the grosser social inequities to be legislated away was that provision of the state militia law of 1792 which required militia service of all white males between the ages of eighteen and forty-five. Certain occupations were exempted (federal officers, mail stage drivers, ferrymen on post roads, postmasters, clergymen, schoolteachers, ships' pilots, judges, sheriffs, and jailers). On the first and second Mondays in May, every year, the state's militiamen were required to drill in company and battalion under their elected officers (election to officership in the militia was a widely used step toward political office). Discipline was theoretically the same as in the regular Army and absence without leave was subject to fine or imprisonment.

The militia requirement was a severe burden to the workingman. He was required to give up two days' pay every year, he had to furnish his own uniform and equipment; and if he was unable to afford the cost, he was subject to fine and ultimately imprisonment. The well-to-do could avoid the whole problem by paying the fine or by organizing their own volunteer companies separately and, after seven years' service in these, becoming exempt from the state system. The inequity was so obvious that absentees were frequently not reported and fines not collected; militia day itself became a day of drinking as much as of marching. At last this system too was abolished, the law being repealed in 1849. No one was really sorry to see it go; and for those who were, the local volunteer companies were still available.

The mechanics lien law was perhaps of more actual importance to artisans than to the factory operatives, but it did apply to the machinists, blacksmiths, masons, and carpenters who worked about a mill. The issue was an economic one. When a building contractor became insolvent while a building was under construction, the mechanic—a mere "wage earner" —who had put in time working on the structure was often left unpaid while "privileged creditors" like banks, moneylenders, tavernkeepers, and merchants were allowed by the court to recover their debts from the remaining assets of the debtor. The mechanics wanted the status of privileged creditor too. The legislature put off action on the measure until 1854, when it passed a law which "gave mechanics first preference, up to one hundred dollars, in the property assignment of insolvent corporations."

Management Skills as the Pathway to Success

In the trades, an indispensable ingredient of success was skill, manifested in manual dexterity, felicity of design, quickness of operation, avoidance of fatigue. The journeyman had to be more skilled than the young apprentice; and the master had to be able to demand a high level of skill both from the apprentices who learned from him and from the journeymen who worked for him. But such a progression of skills did not occur in the cotton mill, except perhaps in the transformation of the young piecer into the adult mule spinner; and this pathway was open to fewer and fewer piecers, as the self-actor made their work less and less necessary. A mule spinner, once installed before his mule (or between his two self-actors), could move to no higher status by skill alone and might, indeed, stand between the very same two mules for all the forty years of his working life, tuning and adjusting them until they spun (so he fancied) like no other two mules in the world.[5]

The way to success was by the development—or the happy possession —of managerial skills. There were essentially three intermediate management positions to which an ordinary operative in a small mill might aspire: carder, spinning-room overseer, and boss weaver. The carder was responsible for the preparation of the cotton for spinning: the picker room, the carding machines, and the drawing and roving frames. Once the bobbins of roving were delivered to the mule or throstle room, the spinning-room overseer was responsible; he performed quality-control checks on the number and strength of the yarns being spun, communicated instructions as to changes in count or degree of twist, and recorded the number of hanks spun by each mule. The boss weaver, similarly, was responsible for overseeing the setting up of the looms, for the receipt of shuttle cops and warp beams, for quality control, and for the recording of the yards of cloth woven by each loom.

These jobs required the overseer not only to know the operatives' work in a technical sense, and have the ability to assess the quality of its product, but also to be able to manage a group of men, women, and children so as to maximize their productivity for the mill. The skills of management were skills in social relationships: being able to command when necessary, to persuade, to mollify, to cajole; to mediate between the human needs of the operatives below him and the economic demands of the directors and owners above him; to coordinate his schedule and organization with that of the overseers adjacent to him in the process. The overseers thus were paid more, much more, sometimes even (as in Riddle's mill) in proportion to the productivity of their department. In January 1844, for instance, the power-loom department at Penn's Grove employed thirty-four people (eighteen men and sixteen women), whose wages amounted to $387.20 (an average per weaver of a little more than $11). For overlooking the looms the overseer received $96.80, calculated at the rate of 25 percent of the weavers' total wages. Since the weavers were paid on a piecework basis, the boss weaver was being paid according to the productivity of his department. The throstle room seems to have had three or four overseers, who like the spinners were paid per diem wages, but at a rate about four times as high as the ordinary machine-minders (one man received $28 per month, and Archibald McDowell—the Riddles' brother-in-law—$24 per month). The five mule spinners, however, seem not to have required an overseer. Six years later, in January 1850, there were still only five mule spinners and still no mule-room supervisor. But there was a carding master (at $48 per month), a throstle-room overseer (at $24 per month), and a man responsible for "overlooking looms" (at $64.50 per month).[6]

It was the policy of at least some of the manufacturers and mill owners (and specifically Crozer and the Smiths) to cultivate and advance this class of foremen or overseers. Abraham Blakeley, an erstwhile Lancashire operative, was Crozer's loom overseer from 1833 to 1846, when he went into business as a manufacturer himself, renting the rebuilt Knowlton Mill from his former employer.[7] He was superintendent at the Sunday School in the little chapel at Knowlton.[8] Hayes P. Griffith, the "loom boss" at the weaving mill owned by Richard S. Smith, was a member of the Calvary congregation and a personal favorite of Clementina; as a a boy he had lived with the Smiths and served them as a waiter.[9] Indeed, the path to worldly success for an aspiring operative would seem to lead from the machine to the overseer's little office to the door of the nearest church or Sunday School.

But such a process of advancement effectively removed from the ranks of the machine-minders many of their natural leaders, the very men who might have organized effective unions and led strikes. Together with the processes of leveling and direct depoliticization, it worked to redefine the cotton mill operative as a semi-skilled laborer, not a craftsman, politically passive, with conventional social views and a limited capacity to organize in opposition to the owners and managers of the mills.

WORKERS AS OBJECTS OF PITY:
THE TEN HOURS LAW

When the struggle between management and labor began in the 1820's, the cotton mill workers, despite their anomalous position in the roster of trades, had generally had a high opinion of themselves as a radical reforming element in society. By the mid-forties, despite a practical improvement in their material conditions, the textile workers had become objects of public sympathy and of the religious reformer's condescending concern. They were now for the most part children, and, as Clementina once put it, "poor girls that work on the looms."[1] The mode of passage and enforcement of the ten hours law symbolizes the transformation.

One of the standing complaints of cotton factory workers was the long working day, on the order of fourteen hours, including about an hour for meals. The Pennsylvania Senate committee's investigation in 1837 had included testimony from operators and manufacturers alike alleging that the protracted hours of work were injurious to the health of children and left them so tired that they could not pay attention in night school or sometimes even in Sunday School. Poor factory children could not of course take advantage at all of the free public schools, which thus, in effect, were reserved for the children of more affluent parents. The turnouts in 1835 and 1836 in Philadelphia had won the journeymen of that city a ten hours agreement with the master tradesmen; but nothing had happened to benefit the operatives as a result of either their own strikes in 1836 and 1842 or the Pennsylvania Senate investigation of 1837.

In 1846, the operatives of Philadelphia, inspired by a brief strike of the factory girls at Pittsburgh in support of a ten hours law, formed their own "Ten Hours Association." They wrote an address to "The Working Classes of the Country," which urged it as beneficial to employers and employees alike that the ten hours system be universally adopted. The address was printed in the *Upland Union.* It described the evil consequences of the long hours in graphic terms:

We see the laborer in the morning approach his toil with a dread of its long protraction and excess, that even a sound night's slumber, and long continued habit have failed to wear away. We see him as the day declines with wearied limbs, and gloomy thoughts, and cheerless spirits, casting upon the setting sun a lingering and heart-sick glance, or after it is gone from view, listening in despondency to hear, through the clattering of machinery, the hour of his delivery from toil. We see him unable to fulfill towards his family the offices and duties of his station, because his wearying labors have substituted petulance and gloom for the feelings of affection; and languor and indifference for the power of instruction. We see him producing wealth by perpetual exertion, yet living a life of unceasing anxiety and want. We see him subjected to continual privations, inconvenience and suffering, and cut off from the ordinary sources of gratification and enjoyment. We see him in ignorance, servility and degradation, and deprived of the time, the taste, the energy, necessary for his elevation and improvement. We see him losing all interest in matters of general importance, and degenerating into a mere machine, with intelligence to guide him in his labor, and compensation enough to keep him in profitable working order and economical repair.

Invoking the welfare of mankind, the spirit of the age, and the evidence of progress in justification, the paper called upon the nation to fix a date for "the general change."

A second, related, complaint was that children of tender years ought not to be employed at all. Although many widows were supported by their children's wages, and although the nimble little fingers of the young were supposedly uniquely qualified for handling delicate yarns, there was a persistent argument in favor of keeping younger children out of the factories. The considerations advanced in support of restrictions on the age of labor included the hazard to health, the threat to morals, and the need for education. These arguments also had been expressed by witnesses before the Senate committee in 1837 but had seen no result.

Precedent existed for government intervention. England had had legislation on the books since 1802 that aimed to protect the health and morals of factory children. In 1834 a new Act of Parliament provided that no person under the age of eighteen was permitted to work at night or to labor more than twelve hours per day or for more than a total of sixty-nine hours per week. In 1840 President Van Buren by executive order had put federal employees on a ten-hour basis. And in 1847 the New Hampshire legislature became the first in the nation to pass a law specifying that ten hours was a legal day's work (although its effectiveness was reduced by a clause permitting special contracts which extended that limit).

The passing of the New Hampshire law served as a signal to Pennsylvanians to renew their demand for a statute defining the length of the working day in textile factories (i.e., the length of time that an employer could *require* an employee to remain at work). In the summer of 1847, editorials began to appear in papers of both Whig and Democratic persuasion, urging the state legislature to take up the matter in its fall sessions. The editor of the *Upland Union* in July urged the passage of a ten hours law in plain terms:

> The Parliament of Great Britain has passed a law enforcing the ten hour system in all manufacturing establishments. This is a highly meritorious act, and will add much to the mental and physical comfort of the men, women and children whose necessities compel them to labor for the support of themselves and others. The State governments here should move early in the adoption of this salutary measure, which gives to the closely defined manufacturer time to revive his physical energies and improve his mind, thus qualifying him to perform more work than when exhausted by long confinement. The adoption of their system even by factory owners, with good moral regulations and facilities for mental improvement will increase the interest and comfort of employers and employed.

In the fall, the mechanics and operatives of Philadelphia held a mass meeting to agitate the question. The keynote address was delivered by a gentleman who claimed to have risen from the ranks of labor. He advanced the main arguments in favor of a ten hours law and advised the workers how to proceed. "You propose," he observed, "to change, in some degree, the position which exists between the employers and employed." It behooved them to act not rashly and hastily but with the caution and deliberation that belong to "a thinking class," to "avoid all unnecessary excitement," and never to "assume personal hostility to your employers." Capitalists and workers were alike creatures of Providence and equally deserving of respect: "It is perfect folly to make war upon either capital or employers as such; for no man would be a laborer could he be an employer, and perhaps it is the duty—certainly it is the right of every operative—to look forward to the time when he will be an employer."

But, caught "in the vortex of speculation and competition," the capitalist, "in the unlimited control of enterprise and capital," could not help but forget the rights of labor now and then. Thus he could not be relied on to correct the evil himself. As a result, "the people" were overworked, and "energies, health, faculties, are enervated, if not destroyed." Furthermore, the employment of children and the long hours both tended to interfere with home life. It was this threat to the *home* that particularly justified the operatives' petition: "if anything can be dearer than *home*—upon this ... depends, almost entirely, the health, the virtue, and the intellect of these *now* 'little ones,' who are hereafter to constitute the Republic." But the operatives could not accomplish the relaxation of factory discipline by themselves. Action by the government was necessary and proper, he argued, because the government had the general right to correct evils in society.

The operatives of Delaware County, like their brothers and sisters in Philadelphia, organized to press the cause. At a meeting toward the end of October at Odd Fellows Hall in Village Green, attended by delegates from all over the county, a resolution urging the legislature to pass a ten hours law was voted unanimously. The argument was based partly on the need to protect the health of the workers, partly on the need of operatives for more free time, and partly on the need to curb overproduction. Long hours were "depriving the operatives of all opportunity for the cultivation of their minds, and unfitting them for mixing socially with the intelligent of other pursuits, as well as for the enjoyment of those literary treasures so liberally bestowed by an enlightened press. . . ." Long hours were also blamed for business cycles:

In a commercial point of view, the evils of the present system are not less clearly seen, in seasons of prosperity, enabling the more grasping to run their mills even for longer than usual time—generally against the wishes or inclination of the operatives, to the disadvantage of their more moderate brethren; thus, in a short time, causing a glut in the market—breaking up manufactories—throwing workmen out of employment—breaking up families and scattering them helpless and dependent upon the community —increasing misery, crime, and pauperism, throughout the land, adding a vast amount to the local taxes, and over-burthening all other pursuits.

And the operatives demanded to be included in the bright Utopian future that lay ahead in America's destiny:

With a population of over twenty millions and an increase which if continued will, in fifty years, swell the number to one hundred millions of human beings, with our vessels floating on every river in this vast land, our railroads running through and almost encircling it, our ships on every ocean, with their sails spread to the wind, carrying our products of industry to every clime, who can fail to be impressed with the conviction that a higher and nobler destiny awaits us than that of being employed fourteen hours a day in obtaining the means of subsistence?[2]

A central executive committee was established, with two representatives from each mill, and a committee of correspondence was set up to coordinate with groups in other counties. A petition was prepared, which was sent to the Delaware County representatives in the Assembly and Senate in Harrisburg. But the senator refused to present it to the Senate and the operatives had to collect the signatures all over again. It was finally presented by a sympathetic senator from Lehigh. The committee met every week for the next several months, developing further petitions and lobbying measures, and providing statements to be reprinted in the newspapers. There was no strike. Passage of the law was achieved in March 1848.[3]

The Pennsylvania Ten Hours Law provided that ten hours in any one day, in all cotton, woolen, and other textile factories (and paper mills), was "a legal day's labor." No minor or adult could be required to work more than ten hours in one day or more than sixty hours in one week; no child under twelve was to be hired. The penalty for each infraction was a $50 "fine." But there were two flaws: the fine had to be recovered by suit "in like manner as debts of like amount are now recovered by law"; and minors between the ages of fourteen and twenty-one could be employed any number of hours "by special contract with their parents or guardians."[4] The law was to take effect on July 4, 1848.

The response of employers varied from place to place. In Philadelphia City and County (including the large concentrations at Manayunk and Kensington) the law was being observed even before the Fourth of July.[5]

In Pittsburgh, where the norm was twelve hours, the manufacturers resolved not to comply with the law and proposed to work out twelve-hour
"special contracts" with their employees. Two thousand operatives who
refused to agree to twelve-hour contracts were laid off. At the end of the
month there was a "riot" when the unemployed workers attempted to close
the twelve-hour mills. But at the end of August a settlement was reached:
the manufacturers agreed to the ten-hour day and the workers who were
paid by the day accepted a 16 percent pay cut.[6] In Delaware County,
however, the law was simply ignored for five years by a band of manufacturers who claimed that the new law would place them in an unfavorable
competitive position in relation to other states and who considered it to be
an unconstitutional interference with the right of employers to hire whoever they wished on whatever terms were mutually agreeable.

What the county historian, Henry Ashmead, called "this little speck of
nullification in the hitherto loyal county of Delaware" was carefully
planned. The manufacturers let it be known in advance that they had
determined to close their factories for several weeks after the Fourth of July,
giving as an excuse the claim that they had large stocks of unsold goods on
hand and, in the presence of a low market, wanted to wait until prices rose.
Many of the operatives who had been active in working for the passage of
the law, realizing what was in store for them, "withdrew and sought other
means to secure a livelihood." After the lockout (which presumably exhausted many of the workers' savings) the mill resumed on the old system.
A few refused to return and in effect went on strike. They too eventually
either had to find other types of employment or move away.

And so, as far as the mills on Chester Creek were concerned, things went
along in the old way, in placid defiance of the law, for five years. But it was
embarrassing to evangelical manufacturers to be patently in violation of the
law while zealously urging obedience to the law upon their employees.
Furthermore, they were unable to argue that the new law put them at a
competitive disadvantage to other Pennsylvania manufacturers, for the
other counties were in compliance, and Delaware County factories were,
in that matter, taking unfair advantage of their fellow manufacturers. But
of course the other states in the Union did not all have a ten hours law—
and Massachusetts in particular did not. So "some of the more conscientious
of the manufacturers" made the astonishing proposal to the operatives that
if they, the operatives, could persuade the New England manufacturers
voluntarily to go on the ten-hour basis, then the Delaware County factories
would obey the laws of their own state! Even more astonishingly, a delegation of Pennsylvania operatives did go up to Boston and attempt to persuade the mill owners of Waltham and Lowell. They met with indifferent

success and returned to present the results to their own manufacturers.

By now public opinion was beginning to turn against the obstinate defiance of law by the richest and most powerful men in the county. A mass meeting was held at the old courthouse in Chester and a resolution passed, urging that "a trial should be made of the effects of the new law." John P. Crozer also now changed his position and urged his fellow employers to comply with the statute.

And so, in 1853, the law of 1848 was actually put into effect in Delaware County. The effects turned out to be much as the operatives had argued. Production did not in fact decline; it rose. After a few years Crozer testified enthusiastically for it, pointing out that in the end both sides had gained: the workers had greater access to opportunities for moral and intellectual improvement; and the manufacturers "got more work done per hour, or at a less rate of expense, than ever before."[7]

With the resolution of the ten-hours controversy, a generation of peace between capital and labor began in Rockdale and the other mill towns of Delaware County. The most obviously noxious aspects of the cotton factory system—the use of the labor of very young children and the excessively long hours—had been reformed; and the workers had for the most part accepted a position of unorganized passivity. In an era of benevolence toward the disadvantaged, with improvements being made in the treatment of the insane, the mentally retarded, the imprisoned, and the indigent, both well and ailing, the cotton mill operatives had come under the protecting shield of reform. But in the process they had abandoned their political ambitions, their organized unions, even their confidence in the effectiveness of the strike. The cotton factory workers had, as a class, become powerless.

THE THEORY OF CHRISTIAN CAPITALISM

The Chester Creek manufacturers, like many of their peers, were subscribers to a developing economic philosophy that may be called "the theory of Christian capitalism." It grew more out of the need to rationalize what was already happening in places like Rockdale than out of existing traditions in political and economic theory. It was formed in part to provide an intellectually satisfying response to Utopian socialists and to southern advocates of free trade; but it also served to reassure the capitalist and worker alike that the British economic system, their principal competitor, was fatally oppressive to workers, to colonial populations, and to developing nations, and that the gloomy English economists, led by Malthus and

Ricardo, were supporting its evils by wrong-headedly claiming that these evils were the inevitable checks and balances. It was a point of view that connected strictly economic variables—rents and wages, capital investment and prices, and so forth—to other dimensions of society, including the general welfare, historical process, and a system of Christian religious values.

A principal local codifier of this body of thought was Henry C. Carey, son of Matthew Carey, the Philadelphia publisher and protectionist pamphleteer. Henry Carey had spent the first forty years of his life working in the successful publishing business of Carey and Lea, then the largest in America. When he retired with a substantial fortune, he began to study political economy, and in 1835 published the first of his eight books and three thousand pamphlets. Carey was something of a system-builder, who tried to develop first a unified science of economics, then a unified social science, and finally a unified body of laws that would bring together the physical, social, mental, and moral sciences in one grand formulation. In this large scheme he was not successful; but his economic theories were very widely read in Europe as well as in the United States. He vigorously denounced the British economists' prescription of free trade and *laissez faire* as the solution to all economic problems and became the most articulate exponent of the economic argument for the protective tariff. Like David Ricardo, he regarded labor as the source of all economic value, and considered that capital and labor were the active and passive partners in an indissoluble marriage in which both must prosper or decline together. Carey was widely consulted by practical men who could look upon the retired successful businessman, with his tendency to strong language and his enthusiasm for their pragmatic view, as one of themselves. Among the Chester Creek manufacturers, he was on visiting terms at least with the Darlingtons, the Smiths, the Sellers family; General Robert Patterson, who bought Lenni Mill when the Lammots moved to the Brandywine, was one of his closest friends.

In 1850 the first edition of Carey's central work on protectionism appeared, with the evocative title *The Harmony of Interests, Agricultural, Manufacturing, and Commercial.* It contained essays previously published by Carey in a periodical, *The Plough, the Loom, and the Anvil,* which he had established a few years before. The book's theme was the basic complementarity of the sectors of the American economy, all of which—and social life in general—would be advanced in unison by the protective tariff. The tone of the book was violently anti-Britain: anti her free trade policy and her economists of despair, Malthus and Ricardo. It was also Utopian, almost but not quite millenarian, in a chauvinistic sort of way, looking forward to a time when the Union should embrace the globe and bring all nations together under the flag of the United States in a Christian empire governed by the holy doctrine, "Do unto others as ye would that others should do unto you." In contrast to the exploitive and militaristic "English system," he described a system of world economy which, he said, "we may be proud to call the American system, for it is the only one ever devised the tendency of which was that of ELEVATING while EQUALIZING the condition of man throughout the world." He went on, in the book's climactic final paragraphs, to describe the American destiny:

To raise the value of labour throughout the world, we need only to raise the value of our own. To raise the value of land throughout the world, it is needed only that we adopt measures that shall raise the value of our own. To diffuse intelligence and to promote the cause of morality throughout the world, we are required only to pursue the course that shall diffuse education throughout our own land, and shall enable every man more readily to acquire property, and with it respect for the rights of property. To improve the political condition of man throughout the world, it is needed that we ourselves should remain at peace, avoid taxation for the maintenance of fleets and armies, and become rich and prosperous. To raise the condition of woman throughout the world, it is required of us only that we pursue that course that enables men to remain at home and marry, that they may surround themselves with happy children and grand-children. To substitute true Christianity for the detestable system known as the Malthusian, it is needed that we prove to the world that it is population that makes the food come from the rich soils, and that food tends to increase more rapidly than population, thus vindicating the policy of God to man. Doing these things, the addition to our population by immigration will speedily rise to millions, and with each and every year the desire for that perfect freedom of trade which results from incorporation within the Union, will be seen to spread and to increase in its intensity, leading gradually to the establishment of an empire the most extensive and magnificent the world has yet seen, based upon the principles of maintaining peace itself, and strong enough to insist upon the maintenance of peace by others, yet carried on without the aid of fleets, or armies, or taxes, the sales of public lands alone sufficing to pay the expense of government. . . .[1]

Probably not all of the manufacturers were as sanguine as Carey about the elevating and equalizing effect of the American economy on other nations. But all subscribed with him to certain basic themes which together make up a coherent theory of Christian capitalism that could be opposed to socialist philosophies. (Indeed, Carey's economics was adopted as an alternative to Marx's by at least one marginal German social theorist, Karl Eugen Dühring, and thus indirectly was influential enough to force Engels to elucidate the Marxist position on the class struggle more clearly in the "anti-Dühring" pamphlet so as to contradict Carey's Utopian "harmony-of-interests" philosophy.)[2] The basic elements of the idealistic theory of Christian capitalism would seem to be the following propositions:

1. Capitalistic enterprise is the supreme creative act, in no wise antithetical to the spirit or the letter of Christian doctrine, and beneficial to the whole community when conducted according to principles of financial probity.

2. The stewardship of wealth on behalf of the community for purposes of social reform and Christian benevolence, not the mere maximization of private profit, is the proper central economic motive of the capitalist.

3. The economic system, like other systems in nature, when functioning properly is governed by an equilibrium principle or "harmony of interests," so that agriculture and manufacturing, capital and labor, are all interdependent and will prosper or suffer together.

4. Government is responsible for allowing the economic system to function in a naturally harmonious way by protecting it from destructive foreign intervention by means of a protective tariff.

5. Although hierarchical relations are necessary in society, between parents and children, between employer and employees, and between the social classes, all men are entitled to earn such advancement in this hierarchy as their natural endowments, moral qualities, and perseverance individually entitle them to.

6. Under such a system economic progress is inevitable and will be unchecked by the Malthusian restraints on population because the productivity of a healthy economic system will always grow faster than the population itself.

7. Economic growth will inevitably be accompanied not only by an improvement in the material standard of living but also by an elevation of the people socially, morally, and spiritually, tending ultimately to a truly Christian commonwealth.

Clearly this theory was more hortatory than descriptive. But, when one examines the lives of the manufacturers, it clearly also was an ideology that gave the manufacturers effective criteria for making decisions. And, for a time at least, the American economic system seemed to be working in just about the way that the theory of Christian capitalism said it should.[3]

Part Four

ROCKDALE FROM 1850 TO 1865 & THE TRANSCENDING OF A WAY OF LIFE

Chapter IX 🗲

MARCHING
TO
MILLENNIUM

Beneath the smooth surface of American prosperity in the years before the Civil War, a vast turbulence was stirring. The northern manufacturers and their workers, in dozens of districts more or less like Rockdale, had created for themselves a comfortable and progressive way of life. After the labor troubles of the 1830's and early 1840's, a settlement had been achieved between the manufacturers and the workers and they had closed ranks in support of the "American System." The continued welfare of this system, they claimed, depended upon a protective tariff and a state-subsidized transportation system for the manufacturers, and for the workers cheap land in the west which could be bought with savings out of wages. But as the decades wore on, the delicate political compromises with the south, the supplier of cotton for the mills, began to break down. These compromises had been worked out in the belief that an awareness of the true harmony of interests would increasingly prevail. Sectional conflict between the manufacturing north and the agricultural south became ever more moralistic in its rhetoric. Eventually evangelical enthusiasm joined forces with economic and political self-interest to form a new Republican Party. And almost simultaneously, the millennialist interpretation of history that was latent in American ideology burst forth in militant glory. To the evangelical, millenarian, Republican manufacturer and worker in towns like Rockdale, the Civil War was not fought merely to preserve the Union from disruption, or even to abolish slavery; far more important than that, it was the first major clash in the war that was predicted in the Book of Revelation. It was the beginning of the greatest and final war, the beginning of the war for the conquest of the world for Christ.

THE ECONOMIC TAKE-OFF

As the depression began to ease in the mid-1840's, and the protective tariff was restored after a decade of lowered rates, the manufacturers and the workers on Chester Creek experienced a dramatic increase in their opportunities. Manufacturers expanded their operations, improved their factories, introduced new machinery; some of the workers invested their savings in machinery and went into manufacturing on their own. Small, precarious enterprises were rapidly transformed into large, secure institutions with plenty of capital available for continuing expansion. The decade from the mid-forties to the mid-fifties was the era of economic take-off for the cotton industry on Chester Creek.

Men of Enterprise and the Chester Project

With the general prosperity of the county and the presence of surplus capital available for investment, in 1845 a number of citizens began to consider whether the old town of Chester might not be revitalized. Chester Borough, which lay immediately around the little fishing harbor, was in many respects a dying town, long ago eclipsed as a port by Philadelphia and Wilmington (and, indeed, even by nearby Marcus Hook), and it had recently been deprived of its status as the county seat in favor of the more centrally located Media. It had long since ceased to grow and in 1840 had a population of only 740 souls, not many more than it had possessed a century before. The surrounding land in Chester Township was occupied by farmers in easy circumstances, who, as the town's historian said, "would not sell a foot of ground at any price, and who looked upon those who would build a city here as visionary men, who would run themselves in debt, and ultimately fail."[1] John Broomall, a business partner of John P. Crozer's, described the borough as it was in 1840:

For a century and a half nothing but its Court house distinguished it from Marcus Hook, its neighboring fishing town. Long since the commencement of the present century, its inhabitants consisted of three or four tavern keepers, a doctor, a few dozen fishermen, two country storekeepers and a custom house-officer, whose arduous duties consisted of signing a receipt for his small salary four times a year.[2]

And Samuel Crozer, who moved into the township with his father a couple of years later, described the place in wry terms:

Chester in the Year 1847 had but about nine hundred and fifty inhabitants, and it was a very old and dried up town. It was stated that only one building had been erected in the town in fifty years, and that one was so long in completion that it had an old appearance before it was finished.[3]

Nevertheless, the township had obvious advantages as a site for industry. The seven-year-old Philadelphia, Wilmington, and Baltimore Railroad ran through it, and there was plenty of land (if only the farmers could be persuaded to sell) where mill workers, merchants, tradesmen, and manufacturers could reside and on which factories, schools, churches, stores, and other institutions could be built. Although water could not provide the power for more than a limited number of mills, the new generation of reliable stationary steam engines could be used instead. With almost all of the promising mill seats taken up in the Rockdale district and in the other manufacturing centers along the Delaware County fall line, the only reasonable place for economic expansion was at a convenient transportation center like Chester.

There were four men who, acting in loose concert, achieved the revitalization of Chester. The first to act was John P. Crozer. Now extremely prosperous from his mills at West Branch, Crozerville, and Knowlton (in his diary he stated matter-of-factly, "I have a large fortune"), he was looking for opportunities to invest his profits. He was attracted to Chester Township because he was growing tired of the long carriage and sleigh ride between Crozerville and the train station at Chester, where he boarded "the cars" that took him and the other manufacturers to Philadelphia at least once a week to conduct business. And he had just had the harrowing experience of a thigh broken by a spill from the sleigh one night on his way home. When part of the Flower estate, including the old seat of Chester Mills, with sixty-six acres and the venerable Caleb Pusey House (built in 1683 and one of the most ancient structures in the commonwealth), came on the market in 1844, Crozer bought it, with some misgivings, for $13,500. He at once set about constructing a cotton factory (five stories, 138 by 50 feet), dozens of surrounding tenement houses, and a mansion on the hillside overlooking the new town, which he named Upland (after the old Swedish name for the area). By 1847, when the Crozers moved into their new mansion, there were forty-six tenement houses on flats below them. The mill was an innovative one, for an eighty-horsepower steam engine had been attached to supplement the water power (which was supplied by a precariously long race extending a mile upstream through other men's properties to a remote dam). It had 11 self-acting mules with 3,864 spindles, 7 or 8 throstles with another 2,000 or so spindles, and 150 power looms. In 1849 the enterprise was incorporated and the commissioners were old friends: George Leiper, Edward Darlington, Samuel Edwards, Daniel Lammot, and John Broomall.[4]

The confidence in the township's future displayed by so successful a businessman and banker as John P. Crozer no doubt inspired the other three principal leaders in the restoration of Chester. Thirty-year-old John M. Broomall, prominent and prosperous Quaker defense attorney, now perceived the advantage of investing in the riverfront properties between Chester and Marcus Hook. After prolonged negotiations, in the course of which Edward Darlington acted as counsel (and Darlington had also been involved as trustee of the Flower estate during its transfer to Crozer), in 1849 Broomall was able to purchase a fifty-acre farm on the west side of Chester Creek with Crozer as his partner. In the next several years he and Crozer bought up a string of riverfront farms, almost to the boundaries of Marcus Hook. Broomall and Crozer planned their South Ward real estate development venture carefully, laying out wide streets, building houses and factories and selling the improvements at cost to those without capital, and taking up to 75 percent mortgages on the land itself (it was on the sale of the land that they planned to realize their profits). They were very successful, and in 1855 Broomall was able to buy out Crozer's interest. Broomall also started the restoration of the old Market Square in Chester itself, buying the burned-out store and dwelling of Preston Eyre (Darlington's father-in-law) and eventually embellishing the site with "fine stores of ample dimensions." As the first official city directory put it a few years later, "from this date others multiplied, and a stimulus seemed to have been given to building and trade." And by the same directory of 1859 it was reported that Broomall and Crozer's South Ward development had prospered exceedingly:

> Upon this purchase there have been built forty-four brick dwellings, two cotton factories, five cotton and wollen [sic] factories, one bleaching and finishing factory, one dyeing factory, one oil mill, one steam saw and planing mill, one sash and door factory, one large seminary, numerous shops, coal and wood yards, three ship yards, and six hundred and ten feet of wharfing, besides other improvements.[5]

The third of the Chester project's entrepreneurs, John Larkin, Jr., had been approached by Broomall with an offer of partnership during the negotiations for the first South Ward farm, but he turned it down. (No hard feelings were involved, evidently, for Broomall a few years later married Larkin's daughter.) Larkin soon after completed the purchase of eighty-three acres of land in the North Ward, including the site of the old racetrack now used as grazing meadows. Like Broomall and Crozer, Larkin laid out and graded the streets and maintained them without township assistance, constructed houses, stores, foundries, shops, and mills, and either sold or leased the properties. By 1881, when he sold the last remaining building lot out of the eighty-three acres, Larkin had built over five hundred houses and places of business (including several large cotton mills).

The fourth of the entrepreneurs was a cotton manufacturer named James Campbell. Campbell was an English weaver, now forty-four, who had emigrated to the United States as a young man. He worked first as loom boss for John S. Phillips at Rockdale and then became manager of James Houghton's factory at Penn's Grove. When Houghton failed in 1837 and removed to New Jersey to re-establish himself in business again, he urged Campbell to go with him. But Campbell declined, no doubt in part because he had married John Garsed's eldest daughter Angelina and they wanted to remain near her family. Angelina's father, who had six new power looms on his hands that insolvent customers had refused to accept, gave his son-in-law the machines and set him up as a manufacturer in one of the vacant buildings at Penn's Grove. He was industrious and successful, even in the midst of the depression, and George G. Leiper (who had earlier helped Crozer to get started in business) now proposed to build a cotton factory at Leiperville on Ridley Creek if Campbell would lease the property. The agreement was made.

Campbell was very successful at Ridley and accumulated "considerable capital." Now, in the early months of 1850, he looked at the central part of Chester and saw the possibility of converting some of the old structures there to manufacturing purposes. In January, when the public buildings were put up for sale after the removal of the county seat to Media, he purchased the old county jail and workhouse. The jail was "a miserable old rat-trap, nearly all the bars of the windows rusted off . . . it could only retain those inmates who were too indolent to make an effort to escape." In March he bought also an old bowling alley adjacent. These buildings he quickly renovated to receive a steam engine and a hundred power looms; in a few years, he had enlarged this factory out to the prison yard walls, and installed Jacquard looms for weaving fancy quilting fabrics. The astonished inhabitants of the borough celebrated the arrival of modern industry with extravagant rhetoric. The *Delaware County Republican* hailed the establishment of Pioneer Mills as a historic event: "In this mill will be the first looms ever set in motion on the spot first occupied as the capital of Pennsylvania, and Mr. Campbell will be the Columbus in manufacturing in Chester." When the machinery was set in motion, a small crowd of Chester's citizens were present. They broke into a cheer and spontaneously sang "Hail Columbia."

Campbell went on to purchase other properties in the borough for cotton weaving and was regarded as the man who made the borough of Chester "into a manufacturing town."

By the eve of the Civil War, the one-time county seat of Chester, with its little fishing village and surrounding township, had indeed been transformed into a major manufacturing center, with an extensive cotton industry, iron foundries, machine shops, furniture factories, and shipyards. Although the persons principally responsible for launching this local economic revolution made money in the process, their motives cannot be regarded as solely economic in the limited sense. The sense of Christian stewardship, and perhaps even a sort of primary creative urge, must have played a part too. Or at least the town liked to think so. When Crozer, for instance, asked, for his share in the South Ward development, only his original investment and 6 percent interest, he was leaving to Broomall a sizable profit. The lands which had been sold by 1855 had brought almost twice what the partners had put in; Crozer could thus have asked for easily double the amount of profit he actually received. When he was reminded of this, he replied "that he had gone into the enterprise not to make money, but to aid in the development of Chester, and that he was quite content that the profits should go to Mr. Broomall, who had done the chief part of the work."[6] Larkin, Broomall, and Campbell also seem to have been motivated as much by a desire to be known by the honorific title of "enterprising men" (to use Broomall's own phrase) as to make a fortune. "Enterprising men" would be praised as those "who made the place what it is." In Crozer's language, they could demonstrate that they had been "good stewards," using their God-given talent for making money in such a way that it benefited the whole community. Broomall's memorialists noted that he always managed his property development program on terms of a liberal character, and although after half a century the company that held the remaining lots eventually sank under a burden of debts abandoned to him by his associates, Broomall left the field with a good name and the gratitude of the community for having created the South Ward. "He battled royally under the load and would have succeeded in carrying it through to a successful conclusion if it had not been for the contraction of values under the slowly gathering financial storm which broke upon the country in 1893."[7]

John Campbell, likewise, lost the Pioneer Mills during the panic of 1857. His eulogist Henry Ashmead, a fellow resident of Chester and county historian, wrote a commendatory account of Campbell's misfortune:

Campbell was very successful, accumulating considerable capital, which he subsequently lost in his effort to develop the borough of Chester into a manufacturing town. His object was attained, hundreds have profited by his endeavours, but in the panic of 1857, when many of the commission-houses with whom he dealt suspended, it embarrassed him, and finally caused his failure. So great had been the struggles to prevent this result that his health broke under the strain, and after several years of almost unintermitting illness, during which his indomitable energy never forsook him, he died, May 14, 1862.[8]

Campbell was not, however, really crushed by the events of 1857, for he continued to operate other mills and continued to serve, along with other men of enterprise, on the town council.[9]

John Larkin's career was uniformly successful. He spent over thirty years developing the North Ward; it was not until 1881 that he sold the last vacant building lot. During much of this time he was a prominent member of the town council and in 1866 he was elected the first mayor of the newly incorporated city. Yet his biographer Ashmead felt obliged to describe him too as a true steward, a man of enterprise struggling to help the people, and suffering mightily in the process.

In the present North Ward, Mr. Larkin, in spite of great opposition, carried out his designs fully. It is related that although he laid out the streets in that part of the town, and dedicated them to the public, the borough authorities refused to keep the highways in repair, and at his own expense he maintained a force of men at work upon them. On one occasion, when a member of the Town Council complained that the streets in the old part of the borough were neglected, contrasting them with those of Larkin-town, which were neat and well kept, and declaring that the public moneys should not all be expended in one locality, another member informed the speaker that Chester had never contributed a dollar for that purpose, and that Mr. Larkin had personally paid for all the highways made, as well as maintaining them in repair. Not only did he do this, but he constantly built houses, stores, foundries, shops, and mills, in conformity with a rule he had adopted at the beginning of his enterprise that every dollar he received from the sale of lands or buildings should be expended in further improvements, and hence, for any person desiring to start in business, he would erect the required structure, and lease it to him or them, with the privilege of purchasing the property at its cost price within ten years. Mr. Larkin has built over five hundred houses and places of business, several being large cotton-mills. In 1881 he sold the last vacant building-lot remaining out of the original eighty-three acres he had bought as an unimproved tract, thirty-one years before.[10]

It is plain that the entrepreneurs who directed the Chester project were not motivated solely by the prospect of personal financial gain. They lived in the communities that they were building; they served the community in public office; they were prepared to accept long delays in realizing limited profits; and in some cases they sacrificed health and wealth together after making substantial contributions to the community's economic progress.

The Rise of Workingmen to Wealth
in the Rockdale District

There was no such dramatic a program of capital investment in the already established Rockdale manufacturing district as there was at Chester; but there was a noticeable expansion of some of the old mills. Daniel Lammot's new mill, of course, had already been built in 1838; his daughter Margaretta du Pont, on visiting it, exclaimed, "I could never imagine a cotton mill to be in such order and cleanliness."[11] Samuel Riddle substantially enlarged the Penn's Grove mill in 1845. Bernard McCready, the Norristown manufacturer, upon purchasing the Old Sable property from Richard S. Smith in 1845, erected a new spinning mill to complement Phillips and Lewis' old weaving mill. And, about 1851, after the death of Peter Hill, Daniel Lammot finally removed his manufacturing operation to another mill on the Brandywine, where so many relatives and friends lived, leaving the mill at Lenni to be leased to the growing textile empire of General Robert S. Patterson.

More significant of the changing times, perhaps, was the fact that in this decade of general prosperity, more and more working people were crossing class lines to become merchants and manufacturers. This was not a new phenomenon, of course. John P. Crozer was not born in poverty; but his father had been a carpenter and an unsuccessful farmer, whose son's wealth and prominence were earned by years of hard work. Similarly the Riddles, although they came of gentle stock in Northern Ireland, had arrived in the United States with no more than a few dollars, and had succeeded in cotton manufacturing by dint of strenuous exertions of their own. And we have already met James Campbell, the Callaghans, the Morrises, Mark Wild, and Archibald McDowell, who by dint of steady application, frugality, and saving ways—and the kindly intervention of friends and kinsmen—had accumulated enough capital to move up from the operative's level to that of the farmer or manufacturer. But let us now look more closely at the cases of two Rockdale operatives, Abraham Blakeley and John B. Rhodes, who rose to degrees of wealth that approached even the Riddles' and the Crozers'.

Abraham Blakeley was a Lancashire weaver who had emigrated to the United States in 1828 at the age of twenty-two. After employment as a weaver in Germantown and Pottsville, in 1833 he came to West Branch as Crozer's weaving foreman. In 1836 he married an Irish woman, who died in about a year, leaving him with an infant son. In 1838 he married Maria Miles, the protégée of Sophie du Pont. He worked diligently for Crozer, saved his money, and in 1846 formed a partnership with Phineas Lownes to manufacture cotton at Knowlton, buying the machinery and leasing the factory from Crozer. The business flourished. In 1853 Blakeley sold his interest and next year removed to a new three-story brick mill, 100 by 45 feet, erected for him by John Larkin in the North Ward development. In this move he again had the assistance of a partner (perhaps Larkin himself) but in 1857 he was able to buy out this gentleman's interest. He now embarked on the manufacture of work cloth—tickings, denims, and stripes —entirely on his own. The business prospered and grew until eventually "Blakeley and Sons" of Arasapha Mills were employing 200 hands in half a dozen buildings with 8,500 spindles and 276 looms, all powered by a Corliss steam engine. Finally he purchased Bishop Potter's mansion and moved into it with his family.

Blakeley followed the classic line of career development. First he was a capable weaver, then a loom boss, then a partner in a small leased factory, and ultimately the owner of a large establishment. When he entered upon manufacturing at Knowlton, he took on the superintendence of the Baptist Sunday School there. Upon his removal to Chester as a successful business-man, he shifted his allegiance to the Methodist Episcopal Church, becoming a leading lay worker, trustee, and steward. In politics he was a Whig and then a Republican, and he served for many years on the Chester City Council. He produced nine children and cared for his wife's sister, Sarah Miles, who was not married and lived with the Blakeleys. A few years before his death in 1886, he received the standard encomium from the city's historian due to a man of enterprise: "Mr. Blakeley has since his residence in Chester been among its most enterprising and public-spirited citizens, and has contributed largely to the building up of its trade and its importance as a manufacturing center."[12]

Maria Miles was, at the time of her marriage, to use her own phrase, a "poor desolate orphan," who recalled with gratitude the instruction she had been given by the benevolent Sophie du Pont and Victorine Bauduy at the Brandywine Manufacturers' Sunday School and the training in sewing and tailoring she and her sister had acquired with their help. Sophie and Clementina kept in touch with the Miles girls, both before and after Maria's marriage, and Maria, and later her daughter Sophia du Pont Blakeley, continued the correspondence. The changing style of the letters reflects the strains involved in the social transformation from a destitute orphan working in a weaving factory to the respected wife of one of Chester's leading citizens.

Maria's first letter to "My dear teacher" was written in 1835 when she was twenty years old. The hand was childish and unformed, the spelling uncertain, punctuation completely absent, and she signed herself "your old hooler Maria Miles." The burden of the message was the gratitude of the "poor desolate orphans" ("we shall never be abel to repay you") and their acceptance of Sophie's plans to send Sarah out to learn "the tayloring trade." The tone was almost obsequious: "you can do what you think best for us."[13] Another letter in 1836 expressed similar dependency and an almost masochistic acceptance of misfortune: "i think on my dear mother often but i have found tis good for me to bear my father rod afflication makes me learn his law. . . ."[14] After that there was a long lapse in the correspondence until she and her husband were established in the business at Knowlton. Then the letters to her "Dear Friend" resumed, now written in a firm and more sharply slanted hand, with almost perfect English grammar and spelling. The Lammots figured as mutual friends; Sophie du Pont was sending presents to her namesake, who was about four years old. And along with family news, a more formal kind of ceremonial religious compliment made its appearance in Maria's communications:

above all I do feel very thankful that you still keep remembering me at a throne of grace—I often think of you in my prayers and hope to see you again soon but if not permitted to see your friendly face in this World I will try by God's assistance to meet you in our Father's kingdom where parting will be no more—[15]

Thereafter through the years of the Civil War she and Sophie exchanged letters, gifts, prayers, and religious sentiments. Maria was determined to raise her children "in the fear of the Lord." Gradually Maria's hand became stronger and the tone more egalitarian. The last letter, in 1862, assumed the idiom of equality that characterized Clementina's correspondence. Maria had found a "suitable girl" to work in Sophie's household, who was "over forty, and very respectable and pious." If Sophie wanted to take her, then either sister Sarah, or namesake Sophie, or Maria herself "will come down with her to see you," and "the family join in sending their love to yourself and sister."[16]

The second case is that of John B. Rhodes, who was born in Rockdale in 1829. His grandfather had come to the United States in 1827 (to be drowned, with two of his daughters, in the flood of 1843) and his father had arrived the year after. The father worked in Phillips' weaving mill and young John commenced working there too at the tender age of six, "with a view" (as his biographer expressed it) "to becoming proficient in that branch of industry." Working in the various departments of the weaving mill, and going to school at night, he gradually acquired both money and knowledge. In 1850, as soon as he attained his majority, he married a local girl (Bishop Potter performed the ceremony) and in the same year became a storekeeper in Crozerville, where his father (although still an operative) had purchased a piece of property. The store prospered, and in 1864 John and his brother Samuel bought Aston Mills (about a mile up the creek from West Branch) and converted it into a cotton and woolen weaving factory. Eventually the Rhodes firm was to acquire both Knowlton and West Branch from the Crozers.

As with the other self-made men in the district, John B. Rhodes did not restrict himself to business associations. He was active in the affairs of the Oddfellows Benevolent Lodge, No. 40, of Aston (founded in 1831 by his father and others prepared to defy the general anti-secret society sentiment of the Anti-Masons). In politics he was, after the war, a Democrat, and he was a delegate to the party's national convention in 1876. Throughout his early years he was active in the affairs of Calvary Church (although later on he joined the Methodists). Indeed, he and Thomas Blackburn, an operative at Rockdale, achieved lasting, if humorous, notoriety in the annals of Calvary Church for having at their own expense installed an old second-hand church clock in the tower. The clock's bell tolled the hour "with commendable exactness" for several months. But then something went wrong:

> . . . one Sunday morning, just as the Rector announced his text, the clock began to strike. It continued to strike until it had tolled off a hundred and gave every evidence that it would strike a thousand. Mr. Rhodes, who was in the congregation, could stand it no longer. Rising from his pew he ran through the church up into the steeple and stopped the untruthful timepiece, bringing to an end its existence, once and for all.[17]

The pattern of success for such working people in Rockdale, including others who were mentioned earlier, is a consistent one. They were highly skilled operatives, who worked hard, saved their money, invested the capital in a farm or business (often with the help of relatives or of a benevolent established merchant or manufacturer), and earned the trust of the community by probity in financial dealings, conspicuous activity in the church, and performing public service when asked. It would be impossible to estimate what proportions of any cohort of young operatives, entering work in the mill in any one year, would eventually succeed as landowners, merchants, or manufacturers in later years. Few, of course, could achieve as high a level of success as the Crozers, the Campbells, the Riddles, the Blakelys, and the Rhodeses. But the high visibility of these few self-made men gave reality to the claim of Christian capitalism that America was an open society where any man of talent, ambition, and good will could make money and contribute to the development of the community. Many more must have succeeded in a lesser way, for the scale of industry and commerce was still small enough to permit a workingman to enter the ranks of the capitalists with no more money than what he and his wife had saved from wages and boarders' rent.

THE POLITICS OF THE MANUFACTURING INTEREST

One issue upon which almost all manufacturers had agreed, from the beginning of the republic, was the need for a protective tariff. It was the continuing dispute between northern cotton manufacturers and southern cotton growers about this tariff which, in various permutations and escalations, for many years maintained the polarization of the states that eventually made the war inevitable.

The Protective Tariff

In Delaware County, the tariff issue was, along with anti-Masonry, the central political theme of the 1820's and early 1830's. The people of the Rockdale manufacturing district were principal figures in the effort to ensure that Congress established and maintained a high tariff on imported cotton goods in order to protect their yarns and fabrics from British competition. The manufacturers bitterly recalled the years after the War of 1812 when the British had attempted to stifle the American textile industry. British goods were dumped on American docks in huge quantities, to be sold at auction at prices so low that American factories could not compete. Hundreds of businesses were ruined. As a result demands were of course made for a more adequately protective schedule of import duties. But merchants and farmers, who profited most in a situation where they could sell American agricultural products and raw materials to England with minimum duties and could purchase English manufactured goods cheaply in return, resisted raising American duties on English goods. After years of controversy, Congress finally passed (with the prodding of Pennsylvania senators and representatives) the significant tariff act of 1824. Henry Clay, in the debates about the issue, coined the phrase "American System" to denote a national policy combining protective tariffs and internal improvements with due concern for the interests of merchants and farmers. It was in 1825, the year after the establishment of the first meaningful protective tariff, that John P. Crozer and John S. Phillips and his brother-in-law commenced their manufacturing of cotton on Chester Creek, thus establishing the Rockdale manufacturing district.

Conflict in Congress over the protective tariff remained at a feverish pitch for the next generation, southern planters and many northern farmers and merchants favoring a low protective tariff, or even a tariff for revenue only, and the manufacturers of textiles, iron, and other products threatened by European competition demanding high protective walls. Although the protective tariff had its ups and downs during the years before the Civil War (when a high protective tariff was again imposed), the rates on cottons mostly fluctuated between about 20 and 30 percent *ad valorem.* This level of protection was adequate to prevent the British from dumping huge quantities of cheap, low-quality goods on the market and in effect restricted importers to the better quality goods, made from mulespun yarns of higher count than were usually produced in American mills. But variations, or threatened variations, even within this range were sufficient to arouse intense political activity.

In the Rockdale district and along the Brandywine, the cotton manufacturers, and as many workers as they could manage to carry with them, were staunch partisans of Henry Clay and his "American System." Clay was an occasional visitor to both the Brandywine and Chester Creek, and one of the mills on the Brandywine was named for him. In December 1833, when agitation over the tariff was at its height, the friends of Henry Clay at Chester learned that their man was making a brief visit to Philadelphia on his way to Washington. At once a committee was appointed "to wait on him, and request him to visit the Borough of Chester, on his way to the seat of Government, to afford themselves and their fellow citizens of Delaware County, an opportunity of personally paying their respects to him, as a testimony of their sense of his private worth and public usefulness." The ten-man invitation committee, which included William Martin and one of Peter Hill's brothers, was successful, and Henry Clay visited Chester, to enjoy a reception organized by a local arrangements committee of thirty that included most of the Chester Creek manufacturers, among them James Willcox, Dennis Kelly, John P. Crozer, Daniel Lammot, and John S. Phillips. Clay, upon alighting from the steamboat, was received at a public house by, as the normally Democratic *Upland Union* noted, "a large assemblage of the citizens of this county, without distinctions of party," and he remained long enough to shake hands with all and partake of the refreshments.[1]

The absence of the Riddles on the occasion of Clay's visit was not evidence of any reluctance on their part to express themselves in favor of the tariff. When in 1832 Secretary of the Treasury Louis McLane (an erstwhile Brandywine cotton manufacturer) made a survey of the nation's manufacturing establishments for the purpose of providing Congress with evidence of the need for a protective tariff, the Riddles wrote a vigorous response to local commissioners agents Matthew Carey and C. C. Biddle:

CHESTER CREEK, March 28, 1832.

GENTLEMEN: Although we believe that some of the queries proposed in the letter which we have received from you, are very improper, inasmuch as they have a direct tendency to expose to public view a person's private affairs; and further, it is easily discovered they have proceeded from a source unfriendly to the manufacturers' interest; yet we hasten to answer them, in consideration of their being sent you, gentlemen, who are well known to have been the long tried friends of our country's best interest. We would, therefore, deem it highly improper to pass by your communication without noticing it. But we would wish to mention a few thoughts that crossed our minds whilst reading these queries that have emanated from the Treasury Department. If we can gather any thing from the apparent bearing of them, the design is, first, to ascertain the least possible profit the manufacturer can, by any means, carry on with. Secondly, to find out the least possible wages the working class can live upon; and thus by measuring out and dividing a bare subsistence to each class connected with manufacturing, the protective duties could be lowered; the system of tyranny that disgraces the factories in England could be introduced; children would have to do the work that young women does now; young women would have to do the work that men does now; and bye and bye petitions would be carried into Congress (similar to the one Mr. Saddler took into the House of Commons a few months ago) "stating the cruelties practised on children in the factories." Gentlemen, the tariff cannot be lowered, unless the working class is reduced to the same state of degradation, poverty, and wretchedness, as they are in England; then, and only then, can the American manufacturer enter into the lists of competition with his foreign rival, or else there can be no manufacturing establishment carried on. Reduce the tariff, and at once you stop every cotton manufactory in our State. . . . Reduce the tariff and unfurl the banner of "free trade," and then we'll have a beggared starving population, without a sufficiency to procure the necessaries of existence; and then we may lay on poor rates, build poor houses, erect penitentiaries, get an armed police, additional constables—standing army—erect gallowses, &c.; all this will follow in the train of the contemplated reductions in the protection of American industry. The spirit of every noble-minded citizen revolts at the idea of sacrificing our working population to the idol of foreign policy, or taking the bread out of the mouths of their children, and giving it to the supporters and menials of aristocratic tyranny. Gentlemen, you'll pardon us for obtruding these remarks upon your time.

> With much deference, we respectfully
> remain your obedient servants,
> SAMUEL & JAMES RIDDLE

To Messrs. MATHEW CAREY, CLEMENT C. BIDDLE

In response to the question, "Would reducing the tariff on cotton to 12.5% cause you to abandon your business or manufacture at reduced prices?" the Riddles replied:

29th.   Most assuredly it would not only cause but force me to abandon my machinery, which would be valueless, as well as my business. Who would take the lease of my mill off my hands? Who would pay a $1,000 a year for a place that had to be abandoned? Who would consume the farmers' productions, &c?

"If you had to abandon your business," they were asked, "how would you employ your capital?" They replied:

30th.   What capital would we have to employ in another business, when it is invested in machinery, water power, buildings, &c? These would be rendered valueless at once. Capital as well as business would be destroyed, and every individual who owned machinery would be ruined. They might take them to England, and try to sell them there, for they would be of no value in America; or, I might say rather in the free States; perhaps the experiment might be tried to work them with the slave population, in order to keep pace with the improvements of England in cheapening labor and grinding the faces of the poor.

And, asked whether they could turn to a more profitable pursuit if the tariff were reduced, they answered sarcastically:

31st.   If we were forced to abandon our business, and consequently our establishments, although there is many businesses as profitable as ours at present, how could we engage in any? We might go with the Indians beyond the Mississippi.

Crozer, who also replied to the same questionnaire, was more temperate, contenting himself with the matter-of-fact observation that if the tariff were reduced to 12 1/2 percent, he would be compelled to abandon his business, his machinery would be of no value (because no one else would be able to manufacture cotton), and "I think there are few pursuits so uninviting as cotton spinning would then become."[2]

Between elections, the conventional way for political advocates to attempt to influence Congress was to present petitions, and this was the course which the Rockdale manufacturers took in concert with others of Delaware County. The years 1832 and 1833, while President Jackson was trying (ultimately successfully) to persuade Congress to reduce the tariffs to a level commensurate with the Treasury's needs for revenue, were a time of intense petitioning. The method employed by the proponents of a position was to call a public meeting at a house or inn, and elect a chairman (or a president and vice-presidents), a secretary, and a committee to draft the resolution. The resolution, quickly composed (more likely prepared in advance), would then pass unanimously and in succeeding days might be carried about the county to collect signatures. Finally, the petition would be carried to Washington to the district's representative, who would submit it to Congress. Tariff petitions were regularly bi-partisan, the request of signatories acting as individuals rather than as representatives of a Democratic, Federalist, Whig, or Anti-Masonic party.

Two pro-tariff petitions were submitted to Congress from Delaware County, the first in June 1832 and the second in February 1833. Daniel Lammot was a member of the first committee on resolutions, along with George W. Hill, Dr. George Smith, and Preston Eyre. The secretaries, who would transmit the resolutions to Congress, were James Willcox and Samuel Edwards.[3] The petition respectfully drew the attention of Congress to the present prosperity of the country under the benevolent protection of the tariff, and urged defeat of the bill currently before Congress that proposed a reduction in the rates—a move "calculated to spread ruin and disaster amongst us."[4] At the second tariff meeting, Daniel Lammot was chairman and George W. Hill secretary; the committee to prepare resolutions consisted of John S. Phillips, John P. Crozer, George G. Leiper, and two other businessmen. This petition, in addition to urging the retention of the moderate import duties provided in the act of 1832, pointedly attacked southern opposition to the very principle of the protective tariff and the imminent danger of abandoning the tariff altogether:

This law, passed after long debate and great deliberation, and not yet in operation, is to be superseded by one of obvious hostility to the best interests of our country. And what is the cause of this ruinous measure now urged upon Congress? Is the violent clamor of South Carolina sufficient cause? Have any facts been adduced to prove that the South is oppressed by the operation of the tariff? It is, however, demanded that the principle of protection be abandoned. The principle of protection had been too distinctly given in the constitution, and affirmed by legislation, for the last forty years, to admit of any doubt or cavil at this time. A sense of justice will at all times cause us to respect the rights of others; but, in doing so, we ask that our rights should be respected also.

The complaining States have lately been clamorous against the tariff as oppressive, unjust, and unequal; the catalogue of opprobious epithets has been exhausted against the manufacturers, a class of citizens called to their present pursuits by the voice of the nation, encouraged to perseverance by every administration from that of Washington to the present; and now, after a lapse of many years, and after investments amounting to more than two hundred millions of dollars, they are to be sacrificed, and for what? To silence the arrogant demands of South Carolina. . . .[5]

The offensive bill was nonetheless passed, reducing the *ad valorem* rates on cottons and woolens to a level below that of 1816.

The tariff issue was powerful enough even to distract the mind of a rejected suitor. When in January 1832 John S. Phillips, after a prolonged series of courting visits to Sophie on the Brandywine, at last "popped the question" (as Eleuthera put it) through Sophie's father, he was refused by Sophie—and the topic of conversation between Phillips and her father then shifted to the tariff! The scene was described in an amusing letter by Eleuthera to her sister Victorine:

. . . After he had sat there some time Mr P. told him that he must be aware that for the last 18 months he had been attached to his daughter that he had not spoken before because he was not in circumstances to marry and that now he was in a situation when he could make a wife happy & comfortable. He then began to give Papa a description of his fortune which Papa interrupted by assuring him that was of no consequence that he never had influenced his children and they were perfectly free to choose for themselves. Mr P still persisting in going on Papa told him Mr P am I to understand that you wish me to communicate yr intention to my daughter "Yes Sir said Mr P.—Papa & he then talked on other matters. . . . [After dinner] Papa with g^t delicacy said "Mr P. I thought best after what you told me this morning to go and see my daughter, She bade me say that she was grateful for the proof of esteem you have given her but that she cannot return the sentiments of attachment you

have for her—Papa paused—he gave a grunt—a dead pause ensued—
"Mr Phillips said Papa I hope that this will not make any difference in
our friendship"—not a word did he say—When Papa saw this he took
up a newspaper and read a few minutes then addressed the knight on
the subject of the tariff on which they talked as if nothing had occured we
soon returned and talked about the roads yr letters &c till Wildfire coming
to the door. . . . He took his leave. . . .

And Eleuthera added, "In all this affair what shocks Sophy most is the
grunt."[6]

The Second Bank of the United States
and the Delaware County Memorial

Equal, for a time, to the tariff in the intensity of emotion it aroused, but
shorter-lived as an issue, was the controversy surrounding Congress's refusal to recharter the Second Bank of the United States, and the Jackson
administration's withdrawal of federal deposits from its vaults. The manufacturers were for the most part in support of the Bank, which seemed to
them to serve as a brake on cycles of irresponsible speculation, and then
depreciation, and thus as some sort of guard against financial panics. In the
early months of 1834, as business generally declined under burden of a
widespread anxiety about the federal bank policy, the Chester Creek manufacturers wrote desperate letters to Edward Darlington, their representative
in Congress, who regularly sent them alarming news from the seat of
government. Samuel and James Riddle expressed themselves, as was their
style, in hyperbolic, even apocalyptic, imagery:

. . . never was a period in the history of our country when it could be
said with more truth "we are in the midst of a revolution" than the
present period. The Demon of the storm is up furiously draging onward
the Revolutionary cart driven by the Spirit of Party the fierce, revengeful,
implacable, unmerciful, unreasonable, Spirit of Party crushing beneath its
angry wheels our Country's boast—our Country's Glory. What makes
her loved at home and never abroad. The good of the people is no longer
the rallying point for which everything of less importance is sacrifice.
High handed measures of vindictive revenge against anti-Partisans seems
to be the order of the day, and upon the altar of this Molock must be
sacrificed the Peace, the happiness, the industry of the people to gratify
the unholy ungovernable vengeance of this incensed *Deity.* . . .[7]

Crozer, less given to dramatic language, merely alluded to "the unhappy experiment of our infatuated president," and sent Darlington a census of unemployment in the Rockdale mills.[8]

In March 1834, "a very large and highly respectable" group of citizens of Delaware County assembled, without distinction of party, to consider "the propriety of the measures adopted by the Executive of the United States in relation to the removal of the deposites [*sic*] of the public money from the Bank of the United States." The usual names of manufacturers occurred among the lists of officers and committee members: John P. Crozer, William Martin, Daniel Lammot, George Escol Sellers. The proceedings drew attention to the financial distress already affecting the county and predicted (correctly) "that still greater and lasting evils are in store for the people." This new memorial pointed out that all classes of persons suffered:

> . . . that the citizens of Delaware county are engaged in trade, agriculture, and manufactures; that, independent of all other capital employed in their various pursuits, there is in the county upwards of $1,500,000 invested in manufactures, producing annually a manufactured property to the value of $2,000,000 and upwards, giving employ to about fifteen hundred people, the whole of which business, in consequence of the present state of the currency and alarm, is on the very brink of total prostration; a number of the manufactories have already stopped, and the hands without employ or the means of support; agricultural produce daily depreciating, and the country swarming with laborers seeking employ.

The petition asked for the rechartering of the Bank and the return of the Treasury deposits, and objected to the tyrannical, vindictive, unconstitutional actions of the chief executive. It also took time to reprove the President for his ignorance of elementary economic principles: *"Resolved,* That the doctrine entertained and expressed by General Jackson, that all who trade on borrowed capital ought to fail, is unworthy and unbecoming a Chief Magistrate of an enlightened, business, and enterprising people."

This time the petition was submitted to Congress with about 2,500 signatures from across the county. The same familiar names appeared again: James Houghton, John S. Phillips, John Garsed, Nathan Sellers, Charles Kelly, Samuel and James Riddle, John P. Crozer, Daniel Lammot. And next to the names of the manufacturers were set the names of their senior male employees, the mule spinners, machinists, loom bosses, and carding masters. Although a pro-Jackson petition was also produced on the same day, it carried few signatures and was evidently the work largely of the Democratic Party faithful. It is clear that the vast majority of the male workers in the Delaware County mills favored the recharter of the Second Bank on the basis of the immediately felt economic distress that followed the removal of the deposits.

To the Senate
and House of Representatives
of the United States:

The memorial of the undersigned, citizens of the county of Delaware, in Pennsylvania,

RESPECTFULLY SHOWETH:

That your memorialists are *farmers, manufacturers, mechanics, merchants,* and *laborers.* That they have heretofore prospered in their several pursuits, and from the sound and healthy state of business amongst them, they had reason to expect continued prosperity. But, in the midst of these expectations, they have suddenly experienced a distressing reverse; a few months ago every branch of trade was active; now, many of our mechanics are without employment, our manufactories some of them closed entirely, others partially suspended operations, and many of them preparing to wind up their business, should Congress do nothing to relieve them. Our merchants unable to collect their bills; the price of agricultural products rapidly declining; a great reduction in wages, and the certainty of many hundreds being left without employment. Thus, in a few short months, your memorialists have passed from a condition of enviable prosperity, to one of distress and threatening ruin.

The number of signatures amounted to about 15 percent of the total population of the county, about 30 percent of the male population of the county, and probably 60 or 70 percent of the adult male population. The Delaware County Memorial was formally presented to Congress by Edward Darlington; it was the first time the county's representative had spoken from the floor of the House.[9]

The methods of some of the manufacturers in securing this appearance of consensus were somewhat exploitive. The Riddles paid their mule spinners $6 apiece (a week's wages) to attend the meeting and sign their names.[10] Others were less gentle in their usages. Six years later, in the depths of the depression that the manufacturers blamed on Jackson's tariff, banking, and hard money policies, and in a presidential election year, the Democratic *Upland Union* charged the manufacturers in the Rockdale district with refusing to hire any but anti-Jackson men. It was a scathing column:

TYRANNY—PROSCRIPTION. A laboring man of this county having heard that a wealthy manufacturer on Chester Creek, wanted to employ hands in his business, offered his services to him. The federalist and manufacturer commenced with the usual cant phrases of hard times: the "government is ruining the manufacturers, paralyzing business, breaking the banks, in favor of a gold and silver currency," &c &c, and we can't afford to hire labor. Very well said the laborer, you do not wish to hire me, so good by. Stop, stop said the manufacturer, we want a hand or two, but what are your politics? We want no hands about us but what are opposed to the Government. The laborer indignant at this insulting attack upon his feelings & principles, the blood boiling in his veins, rose and said, "Sir, I have always voted the democratic ticket, and intend to do so again—so good by to you."

The paper thundered warnings of retribution to come at the polls to this manufacturer ("an unfeeling slave to the old doctrines of Federalism")— a retribution that would fall on all the manufacturers as a result of their "violence and proscription to American citizens." A few months later, the same paper accused the manufacturers on Chester Creek of practicing "white slavery" by forcing their workers to vote against the Democratic ticket. An anecdote was told of "an extensive manufacturer and a bank director" (who could have been none other than John P. Crozer) who "exulted in the declaration that all his hands were against Van Buren except one, and that he should also vote against him in the election. Only think of the humiliating position of a man pretending to some character, who would make such a boast?" Another manufacturer, alleged to have been in his cups at the time, was said to have approved Crozer's boast, and to have given it as his own opinion that workers should be fired if they refused to vote according to their master's will.

Finally in July (as election time neared) the *Union* took direct aim at "The Manufacturers" in an editorial explaining that the Democrats were pro-tariff but anti-Bank (because the Bank was setting itself above the government). And again a certain manufacturer and bank director was arraigned (no doubt Crozer once more):

Shortly before the governor's election, he told his hands with apparent disinterestedness that, "I know you are free men, and have a right to vote for whom you please, but unless you vote as I do, our business will be injured and I will have to discharge you."

The *Union* demanded legislative investigation of such practices.[11]

The Transformation of Issues and the Conservation of Sides:
Tariff, Free Soil, and Slavery

In the 1820's and 1830's, while the northern manufacturers were struggling on weekdays against southern planters about the tariff and against
Democrats about the Bank, they were also, in their evangelical mode, on
Sundays combating the infidels and Utopian socialists, who were likewise
in favor of free trade (because it promised lower prices to the workers) and
against monopolies (like the Second Bank of the United States). Evangelical
capitalism thus found itself fighting at the side of a motley band of allies
against a confusing array of enemies, and experimenting with a variety of
political vehicles, before, in the 1850's, a viable Republican Party was able
to enlist broad popular support for a national policy congenial to the manufacturing interest. The Federalists, the anti-Jackson Democrats, the Anti-
Masons, the National Republicans, and the Whigs all for a time gave
expression to the manufacturers' values. But the values of a dominant
national party had to represent more than the transparent self-interest of the
manufacturer in having a good transportation system, a protective tariff, a
stable currency, and a dependable work force. In order to achieve national
support, the manufacturers' values had to be anchored in a social issue of
paramount national concern. That issue was the politicization of the moral
struggle between north and south over the extension (or contraction) of
slavery.

The northern cotton manufacturer at the beginning of the century
had been able to ignore the moral paradox implicit in his business. He
deplored on principle, either as an evangelical Christian or a free-
enquiring radical, the system of slavery. But that did not mean that he
was an abolitionist or that he liked blacks, whether free or slave. He
knew that the bales of raw cotton he took into his mill were produced
by southern black slaves and that their price would be higher, and his
profits lower, if they were to be produced by white farm labor paid at
northern rates. Furthermore, the southern plantation was a major customer for his own product, which was used (in different qualities, of
course) to clothe both slaves and masters. The cotton-manufacturing industry in the north, employing relatively highly paid white operatives,
was inextricably bound in a reciprocal trade relationship (via intermediary merchant houses) with the slave-operated cotton plantations in the
south. The expansion of the northern industry required, and resulted in,
the expansion of the cotton plantation system and the extension of slavery. Thus it was emotionally necessary to dissociate the moral issue of
slavery from the economic realities of manufacturing cotton.

The initial conflict in this economic compact had to do not with slavery but with the tariff on foreign imports. The plantation owner saw himself as having little to gain from a protective tariff to protect the northern customers for his cotton, for he could dispose of his cotton to English and other foreign markets (and even if rarely done, construct cotton factories run by slave labor himself). The tariff simply raised his costs and invited retaliation against his own export. The long years of debate over the tariff resulted in a series of compromises that permitted both sections to prosper. But the acrimony of the arguments had established, by the early 1830's, an awareness of tension, a choosing of sides on the basis of regional interests, that promised to make other issues more difficult to resolve. And, one may suspect, both sides also had increasingly to deal with a sense of moral dissonance. The southern planter, Christian or Deist, needed to justify slavery; the northern manufacturer, evangelical or Unitarian, needed to justify his ignoring of slavery.

The arrival of increasing thousands of immigrants in America, many of whom served for a time as operatives in cotton mills and then moved on to buy farms and businesses in the west, added a new ingredient to the situation. As the lands in the midwestern states were purchased from the Indian tribes who inhabited them or were acquired by conquest from Mexico, thousands of working people spent their savings to buy land. Workers in cotton mills did not feel chained to their machines for a lifetime of drudgery; they could put up with hard working conditions because they knew that they could, if all went well, move west in a few years as homesteaders on virgin land. The only condition that could block the movement was the pre-emption of large areas for cotton plantations and farms operated by slave labor. Small farmers could not compete with slaveowners in the same markets. Northern opposition to the south thus took on an added economic dimension. Not only were the manufacturers constrained to resist southern demands for lower tariffs; their workers, however they felt about the tariff, wanted to move into states and territories where the soil was free. The struggle over the constitutions of new states, slave or free, was not merely a matter of ensuring balance in the voting power of the sections in Congress. The availability of free soil was functionally necessary to the manufacturing interest because it contributed to the maintenance of a highly productive factory labor force with high morale. Thus the initial transformation of the tariff issue was into a regional issue that involved free soil as well as productive tariffs. By espousing free soil as part of their program, the manufacturers were in fact (whether intentionally or not) bringing to their side politically large numbers of working people whose dream it was to save money from factory wages in order to buy a western farm.

With northern manufacturers and workers solidly aligned on the tariff and free soil issues, with the south as common enemy, all that was needed to cement the alliance was a sense of moral outrage at the south. This was encouraged by the various movements that aimed at improving the status of blacks and reversing the history of slavery. From the highly conservative contributors to the American Colonization Society to the radical Garrisonian abolitionists, there came into existence a spectrum of organizations which had as a common theme the righting of the wrongs done to black slaves by southern planters. Such a moral theme could assure the northern cotton manufacturer and his operatives that they were not responsible for the evils of slavery (even though they indirectly profited from it). And it would provide a common target of displaced resentment (using the south as scapegoat) in a situation of potential labor conflict.

The transformation of political issues from the 1820's to the 1850's, insofar as they were experienced by the cotton manufacturers and their workers, was from disagreement with the south over the tariff, and resentment of the extremely belligerent style of southern rhetoric, to political struggles with the south over free soil, to moral condemnation of the south for the sin of slavery. The functional advantages of this transformation were obvious: it consolidated the workers and the manufacturers in a political and economic alliance and contributed to two decades of relative labor peace. The disadvantage was not foreseen: the continuing escalation of an increasingly moralistic conflict between the regions that placed in jeopardy the whole "American System."

The Manufacturer-Politicians

The manufacturers to a man considered that it was their responsibility to influence events at the seats of government. There were three levels of political activity open to them. The minimal level involved voting, influencing the votes of others (by gentle persuasion or threats), organizing petition meetings, and signing petitions. All of the manufacturers were active on this level. The next step was to engage in political party activities, such as serving as a delegate or a member of a committee, and to accept township and county administrative positions (such as on the school board). At least nine of the cotton manufacturers were active on this level during much of their lives; of these William Martin, Edward Darlington, and James and Samuel Riddle were most prominent. And three of these last four were also, at one time or another, prominent on the third level as candidates for, or holders of, elective office at the state or national level.

Samuel Riddle represents the second level. His political profile was relatively inconspicuous (although one of his biographers inaccurately claimed that he was so busy in promoting the high tariff that he had "presided over all the tariff meetings in Delaware county since the commencement of the agitation").[12] He was appointed U.S. postmaster at Penn's Grove in 1842 (later marrying the daughter of a postmistress from Chester) and retained the post until his death in 1887. From 1844 to 1848 he served as one of the elected directors of the public schools for Middletown Township. (Six others of the manufacturers were elected to the school boards of the two townships.) In 1849 he joined the Hibernian Society, a quasi-political ethnic organization which worked to improve the condition of Irish immigrants, attended its meetings regularly, and for a time served on its committee on finances. (He probably also helped to organize the local chapter of the Society which eventually, in 1892, built a brick hall for its meetings at Rockdale, just across the street from Calvary Church.) And he was active enough in conservative politics to serve as a delegate to the 1856 Whig state convention in Harrisburg, along with his friend Edward Darlington.[13] Samuel Riddle's brother James did not become active politically until he moved to the Brandywine; he was an unsuccessful candidate on the Republican ticket for governor of the State of Delaware.[14]

William Martin had a more illustrious career in politics. He started out as a Federalist, spending the 1827–28 term in the House of Representatives in Harrisburg; thereafter he was prominent in county politics as a chief burgess of the Borough of Chester and an organizer of tariff and bank petitions; after his removal to Philadelphia as director of the Delaware Mutual Insurance Company, he was active in public school affairs, for a time serving as president of the Philadelphia School Board. During Martin's term in the state legislature, the two leading questions were the program of internal improvements by canal and railroad, and a system of free public schools for the children of the state—particularly the children in cotton-manufacturing districts. Martin was, as his voting record shows, a consistent supporter of the extension of the canal system and he voted in favor of issuing a charter for the proposed new Pennsylvania Railroad. He voted regularly in favor of acts to encourage Pennsylvania agriculture and manufactures.[15] The event of which he was most proud, however, was his association with Thaddeus Stevens in introducing a bill to establish "the public school system" in Pennsylvania. According to Martin's son, Stevens asked Martin to prepare such a bill. Martin accordingly drew up "An Act to provide for the education of children employed in manufactories; and also to ascertain the extent and increase of said manufactories in this commonwealth." It was introduced as Bill No. 80 by Thaddeus Stevens. After prolonged debate and agonized opposition by representatives from other manufacturing districts, the bill passed the House, but so late in the session that the Senate did not act on it and it failed to become law. It is said to have served, however, as the basis for the successful act of 1834 establishing a public school system in the State of Pennsylvania.[16]

By all odds the most consistent and successful political career among the early manufacturing group was that of Edward Darlington. We have already noticed some of his activities in the political arena at the time of the furor against Freemasonry. But his career, although not a notable one in political histories of the state, exhibits clearly the transformation of issues, and the evolution of political philosophy, of the economic group whom he represented in a series of elective and appointive offices.

Basically Edward Darlington was a Delaware County Court House lawyer. He read law under Samuel Edwards, a respected Democrat who had himself served terms in both the state and national legislatures. Although Edwards did not hold elective office thereafter, he was, along with the Leiper brothers, one of the Democratic Party leaders in the county, and he was a personal friend of James Buchanan, with whom he had served in the House. Edwards served, like William Martin, as chief burgess of the city for a couple of years, and from 1838 to 1842 he held the sinecure position of Inspector of Customs at the port of Chester (an ancient sinecure indeed, for Chester's international trade had been largely pre-empted by Philadelphia a century before).[17] With Edwards as his mentor and associate in legal practice, Darlington entered county politics as a Democratic Party worker, and by 1825 was serving as secretary at party assemblages. But by 1828 his position had shifted to the right and he participated in a political rally of anti-Jacksonians at Valley Forge in July 1828, where toasts were raised to such heroes of conservatism as Henry Clay ("The intrepid champion of his country's rights, and inflexible advocate of American industry"), Matthew Carey ("Although the friends of Jackson have burnt his effigy, his works have survived the conflagration"), and Darlington's cousin Dr. William Darlington ("The early and efficient advocate of the American system and the policy of Internal Improvement").[18] By 1830 he had joined the crusade against Freemasonry and ran for Congress on a combined Anti-Masonic and Federalist ticket. And, of course, he was elected to Congress in 1832 and 1834 as an Anti-Mason; in 1838, after Pennsylvania Anti-Masonry had received its cruel defeat in the "Buckshot War," when its members were chased by a mob from the chamber and refused the seats necessary to organize the legislature, he was returned as a Whig. Although apparently he did not run again for legislative office and went back to the full-time practice of law, Darlington remained active in the Whig politics of the county and the state until at least 1857, retaining his by now ingrained antipathy to the "loco-foco" wing of the Democratic Party. He was elected district attorney of Delaware County and served in that office from 1851 to 1854. And, of course, he eventually joined the new Republican Party as the Whig organization quietly disintegrated in the years immediately preceding the Civil War.[19]

The evolution of Darlington's political philosophy can be discerned clearly in changing party affiliations. Starting out as a typical Pennsylvania Democrat, favoring the grand old party of Thomas Jefferson but committed to Clay's "American System" of protected manufactures and state-managed internal improvements, he became an anti-Jackson Democrat when he perceived the American System to be threatened by the leadership of his own party. When the revelations of the Masonic conspiracy appeared, and the dangerously liberal tendency of the loco-foco Democrats became even more evident, he joined the Anti-Masonic Party and was sent to Congress. There, anti-Masonry was not a principal object of legislative concern but the American System was, and Darlington voted consistently in favor of the Second Bank of the United States, in favor of high tariffs, in favor of internal improvements, in favor of rules to ensure the safety of boilers on steamboats, and in favor of the encouragement of invention and exploration.[20] He signed a petition in favor of temperance along with other congressional and executive leaders.[21] He corresponded and visited with Henry Carey, Matthew's son and principle economic philosopher of the American System.[22] In these conservative views, he seems to have been consistent and even harsh, joining Thaddeus Stevens and the more radical wing of the Anti-Masonic Party in 1835 in their refusal to endorse Harrison as the party's presidential candidate, and relishing such gossip as the news that some of John Bancroft's relatives in England "say Jackson is the very man they wanted to be President, and if they can only get America into their clutches again, she will have a harder struggle to get free."[23]

But a new dimension was added to Darlington's concerns when he went to Washington: the problem of slavery. He voted consistently with the minority who wanted to outlaw slavery in the District of Columbia, who recognized the right of slaves to petition Congress for the redress of grievances, and who opposed the automatic tabling of all resolutions from citizens opposing slavery. In some of these votes, he was in a highly conspicuous minority: he was one of only eighteen congressmen to vote against a resolution declaring that slaves do not have the right to petition Congress (there were 162 votes in favor). And although he generally voted in favor of national defense measures (such as appropriations bills for fortifications), he would not favor the early annexation of Texas when it appeared that it was certain to become a slave-state. But there was a point at which he would compromise. When a resolution was offered declaring that the United States government has no authority with respect to slavery, he failed to join the six who voted against it; he simply abstained.[24]

John M. Broomall, Crozer's partner in the development of the South Ward, completed the process of political transformation in the manufacturing districts of Delaware County that was begun by Edward Darlington. Like Darlington, he was a birthright Quaker, and after the schism of 1828–29, he was raised in a radical Hicksite household in Chichester Township. Like Darlington, he studied law under Samuel Edwards and began practice in Chester in 1840. He was a trial lawyer and practiced what in later years would be termed "criminal law." It was said that he was engaged for the defense in all the homicide cases in Delaware County for a period of about fifty years after his admission to the bar and that no client of his was ever convicted on a first-degree murder charge. Opposed to capital punishment, and generally disposed in favor of the unfortunate, he prosecuted, so to speak, his defense by shrewd appeals to emotion and by ruthless assaults upon the credibility of prosecution witnesses. As his memorialist observed:

> He had the power of conveying some prominent favorable feature of his case to a jury throughout the trial, even in spite of the rules of evidence, and he was looked upon as an uncurable competitor in a case. His cases were won by selecting beforehand some particularly strong point and by keeping it continually in view. He would use all the other facts in the case as ancillary to the dominant idea.

These aptitudes for public debate were natural qualifications for a political career. By 1850 he was leading the radical Whig faction in the county in a revolt against the hegemony of the Eyres. He was an effective stump speaker and was soon elected to the state House of Representatives. For a time his career as a Whig fell into eclipse because he refused to join the secret order of the Know-Nothing Party, being opposed on principle (like Darlington and Thaddeus Stevens) to secret societies of any kind. But in 1856, when the Republican Party was forming in Pennsylvania, Broomall enthusiastically joined up, primarily because "he saw that it was prepared to take stronger ground on the subject of slavery than its predecessor." He became the nominee of the Delaware County Republicans for the district's congressional seat in 1856 but withdrew in favor of the Chester County delegate. Broomall ran unsuccessfully in 1858, and was finally elected to the House in 1862. In 1860 he attended the Republican National Nominating Convention in Chicago, where despite the unit rule he opposed his own state's nominee, Simon Cameron, and cast his vote for Lincoln. He was a member of the Electoral College which made Lincoln President in 1860 and again in 1872 at the election of Grant.

Broomall served with distinction in the House of Representatives in Washington from 1862 through 1868. He was a radical Republican, a close friend and admirer of Thaddeus Stevens, who saw in the Republican Party the opportunity to bring moral principles to bear upon the affairs of a great nation. He was a vehement abolitionist and was willing to bear arms in that cause; when the war between the states began, although a Quaker, he served as a captain of a regiment of Pennsylvania emergency militia. He worked for the repeal of that clause in the Pennsylvania Constitution of 1837 which denied the suffrage to black citizens of the commonwealth, and during the war and the reconstruction period campaigned tirelessly for a federal law establishing universal suffrage. In this cause he included women as well as men, believing that "civil and political rights should be exercised by all, even without regard to sex."[25]

He worked in close concert with Thaddeus Stevens, and after Stevens's death delivered a eulogy that lauded the "great commoner" for his unremitting labors on behalf of free public education, the abolition of slavery, universal suffrage, and other populist causes. Broomall regarded himself as a radical in Stevens's own tradition and deplored "conservatism":

> Too frequently in men of all stations the generous impulses and noble sentiments of youth give place, with advancing years and prosperity, to that fossil petrefaction of humanity called conservatism, which is nothing more than the want of ability to see the line of progress marked out by the hand of Omnipotence and the want of energy to follow it.[26]

He resisted vigorously the Johnson administration's efforts to ameliorate the conditions of reconstruction and favored the impeachment of the President.

But, like Stevens, he remained a radical in the capitalist evangelical tradition. Although disowned by Friends for his marriage outside the fold, he continued to attend meeting and participated in the affairs of the Society. He continued to administer the South Ward development until nearly the time of his death. He was a strong temperance advocate, and insisted on the strictest standards of financial competence and probity. He contended against government interference in business affairs (having outlived the protectionist era). Broomall represented, in a sense, the acme of evangelical success: the capture of the moral high ground from evangelical capitalism's ideological competitors.[27]

MISSIONS AND THE MILLENNIAL PASSION

The continuing improvement in the worldly situation of the people of the manufacturing districts was impressive enough in an economic sense. But in the decade of the 1850's, it took on, in the eyes of thoughtful observers, a mysterious, almost sacred quality, as though it were a sign from God. To some, the meaning of the sign was plain. The Lord was arming the Christian part of mankind for a final battle with the forces of sin and death.

This theme of conflict was not new. For centuries, Christians had perceived their own spiritual lives as a course of endless struggle against temptation to sin. The prize of victory was salvation; the price of defeat, eternal torment in Hell. Recent years had seen a great increase in the efforts of domestic and foreign missions to save unbelievers from damnation by converting them to Christianity. It would be an easy transition from simple missionary zeal to the conviction that the coming decades were the time foretold in the Book of Revelation when God's people on earth must do battle with the hosts of Hell, with tongue, pen, and sword, to conquer the world for Christ.

The Drama of Salvation and Death

In the Protestant theologies it was generally asserted that at death the body descended into the grave, there to sleep until the Second Coming of Christ, when the dead should rise and their souls be judged. Some would then be saved and enter Heaven, to enjoy endless bliss in the company of the Lord; others would be condemned to endless torment in Hell, the domain of Satan. In common metaphorical usage, however, the souls of the dead who were destined for Heaven were somehow translated there immediately, so that the dying person could be conceived as undergoing a passage directly from one life to another. Yet, much theological uncertainty surrounded the process of assignment. On the one hand, the old-school Calvinists insisted that the event had been decided from the commencement of a depraved mankind's existence by an omniscient, omnipotent, and immutable God, who in effect had condemned the vast majority of mankind to Hell in advance. The elect were saved by God's grace alone and not by good works, or love, or faith on their own part (although these were required); they were to rule the damned, and to ensure that, even though destined by Him for hellfire, these too loved God, lived moral lives, and even enjoyed the prospect of their own torture because it was part of the

Lord's divine plan. On the other hand, the Universalists insisted that God, in an equally deterministic way, had made all men basically good and had decided that all should eventually, albeit with greater or lesser speed, reach Heaven. Most American Protestant denominations in this period taught views somewhere in between, in theory preserving the theological doctrine of predestination but in practice allowing to all but a few the possibility of salvation. Those who sincerely repented and had true faith in God's mercy would be saved.

Given the uncertainties of theology as well as of personal experience, and the enormity of the issue, many sincere Christians experienced severe chronic anxiety about their fate. They continually monitored their overt behavior, private sentiments, and mood, and estimated their prospects for Heaven or Hell according to their introspections. Most highly prized of all were those peak experiences when, in the course of committing oneself unreservedly to faith in Christ the Savior, one experienced a sudden, overwhelming conviction of being loved in return by God. This awareness of the possibility of salvation, achieved during the conversion process, encouraged the believer to go on to commit himself to a life of love and charity and to march toward death with a high hope of Heaven.

Death thus was a highly interesting situation to the Christian observer. It was the final opportunity for mortal man to experience the conviction of being saved and to communicate this knowledge to family and friends. As long as a person regarded himself as dying (a condition which might be as brief as a few minutes or as protracted as several decades), he endeavored to marshal his memories and feelings so as to be able to maintain the assurance of salvation. In order to make sure his mind was clear, he refused to take any more opiates. Those around him helped by singing hymns, praying, reading religious writings aloud, and asking evocative questions to keep the moribund person's mind on his final work. It was not so much the fear, like that of the medieval practitioner of the *ars moriendi,* that he might succumb to a soul-destroying temptation of rage or pride at the last moment. Rather, it was almost a divinatory practice, encouraged by the deterministic Protestant theology, to uncover the intentions of God by observing closely the state of His creature at a time when he knew that his fate was upon him. And it was also a rite of passage designed to ensure that the dying person and his loved ones did indeed take leave of each other with an assurance of meeting again in Heaven and that he go gladly to meet his Maker.[1]

Because of its dramatic significance in the all-important process of salvation, death was a preoccupation of the more religious class of people in Rockdale. At least with those who felt themselves to be in good hope of salvation and who were intimately involved with church affairs, it was not so much a morbid as a professional interest, sometimes warmly tinged with the romantic hues of contemporary fashion, sometimes detached and analytical. As befitted his status, the Reverend Mr. (later Bishop) Lee devoted many of his public utterances to teaching the Christian way of death, and in 1856 he published a hortatory book entitled *A Life Hid with Christ; Being a Memoir of Miss Susan Allibone,* which described the twenty years of illness, and the final exemplary death, of a devout Episcopalian woman in Philadelphia. Based on her diary and letters, it described her progress in piety, the conversations with friends like Bishop Potter, her patience and faith in God's mercy during a long and painful invalidism, her occasional visits to the cemetery where she expected to be buried. There she passed many hours of delightful meditation, looking forward with joy to the period when her flesh should there rest in hope and her spirit be welcomed to its heavenly home. When she was about to die, in September 1854, she called her friends and relatives to her, and with a beautiful smile exclaimed, "I think I am going. Peace! I must go to Jesus!" These were her dying words; it was a perfect dying. As Lee observed, it was plain from the manner of her passing that "the bloodwashed soul of Susan Allibone was added to the glorious company of the spirits of the just made perfect."[2]

The correspondence of the sisterhood was filled with page after page of description of the "interesting situation." When the women knew the person who died, it was important to examine with particular care the evidences of faith and to report to friends the cheerful news that he or she remained confident of God's mercy to the very end. After Alexis du Pont was blown up in the explosion in the powder yard in the summer of 1857, he lingered in great pain for several days; his sisters attended him anxiously, watching for signs that his conversion had been effective. He held firm in faith until he died. Clementina observed, on hearing this good news, "Thank God he was a Christian."[3] A couple of years later, when the young Reverend Mr. Dudley Tyng, who had been so close to the Smiths and the Calvary congregation, died as a result of an accident with a piece of new machinery on his farm, Clementina happily compared him to Alexis:

I think with you dear Sophie that there was a striking resemblance of Christian character and zeal between dear Alexis and Mr. Tyng—and the last of their career; both so earnestly active for their Lord both so calmly meeting their sudden summons in the midst of life and manly vigours! Until a few hours before his death Mr. Tyng expected to recover and spoke of the hope of increased usefulness this trial w^d effect for him— his Father felt it his duty to tell him that he was sinking fast—He then turned to his physician and asked him if that was his opinion he said it was—then he said he had Many loved ones here but he longed to be with Jesus—and turning to his physician Dr. Ablee thanked him for his kindness which had been like a brothers and after "preaching to him Jesus" prayed that he might embrace Him as a brother in Christ. Rev. Mr. Harris said he never saw such perfect abnegation of self.[4]

Tyng's death took on an almost martyr-like quality from the circumstance that he had just been discharged as rector by the vestry at the Church of the Epiphany for condemning slavery from the pulpit as the cause of many of America's problems. His last words were "Stand up for Jesus"—a phrase that became a popular evangelical hymn.[5]

Anna Potts Smith turned to verse when she lost a loved one; and the theme of these deeply felt, if somewhat stilted, elegies was the assurance of a reunion in Heaven. When her daughter Eugenia Victorine died in 1839 at the age of seventeen (three weeks after the birth of Anna's last son and child), she mourned for a long time. She appeared to condolence callers to be properly composed and confident of Eugenia's salvation (she had been in regular attendance at Calvary Church); but next spring, the appearance of the short-lived April flowers that grew on the wooded slopes around Lenni moved her to write a painful poem:

> *Oh! bring me not the wild-flowers—those early flowers of spring!*
> *Ye little think, ye dear ones, of the painful thoughts ye bring—*
> *To you, they speak of coming joy—of sunshine—& of bloom—*
> *But they mind your Mother of the past—of death—& of the tomb.*
>
> *The earliest violets that bloomed beneath the forest trees—*
> *The wood anemonies, that bend their slight stems to the breeze—*
> *And all spring's fairy flowers she brought, when last the season smiled—*
> *And now—the flowers again are here—but oh! where is my child!*
>
> *Not that thy hand no more may cull the blossom & the flowers—*
> *Not that thou may'st no more enjoy this balmy air of ours—*
> *Oh! not for thee, these bitter tears!—In thy bright, blessed sphere,*
> *Immortal spirit! What has earth, that I should wish thee here?*
>
> *Oh! not for thee! And tho' thy death so many hopes has crushed,*
> *At thought of thy surpassing bliss e'en selfish grief is hushed.*
> *And my sad heart is comforted—no more by sorrow riven—*
> *When I think on thee, my gentle child, as an angel now in heaven!*[6]

Perhaps the polarities of an age may be reflected in the different manners of leaving it. Certainly the accounts of the passing of the deistical John

S. Phillips and the evangelical John P. Crozer illustrate the contrast between the Christian *ars moriendi* and that of the cool disciple of the Enlightenment.

After the war's end, Crozer undertook to restore the rent between the northern and southern Baptist churches and to establish philanthropies for the freed slaves. He traveled to the south on this errand of mercy and while on tour was taken gravely ill. He was brought home to Upland, where he died after a few weeks of illness. He refused opiates, which would have eased his pain, in order to remain clear-minded to the last, and he undertook to perform in classic fashion the Christian ritual of dying. Surrounded by family, clergy, and friends, his confidence maintained by the singing of hymns (he had never been known to carry a tune before), he repeatedly gave testimony to his love for Jesus and his confidence in His grace, which was (in the words of a hymn he sang) "the antidote of death." It was, for him, a peak experience, perhaps the supreme emotional experience of his life, a ritual of affirmation of faith that required, for its successful performance, the most genuine conviction. He instructed his family to carry on his work:

> The responsibilities of a large estate are upon you. You are my stewards, my almoners, to carry on the work I have so imperfectly begun; you must take it up where I have left it off, and do it for me. My children, see that you are faithful stewards.

He repeatedly burst out in ecstatic exclamations, "My God doeth all things well. Jesus is my all, he is my Saviour." He responded to questions as to his state of faith with full affirmations of assurance of salvation. When his son-in-law William Bucknell asked, "You feel the everlasting arms beneath you?" he replied, with an expression of joy, "Oh yes, underneath-underneath-underneath me. No more, let me die now."

His last intelligible utterance came when, after suffering a stroke that paralyzed his left side, his daughter inquired, "Dear father, do you still love Jesus?" He raised his right arm and emphatically said, "Yes." He died a few hours later.[7]

John S. Phillips outlived Crozer by ten years. Although he had for the most part lost contact with former associates at Rockdale and the Brandywine, he had become something of a figure in the Philadelphia artists' community. He spent much of his time assembling an extraordinary collection of 65,000 original engravings by European artists, including such masters as Cranach, Dürer, Fragonard, Hogarth, and Rembrandt; when it was bequeathed to the Pennsylvania Academy of the Fine Arts, it was considered to be the largest and most important print collection in the country. During the war he took a severely anti-southern position, going so far as "refusing his hand and even recognition to life-long friends who were disloyal to the government in its peril." In 1864, during the great Sanitary Fair in Philadelphia to raise contributions for the Sanitary Commission, which cared for the sick and wounded, he was responsible for preparing the lighting and machinery for tableau exhibitions. And he was known throughout the city as a kind of eccentric mechanical genius: the inventor of a slide-lathe that cut screws of irregular size, the head of a firm that produced the finest decorative ivory turnings in the country, and the enthusiastic friend of young mechanicians. He particularly enjoyed helping young mechanics to construct machinery for which they lacked the necessary tools—clocks, microscopes, even steam engines.[8]

The artist Cecilia Beaux, as a girl of seventeen, was introduced to Phillips by her cousin and teacher, Katherine Drinker, who painted historical and biblical pictures. She recorded a visit in his later years, when he lived with his sisters and servants in the old house on Clinton Street. Still dressed in black broadcloth, the "old gentlemen" brought them to his attic workshop, where he personally mounted his prints in looseleaf portfolios of his own design, and treated them (as he had the ladies of his youth) to long monologues on technical subjects. "I would not for the world have broken in on our host's soliloquy," Cecilia said, "and took what I could get, by way of feeling, without much mental satisfaction." At ten o'clock, a maid brought Queen's cakes and vintage Madeira. She prized the memory:

> Our old friend's hand trembled a little as he filled the delicate glasses; not from age, but from the emotion of the preceding hour, and my constrained young heart knew and was shaken also.
>
> The evening was over. He accompanied us downstairs; it was our last visit. He put an arm around each of us, bending to look into our faces. "My fine friend, my fair friend," he said.
>
> I never saw him again.[9]

Phillips was anxious to get his prints completely encased in their tamper-proof portfolios before he died and they were turned over to the Academy. And so he worked himself and his assistant Henry Whipple to exhaustion, often until after midnight. Late one Friday night, he told Whipple, "Come early on Saturday, for by Monday we may all be dead." He died before Whipple could reach him, on Saturday morning.[10]

Missionary Zeal

One of the intended functions of the death cult was to terrorize the infidel and the lukewarm Christian. The terrible contrast between the serene death of the convinced believer and the misery of the poor soul approaching the end without having genuinely accepted Christ as his personal Savior was a favorite evangelical theme. It was set before the people of Rockdale in an incessant barrage of sermons, tracts, novels, speeches, editorials, and even short stories and poetry on the front pages of the *Upland Union* and the *Delaware County Republican.* The prince of infidels, Tom Paine, was again and again described in deathbed agonies, too late recanting his deistical principles. The tract societies circulated accounts of how one or another "gentleman of infidel principles," or this or that frivolous woman, died in despair. Stark and grim was the description of the unbeliever's demise. Mrs. Archer, for instance, who succumbed to a fever "after excessive dancing," went to her death in a state of agitated depression, crying: "Torment, torment, torment, is my doom forever and ever, and ever! . . . There is no grace nor mercy for me." And young Antitheus, facing his own end, had a ghastly vision of a fellow Deist, already deceased, who told him, "alas, alas . . . we are in fatal error." Antitheus died in a delirium of fear.[11]

The somber implication of this view of death was that the larger part of mankind were doomed to a terrible eternity of punishment unless they could be saved by Christian missions. Both divine injunction and natural compassion urged that as many souls as possible should be preserved. The task of the missionary was to convince the infidel, the lukewarm Christian, and the heathen that, no matter how wise and upright and just they were in a personal sense, they would be damned forever if they did not recognize their basic human depravity and throw themselves on the mercy of God. The evangelical counterattack against the principles of the Enlightenment had merely cleared the way for an efflorescence of missionary enthusiasm. The congregations gave money to be used to support the work; the religious laymen spent time serving on committees that managed the missionary enterprise.

For Clementina, the work of missions became the central religious interest, absorbing and transcending her teaching role in the parish Sunday School. Indeed, the Calvary Sunday School became not so much a service for an evangelical community as a missionary field in itself (for missions might be both domestic and foreign).[12] Clementina's interest in the spiritual peril of the heathen was awakened in the 1830's by the perusal of a book of "missionary researches" in the Polynesian Islands. She continued her reading and began to realize "how few of the inhabitants of the globe have even the opportunity of hearing of the Christian religion."[13] Her cousin Lucy was the wife of James Beach, the federal agent to the Sac and Fox Indians of Iowa (with some of whom the United States had been lately embroiled in the Black Hawk War).[14] A house visit of the Beaches with the Smiths in Philadelphia began a lifelong interest of Clementina's in the spiritual welfare of the native Americans. Some years later, enjoying the summer season at Saratoga Springs, she was impressed by the local Indian community. At night she watched the campfires of the "poor Indians" and reflected (for Sophie's benefit), "I cannot tell you how strong the contrast suggested by the glorious objects in the Heavens and the poor degraded creatures upon whom they shine so unmindful of the blessings they might enjoy—."[15] It was not, of course, her view that the American Indians were innately any more depraved than the peoples of Oceania, India, China, Africa, or Catholic Europe, or, indeed, that they were less fitted by nature for Heaven than the Rockdalers or she herself. She subscribed to missions to them all. It was just that they, like so many of mankind, were in the degraded condition that ignorance of God inevitably entailed.

"I find," wrote Clementina to her friend, "no subject so exciting as that of foreign missions." Although she was not in circumstances that permitted her to share the work as a missionary's wife or as a missionary herself (and her charge anyway was the Sunday School), she admired women who were participants in the effort to save the "poor perishing heathen." She read the missionary literature constantly, discussed it with her friends, met missionaries returned from abroad, collected (and donated) money to support the cause. Her view was worldwide. Living with a father whose business required him to be in constant receipt of information from foreign lands, and having naval officers and diplomats as family friends, her perspective was global anyway. Now she began to look forward to the time when she might see the whole world Christian.[16]

The Smiths' erstwhile neighbor John P. Crozer had always had a general interest in missions as part of the evangelical field. But it was not until the 1850's, after he had moved to Upland, that his interest crystallized into commitment. Having made his fortune with the help of Providence, he now entered upon the exercise of his stewardship with the same "untiring industry and indomitable perseverance" with which he had addressed the manufacturing of cotton. "In success in business pursuits," he wrote in his autobiography, "I suppose I have very far outstripped any son of Delaware County." Yet he was, he felt, merely an agent of the Divine Plan.

It is safest for me to ascribe my great success to a combination of circumstances, over which I had no control, but which were kindly thrown around me by my Heavenly father for purposes which it becomes me to inquire for; and to seek to feel that I am but his steward in the fortune I have received. In this view of the case—and this I think is the true one

—I rest under a solemn and awful responsibility which no one need covet or desire.[17]

After 1850, most of Crozer's energies were directed to his philanthropic and benevolent enterprises. Every day he rose at 5:00 A.M., prayed and studied the Bible for an hour, then set forth on his errands of mercy. He devoted most of his time and income (and perhaps much of his capital as well) during the remainder of his life to various undertakings of an essentially missionary nature.[18]

One of Crozer's favorite charities was providing churches for operatives in his own and others' cotton mills. In 1851, for instance, a number of residents of the Rockdale manufacturing district, feeling that Mount Hope was too far away for the convenience of the Methodists in the community, proposed to organize a new church to be known as the Rockdale Methodist Episcopal Church. Among the leaders in this movement were John Blackburn and Archibald McDowell, the factory managers at Rockdale proper and at Penn's Grove. The congregation met for a time at Temperance Hall in Lenni; but in November, at the first meeting of their Board of Trustees in Parkmount School House, Crozer stood up to donate a building lot for a new church on Mount Road in Crozerville. Subsequently he contributed generously to the building fund. The church was completed in 1854 and was renamed Crozerville Methodist Episcopal Church in honor of its benefactor. Crozer also in 1856 reserved half a square of ground in his and Broomall's South Ward development for religious purposes; here, more than twenty years later, with the help of an additional donation from his son, a Baptist church was built.[19]

But his principal concern, in the domain of church philanthropy, was the Upland Baptist Church. Crozer was determined to build a Christian industrial village in Upland. When the Upland mills first opened, he made a rule that no work should be done in the mills or in the village (which he owned), not even emergency repairs, between midnight on Saturday and midnight on Sunday. The Baptist church was completed in 1852 and for a few months Sunday School, Sabbath services, and prayer meetings were held there without a congregation being formally organized. But religious interest was awakened in the community and there were several conversions. A congregation was then formally put together, consisting of twenty persons, twelve by dismissal from other Baptist churches and eight by baptism. (Applicants for baptism were required to describe their conversion to the congregation. If the congregation was satisfied that it was genuine, they were immersed in Crozer's millrace by the pastor, John Duncan, who had just arrived from Lowell, Massachusetts, and was used to factory towns.) Of this original congregation of twenty, nine were Crozers and Crozer in-laws, and four more were of the family of Crozer's gardener. By the end of the year, the congregation had increased to sixty-eight (forty-seven of them by baptism). The Sunday School and other services, however, were open to any person who wished to attend, so that actual exposure to the influence of the church was widespread in the town. Crozer believed firmly that it was "a positive duty of all professing Christians to give of their substance," and he accordingly established a schedule of contributions. On the first Sunday of each month a collection was taken for foreign missions; there were four other collections during the year for various other benevolent purposes, including support of the American Baptist Missionary Society, the American Bible Society, the Pennsylvania Convention, the Widows' Fund, and the Baptist Home Mission Society; and at each communion there was a collection for needy church members. The first Sabbath evening of the month was set aside for a "concert of prayer for the success of missions," and the importance of foreign missions in the minds of the congregation is attested by the fact that four times as much money was collected for this purpose as for any other.[20]

Crozer's personal power in the Upland community was of course enormous simply by reason of his ownership of the mills on which virtually every resident depended for his livelihood. But in his role as Christian steward he vastly increased that power and almost made of Upland a theocratic community. Crozer and the Crozer family selected the pastors, who were expected to avoid comment on controversial economic and political topics. As a later memorialist of the church observed:

> It has always insisted that its pastors in their pulpit ministrations confine themselves to strictly Biblical themes, and to the achievement of distinctly spiritual results. If any one of those who have had the honor of being the pastor of this church had deviated from this course to any great extent, if he had undertaken to deliver a series of sermons that were not exclusively spiritual in their aim, something in all likelihood would have happened to him. This church would not have tolerated such exploits, and he would have been obliged to cease from them or to cease from preaching here.[21]

Crozer assumed, also, a responsibility for selective care of the deserving poor, instructing the pastor: "If, in the course of your pastoral visitation, you learn of any families that are in poverty and distress, I would be obliged to you to report them to me."[22] He and his gardener were the two (and only) deacons, and Crozer personally, as deacon, visited the sick and the bereaved. He served as Sunday School superintendent. As deacon and member of the congregation he heard and judged the religious testimonials of applicants for membership, helping to decide whether the speaker was truly aware of his sinful nature and whether he sincerely loved the Heavenly Father. As deacon, he presided over the business meetings of the congregation whenever the pastor was absent. And, as deacon, he administered church discipline.

The Baptist discipline was severe. Members of the congregation were required to attend services regularly and to live moral lives, eschewing alcohol and profanity, loose sexual conduct, "inconsistency," falsehood, and a miscellany of other "disorderly" life styles, such as "separation from wife" and "refusing to live with her husband without satisfying reasons." The cases of persons accused of violating these rules were privately investigated by a committee (and the accused might if he wished testify in public). Those convicted by the congregation were suspended or expelled, in the latter case the name being "erased" from the record. The case of Benjamin Serrill will serve as an example of the process.

> Deacon J. P. Crozer made accusation against Bro. Benjamin Serrill alleging intemperance and falsehood requesting the wish of the church to be expressed as to whether he should make a statement at that time or to committee appointed for the purpose—on motion he was directed to proceed and accordingly laid before the church proofs gathered. After considerable discussion in which Bro. Serrill took part a committee of enquiry consisting of Pastor Brethren Dalton Blakely and Hart was appointed to examine into the matter and report to a special meeting called for the purpose as soon as the committee should have finished its labors.

Two weeks later the committee reported that after a "patient investigation" of the charges, they had found abundant proof that Brother Serrill had been "repeatedly guilty both of the sin of intemperance and falsehood." The sentence, by unanimous vote, was "immediate expulsion."[23]

But Crozer's eye increasingly turned to the wider field of missions. For a time he served on the board of the American Sunday School Union, before he resigned disillusioned with the poor quality of the administration of its affairs.[24] By 1853 he had become a vice-president of the Baptist Publication Society, an organization that produced, printed, and distributed books and tracts in Europe and America. In the activities of this organization he became an associate of Francis Wayland, the noted writer of textbooks on moral philosophy and president of Brown University; of William Bucknell, founder of the University of Lewisburg; and of other leading Baptist clergy and laymen. Crozer's initial role was to serve as chairman of the Committee on Accounts, to make donations, and to recruit his sons and brothers to aid in the Society's work. In 1861 he became chairman of the board.

The Baptist Publication Society fought infidelity and Catholicism in ostensibly Christian nations and was separate from the American Baptist Missionary Society and the Baptist Home Mission Society, to which he also contributed. In the field the Baptist Publication Society relied on "colporteurs"—laymen who distributed publications, formed Baptist Sunday Schools, and made "known the way of salvation to the multitudes who do not visit the Sanctuary."[25] Most of these men worked in ordinary American communities, combating Romanism and modern skepticism; some visited American Indians and some traveled abroad, particularly in Sweden, France, and Germany. The Society had two departments: a "missionary colporteur" department, which collected contributions from the benevolent to support their travels (the goal was "to place in every neighborhood a colporteur"); and a "book" department, which sustained itself "on business principles." The book department financed the preparation and publication of books and tracts to be sold to Sunday Schools and to the general reader, made grants of libraries to poor Sunday Schools and needy ministers, and provided at no charge appropriate religious publications "in all languages" (including hitherto unwritten languages like the American Indian Chippewa). The materials ranged widely over subjects of interest to Protestants young and old. Some of the titles appealed to those eager for descriptions of foreign missions: *Sketches of Life in Burmah, Sophia Brown or the Missionary's Daughter, Travels in South-Eastern Asia, Cox's History of Baptist Missions,* and *Krishna-Pal The First Hindoo Convert.* The works of John Bunyan and Andrew Fuller (the latter being one of Crozer's favorite theologians) were also featured.[26]

Crozer traveled extensively in connection with the meetings of the board, which were held in a different city each year, and he obtained a wide view of the problems of Baptist evangelism and its relation to the education of ministers (and of young men and women generally). He had contributed largely to the building of the new university at Lewisburg, of which the first president William Bucknell was his son-in-law, and in a fine ecumenical spirit had declared, "I do not particularly wish to make Baptists, but I want to make educated young men." A few years later he built an academy in Chester and then a co-educational normal school in Upland (which after his death became the Crozer Theological Seminary). But the Upland institution, constructed and liberally endowed by Crozer and administered along lines advised by the eminent Francis Wayland, was a disappointment. It was intended to provide, in a religious atmosphere and at minimal cost, "a comprehensive, thorough, and practical education for business, teaching, college, and any literal or professional pursuit . . . the dead languages not to have undue prominence." However, it proved difficult to find qualified faculty, the school was expensive to operate, many of the students came from prosperous families and did not need the financial aid Crozer had built into it, and the community was prone to epidemics of scarlet fever and smallpox.

Crozer's most personally satisfying contribution to the cause of education was probably his support of programs for the education of ministers, administered by the Pennsylvania Baptist Education Society (of which he quickly became a board member and then president in 1855). His interest was initially intrigued by the remark of one of its officers that "we had a pious and devoted ministry, but needed also men of liberal culture for prominent points of influence." Crozer caught fire at the idea. He himself was uncomfortable in public speaking, perhaps owing to his sense of the inadequacy of his own education (although in fact he read widely and judiciously and had an excellent library); and in the ideological combat with the infidels, many of whom were erudite, it was obviously important to have the defenders of the faith at least as well educated as their rivals. He was faithful in attendance at gatherings of this board, although his shyness kept him away from the annual meetings of the Society; and, among other gifts, he endowed seven scholarships of $1,500 each. Much of the board's time was spent in evaluating grant applications from needy ministerial students. Crozer was an exemplary reviewer of such requests and of progress reports. The secretary of the Society described his conduct at these meetings:

His counsel was invaluable. . . . The subject-matter was well thought out, and delivered with evident emotion and great spirituality of mind.

So intense was his interest in ministerial students, he could not rest satisfied with ordinary and general statements. He wanted details. On several occasions, after writing a full sheet, and then apologizing for its undue length, I have received the reply, "Do not fear taxing my patience by minute details. You will tax my patience much more by not giving them. I want all these incidents. They go to make up character. Please do not be sparing in letting me know how each beneficiary is advancing, both in spiritual and intellectual pursuits." From time to time he wrote such sentences as the following: "My heart is in this good work. I am glad you are succeeding as well as you are. It must be a work of time. The results will be glorious."[27]

In turning to the support of education for the ministry and to the support of missions themselves, Crozer was not merely applying his money and energies to another sector of the evangelical cause. He was also achieving at last an identification with his well-educated, much-admired, long-dead younger brother Samuel. Crozer had always had a feeling of awed respect for Samuel's Christian zeal, mechanical ingenuity, and intellectual brilliance; he called him "Doctor Crozer" and had even named his first-born son after him. Samuel Crozer had died a martyr's death on the shores of Africa as the first agent of the American Colonization Society. John P. Crozer joined the American Colonization Society in January 1856, donating $1,000 and thereby earning the title of "Life Director."[28]

Apart from his general interest in the benevolent societies of the day, and his further identification with his deceased brother, it is not clear from his biographical remains what at first motivated John Crozer. His opposition to slavery was a matter of public record: he had joined the Pennsylvania Society for Promoting the Abolition of Slavery years before, in 1837. But this did not indicate much more than a general disapproval of an outmoded institution. The Pennsylvania Society was one of the older and less militant abolition societies—founded in 1789 by Benjamin Rush, Robert Morris, Benjamin West, Lafayette, and other worthy liberals in the Enlightenment tradition—and it sought to end the institution of slavery gradually by rational persuasion. It attracted men of substance, many of them mechanicians and manufacturers, including names familiar to Crozer: Nathan Sellers, Abraham Sharpless, Joshua Gilpin, William Martin (the manufacturer's father), Samuel Painter, Matthew Carey, Joseph Trimble, James Ronaldson, the Philadelphia philanthropist and educator Roberts Vaux, Thaddeus Stevens . . .[29] Crozer does not seem to have had much sympathy for Garrison's radical abolition society, founded in Philadelphia in 1832, but the sincerity of his opposition to what he once called "the accursed traffic in human sinews" cannot be doubted.[30]

Of his attitude toward blacks, little information is available. Crozer believed that slavery was wrong but that it was legal in the states that still permitted it. He was opposed to any extension of slavery, but was not necessarily an admirer of free black people. He lived in a place and at a time when the free black population was increasingly being perceived by whites as a social problem. Blacks were being displaced from the positions as unskilled and skilled laborers and even merchants that they had been accustomed to occupy in southeastern Pennsylvania, and they made up a disproportionately large part of the inmates of poorhouses and jails. The Smiths and the Du Ponts complained about the undesirability of black domestic servants and poked fun at the outlandish antics of Philadelphia's colored people. A minister at Middletown Presbyterian Church had been dismissed because he allowed a black man to preach from his pulpit.[31] But the uncanny intensity of the local taboo against contact with blacks is perhaps most vividly conveyed in a gruesome anecdote about Dr. Gideon Humphrey, the homeopathic physician who practiced in the Rockdale district in the 1820's and 1830's. A black man had drowned in Chester Creek and Humphrey procured the body for the purpose of preparing a demonstration skeleton. He borrowed a large iron kettle from a neighbor lady. Ashmead in his county history recounted the story with some relish sixty years later; evidently it was a favorite in the community:

> In the night, while he was at work in the spring-house, a huge fire under the pot, some one passing near saw the light, went to the spring-house, and reported next day that the "Doctor had boiled a darkey's head in the pot." This coming to the ears of the owner of the article, she, when it was sent home, returned it, saying, "Tell the doctor to keep that pot to boil another nigger in. I won't have the nasty thing in my house."[32]

Seen in this context, Crozer was evidently more liberal than most of his neighbors. A biblical allusion in his address on the forty-fifth anniversary of the Pennsylvania Colonization Society is significant of a self-consciously benevolent Christian separatism. He observed that the American Colonization Society and its protégé, the new Republic of Liberia, were smiled upon by Him "who made of one blood all nations of men for to dwell on all the face of the earth, and hath determined the times before appointed and the bounds of their habitation."[33] Presumably also Crozer agreed with the remarks of the other speaker of the evening, who quoted with emphatic approval the proposition on race that allegedly justified the whole program of the American Colonization Society: "two distinct races of people so unlike that amalgamation by intermarriage is impracticable, cannot long dwell in peace on terms of political and social equality."[34]

Crozer was active in the affairs of the Pennsylvania Colonization Society, which was an auxiliary of the national organization, and had become its president. At about the same time (in 1861), perhaps *ex officio,* he became a member of the board of the American Colonization Society. He served on the Committee for Auxiliary Societies, which reviewed income from the auxiliary state organizations, and in 1861, on the eve of the Civil War, was still trying to arrange an embarkation of freedmen from Charleston, South Carolina. More importantly, he was also chairman of the Committee on Foreign Relations. At that date Liberia, although a sovereign nation, was not diplomatically recognized by the government of the United States, and the actual negotiations between the two countries were carried on through the offices of the American Colonization Society. Liberia had been organized by the thousands of freed blacks transported there over the years from the United States and by other thousands of blacks liberated by vessels of the U.S. Navy which patroled the West Coast of Africa to intercept American ships illegally carrying slaves. Crozer's committee lobbied actively and successfully in Washington to persuade Congress and the executive branch to recognize the new nation and to protect it from depredations from the British colony of Sierra Leone to the north. Liberia was recognized in 1862. Crozer also interested himself in such projects as the introduction of coffee trees into Liberia as a cash crop and the encouragement of commercial relations with the United States.[35]

The effort to solve the racial problem in the United States by persuading slaveowners to manumit their slaves and to transport the freedmen to a national home in Africa, with their own consent and at no expense to themselves (costs were met from members' subscriptions and church collections), was doomed from the start. The Colonization Society's accomplishments never even approached the rosy dreams of its members. Many distinguished people, to be sure, lent themselves to the cause: Crozer's associates in the Pennsylvania Colonization Society included such familiar figures as Bishop Potter, Judge Bell, Dr. William Darlington, and James Ronaldson. In Delaware, the names of Charles and Alexis du Pont were enrolled. Nationally, the founders included such figures as Henry Clay (who eventually became the Society's president), Andrew Jackson, Thomas Jefferson, Daniel Webster, John Marshall, James Monroe, James Madison, and Matthew Carey, and later leaders included such celebrated men as the great Lowell cotton manufacturers William Appleton and Abbot Lawrence, the Honorable Louis McLane of Delaware (Jackson's Secretary of the Treasury and erstwhile Brandywine industrialist), and dozens of bishops and university presidents. But despite the impressive array of powerful names, the program foundered. Few slaves were freed (far fewer than the nation's increase by reproduction); few free blacks wanted to go back to Africa anyway; and the effort to resolve the slavery issue by measures that offended no one attracted a withering barrage of Garrisonian accusations of complicity in the maintenance of slavery. The major result, as Crozer noted, was the establishment of the "infant Republic of Liberia" and the abolition of the slave trade along its three hundred miles of African coast. Claimed Crozer proudly:

This Republic is the offspring of the Colonization Society. It is the child of this organization and owns no other parentage. . . . I believe that the Almighty Sovereign of all, the Creator of all, inspired our forefathers to establish this society to aid in elevating the colored race to a position of freedom and equality, and to plant the colony, now the Republic of Liberia, which in the fullness of time is to serve as a beacon to the tribes and nations of Africa, and to introduce the principles of our holy religion amongst these savage people.

It was, in fact, the evangelical opportunity that most inspired Crozer:

The Republic, by its proximity to and frequent intercourse with the interior will, under God, be a great instrument in introducing Christianity into these wide wastes of heathenism and habitations of cruelty. The Christian influence of the Colonization enterprise was not, perhaps, prominent in the minds of its founders, but now its friends look to this result as of primary consequence.

The Society feels that it has a great work on hand. To send colored Christian men and women, not especially as missionaries, but as citizens, who, in cultivating the soil, or in mechanical or mercantile pursuits, will in their frequent mingling with the natives infuse the principles of the Christian religion amongst them working as leaven upon the African mind.[36]

The Millennial Transformation

To recognize oneself as sinner, to throw oneself upon the mercy of God, and to strive for the salvation of one's fellow beings had long been the threefold way of Christian living. It could be, and often was, a rather placid way, resting upon the assumption that the world was going to be pretty much the same for the next generation as it had been for the last. But by the middle of the century, it was plain that while the eternal truths of religion might remain unchanged, the material world was changing very much. People were conscious of the vast advances of machinery: the cotton factories, the railroads, the steamboats were producing a new kind of world; and along with the awareness of a new technological world was arising an awareness of the possibility of a new social world as well, a world entirely Christian. The new wealth, the new technology, made this goal seem suddenly within grasp. And it made also suddenly more real the Christian doctrine of the millennium, when (after some bloody resistance from Satan) the entire world should become Christian and Christ should return to reign for a thousand years. As the Christian nations proceeded rapidly to complete their military and economic conquest of the heathen nations around the globe, everywhere the Christian missionary penetrated. It began to seem as if the millennium were truly at hand.

Militancy in such a holy cause was justified. John P. Crozer's brother Samuel, as he set forth with the aid of the U.S. Navy to establish a beachhead of black Christians on the shores of Africa, had written to his sister explaining his motivations. He first announced his conversion, and then went on to describe his mission in language almost appropriate to a man about to set forth on a dangerous military campaign:

How long have I despised, rejected and trampled under foot the many tender mercies which God has showered on my head with a liberal and unsparing hand, how long have I spurned and crucified my blessed Redeemer. But my sins have found me out, and I have taken refuge under the shadow of the ever blessed the Prince of Peace and oh! exceeding mercy he has stretched forth his hand and rescued me from destruction.

Do not let any painful thought flit across your mind concerning me, consider the banner under which I march with Christ for my buckler. If it be the will of God that I should die in Africa consider how much I shall gain. . . . I feel exceedingly rejoiced at the prospect I have before me of being beneficial to mankind.[37]

To advance Christian missions in the wake of conquest became more explicitly an evangelical policy as the years went on. In 1857 and 1858, Sophie's husband Samuel took command of the new American frigate *Minnesota,* which carried an experimental steam engine for auxiliary power, and sailed her to China. His mission was to carry an American minister to negotiate with the Chinese in concert with the British and French. Although the United States was officially neutral in the hostilities between the Chinese government and the European powers, the overpowering military presence of the Western nations undoubtedly would give added force to American requests. The American diplomat was lawyer and politician William B. Reed of Pennsylvania, a former Anti-Masonic legislator, lately turned Democrat. He had married a daughter of the same Robert Ralston who had sent Samuel Crozer off to Africa. *Minnesota* also had on board a missionary to China. Captain Du Pont carried various charges from Bishop Lee; and, by now a convinced Christian, he studied religious tracts in his cabin on Sundays and read sermons to his crew. All in all it was as much a missionary enterprise as a diplomatic one.

Du Pont's personal observations were cool and clinical. After watching the successful European bombardment of the river ports guarding Peking (which soon after fell to the landing force), and later visiting the ruins littered with dead bodies, he was moved to comment on the poor quality control evident in the manufacture of Chinese gunpowder. He did not agree with Minister Reed's preference for force over negotiation, and hoped for "peaceful relations with China and an extended commerce with her." And he was sufficiently sophisticated to observe: "to judge of Chinese by our standards is altogether fallacious, and to get at their process of reasoning requires a long intercourse with them and a knowledge of their language."[38]

But the *Minnesota* waited patiently in Chinese waters for the European powers to force the Chinese to negotiate—and so at last they did. The upshot of the whole affair was a series of treaties signed the following summer between China and Great Britain, France, Russia, and the United States, which opened eleven more ports to Western trade, legalized the importation of opium, and permitted Christian missionaries to enter the interior of China. It also led to the alliance between British forces under Chinese Gordon and the imperial Chinese troops in prosecuting the civil war against the millennialist, Christian-influenced Taiping rebels, who had taken over much of the country. And, because of his sympathy for Oriental cultures, it resulted in Captain Du Pont's being appointed as escort to the first Japanese embassy in their travels in the United States in 1860.[39]

Observed from the quiet valley of Chester Creek, events such as these were easy to interpret in the fashion of the progressive millennialist theologians. Clementina, already deeply interested in foreign missions, now began to look forward to seeing the whole world Christian.[40] Her millennial aspirations had little in common with those of the vulgar Millerites, who were expecting a sudden apocalyptic intervention by God and were disposing of their worldly goods. She referred to such beliefs as *"crazy doctrines"* and remarked superciliously, "There is a certain class of people almost wild about them."[41] Hers was the more orthodox millennialism, which foresaw a progressive conversion of the world, a continual improvement of the material condition of mankind, perhaps a final test of arms with the forces of Antichrist, and then the Second Coming of the Christ Himself to usher in the thousand years of peace. When all of this would happen was not revealed; it might be a long time away; but now she began to feel that it was imminent. When she learned of the first transatlantic telegraph cable in 1858, like many others she interpreted the event in millennialist terms. Even the first messages reportedly sent—"Glory to God in the highest" and "Peace good will to men—" had a Christian tone. She confided hopefully to Sophie: "The signs of the times do call us to a state of expectation— sometimes I wonder if we shall see the day and coming of the Lord—or whether this is the time of preparation for that great event."[42]

The Smith family's old friend and religious associate, the Reverend Dr. Stephen Tyng, now residing in New York City, perhaps expressed their millennial views most aptly. In an address published in 1848, Tyng had seen that America's great need was to elevate "the moral, relative dignity of labor . . . as the true greatness" of the nation. He went on, in a millennial enthusiasm that combined zealousness toward the conversion of the working class with fervent anticipation of the conversion of heathen everywhere, to describe his view of America's destiny:

> And when the great exalting, leveling system of Christianity gains its universal reign, mountains will be brought down, and valleys will be filled; an highway shall be made for human prosperity and peace—for the elevation and dignity, and security of man—over which no oppressor's foot shall pass; the poorest of the sons of Adam shall dwell unmolested and fearless beneath his own vine and fig tree; the united families of earth shall all compete, to acquire and encourage the arts of peace; nation shall not rise against nation, and men shall learn war no more. Let this . . . be the universal purpose of our people, and the greatness of America shall know no limited zenith, and fear no tendency to decline.[43]

Clementina's friends the Lammots, as members of the Church of the New Jerusalem, were already deeply committed to a millennialist interpretation of current history. Their form of millennialism differed, however, in some respects. The founder, Emmanuel Swedenborg, claimed that the Second Coming had already occurred, in 1757, when the proper mode of interpreting Scripture was revealed to him. Inspired by Swedenborg's writings, the members of the New Church saw their task as a missionary one too, of converting not only the heathen but also the adherents of the old Christian churches to the newly revealed theology of Swedenborg. New Church missionaries were, or soon would be in many countries, preparing the way for the world's redemption.

Baptists, too, were millennialist in their eschatology. Crozer was a careful reader of Andrew Fuller, one of the leading English nonconformist theologians and a favorite of the Baptist Publication Society. Fuller opposed the pessimistic implications of extreme Calvinism and urged an evangelical Christianity. In his essay on the *Nature and Extent of True Conversion,* Fuller also interpreted the present age as being on the brink of redemption:

> The time will come when "all the kindreds of the earth" shall worship. Ethiopia, and all the unknown regions of Africa, shall stretch out their hands to God. Arabia, and Persia, and Tartary, and India, and China, with the numerous islands in the Eastern and Southern Ocean, shall bring an offering before him. Mahomedans shall drop their delusion, papists their cruel superstition, Jews shall be ashamed of their obstinacy, deists of their enmity, and merely nominal Christians of their form of godliness without the power of it. . . .
>
> The last branch of the last of the four beasts is now in its dying

agonies. No sooner will it be proclaimed, "Babylon is fallen!" then the marriage of the Lamb will come. There are no more tyrannical or persecuting powers to succeed; but "the kingdom shall be given to the people of the saints of the Most High." All ranks of men, princes, nobles, and people, becoming real Christians, the government of the world will naturally be in their hands; and love, peace, and universal good shall consequently pervade the whole earth.[44]

But the full flavor of popular millennialist thinking, in its applications to contemporary issues, is perhaps best conveyed in the writings of the popular author Hollis Read, an erstwhile Baptist missionary to India. In 1851 Read was in charge of the Baptist Home Mission effort in New Mexico and Crozer met him in Philadelphia when he visited there to raise money. He was afterward entertained by the Crozers at Upland, where he received a "generous donation" and his wife "an expensive book which she desired to have."[45] Read had already published a two-volume biography of a converted Hindu named Babajee.[46] In the 1850's he rediscovered the American Colonization Society and affiliated himself with its cause, visiting Africa himself as a missionary and eventually (in 1864) publishing a popular work advocating the Society's program as the solution to the "Negro problem." This work was based on the assumption of the impossibility of assimilating the blacks into white American culture, and the consequent desirability of transporting the freed slaves to form Christian colonies on the dark continent. Read was articulate and persuasive in his presentation of this view and (along with Robert Dale Owen) was appointed by Lincoln to a commission to make recommendations on federal policy toward the blacks of the south after emancipation.[47]

Read's views on the millennium were expressed in a series of works beginning in 1859 and continuing at least into the 1870's. The 1859 contribution was a prize essay, published by the Seamen's Friend Society in Philadelphia (its office was at the Bible House in the financial district), entitled *Commerce and Christianity*. The purpose of the book was to increase the importance of the seaman's cause in the eyes of the benevolent by emphasizing the importance of commerce (which was the mission of the sailor) in the progress of mankind toward the millennium. The argument was not unsophisticated, in its way, and anticipated the mode of analysis made popular a century later in the writings of functionalist social scientists. Read demonstrated how international trade necessarily depended upon, and stimulated the diffusion of, ideas or sentiments of civil liberty, honesty, evangelical Christianity, and certain universal standards of decorum. He proceeded from a celebration of the oceans as the binder of nations, via commerce, to a consideration of commerce as a progressive agency, as the process by which the Anglo-Saxon "race" was acquiring worldwide ascendancy, and as a principal agency in the "great awakening." Commerce (and its operatives, the seamen), by promulgating the laws of trade and demonstrating the power of honesty, and by financing from its profits in the hands of Christian stewards the sacred work of missions, was a major instrument in the conversion of the world and the achievement of the millennium.

Read was capable, like Samuel Francis Du Pont, of some degree of cultural relativism. He criticized American false modesty in avoiding the use of the word "leg" and requiring such circumlocutions as "limb" or "lower member." The Hindu, he said, simply said "leg" and displayed it freely, with less "indelicacy in thought and imagination" than in the United States. He urged, "We must not, therefore, suppose that every deviation of the Hindu from *our* standard of propriety, is a transgression of the rules of real decorum." As an example, he described how the "cowardly" Hindu never came to blows but insulted each other instead, when angered, by obscene charges against each other's mother and dead relatives. He pointed out that no offense to these kinsmen of the opponent was really intended; it was merely the *"customary* way of abusing an adversary."[48]

Implicit in Read's functional analysis was a subtle transformation. The worth of an idea or institution was to be measured not merely on gross economic or political or even universal moral dimensions but by its contribution to the advancement of missions. In his evaluation of the commerce with Africa, he pointed out that traffic in other articles would reduce the trade in slaves; this was a peculiarly important functional consequence because the slave trade was *the great obstacle to the conversion of Africans.* In later works, urging the recolonization of Africa with black Christian freedmen from America (with the help of the American Colonization Society, of course), the argument was developed further as we have noted in *The Negro Problem Solved; or, Africa as She Was, As She Is, and As She Shall Be.* In this exposition of "romantic racialism," he saw black participation in the millennium as being neatly contained in a Christian Africa, to which the out-of-place ex-slaves from the United States had been returned as a pious leavening. Here the principle of analysis was even more plainly developed: it was the extent to which an institution or a system of ideas and values contributed to the accomplishment of the millennium that determined its worth. If it advanced the millennium, it was good and the work of God; if it held it back, it was evil and the work of Satan.[49]

The whole cosmic theme was developed to its fullest in a series of eschatological works: *The Coming Crisis of the World, The Hand of God in History, The Palace of the Great King,* and *The Foot-Prints of Satan: or, The Devil in History.* The last work is especially interesting because it so closely parallels the world-conspiracy theme of Robison and the Anti-Masons of the previous generation. Writing after the Civil War, Read blamed Satan as "the great Antagonistic Power," who had been "the instigator of the Slaveholders' Rebellion." Satan might expect a last victory or two before the millennium; but he would have only a short time of triumph, for the Second Coming of Christ was at hand. In the meantime, his vast empire, centered in the Church of Rome (and especially among the Jesuits), was an inconvenience. Satan was responsible for Owenite socialism, Fourierism, communism and the Communist Internationals, free love, the women's rights movement, infidelity and rationalism, spiritualism and rappings, Mormonism, liberal Christianity, the perversions of wealth, the infidel press ("more dangerous because more subtle men never cursed the world in the days of Paine or Voltaire"), and both the Paris Commune and the Tweed Ring in New York. Read deplored (in a not-too-subtle expression of anti-intellectualism) how Satan had subverted such "giants in intellect" as Lord Byron, Voltaire, Hume, Gibbon, Rousseau, and Thomas Paine. For Read, as for the Anti-Masons, all evil was part of one conspiracy; all good would be realized in one millennium.[50]

Read's principal work was *The Coming Crisis of the World; or, The Great Battle and the Golden Age* (1861). In an introductory note, the Reverend Dr. Stephen Tyng lauded the book as "vastly important" because it presented the prospect of "a restored earth—the future everlasting dwelling place of the redeemed of God"—of which Tyng had been convinced for many years. Such support was very significant. Known as the greatest preacher in the Episcopal Church, Tyng was the leader of the evangelical faction in the denomination. He had, like the Smiths, for many years been a devotee and founder of Sunday Schools. Tyng's theme was straightforward. The "golden age of the church" was at hand. One by one the centers of Antichrist and the iniquities of Satan's rule were being overcome. In India and China, pagan priesthoods were being overturned by Christian missionaries. In Europe, the despotism of Rome was being destroyed. In America, the slave system, "this monster of sin," the last stronghold of evil, was now being assailed and the final battle was under way. "Great Babylon is toppling to her fall."

The chapters themselves proceeded in a direct way to document, by reference to the commotions of the times, the near approach of the millennium. In particular, the financial crisis of 1857 and the subsequent revival, the Sepoy Rebellion and the "renovation" of India, the opening of the Far East and of Africa to Christian civilization, and the laying of the transatlantic cable were all cited as indications of the approaching victory of Christianity.

And the American Civil War, now just begun, was seen as one more major confrontation between the power of sin and the dominion of Christ, in which God's chosen people, the Americans, would rise up and forever abolish the satanic institution of slavery. God's people would be sorely tested but they would surely prevail in final victory and redeem the world.[51]

Such a mode of thought transformed all issues. No longer need the south be seen as deserving of opposition because it stubbornly opposed the protective tariff, threatened to outreach with slave labor a legion of white farmers in the west, and attempted to dominate the halls of Congress. The south was evil because it was a region of slaveholders. The slave power opposed the evangelizing of the blacks and the transportation of emancipated Christian blacks to Africa; the south thus was holding back the millennium by interfering with the conversion of the world.

Another purveyor of millennial imagery was Mary Gilpin's brother William, the first governor of Colorado. In his report to the U.S. Senate in 1846 (subsequently amplified in his *Mission of the North American People*), Gilpin painted America's future in imperial purple:

The untransacted destiny of the American people is to subdue the continent—to rush over this vast field to the Pacific Ocean—to animate the many hundreds of millions of its people, and to cheer them upward—to set the principle of self-government at work—to agitate these herculean masses—to establish a new order in human affairs—to set free the enslaved—to regenerate super-annuated nations—to change darkness into light—to stir up the sleep of a hundred centuries—to teach old nations a new civilization—to confirm the destiny of the human race—to carry the career of mankind to its culminating point—to cause the stagnant people to be re-born—to perfect science—to emblazon history with the conquest of peace—to shed a new and resplendent glory upon mankind —to unite the world in one social family—to dissolve the spell of tyranny and exalt charity—to absolve the curse that weighs down humanity, and to shed blessings around the world!
Divine task! Immortal mission!

A geographical and climatic determinist, but mindful of his origins along the Brandywine, he saw Denver as the commercial center of an industrial world. The gold standard and a vigorous program of public works (such as railroads and harbors) "promise to enthrone *industrial organization* as the ruling principle of nations. America leads the host of nations as they ascend to this new order of civilization . . . the industrial conquest of the world."[52]

The millennial imagery was pervasive in Delaware County. Not only did the Lammots, the Smiths, the Crozers know it well; it reached the workers too, in the labor movement as well as in the churches. During the 1850's a labor union of a new style emerged, primarily composed of the spinners, weavers, and dyers who worked the three hundred power and hand looms of the cooperative Carpet Hall Manufacturing Association, situated next door to Christ Church in Philadelphia, and the one hundred looms of the Delaware County Carpet Manufacturing Association, located on Chester Pike in Darby. The union called itself the Associated Working Women and Men, and it regularly published ten thousand copies of a newspaper entitled *The Monthly Jubilee: Published by an Association of the Daughters and the Sons of Toil.* The leaders of the organization were veterans of the constitutional struggle in Rhode Island, where in 1842 Thomas Dorr had led a brief rebellion and established a provisional government. The principal issue there had been the liberalization of archaic suffrage requirements, and although the revolutionary government was suppressed, voting privileges were extended not long afterward. General John Sidney Jones, the manager of Carpet Hall, had held a cabinet post in Dorr's provisional government, and his wife Fannie Lee Townsend, the editor of the *Monthly Jubilee,* had been an associate of Dorr's and an organizer of land and industrial congresses. The Joneses lived in Delaware County and the meeting place of the Association was in Darby.

The Association was a different kind of organization from the trades unions of the 1830's and 1840's. It did, first of all, provide a permanent organization between strikes for workers in textile factories; the trade unions had not done this. It was economically anchored in two successful factory cooperatives. It mustered a 150-man militia company commanded by General Jones. And it had an articulate and extensive social philosophy and political platform that blended somewhat more successfully into the evangelical milieu than had the older associations. The Jubilee Association did not eschew the earlier heroes of labor, to be sure. Its members celebrated the birthday of Tom Paine with speeches and public meetings, and the newspaper published sketches of the life of Fanny Wright and denounced greedy capitalists, sectarian religionists, scheming lawyers, absentee landlords, monopolistic banks, protective tariffs, and all the other *bêtes noires* of the traditional working-class propagandist. But theirs was a populist radicalism that also allowed allusions to the Divine Will and invited addresses by such conservative churchmen as Bishop Potter. And it was avowedly millennial. "Jubilee" was the millennium of labor, the working-man's Utopia, and the paper bore on its cover the progressive motto: "The ideal of the Past, is the actual of the Present; The ideal of the Present, is the actual of the Future." Harbingers of Jubilee had been Tom Paine, George Washington, Andrew Jackson, and the pro-Sunday mail (and anti-evangelical) congressional reports of Richard M. Johnson.

Fannie Lee Townsend, the prophet of the movement (or, as she called herself, the "Edita"), claimed that she was "the first human being of the age to sanction agitation of the Land and Beard question." She was impatient with traditional religious and benevolent causes, banned discussions of sectarian religion and party politics, and proscribed as a waste of time such activities as "Abolition, Temperance, Spirit Rappings, Anti-Slavery, and Women's Rights Conventions." She deplored prudery in sexual mores, favored healthy sexual activity and the reproductive role for women, advocated social equality of men and women, and urged the wearing of beards by men (a growing fashion anyway). She had several pet anti-policies: she opposed the use of petroleum for fuel; she regarded the customary failure to cover human and animal excrement in the fields as one of the causes of soil exhaustion and thus of the "Land Monopoly"; and she complained that "inordinate sexual passion or heat is frequently engendered, as the consequent of a false state of society."

But the fundamental plank in her platform was land reform. Land ownership would usher in the millennium for the workers. Like other free soilers, including such diverse partners as Horace Greeley (whom she claimed as her protégé) and the Fourierist socialists, she felt that every man had a natural right to use land without paying rent, just as he had a right to unlimited personal use of air and water without cost. Rent and the "Land Monopoly" must be brought to an end. To make good these claims, she organized an Emigrating Association which ultimately managed to send some fifty spinners, weavers, and dyers' families to free soil in Iowa and Missouri.

As the "Platform" of the Association asserted, in a working-class parallel to the "conversion of the world" theme of the manufacturing and commercial classes:

The JUBILEE will advocate not the immediate abolition of all useless LAWS, but that public attention should be diverted towards a "good time coming," when a JUBILEE will be the natural result of *public opinion,* endorsing our platform.[53]

ARMAGEDDON

In his vision recorded in the Book of Revelation, St. John witnessed the preparations for the final struggle between Satan and the Holy Redeemer.

(455)

Seven angels emptied vials, loosing terrible catastrophes upon Satan's minions on the earth. After the sixth vial was poured out, unclean spirits began in alarm to assemble the armies of the kings of the whole world, "to gather them to the battle of that great day of God Almighty . . . into a place called in the Hebrew tongue Armageddon" (Revelation XVI: 14, 16). For Protestant evangelicals in the 1860's, Armageddon meant America.

Signs and Portents

To the evangelical Protestants of the north, already schooled in the doctrine of progressive millennialism, it seemed that the deepening confrontation between the north and south, and the economic crises that developed at the same time, were the preliminary skirmishes that presaged the Second Coming of the Lord and the final battle at Armageddon.

In the fall of 1857, after a long period of material prosperity, a financial panic brought on another of the recurrent depressions. John Campbell, the Chester cotton manufacturer, failed in business and some of the mills in the Rockdale district closed down, including the mill at Old Sable. Clementina notified Sophie that it would not be difficult to find servants because "there are so many clever mill people wanting work now." She recommended to Sophie as "most qualified" to be a replacement for her departed domestic "a young man at Rockdale Hayes Griffith who used to live with us as a waiter years ago." Griffith, a loom boss, was actually thirty years old and had a wife and three small children, including a newborn baby boy, "but is now and will probably be for some time out of work. He understands the care of a horse and house work—is . . . a communicant of our church and is I believe a sincere Christian. He is as quiet . . . as Margaret Mullen."[1]

Close on the heels of the financial débâcle came an enthusiastic and protracted revival movement in the cities of the north. It had begun, in fact, before the crash, and as early as February 1857 (more than six months in advance of the bank failures) Clementina had noted an increase in devoutness among some of her acquaintances and expressed hope for "a revival of God's work in the hearts of the people of God." It fed largely on the national sense of crisis, of a sinful America about to be chastised by the Lord as the millennial point of view would predict. The vials of wrath were opening upon the continent and the people experienced a sudden urgency in their need to repent and pray for acceptance by the Redeemer. Prayer meetings were held daily in Philadelphia and other large cities, led by old friends of the Smiths, like the Reverend Kingston Goddard, formerly a reader at Calvary, now pastor of the Church of the Atonement. In the Rockdale district, there was a "a growing interest" in religion, and Clementina and Sophie remarked on a number of "amazing" conversions.[2] Later in the year came the news of the transatlantic telegraph, to which Clementina responded with her expression of hope that "we shall see the day and coming of the Lord."[3] In Upland, Crozer reported: "We have not partaken largely of the blessed revival that has extended so widely over our land but have still much cause for rejoicing that some souls around us have been born again . . . a serious Spirit now prevailing leads us to hope that a blessing is in store and will ere long descend."[4] In Philadelphia, the old patrons of Calvary Church, Bishop Potter and the Reverend Dudley Tyng, as well as the Reverend James Caughey, the revivalist who inspired the Methodists in Rockdale in the 1830's, were extremely active in stirring up the fires of revivalism, not only in Episcopal congregations but among the people of the city at large.[5]

Perhaps the most significant revival effort in Rockdale was made by Harriet Smith. In the winter of 1856–57 some of the better educated and more ambitious young working people, particularly the loom bosses in some of the weaving mills, had formed a nonreligious "literary association." Hattie, who taught the young men's Sunday School class and already knew some of the members of the new association, had exerted herself to turn it in a religious direction. Early in 1857 she organized a well-attended course of lectures by clergymen; the ubiquitous Bishop Potter was one of the speakers and addressed the group on the subject, "Washington the young man's model." Clementina cautiously opined, "I think this effort to engage the interest of the young men in mental improvement must do much good and perhaps lead the way to better things."[6] By 1859 the association had a "reading room," probably in the church, which contained no books but did provide members with some of the daily newspapers (gift subscriptions from the Smiths and other friends), including the *National Intelligencer,* the London *Times,* the *North American Review,* and the *Pennsylvania Inquirer.* Some of the young men were also members of the Delaware County Institute of Science, which had a library that contained books of radical character, and they were in the habit of bringing these borrowed volumes to the reading room.

The conflict was clear. The literary association depended upon Calvary Church and its leaders for support; but many of its members did not want religious oversight in the form of rules and regulations and censorship of the reading matter of its members. As Clementina put it, "It was not a church or even a religious association, indeed I think some of the men were very jealous of its having this character and *we* were afraid of the character of books that might find an entrance among them." Resourceful Harriet handled the problem deftly, said Clementina:

Harriet managed to have a man of good moral character and very leading mind named president and he gave the bias to all that was done. He was very much afraid of admitting any who wd. introduce books of immoral or of infidel tendency—and used great tact and wisdom in this matter— Some who were most fearful of interference of the church of religious people last year in this, are now themselves members of the church.[7]

Apparently the religious sponsors of the association were satisfied, for John P. Crozer quickly donated a building lot in Crozerville to the People's Literary Association of Rockdale and promised a gift of one-quarter the cost of the edifice, on condition that the Association find the other three-quarters.[8] The cornerstone was laid in an impressive ceremony on the Fourth of July, 1860. A band and a company of militia from West Chester arrived at the Lenni depot at 9:00 A.M., where they were met by the members of the Literary Association, and together they marched through the villages in the district until they reached the site at Crozerville. There they heard a Fourth of July oration by Robert L. Martin, the manager of Lenni Mill, attended by Mr. and Mrs. Richard S. Smith, some visiting relatives, and most of the Sunday School teachers.

The oration was followed by dinner in a tent. Then everyone repaired for the afternoon to the picnic grove in the woods where the Sunday School presented the community with its annual supper feast, prepared by Clementina, Harriet, and a few others (the company consumed 55 lbs. of beef, 400 rolls, 20 lbs. of candy, 40 lbs. of cake, 300 lemons for lemonade, and 30 quarts of ice cream).

When the parade marched past the parsonage on Mount Road on its way to the Association grounds, the Sunday School gave it a special salute:

Our school marched to meet . . . and presented to the president of the Association a very handsome wreath which Mother made, also a beautiful bouquet to another of their officers—Both these young men had been in Mother's Infant school—The children then sang the 2d. piece on the paper I enclose and gave three cheers for the literary Assn. of Rockdale. Their offering was responded to by the president in a neat and handsome speech and the band stopped and played "Yankee Doodle" for them. The children then marched back to the woods.[9]

The People's Literary Association of Rockdale was, however, forced to postpone the completion of its edifice. The collection at the time of the cornerstone ceremony was disappointing; and within the year most of the members would be in the Grand Army of the Republic. But after the war the building was completed, with library and meeting rooms on the first floor, and a large hall on the second which was used for "entertainments, lectures, and public meetings." The Association remained in a flourishing condition for many years.

As the months wore on, the sense of foreboding, of a terrible trial to be undergone, increasingly preoccupied the sensitive Christian observer. The cotton industry still languished; many people were still out of work in Rockdale. In Philadelphia, a contract for the making of soldiers' uniforms was being used by a benevolent agency at the Girard House as a relief measure, small subcontracts being let out to the unemployed. The resolute Harriet went there and secured the cloth for the making of forty-eight coats, sixteen pairs of pants, and twenty pairs of Canton flannel drawers. She and Clementina then hired fourteen women to sew up the garments at their house. The parson's sister was a "tayloress"; she instructed the two ladies, who in turn directed the women, as well as feeding them and their children. But it was all discouraging and Clemma complained, to her friend, "Alas! dearest Sophie anxiety and sorrow surround us everywhere our whole social fabric is overturned and my heart sickens with the grieff of all around us—Here there is want and sadness in most of the households and we wonder how the first is to be relieved."[10] She almost despaired of being able to help. "There is so much vice immediately about us in this place . . . I feel there is so much ought to do yet do so little."[11]

By the end of the year, after the secession of North and South Carolina and the first seizures of federal arsenals in the south, it was plain to the people in Rockdale that war was imminent. Clementina bewailed: "We know not literally what a day may bring forth—What sad times are these! We can only look to the God of Nations to relieve us from the woes that threaten. It is grievous to find the peace of families disturbed by differing political opinions."[12]

Rockdale in the Civil War

The war officially began on the morning of April 15 when, two days after the surrender of Fort Sumter in Charleston Harbor, President Lincoln declared publicly that an "insurrection" had occurred and called for three-month volunteers. There had been intense public excitement in the preceding several days, with spontaneous demonstrations against the south and much patriotic flag-waving and badge-wearing in all the mill towns. On the evening of the 15th, after Lincoln's call for volunteers, there were mass meetings in Media and Chester to organize the volunteer companies. Edward Darlington presided over the Media meeting to organize the "Delaware County Union Rifles," and John Broomall made a speech. By the end of the week the company had been mustered into the federal service as Company F, Fourth Regiment of Pennsylvania Volunteers. The same Monday evening, a company of "Union Blues" was organized at a patriotic rally in Chester, and by week's end had been mustered into the Ninth Regiment of Pennsylvania Volunteers. Within the next few weeks, home guards were organized in all the little towns of the county, commanded by scions of the existing local leadership: at Upland by John P. Crozer's son George, at Media by Edward Darlington's son George, at Glenn Mills by one of the younger Willcoxes.

In Chester, early in May, many of the Rockdale men enlisted in Company B, Twenty-sixth Regiment, First Pennsylvania Volunteers, including two of "Hattie's boys," John Newsome and Jones Bradbury, and, serving as chaplain, the Smiths' friend and former rector at Calvary Church, Charles Breck. In the Rockdale district, William Talley, a newspaper editor, was organizing the "Rockdale Rifle Guards," who marched off later in May and were mustered into the service as Company F, Thirtieth Regiment, First Pennsylvania Reserves. Among those who left with Talley was another of "Hattie's boys" from the Sunday School, Hayes P. Griffith, who enlisted as a musician. By the end of summer, most of the young men had gone.[13]

In these early days of the war, many believed that a show of strength and a brief summer's campaign would be enough to overawe the rebels, and that "the horrors of serious conflict might be averted." Enthusiasm among the civilians left at home was intense. Clementina's mother, when she learned that Major Anderson, the hero of Fort Sumter, was visiting Philadelphia, was "crazy" to see him, and dashed off, with Clementina trailing after her, into a dense throng at Independence Hall. Clementina had a close view and was shocked. "I never saw," she said, "a face in which mental conflict was so marked—It was profoundly sad and such a contrast to the frantic delight of the crowd." That night she could not sleep ("my brain was in such a commotion"). Clementina noted that those formerly cautious (like Bishop Potter) were now less reticent and were speaking their views plainly; everywhere she went, even among the young soldiers, she met a spirit of Christian dedication.[14] Inspired by the example of the young volunteers, the community leaders and the women quickly organized a system of war relief. In the crisis the mills had shut down and many families were destitute. Before the end of May, at another mass meeting in Media Courthouse, a county-wide relief organization had formed itself, headed by John P. Crozer, for the purpose of "soliciting funds to equip troops and support the families of volunteers." That very day $2,500 was collected in contributions, and in the two days afterward, in the several collection districts, another $2,700. Crozer himself invested largely in the national loan. The women were active in committee work and as seamstresses, tailoring uniforms. Harriet, as usual, was in the forefront of these relief activities.[15] It was all seen as a thrilling confrontation between a long-suffering, patient, virtuous, and invincible *national* interest and an obstinate, petulant, anarchistic minority of evil slaveholders who had merely *sectional* support. As his biographer described Crozer's attitude in this liminal period of the war: "When the nation's property was seized by force, when hostile batteries were opened upon a national fort, he felt that there was no escape—That force must be met by force, and disobedient wickedness subdued."[16]

It was the first Battle of Bull Run, at the end of July, that made it plain to almost everyone that the troops would not be home in three months. After "the stunning news . . . of the rout of our troops," Richard S. Smith, worried about his son in the service, became chronically depressed about the war; he and Robert Martin, the manager at Lenni Mill, were convinced that Washington, D.C. would soon fall to the enemy. Harriet soon became miserable too. But Clementina's letters took on a tone of hardness. On every front, in every battle, someone she knew was risking his life or his reputation to put down "this wicked rebellion." Rather than admit discouragement, she tried to cheer others up and threw herself into whatever activities she could find that would help the war effort. In August she wrote, "All the mills are stopped now, even Mr. Crozer's." She organized a brigade of women at Lenni to make army shirts and defended with ardor the good name of General Patterson (the owner of Lenni Mill), whose failure to prevent the arrival of southern reinforcements was alleged by some to have given victory to the south at Bull Run. And now that the enormity of the conflict was apparent, she began to find the millennial interpretation congenial:

> I feel more and more that the cause is God's and that He will carry it on in His own way and with what instrumentality he pleases. The folly of our people and their vain boasting and Sabbath breaking was truly punished at Manassas.[17]

Bull Run taught another lesson. The ghastly accounts of the sufferings of the maimed and dying during and after the rout, and of the unpreparedness of either side to cope with the realities of the physical and spiritual needs of the casualties, led directly to the organization of one more benevolent evangelical society. The United States Christian Commission was organized in the fall of 1861 "to promote the spiritual and temporal welfare" of the soldiers in field, camp, and hospital. John P. Crozer was one of the founders, along with John Wanamaker of Philadelphia (experienced in

Y.M.C.A. administration), Stephen Tyng of New York, and other leading evangelical laymen and clergy. The Commission, in the absence of any very effective military system for satisfying the needs of the troops outside battle (and often acting against the wishes of local commanders), took on a role that in later years would be shared by the Red Cross, the United Services Organization, the Chaplain's Office, and various entertainment centers. The goal of the Commission was to ensure that the Grand Army of the Republic was a *Christian* army, that its wounded were properly clothed and fed, that its dying had the opportunity for a Christian death. To this end the Commission, from its offices and warehouse on Bank Street in Philadelphia, equipped and sent out some five thousand "delegates" to various commands. These delegates performed an incredible service: they built 140 chapels and numberless "reading rooms"; they constructed sanitary systems and diet kitchens; they preached 58,000 sermons and wrote 92,000 letters for illiterate or crippled soldiers; they gave out 95,000 packages of food, clothing, and medical supplies; they visited numberless wounded men in hospitals; they distributed (among an army of two million men) a million and a half Bibles, a million hymn books, and eight million tracts or "knapsack books." Crozer remained active in the Commission's work as member of the executive committee, as trustee, and as financial contributor, until the end of the war. The Christian Commission finally received wide public acclaim for its assistance to the armies; President Lincoln met personally with the Commission in January 1866 to express the nation's gratitude.[18]

There was a brief spurt of hope, in the fall, that the war would soon be over, occasioned by Admiral Samuel Francis Du Pont's naval victory at Port Royal, South Carolina. Du Pont was in command of the South Atlantic Blockading Squadron, and in November his vessels, led by the flagship *Wabash,* drove off the Confederate garrison occupying the fort. The town and harbor were then occupied as one of the land bases of the effective Union blockade of the southern coast. The friends of the Du Ponts' were elated (Richard S. Smith was "in an ecstacy with it"); Clementina wrote to Sophie congratulating her on her husband's victory and describing the enthusiasm of the people of Rockdale: "I have just finished writing a letter from a mother to a son, in the army of the Potomac, in which she says, that this news has revived this neighborhood and made the people hope the war will soon be over. . . ."[19] But the war was not soon over and by Christmas news of fatal casualties (two) and men missing in action (three) began to accumulate. Clementina tried to argue herself into optimism. "Out of 200 from our neighbourhood," she said, "this is a small proportion but all feel more like making the season one of exclusively religious services."[20]

Rockdale was almost a ghost town. With the mills closed, "all that can are going away for work and our best young men are nearly all gone" (some no doubt as much motivated by need for military pay and enlistment and re-enlistment bonuses as by patriotism and millennial fervor). The rector gloomily remarked that everywhere he went he found "Ichabod is written." (Ichabod, meaning "inglorious," was the name given to her newborn son by a woman whose husband had died in Israel's great defeat by the Philistines, when the Ark of the Covenant was lost; her last words as she expired in childbirth were: "The glory is departed from Israel.") Those who remained, even the unemployed, were not actually in desperate financial circumstances, because there was "so much govt. work and so much money sent from the camps to fds. at home."[21] But in residence in Lenni, Clementina began to see the wounded limping home. One May, while she was writing to Sophie, "one of our men" who had been taken prisoner at Williamsburg "passed by our door on his way home. He was released on parole, but looks *so* sick, and said he did not feel as if he would get well." Ever cheerful, she remarked to Sophie, "Home may do more than he expects for him."[22] By fall of 1862, after the second Union defeat at Bull Run, and the bloody and inconclusive battle at Antietam, the reports of casualties and the fear of more bad news to come were casting a dark shadow over the community. The last week of September was "the bitterest in this neighbourhood in the war . . . *everything* was so sad, sighs and tears hearts burdened with dread forebodings all around us."[23] In November the rector Mr. Murphy, to allay community concern, made the round of the camps in which "Rockdalers" were stationed. On his return, after the morning sermon, the people lined the road, begging for news. In the afternoon, the custom was for the rector to come to tea at the Smiths, and while they took tea, "the people" would gather and sing hymns. The rector used this occasion to make a public statement about his visit, reassuring the community that their sons and fathers were in health and in reasonably comfortable circumstances. Much moved, Murphy broke down in tears while reading the prayer for those who had "gone out at the call of their country."[24]

As the war went on, more and more names of Rockdalers were reported on the lists of sick and wounded, killed and captured: John Newsome (wounded, captured, and released), Jones Bradbury (wounded, captured, released, and later killed), Hayes P. Griffith (discharged, sick), John Wilde (killed), Henry Odiorne (killed), James Breck (killed), John McDade (wounded) . . . And every mail brought news of the losses suffered by friends in other parts of the country. The women of the managerial class and even some of the men threw themselves into hospital work, visiting the wounded, reading to them and writing letters, teaching the illiterate to read, and bringing the solace of Christian conversation. Clementina's cousin Dan Smith served as a civilian male nurse in a hospital in Philadelphia and told Clemma the affecting story of how an acquaintance of theirs, "poor Snow," died in hope of salvation:

> He said when he saw Snow could not live many hours he asked him what were his views of another life; Snow said he felt he was pardoned—Dan told him he was glad he felt he was "washed in the precious blood of the Lamb of God"—Snow nodded assent and added "write to my Mother" which Dan did the night he died—Poor Dan cried like a child when he died—[25]

Both Harriet and Clementina Smith and Eleanora Lammot spent much time in hospital activity, collecting funds, preparing wound dressings, and making visits. For a time they were busy—along with Maria Blakeley and her daughter Sophia—with the women's auxiliary at the military hospital, which was being set up in Crozer's former normal school at Upland (until, in a dispute with the military commander, the civilians were thrown out there as they had been at Dan's hospital in Philadelphia). Some of their friends, including the wife of the owner of nearby Yearsley's Mill, proposed to enlist as nurses with Miss Dorothea Dix. The Rockdale ladies also served regular schedules as visitors in the big military hospital on South Street in Philadelphia. It was not easy work, but Harriet especially was devoted to serving wounded young men and alternated days with her friend Bessie Baird. Clementina was concerned about her. "I hope she will have strength for it," she said. "I feel a little anxious for I see the depression it causes her."[26] In the summer after the battle at Gettysburg, there was a hot spell, and Clementina described the hospital as being almost "unendurable . . . —the atmosphere so affected by the wounds."[27]

The stress of war was accomplishing another change: it was achieving a final polarization of the people, so that there was no middle ground for compromise, and the two sides were seen, in the millennial interpretation, as hosts of God and Satan. Charity for the enemy was not easy to summon in this time; everyone was suspicious even of friends, finding dark plots in each military and naval reversal. "No one," cried Clementina in the summer of '63, "escapes public censure now, our excited and distressed country is unjust to its best helpers."[28] She was thinking particularly of Sophie's husband, who had recently commanded an ill-fated attack on the forts in Charleston Harbor. After extensive planning and experimentation and the assembling of the most formidable fleet of ironclad naval vessels in history, Admiral Du Pont had failed. He broke off the attack after one day's battle, in the conviction (undoubtedly correct) that continued assault on the virtually untouched land batteries "would have converted a failure into a disaster."[29] The Secretary of the Navy had relieved him of command and he was now surrounded and constantly harassed by hostile newspaper critics and investigation officers. (He was replaced by Admiral Dahlgren, the developer of the powerful guns that were eventually to pound Fort Sumter into rubble.) To be sure, as she said, "we have sinned grievously and God is very angry with us. How much better this, than for us to look to man's mistakes as the cause of our reverses."[30] But it was a difficult philosophy to maintain in the face of the blizzard of rumors, backbiting, and intrigue that filled the air. It was much easier to lay blame, and by 1864 even Clementina was bitter. Writing from Lenni, she told Sophie, "The good element is gone from our population drunken women and copperhead men are left." With evident satisfaction she gave an account of how the mother of one of her Sunday School girls, "Happy Pike," had come to an untimely end:

> Her mother was a very wicked woman who did all she cd. to demoralize this place and some weeks ago went to a soldier's picnic near Chester taking her daughter with her. She left her company when the picnic was over in search of something she had lost and was killed on the R. Road and mangled in the most frightful manner.[31]

And it was with great relish that Clementina quoted at length from a letter from her own and Hattie's friend, Bessie Baird. Mrs. Baird was on the train from New York to Boston when she and her companions, a group of respectable charity women, encountered a group of twelve wounded soldiers on their way home. All during the trip they entertained the men, listening to their battle stories and opinions on the war and exchanging names and promises to write. Her daughter was the first to approach the men, who were much taken with the little girl, cut off a button from her coat and wrote down her name, and accepted her as a kind of mascot for the trip. When they began to pass around a bottle, she begged them not to drink and they actually put the whiskey away, saying, "We cannot take any more after what that child said . . . She spoke the first words of comfort we have had since we left home, and she knows as much as a man about the war." It was in the midst of this scene of romantic patriotism that Bessie suddenly encountered Dr. Lord, the well-known lecturer and advocate of compromise with the south. He sat beside Bessie and never stopped talking. Bessie was outraged and finally exploded:

> We had a regular scene which ended by my saying I regret Dr. Lord that it is not in my power to apportion to you a place in Fort Lafayette as I should be delighted to do so, he got pretty red and said he was only in

fun and wanted to draw me out—He never stopped talking from N.Haven to Hartford. He said my feelings amounted to religious fanaticism and asked what kind of feelings would you like *me* to have—I said oh only respectable manliness I don't ask for courage. He goes for compromise and all that stuff—[32]

The "religious fanaticism" to which Dr. Lord referred was of course the millennial interpretation of the war to which increasing numbers of religious people in the north subscribed. Harriet Beecher Stowe, in *Uncle Tom's Cabin,* had warned of the Second Coming, which was to be a day both of vengeance and redemption. And Julia Ward Howe, in *The Battle Hymn of the Republic,* first published in 1862, had drawn her imagery directly from Revelation, delineating the American Civil War as the final battle to which a mounted Christ in armor would bring his "terrible swift sword."[33] But it was not merely a popular rhetoric, vulnerable to the charge of "fanaticism," that sounded the millennial note. This was also expressed, as we have seen, in more orthodox and measured religious language in the book by Hollis Read, published in 1861, entitled *The Coming Crisis of the World.*

Clementina began to find her chief solace in the feeling that she was playing a part in the greatest event in human history. She wrote to Sophie: "I feel more and more how insignificant this mortal condition except in its bearings upon the great universal plan, and for the *individual,* in its bearing upon Eternal life."[34] After reading Lincoln's Emancipation Proclamation, she reflected on the uncertainty of its effects in a nation better prepared to grant freedom as a military necessity than out of a moral sense. And this uncomfortable train of thought was immediately followed by the expression of a millennialist hope:

May our Heavenly Father grant us His direction and deliver us from wicked men who have certainly been thrown to the surface lately—I cannot think we will be forsaken—and all I desire is that we as a people may be brought to do God's will—Perhaps *we* may be the martyr generation—if so I trust a glorious country will rise from our ashes—and we know that a heavenly one is before all those who seek it—"The time is short"—That is a comfort—[35]

As the end of the war neared, with the help of the rector and the Sunday School teachers Clementina was involving herself in the spreading of the millennial interpretation among all the people of Rockdale. Christmas was coming and she had been listening to the "angelic strains" of the little children practicing their Christmas carols in the church. She was moved to reflect on the pervasiveness of the theme of the Second Coming in the

Christmas services (dedicated to the birth of Jesus) and to declare her wish that everyone might know:

What a solemn season this is dear Sophie when we have set before us the Second coming of our Lord in all our scripture readings and prayers. Oh that we all might be looking for and hasting unto that great day of the Lord when He shall come to be glorified in his Saints and to be admired in all them that believe—[36]

Hattie's Boys

Two of "Hattie's boys" from the young men's Sunday School class and the Literary Association were John Newsome and Jones Bradbury. They were both weavers and close friends, and they enlisted at the same time in the same outfit, Company B of the Twenty-sixth Regiment of the First Pennsylvania Volunteers, where for a time they were army buddies. John Newsome was a man of medium height, blond-haired and gray-eyed, twenty-six years old when the war began. He had been born in Yorkshire and had come to America in 1854, working first in a mill in New Jersey, and then coming to the Rockdale district about 1856. He lived with his parents and five of his brothers and sisters, all of whom except the youngest worked at the looms too. His mother was unable to read or write and his father, also a weaver, seems to have deferred to his oldest son, for John acted as the head of the family and just before the war had bought them a small three-room stone farmhouse at the top of the hill above Rockdale.[37]

Jones Bradbury was 6 feet tall, with blue eyes, auburn hair, and a dark complexion. Twenty-three years old when the war began, he had been born in rural Otsego County, New York. His father was a laborer, born in England; his mother a New York woman. The family had moved to Pennsylvania when Jones was two or three years old and to the Rockdale district about 1855. Now there were nine of them. Jones and his younger brother David worked as weavers in Callaghan's mill in Parkmount, and his sister Alice worked as a spooler. In April, just as the war began, his father, who was about sixty, died and Jones, earning about $7 per week, became the principal support of the family.[38]

John Newsome was a cheerful young man, who breezed through events, carrying people with him and transcending obstacles and personal disasters with a happy self-assurance. Jones Bradbury's nature was of a darker kind, moody and plagued by self-doubt, but determined to endure to the end. John Newsome was the more successful; but Jones Bradbury was Harriet's favorite.

John enlisted as a three-year man in May 1861 and was eventually promoted to first sergeant of Company B. Almost exactly two years later, during the Union defeat at Chancellorsville in Virginia, he suffered a gunshot wound of the right thigh and was captured. (Jones Bradbury wrote home to Hattie mistakenly reporting that John was killed.) He was paroled and sent back to the Union lines two weeks later, eventually reaching the South Street Hospital in Philadelphia. The wound healed slowly and he was suffering from an inguinal hernia that resulted from it, but during the summer he was given a commission as second lieutenant and furloughed to go home to be nursed back to health. He returned to Rockdale and within a couple of months had become engaged to Elizabeth Murphy, the rector's sister. He rejoined Company B in September 1863, although his wound was still suppurating and his rupture was unrepaired, and fought through Grant's Wilderness Campaign until rheumatism and exhaustion wore him down. He was furloughed in March 1864, married Elizabeth Murphy, and then again returned for more. Exhausted and sick, he was discharged in June 1864. He recalled the Wilderness Campaign clearly in the 1890's when he applied for an increase in his invalid pension:

From Bealton to Culpepper Sept. to Dec. 1863 was my first sciatic. But having my gun-shot wound & rupture & my wound still suppurating I attributed my pains to those causes, for I was an ambitious veteran with a commission but not mustered. Our Mine-Run Campaign increased my rheumatism. Nov. 26th 4 P.M. up to my armpits in the Rapahannock, then a sharp engagement and crossed another stream over knee deep, which felt cold as ice. The day we lay in front of the Rebels at Mine Run, very trying day. Feb. 6th/64 was out on the point to relieve Poulter, the streams were swollen & the ground soaked—had a bad time of it & suffered a good deal. April 9th & 10th/64 was on picket on the Rap'ck, the worst rain storm I ever saw, thoroughly drenched & all hands discouraged. May 13th/64 badly exhausted 9 P.M. our Regt. called on to relieve some 6th Corps. Pickets got lost & stood & stood knee-deep in mud till morning, all these things & more caused my rheumatism, but thank God I was ready for discharge.[39]

For a while after leaving the service John worked as a nurse for Caspar Wistar Pennock, M.D., a local physician crippled by sclerosis of the spine. Although Pennock was a distinguished man of medicine, trained in Edinburgh and Paris, and known for his research on diseases of the heart, Clementina was shocked: "John Newsome *nurse* to Dr. Pennock! We think this is a great mistake. John's time is too precious to spend in what cannot elevate or advance him."[40] But in due course John accumulated some money (borrowed, according to family tradition, from Captain Miller of Company B, whose life John had saved). Captain Miller invited John and Elizabeth to live with his family in Middletown after his discharge, and after the war he lent them money to buy a farm. In 1868 John went out west, to the end of the railroad in Iowa, and purchased a farm there, within the sound of train whistles to please his wife, who "wanted to feel she was not entirely outside the bounds of civilization." In 1869 he moved there permanently with his wife, the two children born while they had lived with the Millers, and John's parents and brothers and sisters.[41]

Jones Bradbury was a man tormented by the fear that he did not deserve salvation; and to him Harriet's compassionate nature was strongly drawn. During the summer and fall of 1858 she had taught a Sunday School class for young men, and twenty-one-year-old Jones Bradbury was one. When in January she left Rockdale for the social season in Philadelphia, she held "a sort of Entertainment" for the men at the parsonage. On Sunday evening, at the end of the last class, she saw Jones "taking a *private cry* to himself behind the stove." He pulled himself together and then unexpectedly made a short speech:

Just before they closed he said he had a few remarks to make to them & in a very manly way told them that he cd. not bear to give up their S. ev^g study of the S.S. & he wanted to propose that they should ask Mr. Murphy if there was any one in the parish who could take the class it should be continued I believe Mr. Murphy has determined to give his Sunday evenings to it—[42]

Hattie returned in the spring to her group of devoted young men; her work there, observed Clementina, was "blessed to her own heart as well as all who have been the subjects." During the summer, the family took Harriet off to a vacation in the mountains of Vermont, but she arranged for a substitute teacher, a man, who interested them "exceedingly" and brought in new recruits to the class. Jones progressed in his religious commitment and in the fall was baptized and confirmed at Calvary. Hattie spoke proudly of this and of "his simple childlike faith."

This faith was soon tested. "Poor fellow," wrote Clementina, "he has had a bitter sorrow in his early religious life." Early in January "a very dear brother of his" committed suicide. Jones was sustained, however, by his conviction that his brother could not have surrendered his hope of Heaven by taking his own life deliberately. "Jones says he thinks he should be wild with grief if he did not fully believe it was mental aberration that caused him to take his own life. A post mortem Examination proved that his brain was very much diseased."[43] A year later Jones's father died, and then the war began.

Jones went to Philadelphia with John Newsome and they enlisted together in Company B and served side by side through the first Battle of Bull Run. After Bull Run, Jones came back to Rockdale on furlough for two weeks, and Clementina declared that "his experience has made him a more earnest Christian." Jones and John were together during the subsequent actions in which the Twenty-sixth Pennsylvania was engaged: the Peninsular Campaign, the second Bull Run, and Chancellorsville, where John was wounded and captured. In August 1862, Hattie, Clementina, and Miss Davis the Sunday School teacher went to Washington and visited all over town, including the Navy Department, where they tried to call on the Secretary of the Navy, "good kind Mr. Welles," who unfortunately was not in. They also sought out the Rockdalers in service and found Jones and John: "Hattie had the satisfaction of seeing her two 'boys' John & Jones and of feeling that she could do something to bring them up from careless ways into which this unsettled condition of things has thrown them. They spent Thursday evening with us."[44]

The two men were not separated until John was wounded and captured at Chancellorsville in the spring of 1863. Jones went through the battle at Gettysburg without wounds, although the Twenty-sixth Regiment lost 213 of its 364 enlisted men and 11 of 18 officers, killed or wounded. In the fall they were reunited, with John now promoted to second lieutenant and Jones to sergeant. But their association was looser, with differences in rank and duties and quarters. In November 1863 Jones was wounded (a minnie-ball through the right foot) and hospitalized in Philadelphia. He came out of the hospital after three months with hair prematurely gray. He stayed for a while with the Smiths in their house at 1010 Clinton Street and delighted them by praising Admiral Du Pont's silence before his critics. "I am amazed," said Harriet's mother, "at Jones' improvement. If our army officers were as loyal as well acquainted with the whole condition of our country's civil war, cause to consequences—the rebels would lay down their arms."[45] He re-enlisted for another three years, this time being transferred to another regiment, the Forty-ninth Pennsylvania Volunteers, as third sergeant (and finally as first sergeant).

But Jones's time was running out. In June 1864 he was captured at Mechanicsville, Virginia, while leading his men on a skirmish line. He was sent to the notorious prisoner-of-war camp at Andersonville, Georgia, where he remained for almost six months until he was released on parole for reason of illness. After convalescing in Philadelphia, in March 1865 he returned to his regiment, then pursuing the rebels through Virginia east of Petersburg. He was shot in a small fight between pursuing units of the Ninety-ninth Pennsylvania and the retreating Confederates at Sailors

Creek, Virginia, on April 6, 1865. He lived for a couple of hours and had time to write a note to Hattie before he died. The war ended three days later with Lee's surrender at Appomattox.

Jones's letter reached Rockdale in three weeks' time and Clementina wrote the sad news to Sophie:

> We all feel very deeply Jones Bradbury's death, he was killed on the 6th April before Petersburg while leading his Comy. in a charge—He survived only two hours—A pencil note came to dear Hattie yesterday written with gt. effort when he was dying the paper was stained with his blood! We have the blessed hope that he has entered into Everlasting Life and spared the conflict with sin so dreadful to him.[46]

The Smiths did what they could for Jones's mother, who was living in Philadelphia, trying to support three of her children on the money that Jones had been sending home from his pay. A day or two after the letter arrived, Harriet went to Philadelphia and witnessed Lavinia Bradbury's application for a Mother's Army Pension, testifying that she knew that he had sent home his pay because she had read his letters to his mother. Clementina and her father supported the mother's claim. Harriet also claimed Jones's body and had it shipped to Rockdale, where she waited for it alone in the house in Lenni all through the second week in May. "She went to six trains," said Clementina, "to await the arrival of Jones body before it came and a very rough undertaker tried her sorely." Jones was buried in the cemetery behind Calvary Church.

And Clementina wrote on to Sophie (whose husband was dying), "The weariness of the road here should only make the heavenly home look brighter not lead to repinings for rest & society of those we love. My sweet little book shelf looks beautifully with its patriotic colors & has my bible & P. book in my snug little corner where I wish I had you by me."[47]

ENVOI

In the years after the war, while the grass grew green over the grave of Jones Bradbury, the mill where he had worked at Parkmount, a few hundred yards upstream, returned to normal production. Indeed, the Rockdale manufacturing district grew ever more prosperous and survived as a textile center for another hundred years; the looms at Parkmount, the last of the textile factories to close down, did not cease their clatter until 1970. And the same mills today still house light industry: Westlake Plastics, Sunroc Corporation, Container Research, a lumber mill, machine shops. The Smiths and the Riddles and the Lammots lived on too for many years, gradually dying off in their eighties and nineties as the century came to an end. But only three of the figures in this story made it into the twentieth century: Harriet Smith, who died in 1905 at the age of eighty-seven; Hayes P. Griffith, weaver, servant of the Smiths, and Civil War veteran, who reached eighty and died in 1909; and Lydia, the widow of Samuel Riddle, who died in 1915. The last of the old cohort to survive in the memories of living Rockdalers was Lydia Riddle. She used to watch the passersby as she sat on the porch of the old Leander house (now demolished as unsafe), wearing a black dress and on it a diamond brooch so bright that it flashed all up and down Pennell Road.

But already, a few years after the end of the war, the early growth of the Rockdale manufacturing district, and the lives of its people then, were becoming history even to the remaining participants. Several local histories by local residents appeared in succession, devoted to celebrating the exploits of the "men of enterprise" who had made Delaware County what it was: the first, *History of Delaware County,* in 1862, by George Smith, of the Delaware County Institute of Science; John Broomall's *History of Delaware County for the Past Century,* a product of the call for consciousness of history associated with the Centennial celebrations; then, the history of *Chester (and*

Its Vicinity) by John Hill Martin, the boy who had grown up at Lenni Mill; and, in 1884, the detailed 765-page, double-columned *History of Delaware County* by Henry Graham Ashmead of Chester, which devoted about 25 pages specifically to the Rockdale manufacturing district's mills, churches, schools, and lodges. Published genealogies began to appear, of the Riddles, the Smiths, the Darlingtons. And in Rockdale itself in 1898 William E. Griffith launched the *Rockdale Herald,* a weekly newspaper dedicated to the principles of the Democratic Party, whose first issue carried as its lead article an account, apparently derived from Ashmead, of the history of the Glen Riddle Mills—"A Short Sketch of the flourishing Textile Factory at Glen Riddle, its former management and growth." Noted men like Crozer, Smith, and Bishops Lee, Potter, and Hopkins wrote autobiographical accounts or were the subjects of biographies and memorials. Before the turn of the century, the events of this story had become history to the residents of Rockdale itself.

Today, inevitably, only a few members of the community recall much about these happenings beyond what is available in Ashmead and the *Herald.* Time has flattened out, like the optical perspective of a landscape seen through a telephoto lens, and word-of-mouth transmission of unwritten historical information has slowed to a trickle. With each death of a participant, a whole world of information dies too; for the most part only written records and physical constructions remain. And these dwindle away constantly. Records are lost, paper crumbles, old letters are thrown away, unlabeled photographs become meaningless. And the mills, dams, races, tenements, bridges—all these too are subject to constant erosion. Since beginning this study in 1969, I have seen old Parkmount successively in active use as a rug mill, abandoned, flooded, burned out in a spectacular blaze, and then partly knocked down by wrecking crews. Rotting and hazardous mansions at Lenni and Penn's Grove have been demolished; but Crozer's first mansion at West Branch is still lived in, and the Crozer mansion at Crozerville has been converted into company offices by Container Research. Glen Riddle Dam was washed away in the flood in 1971. Each year less and less information is left of a world that was once as rich and real as the one that is there today.

And yet that world lives on, in a sense, in the customs and beliefs of those who have come after. The people of Rockdale then lived in what they felt was historical time. Their lives spanned the coming of the industrial age to America; they saw themselves as participants in a grand process of development that was bringing technological progress and material prosperity to all mankind, and with it—if the observer was a Christian—salvation and even the millennium; if he was a Deist, then enlightenment and cooperative association. They communicate with us directly through their intentional literary remains; indirectly, through the legacy of beliefs transmitted without consciousness of origin, in classroom, church, political meeting, and union hall, about the social nature of the world. It was in Rockdale, and in dozens of other industrial communities like Rockdale, that an American world view developed which pervades the present—or did so until recently —with a sense of superior Christian virtue, a sense of global mission, a sense of responsibility and capability for bringing enlightenment to a dark and superstitious world, for overthrowing ancient and new tyrannies, and for making backward infidels into Christian men of enterprise.

APPENDIX

NOTES

BIBLIOGRAPHY

INDEX

Paradigmatic Processes
in Culture Change

The following discussion was originally published in 1972 in the *American Anthropologist*. It is reprinted here with some minor changes in wording and without the anticipatory description of the Rockdale study. I had begun the collection of material on the Rockdale manufacturing district in 1969; as the information accumulated, I realized that Rockdale was one of a number of similar villages where the Industrial Revolution began in the United States and that a standard process of cultural and social change was probably common to all of them. This essay was written as a kind of guide for organizing my thoughts about what was happening in Rockdale and deciding what kinds of data would be most relevant.

A second purpose of the essay was to direct attention to, and to delineate more thoroughly, a type of process in culture change which of late has been relatively neglected by anthropologists. Kroeber and his contemporaries over a generation ago emphasized the importance of paradigmatic regularities in historical process in their studies of the growth of culture areas and civilizations.[1] A historian of science, Thomas Kuhn, more recently has formulated in greater detail some of the essential features of the paradigmatic process in his well-known essay on the nature of scientific progress, *The Structure of Scientific Revolutions*.[2] I propose here to amplify their statements, to generalize them still further into a model of a type of culture change (which I shall call "paradigmatic"), and to outline some of the many applications of the model to the study of culture change in domains other than science itself.

Kuhn's Model of Culture Change

Thomas Kuhn argued that contrary to the belief of most scientists and of many historians of science, scientific evolution has not been a steady, continuous accumulation of data and modification of theory. It has proceeded, rather, in alternating phases of normal and revolutionary science. During the course of "normal science," an unchanging paradigm governs the work of most investigators in any given field or discipline. These paradigms are the "recurrent and quasi-standard illustrations of various theories in their conceptual, observational, and instrumental applications."[3] Explicit rules, theories, and assumptions may accompany paradigms but are not necessary for the guidance of research. The student learns the paradigm primarily by repeating as training exercises the very "illustrations" that constitute the paradigm itself, by redoing the laboratory experiments, deriving the equations, intuiting the concepts and findings which are described in the textbooks as classic and fundamental achievements. Later, his professional work as a normal scientist is to discover new applications of the same paradigm, to resolve ambiguities and apparent contradictions in the rules and theories, and to work out the as-yet-undiscovered theorems implicit in its logic. His work is problem solving within the continuously developing domain of interpretations of the paradigm itself. Thus the Greek geometers before Euclid established a paradigm for the study of plane and solid forms based upon constructions that could be accomplished by ruler and compass, by the sectioning of spheres, cones, and cylinders, and by the use of syllogistic reasoning. The formulation of axioms and theorems, and the application of Euclidean geometry to science and technology, was a problem-solving enterprise that occupied the Greek mathematical community for hundreds of years.

In the case of the Greek geometers, no new geometrical paradigm appeared in their own time; truly non-Euclidean geometries did not arrive until the nineteenth century. But inevitably, sooner or later, new paradigms directly confront and replace older ones. This confrontation occurs when the number of nagging, insoluble problems and internal inconsistencies associated with an existing paradigm has accumulated to the point where a whole new way of approaching the problem is seen as necessary by some irritated members of the scientific community. In response to the crisis, a new paradigm is devised, which is able to account for most of the phenomena explicable under the old but which is also able to solve the crucial problems refractory to it. If, after some intellectual conflict, the new paradigm is accepted, and with it a redefinition of the world view of the discipline, a "scientific revolution" may be said to have occurred. Examples of such scientific revolutions are the replacement of Ptolemaic by Galilean astronomy and the overthrow of the phlogiston theory of combustion by the oxygen theory. The development of the oxidation paradigm led directly to the complex set of principles and procedures which constituted the new atomic chemistry.

Both paradigmatic processes—normal science and revolutionary science—involve the activity of a scientific community. Such a community (or discipline, or school, or tradition, or what-have-you) is not usually a community in the ordinary sociological sense, of course, but rather a group of intercommunicating specialists, unrestricted in time or space, who jointly develop the applications of the paradigm. Kuhn does not elaborate on the nature of this community but its existence is explicitly recognized in his argument.

The General Model of Paradigmatic Processes

The paradigmatic process has five essential components: innovation, paradigmatic core development, exploitation, functional consequences, and rationalization. It is possible to think of them as overlapping stages in which each comes to the forefront of attention in due order, but the latter four "tasks" are actually continuous during the life of the paradigm.

This model attempts to embrace a far wider range of culture change processes than Kuhn's, first because Kuhn is centrally concerned with the history of science, and second because he is not attempting to deal at all with exploitation, functional consequences, or rationalization. But my model does not claim to describe *all* sequences of cultural innovations and their consequences. It applies only to those culture change sequences in which a paradigmatic core development process occurs. This restriction is essential to the application of the model.

Innovation of a new paradigm may (as Kuhn emphasizes) entail a conflict with an older one, which it may replace; in this case one may speak of a "revolution," such as the scientific revolutions of which Kuhn writes, or the cultural "revolutions" associated with the development of agriculture, urban life, and industrial technology. Whether the innovation of a new paradigm is always a revolutionary event, in the sense that it immediately challenges the adequacy of existing practice, is debatable; not all innovations basic to a new paradigm necessarily contradict an earlier paradigm, for some may initiate an entirely new line of development. But it is difficult to think of clear-cut examples of this sort of event, and for practical purposes it is probably useful to assume paradigmatic conflict to be the best evidence of fundamental innovation. A more important consideration is that not all innovations are paradigm-forming. Many can best be considered under other headings (core development, functional consequences, and rationalization). And some, perhaps, are simply not relevant to any paradigm process at all.

To qualify as paradigm-forming, an innovation need not be a complete and adequate theory or model; rather, it is an event which solves a limited problem but does so in a way which opens up a whole new line of development. It is a major "break-through." Furthermore, the paradigmatic innovation has a symbolic and charismatic quality. It is often associated with the name of a culture hero (human or divine) and it can be simply represented by some visual image or phrase or manual procedure.

In the history of American anthropology, for instance, one can find a convenient illustration in the origin of the "fieldwork" paradigm. Whether accurately or not, one thinks of Franz Boas stepping off the boat in an Eskimo village with his suitcase in hand, preparing for a long stay in residence. This image *is* the paradigm: the subsequent development of field techniques, standards of ethnographic description, ethnological theory, and training requirements for the Ph.D. stem from, and are implied by, the symbol of Boas as lone fieldworker taking up prolonged residence in a small community. This symbol is opposed in a revolutionary way to a nineteenth century tradition of library scholarship and of uncritical use of the comparative method to derive models of cultural evolution. Of course Boas was not actually the first to do fieldwork; he did not in all respects do adequate fieldwork by the standards of his own paradigm; and he did not really deny the value of library work or of studies of cultural evolution. But all that is beside the point: he did effectively establish the fieldwork paradigm for American academic anthropology.

Paradigmatic core development is the continuous elaboration of the ideas that constitute the original paradigm, according to the rules of the paradigm itself. In science, Kuhn calls this the process of "normal science." Generations of trained workers make "contributions" to the perfection of the paradigm by resolving any surviving internal ambiguities or contradictions and by demonstrating its utility in solving newly discovered problems. Doctoral dissertations, for instance, are expected to be paradigmatic contributions in their own fields. People who are working on the same paradigm tend to be visible as a profession, or a school of thought, or a tradition, and to function as a community whose reference objects are other members of the community rather than the world outside. Such paradigmatic communities in our own culture history are readily recognizable not only in science but outside science as well, in such fields as philosophy, theology, music, art and literature, and technology, and Kuhn has already recognized that humanistic scholarship traditionally assumes a paradigmatic scheme in its approaches to intellectual history and criticism.[4]

Let us briefly consider theology, art, and literature (we shall return to the technology application later in more detail). In the case of religion, almost as soon as the prophet of a revitalization movement has begun to lay down the new paradigm in the form of a code based on his revelations, his disciples begin to discuss, interpret, and apply it. Even within nonliterate or marginally literate cultures, this process of editing, interpreting, and applying the text goes on incessantly, and a body of auxiliary belief and commentary rapidly builds up within the paradigmatic community of disciples, preachers, priests, and other followers. There is a continuing process of defining and redefining the standard symbols and formulas as new historical circumstances arise. Similarly in art, once a new idea or approach has been successfully broached, a "school" is likely to develop, perhaps at first consisting of only a few disciples, who work busily at amplifying and developing their master's paradigm. And again in literature, once a classic work has been created, it provides the format for dozens or hundreds of followers who play with and explore the possibilities implicit in the original.

There is a peculiar arbitrariness in the core development process. It is often remarkably independent in its direction (though not in speed), once launched, from surrounding events, although it influences them. It is as though, once defined, the paradigm must be developed according to its own inner law; like a gyroscope, its attitude remains stable in a shifting historical frame. It is notoriously difficult to censor, suppress, or destroy a process of core development by economic, religious, or political pressures. Furthermore, within the paradigmatic community, new developments are in a sense unpredictable, for to predict the event in any detail is to have anticipated it; the event predicted occurs in the course of its own prediction. Thus, even though core development follows its own inner logic and works to realize latent implications, its course is also accompanied by a constant sense of surprised discovery.

By *exploitation* is meant the recognition and embracing of the paradigm, at some stage in its evolution, by an economic, military, religious, or political organization which sees in its application an opportunity for the protection or advancement of its own interests. The paradigmatic community can, theoretically, exploit its own paradigm, but this in all likelihood rarely happens. More commonly the exploitation is carried out by others, very often in as monopolistic a fashion as possible. The exploiting group may not only wish to apply the paradigm, and be the only applier of it; they may wish to direct in some measure the further development of the core itself, both as to direction and rate. It is in the relationship of the paradigmatic and exploitive community that some of the most interesting features of the process lie, and we shall return to them later in this essay.

By *functional consequences* are meant the new, specific problems which the exploitation of the core development process creates for society and the way in which society responds, at first by expedients, and eventually by cultural change. Recent examples in science are all too obvious: the applications of core development in normal science to the creation of new physical, chemical, and biological weaponry has threatened the survival of mankind, created new industries, developed new patterns of international relations, and so on. Ecological damage from indiscriminate waste disposal, from the incautious use of DDT and other insecticides, and from over-use of natural resources is almost as serious a threat. A result of medical research and improved methods of food production has been a vast increase in the world's population; this increase has entailed further pressure on the ecosystem; and so on *ad infinitum.* It is easy to discover examples of catastrophic problems presented by the innocent development of a core by an oblivious paradigmatic community and a ruthless exploiting group. Typically, core development will create opportunity for some; and if that opportunity is seized, functional consequences will include advantages for some and new problems for others, perhaps even eventually for the opportunist himself. And the solutions to any one problem will produce other problems and the solutions to these problems still more problems. This peculiar Pandora's box quality of the offerings of continuing core development and exploitation almost invariably generates an ambivalence, sometimes even a taboo toward the paradigmatic community by the rest of the society, with some parties interested in exploiting the new developments, others in suppressing them, and many feeling both ways at the same time.

But whether or not there is ambivalence, the problems produced by paradigmatic development are real ones and the policies which political and economic communities concoct to deal with them are an interesting field for cultural analysis, for experimental procedures tend to become policy and, when successful, to harden into conventional practice—ad hoc procedure becomes policy, and policy becomes culture.

By *rationalization* is intended the ethical, philosophical, religious, and political justifications which the paradigmatic community members offer for their participation in the core development process and which general community members offer for their relationship to the paradigm. As Garfinkel[5] and other ethnomethodologists have pointed out, people tend to act in such a way as to validate their theory of the world; but when new actions are made necessary by the challenges of functional consequences of exploiting a paradigm, a new theory must be constructed. The para-community is generally rather monotonous in its rationalizations, saying in effect that working on the paradigm is doing God's work, or that it will lead to a better world, or that basic research is a good thing in itself and will always pay off eventually. The general community has a more interesting problem. In its initial "seizure" of the paradigm for the first application, the exploiting community group may account for its action with familiar and established explanations. Indeed, as Smelser and my student Kasserman indicate, the exploiter may be an essentially conservative person who is simply trying to maintain his footing in a changing world.[6] Later on, however, as more and more expedients must be contrived to cope with spin-off problems, the rationalization must change to take account of the functional changes in the society and in their own lives.

Relations Between the Paradigmatic Community and the Rest of Society

To the historian and sociologist of science, it has long been an appealing hypothesis that the language, the customs, and the values of the general society subtly determine the ideas of supposedly objective fields. The paradigmatic notion looks at the process in another way, concentrating on the evolution of the irrelevant to the point where relevance is discovered. The discovery of relevance is the moment of exploitation. At once the paradigmatic community is confronted by organizations, up to and at times including the sovereign institutions, which make claims upon it. The interaction between these two interest groups is the subject of high drama in our own time—and even in our own profession, where the exploitation of the fieldwork paradigm by government agencies entails serious functional consequences and thus generates intense discussion of ethical issues. There are a number of dimensions along which the relations may vary and for the sake of introductory discussion let us enumerate some of them. In the case of support, the policy of the general community may range from across-the-board support of an entire para-community (e.g., of a discipline like physics) by granting unrestricted research funds and fellowships, by favorable patent and copyright laws, by establishing new research and development communities; or it may restrict support to selected aspects of the field (such as weapons research) and other purely applied projects; or it may make deliberate efforts to destroy the entire para-community (e.g., by accusing them of treason, of being witches, or whatever). In the case of communication, the general community may favor open channels (by avoiding censorship, endorsing freedom of speech, and the like) or it may impose censorship, place embargoes on immigration or emigration or even travel, or restrict foreign trade. In the case of power, the general community may eagerly include the para-community in the power structure, or exclude it from certain sorts of decision-making forums (by requiring a nonpolitical position as a condition of support), or even generally wall off the para-community into a caste-like minority group or ghetto population. In the case of control of applications, the general community may take the initiative and attempt to seduce, hire, or coerce members of the para-community into providing service, or the responsibility for exploitation may be handled jointly, or the para-community may attempt to control the nature, timing, and degree of exploitation of its paradigm, in some cases urging applications, and in others attempting to restrict or control them. And, of course, the reward system for paradigmatic work may vary from material goods, money, and power through symbolic rewards (medals, prizes, and so on) to rewards in the form of status or prestige in the para-community alone.

The development of the relationships between paradigmatic and lay communities is, in a sense, a sideplay, separate from the immediate paradigm development, functional conse-quence, and rationalization problems. It is, however, an important political process whose course will affect the course of the whole society.

The Industrial Revolution

The idea of formulating the theory of paradigmatic process in culture change was originally prompted by the need to develop a frame of thought for the Rockdale project. The model has indeed proved to be useful in guiding the research strategy for that project; and the Rockdale study itself has shown that the way in which the different aspects of a paradigmatic process fit together can be very clearly understood when the aspects are seen in the detail that the intensive ethno-historical study of a small community makes possible. But the paradigmatic process can be illustrated on a grander scale by one of the major events in cultural evolution: the origin of the Industrial Revolution itself. The English Industrial Revolution exemplifies the paradigmatic process very well. Let us consider it according to the five stages that were outlined above: innovation, core development, exploitation, functional consequences, and rationalization.

Innovation and Paradigmatic Core Development—Although many factors combined to create the milieu in which the Industrial Revolution occurred, the most spectacular and symbolically important innovations, by all accounts, were the inventions in the decade of the 1760's of spinning machinery by James Hargreaves and Richard Arkwright in England and of the modern steam engine by James Watt in Scotland. But it is certainly not the case that these gadgets burst unexpectedly upon a surprised world; rather, they—and a number of other innovations in pottery making, metalworking, agriculture, and transportation—represented the first exploitable products of a technological paradigm that had been established at least a century before. Thus Thomas Savery in 1698 had made a workable steam engine for the purpose of pumping ground water from Cornish mines; and Thomas Newcomen in 1708 had developed another type of steam engine for pumping out collieries. Silk-throwing machinery had been introduced from Italy in 1717, and a true factory was developed for its use; the flying shuttle had been invented by John Kay to improve weaving in 1733; and a primitive roller spinning device was produced in 1738. All of this interest in the improvement of mechanical gadgetry had roots in the efforts of millwrights, clockmakers, instrument makers, clergymen, poets, physicians, barbers, and even scientists, to solve various technical problems which had already been conventionally isolated and defined. The notion that mathematical thinking, applied to naturalistic observation and experiment, and expressed in clockwork-like machines, could lead to the solution of practical problems, had so thoroughly taken hold that by 1754 —*before* the critical inventions had been made—there had been founded a Society for the Encouragement of Arts, Manufactures, and Commerce, which offered prizes to inventors.

It is evident then that the inventions of the 1760's, which constituted the classic expressions of the industrial paradigm, were nonetheless the product of several generations of optimistic work by scientists and mechanics. Hargreaves, the millwright; Arkwright, the barber; Watt, the instrument maker, in a sense did for mechanical invention what Euclid did for Greek geometry—they codified and put in a conspicuously applicable form a body of skills and knowledge that had been accumulating for decades. The latent paradigm on which the scientists and engineers had been working was the clock, an intricate system of carefully made and mathematically articulated wheels, gears, and shafts which accepted a source of power at one end and applied it to the performance of a useful and precisely quantifiable task at the other.

Exploitation—What made the machine paradigm into an industrial revolution was its combination with an old concept: the factory. There had been factories since Roman times where large numbers of skilled artisans plied their trade under one roof and under some sort of supervision. The new factory was occupied by large numbers of clockwork-like machines, powered by an external source of energy, that performed precise manual tasks under the supervision of a group of trained operatives. This application of the paradigm, it is said, was achieved first in 1717 by Thomas Lambe in his water-driven silk works in Derby, where three hundred workmen were employed; and Lambe's model was copied by Arkwright in a water-driven cotton factory at Cranford, which by about 1772 employed approximately six hundred. Around the same time Josiah Wedgwood—without major mechanical innovations—introduced the factory method into pottery making when in 1769 he set up the Etruria works.

But before this application could be accomplished, a process of exploitation had to occur. Scientists and mechanics for generations had been producing all kinds of finely made devices which—except for the clocks themselves—were of restricted practical value. The first spinning jennies were made and sold without even the taking of a patent by their inventor, and they were adopted primarily in domestic industries, where they simply amplified the income of household spinning-and-weaving enterprises. Richard Arkwright realized the potential profitability of assembling numbers of improved spinning machines, attaching them to a water wheel as power source, and training and employing factory hands ("operatives") to guide the machines.

The initial conditions for profitable exploitation of the new machinery in England included a capitalist commercial ethic, expanding markets, demand for a higher rate of production than conventional technology could accomplish, and the availability of large sums of money which could be borrowed at relatively low interest rates or which could be attracted as investment in corporate ventures. Thus an economic milieu existed in mid-eighteenth century England which made possible the assembling of the capital required for the exploitation of technical innovations. The industrial exploiter used his capital to perform a complex task; first, to buy, or rent, or develop a mill site, including dam, races, wheel, and mill machinery, a building housing the mill, some associated housing for manager and workers, and transportation facilities; second, to buy, or have made, the desired machines, and to install them in the mill; third, to hire, train, supervise, and pay the operatives.

Functional Consequences—With the securing of capital, the commissioning of machinery, and the employment of operatives, a triad of communities was defined, whose mutual confrontations launched a still-continuing process of social and cultural change. The exploiting community consisted of the owner or owners of the mill, the banks and other lending institutions, the suppliers of raw materials, and the distributors of finished goods. They jointly risked financial loss and jointly hoped for financial gain, and their efforts to make their investment more secure and their profits higher and more certain eventually required society-wide cultural innovations in insurance, in banking, in credit relations, in measures against periodic "panics," in fire and flood control, in labor legislation, local government, and so on.

An interesting analysis of spin-off from the cotton industry's changes during the Industrial

Revolution in Great Britain has been provided by the sociologist Neil J. Smelser in his study, *Social Change in the Industrial Revolution.* He approaches the question with a Parsonian scheme that views culture change as a response to the perception that some technique or institution is not functioning adequately or that there is a bottleneck in a process (e.g., the flying shuttle enabled household weavers to supply more cloth to satisfy foreign markets; this placed a demand on spinners which was eventually met only by the adoption of the jenny). Most of his attention is directed to the families of cotton spinners. Initially, the technical innovations and the early factories merely strengthened the traditional spinner households. Their real income increased, and factory-operative spinners were able to hire and supervise their own children and other kinfolk much as they had earlier in the days of the cottage industries. Thus, despite the massive increase in the production of cotton products resulting from the development of the new machinery and the building of factories, the initial effect on the English cottage family was to confirm its traditional structure. The problem for the spinner family really began in the 1820's (fully two generations after the critical innovations), when spinning machines became so complex that a spinner had to supervise more helpers than his own family could provide and when the availability of efficient steam engines made it possible to locate factories in large towns and cities rather than at the country mill sites. Under these conditions, the authority of the father in many a family was threatened, because his children were able to enter the "free" labor market to work as spinner's helpers for other spinners and also to work as factory-employed hands in machine-weaving rooms. The dissatisfaction with the differentiation of labor within the family was in part responsible for the rise of labor unions, the introduction of factory-hour legislation, the rise of cooperative stores and savings banks, and the rapid spread of state- or industry-supported schools for factory children who could no longer be educated and socialized by their parents.

Rationalization—The initial understanding of what the new machinery and the new factories meant tended to be somewhat Utopian. There was an anticipation of wealth to be gained by merchant adventurers, inventors, and investors; there was an increase in real income among the cottage spinners and weavers; and there was an expectation that the factory system, which required high standards of punctuality and efficiency, would teach the Protestant ethic to the shiftless poor. But these interpretations of the event were made from an optimistic eighteenth-century perspective. By the 1820's the English had had enough experience with the new system to realize what some of the functional consequences of industrialization were. And so, about this time, serious efforts to rationalize the process were begun. Some sought to justify a depersonalization of man (which was implied by a national labor market responding to the prod of starvation) by anticipations of improvement in the general welfare. The Utopian scientists quickly saw both the human costs and benefits; this line of thought received a classic expression in the somewhat romantic, even nostalgic analysis by Karl Marx in *Das Kapital* in 1867. Thinking along somewhat different lines were the *laissez faire* theorists, including Adam Smith, Thomas Malthus, Ricardo, and later the Social Darwinists. Such writers as these, as Polanyi has pointed out,[7] served to make the Industrial Revolution understandable not in simple eighteenth-century "enlightenment" terms, but in terms of the kinds of decisions that industrialists, bankers, government officials and legislators, the clergy, and working people had to make in coping with the deluge of machinery suddenly let loose upon the world. Each of these lines of rationalization, furthermore, became a paradigm for further intellectual work, much as a theological tradition grows up after a new messiah formulates a religious code.

Appendix

Other Applications of the Model

The paradigmatic model is obviously closely related to the revitalization movement model; indeed, one could conceive of revitalization movements as being a special case of paradigm development. In both cases one is dealing with deliberate efforts to innovate continuously over a substantial period of time. Evidently also some of the major leaps in general evolution can be regarded as paradigmatic—not merely the Industrial Revolution, but, if we had the data, probably also the Neolithic and Urban revolutions, and conceivably even earlier processes, such as the development of stone tool traditions. The paradigm model would not, however, be useful in all acculturation studies, for in many situations one suspects that the paradigm is precisely what is *not* communicated across the interface between two cultures. The difficulty of communicating paradigms may have something to do with the problems of development in recently colonial societies and in minority communities. And finally, the paradigm model fits well with such concepts as Kroeber's culture climax and the pattern-fulfillment concepts embodied in most philosophies of history. Culture-historical analysis might be able to use such concepts too, even though the problems usually addressed are those of survival and distribution.

The examples so far cited have tended to lay emphasis largely on scientific and technological cores, with occasional reference to theology and the arts. Perhaps such "hard" domains attract attention because the problems can here be phrased in relatively formal, and therefore finite and solvable, terms. It may be that the aesthetic urge which in part prompts the process of core development is best satisfied in working with systems that permit highly structured, cumulative thinking. But paradigmatic thinking itself does not necessarily address itself to the practical problems of the world; it may appear, to those outside the paradigmatic community, that it is a domain of trivialities, a menagerie of hair-splitting pedants, cranks, and ivory-tower types whose preoccupations are irrelevant to the "real" world. Irrelevant, that is, until the paradigm has been developed to a point where one of its aspects presents a means for solving someone's practical problem. The "practical" problem, of course, may in fact be equally trivial, in comparison with the giant and enduring social and emotional problems of mankind. But it seems to be the case that the world has repeatedly been transformed by the conjunction of trivialities: specifically, by the application of new navigational gadgets to the problem of securing spices for the dining tables and beaver pelts for felt hats, by the application of mechanical rollers to the problem of making enough cotton thread to satisfy the demand for cotton cloth created by the importation of Indian cottons from recently conquered India—and so on. It remains to be seen whether paradigmatic development proceeds in as effective a way in the field of political and economic organization. Indeed, the conditions under which domains of culture become susceptible to paradigmatic change would be an interesting subject for research.

Conclusion

The purpose of this essay has been to draw attention to a pervasive, but not adequately conceptualized, process of culture change which, after Thomas Kuhn, we have called "paradigmatic." A tentative general model of such processes has been presented, delineating as stages or functions the processes of innovation and paradigmatic core development, exploitation, functional consequences, and rationalization. The English Industrial Revolution was considered as a prime example of the process, and finally some general questions were raised about the conditions under which such processes occur, and the relation of the paradigmatic process to other processes in culture change.

Notes

ABBREVIATIONS

MANUSCRIPT COLLECTIONS

ANSP	*Academy of Natural Sciences of Philadelphia*
APS	*American Philosophical Society Library*
BLH	*Baker Library, Harvard*
CCHS	*Chester County Historical Society*
CCR	*Calvary Church, Rockdale*
DCCH	*Delaware County Court House*
DCHS	*Delaware County Historical Society*
DCIS	*Delaware County Institute of Science*
EMHL	*Eleutherian Mills Historical Library*
FI	*Franklin Institute*
HSD	*Historical Society of Delaware*
HSP	*Historical Society of Pennsylvania*
LOC	*Library of Congress*
NA	*National Archives*
NYHS	*New York Historical Society*
PAFA	*Pennsylvania Academy of Fine Arts*
PFL	*Philadelphia Free Library*
PHS	*Presbyterian Historical Society*
PLTA	*Painter Library, John J. Tyler Arboretum*
PSA	*Pennsylvania State Archives*
SSR	*Swedenborgian School of Religion*
UBC	*Upland Baptist Church*
WINH	*Workingmen's Institute, New Harmony*

PERSONS

APL	*Anna Potts Lammot*	JDC	*John D. Carter*
AVDP	*Alfred Victor du Pont*	JPC	*John Price Crozer*
CS	*Clementina Smith*	ML	*Margretta Lammot*
DL	*Daniel Lammot, Jr.*	MLDP	*Margretta (Lammot) du Pont*
EBS	*Elizabeth Beach Smith*	MP	*Minshall Painter*
ED	*Edward Darlington*	RSS	*Richard S. Smith*
EDP	*Eleuthera du Pont*	SDP	*Sophie du Pont*
EIDP	*E. I. du Pont*	SFDP	*Samuel Francis Du Pont*
	VB	*Victorine (du Pont) Bauduy*	

Part One
ROCKDALE IN 1850:
THE CLIMAX OF A WAY OF LIFE

Chapter 1: Sweet, Quiet Rockdale

1. EMHL, W9–21465, SDP to CS, Oct. 5, 1841.
2. Ashmead, 1884, p. 199.
3. *Vide* the discussion in Marx, 1964, of the idealized pastoral compromise between city and wilderness celebrated by many early nineteenth-century American authors.
4. See such advertisements *passim* in the *Upland Union.*

SLEEPY HOLLOW DAYS

1. Griffith's sketches are preserved in EMHL, Longwood MSS, Group 9, Residual, Box 1. According to the genealogical file at CCHS, he was born in 1819 and died in 1900. His later business connections with the Du Ponts on the Brandywine are recorded in the Records of E. I. du Pont de Nemours & Co. (Acc. 500), in Correspondence, Box 127, folder "Griffith, Joseph & Richard S."
2. HSP, Am. 1024, Vol. I, Journal of John Hill Martin, Sept. 24, 1856, p. 179.
3. EMHL, W9–26112, EBS to SDP, Oct. 4, 1857.
4. EMHL, W9–25288, CS to SDP, May, 17, 1838.

THE LORDS OF THE VALLEY

1. Crozer, 1861, pp. 58–60.
2. Interview with Samuel Tryens of Rockdale, July 18, 1969.
3. See Lemieux, 1976, for an extended account of the "culture of dying" in the nineteenth century, with data drawn largely from Delaware County.

THE SISTERHOOD

1. EMHL, W6–20, EBS to VB, Dec. 16, 1828.
2. EMHL, W9–25640, CS to SDP, Jan. 17, 1848.
3. EMHL, Acc. 761, Box 3, APL to MLDP, n.p., n.d.
4. *Ibid.*
5. EMHL, W10, Series E, transcripts 202 (notes on Robert Smith).
6. EMHL, W6, Series A, Box 15.
7. *Ibid.,* Folder 2.
8. EMHL, Acc. 761, Mrs. AVDP, Box 3, APL to MLDP, n.p., n.d.
9. *The Souvenir,* Vol. 2, No. 2, p. 15 (copy at PFL).
10. EMHL, W9–40380, diary of SDP, entry Nov. 28, 1832.
11. EMHL, W9–25532, CS to SDP, Nov. 4, 1845(?).
12. EMHL, W9–21612, SDP to CS, Nov. 14, 1845.
13. EMHL, W9–25580, CS to SDP, Nov. 21, 1846.
14. EMHL, W9–25825 and 25827, CS to SDP, April 8 and 19, 1852.
15. EMHL, W9–25835, CS to SDP, July 13, 1852.

16. EMHL, W9–26117, CS to SDP, Oct. 10, 1857.
17. Undated newspaper clippings from Mary Gilpin file, EMHL.
18. Karnes, 1970, p. 336.
19. The correspondence of CS and SDP at EMHL is of course the source of statements in this section not individually documented.

Chapter II: A Town of Mules and Widows

1. The demographic profile of the Rockdale manufacturing district and its constituent hamlets in 1850 is based, of course, on the manuscript schedules of the Seventh (1850) Census of population and the 1850 Census of Manufactures, both preserved in the National Archives, Washington, D.C. The district does not constitute an enumeration entity; the Delaware County schedules are organized by township, and the Rockdale district lies partly in Aston and partly in Middletown. Dissecting the Rockdale households from the rest of the schedules for these two townships proved to be a relatively simple task, however, because three other complementary bodies of data were available: the property map of Delaware County compiled by Dr. Joshua Ash (a resident of the county) and published in 1848 by Robert Smith of Philadelphia (copies at PSA, DCIS, DCHS, and CCHS); the county tax assessments for 1850 (DCCH), which list the names of workers renting tenements from Crozer and Riddle (in four of the seven hamlets); and Samuel Riddle's paybook for 1844 through March 1850 (DCHS). The boundaries of the Rockdale district were drawn by me on the Ash map (the lines being based on my own knowledge of the terrain, roads, factories, and settlement clusters, and on the ownership of land by mill owners and workers as displayed on the Ash map) and the district was divided among the seven hamlets. The census listed the occupation of males of sixteen or over, and the mill workers are thus identifiable by their designation as "factory man," "operative," "spinner" and "mule spinner," "weaver," "warper," "beamer," "machinist," "clerk," "loom boss," and "factory manager." Persons so identified are found in tight clusters separated by farmers. It is possible to identify many of the farmers on the Ash map, which shows the outlines of the real estate owned by major landowners (whose names are printed on the map). This makes it possible to follow the enumerator through the township to the boundaries of some of the hamlets. The clusters of mill workers can also be identified as occupants of particular hamlets by several other kinds of evidence: the inclusion in the census of some of the owners and manufacturers who are known to be associated with certain mills and therefore certain hamlets; the occurrence of a cluster of names both in the census schedule and also on the tax list; and the presence of a cluster of names in the census that also occur in the Riddle Pay Book for March 1850. These criteria made it possible to identify each operative and his family with a particular hamlet and usually with a particular factory.

The principal uncertainty has to do with the inclusion of farmers in the district. The boundaries of the district, as drawn on the map, include all operatives' households and a number of farms. The boundaries could, by being drawn more tightly, exclude some of these farmers, but not many—perhaps ten households in all—and I decided to draw the lines so as to include most of the farm households along the roads within the immediate watershed. Some small farmers and tradesmen whose properties lay in inter-hamlet areas within the district were sometimes difficult to assign to one hamlet or another.

The area of the district was determined by tracing the outline from the Ash map and transferring it to millimeter graph paper. The total area was then calculated by counting squares and multiplying by the scale factor.

2. See Smith's autobiographical statement in Martin, 1877, p. 460.

3. Callaghan's enterprise is described in a MS treatise of William Bagnall, edited by Victor Clark, entitled "Sketches of Manufacturing and Textile Establishments," and owned by the Baker Library at Harvard. Vol. 4 contains an account of Callaghan's textile factories and those of his sons.

THE SOCIAL STATIONS

1. The Ryedale genealogy (Ridlon, 1884) mentions "a Samuel Riddle residing at Glen-Riddle, in some way connected with the above family, but I have not the genealogy. I was introduced to him at the Family Meeting" (p. 160). The allusion to this man occurs as a footnote to the listing of the elder Samuel Riddle's children. It is no doubt this Samuel Riddle who is listed in the 1870 census as living in Middletown Township, working as a mill manager (presumably for Samuel Riddle), age forty-three, born in Ireland.

2. Richard S. Smith, 1884, pp. 119–20.

3. EMHL, Acc. 761, Box 3, APL to MLDP, n.p., n.d.

4. Martin, 1877, p. 332.

5. EMHL, Longwood MSS, AVDP Letters In, 1817–46, Box 3.

6. Martin, 1877, p. 457.

7. EMHL, Longwood MSS, Group 4, Box 5, notes "Relative to the Election for Directors held at The Columbia Ins. Office, July 2d., 1849."

8. EMHL, W9–26514, CS to SDP, Sept. 10, 1861.

9. EMHL, W9–40380, diary of SDP, Nov. 29, 1832.

10. The events surrounding the death of the wet-nurse's baby are described in EMHL, W9–26033, 26035, and 26037, CS to SDP, Jan. 17, Jan. 22, and Feb. 7, 1857.

11. Charlotte Elizabeth, 1847, p. 517.

12. EMHL, W9–25776, CS to SDP, Feb. 24, 1851. See also W9–25772, CS to SDP, Feb. 3, 1851, W9–26099, CS to SDP, Sept. 3, 1857, and entry in 1850 census for Aston Township listing the Elliot household.

13. EMHL, W9–26099, CS to SDP, Sept. 3, 1857.

14. EMHL, W9–21509, SDP to CS, July 31, 1843.

15. EMHL, W9–25526, CS to SDP, Sept. 16, 1845.

16. EMHL, W9–25910, CS to SDP, March 27, 1854.

17. EMHL, W9–25997, CS to SDP, April 7, 1856.

18. EMHL, W9–26185, CS to SDP, May 31, 1858.

19. PLTA, Letterbook Index B, Letters Rec. by Minshall Painter, 1815–64, No. 75: JPC to MP, Jan. 7, 1841.

20. The "middle class" is more difficult to document than the other two classes. The sketch here presented is based on a miscellany of sources: Ashmead, 1884, which contains a good deal of information about physicians, lawyers, schools, small farmers, and other members of the class; the U.S. census returns for 1850; and the correspondence of the Smith family at EMHL.

21. The social and economic profile of the mill workers in the period 1832–60 is drawn from NA, MS schedules of the U.S. census for Aston and Middletown townships, 1850 and 1860; and DCHS, the Parkmount Day Book, 1832–35, the Penn's Grove Pay Book, 1844–50, and the Penn's Grove Rent Book, 1847–53. Estimates of the cost of food are based on the standard calculations of the nutritional values of food substances published

by the Department of Agriculture (Watt and Merrill, 1963) and on food prices recorded by a nearby farmer, William Reynolds of Upper Chichester Township, who sold food directly to at least one family in Crozerville, and to nearby stores. Also consulted was Walker's study of *Hopewell Village* (1966), an iron-manufacturing community not far away, in the period up to 1841. Assuming a simple high-energy country diet, emphasizing pork and beef, bread and butter, hot cakes, potatoes, and coffee (providing adult males with 3,500 calories per day and adult females 3,000), the estimated daily cost is approximately $0.15 for the male and $0.13 for the female. This figure agrees with the statement that householders could profit from boarders paying $2 per week male and $1.25 per week female.

22. The Morris family's experience is recorded in detail in their letters 1829–46, published in Erickson (1972, pp. 139–74). This source contains detail on rentals and weekly boarding rates which have been used in the general discussion.

Part Two
ROCKDALE FROM 1825 TO 1835:
THE CREATING OF A WAY OF LIFE

Chapter III: *The Assembling of the Industrialists*

1. I am indebted to my former student David Kasserman's insights for the recognition of the conservative innovator as a type of social change agent. See his dissertation, *Conservative Innovation: Introduction of the Cotton Industry into the United States, 1789–1840.*
2. *Proceedings of the Delaware County Institute of Science*, Vol. 3 (1907), pp. 109–11.

THE FIRST ARRIVALS

1. HSP, Wm Martin Receipt Book; DCCH, Deed Book P, p. 257; Ferguson, 1965, p. 107.
2. In addition to the MS of part of his published history, and his father's receipt book, the HSP collection includes John Hill Martin's personal memoirs and journal, detailing the life of a West Point cadet and Philadelphia bachelor, various historical notes and lists, and miscellaneous personal correspondence.
3. See Porter and Livesay, 1971.
4. Martin, 1877, p. 419.
5. *Ibid.,* p. 348.
6. See the volumes of *McElroy's Philadelphia Directory* for the period 1823 to 1835; FI, Report of 1825 Exhibition, p. 30.
7. ANSP, Minutes, 1824 and 1825.
8. Bestor, 1970, p. 158.
9. FI, Report of 1825 Exhibition, p. 30.
10. The agreement is preserved at DCCH.
11. HSP, Lovering Collection, Joseph S. Lovering to Mary Lovering, July 23, 1829.
12. *Pa. Senate Journal,* 1837–38, Part 2, p. 283.
13. Walter M. Phillips and Clifford Lewis III, descendants of the two families, have very kindly allowed me to see the family records, particularly the recollections of John S. Phillips's sister Caroline Biddle of their early life in Philadelphia.
14. Crozer, 1861, p. 71.

15. *Ibid.*, p. 24.
16. Corner, 1972, p. 11.
17. Crozer, 1861, p. 87.
18. *Ibid.*, p. 161.
19. *Ibid.*, p. 53.
20. Crozer's early life is well documented in his autobiography (Crozer, 1861) and in a posthumous biography (J. Wheaton Smith, 1868).
21. Ashmead, 1884, p. 490.
22. EMHL, Pierre S. du Pont Coll., Series D, No. 29, Folder "Auctions" (broadside).
23. Boatman, MS, p. 14.
24. EMHL, Longwood MSS, Group 6, Box 2, JDC to EIDP, June 1, 1822, and June 4, 1822.
25. Boatman, MS, pp. 18–22.
26. EMHL, Acc. 1204, Folder 3 (sheriff's sale announced in the West Chester, Pa., *Village Record*).
27. Boatman, MS, p. 14.
28. EMHL, Longwood MSS, Group 6, Series B, JDC to EIDP, June 1 and 4, 1822, and EIDP to JDC, June 3, 1822.
29. Ashmead, 1884, pp. 620–1; DCCH, Tax Assessments, Middletown Township, 1823–25; Deed Book P, p. 721.
30. Ashmead, 1884, p. 620.
31. DCHS, *Upland Union*, Dec. 27, 1825.

THE FIRST CASUALTIES AND REPLACEMENTS

1. DCCH, Prothonotary's Office.
2. DCCH, Register of Deeds.
3. EMHL, E. B. du Pont Coll., File 143; *American Watchman*, July 4, 1826.
4. DCHS, *Upland Union*, Nov. 14, 1826.
5. EMHL, Acc. 500 (Records of E. I. du Pont de Nemours & Co., 1801–1902).
6. DCCH, Register of Deeds.
7. Cope, 1900.
8. *Biographical Directory of the American Congress,* 1774–1971, p. 777.
9. Ashmead, 1884, p. 249.
10. *Ibid.*, pp. 539–41.
11. *Ibid.*, p. 248.
12. DCHS, *Upland Union*, Nov. 8, 1825.
13. Martin, 1877, pp. 267–8; George E. Darlington, 1909, pp. 10–11, 70–1.
14. APS, Peale-Sellers Papers, Nathan Sellers to Coleman Sellers, n.d.
15. Information on Martin's financial difficulties is to be found in his deed of purchase in 1823 (DCCH, Deed Book P, p. 257), and the Tax Assessments for Aston and Middletown townships, reported on Nov. 17, 1828, also in DCCH; writ to the Sheriff of Delaware County, Prothonotary's Office, in the case of Peter Hill vs. William Martin, April 16, 1829; and HSP, William Martin Receipt Book, AM 1025.
16. DCCH, Prothonotary's Office, Peter Hill vs. William Martin, writ of April 16, 1829.
17. APS, Peale-Sellers Papers (B/P31/50), Coleman Sellers to Nathan Sellers, April 2, 1829.
18. APS, Peale-Sellers Papers (B/P31/50), Peter Hill to Nathan Sellers, Philadelphia, Sept. 10, 1822; Martin, 1877, pp. 141–2.
19. Martin, 1877, pp. 331–4; HSP, William Martin Receipt Books, entries 1829–32.

20. HSP, AM 1024, Vol. 1, Journal of John Hill Martin, pp. 178–9.
21. APS, Peale-Sellers Papers, DL to MLDP, May 26, 1829.
22. APS, Peale-Sellers Papers (B/P31/50), Coleman Sellers to R. C. Marsh, Dec. 29, 1829.
23. DCCH, Tax Assessments, Aston and Middletown townships, 1829–57; APS, Coleman Sellers' power of attorney to Peter Hill, Nov. 2, 1830.
24. DCCH, deed grantor and grantee lists, names of Peter Hill and George W. Hill; similarly Tax Assessments, Aston and Middletown townships, 1829–60.
25. APS, Peale-Sellers Papers, Lease of Lenni Cotton Factory, May 1, 1831; DCCH, Tax Assessments, Aston Township, under name of George W. Hill.
26. EMHL, DL to E. I. du Pont de Nemours & Co., Feb. 26, 1814.
27. Simpson, 1859, pp. 37–49.
28. EMHL, Winterthur MSS, Group 10, Series B, Box 40 (Eleuthera du Pont Smith Autobiography, Vol. 40, pp. 103–4).
29. EMHL, Letterbooks of Daniel Lammot (microfilm M-58.13), DL to Holland Weeks, July 23, 1825.
30. EMHL, Acc. 761, DL to MLDP, Nov. 15, 1824.
31. EMHL, Letterbooks of Daniel Lammot (microfilm M-58.13), DL to Holland Weeks, March 17/April 18, 1825.
32. EMHL, Longwood MSS, DL to EIDP, letters of March 16, April 6, April 9, May 7, May 10, May 17, June 6, June 10, and June 15, 1825.
33. EMHL, Group 7, Series A, Box 2 (1820–77), MLDP to Evelina du Pont, March 23, 1828.
34. EMHL, Acc. 761, Box 3, DL to MLDP, Kensington, May 26, 1829.
35. EMHL, Acc. 761, Box 3, APL to MLDP, n.p., n.d.
36. The date is confirmed by a letter of SDP to CS, Jan. 15, 1830, referring to the recent arrival of the Lammots at Lenni (EMHL, W9–21058).
37. EMHL, Acc. 761, Box 3, APL to MLDP, n.p., n.d. (different letter from note 35).
38. The family birth and baptismal records, preserved at the Swedenborgian Academy in Bryn Athyn, Pa., record no child born to Anna Potts Lammot between 1822 and Sept. 6, 1831. The condition of the roads is described in Sophie du Pont's letter cited in note 36.
39. Ridlon, 1884, p. 155.
40. Most of the information about the emigration of the Riddle family is derived from the Riddle genealogy published in 1884 by Ridlon. Biographical data, with substantially the same information, is also given in several of the biographical encyclopedias: Wiley, 1894, pp. 163–5; *Biographical Encyclopaedia of Pennsylvania in the 19th Century,* 1874; Robson, 1875, pp. 118–19.
41. The role of McDowell in managing the Springfield mill for the Riddles is detailed in the DCHS, Parkmount Day Book 1832–35, *passim.*
42. The details of the financial relations of Peter Hill and the Riddles are given in the DCHS, Parkmount Day Book, 1832–35, *passim.*
43. There is very little information about the earlier lives of Houghton and Garsed. See Ashmead, 1884, pp. 622–3, and the *Biographical Encyclopaedia of Pennsylvania in the Nineteenth Century,* 1874, pp. 289–99.

THE SMITH FAMILY

1. Martin, 1877, p. 456.
2. EMHL, Winterthur MSS (W–6), EBS to VB, October 1832.

3. The account of the Swedish episode is told in detail in Smith's autobiography of his early years (Smith, 1884).

4. See Martin, 1877, pp. 455–60, for a biographical sketch of Smith; see also his own memoirs (Smith, 1884) and the genealogy of the Smith family contained in Leach, 1912.

5. EMHL, W9–26061, RSS to SDP, July 8, 1857.

6. EMHL, W9–26112, EBS to VB [1857].

7. EMHL, W6, EBS to VB, October 1828.

8. Smith, 1884.

9. EMHL, W9–21126, SDP to CS, Jan. 15, 1830.

10. EMHL, W9–40253, obituary of E. B. Smith from *Delaware County Republican,* April 1871.

11. Elizabeth Smith's letters to Victorine Bauduy in EMHL, Winterthur MSS, W6.

12. RSS to C. E. McIlvaine, in [St. Andrew's Church], Alfred Lee, first Bishop of Delaware, 1888, p. 7.

13. CCR, Records, RSS to Missionary Society, April 1838.

14. EMHL, W9–21275, SDP to CS, March 20, 1833.

15. EMHL, W9–40351, diary of SDP, entry of Nov. 24, 1833.

16. Among Sophie du Pont's effects preserved at EMHL is an infant's knit cap labeled in her hand "My baby's cap Sept 25 1835" (Winterthur MSS, Group 9, Series F, Box 189).

17. EMHL, W9–40396, diary of SDP, entry of July 5, 1845.

18. EMHL, W9–21584, SDP to CS, Aug. 22, 1845.

19. EMHL, W9–21300, SDP to CS, May 27, 1834.

20. EMHL, W9–21584, SDP to CS, Aug. 22, 1845.

21. EMHL, W9–25194, CS to SDP, Jan. 2, 1834.

22. EMHL, W9–25369, CS to SDP, March 23, 1841.

23. EMHL, W9–25253, CS to SDP, July 22, 1836.

24. EMHL, W9–25282, CS to SDP, n.p., n.d.

25. EMHL, W9–25335, CS to SDP, March 28, 1840.

26. EMHL, W9–25232, CS to SDP, March 25, 1837 (?).

27. EMHL, W9–25640, CS to SDP, Jan. 17, 1848.

28. EMHL, W9–25231, CS to SDP, Feb. 25, [1837].

29. EMHL, W9–40355, diary of SDP, entry of April 23, 1837.

30. EMHL, W9–25488, CS to SDP, Sept. 18, 1844.

31. EMHL, W9–25642, CS to SDP, Jan. 31, 1848.

32. EMHL, W9–25332, CS to SDP, Jan. 22, 1840.

33. EMHL, W9–21606, SDP to CS, Oct. 24, 1845.

THE MECHANICAL KNOWLEDGE OF THE INDUSTRIALISTS

1. Crozer, 1861, pp. 55–7.

2. Sutcliffe, 1816. (An evaluation of Sutcliffe's career is given in Tann, 1974, pp. 80–9.)

3. For a favorable evaluation of the *Cyclopaedia,* see Harte, 1974.

4. Guest, 1823; Baines, 1835.

5. Nicholson, 1826.

6. James Montgomery, 1833, pp. i–ii.

7. Scott, 1840 (Bancroft's copy is now owned by EMHL), 1851.

8. Ure, 1835.

9. Snell, 1850; Baird, 1851.

10. Gilbert in Singer, 1958, Vol. 4, p. 427.

11. Nicholson, 1826.
12. Buchanan, 1841 (3rd edition).
13. Byrne, 1850, 1853(a), 1853(b), 1853(c).
14. EMHL, Longwood MSS, Bancroft Papers, DL to EIDP, April 9, 1825.
15. Crozer, 1861, p. 54.
16. NA, 1820 Census of Manufactures; Ashmead, 1884, p. 669.
17. EMHL, Longwood MSS, Bancroft Papers, Acc. 467, Items 986 and 987.
18. Jeremy, 1973(b), pp. 35–6.
19. Ashmead, 1884, pp. 399–400; Wiley, 1894, pp. 324–5.
20. Dennis Clark, 1972, pp. 40–9.
21. Ashmead, 1884, pp. 297, 621.

ENTERING THE COTTON MANUFACTURE IN THE 1820'S

1. Ashmead, 1884, p. 295; Sarah Trainer Smith, 1897.
2. Ashmead, 1914.
3. EMHL, Longwood MSS, Group 6, Box 2, DL to EIDP, June 15, 1825.
4. The details of the abortive negotiations are to be found in the correspondence among Daniel Lammot, E. I. du Pont, William Bryan, and Joshua Lippincott at EMHL, Longwood MSS, Group 6, Box 2, between the dates of March 16 and June 15, 1825.

Chapter IV: The Machines, Their Operatives, and the Fabrics

1. Leiper and Martin, 1826.

THE MILLS AND MILL SEATS

1. DCIS, MS map of Delaware County by John Hill, *c.* 1810; Pennsylvania State Land Office, MS map of Delaware County by John Melish, 1817.
2. Bining, 1938, p. 55.
3. General information on these early uses of the mill seats is to be found in Leiper and Martin, 1826, and Ashmead, 1884.
4. Leiper and Martin, 1826.
5. The foregoing account of the dams and races on Chester Creek is based on personal observation of the remains. No description survives (if ever one was written down) from the 1825–35 period.
6. DCHS, Parkmount Day Book, has a running account of expenses incurred in repairing the hydraulic system.
7. The description of the mills is derived in part from personal inspection (particularly of West Branch and Parkmount), in part from early photographs and sketches of mills on Chester Creek and on the Brandywine, and in part from the mill-seat survey (Leiper and Martin, 1826).
8. Data on the power transmission system within the mill must be derived from contemporary published accounts, such as Ure, 1835, and James Montgomery, 1833. The remains of the mills give little information because of subsequent changes in technology. Parkmount Day Book does however give some data corroborative of the above account.
9. See here also such early manuals as Ure, 1835, and James Montgomery, 1833.

THE SPINNING MACHINERY

1. This list of operations is based on William Martin's enumeration of his assets in machinery about 1829 (APS, Peale-Sellers Papers). It agrees in general with the contemporary descriptions in Sutcliffe, 1816, Ure, 1835, and James Montgomery, 1833, although these works described English practice. See also James Montgomery, 1840, for a somewhat later account of American practices in 1836.
2. DCHS, Parkmount Day Book, April 6, 1832.
3. DCIS, 6th Annual Exhibition (1860), list of awards.
4. Charlotte Elizabeth, 1847, pp. 537–8.
5. The account of the machines employed for spinning is derived from the usual early sources, such as Ure, 1835, and Montgomery, 1833; from information in the Parkmount Day Book; and from personal observation of early spinning and weaving machines at the Merrimac Textile Museum (which has a mule from the 1830's whose operation is recorded on film), Upper Canada Village (which has an operating mule from the 1830's spinning woolen yarn), and the National Museum of Science and Technology of the Smithsonian Institution, and of modern spinning and weaving machinery at the South Boston (Va.) Cotton Manufacturing Company, which still takes cotton in by the bale and sends it out as finished cloth.

THE WEAVING MACHINERY

1. McLane, 1833, Vol. 2, p. 200.
2. Erickson, 1972, p. 159.
3. *Ibid.,* pp. 159–61.
4. DCHS, Parkmount Day Book.
5. The description of Phillips' mill is drawn from the Leiper and Martin, 1826, mill-seat survey of Delaware County, pp. 3, 18–19. The general characteristics of power looms of this period are drawn from Batchelder, 1863, pp. 60–72; see also J. L. Bishop, 1904, Vol. 2, and English, 1969.

THE MACHINE SHOPS

1. NYHS, John Rogers Papers, John Rogers, Jr., to John Rogers, Sr., New York, Nov. 28, 1852.
2. Ferguson, 1975, pp. 160–1.
3. David H. Wallace, 1967.
4. NYHS, John Rogers, Jr., to John Rogers, Sr., Manchester, July 19, 1850.
5. Ferguson, 1975, pp. 55, 107, and the John Rogers Papers at NYHS.
6. NYHS, John Rogers, Jr., to John Rogers, Sr., Manchester, Dec. 24, 1850.
7. In this sketch of early machine shop practice, several sources have been particularly valuable: Ferguson, 1975, and APS, MS Memoirs of Nathan and Coleman Sellers; David H. Wallace, 1967; NYHS, Letters of John Rogers; Leavitt, 1969 (the Hollingsworth Letters); and HSD, the Poole letters.
8. DCHS, Parkmount Day Book, *passim.*
9. *Upland Union,* July 21, 1840, announcement of sheriff's sale.
10. DCHS, *Post Boy,* Dec. 3, 1822.

11. McLane, 1833, Vol. 2, p. 211.
12. DCHS, Parkmount Day Book.
13. *Upland Union,* "Assignees Sale," June 15, 1841.
14. *Biographical Encyclopaedia of Pennsylvania in the Nineteenth Century,* 1874, p. 298.
15. *Upland Union,* March 10, 1840.
16. The foregoing account of the Garsed power-loom factory and the associated events at the Penn's Grove mill seat has been put together from a number of sources: advertisements of sales of buildings and machinery in the *Upland Union* for Aug. 22, 1826, March 10, 1840, July 21, 1840, and June 15, 1841 (copies in DCHS), and in the West Chester *American Republican* for June 19, 1817 (copy at CCHS); the Tax Assessments for Aston and Middletown townships, DCCH, in the names of Nathan Sharpless, Peter and George W. Hill, Richard Garsed, and James Houghton; Garsed entries in the Parkmount Day Book; U.S. census schedules for Aston and Middletown townships for 1830 and 1840; the Morris letters in Erickson, 1972, pp. 158–61; the account in Ashmead, 1884, pp. 622–3; the sketch of Garsed in the *Biographical Encyclopaedia of Pennsylvania in the Nineteenth Century,* 1874, pp. 298–9; and *Journal of the Franklin Institute,* Vol. 4 (3rd series), 1847, p. 336.
17. The Hyde contract is at EMHL, Bancroft Papers (Acc. 736), Item 986–7.
18. This description of the use of local suppliers was assembled from data in DCHS, Parkmount Day Book; *McElroy's Philadelphia Directory,* 1837; HSP, William Martin's Receipt Book; *Upland Union,* June 15, 1841.
19. EMHL, Longwood MSS, Group 6, Series B, Daniel Lammot to E. I. du Pont, May 10, 1825.
20. EMHL, Bancroft Papers, Item 182: Journal of Rockford Mill 1831–32.
21. APS, Sellers Papers (B/P31), "Peter Hill Miscellaneous."
22. *Upland Union,* June 22, 1841.
23. *Ibid.*

COMMERCIAL ASPECTS OF COTTON MANUFACTURING

1. DCHS, Parkmount Day Book, is in itself an account of mill office activities. Other Riddle business records at DCHS in the 1840's and 1850's include the rent books and paybooks 1844–50. The Bancroft Papers at EMHL also provide a particularly clear picture of the business aspect of cotton manufacturing in this period.
2. McLane, 1833, Vol. 2, p. 211.
3. See Jeremy, 1971, for a discussion of yarn counts.
4. Leiper and Martin, 1826.
5. McLane, 1833, comments by Crozer (Vol. 2, p. 211), and Samuel and James Riddle (Vol. 2, pp. 225–6).
6. These are the firms from whom the Riddles bought cotton from 1832 to 1835. DCHS, Parkmount Day Book, *passim.*
7. The discussion of buying and selling practice is based on DCHS, Parkmount Day Book, *passim.*
8. McLane, 1833, Vol. 2, p. 211.
9. Erickson, 1972, p. 159.
10. *Ibid.,* p. 161.
11. *Pa. Senate Journal,* 1837–38, Part 2, p. 302.

WORKING IN PARKMOUNT MILL IN 1832

1. McLane, 1833, Vol. 2, p. 225.
2. Insurance survey of Parkmount Mill (courtesy of Aldon Rug Co.); personal inspection.
3. This arrangement, with the mules on the attic floor, the card room and preparation room on the second floor, and the other functions on the ground floor, conforms to the illustrations of English mills of the period, to contemporary description, and to my own observation of the South Boston Manufacturing Company's cotton mill on the Dan River, in southern Virginia, in the spring of 1973.
4. DCHS, Penn's Grove Rent Book (bound with Day Book).
5. The sketches of the workers' households are based on several sources of data: the U.S. censuses for 1830 through 1860 for Aston and Middletown townships, and for 1830 and 1840 for the rest of Delaware County, New Castle County, Delaware, and Philadelphia; the Parkmount Day Book, and the Penn's Grove Pay and Rent Books; Ridlon, 1884, the Ryedale genealogy for McDowell and the Maxwells; and Shaw's testimony in *Pa. Senate Journal*, 1837–38, Part 2, pp. 279–81.
6. *Pa. Senate Journal*, 1837–38, Part 2, p. 289.
7. DCHS, Parkmount Day Book, p. 128, accounting with George Horner, who in December 1833 was paid $18.94 for spinning 702 lbs. of cotton into 10,580 hanks of No. 15 yarn.
8. *Pa. Senate Journal*, 1837–38, Part 2, p. 305.
9. *Ibid.*, p. 301.
10. *Ibid.*, p. 306.
11. *Ibid.*, pp. 347–8, 292.
12. *Ibid.*, pp. 288, 313.
13. *Ibid.*, pp. 329, 280–1.

THE PRODUCT: THE FABRICS OF CHESTER CREEK

1. McLane Report, 1833, Vol. 2, p. 225.
2. DCIS, MS Correspondence, John P. Crozer to Minshall Painter, November 1845.
3. Information about the types of fabrics woven comes from three main sources: the Parkmount Day Book, 1832–35 (DCHS); the Penn's Grove Pay Book, 1844–50 (DCHS); and the 1850 Census of Manufactures (NA). The daybook includes the period when the Riddles were buying looms from the Garseds and first setting up, and gives one instance of cloth construction specifications. The pay book lists piece rates for all the types of cloth woven in the mill. The census lists the types, quantities, and values of the products of all the mills. Ashmead, 1884, gives some information about fabrics and prizes, as do the *Journals* of the Franklin Institute and the annual exhibition records of the Delaware County Institute of Science.

Chapter V: The Inventors of the Machines

1. *Pa. Senate Journal*, 1837–38, Part 2, p. 326.
2. Crozer, 1861, p. 56.
3. McLane, 1833, Vol. 2, p. 211.
4. EMHL, Acc. 761, Box 3: DL to ML, Kensington, May 26, 1829.

5. James Montgomery, 1833, pp. 56–7.
6. Erickson, 1972, p. 161.

THE MAIN SEQUENCE OF INVENTIONS

1. The most authoritative account of the mule and its history is given in Catling, 1970, and the following account is based to a large extent on this work.
2. Ure, 1835, pp. 152–5.
3. Snell, 1850, pp. vi, 184.
4. James Montgomery, 1833, p. 195; see also *Journal of the Franklin Institute,* Vol. 20 (1835), p. 356.
5. BLH, Bagnall MS; Webber, 1879, pp. 51–4.
6. EMHL, Joseph Bancroft "Machinery Account" (ledger 1831–46).
7. DCHS, Day Book, entry p. 128 re George Horner; Pay Book, Jan. 13, 1844.
8. DCIS, vault, Report of 5th Annual Exhibition, 1850.
9. EMHL, "Illustrated Catalogue of Machines Built by Alfred Jenks & Son [1853]," p. 64.
10. Webber, 1879, pp. 66–73.
11. Sandberg, 1970, pp. 120–40. General accounts of improvements in the throstle may be found in Batchelder, 1863, Bishop, 1864, and Clark, 1916.
12. Garsed's biography may be found in the *Biographical Encyclopaedia of Pennsylvania in the Nineteenth Century,* 1874, pp. 298–9.
13. Report of Franklin Institute Exhibition, 1842, pp. 4–5, and 1844, pp. 377–9.
14. *Journal of the Franklin Institute,* 3rd series, Vol. 14 (1847), pp. 170–1. See also U.S. Dept. of Commerce, Patent Office, patent no. 4645, "Looms for twilling, operating treadle cams in."
15. *Biographical Encyclopaedia of Pennsylvania in the Nineteenth Century,* 1874, p. 298.
16. See Richard Garsed's U.S. patent no. 6845.
17. General accounts of loom improvements are to be found in Jeremy, 1973(a), English, 1969, Copeland, 1912, and Lincoln, 1932 and 1933.

THE LESSER INVENTORS OF CHESTER CREEK

1. *Journal of the Franklin Institute,* Vol. 6 (1828), Part 2, p. 263.
2. Silliman, 1833, pp. 70–1.
3. See English, 1969, pp. 99–104, 195, and Jeremy, 1973(a), pp. 54–5, 60–1, 64–6, for an outline of the main sequence of inventions in warping and sizing.
4. The details on the Riddles' sizing trough are drawn from the Riddle Day Book, entries of Nov. 13 and 15, 1833, Jan. 1, 1834, July 18, 1834, and *passim* after November 1833 for purchases of coal (DCHS).
5. Dutton, 1848, pp. 17–18.
6. *Ibid.,* Preface.
7. Bigelow, 1831, p. 264.
8. The account of the Duttons is derived in part from Cope, 1871, pp. 57–9; Dutton, 1848; Ashmead, 1884, pp. 290–3 and 620; Martin, 1877, pp. 247, 251; and NA, Patent Office Records, particularly nos. 3080 (ice accumulation) and 4697 (ice manufacture).
9. Massachusetts Historical Society, Lowell Papers, Thos. Odiorne to Jos. Whipple, Exeter, June 15, 1791.

10. BLH, Boston Manufacturing Company account books.
11. CCHS, Chester and Delaware Co. *Village Record,* Jan. 9, 1811.
12. Sarah Trainer Smith, 1897.
13. Thomas Odiorne, 1792.
14. Leggett, 1874.
15. James C. Odiorne, 1875.
16. Bathe and Bathe, 1943, p. 53.
17. *Ibid.,* pp. 177–8.
18. NA, U.S. Census of Mfrs., 1820, Pennsylvania, "Henry Moore."
19. Chapin, 1860, p. 163.
20. NA, Patent Office Records, Thomas Odiorne patents of Aug. 27 and Sept. 26, 1835.
21. Ferguson, 1965, p. 92.
22. Accounts of Nathan Sellers are to be found in Ferguson, 1965, and in his grandson George Escol Sellers' "Recollections" of his grandfather, in APS, Peale-Sellers Papers.

THE INTERNATIONAL FRATERNITY OF MECHANICIANS

1. Jeremy, 1973(b); Wilkinson, 1963.
2. Ferguson, 1965, p. 112.
3. HSD, Poole Papers; Ferguson, 1965, pp. 46–61; NYHS, Letters of John Rogers, 1850–55.
4. Cantwell, 1961, pp. 143, 234.
5. See the biography of Bishop Hopkins by his son, Hopkins, 1873.
6. Bradley, 1972, p. viii.
7. APS, George Escol Sellers, "Personal Recollections of Coleman Sellers."
8. See Ferguson, 1965, *passim* for an edition of the memoirs of George Escol Sellers, which describe the mechanics' world of Philadelphia in the 1820's and 1830's.
9. See Charles Coleman Sellers, 1939, 1947, for a fine biography of Peale.
10. HSD, Poole Papers, Letters of J. Morton Poole 1830–37.
11. Ferguson, 1965, provides an intimate picture of the relations among the mechanicians.
12. Except as otherwise specified, the materials on the Philadelphia and Brandywine mechanicians are drawn from Ferguson, 1965, Wilkinson, 1963, and Jeremy, 1973(b).
13. In conversation with Eugene Ferguson, it appeared that he and the writer had independently estimated the size of the community at about the same number, in the neighborhood of three hundred.
14. See Kuhn, 1970, and Anthony F. C. Wallace, 1972, for discussions of the concept of paradigmatic community.

THE SELLERS FAMILY

1. The sources of these genealogical details are Ashmead, 1884, pp. 546–50; the biographies of Coleman and William Sellers in Allen Johnson, *et al.,* DAB, 1928–73; and the genealogy in Ferguson, 1965, pp. xiv–xix. See also McCullough, 1972, pp. 485–7.
2. Ferguson, 1965, pp. 7–8.
3. APS, Peale-Sellers Papers, "Personal Recollections of Coleman Sellers," by George Escol Sellers, pp. 1–2, 18–19.
4. *Ibid.,* pp. 24–5.
5. *Ibid.,* pp. 1–2.

6. Ashmead, 1884, p. 549.
7. Allen Johnson, *et al.*, DAB 1928–73, William Sellers; Scharf, 1888, pp. 780–2; Ashmead, 1884, pp. 548–50; HSD, Letters of John Morton Poole to Joseph Bancroft; Sinclair, 1969.
8. Wilkinson, 1963, pp. 4–5; Charles Coleman Sellers, 1947, Vol. 2, pp. 285–6.
9. Charles Coleman Sellers, 1947, Vol. 2., pp. 286–7, 295–6.
10. APS, Peale-Sellers Papers, "Personal Recollections of Coleman Sellers," by George Escol Sellers, pp. 25–7; Charles Coleman Sellers, 1947, Vol. 2, pp. 348–9.
11. Ferguson, 1965, p. 80.

THE FRANKLIN INSTITUTE

1. Ferguson, 1965, p. 38.
2. See, for example, Lyon, 1799, and Claxton, 1839.
3. The definitive study of the founding and early history of the Franklin Institute is Sinclair, 1974.
4. FI, First Annual Report, 1825.
5. Sinclair, 1974, p. 61.
6. Robison, 1822, Vol. 2, pp. vii–viii.
7. Ferguson, 1965, p. 170.
8. FI, Franklin Institute of Exhibitions, Vol. 1, 1825, pp. 8, 30.
9. See the cotton exhibit sections of the *Journal, passim.*
10. FI, Archives, MS Committee on Water Power.
11. See Burke, 1847, and Sinclair, 1974.
12. *Journal of the Franklin Institute,* Vol. 7 (March 1831), pp. 145–6. A thorough study of the history of the science and technology of water wheels is to be found in Reynolds, 1973; this source indicates that the Franklin Institute Committee was seemingly not aware of the extent of the theoretical advances in the understanding of the physics of the subject that had been made in France in the eighteenth century.
13. *Ibid,* p. 147.
14. FI, Archives, MS Committee on Water Power.
15. As noted in Sinclair, 1974, pp. 147–8.

THINKING ABOUT MACHINERY

1. See Kuhn, 1970, and Anthony F. C. Wallace, 1972.

Part Three
ROCKDALE FROM 1835 TO 1850:
THE STRUGGLE FOR CONTROL OF A WAY OF LIFE

Chapter VI: *The Enlightenment's Last Campaign*

THE FREETHINKERS OF CHESTER CREEK

1. John K. Zeilin's notice of the debate on Owen's system is to be found in the *Upland Union,* Jan. 17, 1826; details of his career in Ashmead, 1884, p. 250.

2. *Upland Union,* July 11, 1826.

3. The participation of John S. Phillips in the meetings of the Academy of Natural Sciences of Philadelphia is detailed in the minutes of that organization for 1824 and 1825. Information about his visits to the Brandywine, and the impression he made on the ladies there, came from EMHL, particularly the Tancopanican Chronicle, 1830–33, the diary of Sophie du Pont and her letters to Clementina Smith, and the correspondence of Elizabeth Mackie Smith (Mrs. Francis Gurney Smith) with her daughter-in-law Eleuthera (du Pont) Smith. See also Deacon, 1851, for *Warreniana.*

4. PLTA, Letterbook Index F, Minshall Painter to Ann Tyler, June 23, 1857.

5. PLTA, *Reminiscence; Gleanings and Thoughts,* No. 1 (privately printed by the Painters, 1870).

6. The museum and library of the Institute are still open to the public. DCIS, MSS in vault (membership lists, annual reports, minutes, and correspondence), provided additional information on the early activities of the Institute.

7. Smith, 1868, pp. 97–9.

8. PLTA, Letterbook Index F, Minshall Painter to Ann Tyler, June 23, 1857.

9. CCR, Records, RSS to the Missionary Society of St. James Church, Philadelphia, April 1838.

10. Erickson, 1972, pp. 157, 168.

11. HSP, William Martin's Receipt Book, *passim.*

12. Lima Methodist Church, Antiquities, Minutes by William Fox, 1870–2.

THE CONTEXT OF POST-REVOLUTIONARY RADICALISM
IN THE LOWER DELAWARE VALLEY

1. Selsam, 1971, p. 217.

2. *Ibid.,* p. 211.

3. The discussion of the 1776 constitution is based largely on Selsam, 1971, and Tinkcom, 1950. Fertig, 1926, published the texts of the several constitutions of Pennsylvania.

4. Volney, 1890 (original edition 1791), p. 17.

5. The Jefferson-Maclure-Volney-Paine connection is documented in Chinard, 1923.

6. See Marx, 1964.

7. Hardy, Jensen, and Wolfe, 1966. See also Morton, 1844, for an early appreciation of Maclure's career.

8. Neef, 1808, pp. 2–3.

9. Hagner, 1869, pp. 36–8.

10. Lowell H. Harrison, 1949, pp. 322–5.

11. Farragut, 1879, p. 49.

12. See Hackensmith, 1973, for a detailed biography of Neef.

13. Details of Mme Fretageot's school in Philadelphia are to be found in her correspondence with Maclure, published in Bestor, 1948.

14. B. G. du Pont, 1930, pp. 177–81.

15. EMHL, W9–25129, Ella DP to SDP, Nov. 25, 1823.

16. EMHL, W9–25143, Ella DP to SDP, April 18, 1825.

17. ANSP, Founding Minutes, as quoted in Mautner MS, p. 4.

18. Mautner MS, p. 9.

19. The best general account of the social reformist activities of members of the Academy in its early years is to be found in the 1973 MS of Nancy Mautner. See also APS, MS Acc.

No. 258, "A Biographical Sketch of the late Thomas Say," January 1835.

20. APS, Peale-Sellers Papers, John Wilson to Coleman Sellers, Jan. 24, 1820.
21. Bestor, 1948, p. 303.
22. *Ibid.*, p. 307.
23. WINH, New Harmony MSS, Series S, Folder 11, No. 14, John Speakman to Thomas Speakman, Pittsburgh, *c.* 1823.
24. Bestor, 1948, p. 305.
25. APS, George Ord Papers, George Ord to Charles Waterton, May 15, 1834.

PREACHING THE NEW MORAL WORLD

1. Lafayette's itinerary is given day by day in Nolan, 1934. For events in Chester, see Martin, 1877, pp. 253–9.
2. Details of Fanny Wright's association with Lafayette are given in Perkins and Wolfson, 1939, and Waterman, 1924.
3. Bestor, 1948, pp. 311–12.
4. APS, Peale-Sellers Papers, "Personal Recollections of Coleman Sellers," by George Escol Sellers, pp. 46–7.
5. Bestor, 1948, p. 314.
6. *New Harmony Gazette,* Vol. I, July 30, 1826, as quoted in Bestor, 1970, p. 222.
7. Drinnon, 1972, pp. 220–1.
8. Perkins and Wolfson, 1939, p. 171.
9. The classic study of the New Harmony experiment, cast in the context of other socialist and religious communities of the day, is of course Bestor, 1970.
10. WINH, Ella du Pont to Mme Fretageot, Feb. 10, 1826.
11. WINH, Victor du Pont to Mme Fretageot, Feb. 21, 1826.
12. EMHL, WS-3467, Rey to M. and Mme du Pont, April 14, 1826.
13. John P. Crozer, 186, p. 46.
14. Snedeker, 1942, p. 204.
15. Elizabeth Montgomery, 1851, p. 36.
16. McLane, 1833, Vol. 2, pp. 817–18. See also EMHL, Hancock MS, 1956–58.
17. See Claussen, 1970, for an account of the life of Reuben Haines.
18. Snedeker, 1942, pp. 311–13.
19. *Ibid.*
20. *Ibid.*, p. 209.
21. Bestor, 1970, p. 202; *Niles' Register,* Dec. 31, 1825.
22. HSP, Constitution of the Friendly Association, 1826.
23. WINH, Maclure to Fretageot, July 24 and July 31, 1826; CCHS, *Village Record* of West Chester, Pa., March 15, 1826; Woodman, 1922 (original edition 1850), pp. 100–2.
24. Knight, 1880, pp. 16–18.
25. Robert Dale Owen, 1874, pp. 234–6.
26. White and Taylor, 1871, p. 158; *Niles' Weekly Register,* Dec. 31, 1825.
27. WINH, Diary of William Maclure, August 25, 1825.
28. An early account of the community by a contemporary resident in the area, although not a member of the commune, is found in Woodman, 1922, pp. 100–2.
29. CCHS, *Village Record,* March 15, 1826.
30. Wendall P. Fox, 1911.
31. WINH, Maclure to Fretageot, July 31 and September 19, 1826.

32. Woodman, 1922, pp. 100–2.
33. WINH, Maclure to Fretageot, July 31, 1826.
34. Knight, 1880, pp. 16–17; White and Taylor, 1871, pp. 158–9.
35. The events in this section have been well chronicled by several labor historians in secondary works. Of particular value is Louis H. Arky, "The Mechanics Union of Trade Associations and the Formation of the Philadelphia Workingmen's Movement," 1952. See also Leonard Bernstein, "The Working People of Philadelphia from Colonial Times to the General Strike of 1835," 1950; Edward Pessen, "The Workingmen's Movement of the Jacksonian Era," 1956; Edward Pessen, *Most Uncommon Jacksonians: The Radical Leaders of the Early Labor Movement*, 1967; William A. Sullivan, *The Industrial Worker in Pennsylvania, 1800–1840*, 1955; John R. Commons (ed.), *History of Labor in the United States*, Vol. 1, 1918. Robert Owen's "Address" of June 25, 1827, at the Franklin Institute was printed in Philadelphia in 1827 and a copy is located at the APS. The HSP has an incomplete series of the *Mechanic's Free Press* from 1828 to 1831.

Chapter VII: The Evangelical Counterattack

1. The Presbyterian Historical Society in Philadelphia possesses many of Ely's publications, including his sermons and books, and his MS, *Memoirs of his own life and times.*
2. The sermon was reprinted in Philadelphia in 1828 by W. F. Geddes; a copy is held by the Presbyterian Historical Society.

CALVARY CHURCH IN ROCKDALE

1. Martin, 1877, p. 459.
2. Smith and Cole, 1935, pp. 60, 76.
3. EMHL, W9–25194, CS to SDP, Jan. 2, 1834.
4. EMHL, W9–21299, SDP to CS, Feb. 9, 1834.
5. DCHS, Parkmount Day Book.
6. Erickson, 1972, p. 159.
7. Crozer, 1861, p. 78.
8. EMHL, Genealogy of Smith Family by F. W. Leach.
9. EMHL, SDP to CS, W9–21299, Feb. 9, 1834.
10. DCCH, Register of Deeds, S496, T590.
11. CCR, Records, Letter of RSS, April 1838.
12. *Ibid.*
13. This account of the organization of the church from 1833 to 1841 is derived from a number of sources: R. S. Smith's MS letter of April 1838 in the Records of Calvary Church, in Rockdale; R. S. Smith's letter to B. P. Smith, Aug. 18, 1875, pp. 6–10, in [St. Andrew's Church], Alfred Lee, first Bishop of Delaware, 1888; Smith's account as given to John Hill Martin in Martin's, 1877, *Chester (and Its Vicinity)*, pp. 459–60; and two pamphlet histories of Calvary Church published in 1933 and 1958 on the occasion of the church's 100th and 125th anniversaries.
14. Ferguson, 1965, pp. 40–2.
15. Biographies of Bishop Hopkins are found in DAB and in Hopkins, 1873.
16. This sketch of the composition of the congregation is based on several sets of records: the U.S. census schedules for Aston and Middletown townships for the years 1830–60; the MS book of records of baptisms, marriages, confirmations, and burials of Calvary

Church; the WPA listing of grave markers in Calvary Church cemetery (DCHS, WPA Project #4889, 1936–37); the list of contributors to the wardens and vestrymen. See also John K. Murphy's pamphlet, *To the Communicants and Members of the Congregation of Calvary Church, Rockdale, c.* 1861 (HSP, VoD*/.58 Vol. II).

17. Lee, 1856, pp. 8–9.
18. Lee, 1841.
19. EMHL, W9–25320, CS to SDP, Aug. 20, 1839.
20. EMHL, W9–25368, CS to SDP, March 23, 1841.
21. EMHL, W9–21451, SDP to CS, March 17, 1841.
22. Alfred Lee's life and views have been summarized in a biographical sketch published by the congregation of St. Andrew's Church in Wilmington in 1889. His early career at Rockdale is described in a series of letters from Clementina Smith to Sophie du Pont, 1839 to 1841 (Eleutherian Mills Historical Library, Winterthur Collection, W9–25308 to 25383). A number of his sermons have been published, including a Farewell Discourse to the Rockdale congregation (see Delaware County Historical Society for this); his sermons at St. Andrews in Wilmington are preserved at Eleutherian Mills Historical Library. The early Sunday School is also described in Clementina's letters from 1834 to 1841, W9–25207 to 25383, and in Sophie's letters to Clementina, also at Eleutherian Mills, W9–21301 to 21464.
23. See Potter, 1841(a).
24. CCR, Letter of RSS, April 1838; [St. Andrew's Church] a biography of Bishop Lee, 1888, p. 7 (RSS to C. E. McIlvaine, Aug. 18, 1875).
25. The Brandywine Manufacturers' Sunday School records are at EMHL; particularly valuable is the Receiving Book (Acc. 839, Box 1, Folder 3), which records the particulars of all children and their families (including the Miles and Miller families). Other data on the Miles and the Millers came from the U.S. census of 1850 and from the Penn's Grove Pay Book (DCHS). Sophie's diary contains several valuable accounts of her dealings with Maria Miles.
26. EMHL, W9–40379, diary of SDP, Nov. 18, 1832.
27. *Ibid.*, Nov. 6, 1833.
28. *Ibid.*, July 15, 1839.
29. NA, U.S. census 1850, Pennsylvania, Delaware County, Middletown Township.
30. EMHL, W9–25275, CS to SDP, Aug. 8, 1837.
31. EMHL, W9–25618, CS to SDP, July 28, 1847.
32. EMHL, W9–25523, CS to SDP, Aug. 26, 1845.
33. Govan, 1959, pp. 346–7.
34. EMHL, W9–25462, CS to SDP, March 9, 1844.
35. EMHL, W9–25526, CS to SDP, Aug. 1, 1845.
36. EMHL, W9–25480, CS to SDP, July 2, 1844.
37. EMHL, W9–25810, CS to SDP, Jan. 5, 1852.

THE BENEVOLENT WORK OF OTHER MANUFACTURERS

1. Staughton's career as briefly described in Keen, 1899, and Newman, 1898.
2. Samuel Crozer, 1902, pp. 17–18.
3. Crozer, 1861, p. 72.
4. Samuel Crozer, 1902; see also Charles W. W. Bishop, 1855.

5. Ashmead, 1884, p. 615.
6. Crozer's flirtation with Presbyterianism is revealed in Kruse's "Historical Sketch" of the Middletown Presbyterian Church (September 1920); in Ashmead, 1884, p. 615; in Kruse, 1922; and in Crozer's four letters to Robert Landis, 1833 to 1836, in the Presbyterian Historical Society, Philadelphia.
7. EMHL, W9–25231, CS to SDP. Although the letter is not dated by year, internal evidence makes 1837 the only possible date.
8. Samuel Crozer, 1902.
9. *Pa. Senate Journal*, 1837–38, Part 2, pp. 305–6.
10. The *Upland Union* regularly reported the activities of the benevolent societies in the neighborhood; see for items cited here the issues of Jan. 20, 1829, April 13 and June 1, 1841, and May 7, 1844. Martin, 1877, pp. 235–7, gives an extended account of the Bible Society and the formation of the Tract Society. For an account of the meeting at Calvary Church, see EMHL, W9–25371, CS to SDP, June 1, 1841.
11. Ridlon, 1884, Ryedale genealogy, p. 159.
12. Ashmead, 1884, pp. 300–1; "100th Anniv. Souvenir of Mt. Hope Methodist Church."
13. Ashmead, 1884, p. 300.
14. Ashmead, 1884, p. 617; "100th Anniv. of Lima M.E. Church."
15. Ridlon, 1884, Ryedale genealogy, pp. 158–9.
16. See Anthony F. C. Wallace, 1970, for an account of the early years of this mission.
17. Cope, 1871, pp. 57–9.
18. APS, Peale-Sellers Papers, Correspondence, Box, 1837–44. Peter Hill to Elizabeth Hill, March 27, 1842.
19. Humphrey's practice is commented on in EMHL, Clementina and Sophie's correspondence; his treatment of Riddle employees is remarked in the Parkmount Day Book, DCHS.
20. EMHL, Letterbooks of Daniel Lammot, Jr. (microfilm M-58.13. Acc. 801), DL to James Hargrove, Jan. 1, 1825.
21. *Ibid.*, DL to Howard Weeks, March 8, 1825.
22. EMHL, W9–40392, diary of Sophie du Pont, May 22, 1840.
23. Swedenborgian School of Religion, DL to Chas. Doughty, Penn's Grove, Dec. 28, 1843. For a general account of Philadelphia, and Swedenborgianism in the nineteenth century, see Swank, 1970.

MORAL ORDER IN THE MILLS

1. *Pa. Senate Journal*, 1837–38, Part 2, pp. 280, 302.
2. DCHS, Parkmount Day Book, *passim.*
3. *Pa. Senate Journal*, 1837–38, Part 2, pp. 280, 300, 304.
4. *Hazard's Register of Pennsylvania*, Vol. 12, p. 16 (April 19, 1834).
5. *Pa. Senate Journal*, 1837–38, Part 2, pp. 279–81, 283–5, 299–307.
6. *Ibid.*, p. 305.
7. Snedeker, 1942, p. 195.
8. *Hunt's Merchant's Magazine*, 1846, pp. 370–1.
9. *Pa. Senate Journal*, 1837–38, Part 2, pp. 301–2.
10. *Ibid.*, pp. 304–6.
11. *Pa. Senate Journal*, 1837–38, Part 1, p. 326.
12. Potter, 1841, pp. 258–9, 262–3.

THE RISE OF POLITICAL ANTI-MASONRY

1. For an excellent review of popular freethinkers and their enemies, see Post, 1974.
2. James C. Odiorne, 1830, p. 222.
3. See Post, 1974, pp. 218–19.
4. Speakman's letter to Thomas Say from Pittsburgh, undated, is to be found in the library of the Workingmen's Institute at New Harmony, Indiana.
5. Anne Royall is the subject of an excellent biography (James, 1972). Anne Royall on Ely is quoted on p. 124; the episode in Burlington is described on pp. 211–13; the harassment and trial in Washington, on pp. 250–62.
6. Information on Darlington's career in the House has been culled from a number of scattered sources: records of his speeches and votes in Gale and Seaton's *Register of Debates in Congress,* 23rd, 24th, and 25th Congresses, the *Congressional Globe* (25th Congress), and the *Journal of the House of Representatives;* his political correspondence in CCHS; and letters from his constituents in the Darlington Papers, DCHS.
7. James C. Odiorne, 1830, pp. 224–5.
8. *Ibid.,* pp. 43–44.
9. Robison, 1797 edition, pp. 138–9.
10. Barruel, 1799.

DEFEATING THE INFIDELS ON CHESTER CREEK

1. CCR, Letter of RSS, April 1838.
2. EMHL, W9–21301, 21398, 21473, SDP to CS, Sept. 3, 1834, Oct. 6, 1839, Feb. 6, 1842.
3. CCR, RSS to Alfred Lee, Aug. 1, 1838.
4. CCR, "Sequel" to RSS letter of April 1838. Written about 1843, two years after Lee's departure in 1841.

Chapter VIII: The Emergence of Christian Industrialism

THE RECESSION OF 1834 TO 1842

1. DCHS, George E. Darlington Papers, JPC to ED, April 1, 1834.
2. DCHS, Parkmount Day Book, pp. 152, 247–9.
3. Crozer, 1861, 78–9.
4. DCCH, Deed Books U, p. 263, and V, p. 630.
5. Ashmead, 1914, caption of portrait of J. P. Crozer facing p. 42.
6. Crozer, 1861, p. 80.
7. *Pa. Senate Journal,* 1837–38, Part 2, p. 302.
8. Erickson, 1972, pp. 162, 164.
9. Ashmead, 1884, pp. 621, 623; DCHS, Samuel Riddle's Rent Book (Riddle managed Houghton's estate for Farnum).
10. Ashmead, 1884, p. 296.
11. The details of Daniel Lammot's business affairs in the period 1835 to 1842 are contained in a series of letters to Alfred du Pont at EMHL, Longwood MSS, Group 5, Series A, Box 13. The accounts of the contract weaving arrangement are also at EMHL in business memoranda to E. I. du Pont de Nemours & Co., Aug. 21, 1837, to Nov. 27, 1837.

THE STRIKES OF 1836 AND 1842

1. Ashmead, 1884, p. 109; PLTA, JPC to Minshall Painter, Jan. 7, 1841; Commons, 1918, Vol. 1, p. 476.
2. *Pa. Senate Journal,* 1837–38, Part 2, pp. 279–81.
3. PHS, JPC to R. Landis, Jan. 31, 1836; DCIS, MSS, copy of Hannah Dutton's register, 6 mo 27, 1836.
4. EMHL, Longwood MSS, Group 5, Series A, Box 13, DL to AVDP, May 18, 1836.
5. EMHL, Longwood MSS, Group 4, Series A, Box 3, DL to AVDP, circa June 1836.
6. PLTA, Letterbook Index BJPC to Minshall Painter, Jan. 7, 1841.
7. *Pa. Senate Journal,* 1837–38, Part 2, pp. 280–1, 357–9.
8. *Upland Union,* open letter of Hiram McConnell, June 7, 1842.
9. J. Wheaton Smith, 1868, pp. 77–9.
10. *Upland Union,* open letter of Hiram McConnell, May 3, 1842.
11. J. Wheaton Smith, 1868, p. 78.
12. Ashmead, 1884, p. 235.
13. *Upland Union,* June 7, 1842.
14. Except as otherwise noted, the description of the events of the strike is drawn from the public press. The principal source is the paraphrase of testimony at the trial that was printed in the Philadelphia *Public Ledger,* May 30, May 31, June 1, and June 3, 1842. The *Public Ledger* also published Judge Bell's charge to the jury on July 27; the *Upland Union* published the charge on Aug. 9. The *Upland Union* printed two open letters from Hiram McConnell, May 3, and June 7, 1842, and news of the strike and its aftermath on April 5, April 12, May 31, June 21, and June 28. The *Delaware County Republican* was not sympathetic to the strikers and printed only one straight news story after the trial was over, on June 3, 1842.
15. The principles of organization in the traditional crafts are reviewed in Commons, 1910, 1918, 1926, and in Sullivan, 1955, and both authorities list the unions and strike actions in Pennsylvania in this period. See David Montgomery, 1972, for an account of the Kensington hand-loom weavers. The differing principles of the cotton workers' organization are not clearly formulated in the general surveys but become evident in the data on specific actions, like the strikes in 1836 and 1842.
16. The names of the 1842 strikers charged with conspiracy and riot are given in the records of the case in Court of Sessions, May 1842 (Delaware County Court House), and in the account of the strike in the *Public Ledger.* Dossiers on each of these men were collated from the U.S. census schedules for Aston and Middletown townships, 1790 through 1860; from the Parkmount Day Book, the Penn's Grove Rent Book, the Penn's Grove Pay Book; Delaware County Tax Assessment Records 1825 to 1860; the records of Calvary Church, Middletown Presbyterian Church, Lima Methodist Church, and Mount Hope Methodist Church; and the WPA grave marker survey for these churches.
17. *Upland Union,* June 7, 1842, April 5, 1842, and May 10, 1842 (quoting *Delaware County Republican*).
18. *Delaware County Republican,* July 8, 1842.
19. J. Wheaton Smith, 1868, pp. 80–1.
20. *Delaware County Republican,* July 1, 1842.
21. EMHL, W9–25414, CS to SDP, Rockdale, June 28, 1842.
22. Philadelphia *Public Ledger,* July 27, 1842; *Upland Union,* Aug. 9, 1842.

THE GREAT FLOOD

1. Ashmead, 1884, pp. 99–100.
2. Except as otherwise noted, the account of the flood is drawn primarily from the seventy-nine-page technical paper "The Flood of 1843," prepared in 1843 and 1844 by a committee of the Delaware County Institute of Science, composed of Dr. George Smith, John P. Crozer, and Minshall Painter. This account was republished in the *Proceedings* of the DCIS, Vol. 6, Nos. 1 and 2, 1910. Other details can be found in Ashmead, 1884, pp. 99–108, and in J. Wheaton Smith's 1868 biography of Crozer, which quotes from his letters and diaries (pp. 99–106). In September 1971 a flood occurred along Chester Creek which virtually duplicated the 1843 flood in physical characteristics, damages, and deaths and injuries. The writer's observations of this flood were of help in interpreting the 1843 accounts. The 1971 flood also destroyed the old railroad for the second time and probably permanently.
3. DCIS, "Flood of 1843," No. 1, p. 11.
4. *Ibid.,* p. 42.
5. EMHL, Acc. 801, Letterbooks of Daniel Lammot (microfilm M-58.13, No. 2, p. 3), DL to John Kiefer, Dec. 23, 1856; Swedenborg School of Religion, DL to Chas. Doughty, Penn's Grove, Sept. 20, 1843.
6. J. Wheaton Smith, 1868, pp. 101–2, 104, 107.

THE REDEFINITION OF THE COTTON MILL OPERATIVE

1. *Journal of the Franklin Institute,* Vol. 20 (1835), p. 356; see also Sandberg, 1970.
2. Ure, 1835, pp. 19–21.
3. DCCH, Tax Assessments, Aston Township, 1829.
4. The introduction of the new school system into Delaware County is described in Ashmead, 1884, pp. 95–6, 298–9, 617–19.
5. See Catling, 1970, p. 149, for an account of the conservative role of the English mule spinner. His description probably applies to America as well in this period.
6. DCHS, Parkmount Day Book and Penn's Grove Pay Book.
7. Ashmead, 1884, p. 620.
8. EMHL, W9–25828, Maria Blakely to SDP, April 23, 1852.
9. DCCH, tax lists; EMHL, W9–26153, CS to SDP, February 4, 1858.

WORKERS AS OBJECTS OF PITY: THE TEN HOURS LAW

1. EMHL, W9–26998, CS to SDP, Oct. 29, 1863.
2. *Upland Union,* April 8, 1846, July 14, 1847, Nov. 3, 1847.
3. Ashmead, 1884, pp. 108–12, gives a general account of the ten hours law in Delaware County.
4. Commons, 1910, Vol. 8, p. 200.
5. Ashmead, 1884, p. 110.
6. Commons, 1910, Vol. 8, pp. 200–5.
7. Ashmead, 1884, pp. 108–12.

THE THEORY OF CHRISTIAN CAPITALISM

1. Carey, 1852, p. 229.
2. Mayer, 1936, pp. 236–44, discusses the impact of Carey's economic philosophy on European socialist literature and particularly the pressure which, through Dühring's advocacy of it, it placed on Marx and Engels.
3. For general treatments of Carey's work, and bibliography, see Eiselen, 1932, Elder, 1880, Green, 1951, and Kaplan, 1931.

Part Four
ROCKDALE FROM 1850 TO 1865:
THE TRANSCENDING OF A WAY OF LIFE

Chapter IX. Marching to Millennium

THE ECONOMIC TAKE-OFF

1. Ashmead, 1884, p. 331.
2. Martin, 1877, pp. 313–14.
3. Samuel Crozer, 1902.
4. Ashmead, 1884, pp. 430–1; J. Wheaton Smith, 1868, pp. 120–7; *Laws of the General Assembly of the Commonwealth of Pennsylvania*, 1849, p. 577.
5. Whitehead, 1859, pp. 44–5. See also Ashmead, 1884, p. 331, and Broomall, 1876, p. 5.
6. Ashmead, 1884, pp. 332, 396–8.
7. DCIS, *Memorial of John M. Broomall*, 1894, p. 5.
8. Ashmead, 1884, p. 397.
9. Whitehead, 1859, p. 98.
10. Ashmead, 1884, p. 332.
11. EMHL, MS Group 7, Series A, Box 2, MLDP to Evelina Biderman, Oct. 14, 1838.
12. Ashmead, 1884, pp. 399–400. See also Wiley, 1894, pp. 324–5.
13. EMHL, W9–25225, Maria Miles to SDP, Sept. 6, 1835.
14. EMHL, W9–25241, Maria Miles to SDP, April 16, 1836.
15. EMHL, W9–25625, Maria Blakely to SDP, Oct. 27, 1847.
16. EMHL, W9–26705, Maria Blakely to SDP, July 11, 1862.
17. Calvary Church 100th Anniversary Memorial, 1933. See also Ashmead, 1884, pp. 294–5, 621.

THE POLITICS OF THE MANUFACTURING INTEREST

1. Martin, 1877, p. 325.
2. McLane, 1833, Vol. 2, pp. 224–6, 212.
3. Ashmead, 1884, p. 248.
4. 22nd Congress, 1st Session, House Doc. No. 171, June 25, 1832.
5. 22nd Congress, 2nd Session, House Doc. No. 134, Feb. 18, 1833.
6. EMHL, Winterthur MSS, Series C, Box 24, EDP to VB, Jan. 29, 1832.
7. DCHS, George E. Darlington Papers, Samuel and James Riddle to ED, Feb. 14, 1834.

8. *Ibid.,* JPC to ED, April 1, 1834.
9. 23rd Congress, 1st Session, House Doc. Nos. 282, 280, 287, April 7, 1834.
10. DCHS, Parkmount Day Book, June 6, 1834.
11. *Upland Union,* May 26, June 23, July 21, 1840.
12. Campbell, 1892, pp. 512–13.
13. DCHS *Proceedings,* Vol. 1, pp. 155–70.
14. The political careers of the Riddle brothers are delineated in Campbell, 1892, Ashmead, 1884, and Ridlon, 1884.
15. Martin's voting record is recorded in the *Journal* of the House of Representatives, 1827–28, located in the Pennsylvania State Library (Legislative Reference section).
16. See Martin, 1877, pp. 332–4, and *Pa. House Journal,* Jan. 18 and March 19, 1828.
17. See Ashmead, 1884, p. 248, for an account of Samuel Edwards.
18. CCHS, *Village Record,* July 26, 1828.
19. Details of Edward Darlington's political career are to be found in the regular announcements of political activities in the county in such newspapers as the *Upland Union,* the *Delaware County Republican,* and the *Village Record,* from 1825 on. Some of his political correspondence is preserved in the George E. Darlington Papers, DCHS, and in a series of letters between himself and his cousin William Darlington in CCHS. His voting record in Congress is revealed in the *Congressional Globe* and in the *Journal* of the House. See also some information in the Darlington, 1909, genealogy.
20. See the *Journal* of the House of Representatives, 23rd, 24th, and 25th Congresses, *passim.*
21. HSP, Simon Gratz Collection.
22. HSP, Henry C. Carey Papers, ED to Henry Carey, Nov. 25, 1858.
23. Darlington, 1909, p. 74. See also Zyckowski, 1937, pp. 40–2, for the connection with Stevens.
24. 25th Congress, 3rd Session, *Pa. House Journal,* Dec. 11, 1838.
25. DCIS, *Memorial of John M. Broomall,* 1894, pp. 2, 7, 8.
26. *Congressional Globe,* Dec. 17, 1868, pp. 134–5.
27. In addition to the material provided by the *Memorial of John M. Broomall* (copies of which are located at the Delaware County Institute of Science, the Friends Historical Library, the HSP, and the APS, of which he was a corresponding member), Broomall material can be found in the form of printed speeches at these same libraries, and in manuscript at the HSP, which has a file of his political correspondence amounting to some three hundred items for the years 1867 and 1868. His career has received no attention from such historians of the Republican Party as Foner, 1970, and Myers, 1940.

MISSIONS AND THE MILLENNIAL PASSION

1. See Lemieux, 1976, for a detailed study of the death cult in Delaware County during this period.
2. Lee, 1856, pp. 17, 575, 587.
3. EMHL, W9–26099, CS to SDP, Sept. 3, 1857.
4. EMHL, W9–26174, CS to SDP, April 26, 1858.
5. Francis, 1946, p. 56.
6. EMHL, Longwood MSS, Group 4, Box 10, folder "Lammott, Anna."
7. Wilder, 1866, pp. 25–30.
8. Newspaper obituary of John S. Phillips in the Pennsylvania Academy of Fine Arts.
9. Beaux, 1930, pp. 61–3.

10. Obituary notice in Pennsylvania Academy of Fine Arts. The print collection and part of Phillips' library were transferred to the Philadelphia Museum of Art in 1856. The prints have been removed from Phillips' special folders and combined with other collections.
11. See Lemieux, 1976, pp. 139–42, 246–53.
12. EMHL, W9–25810, CS to SDP, Jan. 5, 1852.
13. EMHL, W9–25263, CS to SDP, Nov. 19, 1830.
14. EMHL, W9–25288, CS to SDP, May 17, 1838.
15. EMHL, W9–25888, CS to SDP, Sept. 10, 1853.
16. EMHL, W9–25355, CS to SDP, Nov. 30, 1840.
17. Crozer, *Autobiography,* 1861, pp. 87–9.
18. Wilder, 1866, p. 22.
19. Ashmead, 1884, pp. 301, 332.
20. Upland Baptist Church, Minutes, Oct. 8, 1852, to March 1865; Samuel Crozer, 1902.
21. Williams, 1902, p. 24.
22. Wilder, 1866, p. 10.
23. Upland Baptist Church, Minutes, Nov. 27 and Dec. 11, 1858.
24. J. Wheaton Smith, 1868, p. 190.
25. *Annual Reports,* May 16, 1859.
26. *Annual Reports, passim,* 1853–66.
27. J. Wheaton Smith, 1868, pp. 141, 171–9.
28. LOC, American Colonization Society Papers, Membership Lists (Microfilm reel 299, List of life directors).
29. HSP, "Ninetieth Anniversary of the Pennsylvania Abolition Society," 1866.
30. Crozer, 1863.
31. Kruse, 1922.
32. Ashmead, 1884, p. 260.
33. Crozer, 1863.
34. Allen, 1863, p. 8.
35. LOC, American Colonization Society Papers, *Annual Reports* for 1861–65; correspondence of JPC in Records, Vols. 167–83 (Microfilm reels 93–98).
36. Crozer, 1863, p. 23.
37. LOC, American Colonization Society Papers, Series 6, Box 5, folder "Crozer, Samuel A."
38. EMHL, W9–1972, SFDP to SDP, May 21, 1858.
39. The cruise of the *Minnesota* is carefully told in "journal letters" from SFDP to SDP in EMHL, W9–1926 to 1999.
40. EMHL, W9–25355, CS to SDP, Nov. 30, 1840.
41. EMHL, W9–25430, CS to SDP, March 15, 1843.
42. EMHL, W9–26203, CS to SDP, Aug. 7, 1858.
43. Tyng, 1848, p. 23.
44. Fuller, 1845, Vol. 1, pp. 552–3.
45. J. Wheaton Smith, 1868, pp. 149–50.
46. Read, 1836.
47. Read, 1864.
48. Read, 1859, p. 219.
49. Read, 1864.
50. Read, 1874.
51. Read, 1861.
52. Gilpin, 1873, pp. 8, 124.

53. The materials describing the Associated Working Women and Men are located in the files of the *Monthly Jubilee* at PLTA.

ARMAGEDDON

1. EMHL, W9–26153, CS to SDP, Feb. 4, 1858; 1860 census, Aston Township.
2. EMHL, W9–26159, 26179, CS to SDP, March 2 and May 3, 1858.
3. EMHL, W9–26203, CS to SDP, Aug. 7, 1858.
4. Upland Baptist Church, Minutes, Sept. 25, 1858.
5. Francis, 1946.
6. EMHL, W9–26039, CS to SDP, Feb. 26, 1857.
7. EMHL, W9–26340, CS to SDP, Jan. 31, 1859.
8. Ashmead, 1884, p. 305.
9. EMHL, W9–26377, CS to SDP, July 5, 1860.
10. EMHL, W9–26360, CS to SDP, April 28, 1860.
11. EMHL, W9–26382, CS to SDP, Aug. 7, 1860.
12. EMHL, W9–26416, Dec. 31, 1860.
13. The general course of events involving Delaware County during the Civil War is provided by Ashmead, 1884; see also the newspaper accounts in the *Delaware County Republican*. Bates, 1869–71, provides valuable information on units and individual soldiers.
14. EMHL, W9–26477, CS to SDP, May 14, 1861.
15. EMHL, W9–26482, CS to SDP, June 6, 1861.
16. J. Wheaton Smith, 1868, p. 183.
17. EMHL, W9–26514, CS to SDP, Sept. 10, 1861.
18. The work of the Christian Commission is described in Moss, 1868; Crozer's participation is also described in J. Wheaton Smith, 1868, pp. 183–5.
19. EMHL, W9–26546, CS to SDP, Nov. 14, 1861.
20. EMHL, W9–26589, CS to SDP, Dec. 7, 1861.
21. EMHL, W9–26514, CS to SDP, Sept. 18, 1861.
22. EMHL, W9–26680, CS to SDP, May 24, 1862.
23. EMHL, W9–26754, CS to SDP, Sept. 30, 1862.
24. EMHL, W9–26774, CS to SDP, Nov. 12, 1862.
25. EMHL, W9–26674, CS to SDP, May 2, 1862.
26. EMHL, W9–26806, CS to SDP, Jan. 8, 1863.
27. EMHL, W9–26970, CS to SDP, Aug. 18, 1863.
28. EMHL, W9–26967, CS to SDP, Aug. 12, 1863.
29. Johnson, 1890, pp. iv–vi.
30. EMHL, W9–26715, CS to SDP, July 23, 1862.
31. EMHL, W9–27121, CS to SDP, Sept. 18, 1864.
32. EMHL, W9–26774, CS to SDP, Nov. 12, 1861.
33. In general see Tuveson, 1968, for an interpretation of the importance of millennialist thinking in popular attitudes toward the war which has greatly helped my understanding of events in the Rockdale district.
34. EMHL, W9–27164, CS to SDP, Jan. 21, 1865.
35. EMHL, W9–26812, CS to SDP, Jan. 16, 1863.
36. EMHL, W9–27147, CS to SDP, Dec. 18, 1864.
37. General information about John Newsome comes from DCCH, Tax Assessment Records, Middletown and Aston townships, 1856–61; the 1860 census, Aston Township; and his

military service record, NA. I am personally indebted to Mr. Samuel Newsome of Media, Pennsylvania, for information from family records. It happens that the writer now occupies John Newsome's house.

38. General information about Jones Bradbury comes from DCCH, Tax Assessment Records, Middletown Township, 1860–62; the 1860 census, Middletown Township; and his military service record, NA.

39. NA, service record of John Newsome, declaration for increase of invalid pension, Dec. 4, 1891.

40. EMHL, W9–27116, CS to SDP, Aug. 24, 1864.

41. An account of John Newsome's career after the war, as described in family records, was given to me in private correspondence by Samuel Newsome.

42. EMHL, W9–26239, CS to SDP, Jan. 9, 1859.

43. EMHL, W9–26340, CS to SDP, Jan. 31, 1860.

44. EMHL, W9–26732, CS to SDP, Aug. 2, 1862.

45. EMHL, W9–27040, EBS to SDP, Feb. 1, 1864.

46. EMHL, W9–27256, CS to SDP, April 28, 1865.

47. EMHL, W9–27260, CS to SDP, May 16, 1865.

APPENDIX

1. See Kroeber, 1939, 1944.

2. Kuhn, 1970.

3. *Ibid.*, 1970, p. 43.

4. *Ibid.*, 1970.

5. Garfinkel, 1967.

6. Smelser, 1959; Kasserman, 1974.

7. Polanyi, 1944.

Bibliography

The Bibliography is intended to serve several purposes: to list the manuscript repositories, and the collections therein, consulted during the research; to list the nineteenth-century newspapers and journals, some issues of which were examined; to list the published genealogies and biographical encyclopedias that yielded useful information; to provide references to the published writings of residents of the Rockdale district who figured in the text, and to other works by nineteenth-century observers, in the fields of technology and social life; and to give references to the scholarly and technical literature. The works cited in the Notes will be found here, but other sources are also listed that are not specifically mentioned yet were of value in giving background data and in stimulating scholarly interpretation. In a work such as this, which attempts to synthesize materials that are conventionally apportioned among several historical specialties—in this case, the Industrial Revolution, the Enlightenment, early nineteenth-century socialism, the history of technology, the new social history, the Jacksonian era, the Civil War, Pennsylvania history, and even economic history—the boundaries of the bibliographical task are difficult to define. In the interest of brevity, no effort is made to cite accounts of other industrial towns that would be of interest in a comparative study, or to provide a bibliography of standard secondary works for places, periods, and events.

MANUSCRIPT COLLECTIONS

Under each repository are listed the principal manuscript collections consulted there.

Academy of Natural Sciences of Philadelphia (Philadelphia, Pa.)
  John S. Phillips, misc. correspondence
  Reuben Haines, copies of papers on loan from Haverford Library
American Philosophical Society Library (Philadelphia, Pa.)
  Peale-Sellers Collection
  Minutes of Concord Monthly Meeting, 1803–28
  Minutes of the Indian Committee, Philadelphia Yearly Meeting, microfilm
  New Harmony Papers, microfilm
Baker Library, Harvard (Cambridge, Mass.)
  William Bagnall, "Sketches of Manufacturing Establishments in
    New York City and of Textile Establishments in the Eastern
    United States." Unpublished MS, 1908
  Account books of the Boston Manufacturing Co., Merrimack Manufacturing Co., Taunton
    Manufacturing Co., Isaac Pierson and Brothers
  Dun and Bradstreet Credit Ratings, Vol. 37, Delaware Co.
Calvary Church, Rockdale (Aston, Pa.)

Records of births, deaths, burials, baptisms, confirmations
Chester County Historical Society (West Chester, Pa.)
  William Darlington Correspondence
Delaware County Court House (Media, Pa.)
  Tax Assessment Books, Aston and Middletown townships, 1825-65
  Register of Deeds
  Register of Wills
Delaware County Historical Society (Chester, Pa.)
  George E. Darlington Papers
  Parkmount Day Book
  Penn's Grove Rent Book
  Penn's Grove Pay Book
  William Reynolds Day Book
  Anna Broomall's Notebooks
  Baker Notebooks
  WPA Grave Marker Surveys
Delaware County Institute of Science (Media, Pa.)
  Minutes, memorials, and correspondence (kept in vault)
Eleutherian Mills Historical Library (Wilmington, Del.)
  Joseph Bancroft Collection
  Correspondence of Sophie du Pont and Clementina Smith
  Smith Family Papers (new accession)
  Tancopanican Chronicle
  Francis Gurney Smith, letterbooks
  Brandywine Manufacturers' Sunday School Papers
  R. S. Griffith Sketches
  Correspondence of a variety of Rockdale residents with members of the Du Pont family (see
    list under Abbreviations, p. 487)
Franklin Institute (Philadelphia, Pa.)
  Minutes of the Committee on Water Power
Historical Society of Delaware (Wilmington, Del.)
  Poole Papers
Historical Society of Pennsylvania (Philadelphia, Pa.)
  John H. Martin Papers
  Gilpin Collection
  Delaware County Poor House Records
  Willcox Papers
  Joseph S. Lovering Collection
  John M. Broomall Correspondence
Library of Congress (Washington, D.C.)
  American Colonization Society Papers
National Archives (Washington, D.C.)
  Patent Office Records
  U.S. Decennial Census Schedules, Population and Manufactures
  Military Service Records
New-York Historical Society (New York, N.Y.)
  John Rogers Papers
Painter Library, John J. Tyler Arboretum (Middletown Township, Delaware Co., Pa.)

Minshall and Jacob Painter Correspondence
Pennsylvania Academy of Fine Arts (Philadelphia, Pa.)
　John S. Phillips Papers
Pennsylvania State Archives (Harrisburg, Pa.)
　U.S. Direct Tax, Pennsylvania, 1798 (microfilm from National Archives)
　Delaware County Election Returns
　Septennial Census
Philadelphia Free Library
　Hexamer General Surveys
Presbyterian Historical Society (Philadelphia, Pa.)
　Robert Landis Correspondence
Swedenborgian School of Religion (Newton, Mass.)
　Daniel Lammot, Jr., Correspondence
Upland Baptist Church (Chester, Pa.)
　Minutes and records of baptism
Workingmen's Institute (New Harmony, Ind.)
　Joseph Neef Papers
　William Maclure Diaries

NEWSPAPERS AND JOURNALS

African Repository (in HSP)
Hazard's Register of Pennsylvania (in DCHS)
Journal of the Franklin Institute (in FI and EMHL)
Niles' Weekly Register (in EMHL)
The Anti-Masonic Register (in PLTA)
The Delaware County Republican (in DCHS)
The Delaware Free Press (in EMHL)
The Free Enquirer (in EMHL and WINH)
The Mechanic's Free Press (in HSP)
The Monthly Jubilee (in PLTA)
The Philadelphia Inquirer (in HSP)
The Philadelphia Liberalist (in HSP)
The Rockdale Herald
The Souvenir (in HSP and PFL)
The Upland Union (in DCHS)
The Village Record, or *Chester and Delaware Federalist* (in CCHS)
The Working Man's Advocate (in HSP)

GENEALOGIES AND BIOGRAPHICAL ENCYCLOPEDIAS

Appleton's Cyclopedia of American Biography. New York: D. Appleton, 1888–1931.
Biographical and Genealogical History of the State of Delaware. Chambersburg, Pa.: Runk, 1899.
Biographical Directory of the American Congress, 1774–1971. Washington, D. C. 1971.
The Biographical Encyclopaedia of Pennsylvania in the Nineteenth Century. Philadelphia: Galaxy,
　1874.
Brown, John Howard (ed.). *The Cyclopedia of American Biographies Comprising the Men and
　Women of the United States Who Have Been Identified with the Growth of the Nation.* Boston:
　Lamb, 1900.
Cope, Gilbert. *Genealogy of the Dutton Family.* West Chester, Pa., 1871.

———— (ed. & comp.). *Genealogy of the Darlington Family.* West Chester, Pa.: Committee for the Family, 1900.

———— and Henry G. Ashmead. *Historic Homes and Institutions and Genealogical and Personal Memoirs of Chester and Delaware Counties, Pennsylvania.* New York: Lewis, 1904.

Darlington, George E. *History of the Eyre and Ashmead Families Who Settled in Chester and Philadelphia, Pennsylvania.* Media, Pa., 1909.

Futhey, J. Smith, and Gilbert Cope. *History of Chester County, Pennsylvania, with Genealogical and Biographical Sketches.* Philadelphia: L. H. Everts, 1881.

Johnson, Allen, *et al.* (eds.). *Dictionary of American Biography.* New York: Charles Scribner's Sons, 1928–73. 23 vols.

Johnson, Rossiter (ed.). *The Biographical Dictionary of America.* Boston, 1906.

Jordan, John W. (ed.). *Encyclopedia of Pennsylvania Biography.* New York: Lewis, 1919.

Leach, Frank Willing. "Old Philadelphia Families (CXXI—Smith [Daniel])," *The North American,* July 28, 1912.

The National Cyclopaedia of American Biography. New York: James T. White Co., 1898–1977. 57 vols. (Vols. 1–49 republished by University Microfilms.)

Odiorne, James C. *Genealogy of the Odiorne Family.* Boston: Rand, Avery, 1875.

Painter, J. *The Gilpin Family from Richard de Goulpyn in 1206, in a Line to Joseph Gilpin.* Lima, Pa., 1870.

Ridlon, G. T. *History of the Ancient Ryedales and their Descendants in Normandy, Great Britain, Ireland, and America, From 860 to 1884. Comprising the Genealogy and Biography, for About One Thousand Years, of the Families of RIDDELL, RIDDLE, RIDLON, RIDLEY, ETC.* Manchester, N.H.: Published by the Author, 1884.

Robson, Charles. *The Manufactories and Manufacturers of Pennsylvania of the Nineteenth Century.* Philadelphia: Galaxy, 1875.

Simpson, Henry. *The Lives of Eminent Philadelphians.* Philadelphia, 1859.

Stephen, Leslie, and Sidney Lee (eds.). *The Dictionary of National Biography . . . from the Earliest Times to 1900.* London: Oxford University Press, 1949–50. 22 vols.

Townsend, Mrs. Stockton. "Phillips Bible Record," *Publications of the Genealogical Society of Pennsylvania,* Vol. 12 (1934), pp. 177–90.

Virkus, Frederick A. (ed.). *The Abridged Compendium of American Genealogy.* Chicago: Marquis, 1925.

Wiley, Samuel T. (ed.). *Biographical and Historical Cyclopaedia of Delaware County, Pennsylvania.* New York: Gresham Publishing Co., 1894.

PUBLISHED WRITINGS BY ROCKDALERS
AND OTHER NINETEENTH-CENTURY OBSERVERS

Part 1: Most Relevant to the History of Technology

Baines, Sir Edward. *History of the Cotton Manufacture in Great Britain . . .* London: Fisher, Fisher & Jackson, 1835.

Baird, Robert H. *The American Cotton Spinner and Managers' and Carders' Guide.* Philadelphia: A. Hart, 1851.

Barfoot, J.R. *The Progress of Cotton.* Helmshore: Helmshore Local History Society, 1973.

Batchelder, Samuel. *Introduction and Early Progress of the Cotton Manufacture in the United States.* Boston, 1863.

Bigelow, Jacob. *Elements of Technology.* 2nd edition, Boston: Hilliard, Gray, Little and Wilkins, 1831.

Buchanan, Robertson. *Practical Essays on Mill-Work and other Machinery, Mechanical and descriptive.* London, 1808 (3rd edition, 1841).

Burke, James. *List of Patents for Inventions and Designs Issued by the United States from 1790 to 1847.* Washington, D.C.: T. and G. S. Gideon, 1847.

Byrne, Oliver. *A dictionary of machines, mechanics, engine-work, and engineering . . .* New York and Philadelphia: Appleton, 1850.

————. *The American engineer, draftsmen, and machinists assistants . . .* Philadelphia: Brown, 1853 (a).

————. *Mechanics: Their principles and practical applications.* New York: Dewitt & Davenport, 1853 (b).

————. *The handbook for the artisan, mechanic, and engineer.* Philadelphia: Collins, 1853 (c).

Chapin, J. R. "Among the Nail-Makers," *Harpers New Monthly Magazine,* Vol. 21 (1860), pp. 145–64.

[Chester, Pa., Board of Trade]. *Chester, Pennsylvania: A History of Its Industrial Progress and Advantages for Large Manufactures. Brief Sketches of Its Representative Business Enterprises.* Chester, Pa., 1899.

Crozer, Samuel A. "The Early Manufactures and Manufacturers of Delaware County," *Proceedings of the Delaware County Historical Society, 1895–1901,* Vol. 1 (1902), pp. 130–6.

Dutton, Jonathan. *The New Planet, Containing a Degree of Novelty: Being an Effort Toward the Pleasure, Comfort, and Convenience of all Citizens.* Philadelphia, 1848.

Evans, Oliver. *The Young Mill-Wright and Miller's Guide.* Philadelphia: Lea and Blanchard, 1840.

————. *The Young Steam Engineer's Guide.* Philadelphia: H. C. Carey and I. Lea, n.d., probably 1826.

Fairbairn, Sir William, Bart. *Mills and Mill-Work.* 2 vols., 2nd edition, London, 1864–65.

Ferguson, Eugene S. (ed.). *Early Engineering Reminiscences (1815–40) of George Escol Sellers.* Washington, D.C.: Smithsonian Institution, 1965.

Francis, James B. *The Lowell Hydraulic Experiments.* New York, 1855.

Guest, Richard. *A Compendious History of the Cotton-Manufacture; with a Disproval of the Claim of Sir Richard Arkwright to the Invention of its Ingenious Machinery.* Manchester, England, 1823.

Howe, Henry. *Memoirs of the Most Eminent American Mechanics.* New York: Harper & Brothers, 1847.

Jenks, Alfred, and Son. *Illustrated Catalogue of Machines built by Alfred Jenks & Son, Manufacturers of Every variety of cotton and wool carding, spinning, and weaving machines, in all its departments. Shafting and mill gearing of the latest and most approved plans.* Bridesburg, Philadelphia Co., Pa., n.d.

Knight, Edward H. *Knight's American Mechanical Dictionary, A description of tools, instruments, machines, processes, and engineering; history of inventions; general technological vocabulary; and digest of mechanical appliances in science and the arts.* Boston: Houghton, Mifflin, 1882.

Leffel, James. *Construction of Mill Dams.* Springfield, Ohio: James Leffel & Co., 1881. Reprinted as History of Technology series, Vol. 1, Park Ridge, N.J.: Noyes Press, 1972.

Leiper, G. G., and W. Martin. *Report of the Committee of Delaware County on the Subject of Manufactories, Unimproved Mill Seats, etc. in said County, 1826.* Chester, Pa.: Lescure, 1826.

McElroy's Philadelphia Directory. 30 vols. Philadelphia. A. McElroy & Co., 1837–1867.

McLane, Louis. *Documents Relating to Manufactures in the United States.* 2 vols., Washington, D.C., 1833. (Reprinted New York: Augustus M. Kelley, 1969.)

Montgomery, James. *The Theory and Practice of Cotton Spinning: or the Carding and Spinning Master's Assistant . . .* 2nd edition, Glasgow: John Niven, 1833.

———. *The Cotton Manufacture of the United States of America and the State of the Cotton Manufacture of that Country Contrasted and Compared with that of Great Britain.* Glasgow: John Niven, 1840.

Nicholson, John. *The Operative Mechanic and British Machinist; being a Practical Display of the Manufactories and Mechanical Arts of the United Kingdom.* 2 vols., Philadelphia: H. C. Carey & I. Lea, 1826.

Rees, Abraham. *Cyclopaedia.* Philadelphia: Bradford, 1805–24.

Robison, John. *A System of Mechanical Philosophy With Notes By David Brewster.* 4 vols., Edinburgh: Printed for John Murray, London, 1822.

Rose, Joshua. *Modern Machine-Shop Practice.* 2 vols., 2nd edition, New York: Scribner's, 1892.

Scott, R. *The Practical Cotton Spinner and Manufacturer.* Preston, England, 1840.

———. *The Practical Cotton Spinner and Manufacturer . . .* Corrected and enlarged with plates of American machines, edited by Oliver Byrne. Philadelphia: Henry Carey Baird, 1851.

Silliman, Benjamin. *Manual on the Cultivation of the Sugar Cane, and the Fabrication and Refinement of Sugar.* Washington, D.C.: Blair, 1833.

Snell, Daniel W. *The Manager's Assistant; being a condensed treatise on Cotton Manufacturing.* Hartford, Conn., 1850.

Sutcliffe, John. *A Treatise on Canals and Reservoirs, and the best Mode of designing and Executing them . . . likewise Observations on the best Mode of Carding, Roving, Drawing, and Spinning all Kinds of Cotton Twist. . . .* Rochdale, England, 1816.

Ure, Andrew. *The Philosophy of Manufactures: or an Exposition of the Scientific, Moral, and Commercial Economy of the Factory system of Great Britain.* London: Charles Knight, 1835.

Webber, Samuel. *Manual of Power for Machines, Shafts and Belts, with the History of Cotton Manufacture in the United States.* Revised edition, New York: Appleton, 1879.

Part II: Most Relevant to Social and Cultural Matters

Allen, William H. "Address to the American Colonization Society," Oct. 25, 1863, in *African Colonization—Its Progress and Prospects,* pp. 5–21. Philadelphia: Pennsylvania Colonization Society, 1863.

[American Colonization Society]. *Annual Reports, 1818–1910.*

[Baptist Publication Society]. *The John P. Crozer Memorial.* Philadelphia: American Baptist Publication Society, 1866.

Barruel, Augustin de. *Memoirs Illustrating the History of Jacobinism.* Hartford, Conn., 1799.

Beaux, Cecilia. *Background with Figures: Autobiography of Cecilia Beaux.* Boston: Houghton Mifflin, 1930.

Bestor, Arthur E. (ed.). *Education and Reform at New Harmony: Correspondence of William Maclure and Marie Duclos Fretageot, 1820–1833.* Indianapolis: Indiana Historical Society, 1948.

Bishop, Charles W. W. *History of the Marcus Hook Baptist Church.* Philadelphia, 1855.

Broomall, John. [Eulogy of Thaddeus Stevens] *Congressional Globe,* 40th Congress, 3rd Session, 1868–69, pp. 134–5.

Broomall, Hon. John M. *History of Delaware County for the Past Century.* Read before the Delaware County Institute of Science. Media, Pa: Vernon and Cooper, Steam Power Book Printers, 1876.

Campbell, John H. *History of the Friendly Sons of St Patrick and the Hibernian Society for the Relief of Emigrants from Ireland, March 17, 1771–March 17, 1892.* Philadelphia: The Hibernian Society, 1892.

Carey, Henry C. *The Harmony of Interests, Agricultural, Manufacturing, and Commercial.* 2nd edition, New York: Finch, 1852.

Charlotte Elizabeth (Tonna, Mrs. Charlotte Elizabeth). *Helen Fleetwood* in *The Works of Charlotte Elizabeth,* Vol. 1, New York: Dodd, 1847.

Claxton, Timothy. *Memoir of a Mechanic. Being a Sketch of the Life of Timothy Claxton, Written by Himself, Together with Miscellaneous Papers.* Boston: George W. Light, 1839.

[Congressional Petitions]. "Memorial . . . For a repeal of the duty on imported raw flax, and an increase of ad valorem duty on thread and twine made from flax," by Garsed, Raines & Co. 22nd Congress, 1st Session, Senate, March 1, 1832.

————. "Resolutions passed at a Meeting of the Citizens of Delaware County, Pennsylvania, in favor of the protective system, and of rechartering the Bank of the United States." 22nd Congress, 1st Session, Senate, June 25, 1832.

————. "Pennsylvania—Delaware County Meeting—Tariff." 22nd Congress, 2nd Session, House, Doc. 134, Feb. 18, 1833.

————. "Proceedings of a Meeting in Delaware County, Against the Bank of the United States." 23rd Congress, 1st Session, House, Doc. 287, April 7, 1834.

————. "Memorial of Citizens of Delaware County, Praying a recharter of the Bank of the United States." 23rd Congress, 1st Session, House, Doc. 280, April 7, 1834.

————. "Proceedings of a Public Meeting of Citizens of Delaware County, in relation to the Bank of the United States." 23rd Congress, 1st Session, House, Doc. 282, April 7, 1834.

Crozer, John P. "Address from the Central Committee (of the Temperance Society) to the Citizens of Delaware County," in *Facts to Think About and What's the Remedy.* Chester, Pa.: Walter, 1850.

————. *Biographical Sketch of John P. Crozer, Written by Himself.* Philadelphia: Grant, Faires & Rodgers, n.d. [1861].

————. [Obituary of William Martin]. In Martin, 1877, pp. 332–4. Published in the *Delaware County Republican,* Oct. 24, 1862.

————. "Address to the American Colonization Society," Oct. 25, 1863, in *African Colonization—Its Progress and Prospects,* pp. 21–4. Philadelphia: Pennsylvania Colonization Society, 1863.

Crozer, Samuel A. "Historical Address," in *Semi-Centennial of Upland Baptist Church 1852–1902.*

Darlington, George E. *History of the Eyre and Ashmead families who Settled in Chester and Philadelphia, Pa.* Media, Pa., 1909.

————. *Recollections of the Old Borough of Chester 1834–1850.* Chester, Pa.: Delaware County Historical Society, 1917.

Deacon, William F. *Warreniana.* Boston: Ticknor, Reed, and Fields, 1851 (reprint of 1824 edition).

[Delaware County Institute of Science]. *Report of a Committee of the Delaware County Institute of Science, on the Great Rain Storm and Flood . . .* August 1843. Chester, Pa.: Walter, 1844.

————. *Memorial of John M. Broomall.* Media, Pa., n.d. [1894].

Ely, Ezra Stiles. *A Contrast Between Calvinism and Hopkinism.* New York, 1811.

————. *The Duty of Christian Freemen to Elect Christian Rulers.* Philadelphia, 1828.

————. *Visits of Mercy or the Journals of the Rev. Ezra Stiles Ely, written while he was stated preacher to the hospital and almshouse, in the city of New York.* 2 vols., Philadelphia: Bradond, 1829.

————. *A Discussion of the Conjoint Question, is the Doctrine of Endless Punishment Taught in the Bible: Or Does the Bible Teach the Doctrine of the Final Holiness and Happiness of all Mankind?* In a Series of Letters Between Ezra Stiles Ely and Abel C. Thomas. New York: P. Price, 1835.

Erickson, Charlotte (ed.). *Invisible Immigrants: The Adaptation of English and Scottish Immigrants in Nineteenth Century America.* Coral Gables, Fla.: University of Miami Press, 1972.

Farragut, Loyall (ed.). *Life of David Glasgow Farragut, First Admiral of the United States Navy. Embodying his Journal and Letters.* New York: D. Appleton & Co., 1879.

Friendly Association for Mutual Interests. *Preamble and Constitution.* Philadelphia, 1826.

Fuller, Andrew. *The Complete works . . . with a memoir of his life by Andrew Gunton Fuller, from the third London edition; revised, with additions by Joseph Belcher, D.D.* 3 vols., Philadelphia: American Baptist Publication Society, 1845.

Gardette, C. D. "Pestalozzi in America," *Galaxy,* Vol. 4 (August 1867), pp. 432–9.

Gilpin, William. *Mission of the North American People, Geographical, Social, and Political.* Philadelphia: Lippincott, 1873.

Gray, John. *A Lecture on Human Happiness . . .* Philadelphia, 1825.

Hagner, Charles V. *Early History of the Falls of Schuylkill, Manayunk, Schuylkill and Lehigh Navagation Companies.* Philadelphia: Claxton, Remsen, and Heffelfinger, 1869.

Harrison, Lowell H. (ed.). "William Duane on Education," *Pennsylvania Magazine of History and Biography,* Vol. 73 (1949), pp. 316–25.

Hawkins, Joseph. *A History of a Voyage to the Coast of Africa, and Travels into the Interior . . . and Interesting Particulars Concerning the Slave Trade.* Philadelphia, 1797.

Hemple, Charles Julius. *The True Organization of the New Church, as indicated in the Writings of Emanuel Swedenborg, and demonstrated by Charles Fourier.* New York: Radde, 1848.

Hiatt, Joel W. (ed.). *Diary of William Owen, 1824–1825.* Indianapolis: Bobbs-Merrill, 1906.

Hopkins, John Henry, Jr. *The Life of the Late Right Reverend John Henry Hopkins, first Bishop of Vermont.* New York: Huntington, 1873.

Howe, M. A. *Memoir of the Life and Services of the Rt. Rev. Alonzo Potter.* Philadelphia: Lippincott, 1871.

Hunter, John Dunn. *Memoirs of a Captivity Among the Indians of North America.* London: Longman, Hursy, Rees, Orme, Brown and Green, 1923.

Hyneman, Leon. *World's Masonic Register.* Philadelphia: Lippincott, 1860.

Jones, John R. *An Address Delivered at a Town-Meeting of the Anti-Masonic Citizens of Philadelphia, October 5th, 1830.* Philadelphia, 1830.

Knight, Jane D. *Brief Narrative of Events Touching Various Reforms.* Albany, N.Y., 1880.

Laws of the General Assembly of the Commonwealth of Pennsylvania. Harrisburg, Pa., published annually by the state printer.

Leavitt, Thomas W. (ed.). *The Hollingsworth Letters: Technical Change in the Textile Industry, 1826–1837.* Cambridge, Mass.: M.I.T. Press, 1969.

Lee, Alfred. *A Life Hid with Christ; Being a Memoir of Miss Susan Allibone.* Philadelphia: J. B. Lippincott, 1856.

———. "A Farewell Discourse Delivered to the congregation of Calvary Church, Rockdale, Penn." Philadelphia: Joseph M. Brown, 1841.

Lyon, Patrick. *The Narrative of Patrick Lyon.* Philadelphia, 1799.

Maclure, William. "An Epitome of the Improved Pestalozzian System of Education, as practised by William Phiquepal and Madam Fretageot, Formerly in Paris, and now in Philadelphia; communicated at the request of the Editor," *American Journal of Science and Arts,* Vol. X (1826), 145–51.

———. *Opinions on various subjects, dedicated to the Industrious Producers.* New Harmony, Ind.: School Press, 1831.

Martin, John Hill. *Chester (and Its Vicinity,) Delaware County, in Pennsylvania.* Philadelphia, 1877.

Montgomery, Elizabeth. *Reminiscences of Wilmington . . .* Philadelphia: Collins, 1851.

Morton, Samuel G. "A Memoir of William MacClure, Esq.," *American Journal of Science* (April–June 1844).

Moss, Lemuel. *Annals of the United States Christian Commission.* Philadelphia: Lippincott, 1868.

Murphy, John K. *To the Communicants and Members of the Congregation of Calvary Church, Rockdale, c.* 1861 (HSP, VoD*/.58 Vol. II).

Neef, Joseph. *Sketch of a Plan and Method of Education.* Philadelphia, 1808.

[Odd Fellows.] *Souvenir History and Program of the Seventy-fifth Anniversary of the Introduction of Odd Fellowship in Delaware County, Pa., Riddle's Grove, Rockdale, September 15, 1906.* Chester, Pa., 1906.

Odiorne, Thomas. *The Progress of Refinement.* Boston: Young and Etheridge, 1792.

Odiorne, James C. (ed.). *Opinions on Speculative Masonry, relative to its Origin, Nature, and Tendency.* Boston: Perkins & Marvin, 1830.

Owen, Robert. *A New View of Society: or Essays on the formation of the Human Character.* New York, 1825 (from 3rd London edition).

————. "Address Delivered . . . at the Franklin Institute . . . June 25, 1827." Philadelphia, 1827.

————. *The Book of the New Moral World.* London, 1849.

Owen, Robert Dale. *Threading My Way: Twenty-Seven Years of Autobiography.* London: Trubner, 1874.

Pendleton, J. M. *Reminiscences of a Long Life.* Louisville, Ky.: Press Baptist Book Concern, 1891.

[Pennsylvania State.] "Report of the Committee by Mr. Peltz, Feb. 7, 1838," *Pennsylvania Senate Journal,* 1837–38, Part I, pp. 322–7.

————. "Testimony of the Witnesses, accompanying the Report of the Committee of the Senate, appointed to investigate the subject of the Employment of Children in Factories," *Pennsylvania Senate Journal,* 1837–38, Part 2, pp. 278–359.

[Pennsylvania Society for Promoting the Abolition of Slavery . . .]. "Celebration of the Nineteenth Anniversary of the Organization." Philadelphia, 1866.

Phillips, John S. "Description of Two New American Species of Helix," *Proceedings of the Academy of Natural Sciences of Philadelphia,* Vol. 1 (1841), pp. 27–8.

————. "Effect of Conflagration on the Atmosphere," *Proceedings of the Academy of Natural Sciences of Philadelphia,* Vol. 1 (1841), p. 46.

————. "Nomenclature of Natural Science," *Proceedings of the Academy of Natural Sciences of Philadelphia,* Vol. 1 (1841), pp. 85–90.

————. "On Helix bidentifera, A Rectification," *Proceedings of the Academy of Natural Sciences of Philadelphia,* Vol. 1 (1841), p. 133.

————. "Description of a new American Species of the genus Helix," *Journal of the Academy of Natural Sciences of Philadelphia,* Vol. 8 (1842), pp. 182–3.

————. "Description of a New Fresh-water Shell and Observations on Glandina obtusa, Pfeif," *Proceedings of the Academy of Natural Sciences of Philadelphia,* Vol. 3 (1846), pp. 66–7.

Potter, Alonzo. *Political Economy.* New York: Harper, 1841(a).

————. *The Principles of Science Applied to the Domestic and Mechanical Arts and to Manufactures and Agriculture.* New York: Harper, 1841(b).

————. *Religious Philosophy; or, Nature, Man, and the Bible . . . Lectures Delivered Before the Lowell Institute Between the Years 1845–1853.* Philadelphia: Lippincott, 1872.

Read, Hollis. *The Christian Brahmun.* 2 vols., New York: Leavitt, Lord & Co., 1836.

————. *Commerce and Christianity.* Philadelphia, Pa.: Seamen's Friend Society, 1859.

———. *The Coming Crisis of the World: or, The Great Battle and the Golden Age.* Columbus, Ohio: Follett, Foster and Co., 1861.

———. *The Negro Problem Solved; or, Africa as She Was, As She Is, and As She Shall Be.* New York: A. A. Constantine, 1864.

———. *The Hand of God in History; or, Divine Providence Illustrated in the Extensions and Establishment of Christianity Throughout the World.* Philadelphia: John E. Potter & Co., 1870.

———. *The Foot-Prints of Satan: or, The Devil in History.* New York: E. B. Treat, 1874.

Robison, John A. M. *Proofs of a Conspiracy against all the Religions and Governments of Europe, carried on in the Secret Meetings of Free Masons, Illuminati, and Reading Societies.* London, 1797.

Royall, Anne. *Mrs. Royall's Pennsylvania.* Washington, D.C., 1829.

[St. Andrew's Church, Wilmington]. *Alfred Lee, first Bishop of Delaware.* Wilmington, Del., 1888.

Silver, Ednah C. *Sketches of the New Church in America on a Background of Civic and Social Life.* Boston: Mass. New Church Union, 1920.

Smith, George, M.D. *History of Delaware County, Pennsylvania, From the Discovery of the Territory Included within its Limits to the Present Time.* Philadelphia: Henry B. Ashmead, 1862. (Facsimile edition published 1976 by Delaware County Institute of Science.)

Smith, J. Wheaton, D.D. *The Life of John P. Crozer.* Philadelphia: American Baptist Publication Society, 1868.

Smith, Richard S. *Reminiscences of Seven Years of Early Life.* Wilmington, Del.: Ferris Bros., 1884.

Snedeker, Carol D. (ed.). *The Diaries of Donald Macdonald, 1824–1826.* Indianapolis: Indiana Historical Society, 1942.

Stille, Charles J. *Memorial of the Great Central Fair for the U.S. Sanitary Commission, held in Philadelphia, June 1864.* Philadelphia: U.S. Sanitary Commission, 1864.

Tyng, Stephen H. *Lectures on the Law and the Gospel.* Philadelphia: Stavely and M'Calla, 1844.

———. *Twenty-first Anniversary Address before the American Institute of the City of New York, at the Tabernacle, on October 12, 1848.* New York, 1848.

———. *Forty Years' Experience in Sunday-Schools.* New York: Sheldon & Company, 1860.

Volney, C. F. *The Ruins, or, Meditation on the Revolutions of Empires: and The Law of Nature.* New York: Twentieth Century Publishing Co., 1890.

White, Anna, and Leila S. Taylor. *Shakerism: Its Meaning and Message.* Columbus, Ohio: Press of Fred J. Herr, 1871.

Whitehead, William. *Directory of the borough of Chester, for the years 1859–60 . . .* West Chester, Pa.: William Whitehead, 1859.

Wilder, Rev. William. *A Discourse, commemorative of John P. Crozer, Preached in Lewisburg, July 22nd, 1866.*

Williams, Charles L. "Address," in *Semi-Centennial of Upland Baptist Church 1852–1902.*

Windle, Mary Jane. *Life in Washington and Life Here and There.* Philadelphia: J. B. Lippincott & Co., 1859.

Woodman, Henry. *The History of Valley Forge.* Oaks, Pa., 1922.

SCHOLARLY AND TECHNICAL BOOKS AND ARTICLES

Arky, Louis H. "The Mechanics' Union of Trade Associations and the Formation of the Philadelphia Workingmen's Movement," *Pennsylvania Magazine of History and Biography*, Vol. 76 (1952), pp. 142–76.

Ashmead, Henry Graham. *Historical Sketch of Chester, on Delaware.* Chester, Pa.: The Republican Steam Printing House, 1883.

———. *History of Delaware County, Pennsylvania.* Philadelphia: L. H. Everts, 1884. (Facsimile edition published 1968 by Concord Township Historical Society.)

———. *History of the Delaware County National Bank.* Chester, Pa., 1914.

Ashton, T. S. *The Industrial Revolution 1760–1830.* London: Oxford University Press, 1948.

Bagnall, William R. *The Textile Industries of the United States.* Vol. 1, *1639–1810.* Cambridge: Riverside Press, 1893.

Bates, Samuel P., *History of the Pennsylvania Volunteers, 1861–1865.* 5 vols. Harrisburg, Pa., 1869–71.

Bathe, Greville and Dorothy. *Oliver Evans: A Chronicle of Early American Engineering.* Philadelphia: Historical Society of Pennsylvania, 1935.

———. *Jacob Perkins: His Inventions, His Times, and His Contemporaries.* Philadelphia: Historical Society of Pennsylvania, 1943.

Benson, Lee. *The Concept of Jacksonian Democracy: New York as a Test Case.* New York: Atheneum, 1969.

Bernstein, Leonard. "The Working People of Philadelphia from Colonial Times to the General Strike of 1835," *Pennsylvania Magazine of History and Biography,* Vol. 74 (1950), pp. 322–39.

Bestor, Arthur E., Jr. "Patent-Office Models of the Good Society: Some Relationships Between Social Reform and Westward Expansion," *American Historical Review,* Vol. 58 (1953), pp. 505–26.

———. "Albert Brisbane, Propagandist for Socialism in the 1840's," *New York History,* Vol. 45 (1947), pp. 128–58.

———. "The Evolution of the Socialist Vocabulary," *Journal of the History of Ideas,* Vol. 9 (1948), pp. 259–302.

———. *American Phalanxes, a Study of Fourierist Socialism in the United States (With Special Reference to the Movement in Western New York).* Ph.D. Thesis, University of Wisconsin, Madison, 1956.

———. *Backwoods Utopias: The Sectarian Origins and the Owenite Phase of Communitarian Socialism in America.* 2nd enlarged edition, Philadelphia: University of Pennsylvania Press, 1970.

Billington, Ray Allen. *The Protestant Crusade, 1800–1860: A Study of the Origins of American Nativism.* New York: Macmillan, 1938.

Bining, Arthur C. *Pennsylvania Iron Manufacture in the Eighteenth Century.* Harrisburg, Pa.: Pennsylvania Historical Commission, 1938.

Bishop, J. L. *History of American Manufactures.* 3 vols., Philadelphia: Edward Young, 1861, 1864, 1868.

Blue, Frederick J. *The Free Soilers: Third Party Politics, 1848–54.* Urbana, Ill.: University of Illinois Press, 1973.

Boatman, Roy M. "The Brandywine Cotton Industry, 1795–1805," MS, 1957. Eleutherian Mills Historical Library.

Bolles, Albert S. *Industrial History of the United States.* Norwich, Conn., 1879.

Bradley, Ian. *A History of Machine Tools.* Hemel Hempstead, England: Model and Allied Publications, 1972.

Calvert, Monte. *The Mechanical Engineer in America, 1830–1910: Professional Cultures in Conflict.* Baltimore: Johns Hopkins Press, 1967.

Cantwell, Robert. *Alexander Wilson, Naturalist and Pioneer.* Philadelphia: Lippincott, 1961.

Carter, Jane Levis. *Edgmont: The Story of a Township.* Kennett Square, Pa.: KNA Press, 1976.

Catling, Harold. *The Spinning Mule.* Newton Abbot, Devon, England: David & Charles, 1970.

Chase, William H. *Five Generations of Loom Builders: A History of the Draper Corporation.* Hopedale, Mass.: Draper Corp., 1950.

Chinard, Gilbert. *Volney et l'Amérique d'après des documents inédits et sa correspondance avec Jefferson.* Baltimore: Johns Hopkins Press, 1923.

Clark, Dennis. "Kellyville. An Immigrant Enterprise," *Pennsylvania History,* Vol. 39 (1972), pp. 40–9.

Clark, V. S. *History of Manufactures in the United States, 1607–1860.* Washington, D.C., 1916.

Claussen, W. Edwards. *Wyck: The Study of a Historic House.* Philadelphia: Privately printed by Mary T. Haines, 1970.

Clifton, Ronald D. *Forms and Patterns: Room Specialization in Maryland, Massachusetts, and Pennsylvania, Family Dwellings, 1725–1834.* Ph.D. Thesis, University of Pennsylvania, 1971.

Cochrane, Thomas C., and William Miller. *The Age of Enterprise: A Social History of Industrial America.* Revised edition, New York: Harper & Row, 1961.

Coleman, John F. *The Disruption of the Pennsylvania Democracy, 1848–1860.* Harrisburg, Pa.: Pennsylvania Historical and Museum Commission, 1975.

Coleman, Peter J. *Debtors and Creditors in America: Insolvency, Imprisonment for Debt, and Bankruptcy, 1607–1900.* Madison, Wis.: State Historical Society of Wisconsin, 1974.

Commons, John R., *et al.* (eds.). *A Documentary History of American Industrial Society.* 10 vols., Cleveland, Ohio: A. H. Clark, 1900–11.

Commons, John Rogers (ed.) *History of Labor in the United States.* 4 vols., New York: The Macmillan Co., 1918–35.

Conway, Jill. "Evangelical Protestantism and Its Influence on Women in North America, 1790–1860," MS, 1972. Paper presented at meeting of American Historical Association.

Copeland, Melvin T. *The Cotton Manufacturing Industry of the United States.* Cambridge: Harvard University Press, 1912.

Corner, George W. *Doctor Kane of the Arctic Seas.* Philadelphia: Temple University Press, 1972.

Curry, Earl R. "Pennsylvania and the Republican Convention of 1860: A Critique of McClure's Thesis," *Pennsylvania Magazine of History and Biography,* Vol. 97 (1973), pp. 183–98.

Drinnon, Richard. *White Savage: The Case of John Dunn Hunter.* New York: Schocken Books, 1972.

Du Pont, B. G. *Lives of Victor and Josephine du Pont.* Wilmington, Del.: Privately printed, 1930.

Eiselen, Malcolm R. *The Rise of Pennsylvania Protectionism.* Ph.D. Thesis, University of Pennsylvania, 1932.

Elder, William. *A Memoir of Henry C. Carey.* Philadelphia, 1880.

English, Walter. *The Textile Industry: An Account of the Early Inventions of Spinning, Weaving, and Knitting Machines.* London: Longmans, 1969.

Ferguson, Eugene S. "The Mind's Eye: Nonverbal Thought in Technology," *Science* 197 (1977), pp. 827–36.

Fertig, John H. *Constitutions of Pennsylvania/Constitutions of the United States.* Harrisburg, Pa.: Legislative Reference Bureau, 1926.

Fletcher, Stevenson W. *Pennsylvania Agriculture and Country Life, 1640–1840, 1840–1940.* 2 vols., Harrisburg, Pa.: Pennsylvania Historical and Museum Commission, 1950, 1955.

Foner, Eric. *Free Soil, Free Labor, Free Men: The Ideology of the Republican Party Before the Civil War.* New York: Oxford University Press, 1970.

Foster, Charles I. *An Errand of Mercy; the Evangelical United Front, 1790–1837.* Chapel Hill,

N.C.: University of North Carolina Press, 1960.

Fox, Early Lee. *The American Colonization Society, 1817–1840.* Baltimore: Johns Hopkins Press, 1919.

Fox, Wendall P. "The Kendall Community," *Ohio Archaeological and Historical Publications,* Vol. 20 (1911), pp. 176–219.

Francis, Russell E. "The Religious Revival of 1858 in Philadelphia," *Pennsylvania Magazine of History and Biography,* Vol. 70 (January 1946), pp. 52–77.

Garfinkel, Harold. *Studies in Ethnomethodology.* Englewood Cliffs, N.J.: Prentice-Hall, 1967.

Geffen, Elizabeth M. *Philadelphia Unitarianism, 1796–1861.* Philadelphia: University of Pennsylvania Press, 1961.

———. "Philadelphia Protestantism Reacts to Social Reform Movements Before the Civil War," *Pennsylvania History,* Vol. 30 (April 1963), pp. 192–211.

Gerrity, Frank. "The Masons, the Antimasons, and the Pennsylvania Legislature, 1834–1836," *Pennsylvania Magazine of History and Biography,* Vol. 99 (April 1975), pp. 180–206.

Gerstner, Patsy. "The Academy of Natural Sciences of Philadelphia," MS, 1973. Conference on Early History of Societies for Promoting Knowledge in the United States.

Gibb, George Sweet. *The Saco-Lowell Shops: Textile Machinery Building in New England, 1813–1849.* Cambridge: Harvard University Press, 1950.

Govan, Thomas P. *Nicholas Biddle.* Chicago: University of Chicago Press, 1959.

Green, Arnold W. *Henry Charles Carey.* Philadelphia: University of Pennsylvania Press, 1951.

Griffin, Clifford S. *Their Brothers' Keepers: Moral Stewardship in the United States, 1800–1865.* New Brunswick, N.J.: Rutgers University Press, 1960.

Gutman, Herbert G. *Work, Culture, and Society in Industrializing America.* New York: Alfred A. Knopf, 1976.

Hackensmith, Charles W. *Biography of Joseph Neef, Educator in the Ohio Valley, 1809–1954.* New York: Carlton Press, 1973.

Hamy, E.-T. *The Travels of the Naturalist Charles A. Lesueur in North America 1815–1837.* Translated by Milton Haber, edited by H. F. Raup. Kent, Ohio: Kent State University Press, 1968.

Hancock, Harold. "The Industrial Worker along the Brandywine," MS, 1956–58. Eleutherian Mills Historical Library.

Hancock, Harold B., and Norman B. Wilkinson. "The Gilpins and Their Endless Papermaking Machine," *Pennsylvania Magazine of History and Biography,* Vol. 81 (October 1957), pp. 391–405.

Hardy, James D., Jr., John H. Jensen, and Martin Wolfe (eds.). *The Maclure Collection of French Revolutionary Materials.* Philadelphia: University of Pennsylvania Press, 1966.

Hareven, Tamara K. (ed.). *Anonymous Americans: Explorations in Nineteenth-Century Social History.* Englewood Cliffs, N.J.: Prentice-Hall, 1971.

Harrison, J. F. C. *Quest for the New Moral World: Robert Owen and the Owenites in Britain and America.* New York: Scribner's, 1969.

Harrison, Lowell H. "William Duane on Education: a Letter to the Kentucky Assembly, 1822." *Pennsylvania Magazine of History and Biography,* 73 (1949), pp. 316–25.

Harte, N. B. "On Rees's *Cyclopaedia* as a Source for the History of the Textile Industries in the Early Nineteenth Century," *Textile History,* Vol. 5 (1974), pp. 119–27.

Hartz, Louis. *The Liberal Tradition in America.* New York: Harcourt, Brace, 1955.

———. *Economic Policy and Democratic Thought: Pennsylvania, 1776–1860.* Cambridge: Harvard University Press, 1948.

Henderson, Helen W. *Pennsylvania Academy of Fine Arts and Other Collections of Philadelphia.* Boston: Page, 1911.

Hindle, Brooke. *Technology in Early America.* Chapel Hill, N.C.: University of North Carolina Press, 1960.

Hobsbawm, E. J. *Primitive Rebels: Studies in Archaic Forms of Social Movements in the Nineteenth and Twentieth Centuries.* New York: Praeger, 1963 (1959).

————. *The Age of Revolution, 1789–1848.* New York: New American Library, 1971.

————. "The Human Results of the Industrial Revolution: 1750–1850," in Y. Cohen, *Man in Adaptation. The Cultural Present.* 2nd edition, Chicago: Aldine, 1974.

Hoye, John. *Staple Cotton Fabrics: Names, Descriptions, Finishes, and Uses of Unbleached, Converted, and Mill Finished Fabrics.* New York and London: McGraw-Hill Book Co., 1942.

Hughes, Thomas P. *Changing Attitudes Toward American Technology.* New York: Harper & Row, 1975.

James, Bessie Rowland. *Anne Royall's U.S.A.* New Brunswick, N.J.: Rutgers University Press, 1972.

Jefferis, Jervas, Jr. "The Chester Mills: The History of the Industrial Development of an Area, with Emphasis upon the Years 1790–1860." M.A. thesis, Temple University, 1965.

Jeremy, David J. "British and American Yarn Count Systems: An Historical Analysis," *Business History Review,* Vol. 45 (1971), pp. 336–8.

————. "Innovation in American Textile Technology During the Early Nineteenth Century," *Technology and Culture,* Vol. 14 (1973[a]), pp. 40–76.

————. "British Textile Technology Transmission to the United States: The Philadelphia Region Experience, 1770–1820," *Business History Review,* Vol. 47 (1973[b]), pp. 24–52.

Johnson, John. *The Defence of Charleston Harbor, 1863–1865.* Charleston, N.C., 1890.

Kaplan, Abraham D. H. *Henry Charles Carey (1793–1879): A Study in American Economic Thought.* Baltimore: Johns Hopkins Press, 1931.

Karnes, Thomas L. *William Gilpin: Western Nationalist.* Austin, Tex.: University of Texas Press, 1970.

Kasserman, David. *Conservative Innovation: Introduction of the Cotton Industry into the United States, 1789–1840.* Ph.D. Thesis, University of Pennsylvania, 1974.

Keen, William W. *The Bi-Centennial Celebration of the Founding of the First Baptist Church of the City of Philadelphia, 1698–1899.* Philadelphia: American Baptist Publication Society, 1899.

Klein, Philip S. *Pennsylvania Politics, 1817–1832: A Game Without Rules.* Philadelphia: Historical Society of Pennsylvania, 1940.

————, and Ari Hoogenboom. *A History of Pennsylvania.* New York: McGraw-Hill Book Co., 1973.

Koch, G. Adolf. *Republican Religion: The American Revolution and the Cult of Reason.* New York: Henry Holt and Company, 1933.

Kranzberg, Melvin, and Carroll W. Pursell, Jr. (eds.). *Technology in Western Civilization.* 2 vols., New York: Oxford University Press, 1967.

Kranzberg, Melvin, and William H. Davenport (eds.). *Technology and Culture: An Anthology.* New York: Schocken Books, 1972.

Kroeber, A. L. *Cultural and Natural Areas of Native North America.* Berkeley, Calif.: University of California Press, 1939.

————. *Configurations of Culture Growth.* Berkeley and Los Angeles: University of California Press, 1944.

Kruse, W. T. "Historical Sketch of the Middletown Presbyterian Church." Elwyn, Pa., September 20, 1920.

———. "Curious Records of an Old Church," *Proceedings of the Delaware County Historical Society*, Vol. 2 (1922), pp. 7–17.

Kuhn, Thomas B. *The Structure of Scientific Revolutions.* 2nd edition, Chicago: University of Chicago Press, 1970.

Layton, Edwin T., Jr. (ed). *Technology and Social Change in America.* New York: Harper & Row, 1973.

Leggett, M. D. *Subject-Matter Index of Patents for Inventions Issued by the United States Patent Office from 1790–1873 Inclusive.* 3 vols., Washington, D.C.: Government Printing Office, 1874.

Lemieux, Christine M. *Living to Die: Nineteenth Century Culture of Death and Dying in Delaware County, Pennsylvania.* Ph.D. Thesis, University of Pennsylvania, 1976.

Lemon, James T. *The Best Poor Man's Country: A Geographical Study of Early Southeastern Pennsylvania.* Baltimore: Johns Hopkins Press, 1972.

Lincoln, Jonathan T. "The Cotton Textile Machine Industry," *Harvard Business Review*, Vol. 11 (October 1932), pp. 88–96.

———. "The Cotton Textile Machine Industry—American Loom Builders," *Harvard Business Review*, Vol. 12 (October 1933), pp. 94–105.

Lipson, Dorothy Ann. *Freemasonry in Connecticut, 1789–1835.* Ph.D. Thesis, University of Connecticut, 1974.

Lynd, Staughton. *Intellectual Origins of American Radicalism.* New York: Random House, 1968.

Maass, John. *The Glorious Enterprise: The Centennial Exhibition of 1876 in Philadelphia, and H. J. Schwarzmann, Architect-in-Chief.* Watkins Glen, N.Y.: American Life Foundation, 1973.

MacMurray, Robert R. *Technological Change in the American Cotton Spinning Industry, 1790–1836.* Ph. D. Thesis, University of Pennsylvania, 1970.

McCadden, Joseph J. *Education in Pennsylvania 1801–1835 and Its Debt to Roberts Vaux.* Philadelphia: University of Pennsylvania Press, 1937.

McCarthy, Charles. "The Anti-masonic Party," in *Annual Report of the American Historical Association*, Vol. 1 (1902).

McCullough, David. *The Great Bridge.* New York: Simon & Schuster, 1972.

McDonough, John E. *Idyls of the Old South Ward.* Chester, Pa: Chester Times, 1932.

McGrane, Reginald C. *The Panic of 1837: Some Financial Problems of the Jacksonian Era.* Chicago: University of Chicago Press, 1924.

McLoughlin, William G. (ed.). *The American Evangelicals, 1800–1900.* New York: Harper & Row, 1968.

Malone, Dumas. *The Public Life of Thomas Cooper, 1783–1839.* New Haven, Conn.: Yale University Press, 1926.

Mann, Julia de L. "The Textile Industry: Machinery for Cotton, Flax, Wool, 1760–1850," in *A History of Technology*, Vol. 4, edited by Charles Singer, E. J. Holmyard, A. R. Hall, and Trevor I. Williams. Oxford: Clarendon Press, 1958.

Manross, William Wilson. *A History of the American Episcopal Church.* New York: Morehouse Publishing Co., 1935.

Mantoux, Paul. *The Industrial Revolution in the Eighteenth Century.* New York: Harper & Row, 1962.

Manufacturers' Mutual Fire Insurance Co. *The Factory Mutuals 1835–1935.* Providence, R.I., 1935.

Marx, Leo. *The Machine in the Garden: Technology and the Pastoral Ideal in America.* London: Oxford University Press, 1964.

Mautner, Nancy L. "Natural Knowledge and Social Reform: A Case Study of the Academy of Natural Sciences of Philadelphia and New Harmony in 1825." Unpublished MS, 1973.

Mayer, Gustav. *Friedrich Engels: A Biography.* New York: Alfred A. Knopf, 1936.

Merrill, Gilbert, Alfred K. Macormac, and G. Herbert R. Mauersberger. *American Cotton Handbook.* New York: Textile Book Publishers, 1941, 1949.

Meyer, D. H. *The Instructed Conscience: The Shaping of the American National Ethic.* Philadelphia: University of Pennsylvania Press, 1972.

Monroe, Will S. *History of the Pestalozzian Movement in the United States.* New York: Arno Press and The New York Times, 1969.

Montgomery, David. "The Shuttle and the Cross: Weavers and Artisans in the Kensington Riots of 1844." Pp. 44–74 in Stearns and Walkowitz, 1974 (originally published in the *Journal of Social Historey* 5 [1972], pp. 411–46.

Mueller, Henry R. *The Whig Party in Pennsylvania.* Ph.D. Thesis, Columbia University, 1922.

Myers, C. Maxwell. *The Rise of the Republican Party in Pennsylvania, 1854–1860.* Ph.D. Thesis, University of Pittsburgh, 1940.

Navin, Thomas R. *The Whitin Machine Works since 1831.* Cambridge: Harvard University Press, 1950.

———. "Innovation and Management Policies in the Textile Machinery Industry: Influence of the Market on Management," *Business History Review,* Vol. 25 (1951), pp. 15–30.

Newman, Albert Henry. *A History of the Baptist Churches in the United States.* Philadelphia: American Baptist Publication Society, 1898.

Nolan, J. Bennett. *Lafayette in America Day by Day.* Baltimore: Johns Hopkins Press, 1934.

Palmer, R. R. *The Age of the Democratic Revolution.* Princeton, N.J.: Princeton University Press, 1964.

———. *The Nineteenth Century World.* New York: Mentor Books, 1963.

Perkins, Alice J., and Theresa Wolfson. *Frances Wright, Free Enquirer.* New York and London: Harper & Brothers, 1939.

Pessen, Edward. "The Ideology of Stephen Simpson, Upper-class Champion of the Early Philadelphia Workingmen's Movement," *Pennsylvania History,* Vol. 22 (1955), pp. 328–40.

———. "The Workingmen's Movement of the Jacksonian Era," *Mississippi Valley Historical Review,* Vol. 43 (1956), pp. 428–43.

———. *Most Uncommon Jacksonians: The Radical Leaders of the Early Labor Movement.* New York: State University of New York Press, 1967.

———. *Jacksonian America: Society, Personality, and Politics.* Homewood, Ill.: The Dorsey Press, 1969.

Pettyjohn, Etta M. *Nineteenth Century Protestant Episcopal Schools in Pennsylvania.* Ph.D. Thesis, University of Pennsylvania, 1951.

Polanyi, Karl. *The Great Transformation.* New York: Farrar and Rinehart, 1944.

Porter, Glenn, and Harold C. Livesay. *Merchants and Manufacturers: Studies in the Changing Structures of Nineteenth Century Marketing.* Baltimore: Johns Hopkins Press, 1971.

Post, Albert. *Popular Freethought in America, 1825–1850.* New York: Octagon Books, 1974.

Pursell, Carroll W., Jr. *Early Stationary Steam Engines in America: A Study in the Migration of a Technology.* Washington, D.C.: Smithsonian Institute Press, 1969.

Rayback, Joseph G. "The American Workingman and the Antislavery Crusade," *Journal of Economic History,* Vol. 3 (1943), pp. 152–63.

Reynolds, Terry S. *Science and the Water Wheel: The Development and Diffusion of Theoretical and*

Experimental Doctrines Relating to the Vertical Water Wheel, c. 1500–c. 1850. Ph.D. Thesis, University of Kansas, 1973.

Rezneck, Samuel. "The Rise and Early Development of Industrial Consciousness in the United States, 1760–1830," *Journal of Economic and Business History,* Vol. 4 (1932), pp. 784–811.
———. "The Social History of an American Depression, 1837–1843," *American Historical Review,* Vol. 40 (1935), pp. 662–87.

Rice, Edwin W. *The Sunday-School Movement, 1780–1917, and the American Sunday-School Union, 1817–1917.* Philadelphia: American Sunday-School Union, 1917.

Rosenberg, Charles E. *The Cholera Years: The United States in 1832, 1849, and 1866.* Chicago: University of Chicago Press, 1962.

Rostow, Walt W. *The Stages of Economic Growth: A Non-Communist Manifesto.* 2nd edition, Cambridge: Cambridge University Press, 1971.

Rothman, David J. *The Discovery of the Asylum: Social Order and Disorder in the New Republic.* Boston and Toronto: Little, Brown, 1971.

Sachse, Julius F. *Old Masonic Lodges of Pennsylvania. "Moderns" and "Ancients" 1730–1800. Which have surrendered their warrants or affiliated with other grand lodges.* Philadelphia, 1912.

[Saco-Lowell Shops]. *A Chronicle of Textile Machinery, 1824–1924. Issued to commemorate the one hundredth anniversary of the Saco-Lowell Shops.* Boston, 1924.

Sandberg, Lars G. "American Rings and English Mules: The Role of Economic Rationality," in Saul (ed.), *Technological Change,* pp. 120–40.

Sandeen, Ernest R. *The Roots of Fundamentalism: British and American Millenarianism, 1800–1930.* Chicago: University of Chicago Press, 1971.

Saul, S. B. (ed.). *Technological Change: The United States and Britain in the Nineteenth Century.* London: Methuen, 1970.

Scharf, John T. *History of Delaware, 1609–1888.* 2 vols., Philadelphia: L. J. Richards, 1888.
——— and Thompson Westcott. *History of Philadelphia: 1609–1884.* Philadelphia: L. H. Everts, 1884.

Schlesinger, Arthur M., Jr. *The Age of Jackson.* Boston: Little, Brown, 1945.

Sellers, Charles Coleman. *The Artist of the Revolution: The Early Life of Charles Willson Peale.* Hebron, Conn.: Feather and Good, 1939.
———. *Charles Willson Peale: Later Life.* Vol. 2 (1790–1827). Philadelphia: American Philosophical Society, 1947.

Selsam, J. Paul. *The Pennsylvania Constitution of 1776: A Study in Revolutionary Democracy.* New York: Octagon Books, 1971.

Sinclair, Bruce. "At the Turn of a Screw: William Sellers, the Franklin Institute and a Standard American Thread," *Technology and Culture,* Vol. 10 (1969), pp. 20–34.
———. *Philadelphia's Philosopher Mechanics.* Baltimore: Johns Hopkins Press, 1974.

Singer, Charles, E. J. Holmyard, A. R. Hall, and Trevor I. Williams (eds.). *A History of Technology.* Vols. 4 and 5, Oxford: Clarendon Press, 1958.

Smelser, Neil J. *Social Change in the Industrial Revolution.* Chicago: University of Chicago Press, 1959.

Smith, Sarah Trainer. *Sketch of Mary Brackett Willcox of Ivy Mills, Pa., 1796–1866.* Privately printed, 1897.

Smith, Timothy L. *Revivalism and Social Reform in Mid-Nineteenth Century America.* New York: Abingdon Press, 1957.

Smith, Walter B., and Arthur H. Cole. *Fluctuations in American Business, 1790–1860.* Cambridge: Harvard University Press, 1935.

Bibliography

Snyder, Charles McCool. *The Jacksonian Heritage: Pennsylvania Politics, 1833–1848.* Harrisburg, Pa.: Pennsylvania Historical and Museum Commission, 1958.

Staudenraus, P. J. *The African Colonization Movement 1816–1865.* New York: Columbia University Press, 1961.

Stauffer, Vernon. "New England and the Bavarian Illuminati," *Studies in History, Economics, and Public Law,* Vol. 82, No. 1. New York: Columbia University Press, 1918.

Stearns, Peter N., and Daniel J. Walkowitz (eds.). *Workers in the Industrial Revolution: Recent Studies of Labor in the United States and Europe.* Edison, N.J.: Transaction Books, 1974.

Sullivan, William A. "The Industrial Revolution and the Factory Operative in Pennsylvania," *Pennsylvania Magazine of History and Biography,* Vol. 78 (1954), pp. 476–94.

————. *The Industrial Worker in Pennsylvania, 1800–1840.* Harrisburg, Pa.: Pennsylvania Historical and Museum Commission, 1955.

Swank, Scott T. *The Unfettered Conscience: A Study of Sectarianism, Spiritualism and Social Reform in the New Jerusalem Church, 1840–1870.* Ph.D. Thesis, University of Pennsylvania, 1970.

Tann, Jennifer. "The Textile Millwright in the Early Industrial Revolution," *Textile History,* Vol. 5 (Oct. 1974), pp. 80–9.

Taussig, Frank W. *Tariff History of the United States.* New York, 1892.

Thernstrom, Stephan, and Richard Sennett (eds.). *Nineteenth-Century Cities: Essays in the New Urban History.* New Haven, Conn.: Yale University Press, 1969.

Tiffany, Charles C. *A History of the Protestant Episcopal Church in the United States . . .* New York, 1895.

Tinkcom, Harry Marlin. *The Republicans and Federalists in Pennsylvania, 1790–1801: A Study in National Stimulus and Local Response.* Harrisburg, Pa.: Pennsylvania Historical and Museum Commission, 1950.

Tryon, R. M. *Household Manufactures in the United States: 1640–1860.* Chicago: University of Chicago Press, 1917.

Tuveson, Ernest Lee. *Redeemer Nation: The Idea of America's Millennial Role.* Chicago: University of Chicago Press, 1968.

[Upland Centennial]. *History of Upland, 1683–1969, on the One Hundredth Anniversary of the Borough Incorporation.*

Usher, A. P. *History of Mechanical Invention.* New York: McGraw-Hill Book Co., 1929.

Vedder, Henry G. *A History of the Baptists in the Middle States.* Philadelphia: American Baptist Publishing Society, 1898.

Walker, Joseph E. *Hopewell Village: A Social and Economic History of an Iron-Making Community.* Philadelphia: University of Pennsylvania Press, 1966.

Wallace, Anthony F. C. *The Death and Rebirth of the Seneca.* New York: Alfred A. Knopf, 1970.

————. "Revitalization Movements," *American Anthropologist,* Vol. 58 (1956), pp. 264–81.

————. *Culture and Personality.* New York: Random House, 1970.

————. "Paradigmatic Processes in Culture Change," *American Anthropologist,* Vol. 74 (1972), pp. 467–78.

Wallace, David H. *John Rogers: The People's Sculptor.* Middletown, Conn.: Wesleyan University Press, 1967.

Wallace, Paul A. W. *Pennsylvania: Seed of a Nation.* New York: Harper & Row, 1967.

Ware, Norman. *The Industrial Worker, 1840–1860.* Boston: Houghton Mifflin, 1924.

Waterman, W. R. *Frances Wright.* Ph.D. Thesis, Columbia University, 1924.

Watson, John R. *Annals of Philadelphia and Pennsylvania, in the Olden Time.* 3 vols., Philadelphia: Stuart, 1898.

Watt, Bernice K., and Annabel L. Merrill. *Composition of Foods: Raw, Processed, Prepared.* Washington, D.C.: U.S. Department of Agriculture, 1963.

Wickersham, James P. *History of Education in Pennsylvania.* Lancaster, Pa.: Inquirer Publishing Co., 1886.

Wilkinson, Norman B. "The Education of Alfred Victor du Pont, Nineteenth Century Industrialist," *Pennsylvania History,* Vol. 28 (1961), pp. 105–20.

———. "Brandywine Borrowings from European Technology," *Technology and Culture,* Vol. 4 (1963), pp. 1–13.

Zyckowski, Stanley S. *The Antimasonic Party in Pennsylvania.* M.A. Thesis, Pennsylvania State University, 1937.

Index

WESTMAR COLLEGE LIBRARY